G000300170

STREET ATLAS

Somerset

www.philips-maps.co.uk

First published in 2002 by

Philip's, a division of
Octopus Publishing Group Ltd
www.octopusbooks.co.uk
2-4 Heron Quays, London E14 4JP
A Hachette Livre UK Company
www.hachettelivre.co.uk

Second edition 2006
Second impression 2008
COMBA

ISBN 978-0-540-08842-3 (spiral)

© Philip's 2006

Ordnance Survey®

This product includes mapping data licensed
from Ordnance Survey® with the permission of
the Controller of Her Majesty's Stationery Office.

© Crown copyright 2006. All rights reserved.
Licence number 100011710.

Contents

III	**Key to map symbols**	
IV	**Key to map pages**	
VI	**Route planning**	
X	**Administrative and Postcode boundaries**	
1	**Street maps** at 3½ inches to 1 mile	
122	**Street maps** at 1¾ inches to 1 mile	
200	**Street maps** at 3½ inches to 1 mile	
226	**Street maps of Bristol and Bath city centres** at 7 inches to 1 mile	
229	**Index** of towns and villages	
233	**Index** of streets, hospitals, industrial estates, railway stations, schools, shopping centres, universities and places of interest	

Digital Data

The exceptionally high-quality mapping found in this atlas is available as digital data in TIFF format, which is easily convertible to other bitmapped (raster) image formats.

The index is also available in digital form as a standard database table. It contains all the details found in the printed index together with the National Grid reference for the map square in which each entry is named.

For further information and to discuss your requirements, please contact james.mann@philips-maps.co.uk

On-line route planner

For detailed driving directions and estimated driving times visit our free route plannner at
www.philips-maps.co.uk

Key to map symbols

III

Motorway with junction number (22a)	
Primary route – dual/single carriageway	
A road – dual/single carriageway	
B road – dual/single carriageway	
Minor road – dual/single carriageway	
Other minor road – dual/single carriageway	
Road under construction	
Tunnel, covered road	
Rural track, private road or narrow road in urban area	
Gate or obstruction to traffic (restrictions may not apply at all times or to all vehicles)	
Path, bridleway, byway open to all traffic, road used as a public path	
Pedestrianised area	
Postcode boundaries DY7	
County and unitary authority boundaries	
Railway, tunnel, railway under construction	
Tramway, tramway under construction	
Miniature railway	
Railway station Walsall	
Private railway station	
Metro station South Shields	
Tram stop, tram stop under construction	
Bus, coach station	

◆	Ambulance station
◆	Coastguard station
◆	Fire station
◆	Police station
✚	Accident and Emergency entrance to hospital
H	Hospital
+	Place of worship
i	Information Centre (open all year)
🛒	Shopping Centre
P P&R	Parking, Park and Ride
PO	Post Office
⚐ 🚐	Camping site, caravan site
▶ ⚐	Golf course, picnic site
Prim Sch	Important buildings, schools, colleges, universities and hospitals
	Built up area
	Woods
River Medway	Water name
	River, weir, stream
	Canal, lock, tunnel
	Water
	Tidal water
Church	Non-Roman antiquity
ROMAN FORT	Roman antiquity
◀ 87	Adjoining page indicators and overlap bands
237	The colour of the arrow and the band indicates the scale of the adjoining or overlapping page (see scales below)

Acad	**Academy**	Inst	**Institute**	Recn Gd	**Recreation**		
Allot Gdns	**Allotments**	Ct	**Law Court**		**Ground**		
Cemy	**Cemetery**	L Ctr	**Leisure Centre**	Resr	**Reservoir**		
C Ctr	**Civic Centre**	LC	**Level Crossing**	Ret Pk	**Retail Park**		
CH	**Club House**	Liby	**Library**	Sch	**School**		
Coll	**College**	Mkt	**Market**	Sh Ctr	**Shopping Centre**		
Crem	**Crematorium**	Meml	**Memorial**	TH	**Town Hall/House**		
Ent	**Enterprise**	Mon	**Monument**	Trad Est	**Trading Estate**		
Ex H	**Exhibition Hall**	Mus	**Museum**	Univ	**University**		
Ind Est	**Industrial Estate**	Obsy	**Observatory**	W Twr	**Water Tower**		
IRB Sta	**Inshore Rescue**	Pal	**Royal Palace**	Wks	**Works**		
	Boat Station	PH	**Public House**	YH	**Youth Hostel**		

■ The small numbers around the edges of the maps identify the 1 kilometre National Grid lines
■ The dark grey border on the inside edge of some pages indicates that the mapping does not continue onto the adjacent page

Enlarged mapping only

	Railway or bus station building
	Place of interest
	Parkland

The scale of the maps on the pages numbered in blue is 5.52 cm to 1 km • 3½ inches to 1 mile • 1: 18103	0 ¼ ½ ¾ 1 mile 0 250 m 500 m 750 m 1 kilometre
The scale of the maps on pages numbered in green is 2.76 cm to 1 km • 1¾ inches to 1 mile • 1: 36206	0 ¼ ½ ¾ 1 mile 0 250m 500m 750m 1 kilometre
The scale of the maps on the pages numbered in red is 11.04 cm to 1 km • 7 inches to 1 mile • 1: 9051	0 220 yards 440 yards 660 yards ½ mile 0 125m 250m 375m ½ kilometre

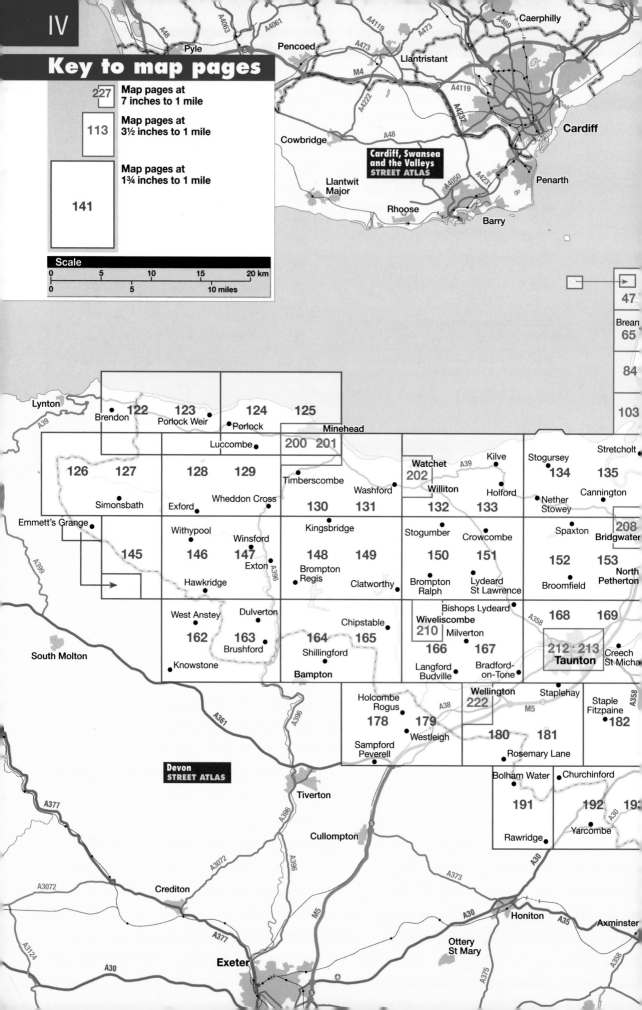

IV

Key to map pages

227	Map pages at 7 inches to 1 mile
113	Map pages at 3½ inches to 1 mile
141	Map pages at 1¾ inches to 1 mile

Scale

0   5   10   15   20 km
0   5   10 miles

Pyle

Pencoed

A48
A4063
A4061
A4119
A473
A473
A469   Caerphilly

Llantristant

M4
A4222
A4119
A4232

Cowbridge

A48

Cardiff

Cardiff, Swansea and the Valleys STREET ATLAS

A4050   A4231   Penarth

Llantwit Major

Rhoose

Barry

47

Brean 65

84

103

Lynton   A39

Brendon   **122**   **123**   Porlock Weir   **124**   **125**   Porlock

Minehead

Luccombe   **200** **201**

126   **127**   **128**   **129**   Timberscombe   **130**   **131**   Washford   Watchet   A39   Kilve   Stogursey   **134**   **135**   Stretcholt

Simonsbath   Exford   Wheddon Cross   **202**   Williton   Holford   Nether Stowey   Cannington

Emmett's Grange   Withypool   Winsford   **148**   Kingsbridge   Stogumber   Crowcombe   Spaxton   **208** Bridgwater

A389   **145**   **146**   **147**   Exton   A396   Brompton Regis   **149**   Brompton Ralph   **150**   **151**   Lydeard St Lawrence   **152**   **153**   North Petherton

Hawkridge   Clatworthy   Broomfield

West Anstey   Dulverton   Chipstable   Bishops Lydeard   A358   **168**   **169**

162   **163**   Brushford   **164**   **165**   Wiveliscombe   **210**   Milverton   **212·213**   Creech St Micha

South Molton   Knowstone   Shillingford   **166**   **167**   Bradford-on-Tone   **Taunton**

Bampton   Langford Budville

A361   Holcombe Rogus   A38   Wellington   Staplehay   Staple Fitzpaine

178   **179**   **222**   M5   **180**   **181**   **182**

Sampford Peverell   Westleigh   Rosemary Lane

A396   **Devon STREET ATLAS**   Bolham Water   Churchinford

A377   Tiverton   **191**   **192**   **19**

Cullompton   Rawridge   Yarcombe   A30

A3072   Crediton   A3072   M5   A373   A30

A377   Honiton   A35   Axminster

A3124   A30   Ottery St Mary   A375   A358

Exeter

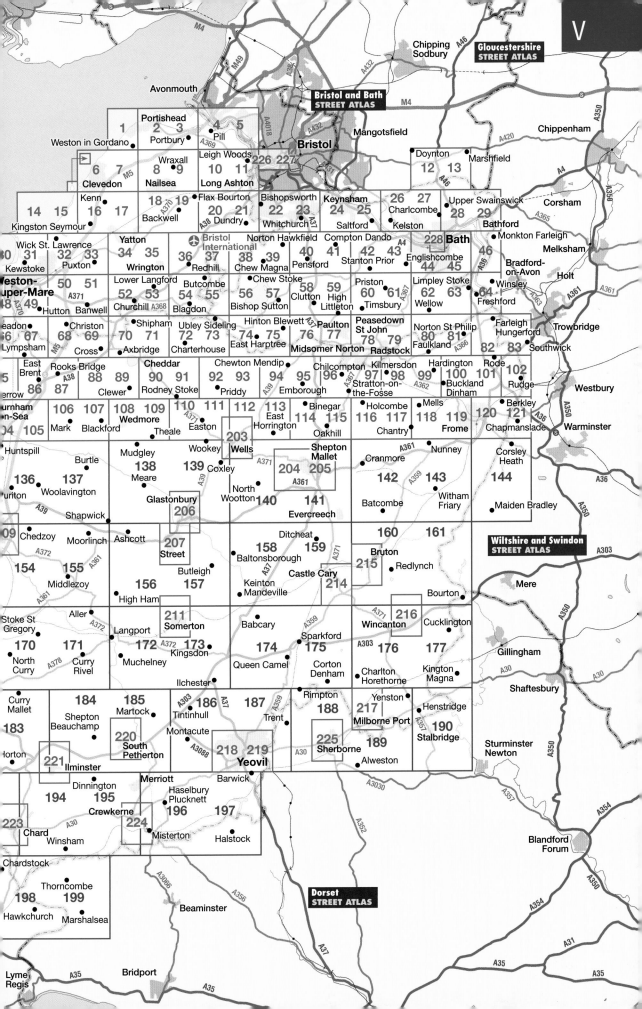

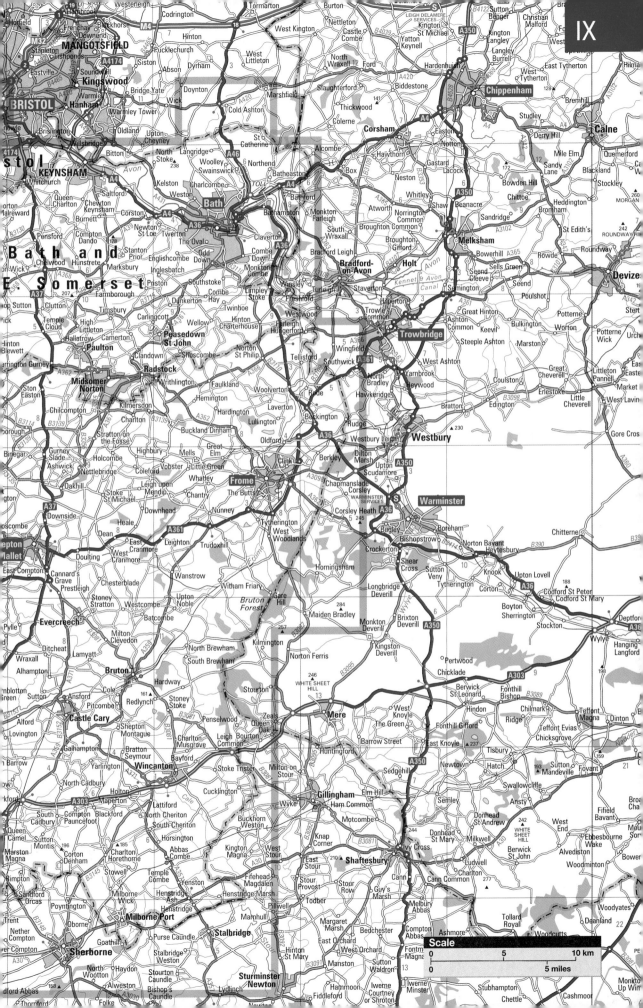

Scale

0   5   10 km

0   5 miles

Major administrative and
Postcode boundaries

County and unitary authority boundaries
District boundaries
Postcode boundaries
Area covered by this atlas

Scale
0   5   10   15 km
0   5   10 miles

City of Bristol
South Gloucestershire
Bath and North East Somerset
North Somerset
Mendip
Sedgemoor
Somerset
Taunton Deane
South Somerset
West Somerset
Wiltshire
Dorset
Devon
Vale of Glamorgan
Cardiff

Portishead, Clevedon, Weston-super-Mare, Nailsea, Congresbury, Banwell, Axbridge, Cheddar, Wedmore, Highbridge, Burnham-on-Sea, Berrow, Bridgwater, Westonzoyland, Catcott, Puriton, Cannington, Nether Stowey, Kilve, Watchet, Stogumber, Elworthy, Wiveliscombe, Wellington, Bishops Lydeard, Kingston St Mary, Taunton, Staplehay, North Curry, Langport, Curry Rivel, Somerton, Glastonbury, Street, Wells, Wookey Hole, East Harptree, Chew Magna, Pensford, Keynsham, Bath, Bathford, Bathford, Timsbury, Radstock, Midsomer Norton, Paulton, Shepton Mallet, Ditcheat, Bruton, Castle Cary, Wincanton, Queen Camel, Martock, South Petherton, Ilminster, Chard, Crewkerne, Yeovil, East Coker, Sherborne, Milborne Port, Abbas Combe, Stalbridge, Tatworth, Churchinford, Horton, Dunster, Minehead, Porlock, Timberscombe, Brompton Regis, Dulverton, Simonsbath, Withypool, Stolford, Frome, Nunney, Beckington, Norton St Philip, Westwood, Horningsham

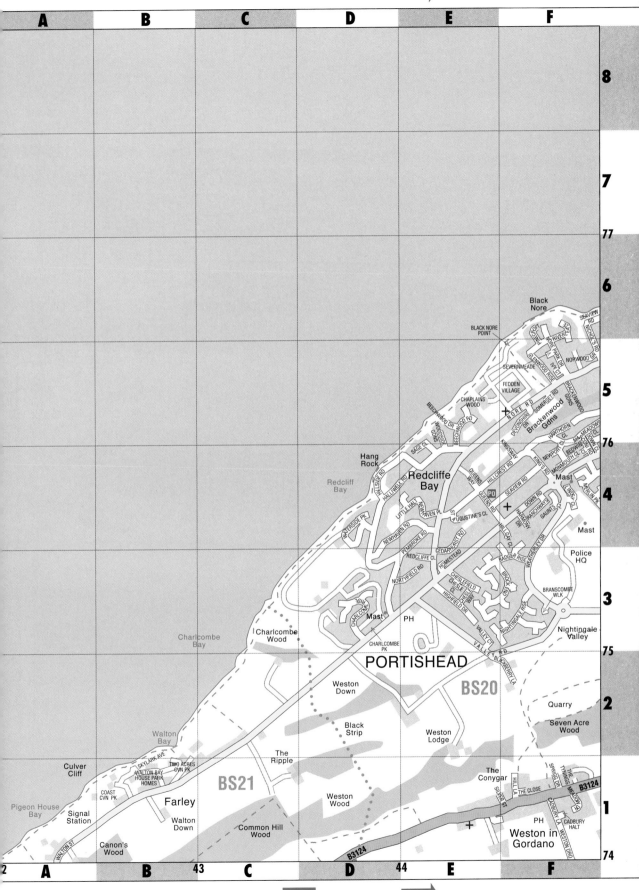

A   B   C   D   E   F

8

7

77

6

Black
Nore

BLACK NORE
POINT

SEVERNMEADE

CHAPLAINS
WOOD

FEDDEN
VILLAGE

N O R E R D

Brackenwood
Gdns

5

76

Hang
Rock

Redcliff
Bay

Redcliffe
Bay

Mast

4

LITTLE HALT

P.O

PORTISHEAD

Police
HQ

Mast

BRANSCOMBE
WLK

Nightingale
Valley

3

Charlcombe
Bay

Charlcombe
Wood

CHARLCOMBE
PK

Mast   PH

PORTISHEAD

75

BS20

Weston
Down

Quarry

2

Walton
Bay

Black
Strip

Weston
Lodge

Seven Acre
Wood

The
Ripple

The
Conygar

Culver
Cliff

WALTON BAY
HOUSE PARK
HOMES

TWO ACRES
CVN PK

BS21

B3124

COAST
CVN PK

Farley

Weston
Wood

1

Pigeon House
Bay

Signal
Station

Walton
Down

Common Hill
Wood

Weston in
Gordano

PH

CADBURY
HALT

74

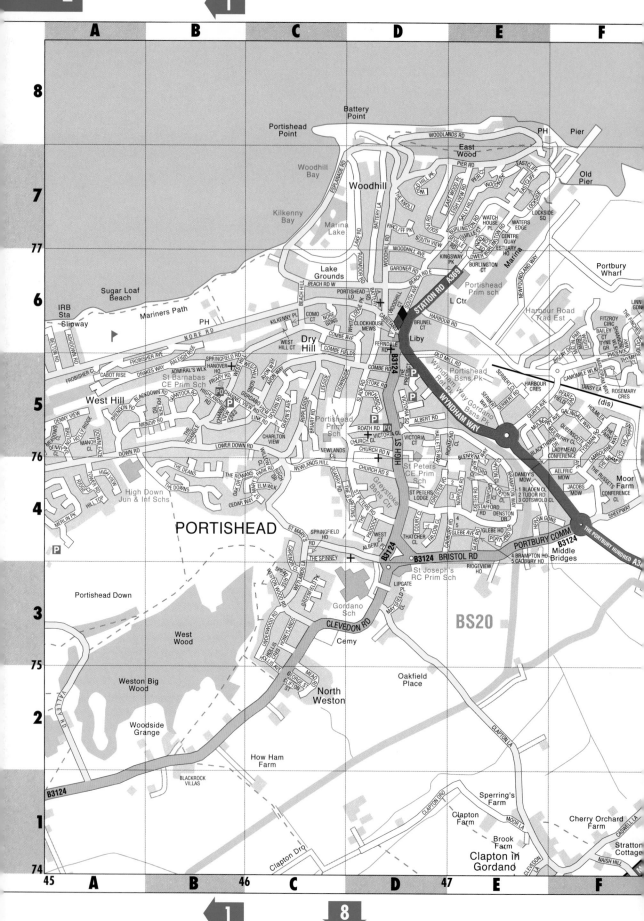

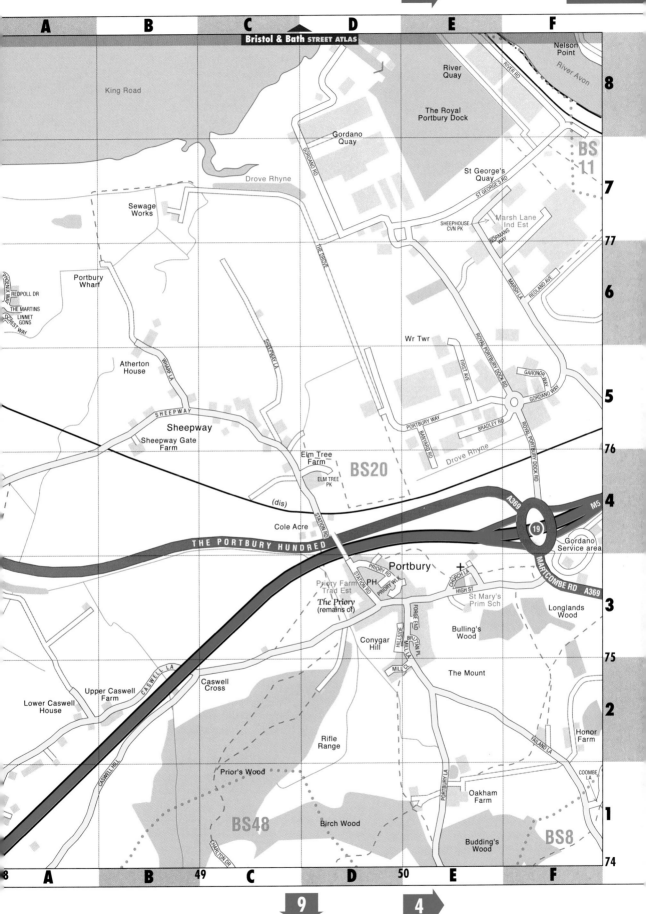

Bristol & Bath STREET ATLAS

Nelson Point

River Avon

River Quay

The Royal Portbury Dock

King Road

Gordano Quay

St George's Quay

BS 11

Drove Rhyne

Sewage Works

SHEEPHOUSE CVN PK

Marsh Lane Ind Est

NORMANS WAY

MARSH LA

REDLAND AVE

Portbury Wharf

REDPOLL DR

THE MARTINS

LINNET GDNS

FOREST WAY

PHEONIX WAY

Atherton House

SHEEPWAY LA

WHARF LA

THE DROVE

GORDANO RD

Wr Twr

ROYAL PORTBURY DOCK RD

FIRST AVE

GARONOR WAY

GORDANO WAY

Sheepway

SHEEPWAY

Sheepway Gate Farm

Elm Tree Farm

ELM TREE PK

BS20

PORTBURY WAY

HANYARD RD

BRADLEY RD

Drove Rhyne

ROYAL PORTBURY DOCK RD

(dis)

Cole Acre

STATION RD

A369

M5

19

Gordano Service area

THE PORTBURY HUNDRED

Priory Farm Trad Est

The Priory (remains of)

PRIORY RD

STATION RD

PH

PRIORY WLK

PRIORY RD

Portbury

CHURCH LA

HIGH ST

St Mary's Prim Sch

MARTCOMBE RD

A369

Longlands Wood

Conygar Hill

HILLSIDE

FORGE END

BRISTOL PL

MILL CL

Bulling's Wood

The Mount

Upper Caswell Farm

CASWELL LA

Caswell Cross

Lower Caswell House

CASWELL HILL

Rifle Range

FAILAND LA

Honor Farm

COOMBE LA

Prior's Wood

CHARLTON DR

PORTBURY LA

Oakham Farm

BS48

Birch Wood

Budding's Wood

BS8

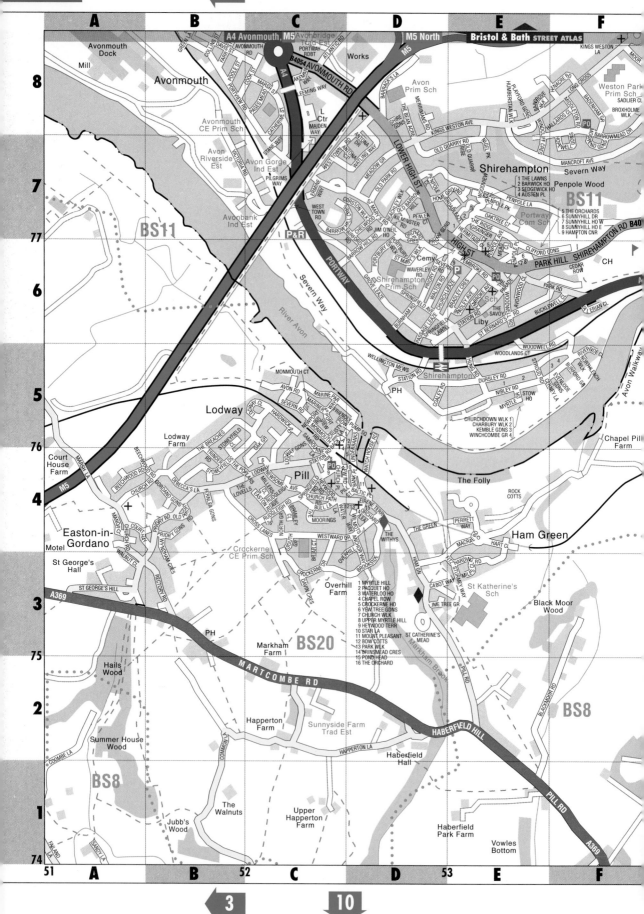

A B C D E F

A4 Avonmouth, M5
M5 North

Avonmouth Dock

Mill

Avonmouth

KINGS WESTON LA

Weston Park Prim Sch
SADLIER CL
BROXHOLME WLK

8

Avonmouth CE Prim Sch

Avon Prim Sch

Works

Shirehampton

Severn Way
Penpole Wood

BS11

Avon Gorge Ind Est

PILGRIMS WAY

Avon Riverside Est

Avonbank Ind Est

7

WEST TOWN RD

HIGH ST

Portway Com Sch

1 THE LAWNS
2 BARWICK HO
3 SEDGEWICK HO
4 AUSTEN PL
5 THE ORCHARDS
6 SUNNYHILL DR
7 SUNNYHILL HO W
8 SUNNYHILL HO E
9 HAMPTON CNR

77

P&R

PARK HILL SHIREHAMPTON RD B40

CH

Cemy

BS11

Shirehampton Prim Sch

PORTWAY

Severn Way

River Avon

6

Liby

MONMOUTH CT

Shirehampton

WOODWELL RD
WOODLANDS CT

RIVERSIDE CL

5

Lodway

MARINE PDE

PH

Avon Walkway

Lodway Farm

Severn Way

STATION RD

CHURCHDOWN WLK 1
CHARBURY WLK 2
KEMBLE GDNS 3
WINCHCOMBE GR 4

76

Court House Farm

THE BREACHES

Pill

The Folly

Chapel Pill Farm

4

M5

Easton-in-Gordano

CHURCH RD

ROCK COTTS

Motel

St George's Hall

Crockerne CE Prim Sch

THE WITHYS

THE GREEN

PERRETT WAY

Ham Green

MACRAE

St George's Hill

Overhill Farm

CABOT WAY

St Katherine's Sch

3

A369

PH

1 MYRTLE HILL
2 PACQUET HO
3 WATERLOO HO
4 CHAPEL ROW
5 CROCKERNE HO
6 YEW TREE GDNS
7 CHURCH WLK
8 UPPER MYRTLE HILL
9 HEYWOOD TERR
10 STAR LA
11 MOUNT PLEASANT
12 BOW COTTS
13 PARK WLK
14 TRINSMEAD CRES
15 POND HEAD
16 THE ORCHARD

St Catherine's Mead

Black Moor Wood

Markham Farm

BS20

75

Hails Wood

MARTCOMBE RD

HABERFIELD HILL

BS8

2

Summer House Wood

COMBE LA

Happerton Farm

Sunnyside Farm Trad Est

Haberfield Hall

HAPPERTON LA

PILL RD

1

The Walnuts

Upper Happerton Farm

Haberfield Park Farm

Jubb's Wood

BS8

Vowles Bottom

A369

74

Bristol & Bath STREET ATLAS

B1
1 CRAWFORD CL
2 SANDFORD CL
3 HEDGES CL
4 SOUTHERN RING PATH
5 LADYCROFT
6 LONGACRE
7 GARSTONS
8 BAKER CL

C1
1 Carey Developments
2 Tweed Rd Ind Est

C2
1 Speedwell Ind Est
2 COLERIDGE VALE RD W
3 WAINS CL
4 HANSON'S WAY
5 CHURCHILL CL
6 COPPACK HO
7 GARLAND HO
8 SHOPLAND HO
9 BRIDGE HO

10 CLIFTON CT

D2
1 COLERIDGE VALE RD E
2 MELBOURNE TERR
3 PENNYWELL EST

E1
1 OTTER RD
2 TIVERTON RD
3 PORLOCK RD
4 PLUMERS CL

F3
1 STREAMSIDE
2 WOODVIEW
3 GREENWAY PK
4 MAYNARD CL
5 HOLLYMAN WLK
6 FRESHMOOR

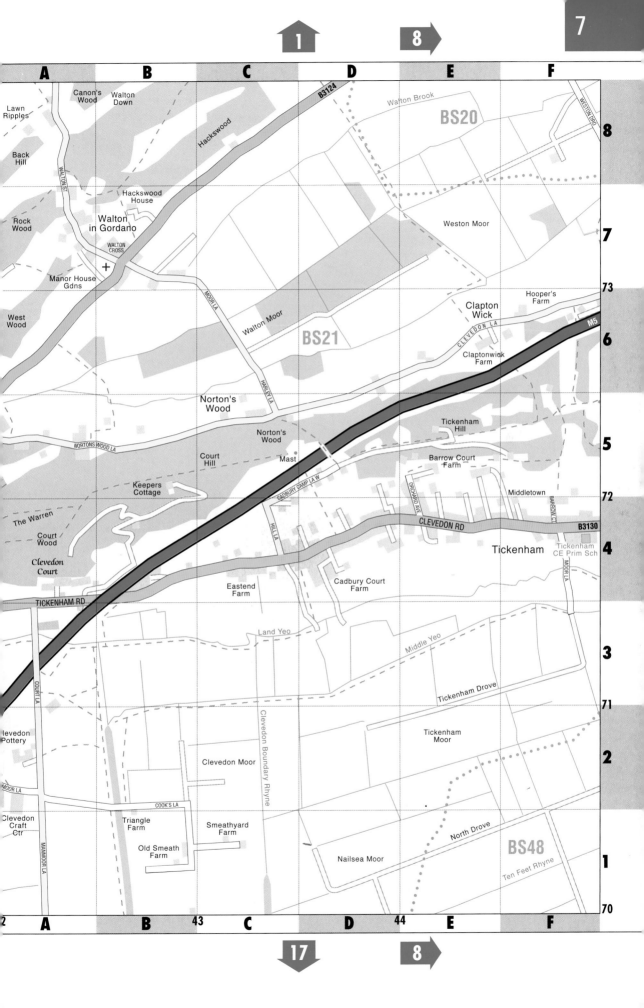

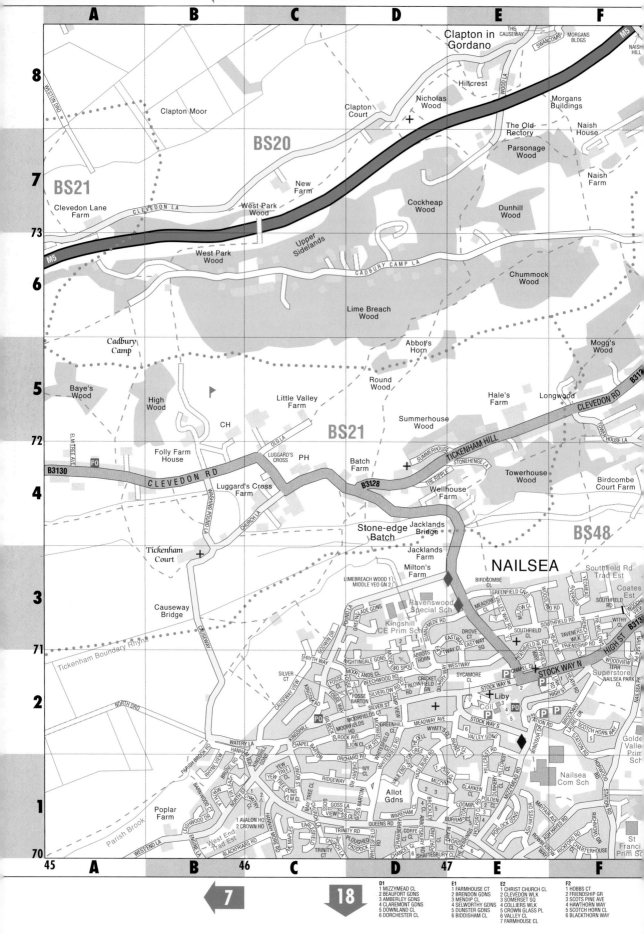

A	B	C	D	E	F

Clapton in Gordano

THE CAUSEWAY

SWANCOMBE

MORGANS BLDGS

NAISH HILL

M5

8

Clapton Moor

Hillcrest

Nicholas Wood

Clapton Court

Morgans Buildings

Naish House

BS20

The Old Rectory

Parsonage Wood

Naish Farm

7

BS21

New Farm

Clevedon Lane Farm

CLEVEDON LA

West Park Wood

Cockheap Wood

Dunhill Wood

73

M5

West Park Wood

Upper Sidelands

CADBURY CAMP LA

Chummock Wood

6

Lime Breach Wood

Abbot's Horn

Mogg's Wood

Cadbury Camp

Round Wood

5

Baye's Wood

High Wood

Little Valley Farm

Summerhouse Wood

Hale's Farm

Longwood

CLEVEDON RD

B312

72

CH

OLD LA

SUMMERHOUSE

TICKENHAM HILL

TOWER HOUSE LA

BS21

ELM TREE AVE

Folly Farm House

Luggard's Cross

PH

Batch Farm

STONEHENGE LA

Towerhouse Wood

Birdcombe Court Farm

B3130

PO

CLEVEDON RD

Luggard's Cross Farm

WASHING POUND LA

CHURCH LA

B3128

THE RIPPLE

Wellhouse Farm

4

Tickenham Court

Stone-edge Batch

Jacklands Bridge

BS48

Jacklands Farm

Milton's Farm

NAILSEA

Southfield Rd Trad Est

Coates Est

3

Causeway Bridge

CAUSEWAY

LIMEBREACH WOOD 1 MIDDLE YEO GN 2

Ravenswood Special Sch

BIRDCOMBE CL

BIRDCOMBE CL

GREENFIELD CRES

MEADOW CL

WOODLAND RD

SOUTHFIELD RD

B3130

71

Tickenham Boundary Rhyne

Kingshill CE Prim Sch

ABBOTS HORN

DROVE

SOUTHFIELD RD

HIGH ST

P

Stock Way N

P

Superstore NAILSEA PARK

2

NORTH DRO

SILVER CT

Cricket Fld

SYCAMORE CL

Liby

Coll

P

PO

P

P

Golde Valle Prim Sch

1

Poplar Farm

WATERY LA

Rock Ave

Allot Gdns

Nailsea Com Sch

St Franci Prim

70

Parish Brook

WESTEND LA

West End Trad Est

BLACKFRIARS RD

TRINITY RD

Queens Rd

70

45	A	B	46	C	D	47	E	F

D1	E1	E2	F2
1 MIZZYMEAD CL	1 FARMHOUSE CT	1 CHRIST CHURCH CL	1 HOBBS CT
2 BEAUFORT GDNS	2 BRENDON GDNS	2 CLEVEDON WLK	2 FRIENDSHIP GR
3 AMBERLEY GDNS	3 MENDIP CL	3 SOMERSET SQ	3 SCOTS PINE AVE
4 CLAREMONT GDNS	4 SELWORTHY GDNS	4 COLLIERS WLK	4 HAWTHORN WAY
5 DOWNLAND CL	5 DUNSTER GDNS	5 CROWN GLASS PL	5 SCOTCH HORN CL
6 DORCHESTER CL	6 BIDDISHAM CL	6 VALLEY CL	6 BLACKTHORN WAY
		7 FARMHOUSE CL	

A B C D E F

8

7

73

6

5

72

4

3

71

2

70

1

Naish Hill

BS20

CASWELL HILL

Bullock's Bottom

Charlton Farm

The Downs Sch

The Cleaves

CHARLTON DR

Windmill Hill

BS20

Old Hill

Racecourse Farm

BS8

Moat House Farm

Breach Wood

PORTBURY LA

New Forest

CADBURY CAMP LA

WHITE HOUSE LA

CUCKOO LA

Moat Cottages

White House

Barn Plantation

The Horse Race

The Ripple

CLEVEDON RD

Higher Farm

Limekiln Cottages

Limekiln Plantation

WEST HILL

West Hill

The Warren

Court Farm

WRAXALL HILL

Sidelands Cottages

Works

BS48

Wraxall Court

The Sidelands

B3128

STONEY STEEP

Rectory

TOWER HOUSE LA

HAM LA

Ham Farm

CLEVEDON RD

Wraxall CE Prim Sch

Home Farm

Tyntesfield

Wraxall House

Cradle Bridge

Wraxall

THE GROVE

BRISTOL RD

PH

FRYTH HO

NORTHAMPTON HO

Truckle Wood

Tyntesfield Park

ynes d Est

Hazel Farm

St John's House

Holly Cottage

Lower Lodge

Gable Farm

CLEVEDON RD

B3130

HOLLY LA

LODGE LA

FOWLES CL

SAWYERS CL

THE HAMLET

THE CHESTNUT CHASE

ELM LODGE RD

CLARK CL RD

MAYFLOWER GDNS

BLACKTHORN WAY

BRIAR CL

ELM FARM

RECTORY CL

CEDAR WAY

LARCH CL

SPINDLEBERRY

BIRCHDENE

THE OAKS

THE BIRCHES

CERNEY GDNS

COATES RD

CHURCH VIEW

CLEEVE PL

WATERCRESS CL

GLASTONBURY CL

WELLS CL

BELL PIT BROW

SCHOOL VIEW

Orchard Farm

Watercress Farm

Brook Farm

BACKWELL BOW

Land Yeo

Watercress Wood

Bathing Pond Wood

East End

1 KEMBLE CL
2 WOODFORD CL
3 SHERSTON CL
4 CRICKLADE CT
5 SUNNINGDALE CL
6 GLENEAGLES CL
7 ST ANDREWS CL
8 NOWHERE LA
9 CHELVEY RISE

SHETLAND WAY

ST AGNES CL

ST IVES RD

TRURO RD

FALMOUTH CL

IDLIP CL

CASEY GR

CAVERSHAM DR

BENDLEWOOD RD

WHITLEY CL

PETRIVEL GDNS

49 C 50 E F

A **B** **C** **D** **E** **F**

8

BS20

Lower Failand Farm

Leigh Wood

Poundbatch Farm

DENNYVIEW RD

PILL RD A3

HARRIS L

FALAND LA

SANDY LA

Lower Failand

Jubbs Court

Home Farm

Mulberry Farm

Old Park

KNIGHTCOT RD

GLEN AVE

Old Park Wood

MANOR LA

7

Failand Court

Failand Court

Three Cornered Wood

Old Park House

Glen Farm

MARKHAM BROOK

SANDY LA

West Tanpit Wood

East Tanpit Wood

Fish Pond Wood

MANOR RD

73

BS8

Scutché's Plantation

Yew Tree Plantation

6

Failand Hill House

Durbans Batch

HORSE RACE LA

OXHOUSE LA

Ox House Bottom

Ferney Row

Failand Farm

Orchard Lodge

Round Hill Clump

Failand Hill Farm

5

Failand Lodge Farm

Manor Farm

Fifty Acre Wood

WEIR LA

72

B3128

PH

Works

PO

CLEVEDON RD

GREEN LA

BEGGAR BUSH LA

CH

B31

4

JUBILEE RD

WOODLAND WAY

WOODLAND RD

FLAX BOURTON RD

BOWDEN WAY

SIXTY ACRES CT

OLD CHELSEA LA

MANOR WAY

HILL DR

Wraxall Piece

North Longwood

LONGWOOD HO

Long Wood

Redwood Lodge Hotel & Country Club

Durnford Quarry

LONGWOOD LA

3

Tyntesfield Plantation

Belmont Combe

BELMONT DR

BIRCHWOOD DR

WESTON RD

Failand Lawn

Failand

Round Plantation

CH

CLARKEN COOME

B31

MONARCH'S WAY

Clifton Lodge

P

71

Iron Plantation

MINERS CL

PROVIDENCE LA

2

Belmont House

Mon

BELMONT HILL

Ashton Hill Plantation

The Brake

BS41

Fenn's Wood

PROVIDENCE RISE

CHERRY RD

ORCHARD HILL

WILLOW CL

KEEDWELL HILL

CEDAR CL

SHORT

1

BS48

CLEVEDON RD

B3130

B3129

Belmont Farm

Belmont Lodge

Kingcot Farm

Cook's Wood

George's Hill Plantation

Shipley Brake

LOVELINCH GDNS 1
BRADVILLE GDNS 2
RAYMORE RISE 3
HOLDERS WLK 4
ELMHURST GDNS 5

FENSWOOD CT

FENSWOOD MEAD

FENSWOOD CL

RAVENS CROSS RD

RAVENS CL

PO

Liby

70

Rudge Farm

Land Yeo

WARREN LA

FENN'S LA

KINGS CR

ARCH CL

WESTON RD

BIRDWELL RD

BIRDWELL LA

IRONGROVE

YEOMEADS

LAMPTON RD

51 **A** **B** **52** **C** **D** **53** **E** **F**

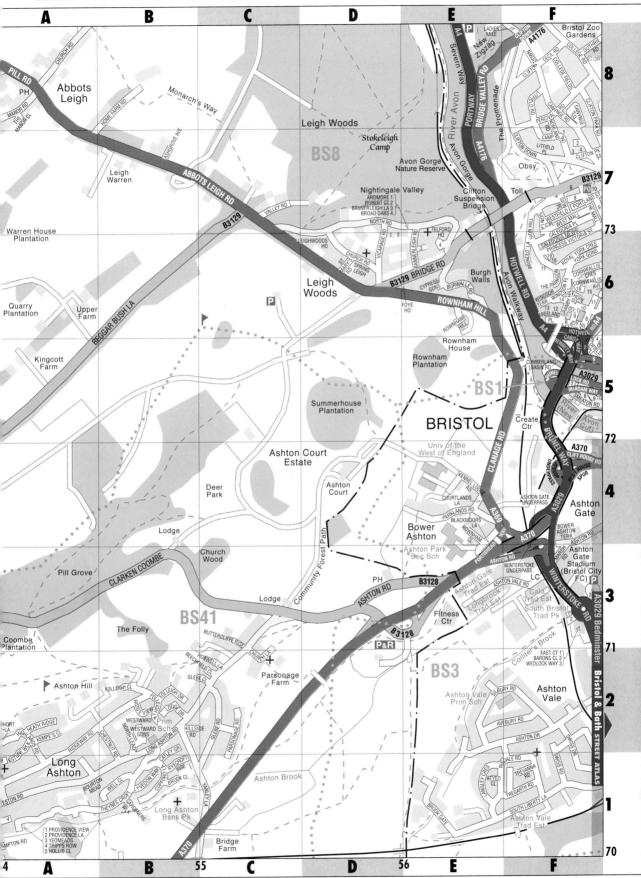

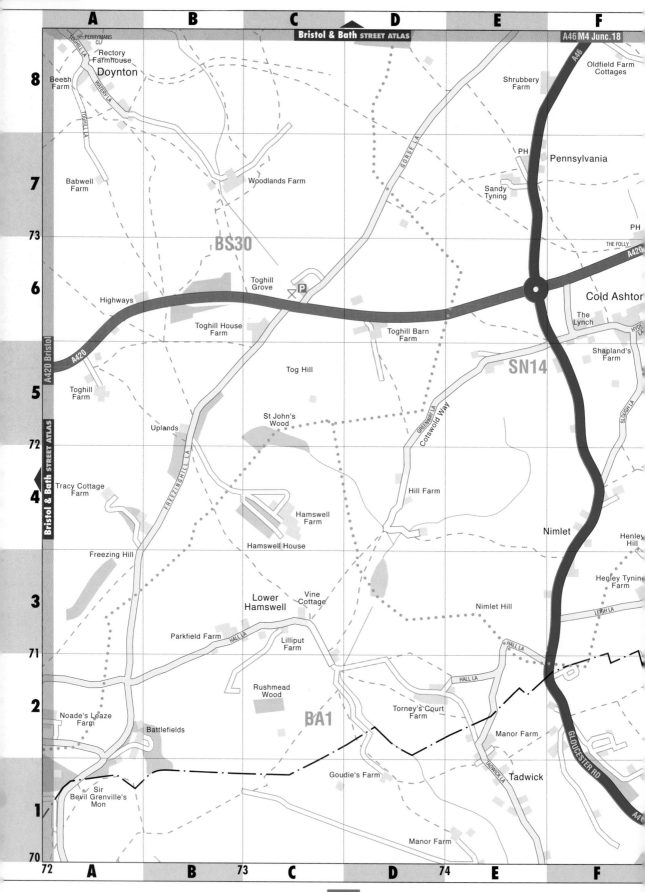

A46 **M4 Junc.18**

Bristol & Bath STREET ATLAS

PERRYMANS CL
Rectory Farmhouse
Doynton
Beech Farm
TOGHILL LA
WATER LA
TOGHILL LA

Oldfield Farm Cottages
Shrubbery Farm
A46
PH
Pennsylvania
Sandy Tyning
PH
THE FOLLY

Babwell Farm
Woodlands Farm

BS30

GORSE LA

A420

Toghill Grove
P

Highways
Toghill House Farm

Toghill Barn Farm

A420 Bristol
Toghill Farm

Tog Hill

Cold Ashton
The Lynch
HYDE LA
Shapland's Farm
SN14

Bristol & Bath STREET ATLAS

72

Uplands

St John's Wood

FREEZINGHILL LA

GREENWAY LA
Cotswold Way

Tracy Cottage Farm

4

Hamswell Farm

Hamswell House

Hill Farm

SLOUGH LA

Nimlet

Henley Hill

Freezing Hill

Henley Tyning Farm

3

Lower Hamswell
Vine Cottage

Nimlet Hill

LEIGH LA

Parkfield Farm
HALL LA
Lilliput Farm

71

HALL LA
HALL LA

Rushmead Wood

BA1

Torney's Court Farm

Noade's Leaze Farm

Battlefields

Manor Farm
GLOUCESTER RD

TADWICK LA

Goudie's Farm

Tadwick

Sir Bevil Grenville's Mon

A46

Manor Farm

27

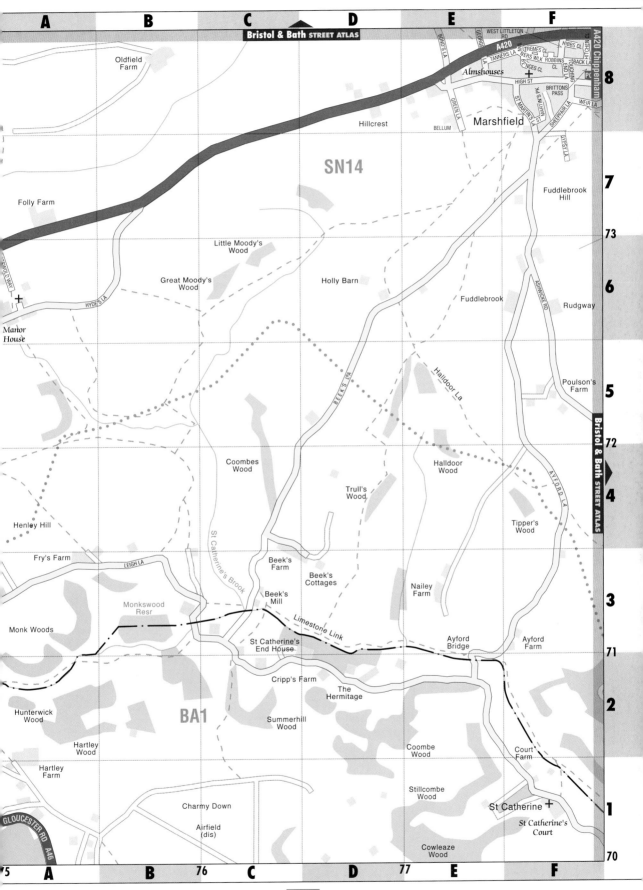

Bristol & Bath STREET ATLAS

A B C D E F

8

Oldfield Farm

WEST LITTLETON RD
GEORGE
BOND'S LA
HIBBS CL
NICHOL
A420
A420 Chippenham
TANNERS LA
TREMES CL
NERS WLK ROBBINS
BACK LA
PO
CL
TOUCHING
END LA
PRINCES CL
Almshouses
HIGH ST
BRITTONS
PASS
ST MARTIN'S PK
SHEPPAIR LA
WEIR LA
BELLUM

Hillcrest
Marshfield
GREEN LA
ST MARTIN'S LA
GYPSY LA

Folly Farm

SN14

7

Fuddlebrook Hill

73

Little Moody's Wood

6

Great Moody's Wood
Holly Barn
Fuddlebrook
Rudgway

HYDE'S LA
ASHWICKE RD

Manor House

Halldoor La

5

BEEK'S LA
Poulson's Farm

72

Coombes Wood
Halldoor Wood

4

Henley Hill
Trull's Wood
AYFORD LA
Tipper's Wood

St Catherine's Brook

LEIGH LA

Fry's Farm
Beek's Farm
Beek's Cottages
Nailey Farm

3

Monkswood Resr
Beek's Mill
Limestone Link

Monk Woods
St Catherine's End House
Ayford Bridge
Ayford Farm

71

Cripp's Farm
The Hermitage

2

Hunterwick Wood
Summerhill Wood

BA1
Coombe Wood

Hartley Wood
Court Farm

Hartley Farm
Stillcombe Wood
St Catherine

1

GLOUCESTER RD A46
Charmy Down
St Catherine's Court

Airfield (dis)
Cowleaze Wood

70

75 A B 76 C D 77 E F

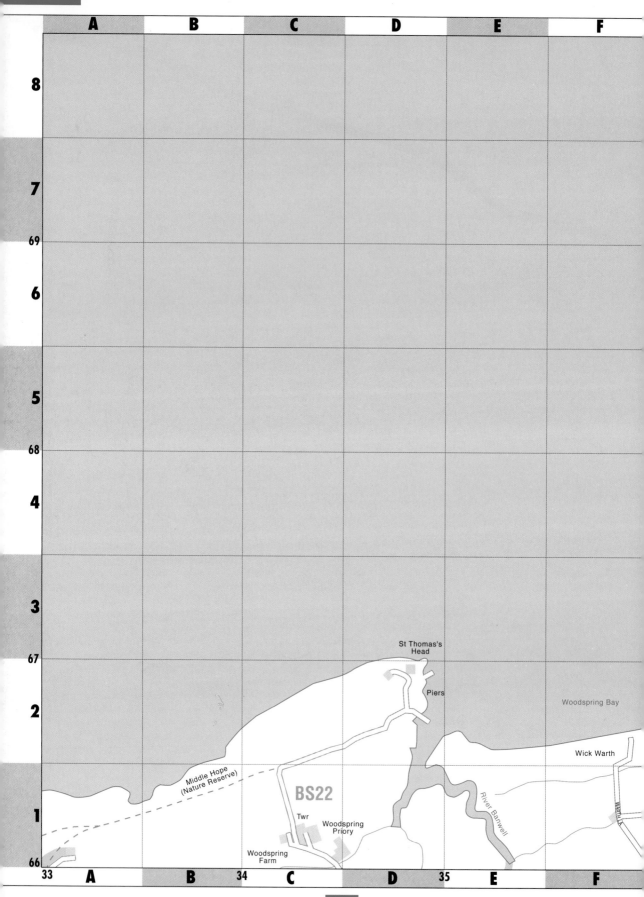

St Thomas's Head

Piers

Woodspring Bay

Wick Warth

Middle Hope
(Nature Reserve)

BS22

River Banwell

WARTH A

Twr

Woodspring
Priory

Woodspring
Farm

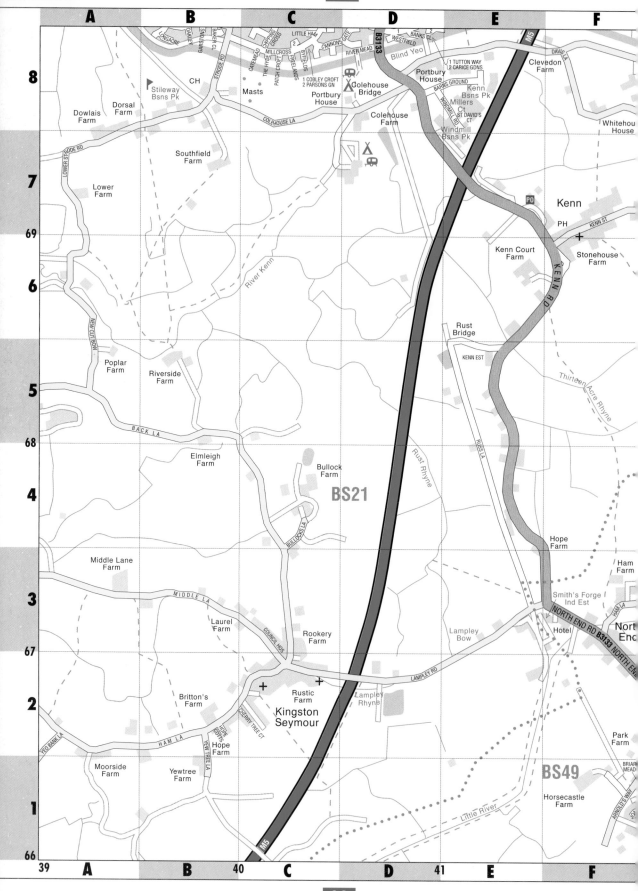

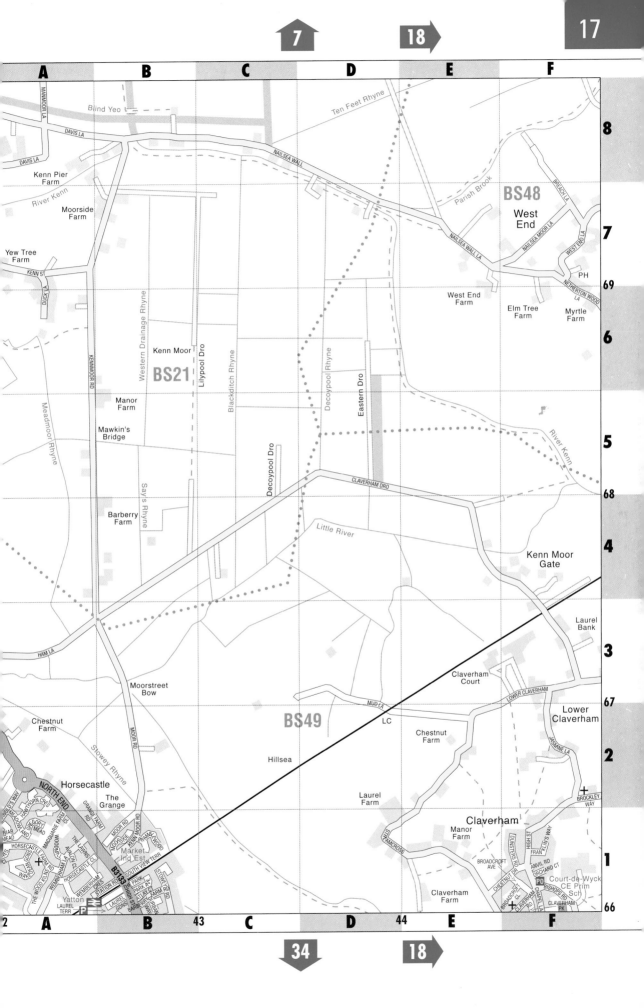

17
8

A **B** **C** **D** **E** **F**

8

BLACKFRIARS RD

Coombe
Farm

West
End

WEST END LA

THE BRAMLEYS

ENGINE LA

Nursebatch
Farm

KINGSTON WAY

NEWTON GN

KINGSTON DR

HANNAH MORE RD

ST MARY'S

THE CHIMES

WORCESTER
GDNS

ALLINGTON GDNS

BLACKLEY TER

FERN GR

RUSSETT GR

ST MARY'S GR

THE UPLANDS

CHURCH LA

OLD CHURCH RD

MORGANS HILL CL

Hannah More
Inf Sch
Grove
Jun Sch

WHITEOAK WAY

HARPTREE CT

MINSTER CL

SHAFTESBURY CL

HASLANDS

1 WHITESFIELD RD
2 CHANCEL CL
3 STRAWBERRY GDNS
4 DORCHESTER CL

White Oak
House

SEDGEMOOR RD

BECKETS LA

WEYMERE

QUEENS WAY

WALNUT CL

BROOK FARM CT

THE PERRINGS

FOUR ACRES CL

EARLER'S END

WOOKEY CL

BUCKLANDS LA

MENDIP CL

CHEDDAR CL

TRENDLEW AY

STATION RD

AVENING

1 LANGPORT GDNS
2 CHURCH HAYES DR
3 CHURCH HAYES CL
4 DINDER CL
5 ASH HAYES RD
6 LITTLE MEADOW END
7 RICKFORD RD
8 BRUTON

BUCKLANDS DR

BUCKLANDS END

BUCKLANDS LA CE

BUCKLANDS GR

NAILSEA

P

7

West
End

Young Wood
Farm

Coombe
Grange

Nailsea
and Backwell

STATION CL

STATION RD

THE BRIARS

69

Bizley
Farm

YOUNGWOOD LA

MOORFIELD RD

Backwell

MOOR LA

PARKSTONE AV

LONG CL

LUNTY
MEAD

6

Baytree
Farm

South Common
Farm

NETHERTON WOOD LA

5

Netherton
Wood

Nailsea
Ford

Chelvey

CHELVEY RD

Grove
Farm

West
Town

Nailsea
Court

BS48

Burnt House
Farm

WEST TOWN RD

THE

68

Midgell
Farm

Brickyard
Wood

KELLWAYS

A370

4

BROCKLEY LA

CHELVEY LA

3

LOWER CLAVERHAM

BROCKLEY WAY

Brockley
Elm

Brockley Elm
Farm

Manor
Farm

CHELVEY BATCH

Tap's Combe

67

Grove
Farm

Claverham Green
Farm

Brockley
Court

Brockley
Hall

BS49

LITTLEWOOD LA

2

ST NICHOLAS WAY

Brockley

Yorkhouse
Cave

MEETINGHOUSE LA

Cleeve House
Farm

PO

MAIN RD

BROCKLEY COMBE RD

Brockley Combe

Brockley
Wood

1

A370

Cleeve
Hill

66

45 **A** **B** **46** **C** **D** **47** **E** **F**

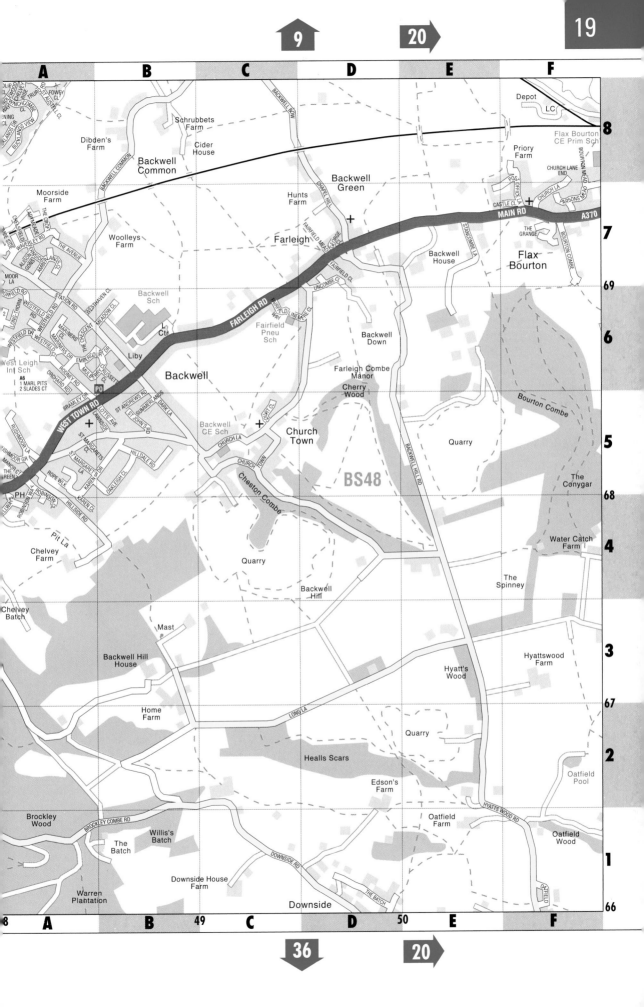

19
10

A B C D E F

8

B3130

Kingcott Mill
Farm

KINGCOTT MILL
FARM CVNS
1 MORGAN PL
2 FARLEIGH CT

Cambridge
Batch

Gatcombe
Court

Ashton
Watering

CLEVEDON RD

Long Ashton
Research Station

FENSHURST GDNS

BRADVILLE GDNS 1
RAYMORE RISE 2
HOLDERS WLK 3
ELMHURST GDNS 4

BS41

STATION RD

ORCHARD CL

HEAD CROFT

ROSEMOUNT RD

Ct

OLD WESTON RD

1
2

WESTON RD

REDWOOD LA

WARREN LA

MONARCH'S WAY

7

PH

A370 MAIN RD

Eastfield

B3130

REDWOOD LA

Redwood
Farm

A37

69

Breach Hill
Wood

Crossgrove
Wood

WILDCOUNTRY LA

Barrow
The Fillies

Barrow
Wood

6

VICARAGE LA

Hillside

Barrow
Mill

Church
Wood

The
Vicarage

Farleigh
Hill

School
Farm

BARROW COURT LA

5

The Triangle

BARROW
CT

BS48

BARROW ST

Barrow
Gurney

HERN LA

Home
Farm

Dead Hill
Wood

SCHOOL LA

Water
Works

68

Park
Cottages

Slade
Wood

BARNS CL

Steps Farm

SLADE LA

HOBBS LA

B3130

A38

4

Batches
Wood

Stevens'
Farm

Resrs

Barrow
Hill

Hill
Farm

Stevens'
Wood

3

Mon

67

Freeman's
Farm

NAISH LA

B3130

2

FREEMANS LA

BRIDGWATER RD

Dial
Farm

PH

Glenville House
Farm

BARROW LA

Elwell Brook

Yewtree
Farm

DIAL LA

1

PH

HILL VIEW
CVN PK

Potters
Hill

NEWDITCH LA

ROCKS LA

Hartcliff
Rocks

ELWELL LA

BS40

B3130

66

A38

CURRELLS LA

A B C D E F
51 52 53

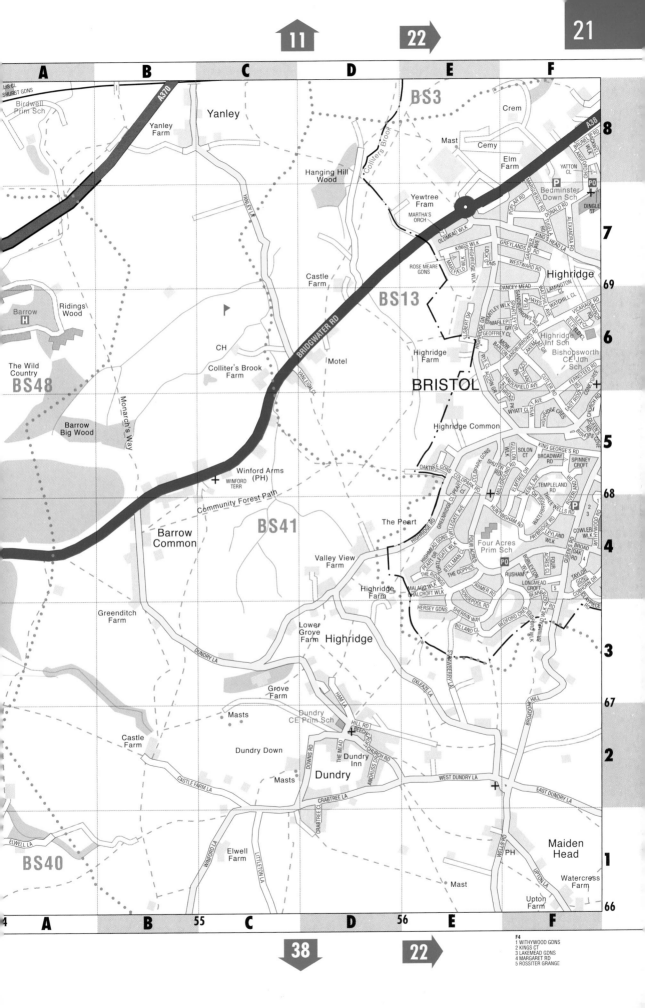

BS3

Crem

Mast

Cemy

Elm
Farm

LHS CL
SHURST GDNS
Birdwell
Prim Sch

A370

Yanley

Yanley
Farm

Hanging Hill
Wood

Colliters Brook

Yewtree
Fram

MARTHA'S
ORCH

YATTON
CL

BRUNEL RD
BRUNEL WLK
LANGFORD RD

A38

P
Bedminster
Down Sch

PO

DINGLE
CT

Castle
Farm

OLDMEAD WLK

KINGS WLK

KINGS HEAD LA

POP. AF RD

DONALD RD

ALEXANDRA RD

TUGELA RD

Highridge

BS13

ROSE MEARE
GDNS

GREYLANDS
RD

WESTWARD RD

GARDNER
RD

DANCEY MEAD

69

BRISTOL

Barrow
Wood

Ridings
Wood

H

BS48

The Wild
Country

CH

Colliter's Brook
Farm

Motel

BRIDGWATER RD

YANLEIGH CL

YANLEY LA

Highridge
Farm

Highridge
Inf Sch

Bishopsworth
CE Jun
Sch

7

6

Barrow
Big Wood

Monarch's Way

Winford Arms
(PH)
WINFORD
TERR

Community Forest Path

BS41

The Peart

Highridge Common

Four Acres
Prim Sch

5

68

Greenditch
Farm

Valley View
Farm

Highridge
Farm

Lower
Grove
Farm

Highridge

OXLEAZE LA

STRAWBERRY LA

Four Acres
PO

4

3

67

Greenditch
Farm

Grove
Farm

HAM LA

Dundry
CE Prim Sch

HILL RD

DOWNS RD

CHURCH RD

BEECH

WEST DUNDRY LA

EAST DUNDRY LA

2

Castle
Farm

Dundry Down

Masts

Masts

Dundry
Inn

Dundry

ANDRUSS D

THE MEAD

BS40

ELWELL LA

WINFORD LA

Elwell
Farm

LITTLETON LA

CRABTREE LA

CASTLE FARM LA

CRABTREE CL

WELLS RD

BROADOAK HILL

PH

UPTON LA

Maiden
Head

Watercress
Farm

Mast

Upton
Farm

1

66

F4
1 WITHYWOOD GDNS
2 KINGS CT
3 LAKEMEAD GDNS
4 MARGARET RD
5 ROSSITER GRANGE

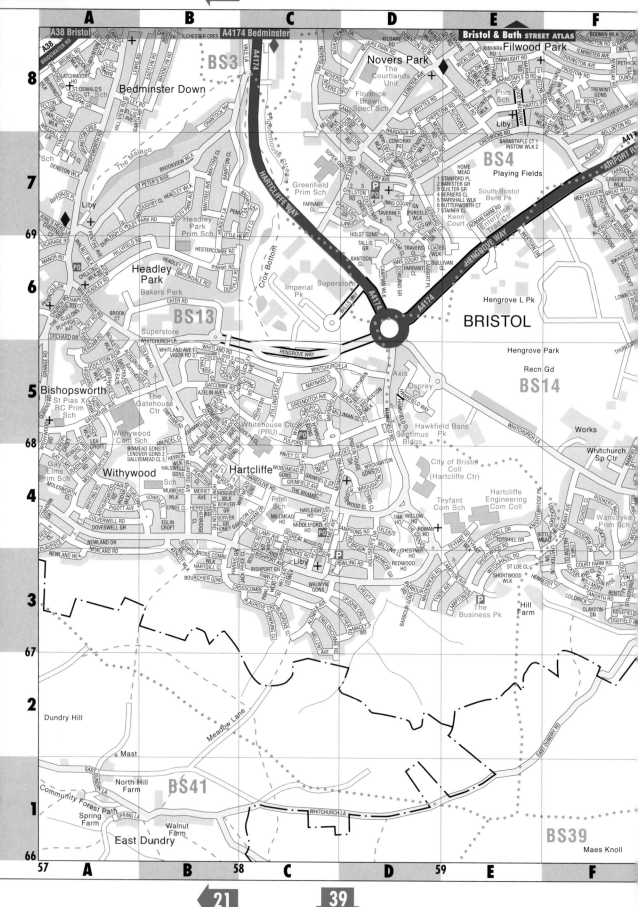

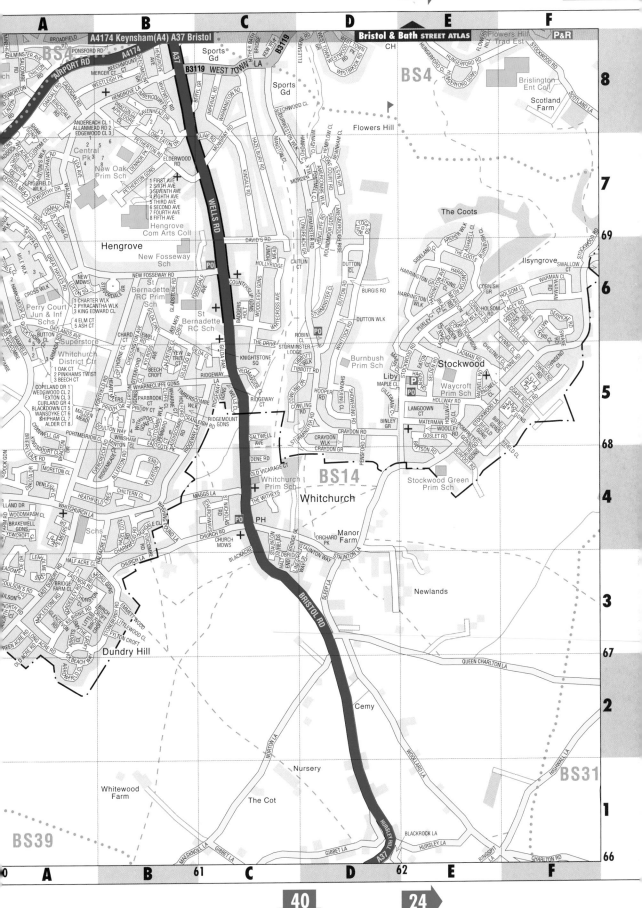

A   **B**   **C**   **D**   **E**   **F**

A4 Bristol

A4174 Bristol Northern Ring Road

Bristol & Bath STREET ATLAS

BS4

Hicks Gate

BS15

BS30

Keysham Hams

8

Avon Walk Way

River Avon

Scotland Bottom

Factory

Somerdale

IRON MOULD LA

A4

BATH RD

DURLEY HILL

A4175

KEYNSHAM BY-PASS

7

Oaklease Farm

Durleypark

Cemy

DURLEY HILL

Recn Gd

69

CH

Stockwood Vale

STOCKWOOD VALE

STOCKWOOD HILL

BRISTOL RD

STATION RD

KEYNSHAM RD

Keynsham

6

BS14

Wood Covert

Charlton Bottom

Sports Ctr

Broadlands Sch

BROADLANDS AVE

The Park

HIGH ST

BATH HILL

Temple/ Prim Sch

The Central Lby

Dragons

BS31

Broadlands House

Wheathill

St Francis Rd

St Margaret's Rd

St Anne's Ave

Cranmore Ave

St Dunstans Cl

Milward Rd

Culvers Rd

St Marks

The Regents

Dragons Ln

5

Heathfield Cl

Westfield Cl

Downfield Cl

Orchard Cl

St George's Rd

Park Cl

St Patricks Ct

Handel Rd

Hawthorns La

Rock Rd

Carpenters La

Temple

River Terr

L Ctr

Fox & Hounds La

BATH RD

B31

Homeavon Ho

Keynsham Prim Sch

Chepstow Walk

St John's CE Prim Sch

Sherwood Rd

St Cadoc Ho

Temple Inf Sch

68

Lays Bsns Ctr

Lays Farm

Monmouth Rd

Arundel Rd

Tintagel Cl

Queens Rd

Albert Rd

Stirling Way

Victoria Ho

Edward Ct

Keynsham

Rockhill Est

4

Box Wlk

Walnut Wlk

Pine Ct

Elm Ct

Firs Ct

Wlk Wallow

Berkeley Gdns

Princess

Windsor Rd

Edinburgh

Amberley Rd

Compton

Chelmer Gr

Chandag Rd

Longmeadow Rd

Lilac Ct

Lime Ct

Birch

Acacia

Cherry

Maple Wlk

Coronation Ave

Castle Prim Sch

Newlands Rd

Dunster Rd

KEYNSHAM

Holmoak Rd

Horbeam Wlk

Laburnum Wlk

May Tree Wlk

Cedar Wlk

Oak Tree Wlk

The Brambles

St Clements Ct

Community Forest Path

River Chew

WELLSWAY

3

Queen Charlton

Parkhouse Farm

Parkhouse La

BS31

Chewton Place

COURTENAY RD

67

Manor Farm

QUEEN CHARLTON LA

Wellfield House

Manor Farm

Chewton Keynsham

2

HIGHWALL LA

PARKHOUSE LA

REDLYNCH LA

1

DAPWELL LA

Poplars Cottage

Warners Farm

Harvey's Ditch

66

63   **A**   **B**   **64**   **C**   **D**   **65**   **E**   **F**

Charlton Field

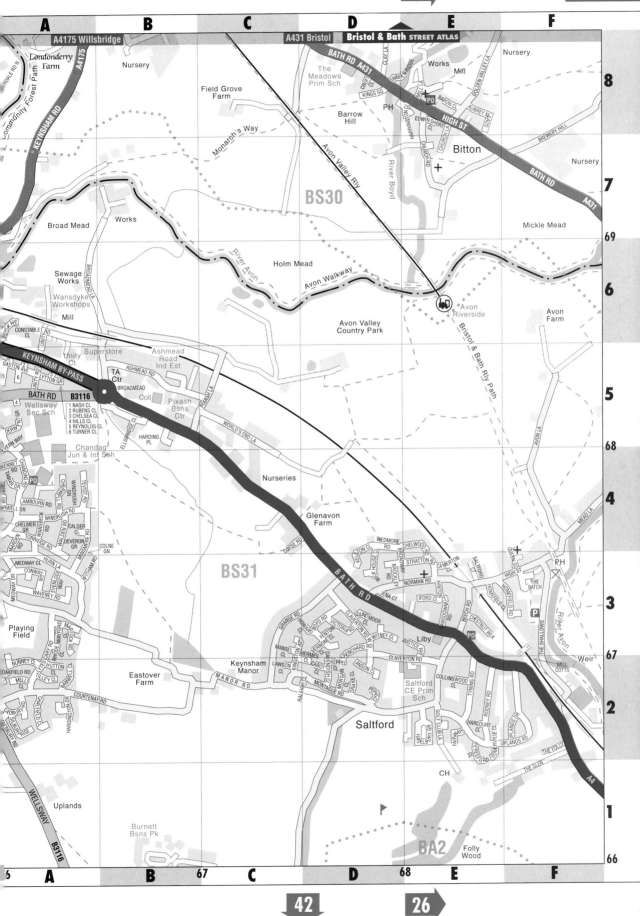

26

Bristol & Bath STREET ATLAS

A4175 Willsbridge

A431 Bristol

BATH RD A431

Londonderry Farm

Community Forest Path

KEYNSHAM RD

Nursery

Field Grove Farm

Monarch's Way

The Meadows Prim Sch

CLAY LA

KINGS SQ

Works

Mfl

Nursery

GOLDEN VALLEY LA

AUBREY MEADS

BARON CL

PO

EDWIN SHORT CL

HOLSONWORTH

PH

CHURCH RD

HIGH ST

Bitton

Barrow Hill

BREWERY HILL

BATH RD

A31

Nursery

BS30

River Boyd

Avon Valley Rly

Mickle Mead

Broad Mead

Works

River Avon

Holm Mead

Avon Walkway

Avon Riverside

Avon Farm

69

6

Sewage Works

BROADMEAD LA

Wansdyke Workshops

Mill

Avon Valley Country Park

Bristol & Bath Rly Path

CONSTABLE CL

KEYNSHAM BY-PASS

Unity Ct

Superstore

Ashmead RD

Ashmead Road Ind Est

TA Ctr

BROADMEAD

PIXASH LA

BATH RD

B3116

Wellsway Sec Sch

Coll

Pixash Bsns Ctr

1 NASH CL
2 RUBENS CL
3 CHELSEA CL
4 HILLS CL
5 REYNOLDS CL
6 TURNER CL

WORLD'S END LA

5

PO

Chandag Jun & Inf Sch

ELLSBRIDGE CL

HARDING PL

Nurseries

68

4

COLNE GN

BS31

CURSE RD

Glenavon Farm

WEDMORE RD

CHELWOOD RD

BROADWAY

SALTFORD RD

MEAD LA

AVON LA

KELSTON CL

STRATTON CL

CAMERTON CL

QUEEN SQ

HIGH ST

PH

Playing Field

MANOR RD

Keynsham Manor

GRANGE RD

Eastover Farm

Saltford

NORMAN RD

IFORD CL

HINTON CL

BEECH RD

CHESTNUT WLK

HONEFIELD RD

THE BATCH

P

River Avon

THE SHALLOWS

Weir

MILL COTTS

67

Liby

PO

Saltford CE Prim Sch

COLLINGWOOD CL

GOLF CLUB LA

FAIRWAYS

HARCOURT CL

SOMERVILLE CL

UPLANDS RD

THE FOLLY

A4

2

Uplands

Burnett Bsns Pk

CH

THE GLEN

BA2

Folly Wood

1

66

WELLSWAY

B3116

Bristol & Bath STREET ATLAS

BS30

Monarch's Way
PH
Upton Cheyney
Springfield Cotts
WICK LA
BREWRY HILL
LANSDOWN LA
NORTH STOKE LA
Nursery
Pipley Bottom
Congrove Wood
LANSDOWN LA
Brockham End
Further Slate
Pipley Wood
Cotswold Way

8

7
PH
Swineford
A431
North Stoke
Little Down
Mast

69
Weir
Saltford Mead
BATH RD
River Avon
Factory
Prospect Stile
Weston Wood
Foxhall Farm

6

BS31
PH
Sewage Works
Weir
MEAD LA

5

68

BA1
Coombe Barn
Kelston Round Hill
Midridge
BROADMOOR LA

4

BLACKSMITH'S LA
Kelston
PH
Roundhill Barn
Cotswold Way

3

67
Manor Farm
Sandpit Shrubbery
Dean Hill
Dean Hill House
DEANHILL LA
Pendean Farm

2

Tennant's Wood
Bristol & Bath Rly Path
River Avon
Avon Walkway
BA2
KELSTON RD
River Avon
Avon Walkway
Oldfield Girls Sch

1
A4
BATH RD
Kelston Park
A431

66

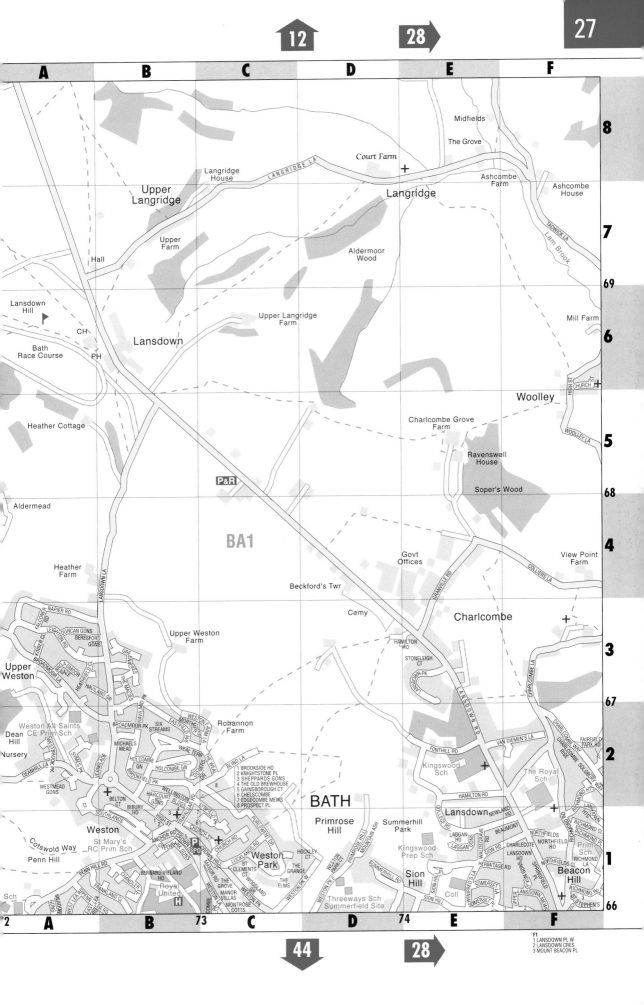

A1
1 MOUNT BEACON ROW
2 BELGRAVE TERR
3 MALVERN VILLAS
4 MALVERN TERR
5 SEYMOUR RD
6 DOVER PL
7 CATHCART HO
8 HIGHBURY COTTS
9 HIGHBURY VILLAS

10 HIGHBURY TERR
11 COBURG VILLAS
12 STANLEY VILLAS
13 CLAREMONT PL
14 EVELYN TERR
15 TYNNING TERR
16 KINGSDOWN VIEW
17 SOLSBURY VIEW
18 COLLEGE VIEW
19 INCHALLOCH

B1
1 BRUNSWICK ST
2 HANOVER ST
3 GILLINGHAM TERR
4 WALMSLEY TERR
5 HANOVER TERR
6 FRANKLEY TERR
7 CHILTON CT
8 BEAUFORT BLDGS
9 GROSVENOR VILLAS

B1
10 ST SAVIOUR'S TERR
11 BEAUFORT W
12 ALEXANDER BLDGS
13 PERCY PL
14 MEZELLION PL
15 LAMBRIDGE MEWS
16 EASTBOURNE AVE
16 VALE VIEW PL
17 BALUSTRADE

C1
1 LAMBRIDGE BLDGS
2 VICTORIA PL
3 BEAUFORT MEWS
4 ST SAVIOURS WAY
5 LAMBRIDGE MEWS
6 LAMBRIDGE
7 LAMONT HO
8 MONTAGUE HO
9 EASTON HO

10 HAMPTON HO
11 BRIDGE HO
C2
1 GARFIELD TERR
2 BROUGHAM PL
3 COTTAGE PL
4 EDEN VILLAS
5 OTAGO TERR
6 LAMBRIDGE GRANGE

SN14

SN14

The Oaks Farm

ROAD HILL

Alcombe Manor

Alcombe

Stoney La

OAKFORD LA

Rodney Farm

Mast

Grubbins Wood

Upper Northend Farm

HOLLIES LA

St Catherine's Brook

Limestone Link

Oldhouse Farm

STEWAY LA

69

Lower Shockerwick Farm

A4 Chippenham

6

Banner Down

Starfall Farm

Shockerwick House

Shockerwick

Sheep Sleight

BANNERDOWN RD

Shockerwick Farm

BROOKSIDE CL

AMBROOK PK

CATHERINE WAY

BA1

The Mount

SHOCKERWICK LA

BATH RD

A4

5

68

Sheylor's Farm

WHITEMORE CT

ELMHURST EST

FOSSE LA

CATHERINE WAY

COALPIT RD

AVON CT

HIGH BANNERDOWN

CLIFF PARK

BANNERDOWN DR

BANNERDOWN CL

WINTERFIELD

Box Bridge

Ashley House

SN13

EDEN PARK DR

BARNFIELD

MORRIS LA

MEADOW PK

EASTWOODS

WORMCLIFF LA

WEST VIEW RD

RIVER TAYLOR

WESTWOODS

MORRIS CL

BOX RD

By Brook

Ashley RD

Kingsdown

LONDON RD E

PH

Mill

Ashley Wood Farm

LOWER KINGSDOWN RD

KINGSDOWN GR

67

A363

BATHFORD HILL

DOVERS LA

TITAN BARROW

PO

NEW RD

GASTON'S RD

Bathampton Farm

PH

CHURCH ST

BATHFORD MANOR

CHAPEL ROW

HIGH ST

Ashley Wood

TYNING RD

LC

CHURCH CL

MANOR RD

DOVERS LA

MOUNTAIN WOOD

PLEASANT PL

PROSPECT PL

River Avon

BRADFORD RD

MOUNTAIN WOOD

DOVERS

BA2

Bathford CE Prim Sch

COURT LA

PUMP LA

Bathford

Limestone Link

Kennet & Avon Canal

Avon Walkway

WARLEIGH LA

Warleigh Lodge

P

BA15

FARLEIGH RISE

HOLCOMBE LA

A363

Brown's Folly

Brown's Folly Nature Reserve

FARLEIGH RISE

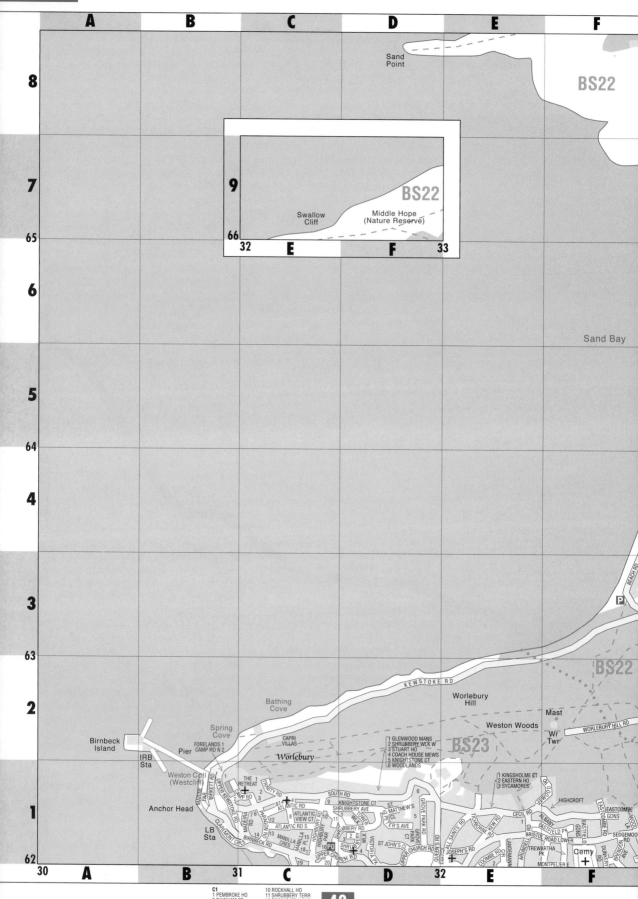

Sand Point

BS22

9

BS22

Swallow Cliff

Middle Hope (Nature Reserve)

66

32 E F 33

Sand Bay

Birnbeck Island

Pier

IRB Sta

Weston Cliff (Westcliff)

Anchor Head

LB Sta

Spring Cove

Bathing Cove

FORELANDS 1
CAMP RD N 2

CAPRI VILLAS

Worlebury

Weston Woods

Worlebury Hill

KEWSTOKE RD

Mast
Wr Twr

WORLEBURY HILL RD

BS23

1 GLENWOOD MANS
2 SHRUBBERY WLK W
3 STUART HO
4 COACH HOUSE MEWS
5 KNIGHTSTONE CT
6 WOODLANDS

1 KINGSHOLME CT
2 EASTERN HO
3 SYCAMORES

HIGHCROFT

THE RETREAT

SOUTH RD
KNIGHTSTONE CT
SHRUBBERY AVE
ST MATTHEW'S

ATLANTIC RD
ATLANTIC VIEW CT
ATLANTIC RD S

GROVE PARK RD
GROVE PARK

CECIL RD

ALBANY

EASTCOMBE RD
EASTCOMBE GDNS

EASTFIELD GDNS

SEDGEMOOR RD

ST JOHN'S CT

UPPER CHURCH RD

ST JOSEPH'S RD

COOMBE RD CIR

TREWARTHA PK

BRISTOL ROAD LOWER

MONTPELIER

Cemy

DUNKERLY RD

62

48

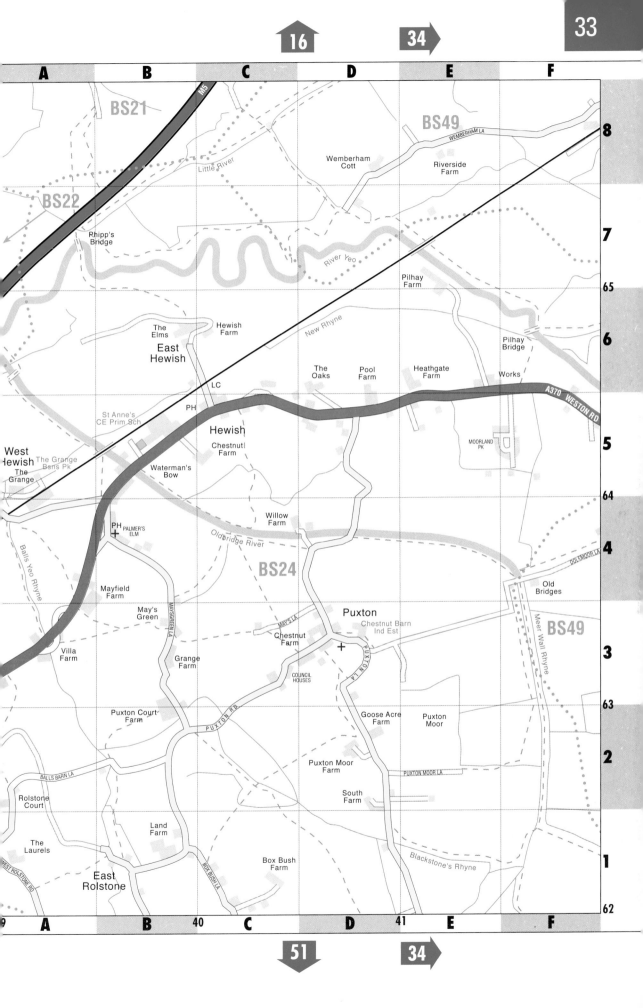

A   B   C   D   E   F

BS21

BS22

M5

Little River

Rhipp's Bridge

River Yeo

BS49

WEMBERHAM LA

Wemberham Cott

Riverside Farm

Pilhay Farm

New Rhyne

Pilhay Bridge

8

7

65

6

The Elms

Hewish Farm

East Hewish

The Oaks

Pool Farm

Heathgate Farm

Works

LC

PH

St Anne's CE Prim Sch

Hewish

Chestnut Farm

Waterman's Bow

A370 WESTON RD

MOORLAND PK

5

West Hewish

The Grange Bsns Pk

The Grange

Willow Farm

64

PH   PALMER'S ELM

Oldbridge River

BS24

DOLEMOOR LA

Old Bridges

4

Balls Yeo Rhyne

Mayfield Farm

May's Green

MAYSGREEN LA

Puxton

Chestnut Barn Ind Est

Meer Wall Rhyne

BS49

3

Villa Farm

Grange Farm

MAY'S LA

Chestnut Farm

PUXTON LA

COUNCIL HOUSES

Puxton Court Farm

PUXTON RD

Goose Acre Farm

Puxton Moor

63

BALLS BARN LA

Puxton Moor Farm

PUXTON MOOR LA

2

Rolstone Court

South Farm

The Laurels

Land Farm

BOX BUSH LA

Box Bush Farm

Blackstone's Rhyne

1

WEST ROLSTONE RD

East Rolstone

62

9   A   B   40   C   D   41   E   F

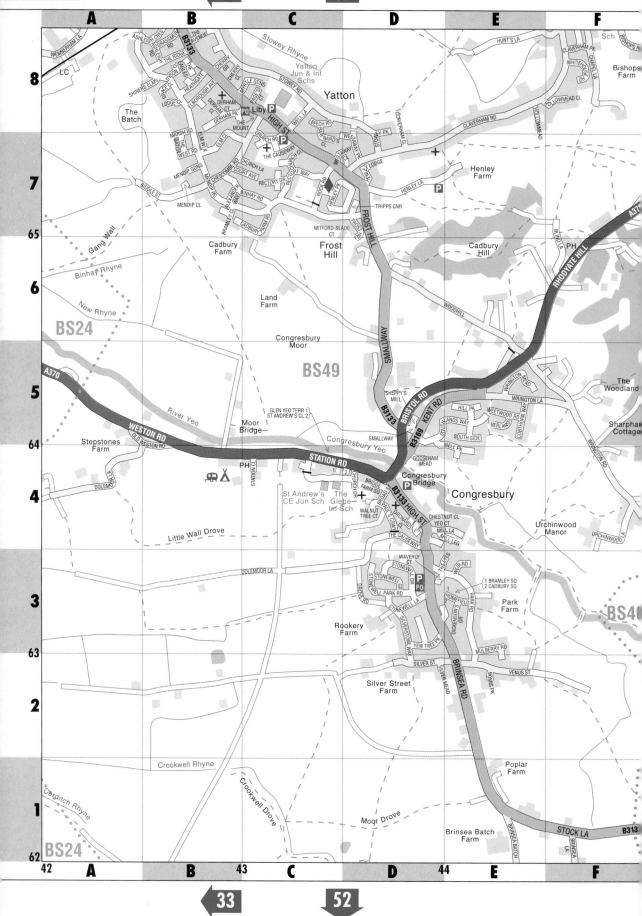

Yatton

The Batch

Frost Hill

Cadbury
Farm

Land
Farm

Congresbury
Moor

BS49

BS24

Gang Wall

Binhay Rhyne

New Rhyne

River Yeo

Stepstones
Farm

Moor
Bridge

Congresbury Yeo

SMALLWAY

STATION RD

St Andrew's
CE Jun Sch

The Glebe
Inf Sch

Little Wall Drove

DOLEMOOR LA

Rookery
Farm

Silver Street
Farm

Crookwell Rhyne

Cardich Rhyne

Crookwell Drove

Moor Drove

BS24

Henley
Farm

Cadbury
Hill

The
Woodland

Sharpham
Cottage

Congresbury
Bridge

Congresbury

Urchinwood
Manor

Park
Farm

BS49

Poplar
Farm

Brinsea Batch
Farm

STOCK LA

BS313

|  A | B | C | D | E | F |

8

Downsi Farm

Cook's Farm

Lulsgate Farm

DOWNSIDE RD

HYATTS WOOD RD

Stone Farm

CH

P

BS48

NORTH SIDE RD

COOKS BRIDLE PATH

Wrington Warren

7

North Hill

Bristol International Airport

65

6

WINTER LA

Cornerpool Farm

A38

Spying Copse

Goblin Combe Farm

Cornerpool Cottage

Broadfield Farm

High Wood

5

Pine Farm

64

Hailstones Farm

NEW RD

ASHFORD RD

Meeting House Farm

Cottage Farm

ROW OF ASHES LA

4

BS40

Worship Farm

Water Catches

Little Horts Wood

Burnt House Farm

Redhill

Tucker's Grove

REDCROFT

REDACRE

Horts Wood

CHURCH CT

CHURCH RD

Scars Wood

Whitley Coppice

THE POUND

PH

Scars Farm

3

CHANCELLORS POUND

63

LONG LA

Chancellor's Farm

LYE HOLE LA

Bottenham Coppice

2

RED HILL

Redhill House

Lye Hole

PUMP LA

Lyehole Farm

UNDER LA

Lye Cross

LYE CROSS RD

PIGEON

1

Pigeon House Farm

SUTTON LA

A38

Lye Cross Farm

CRIBB'S LA

62

| 48 | A | 49 | B | C | 50 | D | E | F |

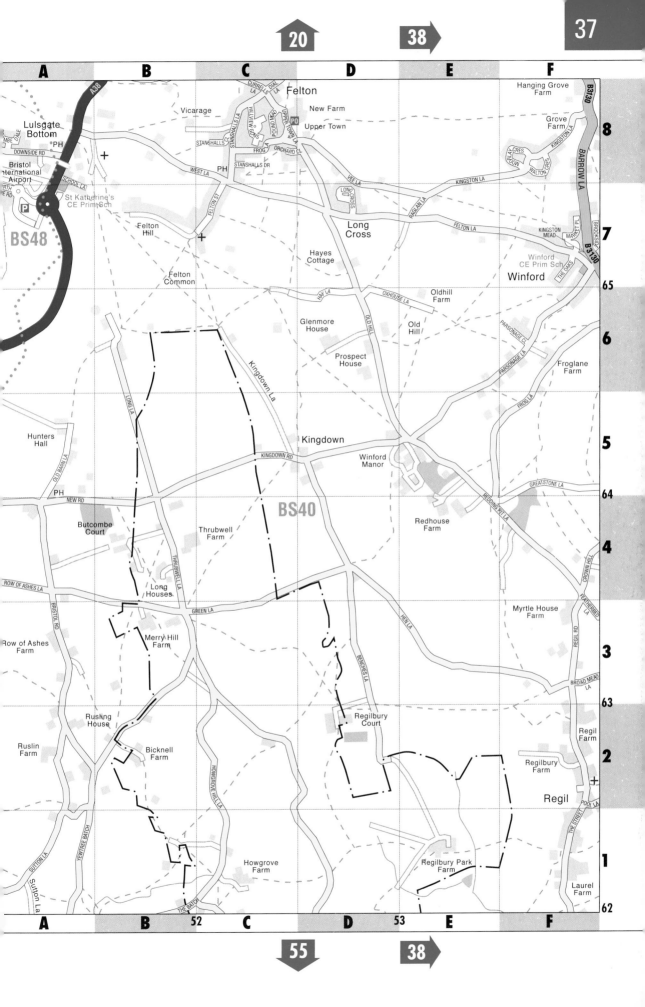

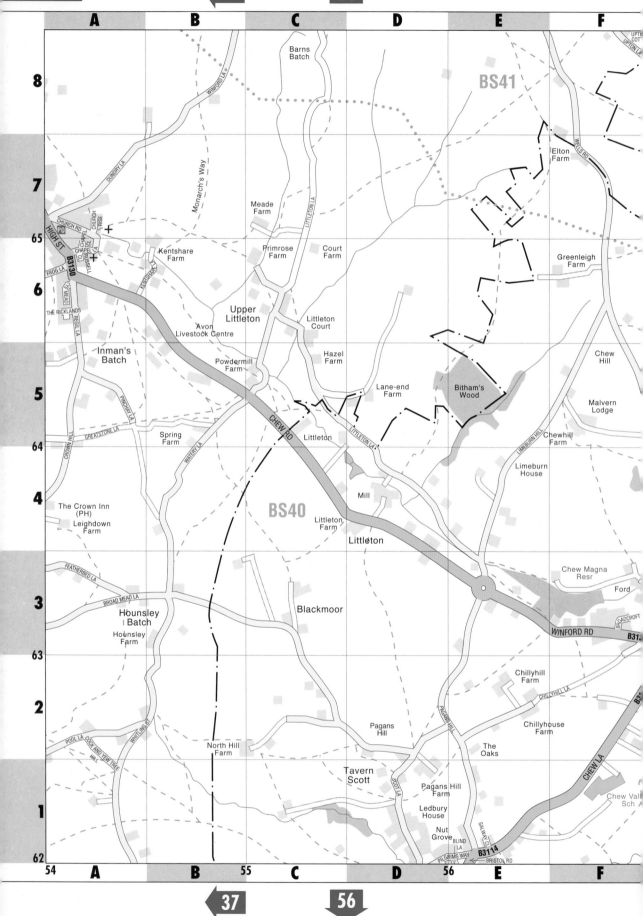

BS41

BS40

Barns
Batch

Monarch's Way

WINFORD LA

DUNDRY LA

CHURCH RD
CHURCH RISE
HIGH ST
CHAPEL CL
RUSSELL
B3130
FROG LA
YE MEAD
THE RICKLANDS
REGIL LA

Kentshare
Farm

KENTSHARE

Meade
Farm

LITTLETON LA

Primrose
Farm

Court
Farm

Upper
Littleton

Avon
Livestock Centre

Littleton
Court

Inman's
Batch

Powdermill
Farm

Hazel
Farm

PINCHAY LA

CROWN HI

GREATSTONE LA

Spring
Farm

WATERY LA

CHEW RD

Littleton

LITTLETON LA

Lane-end
Farm

Bitham's
Wood

Chew
Hill

Malvern
Lodge

LIMEBURN HILL

Chewhill
Farm

Limeburn
House

Mill

The Crown Inn
(PH)

Leighdown
Farm

Littleton
Farm

Littleton

Chew Magna
Resr

Ford

FEATHERBED LA

BROAD MEAD LA

Hounsley
Batch

Hounsley
Farm

Blackmoor

WINFORD RD

B31

BROADCROFT

POOL LA
COCK AND YEW TREE
HILL

WHITLING ST

North Hill
Farm

Pagans
Hill

PAGANS HILL

Chillyhill
Farm

CHILLYHILL LA

Chillyhouse
Farm

B3

The
Oaks

Tavern
Scott

SCOTT LA

Pagans Hill
Farm

Ledbury
House

Nut
Grove

BLIND
LA

PILGRIMS WAY

B3114

SALWAY CL

BRISTOL RD

CHEW LA

Chew Vall
Sch

Elton
Farm

WELLS RD

UPT
COT

UPTON LA

Greenleigh
Farm

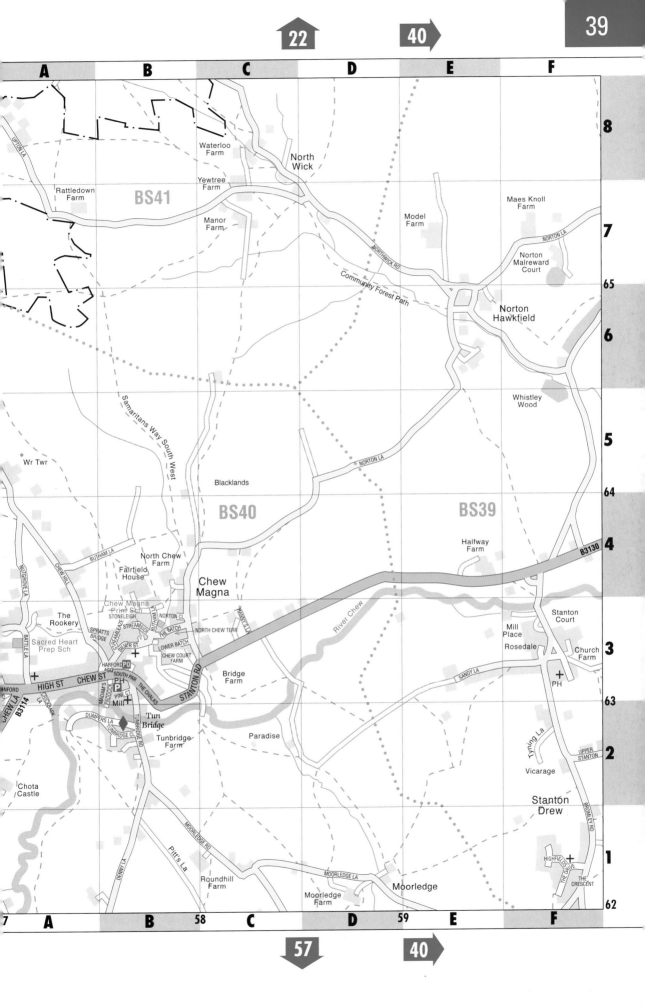

39
23

A B C D E F

8

7

65

6

5

64

4

3

63

2

1

62

60 61 62

MASKNOLL LA
GIBBET LA
CHARLTON RD
WOOLLARD LA
New Barn Farm
BS14
A37
Hursley Hill
Roundlands Farm
Blackrock
The Knoll
HOSPITAL LA
BLACKROCK LA
Publow Hill
NORTON LA
CHURCH RD
Manor Farm
Cottles Farm
CHALK PARDY CL
Norton Malreward
BRISTOL RD
WOOLLARD LA
Settle Hill
Publow Farm
Priest Down
Guy's Hill
Belluton
PARSONAGE LA
Publow
Hammerhill Wood
B3130
BELLUTON VILLAS
BELLUTON LA
Traveller's Rest (PH)
PUBLOW LA
Glebe Farm
PENSFORD HILL
STATION APP
Pensford Prim Sch
Publow Wood
B3130
Byemills Farm
Community Forest Path
River Chew
Hautville's Quoit
PO
CHURCH ST
PH
Pensford
Publow Leigh
STANTON LA
THE ORCHARD
Old Down
HIGH ST
BS39
WICK LA
Leigh Farm
Stanton Drew Stone Circles
NEW RD
Preston Farm
HILLCREST
PENSFORD OLD RD
Broadoak Farm
The Common
OLD RD
Stanton Drew Prim Sch
PENSFORD LA
OLD TARNWELL
TARNWELL
Upper Stanton Drew
THE ORCHARD
South Leigh Farm
UPPER STANTON
BIRCHWOOD LA
Elm Farm
STANTON WICK LA
Whitley Batts
Salter's Brook
Twinway Farm
Carpenters Arms (PH)
Parsons Farm
A37

A B C D E F

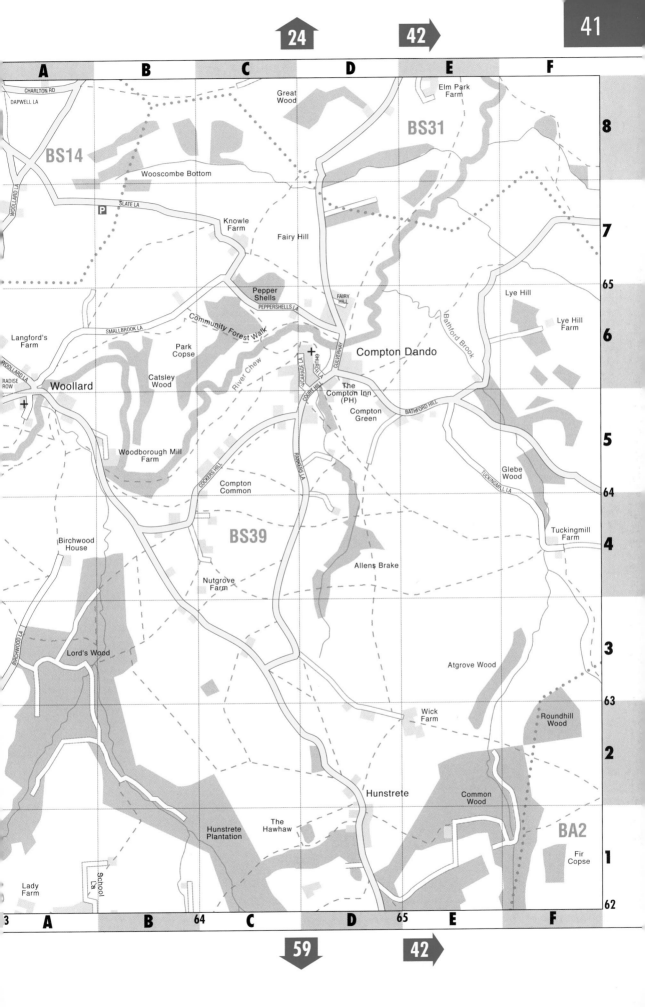

41
25

A **B** **C** **D** **E** **F**

8

Burnett Point

Mast

North Breach

BS31

Ashton Hill

GYPSY LA

BS31

Burnett Hill

B3116 WELLSWAY

Burnett

Manor Farm

7

Batchelor's Farm

Mast

Elm Farm

MIDDLEPIECE LA

A39

65

Corston Field Farm

6

Clay Pits

Caravan Site

Corston Field

PH

Stantonbury House

Long Hill

New Barn

BURY VIEW

South Cleve

B3116

5

Wansdyke House

BA2

64

CROSSPOST LA

BS39

Dog Kennel Wood

STALCOMBE LA

4

Stantonbury Hill

PRINCES LA

3

Winsbury Hill

Washpool La

63

Marksbury Vale

Winsbury House

Stanton Prior

Court Farm

Marksbury CE Prim Sch

2

HILL VIEW

PO

WINSBURY VIEW

CHURCH FARM CL

Marksbury

1

A368

A39

WEST TYNING

62

66 **A** **B** 67 **C** **D** 68 **E** **F**

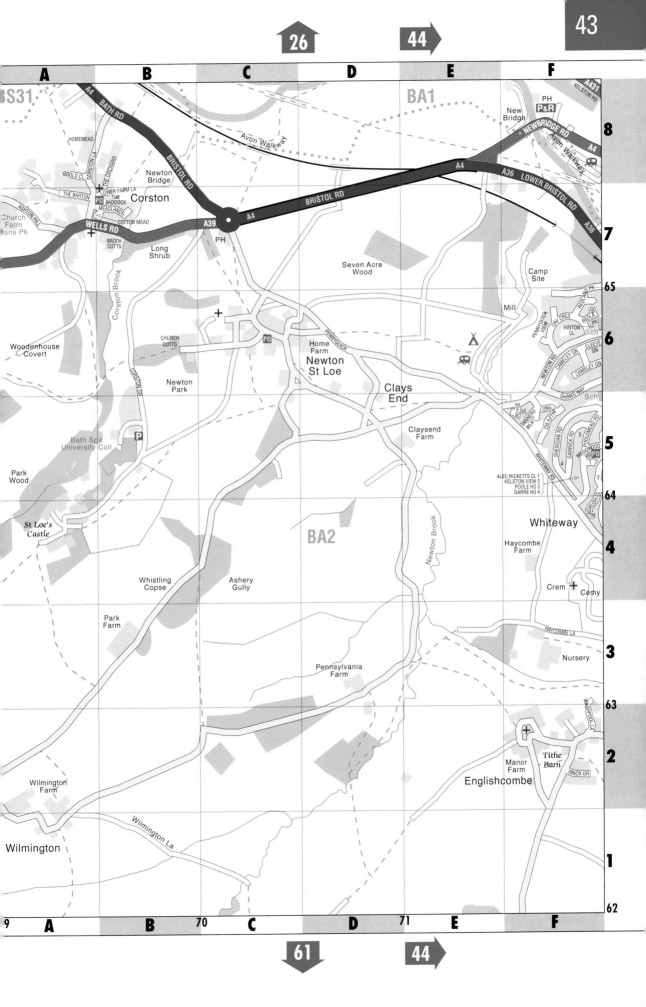

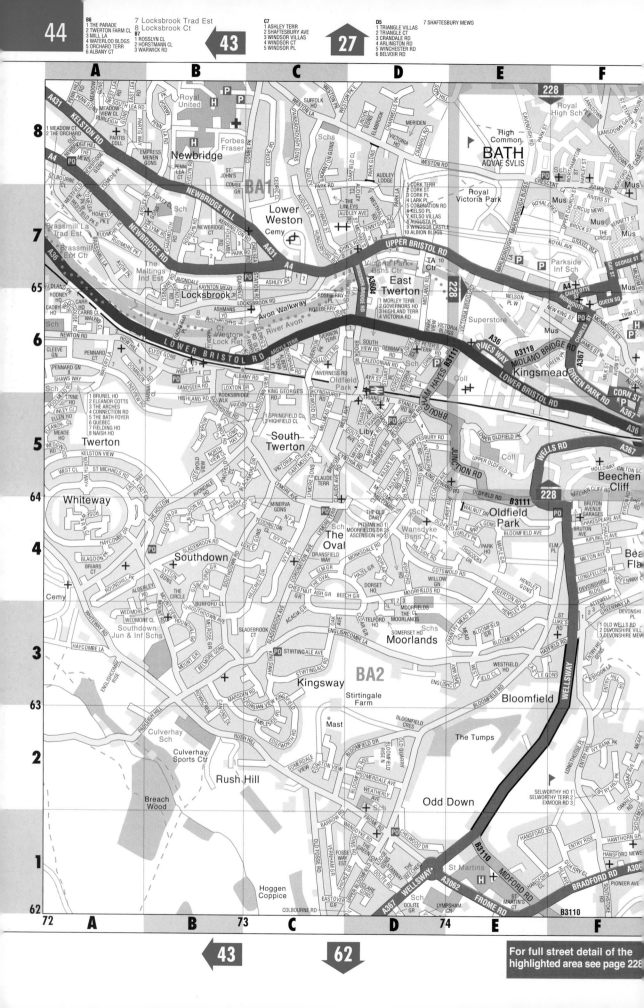

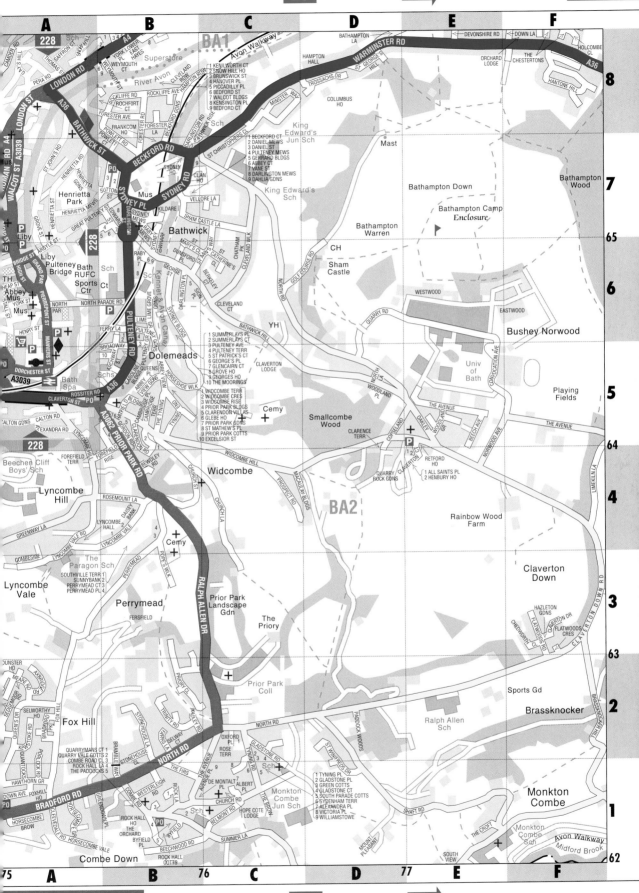

For full street detail of the highlighted area see page 228.

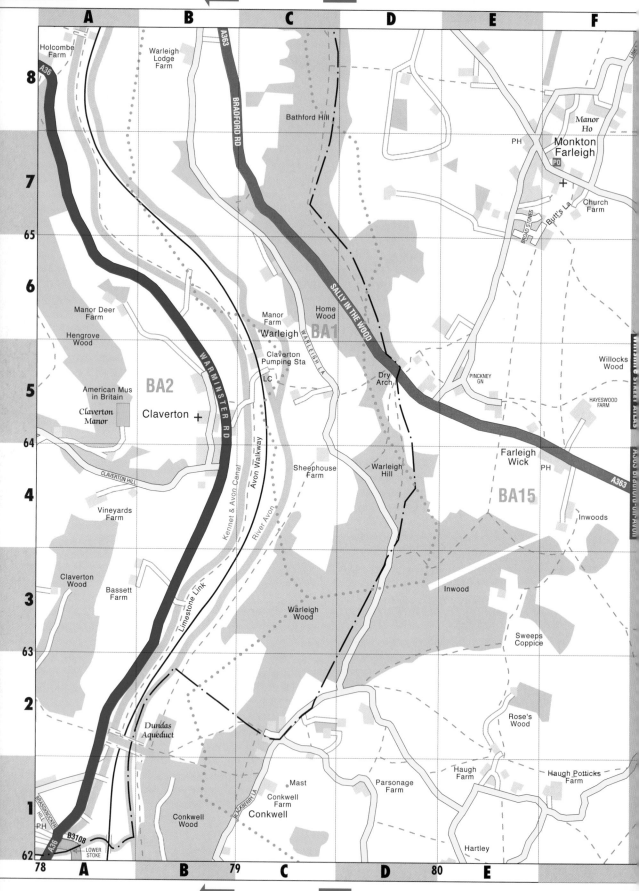

A B C D E F

8

Holcombe Farm

Warleigh Lodge Farm

A363

BRADFORD RD

Bathford Hill

Monkton Farleigh

Manor Ho

PH

PO

Church Farm

Butt's La

BROAD STONES

7

65

SALLY IN THE WOOD

6

Manor Deer Farm

Hengrove Wood

Manor Farm

Warleigh

BA1

Home Wood

WARLEIGH LA

Willocks Wood

PINCKNEY GN

HAYESWOOD FARM

WARMINSTER RD

BA2

Claverton

Claverton Pumping Sta

LC

Dry Arch

5

American Mus in Britain

Claverton Manor

64

CLAVERTON HILL

Kennet & Avon Canal

Avon Walkway

River Avon

Sheephouse Farm

Warleigh Hill

Farleigh Wick

PH

A363

4

Vineyards Farm

Warleigh Wood

Inwoods

BA15

Inwood

Claverton Wood

Bassett Farm

Limestone Link

Sweeps Coppice

3

63

Rose's Wood

2

Dundas Aqueduct

Haugh Farm

Haugh Potticks Farm

BLACKBERRY LA

Mast

Conkwell Farm

Conkwell

Parsonage Farm

BRASSKNOCKER HILL

PH

B3108

A36

LOWER STOKE

Conkwell Wood

Hartley

1

62

78 A B 79 C D 80 E

Wiltshire Street Atlas

A363 Bradford-on-Avon

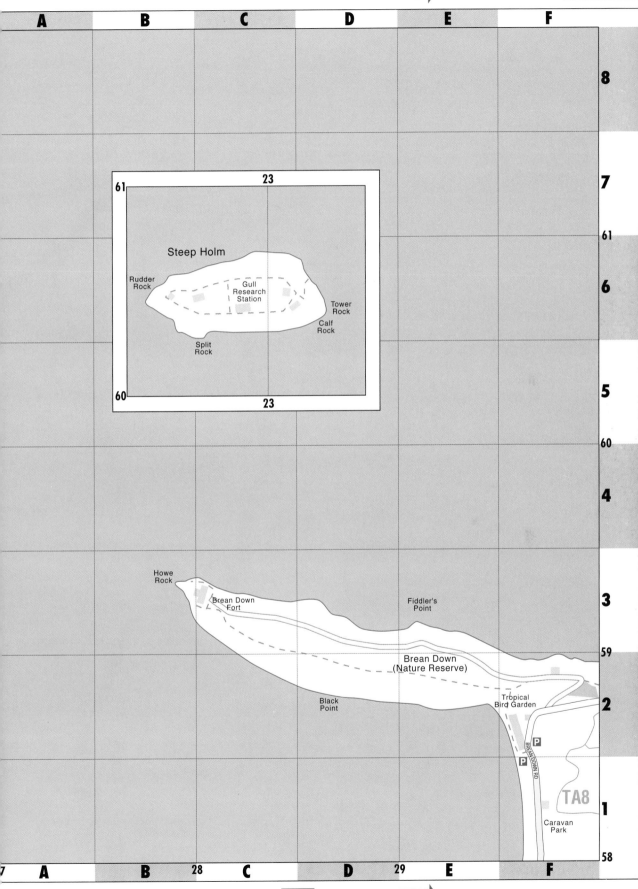

A   B   C   D   E   F

8

7

61

6

23

61

Steep Holm

Rudder
Rock

Gull
Research
Station

Tower
Rock

Calf
Rock

Split
Rock

60

23

5

60

4

Howe
Rock

3

Brean Down
Fort

Fiddler's
Point

59

Brean Down
(Nature Reserve)

Black
Point

Tropical
Bird Garden

2

P

BREAN DOWN RD

P

TA8

1

Caravan
Park

58

47   30

WESTON-SUPER-MARE

Weston Bay

BS23

TA8

Brean Down Farm

Black Rock

Slimeridge Farm

Marina

Uphill

Westhaven Sch

Uphill Manor

Windmill

Hillgrove Terr

West Mendip Way

River Axe

Ferry (P)

Weston Miniature Rly

Weston Bay

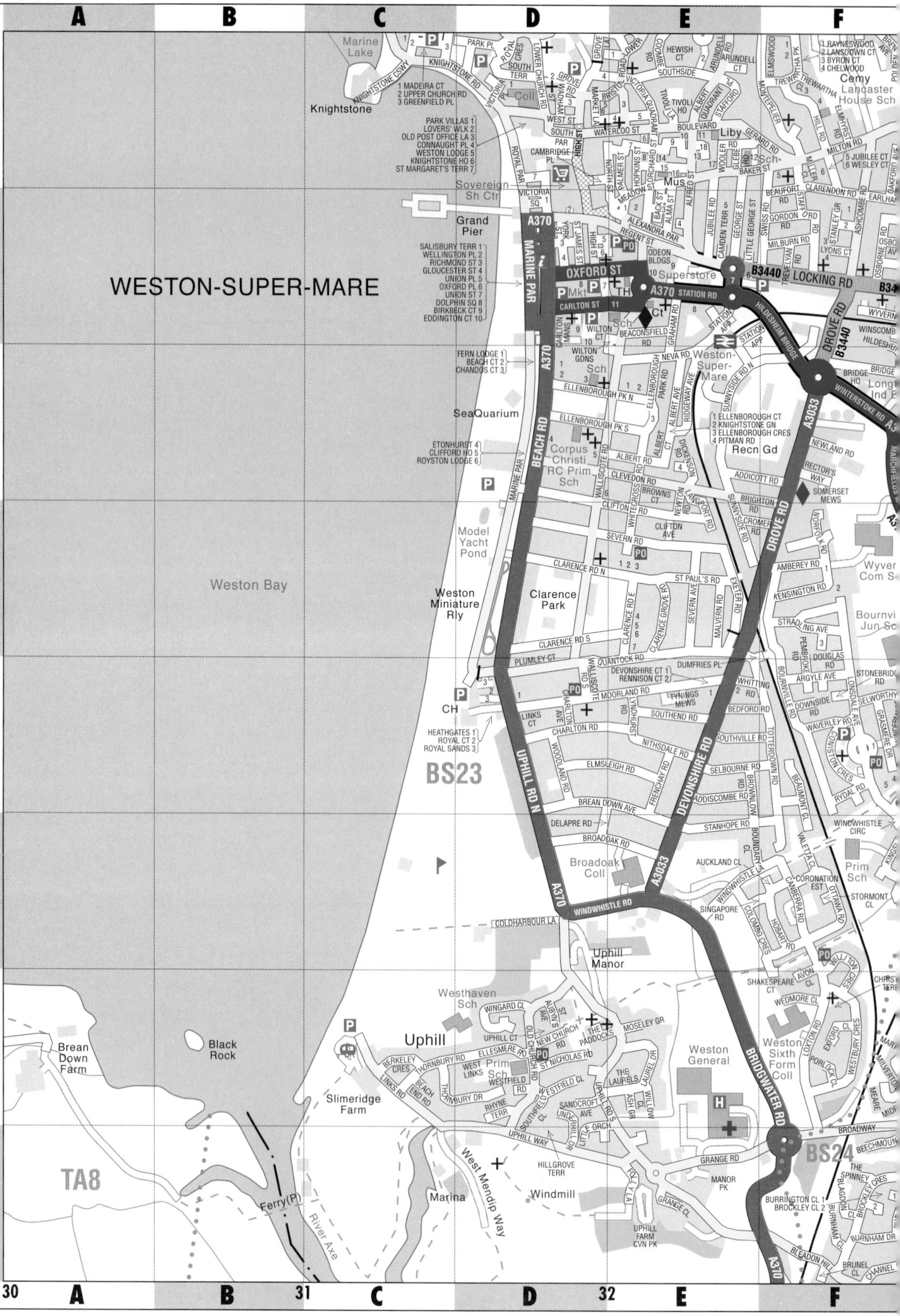

Model Yacht Pond

SeaQuarium

Grand Pier

Knightstone

Marine Lake

Clarence Park

Broadoak Coll

Weston General

Weston Sixth Form Coll

BS24

47   66

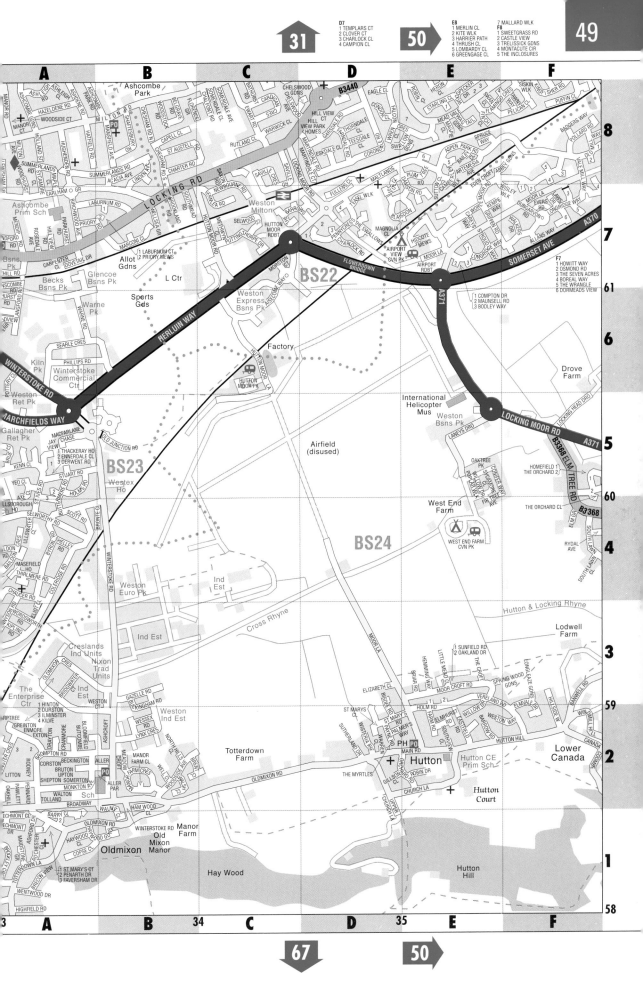

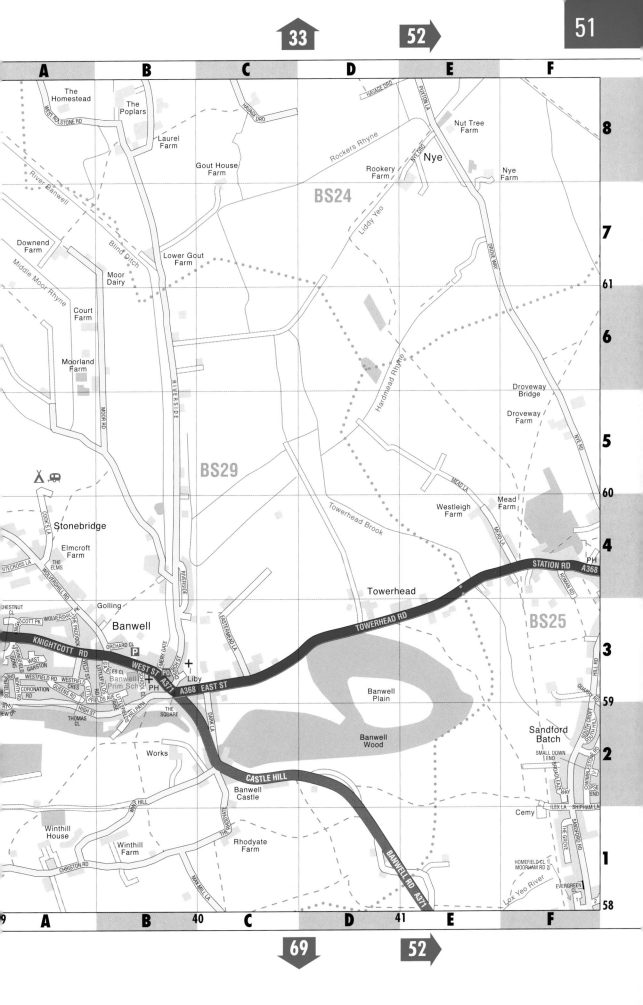

33
52

A · **B** · **C** · **D** · **E** · **F**

8

The Homestead
WEST RD STONE RD
The Poplars
Laurel Farm
Gout House Farm
HAVAGE DRO
Rockers Rhyne
Nut Tree Farm
Nye
NYE DRO
PUXTON LA
Rookery Farm
Nye Farm
BS24
River Banwell
Blind Ditch
Downend Farm
Lower Gout Farm
Liddy Yeo
DROVE WAY

7

Middle Moor Rhyne
Moor Dairy
MOOR RD
RIVERSIDE
61

Court Farm
6
Moorland Farm
Hardmead Rhyne
Droveway Bridge
Droveway Farm
NYE RD

5
BS29
MEAD LA
60
Towerhead Brook
Westleigh Farm
Mead Farm
MEAD LA

Stonebridge
4
Elmcroft Farm
THE ELMS
STATION RD A368
PH
ROMAN RD
WHITECROSS LA
COOK'S LA
WOLVERSHILL RD
WOLVERSHILL PK
Golling
Towerhead
BS25
CHESTNUT CL
WESTCOTT PK
Banwell
ORCHARD CL
P
TOWERHEAD RD
3
KNIGHTCOTT RD
THE PADDOCK
WEST GARSTON
GILES CL
LITTLEFIELDS
EMERY GATE
SCHOOL ST
WEST ST A371
EAST ST A368
Liby
SPRINGFIELD GDNS
WESTFIELD RD
WESTFIELD CRES
QUEENS RD
Banwell Prim Sch
PH
CASTLEMEAD LA
Banwell Plain
QUARRY RD
HILL RD
NORTH RD
CORONATION RD
LITTLEFIELDS AVE
TREE
SMALL PATH
59
SOUTH CROFT
SOUTH HILL
Sandford Batch
HIGH ST
THE SQUARE
DARK LA
2
RIVERVIEW DR
THOMAS CL
Works
Banwell Wood
SMALL DOWN END
WIMBLESTONE RD
BROADLEAZE WAY
COPSE END
CASTLE HILL
Banwell Castle
ILEX LA
SHIPHAM LA
Cemy
THE GROVE
SANDFORD RD
WYTT HILL
THE SHIVAGHRE
MAX MILL LA
Winthill House
Winthill Farm
Rhodyate Farm
HOMEFIELD CL 1
MOORHAM RD 2
EVERGREEN CL
1
CHRISTON RD
BANWELL RD A371
Lox Yeo River
58

A · **B** · **C** · **D** · **E** · **F**

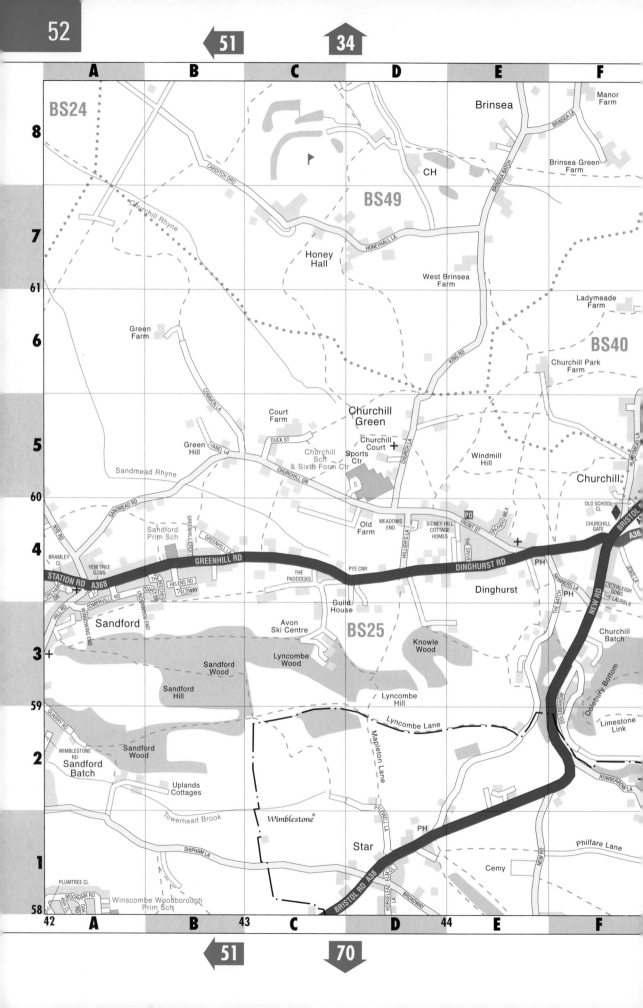

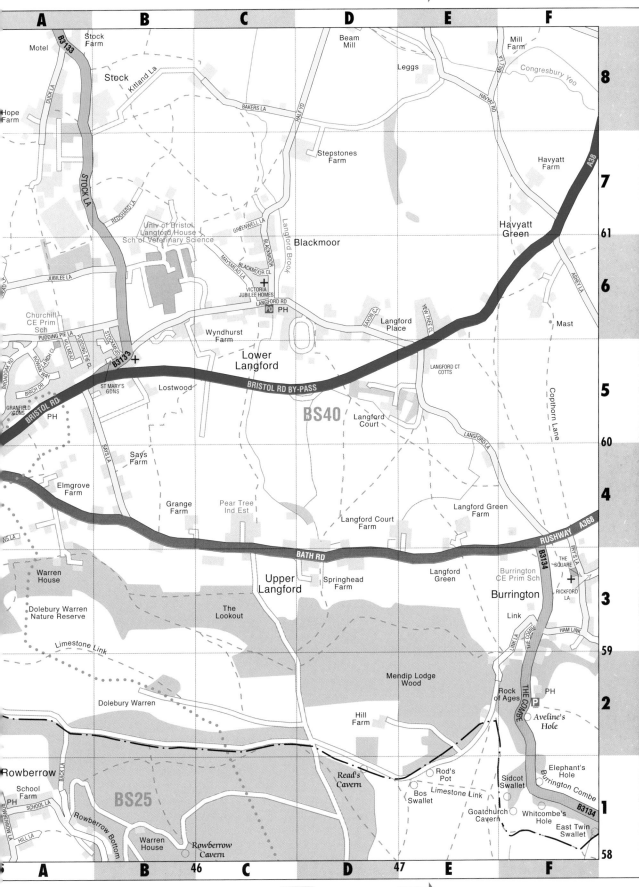

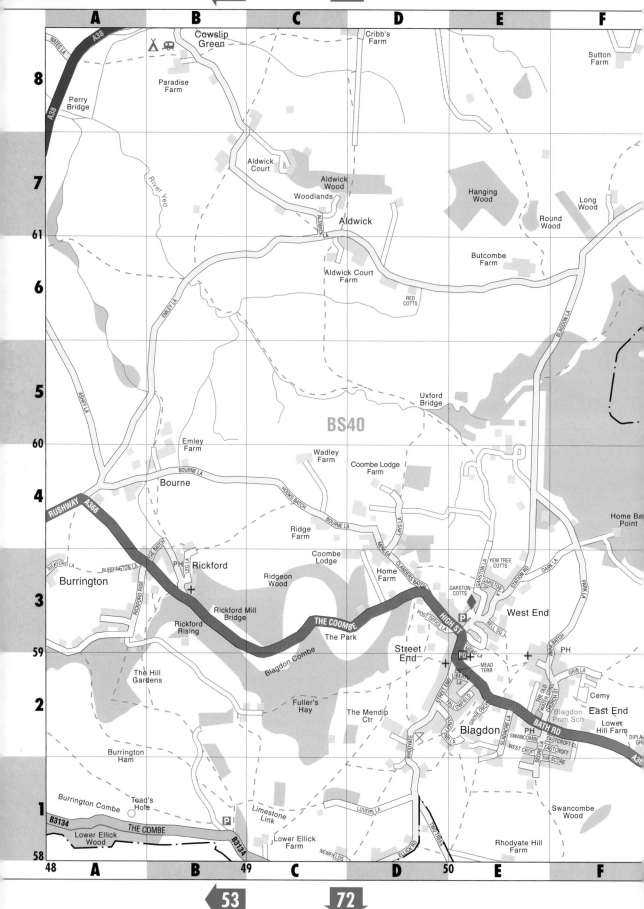

A B C D E F

8

7

61

6

5

60

4

3

59

2

1

58

48 A B 49 C D 50 E F

Cowslip Green

Cribb's Farm

Sutton Farm

Paradise Farm

Perry Bridge

Aldwick Court

Aldwick Wood

Woodlands

Hanging Wood

Long Wood

Round Wood

River Yeo

Aldwick

Butcombe Farm

RED COTTS

BS40

Uxford Bridge

BLAGDON LA

Emley Farm

Wadley Farm

Coombe Lodge Farm

Home Ba Point

RUSHWAY A368

Bourne

BOURNE LA

HOOKS BATCH

BOURNE LA

Ridge Farm

Coombe Lodge

Home Farm

YEW TREE COTTS

STATION RD

DARK LA

PARK LA

West End

THE BATCH

PH LEG LA

Rickford

Ridgeon Wood

CLANDERS BATCH

GARSTON COTTS

GARSTON LA

BELL SQ

Burrington

RICKFORD LA

BURRINGTON LA

RICKFORD RISE

Rickford Mill Bridge

Rickford Rising

THE COOMBE

The Park

Blagdon Combe

POST OFFICE LA

HIGH ST

P

Street End

MEAD TERR

PO

GRIB LA

Cemy

Blagdon Prim Sch

East End

The Hill Gardens

Fuller's Hay

The Mendip Ctr

LIBERTY LA

FALLOWFIELD

GROVE CROFT

Blagdon

BATH RD

SLADACRE LA

WEST CROFT

PH

EASTCROFT CL

EASTCROFT

Lower Hill Farm

A3t

Burrington Ham

RHODYATE

THE SCORE

Swancombe Wood

Burrington Combe

Toad's Hole

B3134

THE COMBE

Limestone Link

LUVERS LA

DIPLA GR

Lower Ellick Wood

P

Lower Ellick Farm

NEWFIELDS

ELLICK RD

TWO TREES

Rhodyate Hill Farm

B3134A

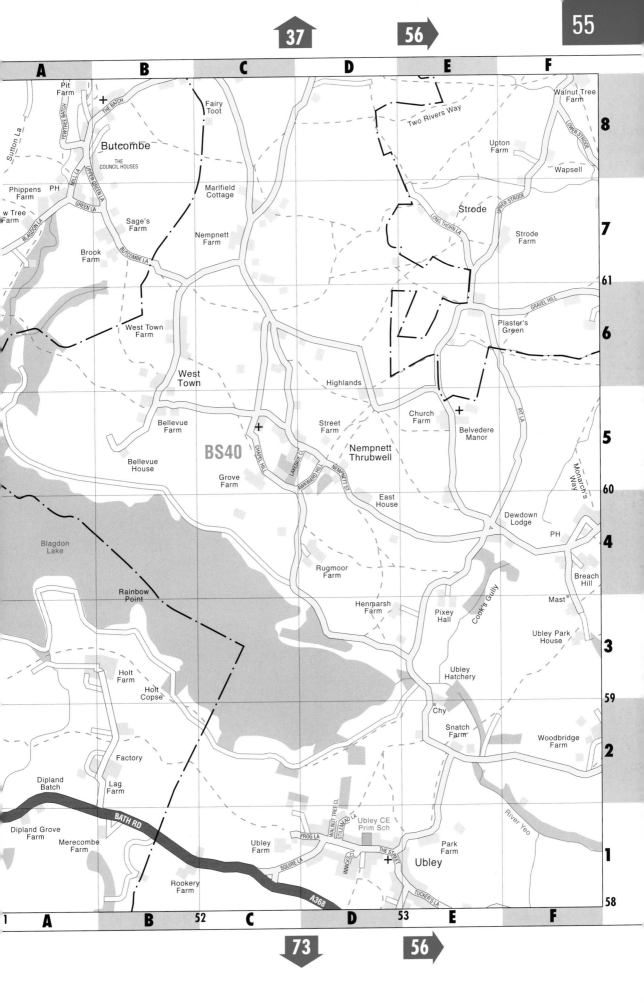

A B C D E F

8

7

61

6

5

60

4

59

3

2

1

58

Sutton La
Pit Farm
THE BATCH
YEWTREE BATCH
Butcombe
THE COUNCIL HOUSES
Fairy Toot
Walnut Tree Farm
LOWER STRODE
Two Rivers Way
Upton Farm
Wapsell
Phippens Farm
PH
MILL LA
UPPER GREEN LA
GREEN LA
Marlfield Cottage
Strode
UPPER STRODE
w Tree Farm
BLAGDON LA
Sage's Farm
Nempnett Farm
LONG THORN LA
Strode Farm
Brook Farm
BUTCOMBE LA
GRAVEL HILL
West Town Farm
Plaster's Green
West Town
Highlands
Church Farm
Belvedere Manor
PIT LA
BS40
Bellevue Farm
Street Farm
Monarch's Way
Bellevue House
CHAPEL HILL
LAKESIDE CL
AWKWARD HILL
NEMPNETT ST
Grove Farm
Nempnett Thrubwell
East House
Dewdown Lodge
PH
Blagdon Lake
Rugmoor Farm
Breach Hill
Rainbow Point
Henmarsh Farm
Pixey Hall
Cook's Gully
Mast
Ubley Park House
Holt Farm
Holt Copse
Ubley Hatchery
Chy
Snatch Farm
Woodbridge Farm
Factory
Dipland Batch
Lag Farm
BATH RD
WALNUT TREE CL
STILEMEAD LA
Ubley CE Prim Sch
River Yeo
Dipland Grove Farm
Merecombe Farm
FROG LA
Ubley Farm
SQUIRE LA
INNICKS CL
THE STREET
Park Farm
Ubley
Rookery Farm
A368
TUCKER'S LA

1 A B 52 C D 53 E F

55 38

A B C D E F

8

The Knoll

Church Farm

Scot La
PH
Church La
Pilgrims Way
The Cedars
Webbs Mead
Works

Chew Stoke CE Prim Sch

Mill La

The Street

Bristol Rd B3114

Lower Strode

Chew Stoke

Quarry Hay

Chapel La

PO

Bilbie Rd
Bilbie Cl
Bushy Thorn

Wally Court Rd

Walley La

Lower Strode Farm

Whitling

Home Orch

School La

Wallis Farm

Fairseat Workshops

7

Manor Farm

Lower Strode

Shoreditch

Scornfield La

Stoke Hill House

Woodford Hill

Stoke Hill

61

Gravel Hill

Breach Hill La

Perry House Farm

Rose Cottage

6

Monarch's Way

Stoke Villice

Woodford Lodge

Obelisk

5

Rookery Farm

Capel La

Manor Farm

BS40

60

Kingshill La

Breach Hill Common

Nunnery Copse

4

Breach Hill

Herons Green Farm

Chew Valley Lake

Herons Green

P

Herons Green Bay

59

Monarch's Way

Moreton Point

3

Moreton La

2

Moat Farm

Bickfield Farm

Villice La

Bickfield La

Newclose La

1

River Yeo

Summerlea Farm

Oldbarn La

Stratford La

B3114

A36

58

54 A B 55 C D 56 E F

55 74

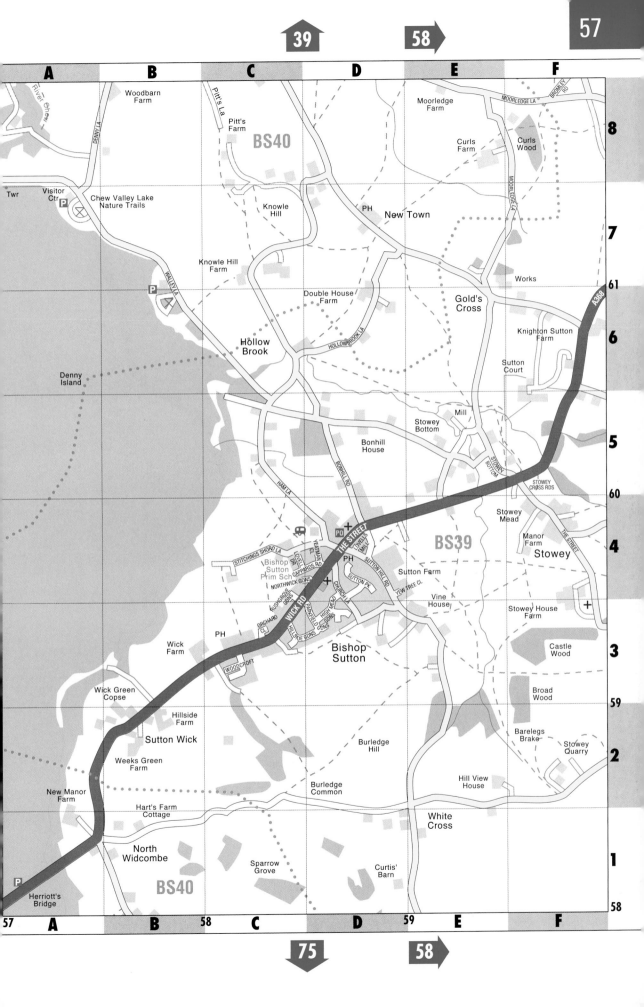

| |  A | B | C | D | E | F |

8

Bromley Farm

Curl's Farm

STANTON WICK LA

Stanton Wick

CHELWOOD RDBT

A37

A368

Utcombe Farm

Chelwood House Hotel

7

Stanton Wick Farm

Park Farm

Fry's Bottom

61

A368

Round Hill

Salter's Brook

FEATHERED LA

6

Folly Wood

Honey Gaston

Red Hill

Breach

BS39

THE FLAT

North End Farm

5

Folly Farm Nature Reserve

Dowling's Wood

North End

60

Taylor's Farm

KING LA

4

Hill Farm

LOWER BRISTOL RD

Cinderlands Brake

Tynemoor Wood

UPPER BRISTOL RD

TYNINGS

TYNINGS WAY

Clutton Prim Sch

BURGHILL CL

GREENRIDGE

Greensbrook

3

Warwick Arms (PH)

WARWICK GDNS

ROGERS CL

BROOMHILL LA

THE MEAD

FURNLEAZE LA

MAYPOLE CL

BATCH LA

CLUTTON HILL

MAYNARD TERR

Tynemore Farm

STATION RD

PO

Clutton

VALLEY VIEW

VENUS LA

MOORSFIELD

CARLINS

59

Church Farm

KINGS OAK MDN

CHURCH RD

CHURCH SQ

Sleight Farm

Cholwell Farm

Bendalls Bridge

2

Cholwell House

New Cholwell Farm

Cholwell

Willow Farm

MARSH LA

CHOLWELL COTTS

Limestone Link

Temple Cloud

THE SQUARE

TEMPLE INN LA

GOLDNEY

GREYFIELD

1

Paul Wood

PAULWOOD RD

OAKLANDS

TILEDOWN

GOLDNEY VIEW

GOLDNEY WAY

FIELDGARDENS RD

HAM CL

NANNY HURN'S LA

PAULMONT RISE

PH

CHERRY TREE

MEADWAY

ASHMEAD

TILEDOWN CL

A37

58

FAIRVIEW ELM VIEW

Cameley CE Prim Sch

| 60 | A | | B | 61 | C | | D | | 62 | E | | F |

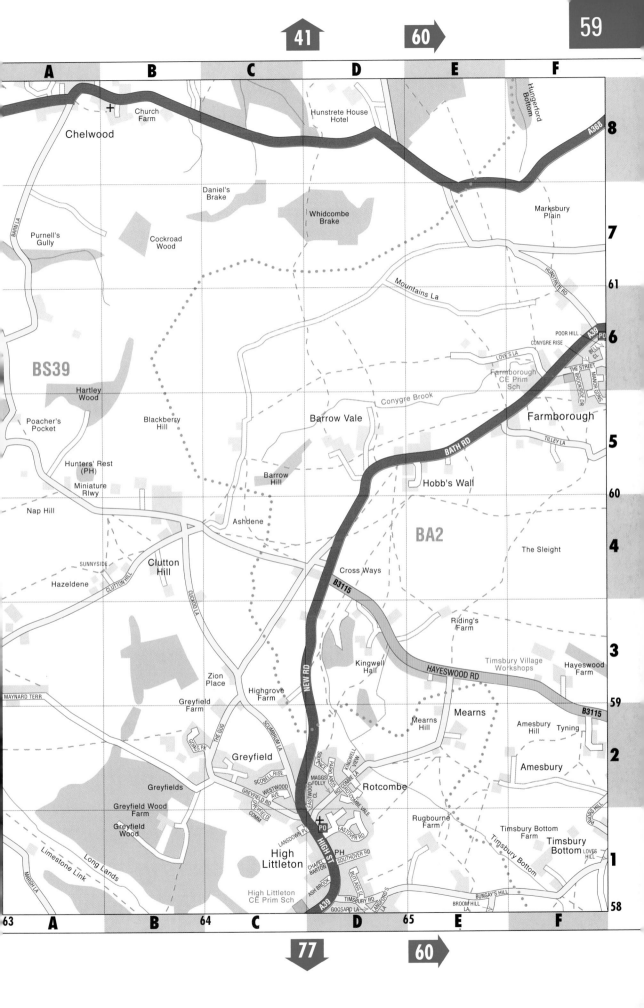

41
60

A   **B**   **C**   **D**   **E**   **F**

A368

Hungerford Bottom

Church Farm

Chelwood

8

Daniel's Brake

Whidcombe Brake

Hunstrete House Hotel

Marksbury Plain

7

Purnell's Gully

BARN LA

Cockroad Wood

Mountains La

HUNSTRETE RD

61

BS39

Hartley Wood

Blackberry Hill

POOR HILL

A39 PO

CONYGRE RISE

BELL CL

THE STREET

MANOR GDNS

BROOKSIDE DR

6

LOVES LA

Farmborough CE Prim Sch

Conygre Brook

Barrow Vale

Farmborough

Poacher's Pocket

BATH RD

TILLEY LA

5

Hunters' Rest (PH)

Barrow Hill

Hobb's Wall

60

Miniature Rlwy

Nap Hill

Ashdene

BA2

The Sleight

4

SUNNYSIDE

Hazeldene

Clutton Hill

CLUTTON HILL

Cross Ways

B3115

Riding's Farm

Timsbury Village Workshops

Hayeswood Farm

3

MAYNARD TERR

CUCKOO LA

Zion Place

Highgrove Farm

NEW RD

Kingwell Hall

HAYESWOOD RD

Mearns Hill

Mearns

Amesbury Hill

Tyning

B3115

59

Greyfield Farm

THE GUG

GORES PK

SCUMBRUM LA

Greyfield

Amesbury

2

Greyfields

SCOBELL RISE

WESTWOOD AVE

GREYFIELD RD

GREYFIELD CL

COMM

MAGGS FOLLY

EASTWOOD CL

PARK ANS

SIXPENCE

KINGWELL VIEW

ROTCOMBE LA

ROTCOMBE VALE

Rotcombe

Rugbourne Farm

Timsbury Bottom Farm

Timsbury Bottom

PB GLADES HILL

LOVES HILL

1

Greyfield Wood Farm

Greyfield Wood

Long Lands

Limestone Link

LANSDOWN PL

HIGH ST

PO

PH

EASTOVER RD

SOUTHOVER RD

High Littleton

CHAPEL BARTON

ASH BROOK

BUTTASS CL

TIMSBURY RD

LANGFORD S LA

BUNGAY'S HILL

Timsbury Bottom

MARSH LA

High Littleton CE Prim Sch

A39

GOOSARD LA

BROOM HILL LA

58

77
60

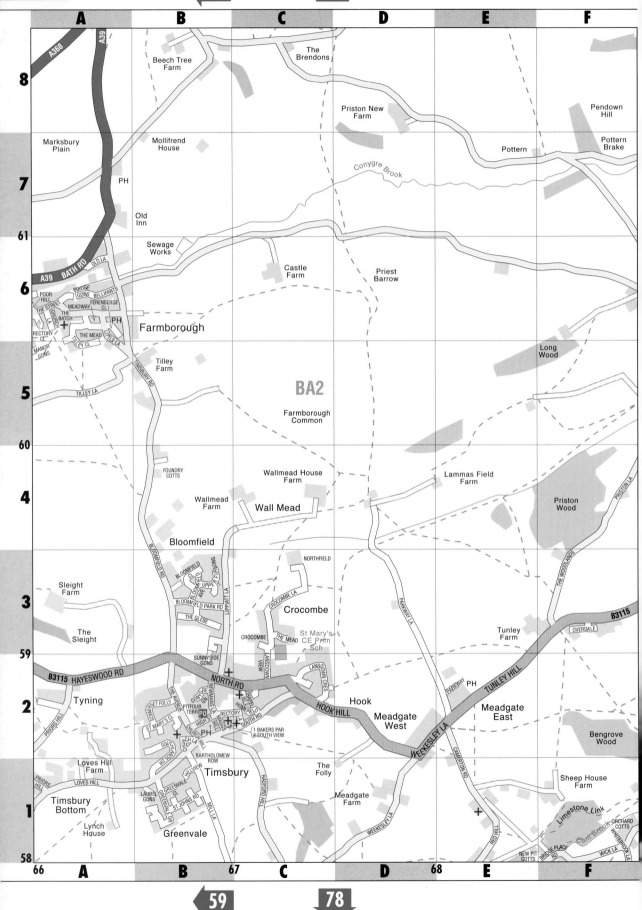

A B C D E F

8

A368 A39

Beech Tree Farm

The Brendons

Priston New Farm

Pendown Hill

Marksbury Plain

Mollifrend House

Conygre Brook

Pottern

Pottern Brake

7

PH

Old Inn

61

A39 BATH RD Old La

Sewage Works

Castle Farm

Priest Barrow

6

POOR HILL BRIDGE GDNS BELLIFANTS
THE STREET MEADWAY FERENBERGE CL
THE BATCH PH
RECTORY CL THE MEAD
MANOR GDNS TILLEY CL TILE LA

Farmborough

Long Wood

Tilley Farm

TILSBURY RD

5

TILLEY LA

BA2

Farmborough Common

60

FOUNDRY COTTS

Wallmead House Farm

Lammas Field Farm

Priston Wood

PRISTON LA

4

Wallmead Farm

Wall Mead

BLOOMFIELD RD

Bloomfield

THE WOODLANDS

Sleight Farm

BLOOMFIELD CL UPPER FURLONG
BLOOMFIELD AVE LIPPIATT LA
BLOOMFIELD PARK RD
THE GLEBE

NORTHFIELD

CROCOMBE LA

Crocombe

Tunley Farm

B3115

OVERDALE

3

The Sleight

CROCOMBE THE MEAD
St Mary's CE Prim Sch

PARKWAY LA

TUNLEY HILL

59

SUNNYSIDE GDNS
LANSDOWN VIEW

B3115 HAYESWOOD RD

NORTH RD

LANSDOWN CRES

Parkway PH

Tyning

THE AVENUE
NEWMANS
CONYGRE PITFOUR TERR
ST MARY'S CL CHURCH HILL RECTORY
SOUTH RD HOMEFIELD

HOOK HILL

Hook

Meadgate West

Meadgate East

2

PRIORS HILL

SOUTH RD CH LA PH
1 BAKERS PAR
2 SOUTH VIEW

CAMERTON RD

Bengrove Wood

Loves Hill Farm

BARTHOLOMEW ROW

The Folly

Sheep House Farm

PRIORS HILL

LOVES HILL

MILL LA RADFORD HILL

Timsbury

Meadgate Farm

WEEKESLEY LA RED HILL

Limestone Link

ORCHARD COTTS

1

Timsbury Bottom

LAUREL GDNS GREENVALE CL
GREENVALE CL ST JOHNS RD

Greenvale

Cam Brook

WHITEBROOK LA

Lynch House

NEW PIT COTTS BRIDGE PLACE

WICK LA

58

66 A B 67 C D 68 E F

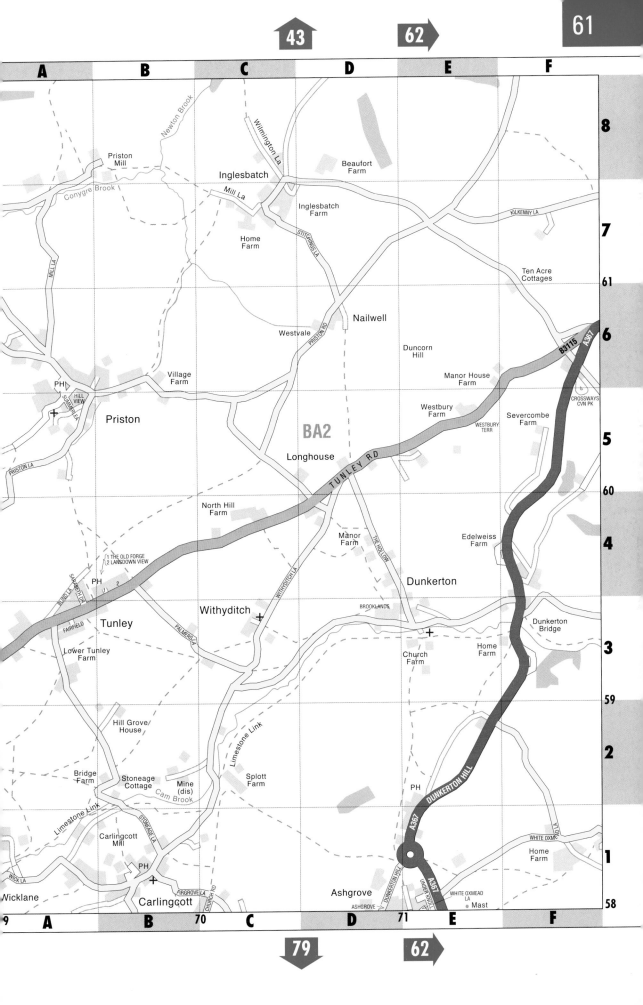

A B C D E F

8

7

61

6

5

60

4

3

59

2

1

58

Priston Mill
Inglesbatch
Beaufort Farm
K.V. KENNY LA
Newton Brook
Wilmington La
Mill La
Inglesbatch Farm
Conygre Brook
Home Farm
STITCHINGS LA
Ten Acre Cottages
MILL LA
Westvale
PRISTON RD
Nailwell
Duncorn Hill
B3115
A367
Manor House Farm
PH
HILL VIEW
SUMMER LA
Village Farm
Westbury Farm
WESTBURY TERR
Severcombe Farm
CROSSWAYS CVN PK
Priston
BA2
Longhouse
TUNLEY RD
PRISTON LA
North Hill Farm
Manor Farm
THE HOLLOW
Edelweiss Farm
1 THE OLD FORGE
2 LANSDOWN VIEW
Dunkerton
PH
SCARLETT DR
BEND LA
2
WITHYDITCH LA
Dunkerton Bridge
FAIRFIELD
Tunley
Withyditch
PALMERS LA
BROOKLANDS
Home Farm
Lower Tunley Farm
Church Farm
59
Hill Grove House
Limestone Link
DUNKERTON HILL
2
Bridge Farm
Stoneage Cottage
Mine (dis)
Cam Brook
Splott Farm
PH
A367
WHITE OXME
WHITE OXMEAD LA
Home Farm
Limestone Link
STONEAGE LA
Carlingcott Mill
PH
AIRGROVE LA
CHURCH RD
Ashgrove
DUNKERTON HILL
A367
UNDER KNOLL
1
WICK LA
Wicklane
Carlingcott
ASHGROVE
WHITE OXMEAD LA
Mast
58

9 A B 70 C D 71 E F

61
44

A   B   C   D   E   F

8

Middle Wood

Vernham Wood

BRISTOL VIEW 1
UPPER BLOOMFIELD RD 2
BURNT HOUSE COTTS 3
FOSSE WAY EST 4

WELLSWAY   A367

OLD FOSSE RD

COOMBE HAY LA

MENDIP GDNS

ABINGDON GDNS

DOLFE

BARWELL RD

FULLERS WAY

CRANMORE PL

LYMPSHAM GN

CRANMORE

Wansdyke Sch

OLD FROME RD

MIDFORD RD

SOUTHSTOKE

B3110

St Gregory's RC Sch

Odd Down

RIDGE GREEN

WILLOW CL

CARDINAL CL

GREGORY'S GR

SULIS MANOR RD

POPLAR RD

HEATHER DR

MOLLY DR

MEADOW DR

ALDER WAY

SPRUCE WAY

HAZEL WAY

Mast

SOUTHSTOKE LA

Nurseri

KILKENNY LA

Woodleaze

Works

BURNT HOUSE RD

BURNT HOUSE RD

Sulis Manor

PACK HORSE LA

OLD SCHOOL

VICTORIA COTTS

PH

COURTMEAD

Southstoke

7

Down Wood

P&R

61

West Wood

A367

Hodshill

HODSHILL

6

A367

COOMBE HAY LA

Fortnight Farm

Rowley Wood

Engine Wood

Fosse Farm

Week Farm

Limestone Link

Rowley House

Rowley Farm

Anchor Farm

5

Rainbow Wood

Cemy

PH

60

Manor House Farm

Cam Brooke

Dunnyham Brake

Combe Hay

Tut's Wood

Brake Wood

Upper Twinhoe Farm

Middl Twinho

4

BA2

Underdown Wood

Upper Twinhoe

3

Limestone Link

Twinhoe Green

59

TWINHOE LA

2

Manor Farm

BATH HILL

White Ox Mead Farm

Upper Hayes

Wellow

WEAVERS ORCH

HIGH ST

THE SQUARE

STAPLE RD

HENLEY VIEW

HUNGERFORD TERR

FARM LA

MILL HILL

BULL'S HILL

St Julian's CE Prim Sch

Church Farm

FORD RD

1

58

Wellow Brook

61
80

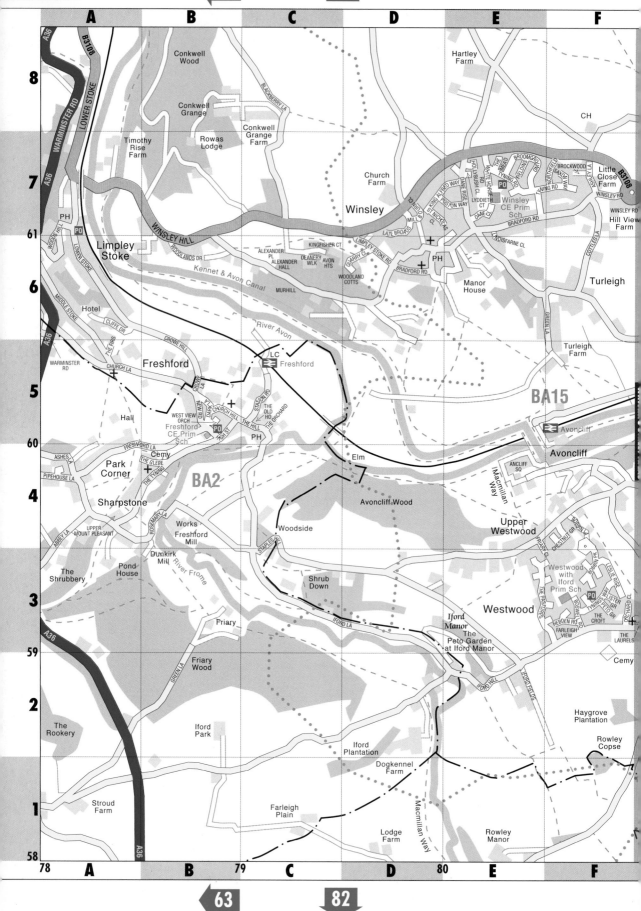

A B C D E F

8

Conkwell Wood

Conkwell Grange

Rowas Lodge

Conkwell Grange Farm

Hartley Farm

CH

7

Timothy Rise Farm

Church Farm

Winsley

Winsley CE Prim Sch

Little Close Farm

PO

BROOMGROVE

BROCKWOOD

SAXON WAY

THE MEAD

KING ALFRED WAY

SAME RISE

PISTON WAY

NORTHFIELD

TYNING RD

Hill View Farm

Winsley Rd

Winsley Rd

HOLLYBUSH CL

ST NICHOLS CL

LYDDIETH CT

DIME CL

BRADFORD RD

LINDISFARNE CL

GREEN LA

COTTLES LA

61

PH

PO

Limpley Stoke

WINSLEY HILL

WOODLANDS DR

Kennet & Avon Canal

Alexander Pl Alexander Hall

Deanery Wlk Avon Hts

Kingfisher Ct

MILL

LATE BROADS

LIMPLEY STOKE RD

QUARRY CL

BRADFORD RD

PH

Manor House

Turleigh

WOODS HILL

A36

B3108

LOWER STOKE

WARMINSTER RD

LOWER STOKE

MURHILL

WOODLAND COTTS

6

Hotel

CLIFFE DR

CROWE HILL

THE FIRS

River Avon

Turleigh Farm

MIDDLE STOKE

A36

Freshford

LC

Freshford

BA15

5

WARMINSTER RD

CHURCH LA

GROVE LA

NEW RD

PARK LA

STATION RD

CHURCH HILL

THE HILL

THE ORCHARD

THE OLD HO

Avoncliff

Avoncliff

Hall

West View Orch

Freshford CE Prim Sch

PO

MILL ST

PH

Elm

ANCLIFF SQ

MACMILLAN WAY

60

ASHES LA

PIPEHOUSE LA

FRESHFORD LA

THE GLEBE

Cemy

THE TYNING

BA2

Upper Westwood

Park Corner

ROSEMARY LA

BOBBIN LA

BOBBIN PK

CHESTNUT GR

LESLIE RISE

PRIORY CL

THE PASTURES

BOSWELL

4

Sharpstone

Works Freshford Mill

Woodside

Avoncliff Wood

Westwood with Iford Prim Sch

PO

TYNING RD

LISTER GR

PETER GR

ORCHARD CL

THE CROFT

ABBEY LA

UPPER MOUNT PLEASANT

Dunkirk Mill

River Frome

STAPLES HILL

Shrub Down

Westwood

HEBDEN RD

FARLEIGH VIEW

THE LAURELS

3

The Shrubbery

Pond House

Iford Manor

The Peto Garden at Iford Manor

Cemy

IFORD LA

59

A36

Friary

GREEN LA

Friary Wood

Iford Plantation

IFORD HILL

FORD FIELDS

2

The Rookery

Iford Park

Haygrove Plantation

Rowley Copse

Iford Plantation

Dogkennel Farm

MACMILLAN WAY

1

Stroud Farm

Farleigh Plain

Lodge Farm

Rowley Manor

58

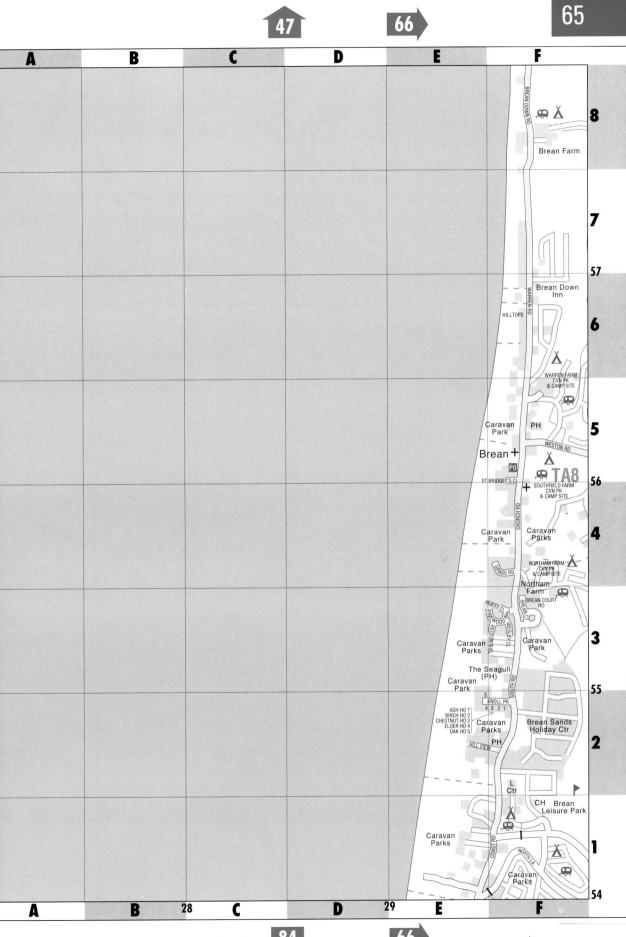

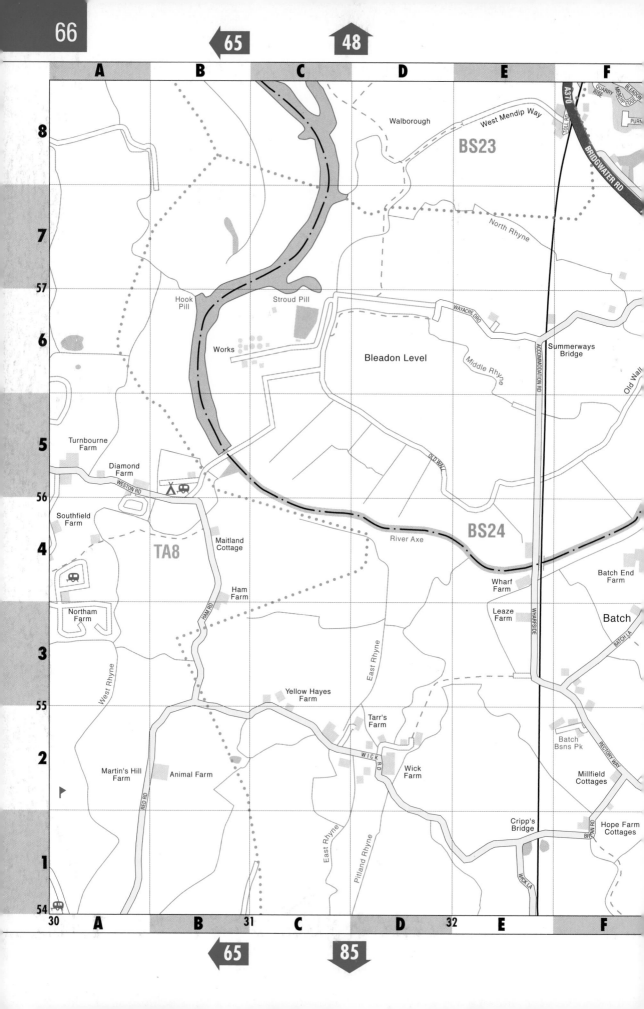

65
48

A B C D E F

8

7

57

6

5

56

4

3

55

2

1

54

30 31 32

Walborough

West Mendip Way

BS23

A370 TOLL RD

QUARRY RISE

BLEADON MENDIP EDGE

PURN

BRIDGWATER RD

North Rhyne

Hook Pill

Stroud Pill

WAYACRE DRO

Summerways Bridge

Works

Bleadon Level

Middle Rhyne

ACCOMMODATION RD

Old Walk

Turnbourne Farm

Diamond Farm

WESTON RD

OLD WALK

BS24

Southfield Farm

TA8

Maitland Cottage

River Axe

Batch End Farm

Northam Farm

Ham Farm

Wharf Farm

Leaze Farm

Batch

WHARFSIDE

BATCH LA

West Rhyne

HAM RD

East Rhyne

Yellow Hayes Farm

Tarr's Farm

Batch Bsns Pk

RECTORY WAY

Millfield Cottages

Martin's Hill Farm

Animal Farm

RED RD

WICK RD

Wick Farm

Cripp's Bridge

BRCN RD

Hope Farm Cottages

East Rhyne

Pitland Rhyne

WICK LA

65
85

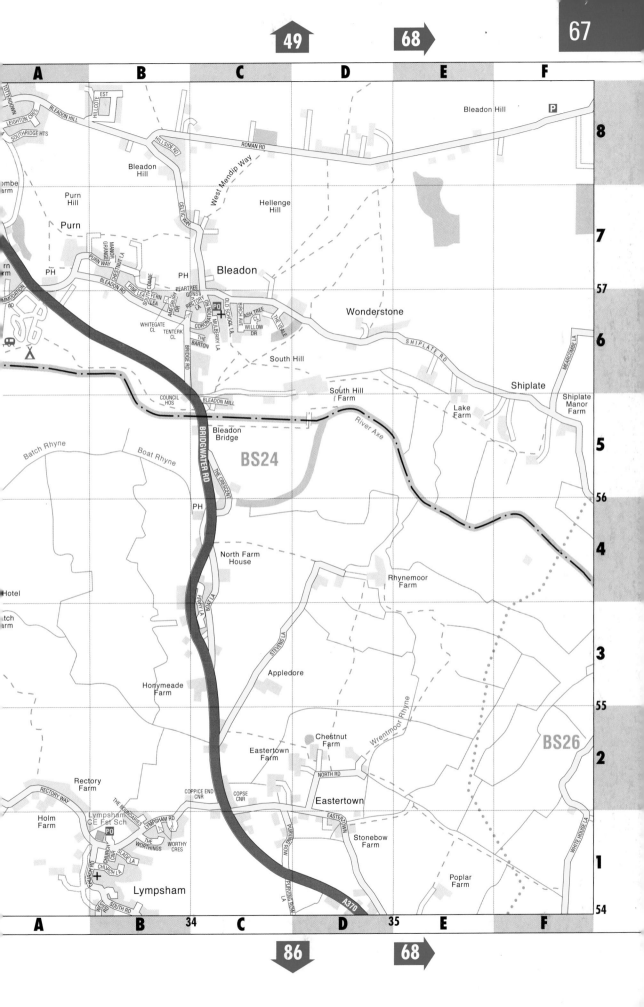

67
50

	A	B	C	D	E	F

CANADA COOMBE

BS29

8

Keeper's Cottage

Barleycombe Lodge

WESTON LA

Manor Farm

BANWELL RD

M5

Yatber Farm

Yatbe

7

BS24

Christon

FLAGSTAFF RD

+

57

Hamwood

Lox Yeo River

Shiplate Slait

MEARCOOMBE LA

6

Oakes Farm

CHRISTON RD

BS25

Loxton Hill

Loxton Wood

West Mendip Way

Long Acre

BARTON RD

5

Shiplate Wood

The Paddock

West Mendip Way

Crook Peak

56

BS26

HILLVIEW RD

CHURCH LA

+

The Lodge

4

Shiplett House Farm

SHIPLATE RD

Loxton

PO

SEVIER RD

COWSLIP LA

Wheelwright & Gypsy Mus

Hotel

Webbington

KENNEL LA

WEBBINGTON RD

White House Farm

Old Lox Yeo

3

WHITE HOUSE LA

HAMS LA

River Axe

55

Poplar Farm

2

North Yeo Farm

Mark Yeo

Crab Hole

BIDISHAM LA

Riverside Farm

Old River Axe

Tile House Farm

1

M5

54

36	A		B	37	C		D	38	E		F

67
87

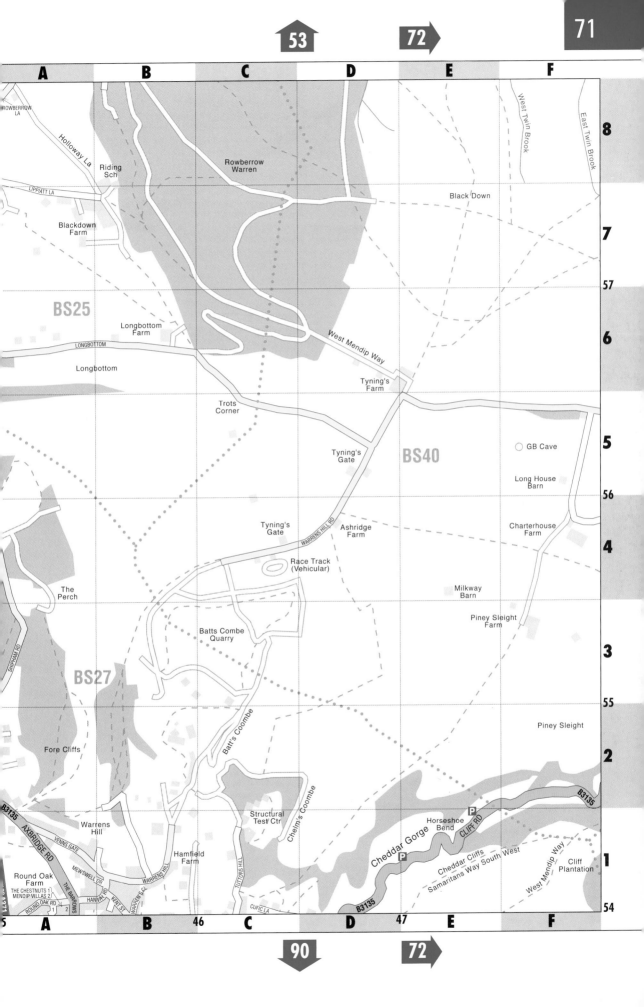

A B C D E F

8
7
57
6
5
56
4
3
55
2
1
54

ROWBERROW LA
Holloway La
Riding Sch
LIPPIATT LA
Blackdown Farm
Rowberrow Warren
Black Down
West Twin Brook
East Twin Brook

BS25
Longbottom Farm
LONGBOTTOM
Longbottom
West Mendip Way
Tyning's Farm
GB Cave

Trots Corner
Tyning's Gate
BS40
Long House Barn

Tyning's Gate
WARRENS HILL RD
Ashridge Farm
Charterhouse Farm

The Perch
Race Track (Vehicular)
Milkway Barn
Piney Sleight Farm

BS27
Batts Combe Quarry
Piney Sleight

Fore Cliffs
Batt's Coombe
Chelm's Coombe

SHIPHAM RD
Warrens Hill
Structural Test Ctr
Horseshoe Bend
CLIFF RD
Cheddar Gorge
Cheddar Cliffs
B3135
West Mendip Way
Cliff Plantation

B3135
AXBRIDGE RD
VENNS GATE
MEWSWELL DR
WARRENS HILL
Hamfield Farm
TUTTORS HILL
Samaritans Way South West

Round Oak Farm
THE CHESTNUTS
MENDIP VILLAS RD
ROUND OAK RD
THE BARROWS
HANNAH
KENT ST
WARRENS CL
CUFIC LA
B3135

46
47

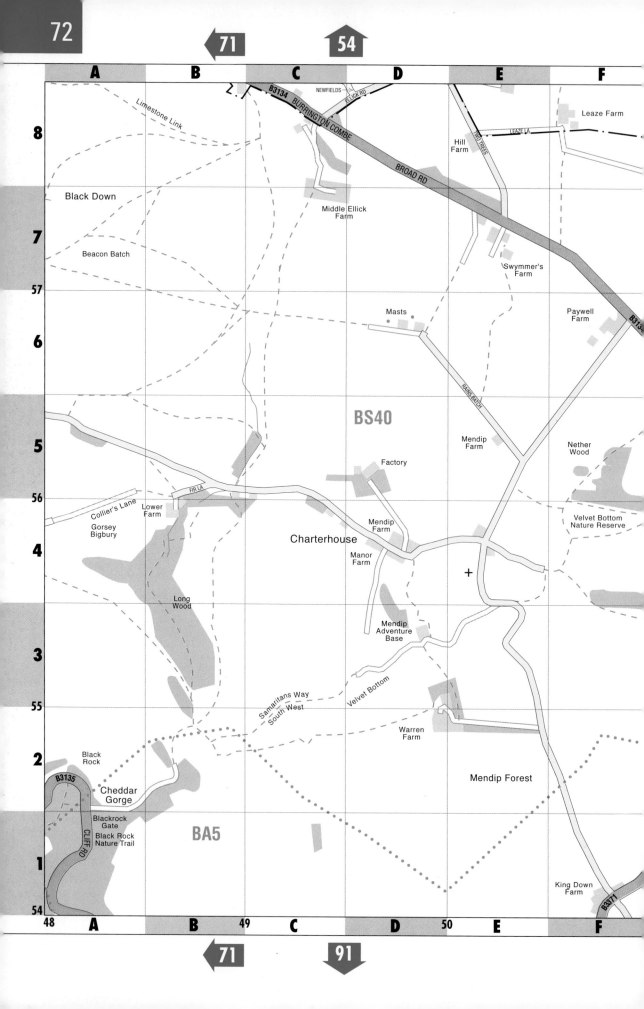

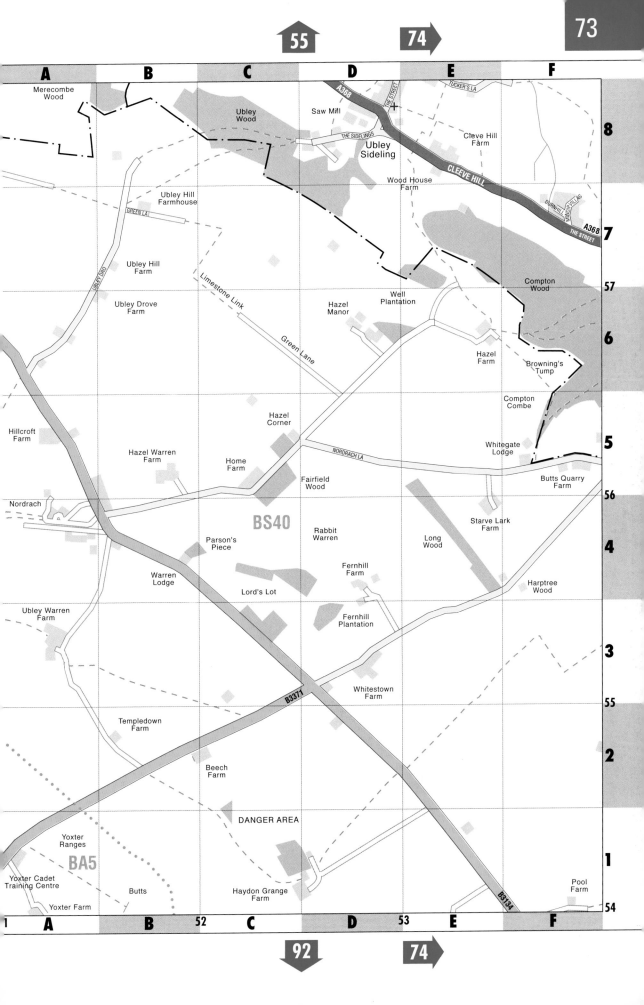

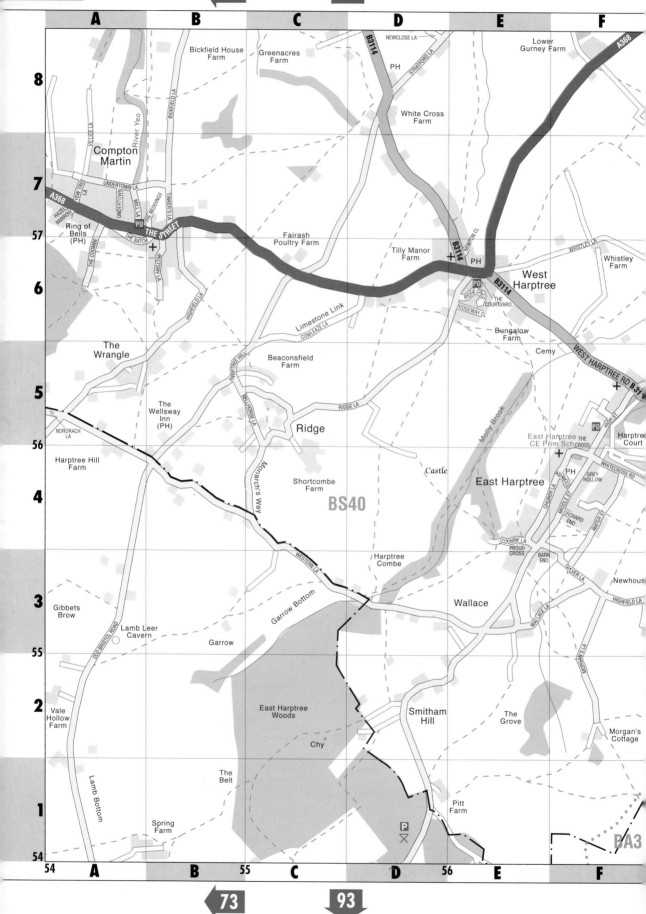

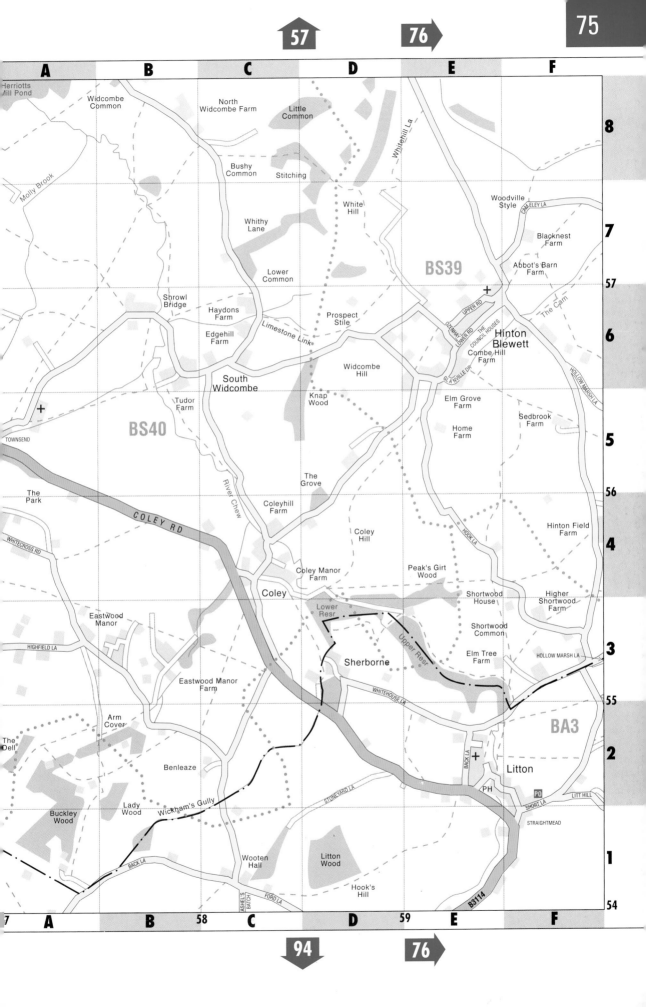

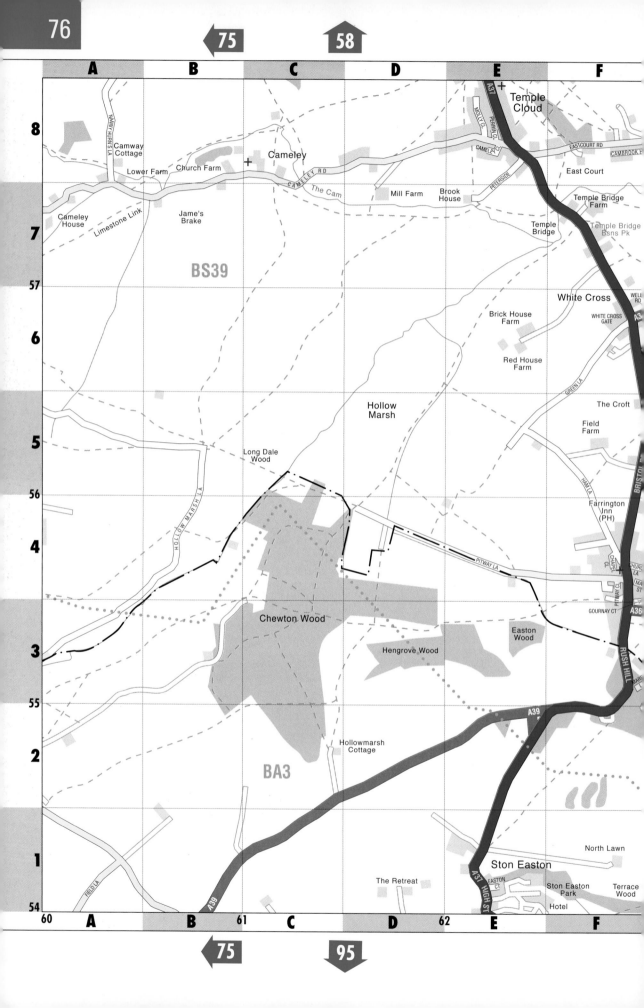

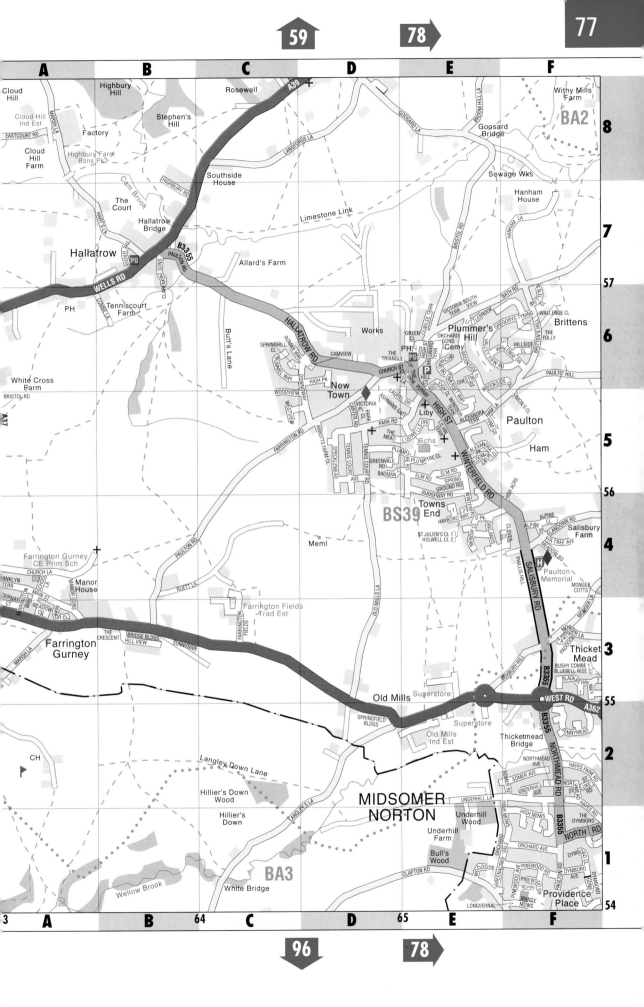

A B C D E F

BA2
8

Cloud Hill
Cloud Hill Ind Est
EASTCOURT RD
Cloud Hill Farm

Highbury Hill
Stephen's Hill
Factory
Highbury Farm Bsns Pk
Cam Brook
HIGHBURY RD
The Court
Hallatrow Bridge
HART'S LA
THE GROVE
PO
Hallatrow
WELLS RD
PH
COMBE LA
Tenniscourt Farm
CLAREM GDNS
PAULTON RD
B3355

Rosewell
A39
Langfords La
Southside House
Limestone Link
Allard's Farm

Goosard Bridge
Goosard La
BROOM HILL LA
Withy Mills Farm

BRISTOL RD
Sewage Wks
Hanham House
HANHAM LA
7
57

White Cross Farm
BRISTOL RD
A437

Butt's Lane

HALLATROW RD
SPRINGHILL CL
ROMAN WAY
ST JAMES WAY
DOWNSIDE
CAMVIEW
HIGH PK
WOODVIEW
WESTVIEW
New Town
Works
The Triangle
CHURCH ST
GREEN CL
HIGH ST
PH
PO
The Mead
PARK RD
VICTORIA PL
CARTER CL
ASHMANS GATE
LAUREL DR
PITWAY
LUDWELLS
ORC
PLUMP PL
PLUMPTRE CL
Liby
Schs
SPRING GROUND RD
ELM RD
ELM RD
RUDGEWAY RD
BADMAN
GREENVALE RD
TENNIS COURT AVE
TENNIS COURT RD
SPECKLEMEAD
ABBOTTS FARM CL
FARRINGTON RD

Plummer's Hill
Cemy
VICTORIA SOUTH TERR
JUBILEE TERR
ORCHARD GDNS
TYTHERI...
BATH RD
GREGORYS TYNING
WALLENGE CL
THE FOLLY
HILLSIDE CL
Brittens
BRITTENS HILL
VALLEY VIEW RD
WALLENGE DR
PAULTO' HILL
BROOKSIDE CL
CHESTNUT CL
SIMON'S CL
HAM LA
Paulton
Ham
ALEXANDRA TERR
WINTERFIELD RD
HIGH ACRE
6
5
56

Farrington Gurney CE Prim Sch
CHURCH LA
FRANKLYN TERR
GURNAY
MARSH LA
SCHOOL CL
MEADOW CL
MANOR GDNS
MAIN ST
MANOR House
Manor House
RUETT LA
PAULTON RD

Meml

Farrington Fields Trad Est
Farrington Fields
OLD MILLS LA

BS39

Towns End
HAYBORO WAY
ST JULIEN'S CL 1
HOLWELL CL 2
MENDIP CL
OAKLANDS
CLOVER CL
ALPINE CL
ALPINE GDNS
GLANDOWN RD
PEAR TREE AVE
MEADOW RD
Salisbury Farm
MONGER COTTS
H
Paulton Memorial
PHILIS HILL
SALISBURY RD
MONGER LA
HEARTS LA
PADDOCKS
4

The Crescent
BRIDGE BLDGS
HILL VIEW
SUNNYSIDE
Farrington Gurney
MARSH LA
CH
Langley Down Lane
Hillier's Down Wood
Hillier's Down
LANGLEY'S LA
Springfield Bldgs
SPRINGFIELD FIELDS

Old Mills
Superstore
Superstore
Old Mills Ind Est
Old Mills Bridge
ROXBURY HILL
West Rd
A362
B3355
SUNNYMEAD
Thicket Mead
BUSHY COMBE 1
BLUEBELL RISE 2
BLACKBERRY WAY
B3355
Thicketmead Bridge
3
55
2

Wellow Brook
White Bridge
CLAPTON RD

MIDSOMER NORTON

Underhill Wood
Underhill Farm
Bull's Wood

BA3

NORTHMEAD AVE
HAYES PARK RD
SOMER AVE
UNDERHILL LA
UNDERHILL AVE
NORTH...
ST LUKE'S RD
HIGH MDWS
NORTHMEAD RD
B3355
THE DYMBORO
NORTH RD
ORCHARD AVE
DYMBORO AVE
DYMBORO GDNS
PAULTON RD
PINEWOOD...
GREENACRES VALE
WOODSIDE
PINEWOOD AVE
Sch
MANDY MDWS
LONGVERNAL
Providence Place
1
54

A B C D E F

8

7

57

6

56

5

4

3

55

2

1

54

HIGH ST
Willow Farm

Gooseberry Cottage

Norton Lane Farm

Wellow Farm

WELLOW RD

Cemy

Stoney Littleton Long Barrow

Brinscombe La

BA2

Greenacres

Baggridge Hill

LITTLETON LA

The Hare Warren

Upper Baggridge Farm

South View Farm

Wellow Brook

Stony Littleton

HANG HILL

GULLEN

Stony Littleton Farm

GRAYS HILL

DAIRY HILL

Baggeridge Belt

Norway Plantation

Dairy Cottage

Littleton Wood

Brigadier's Path

Single Hill

New Plantation

Knoll Wood

Knoll Farm

Ramsgate Wood

FAULKLAND LA

Home Covert

Tenantsfield La

Bladdock Gutter

LIPPIAT HILL

BA3

Oldfield House

A366

Oreston Cottage

Oldfield Cottage

Faulkland Farm

Ruckley Ford

Pond Farm

GROVE LA

THE GREEN

Lower Farm

Limestone Cottage

Rockley Ford Farm

BISHOP ST

POND COTTS

Faulkland

Chapel Farm

HIGH ST

PO
PH

Horsepond Farm

PULWELL CL

FULWELL LA

1 GREENWAY
2 CHURCHWAY
3 LANSDOWN VIEW

TURNER'S TWR

A366

PARK LA

CHICKWELL LA

72 A B 73 C D 74 E F

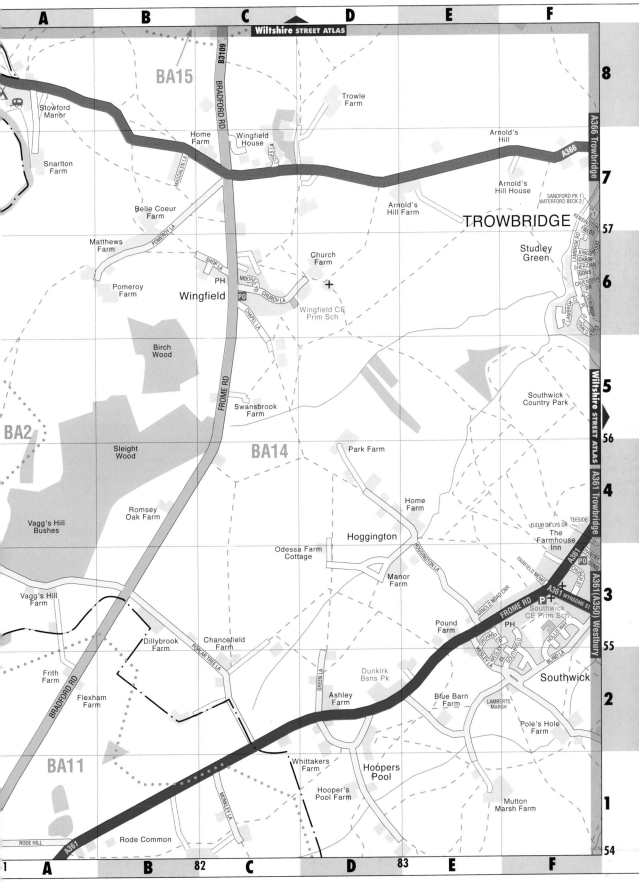

BA15

Stowford Manor

Snarlton Farm

Home Farm

Wingfield House

Trowle Farm

Arnold's Hill

SANDFORD PK 1
WATERFORD BECK 2

A366 Trowbridge

A366

Arnold's Hill House

TROWBRIDGE

Belle Coeur Farm

Matthews Farm

Pomeroy Farm

Wingfield

Arnold's Hill Farm

Church Farm

Wingfield CE Prim Sch

Studley Green

KENSINGTON FIELDS

CAVENDISH DR

ALBURGH

Birch Wood

BA2

Swansbrook Farm

Sleight Wood

BA14

Park Farm

Southwick Country Park

Home Farm

Vagg's Hill Bushes

Romsey Oak Farm

Hoggington

Odessa Farm Cottage

Manor Farm

The Farmhouse Inn

FLEUR DE LYS DR
TEESIDE

FAIRFIELD MEWS

A361 Trowbridge

PO GDNS

A361 (A350) Westbury

Vagg's Hill Farm

Frith Farm

Flexham Farm

Dillybrook Farm

Chancefield Farm

Arnold Moad Cnr

Pound Farm

PH

Southwick CE Prim Sch

HOLLIS WAY

BLIND LA

Southwick

BRADFORD RD

POPLAR TREE LA

Dunkirk Bsns Pk

Ashley Farm

Blue Barn Farm

LAMBERTS MARSH

Pole's Hole Farm

BA11

Whittakers Farm

Hooper's Pool Farm

Hoopers Pool

Mutton Marsh Farm

RODE HILL

A361

Rode Common

Unity Farm

SHRUBBERY CL

HERON PK

HURN LA

Hurn Farm

COAST RD

Mead Farm

Berrow Manor

MANOR CL
MANOR DR
MANOR WAY

CLAREMONT CVN PK

Rose Farm

PINNOCKSCROFT RD
PARSONAGE RD

Westcroft Nurseries

TA8

LITTLE PEN

PENMOOR CL
PENMOOR PL

CHURCH HOUSE RD

BARTON CL

MONKSTONE DR

BROOKE RD

BARTON RD

Sch

Berrow

JULIAN ACRES

FAIRWAY CL

ROSE TREE PADDOCK

ROSENEATH AV

BERROW RD
SANDHILL DR

P

PH

Lark Spit

THE RETREAT CVN PK

A B C D E F

8

7

53

6

5

52

4

3

51

2

1

50

27 28 29

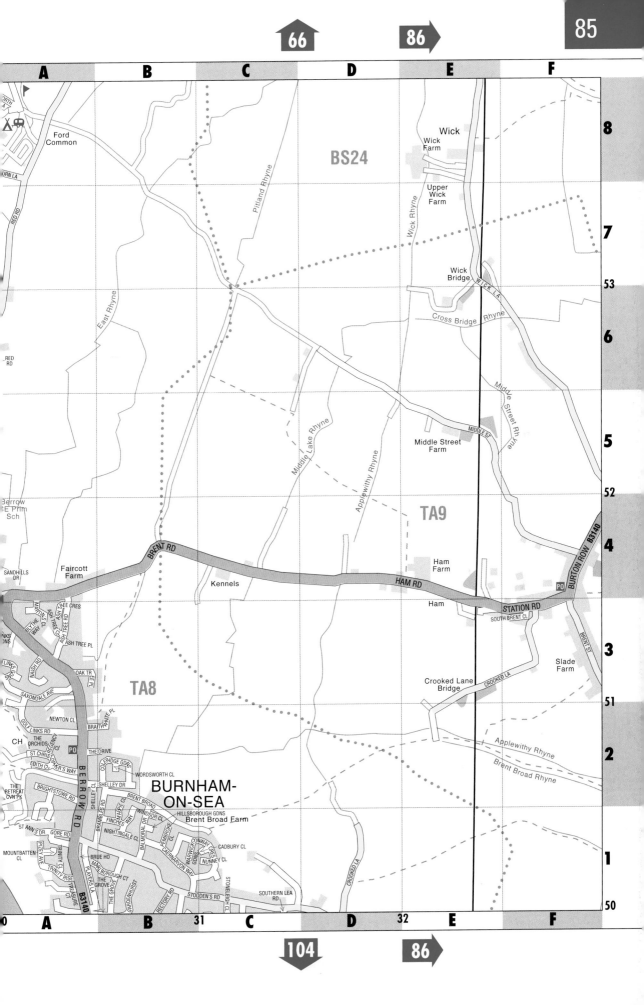

← 85
67 ↑

A **B** **C** **D** **E** **F**

8

BS26

SOUTH CL

Blue Coat Farm

SOUTH RD

PURVING BOW LA

A370

BRIDGWATER RD

EASTERTOWN

WHITE HOUSE LA

Edingworth

7

Lower Farm

WEST RD

DELHORN LA

BS24

Dulhorn Farm

Brent House Farm

EDINGWORTH RD

Manor Farm

Rookery Farm

53

Burton Row Rhyne

WESTON RD

Delhorn Rhyne

STROWLAND LK

Sedgemoor Services

6

Groves Rhyne

STROWLANDS

Motel

BS2

5

Burton Row Farm

East Brent

Manor Farm

BURTON ROW

North Grove Farm

BRENT RD

JOHNSON CL

RED HOUSE RD

POPHAM CL

MANOR EAST DR

THE MEAD

PROSPECT CL

Prospect Farm

Brocks P Rhyne

A38

52

Shrub Farm

WICK LA

B3140

ASH TREES

CHURCH RD

THE OLD RECTORY

WYCHDALE WAY

B3140

MANOR CL

BRENT RD

ORCHARD

Old Bristol Rd

OLD BRISTOL RD

4

East Brent CE Fst Sch

JARVIS LA

BRIDGWATER RD

A370

Mill Batch Farm Ind Est

HILL LA

Elm Tree House

TA9

Chapel Farm

3

The Red Cow (PH)

Manor Farm

Shipton's Copse

BRISTOL RD

A370

M5

Brent Knoll

Lake House

51

LAUREL AVE

Stone

Brent House

2

CHURCH LA

THE WILLOWS

P

CEDAR CL

BRANCH RISE

COOMBE SIDE

BRENT ST

EAST RISE

BRENT CL

South Common Farm

CHURCH LANE CNR

Brent Kngll CE Prim Sch

Battleborough Grange

Brent Knoll

Smithfield Farm

1

BATTLEBOROUGH LA

PO

PORTLAND PL

Battleborough

A38

VOLE RD

M5

50

33 **A** **B** 34 **C** **D** 35 **E** **F**

← 85
105

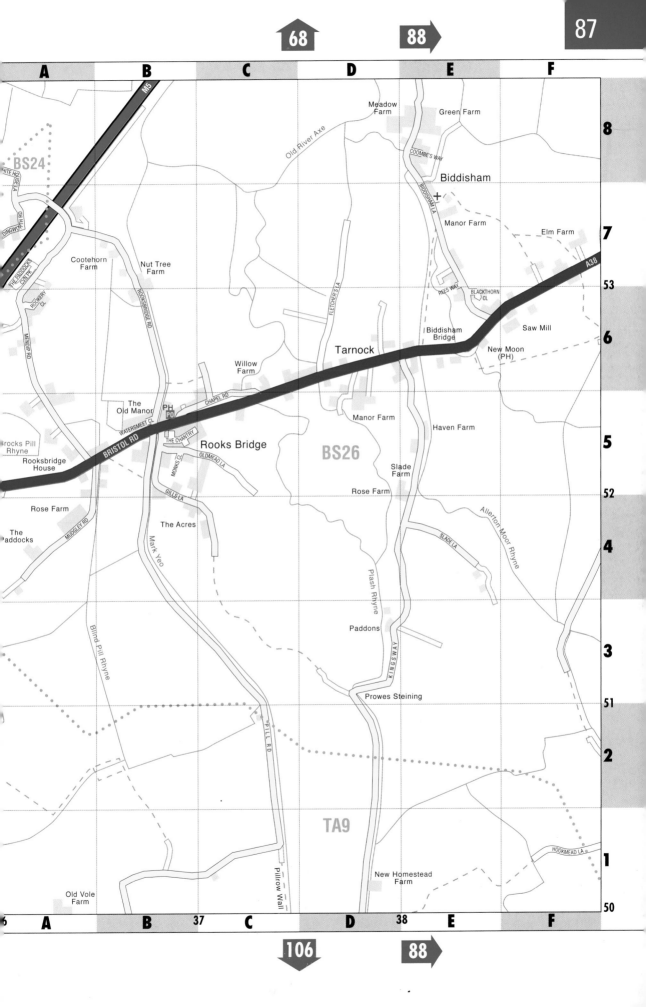

BS24

Meadow Farm

Green Farm

COOMBE'S WAY

Biddisham

BIDDISHAM LA

Manor Farm

Elm Farm

A38

White H'SE LA

DH HO'SE

DINGWOOK

THE PADDOCKS CV'N PK

Cootehorn Farm

Nut Tree Farm

ROOKSBRIDGE RD

FLETCHER'S LA

REES WAY

BLACKTHORN CL

Saw Mill

ROOKERY CL

MENDIP RD

Tarnock

Biddisham Bridge

New Moon (PH)

Willow Farm

Chocks Pill Rhyne

The Old Manor

PH
PO

CHAPEL RD

THE CHANTRY

WATERSMEET CL

BRISTOL RD

Rooks Bridge

Manor Farm

Haven Farm

Rooksbridge House

MONKS CL

OLDMEAD LA

BS26

Slade Farm

Rose Farm

Rose Farm

GILLS LA

The Acres

Mark Yeo

Allerton Moor Rhyne

The Paddocks

MUDGLEY RD

SLADE LA

Plash Rhyne

Paddons

Blind Pill Rhyne

KINGSWAY

Prowes Steining

TA9

PILL RD

New Homestead Farm

HOOKMEAD LA

Old Vole Farm

Pillrow Wall

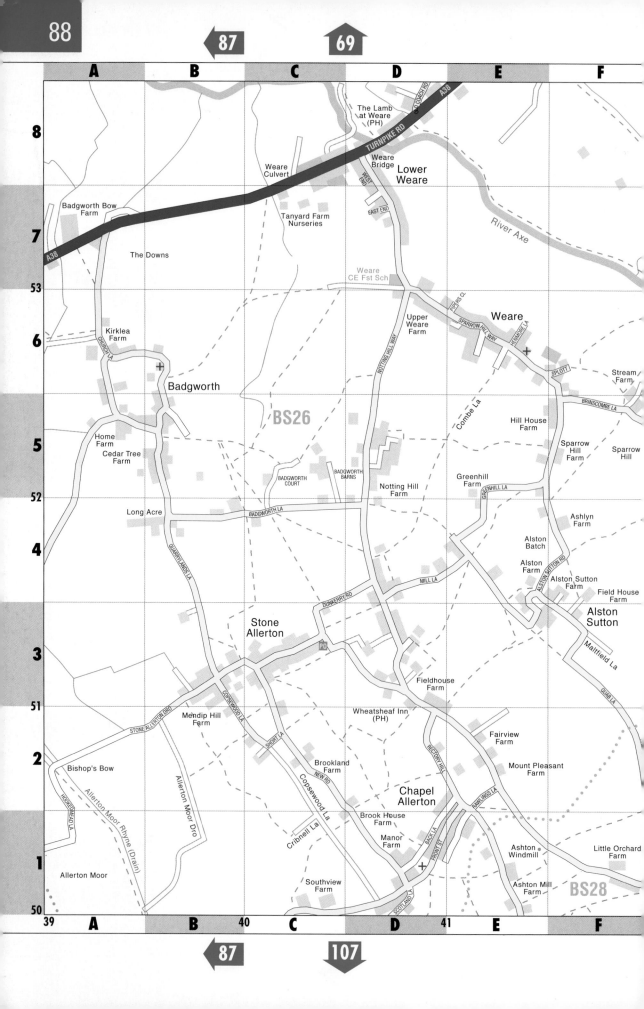

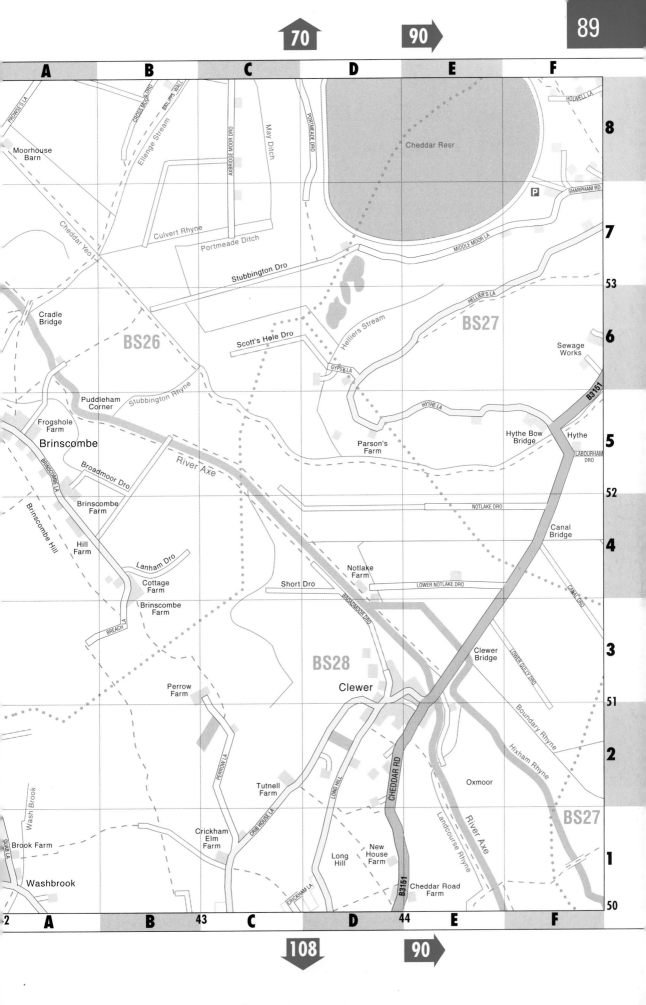

A B C D E F

8

PROWSE LA
HOLWELL LA
Moorhouse Barn
CROSS MOOR DRO
BRILIPPS WALL
Ellenge Stream
AXBRIDGE MOOR DRO
May Ditch
PORTMEADE DRO
Cheddar Resr
P
SHARPHAM RD

7

Cheddar Yeo
Culvert Rhyne
Portmeade Ditch
Stubbington Dro
MIDDLE MOOR LA

53

Cradle Bridge
BS26
Scott's Hole Dro
Helliers Stream
HELLIER'S LA
BS27

6

Puddleham Corner
Stubbington Rhyne
GYPSY LA
Sewage Works
B3151

Frogshole Farm
Brinscombe
River Axe
Parson's Farm
HYTHE LA
Hythe Bow Bridge
Hythe
LABOURHAM DRO

5

BRINSCOMBE LA
Broadmoor Dro
NOTLAKE DRO

52

Brinscombe Farm
Brinscombe Hill
Canal Bridge

Hill Farm
Lanham Dro
Notlake Farm
LOWER NOTLAKE DRO
CANAL DRO

4

BREACH LA
Cottage Farm
Short Dro
BROADMOOR DRO

Brinscombe Farm
BS28
Clewer Bridge
LOWER GULLY DRO

3

Perrow Farm
Clewer
Boundary Rhyne

51

PERROW LA
Hixham Rhyne
BS27

2

QUB LA
Wash Brook
Tutnell Farm
GRIB HOUSE LA
LONG HILL
CHEDDAR RD
Oxmoor
River Axe
Landcourse Rhyne

Brook Farm
Crickham Elm Farm
Long Hill
New House Farm

1

Washbrook
CRICKHAM LA
B3151
Cheddar Road Farm

50

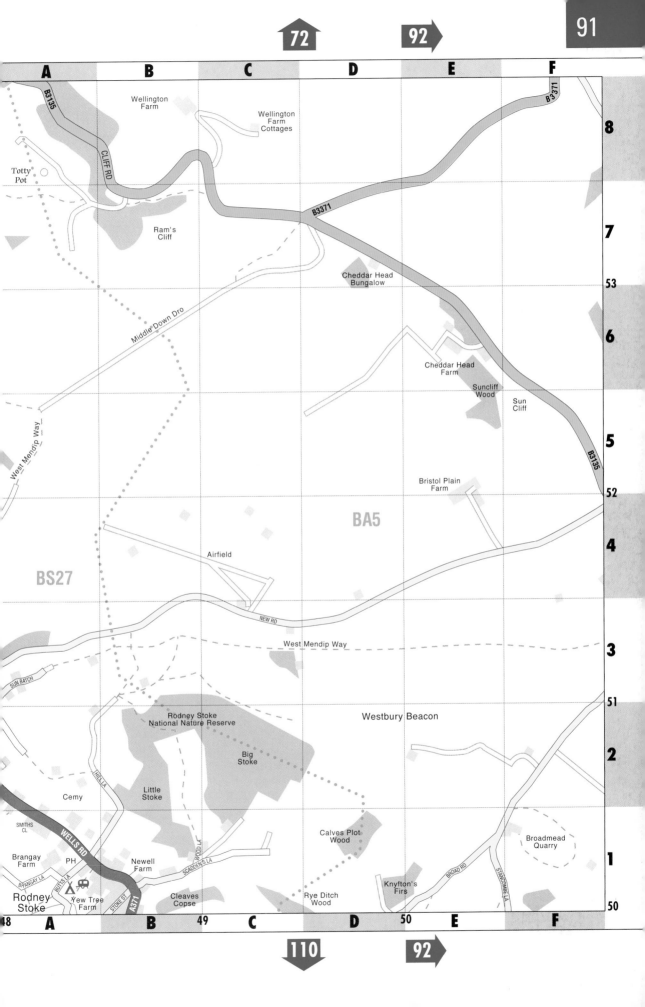

72
92

A B C D E F

8
7
53
6
5
52
4
3
51
2
1
50

B3135
Wellington Farm
Wellington Farm Cottages
CLIFF RD
Totty Pot
Ram's Cliff
B3371
Cheddar Head Bungalow
Middle Down Dro
Cheddar Head Farm
Suncliff Wood
Sun Cliff
West Mendip Way
B3135
Bristol Plain Farm
BA5
BS27
Airfield
NEW RD
West Mendip Way
SUN BATCH
Rodney Stoke National Nature Reserve
Westbury Beacon
Big Stoke
Cemy
HILL LA
Little Stoke
SMITHS CL
WELLS RD
Calves Plot Wood
Broadmead Quarry
Brangay Farm
PH
Newell Farm
SCADDEN'S LA
WOOD LA
Knyfton's Firs
BROAD RD
STANDCOMBE LA
BRANGAY LA
Yew Tree Farm
STOKE ST
A371
Cleaves Copse
Rye Ditch Wood
Rodney Stoke
BUTTS LA

48 A B 49 C D 50 E F

110
92

91
73

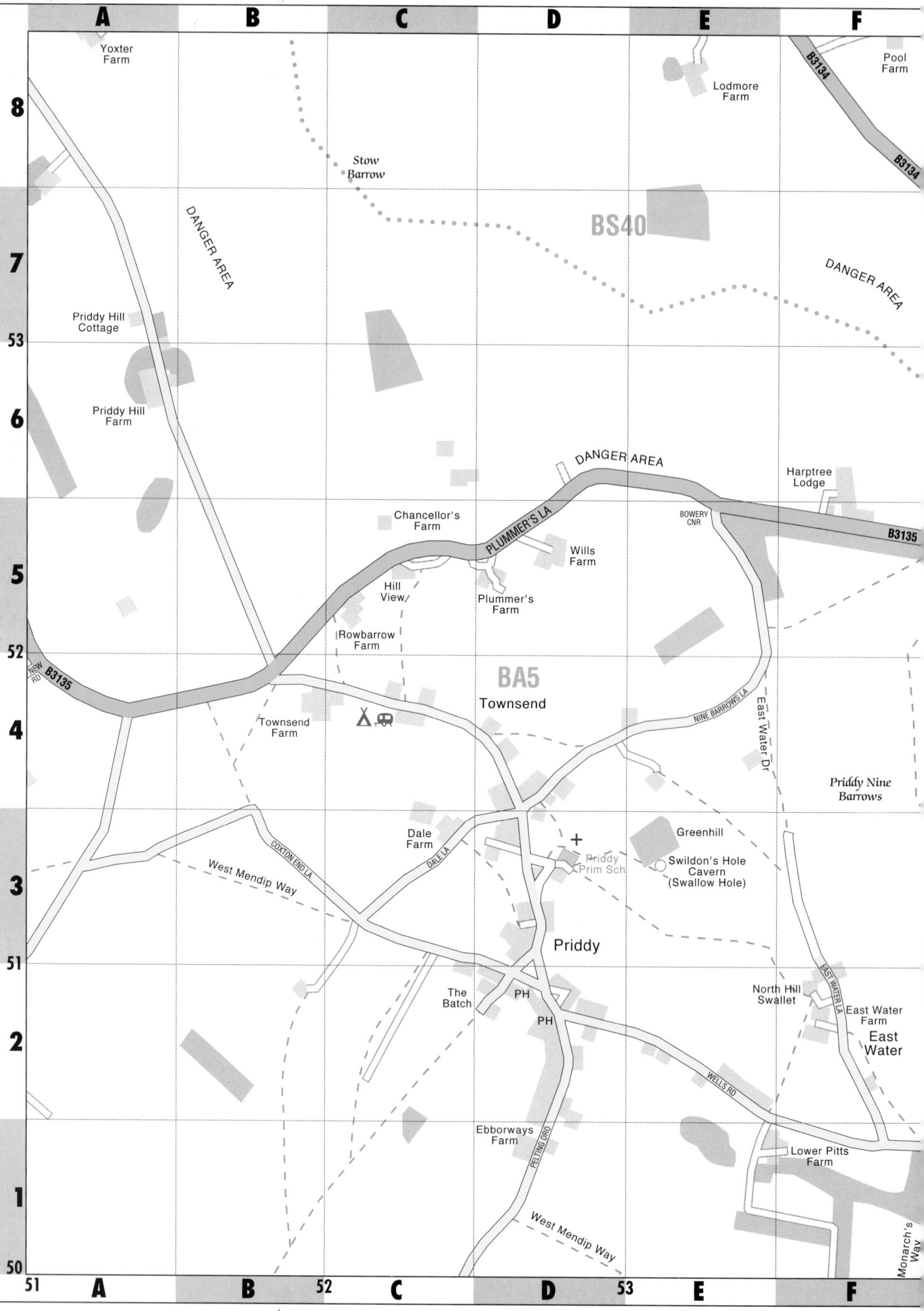

A **B** **C** **D** **E** **F**

Yoxter
Farm

8

DANGER AREA

Stow
Barrow

Lodmore
Farm

B3134

Pool
Farm

B3134

BS40

DANGER AREA

7

Priddy Hill
Cottage

53

Priddy Hill
Farm

6

DANGER AREA

Harptree
Lodge

Chancellor's
Farm

PLUMMER'S LA

Wills
Farm

BOWERY
CNR

B3135

5

Hill
View

Plummer's
Farm

Rowbarrow
Farm

52

NEW RD

B3135

BA5

Townsend

NINE BARROWS LA

East Water Dr

4

Townsend
Farm

Priddy Nine
Barrows

West Mendip Way

COXTON END LA

Dale
Farm

DALE LA

Priddy
Prim Sch

Greenhill

Swildon's Hole
Cavern
(Swallow Hole)

3

51

Priddy

The
Batch

PH

PH

North Hill
Swallet

EAST WATER LA

East Water
Farm

East
Water

2

WELLS RD

Ebborways
Farm

PELTING DRO

Lower Pitts
Farm

1

West Mendip Way

Monarch's Way

50

51 **A** **B** **52** **C** **D** **53** **E** **F**

A   B   C   D   E   F

Monarch's Way

Devil's
Punch Bowl

Wurt Pit
(dis)

Roadside
Clump

Nett Wood
Farm

Greendown Batch

8

Swallet
Farm

Mast

Hill
Grange

Big
Clump

Niver
Hill

B3134

Hill
Farm

BS40

7

53

Castle of Comfort
(PH)

Castle
Farm

Monarch's Way

Bendall's
Grove

Eaker Hill
Farm

West
End

6

Priddy
Circles

OLD BRISTOL RD

The Belt

Wigmore
Farm

BA3

Cranmore
View

Miners' Arms

Eaker
Hill

5

B3134

Red Quarr
Farm

52

TORHOLE BOTTOM

4

BA5

P

North Hill

Monarch's Way

Bendalls
Farm

B3135

3

Priddy
Mineries

51

Stockhill

2

Under Barrow
Farm

Nursery

Cuckoo
Cleeves

Tower
Hill

1

Ash
Plantation

Hunters Lodge
Inn

HILLGROVE RD

50

54   A   B   55   C   D   56   E   F

93 75

A B C D E F

8
Greendown Batch
Holmwood Farm
BACK LA
Green Down
Greendown Farmhouse
Radford Farm
ASHE'S BATCH
Lily Combe
Lily Combe Farm
PRIMMERFIELD LA
FORD LA
B3114
Ford Farm
Ford
KING'S HILL
LOWER ST
FRED LA
B3114

7
Coomb's Grove
Grove Farm
BELL LA
BELL HILL
WATERY COMBE
Grig's Pit Wood
Chewton Mendip
Chewton Mendip CE Prim Sch
PH
CHEWTON H.
A3
COLE'S LA

53
Buddle's Wood
MEARN'S CROSS
Burges's Combe
Grig's Pit
Sage's Farm
Manor House
CHURCH LA
HIGH ST

6
Bendell's Grove
Westend Farm
YORK'S LA
Cole's Farm
Riding Stables
Rookery Farm
SAGE'S LA
WILLET'S LA
Priory Farm
Chewton Cheese Dairy
BACK LA
ORCHARD LA
PUPPY LA
DRIALS LA
The Folly

5
Eaker Hill Wood
Bishop's Pond
Tor Hole
Pedler's Paddock
Preston's Wood
CLAY LA
BROAD ST
CHEDDAR RD
Sperring's Green
Sperring's Green Farm
BA3
B3114
CHAPEL HILL
PO
Bathway
PUPPY CROSS WAYS
Cutler's Green Farm
DUDWELL LA

52
TORHOLE BOTTOM
NEDGE LA
Bathway Farm
Cutler's Green
EAST END LA
HONEY WELL LA
MANNING'S LA
B3114

4
Long Wrangle Plantation
Everard's Farm
NEDGE CNR
Franklyn' Farm

3
Island Plantation
Nedge Farm
NEDGE HILL
East End Farm
East End
EAST END LA
Hippisley Farm

51
B3135
Rookery Farm

2
BA5
Newlands Farm
Shooter's Bottom
Shooter's Bottom Farm

1
Gold Batch
Pinelea Farm
PH
GREEN ORE EST
BRISTOL RD
Green Ore
Mendip Farm

50
Green Ore Farm
A39
B3135
Works

57 A 58 B C 58 D 59 E F

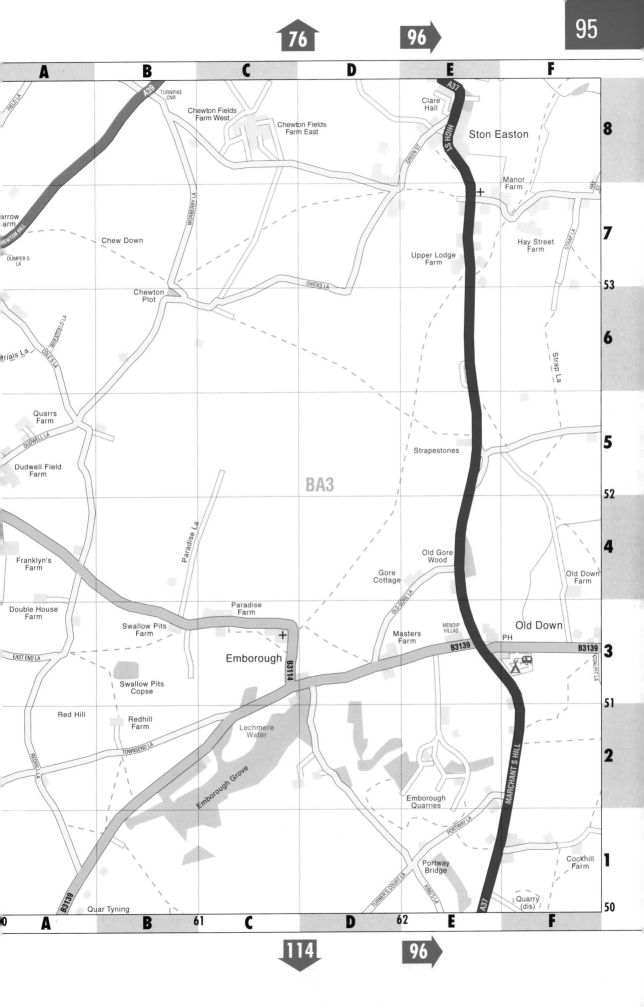

A   B   C   D   E   F

8

Clare Hall

Ston Easton

Manor Farm

7

Hay Street Farm

53

6

5

52

4

3

51

2

1

50

A B C D E F

8
7
53
6
5
52
4
3
51
2
1
50

HAY ST

Lower Hay Street Farm

Whitchurch Farm

LANGLEY'S LA

LANGLEY'S COTTS

Glenwood Farm

CLAPTON RD

ZION HILL

PH

Manor Farm

Clapton

Hillside

SPERRING CT
CLAPTON RD
PAULTON RD
REDFIELD
AMBAR CT
LABURNUM GR
MILLFIELD
SUNRISE PK
HILLSIDE CRES
HILLSIDE AVE
HILLSIDE RD
REDLANDS TERR
WITHIES PK
CASTLE CL
SDALE

Folly Hill
Redfield Wood
SMALLWOOD VIEW
HILLVIEW
UPPER BROOKS
RIVERSIDE RD
RIVERSIDE GDNS
RIVERSIDE WLK
STADILTONS CL
LONG

Riverside

RIVERSIDE WLK

CHILCOMPTON RD

FOLLY CL

CROSSWAY LA

New Whitchurch Farm

GREEN DITCH LA

BA3

River Somer

Sewage Works

Manor Farm

UPPER PITCHING
CORONATION TERR 2

THE PITCHING
THE STREET
CHURCH LA
WOODVIEW
SOMER LEY

Nortondown House

Norton Green Farm

TUNNEL LA

WELLS RD

B31

Tynir Hous

Mount Pleasant

Chilcompton

GOLLEDGE CL
PARSONAGE LA
RAGLAN CL
HIGHFIELD CRES

GREEN DITCH LA
BROADWAY CL

SAWMILL GDNS 1
SHEPPARDS WLK 2
STATION MEAD
1 2
SAWYERS CL

BAKERS LA
PINES CL
VALLEY VIEW
CARTERS WAY
WELL
FRY'S CL
BOSEMHAM HILL
BRITANNIA CL

BENNELL CL
BENNELL BATCH
BENNELL COTTS
NURSERY RISE

St Vigor & St John CE Prim Sch

LYNCH HILL
Rookery Farm
BROADWAY
PH
B3139
PO
B3139
NAISH'S CROSS
NAISH FARM
B3356
WESTMEAD
DOWNSIDE CL
MONTSURE CL

ROCK RD

Downside Abbey Home Farm

FOSSEWAY
A3

SPERRING CT

B3139

Three Tuns Farm

COAL PIT LA

STOCKHILL CL
HOECROFT GDNS
HOECROFT
GREENWAYS
MENDIP FIELDS
STOCKHILL RD

Croft House

ABBEY RD

Downside Abbey

ABBEY RD

Downside Sch

THE MEAD
SUSANNAH MEAD
LINKMEAD
CHURCH ROW
CHURCH LA
PH
THE WILLOW
P

Knitts Farm

Downside

Downside Farm

New Rock Ind Est

South Rock Ind Est

ROCK RD

GREEN LA

Stratton-on-the-Fosse

Winter Top Farm

Blacker's Hill Farm

Blacker's Hill

Green Lane Farmhouse

B3356
THE LODGES

A367
MOUNTMEAD
RAMSHAY
VIEW VIEW
HORNE CL

63 A B 64 C D 65 E F

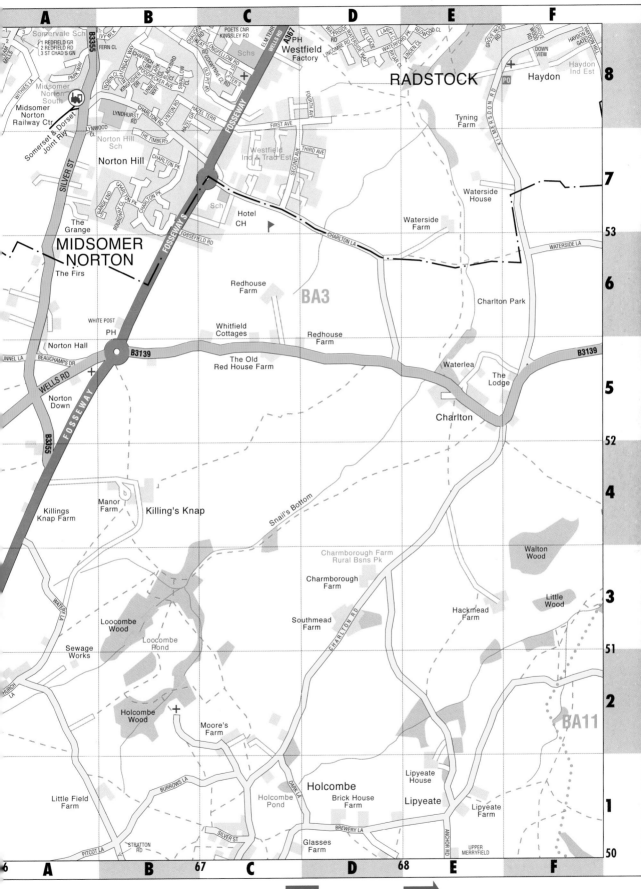

A   B   C   D   E   F

Haydon House

Huish House

FROME RD A362

Peak's Wood

Haywood Wood

Haywood Farm

A36

8

TERRY HILL

AMMERDOWN TERR

HAYDON HILL

Upper Lentney Farm

Upper Lentney Farm Cottage

FROME RD

Lentney Farm

KNOBSBURY LA

Upper Knobsbury

B3139

A366

7

BA3

Terry Hill Plantation

53

Lower Knobsbury

KNOBSBURY HILL

Nap Wood

WATERSIDE LA

Tyning Farm

Home Farm

Gagman Coppice

Ammerdown House

Coldbath Plantation

6

Kilmersdon CE Prim Sch

Sewage Works

AMES LA

SCHOOL LA

CHURCH ST

Kilmersdon

(dis)

Ammerdown Park

The Column

B3139 KILMERSDON HILL

COLES GDNS

Ammerdown Bridge

Manor Farm

P

SILVER ST

Wedingham Copse

Hatchet Hill Coppice

5

52

THE STABLES

Beatle's Wood

Babington Wood

Batch Farm

HATCHET HILL

Walton Farm

NEW RD

Kingsdown Wood

4

HOARE'S LA

South View

Upton's Piece

Mells Down Farm

Lowerfield Farm

Babington Park

Cornish's Grave

Works

3

Babington

Jericho Bridge

51

Babington House

Works

BA11

Lodge

2

Cherry Garden Farm

LUCKINGTON CROSS

DARK LA

Newbury House

CHARITY LA

White Cottage

Edney's Farm

Newbury Farm

INNER'S LA

Luckington Manor Farm

BA3

Newbury

BA3

Works

POPLE'S LA

1

50

69   A   B   70   C   D   71   E   F

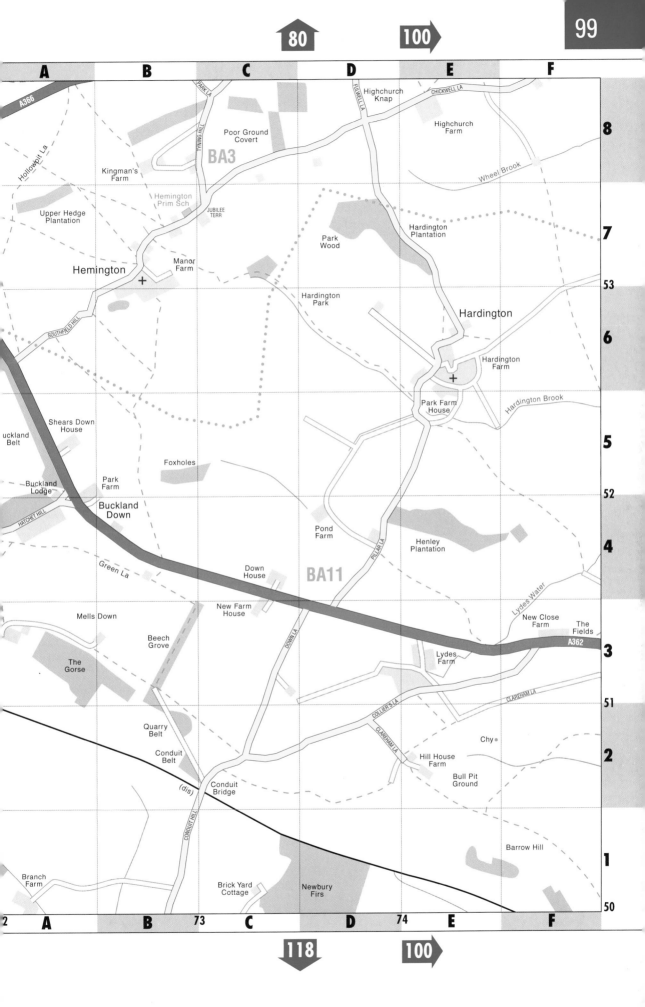

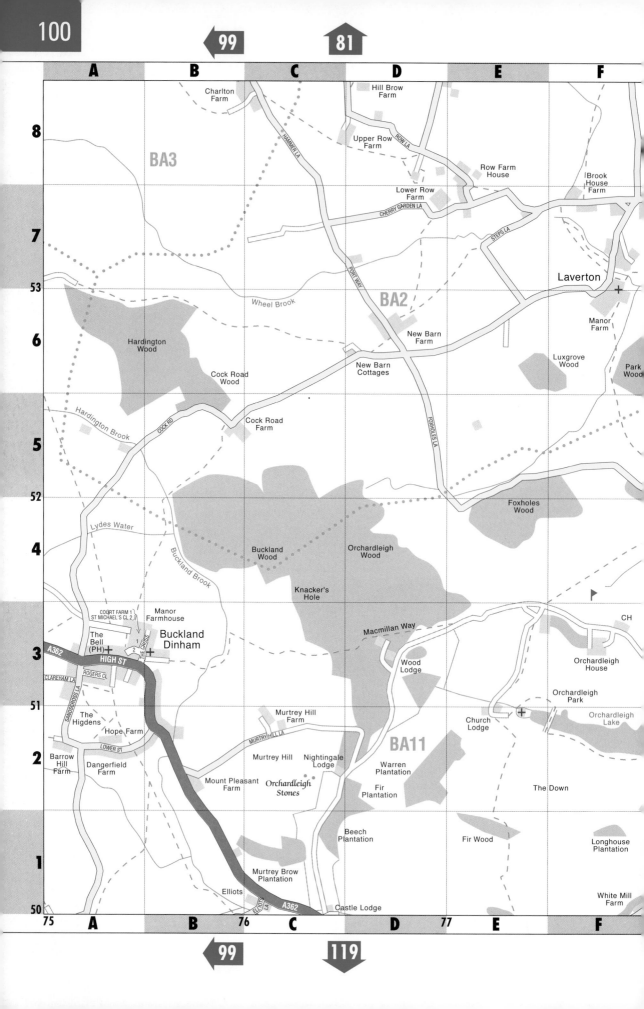

A   B   C   D   E   F

8

BA3

Charlton Farm

Hill Brow Farm

Upper Row Farm

Row Farm House

Lower Row Farm

Brook House Farm

HAMMER LA

ROW LA

CHERRY GARDEN LA

STEPS LA

7

Laverton

Manor Farm

53

Wheel Brook

BA2

PORT WAY

6

Hardington Wood

New Barn Farm

Luxgrove Wood

Park Wood

Cock Road Wood

New Barn Cottages

Hardington Brook

COCK RD

Cock Road Farm

FOXHOLES LA

5

52

Foxholes Wood

Lydes Water

Buckland Brook

4

Buckland Wood

Orchardleigh Wood

Knacker's Hole

CH

COURT FARM 1
ST MICHAEL'S CL 2

Manor Farmhouse

Macmillan Way

Wood Lodge

Orchardleigh House

The Bell (PH)

Buckland Dinham

THE CROSS

Orchardleigh Park

A362

HIGH ST

3

ROGERS CL

Orchardleigh Lake

CLAREHAM LA

51

SANDYSCROSS LA

The Higdens

Murtrey Hill Farm

Church Lodge

BA11

Hope Farm

LOWER ST

MURTRY HILL LA

2

Barrow Hill Farm

Dangerfield Farm

Murtrey Hill

Nightingale Lodge

Warren Plantation

The Down

Mount Pleasant Farm

Orchardleigh Stones

Fir Plantation

Beech Plantation

Fir Wood

Longhouse Plantation

1

Murtrey Brow Plantation

Elliots

ELLIOTS LA

Castle Lodge

White Mill Farm

50

A362

75   A   B   76   C   D   77   E   F

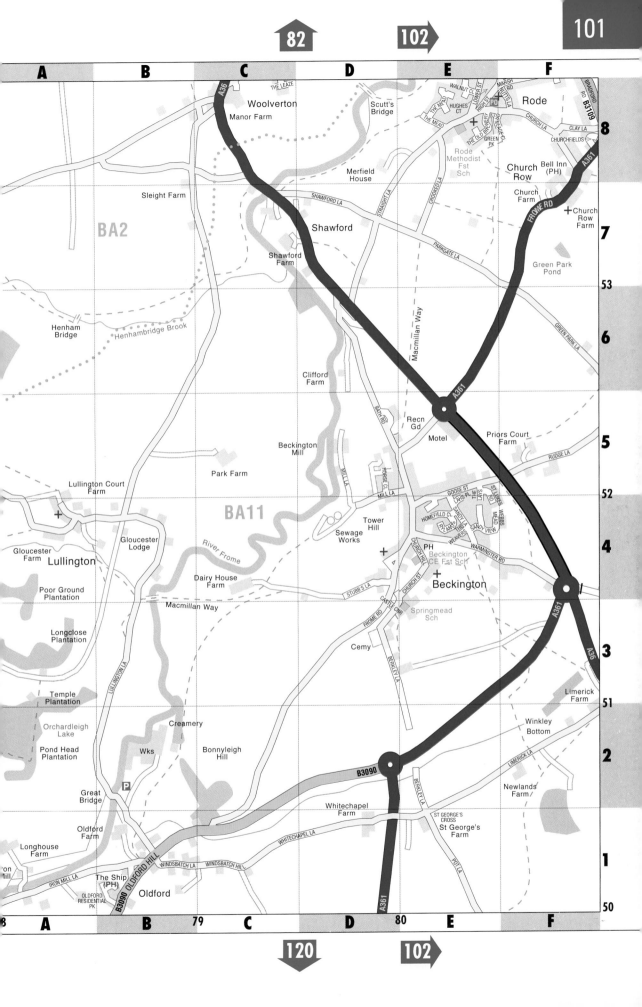

A B C D E F

8

A361
B3109
A361

Parsonage
Farm

Rode Farm

Monkley La

BA14

7

The Devil's
Bed & Bolster

Mount
Pleasant

53

Duck Pool La

6

Seymour's
Court

DUCK POOL LA

RUDGE LA

Duck Pool
Farm

Castley
Farm

CASTLEY LA

Norris Hill
Farm

Overcourt
Farm

Brokerswood
Country Pk

Hazel Wood

5

Waterslade

Upper Castley
Farm

RUDGE HILL

Silver Street
Farm

FAIRWOOD RD

Church
Farm

Round
Wood

52

Lower
Rudge Hill
Farm

SCOTLAND LA

Rudge

Honeybridge
Farm

+

The
Kicking Donkey
(PH)

Brokerswood

BA13

4

BA11

+

Full Moon
(PH)

+

Lower
Rudge

Carter's
Bridge

Stourton
Bushes

3

White Row
Farm

Scotland
Farm

RUDGE LA

51

A36

Court Farm

Standerwick
Court

Trees Farm

Palmer's
Farm

LC

2

Leigh Farm

Bell Inn
(PH)

RUDGE RD

STANDERWICK
CROSS

Standerwick

TENNIS CORNER DRO

Round
Wood

Fairwood
Farm

1

Barber's
Wood

Cuzner's Farm

BERKLEY ST

Frome
Market

B3099

MARSH RD

FOX'S DRO

A36

Westbury
View

Five Lords
Farm

CLIVEY

Clivey

Clivey
Farm

CLEARWOOD

B3099

50

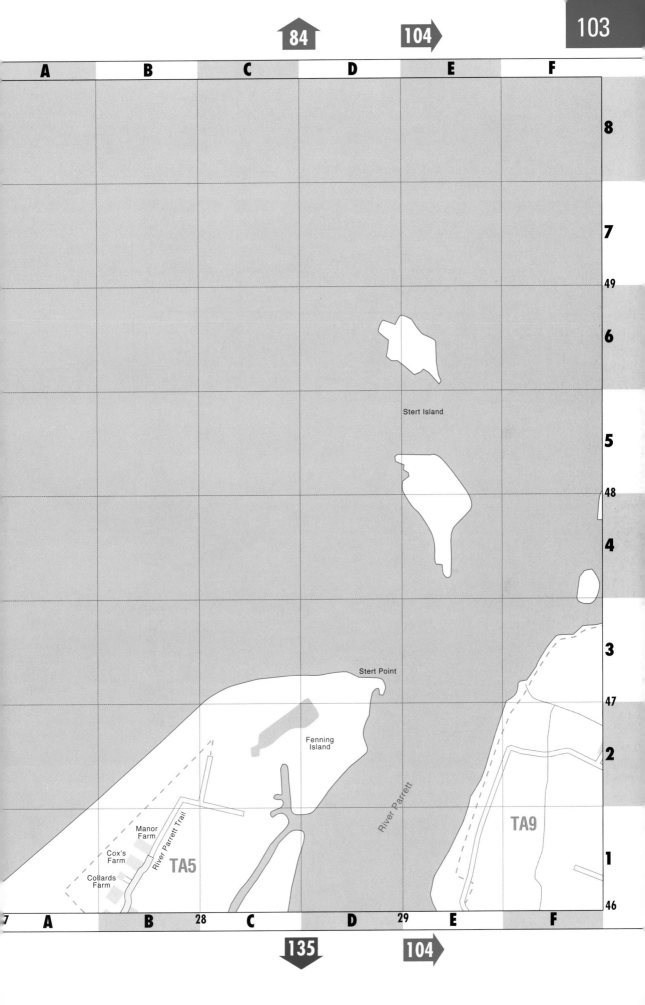

A B C D E F

8

7

49

6

Stert Island

5

48

4

3

47

Stert Point

2

Fenning
Island

River Parrett

TA9

Manor
Farm

River Parrett Trail

Cox's
Farm

TA5

Collards
Farm

1

46

A B 28 C D 29 E F

103
85

A   B   C   D   E   F

8

BURNHAM-
ON-SEA

Middle Burnham

1 SIDMOUTH CL
2 MEADOWCROFT DR
3 WEDMORE CL
4 BUCKLAND CL
5 WILTON CL
6 FROBISHER CL
7 AVEBURY CL
8 EXBURY CL
9 DYRHAM CL
10 COWAN CL
11 VINCENT CL
12 HOWARD CL
13 MADDEN CL
14 DEWAR CL
15 BURNETT CL
16 BERESFORD CL

Edithmead
Bridge

Inner
Farm

Edithmead

Homestead

Chestnut
Farm

7

War
Memorial

Westmans
Est

49

Superstore

Burnham
Level

1 NOEL COWARD CL
2 SHAW PATH
3 RATTIGAN CL
4 AYCKBOURN CL
5 ARCHER DR
6 BRIAR CT

TA8

6

Monks
Way

Prim
Sch

Mill
Mound

Worston
Bridge

Worston
House

5

Holiday
Camp

Playing
Field

Sports
Ctr

BT
Radio Sta

Mast

48

Caravan
Park

The
King Alfred
Sch

Worston
Orch

BRISTOL RD

4

Apex
Leisure Park

Burnham Rd

Cemy

Bristol
Bridge

1 KENNEDY CL
2 FAIRFORD CL

Isleport
Bsns Pk

Abatto

Morlands
Ind Pk

Jun
Sch

Inf
Sch

Springfield

3

Brue Pill

Sewage
Works

Depot

HIGHBRIDGE

Mus

Liby

New Clyce
Bridge

47

Alstone Wildlife
Park

1 VICTORIA PL
2 HOPE COTTS
3 RIVERBED HO
4 QUANTOCK VIEW

Brue
Bridge

MARKET ST   WALROW

Highbridge
& Burnham

MARK RD

Walrow
Ind Est

2

Sewage
Works

North Rhyne

Alstone Court
Farm

Alstone

TA9

Brue
Farm

River Brue

Mill
Farm

1

Maundril's
Farm

West Huntspill
Com Prim Sch

Batts Bow
Bridge

Brent
Farm

Hotel

North Rhyne

New Rd

NEWBRIDGE LA

46

30   A   31   B   C   32   D   E   F

103
136

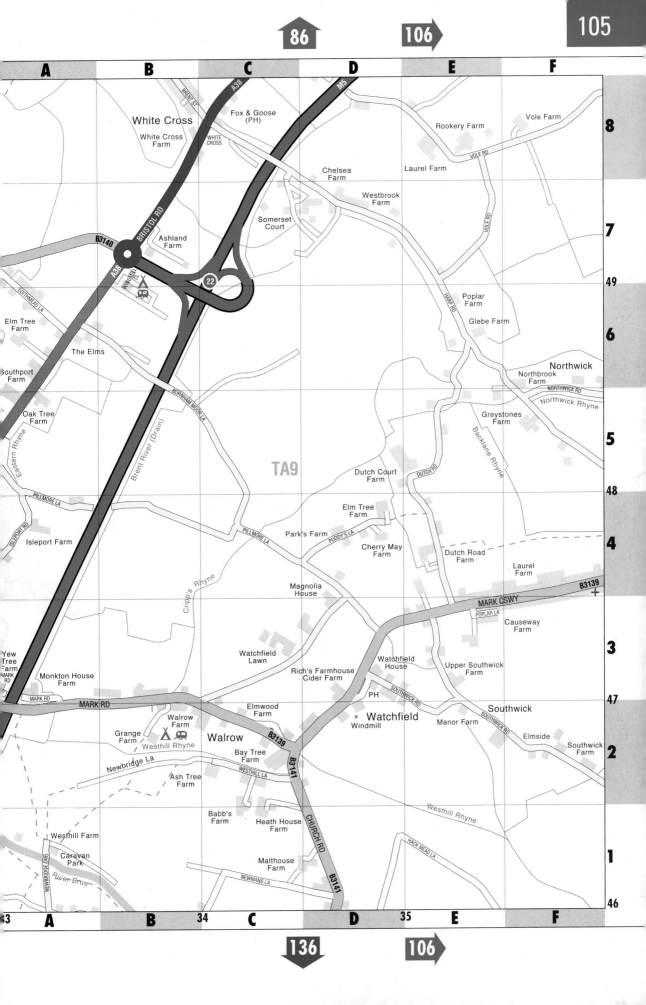

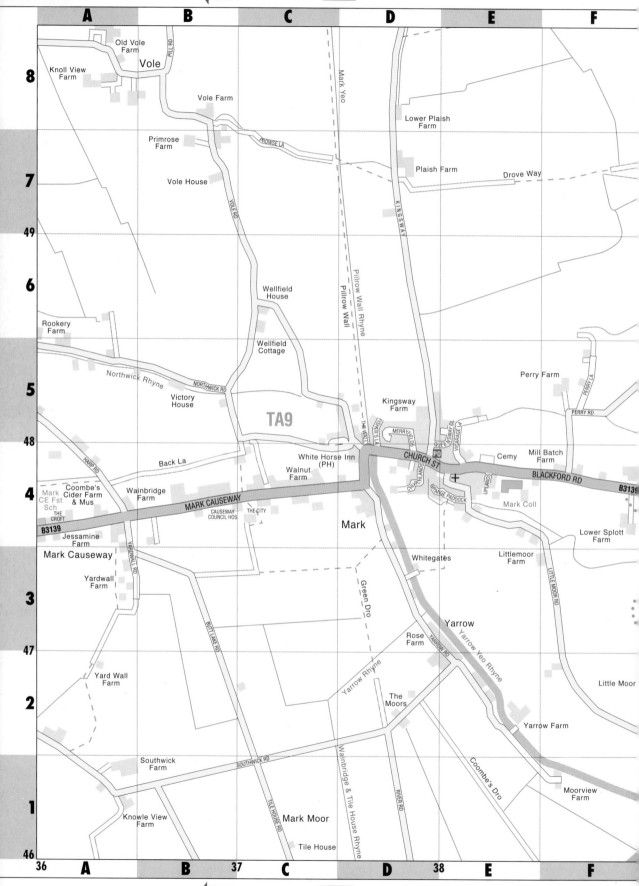

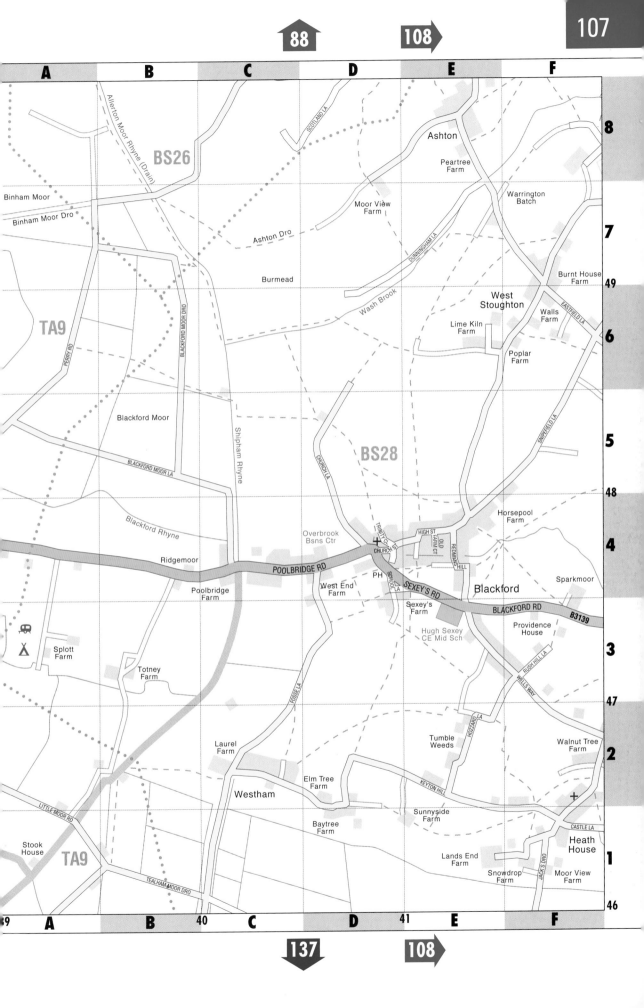

8

7

49

6

5

48

4

3

47

2

1

46

Binham Moor

Binham Moor Dro

Allerton Moor Rhyne (Drain)

BS26

TA9

Perry Rd

Blackford Moor Dro

Scotland La

Ashton

Peartree Farm

Moor View Farm

Ashton Dro

Burmead

Wash Brook

Dunningham La

Warrington Batch

Burnt House Farm

West Stoughton

Walls Farm

Eastfield La

Lime Kiln Farm

Poplar Farm

Blackford Moor

BLACKFORD MOOR LA

Shipham Rhyne

Blackford Rhyne

BS28

Church La

Snipefield La

Horsepool Farm

Ridgemoor

POOLBRIDGE RD

Poolbridge Farm

West End Farm

Overbrook Bsns Ctr

Trinity Cl

Church St

High St

Farm Ct

Old

Redmans Hill

PH

SEXEY'S RD

School La

Sexey's Farm

Blackford

BLACKFORD RD

Sparkmoor

B3139

Splott Farm

Totney Farm

Fosse La

Hugh Sexey CE Mid Sch

Providence House

Rush Hill La

Wells Way

Laurel Farm

Westham

Elm Tree Farm

Tumble Weeds

Hodzard La

Keyton Hill

Walnut Tree Farm

Little Moor Rd

Baytree Farm

Sunnyside Farm

Stook House

TA9

Tealham Moor Dro

Lands End Farm

Snowdrop Farm

Jack's Dro

Castle La

Heath House

Moor View Farm

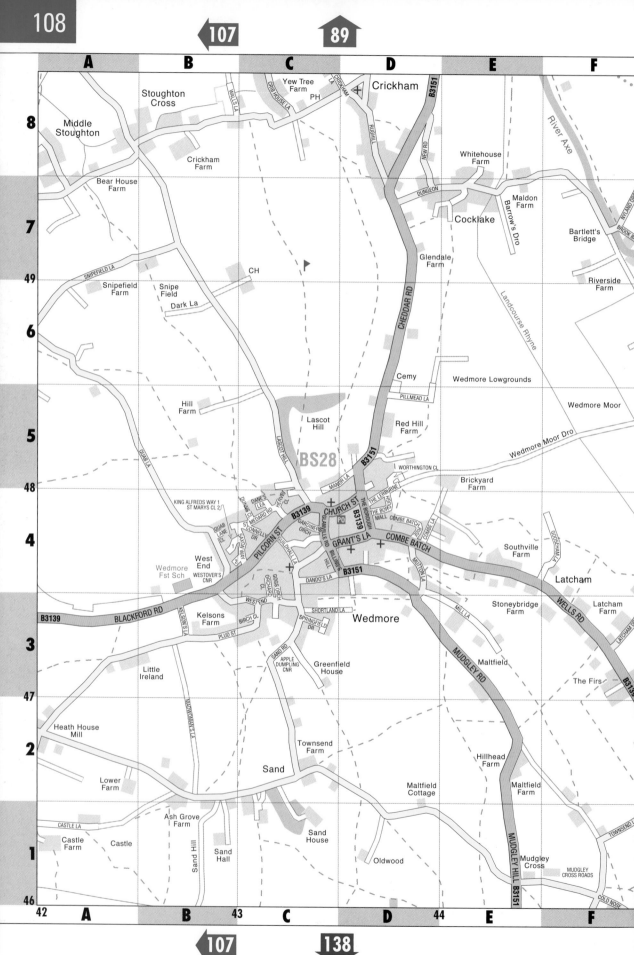

A B C D E F

8

Middle
Stoughton

Stoughton
Cross

Yew Tree
Farm
PH

Crickham

Crickham
Farm

Bear House
Farm

Whitehouse
Farm

River Axe

7

Maldon
Farm

Cocklake

Bartlett's
Bridge

49

Snipefield
Farm

Snipe
Field

CH

Dark La

Glendale
Farm

Riverside
Farm

6

Hill
Farm

Cemy

Wedmore Lowgrounds

Wedmore Moor

5

Lascot
Hill

Red Hill
Farm

Wedmore Moor Dro

48

BS28

Brickyard
Farm

4

King Alfreds Way 1
St Marys Cl 2

West
End

Wedmore
Fst Sch

CHURCH ST

GRANT'S LA

COMBE BATCH

Southville
Farm

Latcham

Latcham
Farm

3

B3139

BLACKFORD RD

Kelsons
Farm

Wedmore

Stoneybridge
Farm

Maltfield

WELLS RD

The Firs

47

Little
Ireland

Apple
Dumpling
Cnr

Greenfield
House

2

Heath House
Mill

Townsend
Farm

Hillhead
Farm

Maltfield
Farm

Sand

1

Lower
Farm

Castle
Farm

Castle

Ash Grove
Farm

Sand
Hall

Sand
House

Maltfield
Cottage

Oldwood

Mudgley
Cross

MUDGLEY HILL

46

42 A 43 B C 44 D E F

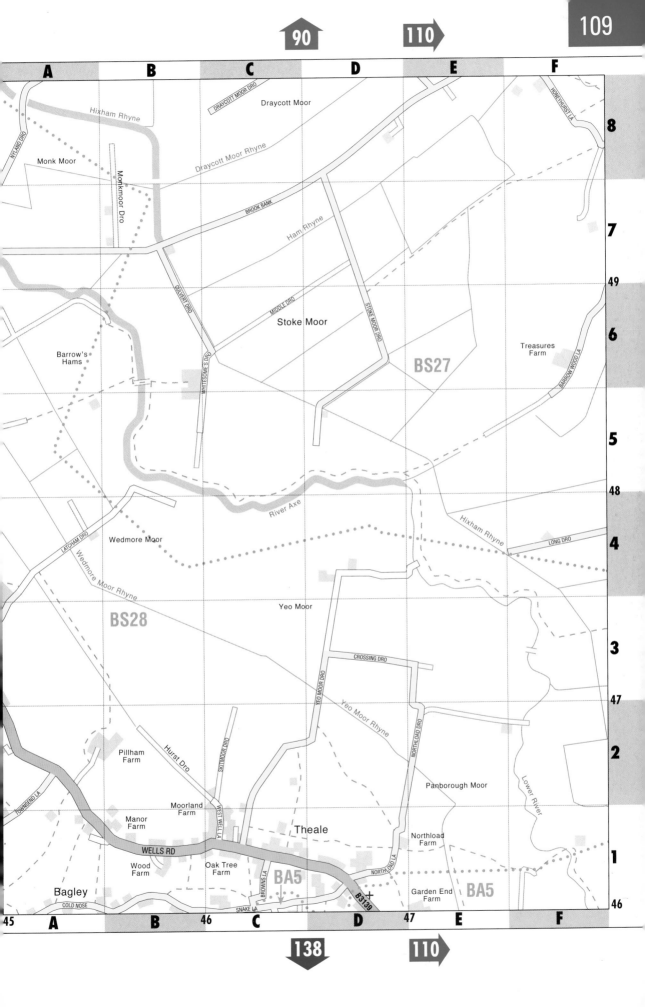

A   **B**   **C**   **D**   **E**   **F**

8

DRAYCOTT MOOR DRO

Draycott Moor

Hixham Rhyne

IVY LAND DRO

Monk Moor

Monkmoor Dro

Draycott Moor Rhyne

HONEYHURST LA

7

BROOK BANK

Ham Rhyne

CALVERT DRO

STOKE MOOR DRO

49

MIDDLE DRO

Stoke Moor

6

Treasures Farm

BARROW WOOD LA

BS27

WHITESOME'S DRO

Barrow's Hams

5

48

River Axe

Hixham Rhyne

LONG DRO

4

LATCHAM DRO

Wedmore Moor

Wedmore Moor Rhyne

BS28

Yeo Moor

3

CROSSING DRO

47

YEO MOOR DRO

Yeo Moor Rhyne

NORTHLOAD DRO

Lower River

2

Pillham Farm

HURST DRO

SKITMOOR DRO

WEST WELL LA

Panborough Moor

TOWNSEND LA

Moorland Farm

Manor Farm

Theale

Northload Farm

WELLS RD

Wood Farm

Oak Tree Farm

BROWNS LA

BA5

NORTH LOAD LA

Garden End Farm

BA5

1

Bagley

COLD NOSE

SNAKE LA

B3139

46

45   **A**   **B**   46   **C**   **D**   47   **E**   **F**

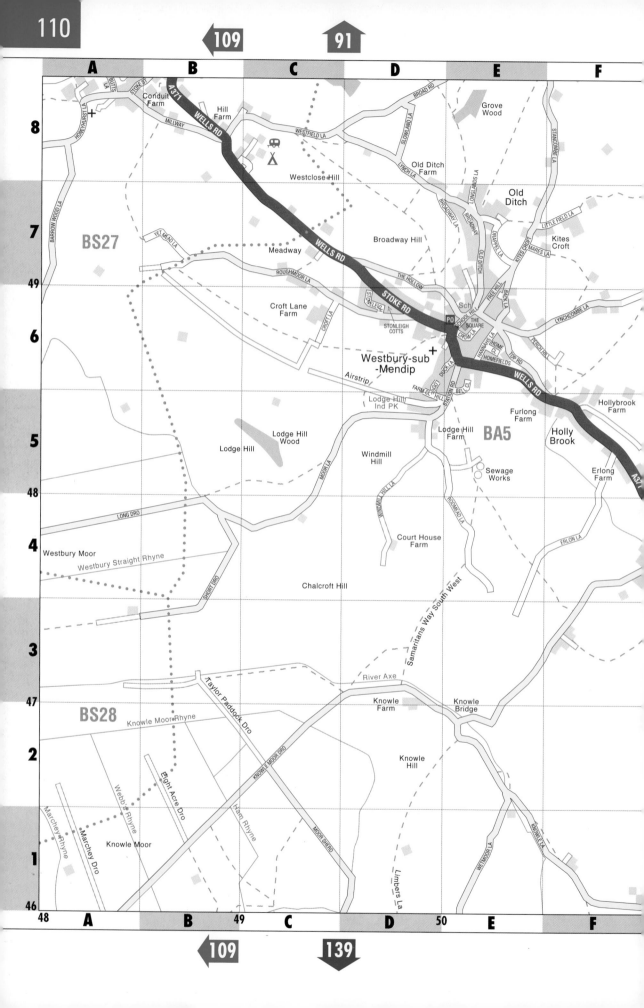

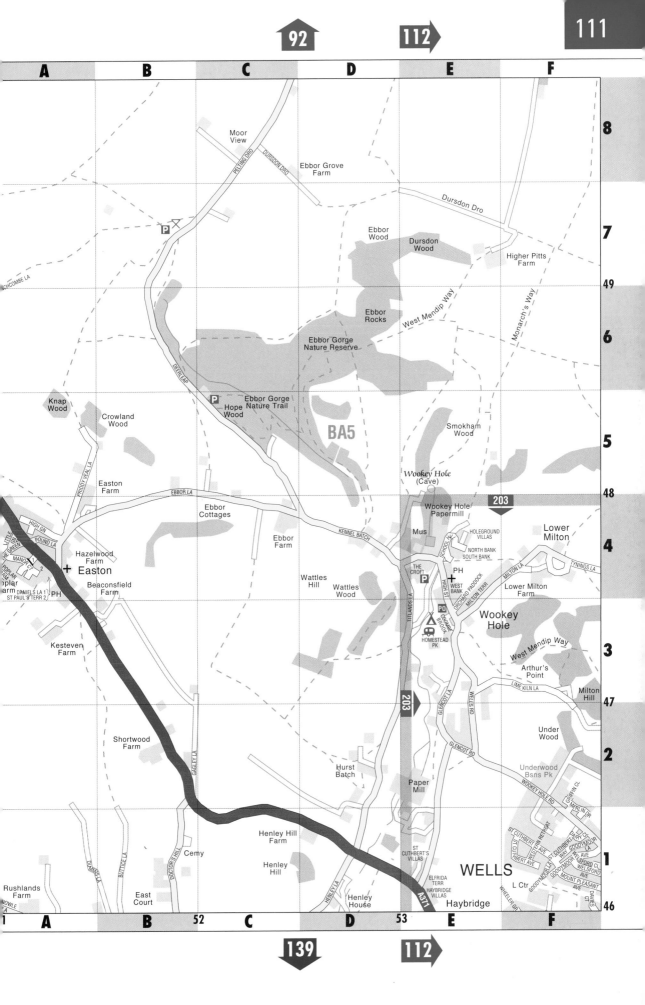

111
93

A B C D E F

8

Southfield Farm

HILLGROVE RD

PRIDDY RD

Rookham House

Drove Cottage

Priddy Road Farm

7

Ores Close Farm

49

6

DURSDON DRO

Mast

Transmitting Sta

Mast Pen Hill

A39

BRISTOL

BA5

Rookham

OLD BRISTOL RD

Rookham Wood

The Round Clump

Ivy Cottage

Pen Hill Wood

Pen Hill Farm

Gollege

Big Plantation

5

Vigo Wood

The Wrangle

Prior's Hill

48

203

Welsh's Green

Welsh's Green La

Walcombe Wood

Gorse Plantation

Biddle Combe

4

TYNINGS LA

NEWCUT

Nibs Hanging

Dairy House Farm

BRISTOL HILL

Manor Farm

Upper Milton

Walcombe Hanging

3

Model Farm

Milton Lodge Garden

Walcombe

Beryl Hanging

Beryl Wood

47

WEST MENDIP WAY

RESERVOIR LA

Milton Lodge

WALCOMBE LA

203

Beryl Farm

2

The Coombe

Stoberry Park

Beryl

Knapp Hill

HILL SIDE LA

FAIR TREE AVE

MILTON LA

ASH GR

ASH LA

NEW ST

ST THOMAS TERR 1
ST THOMAS MEWS 2
OLD SCHOOL PL 3
LORNE PL 4
ST THOMAS' CT 5
ST ANDREW'S CT 6

WELLS

DRAKE RD

KIDDER BANK

COLLES CL

PENN CL

Knapp Hill Farm

B31

WEST CT

GILBERT SC

1

SINGLETON CT

CHERRY ORCHARD DR

MARY RD

KENWOOD RD

SOMERVILLE RD

WELSFORD AVE

WALNUT TREE CL

The Blue Sch

Stoberry Park Sch

STOBERRY AVE

STOBERRY CRES

COLLEGE RD

NORTH RD

LEWMOND AVE

LITTLE ENTRY

KIPPAX AVE

TEAGLE CL

PARAU DR

BERYL LA

DUCO AVE

DROD AVE

HAWKERS LA

EVERETT CL

SEALEY CRES

CHURCHILL RD

HERVEY RD

CHURCHILL CL

CHURCHILL RD E

PO

OLD FROME RD

46

MOUNT PLEASANT AVE

BROOKES CL

BLAKE RD

SLOPE CL

SEYMOUR CL

LOVERS WLK

MOUNTERY RD

A39

NEW ST

B3139

THE LIBERTY

Wells Cathedral Schs

Millers

SNUG

B3139

ST THOMAS ST

TOP WOOD

TOR WOOD VIEW

WOODBURY

Wells & District

H

WOODBURY AVE

BARKHAM RD

PLUMPTRE AVE

MANNING RD

JOHNSON RD

MITCHELL TERR

BEDFORD RD

ALLENS LA

BROAD RD

HOOPER CL

FOSTER CL

BEKYNTON AVE

BATH RD

KINGS CASTLE RD

KINGS RD

54 A B 55 C D 56 E F

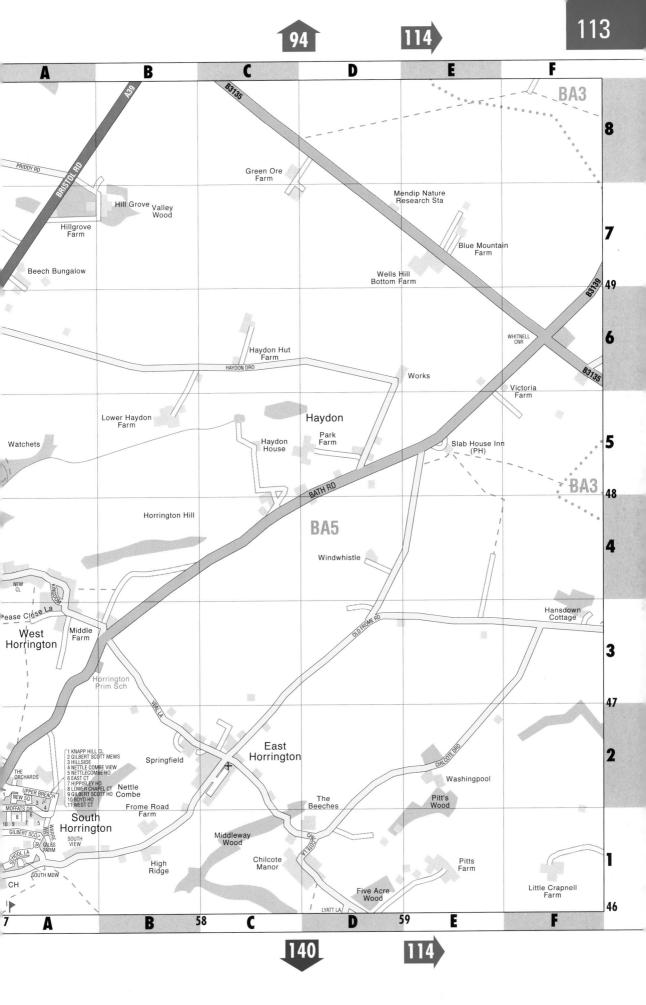

A | B | C | D | E | F

8

Coldharbour Farm

Weaver's Farm

Turner's Court Farm

Church Farm

Cock Hill

Share Hill

WHITNELL LA

Whitnell Farm

Binegar Green

GALLESTON

TURNER'S COURT LA

Binegar CE Prim Sch

TELLIS LA

SALISBURY TERR

Quarry (dis)

B3139

BATH RD

7

Binegar

The Old Rectory

FLOWERSTONE

STATION RD

COLBOURN CL

PH

UNDERHILL

PO

TAPE LA

49

BENNETT'S LA

CHAPEL LA

GRUNTER'S LA

Gurney Slade

Tap Hi

BA5

KINGSCOMBE

6

Whitnell House Farm

Binegar Bottom

Quarry (dis)

Rooker Farm

Whitnell House

BENNETT'S LA

Higher Whitnell Farm

Highcroft Farm

BADGER'S CROSS

B3135

BA3

Gale's Farm

LIMEKILN LA

5

Rookery Farm

ROEMEAD LA

SIMBRISS RD

Simbriss Farm

48

ROEMEAD RD

B3135

GALLEY BATCH

POUND LA

4

BROOMCLOSE CNR

Mead Farm

Roemead Farm

PH

GREEN LA

GALLEY BATCH LA

Nine Acre Wood

Furze Wood

Batts Farm

Little London

BATTS LA

SUMMEAD

GREEN LA

3

Masbury Farm

Marsh Wood

CH

Hansdown Farm

Maesbury Castle

P

GOLF LINKS LA

47

Spring Wood

Castlehill Wood

THRUPE LA

BA5

OLD FROME RD

▶

2

Thrupemarsh Farm

Warren Farm

Mast

OLD BRISTOL RD

A37 LONG HILL

1

CHAPEL LA

Thrupe Farm

BURNTHOUSE DRO

BA4

46

60 | A | | B | 61 | C | | D | 62 | E | | F

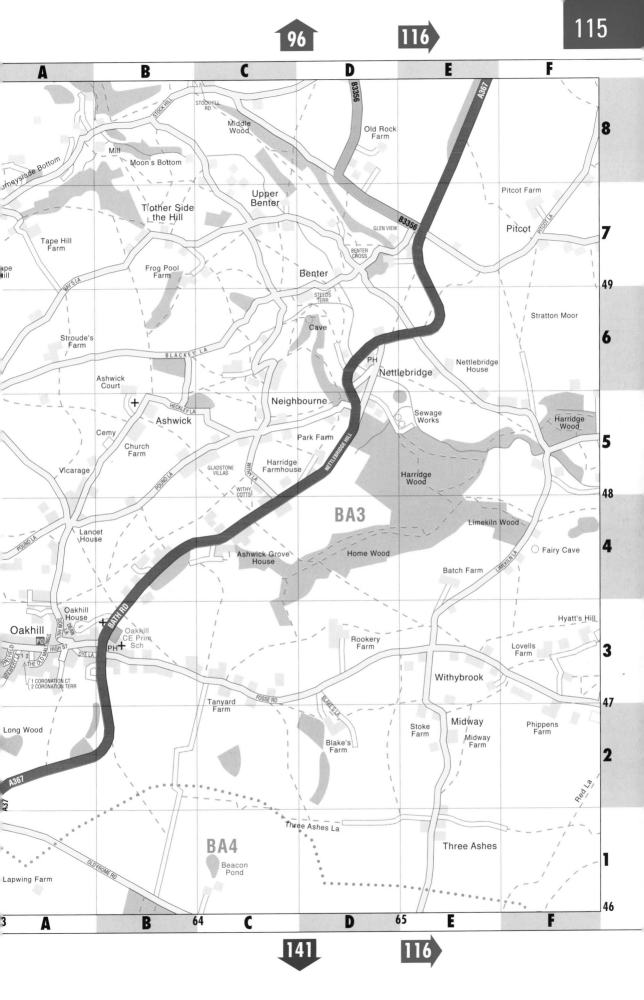

A B C D E F

Burneyside Bottom

Mill

Moon's Bottom

Stockhill Rd

Middle Wood

B3356

Old Rock Farm

Pitcot Farm

Upper Benter

T'other Side the Hill

B3356

GLEN VIEW

Pitcot

Pitcot La

7

Tape Hill Farm

Tape Hill

BAY'S LA

Frog Pool Farm

Benter

BENTER CROSS

49

STEEDS TERR

Stratton Moor

Cave

6

Stroude's Farm

BLACKEY LA

PH

Nettlebridge

Nettlebridge House

Ashwick Court

HECKLEY LA

Neighbourne

Sewage Works

Harridge Wood

Cemy

Ashwick

Park Farm

NETTLEBRIDGE HILL

5

Church Farm

WITHY LA

Harridge Farmhouse

Harridge Wood

Vicarage

POUND LA

GLADSTONE VILLAS

WITHY COTTS

48

Limekiln Wood

Lancet House

POUND LA

BA3

Home Wood

LIMEKILN LA

Fairy Cave

4

Ashwick Grove House

Batch Farm

Hyatt's Hill

Oakhill House

BATH RD

Rookery Farm

Lovells Farm

3

Oakhill

PO

TOW HILL

DEAN

HIGH ST

Oakhill CE Prim Sch

PH

Withybrook

1 CORONATION CT
2 CORONATION TERR

DYE LA

Midway

BRICKKILN LA

THE OLD MALTINGS

FOSSE RD

Tanyard Farm

BLAKE'S LA

Stoke Farm

Midway Farm

Phippens Farm

47

Long Wood

Blake's Farm

2

A367

Red La

Three Ashes La

BA4

Three Ashes

1

A367

OLD FROME RD

Beacon Pond

Lapwing Farm

46

A B C D E F

A B C D E F

8

7

49

6

5

48

4

3

47

2

1

46

66 A B 67 C D 68 E F

Barlake Farm

Pilcot La

The Ring o' Roses (PH)

Manor Farm

Holcombe Manor
1 OLD MANOR EST
2 SCOTTS CL

THE MEAD

CHARLTON RD

CROFT RD

BREWERY LA

Holcombe

LONGLEAT RD

CHAPEL LA

KINGSWAY

LONG LA

HOLCOMBE HILL

JAMES CL

KINGSMEAD CL

BOUNDARY CL

TYNING COTTS

Kilmersdon Common

Ropewalk Farm

ROPE WLK

UPPER MERRIFIELD

RUSH ASH LA

FAIRFIELD

HIGHFIELD

HIGHFIELD VIEW

MERRY-FIELD

FARLEY DR

ANCHOR RD

ANCHOR CL

COAL BARTON

Bishop Henderson CE Prim Sch

MENDIP VALE

BEACON VIEW

CROSSWAYS

HIGHBURY COTTS

HIGHBURY VALE

MENDIP VIEW

PO

P

CAREYS MD

HIGHBURY ST

PREACHERS VALE

DOUGLAS YATES

Barlake House

Barlake House

Spring Farm

WOODS

PADDOCK

WOODLANDS LA

Edford

EDFORD HILL

Wks

Flint House

COMMON LA

BECKS LA

Kilmersdon Common Farm

SPRINGER'S HILL

Coleford

WESLEY VILLAS 1
BARTON VILLAS 2
ROCK TERR 3

ROSE & CROWN COTTS

CHURCH LA

CHURCH ST

Lydford Farm

Hippy Farm

THE GREEN

Edford Green

Duke of Cumberland (PH)

Sewage Works

Ham

Ham Bridge

HAM HILL

Ham Farm

MARSH LA

Bullock's Hill

HIGH ST

Mells Stream

Packsaddle Bridge

Edford Wood

Dunsford's Farm

GREEN LA

Moons Hill Farm

GIDDY LA

MOONS HILL

Stoke Bottom Farm

Folly Wood

Combe Wood

FROG LA

COALPIT LA

Stoke Lane Slocker Hole

RECTOR LA

Whitehole Farm

Leigh Wood

Hurdlestone Wood

WHITEHOLE HILL

BA3

Stoke St Michael Prim Sch

MOONSHILL COTTS 1
STEEPLE VIEW 2
MILLENNIUM CL 3
TOWER CL 4

MOONSHILL

RD

ST MICH'L'S CL

PAYTMAN'S HILL

MILL LA

STONE FIELD CL

MOONSHILL CRES

TOWER HILL

SWEETLEAZE

STOKE HILL

MENDIP RD

CHURCH ST

THE MEAD

THE ST

Cook's Farm

Somer's Farm

Manor House Farm

Chivers Farm

Goldsborough Farm

OAKHILL CT

PITTEN ST

STOCK'S LA

LEIGH ST

Manor Farm

Sparks Farm

PARK HAYES

Town's End

Leigh upon Mendip

Stoke St Michael

Susanna's Cross

BURNT HOUSE LA

DARK LA

Grove Shute Farm

BLACKER'S LA

Red La

SUSANNA'S LA

East End

TADHILL LA

Tadhill

Tadhill Farm

Mendip Farm

LONG CROSS BOTTOM

BURGE'S HILL

BURGE'S LA

FENFALL LA

Moons Hill Quarry

Yellow Marsh Farm

Old Wells Rd

BA4

Tadhill House Farm

LUXTON'S LA

BA4

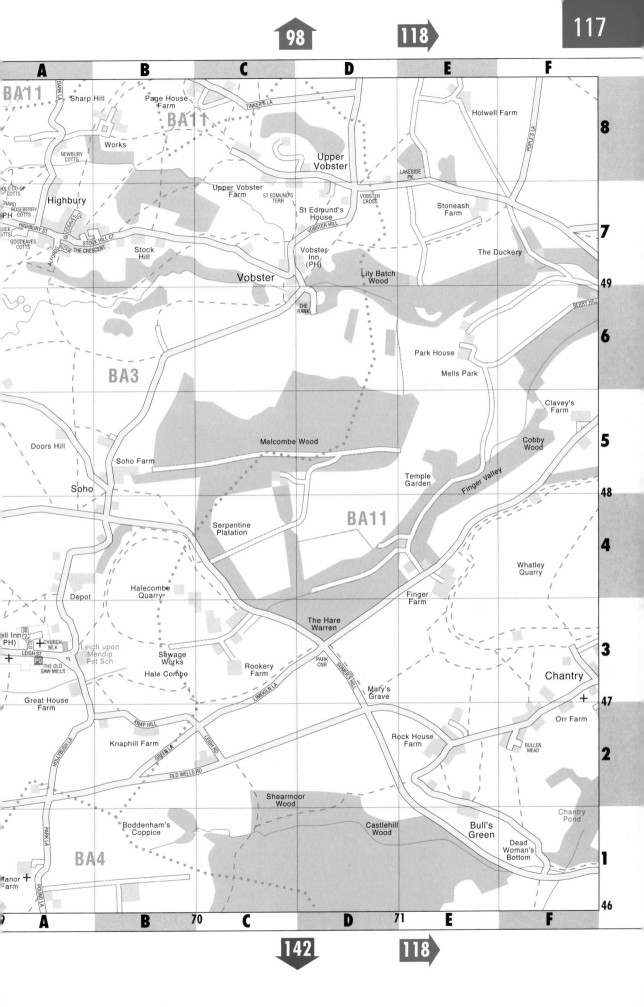

A B C D E F

8

Branch Farm

Newbury Firs

Newbury Hill

(dis)

7

Great Elm

Longfield

PH

SELWOOD ST

NEW ST

FAIRVIEW

PARK HILL

Wadbury

Newlands

Manor Farm

CHURCH CL

ELM LA

Mells

Wadbury Farm

49

Wadbury

Mells Stream

GAY ST

TENT'S HILL

RASHWOOD LA

PO

Woodlands End

Wadbury

BERRY HILL

TOP LA

6

Mells Green

Prospect Farm

HOLES LA

Little Green

KNAPTONS HILL

Wadbury Valley

Tedbury

Fordbury Bottom

Mells CE Fst Sch

Mellsgreen Farm

Murder Combe

5

Whatley Quarry

BA11

Fordbury Water

Whatley Bottom

Macmillan Way

48

Railford Bottom

4

Manor Farm

Whatley Vineyard & Herb Garden

Whatley

RAILFORD HILL

Railford Bridge

Park Farm

Egford Brook

THE OLD SCHOOL HO

Little Acre Farm

Sun Inn (PH)

3

Lower Whatley

Whatley House

47

TARDIS

2

Southfield House

Nunney Combe

Nunney Brook

Bangle Farm

1

COLLIE CNR

46

Combe Farm

72 A B 73 C D 74 E F

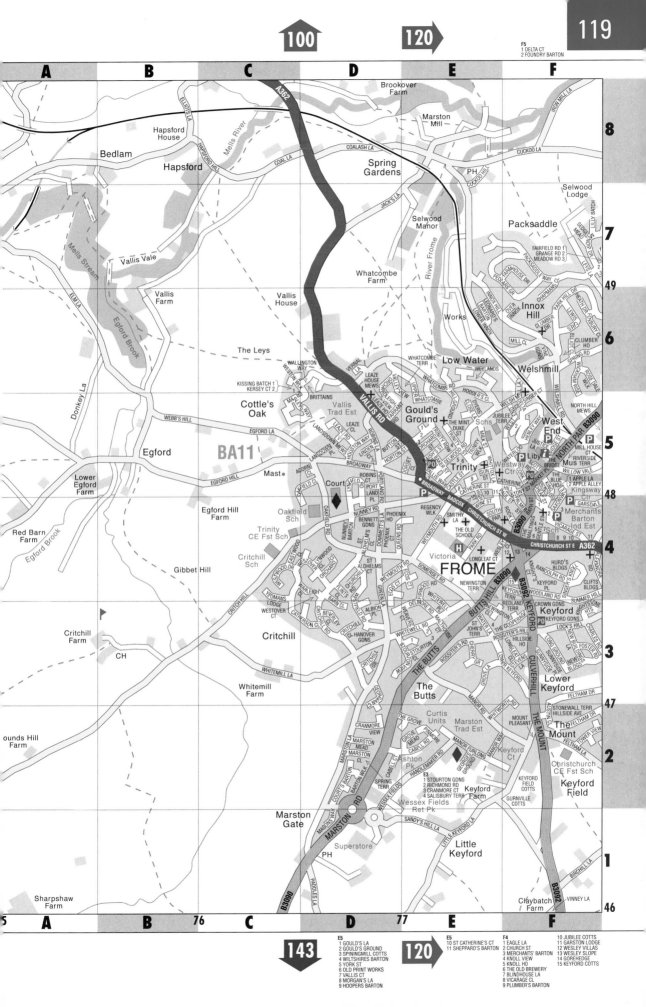

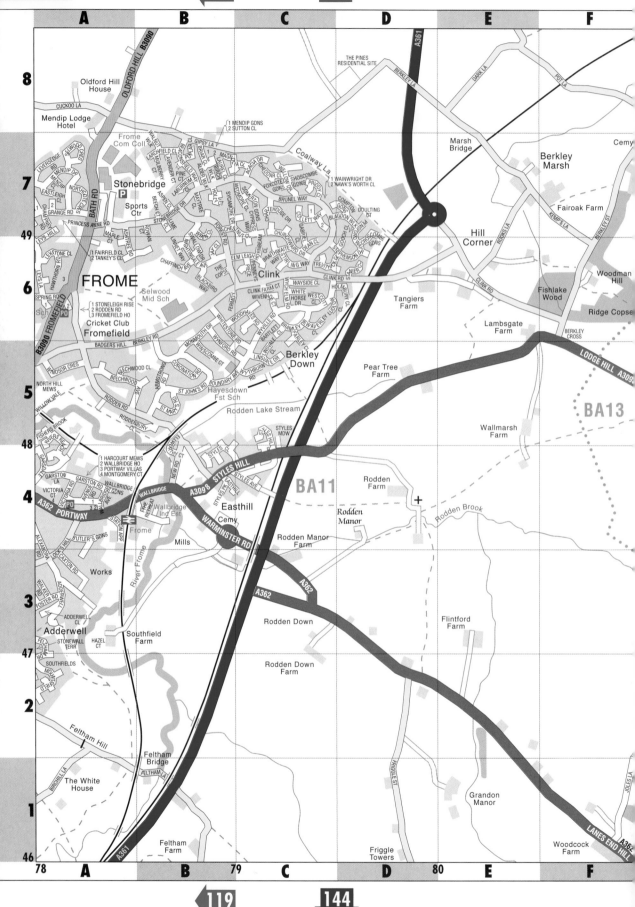

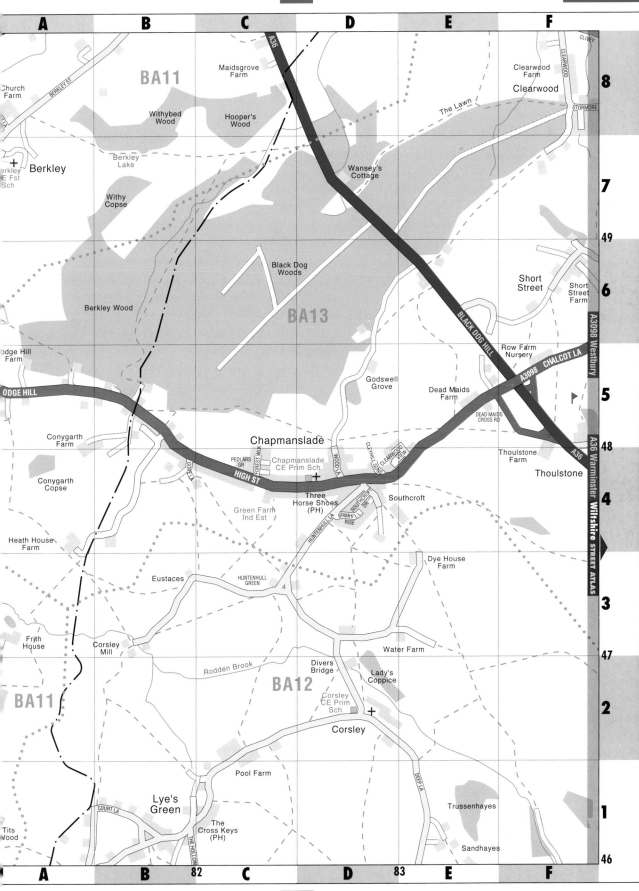

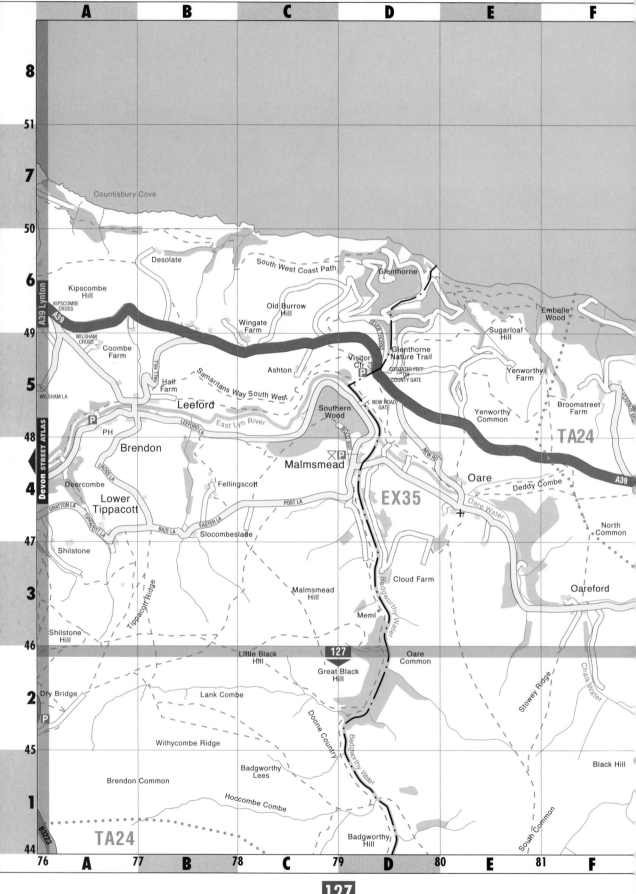

A B C D E F

8
51
7
50
6
49
5
48
4
47
3
46
2
45
1
44

Countisbury Cove

Desolate

Kipscombe Hill

KIPSCOMBE CROSS

A39 Lynton

A39

WILSHAM CROSS

Coombe Farm

WILSHAM LA

HALL HILL

Hall Farm

Leeford

LEEFORD LA

East Lyn River

South West Coast Path

Old Burrow Hill

Wingate Farm

Ashton

Samaritans Way South West

Southern Wood

Glenthorne

SEVEN THORNS

Glenthorne Nature Trail

Visitor Ctr
P

COSGATES FEET OR COUNTY GATE

NEW ROAD GATE

Embelle Wood

Sugarloaf Hill

Yenworthy Farm

Broomstreet Farm

YENWORTHY LA

Yenworthy Common

TA24

Devon STREET ATLAS

P

PH

Brendon

CROSS LA

Deercombe

GRATTON LA

Lower Tippacott

TIPPACOTT LA

BAZE LA

EASTER LA

Slocombeslade

Fellingscott

POST LA

Malmsmead

WOOD WAY

P

NEW RD

EX35

Oare

Deddy Combe

Oare Water

A39

North Common

Shilstone

Tippacott Ridge

Malmsmead Hill

Cloud Farm

Badgworthy Water

Oareford

Shilstone Hill

Little Black Hill

127

Great Black Hill

Meml

Oare Common

Stowey Ridge

ChalkWater

Dry Bridge

P

Lank Combe

Doone Country

Badgworthy Water

Black Hill

Withycombe Ridge

Badgworthy Lees

South Common

Brendon Common

Hoccombe Combe

Badgworthy Hill

B3223

TA24

76 A 77 B 78 C 79 D 80 E 81 F

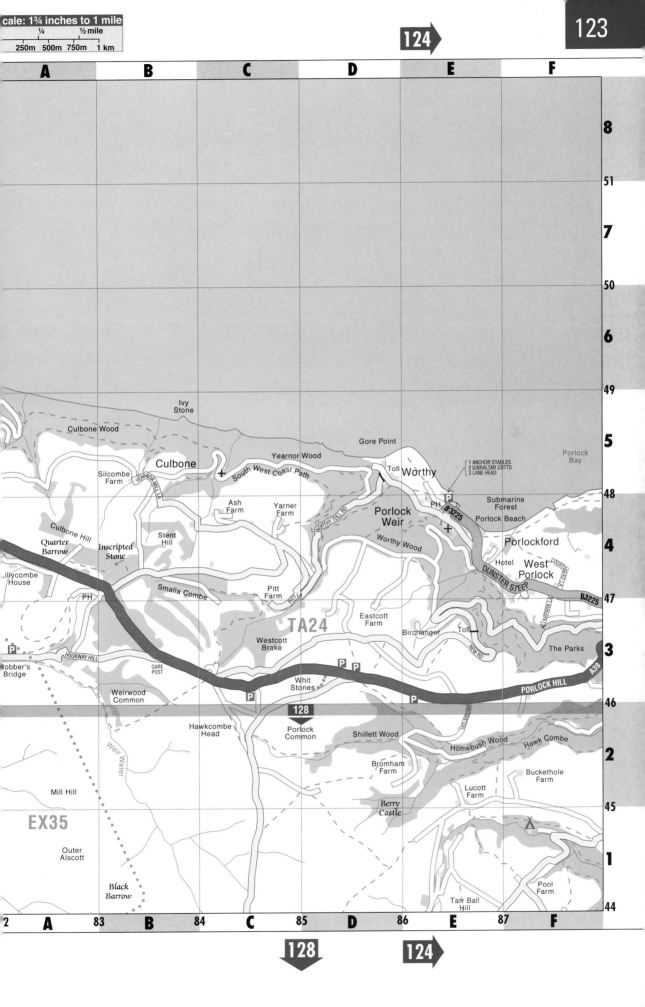

123

Scale: 1¾ inches to 1 mi

0   ¼   ½ mile

0   250m   500m   750m   1 km

A   B   C   D   E   F

8

51

7

50

6
Minehead Bluff

Hurlstone Point
Selworthy
Sand
49
Western
Brockholes
Eastern
Brockholes

5
Porlock Bay
Bossington
Hill
South West Coast Path

48
Meml
Selworthy Beacon
Bossington
Exmoor
Falconry
&
Animal Farm
Lynch
TA24
Memorial
Hut
Hill Rd

4
SYDENHAM
CL
ABINGTON
CROSS
Porlock
HIGH BANK 1
POLLARDS CT 2
RIVERSIDE ROW 3
THE MEADOWS 4
ENGLANDS RD 5
1 PARKS VIEW
2 FURZELAND RD
BAY RD
HEALEYS
HURLSTONE
PK
Bury
Castle

47
B3225
Court
Place
Toll Rd
PH PO
Lby &
Vis Ctr
Mus
DUNSTER
STEEP
THE
RIDGE
Doverhay
RED
POST
Allerford
Mus
Packhorse
Bridge
Brandish
Street
Selworthy
Hindon
Wydon
Farm
DEAN'S
CROSS

3
A39
Mast
Cemy
Sch
THE
POPLARS
HACKETTY WAY
6 RAWLE'S BLDGS
7 LOWERBOURNE TERR
8 MARLEY'S ROW
9 BOND'S ROW
10 THE DRANG
11 COACH RD
12 CHURCH VIEW
13 CRAWTER DR
14 HAWKCOMBE VIEW
Piles Mill
West
Luccombe
Packhorse
Bridge
Holnicote
East
Lynch

46
SUNNYSIDE
COTTS
HUISH
ROW
Hawkcombe
Crawter
Hill
129
Venniford
Cross
HEADON
CROSS

2
Glen Lodge
Packhorse
Bridge
Horner
Horner
Nature
Trails
Doverhay
Down
Blackford
Dovecote
LONG LA
Troyte's
Farm
Tivington
Heights
TIVINGTON
CROSS
Tivington

45
CHISLAND DR
HUISH
STEEP
LANE
FOOT
Ley Hill
Chapel Cross
Knowle Top
Tivington
Knowle

1
Horner
Water
Horner
Hill
CROOK HORN HILL
STOREY ST
Luccombe
Wootton
Knowle
Horner
Wood
Wychanger
HOT BALL STEEP

44
88   **A**   89   **B**   90   **C**   91   **D**   92   **E**   93   **F**

A B C D E F

8
51
7
50
6
49
5
48
4
47
3
46
2
45
1
44

Greenaleigh Point

Burgundy Chapel (remains of)

Greenaleigh Farm

North Hill

South West Coast Path

North Hill Woodland Trail

Bratton Ball

Moor Wood

GREENALEIGH TOWER RD

GREENALEIGH UPPER RD

HILL RD

Higher Town

TIDES REACH

Beacon

IRB Sta

Harbour

NORTH HILL RD

QUAY ST

CULVECLIFFE

BEACON RD

200

P

MINEHEAD

Madbrain Sands

201

Warren Point

Woodcombe

The Strand

CH

ST MICHAEL'S RD

MOOR RD

VICARAGE RD

WHITECROSS LA

Sch

WARREN RD

Bratton Court

BRATTON LA

Cemy

Bratton

BRAFTON MILL LA

SAINSBURY RD

HILLVIEW RD

WHITWORTH RD

POBLOCK RD

THE PARKS

LOWER PK

WEST PK

PARKHOUSE RD

REGENTS WAY

The Parks

PARK ST

PARADE

THE

Minehead

Liby

TH

H

P

PO

The Avenue

QUAY LA

GLENMORE RD

FREGOWELL

INNHAM RD

WARREN RD

Coll

P

LC

Ind Est

130

P

A39

PERITON RD

PERITON WAY

SOUTH PK

OLD FARM RD

WEST ST

POUNDFIELD RD

PAGANEL RD

CHER

WHITEGATE RD

Periton

HOPCOTT RD

TOWNSEND RD

Sch

PONSFORD RD

HAYFIELD RD

Sch

CATS LA

MART RD

200

Great Headon Plantation

Higher Hopcott

Sch

TA24

ALCOMBE RD

STAUNTON RD

PO

ALCOMBE RD

MARSHFIELD RD

SPRING GDNS

TILLARD

Alcombe

Coll

SEAWARD WAY

West Somerset Rly

Holiday Village

Works

The Old Manor

201

Periton Hill

Hopcott Common

Macmillan Way West

Callins

STAUNTON

Quarry

BIRCHAM RD

MANOR RD

CHURCH ST

CUMBERLAND RD

ELLICOMBE LA

DRIFT RD

Marsh Street

LC

Dunster

LC

SEA LA

Tivington Common

Staunton Plantation

Aldersmead

Penny Hill

Hagley

Alcombe Common

Ellicombe

Conygar Tower

DENZIL LA

MARSH LA

MARSH ST

STATION RD

BRIDGES MEAD

A39

Loxhole Bridge

94 A 95 B 96 C 97 D 98 E 99 F

130   131   For full street detail of the highlighted areas see pages 200 and 201.

Scale: 1¾ inches to 1 mil
0   ¼   ½ mile
0 250m 500m 750m 1 km

Barham Hill

Thornworthy

RADSBURY LA
Radsbury

West Lyn River

Stock Common

P   B3223
Farley Hill   P

Shallowford

Ilkerton Ridge

Furzehill

EX35

Two Moors Way
Tarka Trail

Hoaroak Water

Furzehill Common

Farley Water

Cheriton Ridge

Middle Hill

Cannon Hill

8

45

7

44

Butter Hill

Pig Hill

Holcombe Burrows

Saddle Gate

Thorn Hill

Hoaroak

Benjamy

Clannon Ball

6

Long Stone

Longstone Barrow

Winaway

The Chains

Hoaroak Hill

Hoar Oak Tree

43

Wood Barrow

Pinkery Pond

Exe Plain

EX31

5

42

Broad Mead

Pinkworthy

Chains Barrow

Tarka Trail

Exe Head

Yarbury Combe

North Ridge Common

Breakneck Hole

Pinkery Farm

Macmillan Way West

TA24

4

41

Twitchen Farm

B3358   NORTH LA

Old Close Bottom

Edgerley Stone

Goat Hill

Driver

Titchcombe

Dure Down

3

SOUTH LA

Roosthitchen

Hearlake

Tangs Bottom

Duredon Farm

40

Weirs Combe

Kennels

2

Shoulsbarrow Common

Sloley Stone

Mole's Chamber

Acklands

Great Vintcombe

River Barle

Cornham Farm

B3358

Shoulsbury Castle

Smallacombe

39

EX32

Henthitchen

Ricksy Ball

Two Moors Way

1

ROCKLEY LA

Rockley Farm

Bray Common

Setta Barrow

Squallacombe

Horcombe

38

70   A   71   B   72   C   73   D   74   E   75   F

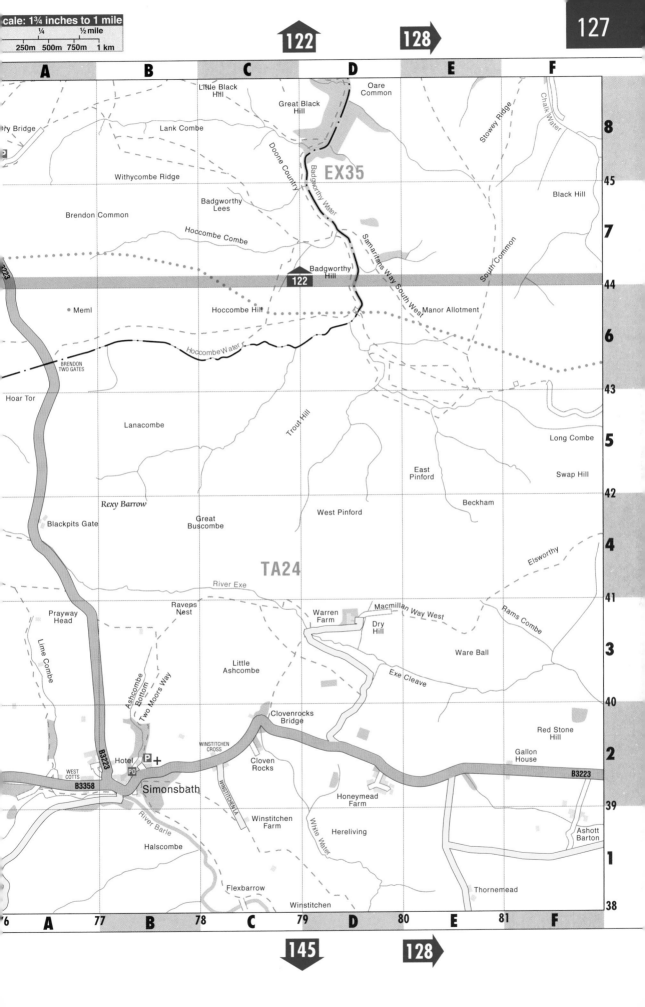

Scale: 1¾ inches to 1 mi

0   ¼   ½ mile
0 250m 500m 750m 1 km

A B C D E F

123

8

45

7

44

6

43

5

42

4

41

3

40

2

39

1

38

82 A 83 B 84 C 85 D 86 E 87 F

Mill Hill

EX35

Outer Alscott

Weir Water

Black Barrow

Meads

Hawkcombe Head

Porlock Common

Shillett Wood

Bromham Farm

Berry Castle

Lucott Moor

Lucott Cross

Homebush Wood

Hawk Combe

Buckethole Farm

Lucott Farm

HOLMBUSH

Tarr Ball Hill

Pool Farm

Wilmersham

Babe Hill

Nutscale Water

Nutscale Reservoir

Stoke Pero

Stoke Ridge

Stoke Pero Common

Lang Combe

Larkbarrow (ruin)

Madacombe

Alderman's Barrow

Almsworthy Common

Wellshead Allotment

Greenlands

Chetsford Water

Wilmersham Common

Ember Combe

TA24

Macmillan Way West

Rowbarrows

Allcombe Water

Greenland Water

Pitsworthy Farm

Exford Common

Hillhead Cross

Hoar Moor

Codsend Moors

River Quarme

Kitnor Heath

WELLSHEAD LA

Hill Farm

Wellshead Farm

THE TUNNEL

Westermill Farm

Riscombe

Downscombe

BONNY LA

River Exe

MILL LA

Samaritans Way South West

Sharcott

Higher Riscombe Farm

B3223

MUDDICOMBE LA

MUDDICOMBE CROSS

YEALSCOMBE LA

WHITE CROSS

Coombe Farm

COOMBE LA

Edgcott

Stone

STONE LA

STONE CROSS

Langdon Way

B322

Larcomb Farm

Pennycombe Water

Newland

NEWLAND CROSS

Higher Thorne

North & South Ley

B3224

EDGCOTT RD

TUDBALLS

Kennels

Hotel

PO

CORNER CL.

CHURCH HILL

Exford

Exford CE Fst sch

Stetfold Rocks

STADDON MILL RD

Higher Combe

Withycombe

Lower Thorne

B3223

MONK CROSS

ROCK LA

CHAPEL LA

YH

P

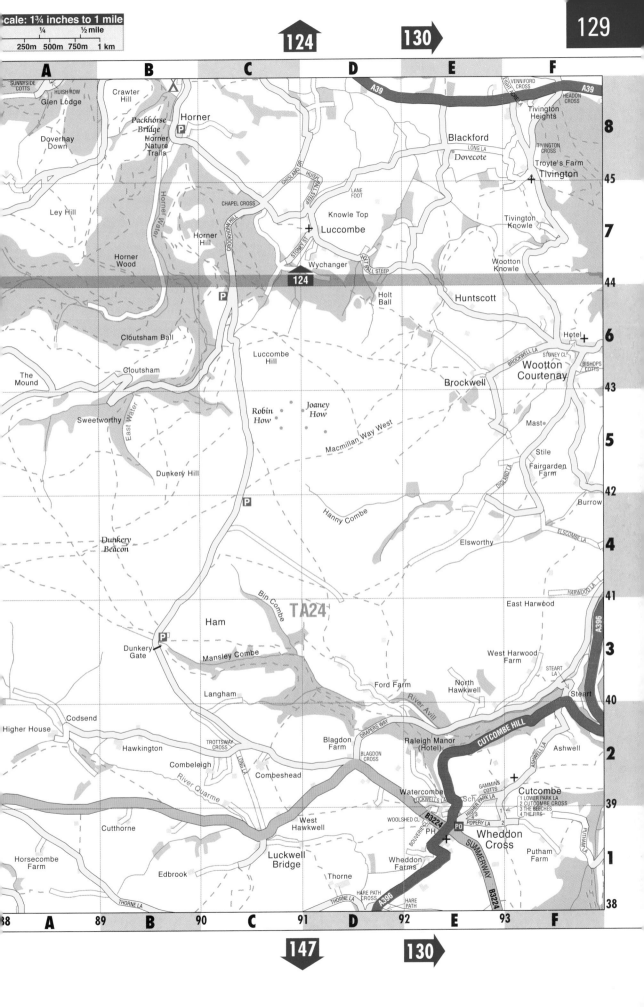

129
125

Scale: 1¾ inches to 1 mil

0   ¼   ½ mile

0   250m   500m   750m   1 km

A   B   C   D   E   F

8

A39
PORLOCK RD
PERITON LA
PERITON WAY
PARKHOUSE RD
REGENTS WAY
OLD FARM RD
SOUTH FK
PERITON RD
WEST ST
Periton
POUNDFIELD RD
PAGANEL RD
BAMPTON ST
CHE... RD
WHITEGATE RD
TOWNSEND RD
Sch
HOPCOTT RD
MART RD
PONSFORD RD
CATS LA
Ind Est
P
P
Sch
Sch
MARSHFIELD RD
HAYFIELD RD
PO
Alcombe
SEAWARD WAY
Coll
MILLARD RD
SPRING GDNS
CHURCH ST
BIRCHAM RD
West Somerset Rly
Holiday Village
The Old Manor
Works
Dunster LC
LC

45

Great Headon Plantation
Higher Hopcott
STAUNTON RD
MANOR RD
QUARRY CL
CUMBERLAND RD
DRIFT RD
ELLICOMBE RD
Marsh Street
STATION RD
SEA LA
MARSH LA
BRIDGES MEAD

7

200
Tivington Common
Periton Hill
Hopcott Common
Macmillan Way West
Callins
STAUNTON LA
Penny Hill
Ellicombe
DEAN LA
Conygar Tower
MARSH ST
Loxhole Bridge

44

Wootton Common
Staunton Plantation
125
Hagley
Alcombe Common
Aldersmead
Macmillan Way West
St Leonards Well
ST GEORGE'S RD
HIGH ST
Butter Cross
A396
Yarn Market
PO
DUNSTER STEEP
P

6

Dunkery Vineyard
Ranscombe
Knowle Hill
Burnells
TA24
Grabbist Hill
Sch
Cemy
WEST CL
CASTLE
HILL
MILL LA
Dunster
Dunster Castle
Mill
The Lawns
Kennels
200
Knowle
Aville Farm
KNOWLE LA WEST ST
Gallox Bridge

43

Cowbridge
River Avill
KNOWLE LA
201
BONNITON LA
Vinegar Hill
BONNITON NEW RD
P

5

MEADOW VIEW
VIGARAGE CT
Well Farm
WELL LA
BEMBERRY BANK
Totterdown Farm
KITSVALL LA
Whits Wood
Dunster Wood Forest Trails
BROADWOOD RD
Black Ball
Dunster Park
Bat's Castle
P

42

HORSEPARK LA
ORCHARD RD
BROOK ST
WATLI ST
HOLES SQ
WILLOWBANK
CHURCH ST
P
Sch
JUBILEE TERR
THE GLEBE
Bickham
THE KNAPP
Timberscombe
WAYDOWN LA
WHITSWOOD STEEP
P
Hur Wood
WITHYCOMBE HILL GATE
HORSE RD
Aller Hill
PARK LA

4

WAYDOWN CROSS
ELSCOMBE LA
HARWOOD CROSS
HARWOOD LA
A396
Pitt Bridge
Slade
Slade Lane
Broadwood Farm
Withycombe Scruffets
Gupworthy Farm
STAPLING LA
BOWDEN LA
Bowden

41

Oaktrow Wood
Oaktrow Farm
Beasley
Croydon House
Croydon Hill
Black Hill
OAK LA

3

40

A396
GUPWORTHY... CROSS
Sully
Allercott
Well
TA23
Rodhuish Common

2

Stowey Farm
Kersham
PUTHAM LA
KERSHAM LA
Couple Cross
Nurcott Farm
Monkham Hill
Slowley Farm

1

39

Kersham Hill
Old Stowey
BEECH TREE LA
Churchtown
Luxborough
WESTCOTT CROSS
STOUT'S WAY LA
Slowley Wood
STOUT'S WAY L...

38

94   A   95   B   96   C   97   D   98   E   99   F

For full street detail of the highlighted areas see pages 200 and 201.

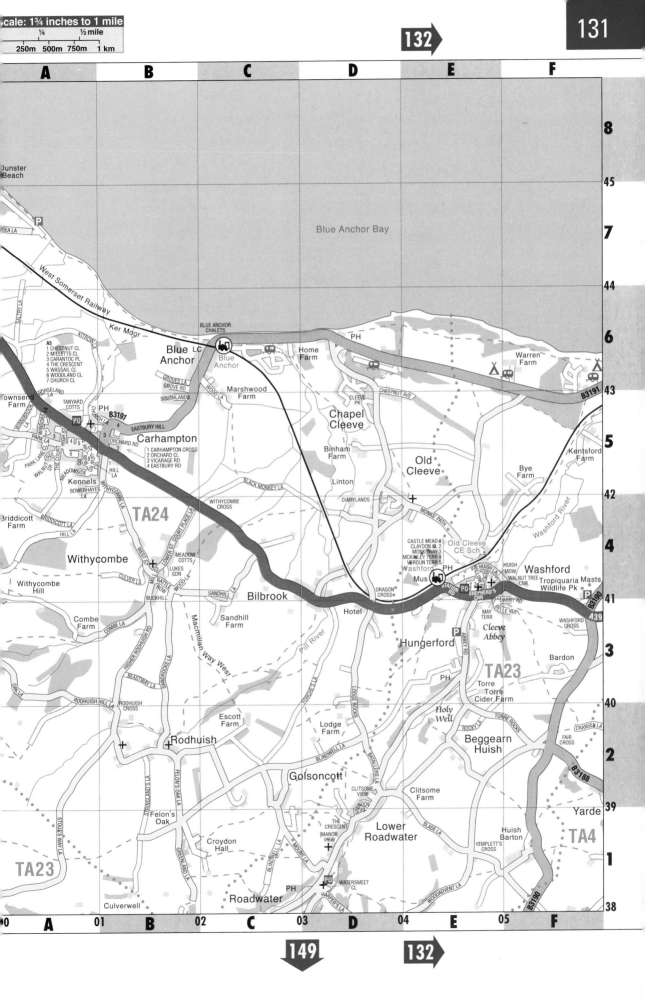

131

Scale: 1¾ inches to 1 mile

0	¼	½ mile

0	250m	500m	750m	1 km

A **B** **C** **D** **E** **F**

8

45

7

44

202

WATCHET

6

WEST ST
PO
P
Watchet
P
MARKET
HARBOUR RD
ST DECUMAN'S RD
SOUTH RD
LIDDYMORE RD

43
B3191
Mill
BRENDON RD
Sch
Sch
DONIFORD RD
Doniford Beach Halt
Doniford
NORMANDY AVE

St Audrie's Bay

Holiday Village

Holiday Park
The Belt

The Home Farm

Perry Farm

St Decumans
WASHFORD HILL
Five Bells
Liddymore Farm
LIDDYMORE LA
TA23
Rydon Farm

St Audrie's House

5

B3190
B3191
FIVE BELLS

West Wood

A39

42
202
B3190
DONIFORD RD
NORTH CROSS
UNION LA
STATION RD
Williton LC
Wibble Farm
STAPLE CL
BRACKEN EDGE
THE PARK
STAPLE LA
HILL LA
PO
PH
Stowborrow Hill

4
SMITHYARD LA
Schs
NORTH RD
B3191
Williton & District
H
LONG ST
High Bridge
West Quantoxhead
Staple Plantation
P

Williton
PRIEST ST
BANK
PO
P
HIGH ST
FORE ST
BRIDGE ST
Castle Hill
Torweston Farm
LUCKES LA
TA4
Weacombe

41
A39
Mus
BURROW ROCKS
TOWER HILL
A358
SAMPFORD ROCKS
West Somerset Railway
Lower Weacombe

3
Sampford Brett
HONEY ROW LA

202
Stream
Orchard Wyndham
Woolston
Bicknolle Hill
Bicknoller

40
CRANSEY
Macmillan Way West
DASHWOODS LA
GATCHELLS LA
Trendle Ring

2
Black Down Wood
Capton
Capton Cross
Yellow Wood Cross
COMBE LA
CHURCH LA
PARSONS CLOSE
TRENDLE LA
PH
B3188
Yarde
YELLOW WOOD LA
Chilcombe
Quantoc Moor Farm
CHILCOMBE LA

39
Woodford Gotts
NETTLECOMBE PARK LA
Yellow Wood Farm
YELLOW WOOD LA
Lower Yellow
Newton
Culverhays
COOKLEY LA

1
Cemy
Woodford
BEECH TREE CROSS
COMBECROSS LA
Rowdon Farm
ESCOTT LA
FENTON LA
VILLOUGH
HALSWAY HILL A358
CULVERHAYS LA

B3188
Yard Farm

38
06
A
07
B
08
C
09
D
10
E
11
F

For full street detail of the highlighted area see page 202.

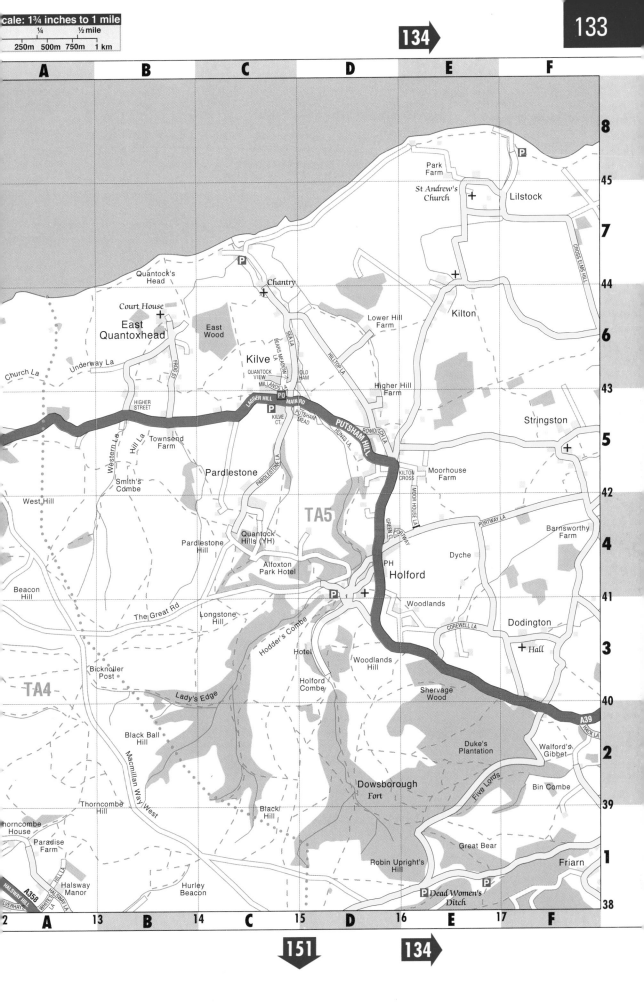

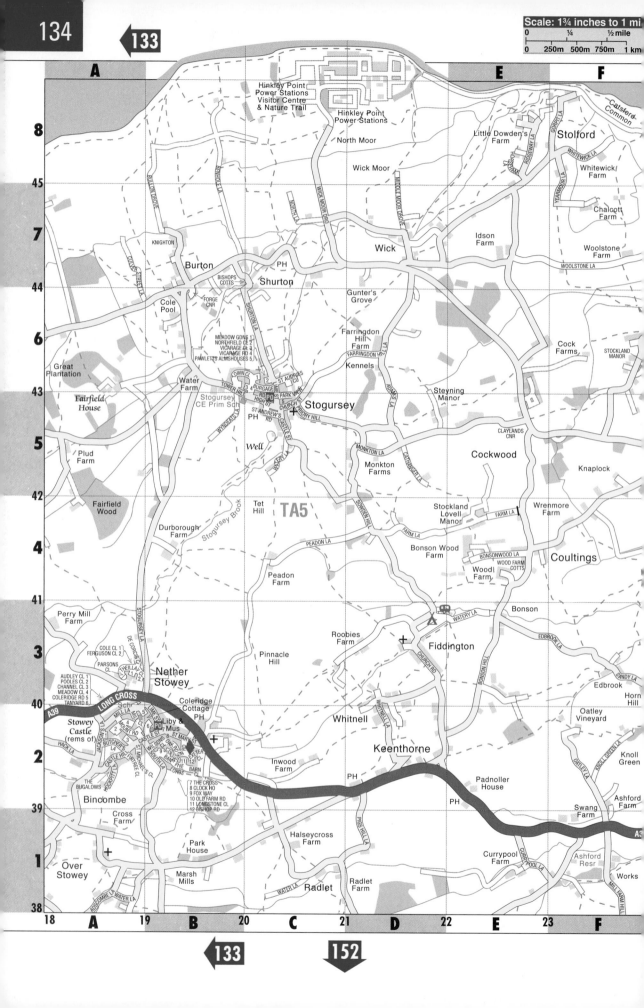

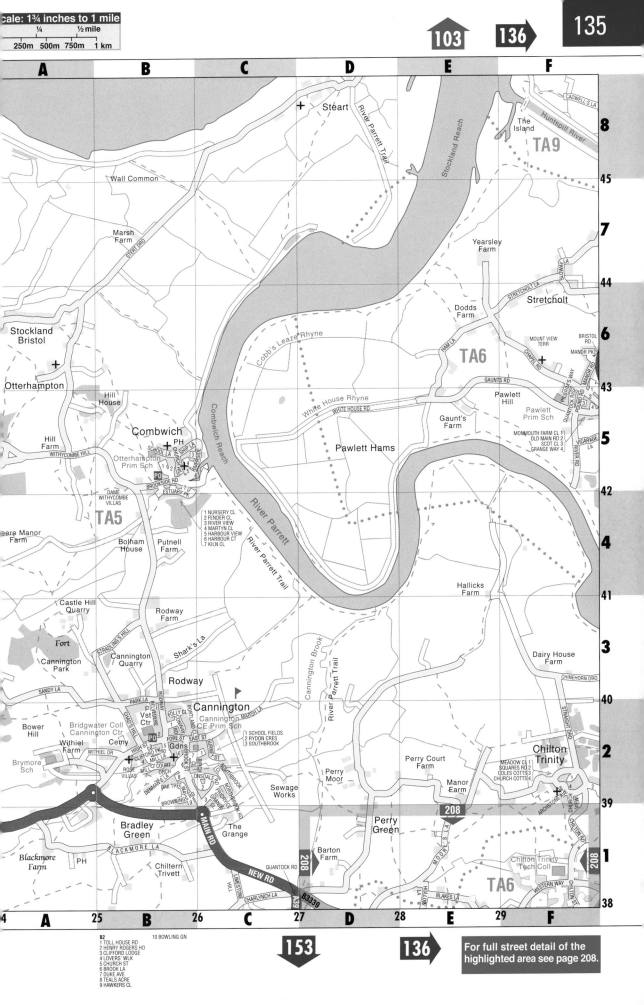

A   B   C   D   E   F

8

45

7

44

6

43

5

42

4

41

3

40

2

39

1

38

24 A 25 B 26 C 27 D 28 E 29 F

Steart

River Parrett Trail

Stockland Reach

Huntspill River

CADWELL'S LA

The Island

TA9

Wall Common

Marsh Farm

STEART DRO

Yearsley Farm

SOLWAY LA

Stretcholt

Dodds Farm

STRETCHOLT LA

Stockland Bristol

Cobb's Leaze Rhyne

TA6

HAM LA

Mount View Terr

CHAPEL RD

BRISTOL RD

MANOR PK

Otterhampton

Hill House

Gaunts Rd

GAUNTS RD

Pawlett Hill

Pawlett Prim Sch

PILGRIMS WAY

QUANTOCK RISE

POUND RD

MANOR RD

Hill Farm

WITHYCOMBE HILL

White House Rhyne

WHITE HOUSE RD

Gaunt's Farm

MONMOUTH FARM CL 1
OLD MAIN RD 2
SCOT CL 3
GRANGE WAY 4

VICARAGE LA

RIVER RD

Combwich

PH

SCHOOL LA

SHIP LA

CHURCH HILL

RIVERSIDE

Otterhampton Prim Sch

Pawlett Hams

Combwich Reach

PO

BROOKSIDE RD

ESTUARY PK

1 NURSERY CL
2 FENDER CL
3 RIVER VIEW
4 MARTYN CL
5 HARBOUR VIEW
6 HARBOUR CT
7 KILN CL

DAME WITHYCOMBE VILLAS

TA5

Deere Manor Farm

Bolham House

Putnell Farm

River Parrett

River Parrett Trail

Hallicks Farm

Castle Hill Quarry

Rodway Farm

Fort

STRADLING'S HILL

Cannington Quarry

Shark's La

Cannington Brook

River Parrett Trail

Dairy House Farm

CHINEHORN DRO

Cannington Park

RODWAY

Rodway

SANDY LA

PARK LA

BELGROVE

Vstr Ctr

Cannington CE Prim Sch

Cannington MARSH LA

1 SCHOOL FIELDS
2 RYDON CRES
3 SOUTHBROOK

STRAIGHT DRO

Chilton Trinity

Bridgwater Coll Cannington Ctr

CHAD'S HILL

HIGH ST

PO

FOLLY CL

PORTLAND CL

CONWAY

FORE ST

EAST ST

GURNEY ST

BIRCH

SOUTHBROOK

Perry Court Farm

MEADOW CL 1
SQUARES RD 2
COLES COTTS 3
CHURCH COTTS 4

Bower Hill

Withiel Farm

WITHIEL DR

Cemy

CLIFFORD PK

MILL LA

Gdns

MILL'S COURT

ORCH

ROSE VILLAS

DENMAN CL

OAK TREE

BROWNINGS

LONSDALE CL

NORTHBROOK

EBDON CL

WAY

GRANGE

Perry Moor

Sewage Works

Perry Court Farm

Manor Farm

ARCHSTONE AVE

CHURCH VIEW

CHILTON RD

208

Brymore Sch

Bradley Green

The Grange

MAIN RD

BLACKMORE LA

Blackmore Farm

PH

Chiltern Trivett

NEW RD

LIMESTONE HILL

QUANTOCK RD

CHARLYNCH LA

208

B3339

A39

Barton Farm

Perry Green

MOORE'S LA

HOLLOW LA

BLAKES LA

208

Chilton Trinity Tech Coll

WESTERN WAY

TA6

B2
1 TOLL HOUSE RD
2 HENRY ROGERS HO
3 CLIFFORD LODGE
4 LOVERS' WLK
5 CHURCH ST
6 BROOK LA
7 DUKE AVE
8 TEALS ACRE
9 HAWKERS CL
10 BOWLING GN

A B C D E F

8 45 7 44 6 43 5 42 4 41 3 40 2 39 1 38

Huntspill

CADWELL'S LA
CHURCH RD
GROVE
MILLGREEN CL
SILVER LA
SWELL
SEALEYS
LABURNUM LODGES
ALEX CL
RINGSTONE
MAIN RD
A38

1 PLYMOR RD
2 CARAMIA PK
3 CHAPEL FORGE CL
4 SUNNY CL
5 GREENWOOD CL

NEWBRIDGE LA
NEW RD
CATHERINE ST
Secret World
Hackness

M5

East Huntspill Prim Sch
B3141
FACTORY LA
PO
Brue Bsns Pk
Moor Row
MEAD LA
ORCHARD CL
CHAPEL LA
HACKNESS
COMBE TERR
CHURCHLEA PK
MERRY LA
HACK MEAD LA

Huntspill Level
West Huntspill
East Huntspill
Cote
CHURCH LA
CHURCH RD
WILLOW
MILL LA
PH
1 NUT TREE CL
2 CHURCH CL

Bleak Bridge
OLD PAWLETT RD
PAWLETT RD
STRAIGHT DRO
PURITON RD
RUGG'S DRO
HARDY MEAD DRO
LC
WITHY RD
WITHY GR
Withy Grove Farm
WEST CORNMOOR DRO
TA9
Huntspill River
Cornmoor Farm
CORNMOOR CRES
CORNMOOR LA
WHITE HOUSE LA
BURTLE RD
COTE RD
COTE CNR

Withy Farm
Huntspill Moor
GOLD CORNER DRO

Pawlett
OLD MAIN RD
PO
VICARS LA
North Farm
PAWLETT MEAD DRO
PURITON RD
Landfill Site
LC
BANNOCK DRO
BATCH RD
NORTH MEAD DRO
Black Ditch
Moormead Dro
MOORMEAD DRO
CAUSEWAY
PYDE DRO
Middle Moor Dro
Middlemoor Water Park
Woolavington Level

PARSONAGE CT 1
PURITON MANOR 2
COURT GR 3
POOL CL 4
ROOKERY CL 5
PUREWELL 6
CULVERHAY CL 7
WALNUT CL 8

Factory
Puriton Level

Walpole
Motte & Baileys
DOWNEND TERR
DOWNEND RD
DOWNEND CRES
END RD
PAWLETT RD
CHURCH FIELD LA
BATCH CL
RYE
RIVERTON RD
MIDDLE DOWNS
WATERLOO CL
WATERLOO CL
Puriton
WEST APPROACH RD
EAST APPROACH RD
WOOLAVINGTON RD
CROCKERS
MORTIMER
HECTORS STONES
LOWER
HIGHER
CAUSEWAY CL
REEDS CL
CHILPITTS
1 THE DRIVE
2 THE SQUARE
3 CHURCH ST
4 VICARAGE RD
Woolavington

Down End
Dunball Ind Est
Factory
A39
23
A39
WEBBERS WAY
STATION RD
BRISTOL RD
PURITON HILL
ROWLANDS RISE
PURITON PK
HILLSIDE DR
CYPRESS
SPRING RISE
9 HILLSIDE DR
10 HILLSIDE CRES
11 ROWAN CL
12 BIRCH AVE
13 MAPLE CL
14 MANSE LA
15 SPRING RISE
16 ELM LEA CL
Puriton Prim Sch
Woolavington Village Prim Sch
MEADOW
BAWDEN
HIGHCROFT
WOOLAVINGTON HILL
TOR VIEW
LOCKWELL
EDGEBURY
COMBE LA

Dunball
PURITON HILL
TA7
CRANCOMBE LA
KNOWLE LA
SEDGEMOOR CL
1 THE COPSE 2
MARTLAND CL 10
POEDEN WLK 11
WINDMILL CRES 12
BITHAM WLK 13
MILL WLK 14
MAPLE TREE CT 1
MANOR CT 3
BRENT RD
PARK CRES
ST MARY'S CL
Gardiners Bsns Pk
STATION RD
5 CROSSMEAD
6 CLARK CL
7 BROADLAWN
8 MOUNT VIEW
9 HILLSBORO
10 ORCHARD WAY
WALNUT LA
MIDDLE RD
PO
B3141
Cossington
Cossington Prim Sch

TA6
River Parrett
Horsey Pill
The Polden Bsns Ctr
Knowle Hall
FAIRWAYS CVN PK
BATH RD
PH
Little Wall La
NEW RD
BAWDRIP LA
CHURCH WLK
GREENFIELD
ST MICHAELS CT
King's Farm
EAST SVE LA
Brook La
THISTLEDOO VINE
WOOD LA

TA5
CHINEHAM
Express Pk
SQUARES RD
The Wireworks Est
Sedgemount Ind Pk
HORSEY LA
Manor Farm
Horsey Level
Crandon Bridge
A39
King's Sedgemoor Drain
MARSH LA
Knowle
Kingsmoor Prim Sch
Bawdrip
STONE DRO
Bawdrip Level
Peasey Farm

Sewage Works
CRYPTON TECH BSNS PK
IND EST
WYLDS RD
209
A38
209
M5
WILFRED RD
BOWER LA
SHERWOOD RD
GREDGLEY LA
Horsey
BRADNEY LA
BRIDGWATER
Bradney
Slape Cross
A39
209
WEST END CT
Pendon Hill
Works

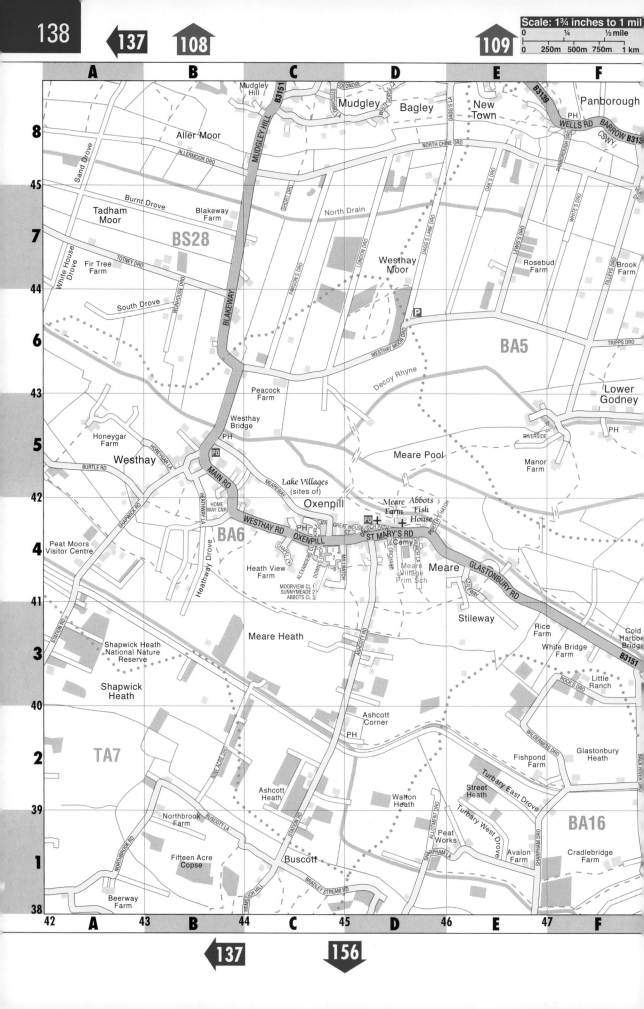

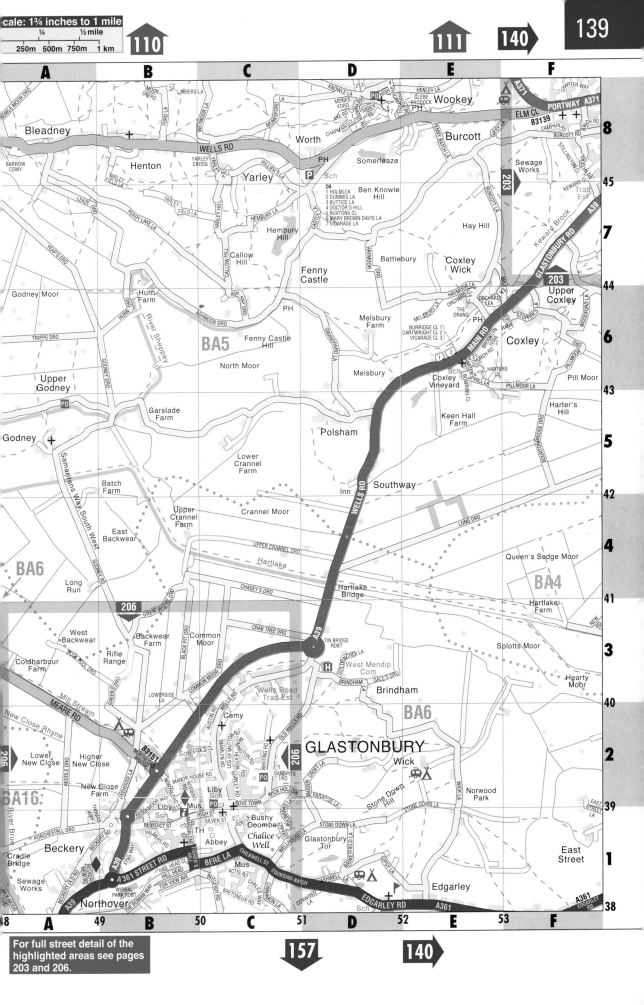

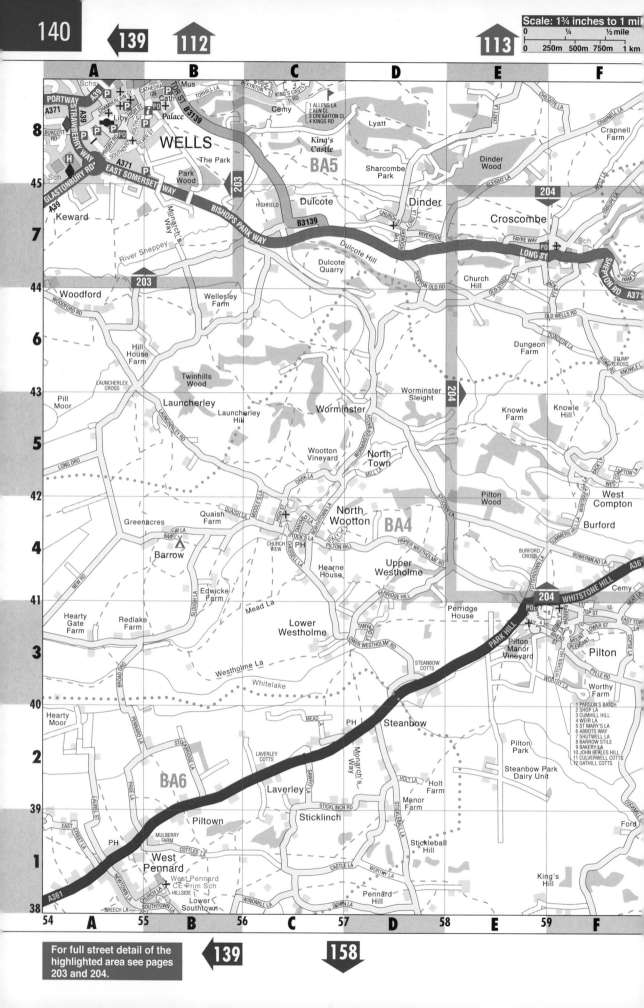

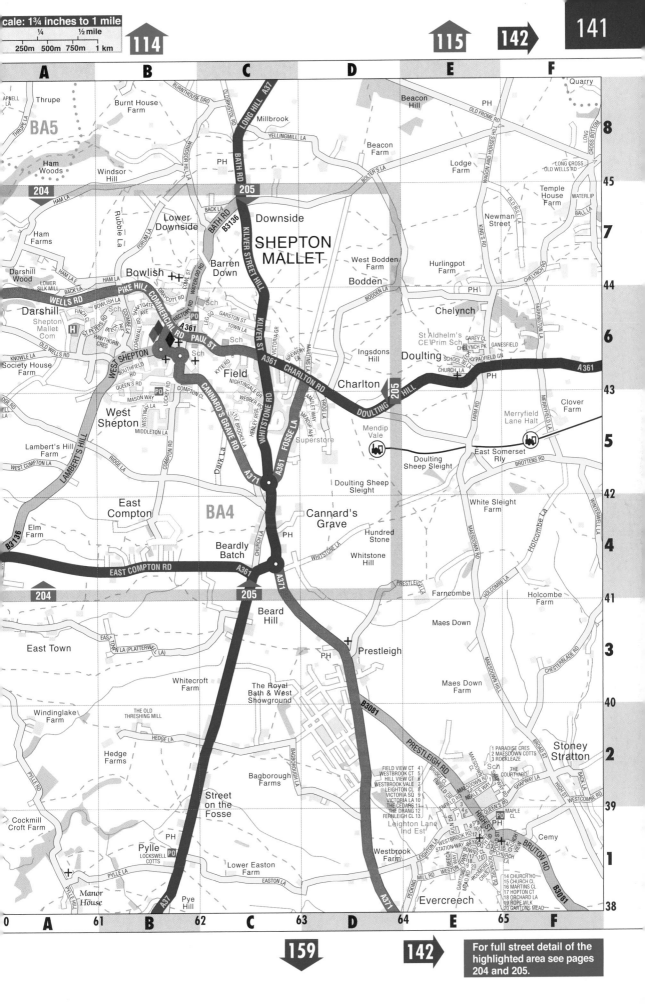

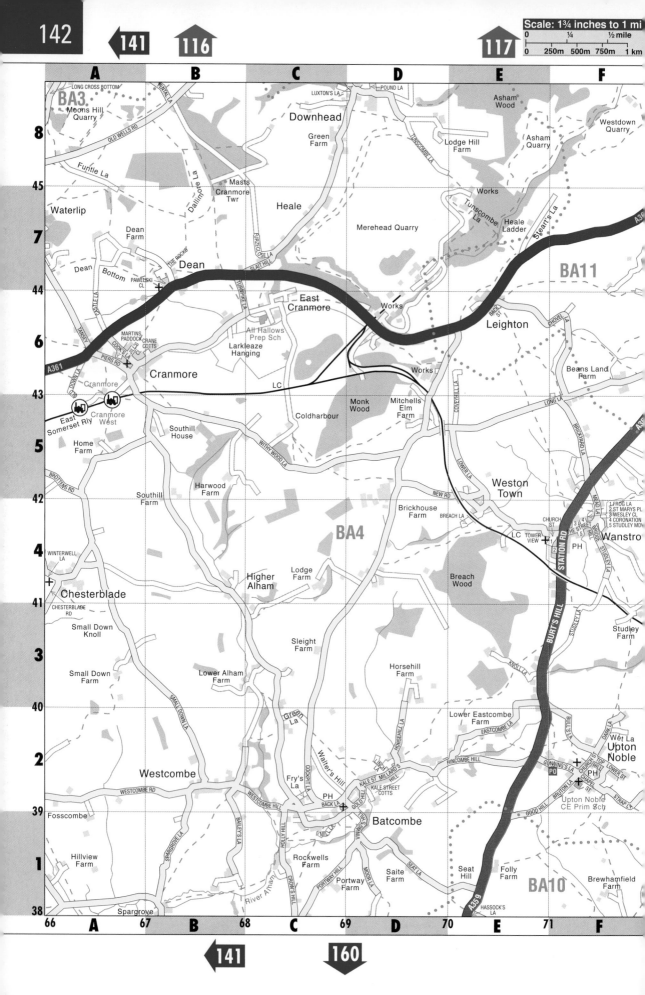

A B C D E F

BA3

LONG CROSS BOTTOM

Moons Hill
Quarry

LUXTON'S LA POUND LA

Downhead

Asham
Wood

Westdown
Quarry

8

Funtle La

OLD WELLS RD

Green
Farm

Lodge Hill
Farm

Asham
Quarry

45

Masts
Cranmore
Twr

Heale

Works

Tunscombe
La

7

Waterlip

Dean
Farm

THE ROCKS

Dean

Merehead Quarry

Heale
Ladder

BA11

44

Dean
Bottom

Dean

PAWELSKI
CL

East
Cranmore

Works

Leighton

6

CASTLE LA

TANSEY

MARTINS
PADDOCK

CRANE
COTTS

COOK'S LA

PIERS RD

All Hallows
Prep Sch

Larkleaze
Hanging

Works

BACK ST

CHOVEL LA

Beans Land
Farm

43

A361

Cranmore

Cranmore

LC

Coldharbour

Monk
Wood

Mitchells
Elm
Farm

COVEHILL LA

LONG LA

East
Somerset Rly

Cranmore
West

Southill
House

WITHY WOOD LA

LOWER LA

Weston
Town

BRICKYARD LA

5

Home
Farm

Southill
Farm

Harwood
Farm

NEW RD

BREACH LA

CHURCH
ST

1 FROG LA
2 ST MARYS PL
3 WESLEY CL
4 CORONATION
5 STUDLEY MDW

42

BROTTENS RD

Brickhouse
Farm

STATION RD

THE STREET

MEAD LA

BRIDGE

Wanstro

WINTERWELL
LA

Higher
Alham

Lodge
Farm

Breach
Wood

LC

TOWER
VIEW

PH

STUDLEY LA

4

Chesterblade

Small Down
Knoll

CHESTERBLADE
RD

Breach
Wood

BURT'S HILL

BA4

KNOLL LA

Studley
Farm

41

3

Small Down
Farm

SMALL DOWN LA

Lower Alham
Farm

Sleight
Farm

Horsehill
Farm

40

Green
La

Lower Eastcombe
Farm

EASTCOMBE LA

BULL'S LA

DARK LA

Wet La

Upton
Noble

2

Westcombe

WALTER'S HILL

COCKPIT LA

Fry's
La

KALE ST

THE LYNCH

MILLARD'S
HILL

HORSEHILL LA

HINCOMBE HILL

GUNNING'S LA

PO

PH

1ST TOP

CHURCH
ST

LOWER ST

STRAP LA

Upton Noble
CE Prim Sch

39

WESTCOMBE RD

BAILEY'S LA

WESTCOMBE HILL

Kale Street
Cotts

BACK LA

GOLD

PH

Batcombe

GOOD HILL

BRUTON LA

CHAPEL LA

1

Fosscombe

SPARGROVE LA

CROW'S HILL

Rockwells
Farm

PORTWAY HILL

Saite
Farm

SEAT LA

MOOR LA

Seat
Hill

Folly
Farm

BA10

Brewhamfield
Farm

Hillview
Farm

River A'lham

Portway
Farm

A359

HASSOCK'S
LA

38

66 A 67 B 68 C 69 D 70 E 71 F

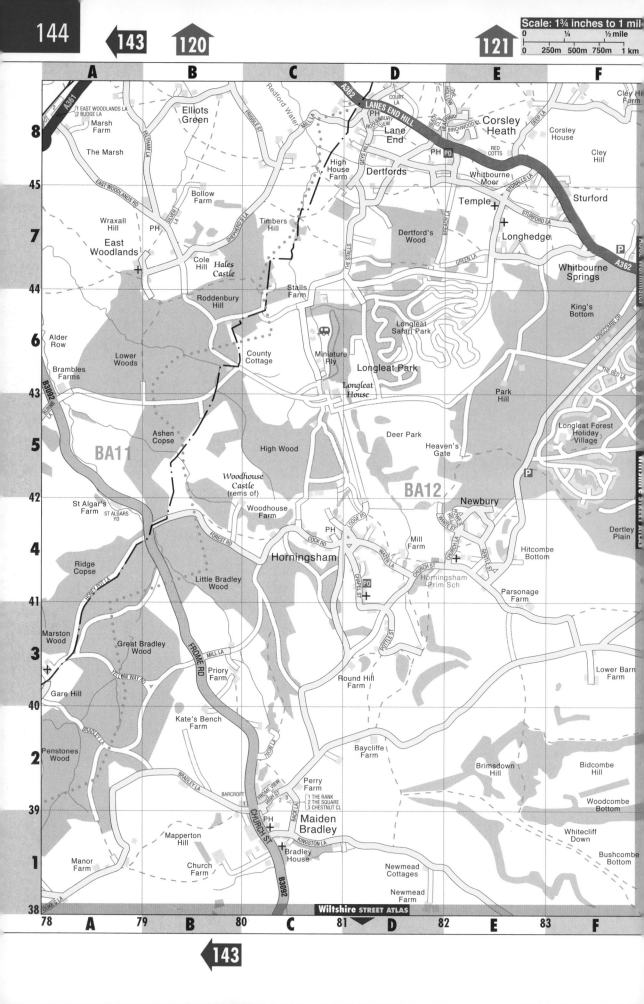

143
120
121

Scale: 1¾ inches to 1 mile

0 ¼ ½ mile
0 250m 500m 750m 1 km

A B C D E F

8
1 EAST WOODLANDS LA
2 BUDGE LA
Marsh Farm
The Marsh
Elliots Green
Redford Water
A362
LANES END HILL
Court
Lane End
Corsley Heath
Cley Hill Farm

45
EAST WOODLANDS RD
Bollow Farm
High House Farm
Dertfords
Whitbourne Moor
RED COTTS
Corsley House
Cley Hill

7
Wraxall Hill
PH
SILVER LA
FELTHAM LA
Timbers Hill
SHEPHERDS LA
THE STALLS
Dertford's Wood
BEECH LA
GREEN LA
Temple
Longhedge
SYDNALLS LA
STURFORD LA
Sturford
A362
P

East Woodlands
Cole Hill
Hales Castle
Roddenbury Hill
Stalls Farm
Whitbourne Springs

44
King's Bottom
LONGCOMBE DR
THE RED LA

6
Alder Row
Brambles Farms
Lower Woods
County Cottage
Miniature Rly
Longleat Safari Park
Longleat Park
Park Hill

43
B3092
BURNS LA
Ashen Copse
High Wood
Longleat House
Deer Park
Heaven's Gate
Longleat Forest Holiday Village

5
BA11
Woodhouse Castle (rems of)
BA12
Newbury
P

42
St Algar's Farm
ST ALGARS YD
Woodhouse Farm
PH
WHITE ST
ROME LA
Dertley Plain

4
Ridge Copse
HONEY BOTTLE LA
FOREST RD
Little Bradley Wood
COCK RD
LODGE RD
Horningsham
Mill Farm
CHURCH ST
GENTLE ST
CHURCH LA
Horningsham Prim Sch
Hitcombe Bottom
Parsonage Farm

41
CHAPEL ST
PO
WATER LA

3
Marston Wood
Great Bradley Wood
YELLOW WAY RD
Priory Farm
MILL LA
FROME RD
POTTLE ST
Round Hill Farm
Lower Barn Farm

40
Gare Hill
BRADLEY LA
Kate's Bench Farm

2
Penstones Wood
BRADLEY LA
BARCROFT
FROME VIEW
HIGH ST
PROW LA
Perry Farm
1 THE RANK
2 THE SQUARE
3 CHESTNUT CL
Baycliffe Farm
Brimsdown Hill
Bidcombe Hill
Woodcombe Bottom

39
CHURCH ST
PH
BACK LA
Maiden Bradley
Whitecliff Down

1
Manor Farm
Mapperton Hill
Church Farm
KINGSTON LA
Bradley House
B3092
Newmead Cottages
Newmead Farm
Bushcombe Bottom

38
DUKES LA

78 A 79 B 80 C 81 D 82 E 83 F

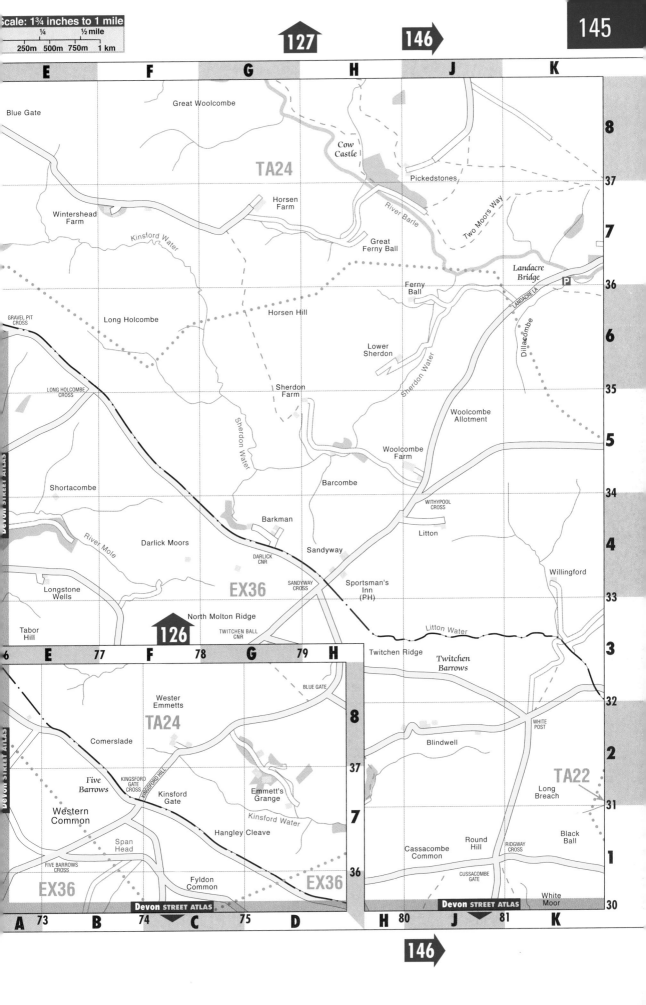

Scale: 1¾ inches to 1 mile

¼   ½ mile

250m 500m 750m 1 km

E   F   G   H   J   K

Blue Gate

Great Woolcombe

Cow Castle

TA24

Pickedstones

8

37

Horsen Farm

River Barle

Two Moors Way

Wintershead Farm

Kinsford Water

Great Ferny Ball

7

Landacre Bridge

P

36

GRAVEL PIT CROSS

Long Holcombe

Horsen Hill

Ferny Ball

LANDACRE LA

Dillacombe

6

Lower Sherdon

Sherdon Water

LONG HOLCOMBE CROSS

Sherdon Farm

35

Woolcombe Allotment

Shortacombe

Sherdon Water

Woolcombe Farm

Barcombe

5

WITHYPOOL CROSS

34

Barkman

Litton

River Mole

Darlick Moors

Sandyway

4

DARLICK CNR

Willingford

Longstone Wells

EX36

SANDYWAY CROSS

Sportsman's Inn (PH)

Litton Water

33

Tabor Hill

North Molton Ridge

TWITCHEN BALL CNR

Twitchen Ridge

Twitchen Barrows

3

126

32

6   E   77   F   78   G   79   H

WHITE POST

Wester Emmetts

BLUE GATE

Blindwell

2

Comerslade

TA24

8

TA22

37

Five Barrows

KINGSFORD GATE CROSS

KINGSFORD HILL

Emmett's Grange

Long Breach

31

Western Common

Kinsford Gate

Kinsford Water

7

Black Ball

Span Head

Hangley Cleave

Cassacombe Common

Round Hill

RIDGWAY CROSS

1

FIVE BARROWS CROSS

36

EX36

Fyldon Common

EX36

CUSSACOMBE GATE

White Moor

30

Devon STREET ATLAS

Devon STREET ATLAS

A   73   B   74   C   75   D   H   80   J   81   K

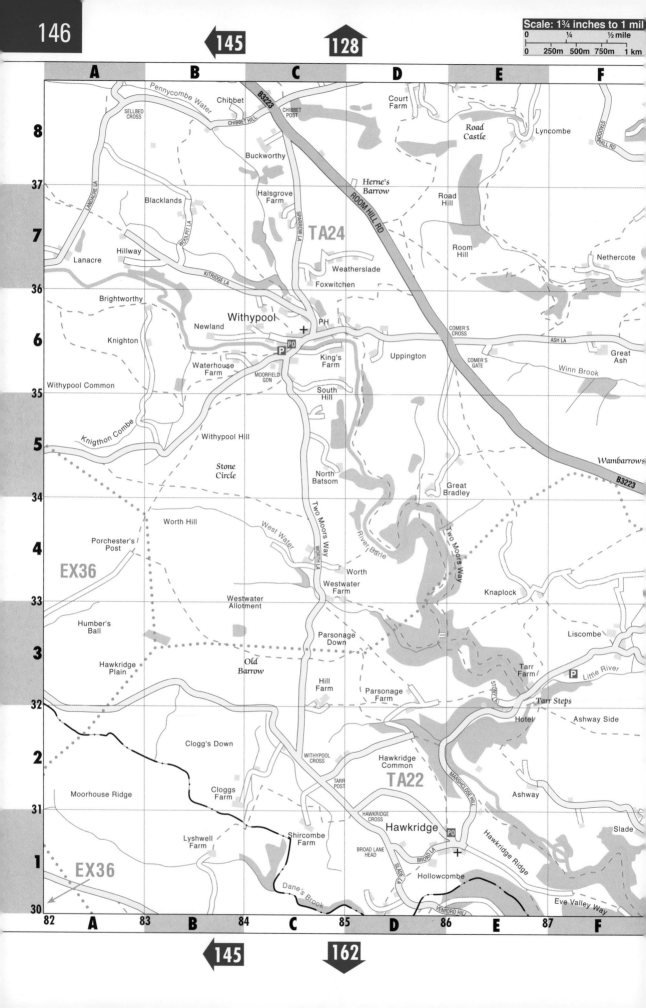

Scale: 1¾ inches to 1 mil
0   ¼   ½ mile
0   250m   500m   750m   1 km

A   B   C   D   E   F

Pennycombe Water
Chibbet
B3223
Chibbet Post
Chibbet Hill
Court Farm
Sellbed Cross
Road Castle
Lyncombe
STADDON HILL RD
8

Buckworthy
Herne's Barrow
ROOM HILL RD
37

Blacklands
Halsgrove Farm
Road Hill
Road Castle

LANDACRE LA
SPARROW LA
TA24
Room Hill
Nethercote
7

Hillway
Weatherslade
WOOLPIT LA
KITRIDGE LA
Foxwitchen
Lanacre

Brightworthy
Withypool
PH
COMER'S CROSS
ASH LA
Great Ash
6

Newland
King's Farm
Uppington
Comer's Gate
Knighton
PO
Waterhouse Farm
MOORFIELD GDN
Withypool Common
South Hill
Winn Brook
35

Knigthon Combe
Withypool Hill
Wambarrows
B3223
5

Stone Circle
North Batsom
Great Bradley
34

Worth Hill
West Water
River Barle
Two Moors Way
Porchester's Post
WORTH LA
Worth
Knaplock
EX36
4

Westwater Farm
Two Moors Way
Westwater Allotment
Liscombe
33

Humber's Ball
Parsonage Down
Tarr Farm
Little River
P
3

Hawkridge Plain
Old Barrow
Hill Farm
Parsonage Farm
Tarr Steps
Ashway Side
32

Clogg's Down
Withypool Cross
Hawkridge Common
MARSHCLOSE HILL
Hotel
STOWEY
Cloggs Farm
Tarr Post
TA22
Ashway
Moorhouse Ridge
31

Hawkridge Cross
Hawkridge
PO
Slade
Lyshwell Farm
Shircombe Farm
Hawkridge Ridge
EX36
Broad Lane Head
SLADE LA
BROND LA
Hollowcombe
Eve Valley Way
Dane's Brook
VENFORD HILL
30

82   A   83   B   84   C   85   D   86   E   87   F

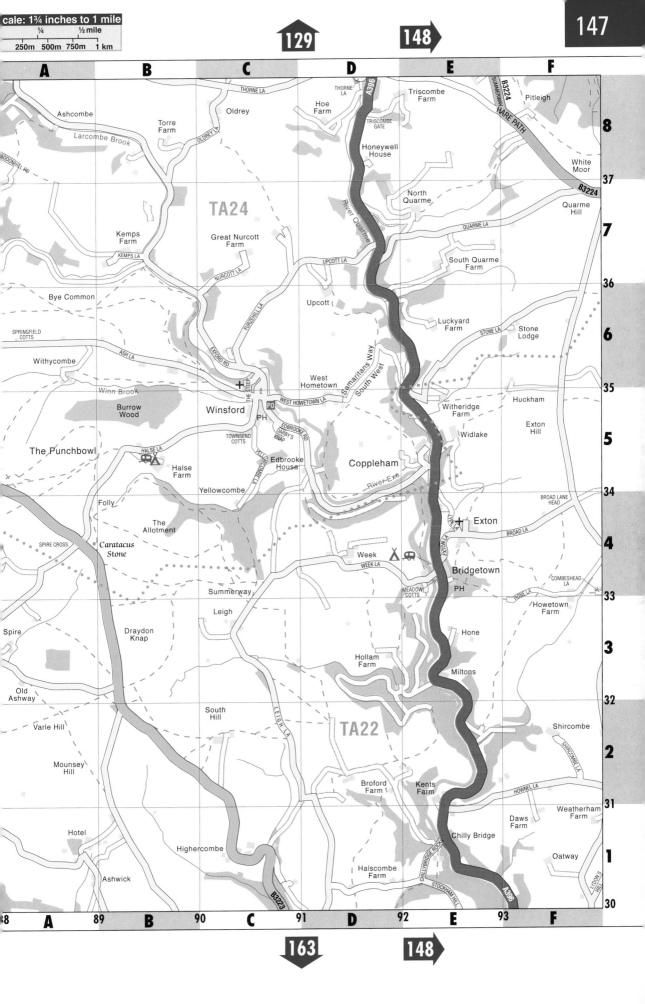

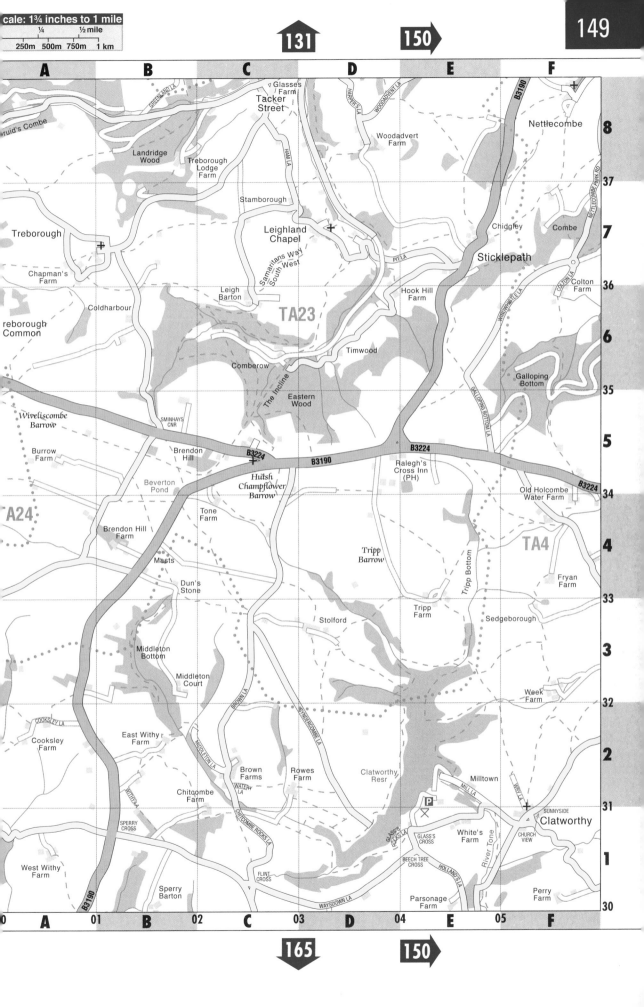

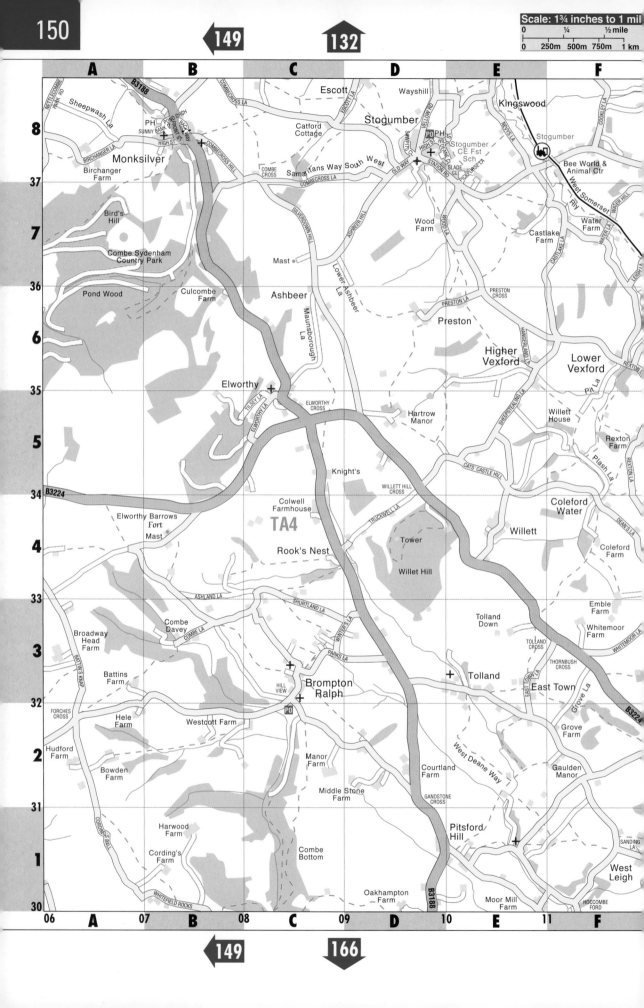

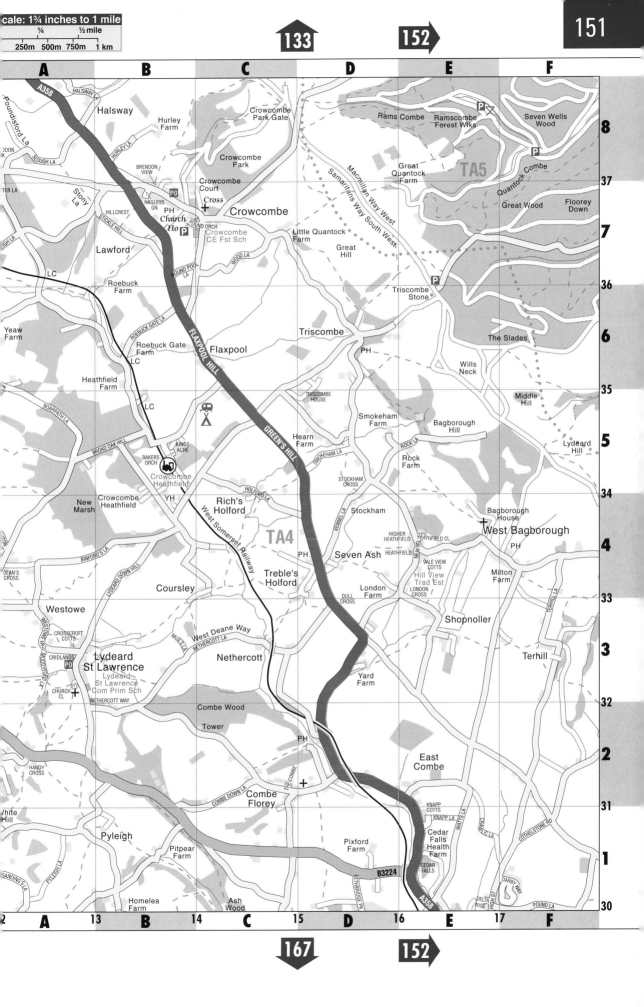

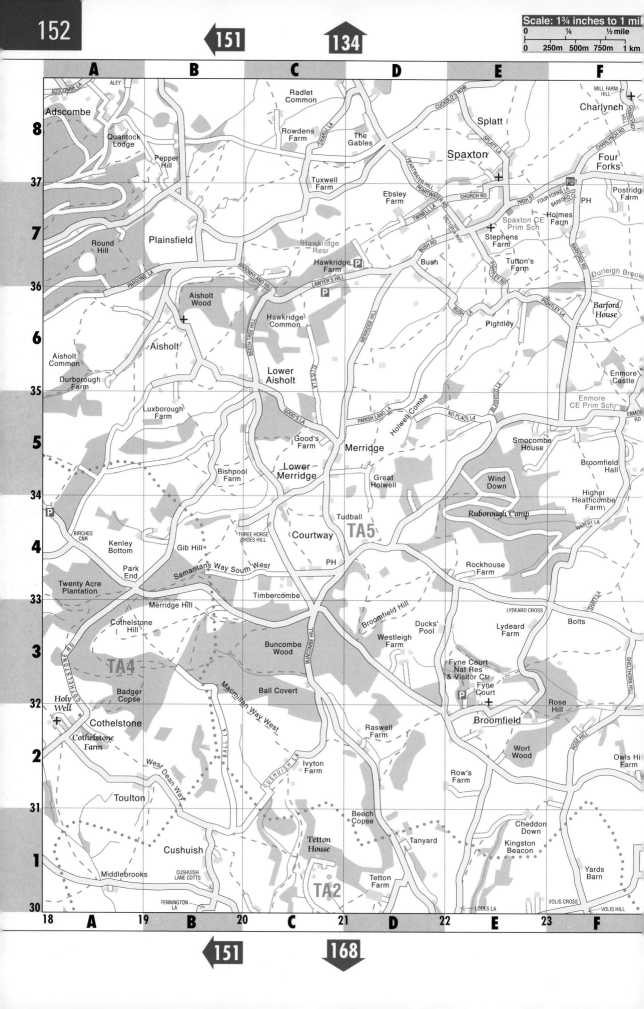

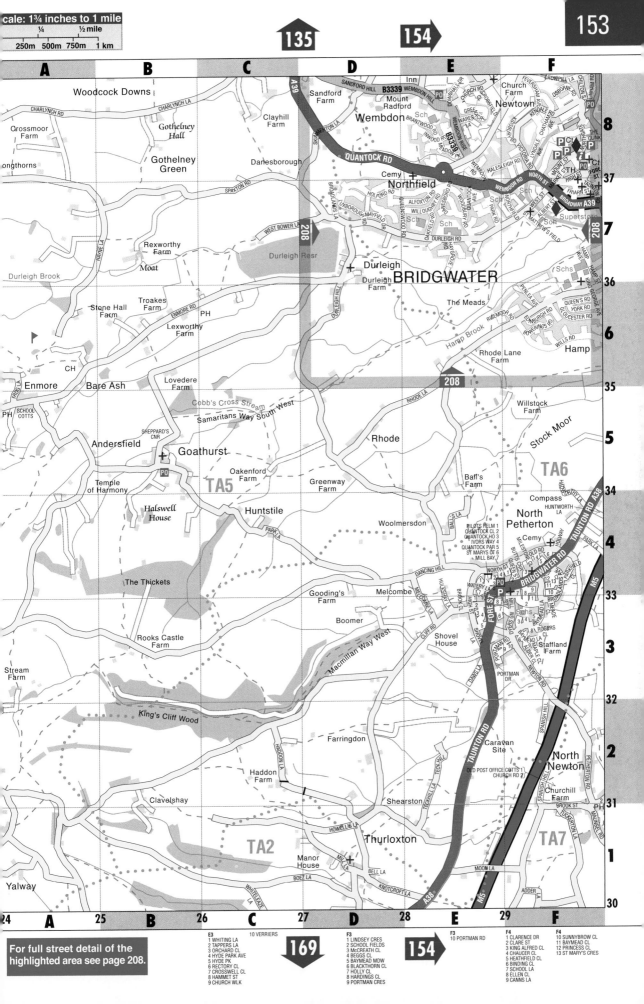

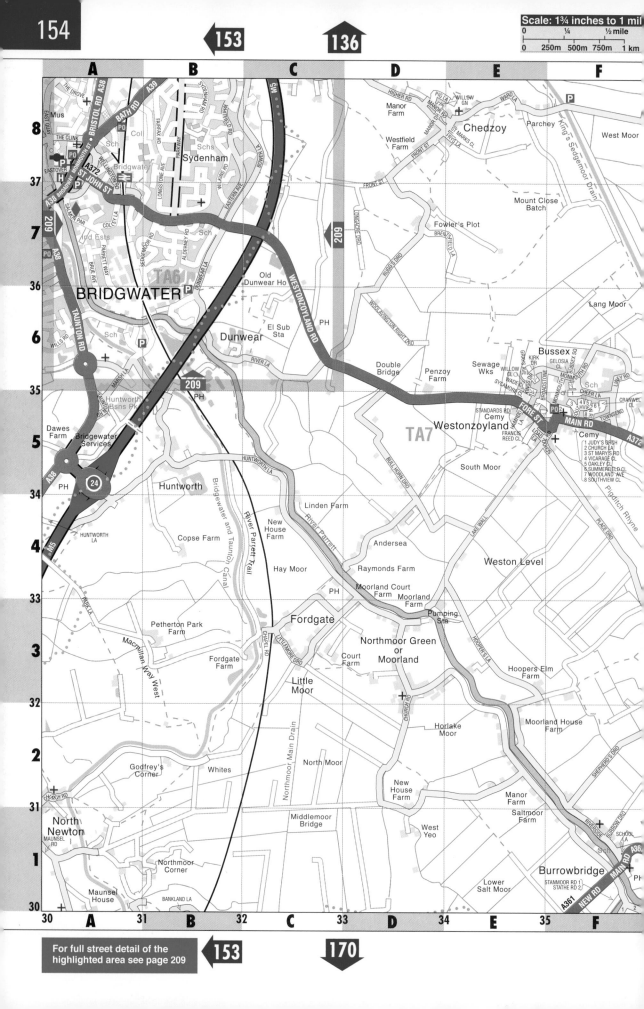

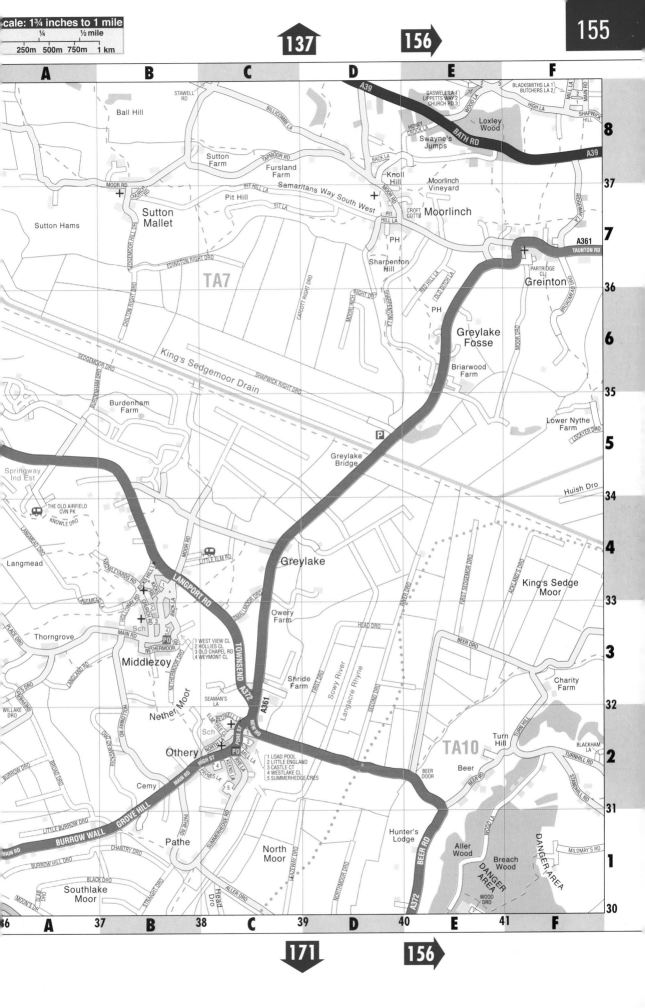

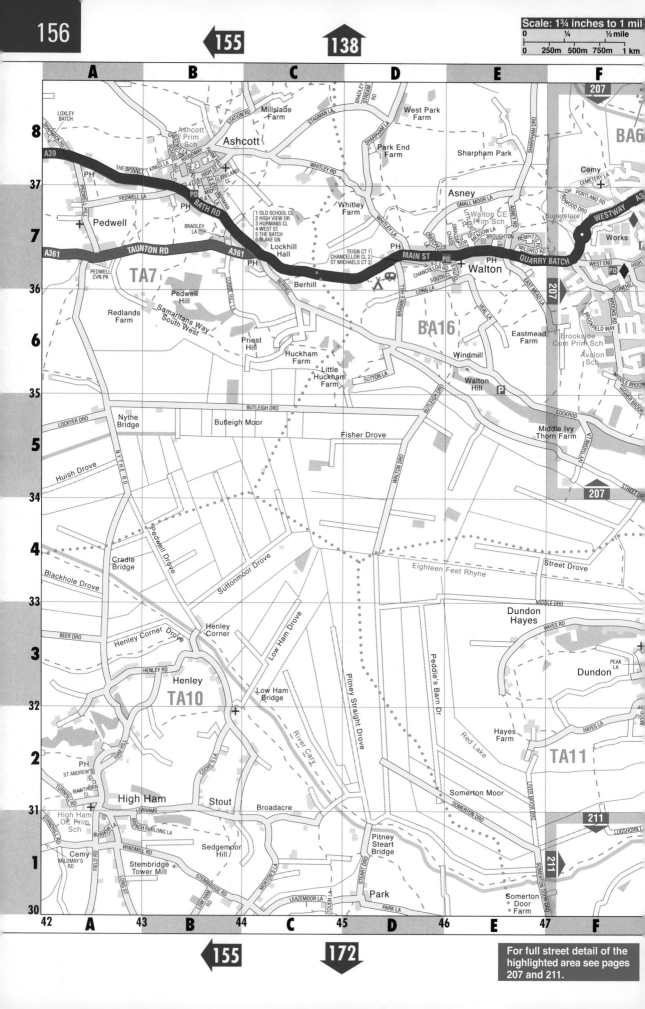

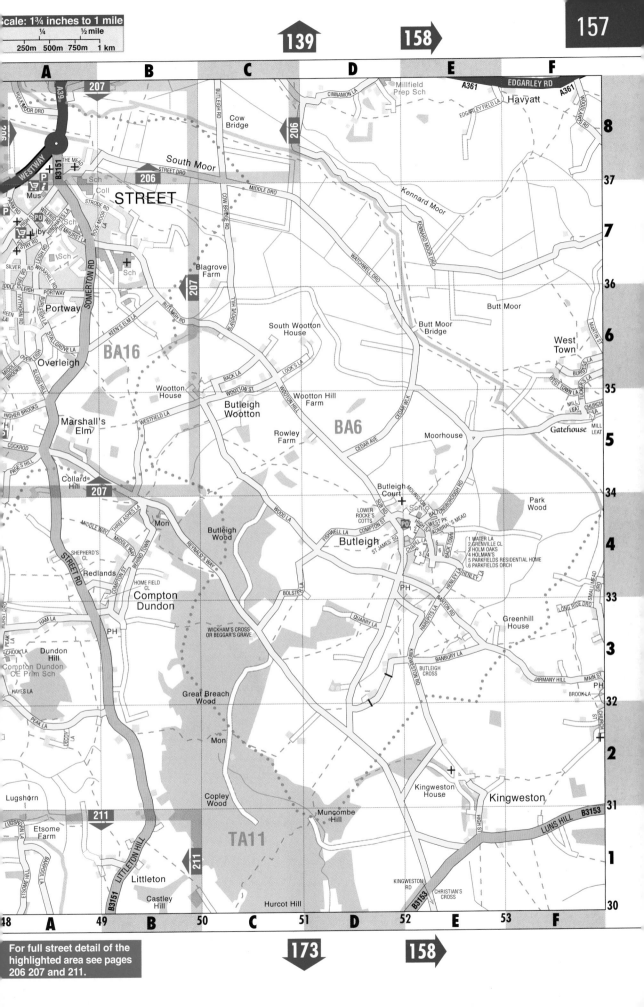

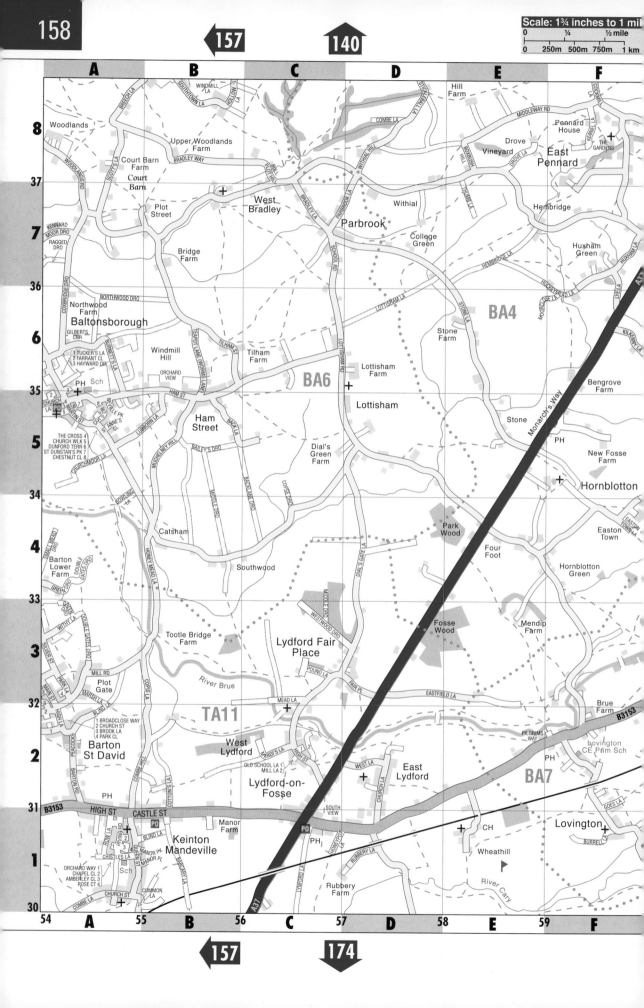

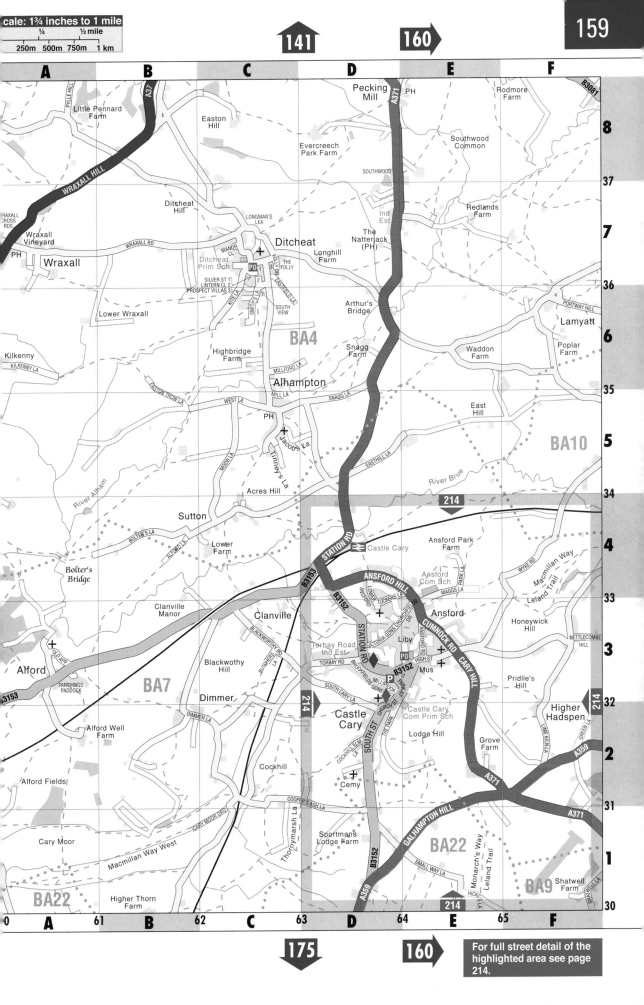

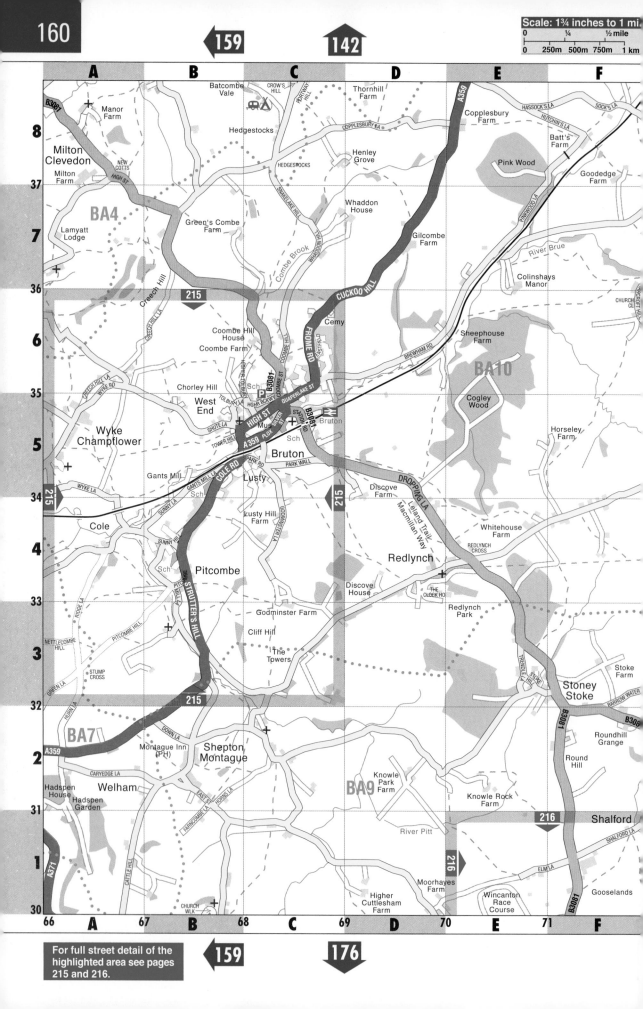

159

142

Scale: 1¾ inches to 1 ml.
0   ¼   ½ mile
0   250m   500m   750m   1 km

A   B   C   D   E   F

8

Manor
Farm
Milton
Clevedon
Milton
Farm
NEW
COTTS
HIGH ST

Batcombe
Vale

CROW'S
HILL

Hedgestocks
HEDGESTOCKS

Thornhill
Farm

A359
Copplesbury
Farm
HASSOCK'S LA
HUTCHIN'S LA
SOCK'S LA

Batt's
Farm

Pink Wood
Goodedge
Farm

37

BA4

Green's Combe
Farm

Henley
Grove

Whaddon
House

Gilcombe
Farm

PINKWOOD LA

River Brue

Colinshays
Manor

7

Lamyatt
Lodge

Creech Hill

Combe Brook

CUCKOO HILL

Sheephouse
Farm

BA10

CHURCH
CL

36

215

Coombe Hill
House
Coombe Farm

Cemy

BREWHAM RD

6

Chorley Hill
West
End

FROME RD
B3081
Sch
HIGH ST
P
COOMBE ST
QUAPERLAKE ST

Cogley
Wood

35

Wyke
Champflower
TOLBURY LA
SHUTE LA
TOWER HILL
HIGH ST
Mus
PLOX
SILVER ST
Sch
A359
B3081
STATION RD
Bruton

Horseley
Farm

5

Gants Mill
COLE RD
GANTS MILL LA
PARK RD
Lusty
Park Wall
DROPPING LA

Discove
Farm

Leland Trail
Macmillan Way

Whitehouse
Farm

34

215

Cole
WYKE LA
SUNNY LA
Sch
Lusty Hill
Farm
GODMINSTER LA
215
Discove
House

Redlynch
Cross

4

SUNNY HILL
Sch
Pitcombe
PITCOMBE
MILL LA
STRUTTER'S HILL
Redlynch
THE
CLOCK HO
Redlynch
Park

TRENDLE LA
STOKE
HILL

33

NETTLECOMBE
HILL
PITCOMBE HILL
Godminster Farm
Cliff Hill

3

RIDGE LA
GREEN LA
STUMP
CROSS
The
Towers

Stoney
Stoke
Stoke
Farm

B3081
B306

32

215
BA7
A359
DOWN LA
Montague Inn
(PH)
Shepton
Montague

Knowle
Park
Farm

Roundhill
Grange

2

CARYEDGE LA
Welham
EAST LA
HORNS LA
BA9
Knowle Rock
Farm
Round
Hill

Hadspen
House
Hadspen
Garden

FARNCOMBE LA
River Pitt

216

Shalford

SHALFORD LA

1

A371
CATTLE HILL
Moorhayes
Farm
216
ELM LA
B3081
Gooselands

30

Higher
Cuttlesham
Farm
CHURCH
WLK
Wincanton
Race
Course

66   A   67   B   68   C   69   D   70   E   71   F

159

176

For full street detail of the
highlighted area see pages
215 and 216.

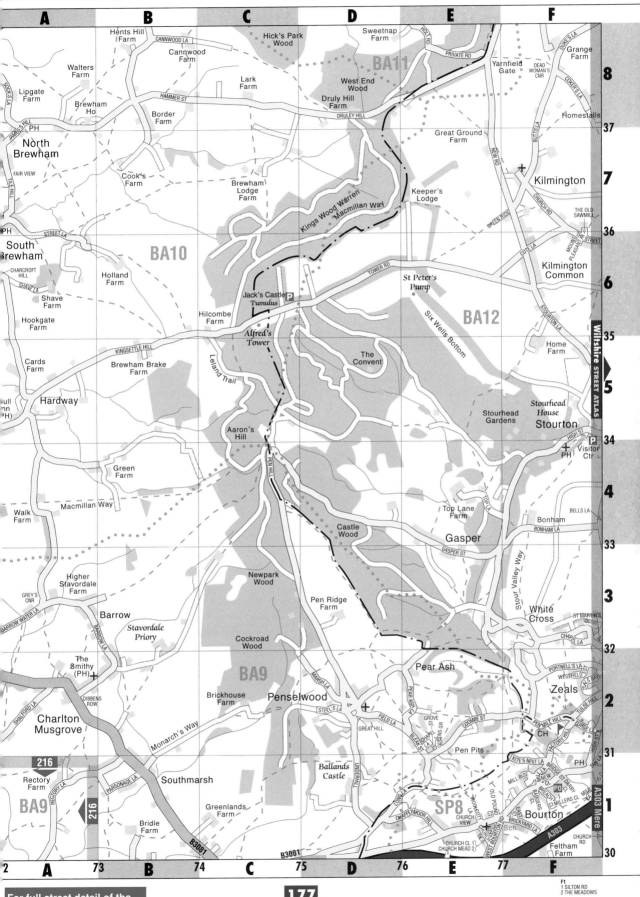

cale: 1¾ inches to 1 mile

¼   ½ mile

250m 500m 750m 1 km

Wiltshire STREET ATLAS

A **B** **C** **D** **E** **F**

8

Hents Hill Farm
CANNWOOD LA
Cannwood Farm
Hick's Park Wood
Sweetnap Farm
HOLT RD
PRIVATE RD
BA11
Yarnfield Gate
DEAD WOMAN'S CNR
Grange Farm
DUKE'S LA
COKER'S LA

Walters Farm
Lark Farm
West End Wood
Druly Hill Farm
Homestalls

37

Lipgate Farm
JAMES'S HILL
PH
Brewham Ho
HAMMER ST
Border Farm
Great Ground Farm
NEW RD
BUTTS LA
Kilmington

7

North Brewham
Cook's Farm
Brewham Lodge Farm
Keeper's Lodge
GREEN RIDGE
CHURCH RD
THE OLD SAWMILL

FAIR VIEW
STREET LA
BA10
Kings Wood Warren
Macmillan Way
COTE LA
THE STREET
MOUNT PLEASANT

36

PH
South Brewham
Holland Farm
Brewham Lodge Farm
TOWER RD
St Peter's Pump
Kilmington Common

6

CHARCROFT HILL
SHAVE LA
Shave Farm
Hilcombe Farm
Jack's Castle Tumulus
P
Six Wells Bottom
BA12
STOURTON LA

Hookgate Farm
KINGSETTLE HILL
Alfred's Tower
The Convent
Home Farm

35

Cards Farm
Brewham Brake Farm
Leland Trail
Stourhead Gardens
Stourhead House
Stourton

5

Hardway
Aaron's Hill
PEN HILL
Stourhead House
HIGH ST
P
Visitor Ctr
PH

34

Green Farm
Macmillan Way
Top Lane Farm
TOP LA
Bonham
BELLS LA

4

Walk Farm
Castle Wood
Gasper
BONHAM LA
GASPER ST

33

Higher Stavordale Farm
GREY'S CNR
Newpark Wood
Pen Ridge Farm
Stour Valley Way
White Cross
ST MARTIN'S CL

3

BARROW WATER LA
Barrow
Stavordale Priory
BARROW LA
Cockroad Wood
CHAPEL LA

32

The Smithy (PH)
DIBBENS ROW
BA9
MARSH LA
Pear Ash
PORTNELL'S LA
WESTFIELD
ZEAL'S RISE
Zeals

2

Charlton Musgrove
SHALFORD LA
Brickhouse Farm
STEEL'S LA
Penselwood
FIELD LA
PEAR ASH LA
GROVE CL
COOMBE ST
PEN MILL HILL
TULSE HILL
CH

SHALFORD LA
Monarch's Way
PARSONAGE LA
Southmarsh
Great Hill
BLEAK CL
CHAPEL
QUEEN'S GR
Pen Pits
FACTORY LA
KITE'S NEST LA
PH
PO

31

216
Rectory Farm
216
Bridle Farm
Greenlands Farm
Ballands Castle
UNDERHILL
LONG LA
OMAREY MOOR HILL
SP8
PROPCOTT LA
OLD POUND
Bourton
BRICKYARD LA
BADGERS
MILLERS CL
A303 Mere

BA9
B3081
B3081
CHURCH VIEW
CHURCH CL 1
CHURCH MEAD 2
Sch
WEST BOURTON RD
A303
Feltham Farm
CHURCH RD

30

A **B** **C** **D** **E** **F**

2 73 74 75 76 77

For full street detail of the highlighted area see page 216.

F1
1 SILTON RD
2 THE MEADOWS

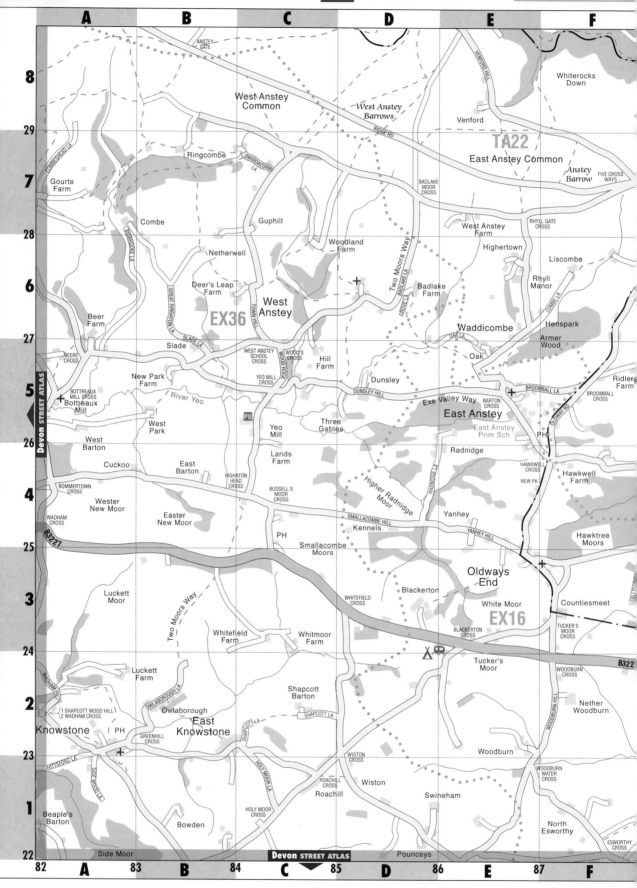

Scale: 1¾ inches to 1 mile

West Anstey Common
West Anstey Barrows
Whiterocks Down
Venford
VENFORD HILL
TA22
East Anstey Common
Anstey Barrow
FIVE CROSS WAYS
Ringcombe
SWIDDACOMBE LA
Gourte Farm
COMBESHEAD LA
Combe
Guphill
Woodland Farm
West Anstey Farm
RHYLL GATE CROSS
Highertown
Liscombe
Netherwell
BIDBROOKE LA
Deer's Leap Farm
West Anstey
EX36
TOWN HILL
BADLAKE MOOR CROSS
Two Moors Way
BADLAKE LA
GROVE LA
Badlake Farm
Waddicombe
Rhyll Manor
Hensbark
COMBE LA
Beer Farm
GREAT RINGCOMB LA
Slade
SLADE LA
West Anstey School Cross
WOOD'S CROSS
WOOD ROCK
Hill Farm
OAK LA
Oak
Armer Wood
Ridlers Farm
Beere Cross
New Park Farm
River Yeo
YEO MILL CROSS
Dunsley
Exe Valley Way
BARTON CROSS
East Anstey
BROOMBALL LA
Broomball Cross
Bottreaux Mill Cross
Bottreaux Mill
PO
Yeo Mill
Three Gables
Dunsley Hill
East Anstey Prim Sch
OLDWAY RD
PH
West Barton
West Park
Lands Farm
Radnidge
HAWKWELL CROSS
NEW PK
Hawkwell Farm
Cuckoo
East Barton
HIGHATON HEAD CROSS
BUSSELL'S MOOR CROSS
Higher Radnidge Moor
RADNIDGE LA
Bommertown Cross
Wester New Moor
Easter New Moor
PH
SMALLACOMBE HILL
Yanhey
YANHEY HILL
Hawktree Moors
WADHAM CROSS
B3227
Smallacombe Moors
Kennels
Oldways End
EX16
Countiesmeet
Luckett Moor
Two Moors Way
Whitefield Cross
Blackerton
White Moor
TUCKER'S MOOR CROSS
Whitefield Farm
Whitmoor Farm
BLACKERTON CROSS
B322
WADHAM HILL
Luckett Farm
OWLABOROUGH LA
Tucker's Moor
WOODBURN CROSS
Nether Woodburn
WOODBURN HILL
1 SHAPCOTT WOOD HILL
2 WADHAM CROSS
Owlaborough
East Knowstone
Shapcott Barton
SHAPCOTT LA
Knowstone
PH
GREENHILL CROSS
SHAPCOTT LA
Woodburn
HITTSFORD LA
SIDE WOOD LA
WISTON CROSS
Wiston
Swineham
WOODBURN WATER CROSS
HOLY MOOR LA
ROACHILL CROSS
Roachill
Beaple's Barton
HOLY MOOR CROSS
Bowden
North Esworthy
ESWORTHY CROSS
Side Moor
Pounceys

Devon STREET ATLAS

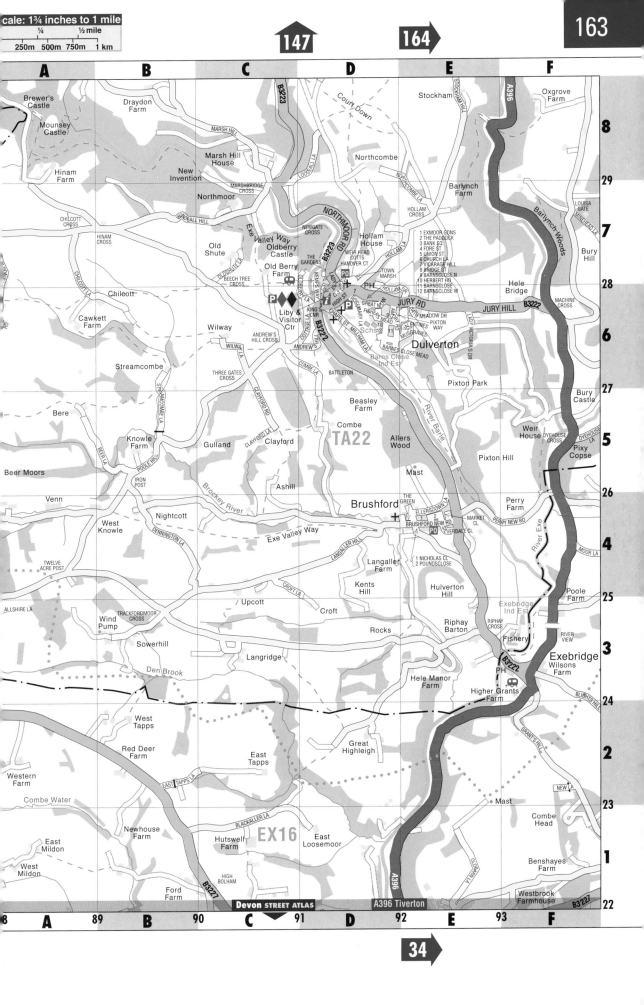

Lyncombe Farm

Hartford Bottom
LADY HARRIET ACLAND'S DR
River Haddeo
Hartford
Hadborough
West Hill Wood
Wimbleball Lake
Upton Farm
St Jame's Church (rems of)
Hayne Farm
EASTMOOR LA
HANSETOWN RD
Upton
B319

Clammer
Haddon Hill
LADY HARRIET ACLAND'S DR
TA4

Haddon Farm
HADDON LA
Chapple Farm
Frogwell Farm
WINDWAY HILL
Surridge Farm
Blindwell Farm
BLINDWE
ST JOHN'S CL

South Haddon
HADDON LA
Frogwell Cross
POST LA

Bury
DYEHOUSE CNR
Leigh Barton
ORANGE LA
Skilgate
PITSHAM LA
CROFT LA
GAMBLYN CROSS

TA22
DYEHOUSE LA
PORT LA
Withywine Farm
WITHYWINE LA
Skilgate Wood
CHALCOMBE ROCKS LA
Gamblyn Farm

Combeland
Brockhole Farm
Haynes Down Farm
HONE CROSS

Warmore
COMBELAND LA
Willishayes Farm
HAYNE CROSS
Hayne Farm
Timewell
Morebath Manor
Combe
East Combe
QUARTLEY HILL

Burston Farm
MOOR LA
BURSTON LA
MORRELL'S CROSS
TIMEWELL HILL
Claypits
COURT LA
Court
COMBE CROSS
Quartley Farm
East Holcombe
B322

ASHTOWN CROSS
Ashtown Farm
VALLEY VIEW
Morebath
Loyton
HOOPERS CROSS
Eastwoods
BOWDENS LA
Westwoods
Hayne Barton

Keens
Ben Brook
EX16
SAWYERS HILL
BAKERS
Lower Rill
Great R Farm

Surridge Farm
Moor Farm
BONNY CROSS
FIRWAY CROSS
HUKELEY HEAD CROSS
PH
Shillingford
Haynemoor Wood

BLIGHTS HILL
Blight's Farm
LOWER LODFIN
CHILTERN CROSS
Mast
Hukeley Farm
Doddiscombe

Coldharbour Farm
Lodfin Farm
Chapel (rems of)
RIDGEWAY LA
South Hayne Farm

Exe Valley Way
ROWS LA
Birchdown
B3190
FROG ST
River Batherm
FORD RD
FORDMILL CROSS
Sunderleigh Farm
Zea Far

Rows Farm
HIGH CROSS
Gumbland
HIGH ST
SOUTH MOLTON RD
Liby
BRICK CASTLE
PH PO
Bampton
Pipshayne
OLD TIVERTON RD
Borough House

B3227
Bampton CE Prim Sch
SCHOOL
WEST
Devon STREET ATLAS

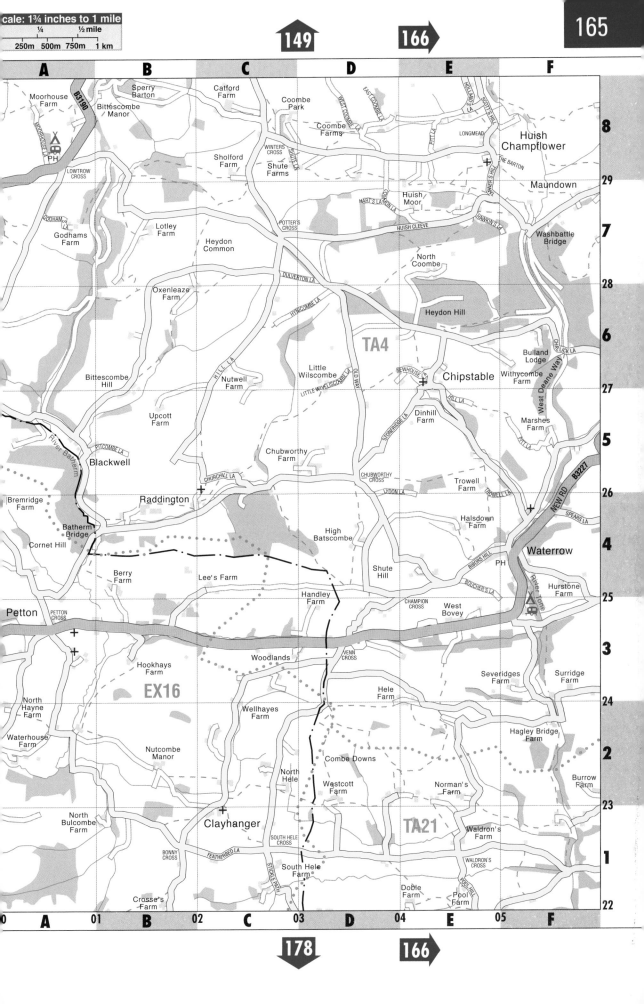

165
150

Scale: 1¾ inches to 1 mi

0   ¼   ½ mile
0   250m 500m 750m 1 km

A   B   C   D   E   F

8

Chorleys Farm House
WHITEFIELD ROCKS
Whitefield
210
Oakhampton Farm
Burrow Hill Farm
BLACK LA
COMBE LA
Billy Farm
B3188
TIPNOLLER HILL

29

Works
PH
DEEP LEIGH LA
Langley
SANDY LA
Brewers Farm
BAGN CL
Langley Marsh
GRANT'S LA
YARD LA
BILLY LA
Ford
CHURCH RD

7

Maundown Hill
Greenway Farm
Northgate
West Deane Way
RIDGE HILL
HEATHSTOCK HILL
Castle Hill fort
Knight's Farm
Fitzhead
GREENWAY LA
CAT'S ASH
Croford House
CAT'S ASH LA
Wiveliscombe
210
Sch
STYLE RD
FORD RD
Castle
210
Croford

28

Challick Farm
JEWS LA
BURGES LA
B3188
TAUNTON RD
CROFORD HILL
BEACH TREE CROSS
KITS LA
CHALLICK LA
COATE TURN
CROFT WAY
CHURCH ST
SOUTH LA
HARTSWELL LA
River's Farm

6

Fleed Farm
FLEED CROSS
Coate Farm
Hartswell
Manor Farm
Slape Moor
CULVERHAY LA
Sch
TA4
NEW RD

27

PYNCOMBE LA
Westbrooks Farm
B3187
B3227
North Down Farm
Fry's Farm
QUAKINGHOUSE LA

5

Pyncombe Farm
Nunnington Park Farm
Holme Moor
Quaking House
LOWER FAIRFIELD
WALRIDGE CROSS
210
FAIRFIELD TERR
SPEARS LA
BICKING'S CLOSE LA
HIGH ST

26

Sharps Farm
Manworthy Cross
Farthing's Farm
Milverton
Gummer Cleeve LA
WOODBARTON
SAND ST
Ridge Farm
Screedy
NEWFIELD
BUTTS WAY

4

Hellings Farm
Auton Dolwells
COURTFIELD LA
HELLING'S CROSS
Woodlands Farm
Lower Lovelynch
HUNT LA

25

Hawthorn Farm
ROAD HILL
Cobhay Farm
Spring Grove House
Higher Lovelynch Farm
BURN HILL

3

Yeancott Farm
Bathealton Court
STONE HILL LA
RIDGE HIGHWAY
Bindon Farm
Stone Hill La

24

Bathealton
Leigh Farm
GIPSY CROSS
WATERY LA
Langford Heathfield
Langford Gate

2

Kittisford Farm
Greenvale Farm
CARRIER'S LA
Chipley
CHURWELL LA
BUTTS LA
LANGFORD
Langford Budville
REYNOLDS

23

Stawley Wood Farm
BULLOCK FIELD HILL
Kittisford Barton
Poleshill
Sch
SWIFTS
Langford La
WEST DEANE WAY
BOCKLAND HILL
TA21
PH
WATERY LA

1

Stawley
Stancombe Farm
HAM HILL
River Tone
Kittisford

22

06   **A**   07   **B**   08   **C**   09   **D**   10   **E**   11   **F**

165
179

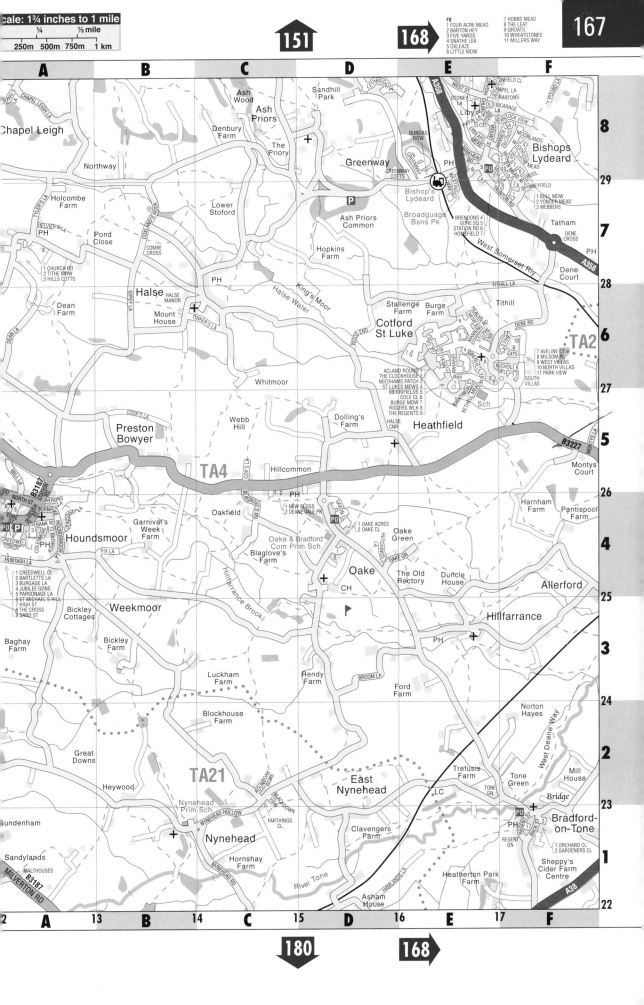

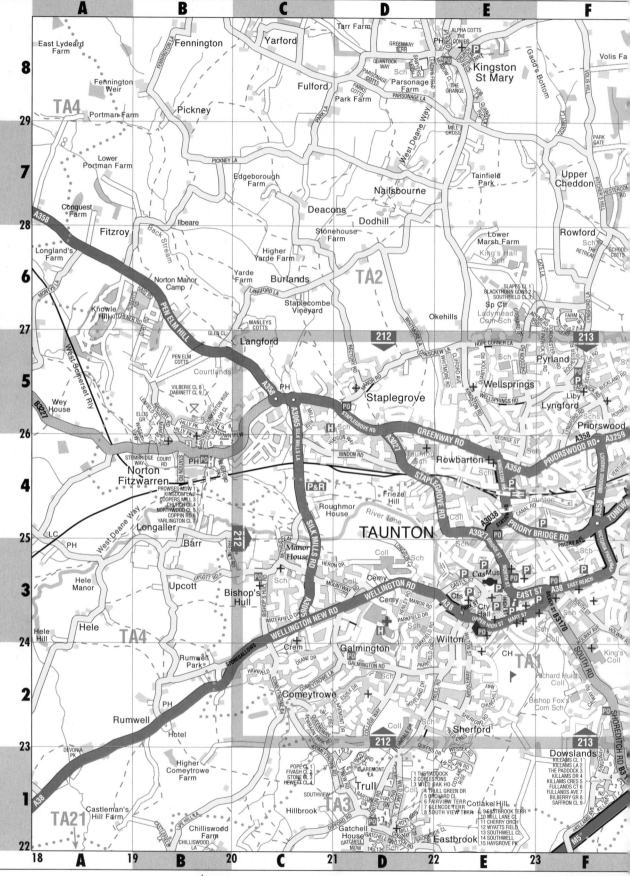

Scale: 1¾ inches to 1 mi
0   ¼   ½ mile
0 250m 500m 750m 1 km

A B C D E F

8
29
7
28
6
27
5
26
4
25
3
24
2
23
1
22

East Lydeard Farm
Fennington
Yarford
Tarr Farm
GREENWAY TERR
Alpha Cotts THE CONES
PH
Kingston St Mary
Volis Fm

TA4
Fennington Weir
Pickney
Fulford
QUANTOCK WAY
Parsonage Farm
THE GRANGE
P
WINDMILL ST
CHURCH
Sch
SAWYERS LEIGH
PARSONAGE COTTS
Park Farm
PARSONAGE LA
MILL CROSS

Portman Farm
Park Farm
PARK LA
WEST DEANE WAY
Tainfield Park
Upper Cheddon

Lower Portman Farm
PICKNEY LA
Edgeborough Farm
Nailsbourne
Dodhill
Lower Marsh Farm
King's Hall Sch
Rowford
Sch
THE RETREAT

A358
Conquest Farm
Fitzroy
Ilbeare
Deacons
Stonehouse Farm
SLAPES CL 1
BLACKTHORN GDNS 2
SOUTHFIELD CL 3

Longland's Farm
Back Stream
Higher Yarde Farm
TA2
Okehills
Sp Ctr
Ladymead Com Sch

B3227
Wey House
Knowle Hill
Norton Manor Camp
Yarde Farm
LANGFORD LA
Burlands
Staplecombe Vineyard
212
Pyrland
213

West Somerset Rly
PEN ELM HILL
GLEN CL
Langford
Staplegrove
Wellsprings
Lyngford
Priorswood

PEN ELM COTTS
Courtlands
VILBERIE CL 8
DABINETT CL 9
A358
PH
Manor Rd
STAPLEGROVE RD
Rowbarton
A358 A3259

Stembridge Way
COURT RD
Norton Fitzwarren
BINDON RD
GREENWAY RD
A3027
PRIORSWOOD RD

PROWSES MDW 1
KINGDON LA 2
COOPERS MILL 3
CHURCH CL 4
NORTHWOOD CL 5
COPPIN RD 6
YARLINGTON CL 7
P&R
Frieze Hill
Taunton
A358
Taunton
OBRIDGE VIADUCT

Longaller
Barr
212
FRIEZE RD
SILK MILLS RD
Roughmor House
River Tone
TAUNTON
A3027
PRIORY BRIDGE RD
TONE

Hele Manor
Upcott
UPCOTT RD
Bishop's Hull
Manor House
HERON DR
Cemy
A38
EAST ST
EAST REACH

Hele Hill
Hele
TA4
Rumwell Park
WELLINGTON RD
Cemy
Wilton
TA1
King's Coll

Rumwell
PH
STONEGALLOWS
Crem
Galmington
GALMINGTON RD
Sherford
Bishop Fox's Com Sch

Hotel
Higher Comeytrowe Farm
Comeytrowe
212
Sherford
213
Dowslands

A38
Castleman's Hill Farm
Chilliswood Farm
Trull
Hillbrook
TA3
Eastbrook
Cotlake Hill
M5

TA21

18 A 19 B 20 C 21 D 22 E 23 F

For full street detail of the highlighted area see pages 212 and 213.

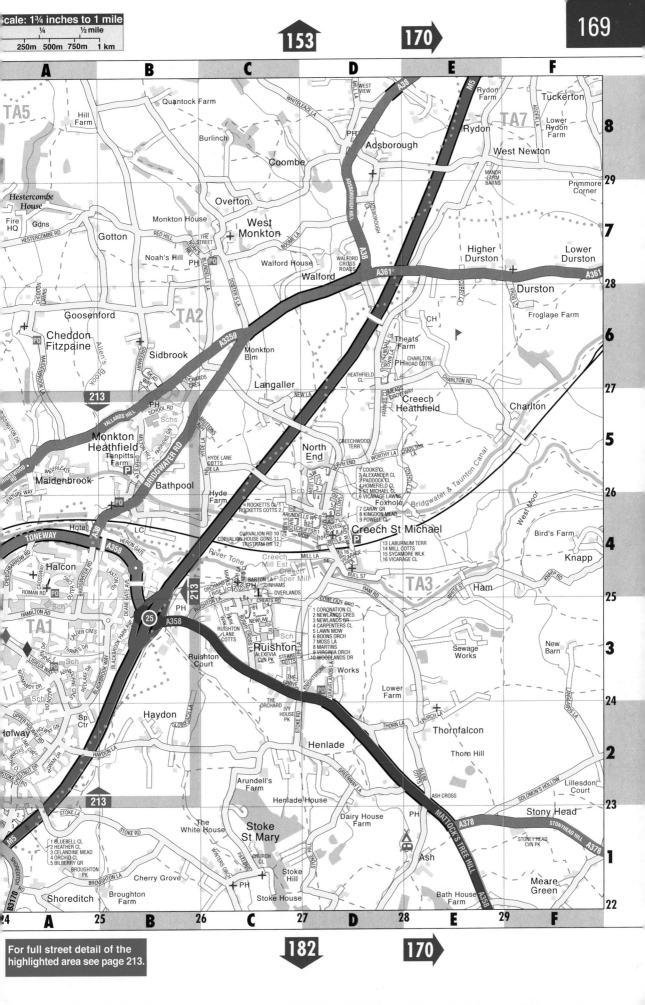

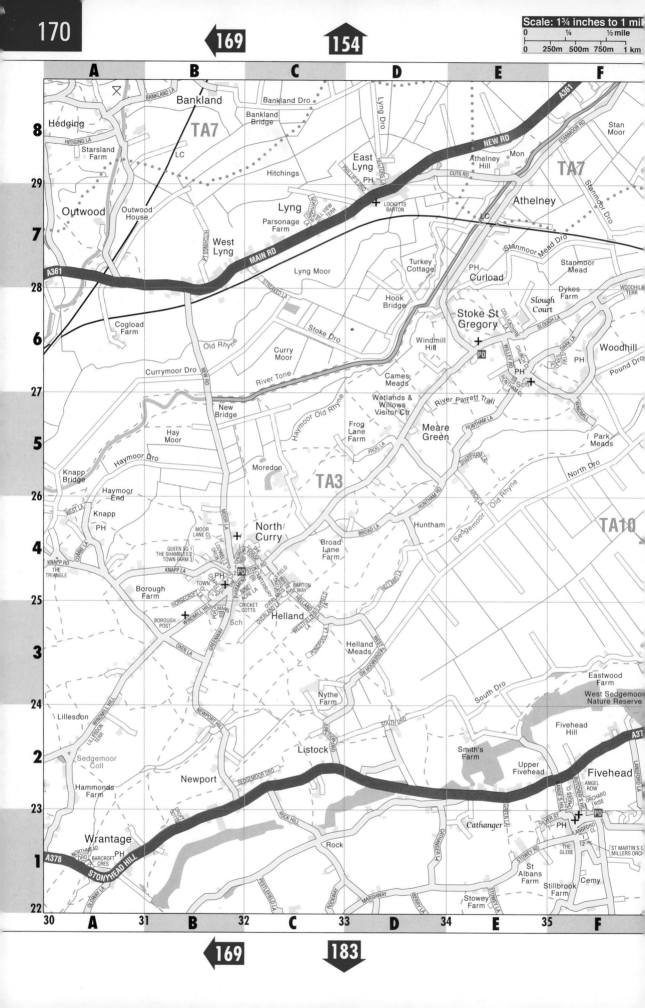

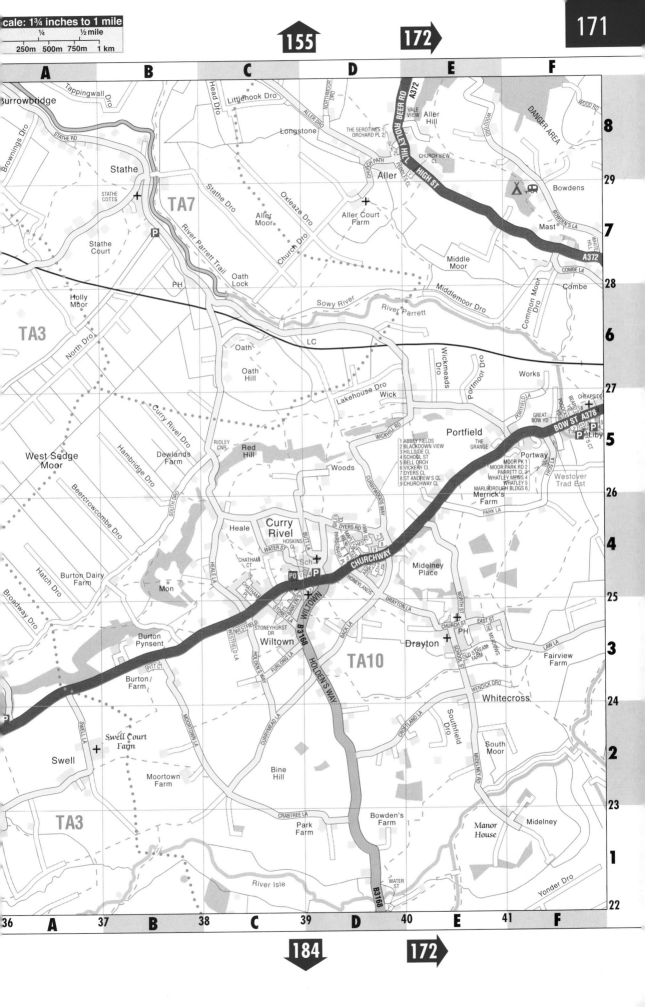

Scale: 1¾ inches to 1 mile
0   ¼   ½ mile
0 250m 500m 750m 1 km

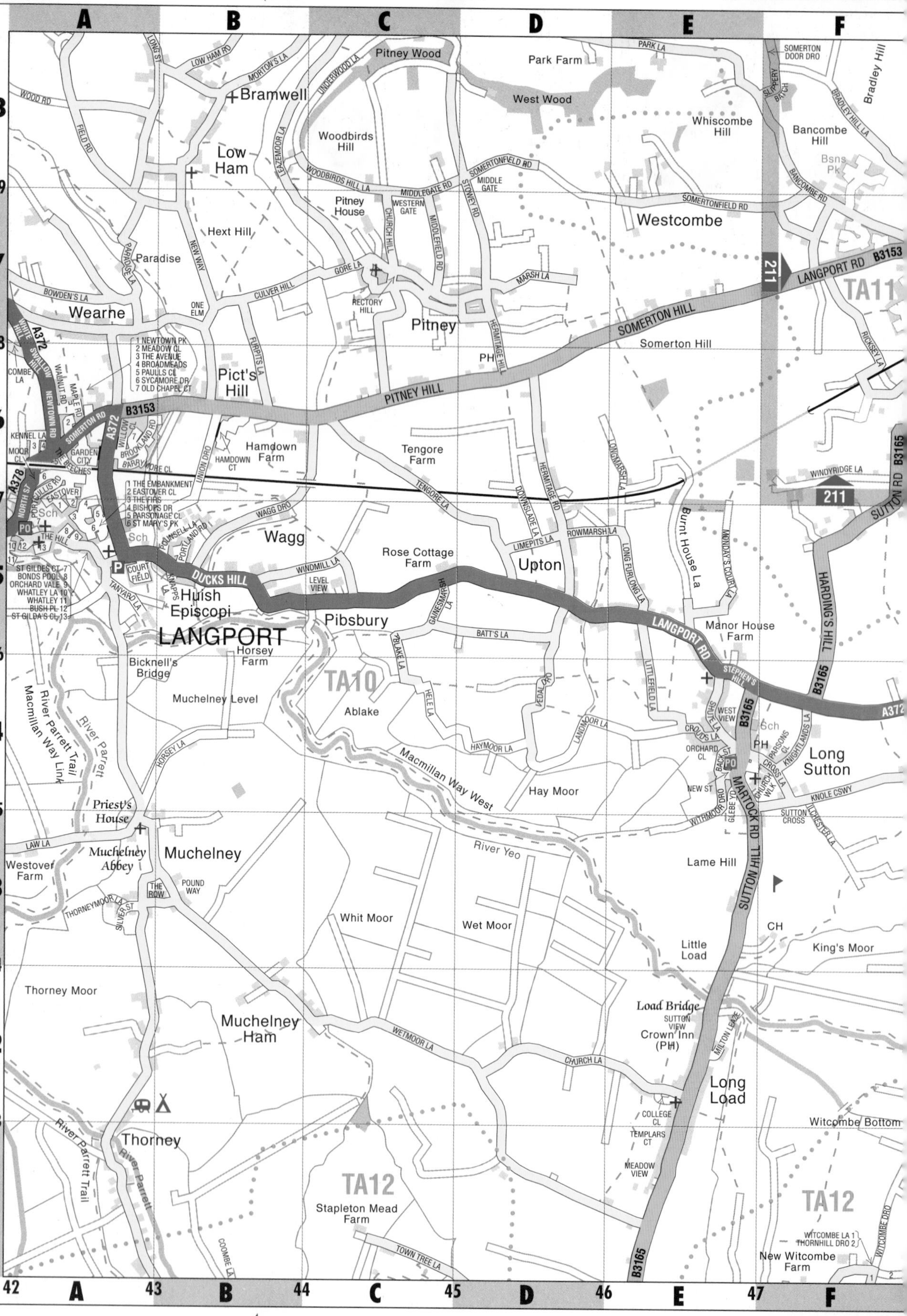

Grid columns: A B C D E F
Grid rows: 8 29 7 28 6 27 5 26 4 25 3 24 2 23 1 22

WOOD RD
LONG ST
LOW HAM RD
MORTON'S LA
UNDERWOOD LA
Pitney Wood
Park Farm
PARK LA
SOMERTON DOOR DRO
Bradley Hill
+ Bramwell
West Wood
Whiscombe Hill
Bancombe Hill
Bsns Pk
Low Ham
Woodbirds Hill
FIELD RD
LEZEMOOR LA
WOODBIRDS HILL LA
Pitney House
SOMERTONFIELD RD
MIDDLE GATE
MIDDLEGATE RD
STONEY RD
SOMERTONFIELD RD
Westcombe
BANCOMBE RD
Hext Hill
NEW WAY
Paradise
Pitney
GORE LA
CULVER HILL
RECTORY HILL
MARSH LA
HENMEAD RD
LANGPORT RD B3153
TA11
Wearhe
BOWDEN'S LA
ONE ELM
SOMERTON HILL
211
RICKSEY LA
A372
WHITE SWALLOW
FARPITTS LA
Pict's Hill
PITNEY HILL
Somerton Hill
PH
COMBE LA
WALNUT RD
NEWTOWN RD
1 NEWTOWN PK
2 MEADOW CL
3 THE AVENUE
4 BROADMEADS
5 PAULLS CL
6 SYCAMORE DR
7 OLD CHAPEL CT
MAPLE RD
WILLOW
B3153
SOMERTON RD
KENNEL LA
MOOR CL
GARDEN CITY
BEECHES
BROCKWELL
PARRY MORE CL
Hamdown Farm
HAMDOWN CT
Tengore Farm
LONDRMARSH LA
WINDYRIDGE LA
B3165
211
SUTTON RD B3165
NORTH ST
EASTOVER
1 THE EMBANKMENT
2 EASTOVER CL
3 THE FIRS
4 BISHOPS DR
5 PARSONAGE CL
6 ST MARY'S PK
Sch
UNION DRO
HAMDOWN LA
WAGG DRO
TENGORE LA
DOWNSLADE LA
HERMITAGE RD
Burnt House La
HARDING'S HILL
PO
Sch
THE HILL
Wagg
WAGG DRO
Windmill La
Rose Cottage Farm
LIMEPITS LA
ROWMARSH LA
Upton
MONDAY'S COURT LA
Manor House Farm
ST GILDES 6 1-7
BONDS POOL
ORCHARD VALE 9
WHATLEY LA 10
WHATLEY 11
BUSH PL 12
ST GILDA'S CL 13
DUCKS HILL
COURT FIELD
P
TANYARD LA
Sch
LEVEL VIEW
Pibsbury
GAINSMARSH LA
BLAKE LA
HELE LA
BATT'S LA
LONG FURLONG LA
LITTLEFIELD LA
STEPHEN'S LA
B3165
WEST VIEW
Sch
A372
Huish Episcopi
LANGPORT
Horsey Farm
TA10
Ablake
LANGPORT RD
Bicknell's Bridge
Muchelney Level
HAYMOOR LA
LANDA DOR LA
PEDAL DRO
ORCHARD CL
NEW ST
CR2/05 LA
BACK LA
PH
Long Sutton
River Parrett Way Link
Macmillan Way Trail
River Parrett
HORSEY LA
Hay Moor
KNIGHTAMS LA
CROSS LA
CHURCH WLK
WITHY WK
KNOLE CSWY
SUTTON CROSS
CHESTER LA
Priest's House
LAW LA
Muchelney Abbey
Muchelney
THE ROW
SILVER ST
Macmillan Way West
River Yeo
WEST VIEW
MARTOCK RD
SUTTON ROAD
WITHNORTH DRO
GLEBE RD
Lame Hill
CH
King's Moor
Westover Farm
THORNEYMOOR LA
POUND WAY
Whit Moor
Wet Moor
Little Load
Thorney Moor
Muchelney Ham
WETMOOR LA
CHURCH LA
Load Bridge
SUTTON VIEW
Crown Inn (PH)
MILTON LANE
Long Load
River Parrett Trail
Thorney
COOMBE LA
COLLEGE CL
TEMPLARS CT
MEADOW VIEW
Witcombe Bottom
TA12
Stapleton Mead Farm
TOWN TREE LA
B3165
TA12
WITCOMBE LA 1
THORNHILL DRO 2
New Witcombe Farm

Bottom grid columns: A 42 A 43 B 44 C 45 D 46 E 47 F

For full street detail of the highlighted area see page 211.

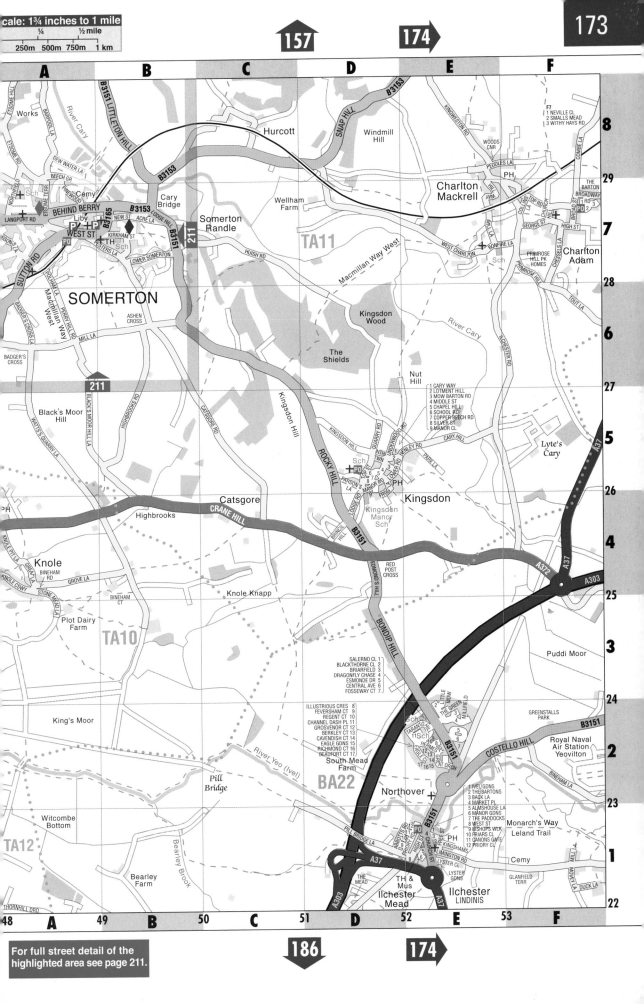

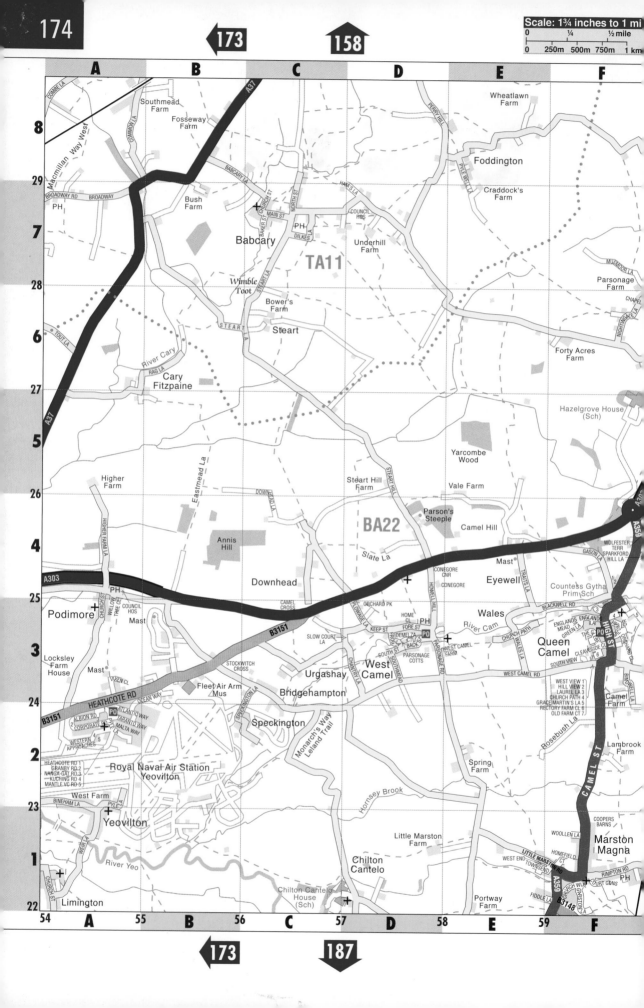

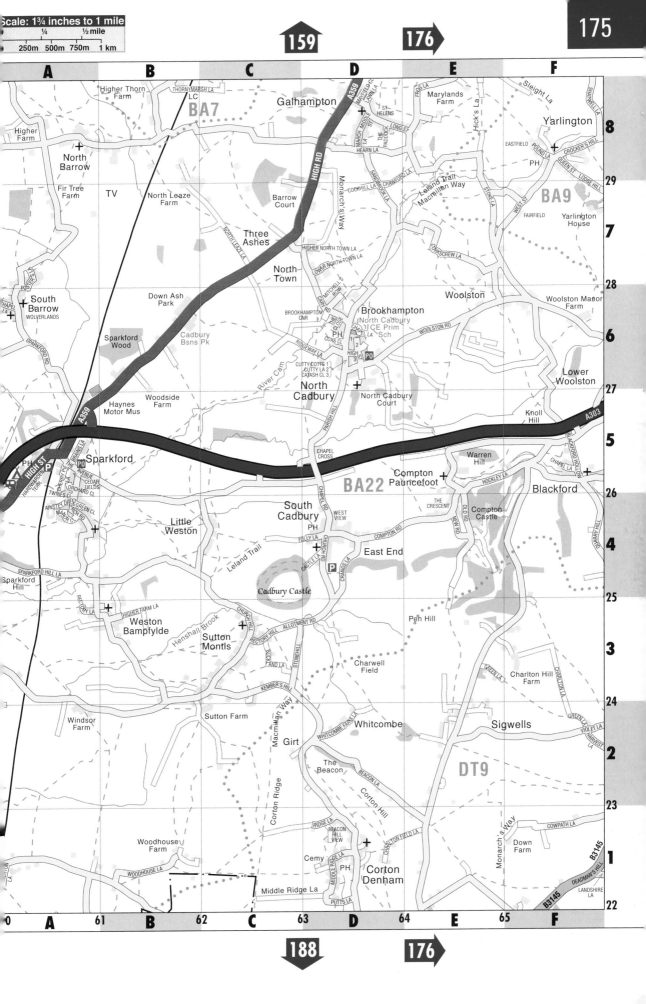

175
160

Scale: 1¾ inches to 1 mile

| 0 | ¼ | ½ mile |
| 0 | 250m | 500m 750m | 1 km |

A B C D E F

8 29 7 28 6 27 5 26 4 25 3 24 2 23 1 22

A371
God's Hill
CATTLE HILL
BA7
GREEN LANE GATE
Bratton Hill
UPLANDS 1
BRATTON HO 2
CHURCH VW
Bratton Seymour
Wincanton Race Course
CH
B3081
RECTORY LA

Eastwood Farm
LODGE HILL
Jack White's Gibbet
Masts
Higher Holbrook Farm
Westleaze Farm
Verrington
VERRINGTON LA
Windmill Hill
GRANTS CL

Hosp
H
West Hill
DANCING LA
SPRINGFIELD RD
NORTH ST
CHURCH ST
SILVER MILL ST
WEST HILL
Sch
Liby
HIGH ST
Mus
BAYFORD HILL
P
COMMON RD

Higher Clapton Farm
GIBBET RD
CLAPTON LA
ELLISCOMBE PK
Hunger Hill
Suddon Grange
Holbrook House Hotel
216
Sch
PORCH ST
STATION RD
Cemy
SOUTHGATE RD
WINCANTON
B3081
SOUTHGATE RD
A303

BA9
Hook Valley Farm
A371
LAWRENCE HILL
A371
Hatherleigh Farms
Sewage Works
Brains Farm
MOOR LA
River Cale

A303
HOLTON CROSS
Dancing Cross
Holton St
PH
Holton
Higher Holton
ANCHOR CNR
A357
ANCHOR HILL
216

Maperton
HOOK LA
Lattiford Farm
Lattiford
B3145
SLOPERS LA
GROVE LA
Grove Farm
Maltkin Hill Farm

BA22
SHEPHERDS CROSS
HARDINGS LA
Marchant-Holliday Sch
North Cheriton
Landseer
LOWER CHERITON LA
WOOD LA
BLACKACRE HILL

Charlton Hill
CHARLTON HILL
Silver Knap
DAW'S LA
GREEN LA
HULL LA
Hull Farm
GOATHILL LA
CABBAGE LA
South Cheriton
BARBARY CL
CHERITON CL
BEHIND HAYES
PH
BROOKSIDE
Cemy
LOWER RD
Monarch's Way
MARSH LA
Horsington Marsh
BATCHPOOL LA
Marshbarr Farm

QUARRY HILL
Windmill Hill
Darkharbour Farm
TOWER VIEW
COLDHILL LA
HIGHER RD
Horsington CE Prim Sch
WHITE COT COTTS
DUCK LA
BROADMEAD LA

BLACKFORD WAY
MAPERTON RD
NORTH RD
BLACKFORD RD
LESTER LA
GUNVILLE LA
Charlton Horethorne
HANGLANDS LA
BA8
MANOR CT
Horsington
PH
RECTORY LA
Horsington HO
HOUND'S HILL

VIOLET LA
NORTH END
HARVEST LA
PH
5
1
4
2
PO
3
Sch
Kennels
1 CLEEVEWAYS
2 WARREN CL
3 MANOR CL
4 BRAMLEY CL
5 ORCHARD WAY
Wilkinthroop
TOWER HILL
TRISCOCK'S LA
Combe Throop
PH

COWPATH LA
CENTENARY COTTS
DEADMAN'S LA
HORSE LA
SOUTHDOWN
CATHILL LA
ENCOMBE LA
Abbas Combe
SLADES HILL
SCHOOL LA
BLACKMORE VALE CL
THE SHAPLANDS
Abbas & Templecombe CE Prim Sch
THROOP RD

B3145
LANDSHIRE LA
MOUNT LA
Stowell
STOWELL HILL
WATERY LA
North Side Wood
WESTWOOD COTTS
LILY LA
Templecombe
PO
SAMUEL CT
HIGH ST
EAST ST
TEMPLE LA

DT9
Waterloo Cres
HILL CRES
WEST WESTCOMBE
STATION RD
A357
1 YARNBARTON
2 THE KNAP
3 TEMPLARS PL
4 CORONATION VILLAS
5 BRINES ORCH
6 WEST CT
7 TEMPLARS BARTON
8 MERTHYR GUEST CL
9 KINGTON VIEW

66 A 67 B 68 C 69 D 70 E 71 F

175
189

For full street detail of the highlighted area see page 216.

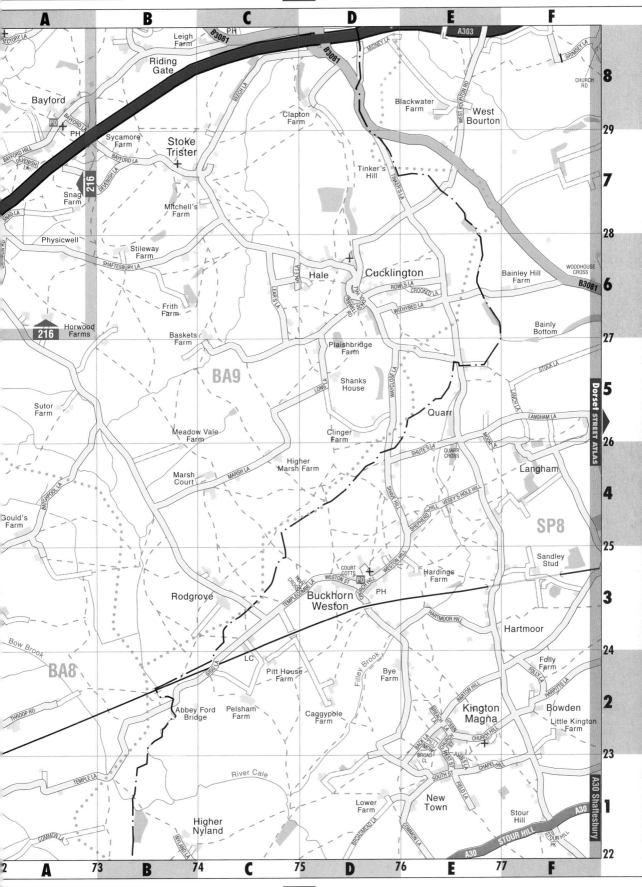

cale: 1¾ inches to 1 mile
¼ ½ mile
250m 500m 750m 1 km

A **B** **C** **D** **E** **F**

RECTORY LA

B3081

PH

A303

Leigh Farm

Riding Gate

Bayford

8

CHURCH RD

PO
PH

BAYFORD HILL
DEVENISH LA
BAYFORD LA

Sycamore Farm

Stoke Trister

Clapton Farm

Blackwater Farm

West Bourton

29

216

BEECH LA

MIDNEY LA

WESTON RD

WEST BOURTON RD

GRINSEY LA

Snag Farm

DEVENISH LA
BAYFORD LA

7

SNAG LA

Mitchell's Farm

Tinker's Hill

TINKER'S LA

28

Physicwell

SHAFTESBURY LA

Stileway Farm

Hale

Cucklington

Bainley Hill Farm

WOODHOUSE CROSS

6

LEAR'S LA

PINE LA

CHURCH RD
RUN LA

ROWLS LA

CROOKED LA

B3081

Frith Farm

WITHYBED LA

Bainly Bottom

27

Baskets Farm

Plaishbridge Farm

BA9

LONG LA

Shanks House

STOCK LA

5

Sutor Farm

Meadow Vale Farm

WAYCLOSE LA

Quarr

LANGHAM LA

LANCH LA

MOOR LA

26

Clinger Farm

QUARR CROSS

Langham

Marsh Court

MARSH LA

Higher Marsh Farm

SHUTE'S LA

SP8

4

Gould's Farm

BATCHPOOL LA

SHAVE HILL

SHEPHERD HILL

Vesey's Hole Hill

25

BA8

Bow Brook

Rodgrove

GIGG LA

LC

Pitt House Farm

THORPE CROSS
TEMPLECOMBE LA

WESTON ST
COURT COTTS
PO
CHURCH HILL
PH

WESTON HILL

Hardings Farm

Sandley Stud

3

THROOP RD

Buckhorn Weston

HARTMOOR HILL

Hartmoor

24

Abbey Ford Bridge

Pelsham Farm

Caggypole Farm

Filler Brook

Bye Farm

BARTON HILL

Kington Magna

FOLLY LA

Folly Farm

HARPITTS LA

Bowden

Little Kington Farm

2

TEMPLE LA

River Cale

Lower Farm

BREACH LA
BACK LA
MOW
BROAD
CL
PILL
CHURCH HILL
SOUTH ST
WEST ST
JEAN S LA
FIELD LA
CHAPEL HILL

23

Higher Nyland

NYLAND LA

BROADMEAD LA

New Town

Stour Hill

STOUR HILL PK

A30

A30 Shaftesbury

1

COMMON LA

COMMON LA

STOUR HILL

A30

22

A **73** **B** **74** **C** **75** **D** **76** **E** **77** **F**

For full street detail of the highlighted area see page 216.

Dorset STREET ATLAS

165

Devon STREET ATLAS

EX16

TA21

EX1

Cudmore Farm
Hearne Farm
BRODEN GATE
DARK LA
HENDON CROSS
DOG DOWN CROSS
Huntsham Barton
Kerswell Barton
East Holelake Farm
Heniton Hill
Ashbrittle
West Deane Way
Pytt Farm
River Tone
POOL HILL
BAMPTON DOWN RD
STICKLE PATH
THORNE CROSS WAY
Thornland
BURROW LA
Stallenge-Thorne Farm
Hole La
Hole Farm
Marcombe Lake
ROWCLIFFE COTTS
Court Place
RECTORY RD
Huntsham
PO
Hockford Waters
Staple Court
Burrow Farm
Staple Cross
Lea Barton
Cowlings Farm
Bences Barton
Chimney Down
Hockworthy
Turnham
MORRELL'S LA
Slantycombe Farm
Court Hall Farm
BLACK LA
Holcombe Court
Webbers CE Prim Sch
Hill
Morrell's Farm
Redwoods Farm
Waterslade
Holcombe Rogus
FORE ST
SOUTH ST
PROA LA
Huntsham Wood
Redgate La
Higher Besley Farm
WHITEBROOK TERR
Beer Down
Fair Oak
Lower Besley Farm
Ford
River Lowman
BAILEY'S KNAPP
Beer Down Farm
Great Ridge Farm
DURLEYMOOR CROSS
Coombe
Hill Farm
Spalsbury Farm
Murley
Churchwalls
Westleigh Quarry
Kennels Dairy
Lower Beer
STONEY LANE CROSS
Newmill Farm
Pitt
Stagg Mill
GOLDSMOOR CROSS
Trumps
Rocknell Farm
STAG MILL CROSS
Wood
Cott
Great Landside
TRUMPS CROSS
Westcott Farm
STAPLEGATE
Higher Chieflowman
EAST MERE CROSS
Whitnage
WHITNAGE LA
Little Landside
Uplowman CE Prim Sch
Ayshford Chapel
BRIMSTONE LA
Grand Western Canal (Country Park)
Pugham Farm
GREEN GATE
Uplowman
PH
Green Gate
Boehill
WHITNAGE RD
Holbrooke Farm
PO
LOWMAN CROSS
Paullet Hill
UPLOWMAN RD
Widhayes Farm
A361 Tiverton
A361
Sampford Peverell CE Prim Sch
BLACKDOWN VIEW
HIGHER TOWN
PAULLET
TURNPIKE
CHAINS RD
THE BRENDONS
BROBERY
CORNLANDS
FAIRFIELD
EASTONIA
FORD ORCH
RICHMOND CT
LOWER TOWN
1 COOT HIDE
2 BEAUFORT CL
3 COURT WAY
Sampford Peverell
A361
M5
27
M5 Exeter
Jersey Farm
Swallow Ct
PO

Devon STREET ATLAS

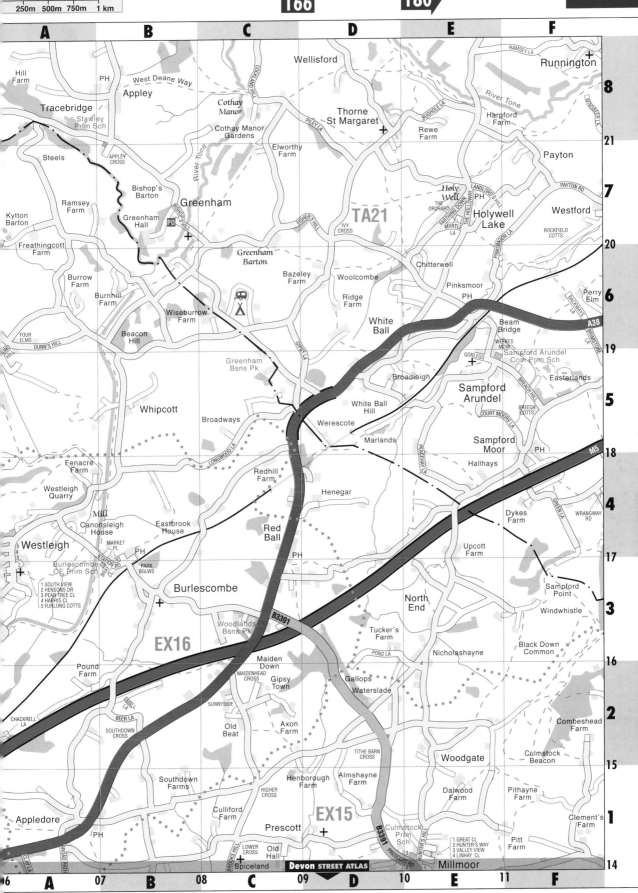

179
167

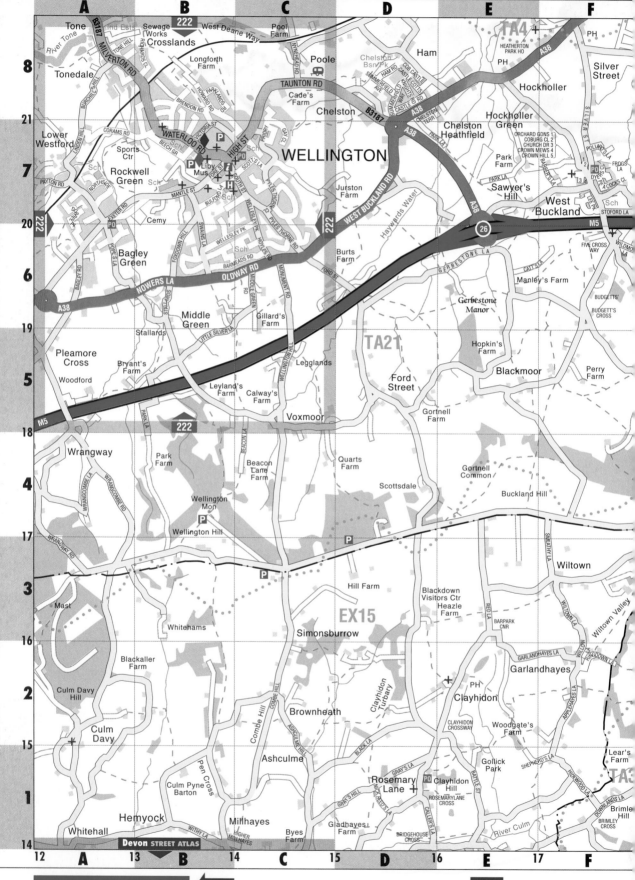

A   B   C   D   E   F

8

Tone
River Tone
Tonedale
B3187
Ind Ests
MILVERTON RD
TONE HILL
BURGHILL HILL
RICHARDS CL
Sewage Works
Crosslands
222
West Deane Way
Pool Farm
Poole
Chelston Bsn Pk
Ham
TA4
HEATHERTON PARK HO
PH
A38
PH
Silver Street
Hockholler

21

Lower Westford
LINDEN HILL
CORAMS RD
LONGFORTH FARM
HOWARD RD
BRENDON RD
PARKLANDS GR
VICTORIA ST
Waterloo RD
TAUNTON RD
Cade's Farm
Chelston
B3187
A38
Chelston Heathfield
Hockholler Green
SILVER ST
POLLARD'S LA
ORCHARD GDNS 1
COBURG CL 2
CHURCH DR 3
CROWN MEWS 4
CROWN HILL 5

7

PAYTON RD
NORTHWAY RD
EXETER RD
Sports Ctr
Sch
Rockwell Green
BEECH GR
Sch
Liby
Mus
P
PO
HIGH ST
SCOTT'S LA
WELLINGTON
Park Farm
Sawyer's Hill
ROBERT'S LA
DYER'S
4 COCKS CL
FROGS LA
P
PO
West Buckland
Sch
STOFORD LA

20

222
PO
MANTLE ST
BULFORD
Sch
WELLESLEY PK
HOLLIS RD
SOUTH ST
FORE ST
PILE ST
PILES THORNE RD
Jurston Farm
WEST BUCKLAND RD
Hawkers Water
A38
26
M5

6

A38
NOWERS LA
Cemy
FOXDOWN HILL
WELLESLEY LA
SWAINS LA
BARMEADS RD
OLDWAY RD
STALLARDS
MIDDLE GREEN
MONUMENT RD
Gillard's Farm
Burts Farm
Ford St
GERBESTONE LA
Gerbestone Manor
CATT'S LA
Manley's Farm
BUDGETTS' CROSS
BUDGETTS'

19

Bagley Green
POPES LA
Middle Green
Stallards
LITTLE SILVER LA
TA21
Hopkin's Farm
Blackmoor
Perry Farm

5

M5
Pleamore Cross
Woodford
Bryant's Farm
PARK LA
Leyland's Farm
Calway's Farm
WELLINGTON HILL
Legglands
Voxmoor
Ford Street
Gortnell Farm

18

Wrangway
WRANGHAY RD
WRANGCOMBE LA
WRANGCOMBE RD
222
Park Farm
BEACON LA
Beacon Lane Farm
Quarts Farm
Scottsdale
Gortnell Common
Buckland Hill

4

Wellington Mon
P
Wellington Hill
SMEATHY LA

17

Mast
P
P
Hill Farm
Blackdown Visitors Ctr
Heazle Farm
RED LA
BARPARK CNR
WILTOWN LA
KINGSDOWN LA
Wiltown
Wiltown Valley

3

Whitehams
EX15
Simonsburrow
GARLANDHAYES LA
APPLEGRASS LA
Garlandhayes

16

Blackaller Farm
COMBE HILL
DODGE HILL
ASHCULME HILL
Brownheath
Clayhidon Turbary
BLACK LA
GRAY'S LA
PH
Clayhidon
CLAYHIDON CROSSWAY
Woodgate's Farm
Gollick Park
SHEPHERD'S LA
HINGKWOOD LA
TA3

2

Culm Davy Hill
Culm Davy
PEN CROSS
Culm Pyne Barton
Ashculme
BATTLE ST
PO
GRAY'S HILL
REDS LA
CALLER LA
Rosemary Lane
Clayhidon Hill
ROSEMARYLANE CROSS
Lear's Farm
DOWNLANDS LA
Brimley Hill
BRIMLEY CROSS

15

Whitehall
Hemyock
WITHY LA
HIGHER MILLHAYES
Millhayes
Byes Farm
Gladhayes Farm
BRIDGEHOUSE CROSS
River Culm

1

14

12   A   13   B   14   C   15   D   16   E   17   F

For full street detail of the highlighted area see page 222.
179
191

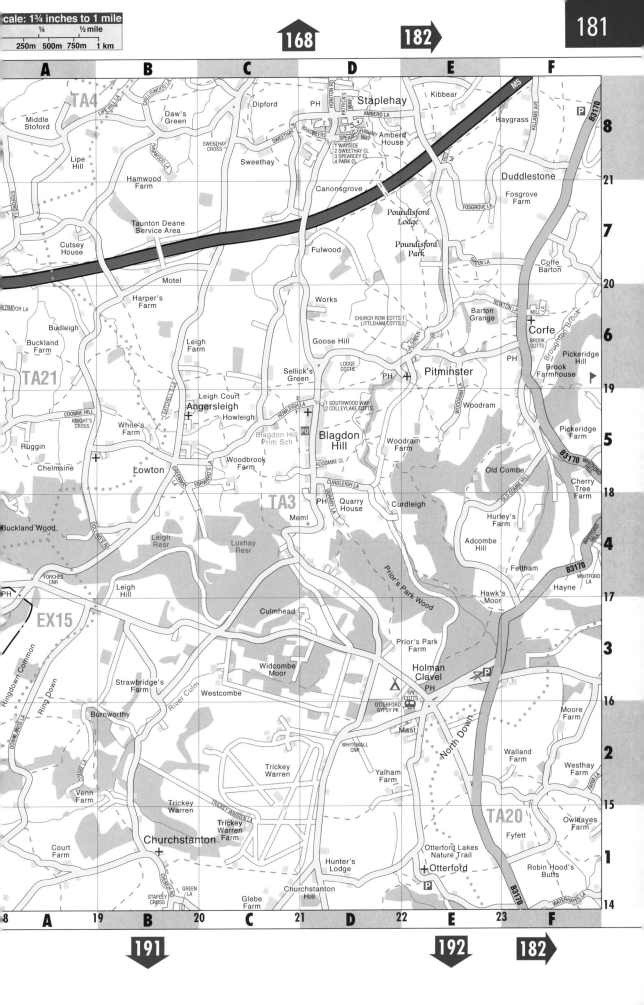

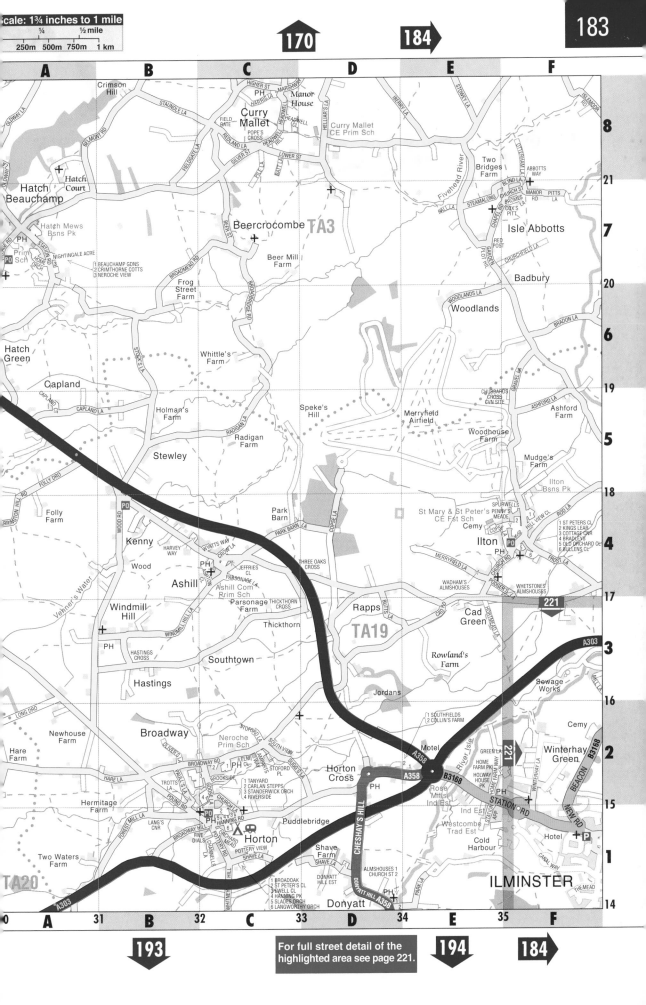

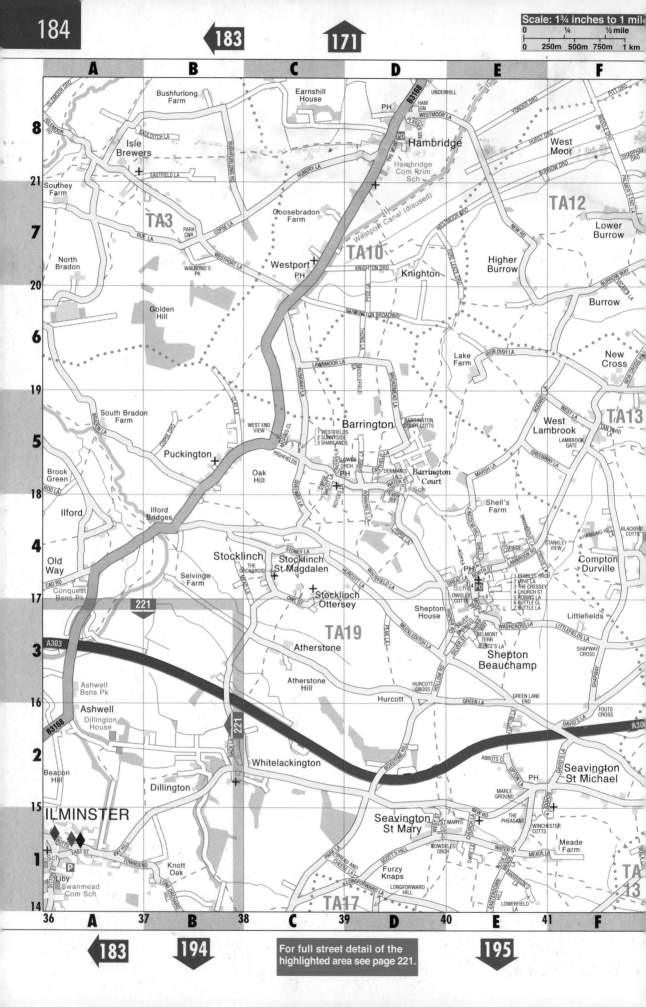

Scale: 1¾ inches to 1 mile

0   ¼   ½ mile
0 250m 500m 750m 1 km

A   B   C   D   E   F

8

21

TA3

7

North
Bradon

20

6

Golden
Hill

19

Brook
Green

South Bradon
Farm

5

Puckington

Ilford

Oak
Hill

18

Ilford
Bridges

Old
Way

4

Selvinge
Farm

Stocklinch

Stocklinch
St Magdalen

Conquest
Bsns Pk

221

Stocklinch
Ottersey

OWL ST

3

A303

Ashwell
Bsns Pk

Atherstone

TA19

Atherstone
Hill

16

Ashwell

Dillington
House

Hurcott

221

2

Beacon
Hill

Dillington

Whitelackington

15

ILMINSTER

Seavington
St Mary

1

Sch

P
Liby

Swanmead
Com Sch

Knott
Oak

Furzy
Knaps

14

TA17

36   A   37   B   38   C   39   D   40   E   41   F

Isle
Brewers

Bushfurlong
Farm

Earnshill
House

Goosebradon
Farm

Westport
PH

Westport Canal (disused)

Barrington

Barrington
Court

Shell's
Farm

Hambridge

Hambridge
Com Prim
Sch

UNDERHILL

B3168

West
Moor

TA12

Lower
Burrow

Higher
Burrow

Knighton

Lake
Farm

Burrow

New
Cross

West
Lambrook

TA13

Compton
Durville

Shepton
House

Shepton
Beauchamp

Littlefields

Seavington
St Michael

Meade
Farm

TA
13

For full street detail of the
highlighted area see page 221.

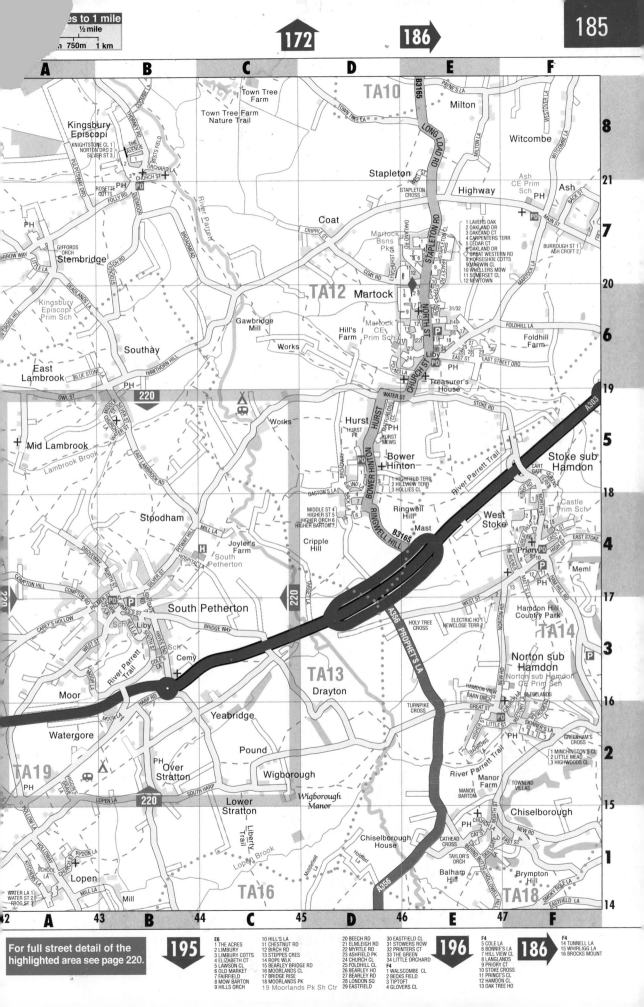

For full street detail of the highlighted area see page 220.

195 196 186

← 185
173 ↑

Scale: 1¾ in
0   ¼
0   250m   500m

A   B   C   D   E   F

8
Ash Dro
Bearley Brook
Burlingham's Farm
BURLINGHAM'S LA
Sock Dennis Farm
A303
A37
Oakley Brook

21
BACK ST
Ash
LAVERS CT
Broadleaze Farm
BEARLEY LA
Higher Oakley Farm
Oakley Farms

7
MIDDLE LEAZE DRO
TA12
Durnfield
Stonecroft Manor Farm
Rushley Farm

20
FOLDHILL LA
LITTLE TRUMPS
QUEEN ST
Tintinhull Garden
Tintinhull House
Shortland Farm
OAKLEY LA
HALFWAY PH
ILCHESTER RD

6
SOUTHCOMBE WAY 1
THE OLD GLOVE FACTORY 2
LEACHES CL 3
CHURCH ST
FARM ST
PH
St Margaret's Sch
SCHOOL CL
Sock Farm
KINGS HILL
A37

Halfway House Farm
HALLETS ORCH
ST MARGARET'S
MEAD ST
YEOVIL RD
CHILTHORNE LA
MAIN ST
Chilthorne Domer CE Sch
Chilthorne Domer
BA21

19
A3088
A303
THURLOCKS
PO
Tintinhull
COLE CROSS
LITTLE SAMMONS PH
VAGG LA

Caravan Pk
MARSH LA
Perren's Hill Farm
Monarch's Way
Leland Trail
Axesclose Farm
VAGG HILL
TINTINHULL RD
Vagg

5
Wellham's Mill
Wellhams Brook
Vagg Farm
Vagg Pk

18
East Stoke
MULBERRY LA
Stanchester Sports Com Sch Ctr
LOWER HYDE RD
WINDMILL LA
Windmill Farm
BA22
Thorne Coffin
218

4
WINDSOR LA
STONEHILL LA
EAST STOKE
MONTACUTE RD
HYDE RD
LOWER TOWN
MARSH LA
Gaundle Farm
Windmill Cotts
BALL'S HILL
Lufton Coll of FE
HIGSON CL
THORNE LA
WESSEX R
Trad Est
BOUNDARY WAY
COPSE RD

17
Hedgecock Hill
St Michael's Hill
SMITH'S ROW
ST MICHAEL'S VIEW
BISHOPSTON LA
TV & Radio Mus
PO
Montacute House
TA15
Lufton
Houndstone
P Huish Park
MEMORIAL
ARTILLERY RD

3
Ham Hill Ctry Pk
Twr
MIDDLE ST 1
THE BOROUGH 2
SOUTH ST 3
Montacute
All Saints CE Prim Sch
HOLLOW LA
Woodhouse Farm
NEW RD
High Leaze Farm
Crem
PRESTON RD
Tithe Barn
Preston Sch

16
Monarch's Way
TA14
PARK LA
FIVE ASHES
DRAY RD
BOUNDARY LA
LOWER ODCOMBE LA
Lower Odcombe PH
218
ALVINGTON
Alvington
A3088
Preston Plucknett
Yeovil Airfield
BUNFORD LA

2
Little Norton
Liberty Trail
Westbury Farm
CHERRY LA
DONNE LA
HOLLY TERR 1
ORCHARD CL 2
BROADWAY 3
CORYATE CL 4
CHURCH TERR 5
HAM HILL RD
CHAPEL HILL
OLD RD
Odcombe
Brympton House
Brympton D'Evercy
BA20
WATERCOMBE LA
Trad Est
A3088

15
Bagnell Farm
STREET LA
LANDSHIRE LA
WESTBURY RD
LONG ST
Higher Odcombe
Pye Corner Farm
Broadleaze Farm
RUSSET WAY
LABURNUM WAY
LYSANDER RD

1
Chiselborough Hill
TA18
Eastfield
EASTFIELD LA
GREEN LA
East Chinnock Hill
Cloverleaf Farm
DIBBLES LA
CAMP RD
Camp Hill
Feebarrow
WEST COKER RD A30
A3088

14
48   A   49   B   50   C   51   D   52   E   53   F

← 185
196 ↓
197 ↓

For full street detail of the highlighted area see page 218.

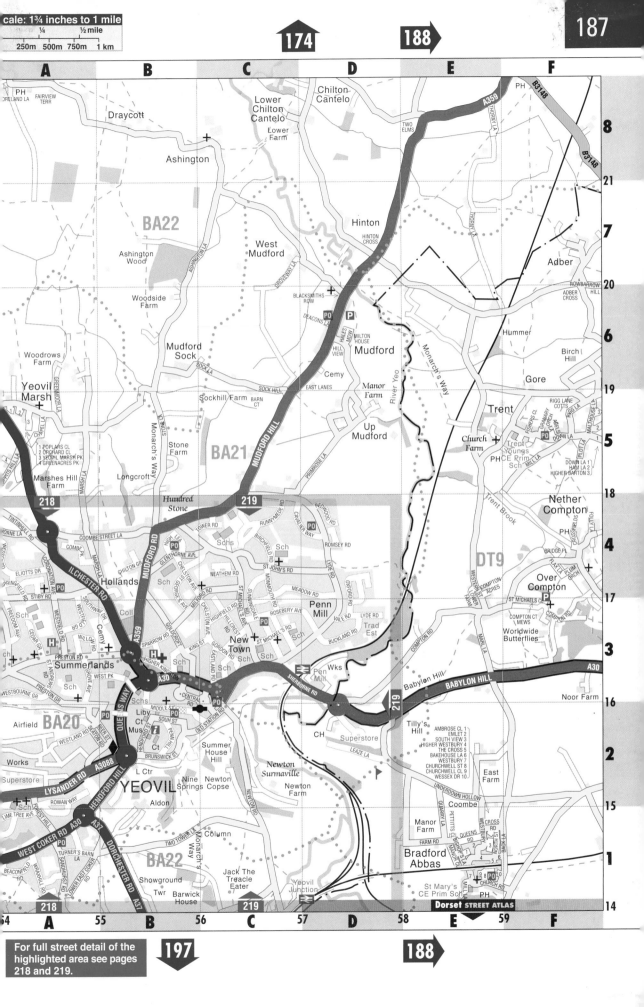

Scale: 1¾ inches to 1 mil
0   ¼   ½ mile
0 250m 500m 750m 1 km

A   B   C   D   E   F

8

Rimpton

BA22

Heaven's
Door

Weathergrove
Farm

PINK KNOLL
HOLLOW

Windmill
Hill

Stafford's
Green

Wheat Sheaf
Hill

Seven Wells
Down

Poyntington
Down

Milborne
Down

B3145

HOME FARM LA
DAISYFIELD
MID LA
HIGH ST
CHURCH LA
BACK LA
ROE LA

21

B3148

PH   White Post

CAR.
PITFIELD
SLADE LA
GREAT PIT LA

Sandford Orcas
Manor House

DARK LA
FARM
ORCH
PH
SHILLER'S LA

Holway
Hill

THE
BUNGALOWS
WASHINGPOOL

THE RIDGE

Poyntington Hill

7

Sandford Orcas

Higher
Sandford

SPRING LA

Holway

Red Post

Poyntington

LOWER BOYSTON LA

20

RONBARROW HILL
PENMORE RD
MIDDLE FIELD LA
MOORWAY LA

HAM LA

19

Patson
Hill

COOMBE LA

Higher
Clatcombe Farm

CH
CLATCOMBE LA

WHITEPOST
GATE

225

Ambrose
Hill

REDHOLE LA

SANDFORD ORCAS RD

Oborne

5

DOWN
LA
LOWSOME LA

Monarch's Way

Trent
Barrow

Charlock
Hill

CRECOMBE LA

Coombe
Farm

Coombe
Farm

Sch
Ctr

CASTLE TON RD
OWN WAY
GRANVILLE WAY

Blackmarsh
Farm

BANYERS

A3

18

TUCKER'S
CROSS
KITTON LA
GUINEAGORE LA

PATSON HILL LA

QUABB LA
ST. ALDHELM'S RD

Sch

A3

4

HART'S LA
RATLEIGH LA

SHERBORNE

MARSTON RD

TRENT PATH LA

COOMBE

BRISTOL RD
KINGS RD

P   PO

COLD HARBOUR

OBORNE RD B3145

225

17

Stallen

225

SHEPLANDS LA
MILL HILL

YEOVIL RD

B3148
Sch

GREENHILL

CHEAP ST

THE AV
NEWLAND
TINNEYS LA
CAST LE RD

PINFORD LA

Liby

Sherborne
Old Castle

Sherborne
Lake

3

A30

Halfway House
Farm

LOW'S HILL LA

Hotel

A352

BRADFORD RD
RIDGEWAY

HORSECASTLES LA
RICHMOND RD

ACREMAN ST

Sch

B3148
Sch
Abbey
H
P   PO
Mus
i   Ct

LONG ST

P

LC

NEW RD

Sherborne
Castle

Sherborne

Home Farm

16

SILVERLAKE
COTTS

Lenthay
Dairy
House

WEST BRIDGE PK
SOUTH AVE
LENTHAY RD

Cemy

OTTERY LA
HORSECASTLES LA
WESTBURY

SOUTH ST

Sherborne

Dancing
Hill

The
Kennels

2

Bedmill
Farm

Silverlake
Farm

Lenthay
Common

Sch

LC

WEST MILL LA

Sewage
Works

Limekiln
Farm

B3145

SHERBORNE HILL

COOMBE HILL

15

225

1

LC
Wyke Farm

Honeycombe
Farm

Court House
Dairy

Honeycombe
Wood

MACMILLAN WAY

A3030

Westhill
Lodge

GREEN LA

A352

CLOTHIER LONG LA
PH

North
Wootto

A3030

14

60   A   61   B   62   C   63   D   64   E   65   F

For full street detail of the
highlighted area see page 225.

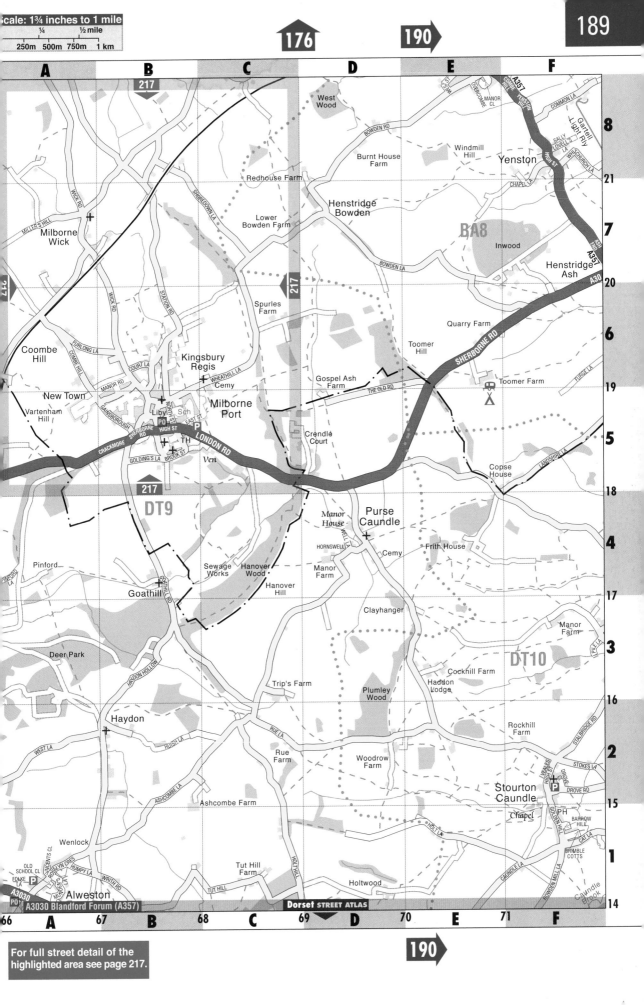

Scale: 1¾ inches to 1 mile
¼ ½ mile
250m 500m 750m 1 km

A B C D E F

217

West Wood

Bowden Rd

Burnt House Farm

Windmill Hill

A357

Manor Cl

Common La

Garrell Light Riv

Yenston

Redhouse Farm

Henstridge Bowden

Chapel

BA8

Milborne Wick

Miller's Hill

Lower Bowden Farm

Sherdown La

Bowden La

Inwood

Henstridge Ash

A357

A30

Coombe Hill

Furlong La

Wick Rd

Station Rd

Spurles Farm

Quarry Farm

Sherborne Rd

Toomer Hill

Toomer Farm

Forge La

217

Kingsbury Regis

Court La

Wheathill La

Cemy

Gospel Ash Farm

The Old Rd

New Town

Manor Rd

Gainsborough

Sherborne Rd

Milborne Port

Copse House

Landshire La

Vartenham Hill

Liby Sch

PO

High St

North St

East St

Crackmore

P

London Rd

Ven

Crendle Court

Golding's La

Brook St

TH

DT9

Manor House

Purse Caundle

Frith House

Hornswell

Cemy

Well La

Pinford

Sewage Works

Hanover Wood

Hanover Hill

Manor Farm

Goathill

Goathill Rd

Clayhanger

Manor Farm

Piv La

Deer Park

Haydon Hollow

DT10

Cockhill Farm

Haddon Lodge

Rockhill Farm

Stalbridge Rd

Haydon

Trip's Farm

Plumley Wood

Rue La

Ruishl La

West La

Rue Farm

Woodrow Farm

Stourton Caundle

High St

Stokes La

Drove

Drove Rd

P

PH

Ashcombe La

Ashcombe Farm

Holt La

Chapel

Golden Hill

Barrow Hill

Cat La

Brimble Cotts

Wenlock

Rosslyn Cres

Humpy La

Vincents Cl

Writth Rd

Old School Cl

Folke La

P

PO

Tut Hill Farm

Tut Hill

Holt Hill

Holtwood

Candle La

Rowden Mill La

Caundle Brook

A3030

Alweston

A3030 Blandford Forum (A357)

Dorset STREET ATLAS

66 A 67 B 68 C 69 D 70 E 71 F

For full street detail of the highlighted area see page 217.

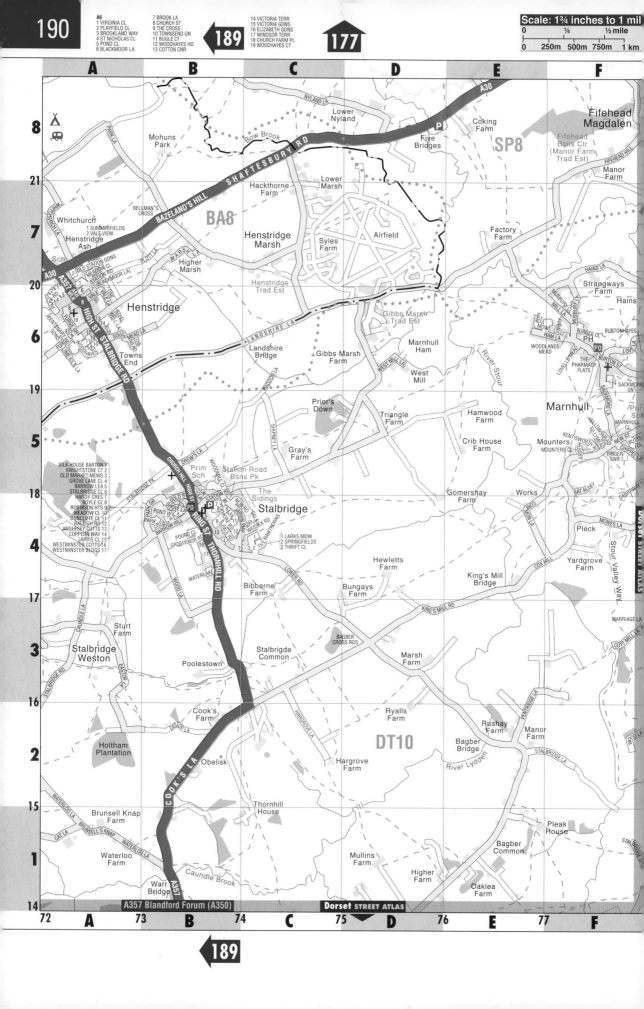

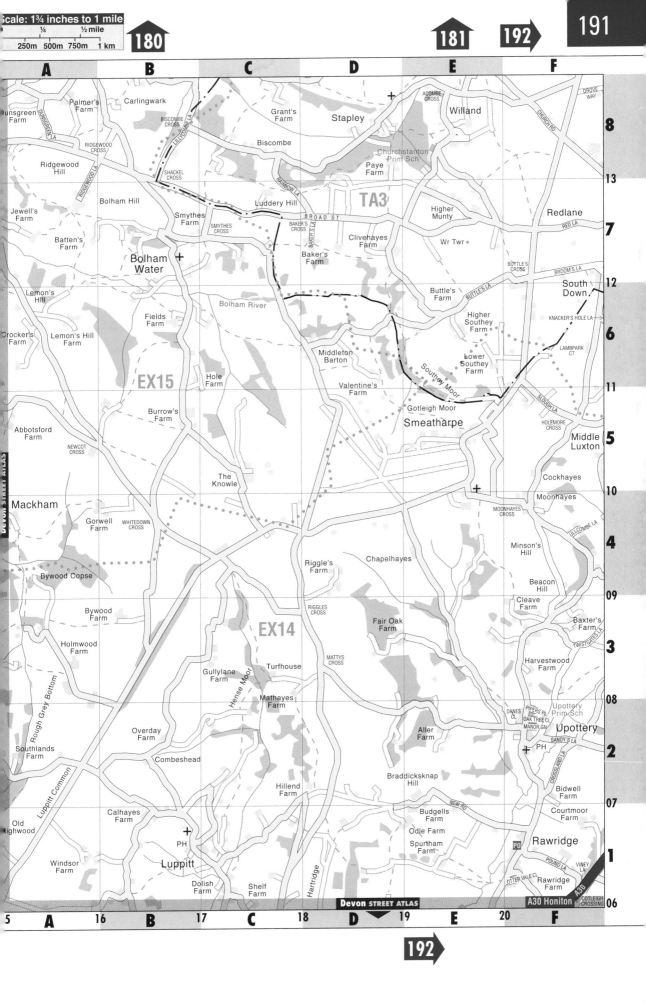

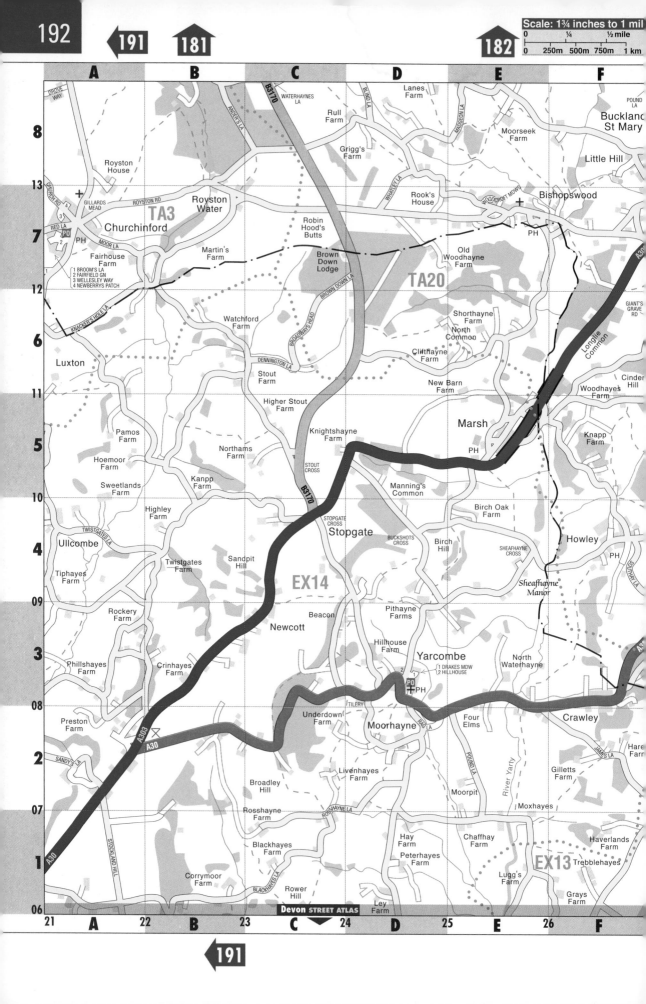

For full street detail of the highlighted area see page 223.

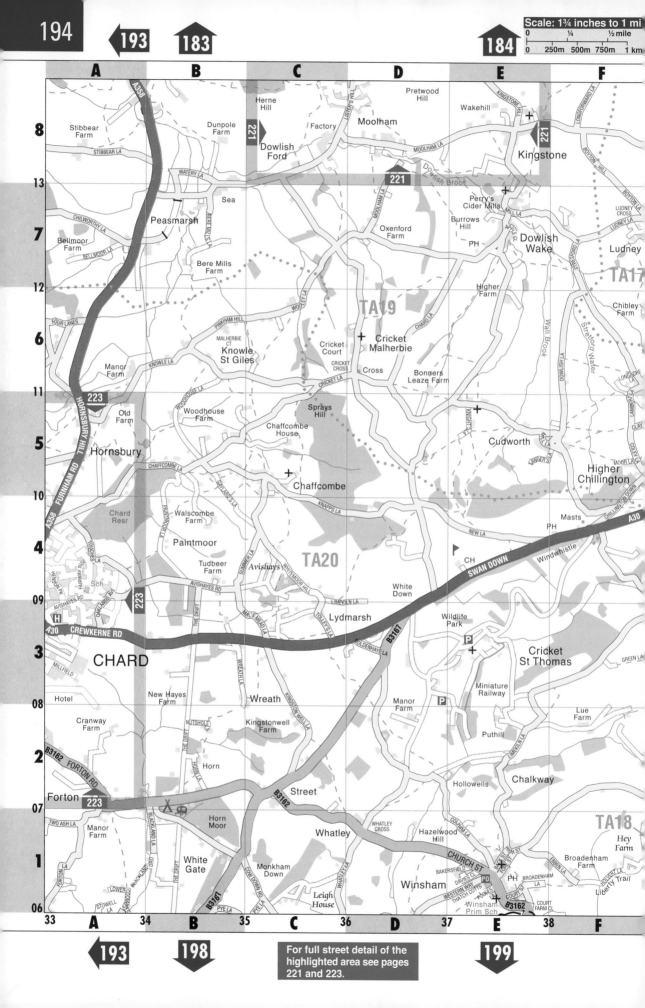

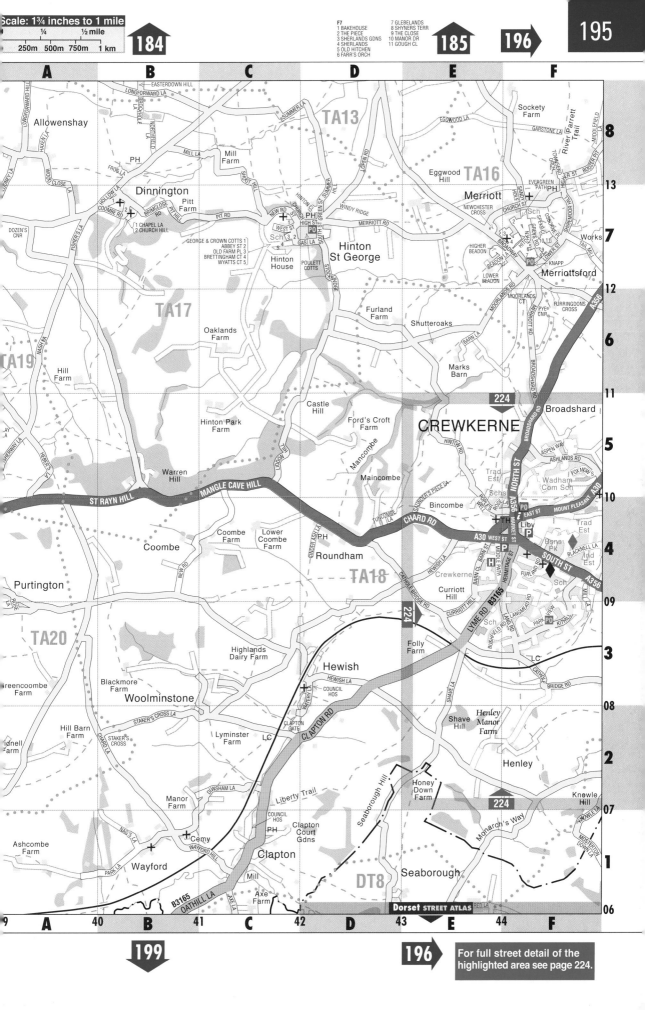

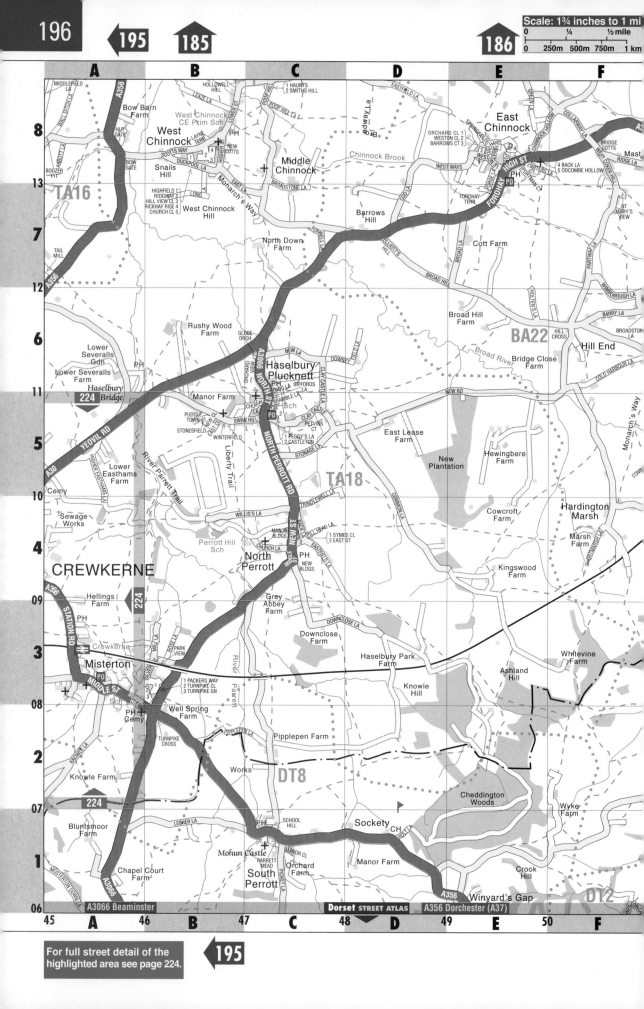

Scale: 1¾ inches to 1 mile

¼ ½ mile
250m 500m 750m 1 km

186

187

197

F8
1 HILLSIDE VIEW
2 YEO VALLEY
3 FIVE ACRES
4 MEADOW VIEW
5 HAMPTON CL
6 COURT ACRES
7 COURT LA
8 THE GREEN
9 CLIFTON VIEW
10 WHITCROSS
11 MOWLEAZE
12 SOUTH VIEW
13 SCHOOL COTTS

A B C D E F

8
13
7
12
6
11
5
10
4
09
3
08
2
07
1
06

A 52 B 53 C 54 D 55 E 56 F

Hotel
DIBBLES LA
HIGH ST
West Coker CE Prim Sch
West Coker
CHURLANDS
Hardington Moor
St James Terr
Monarch's Way
Lyatts
PEN CROSS
Hardington Mandeville
Windmill Hill
Pen Hill Farm
COMMON LA
PENDOMER RD
Pendomer
Pen Moor
Grove Farm

A30
GREEN LA
Nash
Burton
Holywell
BERYL KNAPP
Westfield Farm
East Coker Sawmills
Coker Court
Isles Farm
Isles La
Wickets Beer
BA22
Kit Hill
Coker Wood

Meadow View
CULLIVER'S GRAVE
GARDEN ROW
COKER HOUSE
BURTON BARTON
North Coker
East Coker Com Prim Sch
East Coker
Cemy
THE MEWS
CHURCH TERR
Stoney La
Hyde Farm
Sutton Bingham
Sutton Bingham Resr

BA20
Redlands
Monarch's Way
Lower Key
Pavyotts Farm
PINCUSHION CNR
PH
Darvole
Coker Marsh
Works
Netherton
NETHERTON CROSS
PROWLE'S CROSS
Weston Farm
WESTON LA
NETHERTON LA

PH
PAVYOTTS LA
TARRATT LA
Barwick
Stoford
Obelisk
KEY HILL
DORCHESTER RD
Whistle Bridge
DT9
A37 Dorchester
Dorset STREET ATLAS
A37
Closworth
Manor Farm

Macmillan Way Link
Abbot's Hill Farm
Abbot's Hill
Pen Wood
Birts Hill
Locke Farm
BACK LA
Mill Cross
LEIGH LA
Halstock
MEREDITH CL
Winford Rural Workshops
Higher Halstock Leigh
Lower Halstock Leigh
CH
Merrylands Farm
Wood Fold Hill
LOVELANDS
RYE WATER LA
CURRY HILL LA
Dogwell Farm
DT2

NETHERSTONE LA
Netherstoke
Harvard Farm
BULL BRIDGE MEAD
HOLLIS WAY
HOLLIS CL
ST JUTHWARE CL
BRANSFORD
Abbot's Hill Farm
Adam's Green
Wood Farm
Crockermoor Farm

Pondclose Farm
Liberty Farm
Clarkham Cross
CLARKHAM CROSS
Lewcombe
Holts Farms
HOLT LA

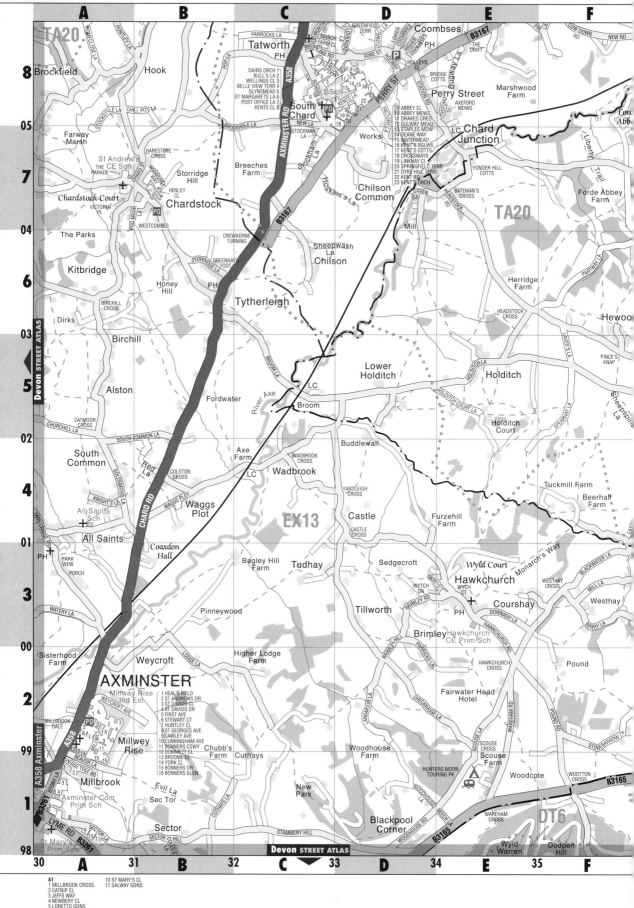

A1
1 MILLBROOK CROSS
2 CATNIP CL
3 JEFFS WAY
4 NEWBERY CL
5 LORETTO GDNS
6 MONKSTONE GDNS
7 CRIDLAKE
8 VALLEY VIEW
9 PRESTOR
10 ST MARY'S CL
11 SALWAY GDNS

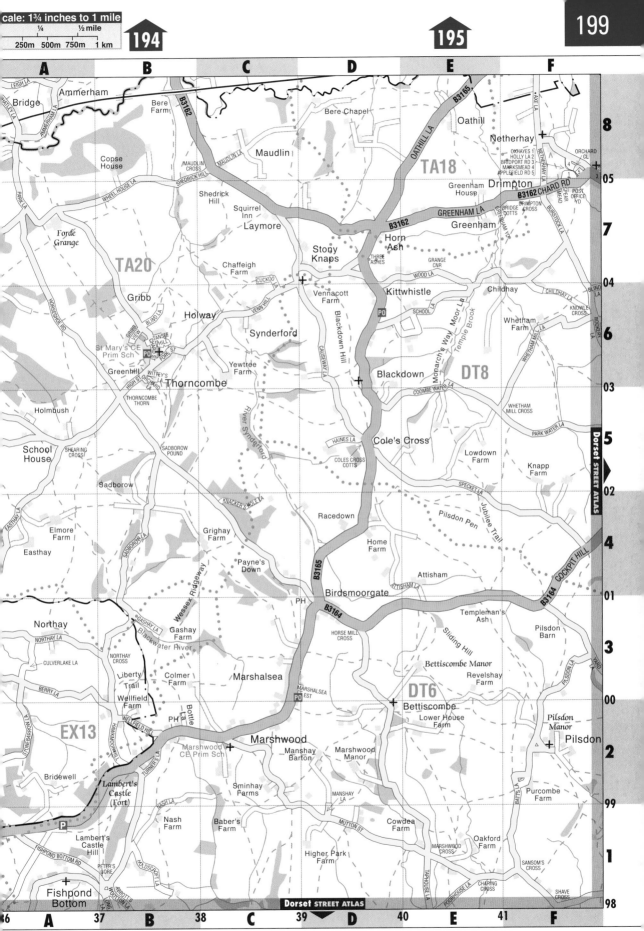

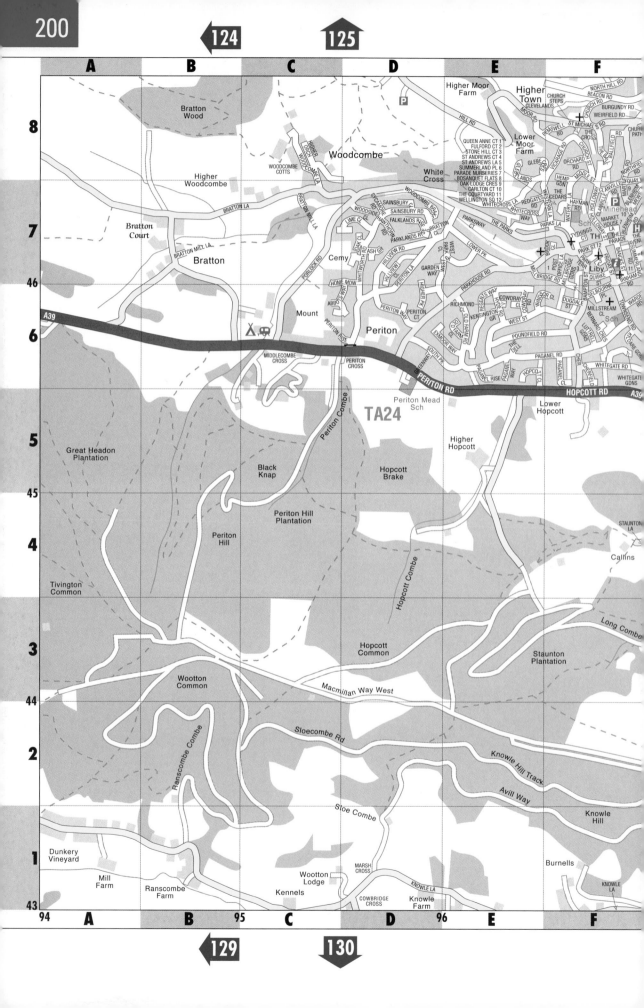

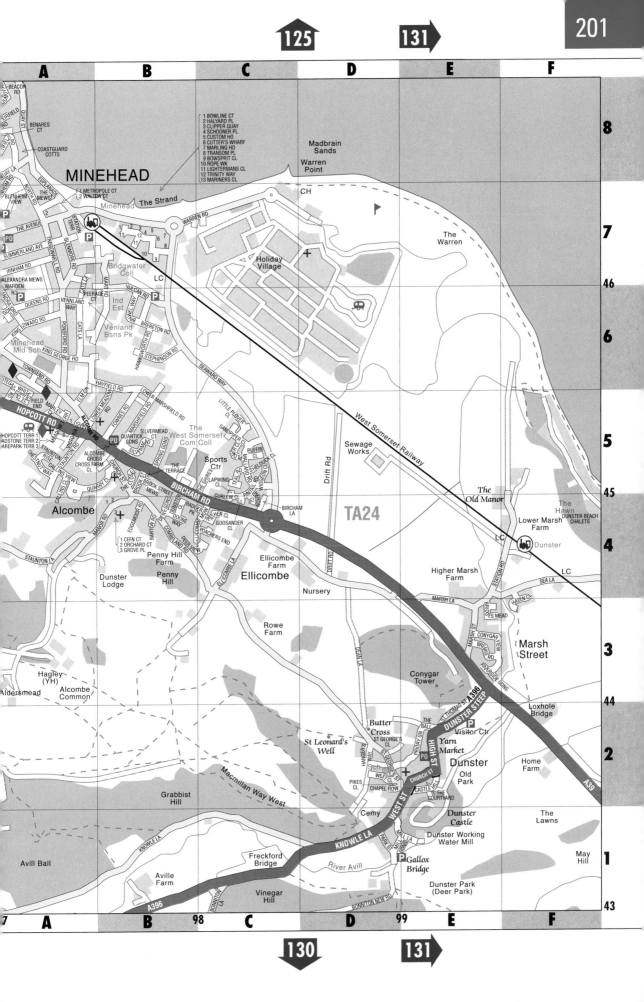

125
131

A **B** **C** **D** **E** **F**

8

1 BOWLINE CT
2 HALYARD PL
3 CLIPPER QUAY
4 SCHOONER PL
5 CUSTOM HO
6 CUTTER'S WHARF
7 MARLING HO
8 TRANSOM PL
9 BOWSPRIT CL
10 ROPE WK
11 LIGHTERMANS CL
12 TRINITY WAY
13 MARINERS CL

Madbrain
Sands

Warren
Point

CH

The
Warren

7

MINEHEAD

1 METROPOLE CT
2 WALTON CT

Minehead The Strand

WARREN RD

Holiday
Village

46

BLENHEIM
VIEW

THE MEWS

ESPLANADE

NORTH RD

THE AVENUE

PO

P

SUMMERLAND AVE

IRNHAM RD

BRIDGWATER
Coll

LC

6

ALEXANDRA MEWS
WARDEN
RD

P

QUEENS RD

KING EDWARD RD

VENNLAND
WAY

VULCAN RD

Ind
Est

NEW WAY

P

BRERETON RD

Venland
Bsns Pk

Minehead
Mid Sch

KING GEORGE RD

HAWKSWORTH RD

STEPHENSON RD

SEAWARD WAY

TOWNSEND RD

HAYFIELD RD

LOWER MARSHFIELD RD

LITTLE PLOVER
CL

SANDPIPER CL

PUFFIN
CL

West Somerset Railway

5

HOPCOTT RD

ALCOMBE RD

HOPCOTT TERR 1
ADSTONE TERR 2
AREPARK TERR 3

The
West Somerset
Com Coll

SILVERMEAD
GDNS

Sports
Ctr

LAPWING
CL

TEAL RD

MALLARD RD

WIDGEON CL

Sewage
Works

The
Old Manor

Lower Marsh
Farm

The
Hawn

DUNSTER BEACH
CHALETS

45

Alcombe

ALCOMBE
CROSS
CROSS
FARM
CL

CHURCH ST

BIRCHAM RD

THE
HEDGES

CURLEW CL

BIRCHAM
LA

TA24

LC

Dunster

4

1 CEFN CT
2 ORCHARD CT
3 GROVE PL

EDGEMOOR LA

BARTON RD

DEER VIEW

POACHERS END

Penny Hill
Farm

Ellicombe
Farm

GOOSANDER
CL

Ellicombe

Higher Marsh
Farm

MARSH LA

STANTON RD

SEA LA

HAVEN CL

LC

STAUNTON LA

Dunster
Lodge

Penny
Hill

Nursery

BR...ES MEAD

CONYGAR
VIEW

BRAMS RD

Marsh
Street

3

Hagley
(YH)

Aldersmead

Alcombe
Common

Rowe
Farm

DEAN LA

Conygar
Tower

RIVERSIDE GDNS

Loxhole
Bridge

44

Butter
Cross

ST GEORGE'S
CL

THE
BALL

ST THOMAS ST

DUNSTER STEEP

A396

Visitor Ctr

P

Home
Farm

A39

2

Macmillan Way West

St Leonard's
Well

SUGENHILL

ST GEORGE'S WAY

PRIORY GN

PO

Yarn
Market

THE
WEST
ST

CHURCH ST

Dunster
Old Park

HIGH ST

Grabbist
Hill

PIKES
CL

CHAPEL ROW

WEST ST

CASTLE HILL

THE
COURTYARD

Dunster
Castle

The
Lawns

Avill Ball

KNOWLE LA

Cemy

PARK ST

MILL LA

Dunster Working
Water Mill

May
Hill

1

Freckford
Bridge

River Avill

P

Gallox
Bridge

Dunster Park
(Deer Park)

43

Aville
Farm

Vinegar
Hill

A396

BONNITON LA

BONNITON NEW RD

A 98 **B** **C** **D** 99 **E** **F**

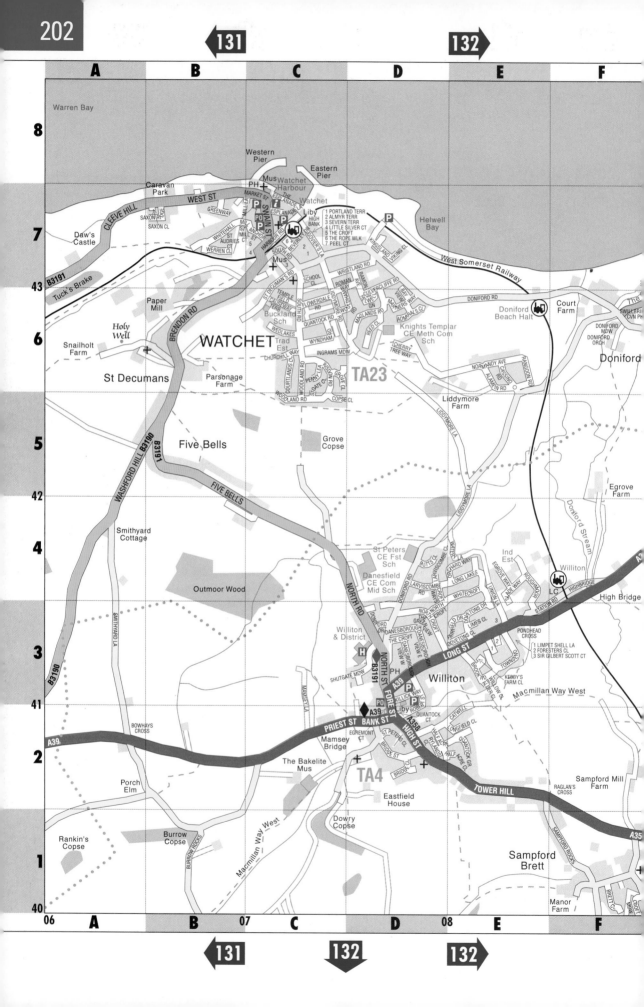

A B C D E F

8

Warren Bay

Western Pier

Eastern Pier

Mus
Watchet Harbour
Watchet

PH

Caravan Park

Helwell Bay

WEST ST

CLEEVE HILL

Daw's Castle

7

SAXON RS
SAXON CL

GREENWAY

MARKET ST
PO
P
P
ANCHOR ST

Liby
High BANK

1 PORTLAND TERR
2 ALMYR TERR
3 SEVERN TERR
4 LITTLE SILVER CT
5 THE CROFT
6 THE ROPE WLK
7 PEEL CT

P

West Somerset Railway

B3191

Tuck's Brake

WHITEHALL ST
AUDRIES CT
WERREN CL
MILL
ST

Mus

43

Paper Mill

BRENDON RD

ST DECUMAN'S RD
TEMPLE
FIELD
GATEWAY
TERR

SCHOOL CL

ROMAN WAY

DONIFORD RD

Doniford Beach Halt

Court Farm

The SWILLBRI CVN PH

Holy Well

FLOWERDALE RD

CULVERCLIFFE RD

Knights Templar CE Meth Com Sch

DONIFORD MDW
DONIFORD ORCH

6

Snailholt Farm

Buckland Sch
MEDLAKES

WATCHET

WYNDHAM

REED CL

MAGLANDS RD

ADMIRALS CT

NORMANDY AVE

CRESSING RD
ALAMEIN RD

HANGOOR RD

Doniford

St Decumans

Parsonage Farm

COURTLANDS CL
WOODLAND RD

PENNY LEA
SLADE CL

RISDON RD
GROVE CL

TA23

CHERRY TREE WAY

Liddymore Farm

COPSE CL

WOODLAND RD

5

Five Bells

WASHFORD HILL B3190

B3191

Grove Copse

LIDDYMORE LA

Egrove Farm

42

FIVE BELLS

Smithyard Cottage

St Peters CE Fst Sch

BUTTS CL
LAVINGCOMBE RD
ORCHARD WAY
LONG LAKES

WATER LA

Ind Est

Williton

LC

HIGHBRIDGE

Doniford Stream

A3

4

Outmoor Wood

Danesfield CE Com Mid Sch

DONIFORD RD

LARVISCOMBE RD

NORTH
CROFT
WHITECROFT

LINION LA

EGROVE
WAY
INE WAY

STATION RD

ROUGHMOOR

High Bridge

SMITHYARD LA

NORTH RD

NORTH
GATE
VIEW

DOYETONS DR
LIMES CL

3

B3190

Williton & District

H

SHUTGATE MDW

THE CROFT
DANESBOROUGH VIEW
DANESBOROUGH VIEW W

LONG ST

Williton

1 LIMPET SHELL LA
2 FORESTERS CL
3 SIR GILBERT SCOTT CT

PONDHEAD CROSS

KEBBY'S FARM CL

Macmillan Way West

41

B3190

Bowhays Cross

MAMSEY LA

NORTH ST
B3191

PH

PO
P
P

A39

Liby

KILLICK WAY
ROBERTS

QUANTOCK CT

CATWELL

KINGFIELD CL

MacMillan Way West

A39

PRIEST ST
BANK ST

A39
FORE ST

A358
HIGH ST

HALE RD
HALF ACRE

QUANTOCK GR

RAGLAN'S CROSS

2

Mamsey Bridge

EGREMONT CT

ST PETERS CL

BRIDGE ST
BRIDGE

TA4

TOWER HILL

Sampford Mill Farm

A39

The Bakelite Mus

Porch Elm

Eastfield House

Dowry Copse

A35

1

Rankin's Copse

Burrow Copse

BURROW ROCKS

Macmillan Way West

SAMPFORD ROCKS

Sampford Brett

Manor Farm

BRETT CL

40

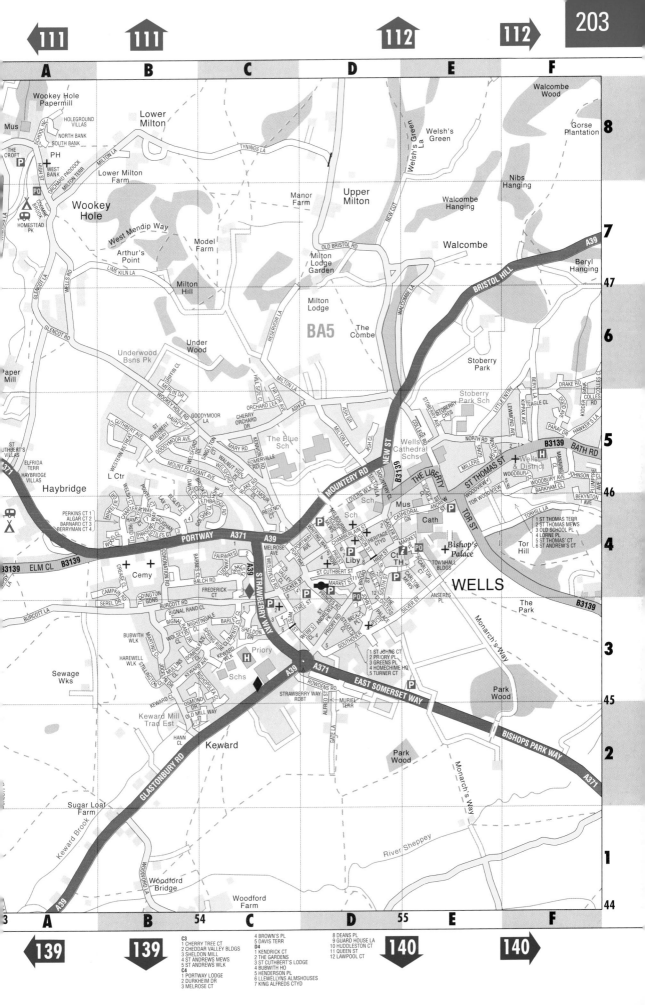

C3
1 CHERRY TREE CT
2 CHEDDAR VALLEY BLDGS
3 SHELDON MILL
4 ST ANDREWS MEWS
5 ST ANDREWS WLK
C4
1 PORTWAY LODGE
2 DURKHEIM DR
3 MELROSE CT

4 BROWN'S PL
5 DAVIS TERR
D4
1 KENDRICK CT
2 THE GARDENS
3 ST CUTHBERT'S LODGE
4 BUBWITH HO
5 HENDERSON PL
6 LLEWELLYNS ALMSHOUSES
7 KING ALFREDS CTYD

8 DEANS PL
9 GUARD HOUSE LA
10 HUDDLESTON CT
11 QUEEN ST
12 LAWPOOL CT

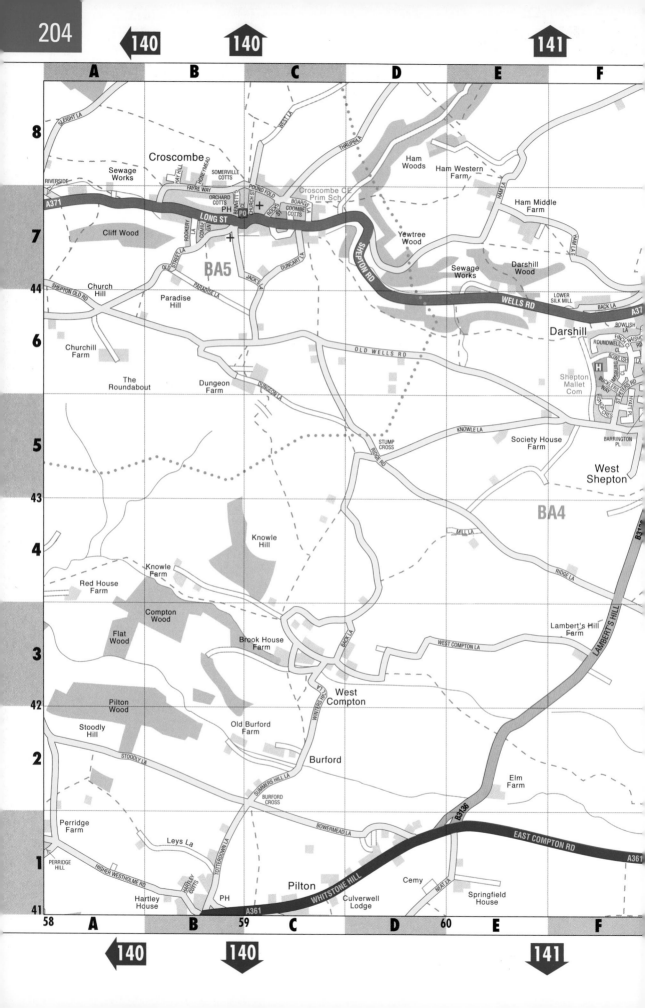

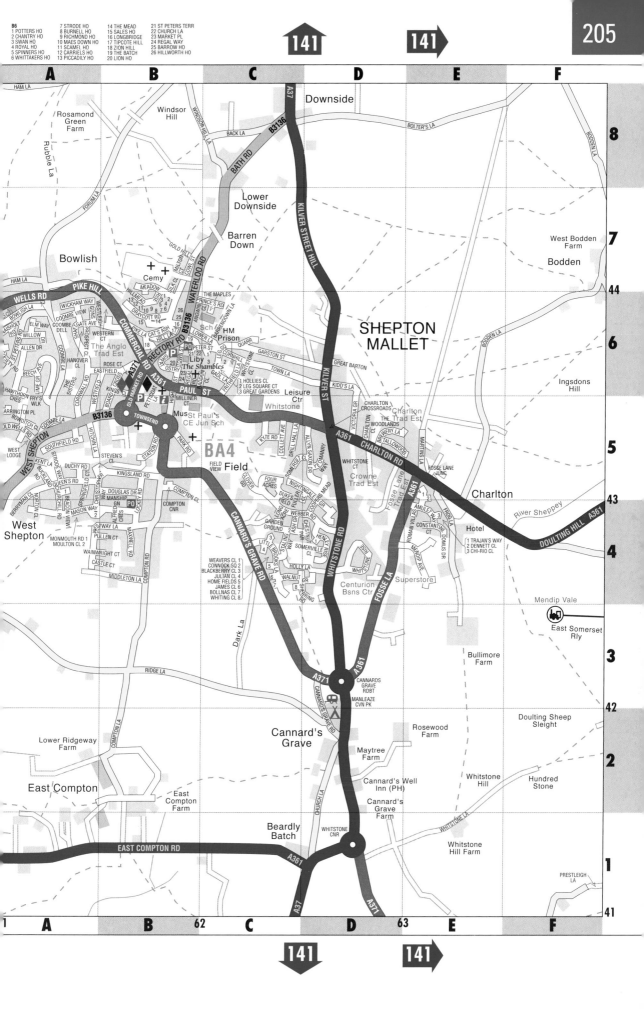

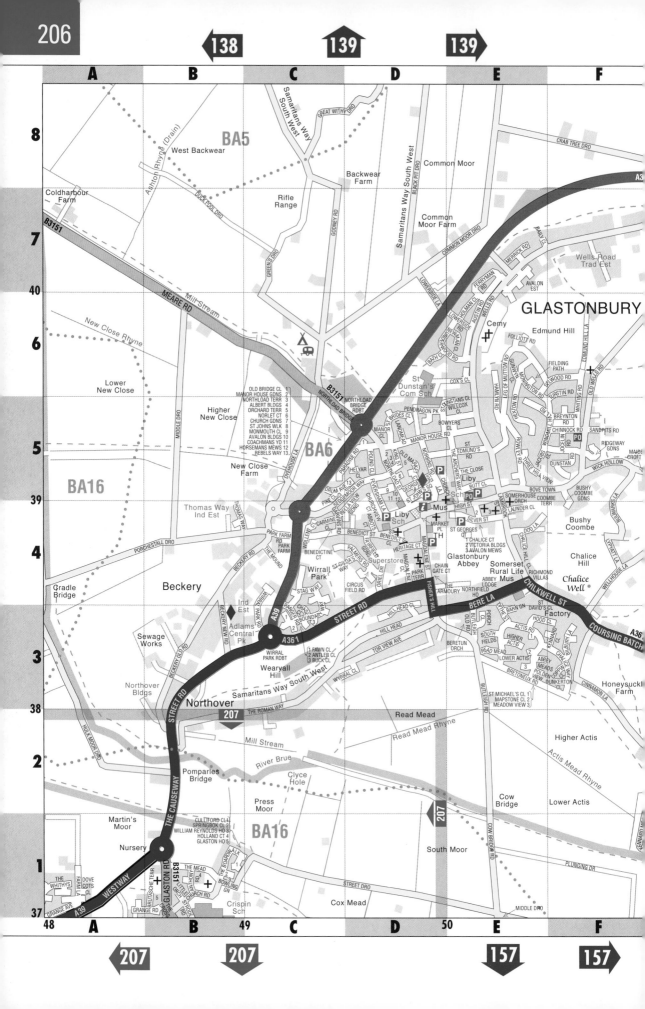

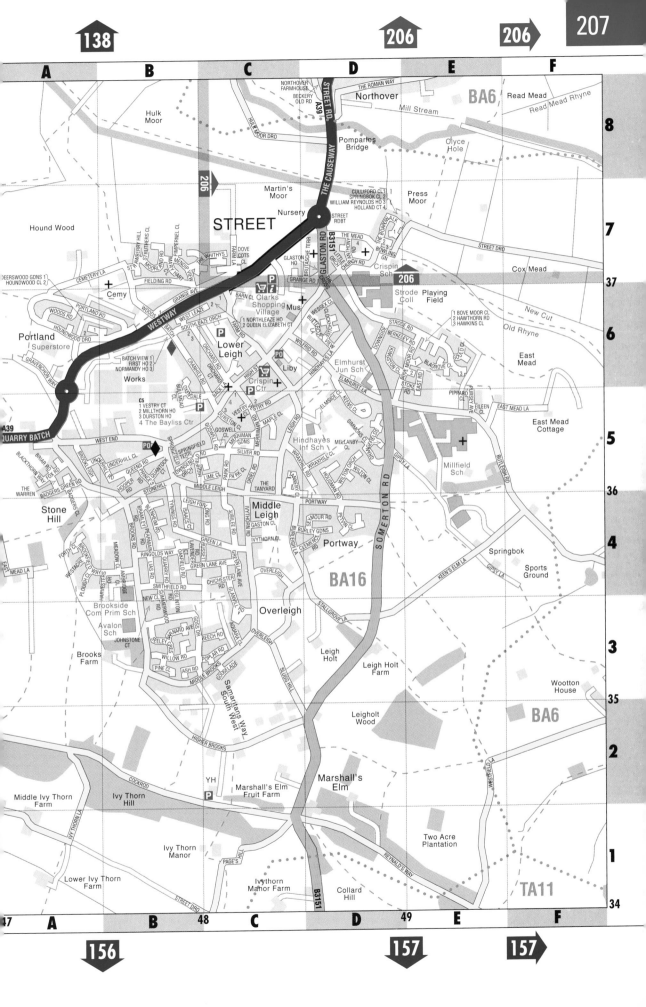

135 135

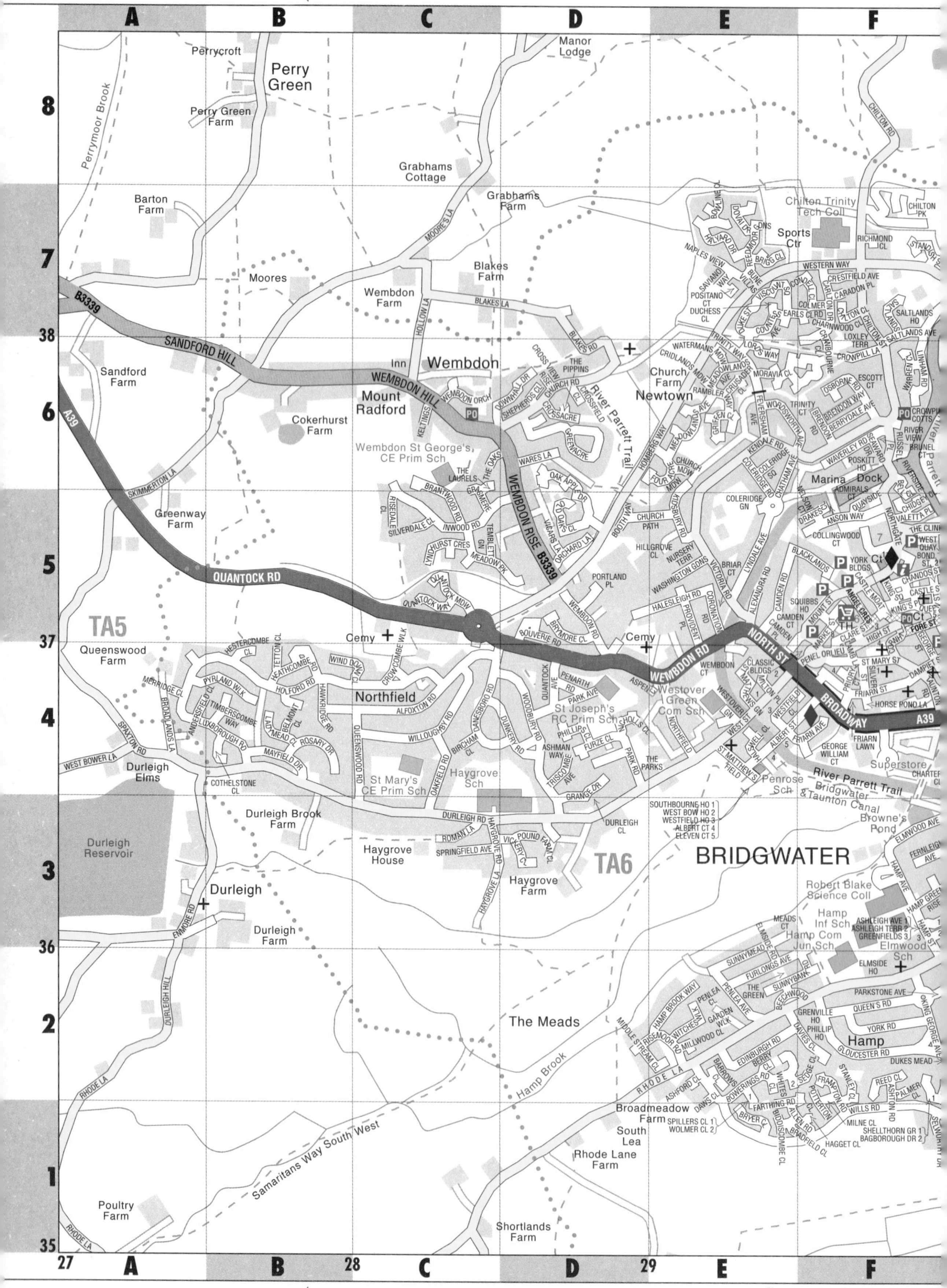

F4
1 ST MARY'S CT
2 BLAKE ST
3 OLD TAUNTON RD
4 GREEN DRAGON CT

F5
1 CHALICE MEWS
1 HOMECASTLE HO
3 THE AVENUE
4 CHURCH PASS
5 COURT ST
6 ANGEL PLACE SH CTR
7 BRIDGWATER ENT CTR
8 MARKET CT

BRIDGWATER

SOUTHBOURNE HO 1
WEST BOW HO 2
WESTFIELD HO 3
ALBERT CT 4
ELEVEN CT 5.

SPILLERS CL 1
WOLMER CL 2

SHELLTHORN GR 1
BAGBOROUGH DR 2

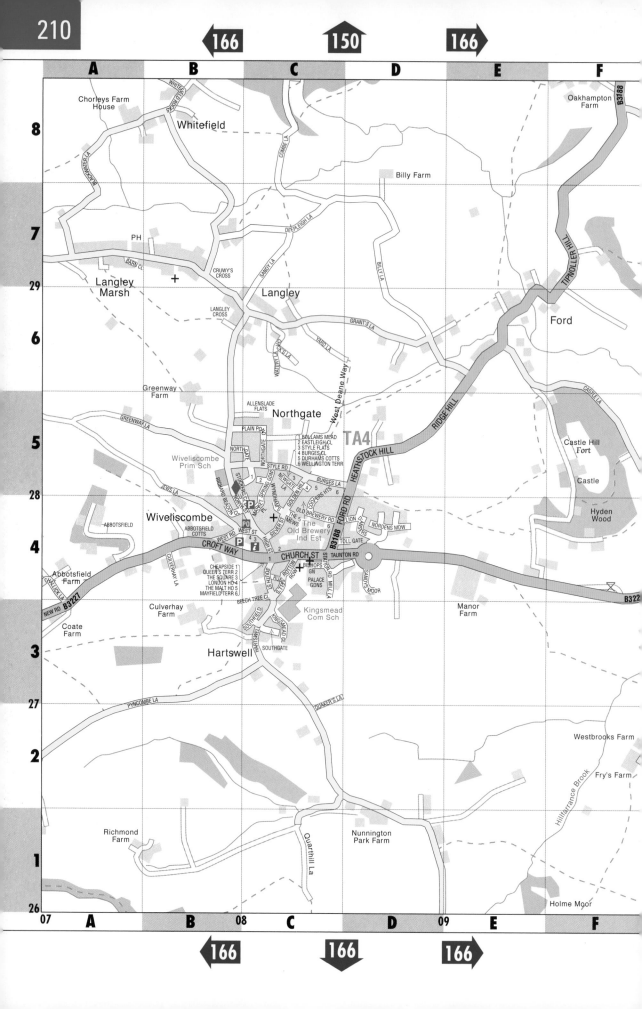

A B C D E F

8 Chorleys Farm House
Whitefield
Oakhampton Farm
B3188

Billy Farm

7 PH
DEEPALEIGH LA
WHITE FIELD ROAD
CRUWY'S CROSS
SANDY LA
TIPNOLLER HILL

29 Langley Marsh
Langley
Ford

6 LANGLEY CROSS
GRANT'S LA
YARD LA
WATERY LA
OAKS LA

Greenway Farm
West Deane Way
RIDGE HILL
CASTLE LA

5 ALLENSLADE FLATS
Northgate
TA4
Castle Hill Fort

PLAIN PO
1 BOLLAMS MEAD
2 EASTLEIGH CL
3 STYLE FLATS
4 BURGES CL
5 DURHAMS COTTS
6 WELLINGTON TERR

Wiveliscombe Prim Sch
NORTH GATE
NORTHGATE
STYLE RD
HEATHSTOCK HILL
Castle

GREENWAY LA
JEWS LA
RICHARD BEACON CL
STOCKERS LA
MARKET SPRING GDNS
WINDHAM LA
NEWGATE LA
GOLDEN HILL
BURGES LA
COOPERS HTS
FORD RD

28 ABBOTSFIELD
ABBOTSFIELD COTTS
WEST RD
WEST ST
SILVER ST
HIGH ST
OLD BREWERY RD
THE MEWS
The Old Brewery Ind Est
LION D
MEWKERS
NORDENS MDW
Hyden Wood

4 CROFT WAY
CULVERHAY LA
P
CHURCH ST
TAUNTON RD
B3188
TOLL GATE
B3227

Abbotsfield Farm
CHADWICK LA
NEW RD B3227
CHEAPSIDE 1
QUEEN'S TERR 2
THE SQUARE 3
LONDON HO 4
THE MALT HO 5
MAYFIELD TERR 6
BISHOPS GN
PALACE GDNS
STATION RD
SANDYS MOOR
Manor Farm
B322

Coate Farm
Culverhay Farm
BEECH TREE CL
Kingsmead Com Sch

3 Hartswell
SOUTHFIELD
HARTSWELL
KINGSMEAD CL
SOUTHGATE

27 PYNCOMBE LA
QUAKER'S LA

2 Westbrooks Farm
Fry's Farm
Hillfarrance Brook

Richmond Farm
Quarthill La
Nunnington Park Farm

1

26 Holme Moor

07 A B 08 C D 09 E F

A   B   C   D   E   F

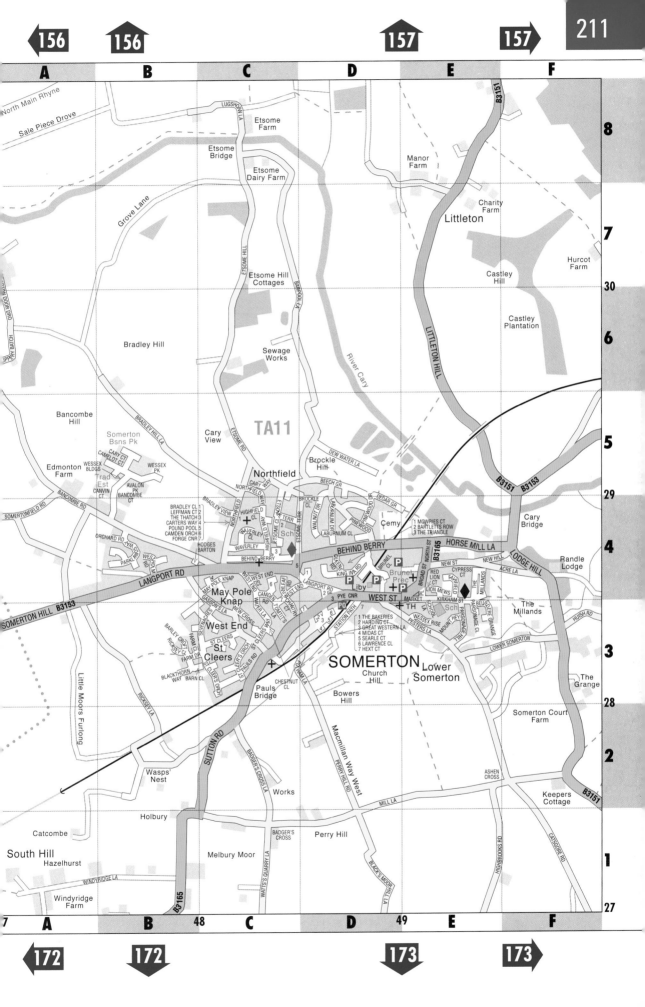

North Main Rhyne
Sale Piece Drove
Lugshorn La
Etsome Farm
Etsome Bridge
Etsome Dairy Farm
Manor Farm
Charity Farm
Littleton
Hurcot Farm
Castley Hill
Castley Plantation
Grove Lane
Etsome Hill
Barpool La
Etsome Hill Cottages
Littleton Hill
B3151
8
30
7
6

Bradley Hill
Sewage Works
River Cary
TA11

Bancombe Hill
Somerton Bsns Pk
Cary View
Brockle Hill
Northfield
Dew Water La
B3151 B3153
Cary Bridge
5
29

Edmonton Farm
Wessex Bldgs
Camelot Ct
Cary Ct
Avalon Pk
Canvin Ct
Bancombe Ct
Wessex Pk
Trad Est
Somertonfield Rd
Bancombe Rd
Bradley Hill La

Bradley Cl 1
Leffman Ct 2
The Thatch 3
Carters Way 4
Pound Pool 5
Camden Orch 6
Forge Cnr 7
Bradley View
Highfield
Northfield Way
Cary Way
Etsome Cross
Etsome Terr
Beech Gr
Walnut Dr
Laburnum Dr
Pinewood
Cedar Gr
Brockle Cl
Redwood Dr
Laburnum Cl
Cemy
1 Mowries Ct
2 Bartletts Row
3 The Triangle
Horse Mill La
Orchard Rd
Park La
Langport Rd
B3153
Somerton Hill
Waverley
Behind Berry
Hodges Barton
Sch
Behind Berry
Brunel Cl
King La Rd
Queens Rd
Broad St
North St
B3165
New St
Red Lion
Lion Mews
New St
Cypress Ct
New Hill
Acre La
Lodge Hill
Randle Lodge
4

May Pole Knap
West End
St Cleers
Barley Croft
Rixsey Cl
St Cleers Orch
St Cleers Rd
St Cleers Orch
Blackthorn Way
Barn Cl
Gasson's La
New Croses
Camden Orch
Sivells Rd
Pauls Rd
Chestnut Cl
Poltimore Rd
West St
Market
Kirkham St
School
Sch
The
Mount
Parsonage Cl
Hey Mead
The Link
Belvedere Grange
Lower Somerton
Hursh Rd
The Millands
3
28

May Pole Knap
Brunel Prec
P P P
Liby
TH
SOMERTON
Lower Somerton
Church Hill
Wessex Rise
Pesters La
Station Path
1 The Bakeries
2 Harding St
3 Great Western La
4 Midas Ct
5 Searle Ct
6 Lawrence Cl
7 Hext Ct
PO
Pye Cnr

Little Moors Furlong
Rixsey La
Pauls Bridge
Bowers Hill
Church Hill
The Grange
Somerton Court Farm

Wasps' Nest
Sutton Rd
Badgers Cross La
Works
Macmillan Way West
Perry Hill Rd
Mill La
Ashen Cross
Keepers Cottage
B3151
2

Holbury
Catcombe
South Hill
Hazelhurst
Windyridge La
Windyridge Farm
B3165
Melbury Moor
Watts's Quarry La
Badger's Cross
Perry Hill
Black's Moor Hill La
Highbrooks Rd
Catsgore Rd
1
27

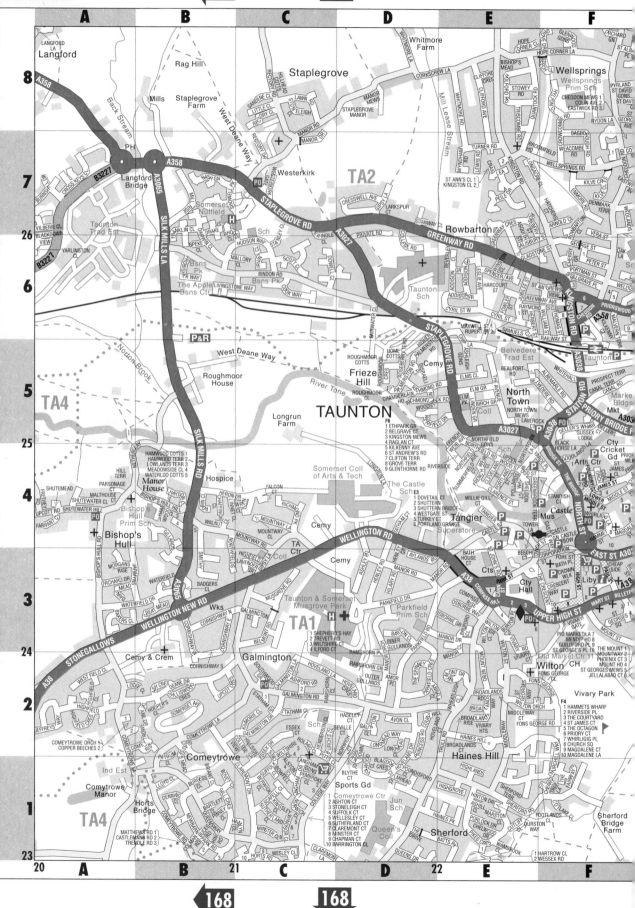

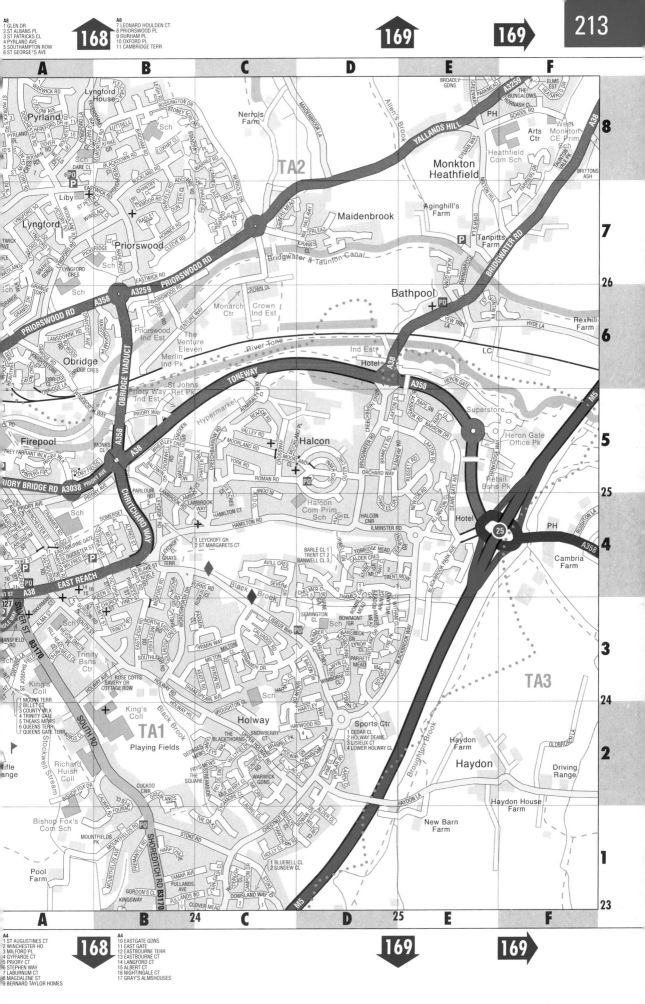

159 159

A B C D E F

8
BA10

River Brue

Ansford
Bridge
Castle Cary
Ansford Park
Farm

A371
STATION RD

7
Hillcrest
Farm
ANSFORD HILL
ELM LA
Leland Trail
Macmillan Way
WYKE RD

B3153

33
B3152
ST ANDREWS CL
ORCHARD
HALLETT RD
TUCKERS LA
MULLINS WAY
PARSONAGE CRES
CHURCHFIELDS DR
1 ASHLEA
2 PARSONS GATE
Ansford
Com Sch
MAGGS LA
Bottom Barn
Farm

Wayside
Farm
LOWER ANSFORD
WOODFORDS GN
PRIORY VIEW
YEABSLEYS WAY
BROCK CT
Ansford
Honeywick
Hill

6
FLORIDA FIELDS
CLOTHIER RD
WEST PK
VICTORIA GDNS
PRIORYGATE CT
GREENWAY
COOMBE CL
COOMBE CL
CATHERINES CL
CUMNOCK TERR
CUMNOCK RD
NORTH SIDE
ARNCASTLE TERR
ANCASTLE RD
CUMNOCK CRES
Sunnydene
Farm
FOURWAYS CL
Knapp
Farm
NETTLECOMBE HILL
Hadspe

Torbay Road
Ind Est
STATION RD
TORBAY CT
VICTORIA GDNS
VICTORIA PK
KINGSACRE
SALISBURY TERR
P
KNIGHTS YD
Liby
PO
NORTH ST
MOUNT PLEASANT
Cary Hill

Torbay
Villas
TORBAY RD
BROCKFIELDS
BRIDGERS
POLLY
VICTORIA CT
VICTORIA CT
HANOVER CT
CHAPEL
UPPER HIGH ST
HIGH ST
Mus

5
DONNES TERR 1
BRIDGWATER BLDGS 2
REMALARD CT
MILLBROOK GDNS
WOODCOCK ST
FORE ST
P
CASTLE RISE
1 VICTORIA MEWS
2 MONTAGUE GDNS
3 PRIORY PATH
4 BAILEY HILL
5 MARKET PL
6 THE PITCHING
7 LOWER WOODCOCK ST
8 ASHBY PL
9 THE TRIANGLE
BA7
Priddle's
Hill

Castle
Cary
SOUTH CARY LA
PARK ST
PARK PL
Hadspen
Farm
Higher
Hadspen

32
CHURCH ST
ANNANDALE
THE PARK
Castle Cary
Com Prim Sch
HELL LADDER LA
LIME KILN LA
GREEN LA

4
Sewage
Works
ALMA RD
SOUTH ST
CHAPEL YD
LODGE CT
Castle Cary
Park
Lodge Hill
Farm
Hill
A35

COCKHILL ELM LA
SOUTH BANK PARK AVE
Monarch's Way
Grove
Farm

3
Higher
Cockhill Farm
Cemy
Abbey
Gardens
Manor
Farm
Mast
Grove
Mead
A371
Hadspen
Wood

31
COOPER'S ASH LA
BROADWAY LA
A371
Hadsp
Hous

2
GALHAMPTON HILL
Sportsman's
Lodge Farm
Small
Way
BA22
Tor View
Farm
Macmillan Way
Leland Trail
A37

B3152

1
Ferndale
Farm
Redlands
Farm
Mount Pleasant
Farm
SMALL WAY LA
HICKS'S LA
Sleight La
BA9
Shatwell
Farm
SHATWELL LA

30
A359

63 A B 64 C D 65 E F

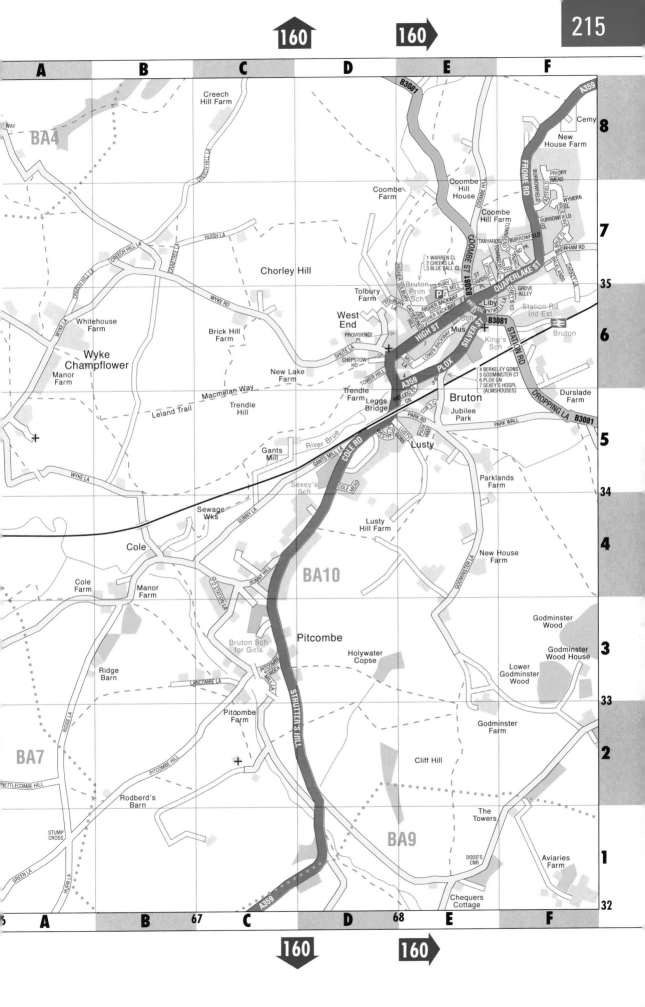

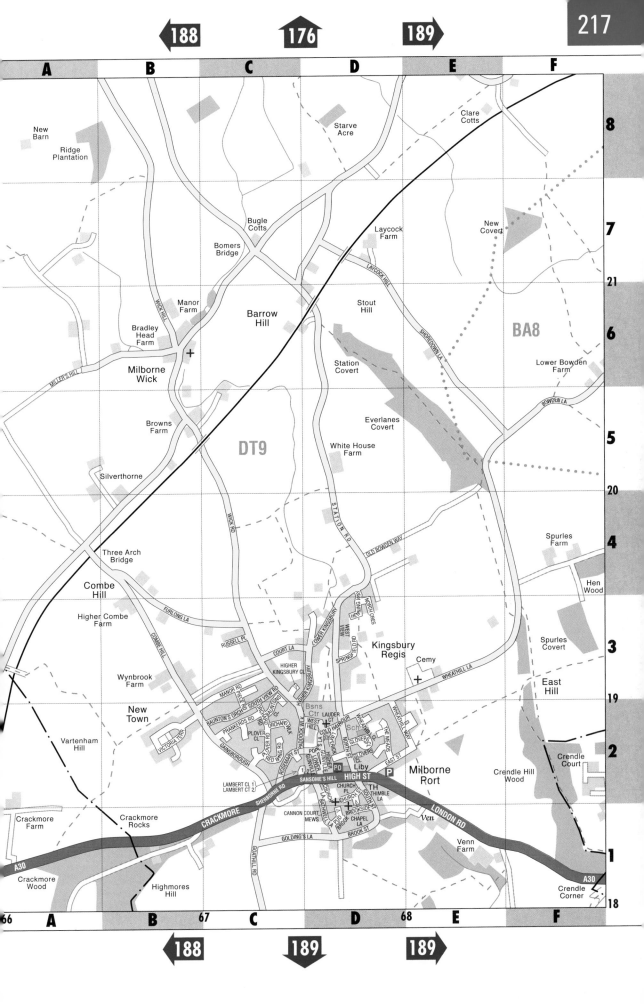

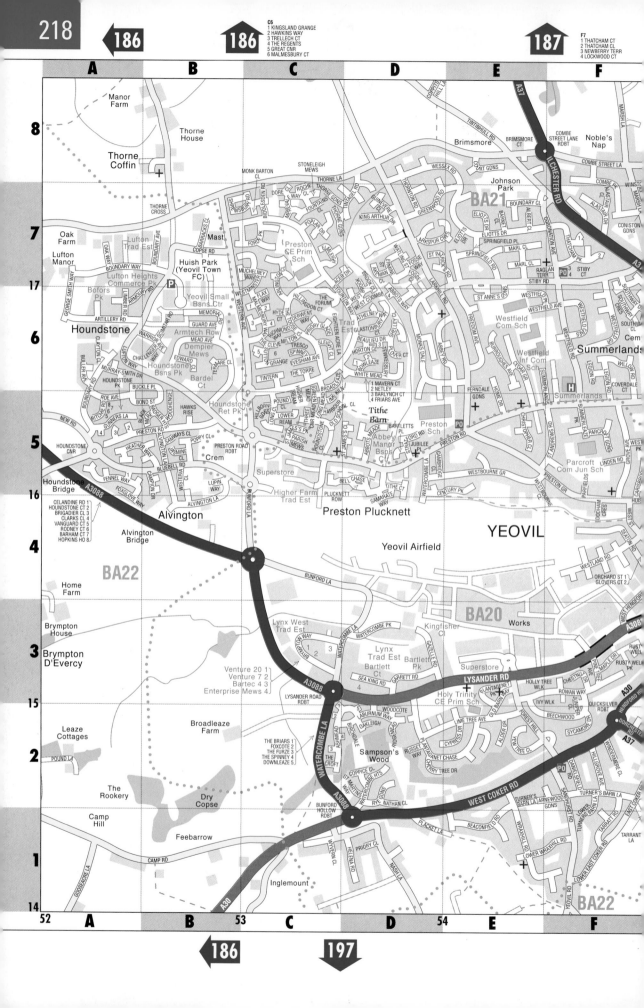

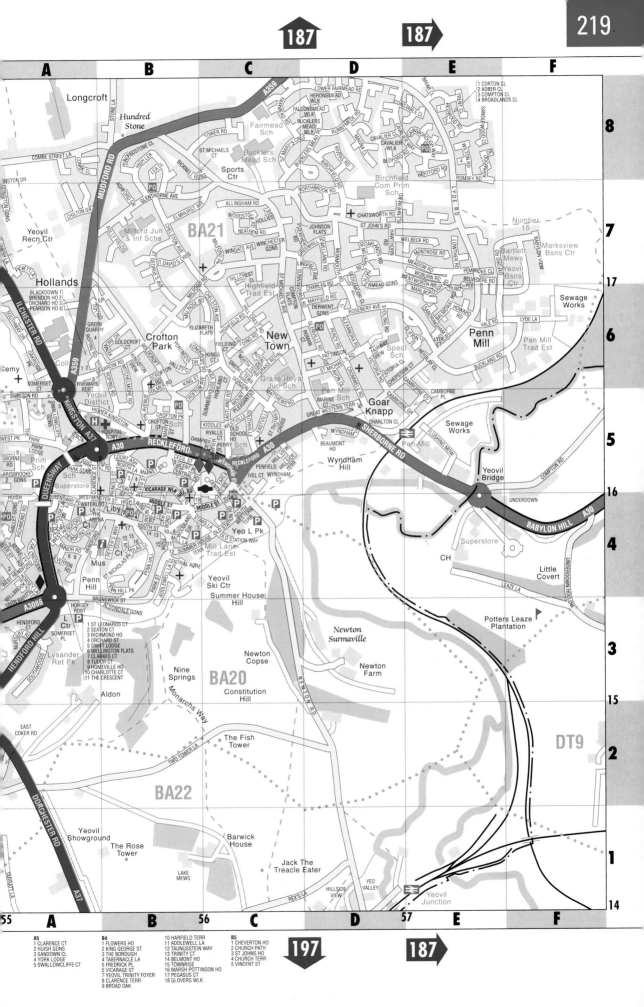

187 187

Longcroft

Hundred
Stone

COMBE STREET LA

Yeovil
Recn Ctr

Hollands

BLACKDOWN 1
BRENDON HO 2
ORCHARD HO 3
PEARSON HO 4

Green
Quarry

Crofton
Park

Yeovil
District

BA21

Fairmead
Sch

Bucklers
Mead Sch

Sports
Ctr

Birchfield
Com Prim
Sch

1 CORTON CL
2 ADBER CL
3 COMPTON CL
4 BROADLANDS CL

Number
15

Marksview
Bsns Ctr

Yeovil
Bsns
Ctr

New
Town

Sewage
Works

Penn
Mill

Pen Mill
Trad Est

Goar
Knapp

Sewage
Works

Somerset
Ct

Preston Rd

Hospital

Superstore

Queensway

Park
Lodge

ARISBROOKE
GDNS

Reckleford

Reckleford

Pen Mill

Yeovil
Bridge

UNDERDOWN

BABYLON HILL   A30

Wyndham
Hill

Wyndham

Beaumont
Ho

Superstore

CH

Little
Covert

The Arena

Liby

Yeo L Pk

Mill Lanes
Trad Est

Central Acre

Potters Leaze
Plantation

Mus

Penn
Hill

Yeovil
Ski Ctr

Summer House
Hill

Newton
Surmaville

Newton
Copse

Newton
Farm

1 ST LEONARDS CT
2 SEATON CT
3 RICHMOND HO
4 ORCHARD ST
5 SWIFT LODGE
6 WELLINGTON FLATS
7 CLARKES CT
8 TUDOR CT
9 HOMEVILLE HO
10 CHARLOTTE HO
11 THE CRESCENT

L Ctr

SOMERSET
PL

Lysander
Ret Pk

Aldon

Nine
Springs

BA20

Constitution
Hill

Monarchs Way

EAST
COKER RD

The Fish
Tower

DT9

BA22

Yeovil
Showground

The Rose
Tower

Barwick
House

Jack The
Treacle Eater

Yeo
Valley

Yeovil
Junction

LAKE
MEWS

HILLSIDE
VIEW

REX'S LA

55   A   56   C   57   E   F

197 187

A5
1 CLARENCE CT
2 HUISH GDNS
3 SANDOWN CL
4 YORK LODGE
5 SWALLOWCLIFFE CT

B4
1 FLOWERS HO
2 KING GEORGE ST
3 THE BOROUGH
4 TABERNACLE LA
5 FREDRICK PL
6 VICARAGE ST
7 YEOVIL TRINITY FOYER
8 CLARENCE TERR
9 BROAD OAK

10 HARFIELD TERR
11 ADDLEWELL LA
12 TAUNUSSTEIN WAY
13 TRINITY CT
14 BELMONT HO
15 TOWNRISE
16 MARSH POTTINSON HO
17 PEGASUS CT
18 GLOVERS WLK

B5
1 CHEVERTON HO
2 CHURCH PATH
3 ST JOHNS HO
4 CHURCH TERR
5 VINCENT ST

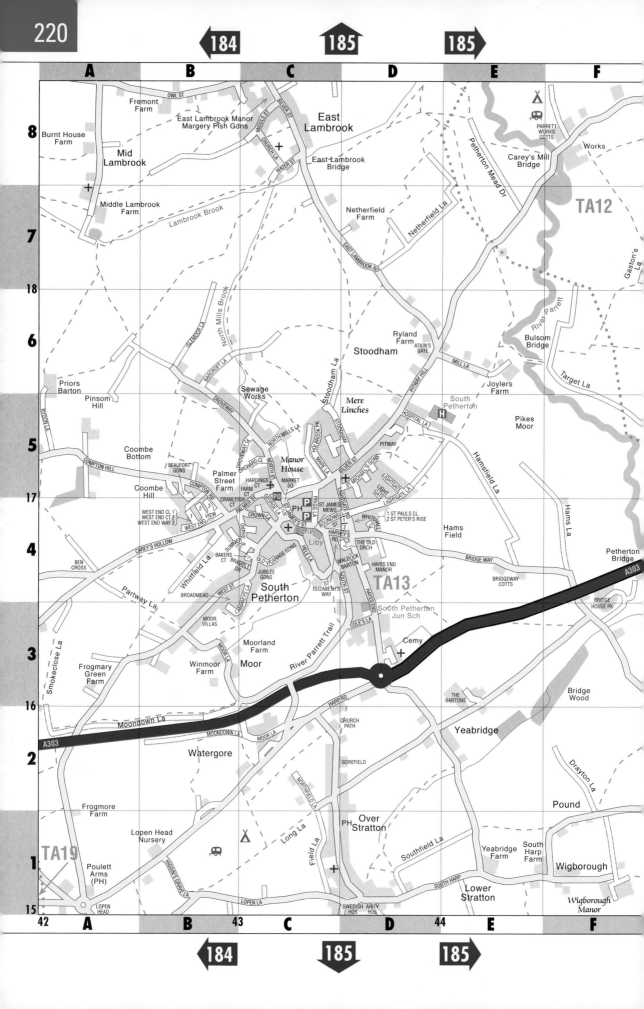

A **B** **C** **D** **E** **F**

8

Burnt House Farm

Fremont Farm

OWL ST

Mid Lambrook

East Lambrook Manor Margery Fish Gdns

MIDDLE ST

SILVER ST

East Lambrook

CHURCH LA

WATER ST

East Lambrook Bridge

PARRETT WORKS COTTS

Petherton Mead Dr

Carey's Mill Bridge

Works

TA12

Middle Lambrook Farm

Lambrook Brook

7

Netherfield Farm

Netherfield La

EAST LAMBROOK RD

River Parrett

Gaston's La

18

North Mills Brook

Bulsom Bridge

6

Priors Barton

Pinsom Hill

BARCROFT LA

ISEMOOR LA

DROVEWAY

Sewage Works

Stoodham La

Ryland Farm

ATKIN'S GATE

Stoodham

MILL LA

PITWAY HILL

Joylers Farm

Target La

Pikes Moor

South Petherton

H

5

Coombe Bottom

COMPTON HILL

NORTH MILLS LA

DROVEWAY

ORCHARD CL

Manor House

HOLYROOD LA

MARE LA

STOODHAM

SILVER ST

HOSPITAL LA

PITWAY

PITWAY

ST MICHAEL'S GDNS

LIGHTGATE

Hamsfield La

Hams La

17

BEAUFORT GDNS

Coombe Hill

COMPTON RD

Palmer Street Farm

HARDINGS FARM CT

CRANLEIGH CT

FARM CT

MARKET SQ

PALMER ST

GEORGE LA

PO

ST JAMES ST

PRIGG LA

P P

LIGHTGATE LA

LIGHTGATE

LIGHT GATE

ST JAMES MEWS

1 ST PAULS CL
2 ST PETER'S RISE

Hams Field

WEST END CL 1
WEST END CT 2
WEST END WAY 3

1 2 3 VIEW

WEST END

CHURCH ST

CROWN LA

PH

Sch

ROUNDWELL ST

WHITEHALL

WHITE HALL CT

4

BEN CROSS

CAREY'S HOLLOW

Whitfield La

SUMMER LA

BAKERS CT

BRAMBLE DR

OLD VICARAGE GDNS

HELE LA

Liby

HARVEY'S RD

THE OLD ORCH

WALDOCK BARTON

Hayes End Manor

HAYES END

ST ELIZABETH'S WAY

BRIDGE WAY

BRIDGEWAY COTTS

Petherton Bridge

A303

BRIDGE HOUSE PK

Partway La

BROADMEAD

WEST ST

CAMPRE'S LA

JUBILEE GDNS

South Petherton

TA13

South Petherton Jun Sch

COLE'S LA

3

Smokeclose La

Frogmary Green Farm

Winmoor Farm

MOOR LA

Moor

MOOR VILLAS

Moorland Farm

River Parrett Trail

Cemy

THE BARTONS

Bridge Wood

16

Moondown La

MOONDOWN LA

MOOR LA

HARP RD

CHURCH PATH

Yeabridge

2

A303

Watergore

NORTHFIELD LA

GOREFIELD

Drayton La

Pound

Frogmore Farm

Lopen Head Nursery

HIGGIN'S GRAVE LA

Long La

Field La

PH

Over Stratton

Southfield La

Yeabridge Farm

South Harp Farm

Wigborough

1

TA19

Poulett Arms (PH)

LOPEN LA

SWEDISH HOS

ABBEY HO

SOUTH HARP

Lower Stratton

Wigborough Manor

15

Lopen Head

42 **A** **B** **43** **C** **D** **44** **E** **F**

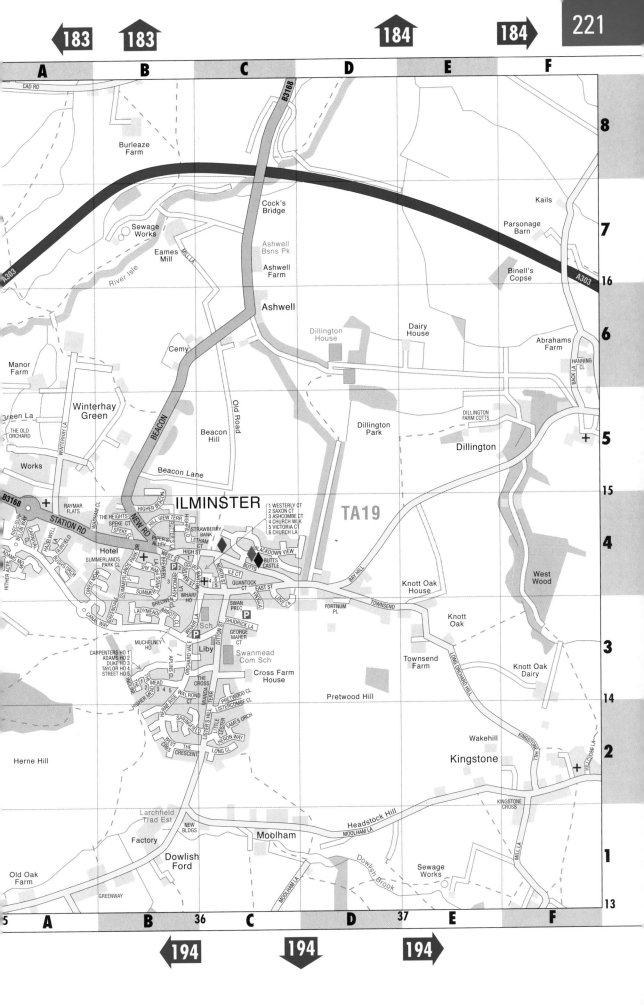

CAD RD

B3168

Burleaze Farm

Cock's Bridge

Kails

Parsonage Barn

A303

Sewage Works

Eames Mill

MILL LA

River Isle

Ashwell Bsns Pk

Ashwell Farm

Binell's Copse

A303

16

8

7

Ashwell

Dillington House

Dairy House

Abrahams Farm

6

Cemy

HANNING CL

BACK LA

Manor Farm

Winterhay Green

WINTERHAY LA

Green La

THE OLD ORCHARD

Old Road

Beacon Hill

Dillington Park

Dillington FARM COTTS

Dillington

✝

5

BEACON

Works

Beacon Lane

15

B3168

RIEC SUR BELON WAY

CARNIVAL
HAZELWELL LA
FAIRFIELD

ADAMS MD

HITHER ACRE

STATION RD

RAYMAR FLATS

THE HEIGHTS
SPEKE CT

WADHAM CL

HIGHER BEACON

HILL VIEW TERR

NEW RD

SUMMERLANDS PARK CL

SUMMERLANDS PARK AV

SUMMERLANDS PARK DR

SUMMER...

LOWER MDW

GREENDALE

ABBOTS CL

LADYMEADE

THE...

HIGH ST

WEST ST
BREWERY

HIGHFIELD
RUTTERS

PIPER'S ALLEY

Strawberry Bank
LETHAM CT

NORTH ST

BARTON

ILE CT

COURT...

BUTTS

BLACKDOWN VIEW

BUTTS CASTLE

ILMINSTER

1 WESTERLY CT
2 SAXON CT
3 ASHCOMBE CT
4 CHURCH WLK
5 VICTORIA CT
6 CHURCH LA

TA19

West Wood

4

Hotel

✝

P

P

QUANTOCK CT

EAST ST

FRY LA

LOVE LA

WHARF HO

FORTNUM PL

TOWNSEND

Knott Oak House

BAY HILL

Knott Oak

SWAN PREC

SHUDRICK LA

GEORGE MAHER CT

3

MUCHELNEY HO

APLINS CL

ORCHARD VALE

DITTON LA

WHARF LA

Sch

Liby

Swanmead Com Sch

Cross Farm House

Townsend Farm

Knott Oak Dairy

LONG ORCHARD HILL

CARPENTERS HO 1
ADAMS HO 2
DUKE HO 3
TAYLOR HO 4
STREET HO 5

THE INCLINE
HIGHER MD

THE
MEAD
3 4 5

WAL ROND CT

THE CROSS

MIRANDA
TERR

Pretwood Hill

PRETWOOD CL

LISTERCOMBE CL

KINGSTONE HILL

14

HERNE RISE

SPRINGFIELD

LISTER'S HILL

LITTLE LESTER

HERON WAY

EAMES ORCH

Wakehill

Kingstone

2

Herne Hill

WEST CRES

THE CRESCENT

LONG CL

HILLCLOSE LA

✝

KINGSTONE CROSS

Larchfield Trad Est

NEW BLDGS

Moolham

Headstock Hill

MOOLHAM LA

MILL LA

1

Factory

Dowlish Ford

GREENWAY

MOOLHAM LA

Dowlish Brook

Sewage Works

Old Oak Farm

13

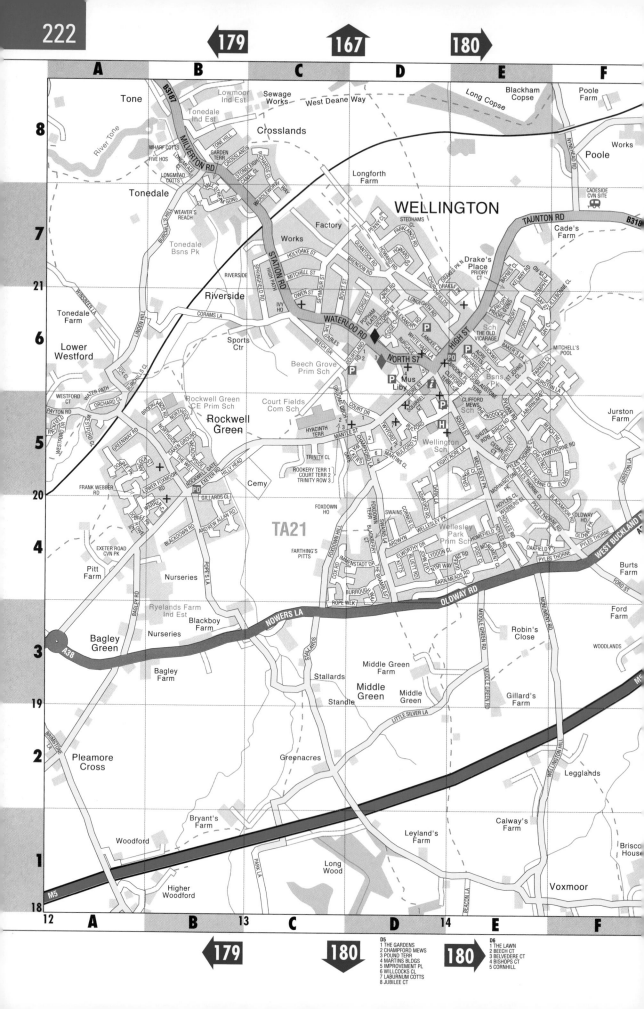

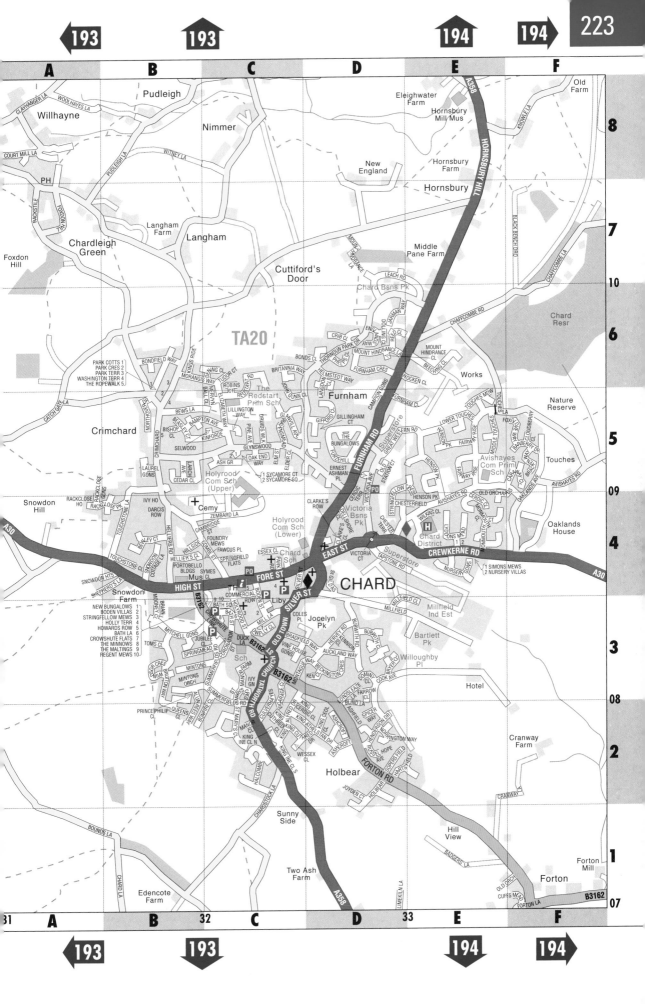

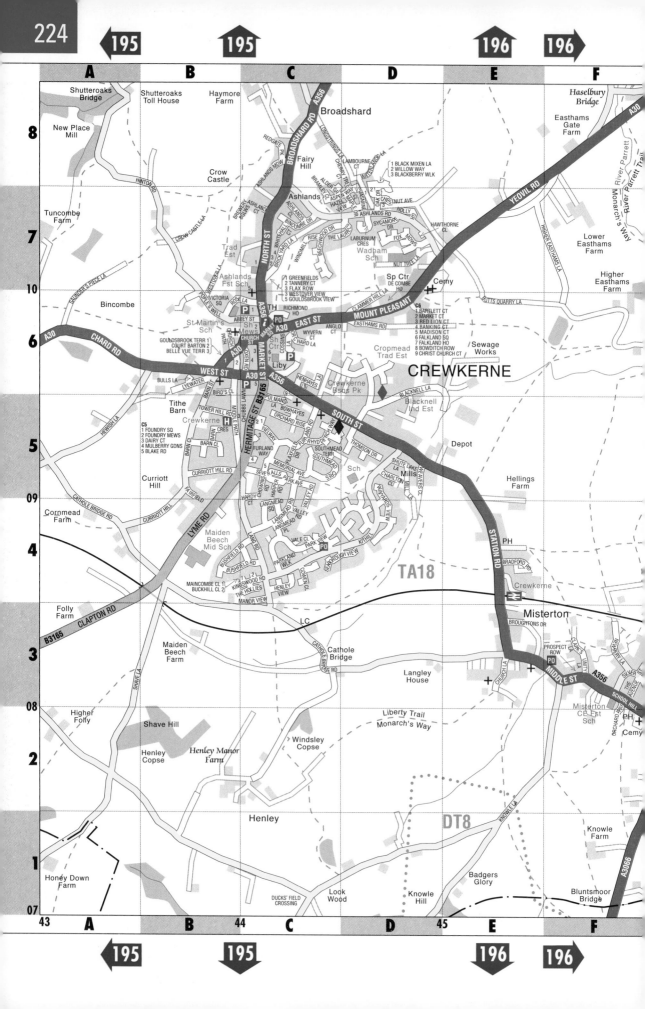

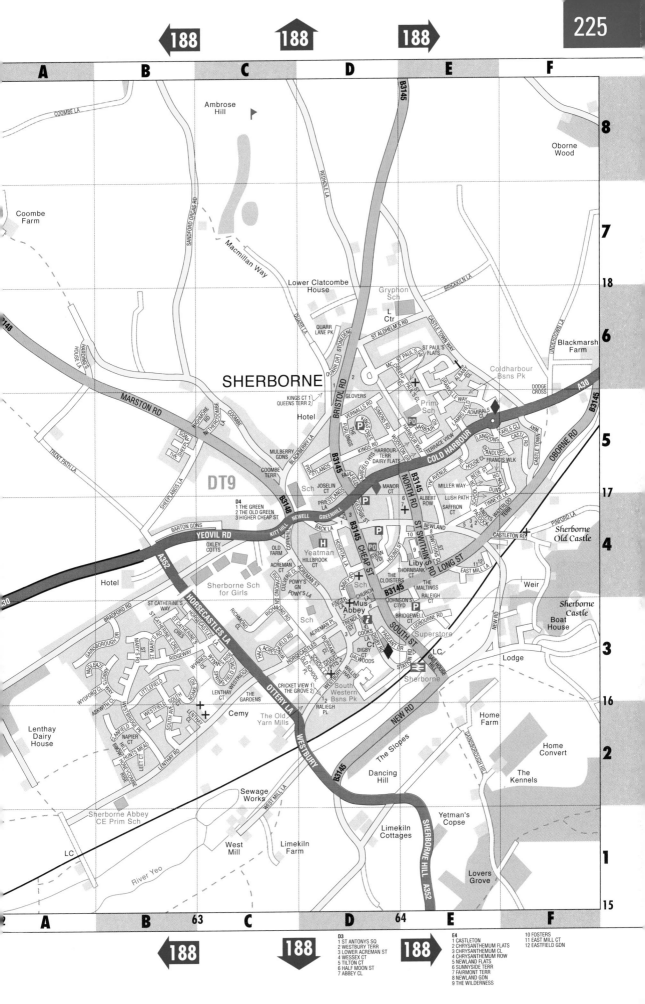

8
7
18
6
5
17
4
3
16
2
1
15

SHERBORNE

DT9

COOMBE LA
Coombe Farm
Ambrose Hill
Macmillan Way
Lower Clatcombe House
B3145
Oborne Wood
Blackmarsh Farm
SANDFORD ORCAS RD
REDHILL LA
QUARR LA
QUARR DRI
STONEHENGE
Gryphon Sch
L Ctr
BRICKKILN LA
UNDERDOWN LA
A148
HARDING'S
HOUSE LA
MARSTON RD
ST ALDHELM'S RD
MC.CREERY RD
ST PAUL'S
St PAUL'S FLATS
ALBANY
CASTLE TOWN WAY
Coldharbour Bsns Pk
DODGE CROSS
A30
B3145
OBORNE RD
TRENT PATH LA
SHEEPLANDS LA
BIGTHROPE RD
McHERCOMBE RD
COOMBE
BLACKBERRY LA
THE SHEPL...
SON
A
THE SHEPL
MULBERRY GDNS
COOMBE TERR
PRI...LANDS
Sch
JOSELIN CT
PRIESTLY LA
GREENHILL
BRISTOL RD
VERNALLS RD
SIMONS RD
KINGS CRES
WOOTTON RD
AIRFIELD HTS
KINGS RD
HARBOUR WA
HARBOUR TERR
DAIRY FLATS
Hotel
KINGS CT 1
QUEENS TERR 2
GLOVERS
THE FURLONGS
Prim Sch
GRANVILLE WAY
LAMBS FIELD
ADMIRALS
TERRACE VIEW
COLD HARBOUR
LANGDONS
HOUSE CT
KEY AVENUE
BEDE ST
MILLER WAY
LUSH PATH
SAFFRON
FRANCIS WLK
LANGDONS
EARLS CL
CASTLE RD
CASTLE TOWN WAY
DUNS
KNOTTS PADDOCK
WATERLOO
TINNEYS LA
PINFORD LA
CASTLETON RD
Sherborne Old Castle
MANOR CT
NORTH RD
ALBERT ROW
NEWLAND
ST SWITHINS RD
SWAN
HOUND ST
LONG ST
ST SWITHIN'S RD
THORNBANK
EAST MILL LA
THE CLOISTERS
RALEIGH CT
THE MALTINGS
JOHNSON'S CTYD
BRIDGEWELL CT
LUDBOURNE RD
SOUTH ST
NEW RD
Sherborne Castle
Boat House
Weir
Sherborne Castle
Lodge
Home Farm
Home Convert
The Kennels
Yetman's Copse
Lovers Grove
Limekiln Cottages
SHERBORNE HILL A352
GAINSBOROUGH HILL
Superstore
LC
Sherborne
PAGEANT DR
STATION RD
NEW RD
WESTBURY
B3145
The Slopes
Dancing Hill
Limekiln Farm
West Mill
LC
River Yeo
WEST MILL LA
Sewage Works
Sherborne Abbey CE Prim Sch
West Mill
The Old Yarn Mills
Cemy
Lenthay Dairy House
Lenthay CT
The Gardens
South Western Bsns Pk
CRICKET VIEW 1
THE GROVE 2
RALEIGH PL
OTTERY LA
HORSECASTLES LA
A352
YEOVIL RD
MARSTON RD
A30
Hotel
Sherborne Sch for Girls
BARTON GDNS
KITT HILL
NEWELL
CORNHILL
OLD FARM
ACREMAN
CULVERS CL
GREENHILL
RICHMOND GRN
RICHMOND RD
POWY'S GN
POWY'S LA
Sch
ACREMAN PL
DURHAM CT
GRANVILLE
OLD SCHOOL LA
COOKS LANE
HORSECASTLES
WESTBURY
South
DIGBY
DALWOODS
PAGEANT DR
BRADFORD RD
ST CATHERINE'S WAY
GAINSBOROUGH RD
MARY'S RD
ST CATHERINE'S CRES
ST LATHERINE'S CRES
RIDGEWAY
WYNNES CT
SPRING WESTBRIDGE
ST MARY'S
MAPLEAZE
WYFORD CT
ASKWITH RD
SOUTH AVE
HONEYCOMBE
BRUNT
HUNT'S MEAD
LEFT CT
LENTHAY RD
NAPIER CT
CLANFIELD PK
LITTLEFIELD
WESTFIELD RD
WESTFIELD
WESTBRIDGE PK
MONKS CL
LENTHAY CT
BROWN
B3148
B3145
NORTH RD
MANOR CT
CHEAP ST
HOSPITAL LA
GEORGE ST
ACREMAN ST
BACK LA
Yeatman
HILLBROOK CT
H
Liby
Mus
Abbey
i
Sch
PRIESTLY LA
FINGER LA
TRENDLE ST
ABBEY
SWAN
Sch
COLDHARBOUR
PO
PO
P
P
P
P
PO
Sch
GREAVES
WILLIS
CASTLE RD

D4
1 THE GREEN
2 THE OLD GREEN
3 HIGHER CHEAP ST

D3
1 ST ANTONYS SQ
2 WESTBURY TERR
3 LOWER ACREMAN ST
4 WESSEX CT
5 TILTON CT
6 HALF MOON ST
7 ABBEY CL

E4
1 CASTLETON
2 CHRYSANTHEMUM FLATS
3 CHRYSANTHEMUM CL
4 CHRYSANTHEMUM ROW
5 NEWLAND FLATS
6 SUNNYSIDE TERR
7 FAIRMONT TERR
8 NEWLAND GDN
9 THE WILDERNESS
10 FOSTERS
11 EAST MILL CT
12 EASTFIELD GDN

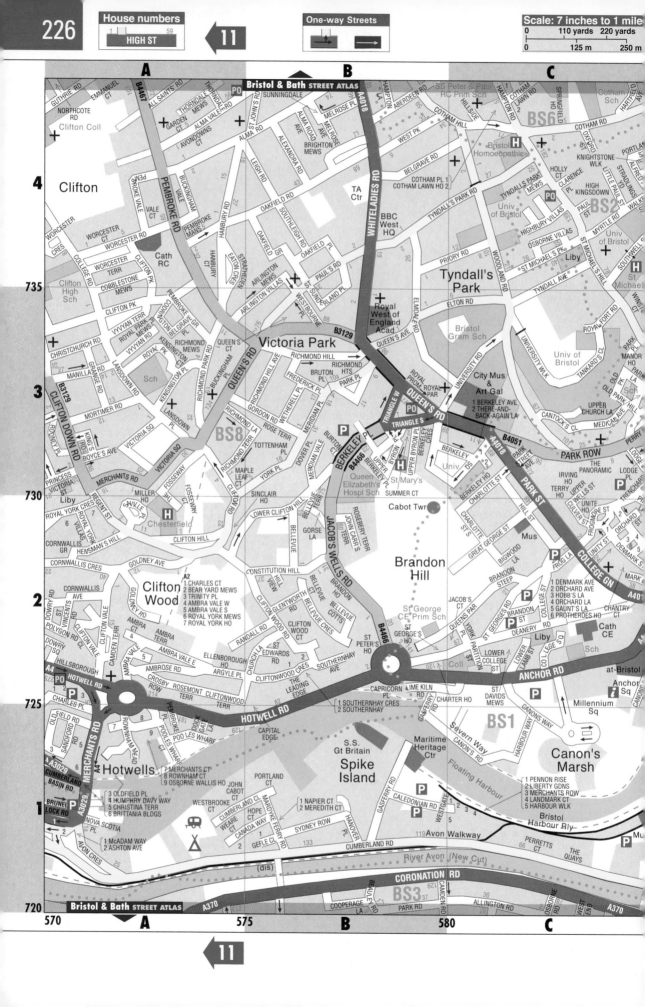

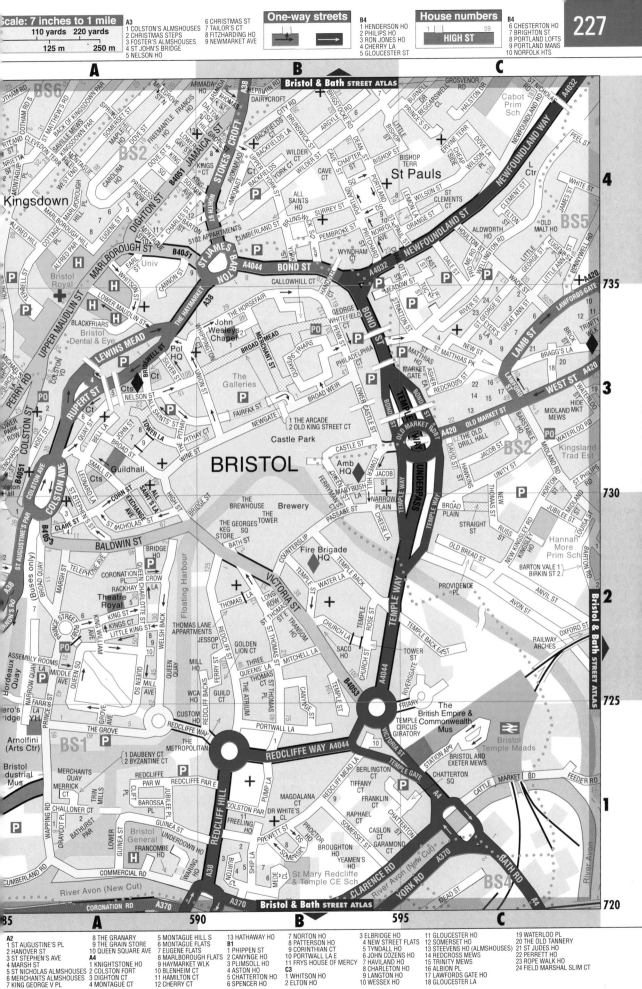

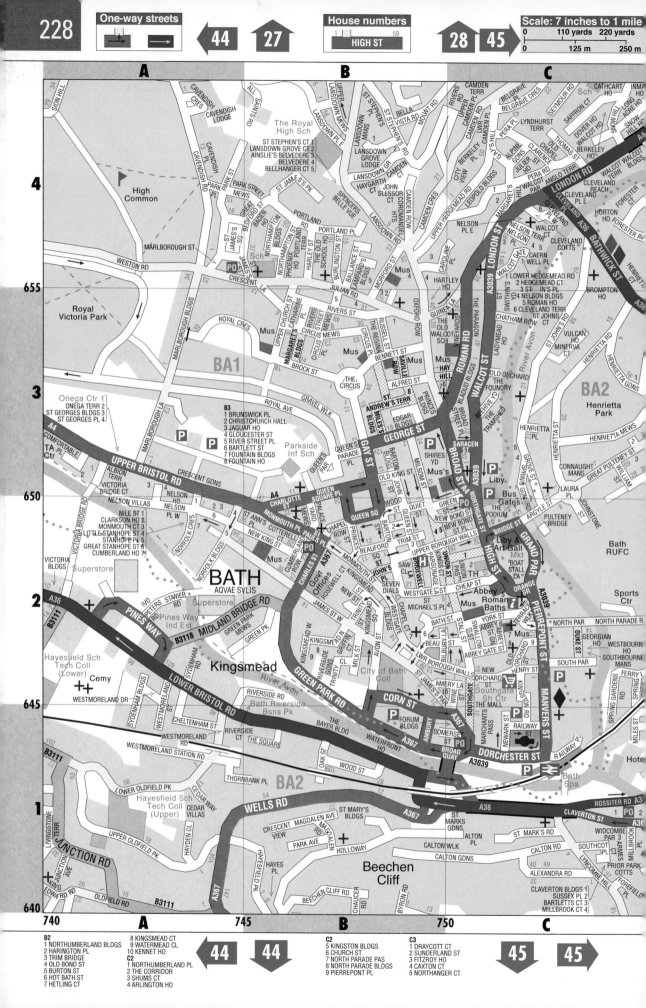

Index

Place name May be abbreviated on the map	→ Church Rd **6** Beckenham BR2..........**53** C6
Location number Present when a number indicates the place's position in a crowded area of mapping	
Locality, town or village Shown when more than one place has the same name	
Postcode district District for the indexed place	
Page and grid square Page number and grid reference for the standard mapping	

Public and commercial buildings are highlighted in magenta   **Places of interest** are highlighted in blue with a star★

Abbreviations used in the index

Acad	**Academy**	Comm	**Common**	Gd	**Ground**	L	**Leisure**	Prom	**Promenade**
App	**Approach**	Cott	**Cottage**	Gdn	**Garden**	La	**Lane**	Rd	**Road**
Arc	**Arcade**	Cres	**Crescent**	Gn	**Green**	Liby	**Library**	Recn	**Recreation**
Ave	**Avenue**	Cswy	**Causeway**	Gr	**Grove**	Mdw	**Meadow**	Ret	**Retail**
Bglw	**Bungalow**	Ct	**Court**	H	**Hall**	Meml	**Memorial**	Sh	**Shopping**
Bldg	**Building**	Ctr	**Centre**	Ho	**House**	Mkt	**Market**	Sq	**Square**
Bsns, Bus	**Business**	Ctry	**Country**	Hospl	**Hospital**	Mus	**Museum**	St	**Street**
Bvd	**Boulevard**	Cty	**County**	HQ	**Headquarters**	Orch	**Orchard**	Sta	**Station**
Cath	**Cathedral**	Dr	**Drive**	Hts	**Heights**	Pal	**Palace**	Terr	**Terrace**
Cir	**Circus**	Dro	**Drove**	Ind	**Industrial**	Par	**Parade**	TH	**Town Hall**
Cl	**Close**	Ed	**Education**	Inst	**Institute**	Pas	**Passage**	Univ	**University**
Cnr	**Corner**	Emb	**Embankment**	Int	**International**	Pk	**Park**	Wk, Wlk	**Walk**
Coll	**College**	Est	**Estate**	Intc	**Interchange**	Pl	**Place**	Wr	**Water**
Com	**Community**	Ex	**Exhibition**	Junc	**Junction**	Prec	**Precinct**	Yd	**Yard**

Index of localities, towns and villages

A

Abbas Combe.......... 176 E1
Abbey Hill 182 E5
Abbots Leigh 11 A8
Adam's Green......... 197 D2
Adber 187 F7
Adderwell 120 A3
Adsborough 169 D8
Adscombe 152 A8
Aisholt 152 B6
Alcombe
  Kingsdown.............. 29 F7
  Minehead............. 201 A4
Aldwick 54 D7
Alford 159 A3
Alhampton 159 C6
Aller 171 D8
Allerford
  Porlock 124 C4
  Taunton 167 F4
Allowenshay 195 A8
All Saints 198 A4
Alston 198 A5
Alston Sutton 88 F3
Alvington 218 B4
Alweston 189 A1
Amesbury 59 F2
Ammerham 199 A8
Andersfield 153 B5
Angersleigh 181 C5
Ansford 214 C6
Appledore 179 A1
Appley 179 B8
Ash
  Martock............. 185 F7
  Taunton 169 E1
Ashbeer 150 C6
Ashbrittle 178 F8
Ashcott 156 B8
Ashculme 180 C1
Ashgrove 79 D8
Ashill................ 183 B4
Ashington 187 B8
Ash Priors 167 C8
Ashton 107 E8
Ashton Gate 11 F4
Ashton Vale 11 F2
Ashwell 221 C6
Ashwick 115 B5
Asney 156 E7
Atherstone 184 C3
Avoncliff 64 F4
Avonmouth 4 B8
Axbridge 70 B1

Axminster 198 B2
Ayshford 178 E2

B

Babcary 174 C7
Backwell 19 B6
Backwell Common 19 B8
Backwell Green 19 D8
Badbury 183 F7
Badger Street......... 182 B6
Bagley............... 109 A1
Bagley Green 222 A3
Bailbrook............. 28 D3
Baltonsborough....... 158 A6
Bampton 164 C1
Banwell 51 B3
Bare Ash 153 B6
Barr................. 168 B3
Barren Down 205 C4
Barrington 184 D5
Barrow
  Wells 140 B4
  Wincanton 161 B3
Barrow Common 21 B4
Barrow Gurney......... 20 E5
Barrow Vale 59 D5
Barton 69 B6
Barton St David 158 A2
Barwick 197 F8
Batch 66 F3
Batcombe 142 D1
Bath................. 228 A2
Bathampton 28 F1
Bathealton 166 B3
Batheaston 28 F4
Bathford 29 C1
Bathpool 213 E6
Bathway 94 E5
Bathwick 45 B7
Batten's Green 182 F5
Battleborough 86 C1
Bawdrip 136 E2
Bayford 216 F5
Beacon Hill 27 F1
Beard Hill 141 C3
Beardly Batch........ 205 C1
Bear Flat 44 F4
Beckery 206 B4
Beckington 101 E4
Bedlam 119 B8
Bedminster Down....... 22 B8
Beechen Cliff 228 B1
Beggearn Huish....... 131 E2

Belle Vue............. 78 B3
Belluton.............. 40 D6
Benter............... 115 D7
Berkley.............. 121 A7
Berkley Down......... 120 C5
Berkley Marsh 120 F7
Berrow 84 E5
Bettiscombe 199 E2
Bickenhall 182 E5
Bicknoller 132 F2
Biddisham 87 E8
Bilbrook............. 131 C4
Bincombe 134 A2
Binegar 114 C2
Birchill 198 A5
Birchwood 182 A1
Birdsmoorgate........ 199 D4
Bishop's Hull 212 A4
Bishops Lydeard 167 F8
Bishop Sutton 57 D3
Bishopswood 192 F7
Bishopsworth 22 A5
Bitton 25 E7
Blackdown 199 D6
Blackford
  Minehead............ 129 E8
  Wedmore............. 107 E4
  Wincanton 175 F5
Blackmoor
  Chew Stoke 38 C3
  Churchill 53 D6
  Wellington 180 E5
Blackpool Corner 198 D1
Blackrock 40 E8
Blackwater 182 C2
Blackwell 165 B5
Blagdon 54 E2
Blagdon Hill 181 D5
Blatchbridge 143 F8
Bleadney 139 A8
Bleadon 67 C7
Bloomfield
  Bath 44 E3
  Timsbury 60 B4
Blue Anchor 131 B6
Bodden 205 F7
Bolham Water 191 B7
Bossington 124 B4
Bourne 54 B4
Bourton
  Gillingham 161 F1
  Weston-super-Mare .. 32 E6
Bowden 177 F2
Bower Ashton 11 E4
Bower Hinton 185 D5
Bowlish 205 A7

Bradford Abbas 187 E1
Bradford on Tone 167 F1
Bradley Green 135 B1
Bradney 136 D1
Bramwell 172 B8
Brandish Street 124 C3
Brandon Hill 226 B2
Brassknocker 45 F2
Bratton 200 B7
Bratton Seymour 176 C8
Breach 58 F6
Brean 65 F5
Brendon 122 A4
Brent Knoll 86 A1
Bridge 199 A8
Bridgehampton 174 C3
Bridgetown 147 E4
Bridgwater 208 D4
Brimley 198 D3
Brindham 139 D3
Brinscombe 89 A5
Brinsea 52 E8
Bristol............. 227 B3
Brittens 77 F6
Broadway 183 B2
Brockfield 198 A8
Brockley 18 C2
Brockwell 129 E6
Brokerswood 102 F5
Brompton Ralph 150 C3
Brompton Regis 148 B2
Brookhampton 175 D6
Broomfield 152 E2
Brownheath 180 C2
Brushford 163 D4
Bruton 215 E5
Brympton D'Evercy .. 218 A3
Buckhorn Weston 177 D3
Buckland Dinham 100 A3
Buckland Down 99 B4
Buckland St Mary ... 192 F8
Bulford 182 C4
Bull's Green 117 E1
Burcott 139 E8
Burford 204 C2
Burlands 168 C6
Burlescombe 179 B3
Burnett 42 B7
Burnham-on-Sea 104 D8
Burrington 53 D2
Burrow 184 F6
Burrowbridge 154 F1
Burtle 137 D6
Burton
  Stogursey 134 B7
  Yeovil 197 C8

Bury................. 164 A6
Buscott............. 138 C1
Bushey Norwood....... 45 F6
Bussex 154 F6
Butcombe 55 B8
Butleigh 157 D4
Butleigh Wotton 157 C5
Butt's Batch 35 D1

C

Cad Green............ 183 E3
Cambridge Batch 20 C8
Cameley.............. 76 C8
Camerton............. 78 E8
Cannard's Grave 205 D2
Cannington 135 C2
Cannon's Marsh 226 C1
Capland 183 A6
Capton 132 C2
Carhampton 131 B5
Carlingcott 61 B1
Cary Fitzpaine 174 B6
Castle 198 D4
Castle Cary 214 B5
Catcott 137 D2
Catsgore 173 C4
Chaffcombe 194 C5
Chalkway 194 E2
Chantry 117 F3
Chapel Allerton 88 D2
Chapel Cleeve 131 D5
Chapel Leigh 167 A8
Chapmanslade 121 C5
Chard 223 D4
Chard Junction 198 E7
Chardleigh Green ... 223 A7
Chardstock 198 B7
Charlcombe 27 E3
Charlton
  Creech St Michael .. 169 F5
  Radstock 97 E5
  Shepton Mallet 205 E5
Charlton Adam....... 173 F7
Charlton Horethorne . 176 B2
Charlton Mackrell .. 173 E7
Charlton Musgrove... 161 A2
Charlynch 152 F8
Charterhouse 72 C4
Cheddar 90 D8
Cheddon Fitzpaine .. 169 A6
Chedzoy 154 E8
Chelston............ 180 D8
Chelston Heathfield. 180 E7
Chelvey 18 D5

Chelwood 59 A8
Chelynch 141 E6
Chesterblade 142 A4
Chew Magna 39 C4
Chew Stoke 56 D8
Chewton Keynsham . . . 24 E2
Chewton Mendip 94 E7
Chilcombe 132 F1
Chilcompton 96 C4
Chilson 198 C6
Chilson Common 198 D7
Chilthorne Domer 186 E5
Chilton Cantelo 174 D1
Chilton Polden 137 B2
Chilton Trinity 135 F2
Chipley 166 F2
Chipstable 165 E4
Chiselborough 185 F1
Cholwell 58 D2
Christon 68 D7
Churchill 52 F5
Churchill Green 52 D5
Churchinford 192 A7
Church Row 101 F8
Churchstanton 181 B1
Church Town 19 C5
Clandown 78 E4
Clanville 159 C3
Clapton
  Crewkerne 195 C1
  Midsomer Norton 96 C7
Clapton In Gordano 2 E1
Clapton Wick 7 E6
Clarkham Cross 197 E2
Clatworthy 149 F1
Claverham 17 E1
Claverton 46 B5
Claverton Down 45 F3
Clayhanger 165 C1
Clayhidon 180 E2
Claypits 164 C4
Clays End 43 D6
Clearwood 121 F8
Cleeve 35 B8
Clevedon 6 B3
Clewer 89 D3
Clifton 226 A4
Clifton Wood 226 A2
Clink 120 C6
Cloford 143 C7
Cloford Common 143 B6
Closworth 197 F5
Clutton 58 E3
Clutton Hill 59 B4
Coat 185 D7
Cocklake 108 E7
Cockwood 134 E5
Cold Ashton 12 F6
Coleford 116 F7
Coleford Water 150 F4
Cole's Cross 199 D5
Coley 75 C4
Combe Down 45 B1
Combe Florey 151 C2
Combe Hay 62 D4
Combe Hill 217 A4
Combe St Nicholas . . . 193 D6
Combe Throop 176 F2
Combwich 135 B5
Comeytrowe 212 B1
Compton Bishop 69 A3
Compton Dando 41 D6
Compton Dundon 157 B4
Compton Durville 184 F4
Compton Martin 74 A7
Compton Pauncefoot . . 175 E5
Congresbury 34 E4
Conkwell 46 C1
Coombe
  Crewkerne 195 B4
  Sampford Peverell . . . 178 A4
  Taunton 169 C8
Coombe Dingle 5 C8
Coppleham 147 D5
Corfe 181 F6
Corsley 121 D2
Corsley Heath 144 B7
Corston 43 B7
Corton Denham 175 D1
Cossington 136 F3
Cotford St Luke 167 E6
Cothelstone 152 A2
Cottle's Oak 119 C5
Coultings 134 F4
Courshay 198 E3
Coursley 151 B4
Courtway 152 C4
Cowbridge 130 B5
Cowslip Green 54 B8
Coxley 139 F6
Coxley Wick 139 E7
Cox's Green 35 E1
Cranmore 142 B6
Crawley 192 F2
Creech Heathfield 169 E5
Creech St Michael 169 D4
Crewkerne 224 D6
Cricket Malherbie 194 D6
Cricket St Thomas . . . 194 E3
Crickham 108 D8
Crimchard 223 B5
Critchill 119 C3
Crocombe 60 C3
Crofton Park 219 B6
Croscombe 204 B8
Cross 69 E2
Crosslands 222 C8
Crowcombe 151 C7

Cucklington 177 D6
Cudworth 194 E5
Culbone 123 B5
Culm Davy 180 A2
Culverhays 132 F1
Curland 182 D4
Curland Common 182 D4
Curload 170 E7
Curry Mallet 183 C8
Curry Rivel 171 C4
Cushuish 152 B1
Cutcombe 129 F2
Cutler's Green 94 F4
Cuttiford's Door 223 C7

D

Darshill 204 F6
Deacons 168 C7
Dean 142 B7
Dertfords 144 D8
Dillington 221 E5
Dimmer 159 C3
Dinder 140 D7
Dinghurst 52 E4
Dinnington 195 B7
Ditcheat 159 C7
Dodhill 168 D7
Doddington 133 F3
Dolebury 53 B5
Dolemeads 45 B5
Dommett 182 D1
Doniford 202 F6
Donyatt 183 D1
Doulting 141 E6
Doverhay 124 B3
Dowlish Ford 221 B1
Dowlish Wake 194 E7
Downhead
  Stoke St Michael 142 C8
  Yeovilton 174 C4
Downside
  Chilcompton 96 C1
  Felton 19 D1
  Shepton Mallet 205 D8
Dowslands 168 F1
Doynton 12 A8
Draycott
  Cheddar 90 E2
  Yeovil 187 B8
Drayton
  Curry Rival 171 E3
  Southerton 185 D3
Drimpton 199 F7
Dry Hill 2 C6
Duddlestone 181 F8
Dulcote 140 C7
Dulverton 163 E6
Dunball 136 A3
Dundon 156 F3
Dundon Hayes 156 E3
Dundry 21 D2
Dundry Hill 23 B3
Dunkerton 61 E4
Dunster 201 E2
Dunwear 209 D1
Durleigh 208 B3
Durnfield 186 B7
Durston 169 F6

E

East Anstey 162 E5
East Bower 209 E6
East Brent 86 D5
Eastbrook 168 L1
East Chinnock 196 E8
East Clevedon 6 F3
East Coker 197 D7
East Combe 151 E2
East Compton 205 A2
East Cranmore 142 C6
East Dundry 22 A1
East End
  Blagdon 54 F2
  Chewton Mendip 94 E4
  Nailsea 9 A1
  South Cadbury 175 D4
  Stoke St Michael 116 C2
Eastertown 67 D2
East Harptree 74 E4
East Hewish 33 B6
Easthill 120 B4
East Huntspill 136 E7
East Knowstone 162 B2
East Lambrook 220 C8
East Lydford 158 D2
East Lyng 170 D8
East Nynehead 167 D2
Easton 111 A4
Easton-in-Gordano 4 A4
Eastover 209 B5
East Pennard 158 F8
East Quantoxhead . . . 133 B6
East Rolstone 33 B1
East Stoke 186 A4
East Street 139 F1
East Town
  Lydeard St Lawrence . 150 E3
  Shepton Mallet 141 A3
East Twerton 44 D7
East Water 92 F2
East Woodlands 144 A7
Ebdon 32 B6
Edford 116 C7
Edgarley 139 C1
Edgcott 128 C1

Edington 137 C3
Edingworth 86 F7
Edithmead 104 F7
Egford 119 B5
Ellicombe 201 C4
Elliots Green 144 B8
Elworthy 150 C6
Emborough 95 C3
Englishcombe 43 F7
Enmore 153 A6
Escott 150 C8
Evercreech 141 E1
Exebridge 163 F3
Exford 128 C1
Exton 147 E4
Eyewell 174 E4

F

Failand 10 C3
Fairfield Park 28 A2
Farleigh 19 D7
Farleigh Hungerford . . . 82 E8
Farleigh Wick 46 E4
Farley 1 B1
Farmborough 60 B6
Farrington Gurney 77 A3
Faulkland 80 E2
Felton 37 C8
Fennington 168 B8
Fenny Castle 139 D7
Fiddington 134 D3
Field 205 C5
Fifehead Magdalen . . . 190 F8
Filwood Park 22 E8
Firepool 213 A5
Fishpond Bottom 199 A1
Fitzhead 166 F7
Fitzroy 168 A6
Five Bells 202 B5
Fivehead 170 F2
Flax Bourton 19 F7
Flaxpool 151 C6
Foddington 174 E8
Ford
  Chewton Mendip 94 E8
  Holcombe Rogus 178 F5
  Wiveliscombe 210 F6
Fordgate 154 C3
Ford Street 180 D5
Forton 223 F1
Four Forks 152 F8
Foxcote 79 F4
Fox Hill 45 A2
Fox Hills 79 A1
Freshford 64 B5
Friarn 133 F1
Frieze Hill 212 D5
Frome 119 E4
Fromefield 120 A6
Frost Hill 34 C6
Fulford 168 C8
Furnham 223 D5

G

Galhampton 175 D8
Galmington 212 C2
Garlandhayes 180 F2
Gasper 161 E4
Girt 175 C2
Glastonbury 206 F6
Goar Knapp 219 D5
Goathill 189 B4
Goathurst 153 B5
Godney 139 A5
Gold's Cross 57 E6
Golsoncott 131 D2
Goosenford 169 A6
Gore 187 F6
Gothelney Green 153 B8
Gotton 169 B7
Gould's Ground 119 E5
Great Elm 118 F7
Green Down 94 B8
Green Gate 178 B2
Greenham
  Drimpton 199 E7
  Wellington 179 B7
Greenhill 78 A3
Green Ore 94 C1
Green Parlour 79 D2
Greensbrook 58 F3
Greenvale 60 B1
Greenway 167 D8
Greinton 155 F7
Greylake 155 C4
Greylake Fosse 155 B6
Gribb 199 B6
Grosvenor 28 C1
Gupworthy 148 C6
Gurney Slade 114 F7

H

Hackness 136 D8
Hadspen 214 F6
Haines Hill 212 E2
Halcon 213 D5
Hale 177 D6
Hallatrow 77 B7
Halse 167 B6
Halstock 197 C3
Halsway 151 B8

Ham
  Creech St Michael 169 E4
  Holcombe 116 D6
  Paulton 77 F5
  Wellington 180 D8
Hambridge 184 D8
Ham Green 4 E1
Hamp 208 F2
Ham Street 158 B5
Hamwood 68 C2
Hapsford 119 B8
Hardington 99 E6
Hardington Mandeville . 197 A6
Hardington Marsh 196 F4
Hardington Moor 197 A7
Hardway 161 A5
Hare 182 F2
Hartcliffe 22 C4
Hartford 164 C8
Hartmoor 177 F3
Hartswell 210 B3
Haselbury Plucknett . . 196 C6
Hastings 183 B3
Hatch Beauchamp . . . 183 A7
Hatch Green 183 A6
Havyatt 157 F8
Havyatt Green 53 F7
Hawkchurch 198 E3
Hawkcombe 124 A3
Hawkridge 146 D1
Haybridge 203 A5
Haydon
  Milborne Port 189 B2
  Radstock 97 F8
  Taunton 213 E2
  Wells 113 D5
Hayes Park 78 A2
Headley Park 22 B6
Heale 142 C7
Heathfield 167 E5
Heath House 107 F1
Heaven's Door 188 A8
Hedging 170 A8
Hele 168 A3
Helland 170 C3
Hemington 99 B7
Hemyock 180 B1
Hengrove 23 B6
Henlade 169 D2
Henley 156 B3
Henstridge 190 A6
Henstridge Ash 189 F7
Henstridge Bowden . . 189 D7
Henstridge Marsh 190 C7
Henton 139 B8
Herons Green 56 C3
Hewish
  Crewkerne 195 D3
  Weston-super-Mare . . . 33 C5
Hicks Gate 24 B8
Highbridge 104 E3
Highbury 117 A7
Higher Alham 142 C4
Higher Burrow 184 E7
Higher Chillington . . . 194 F5
Higher Durston 169 E7
Higher Hadspen 214 E4
Higher Halstock Leigh . 197 A2
Higher Nyland 177 C1
Higher Odcombe 186 C2
Higher Sandford 188 C7
Higher Town 200 E8
Higher Vexford 150 E6
High Ham 156 A2
High Littleton 59 C1
Highridge
  Bristol 21 F7
  Dundry 21 D3
Highway 185 E7
Hill Corner 120 E6
Hill End 196 F6
Hillfarrance 167 E3
Hillside
  Axbridge 70 C2
  Midsomer Norton 96 E8
Hinton 187 D7
Hinton Blewett 75 D4
Hinton Charterhouse . . 63 E1
Hinton St George 195 D7
Hobb's Wall 59 E5
Hockholler 180 E8
Hockholler Green 180 E8
Hockworthy 178 D6
Hoggington 83 D4
Holbear 223 D2
Holcombe 116 C8
Holcombe Rogus 178 F5
Holford 133 D4
Hollands 219 A7
Hollow Brook 57 C6
Holly Brook 110 F5
Holman Clavel 181 E3
Holton 176 C5
Holway
  Sherborne 188 D7
  Taunton 213 C2
  Thorncombe 199 C6
Holwell 143 B8
Holywell 197 C8
Holywell Lake 179 E7
Honey Hall 52 C7
Hook
  Chard 198 B8
  Timsbury 60 D2
Hoopers Pool 83 D1
Horn Ash 199 D7
Hornblotton 158 F5
Horner 129 B8

Horningsham 144 C4
Hornsbury 223 E7
Horrington 113 A1
Horsecastle 17 A2
Horsey 136 C2
Horsington 176 D2
Horton 183 C1
Horton Cross 183 D2
Hotwells 226 A1
Houndsmoor 167 A4
Houndstone 218 A6
Hounsley Batch 38 A3
Howley 192 F4
Huish Champflower . . . 165 F8
Huish Episcopi 172 B5
Hungerford 131 E3
Hunstrete 41 D2
Huntscott 129 E6
Huntsham 178 A7
Huntspill 136 B8
Huntstile 153 C4
Huntworth 154 B5
Hurcott 173 C8
Hurst 185 D5
Hutton 49 E2

I

Icelton 32 C8
Ilchester 173 E1
Ilchester Mead 173 D1
Ilford 184 A4
Ilminster 221 C4
Ilton 183 E4
Inglesbatch 61 C8
Inman's Batch 38 A5
Innox Hill 119 F6
Isle Abbotts 183 F1
Isle Brewers 184 A8
Iwood 35 A3

K

Keenthorne 134 D2
Keinton Mandeville . . . 158 B1
Kelston 26 C3
Kenn 16 F7
Kenn Moor Gate 17 F4
Kenny 183 B4
Keward 203 C2
Kewstoke 31 B4
Keyford 119 F3
Keyford Field 119 F2
Keynsham 24 E3
Killing's Knap 97 B4
Kilmersdon 98 B5
Kilmington 161 F7
Kilmington Common . . 161 E6
Kilton 133 E6
Kilve 133 C6
Kingdown 37 D5
Kingsbridge 148 E8
Kingsbury Episcopi . . . 185 A8
Kingsbury Regis 217 D3
Kingsdon 173 E1
Kingsdown
  Box 29 E4
  Bristol 227 A4
Kingsmead 228 A2
Kingstone 221 E2
Kingston St Mary 168 E8
Kingston Seymour 16 C2
Kingsway 44 C3
Kingswood 150 E8
Kington Magna 177 E2
Kingweston 157 E2
Kitbridge 198 A6
Kittisford 166 B1
Kittwhistle 199 D6
Knapp 169 F4
Knightcott 50 F3
Knighton 184 D7
Knole 173 A4
Knowle 136 D2
Knowle St Giles 194 B6
Knowstone 162 A2

L

Lambridge 28 C2
Lamyatt 159 F6
Lane End 144 D8
Langaller 169 C6
Langford 212 A6
Langford Budville 166 E2
Langham
  Chard 223 C2
  Gillingham 177 F4
Langley 210 C6
Langley Marsh 210 A7
Langport 172 B5
Langridge 27 E2
Lansdown
  Bath 27 E1
  Langridge 27 B6
Larkhall 28 C2
Latcham 108 F4
Lattiford 176 D5
Launcherley 140 B5
Laverley 140 C2
Laverton 100 F7
Lawford 151 B7
Laymore 199 C7
Leeford 122 B5
Leighland Chapel 149 C7

Leighton 142 E6
Leigh upon Mendip 116 F3
Leigh Woods. 11 D6
Lewcombe 197 E2
Lilstock 133 F7
Limington 174 A1
Limpley Stoke 64 A6
Lipyeate 97 E1
Listock 170 C2
Little Green 118 B6
Little Hill 192 F8
Little Keyford 119 E1
Little London 114 F3
Little Norton 186 A2
Littleton 38 D4
Little Weston 175 B4
Litton 75 F2
Locking 50 A4
Locksbrook 44 B6
Lodway 4 B5
Longaller 168 B4
Long Ashton 11 A1
Longcroft 219 A8
Long Cross 37 D7
Longhedge 144 E7
Longhouse 61 D7
Long Load 172 E2
Long Sutton 172 F4
Lopen 185 A1
Lottisham 158 D5
Lovington 158 F1
Lower Aisholt 152 C6
Lower Burrow 184 F7
Lower Canada 49 F2
Lower Chilton Cantelo . 187 C8
Lower Claverham 17 F2
Lower Downside 205 C7
Lower Durston 169 F7
Lower Failand 10 A8
Lower Godney 138 F5
Lower Halstock Leigh . . 197 B2
Lower Harmswell 12 C3
Lower Holditch 198 D5
Lower Keyford 119 F3
Lower Langford 53 C5
Lower Leigh 207 C6
Lower Marston 143 E7
Lower Merridge. 152 C5
Lower Milton 203 B8
Lower Odcombe 186 D2
Lower Peasedown 79 B8
Lower Roadwater 131 D4
Lower Rudge 102 D4
Lower Somerton 211 E3
Lower Stratton 220 E1
Lower Strode 56 A8
Lower Swainswick 28 C3
Lower Tippacott 122 A4
Lower Vellow 132 D1
Lower Vexford 150 F6
Lower Weacombe 132 E4
Lower Weare 88 D8
Lower Westford 222 A6
Lower Westholme 140 C3
Lower Weston 44 C7
Lower Whatley 118 D3
Lower Woolston 175 F6
Lower Writhlington . . . 79 C3
Low Ham 172 B8
Lowton 181 B5
Low Water 119 E6
Loxton 68 C4
Luccombe 129 D7
Luckwell Bridge 129 C1
Ludney 194 F7
Lufton 186 D3
Lullington 101 A4
Lulsgate Bottom 37 A8
Luppitt 191 B1
Luxborough 148 E8
Luxton 192 A6
Lyatts 197 E3
Lydeard St Lawrence . . 151 B3
Lydford Fair Place 158 C3
Lydmarsh 194 C3
Lye Cross 36 C1
Lye Hole 36 E2
Lye's Green 121 B1
Lympsham 67 B1
Lyncombe Hill 45 A4
Lyncombe Vale 45 A3
Lynford-on-Fosse 158 C2
Lyng 170 C7
Lyngford 213 A7

M

Mackham 191 A4
Maiden Bradley 144 C1
Maidenbrook 213 D7
Maiden Head 21 F1
Malmsmead 122 C4
Maperton 176 B5
Mark 106 D4
Mark Causeway 106 A3
Marksbury 42 B1
Marnhull 190 F5
Marsh 192 E5
Marshall's Elm 207 D2
Marshalsea 199 C3
Marshfield 13 E8
Marsh Street 201 F3
Marshwood 199 C2
Marston Bigot 143 D7
Marston Gate 119 C1
Marston Magna 174 F1

Martock 185 D6
Maudlin 199 C8
Maundown 165 F7
May Pole Knap 211 C4
Meadgate East 60 E2
Meadgate West 60 D2
Meare 138 D4
Meare Green
  Hatch Beauchamp . . . 169 F1
  Stoke St Gregory 170 D5
Mearns 59 E2
Mells 118 B7
Mells Green 118 A6
Merridge 152 D5
Merriott 195 E7
Merriottsford 195 F7
Middle Burnham 104 D8
Middle Chinnock 196 C6
Middle Green 222 D3
Middle Leigh 207 C4
Middle Luxton 191 F5
Middle Stoughton 108 A8
Middlezoy 155 B3
Midford 63 C6
Mid Lambrook 220 A8
Midsomer Norton 78 B3
Midway 115 E2
Milborne Port 217 E2
Milborne Wick 217 B6
Millbrook 198 A1
Millhayes 180 C1
Millhouse 179 E1
Millwey Rise 198 A2
Milton
  Martock 185 E8
  Weston-Super-Mare . . . 31 C2
Milton Clevedon 160 A8
Milverton 166 F4
Minehead 201 A8
Misterton 224 E3
Monksilver 150 A8
Monkton Combe 45 F1
Monkton Farleigh 46 F7
Monkton Heathfield . . 213 E8
Montacute 186 B3
Moolham 221 C1
Moor 220 C3
Moorhayne 192 D2
Moorlands 44 D3
Moorledge 39 E1
Moorlinch 155 C7
Morebath 164 B3
Mount Radford 208 C6
Muchelney 172 B3
Muchelney Ham 172 B2
Mudford 187 D6
Mudford Sock 187 B6
Mudgley 138 D8

N

Nailsbourne 168 D7
Nailsea 8 E3
Nailwell 61 D6
Narford's 193 C1
Nash 197 C8
Neighbourne 115 C5
Nempnett Thrubwell . . 55 D5
Netherclay 182 B7
Nether Compton 187 F4
Nethercott 151 C3
Netherhay 199 F8
Netherstoke 197 D3
Nether Stowey 134 B3
Nettlebridge 115 D6
Nettlecombe 149 F8
Newbridge 44 B8
Newbury
  Coleford 98 B1
  Horningsham 144 E4
Newcott 192 C3
New Cross 184 F6
Newport 170 B2
Newton
  Combe St Nicholas . . . 193 A7
  Watchet 132 E1
Newton St Loe 43 D6
Newtown
  Axbridge 69 D2
  Bridgwater 208 E6
New Town
  Bishop Sutton 57 D7
  Freshford 81 F8
  Hatch Beauchamp . . . 182 E4
  Kington Magna 177 E1
  Milborne Port 217 B2
  Paulton 77 D6
  Wedmore 138 E8
  Yeovil 219 C6
Nimmer 223 C8
Northay
  Combe St Nicholas . . . 193 B6
  Hawkchurch 199 A3
North Barrow 175 A8
North Brewham 161 A7
North Cadbury 175 D6
North Cheriton 176 C4
North Coker 197 D8
North Curry 170 C4
Northend 28 F5
North End
  Clutton 58 E5
  Millmoor 179 E3
  Taunton 169 D5
  Yatton 16 F1
Northfield
  Bridgwater 208 C4

Radstock 79 B1
  Somerton 211 C5
Northgate 210 C5
North Newton 153 F2
Northover
  Glastonbury 206 B3
  Ilchester 173 E2
North Perrott 196 C4
North Petherton 153 F4
North Stoke 26 C6
North Town
  North Cadbury 175 C7
  North Wootton 140 D5
  Taunton 212 E5
North Weston 2 C2
Northwick 105 F6
North Wick 39 D8
North Widcombe 57 B1
North Wootton
  Sherborne 188 F1
  Wells 140 C4
Norton 31 D4
Norton Fitzwarren 168 B4
Norton Hawkfield 39 F6
Norton Hill 97 B7
Norton Malreward 40 B7
Norton St Philip 81 F4
Norton Sub Hamdon . . 185 F3
Norton's Wood 7 C5
Novers Park 22 D8
Nunney 143 C8
Nunney Catch 143 B7
Nye 51 E8
Nyland 90 C1
Nynehead 167 C1

O

Oake 167 D4
Oakhill 115 A3
Oare 122 E4
Oareford 122 F3
Oathill 199 E8
Obridge 213 A6
Odcombe 186 D2
Odd Down 44 D2
Old Cleeve 131 E5
Old Ditch 110 E7
Old Down 95 F3
Oldfield Park 44 E4
Oldford 101 B1
Old Mills 77 D3
Oldmixon 49 B1
Old Way 184 A4
Oldways End 162 E3
Orchard Common 182 A8
Othery 155 B2
Otterford 181 E1
Otterhampton 135 A6
Over Compton 187 F4
Overleigh 207 C3
Over Stowey 134 A1
Over Stratton 220 D1
Overton 169 C7
Oxenpill 138 C4

P

Packsaddle 119 F7
Paintmoor 194 B4
Panborough 138 F8
Parbrook 158 D7
Pardlestone 133 C5
Park 156 D1
Park Corner 64 A4
Paulton 77 F5
Pawlett 136 A5
Payton 179 F7
Pear Ash 161 E2
Peasedown St John . . . 79 C8
Peasmarsh 194 B7
Pecking Mill 159 D8
Pedwell 156 A7
Pendomer 197 B5
Penn Mill 219 E6
Pennsylvania 12 F7
Penselwood 161 C2
Pensford 40 E4
Periton 200 D6
Perry Green 208 B8
Perrymead 45 B3
Perry Street 198 E8
Petton 165 A3
Pibsbury 172 C5
Pickney 168 B8
Pict's Hill 172 B6
Pill 4 C4
Pilsdon 199 F2
Pilton 140 F3
Pitcombe 215 D3
Pitcot 115 F7
Pitminster 181 E6
Pitney 172 C7
Pitsford Hill 150 E1
Plainsfield 152 B7
Pleamore Cross 222 A2
Plummer's Hill 77 E6
Podimore 174 A3
Poleshill 166 C1
Polsham 139 D5
Poole 222 F8
Pooltown 148 E8
Porlock 124 A4
Porlockford 123 F4
Porlock Weir 123 D4
Portbury 3 D3

Portfield 171 E5
Portishead 2 B4
Portland 207 A6
Portway 207 D4
Potters Hill 20 B1
Pound 220 F2
Poyntington 188 B6
Prescott 179 C1
Prestleigh 141 D3
Preston 150 E6
Preston Bowyer 167 B5
Preston Plucknett 218 D4
Priddy 92 D3
Primrose Hill 27 D1
Priorswood 213 B7
Priston 61 B5
Providence Place 77 F1
Publow 40 F5
Puckington 184 B5
Pudleigh 223 B8
Puriton 136 C4
Purn 67 A7
Purse Caundle 189 D4
Purtington 195 A4
Puxton 33 D3
Pyleigh 151 B1
Pylle 141 B1
Pyrland 213 A8

Q

Quarr 177 E5
Queen Camel 174 F3
Queen Charlton 24 B3

R

Raddington 165 B4
Radford 78 C8
Radlet 134 C1
Radstock 78 E1
Rapps 183 D3
Rawridge 191 F1
Red Ball 179 C4
Redcliffe Bay 1 E4
Redhill 36 D3
Redlane 191 F7
Redlynch 160 D4
Red Post 79 B7
Regil 37 F2
Rhode 153 D5
Rich's Holford 151 C4
Rickford 54 B3
Ridge 74 C5
Ridgeway 143 C7
Riding Gate 177 B8
Rimpton 188 A8
Riverside
  Midsomer Norton 96 F7
  Wellington 222 B6
Roadwater 131 C4
Rockwell Green 222 B5
Rode 101 F8
Rodgrove 177 C3
Rodhuish 131 B2
Rodney Stoke 91 A1
Rodway 135 B3
Rolstone 32 F2
Rookham 112 B5
Rooks Bridge 87 C5
Rook's Nest 150 C4
Rosemary Lane 180 D1
Rotcombe 59 D2
Roundham 195 D4
Rowbarton 212 E7
Rowberrow 53 A1
Rowford 168 F6
Royston Water 192 F3
Rudge 102 D5
Ruishton 169 C3
Rumwell 168 B2
Runnington 179 F8
Rush Hill 44 B2
Rydon 169 E6

S

St Catherine 13 F1
St Cleers 211 C3
St Decumans 202 B6
St Georges 32 D3
St Pauls 227 C4
Saltford 25 C2
Sampford Arundel 179 E5
Sampford Brett 202 E1
Sampford Moor 179 F5
Sampford Peverell 178 E1
Sand 108 C2
Sandford 52 A3
Sandford Batch 51 F2
Sandford Orcas 188 C2
Sawyer's Hill 180 E7
School House 199 A5
Seaborough 199 E8
Sea Mills 5 B6
Seavington St Mary . . 184 D1
Seavington St Michael . 184 F2
Sector 198 B1
Selworthy 124 D3
Seven Ash 151 D4
Shalford 216 D8
Shapwick 137 F1
Sharpstone 64 A4
Shawford 101 D7
Sheepway 3 B5

Shepton Beauchamp . . 184 E3
Shepton Mallet 205 D6
Shepton Montague . . . 160 B2
Sherborne
  Litton 75 D3
  Milborne Port 225 C6
Sherford 212 E1
Shillingford 164 E2
Shipham 70 F7
Shiplate 67 F6
Shirehampton 4 E7
Shockerwick 29 F5
Shopnoller 151 E3
Shoreditch 169 A1
Short Street 121 F6
Shoscombe 79 E6
Shoscombe Vale 79 E5
Shurton 134 C7
Sidbrook 169 B6
Sidcot 70 C7
Sigwells 175 E2
Silver Street 180 F8
Simonsbath 127 B2
Simonsburrow 180 C3
Single Hill 80 A5
Sion Hill 27 E1
Skilgate 164 E6
Slape Cross 209 F6
Slough Green 182 D7
Small Way 214 B2
Smeatharpe 191 E5
Smitham Hill 74 D2
Sneyd Pk 5 D3
Sockety 196 D1
Soho 117 A5
Somerdale 24 E7
Somerton 211 D3
Somerton Randle 173 C7
Southay 185 B6
South Barrow 175 A6
South Brewham 161 A6
South Cadbury 175 C4
South Chard 198 C8
South Cheriton 176 D3
South Common 198 A4
Southdown 44 B4
South Down 191 F6
Southfield 79 A2
South Hill 211 A1
Southmarsh 161 B1
South Perrott 196 C1
South Petherton 220 C4
Southstoke 62 E7
South Twerton 44 C5
Southtown 183 C3
Southway 139 D5
Southwick
  Trowbridge 83 F2
  Watchfield 105 E2
South Widcombe 75 C6
Sparkford 175 A5
Spaxton 152 E8
Speckington 174 C2
Spike Island 226 B1
Splatt 152 E8
Spring Gardens 119 D8
Stafford's Green 188 D8
Stalbridge 190 C4
Stalbridge Weston . . . 190 A3
Stallen 188 A3
Standerwick 102 C2
Stanton Drew 39 F2
Stanton Prior 42 E2
Stanton Wick 58 B8
Staple Fitzpaine 182 C5
Staplegrove 212 C6
Staplehay 181 D8
Staple Lawns 182 B5
Stapleton 185 E8
Stapley 191 D8
Star 52 D1
Stathe 171 B8
Stawell 137 A1
Stawley 166 A1
Steanbow 140 D2
Steart
  Babcary 174 C6
  Combwich 135 D8
Stembridge 185 A7
Stewley 183 B5
Sticklepath
  Combe St Nicholas . . . 193 D7
  Monksilver 149 E7
Sticklinch 140 C1
Stileway 138 E3
Stock 53 B8
Stockland Bristol 135 A6
Stocklinch 184 B4
Stocklinch Ottersey . . 184 C4
Stocklinch St
  Magdalen 184 C4
Stockwood 23 E5
Stockwood Vale 24 C6
Stoford 197 F8
Stogumber 150 D8
Stogursey 134 C5
Stoke Bishop 5 E5
Stoke Pero 128 F6
Stoke St Gregory 170 E6
Stoke St Mary 169 C1
Stoke St Michael 116 B2
Stoke sub Hamdon . . . 185 F5
Stoke Trister 177 B7
Stolford 134 F8
Stone Allerton 88 C3
Ston Easton 95 E8
Stonebridge
  Banwell 51 A4

Frome 120 A7
Stone-edge Batch 8 D4
Stone Hill 207 A4
Stoney Stoke 160 F3
Stoney Stratton 141 F2
Stony Head 169 F1
Stony Knaps 199 D7
Stony Littleton 80 B6
Stoodham 220 D6
Stopgate 192 C4
Stoughton Cross 108 B8
Stourton 161 F5
Stourton Caundle 189 F2
Stout 156 B2
Stowell 176 C1
Stowey 57 F4
Stratton-on-the-Fosse . . 96 F1
Stream 132 A2
Street
  Chard 194 C2
  Glastonbury 207 C7
Street Ash 193 C8
Street End 54 D3
Street on the Fosse 141 C2
Stringston 133 F5
Strode 55 E7
Studley Green 83 F6
Sturford 144 F7
Summerlands 218 F6
Sutton 159 B4
Sutton Bingham 197 D6
Sutton Mallet 155 B7
Sutton Montis 175 C3
Sutton Wick 57 B2
Swell 171 A2
Swineford 26 A7
Sydenham 209 C5
Synderford 199 C6

T

Tacker Street 149 C8
Tadhill 116 F2
Tadwick 12 E1
Tangier 212 E4
Tarnock 87 D6
Tatworth 198 C8
Taunton 212 D5
Tavern Scott 38 D1
Tellisford 82 E4
Temple 144 E7
Temple Cloud 58 E1
Templecombe 176 E1
Terhill 151 F3
Theale 109 C1
The Butts 119 E3
The Folly 94 F6
The Mount 119 F2
The Oval 44 C4
The Wrangle 74 A5
Thicket Mead 77 F3
Thorncombe 199 B6
Thorne Coffin 218 A8
Thorne St Margaret . . . 179 D8
Thorney 172 A1
Thornfalcon 169 E2
Thoulstone 121 F4
Three Ashes
  North Cadbury 175 C7
  Oakhill 115 E1
Thurlbear 182 C8
Thurloxton 153 D1
Tickenham 7 F4
Tillworth 198 D3
Timberscombe 130 C4
Timsbury 60 B1
Timsbury Bottom 60 A1
Tintinhull 186 C6
Tivington 129 F8
Tolland 150 E3

Tone 222 A8
Tonedale 222 B7
T'other Side the Hill . . . 115 B7
Toulton 152 A2
Towerhead 51 D4
Townsend 92 D4
Towns End 77 E4
Town's End 116 E3
Tracebridge 179 A8
Treble's Holford 151 C4
Treborough 149 A7
Trent 187 F5
Trinity 119 E5
Triscombe 151 D6
Trowbridge 83 F7
Trudoxhill 143 C6
Trull 168 D1
Tuckerton 169 F8
Tucking Mill 63 C8
Tudhay 198 C3
Tunley 61 B3
Turleigh 64 F6
Twerton 44 A5
Tyndall's Park 226 C4
Tyning
  Radstock 79 B3
  Timsbury 60 A2
Tytherington 143 E8
Tytherleigh 198 C6

U

Ubley 55 E1
Ubley Sideling 73 D8
Udley 35 C4
Ullcombe 192 A4
Upcott 168 B3
Uphill 48 C2
Uplowman 178 B2
Up Mudford 187 D5
Upottery 191 F2
Upper Benter 115 C7
Upper Cheddon 168 F7
Upper Coxley 139 F6
Upper Godney 139 A6
Upper Langford 53 C3
Upper Langridge 27 B7
Upper Littleton 38 B6
Upper Milton 203 D7
Upper Radford 78 B8
Upper Stanton Drew . . . 40 B2
Upper Swainswick 28 B5
Upper Vobster 117 D8
Upper Westholme 140 D4
Upper Weston 27 A3
Upper Westwood 64 E4
Upotery 191 F2
Upton
  Langport 172 D5
  Skilgate 164 F8
Upton Cheyney 26 B8
Upton Noble 142 F2
Urgashay 174 C3

V

Vagg 186 F5
Verrington 216 A5
Victoria Park 226 B3
Vobster 117 C7
Vole 106 B8
Voxmoor 222 F1

W

Wadbrook 198 C4
Wadbury 118 D7
Waddicombe 162 E6

Wadeford 193 D5
Wagg 172 B5
Waggs Plot 198 B4
Walcombe 203 E7
Wales 174 E3
Walford 169 D7
Wallace 74 E3
Wall Mead 60 C4
Walpole 136 B4
Walrow 105 C2
Walton 156 E7
Walton in Gordano 7 B7
Walton St Mary 6 E5
Wambrook 193 C3
Wanstrow 142 F4
Warleigh 46 C6
Washbrook 89 A1
Washford 131 F4
Watchet 202 B6
Watchfield 105 D2
Watergore 220 B2
Waterlip 142 A7
Waterrow 165 F4
Waterside 78 E1
Wayford 195 B1
Way Wick 32 E1
Weacombe 132 F3
Weare 88 E6
Wearne 172 A7
Webbington 68 E4
Wedmore 108 D3
Weekmoor 167 B3
Welham 160 A2
Wellington 222 D7
Wellisford 179 D8
Wellow 62 D1
Wells 203 E4
Wellsprings 212 F8
Welshmill 119 F6
Welton 78 B2
Welton Hollow 78 D2
Wembdon 208 C6
West Anstey 162 C6
West Bagborough 151 F4
West Bourton 177 E8
West Bradley 158 C7
West Buckland 180 F7
Westbury on Trym 5 F7
Westbury-sub-Mendip . . 110 D6
West Camel 174 D3
West Chinnock 196 B8
West Coker 197 A8
Westcombe
  Batcombe 142 B2
  Somerton 172 E7
West Compton 204 C3
West End
  Blagdon 54 E3
  Chewton Mendip 93 F6
  Clevedon 6 B2
  Frome 119 F5
  Nailsea 17 F7
  Somerton 211 C3
Westfield 97 C8
Westford 179 F7
Westham 107 C2
West Harptree 74 E6
West Hatch 182 E7
Westhay 138 A5
West Hewish 33 A5
West Hill
  Nailsea 9 A5
  Portishead 2 A5
  Wincanton 216 B4
West Hill Gardens 78 E1
West Huntspill 136 A7
West Lambrook 184 F5
Westleigh 179 A4
West Leigh 150 F1
West Luccombe 124 C3
West Lydford 158 C2

West Lyng 170 B7
West Monkton 169 C7
West Mudford 187 C7
West Newton 169 F8
Weston 27 B1
Weston Bampfylde 175 B3
Weston in Gordano 1 F1
Weston Park 27 C1
Weston-Super-Mare . . . 48 B7
Weston Town 142 E5
Westonzoyland 154 E5
Westowe 151 A3
West Pennard 140 B1
West Porlock 123 F4
Westport 184 C7
West Quantoxhead 132 E4
West Shepton 205 A4
West Stoke 185 E4
West Stoughton 107 E6
West Town
  Backwell 18 F5
  Baltonsborough 157 F6
  Ubley 55 B6
West Wick 32 C1
Westwood 64 E3
West Woodlands 143 F6
Weycroft 198 B2
Whatley
  Frome 118 D4
  Winsham 194 C1
Wheddon Cross 129 E1
Wheeler's Hill 78 C2
Whipcott 179 B5
Whitbourne Springs . . . 144 F7
Whitchurch 23 D4
Whitcombe 175 D2
White Ball 179 D6
Whitecross 171 E3
White Cross
  Bishop Sutton 57 E1
  Burnham-on-Sea 105 B8
  Hallatrow 76 F6
  Zeals 161 F3
Whitefield 210 B8
White Gate 194 B1
Whitehall 180 A1
White Hill 79 F6
Whitelackington 184 C2
Whitestaunton 193 B5
Whiteway 44 A4
Whitley Batts 40 F2
Whitnage 178 C2
Whitnell 134 D2
Wick
  Burnham-on-Sea 85 E8
  Glastonbury 139 E2
  Stogursey 134 D7
Wicklane 61 A1
Wick St Lawrence 32 B7
Widcombe 45 C4
Wigborough 220 F1
Wilkinthroop 176 C2
Willand 191 E8
Willett 150 E4
Willhayne 223 A8
Williton 202 D3
Wilmington 43 A1
Wilton 212 F2
Wiltown
  Curry Rivel 171 C3
  Wellington 180 F3
Wincanton 216 B3
Windmill Hill 183 B3
Winford 37 F7
Wingfield 83 C6
Winscombe 69 F7
Winsford 147 C5
Winsham 194 D1
Winsley 64 D7
Winterhay Green 221 A5
Winterhead 70 D8

Winter Well 182 C7
Winyard's Gap 196 E1
Witcombe 185 F8
Witham Friary 143 C3
Withiel Florey 148 E4
Withybrook 115 E3
Withycombe 131 B4
Withyditch 61 C3
Withy Mills 78 A7
Withypool 146 C6
Withywood 22 A4
Wiveliscombe 210 B4
Wonderstone 67 D6
Woodborough 70 B8
Woodcombe 200 C8
Woodford
  Watchet 132 A1
  Wells 140 A6
Woodgate 179 E2
Woodhill
  Portishead 2 D7
  Stoke St Gregory 170 F6
Woodlands 183 E6
Wookey 139 E8
Wookey Hole 203 E8
Woolavington 136 F4
Woollard 41 A6
Woolley 27 F5
Woolminstone 195 B3
Woolston
  North Cadbury 175 E6
  Watchet 132 C2
Woolverton 82 C1
Wootton Courtenay . . . 129 F6
Worle 31 F2
Worlebury 31 A2
Worminster 140 C5
Worth 139 D8
Worthy 123 E5
Wrangway 180 A4
Wrantage 170 A1
Wreath
  Ditcheat 159 A7
  Nailsea 9 C3
Wreath 194 C3
Wrington 35 E1
Writhlington 79 C2
Wyke Champflower 215 A6

Y

Yalway 153 A1
Yanley 21 C8
Yarcombe 192 D3
Yarde 132 A2
Yarford 168 C8
Yarley 139 C8
Yarlington 175 F8
Yarrow 106 E3
Yatton 34 C8
Yeabridge 220 E2
Yenston 189 F8
Yeovil 218 E4
Yeovil Marsh 187 A6
Yeovilton 174 A1

Z

Zeals 161 F2

5102 Appartments BS1.. 227 B4

A

Abbas & Templecombe CE
  Prim Sch BA8 ....176 E1
Abbey Cl
  Curry Rivel TA10 ....171 D4
  Keynsham BS31........ 24 F6
  7 Sherborne DT9....225 D3
  Tatworth TA20 ....198 D8
  Wookey BA5 ....139 D8
Abbey Ct BA2..........45 B7
Abbey Fields TA10 ......171 D4
Abbey Gate St BA1......228 C2
Abbey Gdns BS22...... 49 E8
Abbey Gn BA1.........228 C2
Abbey Hill Dro TA3......182 B5
Abbey La BA3..........64 A4
Abbey Lodge BA6.......206 E4
Abbey Manor Bsns Ctr
  BA21.................218 D5
Abbey Meads BA6.......206 E3
Abbey Mews TA20 ......198 D8
Abbey Pk BS31........ 24 F6
Abbey Rd
  Bristol BS9..............5 F7
  Chilcompton BA3 .... 96 D2
  Sherborne DT9.........225 D4
  Stratton-on-t F BA3...... 96 F2
  Washford TA23 ....131 E3
  Yeovil BA21 ....218 D6
Abbey St
  Bath BA1 ....228 C2
  Crewkerne TA18 ....224 C6
  Hinton St George TA17 ...195 C7
Abbey Trad Est BA21....218 D6
Abbey View
  Bath BA2 ....45 B5
  Radstock BA3 ....79 A3
Abbey View Gdns BA2... 45 B5
Abbeywood Dr BS9 ......5 C5
Abbot's Cl BS22........32 A3
Abbotsbury Rd BS48 .....8 D1
Abbots Cl
  Bristol BS14..........23 A3
  Burnham-on-S TA8.....104 B6
  Ilminster TA19 ....221 B3
  Oxenpill BA6 ....138 C4
  Seavington St Michael
    TA19.................184 E2
Abbots Ct BA6.........206 D4
Abbotsfield TA4 ....210 A4
Abbotsfield Cotts TA4...210 B4
Abbots Fish Ho★ BA6...138 D4
Abbots Horn BS48 ....8 D2
Abbots Leigh Rd BS8....11 C7
Abbots Meade BA21.....218 D5
Abbots Way
  Minehead TA24 ....200 C6
  Pilton BA4 ....140 E3
  Sherborne DT9 ....225 B3
  Yeovil BA21 ....218 D6
Abbott's Wootton La
  DT6..................199 B1
Abbott La TA16 ....196 A8
Abbotts Farm Cl BS39....77 D5
Abbotts Rd BA22 ....173 D1
Abbotts Way TA3 ....183 F7
Abels Cl TA19 ....187 F5
Aberdeen Rd BS6.......226 B4
Abingdon Gdns BA2.....62 D8
Abingdon St TA8........104 B6
Abington Cross TA24....124 B4
Ablake La TA10 ....172 C5
Ableton Wlk BS9.........5 C5
Abon Ho BS9 ....5 C4
Acacia Ave BS23 ....49 B8
Acacia Ct BS31 ....24 C4
Acacia Dr BA11 ....120 C7
Acacia Gdns TA2........213 E2
Acacia Gr BA2..........44 C3
Acacia Rd BA3..........78 E1
Accommodation Rd BS24. 66 E6
Acer Dr BA21 ....218 C7
Ackland's Dro TA10 ....155 F4
Acland Round TA4 ......167 E6
Acombe Cross TA3......191 E8
Aconite Cl BS22........ 32 B5
Acorn Cl
  Frome BA11...........119 C5
  Highbridge TA9 ....104 D4
Acorn Gr BS13.........21 E6
Acre Cotts BS21 ....222 E6
Acre La TA11 ....211 F4
Acreman Ct DT9 ....225 C4
Acreman Pl DT9 ....225 D3
Acreman St DT9 ....225 D4
Acresbush Cl BS13......22 A5
Acres Ct BA22 ....197 F8
Acres The **1** TA12 ....185 E6
Actis Rd BA6 ....206 E3
Adam's La TA5..........134 D6
Adams Cl
  Highbridge TA9 ....104 C2
  Peasedown St John BA2...79 D8
Adams Ct **5** BS8.......11 F6
Adams Ho TA19.........221 B3
Adams Mdw TA19.......221 A4
Adam St TA8 ....104 B6
Adastral Rd BS24 ....50 D4

Adber Cl BA21 ....219 E8
Adber Cross DT9.......187 F6
Adcombe Cl TA3........181 D5
Adcombe Rd TA2 ....213 B8
Adder La TA7...........169 F8
Adderwell BA11.........120 A3
Adderwell Cl BA11......120 A3
Addicott Rd BS13 ....48 E6
Addiscombe Rd
  Bristol BS14............23 B5
  Weston-Super-Mare BS23.. 48 E4
Addison Gr TA2.........212 E6
Addlewell La **11** BA20 ...219 B4
Admiral's Mead BA6 ....157 E4
Admiral's Wlk BS20......2 B5
Admiral Blake Mus★
  TA6..................209 A4
Admirals Cl
  Sherborne DT9 ....225 E5
  Watchet TA23.........202 D6
Admirals Ct TA6 ....208 F5
Admiralty Way TA1......213 C5
Adsborough Hill TA2....169 D7
Adsborough La TA2 ....169 D7
Adscombe Ave TA6 .....209 C6
Adscombe La TA5 ......134 A1
Aelfric Mdw BS20.......2 F4
Ainslie's Belvedere BA1.228 B4
Ainstey Dr BA22 ....175 A4
Airey Hos TA13 ....220 D1
Airport Rd BS14.........23 A8
Airport Rdbt BS24.......49 D7
Airport View Cvn Pk BS24 49 D7
Aisecome Way BS22.....49 C6
Akeman Cl BA21 ....218 D7
Akeman Way BS11 ....4 C8
Alamein Rd TA23 ....202 E6
Alard Rd BS4...........22 F7
Alastair Cl BA21 ....218 F7
Alastair Dr BA21 ....218 F7
Albany BS23 ....30 F1
Albany Cl DT9 ....225 E6
Albany Ct **6** BA1 ....44 B6
Albany Rd BA2.........44 C6
Albemarle Rd TA1 ......212 F5
Albemarle Row **9** BS8 ..11 F6
Albert Ave
  Peasedown St John BA2... 79 C7
  Weston-Super-Mare BS23.. 48 E6
Albert Bldgs BA6.......206 D5
Albert Cl BA21 ....218 E7
Albert Ct
  Bridgwater TA6 ....208 E4
  15 Taunton TA1 ....213 A4
  Weston-Super-Mare BS23.. 48 E6
Albert Pl
  Bath BA2 ....45 C1
  Portishead BS20 ....2 D4
Albert Quadrant BS23 ...48 E8
Albert Rd
  Clevedon BS21...........6 C3
  Keynsham BS31.........24 E5
  Portishead BS20 ....2 D5
  Weston-Super-Mare BS23.. 48 E6
Albert Row DT9 ....225 E4
Albert St TA6 ....208 E4
Albert Terr BA1.........44 C6
Albion Bldgs BA1.......44 D7
Albion Cl TA6..........209 B5
Albion Pl
  16 Bristol BS2.......227 C3
  Frome BA11...........119 D3
Albion Rd BA22 ....174 A2
Albion Terr
  Bath BA1 ....228 A3
  Cheddar BS27 ....90 B7
Alburys BS40 ....35 D3
Alcombe Cross TA24 ....201 B5
Alcombe Rd TA24 ......201 A5
Aldeburgh Pl BA14......83 F6
Alder Cl
  North Petherton TA6 ...153 F3
  Taunton TA1 ....213 D1
  Williton TA4 ....202 E3
Aldercombe Rd BS9.....5 C8
Alder Ct BS14..........23 B5
Alderdown Cl BS11 ......5 A8
Alder Gr
  Crewkerne TA18 ....224 C7
  Yeovil BA20 ....218 E2
Alderley Rd BA2........44 B4
Alderney Rd TA6........209 C3
Alder Terr BA3.........78 E2
Alder Way BA2.........62 D8
Alder Wlk BA11 ....120 B7
Aldondale Gdns BA20 ...219 B3
Aldwick Ave BS13.......22 C3
Aldwick Cl BS40........54 C7
Aldworth Ho BS2.......227 C4
Aldwych Cl TA8........104 C6
Alec Ricketts Cl BA2 ....43 F5
Alexander Bldgs **12** BA1.. 28 B1
Alexander Cl TA3.......169 D5
Alexander Hall BA3.....64 C6
Alexander Ho **5** BS23...48 F4
Alexander Mews **5** BS23.. 48 E7
Alexander Pl BA3.......64 C6
Alexanders Cl BA6......138 C4
Alexander Way BS49 ....34 B7
Alexandra Cl BS21 ......6 C4
Alexandra Gdns TA24 ...201 A6

Alexandra Mews TA24...201 A7
Alexandra Par BS23 .....48 E7
Alexandra Pk BS39......77 E5
Alexandra Pl BA2 ....45 C1
Alexandra Rd
  Bath BA2 ....228 C1
  Bridgwater TA6 ....208 E5
  Bristol BS8............226 B4
  Bristol, Highridge BS13 ...21 F7
  Clevedon BS21...........6 D6
  Frome BA11...........119 F4
  Minehead TA24 ....201 A6
  Wellington TA21.......222 D6
  Yeovil BA21 ....219 D6
Alexandra Terr BS39 .....77 E5
Alexevia Cvn Pk TA3 ...169 C3
Aley TA5 ....152 A8
Alford La BA4, BA7.....159 B4
Alfords Ridge BA3 ......117 A7
Alfoxton Rd TA6........208 C4
Alfred's Way BA9 ......216 B3
Alfred's Twr★ BA10 ....161 C6
Alfred Cl **4** BS23 ......48 E7
Alfred Cres BA4........205 B4
Alfred Hill BS2.........227 A4
Alfred Par BS2.........227 A4
Alfred Pl BS2 ....226 C4
Alfred St
  Bath BA1 ....228 B3
  Taunton TA1 ....213 B4
  Wells BA5 ....203 D3
  Weston-Super-Mare BS23.. 48 E8
Algar Cl BS25.........203 B4
Alice St BA11 ....143 A6
Alison Gdns BS48 ....19 A7
Allandale Cl TA8........104 B8
Allandale Rd TA8 ....104 A8
Allanmead Rd BS14 .....23 B8
Allans Way BS24 ....49 F7
Allen Dr BA5 ....205 A6
Allen Rd TA6 ....208 F1
Allens La
  Shipham BS25 ....70 F8
  Wells BA5 ....112 E1
Allenslade Flats TA4 ....210 C5
Aller BS24 ....49 B2
Aller Dro
  Aller TA10 ....171 D8
  Othery TA7 ....155 C1
Allermoor Dro BS28....138 B8
Aller Par BS24 ....49 B2
Allerpark La TA4 ....123 F3
Allerton Cres BS14 .....23 B4
Allerton Gdns BS14 ....23 B5
Allerton Rd
  Bridgwater TA6 ....209 B7
  Bristol BS14...........23 B4
All Hallows Prep Sch
  BA4..................142 C6
Allingham Rd BA21 .....219 C7
Allington Cl TA1 ....213 E4
Allington Gdns BS48 ....18 C8
Allington Rd BS3.......226 C1
Allotment Dro
  Combe St Nicholas TA20 .193 C5
  Glastonbury BA16 .....138 D1
Allotment Rd BA22 .....175 C3
All Saints' La BS1 ......227 A2
All Saints' Rd
  Bristol BS8............226 A4
  Weston-Super-Mare BS23.. 30 E1
All Saints' St BS1 ......227 A3
All Saints' Terr TA6 ....209 B4
All Saints CE Prim Sch
  Dulverton TA22 ....163 D6
  Montacute TA15.......186 B3
All Saints CE Sch LA13 ..198 A4
All Saints East Clevedon CE
  Prim Sch BS21...........6 F4
All Saints Ho BS2 ......227 B4
All Saints La BS21.......6 F4
All Saints Pl BA2 ....45 E4
All Saints Rd BA1 ......228 B4
Allshire La EX16 ....162 F3
Allyn Saxon Dr BA4 ....205 D5
Alma Field BA7........214 B4
Alma Rd BS8 ....226 B4
Alma Road Ave BS8 ....226 B4
Alma St
  Taunton TA1 ....213 A3
  Weston-Super-Mare BS23.. 48 E7
Alma Vale Rd BS8......226 A4
Almond Cl BS22........32 A1
Almond Tree Cl TA6.....209 D4
Almshouse La BA22 ....173 D1
Almshouses
  Donyatt TA19..........183 D1
  Marshfield SN14 ....13 E8
Almyr Terr TA23........202 C7
Alpha Cotts TA2........168 E8
Alpha Ho TA9..........104 E3
Alpine Cl BS39.........77 F4
Alpine Gdns BA1.......228 C4
Alpine Rd BS39........77 F4
Alston Cl TA1..........212 C1
Alstone Gdns TA9......104 C2
Alstone La TA9.........104 C2
Alstone Wildlife Pk★
  TA9..................104 C3
Alston Sutton Rd BS26...88 F4
Alton Pl BA2...........228 C1

Alun Rees Way TA20 ...223 B3
Alverstoke BS14 ....22 F7
Alveston Wlk BS9 ....5 B7
Alvington La BA22 ......218 B5
Alweston DT9..........189 A1
Ambares Ct BA3 ....96 F8
Amberd La TA3 ....181 D8
Amberey Rd BS23.......48 F5
Amberlands Cl BS48 ....19 A7
Amberley Cl
  Keinton Mandeville TA11..158 A1
  Keynsham BS31........24 E4
Amberley Gdns **3** BS48 .. 8 D1
Amber Mead TA1 ....213 D3
Ambleside Rd BA2 ......44 C2
Ambra Ct BS8 ....226 A2
Ambra Terr BS8 ....226 A2
Ambra Vale BS8 ....226 A2
Ambra Vale E BS8.......226 A2
Ambra Vale S **5** BS8....226 A2
Ambra Vale W **4** BS8....226 A2
Ambridge Cl BA16......207 B4
Ambrose Cl DT9 ....187 E1
Ambrose Rd BS8........226 A2
Ambury BA1 ....228 B1
Amercombe Wlk BS14....23 D7
American Mus in Britain★
  BA2..................46 A5
Amery La BA1..........228 C2
Amesbury Dr BS24......67 B6
Ames La BA3...........98 B6
Ammerdown Terr BA3 ...98 F3
Ammerham La TA20.....199 A8
Amor Pl TA1...........212 D2
Amory Rd TA22 ....163 D6
Amulet Way BA4........205 E4
Ancastle Ave BA7 ......214 D6
Ancastle Terr BA7 ......214 C6
Anchor Cl BA3 ....116 E8
Anchor Cnr BA9 ....176 D6
Anchor Hill BA9........176 D6
Anchor Rd
  Bath BA1 ....27 B1
  Bristol BS1............226 C2
  Coleford BA3 ....116 E8
Anchor Sq BS1 ....226 C2
Anchor St TA23 ....202 C7
Anchor Stables TA24....123 E4
Anchor Way BS20.......4 D4
Ancliff Sq BA15........64 E4
Ander's La TA3 ....192 B8
Andereach Cl BS14.....23 B8
Andersfield Cl TA6 .....208 A4
Andrew's Hill TA22 ....163 C6
Andrew's Hill Cross
  TA22 ....163 C6
Andrew Allan Rd TA21 ..222 B4
Andruss Dr BS41.......21 D2
Angela Cl TA1 ....212 D2
Angel Cres TA6 ....208 F5
Angel La BA9 ....216 C4
Angel Place Sh Ctr **6**
  TA6 ....208 F5
Angel Row TA3 ....170 F2
Anglesey Cotts DT10 ...190 B4
Anglo Ct TA18 ....224 C6
Anglo Terr BA1 ....228 C4
Anglo Trad Est The BA4..205 B6
Angwin Cl BA4.........205 B6
Animal Farm★ TA8......66 B2
Annaly Rd BS27........90 A7
Annandale BA7 ....214 B4
Annandale Ave BS22 ....31 E1
Anseres Pl BA5 ....203 E4
Ansford Com Sch BA7...214 C7
Ansford Hill BA7 ....214 C6
Ansford Rd BA7........214 C6
Anson Cl BS31 ....25 D2
Anson Rd
  Locking BS24.........50 B6
  Weston-Super-Mare BS22.. 31 D4
Anson Way TA6 ....208 F5
Anstey Gate TA22 ......162 B8
Anthony Rd BA16 ......207 D7
Antler Cl BA6 ....206 C3
Antona Ct BS11........4 D7
Antona Dr BS11........4 D7
Anvil Rd BS49.........17 F1
Anvil St BS2 ....227 C2
Apex Dr TA9...........104 C4
Aplins Cl TA19 ....221 B3
Apple Alley BA11.......119 F5
Apple Bsns Ctr The TA2..212 B6
Appleby Wlk BS4 ......22 D7
Apple Cl TA19 ....194 E7
Applecroft BA2 ....79 E6
Appledore **4** BS22.....31 F2
Appledore Cl BS14......23 B8
Apple Dumpling Cnr
  BS28 ....108 C3
Applefield Rd DT8 .....199 F8
Applehayes La EX15....180 C2
Apple La BA11 ....119 F5
Apple Tree Cl TA6 .....209 D4
Appletree Cl BS22 ......32 B2
Apple Tree Dr BS25 .....70 A8
Appletree Mews BS22....32 B2
Appley Cross TA21 .....179 B7
Appsley Cl BS22 ....31 C1
Apricot Tree Cl TA6.....209 D5
Apsley Rd BA1..........44 A7
Aquara Cl BA16 ....207 C3

Arbutus Dr BS9..........5 C8
Arcade The BS1 ....227 B3
Archbishop Cranmer CE Com
  Prim Sch TA1 ....213 A4
Arch Cl BS41 ....10 F1
Archer Ct BS21 ....6 D4
Archer Dr TA8 ....104 C6
Archers Way The BA6 ...206 E5
Archer Wlk BS14.......23 E6
Arches The BA2........44 A6
Archgrove BS41 ....10 F1
Arch La TA3 ....170 E4
Archstone Ave TA5.....135 F2
Archway St BA2........45 B5
Arden Cl BS22.........31 F3
Ardern Cl BS9 ....5 B8
Ardmore BS8 ....11 D7
Ardwyn TA21 ....222 D4
Arena The BA20........219 A4
Argyle Ave BS23 ....48 F4
Argyle Pl BS8..........226 A2
Argyle Rd
  Bristol BS2............227 B4
  Clevedon BS21..........6 D6
Argyle St BA2.........228 C2
Argyle Terr BA2........44 C6
Arlington Cl
  Bridgwater TA6 ....209 A2
  Yeovil BA21 ....218 C7
Arlington Ho **4** BA1....228 C2
Arlington Mans BS8.....226 B4
Arlington Rd **4** BA1....44 D5
Arlington Villas BS8.....226 B3
Armada Ho BS2........227 A4
Armada Pl BS1.........227 B4
Armada Rd BS14.......23 A6
Armes Ct BA2.........228 C1
Armoury Rd BA22 ......218 A6
Armoury The BA6......206 D4
Armstrong Rd BA11 ....120 B5
Armtech Row BA22 .....218 B6
Arnewood Gdns BA20 ..218 F2
Arnold's Way BS49 .....17 A2
Arnold Cl TA2 ....212 F7
Arnold Noad Cnr BA14...83 E3
Arnolfini (Arts Ctr)★
  BS1..................227 A1
Arnor Cl BS22 ....32 A4
Arrowfield Cl BS14 .....23 A2
Artemesia Ave BS22....49 E8
Arthurswood Rd BS13 ...22 A4
Artillery Rd BA22 ......218 A6
Arundel Cl BS13 ....22 B5
Arundel Ct BS23 ....48 E8
Arundel Rd BS23 ....30 E1
Arundells Way TA3.....169 D4
Arundel Rd
  Bath BA1 ....28 A1
  Clevedon BS21..........6 D3
  Yeovil BA21 ....219 E6
Arundel Wlk BS31......24 D5
Arun Gr TA1 ....213 D4
Ascension Ho BA2 .....44 D4
Ashbeer Hill TA4.......150 D7
Ashbourne Cres TA1 ...213 D3
Ash Brook BS39........59 D1
Ashbrooke House Sch
  BS23 ....48 D6
Ashbury Dr BS22.......31 B2
Ashby Rd BA7 ....214 C5
Ash CE Prim Sch TA12...185 F7
Ash Cl
  Bridgwater TA6 ....209 D4
  Wells BA5 ....203 D5
  Weston-Super-Mare BS22.. 32 D2
  Winscombe BS25.......52 A1
Ashcombe Ct
  Ilminster TA19 ....221 B4
  1 Weston-Super-Mare
    BS23 ....48 F7
Ashcombe Gdns BS23 ...49 A8
Ashcombe La
  Alweston DT9 ....189 B2
  Ilminster TA19 ....221 B4
Ashcombe Park Rd BS23 .31 A1
Ashcombe Pl **4** BS23...48 F7
Ashcombe Prim Sch BS23 49 A7
Ashcombe Rd BS23 .....48 F7
Ashcott BS14 ....22 F7
Ashcott Cl TA8.........104 C6
Ashcott Dr TA8 ....104 C6
Ashcott Pl TA8.........104 C6
Ashcott Prim Sch TA7...156 B8
Ashcott Rd BA6........138 D3
Ash Cres TA1 ....212 D2
Ashcroft
  Chard TA20............223 D2
  Weston-Super-Mare BS24.. 49 B2
Ash Croft TA12.........185 F7
Ashcroft Ave BS31 .....24 D5
Ashcroft Rd BS9 ....5 C7
Ash Cross TA3 ....169 E2
Ash Ct BS14 ....23 A6
Ashculme Hill EX15....180 C2
Ashdene Ct BS23 ......49 A8
Ashdown Ct BS9 ....5 E5
Ashdown Rd BS20 ......2 A6
Ashel's Batch BA3 ......94 C8
Ashen Cross TA11......211 E2

Ash End BA8............**189** F7
Asher La BS2............**227** C3
Ashes La BA3............**64** A4
Ashey La
  Burrington BS40............**54** A5
  Cheddar BS27............**90** B8
Ashfield TA20............**223** D2
Ashfield Cl BA11............**143** C6
Ashfield Pk 28 TA12....**185** E6
Ashford Cl
  Bridgwater TA6............**208** E2
  Milverton TA4............**167** A4
Ashford Dr BS24............**49** A1
Ashford Gr BA21............**219** B7
Ashford La TA19............**183** F5
Ashford Rd
  Bath BA2............**44** D4
  Redhill BS40............**36** E4
  Taunton TA1............**212** C2
  Wellington TA21............**222** D4
Ash Gr
  Bath BA2............**44** C4
  Chard TA20............**223** C5
  Clevedon BS21............**6** E4
  Minehead TA24............**200** D7
  Shepton Mallet BA4............**205** C4
  Wells BA5............**203** D5
  Weston-Super-Mare BS23..**48** E2
Ashgrove BA2............**79** D8
Ashgrove Ave BS8............**11** B7
Ashgrove Ct BA2............**79** D8
Ash Grove Way TA6............**209** D7
Ash Hay Dro BA5............**139** C6
Ash Hayes Dr BS48............**8** E1
Ash Hayes Rd BS48............**8** F1
Ash Ho TA8............**65** F2
Ashill Cl TA1............**212** E1
Ashill Com Prim Sch
  TA19............**183** C4
Ashington La BA21............**187** B7
Ash La
  Shepton Beauchamp
  TA19............**184** E4
  Wells BA5............**203** C5
  Winsford TA24............**147** B6
Ashland Ct TA18............**224** C7
Ashland La TA4............**150** B4
Ashland Rd BS13............**22** A4
Ashlands Cl TA18............**224** C7
Ashlands Fst Sch TA18..**224** C7
Ashlands Mdw TA18....**224** C8
Ashlands Rd TA18............**224** D7
Ashlea BA7............**214** B6
Ashlea Pk TA9............**136** E8
Ashleigh Ave TA6............**209** A3
Ashleigh Cl
  Paulton BS39............**77** E6
  Weston-Super-Mare BS23..**49** A8
Ashleigh Cres BS49......**34** B8
Ashleigh Gdns TA1............**212** E5
Ashleigh Rd
  Weston-Super-Mare BS23..**49** A8
  Yatton BS49............**34** B8
Ashleigh Terr TA6............**209** A3
Ashley Ave
  Bath BA1............**44** C7
  Burnham-on-S TA8............**104** B6
Ashley Cl BS25............**70** A7
Ashley La BA15............**64** F7
Ashley Rd
  Bathford BA1............**29** E3
  Clevedon BS21............**6** B1
  Taunton TA1............**212** D3
Ashley Terr 1 BA1............**44** C7
Ashmans Cl BA1............**44** B6
Ashmans Gate BS39......**77** E5
Ashmans Yd BA1............**44** B6
Ashman Way TA6............**208** D4
Ashmead
  Temple Cloud BS39............**58** E1
  Yeovil BA20............**218** C2
Ashmead Rd BS31............**25** B5
Ashmead Road Ind Est
  BS31............**25** B5
Ashmead Way 8 BS1....**11** F5
Ashmoor Dro BA5............**139** C6
Ash Rd
  Banwell BS29............**50** E4
  Street BA16............**207** B3
Ashton Ave BS1............**226** A1
Ashton Cl
  Ashill TA19............**183** C4
  Clevedon BS21............**6** B1
Ashton Court Est* BS41..**11** C4
Ashton Cres BS48............**8** D1
Ashton Ct TA1............**212** C1
Ashton Dr BS3............**11** F2
Ashton Gate Stadium (Bristol
  City FC)* BS3............**11** E3
Ashton Gate Trad Est BS3 **11** E3
Ashton Gate Underpass
  BS3............**11** F3
Ashton Hill BA2............**43** A7
Ashton Park Sec Sch BS3 **11** F1
Ashton Pk BA11............**119** E2
Ashton Rd
  Bridgwater TA6............**208** E2
  Bristol, Ashton Gate BS3..**11** F4
  Bristol, Bower Ashton BS3..**11** D3
Ashton Vale Prim Sch
  BS3............**11** F2
Ashton Vale Rd BS3............**11** E3
Ashton Vale Trad Est BS3 **11** F1
Ashton Way BS31............**24** E6
Ashton Windmill* BS28..**88** E1

Ashtown Cross EX16....**164** A3
Ash Tree Cl
  Bleadon BS24............**67** C6
  Burnham-on-S TA8............**85** A3
Ash Tree Cres TA8............**85** A3
Ash Tree Ct BA3............**78** E1
Ash Tree Rd TA8............**85** A3
Ash Trees TA9............**86** C5
Ashvale Cl BS48............**9** A2
Ashwell Bsns Pk TA19..**221** C7
Ashwell Cl BS14............**23** E6
Ashwell La
  Glastonbury BA6............**139** D1
  Wheddon Cross TA24....**129** F2
Ashwicke BS14............**23** A6
Ash Wlk BA8............**190** A6
Ashwood BS40............**74** F4
Ashwood Dr BA21............**219** E8
Askwith Cl DT9............**225** B3
Asney Rd BA16............**156** E7
Aspen Cl BA11............**120** B7
Aspen Ct TA6............**208** E4
Aspen Park Rd BS22......**49** E8
Aspen Way TA18............**224** D7
Aspley Cl BA1............**44** B7
Asquith St TA1............**212** E6
Assembly Rooms La BS1 **227** A2
Aston Ho 4 BS1............**227** B1
at-bristol* BS1............**226** C1
Athelney Way BA21............**218** D6
Athlone Rd TA6............**209** A2
Atholl Cl BS22............**31** F3
Atkin's Gate TA13............**220** D6
Atkins Cl BS14............**23** E6
Atlanta Key TA8............**104** A8
Atlantic Cres TA8............**104** B5
Atlantic Rd
  Bristol BS11............**4** C8
  Weston-Super-Mare BS23..**30** C1
Atlantic Rd S BS23............**30** C1
Atlantic View TA8............**30** C1
Atlantic Way BA22............**174** A2
Atlay Ct BS49............**17** B1
Atrium The BS1............**227** B2
Attewell Ct BA2............**44** F4
Attisham La DT6............**199** D4
Atyeo Cl
  Bristol BS3............**11** E1
  Burnham-on-S TA8............**104** C8
Aubrey Meads BS30......**25** E8
Auckland Cl BS23............**48** F3
Auckland Way TA20............**223** D3
Audley Ave BA1............**44** D7
Audley Cl
  Bath BA1............**44** D7
  Nether Stowey TA5............**134** A2
Audley Gr BA1............**44** C7
Audley Lodge BA1............**44** C7
Audley Park Rd BA1............**44** C7
Audley Pl BA1............**44** D7
Augusta Pl BA1............**44** D7
Augustine's Cl BS20............**1** E4
Austen Dr BS22............**32** B4
Austen Pl BS11............**4** E7
Austin Cl BA11............**119** F2
Austin Rd BA6............**206** E6
Autumn Mews BS24......**50** A8
Avalon Bldgs BA6............**206** D5
Avalon Cl BS49............**17** A1
Avalon Est BA6............**206** E7
Avalon Ho BS48............**8** C1
Avalon Mews BA6............**206** E4
Avalon Pk TA11............**211** B5
Avalon Rd
  Bridgwater TA6............**209** D5
  Highbridge TA9............**104** E4
Avalon Sch BA16............**207** B3
Avebury Cl TA8............**104** D8
Avebury Dr TA6............**209** D5
Avebury Rd BA3............**11** F2
Aveline Ct TA4............**167** F6
Avening Cl BS48............**19** A8
Avenue Pl BA2............**45** B1
Avenue Rd BA11............**120** A4
Avenue The
  Backwell BS48............**19** A7
  Bath, Bushey Norwood BA2 **45** E5
  Bath, Combe Down BA2..**45** C1
  Bicknoller TA4............**132** F4
  3 Bridgwater TA6............**208** F5
  Bristol, Sneyd Park BS9..**5** E3
  Chard TA20............**193** F7
  Clevedon BS21............**6** E6
  Keynsham BS31............**6** E6
  Kingsbury Episcopi TA12 **185** B8
  Langport TA10............**172** A6
  Minehead TA24............**201** A7
  Misterton TA18............**224** F3
  Sherborne DT9............**225** E6
  Sparkford BA22............**175** A5
  Stoke sub Hamdon TA14..**185** F4
  Taunton TA1............**212** E6
  Timsbury BA2............**60** B2
  Weston-Super-Mare BS22..**32** C3
  Wincanton BA9............**216** D3
  Winscombe BS25............**70** C8
  Yatton BS49............**34** B8
  Yeovil BA21............**219** B5
Averill Ct BS21............**6** D4
Avill Cres TA1............**213** C4
Avishayes Com Prim Sch
  TA20............**223** E5
Avishayes Rd TA20............**223** E4
Avonbank Ind Est BS11..**4** B7
Avonbridge Trad Est BS11..**4** C8
Avon Cl
  Keynsham BS31............**24** F6

Avon Cl continued
  Taunton TA12............**212** D2
  Weston-Super-Mare BS23..**48** F2
  Yeovil BA21............**219** D6
Avoncliff Halt BA15......**64** F5
Avon Cres BS1............**226** A1
Avon Ct BA1............**29** A4
Avondale Bldgs BA1......**28** B2
Avondale Ct
  Bath BA1............**44** B7
  Bristol, Sneyd Park BS9..**5** D3
Avondale Ho
  Bath BA2............**44** B5
  Bridgwater TA6............**209** A2
Avondale Rd BA1............**44** B6
Avondowns Ct BS8......**28** B2
Avon Gorge Ind Est BS11..**4** C7
Avon Gorge Nature Reserve*
  BS8............**11** E7
Avon Gr BS9............**5** D2
Avon Hts BA3............**64** C6
Avon La BS31............**25** F5
Avonleaze BS9............**5** B5
Avonmead BS2............**227** B4
Avon Mill La BS31............**24** F6
Avonmouth CE Prim Sch
  BS11............**4** C8
Avonmouth Rd BS11......**4** C8
Avon Pk BA1............**44** A7
Avon Prim Sch BS11......**4** D8
Avon Rd
  Bristol BS13............**22** A4
  Keynsham BS31............**24** F5
  Pill BS20............**4** C5
Avon Riverside Est BS11..**4** B7
Avon Riverside Sta* BS30 **25** E6
Avon Ski Ctr* BS25......**52** C3
Avon & Somerset Pol HQ
  BS20............**1** F3
Avon St
  Bath BA1............**228** B2
  Bristol BS2............**227** C2
Avon Vale BS9............**5** D4
Avonvale Pl BA1............**28** F3
Avon Way
  Bristol, Sneyd Park BS9..**5** C4
  Portishead BS20............**2** C5
Avonwood Cl BS11............**4** E6
Awkward Hill BS40......**55** D5
Axbridge CE Fst Sch BS26 **70** C1
Axbridge Cl
  Burnham-on-S TA8............**104** C8
  Nailsea BS48............**8** E1
Axbridge Moor Dro BS26 **70** C1
Axbridge Mus* BS26....**70** C2
Axbridge Rd
  Bath BA2............**45** A2
  Cheddar BS27............**70** F2
  Taunton TA1............**212** B3
Axe Cl BS23............**49** A5
Axeford TA20............**198** E8
Axeford Mdws TA20....**198** E8
Axe La
  Clapton DT8............**195** C1
  Drimpton DT8............**199** F8
Axe Rd
  Bridgwater TA6............**209** B3
  Wookey BA5............**139** D8
Axe Valley Com Coll The
  EX13............**198** A1
Axford Way BA2............**79** D8
Axis BS14............**22** B5
Axminster Com Prim Sch
  EX13............**198** A1
Axminster Rd TA20............**198** C7
Ayckbourn Cl TA8............**104** C6
Aycote Cl BS22............**31** C2
Ayford La SN14............**13** F4
Aylands Rd TA1............**212** D3
Aylmer Cres BS14............**23** B6
Ayr St BA2............**44** D6
Azalea Rd BS22............**32** A5
Azelin Ave BS13............**22** B5

B

Babcary La BA22............**174** B8
Babwell Rd BA9............**177** D6
Babylon Hill
  Sherborne DT9............**188** A3
  Yeovil BA21............**219** F4
Babylon View BA21............**219** F7
Backfields BS2............**227** B4
Backfields Ct BS2............**227** B4
Backfields La BS2............**227** B4
Back La
  Axbridge BS26............**70** C2
  Baltonsborough BA6....**158** B5
  Batcombe BA4............**142** C2
  Bradford Abbas DT9......**187** F1
  Chapel Allerton BS26......**88** D1
  Cheddar BS27............**90** A7
  Chewton Mendip BA3......**75** B1
  Curry Rivel TA10............**171** D3
  Draycott BS27............**90** F2
  East Chinnock BA22......**196** E8
  East Coker BA22............**197** C7
  Halstock BA22............**197** C3
  Ilchester BA22............**173** E1
  Keynsham BS31............**24** E6
  Kingston Seymour BS21..**16** A5
  Kington Magna SP8......**177** E2
  Litton BA3............**75** E2
  Maiden Bradley BA12....**144** C2
  Marshfield SN14............**13** F8

Back La continued
  Martock TA12............**185** D4
  Middlezoy TA7............**155** B3
  Montacute TA15............**186** B3
  Moorlinch TA7............**155** D8
  North Perrott TA18......**196** C4
  Pill BS20............**4** C5
  Pilton BA4............**204** D3
  Rimpton BA22............**188** A8
  Rowberrow BS25............**53** A1
  Shepton Mallet, Darshill
  BA4............**204** F6
  Shepton Mallet, Downside
  BA4............**205** D8
  Sherborne DT9............**225** D4
  Stoney Stratton BA4......**141** F2
  Street BA16............**207** C6
  Street, Butleigh Wootton
  BA6............**157** C6
  Westbury-sub-Mendip BA5 **110** E6
  Whitelackington TA19....**221** F6
Backlane Dro BA6............**158** C5
Back Of Kingsdown Par
  BS6............**227** A4
Back St
  Ash TA12............**186** A7
  Bampton EX16............**164** B1
  Bradford On Tone TA4....**167** F1
  Leighton BA11............**142** E6
  Long Sutton TA10............**172** E4
  Martock TA12............**185** F7
  West Camel BA22............**174** D3
  Weston-Super-Mare BS23..**48** E7
  Winsham TA20............**194** E1
Back Stoke La BS9............**5** D7
Back Town BA6............**157** E4
Back Way TA4............**150** B8
Backways La TA21............**179** F6
Backwell Bow BS48......**9** C1
Backwell CE Jun Sch
  BS48............**19** C5
Backwell Comm BS48....**19** B8
Backwell Hill Rd BS48....**19** E5
Backwell Sch BS48............**19** B6
Backwell Wlk BS13............**21** F8
Bacon Dr TA1............**213** D3
Badcox BA11............**119** E4
Badenham Gr BS11............**4** E8
Baden Ho BA1............**228** B4
Badger's Cross
  Oakhill BA3............**114** F5
  Somerton TA11............**211** C1
Badger's Cross La TA11 **211** C2
Badger Hts BA22............**218** B5
Badger Pk TA24............**201** C4
Badger Rise BS20............**1** F3
Badgers' La TA20............**223** E1
Badgers Cl
  Bourton SP8............**161** F1
  Street BA16............**207** C6
  Taunton TA1............**212** B3
Badgers Folly BA7............**214** B5
Badgers Green Rd BA16 **207** B6
Badgers Hill BA11............**120** A5
Badgers Holt BS14............**23** C6
Badgers The BS22............**32** D3
Badgers Way BS24............**49** F8
Badgworth Barns BS26...**88** D5
Badgworth Ct BS26......**88** C5
Badgworth La BS26......**88** C4
Badlake La EX36............**162** D6
Badlake Moor Cross
  TA22............**162** D7
Badman Cl BS39............**77** D5
Badminton Ct 17 BS23..**30** C1
Badminton Gdns BA1....**44** C8
Bagber Cross Rds DT10 **190** D3
Bagborough Dr TA6......**208** F2
Bagborough Rd TA2......**212** F7
Bagborough La BA4......**141** C2
Baggridge Hill BA2......**80** F7
Baggs La BS27............**90** F2
Bagley Rd TA21............**222** A3
Bagnell Cl BS14............**23** E5
Bagnell Rd BS14............**23** E5
Bailbrook Coll BA1............**28** D2
Bailbrook Gr BA1............**28** C3
Bailbrook La BA1............**28** D3
Baildon Cres BS23............**49** A4
Baildon Ct 2 BS23............**48** F4
Baildon Rd BS23............**49** A4
Bailey's Dro BA6............**158** B5
Bailey's Knapp EX16....**178** B4
Bailey's La BA4............**142** B1
Bailey Cl BS22............**49** E8
Bailey Ct BS20............**2** F6
Bailey Hill BA2............**214** C5
Baileys Gate TA4............**167** F6
Bailey St TA6............**209** B5
Bailiffs' Wall BS26............**70** B1
Bailiffs Cl BS26............**70** C1
Baily Cl BA6............**206** E7
Bainsbury View BA3......**96** F1
Bakehouse 1 TA16............**195** F7
Bakehouse La DT9............**187** E1
Bakelite Mus Sec* TA4..**202** C2
Baker's Bldgs BS40......**35** D2
Baker's Cross TA3............**191** D7
Baker's La
  Churchinford TA3............**191** D7
  Wellington TA21............**222** E6
Baker Cl 8 BS21............**6** B1
Bakeries The TA11............**211** D3
Bakers Cl TA1............**212** A3
Bakers Ct TA13............**220** C4
Bakersfield TA20............**194** E1

Bakers La
  Barrington TA19............**184** C5
  Chilcompton BA3............**96** D3
  Lower Langford BS40......**53** C8
Bakers Orch TA4............**151** B5
Bakers Par BA2............**60** B2
Bakers Pk BS13............**22** B6
Baker St
  Babcary TA11............**174** C7
  Frome BA11............**119** E5
  Weston-Super-Mare BS23..**48** E8
Bakery La BA4............**140** F3
Balch Rd BA5............**203** C4
Baldwin La BA4............**213** B5
Baldwin Rd TA1............**213** B5
Baldwin St BS1............**227** A2
Ball's Hill BA22, TA15..**186** C4
Ball's La TA5............**153** E4
Ballance St BA1............**228** B4
Ballfield Rd TA24............**200** F8
Ballhill La EX16............**164** B1
Ball La
  Doulting BA4............**141** F7
  Isle Abbotts TA3............**183** E7
  Spaxton TA2, TA5............**152** B2
Balls Barn La BS24......**33** A2
Ball The
  Dunster TA24............**201** E2
  Minehead TA24............**200** F8
Balmoral Dr TA8............**85** B1
Balmoral Ho TA6............**209** C4
Balmoral Rd
  Keynsham BS31............**24** E4
  Yeovil BA21............**219** E6
Balmoral Way BS22......**31** D2
Balsam Cl BA9............**216** D3
Balsam Fields BA9............**216** D3
Balsam La BA9............**216** E3
Balsam Pk BA9............**216** C3
Baltic Pl BS20............**4** D4
Baltonsborough CE Prim Sch
  BA6............**158** A6
Baltonsborough Rd BA6 **157** F4
Balustrade 17 BA1............**28** B1
Bamfield BS14............**23** A6
Bampton 5 BS22............**31** F2
Bampton TA20............**223** B5
Bampton Cl BS13............**22** B7
Bampton Down Rd EX16 **178** A7
Bampton Prim Sch EX16 **164** B1
Bampton St TA20............**200** F6
Banbury La BA6............**157** E3
Bancks St TA24............**200** F7
Bancombe Ct TA11............**211** B5
Bancombe Rd TA11............**211** A4
Banfield Cl BS11............**5** A8
Bangers DT9............**188** F5
Bangrove Wlk BS11............**4** E8
Banister Gr BS4............**22** D7
Banking Ct 4 TA18............**224** C6
Bankland La TA7............**154** B1
Bank Pl BS20............**2** D4
Banks Cl BS21............**16** D8
Bank Sq TA22............**163** E5
Bank St
  Highbridge TA9............**104** D3
  Williton TA4............**202** D2
Bannerdown Cl BA1......**29** B4
Bannerdown Dr BA1......**29** A4
Bannerdown Rd BA1......**29** C3
Bannerleigh La BS8......**11** E6
Bannerleigh Rd BS8......**11** E6
Banneson Rd TA5............**134** B2
Bantock Cl BS4............**22** D6
Bantry Rd BS4............**22** E8
Banwell Cl
  Bristol BS13............**22** A4
  Keynsham BS31............**25** A2
  Taunton TA1............**213** D4
Banwell Prim Sch BS29..**51** B3
Banwell Rd
  Banwell BS26, BS29......**68** E8
  Bath BA2............**62** D8
  Locking BS24............**50** B3
  Winscombe BS25, BS29..**69** E8
Banyard Rd BS20............**3** E5
Barbary Cl BA8............**176** D3
Barber's La TA21............**180** F7
Barberry Dr TA20............**223** E5
Barberry Farm Rd BS49..**17** B1
Barbers Mead TA2............**213** C5
Barbour Gdns BS13......**22** D3
Barbour Rd BS13............**22** D3
Barclay St TA6............**209** A5
Barcroft BA12............**144** B2
Barcroft Cres TA3............**170** A1
Barcroft La TA13............**220** B6
Bardel Ct BA22............**218** B6
Barford Cl TA5............**152** F7
Barford Ho* TA5............**152** F6
Barford Rd TA5............**152** F7
Barham Ct BA22............**218** A5
Barhams Cl TA6............**209** A7
Barkham Cl BA5............**203** C5
Barle Cl TA1............**213** C4
Barley Cl BA5............**213** C4
Barley Croft
  Bristol BS9............**5** F5
  Somerton TA11............**211** B3
Barley Cross BS22............**32** E3
Barley Wood Walled Gdn*
  BS40............**35** F3
Barlinch Cl TA1............**213** B7
Barlynch Ct BA21............**218** D6
Barnabas Cl BS26............**70** D2
Barnaby Cl BA3............**78** B2
Barnard's Cl BS49............**34** C7
Barnard Ave BA16............**207** B3
Barnard Ct BA5............**203** B4

Barnard Wlk BS31 . . . . 24 D4
Barn Cl
  Crewkerne TA18 . . . . 224 B5
  Frome BA11 . . . . 119 D3
  Nether Stowey TA5 . . . . . 134 B2
  Somerton TA11 . . . . 211 B3
  Street BA16 . . . . 207 C6
  Wiveliscombe TA4 . . . . . . 210 A7
Barn Cres TA18 . . . . 224 B5
Barn Ct BA21 . . . . 187 C5
Barn End BS40 . . . . 74 E3
Barnes Cl
  Castle Cary BA7 . . . . 214 C6
  Wells BA5 . . . . 203 B4
Barnes Close Mead
  TA22 . . . . 163 D6
Barnet BA21 . . . . 218 E7
Barnetts Well BS27 . . . . 90 F2
Barnfield Way BA1 . . . . 29 B3
Barn Gn BA6 . . . . 206 D3
Barnhay 6 EX16 . . . . 164 B1
Barn Hill BA2 . . . . 79 F5
Barn La
  Clutton BS39 . . . . 59 A7
  Crewkerne TA18 . . . . 195 E6
Barn Meads Rd TA21 . . . . . 222 E4
Barn Orch TA14 . . . . 185 E3
Barn Pool BS25 . . . . 70 F8
Barns Cl
  Barrow Gurney BS48 . . . . . 20 E4
  Nailsea BS48 . . . . 8 E2
Barnsclose TA22 . . . . 163 D6
Barns Close Ind Est
  TA22 . . . . 163 D6
Barnsclose N TA22 . . . . 163 D6
Barnsclose W TA22 . . . . . . 163 D6
Barns Gd BS21 . . . . 16 E8
Barn St TA18 . . . . 224 B6
Barnstaple Ct BS4 . . . . 22 E8
Barnstaple Rd BS4 . . . . 22 E8
Barnstaple Wlk BS4 . . . . 22 F8
Barnwood BS48 . . . . 8 E1
Baron Cl BS30 . . . . 25 E8
Barons Cl BS3 . . . . 11 F3
Barossa Pl BS1 . . . . 227 A1
Barpark Cnr EX15 . . . . 180 E3
Barpool La TA11 . . . . 211 D6
Barrack's La BS11 . . . . 4 D8
Barracks Cl BA22 . . . . 218 B7
Barrendown La BA4 . . . . . . 205 C6
Barrie Way TA8 . . . . 104 C6
Barrington Broadway
  TA10 . . . . 184 D6
Barrington Cl TA1 . . . . 212 C1
Barrington Ct* TA19 . . . . . 184 D5
Barrington Court Cotts
  TA19 . . . . 184 D5
Barrington Hill Rd TA19 . 182 F4
Barrington Pl BA4 . . . . 204 F5
Barrington Rd TA8 . . . . 104 C8
Barrow Court La BS19 . . . . . 20 B5
Barrow Cswy BA5 . . . . 138 F8
Barrow Ct
  Barrow Gurney BS48 . . . . . 20 A5
  Tickenham BS21 . . . . 7 F4
Barrow Dr TA3 . . . . 213 E5
Barrow Hill
  Stalbridge DT10 . . . . 190 B4
  Stourton Caundle DT10 . . 189 F1
Barrow Hill Cres BS11 . . . . . 4 C7
Barrow Hill Rd BS11 . . . . . . 4 D6
Barrow Ho 25 BA4 . . . . 205 B6
Barrow Hospl
  Barrow Gurney BS48 . . . . . 20 F6
  Dundry BS48 . . . . 21 A6
Barrow La
  Charlton Musgrove BA9 . . 161 B3
  North Wootton BA4 . . . . . 140 B4
  Pilton BA4 . . . . 140 F3
  Winford BS40 . . . . 20 F1
Barrow Lea DT10 . . . . 190 B4
Barrowmead Dr BS11 . . . . . 4 F7
Barrow Pk BS27 . . . . 90 A8
Barrow Rd
  Bath BA2 . . . . 44 C1
  Hutton BS24 . . . . 49 E2
Barrows Cl TA6 . . . . 208 C2
Barrows Croft BS27 . . . . . . 90 A8
Barrows Ct BA22 . . . . 196 E8
Barrows La TA14 . . . . 185 E2
Barrows Rd BS27 . . . . 90 A8
Barrow St BS48 . . . . 20 D5
Barrows The
  Cheddar BS27 . . . . 90 A8
  Weston-Super-Mare BS22. . 49 C7
Barrow Stile BA4 . . . . 140 F3
Barrow Water La BA9 . . . . 161 A3
Barrow Wood La BS27. . . . 110 A7
Barry Cl BS24 . . . . 49 A1
Barry La BA22 . . . . 196 F6
Barrymore Ct TA10 . . . . . . 172 A6
Barstable Ho BS2 . . . . 227 C3
Bartec 4 BA20 . . . . 218 C3
Bartholomew Row BA2. . . . 60 B2
Bartlett Cl
  Frome BA11 . . . . 120 C4
  Taunton TA1 . . . . 212 B1
Bartlett Ct
  1 Crewkerne TA18 . . . . . 224 C6
  Yeovil BA20 . . . . 218 D3
Bartlett Mews BA21 . . . . . 219 F7
Bartlett Pk
  Chard TA20 . . . . 223 E3
  Yeovil BA20 . . . . 218 D3
Bartletts Ct BA2 . . . . 228 C1
Bartletts La TA4 . . . . 167 A4
Bartletts Pl BA21. . . . . 218 D5
Bartletts Row TA11 . . . . . . 211 D4

Bartlett St 6 BA1 . . . . 228 B3
Bartletts Way BS24 . . . . . . 50 A4
Barton Bldgs BA1 . . . . 228 B3
Barton Cl
  Berrow TA8 . . . . 84 F5
  Taunton TA1 . . . . 212 D3
Barton Cross EX16 . . . . . . 162 E5
Barton Dro BS25 . . . . 69 D5
Barton Gn TA3 . . . . 168 D1
Barton Hey 2 TA4 . . . . 167 F8
Barton Hill SP8 . . . . 177 E2
Barton La TA1 . . . . 169 C4
Barton Rd
  Barton St David TA11 . . . 158 A2
  Berrow TA8 . . . . 84 F4
  Bristol BS2 . . . . 227 C2
  Butleigh BA6 . . . . 157 E3
  Minehead TA24 . . . . 201 B4
  Winscombe BS26 . . . . 69 C6
Barton Rise TA7 . . . . 137 B3
Barton St
  Bath BA1 . . . . 228 B2
  Bristol BS1 . . . . 227 A4
Bartons The
  Bishops Lydeard TA4 . . . . 167 E8
  Ilchester BA22 . . . . 173 E1
  South Petherton TA13 . . . 220 E3
Barton The
  Bleadon BS24 . . . . 67 C6
  Charlton Adam TA11 . . . . 173 F7
  Corston BA2 . . . . 43 A7
  Huish Champflower TA4 . . 165 E8
  Norton St Philip BA2 . . . . 81 E4
Barton Vale BS2 . . . . 227 C2
Barton Villas BA3 . . . . 116 F6
Barton Way TA3 . . . . 170 C4
Barton Wlk BA11 . . . . 119 D2
Barwick Ho BS11 . . . . 4 E7
Barwick & Stoford Com Prim
  Sch BA22 . . . . 197 F8
Basketfield La BA6 . . . . . . 139 D1
Batallers La TA23 . . . . 131 D1
Bat Alley DT10 . . . . 190 F5
Batch Bsns Pk BS24. . . . . . 66 F2
Batch Cl TA7 . . . . 136 C4
Batch La
  Clutton BS39 . . . . 58 F3
  Lympsham BS24 . . . . 66 F3
Batchpool La BA8 . . . . 176 F3
Batch Rd TA7 . . . . 136 B5
Batch The
  Ashcott TA7 . . . . 156 B7
  Backwell BS48 . . . . 19 D1
  Batheaston BA1 . . . . 28 F3
  Burrington BS40 . . . . 54 B3
  Butcombe BS40 . . . . 55 B8
  Chew Magna BS40. . . . . . . 39 B3
  Churchill BS25 . . . . 52 F4
  Draycott BS27 . . . . 90 F2
  Farnborough BA2 . . . . 60 A6
  Hinton Charterhouse BA2 . 63 E1
  Saltford BS31 . . . . 25 F3
  19 Shepton Mallet BA4 . . 205 B6
  Wincanton BA9 . . . . 216 B4
  Yatton BS49 . . . . 34 B7
Batch View BA16 . . . . 207 B6
Bateman's Cross TA20 . . . 198 E7
Bath Abbey* BA1 . . . . 228 C2
Bathampton La BA2 . . . . . . 28 E1
Bathampton Prim Sch
  BA2 . . . . 28 F2
Bath Bridge Bsns Pk
  TA6 . . . . 209 B6
Bath Cl BA6 . . . . 206 D6
Batheaston CE Prim Sch
  BA1 . . . . 28 F4
Bathford CE Prim Sch
  BA1 . . . . 29 C2
Bathford Hill
  Bathford BA1 . . . . 29 B2
  Compton Dando BS39 . . . . 41 E5
Bathford Manor BA1 . . . . . 29 C2
Bath Foyer The BA2 . . . . . . 44 A6
Bath Hill
  Keynsham BS31 . . . . 24 F5
  Wellow BA2 . . . . 62 D2
Bath House Ct TA1 . . . . . . 212 E3
Bath La TA20 . . . . 223 C3
Bath Meadow Dr TA22 . . 163 E6
Bath New Rd BA3 . . . . 78 F4
Bath Old Rd BA3 . . . . 78 F4
Bath Pl TA1 . . . . 212 F5
Bath Postal Mus* BA1 . . . 228 C3
Bath Race Course* BA1. . . 27 A6
Bath Rd
  Ashcott TA7 . . . . 156 B7
  Bawdrip TA7. . . . . 136 D2
  Beckington BA11 . . . . 101 D5
  Bitton BS30 . . . . 25 D8
  Blagdon BS40 . . . . 55 B1
  Bridgwater TA6 . . . . 209 C7
  Bristol BS2 . . . . 227 C1
  Farmborough BA2 . . . . 59 E5
  Frome BA11 . . . . 120 A7
  Horrington BA3, BA5 . . . . 113 D5
  Kelston BA1, BS30. . . . . . . 26 B6
  Kingsdown SN13 . . . . 29 F5
  Moorlinch TA7 . . . . 155 E8
  Norton St Philip BA2 . . . . 81 E5
  Oakhill BA3 . . . . 115 B3
  Paulton BS39 . . . . 77 F6
  Peasedown St John BA2 . . 79 C7
  Saltford BS31 . . . . 25 D3
  Shepton Mallet BA4. . . . . 141 C8
  Stawell TA7 . . . . 137 B1
  Upper Langford BS40 . . . . 53 D3
  Wells BA5 . . . . 112 L1

Bath Riverside Bsns Pk
  BA2 . . . . 228 B1
Bath Spa Sta BA1 . . . . 228 C1
Bath Spa Univ Coll BA1 . . . 27 E1
Bath Spa University Coll
  (Newton Pk Campus)
  BA2 . . . . 43 B5
Bath Sq TA20 . . . . 223 C3
Bath St
  Bath BA1 . . . . 228 C2
  Bristol BS1 . . . . 227 B2
  Chard TA20 . . . . 223 C3
  Cheddar BS27 . . . . 90 B7
  Frome BA11 . . . . 119 F4
Bathurst Cl TA8 . . . . 104 D8
Bathurst Par BS1 . . . . 227 A1
Bathurst Rd BS22 . . . . 49 C8
Bath View BA3 . . . . 96 F1
Bathwell La DT9 . . . . 217 D1
Bathwick Hill BA2 . . . . 45 C6
Bathwick Rise BA2 . . . . 45 B7
Bathwick St BA1, BA2. . . . 228 C4
Batstone Cl BA1 . . . . 28 B2
Batt's La TA10 . . . . 172 D5
Battery La BS20 . . . . 2 D7
Battery Rd BS20 . . . . 2 D6
Battin's Knap TA4. . . . . . . 150 A3
Batt La TA3 . . . . 183 C8
Battleborough La TA9. . . . . 86 B1
Battle La BS40 . . . . 39 A3
Battle St EX15 . . . . 180 E1
Battleton TA22 . . . . 163 D6
Batts Bow Bridge TA9. . . 104 E1
Batts La
  Oakhill BA3 . . . . 114 E3
  Pilsdon DT6 . . . . 199 F2
Battson Rd BS14 . . . . 23 E4
Batts Pk TA1 . . . . 212 E1
Baulditch La TA3 . . . . 184 B8
Baunton's Orch DT9. . . . . 217 C2
Bauntons Cl DT9 . . . . 217 C2
Bawden Cl TA7 . . . . 136 E4
Bawdrip La TA7 . . . . 136 E2
Bawler's La TA10 . . . . 171 C3
Bay's La BA14 . . . . 115 A7
Bayer Bldg The BA2. . . . . 228 B1
Bayford BA9 . . . . 216 E4
Bayford La BA9 . . . . 177 B7
Bayford Rd TA6 . . . . 209 C6
Bay Hill TA19 . . . . 221 D4
Bay La BS27 . . . . 90 F2
Bayliss Ctr The 4 BA16 . 207 C5
Baymead Cl 11 TA6 . . . . . 153 F4
Baymead La TA6 . . . . 153 F3
Baymead Mdw 5 TA6. . . 153 F3
Baynes Cl TA21 . . . . 222 E7
Bay Rd
  Clevedon BS21. . . . . 6 D6
  Porlock TA24 . . . . 124 A4
Bays The BS27 . . . . 90 C8
Baytree Ct BS22 . . . . 31 D1
Baytree Rd BS22 . . . . 31 C1
Bay Tree Rd
  Bath BA1 . . . . 28 B2
  Clevedon BS21. . . . . 6 E1
Baytree Sch BS24 . . . . 50 A8
Baytree View BS22 . . . . . . 31 D1
Bay Tree View BS22. . . . . . 31 D1
Bay View TA23 . . . . 202 D6
Bay View Gdns TA8 . . . . . 104 B5
Baze La EX35 . . . . 122 B4
Bazelands Hill BA8. . . . . . 190 B7
Beach Ave BS21 . . . . 6 C2
Beach Ct BS23 . . . . 48 D6
Beach End Rd BS23 . . . . . . 48 C2
Beach Hill BS20. . . . . 2 C4
Beachlands Pk BS24. . . . . . 31 A6
Beachley Wlk BS11 . . . . 4 D7
Beach Mews BS21 . . . . 6 C4
Beach Rd
  Weston-Super-Mare BS23. . 48 D6
  Weston-Super-Mare, Kewstoke
  BS22. . . . . 31 A5
Beach Rd E BS20 . . . . 2 D6
Beach Rd W BS20 . . . . 2 C6
Beach The BS21 . . . . 6 C4
Beach Tree Cross TA4. . . 166 F6
Beacon TA19 . . . . 221 B5
Beaconfield Ho TA6. . . . . 209 A2
Beaconfield Rd BA20. . . . 218 E4
Beacon Hill View DT9 . . 175 D1
Beacon La
  Corton Denham DT9 . . . . 175 D2
  Wellington TA21 . . . . 180 C4
Beacon Rd
  Bath BA1 . . . . 28 A1
  Minehead TA24 . . . . 200 F8
Beaconsfield Rd
  Clevedon BS21 . . . . 6 D2
  Weston-Super-Mare BS23. . 48 E7
Beaconsfield Way BA11 . 120 B7
Beacon View
  Coleford BA3 . . . . 116 E7
  Shepton Mallet BA4. . . . . 205 A4
Beadon La TA16 . . . . 195 F7
Beadon Rd TA1 . . . . 213 C5
Beafort BS24. . . . . 50 C3
Beale Cl BS14. . . . . 23 E6
Beale Way TA8 . . . . 104 D5
Bean Acre The BS11 . . . . . . 4 D8
Bearbridge Rd BS13. . . . . . 21 F4
Beard's Yd TA15 . . . . 171 F5
Bearley Bridge Rd 15
  TA12 . . . . 185 E6
Bearley Ho 26 TA12 . . . . 185 E6
Bearley La BA22 . . . . 186 B3
Bearley Rd 27 TA12 . . . . 185 E6
Bears Meadow La TA5. . 133 C6

Bear Yard Mews 2 BS8 226 A2
Beasley Ct TA20 . . . . 223 B5
Beastway La TA24. . . . . . . 131 B3
Beatty Way TA8. . . . . 104 C7
Beauchamp Gdns TA3. . . 183 A7
Beauchamps Dr BA3 . . . . . 97 A5
Beaufitz Pl TA20 . . . . 193 F1
Beauford Pk TA2. . . . . 168 B4
Beauford Sq BA1 . . . . 228 B2
Beaufort Ave BA3. . . . . 78 A2
Beaufort Bldgs 7 BS8 . . . 11 F7
Beaufort Cl EX16. . . . . 178 D1
Beaufort Ct
  Clevedon BS21. . . . . 6 C5
  Ilchester BA22 . . . . 173 E2
Beaufort E BA1 . . . . 28 C1
Beaufort Gdns
  2 Nailsea BS48 . . . . 8 D1
  South Petherton TA13 . . . 220 B5
Beaufort Mews
  3 Bath BA1 . . . . 28 C1
  10 Bristol BS8 . . . . 11 F7
Beaufort Pl BA1 . . . . 28 C1
Beaufort Rd
  Taunton TA1 . . . . 212 E5
  Weston-Super-Mare BS23. . 48 F7
Beaufort Villas 8 BA1 . . . 28 B1
Beaufort W 1 BA1. . . . . . . 28 B1
Beauley Rd BS3 . . . . 226 B1
Beaulieu Dr BA21 . . . . . . 218 D6
Beaumont BA1. . . . . 27 F1
Beaumont Cl BS23 . . . . . . 48 F4
Beaumont Ho BA21 . . . . . 219 D5
Beau St BA1. . . . . 228 B2
Beavor La EX13 . . . . 198 A1
Beck's La BA3 . . . . 116 D6
Beckery New Rd BA6. . . . 206 B3
Beckery Old Rd BA6. . . . . 206 B3
Beckery Rd BA6 . . . . 206 B4
Becket's La BS48 . . . . 18 E8
Becket Dr BS22 . . . . 32 A3
Becket Pl BA5 . . . . 203 D3
Becket Prim Sch BS22 . . . 32 A3
Becket Rd BS22. . . . . 32 A4
Beckford's Twr* BA1. . . . . 27 D4
Beckford Ct BA2 . . . . 45 B7
Beckford Gdns
  Bath BA2 . . . . 45 B8
  Bristol BS14 . . . . 23 A3
Beckford Rd BA2 . . . . 45 B7
Beckhampton Rd BA2. . . . . 44 D5
Beckington BS24. . . . . 49 A2
Beckington CE Fst Sch
  BA11. . . . . 101 E4
Beckington Cres TA20. . . 223 D3
Becks Bsns Pk BS23. . . . . . 49 A7
Becks Field 2 TA14. . . . . 185 E4
Beckworth Cl TA6. . . . . . . 209 C3
Bector La BA3 . . . . 116 C3
Bede St DT9 . . . . 225 E5
Bedford Cl TA6 . . . . 209 C3
Bedford Ct BA1 . . . . 45 B8
Bedford Rd
  Wells BA5 . . . . 112 E1
  Weston-Super-Mare BS23. . 48 E4
  Yeovil BA21 . . . . 219 D8
Bedford St BA1 . . . . 45 B8
Bedminster Down Sch
  BS13. . . . . 21 F7
Bedwell La TA7 . . . . 155 C2
Bedwin Cl BS20. . . . . 1 F4
Beech Ave
  Bath BA2 . . . . 45 E5
  Shepton Mallet BA4. . . . . 205 A6
Beech Cl
  Doulting BA4 . . . . 141 E6
  Shipham BS25 . . . . 70 F8
  Taunton TA2 . . . . 212 F8
Beechcroft BS41. . . . . 21 D2
Beech Croft BS14 . . . . 23 B5
Beech Ct
  Bristol BS14. . . . . 23 A5
  Frome BA11. . . . . 120 B7
  Taunton TA1. . . . . 212 E3
  2 Wellington TA21 . . . . 222 D6
Beech Dr
  Bridgwater TA6 . . . . 209 D5
  Nailsea BS48. . . . . 9 A3
  Shipham BS25 . . . . 70 E8
Beechen Cliff Boys' Sch
  BA2. . . . . 44 D1
Beechen Cliff Rd BA2 . . . 228 B1
Beeches The
  Bath BA2 . . . . 44 D1
  Langport TA10 . . . . 172 A6
  Sandford BS25 . . . . 52 B4
  Wheddon Cross TA24. . . . 129 E1
Beechfield Cl BS41. . . . . . . 11 C2
Beechfield Gr BS9 . . . . 5 C8
Beechfield Inf Sch TA9. . 104 D4
Beech Gr
  Bath BA2 . . . . 44 D4
  Somerton TA11 . . . . 211 D5
  Wellington TA21 . . . . 222 C6
Beech Grove Prim Sch
  TA21 . . . . 222 C6
Beech Hill TA21 . . . . 222 F6
Beeching Cl TA20 . . . . . . 223 E6
Beech La
  Axminster EX13 . . . . 198 E1
  Stoke Trister BA9. . . . . . . 177 C8
Beechmont Cl BS24. . . . . . 49 A1
Beechmount Cl BS14. . . . . 23 B8
Beechmount Gr BS14 . . . . 23 B8
Beech Rd
  Bridgwater TA6 . . . . 209 D5
  20 Martock TA12 . . . . . 185 E6

Beech Rd continued
  Saltford BS31 . . . . 25 E3
  Shipham BS25 . . . . 70 F8
  Street BA16 . . . . 207 C3
  Yatton BS49 . . . . 34 C8
Beech Terr BA3 . . . . 78 E1
Beech Tree TA23. . . . . 130 D1
Beech Tree Cl TA4 . . . . . . 210 C4
Beech Tree Cross
  Clatworthy TA4 . . . . 149 E1
  Dulverton TA22 . . . . 163 C7
  Monksilver TA4 . . . . 132 B1
Beech Tree Hill TA5. . . . . 152 C6
Beech Way BA4 . . . . 141 E1
Beechwood
  Bridgwater TA6 . . . . 208 E2
  Yeovil BA20 . . . . 218 F2
Beechwood Ave
  Frome BA11. . . . . 120 A5
  Locking BS24 . . . . 50 A5
Beechwood Cl
  Bristol BS14. . . . . 23 C8
  Frome BA11. . . . . 120 A5
Beechwood Dr
  Crewkerne TA18 . . . . 224 C7
  Portishead BS20. . . . . 1 E5
Beechwood Rd
  Bath BA2 . . . . 45 B1
  Easton-in-G BS20. . . . . 4 A4
  Nailsea BS48. . . . . 8 D2
  Portishead BS20. . . . . 1 E5
Beehive Yd BA1. . . . . 228 C3
Beek's La SN14, BA1 . . . . . 13 D5
Beer Door TA10. . . . . 155 E2
Beer Dro TA10 . . . . 155 E1
Beere Cross EX36 . . . . . . 162 A5
Beer La
  Burlescombe EX16. . . . . . 179 B2
  Dulverton TA22 . . . . 163 B5
Beer Rd TA10 . . . . 155 E1
Beer St
  Curry Mallet TA3 . . . . . . 183 C7
  Yeovil BA20 . . . . 219 A4
Bees Ho BS21. . . . . 6 C2
Beetham La TA20 . . . . 193 B6
Bee World & Animal Ctr*
  TA4 . . . . 150 F8
Beggar Bush La BS8 . . . . . 11 B6
Beggarswell Cl BS2 . . . . . 227 C4
Beggs Cl 4 TA6 . . . . 153 F3
Behind Berry TA11 . . . . . . 211 D4
Behind Butts TA14 . . . . . . 185 E1
Behind Hayes BA8 . . . . . . 176 D3
Behind Town TA11. . . . . . 157 B4
Bekynton Ave BA5 . . . . . . 203 F4
Belcombe Dro TA20. . . . . 193 B7
Belfast Wlk BS4. . . . . 22 E8
Belfield Ct TA8 . . . . 104 A8
Belgrave Cres BA1 . . . . . . 228 C4
Belgrave Ct 2 TA2. . . . . . 212 F6
Belgrave Pl
  Bath BA1 . . . . 228 C4
  Bristol BS8. . . . . 226 A3
  Taunton TA2 . . . . 212 F6
Belgrave Rd
  Bath BA1 . . . . 28 B1
  Bristol BS8. . . . . 226 A3
  Weston-Super-Mare BS22. . 49 B8
Belgrave Terr 2 BA1 . . . . 28 A1
Bellamy Ave BS13. . . . . . . 22 C4
Belland Dr BS14 . . . . 22 F4
Bella View Gdns BA6. . . . 206 D4
Bella Vista Rd BA1 . . . . . 228 B4
Bell Barn Rd BS9 . . . . 5 D6
Bell Chase BA20 . . . . 218 D5
Bell Cl
  Bridgwater TA6 . . . . 208 F6
  Farmborough BA2 . . . . 59 F6
  Westbury-sub-Mendip BA5 110 E6
Belle View Terr TA20. . . . 198 C8
Bellevue BS8 . . . . 226 B2
Belle Vue
  Midsomer Norton BA3. . . . 78 B3
  Washford TA23 . . . . 131 E3
Belle Vue Cl BA2. . . . . 79 D7
Bellevue Cotts BS8. . . . . . 226 B2
Bellevue Cres BS8 . . . . . . 226 B2
Bellevue Ct
  Bristol BS8. . . . . 226 B2
  Clevedon BS21. . . . . 6 D4
Bellevue Mans BS21 . . . . . 6 D4
Bellevue Rd BS21 . . . . 6 D4
Bellevue Terr BS8. . . . . . . 226 B2
Belle Vue Terr TA18. . . . . 224 B6
Bellfield BA3 . . . . 117 A3
Bellhanger Ct BA1 . . . . . . 228 B4
Bell Hill
  Chewton Mendip BA3 . . . . 94 B7
  Norton St Philip BA2 . . . . 81 E4
Bellhorse La BS40. . . . . . . 74 C5
Bellifants BA2. . . . . 60 A6
Bell La
  Bristol BS1. . . . . 227 A3
  Chard TA19, TA20. . . . . . 193 F7
  Chewton Mendip BA3 . . . . 94 B7
  Cossington TA7 . . . . 137 A3
  Thurloxton TA2 . . . . 153 D1
Bell Language Sch The
  BA1. . . . . 44 C4
Bellman's Cross BA8. . . . 190 E2
Bellmoor La TA19 . . . . . . 194 A7
Bell Orch TA10 . . . . 171 D4
Bellotts Rd BA2 . . . . 44 C6
Bell Pit Brow BS48. . . . . . . 9 B2
Bell Sq BS40 . . . . 54 E3

Bellum SN14 . . . . 13 E8
Belluton La BS39 . . . . 40 D5
Belluton Villas BS39 . . . . 40 D5
Bell Wlk BS40 . . . . 35 E2
Belmont Cl TA6 . . . . 208 B4
Belmont Dr
  Failand BS8 . . . . 10 B3
  Taunton TA1 . . . . 212 E2
Belmont Hill BS48 . . . . . . 10 B1
Belmont Ho **14** BA20 . . 219 B4
Belmont Rd
  Bath BA2 . . . . 45 C1
  Hatch Beauchamp TA3 . 183 A8
  Taunton TA1 . . . . 212 C3
  Winscombe BS25 . . . . . . 70 A8
Belmont Terr TA19 . . . . 184 E3
Belmont The BS21 . . . . 6 D3
Belmore Gdns BA2 . . . . . . 44 B3
Belstone Wlk BS4 . . . . . . 22 C8
Belton Ct BA1 . . . . 27 B2
Belton Rd BS20 . . . . 2 A6
Belvedere BA1 . . . . 228 B4
Belvedere Cl TA5 . . . . . 135 B2
Belvedere Cres BS22 . . . 31 C1
Belvedere Ct **3** BA2 . . 222 D6
Belvedere Grange TA11 . 211 E3
Belvedere Rd
  Taunton TA1 . . . . 212 F5
  Yeovil BA21 . . . . 219 E7
Belvedere Trad Est TA1 . 212 F5
Belvoir Rd **6** BA2 . . . . . 44 D5
Bemberry Bank TA24 . . . 130 B5
Benares Ct TA24 . . . . . . 201 A8
Bences Cl SN14 . . . . 13 F8
Benches La BS40 . . . . 37 D3
Bench La TA20 . . . . 193 D5
Ben Cross TA13 . . . . 220 A4
Benedictine Ct BA6 . . . . 206 C4
Benedict St BA6 . . . . 206 D4
Benhole La TA5 . . . . 134 B8
Bennell Batch BA3 . . . . . 96 E4
Bennell Cl BA3 . . . . 96 E4
Bennell Cotts BA3 . . . . . 96 E4
Bennett's Cl BA5 . . . . . . 204 B7
Bennett's La BA3, BA5 . . 114 B7
Bennett's Rd BA1 . . . . . . 28 C3
Bennett Gdns BA11 . . . . 119 C4
Bennett La BA1 . . . . 28 A1
Bennett Rd TA9 . . . . 104 F4
Bennetts Field Trad Est
  BA9 . . . . 216 C2
Bennett St BA1 . . . . 228 B3
Bennetts Way BS21 . . . . . 6 E5
Bennett Way BS1, BS8 . . 11 F5
Benter Cross BA3 . . . . . . 115 D7
Bentley Cl BS14 . . . . 22 F3
Bentley Rd BS22 . . . . 32 B3
Ben Travers Way TA8 . . 104 C6
Bere La BA6 . . . . 206 E4
Bere Mills La TA19 . . . . . 194 B7
Benville Ave BS9 . . . . 5 C8
Beresford Cl
  Burnham-on-S TA8 . . . . 104 C7
  Saltford BS31 . . . . 25 E2
Beresford Gdns BA1 . . . . 27 A3
Beretun Orch BA6 . . . . . 206 E3
Berhill TA7 . . . . 156 C7
Berkeley Ave
  Bristol BS8 . . . . 226 C3
  Midsomer Norton BA3 . . . 78 A2
Berkeley Cres
  Bristol BS8 . . . . 226 B3
  Weston-Super-Mare BS23 . 48 C2
Berkeley Ct BA2 . . . . 45 C6
Berkeley Gdns
  Bruton BA10 . . . . 215 E6
  Keynsham BS31 . . . . 24 E4
Berkeley Ho
  Bath BA1 . . . . 228 C4
  Bristol BS1 . . . . 226 C3
Berkeley Pl
  Bath BA1 . . . . 228 C4
  Bristol BS8 . . . . 226 B3
Berkeley Rd
  Street BA16 . . . . 207 E6
  Yeovil BA20 . . . . 219 A4
Berkeley Sq BS8 . . . . . . 226 B3
Berkeley Way BS8 . . . . . 226 B3
Berkley CE Fst Sch BA11 121 A7
Berkley Cross BA11 . . . . 120 F6
Berkley Ct BA22 . . . . . . 173 E2
Berkley La
  Beckington BA11 . . . . . . 101 D3
  Frome BA11 . . . . 120 D8
Berkley Rd BA11 . . . . . . 120 B6
Berkley St BA11 . . . . . . 121 A8
Berlington Ct BS1 . . . . . 227 B1
Bernard Cres TA24 . . . . 200 F6
Bernard Herridge Ct
  BA9 . . . . 216 D4
Bernard Ireland Ho BA1 . 27 B1
Bernard Taylor Homes **9**
  TA1 . . . . 213 A4
Berners Cl BS4 . . . . 22 D7
Berrow CE Prim Sch TA8 . 84 F4
Berrow Lodge **7** BS23 . 48 E5
Berrow Rd TA8 . . . . 85 A2
Berry Cl TA6 . . . . 208 C4
Berrydale Ave TA6 . . . . 208 F6
Berry Hill
  Mells BA11 . . . . 118 A6
  Nunney BA11 . . . . 143 B8
Berry La EX13 . . . . 198 F3
Berryman Cl BA4 . . . . . . 205 A5
Berryman Ct BA5 . . . . . . 203 B4

Bertha Terr TA9 . . . . . . 104 D3
Berwick Cl TA1 . . . . 212 C1
Beryl Gr BS14 . . . . 23 C8
Beryl Knapp BA22 . . . . . 197 B8
Beryl La BA5 . . . . 203 F6
Besley Ct BA5 . . . . 203 B4
Bests Field TA12 . . . . . . 185 B8
Bethell Mead TA4 . . . . . 167 E6
Beverley Cl
  Frome BA11 . . . . 119 D3
  Taunton TA2 . . . . 212 E6
Beverley Ct BA23 . . . . . . 202 C7
Beverley Gdns BS9 . . . . . . 5 D7
Beverley Rd BA2 . . . . 45 B4
Bewley Ct TA20 . . . . 223 B4
Bews La TA20 . . . . 223 B5
Bibors Hill TA4 . . . . 165 E4
Bibury Cl BS48 . . . . 9 A1
Bibury Ho BA1 . . . . 27 B2
Bickenhall La TA3 . . . . . 182 F6
Bickfield La BS40 . . . . . . 74 B8
Bicking's Close La TA4 . . 166 A4
Bicknell Gdns BA21 . . . . 219 B8
Biddiscombe Cl TA6 . . . 208 E1
Biddisham Cl **6** BS48 . . . 8 E1
Biddisham La BS26 . . . . . 87 E7
Biddlecombe Rd BA21 . . 218 C7
Biddle St BS49 . . . . 34 B7
Bideford Cres BS4 . . . . . 22 F8
Bideford Rd BS22 . . . . . 31 F2
Bifield Cl BS14 . . . . 23 F5
Bifield Gdns BS14 . . . . . 23 F5
Bifield Rd BS14 . . . . 23 F5
Bignal Rand Cl BA5 . . . . 203 B3
Bignal Rand Dr BA5 . . . 203 B3
Bignell Cl BS25 . . . . 69 F8
Big Tree Cl BS26 . . . . . . 69 C3
Bigwood La BS1 . . . . . . 226 C2
Bilberry Cl BS9 . . . . 5 C8
Bilberry Gr TA1 . . . . 168 F1
Bilbie Cl BS40 . . . . 56 E8
Bilbie Rd
  Chew Stoke BS40 . . . . . . 56 E8
  Weston-Super-Mare BS22 . 32 B3
Bilbury La
  Bath BA1 . . . . 228 B2
  Glastonbury BA6 . . . . . . 206 F3
Billand Cl BS13 . . . . 21 E3
Billetfield TA1 . . . . 212 F3
Billet St TA1 . . . . 212 F3
Billicombe La TA7 . . . . . 155 C8
Billing's Hill BS28 . . . . . 108 C4
Billy La TA4 . . . . 210 D7
Bince's Lodge La BA3 . . . 78 B3
Binces La BA2 . . . . 42 E3
Bincombe Dr TA18 . . . . 224 C7
Bincombe Rd TA6 . . . . . 209 C4
Binding Cl **6** TA6 . . . . 153 F4
Bindon La BA11 . . . . . . 143 B2
Bindon Rd TA2 . . . . 212 C6
Bindwell La BA22 . . . . . 174 C3
Binegar CE Prim Sch
  BA3 . . . . 114 D8
Bineham Ct TA10 . . . . . 173 B4
Bineham La
  Ilchester BA22 . . . . 173 F2
  Yeovilton BA22 . . . . 174 A2
Bineham Rd TA10 . . . . . 173 A4
Binford's La TA4 . . . . . . 151 A4
Binhay Rd BS49 . . . . 34 C7
Binley Gr BS14 . . . . 23 D5
Binmead Gdns BS13 . . . . 22 B4
Binnings The BS27 . . . . . 90 F3
Bircham Cl TA6 . . . . 208 C4
Bircham La TA24 . . . . . . 201 C4
Bircham Rd
  Minehead TA24 . . . . . . 201 B5
  Taunton TA2 . . . . 213 B8
Birchanger La TA4 . . . . 150 A8
Birch Ave
  Bleadon BS24 . . . . 67 C6
  Clevedon BS21 . . . . 6 E4
  Puriton TA7 . . . . 136 C4
Birch Cl
  Bridgwater TA6 . . . . . . 209 D5
  Cannington TA5 . . . . . . 135 B2
  Cheddar BS27 . . . . 90 C8
  Locking BS24 . . . . 50 B4
  Wedmore BS28 . . . . 108 C3
Birch Croft BS14 . . . . . . 23 A3
Birch Ct BS31 . . . . 24 C4
Birchdale BA20 . . . . 218 D2
Birchdale Rd BS14 . . . . . 23 A8
Birchdene BS48 . . . . 9 A2
Birch Dr BS40 . . . . 53 A5
Birches Cnr TA4 . . . . . . 152 A4
Birches The BS48 . . . . . . 9 A2
Birchfield Com Prim Sch
  BA21 . . . . 219 D7
Birchfield Rd BA21 . . . . 219 D8
Birch Gr
  Portishead BS20 . . . . 2 C4
  Taunton TA1 . . . . 212 E5
Birch Hill BS27 . . . . 90 C8
Birch Ho TA8 . . . . 65 F2
Birchill Cross EX13 . . . . 198 A6
Birchill La BA11 . . . . . . 120 A1
Birch Lawn TA8 . . . . . . 104 B6
Birch Rd
  12 Martock TA12 . . . . 185 E6
  Radstock BA3 . . . . 78 E1
  Wellington TA21 . . . . . . 222 E5
Birch Wlk BA11 . . . . 120 B7
Birchwood Ave BS23 . . . 49 A7
Birchwood Dr BS8 . . . . . 10 B3
Birchwood La BS39 . . . . 40 F2
Bird's Cl TA18 . . . . 224 B6
Birdcombe Cl BS48 . . . . . 8 E3
Birdlip Cl BS48 . . . . 9 A1
Birdwell La BS41 . . . . . . 10 F1
Birdwell Prim Sch BS41 . 21 A8
Birdwell Rd BS41 . . . . . . 10 F1
Birkbeck Ct BS23 . . . . . . 48 D7
Birkett Rd BS23 . . . . 30 B1
Birnbeck Rd BS23 . . . . . 30 C1
Biscay Dr BS20 . . . . 2 F6
Biscombe Cross TA3 . . . 191 B8
Bisdee Rd BS24 . . . . 49 D2
Bishop's Hill TA21 . . . . . 179 B7
Bishop's Hull Hill TA1 . . 212 B4
Bishop's Hull Prim Sch
  TA1 . . . . 212 B4
Bishop's Hull Rd TA1 . . . 212 A3
Bishop's La DT9 . . . . . . 187 F3
Bishop's Lydeard Sta
  TA4 . . . . 167 E7
Bishop's Mead TA2 . . . . 212 E8
Bishop's Pal* BA5 . . . . . 203 E4
Bishop's Path TA8 . . . . . 104 B6
Bishop Ave BS22 . . . . . . 32 A3
Bishop Cl TA20 . . . . 223 B5
Bishop Cres BA4 . . . . . . 204 F5
Bishop Fox's Com Sch
  TA1 . . . . 213 A1
Bishop Fox Dr TA1 . . . . 213 A2
Bishop Henderson CE Prim
  Sch
  Coleford BA3 . . . . 116 E8
  Taunton TA1 . . . . 212 C2
Bishop Rd TA5 . . . . 134 B2
Bishops Cl BS9 . . . . 5 E3
Bishops Cotts
  Stogursey TA5 . . . . 134 B7
  Wootton Courtenay TA24 . 129 F6
Bishops Cove BS13 . . . . 21 F5
Bishops Ct **4** TA21 . . . 222 D6
Bishops Dr TA10 . . . . . . 172 A5
Bishops Gn TA4 . . . . . . 210 C4
Bishops Knoll BS9 . . . . . 5 C3
Bishops La BA22 . . . . . . 197 A6
Bishopslea Cl BA5 . . . . . 203 C3
Bishops Lydeard CE Prim
  Sch TA4 . . . . 167 E8
Bishops Mead BS49 . . . . 35 A8
Bishops Park Way BA5 . 203 F2
Bishops Rd BS49 . . . . . . 35 A8
Bishop St
  Bristol BS2 . . . . 227 B4
  Faulkland BA3 . . . . 80 D2
Bishopston TA15 . . . . . . 186 B4
Bishop Sutton Prim Sch
  BS39 . . . . 57 D4
Bishops Wlk BA22 . . . . . 173 D1
Bishopsworth CE Jun Sch
  BS13 . . . . 21 F6
Bishopsworth Rd BS13 . . 22 A7
Bishop Terr BS2 . . . . 227 C4
Bishport Ave BS13 . . . . . 22 C3
Bishport Cl BS13 . . . . . . 22 B4
Bishport Gn BS13 . . . . . . 22 C3
Bitham Wlk TA7 . . . . . . 136 E3
Bittern Cl BS22 . . . . 31 F1
Bittlemead BS13 . . . . . . 22 F4
Black's Moor Hill La
  TA11 . . . . 173 A5
Blackacre BS14 . . . . 23 C4
Blackacre Hill BA8 . . . . . 176 D4
Blackaller La EX16 . . . . 163 C1
Black Bench Dro TA20 . . 223 F7
Blackberry Cl BA4 . . . . . 205 C4
Blackberry Ct TA21 . . . . 222 D4
Blackberry Dr BS22 . . . . 32 A2
Blackberry La
  Portishead BS20 . . . . 1 F2
  Sherborne DT9 . . . . 225 D5
  Winsley BA3, BA15 . . . . . 64 C8
Blackberry Way BA3 . . . 77 F3
Blackberry Wlk TA18 . . . 224 D7
Blackbird Cl BA3 . . . . . . 97 B8
Blackbird Way BA11 . . . 120 B6
Blackbrook Park Ave
  TA1 . . . . 213 E4
Blackbrook Prim Sch
  TA1 . . . . 213 D3
Blackbrook Rd TA1 . . . . 213 E5
Blackbrook Way TA1 . . . 213 E6
Black Dog Hill BA13 . . . 121 E6
Blackdown BA21 . . . . . . 219 A6
Blackdown Bsns Pk
  TA21 . . . . 222 E6
Blackdown Ct TA18 . . . . 23 B5
Blackdown Mead BS22 . . 90 C6
Blackdown Rd
  Bridgwater TA6 . . . . . . 209 D4
  Portishead BS20 . . . . 2 B5
  Rockwell Green TA21 . . . 222 B4
  Taunton TA1 . . . . 213 B8
Blackdown View
  Curry Rivel TA10 . . . . . 171 D4
  Ilminster TA19 . . . . 221 C4
  Norton Fitzwarren TA2 . . 168 B5
  Nynehead TA21 . . . . . . 167 C2
  Sampford Peverell EX16 . 178 C1
Blackdown Visitors Ctr*
  EX15 . . . . 180 D3
Black Dro TA7 . . . . 155 A1
Blacker's La BA3 . . . . . . 116 E4
Blackerton Cross EX16 . 162 E3
Blackey La BA3 . . . . 115 B6
Blackford Hollow BA22 . 175 F5

Blackford Moor Dro BS26,
  BS28 . . . . 107 B6
Blackford Moor La TA9,
  BS28 . . . . 107 B5
Blackford Rd
  Charlton Horethorne
    DT9 . . . . 176 A2
  Mark TA9 . . . . 106 F4
  Wedmore BS28 . . . . 108 A3
Blackford Way DT9 . . . . 176 A3
Blackfriars BS1 . . . . 227 A3
Blackfriars Rd BS48 . . . . 8 B1
Blackham La TA10 . . . . . 155 F2
Blackhayes La EX14 . . . . 192 C1
Black Horse La TA1 . . . . 212 F5
Black La
  Axbridge BS26 . . . . 70 E2
  Hemyock EX15 . . . . 180 D2
  Holcombe Rogus TA21 . . 178 E6
Blackland Dro TA20 . . . . 194 A1
Blackland La TA20 . . . . . 194 B1
Blacklands TA6 . . . . 208 F5
Black Mere BA22 . . . . . . 218 B5
Black Mixen La TA18 . . . 224 C7
Black Monkey La TA24 . . 131 C5
Blackmoor
  Clevedon BS21 . . . . 6 C1
  Lower Langford BS40 . . . 53 C6
  3 Weston-Super-Mare
    BS22 . . . . 31 F2
Blackmoor Cl BS40 . . . . 53 C6
Blackmoor La **6** BA8 . . 190 A6
Blackmoor Rd
  Abbots Leigh BS8 . . . . . . 4 E2
  Taunton TA2 . . . . 213 B7
  Wellington TA21 . . . . . . 222 F4
Blackmoors La BS3 . . . . 11 E4
Blackmore Chase BA9 . . 216 D3
Blackmore Dr BA2 . . . . . 44 C5
Blackmore La TA5 . . . . . 135 B1
Blackmore Rd DT10 . . . 190 B4
Blackmore Vale Cl BA8 . 176 E1
Blacknell Ind Est TA18 . . 224 C5
Blacknell La TA18 . . . . . 224 D6
Black Nore Point BS20 . . 1 F5
Black Pit Dro BA6 . . . . . 206 D8
Blackrock La BS39 . . . . . 40 E7
Black Rock Nature Trail*
  BA5 . . . . 72 A1
Blackrock Villas BS20 . . 2 B1
Blackrod Cotts TA13 . . . 184 F4
Blacksmith's La BA1 . . . 26 B3
Blacksmith La BA1 . . . . . 28 B6
Blacksmiths La TA4 . . . . 155 F8
Blacksmiths Row BA21 . 187 D6
Blackthorn Cl
  Biddisham BS26 . . . . . . 87 E6
  Bristol BS13 . . . . 22 D5
  6 North Petherton TA6 . 153 F3
Blackthorn Dr BS20 . . . . 2 E5
Blackthorne Cl BA22 . . . 173 E2
Blackthorn Gdns
  Taunton TA2 . . . . 168 F6
  Weston-Super-Mare BS22 . 32 A1
Blackthorn Rd BS13 . . . . 22 D5
Blackthorn Sq BS21 . . . . 6 D1
Blackthorns The TA1 . . . 213 C2
Blackthorn Terr BS22 . . . 32 A1
Blackthorn Way
  Nailsea BS48 . . . . 9 A2
  Somerton TA11 . . . . 211 B3
  Street BA16 . . . . 207 A5
Blackwater La
  Axminster EX13 . . . . . . 198 F3
  Wiveliscombe TA4 . . . . . 210 A8
Blackwell Rd BA22 . . . . 174 F3
Blackworthy Rd BA7 . . . 159 C3
Bladen Cl BS20 . . . . 2 E4
Bladud Bldgs BA1 . . . . . 228 C3
Blagdon Cl BS24 . . . . . . 48 F1
Blagdon Cres TA1 . . . . . 212 D1
Blagdon Cross TA1 . . . . 129 D2
Blagdon Hill Prim Sch
  TA3 . . . . 181 C5
Blagdon La
  Blagdon BS40 . . . . 54 F6
  Brompton Regis TA22,
    TA24 . . . . 148 D4
Blagdon Pk BA2 . . . . 44 A4
Blagdon Prim Sch BS40 . 54 F2
Blagdon Wlk BA11 . . . . 120 D7
Blagrove's Rd TA4 . . . . . 167 C4
Blagrove Cl
  Bristol BS13 . . . . 22 C3
  Street BA16 . . . . 207 E6
Blagrove Cres BS13 . . . . 22 C3
Blagrove Hill BA6 . . . . . 157 C6
Blaisdon **2** 49 D7
Blaise Wlk BS9 . . . . 5 C6
Blake's Cres TA9 . . . . . . 104 E5
Blake's La BA3 . . . . 115 D2
Blake End BS22 . . . . 31 E4
Blake Gn TA7 . . . . 156 B7
Blake Ind Est TA6 . . . . . 209 A3
Blakeney Gr BS48 . . . . . 18 C8
Blake Pl TA6 . . . . 209 A5
Blake Rd
  5 Crewkerne TA18 . . . 224 C5
  Wells BA5 . . . . 203 C5
Blakes La TA5, TA6 . . . . 208 C6
Blakes Rd TA6 . . . . 208 D6
Blake St
  2 Bridgwater TA6 . . . 208 F4
  Taunton TA1 . . . . 213 B4
Blakeway BS28 . . . . 138 B6
Blandford Cl BS48 . . . . . 8 E1
Blaxhold La TA5 . . . . . . 152 E5
Bleadon Hill BS23, BS24 . 67 A8

Bleadon Mill BS24 . . . . . 67 C5
Bleadon Rd BS24 . . . . . . 67 B7
Bleak St BA9 . . . . 161 E2
Blencathra Ct TA8 . . . . . 104 A8
Blenheim Cl
  Peasedown St John BA2 . 79 D7
  Weston-Super-Mare BS22 . 32 A2
Blenheim Ct **10** BS1 . . 227 A4
Blenheim Gdns BA1 . . . . 28 A2
Blenheim Mews TA24 . . 200 F7
Blenheim Rd
  Bridgwater TA6 . . . . . . 209 D7
  Minehead TA24 . . . . . . 201 A7
  Street BA16 . . . . 207 B4
  Taunton TA1 . . . . 213 D5
  Yeovil BA21 . . . . 219 D7
Blenheim View TA1 . . . . 201 A7
Blenheim Way BS20 . . . . 2 E5
Blights Hill EX16, TA22 . 163 F3
Blindhouse La **7** BA11 . 119 F4
Blind La
  Barton St David TA11 . . 158 A2
  Bath BA1 . . . . 27 C2
  Buckland St Mary TA20 . 182 A1
  Chard TA20 . . . . 223 D2
  Chew Stoke BS40 . . . . . . 56 E8
  Congresbury BS49 . . . . . 34 F6
  Drimpton DT8 . . . . 199 F6
  Isle Abbotts TA3 . . . . . . 183 F8
  Keinton Mandeville TA11 . 158 B1
  Martock TA12 . . . . 185 D5
  Southwick BA14 . . . . . . 83 F2
  Thorncombe TA20 . . . . . 199 B6
  Tunley BA2 . . . . 61 A4
Blindwell La
  Golsoncott TA23, TA24 . . 131 C1
  Skilgate TA4 . . . . 164 E6
Bloomfield BA11 . . . . . . 49 A2
Bloomfield Ave
  Bath BA2 . . . . 44 E4
  Timsbury BA2 . . . . 60 B3
Bloomfield Cl
  Taunton TA1 . . . . 213 C5
  Timsbury BA2 . . . . 60 B3
Bloomfield Cotts BA2 . . 79 C7
Bloomfield Cres BA2 . . . 44 D2
Bloomfield Dr BA2 . . . . . 44 D2
Bloomfield Gr BA2 . . . . . 44 E3
Bloomfield La BS39 . . . . 77 E5
Bloomfield Park Rd BA2 . 44 E3
Bloomfield Pk BA2 . . . . . 44 E3
Bloomfield Rd
  Bath BA2 . . . . 44 E3
  Timsbury BA2 . . . . 60 B3
Bloomfield Rise BA2 . . . 44 D2
Bloomfield Rise N BA2 . . 44 D2
Bloomfield Terr BA2 . . . 79 C7
Bloom Row TA6 . . . . . . 209 D5
Blossom Cl TA6 . . . . 208 D5
Blue Anchor Chalets
  TA24 . . . . 131 C6
Blue Anchor Sta TA24 . . 131 C6
Blue Ball Cl BA10 . . . . . 215 E6
Bluebell Cl
  Bristol BS9 . . . . 5 B6
  Taunton TA1 . . . . 213 C5
Bluebell Rd
  Weston-Super-Mare BS22 . 32 A6
  Yeovil BA22 . . . . 218 B5
Bluebell Rise BA3 . . . . . 77 F3
Blueberry Way BS22 . . . 31 F1
Blue Gate TA24 . . . . 145 D8
Blue Ho The BA11 . . . . . 119 F5
Blue Sch The BA5 . . . . . 203 C5
Blue Stone La TA13 . . . . 185 B6
Bluett Rd TA21 . . . . 222 F4
Blue Water Dr BS24 . . . . 50 D3
Blundells La TA2 . . . . . . 169 C4
Blythe Ct TA1 . . . . 212 D1
Blythe Gdns BS22 . . . . . 32 A3
Blythe Way TA8 . . . . 85 A3
Board Cross BA4 . . . . . . 205 B6
Boards Rd TA6 . . . . 209 A6
Boardwalk The BA16 . . . 207 D8
Boarpath La TA4 . . . . . . 151 A5
Boat La BS24 . . . . 67 C3
Boat Stall La BA2 . . . . . 228 C2
Bobbin La BA15 . . . . 64 F4
Bobbin Pk BA15 . . . . 64 F3
Bodden La BA4 . . . . 205 E6
Boden St TA20 . . . . 223 C3
Boden Villas TA20 . . . . . 223 C3
Bodley Way BS24 . . . . . . 49 E7
Bodmin Rd TA2 . . . . 213 A8
Bodmin Wlk BS4 . . . . . . 22 F8
Boez La TA12 . . . . 153 D1
Bofors Pk BA22 . . . . 218 A6
Bollams Mead TA4 . . . . 210 C5
Bollnas Cl BA4 . . . . 205 C4
Bolster La BA4 . . . . 157 C4
Bolter's La
  Alhampton BA4, BA7 . . . 159 B4
  Shepton Mallet BA4 . . . . 141 D8
Bolton Cl TA9 . . . . 104 F4
Bommertown Cross
  EX36 . . . . 162 A4
Bond's La SN14 . . . . 13 E8
Bond's Row TA24 . . . . . 124 A3
Bondfield Way TA20 . . . 223 B6
Bondip Hill BA22, TA11 . 173 D3
Bonds Cl TA20 . . . . 223 D6
Bonds Pool TA10 . . . . . . 172 A5
Bond St
  Bridgwater TA6 . . . . . . 208 F5
  Bristol BS1 . . . . 227 B4
  Yeovil BA20 . . . . 219 B4
  Yeovil, Houndstone BA22 . 218 B5

Bonfire Cl TA20 . . . . 223 C2
Bonfire La TA11 . . . . 173 E7
Bonham La BA12 . . . . 161 F4
Bonhill Rd BS39 . . . . 57 D5
Boniface Wlk TA8 . . . . . . 104 B6
Bonners Cswy EX13 . . . . . 198 A2
Bonners Dr EX13 . . . . 198 A1
Bonners Glen EX13 . . . . . 198 A1
Bonnie's La 6 TA14 . . . . . 185 F4
Bonning's La TA19 . . . . . . 184 D4
Bonniton La TA24 . . . . . . 130 E5
Bonniton New Rd TA24 . . . 201 D1
Bonny Cross
  Clayhanger EX16 . . . . . . 165 B1
  Morebath EX16 . . . . 164 B3
Bonny La TA24 . . . . 128 B2
Bonson Hill TA5 . . . . 134 E3
Bonsonwood La TA5 . . . . 134 E4
Boobery EX16 . . . . 178 D1
Boome La TA2 . . . . 169 C7
Boons Orch TA3 . . . . 169 C3
Booth Way TA6 . . . . 208 D5
Boozer Pit TA16 . . . . 195 F8
Borden Gate EX16 . . . . . . 178 B8
Bordesley Rd BS14 . . . . . . 23 A3
Boreal Way 4 BS24 . . . . . . 49 F7
Boreland La BA22 . . . . . . 187 A8
Borgie Pl BS22 . . . . 31 F3
Borleyton Wlk BS13 . . . . . . 21 F4
Borough Mall The BS28 . . 108 D4
Borough Post TA3 . . . . . . 170 B3
Borough The
  Montacute TA15 . . . . . . 186 B3
  Wedmore BS28 . . . . 108 D4
  3 Yeovil BA20 . . . . 219 B4
Borver Gr BS13 . . . . 22 B4
Bosanquet Flats TA24 . . . . 200 F7
Bossington Dr TA2 . . . . . . 213 B8
Bossington La TA24 . . . . . 124 B4
Boswell Rd BA15 . . . . 64 F3
Botham Cl BS22 . . . . 32 A4
Bottreaux Mill Cross
  EX36 . . . . 162 A5
Boucher's La TA4 . . . . 165 E4
Boulevard BS23 . . . . 48 E8
Boulters Rd BS13 . . . . 22 C4
Boundaries The BS24 . . . . . 67 B1
Boundary Ave
  Frome BA11 . . . . 120 B5
  Yeovil BA22 . . . . 218 B7
Boundary Cl
  Holcombe BA3 . . . . 116 C8
  Midsomer Norton BA3 . . . 97 B7
  Weston-Super-Mare BS23 . . 48 E3
  Yeovil BA21 . . . . 218 B7
Boundary Rd
  Weston-Super-Mare BS24 . . 50 A4
  Yeovil BA22 . . . . 218 A5
Boundary Way
  Glastonbury BA6 . . . . . . 206 C3
  Yeovil BA22 . . . . 218 A7
Boundhay BA22 . . . . 186 C2
Bounds La TA20 . . . . 223 A1
Bourchier Cl 13 EX16 . . . . 164 B1
Bourchier Dr 12 EX16 . . . . 164 B1
Bourchier Gdns BS13 . . . . . 22 B3
Bourne Gr TA1 . . . . 213 D4
Bourne La
  Blagdon BS40 . . . . 54 C4
  Burrington BS40 . . . . 54 B4
Bournville Inf Sch BS23 . . . 49 A4
Bournville Jun Sch BS23 . . . 48 F5
Bournville Rd BS23 . . . . . . 48 F4
Bourtonbridge Dro BA5 . . 139 F5
Bourton Combe BS48 . . . . . 19 F7
Bourton La
  Cross BS26 . . . . 69 E3
  Weston-Super-Mare BS22 . . 32 C4
Bourton Mead
  Flax Bourton BS48 . . . . . . 19 E8
  Long Ashton BS41 . . . . . . 11 A1
Bourton Wlk BS13 . . . . 22 A8
Bouverie Cl TA24 . . . . . . 129 E1
Bouverie Rd TA6 . . . . 208 D5
Bove Moor Cl BA16 . . . . . 207 E6
Bove Moor Rd BA16 . . . . . 207 E6
Bovet Cl TA1 . . . . 212 B1
Bove Town BA6 . . . . 206 E5
Bovet St TA21 . . . . 222 C6
Bow Cotts BS20 . . . . 4 C4
Bowden's La TA10 . . . . . . 171 F7
Bowden Hill BA3 . . . . 96 D4
Bowden La
  Milborne Port BA8 . . . . . 217 F5
  Rodhuish TA24 . . . . 130 F3
  Yenston BA8 . . . . 189 D7
Bowden Rd BA8 . . . . 189 D8
Bowdens La EX16 . . . . . . 164 E3
Bowden Way BS8 . . . . 10 B3
Bowditch Cl BA4 . . . . . . 205 A5
Bowditch Row 8 TA18 . . . 224 C6
Bowen Rd BS24 . . . . 50 C5
Bower Ashton Terr BS3 . . . 11 F4
Bower Ave TA6 . . . . 209 C6
Bower Fields TA6 . . . . . . 209 D6
Bowerhayes La TA4 . . . . . 131 A5
Bower Hinton TA12 . . . . . 185 D5
Bowerings Rd TA6 . . . . . . 208 E2
Bower La TA6 . . . . 209 E6
Bowerleaze BS9 . . . . 5 C5
Bower Manor Sh Ctr
  TA6 . . . . 209 D6
Bowermead La BA4 . . . . . 204 C1
Bowery Cnr BA5 . . . . 92 E5
Bowfell Cl TA1 . . . . 212 C1
Bow Gate TA18 . . . . 196 A8
Bowhayes TA18 . . . . 224 C5

Bowhays Cross TA4 . . . . . 202 A2
Bowlditch La BA3 . . . . 78 A5
Bowleaze BA21 . . . . 218 D6
Bowline Cl TA6 . . . . 208 E7
Bowline Ct TA24 . . . . . . 201 B7
Bowling Gn
  10 Cannington TA5 . . . . 135 B2
  Street BA16 . . . . 207 D7
Bowlish Inf Sch BA4 . . . . 205 A6
Bowlish La BA4 . . . . 205 A6
Bowmont Gr TA1 . . . . . . 213 D3
Bowns Cl BA4 . . . . 141 E1
Bowood Rd TA2 . . . . 213 A6
Bowring Cl
  Bristol BS13 . . . . 22 C3
  Coxley BA5 . . . . 139 E6
Bowsprit Cl TA24 . . . . . . 201 B7
Bow St TA10 . . . . 171 F5
Bowyers Cl BA6 . . . . 206 E5
Boxbury Hill BS39 . . . . 77 F3
Boxbush Hill BA4 . . . . . . 158 E8
Box Bush La BS40 . . . . 33 C1
Box Rd BA1 . . . . 29 C3
Boxstone Hill TA19 . . . . . 184 D2
Box Wlk BS31 . . . . 24 C4
Boyce's Ave BS8 . . . . 226 A3
Boyce Cl BA2 . . . . 43 F5
Boyd Ho BA5 . . . . 113 A1
Boyd St BA5 . . . . 25 D3
Boyle Cl DT10 . . . . 190 B4
Boyton Hill TA19 . . . . . . 194 F8
Boyton La TA19 . . . . 194 F7
Bracey Rd TA21 . . . . 185 E7
Bracken Edge TA4 . . . . . . 132 E4
Bracken Way TA20 . . . . . . 223 F5
Brackenwood Gdns* BS20 . 1 F5
Brackenwood Rd BS21 . . . . . 6 E6
Bracton Dr BS14 . . . . 23 A5
Bradbeers TA3 . . . . 181 D8
Bradfield Cl TA6 . . . . 208 E1
Bradfield Way TA20 . . . . . 223 C3
Bradford Cl
  Clevedon BS21 . . . . 6 C1
  Taunton TA1 . . . . 168 D1
Bradford Pk BA2 . . . . 45 A2
Bradford Rd
  Bath BA2 . . . . 45 A1
  Bathford BA1 . . . . 29 B2
  Misterton TA18 . . . . . . 224 E4
  Rode BA11, BA14 . . . . . . 83 A2
  Sherborne DT9 . . . . 225 B3
  Wingfield BA14, BA15 . . . 83 C8
  Winsley BA15 . . . . 64 D6
  Winsley BA15 . . . . 64 E7
Bradley Ave BS11 . . . . 4 E6
Bradley Cl TA11 . . . . 211 C4
Bradley Cres BS11 . . . . 4 E6
Bradley Cross BS27 . . . . . . 90 D7
Bradley Hill La TA11 . . . . 211 B5
Bradley La
  Ashcott TA7 . . . . 156 B7
  Maiden Bradley BA11,
    BA12 . . . . 144 B2
  Parbrook BA6 . . . . 158 C7
Bradley Rd BS20 . . . . 3 E5
Bradley View TA11 . . . . . 211 C4
Bradley Way BA6 . . . . . . 158 B8
Bradney La TA7 . . . . 136 D1
Bradon La
  Isle Abbotts TA3 . . . . . 183 F6
  Stocklinch TA19 . . . . . . 184 A5
Bradville Gdns BS41 . . . . . 27 B8
Brae Rd BS25 . . . . 70 B8
Brae Rise BS25 . . . . 70 A8
Bragg's La BS2 . . . . 227 C3
Braikenridge Cl BS21 . . . . . 6 C1
Brain's Cnr BA9 . . . . 216 E1
Brainsfield BS9 . . . . 5 F6
Brains La BS21 . . . . 175 A5
Braithwaite Pl TA8 . . . . . . 85 A2
Braithwaite Way BA11 . . . 120 C6
Brakewell Gdns BS14 . . . . . 23 A4
Bramble Dr
  Berrow TA8 . . . . 84 F5
  Bristol BS9 . . . . 5 D3
  South Petherton TA13 . . . 220 C4
Bramble Hill BA16 . . . . . 156 D6
Bramble La
  Bristol BS9 . . . . 5 C3
  Haselbury Plucknett TA18 . 196 C5
Bramble Pk TA1 . . . . 213 C2
Brambles Rd TA8 . . . . 85 B1
Brambles The
  Bristol BS13 . . . . 22 C4
  Hinton Charterhouse BA2 . . 63 E1
  Keynsham BS31 . . . . 24 D3
  Wellington TA21 . . . . . . 222 D4
  Weston-Super-Mare BS22 . . 32 E2
Bramble Way BA2 . . . . 45 B1
Bramblewood TA3 . . . . . . 17 B1
Bramblewood Rd BS22 . . . . 31 E3
Bramley Cl
  Charlton Horethorne
    DT9 . . . . 176 A2
  Crewkerne TA18 . . . . . . 224 F4
  Locking BS24 . . . . 50 A5
  Peasedown St John BA2 . . . 79 D7
  Pill BS20 . . . . 4 C4
  Sandford BS25 . . . . 52 A4
  Yatton BS49 . . . . 34 B7
Bramley Dr
  Backwell BS48 . . . . 19 A5
  Frome BA11 . . . . 120 C6
Bramley Rd
  Street BA16 . . . . 207 B4

Bramley Rd continued
  Taunton TA1 . . . . 213 D5
Bramley Sq BS49 . . . . 34 B3
Bramleys The
  Nailsea BS48 . . . . 18 B8
  Portishead BS20 . . . . 2 F5
Brampton Ho BS20 . . . . 2 E4
Brampton Way BS20 . . . . . . 2 E4
Bramshill Dr BS22 . . . . 31 F3
Branche Gr BS13 . . . . 22 D3
Branches Cross BS40 . . . . . 35 E3
Branch Rd BA2 . . . . 63 F2
Brandon Ho BS8 . . . . 226 B2
Brandon St BS1 . . . . 226 C2
Brandon Steep BS1 . . . . . 226 C2
Brangay La BS27 . . . . 91 A1
Brangwyn Sq BS22 . . . . . . 31 F2
Branksome Ave TA6 . . . . . 209 B5
Bransby Way BS24 . . . . . . 50 A8
Branscombe Rd BS9 . . . . . . 5 C4
Branscombe Wlk BS20 . . . . 1 F3
Bransford BA22 . . . . 197 D3
Brantwood Rd TA6 . . . . . . 208 C5
Brasknocker Hill BA2 . . . . . 45 F2
Brassmill Ent Ctr BA1 . . . . 44 A7
Brassmill La BA1 . . . . 44 A7
Brassmill Lane Trad Est
  BA1 . . . . 44 A7
Bratton Cl TA24 . . . . 200 D7
Bratton Ho BA9 . . . . 176 B8
Bratton La TA24 . . . . 200 B7
Bratton Mill La
  Minehead, Bratton TA24 . . 200 B7
  Minehead, Woodcombe
    TA24 . . . . 200 C7
Bratton Rd BS4 . . . . 22 D7
Bray Cl TA24 . . . . 179 B3
Braysbridge BS27 . . . . 90 C7
Braysdown Cl BA2 . . . . . . 79 B6
Braysdown La BA2 . . . . . . 79 C7
Breach Cl SP8 . . . . 161 F1
Breaches The BS20 . . . . . . 4 B5
Breach Furlong La TA10 . . 156 A1
Breach Hill TA21 . . . . 179 F5
Breach Hill La BS40 . . . . . . 56 C6
Breach La
  Brinscombe BS26 . . . . . . 89 B3
  Corsley Heath BA12 . . . . 144 E7
  Kington Magna SP8 . . . . 177 E2
  Nailsea BS48 . . . . 17 F7
  Weston Town BA4 . . . . . 142 E4
Bread & Cheese La TA19 . . 184 C1
Bread St BA4 . . . . 140 F3
Brean Court Ho TA8 . . . . . 65 F3
Brean Ct TA8 . . . . 65 F3
Brean Down Ave BS23 . . . . 48 E4
Brean Down Rd TA8 . . . . . 47 F1
Brean Rd BS24 . . . . 49 A1
Brecon View BS24 . . . . . . 49 A1
Breech Cotts TA21 . . . . . . 179 F5
Bree Cl BS22 . . . . 32 A4
Breech La BA6 . . . . 158 A8
Bremis Rd TA24 . . . . 201 E3
Brendon Ave BS23 . . . . . . 48 F8
Brendon Cl TA23 . . . . 131 D2
Brendon Gdns 2 BS48 . . . . 8 E1
Brendon Ho BA21 . . . . . . 219 A6
Brendon Rd
  Bridgwater TA6 . . . . . . 208 F6
  Portishead BS20 . . . . 2 A5
  Watchet TA23 . . . . 202 B6
  Wellington TA21 . . . . . . 222 D7
Brendons TA4 . . . . 167 E8
Brendons The EX16 . . . . . 178 D1
Brendon Two Gates
  TA24 . . . . 127 A6
Brendon View TA4 . . . . . . 151 B7
Brendon Way
  Bridgwater TA6 . . . . . . 208 F6
  Cheddar BS27 . . . . 90 C8
Brent Broad TA8 . . . . 85 B2
Brent Cl
  Brent Knoll TA9 . . . . 86 B1
  Weston-Super-Mare BS24 . . 49 B2
Brent Knoll CE Prim Sch
  TA9 . . . . 86 A2
Brent Rd
  Burnham-on-S TA8, TA9 . . . 85 B4
  Cossington TA7 . . . . . . 136 F3
  East Brent TA9 . . . . 86 C5
Brentsfield La TA7 . . . . . . 154 E7
Brent St TA9 . . . . 86 A2
Breowen Cl TA19 . . . . . . 221 B3
Brereton Rd TA24 . . . . . . 201 B6
Bretoneux Rd BA6 . . . . . . 206 E3
Brett Cl TA4 . . . . 202 F1
Brettingham Ct TA17 . . . . 195 C7
Brewery Bglws TA18 . . . . 224 C7
Brewery Hill BS30 . . . . . . 25 F7
Brewery La
  Holcombe BA3 . . . . 97 D1
  Ilminster TA19 . . . . 221 B4
  Oakhill BA3 . . . . 115 A3
  Shepton Mallet BA4 . . . . 205 D5
Brewham Rd BA10 . . . . . . 160 D6
Brewhouse The TA6 . . . . . 209 A5
Brewhouse Theatre & Arts
  Ctr* TA1 . . . . 212 F4
Breynton Rd BA6 . . . . . . 206 F5
Brian Mooney Cl TA20 . . . 223 B3
Briant Cl TA1 . . . . 212 B1
Briar Cl
  Burnham-on-S TA8 . . . . . 104 C6
  Frome BA11 . . . . 120 B7
  Nailsea BS48 . . . . 9 A2
  Radstock BA3 . . . . 97 D8
  Yeovil BA21 . . . . 219 E8

Briar Ct
  Bridgwater TA6 . . . . . . 208 E5
  Burnham-on-S TA8 . . . . . 104 C6
  Pill BS20 . . . . 4 C4
Briarfield BA22 . . . . 173 E2
Briar Mead BS49 . . . . 17 A1
Briar Rd
  Hutton BS24 . . . . 49 E3
  Street BA16 . . . . 207 A5
Briars Ct BA2 . . . . 44 A4
Briars The
  Backwell BS48 . . . . 18 F7
  Yeovil BA20 . . . . 218 C2
Briarwood BS9 . . . . 5 F6
Briary Rd BS20 . . . . 2 C5
Brick Cotts BA3 . . . . 117 A7
Brickkiln La DT9 . . . . 225 E7
Brick St BS2 . . . . 227 C3
Brickyard La
  Bourton SP8 . . . . 161 F1
  Wanstrow BA4 . . . . 142 F5
Brick Yard La TA18 . . . . . 224 C7
Briddicott La TA24 . . . . . 131 A4
Bridewell La
  Bath BA1 . . . . 228 B2
  Hutton BS24, BS26, BS29 . . 50 D1
  Shapwick TA7 . . . . 137 F1
Bridewell St BS1 . . . . . . 227 A3
Bridge Bldgs BS39 . . . . . . 77 B3
Bridge Cl
  Evercreech BA4 . . . . . . 141 E2
  Whitchurch BS14 . . . . . . 23 C4
  Williton TA4 . . . . 202 D2
Bridge Cotts
  Chard Junction TA20 . . . 198 D8
  Drimpton DT8 . . . . 199 F7
  East Chinnock BA22 . . . . 196 F8
Bridge Farm Cl BS14 . . . . 23 A3
Bridge Farm Inf Sch BS14 . 23 A4
Bridge Farm Jun Sch
  BS14 . . . . 23 A4
Bridge Farm Sq BS49 . . . . 34 D4
Bridge Gdns BA2 . . . . . . 60 A6
Bridge Hill BA4 . . . . 142 F4
Bridge Ho
  11 Bath BA1 . . . . 28 C1
  Bristol BS1 . . . . 227 A2
  9 Clevedon BS21 . . . . . . 6 C2
  Weston-Super-Mare BS23 . . 48 E6
Bridgehouse Cross EX15 . . 180 D1
Bridge House Pk TA13 . . . 220 F4
Bridge Pl DT9 . . . . 187 F4
Bridge Place Rd BA2 . . . . . 78 E8
Bridge Rd
  Bath BA2 . . . . 44 C5
  Bleadon BS24 . . . . 67 B6
  Leigh Woods BS8 . . . . . . 11 E6
  Weston-Super-Mare BS23 . . 48 F6
Bridge Rise 17 TA12 . . . . 185 E6
Bridges Mead TA24 . . . . . 201 E3
Bridge St
  Bath BA2 . . . . 228 C2
  Bourton SP8 . . . . 161 F1
  Bristol BS1 . . . . 227 A2
  Dulverton TA22 . . . . . . 163 D6
  Frome BA11 . . . . 119 F5
  Taunton TA1 . . . . 212 F4
  Williton TA4 . . . . 202 D2
Bridge Terr EX16 . . . . . . 164 B1
Bridge The
  Frome BA11 . . . . 119 F5
  Taunton TA1 . . . . 212 F4
Bridge Valley Rd BS8 . . . . . 11 E4
Bridgwater Coll Cannington
  Ctr TA5 . . . . 135 B2
Bridgwater Ent Ctr 7
  TA6 . . . . 208 F6
Bridge Way TA13 . . . . . . 220 F4
Bridgeway Cotts TA13 . . . 220 E4
Bridgewell Ct DT9 . . . . . 225 E3
Bridgwater TA6 . . . . 208 F4
Bridgwater Bldgs BA7 . . . 214 B5
Bridgwater Coll
  Bridgwater TA6 . . . . . . 209 B5
  Minehead TA24 . . . . . . 201 A7
Bridgwater Ct BS24 . . . . . 49 A3
Bridgwater General Hospl
  TA6 . . . . 209 A5
Bridgwater Rd
  Dundry BS41, BS13, BS48 . . 21 D6
  East Brent TA9 . . . . 86 D4
  Lympsham BS24 . . . . . . 67 C5
  North Petherton TA6 . . . 153 F4
  Taunton, Bathpool TA2 . . . 213 F7
  Taunton TA1 . . . . 213 D5
  Weston-Super-Mare BS23,
    BS24 . . . . 48 F2
  Winscombe BS25 . . . . . . 70 A5
Bridle Way BA22 . . . . . . 197 F8
Bridport Rd DT8 . . . . 199 F8
Briercliffe Rd BS9 . . . . 5 D7
Briery Leaze Rd BS14 . . . . 23 A5
Brigadier Cl BA22 . . . . . . 218 A5
Brigg Cl TA2 . . . . 208 E7
Brighton Mews BS8 . . . . . 226 B4
Brighton Rd BS23 . . . . . . 48 E6
Brighton St 7 BS2 . . . . . 227 B4
Brightstowe Rd TA8 . . . . . 85 A2
Brigstocke Rd BS2 . . . . . . 227 B4
Brimble Cotts DT10 . . . . . 189 F1
Brimblecombe Cl BA22 . . . 32 C3
Brimclose Rd TA17 . . . . . 195 C7
Brimgrove La TA19 . . . . . 184 E4
Brimhill Rise BA13 . . . . . 121 D4
Brimley Cross TA3 . . . . . 180 F1
Brimley Hill EX13 . . . . . . 198 D3
Brimley Rd EX13 . . . . . . 198 D3

Briar Ct
  Bridgwater TA6 . . . . . . 208 E5

Bon–Bro 237

Brimridge Rd BS25 . . . . . . 70 A8
Brimsmore Ct BA21 . . . . . 218 E8
Brimstone La
  Rockwell Green TA21 . . . 222 A2
  Sampford Arundel TA21 . . 179 F6
  Sampford Peverell EX16 . . 178 E2
Brincil Hill TA11 . . . . 173 D4
Brindham La BA6 . . . . . . 139 D3
Brindle Cl TA2 . . . . 212 C7
Brines Orch BA8 . . . . . . 176 E1
Brinmead Wlk BS13 . . . . . . 21 F3
Brinscombe La BS26 . . . . . 89 A5
Brinsea Batch BS49 . . . . . . 52 E8
Brinsea La BS49 . . . . 52 F8
Brinsea Rd BS49 . . . . 34 E2
Brinsmead Cres BS20 . . . . . 4 D4
Briscoes Ave BS13 . . . . . . 22 D4
Brislington Ent Coll BS4 . . . 23 F8
Bristol Cathedral Sch
  BS1 . . . . 226 C2
Bristol Dental Hospl
  BS1 . . . . 227 A3
Bristol & Exeter Mews
  BS1 . . . . 227 C1
Bristol Eye Hospl BS1 . . . 227 A3
Bristol Gate 1 BS8 . . . . . 11 F5
Bristol General Hospl
  BS1 . . . . 227 A1
Bristol Gram Sch BS8 . . . 226 C3
Bristol Harbour Rly*
  BS1 . . . . 226 C1
Bristol Hill BS4 . . . . 112 E3
Bristol Homeopathic Hospl
  BS8 . . . . 226 C4
Bristol Ind Mus* BS1 . . . 227 C1
Bristol International Airport
  BS48 . . . . 36 E7
Bristol Rd
  Bridgwater TA6 . . . . . . 209 B7
  Chew Stoke BS40 . . . . . . 56 E8
  Chewton Mendip BA5 . . . 113 A8
  Churchill BS25 . . . . 53 A5
  Congresbury BS49 . . . . . 34 D5
  Farrington Gurney BS39 . . 76 F5
  Highbridge TA9 . . . . . . 104 F4
  Horrington BA5 . . . . . . 112 F6
  Keynsham BS31 . . . . 24 E6
  Newton St Loe BA2 . . . . 43 D7
  Paulton BS39 . . . . 77 E7
  Pensford BS39 . . . . 40 D6
  Portishead BS20 . . . . 2 E4
  Radstock BA3 . . . . 78 F3
  Redhill BS40 . . . . 37 A3
  Rooks Bridge BS26, TA9 . . 87 B5
  Sherborne DT9 . . . . . . 225 D6
  Walpole TA6 . . . . 136 B3
  Weston-Super-Mare BS22 . . 32 C2
  Whitchurch BS14 . . . . . . 23 D3
  Winscombe BS25 . . . . . . 70 C8
  Wraxall BS48 . . . . 9 D4
Bristol Rd By-pass BS40 . . . 53 C5
Bristol Rd Lower BS23 . . . . 30 E1
Bristol Rd Lower BS23 . . . . 30 E1
Bristol Royal Infmy BS2 . . 227 A4
Bristol Temple Meads Sta
  BS1 . . . . 227 C1
Bristol View BS4 . . . . 62 C8
Bristol Zoo Gdns* BS8 . . . . 5 F1
Britannia Cl BA3 . . . . 96 D4
Britannia Way
  Chard TA20 . . . . 223 C6
  Clevedon BS21 . . . . 6 C1
British Empire &
  Commonwealth Mus The*
  BS1 . . . . 227 C1
Briton St 2 EX16 . . . . . . 164 C1
Brittains BA11 . . . . 119 D6
Brittania Bldgs BS8 . . . . . 226 A1
Brittan Pl BS20 . . . . 3 E3
Britten's Cl BS39 . . . . 77 F6
Britten's Hill BS39 . . . . . . 77 F6
Brittons Ash TA2 . . . . . . 213 F8
Brittons Pass SN14 . . . . . . 13 F8
Broadacres BA22 . . . . . . 197 C8
Broadbridge Rd TA3 . . . . 183 C6
Broadbury Rd BS4 . . . . . . 22 E8
Broad Cl
  Kington Magna SP8 . . . . 177 E1
  Wells BA5 . . . . 112 E1
Broadclose Way TA11 . . . 158 A2
Broadcroft BS40 . . . . 38 F3
Broadcroft Ave BS49 . . . . . 17 F1
Broadcroft Cl BS49 . . . . . . 17 F1
Broad Dro
  Burrowbridge TA7 . . . . . 155 A2
  North Wootton BA4 . . . . 140 A3
Broadenham La TA20 . . . . 194 E1
Broadfield Rd BS4 . . . . . . 23 A8
Broadguage Bsns Pk
  TA4 . . . . 167 E7
Broadhay BA5 . . . . 110 E2
Broad Hill BA22 . . . . 196 D7
Broadhurst Gdns TA8 . . . . 104 B5
Broad La
  East Chinnock BA22 . . . . 196 E7
  Hawkridge TA22 . . . . . . 146 D1
  North Curry TA3 . . . . . . 170 D4
  Winsford TA24 . . . . 147 F4
Broadlands BS21 . . . . 6 F3
Broadlands Ave
  Keynsham BS31 . . . . 24 D6
  North Petherton TA6 . . . 153 F4
Broadlands Cl BS21 . . . . . 219 E8
Broadlands Ct TA1 . . . . . 212 E2
Broadlands Dr BS11 . . . . . . 5 A8

Broadlands La TA5 . . . . . **208** A4
Broadlands Rd TA1 . . . . **212** E2
Broadlands Rise TA1 . . . **212** E2
Broadlands Sch BS31 . . . **24** D6
Broadlands Way TA1 . . . **212** E2
Broad Lane Head
Hawkridge TA22 . . . . . . **146** D1
Winsford TA22 . . . . **147** F4
Broadlawn TA7 . . . . . . **136** E4
Broadleas BS13 . . . . **22** C7
Broadleaze
Bristol BS11 . . . . **4** E7
Yeovil BA21 . . . . **218** C6
Broadleaze Way BS25 . . . **51** F2
Broadly Gdns TA2 . . . . . **213** E8
Broadmead
Bristol BS1 . . . . **227** B3
Keynsham BS31 . . . . **25** B5
Kingsbury Episcopi TA12 . **185** B7
South Petherton TA13 . . **220** B4
Broadmead Dro TA7 . . . **155** F6
Broadmead La
Barrington TA19 . . . . . . **184** D6
Catcott TA7 . . . . **137** D2
Edington TA7 . . . . **137** C3
Keynsham BS31 . . . . **25** A6
Kington Magna SP8 . . . . **177** D1
Norton Sub Hamdon TA14 . **185** F2
Broadmead Rd TA3 . . . . **183** B1
Broadmeads TA10 . . . . . **172** A6
Broadmoor Dro BS28 . . . . **89** D3
Broadmoor La
Bath BA1 . . . . **27** A3
Horsington BA8 . . . . . . **176** E2
Broadmoor Pk BA1 . . . . . **27** B2
Broadmoor Vale BA1 . . . . **27** A2
Broadoak TA19 . . . . **183** C1
Broad Oak **9** BA20 . . . . **219** B4
Broadoak Hill BS41 . . . . . **21** F2
Broad Oak Hill TA4 . . . . **151** B5
Broadoak Mathematics &
Computing Coll BS23 . . . . **48** E3
Broadoak Rd
Bridgwater TA6 . . . . **209** D5
Churchill BS40 . . . . **53** A5
Weston-Super-Mare BS23 . . **48** D3
Broad Oak Rd BS13 . . . . . **21** F4
Broad Oaks BS8 . . . . **11** E6
Broad Path EX15 . . . . . . **179** A1
Broad Plain BS2 . . . . . . **227** C2
Broad Quay
Bath BA1 . . . . **228** C1
Bristol BS1 . . . . **227** A2
Broad Rd
Blagdon BS40 . . . . **72** D8
Rodney Stoke BA5 . . . . . . **91** E1
Broadshard Rd TA18 . . . **224** C8
Broad St
Bath BA1 . . . . **228** C3
Bristol BS1 . . . . **227** A3
Charlton Adam TA11 . . . **173** F7
Chewton Mendip BA3 . . . . **94** C5
Churchinford TA3 . . . . . **191** D7
Congresbury BS49 . . . . . . **34** D4
Somerton TA11 . . . . **211** E4
Stoney Stratton BA4 . . . . **141** F2
Wells BA5 . . . . **203** D4
Wrington BS40 . . . . **35** D2
Broadstone TA7 . . . . . . **154** E6
Broadstone La
Hardington Mandeville
BA22 . . . . **197** A6
Kingston Seymour BS21 . . . **15** F3
West Chinnock TA18 . . . . **196** C7
Broad Stones BA15 . . . . . **46** E7
Broadstone Wlk BS13 . . . **22** D5
Broad Street Pl BA1 . . . **228** C3
Broadway
Bath BA2 . . . . **45** B6
Bridgwater TA6 . . . . . . **208** F4
Charlton Adam TA11 . . . **174** A7
Chilcompton BA3 . . . . **96** C3
Chilton Polden TA7 . . . . **137** B2
Frome BA11 . . . . **119** D5
Locking BS24 . . . . **50** D4
Merriott TA16 . . . . **195** F7
Odcombe BA22 . . . . . . **186** C2
Saltford BS31 . . . . **25** D3
Shipham BS25 . . . . **70** E8
Weston-Super-Mare BS24 . . **49** A2
Broad Way TA12 . . . . . . **185** D5
Broadway Acres BS27 . . . **70** F1
Broadway Ave TA7 . . . . **137** B2
Broadway Cl BA3 . . . . . . **96** C3
Broadway Hill TA19 . . . . **183** B1
Broadway La
Castle Cary BA22 . . . . . **214** B3
Midsomer Norton BA3 . . . **78** B5
Westbury-sub-Mendip
BA5 . . . . **110** D7
Broadway Rd
Bristol, Bishopsworth
BS13 . . . . **21** F5
Charlton Adam TA11 . . . **173** F7
Horton TA19 . . . . **183** C2
Broadways Head EX14,
TA20 . . . . **192** C6
Broad Weir BS1 . . . . **227** B3
Broadwell Cl TA20 . . . . . **193** D6
Broadwood Rd TA24 . . . **130** B4
Brock Ct BA7 . . . . **214** C6
Brock End BS20 . . . . **1** F3
Brockhole La
Dinnington TA17 . . . . . . **195** B8

Brockhole La continued
Tatworth TA20 . . . . **198** B7
Brockle Cl TA11 . . . . . . **211** D4
Brockley Cl
Nailsea BS48 . . . . **8** D1
Weston-Super-Mare BS24 . . **48** F1
Brockley Combe Rd BS48 . **19** B1
Brockley Cres BS24 . . . . . **48** F1
Brockley La BS48 . . . . . . **18** D4
Brockley Mini Farm (Open
Farm)★ BS48 . . . . **35** F7
Brockley Rd BS31 . . . . . . **25** D3
Brockley Way BS49 . . . . . **18** B3
Brockley Wlk BS13 . . . . . **22** A8
Brocks La BS41 . . . . **10** F1
Brocks Mount **16** TA14 . . **185** F4
Brocks Rd BS13 . . . . **22** C3
Brock St BA1 . . . . **228** B3
Brockway BS48 . . . . **8** F2
Brockwell La TA24 . . . . **129** F6
Brockwood BA15 . . . . . . **64** F7
Brocole La TA20 . . . . . . **193** D5
Broderip TA4 . . . . **136** F3
Brokerswood Country Pk★
BA13 . . . . **102** F6
Bromes La TA3 . . . . **183** F7
Bromley Rd BS39 . . . . . . **39** F1
Brompton Ho BA2 . . . . . **228** C4
Brompton Mdws TA22 . . **148** B2
Brompton Rd BS24 . . . . . **49** A2
Bronte Cl BS23 . . . . **49** B4
Brook's Hill EX15 . . . . . **179** C1
Brook Bank
Draycott BS27 . . . . **90** F2
Rodney Stoke BS27 . . . . **109** C7
Brook Cl
Long Ashton BS41 . . . . . . **11** B1
Minehead TA24 . . . . . . **200** F7
North Petherton TA6 . . . **153** E3
Yeovil BA21 . . . . **218** D7
Brook Cotts
Corfe TA3 . . . . **181** F6
Corston BA2 . . . . **43** B7
Brook Ct BS13 . . . . **22** A6
Brookdale Rd BS13 . . . . . **22** B6
Brooke Rd
Berrow TA8 . . . . **84** F4
Taunton TA1 . . . . **213** B4
Brookes Cl BA5 . . . . . . **203** C5
Brookfield Pk BA1 . . . . . **27** B2
Brookfields BA7 . . . . . . **214** B5
Brookfield Way BA16 . . . **207** A4
Brookfield Wlk BA21 . . . . . **6** F3
Brook Gate BS13 . . . . . . **11** E1
Brookhampton Cnr
BA22 . . . . **175** D6
Brook La
Barton St David BA6 . . . **157** F3
6 Cannington TA5 . . . . **135** B2
Catcott TA7 . . . . **137** D2
7 Henstridge BA8 . . . . **190** A6
Brookland Rd
Langport TA10 . . . . **172** A6
Weston-Super-Mare BS22 . . **49** B7
Brooklands
Bridgwater TA6 . . . . . . **209** C5
Dunkerton BA2 . . . . **61** D3
Brooklands Rd TA21 . . . **222** B5
Brookland Way **3** BA8 . . **190** A6
Brookleaze BS9 . . . . **5** C5
Brookleaze Bldgs BA1 . . . **28** B2
Brookleigh BA16 . . . . . . **207** A5
Brooklyn BS40 . . . . **35** D2
Brooklyn Rd
Bath BA1 . . . . **28** C2
Bristol BS13 . . . . **22** B8
Brooklyn Terr BA5 . . . . **139** E6
Brook Rd
Bath BA2 . . . . **44** D6
Williton TA4 . . . . **202** E3
Brookside
Broadway TA19 . . . . . . **183** C2
Milborne Port DT9 . . . . **217** D1
Paulton BS39 . . . . **77** E6
Pill BS20 . . . . **4** D3
South Cheriton BA8 . . . . **176** D3
West Coker BA22 . . . . . **197** A8
Brookside Cl
Batheaston BA1 . . . . **28** F5
Paulton BS39 . . . . **77** E6
Taunton TA1 . . . . **168** D1
Brookside Com Prim Sch
BA16 . . . . **207** B4
Brookside Dr BA2 . . . . . . **59** F6
Brookside Ho BA1 . . . . . . **27** B1
Brookside Rd TA5 . . . . . **135** B5
Brooks Pl TA21 . . . . **222** E6
Brooks Rd BA16 . . . . . . **207** B4
Brook St
Bampton EX16 . . . . **164** B1
Cannington TA5 . . . . . . **135** B2
Milborne Port DT9 . . . . **217** D1
Minehead TA24 . . . . . . **201** B5
North Newton TA7 . . . . **153** F1
Timberscombe TA24 . . . **130** B5
Brook Street Mews TA24 **201** B5
Brookview Wlk BS13 . . . . **22** B7
Broom's La TA3 . . . . . . **191** F7
Broomball Cross TA22 . . **162** F5
Broomball La EX16 . . . . **162** E5
Broomclose Cnr BA3 . . . **114** B4
Broome Cl EX13 . . . . . . **198** A1
Broom Farm Cl BS48 . . . . **18** E8
Bromfield Ho TA2 . . . . . **212** E7
Broomground BA15 . . . . . **64** E7
Broomhill La BS39 . . . . . **58** E3
Broom Hill La BS39 . . . . **77** E8

Broom La
Chardstock EX13 . . . . . **198** C5
Oake TA4 . . . . **167** A2
Broomyland Hill TA5 . . . **152** C7
Brottens Rd
Cranmore BA4 . . . . **142** A5
Doulting BA4 . . . . **141** F5
Brougham Hayes BA2 . . **44** D6
Brougham Pl **2** BA1 . . . **28** C2
Broughton Cl
Taunton TA1 . . . . **213** C2
Walton BA16 . . . . **156** E7
Broughton Ho BS1 . . . . **227** B1
Broughton La BS1 . . . . . **169** B1
Broughton Pk TA3 . . . . . **169** A1
Broughtons Dr TA18 . . . **224** E3
Brow Hill BA2 . . . . **28** F4
Brow The
Bath BA2 . . . . **44** B5
Bath, Combe Down BA2 . . **45** C1
Broxholme Wlk BS11 . . . . . **4** F8
Brue Ave
Bridgwater TA6 . . . . . . **209** B3
Bruton BA10 . . . . **215** F7
Brue Bsns Pk TA9 . . . . . **136** E8
Brue Cl
Bruton BA10 . . . . **215** F7
Weston-Super-Mare BS23 . . **49** A5
Brue Cres TA8 . . . . **104** B5
Brue Ho TA8 . . . . **85** A1
Bruelands BA10 . . . . . . **215** F7
Brue Way TA9 . . . . **104** F3
Bruford Cl TA1 . . . . **212** E3
Brummel Way BS39 . . . . **77** C6
Brunel's Way TA9 . . . . . **104** F3
Brunel Cl
Somerton TA11 . . . . **211** D4
Weston-Super-Mare BS24 . . **48** F1
Brunel Ct
Bridgwater TA6 . . . . . . **208** F6
Portishead BS20 . . . . **2** D6
Brunel Ho BA2 . . . . **44** A6
Brunel Lock Rd BS1 . . . . **11** F5
Brunel Prec TA11 . . . . . **211** D4
Brunel Rd
Bristol BS13 . . . . **22** A8
Nailsea BS48 . . . . **8** B1
Brunel Way
Bristol BS1, BS3 . . . . . . **11** F4
Frome BA11 . . . . **120** C2
Minehead TA24 . . . . . . **201** B6
Brunsell's Knap DT10 . . **190** A1
Brunswick Pl
1 Bath BA1 . . . . **228** B3
10 Bristol BS2 . . . . **11** F5
Brunswick Sq BS2 . . . . **227** B4
Brunswick St
1 Bath BA1 . . . . **28** B1
Bristol BS2 . . . . **227** B4
Yeovil BA20 . . . . **219** A4
Brushford New Rd TA22 . **163** E4
Brutasche Terr BA16 . . . **207** D7
Bruton BS24 . . . . **49** A2
Bruton Ave
Bath BA2 . . . . **44** F4
Portishead BS20 . . . . **2** A5
Bruton Avenue Garages
BA2 . . . . **44** F4
Bruton Cl BS48 . . . . **18** E8
Bruton La BA4 . . . . **142** F2
Bruton Mus★ BA10 . . . . **215** E6
Bruton Pl BS8 . . . . **226** B3
Bruton Prim Sch BA10 . . **215** E6
Bruton Rd BA4 . . . . **141** F1
Bruton Sch for Girls
BA10 . . . . **215** C3
Bruton Sta BA10 . . . . . **215** F6
Brutton Way TA20 . . . . **223** B3
Bryant's Hill TA22 . . . . **148** C3
Bryant Ave BA3 . . . . **78** D1
Bryant Gdns BS21 . . . . . . **6** C1
Bryer Cl
Bridgwater TA6 . . . . . . **208** E1
Chard TA20 . . . . **223** D3
Brymore Cl TA6 . . . . . . **208** D5
Brymore Sch TA5 . . . . . **135** A2
Brympton Ave BA22 . . . **186** D2
Brympton Way BA20 . . . **218** C3
Bsns Courtyard The
BA11 . . . . **143** C7
Bubwith Cl TA20 . . . . . **223** B3
Bubwith Ho **4** BA5 . . . **203** D4
Bubwith Rd TA20 . . . . . **223** D3
Bubwith Wlk BA5 . . . . . **203** B3
Buces Rd TA1 . . . . **212** B1
Buck Cl BA6 . . . . **206** C3
Buckhill TA24 . . . . **131** B4
Buckhill Cl TA18 . . . . . . **224** C4
Buckingham Cl TA6 . . . . **209** A2
Buckingham Pl BS8 . . . . **226** A3
Buckingham Rd BS24 . . . **49** B2
Buckingham Vale BS8 . . . **226** A4
Buckland Cl TA8 . . . . . . **104** C8
Buckland Gn BA22 . . . . . **32** A5
Buckland La BA22 . . . . . **175** C3
Buckland Rd
Shepton Mallet BA4 . . . . **205** A5
Taunton TA2 . . . . **213** B8

Buckland Rd continued
Yeovil BA21 . . . . **219** E6
Buckland St Mary CE Prim
Sch TA20 . . . . **193** A8
Bucklands Batch BS48 . . . **18** F8
Buckland Batch TA23 . . . **202** C6
Bucklands Dr BS48 . . . . . **19** A8
Bucklands End BS48 . . . . **18** F8
Bucklands Gr BS48 . . . . . **18** F8
Bucklands La BS48 . . . . . **18** F8
Bucklands View BS48 . . . **19** A8
Buckle Pl BA22 . . . . **218** B6
Bucklers Mead Rd BA21 **219** D8
Bucklers Mead Sch
BA21 . . . . **219** C8
Bucklers Mead Wlk
BA21 . . . . **219** D8
Bucklers Way BA4 . . . . . **204** F6
Bucklewell Cl BS11 . . . . . . **4** F6
Buckshaw Cl BA21 . . . . **222** E6
Buckshots Cross EX14 . . **192** D4
Buckwell TA21 . . . . **222** E6
Bude Cl BS48 . . . . **9** B1
Budge La BA11 . . . . **144** A8
Budgett's Cross TA21 . . **180** F6
Budgetts TA21 . . . . **180** F6
Bughole La TA21 . . . . . . **179** E8
Bugle Ct **11** BA8 . . . . . . **190** A6
Building of Bath Mus★
BA1 . . . . **228** C3
Bulford BA21 . . . . **222** D5
Bulford La TA21 . . . . . . **222** D5
Bull's Hill BA2 . . . . **62** E1
Bull's La
Tatworth TA20 . . . . **198** C8
Upton Noble BA4 . . . . . **142** F2
Bull's Quarr BA11 . . . . . **143** E8
Bull's Quarries Rd BA11 . **143** F7
Bull Bridge Mead BA22 . **197** D3
Bullen Mead BA11 . . . . . **117** F2
Bullens Cl TA19 . . . . . . **183** F4
Buller Ave BA22 . . . . . . **218** A6
Bull Horn Dro TA7 . . . . **154** D5
Bull La BS20 . . . . **4** C4
Bull Mdw TA4 . . . . **167** F7
Bullmead BA16 . . . . **207** B5
Bullmead La BA11 . . . . . **143** C7
Bullock Field Hill TA21 . **166** B2
Bullocks La BS21 . . . . . . **16** C4
Bullon Dro TA5 . . . . **134** B7
Bull Plot Hill BA6 . . . . . **158** C8
Bulls La TA18 . . . . **224** B6
Bull St TA3 . . . . **169** D4
Bulwarks La BA6 . . . . . . **206** F4
Bumper's Batch BA2 . . . . **63** A8
Bunce's La TA19 . . . . . . **184** E3
Buncombe Hill TA5 . . . . **152** C3
Bune Villas TA6 . . . . . . **208** E7
Bunford Hollow Rdbt
BA20 . . . . **218** D1
Bunford La BA20, BA21 . **218** C4
Bungalows The
Axbridge BS26 . . . . **70** C2
Chard TA20 . . . . **223** D5
Monkton Heathfield TA2 . **213** D8
Nether Stowey TA5 . . . . **134** A2
Poyntington DT9 . . . . . **188** E7
Bungay's Hill BA2, BS39 . **59** E1
Bunker Military Mus The★
TA9 . . . . **104** D3
Bunns La
Horningsham BA11 . . . . **144** A5
Witham Friary BA11 . . . **143** F5
Bunting Ct BS22 . . . . **31** E1
Burch's Cl TA1 . . . . **212** C2
Burchill's Hill TA21 . . . . **222** B7
Burchill Cl BS39 . . . . **58** F3
Burchills Cl TA21 . . . . . **222** A6
Burcott La
Coxley BA5 . . . . **139** E2
Wells BA5 . . . . **203** A3
Burcott Rd BA5 . . . . . . **203** B3
Burdenham Dro TA7 . . . **155** A6
Burfoote Gdns BS14 . . . . **23** E4
Burfoot Rd BS14 . . . . . . **23** E4
Burford Cl
Bath BA2 . . . . **44** B3
Portishead BS20 . . . . **2** E4
Burford Cross BA4 . . . . **204** C2
Burford Gr BS11 . . . . **4** F5
Burgage TA21 . . . . **222** D6
Burgage La TA4 . . . . . . **167** A4
Burgage Rd TA5 . . . . . . **134** C6
Burge's Hill BA3 . . . . . . **116** B1
Burge's La BA3 . . . . **116** B1
Burge Cres TA4 . . . . . . **167** E6
Burge Mdw TA4 . . . . . . **167** E6
Burges Cl
Marnhull DT10 . . . . **190** F6
Wiveliscombe TA4 . . . . . **210** C5
Burges La TA4 . . . . **210** C5
Burgess Cl TA1 . . . . **212** B1
Burgess La BA6 . . . . . . **157** F6
Burgis Rd BS14 . . . . **23** D6
Burgundy Rd TA24 . . . . **201** A8
Burleigh Gdns BA1 . . . . . **44** A8
Burleigh La BA16 . . . . . **207** C4
Burlescombe CE Prim Sch
EX16 . . . . **179** B3
Burley Gdns BA16 . . . . . **207** D4
Burlingham's La BA22 . . **186** C8
Burlington Ct BS20 . . . . . **2** E6
Burlington Rd
Midsomer Norton BA3 . . . **78** C2
Portishead BS20 . . . . **2** E7
Burlington St
Bath BA1 . . . . **228** B4
15 Weston-Super-Mare
BS23 . . . . **48** E8

Burnbush Cl BS14 . . . . . . **23** E6
Burnbush Prim Sch BS14 . **23** E6
Burnell Dr BS2 . . . . **227** C4
Burnell Ho **8** BA4 . . . . **205** B6
Burnett's La BA6 . . . . . . **158** A6
Burnett Bsns Pk BS31 . . . **25** B1
Burnett Cl TA8 . . . . **104** C7
Burnett Ind Est BS40 . . . . **35** E1
Burnham Cl BS24 . . . . . . **48** F1
Burnham Dr BS24 . . . . . . **48** F1
Burnham Moor La TA9 . . **105** B5
Burnham-on-Sea Inf Sch
TA8 . . . . **104** C8
Burnham Rd
Bath BA2 . . . . **44** C6
Bristol BS11 . . . . **4** D3
Highbridge TA9 . . . . . . **104** D4
Burn Hill TA4, TA21 . . . **166** F3
Burnshill Dr TA2 . . . . . . **212** A4
Burns Rd TA1 . . . . **213** C4
Burnt House Cotts BA2 . . **62** C8
Burnthouse Dro BA5 . . . **141** B8
Burnt House La BA3 . . . . **116** C2
Burnt House Rd BA2 . . . . **62** D8
Burrell La BA7 . . . . **158** F1
Burrells BA22 . . . . **197** B8
Burridge Cl BA5 . . . . . . **139** E6
Burridge Cross TA20 . . . **193** C1
Burrington Ave BS24 . . . . **48** F1
Burrington CE Prim Sch
BS40 . . . . **53** E3
Burrington Cl
Nailsea BS48 . . . . **8** D1
Weston-Super-Mare BS24 . . **48** F1
Burrington Combe BS40 . . **72** C3
Burrington Coombe★
BS40 . . . . **54** A1
Burrington La BS40 . . . . . **54** A3
Burrington Wlk BS13 . . . **22** A8
Burroughes Ave BA21 . . **218** E6
Burrough St TA12 . . . . . **185** F7
Burrough Way TA21 . . . **222** D4
Burrowbridge CE Sch
TA7 . . . . **154** F1
Burrow Dro
Burrowbridge TA7 . . . . . **154** F1
Hambridge TA12 . . . . . . **184** F8
Burrowfield BA10 . . . . . **215** F7
Burrowfield Cl BA10 . . . **215** F7
Burrow Hill Dro TA7 . . . **155** A1
Burrow La
Ashbrittle TA21 . . . . . . **178** D8
High Ham TA10 . . . . . . **156** A1
Burrow Rocks TA4 . . . . **202** B1
Burrows La BA3 . . . . **97** B1
Burrow Wall TA7 . . . . . **155** A1
Burrow Way
Hambridge TA12 . . . . . . **184** F7
Kingsbury Episcopi TA12 . **185** A7
Burstock La DT8 . . . . . . **199** F7
Burston La EX16 . . . . . **164** A4
Burt's Hill BA4 . . . . **142** F3
Burtle Rd
Burtle TA7 . . . . **137** D6
East Huntspill TA9 . . . . **136** E7
Westhay BA6 . . . . **138** A5
Burton Barton BA22 . . . **197** B8
Burton Ct BS1 . . . . **227** B1
Burton Ct BS8 . . . . **226** B3
Burtonhayes DT10 . . . . **190** F6
Burton La BA22 . . . . . . **197** C8
Burton Pl TA1 . . . . **212** E3
Burton Row TA9 . . . . . . **86** A5
Burton St
5 Bath BA1 . . . . **228** B2
Marnhull DT10 . . . . **190** F6
Burwalls Rd BS8 . . . . . . **11** E6
Bury The TA5 . . . . **50** A3
Bury View BA2 . . . . **42** C5
Buscott La TA7 . . . . **138** B1
Bush La
Bush La TA5 . . . . **152** E6
Bush Pl TA10 . . . . **172** A5
Bush Rd TA5 . . . . **152** D7
Bushs Orch TA19 . . . . . **221** A4
Bushy Combe BA3 . . . . . **77** F3
Bushy Coombe Gdns
BA6 . . . . **206** F5
Bushy Cross La TA3 . . . . **169** C3
Bushy Thorn Rd BS40 . . . **56** E8
Business Pk The BS13 . . . **22** E3
Bussell's Moor Cross
EX36 . . . . **162** C4
Bussex Sq TA7 . . . . **154** F6
Butcher's Hill TA3 . . . . . **170** F2
Butcher's La TA5 . . . . . **134** A2
Butchers La
Castle Cary BA7 . . . . . . **159** C3
Shapwick TA7 . . . . **155** F8
Butcombe BS24 . . . . **49** A2
Butcombe La BS40 . . . . . **55** B7
Butcombe Wlk BS14 . . . . **23** B5
Butham La
Chew Magna BS40 . . . . . **39** A4
Chew Magna BS40 . . . . . **39** B3
Butlass Cl BS39 . . . . **59** D1
Butleigh CE Prim Sch
BA6 . . . . **157** E4
Butleigh Cl TA6 . . . . . . **209** D4
Butleigh Cross BA6 . . . . **157** E3
Butleigh Dro
Ashcott TA7, TA6 . . . . . **156** C1
Walton BA16 . . . . **156** D6
Butleigh Old Rd BA6 . . . **206** E3

Butleigh Rd
Glastonbury BA6 . . . . . **206** E5
Street BA16 . . . . **207** E5
Butler's Gdns BA11 . . . . **120** A4
Butt's Batch BS40 . . . . . . **35** D1
Butt Cl BA6 . . . . **206** E5
Buttercliffe Rise BS41 . . . **11** C3
Buttercup La BA16 . . . . . **207** D6
Butterfield Pk BS21 . . . . . **6** A5
Buttermere Rd BS23 . . . . **49** A5
Butterworth Ct BS4 . . . . . **22** D7
Buttice La BA5 . . . . **111** B1
Butt La TA10 . . . . **171** D4
Butt Lake Rd TA9 . . . . . **106** B3
Butt's Cross TA3 . . . . . . **191** F7
Buttle's La TA3 . . . . **191** E6
Buttle Cl TA19 . . . . **184** E4
Buttle La TA19 . . . . **184** E3
Button Cl BS14 . . . . **23** A6
Button St BA11 . . . . **119** D5
Butts TA19 . . . . **221** C4
Butts Batch BS26 . . . . . . **69** B3
Butts Castle TA19 . . . . . **221** C4
Butts Cl
Marnhull DT10 . . . . . . **190** F5
Williton TA4 . . . . **202** D4
Butts Cnr TA6 . . . . **153** F4
Butts Hill BA11 . . . . **119** E3
Butts La
Ilton TA19 . . . . **183** D3
Kilmington BA12 . . . . . **161** F7
Langford Budville TA21 . . **166** F2
Rodney Stoke BS27 . . . . **91** A1
Butts Orch BS40 . . . . **35** D1
Butts Quarry La TA18 . . . **224** E6
Butts The BA11 . . . . **119** E3
Butts Way TA4 . . . . **166** F4
Buxtons Cl **5** BA5 . . . . . **139** D8
Byfield BA2 . . . . **45** B1
Byfield Pl BA2 . . . . **45** B1
Byfields BS21 . . . . **16** C8
Byron Cl BS24 . . . . **50** A4
Byron Ct BS23 . . . . **48** F8
Byron Pl BS8 . . . . **226** B3
Byron Rd
Bath BA2 . . . . **44** F4
Locking BS24 . . . . **50** A4
Taunton TA1 . . . . **213** C3
Weston-Super-Mare BS23 . . **49** A4
Byways Cvn Pk BS21 . . . . . **6** C1
Byzantine Ct BS1 . . . . . . **227** A1

C

Cabbage La BA8 . . . . **176** C3
Cabell Ct BA11 . . . . **119** D2
Cabell Rd BA11 . . . . **119** E2
Cabot Cl BS31 . . . . **25** D2
Cabot Prim Sch BS2 . . . . **227** C4
Cabot Rise BS20 . . . . **2** A5
Cabot Twr* BS8 . . . . . . **226** B2
Cabot Way
Bristol BS8 . . . . **11** F5
Pill BS20 . . . . **4** D3
Weston-Super-Mare BS22 . . **32** A3
Cabstand BS20 . . . . **2** D6
Cadbury Bsns Pk BA22 . . **175** B6
Cadbury Camp La BS20 . . . **8** D6
Cadbury Camp La W BS21 . . **7** C5
Cadbury Castle* BA22 . . **175** C4
Cadbury Cl TA8 . . . . **85** C1
Cadbury Farm Rd BS49 . . . **34** C7
Cadbury Halt BS20 . . . . . . **1** F1
Cadbury Ho BS20 . . . . **2** E4
Cadbury La BS20 . . . . **1** F1
Cadbury Rd
Keynsham BS31 . . . . . . **25** A2
Portishead BS20 . . . . . . **2** E4
Cadbury Sq BS49 . . . . . . **34** E3
Cadby Ho BA2 . . . . **44** A6
Cadeside Cvn Site TA21 . **222** F7
Cadogan Rd BS14 . . . . . . **23** A8
Cad Rd
Ilminster TA19 . . . . . . **221** A8
Ilton TA19 . . . . **183** C3
Cadwell's La TA9 . . . . . . **136** A8
Caernarvon Rd BS31 . . . . **24** C4
Caernarvon Way TA8 . . . . **85** B1
Caern Well Pl BA1 . . . . . **228** C4
Cairn Cl BS48 . . . . **9** A1
Cairo Ct **18** BS23 . . . . . . **30** C1
Caitlin Ct BS14 . . . . **23** D6
Cala Trad Est BS3 . . . . . . **11** F3
Calder Cl BS31 . . . . **25** A4
Calder Cres TA1 . . . . . . **213** D4
Cale Cl DT10 . . . . **190** C4
Caledonia Mews BS8 . . . . **11** F6
Caledonian Rd
Bath BA2 . . . . **44** D6
Bristol BS1 . . . . **226** B1
Caledonia Pl BS8 . . . . . . **11** F7
Cale Way BA9 . . . . **216** B4
Caller's La EX15 . . . . . . **180** D1
Callins Cl TA24 . . . . **201** A5
Callins View TA24 . . . . . **201** A5
Callow Hill BA5 . . . . **139** C7
Callowhill Ct BS1 . . . . . **227** B3
Calluna Cl BS22 . . . . **32** A5
Calton Gdns BA2 . . . . . . **228** C1
Calton Rd BA2 . . . . **228** C1
Calton Wlk BA2 . . . . **228** B1
Calvados Rd TA1 . . . . . . **213** C3
Calway Rd TA1 . . . . **213** B2
Camberley Rd BS4 . . . . . . **22** D8
Camberley Wlk BS22 . . . . **49** E8
Camborne Gr BA21 . . . . . **219** E5
Camborne Pl BA21 . . . . . **219** E5

Camborne St BA21 . . . . . **219** E5
Cambridge Cl BA20 . . . . . **218** D5
Cambridge Ct BS40 . . . . . **35** D2
Cambridge Gr BS21 . . . . . . **6** D5
Cambridge Pl
Bath BA2 . . . . **45** B5
Weston-Super-Mare BS23 . . **48** D8
Cambridge Rd BS21 . . . . . . **6** D5
Cambridge St TA20 . . . . . **223** C4
Cambridge Terr
11 Taunton TA2 . . . . . **213** A8
Cam Brook Cl BA2 . . . . . . **78** D8
Cambrook Ho BS39 . . . . . **76** F8
Camden Cres BA1 . . . . . **228** B4
Camden Ct
Bath BA1 . . . . **228** B4
Bridgwater TA6 . . . . . **208** E5
Camden Orch TA11 . . . . . **211** C4
Camden Pl TA6 . . . . **208** E5
Camden Rd
Bath BA1 . . . . **28** A1
Bridgwater TA6 . . . . . **208** E5
Bristol BS3 . . . . **226** B1
Somerton TA11 . . . . . . **211** C4
Camden Row BA1 . . . . . **228** B4
Camden Terr
Bath BA1 . . . . **228** C4
Bristol BS8 . . . . **226** A2
Weston-Super-Mare BS23 . . **48** E7
Camel Cross BA22 . . . . . **174** C3
Cameley CE Prim Sch
BS39 . . . . **58** E1
Cameley Cl BS39 . . . . . . **76** E8
Cameley Gn BA2 . . . . **43** F6
Cameley La BS39 . . . . . . **75** F7
Cameley Rd BS39 . . . . . . **76** C8
Camelot Ct TA11 . . . . . . **211** B5
Camelot Sh Ctr BA9 . . . . **216** C4
Camel St BA22 . . . . **174** F2
Cameroons Cl BS31 . . . . . **24** E4
Camerton CE Prim Sch
BA2 . . . . **78** E8
Camerton Cl BS31 . . . . . . **25** E3
Camerton Hill BA2 . . . . . **78** E8
Camerton Rd BA2 . . . . . . **60** C1
Camomile Wlk BS20 . . . . . **2** F5
Campian Wlk BS4 . . . . . . **22** D6
Campion Cl **4** BS22 . . . . **49** D7
Campion Dr
Taunton TA1 . . . . **213** C1
Yeovil BA22 . . . . **218** B5
Campion Gdns TA20 . . . . **223** D5
Campkin Rd BA5 . . . . . . **203** B4
Camplins BS21 . . . . **6** C1
Camp Rd
Bristol BS8 . . . . **11** F7
Weston-Super-Mare BS23 . . **30** C1
Yeovil BA22 . . . . **186** D1
Camp Rd N BS23 . . . . . . **30** B1
Camp View BS48 . . . . **8** D2
Camvale BA2 . . . . **79** B8
Camview BS39 . . . . **77** D6
Canada Coombe BS24 . . . . **50** A1
Canada Way BS1 . . . . . . **226** B1
Canal Cl TA21 . . . . **222** B8
Canal Dro BS27, BS28 . . . . **90** A3
Canal Rd TA1 . . . . **212** F5
Canal Terr
Bathampton BA2 . . . . . . **28** C1
Taunton TA1 . . . . **212** F5
Canal View TA6 . . . . **209** A4
Canal Way TA19 . . . . . . **221** A3
Canberra Cres BS24 . . . . . **50** B6
Canberra Rd BS23 . . . . . . **48** F3
Canford La BS9 . . . . **5** E8
Canford Rd BS9 . . . . **5** E8
Cannard's Grave Rd BA4 **205** C4
Cannards Grave Rdbt
BA4 . . . . **205** D3
Cannington CE Prim Sch
TA5 . . . . **135** C2
Cannington College Gdns*
TA5 . . . . **135** B2
Cannington Countryside Vst
Ctr* TA5 . . . . **135** B2
Cannon Cl TA6 . . . . **209** B5
Cannon Court Mews
DT9 . . . . **217** D1
Cannons Gate BS21 . . . . . **16** C8
Cannon St BS1 . . . . **227** A4
Canns La
9 North Petherton TA6 . **153** F4
Puriton TA7 . . . . **136** E4
Cann St TA1 . . . . **212** E3
Cannwood La BA10 . . . . . **161** B8
Canon's Rd BS1 . . . . **226** C1
Canons Cl BA2 . . . . **44** B2
Canons Gate BA22 . . . . . **173** E1
Canons Rd BS1 . . . . **226** C2
Canon St TA1 . . . . **213** A4
Canons Way BS1 . . . . . . **226** C1
Canons Wlk BS22 . . . . . . **31** D2
Cantell Gr BS14 . . . . **23** F5
Canterbury Cl BS22 . . . . . **32** B3
Canterbury Dr TA3 . . . . . **170** C4
Canterbury Rd BA2 . . . . . **44** D5
Cantock's Cl BS8 . . . . . . **226** C3
Canvin Ct TA11 . . . . **211** B5
Canworth Way TA6 . . . . **209** C4
Canynge Ho **2** BS1 . . . . **227** B1
Canynge Rd BS8 . . . . **11** F8
Canynge Sq BS8 . . . . **11** F8
Canynge St BS1 . . . . . . **227** B2
Capell Cl BS22 . . . . **49** E8
Capenor Cl BS20 . . . . **2** C4
Capes Cl TA6 . . . . **209** A5
Capital Edge BS8 . . . . . . **226** B1

Capland Ct TA3 . . . . **183** A5
Capland La TA3 . . . . **183** A5
Caple La BS40 . . . . **56** B5
Cappards Rd BS39 . . . . . . **57** D5
Capricorn Pl BS8 . . . . . . **226** B2
Capri Villas BS23 . . . . . . **30** C2
Capton TA4 . . . . **132** C2
Capton Cross TA4 . . . . . **132** C2
Caradon Rd TA4 . . . . . . **208** F7
Caramia Pk TA9 . . . . . . **136** A8
Caraway Ct TA20 . . . . . . **223** F5
Caray Gr TA3 . . . . **169** D3
Carberry View BS24 . . . . . **50** A8
Card Cl BS27 . . . . **90** F3
Cardigan Cres BS22 . . . . . **49** C8
Cardill Cl BS13 . . . . **22** A8
Carditch Dro BS49 . . . . . . **52** B8
Carey's Cl BS21 . . . . **6** F4
Carey's Hollow TA13 . . . **220** B4
Carey Cl BA4 . . . . **141** E6
Carey Developments **1**
BS21 . . . . **6** C1
Careys Mead BA3 . . . . . **116** F7
Careys Way BS24 . . . . . . **49** E7
Carhampton Cross TA24 . **131** B5
Carice Gdns BS21 . . . . . . **16** D8
Carisbrooke Gdns BA20 . **218** F5
Carisbrooke Rd BS4 . . . . . **22** D7
Carlan Stepps TA19 . . . . **183** C2
Carlingford Terr BA3 . . . . **79** A2
Carlingford Terrace Rd
BA3 . . . . **79** A2
Carlow Rd BS4 . . . . **22** E8
Carlton Cl BS39 . . . . **58** F3
Carlton Ct
Minehead TA24 . . . . . **200** F7
Wells BA5 . . . . **203** E4
Carlton Dr TA6 . . . . **208** F7
Carlton Mans BS23 . . . . . **48** E7
Carlton Mews BA5 . . . . . **203** E4
Carlton St BS23 . . . . **48** D7
Carmine Cl BA6 . . . . **206** C4
Carnival Cl TA19 . . . . . . **221** B4
Carolina Ho BS2 . . . . . . **227** A4
Caroline Bldgs BA2 . . . . . **45** B5
Caroline Cl BS31 . . . . **24** C4
Caroline Pl BA1 . . . . **228** B4
Carpenter Cl BS23 . . . . . . **49** A7
Carpenters Cl TA3 . . . . . **169** C3
Carpenters Ho TA19 . . . . **221** B3
Carpenters La BS31 . . . . . **24** E5
Carpenters Terr TA12 . . . **185** E7
Carraway La DT10 . . . . . **190** F5
Carre Gdns BS22 . . . . **31** F4
Carrick Ho **7** BS8 . . . . . **11** F6
Carriels Ho **12** BA4 . . . . **205** B6
Carrier's La TA21 . . . . . **166** C2
Carrington Way BA9 . . . . **216** C4
Carrs Cl BA22 . . . . **44** A6
Carstons Cl BS48 . . . . **18** F6
Carter Rd BS39 . . . . **77** D5
Carters La BA22 . . . . . . **196** E8
Carters Way
Chilcompton BA3 . . . . . . **96** D3
Somerton TA11 . . . . . . **211** C4
Cart Gate TA14 . . . . **185** F5
Cartwright Cl BA5 . . . . . **139** E6
Carvers Rd TA6 . . . . **209** A4
Cary Ct TA11 . . . . **211** B5
Caryedge La BA7 . . . . . . **160** A2
Cary Hill
Castle Cary BA7 . . . . . **214** D5
Kingsdon TA11 . . . . . . **173** E5
Cary Moor Dro BA7 . . . . **159** C1
Cary Rd BA22 . . . . **175** D6
Cary Way
Kingsdon TA11 . . . . . . **173** D5
Somerton TA11 . . . . . . **211** C5
Cashford Gate TA2 . . . . . **213** C4
Casion Ct BS1 . . . . **227** B1
Casley La BA11 . . . . **102** D6
Cassino Rd TA23 . . . . . . **202** E6
Cassis Ct TA8 . . . . **104** C5
Castlake La TA4 . . . . . . **150** F7
Castle Batch Prim Sch
BS22 . . . . **32** A5
Castle Bow TA1 . . . . **212** F4
Castle Cary Com Prim Sch
BA7 . . . . **214** C4
Castle Cary Mus* BA7 . . **214** C5
Castle Cary Sta BA7 . . . . **214** B8
Castle Cl BS48 . . . . **19** F7
Castle Cnr BA11 . . . . . . **101** D3
Castle Cotts TA21 . . . . . **180** C5
Castle Cross EX13 . . . . . **198** D4
Castle Ct
Othery TA7 . . . . **155** C2
Shepton Mallet BA4 . . . **205** A4
Castle Farm La BA11 . . . . **21** B2
Castlefield La TA4 . . . . . **168** B1
Castle Gdns BA2 . . . . **44** E3
Castle Gn TA1 . . . . **212** F4
Castle Hill
Banwell BS29 . . . . **51** C2
Dunster TA24 . . . . **201** E2
Nether Stowey TA5 . . . . **134** B2
Nunney BA11 . . . . **143** B8

Castlemans Rd TA1 . . . . . **212** B1
Castle Mead TA23 . . . . . **131** E4
Castle Moat TA6 . . . . . . **208** F5
Castle Neroche Forest Trail*
TA20 . . . . **182** D2
Castle Prim Sch BS31 . . . . **24** D4
Castle Rd
Clevedon BS21 . . . . **6** E6
Sherborne DT9 . . . . . . **225** F5
Wellington TA21 . . . . . **180** D8
Weston-Super-Mare BS22 . . **31** E3
Castle Rise BA7 . . . . **214** C5
Castle Sch The TA1 . . . . . **212** C4
Castle St
Bampton EX16 . . . . . . **164** B1
Bridgwater TA6 . . . . . **208** F5
Bristol BS1 . . . . **227** B3
Frome BA11 . . . . **119** E5
Keinton Mandeville TA11 . . **158** B1
Nether Stowey TA5 . . . . **134** B2
Nunney BA11 . . . . **143** B8
Stogursey TA5 . . . . . . **134** C5
Stoke sub Hamdon TA14 . **185** F4
Taunton TA1 . . . . **212** F4
Castleton
Haselbury Plucknett
TA18 . . . . **196** C5
1 Sherborne DT9 . . . . **225** E4
Castleton Rd DT9 . . . . . . **225** E4
Castle Town Way DT9 . . . **225** E6
Castle View **2** BS24 . . . . **49** E6
Castle View Rd BS21 . . . . . **6** D5
Castle Way TA1 . . . . **212** F4
Castlewood Cl BS21 . . . . . . **6** D4
Castle Wood La EX13,
TA20 . . . . **193** C1
Caswell Hill BS20 . . . . **3** B1
Caswell La BS20 . . . . **3** B2
Cat's Ash
Fitzhead TA4 . . . . **166** F7
Shepton Mallet BA4 . . . **205** B6
Catash Cl BA22 . . . . **175** D6
Catch Gate La TA20 . . . . **223** A5
Catch Rd BA11 . . . . **143** B7
Catcott Broad Dro TA7 . . **137** D5
Catcott Prim Sch TA7 . . . **137** D2
Catcott Right Dro TA7 . . . **155** D6
Catemead BS21 . . . . **16** C8
Cater Rd BS13 . . . . **22** B6
Cathanger La
Fivehead TA3 . . . . **170** D1
Stogursey TA5 . . . . . . **134** D5
Catharine Pl BA1 . . . . . . **228** B3
Cathay La BS27 . . . . **90** B7
Cathcart Ho **7** BA1 . . . . . **28** A1
Cathead Cross TA14 . . . . **185** E1
Cathedral Church of The
Holy & Undivided Trinity*
BS1 . . . . **226** C2
Cathedral Gn BA5 . . . . . **203** E4
Catherine Hill BA11 . . . . **119** F5
Catherines Cl BA7 . . . . . **214** C6
Catherine St
Avonmouth BS11 . . . . . . **4** C8
East Huntspill TA9 . . . . **136** D8
Frome BA11 . . . . **119** E5
Catherine Way BA1 . . . . . **29** A5
Catherson Cl BA11 . . . . . **119** D3
Cathill La DT9 . . . . **176** A2
Cathole Bridge Rd BA18 . **224** A4
Cat La
Stalbridge DT10 . . . . . **190** A1
Stourton Caundle DT10 . **189** A1
Catley Gr BS41 . . . . **11** B2
Catmoor Cross EX13 . . . . **198** A5
Catnip Cl **2** EX13 . . . . . **198** A1
Cats' Castle Hill TA4 . . . . **150** E5
Catsgore Rd TA11 . . . . . **173** C5
Cats La
Minehead TA24 . . . . . **201** A6
Taunton TA2 . . . . **168** F6
Cat St TA14 . . . . **185** E1
Catt's La TA21 . . . . **180** E6
Cattle Hill
Bratton Seymour BA9 . . **176** A8
Welham BA7 . . . . **160** A1
Cattle Market Rd BS1 . . . **227** C1
Catwell TA4 . . . . **202** E2
Caulfield Rd BS22 . . . . . . **32** B4
Caundle La
Stalbridge Weston DT10 . **190** A3
Stourton Caundle DT10 . **189** F1
Causeway
Nailsea BS48 . . . . **8** B3
Woolavington TA7, TA9 . . **136** E4
Causeway Cl TA7 . . . . . . **136** E4
Causeway Council Hos
TA9 . . . . **106** B4
Causeway La DT8 . . . . . . **199** D6
Causeway Terr TA23 . . . . **202** C6
Causeway The
Congresbury BS49 . . . . . **34** D4
Nailsea BS20 . . . . **8** F8
Street BA16 . . . . **207** D8
Yatton BS49 . . . . **34** C2
Causeway View BS48 . . . . **8** C2
Cautletts Cl BA3 . . . . **96** F8
Cavalier Cl BA21 . . . . . . **219** D8
Cavalier Way
Wincanton BA9 . . . . . **216** C3
Yeovil BA21 . . . . **219** E8
Cavalier Wlk BA21 . . . . . **219** D8
Cave Ct BS2 . . . . **227** B4
Cavell Ct BS21 . . . . **6** C1
Cavendish Cl BS31 . . . . . **25** D2
Cavendish Cres BA1 . . . . **228** A4
Cavendish Ct BA22 . . . . . **173** E2
Cavendish Dr BA14 . . . . . **83** F6

Cavendish Gdns BS9 . . . . . **5** C4
Cavendish Lodge BA1 . . . **228** A4
Cavendish Pl BA1 . . . . . . **228** A4
Cavendish Rd BA1 . . . . . **228** A4
Caveners Ct BS22 . . . . . . **31** B1
Caversham Dr BS48 . . . . . . **9** A2
Cave St BS2 . . . . **227** B4
Cawley Ave EX13 . . . . . . **198** A2
Caxton Ct **4** BA2 . . . . . **228** C3
Caxton Rd BA11 . . . . . . **120** A3
Cecil Rd
Bristol, Clifton BS8 . . . . **11** F8
Weston-Super-Mare BS23 . . **30** E1
Cecil St BA20 . . . . **219** B5
Cecil Terr TA6 . . . . **209** B4
Cedar Ave
Butleigh BA6 . . . . **157** D5
Weston-Super-Mare BS22 . . **31** C1
Cedar Cl
Brent Knoll TA9 . . . . . . **86** B2
Bridgwater TA6 . . . . . **209** C3
Chard TA20 . . . . **223** B5
Long Ashton BS41 . . . . . **10** F1
Taunton TA1 . . . . **213** D2
Cedar Ct
Bristol, Combe Dingle BS9 . . **5** C4
Bristol, Sneyd Park BS9 . . . . **5** C4
Bristol, Westbury on T BS9 . . **5** F8
Martock TA12 . . . . . . **185** E7
Wellington TA21 . . . . . **222** E5
Cedar Dr BS31 . . . . **24** D4
Cedar Falls TA4 . . . . **151** E1
Cedar Fields
Sparkford BA22 . . . . . **175** A5
West Coker BA22 . . . . . **197** A8
Cedar Gr
Bath BA2 . . . . **44** D3
Bristol BS9 . . . . **5** D5
Somerton TA11 . . . . . . **211** D4
Yeovil BA21 . . . . **218** E6
Cedarhurst Rd BS20 . . . . . **1** E4
Cedarn Ct BS22 . . . . **31** B4
Cedar Pk BS9 . . . . **5** D5
Cedar Row BS11 . . . . **4** F6
Cedars The
Chew Stoke BS40 . . . . . **56** D8
Evercreech BA4 . . . . . **141** E1
Minehead TA24 . . . . . **200** F7
Cedar Terr BA3 . . . . **78** D1
Cedar Villas BA2 . . . . . . **228** A1
Cedar Way
Bath BA2 . . . . **228** A1
Nailsea BS48 . . . . **9** A2
Portishead BS20 . . . . . . **2** C4
Cedar Wlk BA6 . . . . **157** E5
Cedern Ave BS24 . . . . . . **50** C3
Cedric Cl BA1 . . . . **44** C7
Cedric Rd BA1 . . . . **44** C8
Cefn Ct TA24 . . . . **201** B4
Celandine Mead TA1 . . . . **169** A1
Celandine Rd BA22 . . . . . **218** A5
Celtic Way BS24 . . . . **67** B7
Cemetery La
Street BA16 . . . . **207** A4
Wincanton BA9 . . . . . **216** B3
Centenary Cotts DT9 . . . **176** A1
Centenary Gdns BA8 . . . . **190** A6
Centenary Way BS27 . . . . **90** A7
Central Acre BA20 . . . . . **219** B4
Central Ave BA22 . . . . . . **173** E2
Central Pk BS14 . . . . **23** B7
Central Rd BA20 . . . . . . **219** B5
Central Way BS21 . . . . **6** E1
Centre Dr BS29 . . . . **50** E4
Centre Quay BS20 . . . . **2** E7
Centre Rd TA7 . . . . **137** C2
Centre The
Keynsham BS31 . . . . . . **24** F5
10 Weston-Super-Mare
BS23 . . . . **48** E7
Centurion Bsns Ctr BA4 **205** D4
Century Pk BA20 . . . . . . **218** E5
Cerdic Cl TA20 . . . . **223** E4
Cerdic Terr TA20 . . . . . . **223** D4
Cerney Gdns BS48 . . . . . . **9** A2
Cerney La BS11 . . . . **4** E5
Chackrell La EX16 . . . . . **178** F2
Chad's Hill TA5 . . . . **135** B2
Chadleigh Gr BS4 . . . . . . **22** D7
Chaffcombe La TA20 . . . . **194** B5
Chaffcombe Rd TA20 . . . **223** E6
Chaffeymoor Hill SP8 . . . **161** E1
Chaffinch Ave BA11 . . . . **120** B6
Chaffinch Cl TA1 . . . . . . **212** B6
Chaffinch Dr BA3 . . . . . . **97** B8
Chaffins The BS21 . . . . . . **6** E2
Chain Gate Ct BA6 . . . . . **206** D4
Chains Rd EX16 . . . . **178** D1
Chalcombe Rocks La
TA4 . . . . **164** E5
Chalcot La BA13 . . . . . . **121** F5
Chalcroft Wlk BS13 . . . . . **21** E4
Chalfield Cl BS31 . . . . . . **25** A2
Chalfont Rd BS22 . . . . . . **49** C8
Chalice Cl BA6 . . . . **206** F4
Chalice Hill Cl BA6 . . . . . **206** E4
Chalice Mews **1** TA6 . . . **208** F5
Chalice Way BA6 . . . . . . **206** F3
Chalice Well* BA6 . . . . . **206** F4
Chalk Farm Cl BS39 . . . . . **40** A7
Chalks The BS40 . . . . **39** B3
Challenger Way BA22 . . . **218** B6
Challick La TA4 . . . . **166** A6
Challoner Ct BS1 . . . . . . **227** A1
Challow Dr BS22 . . . . **31** B2

Chamberlain Ho TA1 . . . . **212** D5
Chamberlain St BA5 . . . . **203** D4
Chamberlin Ave TA6 . . . **209** C6
Champford La TA21 . . . . **222** D5
Champford Mews 2
TA21 . . . . **222** D5
Champion Cross TA4 . . . . **165** E3
Champney Rd BA11 . . . . **120** A7
Chancel Cl
Bristol BS9 . . . . **5** D3
Nailsea BS48 . . . . **8** D1
Chancellor's Pound BS40 . **36** D3
Chancellor Cl BA16 . . . . . **156** D7
Chancellor Rd BA16 . . . . **156** D7
Chandag Inf Sch BS31 . . . **25** A4
Chandag Jun Sch BS31 . . **25** A4
Chandag Rd BS31 . . . . . . **25** A4
Chandler Cl BA1 . . . . **27** B1
Chandlers DT9 . . . . **225** E5
Chandlers La TA7 . . . . . . **137** C3
Chandos Ct BS23 . . . . **48** D6
Chandos Rd BS31 . . . . . . **24** E7
Chandos St TA6 . . . . **208** F5
Change La TA4 . . . . **164** D6
Channel Cl TA5 . . . . **134** A2
Channel Ct
Burnham-on-S TA8 . . . . . . **104** B5
Weston-Super-Mare BS22 . . **31** B3
Channel Dash Pl BA22 . . . **173** E2
Channel Hts BS24 . . . . **48** F1
Channells La TA19 . . . . . **183** C1
Channel Rd BS21 . . . . **6** D4
Channel View Cres BS20 . . .**2** B5
Channel View Rd BS20 . . . .**2** B5
Channing Cl TA8 . . . . **104** B5
Chantry Cl
Nailsea BS48 . . . . **8** C1
Taunton TA2 . . . . **213** B7
Chantry Ct
Bristol BS1 . . . . **226** C2
Somerton TA11 . . . . **211** C3
Chantry Dr BS22 . . . . **32** A4
Chantry Dro TA7 . . . . **155** B1
Chantry Gdns BA14 . . . . . **83** F3
Chantry Ho 2 BA4 . . . . . **205** B6
Chantry La BA22 . . . . **174** D3
Chantry Mead Rd BA2 . . . **44** E3
Chantry The BS26 . . . . **87** B5
Chantry View BA22 . . . . . **197** D8
Chapel Barton
High Littleton BS39 . . . . . . **59** D1
Nailsea BS48 . . . . **8** C2
Chapel Cl
Castle Cary BA7 . . . . **214** C5
Chew Stoke BS40 . . . . **56** E8
Chilton Polden TA7 . . . . . **137** B2
Farrington Gurney BS39 . . . **76** F4
Keinton Mandeville TA11 . . **158** A1
Nailsea BS48 . . . . **8** E2
North Curry TA3 . . . . **170** B4
Winford BS40 . . . . **38** A6
Chapel Cross
North Cadbury BA22 . . . . . **175** D5
Porlock TA24 . . . . **129** C7
Chapel Ct
Bath BA1 . . . . **228** B2
Clandown BA3 . . . . **78** E4
Clevedon BS21 . . . . **6** D3
Chapelfield BA3 . . . . **115** A3
Chapel Field BA2 . . . . **79** E8
Chapel Forge Cl TA9 . . . **136** B8
Chapel Hill
Ashcott TA7 . . . . **156** B8
Backwell BS48 . . . . **19** D7
Chewton Mendip BA3 . . . . **94** E5
Clevedon BS21 . . . . **6** D3
Kingsdon TA11 . . . . **173** D5
Kington Magna SP8 . . . . . **177** E1
Odcombe BA22 . . . . **186** C2
Ubley BS40 . . . . **55** C5
Wrington BS40 . . . . **35** D3
Chapel La
Bishops Lydeard TA4 . . . . . **167** E8
Butleigh BA6 . . . . **157** E4
Chew Stoke BS40 . . . . **56** D8
Claverham BS49 . . . . **34** F8
Cleeve BS49 . . . . **35** B7
Dinnington TA17 . . . . **195** B7
East Huntspill TA9 . . . . . . **136** E8
Gurney Slade BA3 . . . . **114** E7
Holcombe BA3 . . . . **116** C8
Milborne Port DT9 . . . . . . **217** D2
North Cadbury BA22 . . . . . **175** D6
Oxenpill BA6 . . . . **138** C4
Penselwood BA9 . . . . **161** E2
South Cadbury BA22 . . . . . **175** F5
Sparkford BA22 . . . . **175** A6
Winford BS40 . . . . **38** A6
Wingfield BA14 . . . . **83** C6
Yenston BA8 . . . . **189** F7
Yeovil Marsh BA21 . . . . . . **187** A5
Zeals BA12 . . . . **161** F3
Chapel Lawns BA3 . . . . . . **78** E4
Chapel Leigh La TA4 . . . . **167** A8
Chapel Rd
Bristol, Bishopsworth
BS13 . . . . **22** A6
Clandown BA3 . . . . **78** E4
Fordgate TA7 . . . . **154** C3
Isle Abbotts TA3 . . . . **183** E7
Pawlett TA6 . . . . **135** F6
Rooks Bridge BS26 . . . . . . **87** C5
South Cadbury BA22 . . . . . **175** D4
Chapel Row
Bath BA1 . . . . **228** B2

Chapel Row continued
Bathford BA1 . . . . **29** C2
Dunster TA24 . . . . **201** D2
Norton St Philip BA2 . . . . . **81** F4
Pill BS20 . . . . **4** C4
Chapel St
Bridgwater TA6 . . . . **209** A5
Burnham-on-S TA8 . . . . . **104** A7
Dulverton TA22 . . . . **163** D6
Exford TA24 . . . . **128** D1
Horningsham BA12 . . . . . . **144** D4
Upton Noble BA4 . . . . . . **142** F2
Chapel Wlk BA2 . . . . **60** C2
Chapel Yd BA7 . . . . **214** B4
Chaplains Wood BS20 . . . . .**1** E5
Chapman Ct TA1 . . . . **212** C1
Chapmans Cl
Frome BA11 . . . . **119** F6
Wookey BA5 . . . . **139** D8
Chapmanslade CE Prim Sch
BA13 . . . . **121** D4
Chapter St BS2 . . . . **227** B4
Charbury Wlk BS11 . . . .**4** E5
Charcroft Hill BA10 . . . . . **160** F6
Chard Bsns Pk TA20 . . . . **223** D6
Chard Cl BS48 . . . . **18** F8
Chard Ct BS14 . . . . **23** B6
Chard & District Hospl
TA20 . . . . **223** E4
Chard La
Chard TA20 . . . . **223** B1
Drimpton DT8 . . . . **199** F8
Ilminster TA19 . . . . **194** D6
Tatworth EX13, TA20 . . . . **193** E1
Woolminstone TA18, TA20 . **195** B2
Chard Mus★ TA20 . . . . . . **223** B4
Chard Rd
Axminster EX13 . . . . **198** B4
Clevedon BS21 . . . . **6** E1
Crewkerne TA18 . . . . **224** A6
Drimpton DT8 . . . . **199** F7
Chard Sch TA20 . . . . **223** C4
Chard St
Chardstock EX13 . . . . **198** B7
Thorncombe TA20 . . . . . . **199** B6
Chardstock Ave BS9 . . . .**5** D8
Chardstock La TA20 . . . . . **223** C2
Chardyke Dr BS39 . . . . **58** E1
Charing Cross DT6 . . . . . . **199** E1
Charity La BA11 . . . . **98** C1
Charlcombe La BA1 . . . . . . **27** F3
Charlcombe Pk BS20 . . . . . .**1** D3
Charlcombe Rise BA1 . . . . **27** F2
Charlcombe View Rd BA1 . **28** A2
Charlcombe Way BA1 . . . . **27** F2
Charlcome Rise BS20 . . . . . .**1** D3
Charlecombe Ct BS9 . . . .**5** F6
Charlecombe Rd BS9 . . . . . .**5** F6
Charlecote BA1 . . . . **27** F1
Charles Cres TA1 . . . . **213** D4
Charles Ct 1 BS8 . . . . **226** A2
Charles Pl BS8 . . . . **226** A2
Charles Rd
Frome BA11 . . . . **119** F3
Yeovil BA21 . . . . **219** D6
Charles St
Bath BA1 . . . . **228** B2
Bristol BS1 . . . . **227** A4
Charlestone Rd TA8 . . . . . **104** B8
Charleton Ho 8 BS2 . . . . . **227** C3
Charlock Cl 3 BS22 . . . . . **49** D7
Charlock Rd BS22 . . . . **49** D7
Charlotte Ct BA20 . . . . . . **219** A4
Charlotte St S BS1 . . . . . . **226** C2
Charlotte St
Bath BA1 . . . . **228** B2
Bristol, Brandon Hill BS1 . . **226** C3
Bristol, St Pauls BS2 . . . . . **227** C4
Charlton Ave BS23 . . . . . . **48** D4
Charlton Cl
Bridgwater TA6 . . . . **209** C4
Crewkerne TA18 . . . . **224** D6
Shepton Mallet BA4 . . . . . **205** D5
Yeovil BA21 . . . . **219** D6
Charlton Crossroads
BA4 . . . . **205** D5
Charlton Dr BS48 . . . .**9** C7
Charlton Field La DT9 . . . **175** D1
Charlton Hill DT9, BA8 . . . **176** B3
Charlton Horethorne CE
Prim Sch DT9 . . . . **176** A1
Charlton La
Creech St Michael TA3 . . . **169** C5
Radstock BA3 . . . . **97** D6
Sparkford DT9 . . . . **175** F3
Charlton Mackrell CE Prim
Sch TA11 . . . . **173** E7
Charlton Pk
Keynsham BS31 . . . . **24** D5
Midsomer Norton BA3 . . . . **97** B7
Charlton Rd
Creech St Michael TA3 . . . **169** E6
Holcombe BA3 . . . . **97** D3
Keynsham BS31, BS14 . . . . **24** C3
Midsomer Norton BA3 . . . . **97** B7
Shepton Mallet BA4 . . . . . **205** D5
Weston-Super-Mare BS23 . . **48** D4
Charlton Road Cotts
TA3 . . . . **169** D6
Charlton Trad Est BA4 . . . **205** E5
Charlton View BS20 . . . .**2** C5
Charlynch Hill TA5 . . . . . . **152** F8
Charlynch La TA5 . . . . **153** B8
Charlynch Rd TA5 . . . . . . **153** B8
Charmborough Farm Rural
Bsns Pk BA3 . . . . **97** D3
Charmoor Dro TA20 . . . . . **182** F1
Charmoor La TA20 . . . . . . **182** F1

Charmouth Rd BA1 . . . . . . **44** B7
Charnwood Cl TA6 . . . . . . **208** F7
Charnwood Dr BS27 . . . . . **90** B7
Charnwood Rd BS14 . . . . . **23** B4
Charter Cl TA6 . . . . **209** A4
Charter Ho BS1 . . . . **226** B2
Charterhouse Cl
Cheddar BS27 . . . . **90** C6
Nailsea BS48 . . . .**8** F1
Charterhouse Dr BA11 . . . **120** C7
Charterhouse Rd TA2 . . . . **49** B8
Charter Way BA5 . . . . **203** B4
Charter Wlk
Bristol BS14 . . . . **23** A4
Taunton TA1 . . . . **213** C5
Chartley BS9 . . . .**5** D2
Chase Cl BA6 . . . . **206** C3
Chasey's Dro BA6 . . . . . . **139** C4
Chatham Ave TA6 . . . . . . **208** E6
Chatham Ct TA10 . . . . **171** C4
Chatham Pk BA2 . . . . **45** C6
Chatham Pl TA10 . . . . **171** C4
Chatham Row BA1 . . . . . . **228** C3
Chatley Furlong BA2 . . . . **81** F3
Chatsworth Rd BA21 . . . . **219** D7
Chattenden Ho BS9 . . . .**5** F3
Chatterton Gn BS14 . . . . . **22** F3
Chatterton Ho 6 BS1 . . . . **227** B1
Chatterton Sq BS1 . . . . . . **227** C1
Chatterton St BS1 . . . . . . **227** C1
Chaucer Cl 4 TA6 . . . . . . **153** F4
Chaucer Rd
Bath BA2 . . . . **44** F4
Midsomer Norton BA3 . . . . **97** B8
Weston-Super-Mare BS23 . . **49** A4
Chaundey Gr BS13 . . . . . . **22** B5
Cheapside
Bristol BS2 . . . . **227** C4
Langport TA10 . . . . **171** F5
Taunton TA1 . . . . **212** F3
Wiveliscombe TA4 . . . . . . **210** C4
Cheap St
Bath BA1 . . . . **228** C2
Frome BA11 . . . . **119** F5
Sherborne DT9 . . . . **225** D4
Cheats Rd TA3 . . . . **169** C3
Checcombe La DT9 . . . . . **188** B4
Checkridge La EX13 . . . . . **198** D2
Cheddar Bsns Pk BS27 . . . **90** A6
Cheddar Cl
Burnham-on-S TA8 . . . . . **104** C8
Frome BA11 . . . . **120** C7
Nailsea BS48 . . . . **18** F8
Cheddar Ct BS27 . . . . **90** B7
Cheddar Fields BS27 . . . . . **90** A7
Cheddar Fst Sch BS27 . . . . **90** B7
Cheddar Gorge★ BS27 . . . . **71** E1
Cheddar Gorge Rural
Village★ BS27 . . . . **90** C8
Cheddar Gr BS13 . . . . **22** A8
Cheddar Grove Prim Sch
BS13 . . . . **22** A8
Cheddar Moor Dro BS27 . . **90** C4
Cheddar Rd
Axbridge BS26 . . . . **70** E2
Chewton Mendip BA3 . . . . **94** D6
Clewer BS28 . . . . **89** D2
Wedmore BS28 . . . . **108** D6
Cheddar Valley Bldgs 2
BA5 . . . . **203** C3
Cheddon Fitzpaine CE Prim
Sch TA2 . . . . **168** F6
Cheddon Lawns TA2 . . . . . **169** A6
Cheddon Mews TA2 . . . . . **212** F7
Cheddon Rd TA2 . . . . **212** F7
Chedworth Cl BA2 . . . . . . **45** F3
Chedzoy La TA7 . . . . **209** F7
Cheeks La BA10 . . . . **215** E6
Cheer La TA7 . . . . **154** F5
Cheese Hill BA11 . . . . **143** D8
Cheese La BS2 . . . . **227** B2
Chelmer Cl TA1 . . . . **213** D4
Chelmer Gr BS31 . . . . **24** F4
Chelscombe BA1 . . . . **27** B1
Chelsea Cl BS31 . . . . **25** A5
Chelsea Rd BA1 . . . . **44** C7
Chelsfield BS48 . . . . **19** A7
Chelston Ave BA21 . . . . . **219** B7
Chelston Bsns Pk TA21 . . **180** C8
Chelston Rd BS4 . . . . **22** D7
Chelston Terr TA21 . . . . . **180** D8
Chelswood Ave BS22 . . . . **49** C8
Chelswood Gdns BS22 . . . . **49** D8
Cheltenham St BA2 . . . . . **228** A1
Chelvey Batch BS48 . . . . . **18** F3
Chelvey La BS48 . . . . **18** E4
Chelvey Rd BS48 . . . . **18** D5
Chelvey Rise BS48 . . . .**9** A1
Chelvy Cl BS13 . . . . **22** D3
Chelwood BS23 . . . . **48** F8
Chelwood Dr
Bath BA2 . . . . **44** D1
Taunton TA1 . . . . **212** C1
Chelwood Rd
Bristol BS11 . . . .**4** D7
Saltford BS31 . . . . **25** E4
Chelwood Rdbt BS39 . . . . . **58** E8
Chelynch Pk BA4 . . . . **141** E6
Chelynch Rd BA4 . . . . **141** F7
Chepstow Ave TA6 . . . . . . **209** A2
Chepstow Ct BA21 . . . . . . **219** D6
Chepstow Ho BA10 . . . . . . **215** D6
Chepstow Rd BS4 . . . . **22** D8
Chepstow Wlk BS31 . . . . . **24** D5
Cher TA24 . . . . **200** F6
Cherfield TA24 . . . . **200** F6
Cherington Rd BS48 . . . .**9** A2
Cheriton St BA8 . . . . **176** D3

Cherry Ave BS21 . . . .**6** E2
Cherry Cl
Bridgwater TA6 . . . . **209** C3
Yatton BS49 . . . . **34** B8
Cherry Ct 12 BS1 . . . . **227** A4
Cherry Garden La BA2 . . . **100** D7
Cherry Gr
Frome BA11 . . . . **119** E3
Taunton TA2 . . . . **212** F6
Yatton BS49 . . . . **34** B8
Cherry Hay BS21 . . . .**6** D1
Cherry La
4 Bristol BS1 . . . . **227** B4
Odcombe BA22 . . . . **186** C2
Cherry Orch TA3 . . . . **168** D1
Cherry Orchard Dr BA5 . . **203** C5
Cherry Pie La BA22 . . . . . **175** A5
Cherry Rd
Long Ashton BS41 . . . . **10** F1
Nailsea BS48 . . . .**8** D1
Cherry Tree Cl
Keynsham BS31 . . . . **24** C4
Radstock BA3 . . . . **78** E1
Cherry Tree Ct
Crewkerne TA18 . . . . **224** D8
Kingston Seymour BS21 . . . **16** C2
Wells BA5 . . . . **203** C3
Wincanton BA9 . . . . **216** D4
Cherry Tree Dr BA20 . . . . **218** D2
Cherry Tree La TA1 . . . . . **212** F1
Cherry Tree Rd EX13 . . . . **198** A1
Cherry Tree Way TA23 . . . **202** D6
Cherrywood Rd BS22 . . . . **31** F2
Cherrywood Rise BS22 . . . **31** F2
Chertsey Cl TA7 . . . . **136** E4
Cherwell Rd BS31 . . . . **25** A4
Chescombe Rd BS49 . . . . . **34** B7
Chesham Rd N BS22 . . . . . **49** B8
Chesham Rd S BS22 . . . . . **49** B8
Cheshay's Hill TA19 . . . . . **183** C1
Chesle Cl BS20 . . . .**1** E3
Cheslefield BS20 . . . .**1** E3
Chesle Way BS20 . . . .**1** E3
Chessell La BA4 . . . . **140** C4
Chessels Cl BA22 . . . . **197** B8
Chessels La TA11 . . . . **173** F7
Chessington Ave BS14 . . . **23** B5
Chesterblade Rd
Chesterblade BA4 . . . . **142** A4
Evercreech BA4 . . . . **141** F3
Chester Cl BS24 . . . . **50** A8
Chester Cres BS13 . . . . **22** B8
Chesterfield Cl BS29 . . . . . **50** F3
Chesterfield Ho BA3 . . . . . **78** B1
Chesterfield Hospl BS8 . . **226** A2
Chester Terr TA20 . . . . . . **223** D4
Chesterton Dr BS48 . . . .**9** A2
Chesterton Ho 6 BS2 . . . . **227** B4
Chestertons The BA2 . . . . . **45** E4
Chestnut Ave
Axbridge BS26 . . . . **70** C2
Chapel Cleeve TA24 . . . . . **131** D5
Crewkerne TA18 . . . . **224** D7
Weston-Super-Mare BS22 . . **32** A1
Chestnut Barn Ind Est
BS24 . . . . **33** D3
Chestnut Chase BS48 . . . . . .**9** A3
Chestnut Cl
Baltonsborough BA6 . . . . . **158** A5
Banwell BS29 . . . . **51** A3
Bridgwater TA6 . . . . **209** C4
Bristol BS14 . . . . **23** F5
1 Carhampton TA24 . . . . **131** A5
Congresbury BS49 . . . . **34** D4
Frome BA11 . . . . **120** C7
Maiden Bradley BA12 . . . . **144** C2
Paulton BS39 . . . . **77** E6
Radstock BA3 . . . . **78** E1
Somerton TA11 . . . . **211** C3
Wellington TA21 . . . . **222** B5
Chestnut Ct BS13 . . . . **22** A7
Chestnut Dr
Claverham BS49 . . . . **17** F1
Taunton TA1 . . . . **213** C1
Yeovil BA20 . . . . **218** F3
Chestnut Gr
Bath BA2 . . . . **44** C4
Clevedon BS21 . . . . **6** E4
Westwood BA15 . . . . **64** F4
Chestnut Ho
Brean TA8 . . . . **65** F7
Bristol BS13 . . . . **22** D3
Chestnut Par BA4 . . . . **205** B4
Chestnut Rd
Long Ashton BS41 . . . . **11** B2
11 Martock TA12 . . . . . . **185** E6
Chestnuts The
Cheddar BS27 . . . . **71** A1
Winscombe BS25 . . . . **70** A7
Chestnut Way TA24 . . . . . **201** A6
Chestnut Wlk
Bristol BS13 . . . . **22** A6
Saltford BS31 . . . . **25** E3
Chever's La BA2 . . . . **81** E5
Cheverton Ho 1 BA21 . . . **219** B5
Chew Cotts BS31 . . . . **24** F5
Chew Court Farm BS40 . . . **39** B3
Chew Hill BS40 . . . . **39** A4
Chew La BS40 . . . . **38** F1
Chew Magna Prim Sch
BS40 . . . . **39** B3
Chew Rd BS40 . . . . **38** C5
Chew St BS40 . . . . **39** A3

Chew Stoke CE Prim Sch
BS40 . . . . **56** D8
Chewton Cheese Dairy★
BA3 . . . . **94** E6
Chewton Hill BA3 . . . . **95** A7
Chewton Mendip CE Prim
Sch BA3 . . . . **94** F7
Chewton Rd BS31 . . . . **24** F2
Chew Valley Lake Nature
Trails★ BS39 . . . . **57** B7
Chew Valley Sch BS40 . . . . **38** F1
Cheyne Rd BS9 . . . .**5** D6
Chibbet Hill TA24 . . . . **146** B8
Chibbet Post TA24 . . . . . . **146** C8
Chichester Cl TA8 . . . . . . **104** B8
Chichester Pl BA3 . . . . **79** A2
Chichester Rd BA16 . . . . . **207** C4
Chichester Way BS24 . . . . **50** A8
Chick's La TA4 . . . . **210** C6
Chicks La BA3 . . . . **95** D7
Chickwell La BA3 . . . . **81** A1
Chidgey Cl TA6 . . . . **208** F5
Chilcombe La TA4 . . . . **132** C3
Chilcompton Rd BA3 . . . . . **96** E7
Chilcote Dro BA5 . . . . **113** C2
Chilcote La BA5 . . . . **113** D1
Chilcott Cross TA22 . . . . . **163** A7
Chilcott La TA22 . . . . **163** A7
Childhay La DT8 . . . . **199** F6
Chilkwell St BA6 . . . . **206** E4
Chillington Down TA19,
TA20 . . . . **194** F4
Chilliswood Cres TA1 . . . . **212** B2
Chilliswood La
Staplehay TA3 . . . . **181** B8
Taunton TA3 . . . . **168** B1
Chill Pits La EX13 . . . . . . **198** B8
Chillybridge Rocks TA22 **147** E1
Chillyhill La BS40 . . . . **38** F2
Chilpitts TA7 . . . . **136** F4
Chiltern Cl BS14 . . . . **23** B4
Chiltern Cross EX16 . . . . . **164** B2
Chilthorne Domer CE Sch
BA22 . . . . **186** E5
Chilthornehill La BA22 . . . **186** E5
Chilton Cantelo House (Sch)
BA22 . . . . **174** C1
Chilton Cl TA6 . . . . **208** F7
Chilton Ct 7 BA1 . . . . **28** B1
Chilton Dro TA7 . . . . **137** C6
Chilton Gr BA21 . . . . **219** A4
Chilton Pk TA6 . . . . **208** F7
Chilton Rd
Bath BA1 . . . . **28** B1
Bridgwater TA5, TA6 . . . . **208** F8
Bristol BS4 . . . . **23** A8
Chilton Polden TA7 . . . . . **137** B4
Chilton Right Dro TA7 . . . **155** B6
Chilton St TA6 . . . . **208** F7
Chilton Trinity Tech Coll
TA6 . . . . **208** F8
Chilworthy La TA19, TA20 **193** F7
Chimes The BS48 . . . . **18** C8
Chinehorn Dro TA5 . . . . . . **135** F3
Chinnock Hollow BA22 . . . **196** B6
Chinnock Rd BA6 . . . . **206** F5
Chip La TA1 . . . . **212** E5
Chippel La DT10 . . . . **190** F5
Chipping Cross BS21 . . . . . **16** C8
Chi-Rio Cl BA4 . . . . **205** E4
Chisland Dr TA24 . . . . **129** C8
Chistles La TA11 . . . . **158** A1
Chitcombe Rocks La
TA4 . . . . **149** C1
Cholwell Cotts BS39 . . . . . **58** D2
Chorwell La TA21 . . . . **166** E2
Chovel La BA11 . . . . **142** F6
Chowins Rd TA18 . . . . **224** C5
Christchurch CE Fst Sch
BA11 . . . . **119** F2
Christ Church CE Prim Sch
Bristol BS8 . . . . **226** A3
Weston-Super-Mare BS23 . . **48** E8
Christ Church Cl 1 BS48 . . .**8** E2
Christ Church Ct 9
TA18 . . . . **224** D6
Christchurch Hall 2
BA1 . . . . **228** B3
Christ Church Path S 12
BS23 . . . . **48** E8
Christchurch Rd BS8 . . . . **226** A3
Christchurch St E BA11 . . **119** F4
Christchurch St W BA11 . . **119** F4
Christian's Cross BA6 . . . **157** E1
Christian Cl BS22 . . . . **32** A3
Christina Terr BS8 . . . . . . **226** A1
Christmas St 6 BS1 . . . . . **227** A3
Christmas Stps 2 BS1 . . . **227** A3
Christon Rd
Banwell BS29 . . . . **51** A1
Loxton BS26 . . . . **68** C6
Christon Terr BS23 . . . . . . **48** F2
Christopher Cl BA20 . . . . **218** E5
Christopher Way BA4 . . . . **205** A5
Chritchard Way TA1 . . . . . **213** B4
Chrysanthemum Cl 3
DT9 . . . . **225** E4
Chrysanthemum Flats 2
DT9 . . . . **225** E4
Chrysanthemum Row 4
DT9 . . . . **225** E4
Chubbards Cross Cvn Site
TA19 . . . . **183** E5
Chubbs Lawn TA18 . . . . . **224** C5
Chubworthy Cross TA4 . . **165** D5
Church Ave BS9 . . . .**5** E4
Church Cl
Bathampton BA2 . . . . **28** F2

Church Cl *continued*
Bathford BA1 . . . . **29** B2
Bourton SP8 . . . . **161** E1
7 Carhampton TA24 . . **131** A5
Clevedon BS21. . . . . **6** A2
East Huntspill TA9 . . . . **136** E8
Evercreech BA4 . . . . . . **141** E1
Great Elm BA11 . . . . . . **118** F7
Lydeard St Lawrence TA4 . **151** A3
24 Martock TA12 . . . . . . **185** E6
Norton Fitzwarren TA2 . . **168** B4
Portishead BS20 . . . . **2** D5
Shapwick TA7 . . . . **137** F1
South Brewham BA10 . . . **160** F6
Stoke St Gregory TA3 . . . **170** E6
Stoke St Mary TA3 . . . . . **169** C1
West Chinnock TA18 . . . **196** B8
Yatton BS49 . . . . **34** C7
Church Cnr BS24 . . . . . . **67** B1
Church Cotts
Chilton Trinity TA5 . . . . **135** F2
Monkton Combe BA2 . . . . **63** E8
Newton St Loe BA2 . . . . **43** B6
Church Ct
Midsomer Norton BA3 . . . **78** A1
Redhill BS40 . . . . **36** D3
Churchdown Wlk BS11 . . . .**4** E5
Church Dr
Congresbury BS49 . . . . . . **34** D4
West Buckland TA21 . . . **180** F7
Church Farm Bsns Pk
BA2 . . . . **43** A7
Church Farm Cl
Marksbury BA2 . . . . **42** B1
Stawell TA7 . . . . **137** A1
Church Farm Pl **18** BA8 . . **190** A6
Church Field La TA7 . . **136** C4
Churchfields
Rode BA11 . . . . **101** F8
Wellington TA21 . . . . . . **222** D7
Church Fields
Wellington TA21 . . . . . . **222** E6
Wincanton BA9 . . . . . . **216** C3
Churchfields Dr BA7 . . **214** C6
Church Gdns BA6 . . . . . **206** D5
Church Hayes Cl BS48 . . **18** E8
Church Hayes Dr BS48 . . **18** E8
Church Hill
Beckington BA11 . . . . . **101** E4
Buckhorn Weston SP8 . . **177** D3
Charlton Adam TA11 . . . **173** F7
Combwich TA5 . . . . . . **135** B4
Dinnington TA17 . . . . . **195** B7
Exford TA24 . . . . **128** D1
Freshford BA3 . . . . **64** B5
Kington Magna SP8 . . . **177** E2
Pitney TA10 . . . . **172** C7
Radstock BA3 . . . . **79** C3
South Cadbury BA22 . . . **175** C3
Stalbridge DT10 . . . . . . **190** B5
Templecombe BA8 . . . . **176** E1
Timsbury BA2 . . . . **60** B2
Church Ho BA4 . . . . **141** F4
Church House Rd TA8 . . . **84** F5
Churchill Ave
Clevedon BS21 . . . . **6** C2
Wells BA5 . . . . **112** E1
Churchill Bsns Pk BS23 . **49** A7
Churchill CE Prim Sch
BS40 . . . . **53** A5
Churchill Cl
Burnham-on-S TA8 . . . . **104** C5
5 Clevedon BS21 . . . . . . **6** C2
Wells BA5 . . . . **112** E1
Churchill Dr BS9 . . . . **5** D7
Churchill Gate BS25 . . . . **52** F4
Churchill Gn BS25 . . . . . **52** C5
Churchill La
Axminster EX13 . . . . . . **198** A5
Chipstable TA4 . . . . . . **165** C5
Churchill Rd
Frome BA11 . . . . **119** D4
Shepton Mallet BA4 . . . **205** A5
Wells BA5 . . . . **112** E1
Weston-Super-Mare BS23 . **49** A7
Churchill Rd E BA5 . . . . **112** E1
**Churchill Sch & Sixth Form
Ctr** BS25 . . . . **52** D5
Churchill Way
Taunton TA1 . . . . **212** F1
Watchet TA23 . . . . **202** C6
Church La
Axbridge BS26 . . . . **70** C2
Backwell BS48 . . . . **19** C5
Badgworth BS26 . . . . . . **88** A6
Baltonsborough BA6 . . . **158** A5
Bath BA2 . . . . **45** C4
Batheaston BA1 . . . . **28** F4
Bicknoller TA4 . . . . **132** F2
Bishop Sutton BS39 . . . . **57** D4
Bitton BS30 . . . . **25** E7
Blackford BS28 . . . . . . **107** D5
Brent Knoll TA9 . . . . **86** A2
Bristol BS1 . . . . **227** B2
Bristol, Clifton Wood BS8 . **226** B2
Bristol, Dundry Hill BS14 . . **23** B3
Carhampton TA24 . . . . . **131** B5
Chew Stoke BS40 . . . . . . **56** D8
Chewton Mendip BA3 . . . **94** F7
Chilcompton BA3 . . . . . . **96** D5
Chilton Polden TA7 . . . . **137** B2
Churchill BS25 . . . . **52** D5
Clutton BS39 . . . . **58** E3
Coleford BA3 . . . . **116** F7
Compton Bishop BS26 . . . **69** B3
Compton Dando BS39 . . . **41** D6
Doulting BA4 . . . . **141** E6

Church La *continued*
Dulverton TA22 . . . . . . **163** D6
East Coker BA22 . . . . . . **197** E8
East Harptree BS40 . . . . . **74** E4
East Huntspill TA9 . . . . **136** E8
East Lambrook TA13 . . . **220** C8
Evercreech BA4 . . . . . . **141** E1
Farmborough BA2 . . . . . . **60** A6
Farrington Gurney BS39 . . **77** A4
Flax Bourton BS48 . . . . . . **19** F7
Glastonbury BA6 . . . . . . **206** D5
Haselbury Plucknett TA18 . **196** C5
Hatch Beauchamp TA3 . . **182** B5
Horningsham BA12 . . . . **144** E4
Horton TA19 . . . . **183** C2
Hutton BS24 . . . . **49** E2
Ilminster TA19 . . . . **221** C4
Kingston St Mary TA2 . . **168** E8
Limpley Stoke BA3 . . . . . **64** A5
Long Ashton BS41 . . . . . . **11** C2
Long Sutton TA10 . . . . . **172** D2
Loxton BS26 . . . . **68** D4
Lympsham BS24 . . . . **67** B1
Lynford-on-F TA11 . . . . . **158** D2
Meare BA6 . . . . **138** D4
Midsomer Norton BA3 . . . **78** A1
Milborne Port DT9 . . . . **217** D2
Misterton TA18 . . . . . . **224** E3
Nailsea BS21 . . . . **8** C4
Nailsea BS48 . . . . **8** C1
North Perrott TA18 . . . . **196** C4
Norton Sub Hamdon,
 Chiselborough TA14 . . **185** E1
Norton Sub Hamdon TA14 . **185** F2
Paulton BS39 . . . . **77** E6
Portbury BS20 . . . . **3** E3
Rimpton BA22 . . . . **188** B8
Rode BA11 . . . . **101** F8
Ruishton TA3 . . . . **169** C4
Ruishton, Thornfalcon TA3 . **169** D4
Seavington St Mary TA19 . **184** E1
22 Shepton Mallet BA4 . . **205** B6
Shepton Mallet, Cannards Grave
 BA4 . . . . **205** D2
Stratton-on-t F BA3 . . . . . **96** F2
Timsbury BA2 . . . . **60** B2
Westonzoyland TA7 . . . . **154** F5
West Pennard BA6 . . . . **140** B1
Wingfield BA14 . . . . **83** C6
Winscombe BS25 . . . . . . **69** E6
Yatton BS49 . . . . **34** C7
Churchlands TA9 . . . . . **106** D4
Churchlands Ct TA8 . . . **104** A7
Churchland Way BS22 . . **50** B8
Church Lane Cnr TA9 . . . **86** A2
Church Lane End BS48 . . **19** F8
Church Leaze BS11 . . . . . **4** D6
Church Mdw TA6 . . . . . . **208** E6
Church Mdws BS14 . . . . . **23** C4
Church Mead SP8 . . . . . **161** E1
Churchmoor La BA6 . . . **158** A5
Church Pass **4** TA6 . . . **208** F5
Church Path
Aller TA10 . . . . **171** D8
Bridgwater TA6 . . . . . . **208** E5
Crewkerne TA18 . . . . . . **224** B6
Meare BA6 . . . . **138** D4
Minehead TA24 . . . . . . **200** F8
Queen Camel BA22 . . . **174** F3
South Petherton TA13 . . **220** C2
2 Yeovil BA20 . . . . **219** B5
Church Path Rd BS20 . . . . **4** C4
Church Pl
Milborne Port DT9 . . . . **217** D2
Pill BS20 . . . . **4** C4
Church Rd
Abbots Leigh BS8 . . . . . . **11** A8
Bath, Combe Down BA2 . . **45** C1
Bath, Weston Park BA1 . . . **27** C1
Bawdrip TA7 . . . . **136** E2
Bitton BS30 . . . . **25** E7
Bourton SP8 . . . . **177** F8
Bradford Abbas DT9 . . . **187** E1
Brean TA8 . . . . **65** F4
Bristol, Bishopsworth BS13 . **22** A6
Bristol, Sneyd Park BS9 . . . **5** D3
Chapel Leigh TA4 . . . . . **167** A7
Churchinford TA3 . . . . . **191** F8
Churchstanton TA3 . . . . **181** B1
Coxley BA5 . . . . **139** E6
Dundry BS41 . . . . **21** D2
East Brent TA9 . . . . **86** C4
Easton-in-G BS20 . . . . . . **4** A4
Edington TA7 . . . . **137** C2
Fitzhead TA4 . . . . **166** F7
Fordgate TA7 . . . . **154** D3
Huntspill TA9 . . . . **136** A8
Ilton TA19 . . . . **183** E4
Keenthorne TA5 . . . . . . **134** D3
Kilmington BA12 . . . . . . **161** F7
Leigh Woods BS8 . . . . . . **11** D6
Lympsham BS24 . . . . **67** B1
Middlezoy TA7 . . . . **155** B3
Minehead TA24 . . . . . . **200** F8
North Curry TA3 . . . . . . **170** B4
North Newton TA7 . . . . **154** A2
Peasedown St John BA2 . . **79** B8
Pensford BS39 . . . . **40** A7
Redhill BS40 . . . . **36** D3
Shapwick TA7 . . . . **137** F1
South Cadbury BA22 . . . **175** D4
Sparkford BA22 . . . . . . **175** A4
Spaxton TA5 . . . . **152** E2
Street BA16 . . . . **207** D7
Sutton Mallet TA7 . . . . **155** B7
Taunton TA3 . . . . **168** D1
Wembdon TA6 . . . . **208** D6

Church Rd *continued*
Weston-Super-Mare BS22 . . **31** E2
Whitchurch BS14 . . . . . . **23** C4
Winford BS40 . . . . **38** A7
Winscombe BS25 . . . . . . **69** E7
Yatton BS49 . . . . **34** C7
Church Rd N BS20 . . . . . . **2** D5
Church Rd S BS20 . . . . . . **2** D4
Church Rise BS40 . . . . . . **38** A7
Church Row BA3 . . . . **96** F2
Church Row Cotts TA3 . . **181** E6
Church Sq
Clutton BS39 . . . . **58** E2
Midsomer Norton BA3 . . . **78** A1
8 Taunton TA1 . . . . **212** F4
Church St
Babcary TA11 . . . . **174** C7
Banwell BS29 . . . . **51** B3
Barton St David BA6 . . . **157** F2
6 Bath BA1 . . . . **228** C2
Bathford BA1 . . . . **29** B2
Bath, Weston park BA1 . . . **27** B1
Bath, Widcombe BA2 . . . . **45** B4
Beckington BA11 . . . . . . **101** E4
Bishops Lydeard TA4 . . . **167** E8
Blackford BS28 . . . . . . **107** D4
Blagdon BS40 . . . . **54** F2
Bridgwater TA6 . . . . . . **209** A5
Bristol BS1 . . . . **227** B2
5 Cannington TA5 . . . . . **135** B2
Castle Cary BA7 . . . . . . **214** B4
Chard TA20 . . . . **223** C3
Cheddar BS27 . . . . **90** B7
Coleford BA3 . . . . **116** F7
Crewkerne TA18 . . . . . . **224** C6
Croscombe BA5 . . . . . . **204** C7
Dinder BA5 . . . . **140** D7
Donyatt TA19 . . . . **183** D1
Drayton TA10 . . . . **171** E3
Dunster TA24 . . . . **201** E2
2 Frome BA11 . . . . **119** F4
Halstock BA22 . . . . **197** C3
8 Henstridge BA8 . . . . **190** A6
Highbridge TA9 . . . . . . **104** E4
Hinton St George TA17 . . **195** C7
Horningsham BA12 . . . . **144** D4
Ilchester BA22 . . . . **173** E1
Isle Abbotts TA3 . . . . . . **183** F7
Keinton Mandeville TA11 . **158** A1
Kilmersdon BA3 . . . . **98** B5
Kingsbury Episcopi TA12 . **185** B8
Kington Magna SP8 . . . . **177** E2
Lopen TA13 . . . . **185** A1
Maiden Bradley BA12 . . . **144** C1
Mark TA9 . . . . **106** D4
Martock TA12 . . . . **185** E6
Merriott TA16 . . . . **195** F7
Milborne Port DT9 . . . . **217** D2
Minehead, Alcombe TA24 . **201** B5
Minehead TA24 . . . . . . **200** F8
Norton St Philip BA2 . . . . **81** E4
Nunney BA11 . . . . **143** B8
Paulton BS39 . . . . **77** D6
Pensford BS39 . . . . **40** D4
Podimore BA22 . . . . . . **174** A3
Radstock BA3 . . . . **78** F2
Shepton Beauchamp TA19 . **184** E4
Southwick BA14 . . . . **83** F3
Stogursey TA5 . . . . **134** C5
Stoke St Michael BA3 . . . **116** A2
Taunton TA1 . . . . **213** B3
Timberscombe TA24 . . . **130** B5
Tintinhull BA22 . . . . . . **186** B6
Upton Noble BA4 . . . . . **142** F2
Wanstrow BA4 . . . . **142** F4
Wedmore BS28 . . . . . . **108** D4
West Coker BA22 . . . . . **197** A8
Wincanton BA9 . . . . . . **216** C4
Winsham TA20 . . . . **194** E1
Wiveliscombe TA4 . . . . **210** C4
Woolavington TA7 . . . . **136** E4
Woolley BA1 . . . . **27** F6
Yeovil BA20 . . . . **219** B5
Yeovilton BA22 . . . . . . **174** A1
Churchstanton Prim Sch
TA3 . . . . **191** B8
Church Stps TA24 . . . . . **200** F8
Church Terr
7 Bampton EX16 . . . . . **164** B1
East Coker BA22 . . . . . . **197** C7
Odcombe BA22 . . . . . . **186** C2
4 Yeovil BA20 . . . . **219** B5
Church Tk SP8 . . . . **161** E1
Church Town BS48 . . . . . **19** C5
Church View
Bourton SP8 . . . . **161** E1
Chilton Trinity TA5 . . . . **135** F2
Clatworthy TA4 . . . . . . **149** F1
Evercreech BA4 . . . . . . **141** E1
North Wootton BA4 . . . **140** C4
Porlock TA24 . . . . **124** A3
Wraxall BS48 . . . . **9** B2
Church View Cl TA10 . . . **171** E8
Churchview Ct BA6 . . . . **206** D4
Churchward Dr BA11 . . . **120** C6
Churchward Rd BS22 . . . **32** B3
Churchway
Curry Rivel TA10 . . . . . **171** D4
Faulkland BA3 . . . . **80** D1
Church Way TA7 . . . . . . **137** D2
Churchway Cl TA10 . . . . **171** D4
Churchways BS14 . . . . . . **23** C4
Churchwell Cl DT9 . . . . **187** E1
Churchwell St DT9 . . . . **187** E1
Church Wlk
Baltonsborough BA6 . . . **158** A5
Bawdrip TA7 . . . . **136** E2
Bratton Seymour BA9 . . . **176** B8

Church Wlk *continued*
Ilminster TA19 . . . . **221** C4
Leigh u M BA3 . . . . **117** A3
Long Sutton TA10 . . . . . **172** F4
Marston Magna BA22 . . . **174** F1
9 North Petherton TA6 . **153** E3
Pill BS20 . . . . **4** C4
Wrington BS40 . . . . **35** D2
Chur BA2 . . . . **197** A8
Churlands Cl BA22 . . . . **197** A8
Churston Cl BS14 . . . . . . **23** A3
Cinder Ash La TA18 . . . **195** D4
Cinnamon La BA6 . . . . . **206** F3
Circle The BA2 . . . . **44** B3
Circular Rd BS9 . . . .**5** E1
Circus Field Rd BA6 . . . **206** D4
Circus Mews BA1 . . . . . **228** B3
Circus Pl BA1 . . . . **228** B3
Circus The BA1 . . . . **228** B3
City Mus & Art Gal BS8 **226** C3
City of Bath Coll BA1 . . **228** B2
City of Bristol Coll BS1 . **226** C2
**City of Bristol Coll (Hartcliffe
 Ctr)** BS13 . . . . **22** D4
City Rd BS2 . . . . **227** B4
City The TA9 . . . . **106** C4
City View BA1 . . . . **228** C4
Clammer Hill La TA18 . . **224** D6
Clanage Rd BS3 . . . . **11** E4
Clanders Batch BS40 . . . **54** D3
Clandown CE Prim Sch
BA3 . . . . **78** E4
Clandown Rd BS39 . . . . . **77** F4
Clanfield DT9 . . . . **225** B2
Clan Ho BA2 . . . . **45** C7
Clanville TA24 . . . . **200** F7
Clanville Rd TA24 . . . . . **200** F7
Clapton Court Gdns
TA18 . . . . **195** D1
Clapton Dro BS20 . . . . . . **2** C1
Clapton Gate TA18 . . . . **195** C2
Clapton La
Holton BA9 . . . . **176** B6
Portishead BS20 . . . . **2** E2
Clapton Rd
Hewish TA18 . . . . **195** D2
Midsomer Norton BA3 . . . **77** D1
Clapton Wlk BS9 . . . . **5** C5
Clare Gdns BA2 . . . . **44** D1
Clareham La
Buckland Dinham BA11 . . **99** D2
Buckland Dinham BA11 . . **99** F3
Claremont Bldgs BA1 . . . **28** A1
Claremont Cres BS23 . . . **30** B1
Claremont Ct TA1 . . . . . **212** C1
Claremont Cvn Pk TA8 . . **84** F6
Claremont Dr TA1 . . . . . **212** C1
Claremont Gdns
Clevedon BS21 . . . . **6** C1
Hallatrow BS39 . . . . **77** B7
4 Nailsea BS48 . . . . **8** D1
Claremont Gr TA6 . . . . **209** D4
Claremont Hall BS21 . . . . **6** E4
Claremont La TA1 . . . . . **212** C1
Claremont Pl **13** BA1 . . **28** A1
Claremont Rd BA1 . . . . . **28** A1
Claremont Wlk BA1 . . . . **28** A1
Clarence Ct **1** BA22 . . **219** A5
Clarence Dr **1** TA6 . . . **153** F4
Clarence Grove Rd BS23 . **48** E5
Clarence Pl
Bath BA1 . . . . **44** B6
Bristol BS2 . . . . **226** C4
Clarence Rd BS1 . . . . . . **227** B1
Clarence Rd E BS23 . . . . **48** E5
Clarence Rd N BS23 . . . . **48** D5
Clarence Rd S BS23 . . . . **48** D5
Clarence St
Bath BA1 . . . . **228** C4
Taunton TA1 . . . . **212** E4
Yeovil BA22 . . . . **219** A5
Clarence Terr
Bath BA2 . . . . **45** D5
8 Yeovil BA20 . . . . **219** B4
Clarendon Rd
Bath BA2 . . . . **45** B5
Weston-Super-Mare BS23 . **48** F8
Clarendon Villas BA2 . . . **45** B5
Clare St
Bridgwater TA6 . . . . . . **208** F5
Bristol BS1 . . . . **227** A2
2 North Petherton TA6 . **153** F4
Clark's La TA18 . . . . . . **224** F3
Clark Cl
Woolavington TA7 . . . . **136** E4
Wraxall BS48 . . . . **9** B2
Clarke's Cl TA20 . . . . . . **223** D4
Clarke's Row TA20 . . . . **223** D4
Clarken Coombe BS41 . . **11** B3
Clarken Cl BS48 . . . .**8** E1
Clarkes Ct BA20 . . . . . . **219** A4
Clarkham Cross BA22 . . **197** E2
Clarks Cl BA22 . . . . **218** A5
Clarkson Ave BS22 . . . . . **31** C1
Clarkson Ho BA1 . . . . . . **228** A2
Clarks Rd TA6 . . . . **209** C4
Clarks Shopping Village
BA16 . . . . **207** C6
Classic Bldgs TA6 . . . . . **208** F4
Clatcombe La DT9 . . . . . **188** D6
Clatworthy Dr BS14 . . . . **23** A7
Clatworthy Resr TA4 . . **149** D2
Claude Ave BA2 . . . . **44** C5
Claude Terr BA2 . . . . **44** C5
Claverham Cl BS49 . . . . . **34** D7
Claverham Dro BS49 . . . . **17** D5
Claverham Rd BS49 . . . . **34** E4

Claverton Bldgs BA2 . . . **228** C1
Claverton Ct BA2 . . . . . . **45** E4
Claverton Down Rd BA2 . **45** F3
Claverton Dr BA2 . . . . . . **45** F3
Claverton Hill BA2 . . . . . **46** A4
Claverton Lodge BA2 . . . **45** C5
Claverton Pumping Sta
BA2 . . . . **46** C5
Claverton Rd BS31 . . . . . **25** E2
Claverton Rd W BS31 . . . **25** D3
Claverton St BA2 . . . . . **228** C1
Clay Castle TA18 . . . . . . **196** C5
Clay Castle La TA18 . . . **196** C6
Claydon Cl TA23 . . . . . . **131** E4
Claydon Gn BS14 . . . . . . **22** F3
Clayford La TA22 . . . . . **163** C5
Clayford Rd TA22 . . . . . **163** C5
Clayhanger Cross TA20 . **193** E6
Clayhanger La
Chard TA20 . . . . **223** A8
Combe St Nicholas TA20 . **193** E6
Clayhidon Crossway
EX15 . . . . **180** E2
Clay La
Barrington TA19 . . . . . . **184** B5
Bitton BS30 . . . . **25** D8
Chewton Mendip BA3 . . . **94** C5
Higher Chillington TA19 . **194** F5
Millmoor EX15 . . . . . . **179** A1
Rode BA11 . . . . **101** F8
Claylands Cnr TA5 . . . . **134** E5
Claypiece Rd BS13 . . . . . **22** A4
Clayton Cl
Portishead BS20 . . . . **2** E4
Yeovil BA22 . . . . **218** A6
Clearwood BA13 . . . . . . **121** E8
Clearwood View BA13 . . **121** E4
Cleaveside Cl BA22 . . . . **174** F3
Cleeve Abbey TA23 . . . . **131** E3
Cleevedale Rd BA2 . . . . . **45** A1
Cleeve Dr BS49 . . . . **35** B8
Cleeve Gn BA2 . . . . **44** A6
Cleeve Gr BS31 . . . . **24** D5
Cleeve Hill
Ubley BS40 . . . . **73** E8
Watchet TA23 . . . . **202** A7
Cleeve Hill Rd BS40 . . . . **35** C7
Cleeve Pk TA24 . . . . . . **131** D5
Cleeve Pl BS48 . . . . **9** A1
Cleeve Rd TA2 . . . . **213** B7
Cleeveways DT9 . . . . . . **176** A2
Clemence Rd BA16 . . . . **207** D4
Clements Cl BA5 . . . . . . **203** C3
Clement St BS2 . . . . **227** C4
Cleve Ct **3** BS8 . . . . . . **11** F6
Clevedon Com Sch BS21 . **6** F5
Clevedon Craft Ctr BS21 . **7** A1
Clevedon Ct BS21 . . . . . . **7** A4
Clevedon Hospl BS21 . . . . **6** E3
Clevedon Min Rly BS21 . . **6** B3
Clevedon Pier BS21 . . . . . **6** C4
Clevedon Rd
Flax Bourton BS48 . . . . . . **9** F2
Midsomer Norton BA3 . . . **78** A2
Nailsea BS21 . . . . **8** B4
Portishead BS20 . . . . **2** D3
Weston-Super-Mare BS23 . **48** E6
Wraxall BS48 . . . . **9** B4
Wraxall BS48 . . . . **9** D6
Clevedon Terr BS6 . . . . . **227** A4
Clevedon Wlk **2** BS48 . . **8** E2
Cleveland Cotts BA1 . . . **228** C4
Cleveland Ct BA2 . . . . . . **45** C6
Cleveland Pl BA1 . . . . . **228** C4
Cleveland Pl E BA1 . . . . **228** C4
Cleveland Pl W BA1 . . . **228** C4
Cleveland Reach BA1 . . **228** C4
Cleveland Row BA1 . . . . **45** B8
Clevelands TA24 . . . . . . **200** F8
Cleveland St TA1 . . . . . **212** E4
Cleveland Terr BA1 . . . **228** C4
Cleveland Wlk BA2 . . . . **45** C6
Cleve The BA21 . . . . . . **218** C6
Clewson Rise BS14 . . . . . **22** F3
Cleyhill Gdns BA13 . . . . **121** D4
Cliffe Dr BA3 . . . . **64** A6
Clifford Ave TA2 . . . . . . **212** E8
Clifford Cres TA2 . . . . . **212** E8
Clifford Gdns BS11 . . . . . .**4** E6
Clifford Ho BS23 . . . . . . **48** D6
Clifford Lodge **3** TA5 . **135** B2
Clifford Mews TA21 . . . **222** E6
Clifford Pk TA5 . . . . . . **135** B2
Clifford Terr TA21 . . . . **222** E6
Cliff Rd
Cheddar BS27 . . . . **71** E1
North Petherton TA6 . . . **153** E3
Weston-Super-Mare BS22 . **31** A2
Cliff St BS27 . . . . **90** C8
Cliffs The BS27 . . . . **90** C8
Clift House Rd BS3 . . . . . **11** F4
Clift House Spur BS3 . . . . **11** F4
Clifton Ave BS23 . . . . . . **48** E5
Clifton Cl
1 Bristol BS8 . . . . **11** F7
Yeovil BA21 . . . . **219** E6
Clifton Coll BS8 . . . . . . **226** A4
Clifton College Prep Sch
BS8 . . . .**5** F1
Clifton Ct **10** BS21 . . . . . **6** C2
Clifton Down BS8 . . . . . . **11** F7
Clifton Down Rd BS8 . . . **226** A3
Clifton High Gr BS9 . . . . . **5** E5
Clifton High Sch BS8 . . . **226** A4

Clifton Hill
Barwick BA22 . . . . **197** F8
Bristol BS8 . . . . **226** A2
Clifton Park Rd BS8 . . . . **11** F8
Clifton Pk BS8 . . . . **226** A3
Clifton Rd
Bristol BS8 . . . . **226** A2
Weston-Super-Mare BS23 . . **48** E5
Clifton St BS20 . . . . **2** C2
Clifton Suspension Bridge★
BS8 . . . . **11** E7
Clifton Terr 7 TA2 . . . . . **212** F6
Clifton Vale BS8 . . . . **226** A2
Clifton Vale Cl BS8 . . . . . . **226** A2
Clifton View 9 BA22 . . . **197** F8
Cliftonwood Cres BS8 . . . **226** B2
Clifton Wood Cres BS8 . . **226** B2
Clifton Wood Ct BS8 . . . . **226** B2
Clifton Wood Rd BS8 . . . . **226** B2
Cliftonwood Terr BS8 . . . . **226** A2
Clift Pl BS1 . . . . **227** A1
Clifts Bldgs BA11 . . . . . . **119** F4
Clink Farm Ct BA11 . . . . . **120** C6
Clink Rd BA11 . . . . **120** D6
Clink The TA6 . . . . **209** A6
Clipper Cl TA5 . . . . **209** C4
Clipper Quay TA24 . . . . . **201** B7
Clitsome View TA23 . . . . **131** D2
Clive Rd BS14 . . . . **23** C8
Clivey BA13 . . . . **102** E1
Clock Ho TA5 . . . . **134** B2
Clock Ho The BA10 . . . . **160** E7
Clockhouse Mews BS20 . . . **2** D6
Clockhouse The TA4 . . . . **167** E6
Clockhouse Way BA16 . . . **207** D6
Cloisters Croft TA8 . . . . . **104** B6
Cloisters The BA5 . . . . . . **203** D3
Cloister The DT9 . . . . . . **225** D4
Closemead BS21 . . . . **6** D1
Close The
Glastonbury BA6 . . . . . . **206** E5
9 Merriott TA16 . . . . . . **195** F7
Minehead TA24 . . . . . . **201** B5
North Cadbury BA22 . . . **175** D6
Portishead BS20 . . . . **1** F1
Clotfurlong La DT9 . . . . . **188** F1
Clothier Mdw BA7 . . . . . **214** B6
Cloudberry Cl TA20 . . . . . **223** F5
Cloud Hill Ind Est BS39 . . **77** A8
Clovelly Rd BS22 . . . . **32** A2
Clover Cl
Clevedon BS21 . . . . **6** F3
Paulton BS39 . . . . **77** E4
Clover Ct 2 BS22 . . . . . . **49** D7
Clover Gd BA4 . . . . **205** C5
Clover Mead TA1 . . . . . . **213** C1
Clover Rd BS22 . . . . **32** A6
Clover Way TA4 . . . . **104** E4
Clumber Dr BA11 . . . . . . **119** F6
Clumber Ho BA11 . . . . . . **119** F6
Clutton Hill BS39 . . . . . . **59** B4
Clutton Prim Sch BS39 . . . **58** E3
Clyce Rd TA9 . . . . **104** D3
Clyde Ave BS31 . . . . **24** F4
Clyde Gdns BA2 . . . . **44** B6
Clydesdale Cl BS14 . . . . . . **23** A6
Clynder Gr BS21 . . . . **6** E6
Clyntonville BS22 . . . . . . **31** A4
Coach House Mews BS23 . **30** D1
Coachmans Yd BA6 . . . . . **206** D5
Coach Rd TA24 . . . . **124** A3
Coalash La BA11 . . . . **119** D8
Coal Barton BA3 . . . . **116** E8
Coalbridge Cl BS22 . . . . . . **31** F2
Coaley Rd BS11 . . . . **4** D5
Coal La BA11 . . . . **119** C8
Coal Orch TA1 . . . . **212** F4
Coalpit La
Chilcompton BA3 . . . . . . **96** A2
Stoke St Michael BA3 . . . **116** B3
Coalpit Rd BA1 . . . . **29** A4
Coape Rd BS14 . . . . **23** F5
Coast Cvn Pk BS21 . . . . . . **1** B1
Coastguard Cotts TA24 . . **201** A8
Coast Rd TA8 . . . . **84** F7
Coates Est BS48 . . . . **8** F3
Coates Gr BS48 . . . . **9** A2
Coates Wlk BS4 . . . . **22** D6
Coate Turn TA4 . . . . **166** A6
Coat Rd TA12 . . . . **185** D7
Cobblestone Mews BS8 . . **226** A4
Cobhorn Dr BS13 . . . . **21** F4
Cobley Croft BS21 . . . . . . **16** C8
Cobthorn Way BS49 . . . . . **34** E5
Coburg Villas 11 BA1 . . . . **28** A1
Cock-Crowing Stone
TA20 . . . . **193** D4
Cockers Hill BS39 . . . . . . **41** C5
Cockhill Elm La BA7 . . . . **214** D4
Cockhill La BA22 . . . . . . **175** D7
Cockland Hill TA21 . . . . . **166** C1
Cockmill La BA4 . . . . . . **140** F1
Cockpit Hill DT6, DT8 . . . **199** F4
Cockpit La BA4 . . . . **142** C2
Cock Rd
Buckland Dinham BA2,
BA11 . . . . **100** B5
Horningsham BA12 . . . . **144** A4
Cockrod BA16 . . . . **207** B2
Cock & Yew Tree Hill
BS40 . . . . **38** A2
Cod La BA22 . . . . **196** D7
Codrington Pl BS8 . . . . . **226** A3

Cogsall Rd BS14 . . . . **23** F6
Coity Pl BS21 . . . . **6** C4
Coker's La BA12 . . . . **161** F8
Coker Hill BA22 . . . . **196** F8
Coker Hill La BA22 . . . . . **197** A7
Coker Ho BA22 . . . . **197** C8
Coker Marsh BA22 . . . . . **197** D7
Coker Rd BS22 . . . . **32** B2
Colbourn Cl BA3 . . . . . . **114** E7
Colchester Cres BS4 . . . . . **22** D7
Cold Harbour
Milborne Port DT9 . . . . **217** D2
Sherborne DT9 . . . . **225** E5
Coldharbour Bsns Pk
DT9 . . . . **225** E6
Coldharbour La BS23 . . . . **48** D3
Cold Harbour La BA22 . . **196** F6
Coldhills La BA8 . . . . **176** D2
Cold Nose BS28 . . . . **138** D8
Coldpark Gdns BS13 . . . . . **21** E5
Coldpark Rd BS13 . . . . **21** E5
Cold Rd TA3 . . . . **182** D6
Cole Cl BA22 . . . . **186** C6
Cole La 5 TA14 . . . . **185** F4
Cole Mead BA10 . . . . **215** D5
Cole Rd BA10 . . . . **215** D5
Coleridge Cottage★ TA5 . . **134** B2
Coleridge Cres TA1 . . . . . **213** B3
Coleridge Gdns TA8 . . . . . **85** B3
Coleridge Gn TA6 . . . . . . **208** E5
Coleridge Rd
Bridgwater TA6 . . . . . . **208** E6
Clevedon BS21 . . . . **6** C3
Nether Stowey TA5 . . . . **134** A2
Weston-Super-Mare BS23 . . **49** A4
Coleridge Sq TA6 . . . . . . **208** E6
Coleridge Vale Rd E 1
BS21 . . . . **6** D2
Coleridge Vale Rd N BS21 . . **6** C2
Coleridge Vale Rd S BS21 . . **6** D2
Coleridge Vale Rd W 2
BS21 . . . . **6** C2
Coles's La EX13 . . . . **198** B1
Coles Cotts TA5 . . . . **135** F2
Coles Cross Cotts DT8 . . . **199** D5
Coleshill La BS13 . . . . **22** B5
Colesmore TA4 . . . . **167** A4
Coles Pl TA20 . . . . **223** C3
Coley La TA19 . . . . **194** F5
Coley Rd BS40 . . . . **75** B4
Colham La TA20 . . . . **194** E1
Colin Ave TA2 . . . . **212** F7
Colin Rd TA2 . . . . **213** A7
Collarway La BA22 . . . . . **196** F8
College BA22 . . . . **196** E8
College Cl TA10 . . . . **172** E2
College Ct TA8 . . . . **104** A7
College Fields BS8 . . . . . . **11** F8
College Gn
Bristol BS1 . . . . **226** C2
Yeovil BA21 . . . . **219** B6
College Rd
Bath BA1 . . . . **27** E1
Bristol, Clifton BS8 . . . . . **11** F8
Taunton TA2 . . . . **212** D6
Wells BA5 . . . . **203** E5
College Sq BS1 . . . . **226** C2
College St
Bristol BS1 . . . . **226** C2
Burnham-on-S TA8 . . . . **104** A7
College View
18 Bath BA1 . . . . **28** A1
Taunton TA1 . . . . **212** C2
College Way
Bridgwater TA6 . . . . . . **209** C6
Taunton TA1 . . . . **212** C1
Colles Cl BA5 . . . . **203** F5
Colles Rd BA5 . . . . **203** F5
Collett Ave BA4 . . . . **205** C5
Collett Cl BS22 . . . . **32** C4
Collett Way BA11 . . . . . . **120** C7
Colley La TA6 . . . . **209** B4
Colley Lane Ind Est TA6 . **209** B3
Collickshire La TA3 . . . . . **170** E6
Collie Cnr BA11 . . . . **118** A1
Collier's La BA11 . . . . . . **99** D2
Collier Cl BA2 . . . . **78** D8
Colliers La BA1 . . . . **27** F4
Colliers Rise BA3 . . . . **79** A3
Colliers Wlk 4 BS48 . . . . **8** E2
Collin's Farm TA19 . . . . . **183** E4
Collingwood Cl
Saltford BS31 . . . . **25** D2
Weston-Super-Mare BS22 . . **31** E4
Collingwood Ct TA6 . . . . **208** F5
Collins' La TA13 . . . . **173** F7
Collinson Rd BS13 . . . . . . **22** B5
Collins St BS11 . . . . **4** B8
Collum La BS22 . . . . **31** E6
Colman Rd TA1 . . . . **212** B1
Colmer Rd
Bridgwater TA6 . . . . . . **208** F7
Yeovil BA21 . . . . **219** B6
Colne Gn BS31 . . . . **25** A4
Colombo Cres BS23 . . . . . **48** E3

Colston's Almshouses 1
BS1 . . . . **227** A3
Colston Ave BS1 . . . . **227** A2
Colston Cross EX13 . . . . . **198** B4
Colston Fort 2 BS2 . . . . . **227** A4
Colston Par BS1 . . . . **227** B1
Colston St BS1 . . . . **227** A3
Colston Yd BS1 . . . . **227** A3
Colton La TA4 . . . . **149** F7
Columbus Ho BA2 . . . . . . **45** D8
Colyton 11 BS22 . . . . **32** A2
Combe Ave BS20 . . . . **2** C6
Combe Batch BS28 . . . . . **108** D4
Combe Batch Rise BS28 . . **108** D4
Combe Beacon La TA20 . . **193** C7
Combe Cl
Bicknoller TA4 . . . . **132** E2
Yeovil BA21 . . . . **219** A8
Combe Cross
Halse TA4 . . . . **167** B7
Monksilver TA4 . . . . . . **150** C8
Shillingford EX16 . . . . . **164** D4
Combecross Hill TA4 . . . . **150** B8
Combecross La
Monksilver TA4 . . . . . . **150** C8
Stogumber TA4 . . . . . . **150** C8
Combe Down CE Prim Sch
BA2 . . . . **45** B1
Combe Down La TA4 . . . . **151** C2
Combe Fields BS20 . . . . . . **2** C6
Combe Gn BA5 . . . . **204** B7
Combe Gr BA1 . . . . **44** B8
Combe Hay La BA2 . . . . . . **62** B6
Combe Hill
Barton St David TA11 . . . **158** A2
Combe St Nicholas TA20 . **193** D5
Hemyock EX15 . . . . **180** C2
Milborne Port DT9 . . . . **217** B3
Templecombe BA8 . . . . . **176** E1
Yenston BA8 . . . . **189** F8
Combe Hill Dro TA20 . . . **193** C5
Combe Hill La TA7 . . . . . **156** B7
Combe La
Brompton Ralph TA4 . . . **150** B3
Charlton Adam TA11 . . . **173** F8
Chilton Polden TA7 . . . . **137** B3
Churchstanton TA3 . . . . **181** A2
Combe St Nicholas TA20 . **193** B5
Dulverton TA22 . . . . . . **163** D6
East Anstey TA22 . . . . . **162** F6
Exford TA24 . . . . **128** D1
Hallatrow BS39 . . . . **77** B6
Langport TA10 . . . . **171** F7
North Curry TA3 . . . . . **170** A4
Parbrook BA4 . . . . **158** D8
Rodhuish TA24 . . . . . . **131** B3
Wedmore BS28 . . . . . . **108** D4
Wiveliscombe TA4 . . . . . **210** C8
Woolavington TA7 . . . . . **136** F4
Combeland La TA22 . . . . . **164** A5
Combeland Rd TA24 . . . . **201** B4
Combe Pk
Bath BA1 . . . . **44** C8
Yeovil BA21 . . . . **218** F8
Combe Rd
Bath BA2 . . . . **45** B1
Portishead BS20 . . . . **2** D5
Combe Road Cl BA2 . . . . . **45** B1
Combeshead Hill TA22 . . **148** A3
Combeshead La
Brompton Regis TA22 . . **148** A4
West Anstey EX36 . . . . . **162** A7
Combeside BA2 . . . . **45** A3
Combe Side BS48 . . . . **19** A7
Combe St TA20 . . . . **223** C4
Combe Street La BA21 . . . **219** A8
Combe Street Lane Rdbt
BA21 . . . . **218** F8
Combe Sydenham Ctry Pk★
TA4 . . . . **150** A7
Combe Terr TA9 . . . . **136** E8
Combe The
Burrington BS40 . . . . . . **53** F2
Lydeard St Lawrence TA4 . **151** C2
Comer's Cross TA24 . . . . . **146** A2
Comer's Gate TA24 . . . . . **146** A6
Comer Rd BS27 . . . . **90** A7
Comeytrowe Ctr TA1 . . . **212** C1
Comeytrowe La TA1 . . . . **212** A2
Comeytrowe Orch TA1 . . . **212** A2
Comeytrowe Rd TA1 . . . . **212** B1
Comeytrowe Rise TA1 . . . **212** B2
Comfortable Pl BA1 . . . . . **228** A3
Commerce Way TA9 . . . . **104** F2
Commercial Rd
Bristol BS1 . . . . **227** A1
Shepton Mallet BA4 . . . . **205** B6
Commercial Row BA22 . . . **223** C4
Commercial Way BS22 . . . **32** B2
Common La
Charlton Adam TA11 . . . **174** A8
Churchill Green BS25 . . . **52** B5
Easton-in-G BS20 . . . . . . **4** C2
Halstock BA22 . . . . **197** C2
Hardington Mandeville
BA22 . . . . **197** A5
Holcombe BA3 . . . . **116** D7
Huish Champflower TA4 . **165** D7
Kington Magna SP8 . . . . **177** E1
Marnhull DT10 . . . . **190** E4
North Perrott TA18 . . . . **196** D4
Templecombe BA8 . . . . . **177** A1
Wincanton BA9 . . . . . . **216** D3
Yenston BA8 . . . . **189** F8
Common Moor Dro BA6 . . **206** E6
Common Rd BA9 . . . . . . **216** E3
Como Ct BS20 . . . . **2** C6
Compass Hill TA1 . . . . . . **212** E3

Compass Rise TA1 . . . . . **212** E3
Compton Acres DT9 . . . . . **187** E4
Compton Cl
Shepton Mallet BA4 . . . . **205** B5
Taunton TA2 . . . . **213** A6
Yeovil BA21 . . . . **219** E8
Compton Cnr BA4 . . . . . . **205** B5
Compton Ct Mews DT9 . . **187** F3
Compton Dr
Bristol BS9 . . . . **5** C7
Weston-Super-Mare BS24 . . **49** E7
Compton Dundon CE Prim
Sch TA11 . . . . **157** A3
Compton Flats BA21 . . . . **219** C6
Compton Gdns BA11 . . . . **120** D7
Compton Gn BS31 . . . . . . **24** E4
Compton Hill TA13 . . . . . **220** A5
Compton La
Axbridge BS26 . . . . **70** B1
Shepton Mallet BA4 . . . . **205** B2
Compton Rd
Shepton Mallet BA4 . . . . **205** B2
South Cadbury BA22 . . . **175** D4
South Petherton TA13 . . **220** B5
Yeovil BA21 . . . . **187** E3
Compton St
Butleigh BA6 . . . . **157** D4
Compton Dundon TA11 . . **157** B4
Comrade Ave BS25 . . . . . **70** E8
Concorde Dr BS21 . . . . **6** B1
Condell Cl TA6 . . . . **208** F7
Condor Cl BS22 . . . . **49** D8
Conduit Hill BA11 . . . . . . **99** B1
Congore BA22 . . . . **174** D4
Congore Cnr BA22 . . . . . **174** D4
Coneygree BS13 . . . . **21** F6
Conference Ave BS20 . . . . . **2** F5
Conference Cl BS20 . . . . . . **2** F5
Conies The TA2 . . . . **168** E8
Conifer Cl TA24 . . . . **128** D1
Conifer Way BS24 . . . . . . **49** E5
Coniston Ave BS9 . . . . **5** E6
Coniston Cres BS23 . . . . . **48** F4
Coniston Gdns BA21 . . . . **219** A7
Connaught Ho TA6 . . . . . **209** C5
Connaught Mans BA2 . . . **228** C3
Connaught Pl BS23 . . . . . . **48** D8
Connaught Rd BS4 . . . . . . **22** E8
Connection Rd BA2 . . . . . **44** A6
Connelly Dr BS28 . . . . . . **108** C4
Connock Sq BA4 . . . . . . **205** C4
Conquest Bsns Pk TA19 . . **184** A4
Constable Cl
Keynsham BS31 . . . . **24** F6
Yeovil BA21 . . . . **219** E8
Constable Dr BS22 . . . . . . **31** F3
Constantine Ct BA4 . . . . . **205** E4
Constitution Hill BS8 . . . . **226** B2
Convocation Ave BA2 . . . . **45** E5
Conway Cres TA8 . . . . . . **85** C1
Conway Gn BS31 . . . . **25** A3
Conway Rd TA5 . . . . **135** B2
Conygar Cl BS21 . . . . **6** F5
Conygar View TA24 . . . . . **201** E3
Conygre Gn BA2 . . . . **60** B2
Conygre Rise BA2 . . . . . . **59** F6
Cook's Folly Rd BS9 . . . . . **5** D3
Cook's La
Banwell BS29 . . . . **51** A4
Clevedon BS21 . . . . **7** B2
Cranmore BA4 . . . . **142** A6
Milverton TA4 . . . . **167** B5
Stalbridge DT10 . . . . . . **190** B2
Cook Ave TA20 . . . . **223** D3
Cooke's La TA10 . . . . **156** B2
Cookley La TA4 . . . . **150** F8
Cooks Bridle Path BS48 . . **36** D8
Cooks Cl TA3 . . . . **169** D5
Cooks Gdns BS48 . . . . **9** A2
Cooksley La TA4 . . . . **149** A2
Cookson Cl TA8 . . . . **104** D5
Cook St BS11 . . . . **4** C8
Cook Way TA2 . . . . **212** C6
Coombe's Cider Farm &
Mus★ TA9 . . . . **106** A4
Coombe's Way BS26 . . . . . **87** E8
Coombe DT9 . . . . **225** C5
Coombe Bridge Ave BS9 . . **5** D6
Coombe Brook BA5 . . . . . **203** A4
Coombe Cl BA7 . . . . **214** C6
Coombe Cotts BA5 . . . . . **204** C7
Coombe Dale
Backwell BS48 . . . . **37** A8
Bristol BS9 . . . . **5** C6
Coombe Dell BA4 . . . . . . **205** A6
Coombe Gdns BS9 . . . . . . **5** E6
Coombe Hill
Blagdon Hill TA21 . . . . . **181** A5
Bruton BA10 . . . . **215** E7
Coombe La
Bristol BS9 . . . . **5** E6
Compton Bishop BS26 . . . **69** B4
East Harptree BS40 . . . . . **74** E4
Easton-in-G BS8 . . . . **4** A2
Kingsbury Episcopi TA12 . **185** B8
Shepton Mallet BA4 . . . . **205** A6
Coomb End BA3 . . . . **78** F3
Coombend Ho BA3 . . . . . . **78** F3
Coombe Rd
Dinnington TA17 . . . . . **195** B7
Nailsea BS48 . . . . **8** E1
Weston-Super-Mare BS23 . . **30** C1
Coombe Side TA9 . . . . . . **86** B2
Coombe St
Bruton BA10 . . . . **215** E7
Penselwood BA9 . . . . . . **161** E2

Coombe Terr
Glastonbury BA6 . . . . . **206** E5
Sherborne DT9 . . . . **225** C5
Coombe The
Blagdon BS40 . . . . **54** C3
Compton Martin BS40 . . . **74** A6
Coombe View BA4 . . . . . **205** A6
Coombe Water La DT8 . . . **199** E5
Coomb Rocke BS9 . . . . . . **5** D6
Cooper's Ash La BA7,
BA22 . . . . **214** A2
Cooperage La BS3 . . . . . . **226** B1
Cooperage The BA11 . . . . **119** F3
Cooper Rd BS9 . . . . **5** F7
Coopers Barns BA22 . . . . **174** F1
Coopers Hts TA4 . . . . . . **210** C4
Coopers Mead BA4 . . . . . **205** D4
Coopers Mill TA2 . . . . . . **168** B4
Coot Hide EX16 . . . . **178** D1
Coots The BS14 . . . . **23** D6
Copeland Dr BS14 . . . . . . **23** B5
Copford BS41 . . . . **11** B1
Copis La TA11 . . . . **158** B3
Coplestons BS13 . . . . **168** D1
Copley Gdns BS22 . . . . . . **31** F2
Coppack Ho 6 BS1 . . . . . . **6** C2
Copper Beeches TA1 . . . . **212** A2
Copper Beech Rd TA11 . . **173** D5
Copper Cl BS27 . . . . **90** A8
Copperfield Dr BS22 . . . . . **31** F4
Coppern Way DT10 . . . . . **190** B4
Coppice Cl BA20 . . . . **218** D2
Coppice End Cnr BS24 . . . **67** C2
Coppice Mews BS21 . . . . . **6** C4
Coppice The BS13 . . . . . . **21** E4
Coppin Cl BA6 . . . . **206** F3
Coppin Rd TA2 . . . . **168** B4
Coppits Hill La
Yeovil BA21 . . . . **218** D3
Yeovil Marsh BA21 . . . . **187** A3
Copplesbury La BA4,
BA10 . . . . **160** D8
Copse Cl
Watchet TA23 . . . . **202** C5
Weston-Super-Mare BS24 . . **49** A1
Copse Cnr BS24 . . . . **67** C2
Copse Dro
Baltonsborough BA6 . . . **158** C5
Barrington TA19 . . . . . . **184** B5
Copse End BS25 . . . . **51** F2
Copse La
Ashill TA19 . . . . **183** D4
Barrington TA19 . . . . . . **184** D4
Hambridge TA3 . . . . . . **184** B7
Ilton TA19 . . . . **183** F4
Pilton BA4 . . . . **140** F3
Copseland BA2 . . . . **45** D5
Copse Rd
Clevedon BS21 . . . . **6** C4
Keynsham BS31 . . . . **25** C4
Yeovil BA22 . . . . **218** B7
Copse Shoot La TA19 . . . . **184** C5
Copse Stile TA20 . . . . . . **193** C2
Copse The
Bridgwater TA6 . . . . . . **209** C6
Cossington TA7 . . . . . . **136** F3
Frome BA11 . . . . **120** B6
Weston-Super-Mare BS22 . . **32** D2
Copsewood La BS26 . . . . . **88** B2
Copthorne Cl BS14 . . . . . . **23** B5
Coralberry Dr BS22 . . . . . **31** F1
Corams La TA21 . . . . **222** B6
Cording's Ball TA4 . . . . . **150** A1
Corewell La TA5 . . . . **133** E3
Corfe Cl BS48 . . . . **8** D1
Corfe Cres BS31 . . . . **24** E4
Corfe Rd BS4 . . . . **22** D7
Corinthian Ct 9 BS1 . . . . **227** B1
Cork Pl BA1 . . . . **44** D7
Corkscrew La
North Cadbury BA22 . . . **175** A5
Staplegrove TA2 . . . . . . **212** D8
Cork St
Bath BA1 . . . . **44** D7
Frome BA11 . . . . **119** F5
Cork Terr BA1 . . . . **44** D7
Cormorant Cl
Bridgwater TA6 . . . . . . **209** C4
Weston-Super-Mare BS22 . . **31** F1
Cornborough Pl TA6 . . . . **209** B5
Corner Cl TA21 . . . . **222** D4
Corner Croft BS21 . . . . **6** D1
Cornfields The BS22 . . . . . **31** F5
Cornhill
Bridgwater TA6 . . . . . . **208** F5
Shepton Mallet BA4 . . . . **205** C6
Sherborne DT9 . . . . **225** C4
5 Wellington TA21 . . . . **222** D6
Cornhill Dr BS14 . . . . **23** A7
Cornish Gr BS14 . . . . **23** E6
Cornish Rd BS14 . . . . **23** E6
Cornishway E TA1 . . . . . . **212** B3
Cornishway N TA1 . . . . . **212** B3
Cornishway S TA1 . . . . . **212** B2
Cornishway W TA1 . . . . . **212** B2
Cornish Wlk BS14 . . . . . . **23** E6
Cornlands EX16 . . . . **178** D1
Cornleaze BS13 . . . . **22** A5
Cornmoor Cres TA9 . . . . **136** E2
Cornmoor La TA9 . . . . . . **136** E2
Corn St
Bath BA1 . . . . **228** B2
Bristol BS1 . . . . **227** A3
Cornwallis Ave
Bristol BS8 . . . . **226** A2
Weston-Super-Mare BS22 . . **31** F4
Cornwallis Cres BS8 . . . . . **11** F6
Cornwallis Gr BS8 . . . . . . **226** A2

Cornwall Rd BA4........205 A6
Coromandel Hts BA1....228 B4
Coronation Ave
  Bath BA2.............44 C4
  Keynsham BS31......24 D4
  Yeovil BA21..........218 F7
Coronation Cl
  Ruishton TA3.........169 C3
  Wanstrow BA4........142 F4
Coronation Ct BA3.....115 A3
Coronation Est BS23....48 F3
Coronation Ho TA6....209 C6
Coronation Pl BS1.....227 A2
Coronation Rd
  Banwell BS29.........51 A3
  Bath BA1.............44 D7
  Bleadon BS24........67 C6
  Bridgwater TA6......208 E5
  Bristol BS3..........226 B1
  Frome BA11..........120 B5
  Highbridge TA9......104 D4
  Wells BA5...........203 B4
  Weston-Super-Mare BS22..31 E2
Coronation St TA20....223 C3
Coronation Terr
  Chilcompton BA3......96 D5
  Oakhill BA3..........115 A3
Coronation Villas BA8..176 E1
Corondale Rd BS22......49 D8
Corporate Rd BA22.....174 A2
Corporation St TA1....212 F3
Corpus Christi RC Prim Sch
  BS23................48 D6
Corrick Cl BS27........90 F2
Corridor The ❷ BA1...228 C2
Corsham Dr TA8........104 C8
Corsley CE Prim Sch
  BA12................121 D2
Corsley Wlk BS4........22 F8
Corston BS24...........49 A2
Corston Dr BA2.........43 B6
Corston La BA2.........43 A8
Corston View BA2.......44 C2
Corston Wlk BS11.......4 D7
Corton Cl BA21........219 E8
Coryate Cl BA22.......186 C2
Cory Rd TA2...........213 A8
Cosgates Feet or County
  Gate EX35...........122 D5
Cossington La TA7.....136 E3
Cossington Prim Sch
  TA7.................136 F3
Cossington Rd BS4......22 F8
Cossins La TA18.......224 C6
Costello Hill BA22....173 F2
Costiland Dr BS13......21 F6
Cote Cnr TA9..........136 F7
Cote House La BS9......5 F5
Cote La BA12..........161 F6
Cote Paddock BS9.......5 E6
Cote Pk BS9............5 E6
Cotford St Luke Prim Sch
  TA4.................167 E5
Cotham Hill BS6.......226 C4
Cotham Lawn Ho BS6...226 C4
Cotham Lawn Rd BS6...226 C4
Cotham Pl BS6.........226 C4
Cotham Rd BS6.........226 C4
Cotham Rd S BS6......227 A4
Cotham Sch BS6........226 C4
Cothay Manor Gdns★
  TA21...............179 C8
Cothelstone Cl TA6...208 B4
Cothelstone Rd TA4...151 F1
Cotlake Cl TA1........212 F1
Cotlake Rise TA1.....168 E1
Cotleigh Crossing EX14..191 F1
Cotley La TA20........193 D2
Cotman Wlk ❶ BS22....31 F2
Cotswold Cl BS20......2 E4
Cotswold Rd BA2.......44 E4
Cotswold View BA2.....44 B5
Cotswold Way SN14....13 A6
Cottage Cnr TA19.....183 F4
Cottage La TA22.......163 D6
Cottage Pl
  ❸ Bath BA1..........28 C2
  Bristol BS2.........227 A4
Cottage Row TA8......104 A6
Cottages The BS40.....35 D2
Cotterell Ct BA1......228 B2
Cottle Gdns BS14......23 F6
Cottle Rd BS14........23 F6
Cottles La
  West Pennard BA6....140 B1
  Winsley BA15........64 F6
Cotton's La TA11......158 B2
Cotton Cnr ❽ BA8.....190 A6
Cotton Mead BA2......43 B7
Coulson's Cl BS14.....23 A3
Coulson's Rd BS14....23 A3
Coulson Dr BS22.......32 B3
Council Hos
  Babcary TA11........174 D7
  Bleadon BS24........67 B5
  Clapton TA18........195 C1
  Hewish TA18.........195 D3
  Kingston Seymour BS21..16 C3
  Podimore BA22.......174 A4
  Wick St Lawrence BS22..32 B8
Council Houses BS24...33 C3
Council Houses The
  Butcombe BS40........55 B8
  Hinton Blewett BS39..75 E6
Counterslip BS1......227 B2
Countersslip Gdns BS14..23 C6
Countess Ave TA6....208 E7

Countess Gytha Prim Sch
  BA22...............174 F3
County Wlk TA1.......213 A3
Couple Cross TA24....130 B1
Coursing Batch BA6...206 F3
Court's Barton BA11...119 D2
Court Acres ❻ BA22...197 F8
Court Ash BA20.......219 B5
Court Ave BS49........34 C7
Court Barton
  Crewkerne TA18......224 B6
  Ilminster TA19......221 C4
Court Cl
  Backwell BS48........19 C5
  Portishead BS20......2 D4
Court Cotts SP8......177 D3
Court-de-Wyck CE Prim Sch
  BS49...............17 F1
Court Dr
  Sandford BS25........52 B4
  Wellington TA21.....222 D5
Courtenay Cres BS4....22 D7
Courtenay Rd BS31.....25 B2
Courtenay Wlk BS22....32 A3
Court Farm BA11......100 A3
Court Farm Cl TA20...194 E1
Court Farm Pk★ BS29...50 F5
Court Farm Rd BS14....22 F3
Courtfield
  Langport TA10.......172 A5
  Milverton TA4.......166 F4
Court Field La TA20...193 B5
Court Fields Com Sch
  TA21...............222 C5
Court Gdns
  Batheaston BA1.......29 A4
  Marston Magna BA22..174 F1
  Yeovil BA21.........218 E8
Court Gr TA7.........136 C4
Court Hay BS20.........4 A4
Court Hill
  Compton Dando BS39...41 D5
  Taunton TA1.........212 D2
Court Ho BS26.........70 B2
Court La
  ❼ Barwick BA22.....197 F8
  Bathford BA1........29 B2
  Clevedon BS21........7 A3
  Lye's Green BA12....121 B1
  Milborne Port DT9...217 C3
  Morebath EX16.......164 D4
  Shipham BS25.........70 F8
Courtland Rd TA21....222 D6
Courtlands
  Keynsham BS31........24 E5
  Norton Fitzwarren TA2..168 B5
Courtlands Cl TA23...202 C6
Courtlands La BS3.....11 E4
Courtlands Unit BS4...22 D8
Courtmead BA2........62 F7
Courtmead La TA24...123 F4
Court Mill La TA20...223 A8
Court Moors La TA21..179 E5
Court Orch TA5.......135 B2
Court Pl BS22.........31 F2
Court Place La TA24...131 B4
Court Rd
  Norton Fitzwarren TA2..168 B4
  Weston-Super-Mare BS22..31 A5
Court St
  ❺ Bridgwater TA6....208 F5
  Winsham TA20.......194 E1
Court Terr TA21.......222 C5
Court The TA24.......131 A5
Court Way TA4.........131 B4
Courtway Ave TA6.....209 C4
Courtyard The
  Dunster TA24........201 E2
  Evercreech BA4......141 F2
  Minehead TA24.......200 F7
  Shapwick TA7........137 F1
  ❸ Taunton TA1......212 F4
  West Harptree BS40...74 E6
Coverdale Ct BA21....218 F6
Coveyhill La BA4......142 E5
Cowan Cl TA4.........124 C7
Cowbridge Cross TA24..200 D1
Cow Bridge Rd BA6....157 C7
Cow Down Rd TA20....194 C1
Cowdray Cl TA24.....200 E6
Cowdray Rd
  Bristol BS4..........22 D7
  Minehead TA24.......200 E6
Cowen Cl TA18........224 C4
Cowleaze Dro TA3.....169 D3
Cowleaze La BS40......74 C6
Cowler Wlk BS13.......21 F4
Cowling Dr BS14.......23 C5
Cowling Rd BS14.......23 D5
Cowl St BA4..........205 B7
Cowpath La DT9.......176 A1
Cowslip La BS26.......68 D3
Cox's Cl
  Bruton BA10.........215 E5
  Glastonbury BA6.....206 E6
Cox's Dr BA6.........158 A5
Cox's Gn BS40.........35 E1
Cox's La TA4.........167 C5
Coxbridge Dro BA6....158 A6
Cox Hill DT10.........190 C4
Coxland's Rock TA4...167 B7
Coxley Dr BA2.........28 B2
Coxley Prim Sch BA5...139 E6
Coxley Vineyard★ BA5..139 E6
Cox Rd TA1...........222 C4
Coxs Cl BA22.........175 D6
Coxton End La BA5.....92 B3
Coxway BS21...........6 F2

Coxwithy La BA6......139 D1
Coxwynne Cl BA3.......97 C8
Crabtree Cl BS41.......21 D1
Crab Tree Dro BA6....206 F8
Crabtree La
  Curry Rivel TA10....171 C1
  Dundry BS41.........21 D2
  Wyke Champflower BA10..215 B7
Crackmore DT9.......217 C1
Craig Lea TA2........212 E7
Cranberry Wlk BS9......5 C8
Cranbourne Chase BS23..31 A1
Cranbourne Cl TA6....208 F6
Crancombe La TA7....136 D3
Crandale Rd ❸ BA2....44 D5
Crane Cnts BA4.......142 B6
Crane Hill TA10, TA11..173 C4
Cranes Cl TA13.......213 D7
Cranford Cl BS22......31 D1
Crangs La BA22.......175 D4
Cranhill Rd
  Bath BA1............44 D8
  Street BA16.........207 B6
Cranleigh BA2.........62 F8
Cranleigh Ct TA13....220 B8
Cranleigh Gdns
  Bridgwater TA6......209 A4
  Bristol BS9...........5 E4
Cranleigh Rd BS14.....23 B5
Cranmer Rd TA1......213 A4
Cranmore BS24........49 A2
Cranmore Ave BS31....24 E6
Cranmore Ct ❸ BA11..119 E3
Cranmore Pl BA2......62 E8
Cranmore Sta★ BA4...142 A5
Cranmore View BA11...119 D2
Cranmore West Sta★
  BA4................142 A5
Cransey La
  Washford TA4, TA23..131 F2
  Williton TA4........132 A2
Crantock Ave BS13.....22 B8
Cranway La TA20......223 F2
Cranwell CE Fst Sch
  TA4................154 F5
Cranwell Gr BS14......23 A5
Cranwell Rd BS24......50 C5
Cranwells Pk BA1......44 D8
Crapnell La BA5......140 F8
Crawford Cl ❶ BS21....6 B1
Crawford La BA22.....175 D7
Crawlic La TA4.......151 E1
Crawl La BA3..........78 C4
Crawter Dr TA24.....124 A3
Craydon Gr BS14......23 D4
Craydon Rd BS14......23 D5
Craydon Wlk BS14.....23 D5
Crease Cl BA5........203 B4
Create Ctr★ BS1......11 F5
Crediton ❺ BS22.......32 A2
Creechbarrow Rd TA1..213 C5
Creechberry Orch TA1..213 D5
Creeches La BA16.....156 D7
Creech Hill La BA10...215 B7
Creech Mill Est TA3..169 C4
Creech Paper Mill TA3..169 C4
Creech St Michael CE Prim
  Sch TA3............169 D4
Creechwood Terr TA3..169 C4
Creedwell Cl TA4.....167 A4
Creedwell Orch TA4...167 A4
Creighton Cl BA5.....140 C8
Crescent Gdns BA1....228 A3
Crescent La BA1......228 B4
Crescent The
  Backwell BS48........19 A6
  Bristol, Sea Mills BS9..5 C6
  ❹ Carhampton TA24...131 A5
  Coleford BA3........117 A7
  Farrington Gurney BS39..77 B3
  Golsoncott TA23.....131 D1
  Ilminster TA19......221 B2
  Lympsham BS24.......67 C5
  South Cadbury BA22..175 E4
  Stanton Drew BS39....39 F1
  Taunton TA1.........212 F3
  Weston-Super-Mare BS22..31 B1
  Yeovil BA20.........219 A4
Crescent View BA2....228 B1
Crescent View Ct BS22..31 B1
Crescent Way TA1....212 F3
Creslands Ind Units BS24..49 A3
Cressey The TA19.....184 E4
Cresswell Ave TA2....212 D7
Cresswell Cl BS22.....32 A2
Crestfield Ave TA6...208 F7
Creswicke Rd BS4......22 E7
Creswick Way TA8....104 C8
Crewkerne Bsns Pk
  TA18...............224 D6
Crewkerne CE Fst Sch..9 B1
Crewkerne Hospl TA18..224 B5
Crewkerne Rd TA20...223 E4
Crewkerne Sta TA18...224 E4
Crewkerne Turning
  EX13...............198 C6
Cribb's La BS40.......36 D1
Crib Cl TA20.........223 D6
Crib House La BS28....89 C1
Crickback La BS40.....39 A3
Cricket Cotts TA3....170 B3
Cricket Cross TA19...194 C6
Cricket Field Gn BS48...8 D2
Cricket La TA19, TA20..194 C6
Cricket St Thomas Miniature
  Rly★ TA20..........194 E3
Cricket St Thomas Wildlife
  Pk★ TA20..........194 E3
Cricket View DT9.....225 D3

Crickham La BS28.....108 D8
Cricklade St BS48......9 A1
Cridlake ❼ EX13.....198 A1
Cridlands Mdw TA6...208 E6
Crimchard TA20.......223 B5
Cripple St TA12.......185 D7
Crispin Ctr BA16.....207 C6
Crispin Sch BA16.....207 D7
Critch Hill BA11.....119 C3
Critchill Cl BA11....119 D3
Critchill Gr BA11....119 D3
Critchill Rd BA11....119 D3
Critchill Sch BA11...119 C4
Crocker's Hill BA9...175 F8
Crockerne CE Prim Sch
  BS20...............4 C4
Crockerne Dr BS20......4 C3
Crockerne Ho BS20......4 D4
Crockers Hill TA7....136 E4
Crocombe BA2.........60 C3
Crocombe La BA2......60 C3
Croford Hill TA4.....166 E6
Croft Cl BS30.........25 D8
Croft Cotts
  Moorlinch TA7......155 E7
  Wrantage TA3.......170 B1
Croft La
  Brushford TA22......163 C4
  Skilgate TA4........164 E6
  Westbury-sub-Mendip BA5..110 C6
Croftland La TA10....171 E2
Croft Mdw TA4.......202 F1
Crofton Ave BA21....219 B6
Crofton Ct BA21.....219 B5
Crofton Pk BA21.....219 B5
Crofton Rd BA21.....219 B6
Croft Rd
  Bath BA1............28 B1
  Holcombe BA3.......116 C8
Crofts Mead BA9.....216 C2
Croft The
  Backwell BS48........19 A7
  Cheddar BS27........90 C8
  Clevedon BS21.........6 C4
  Hutton BS24..........49 E3
  Mark TA9...........106 A4
  Monkton Combe BA2...45 E1
  Watchet TA23........202 C7
  Westwood BA15.......64 F3
  Williton TA4........202 D3
  Wookey Hole BA5....203 A8
  Yeovil BA21.........218 C2
Croft Way TA4.......210 C4
Croftways TA4........202 D4
Cromer Cl BA21......219 D6
Cromer Rd BS23........48 E5
Cromwell Dr BS22.....32 A4
Cromwell Rd
  Bridgwater TA6......209 A2
  Taunton TA1.........213 B6
  Yeovil BA21.........219 D6
Crooked La
  Brent Knoll TA9......85 E3
  Burnham-on-S TA8....85 D1
  Cucklington SP8....177 E6
  Rode BA11..........101 E7
Crookes La BS22.......31 A4
Crookhorn Hill TA24..129 C7
Cropmead Trad Est
  TA18...............224 D6
Crosby Row BS8.......226 A2
Croscombe CE Prim Sch
  BA5................204 C7
Croscombe Gdns BA11..120 D6
Crossacre TA6........208 D6
Crosscombe Dr BS13....22 C3
Crosscroft Cotts TA4..151 A3
Cross Elms Hill TA5...133 F7
Cross Elms La BS9......5 E5
Cross Farm Cl TA24...201 A5
Cross Farm Rd BS27....90 F3
Crossfield Cl TA6....208 D6
Crossfields DT9......187 F4
Crossing Dro TA20....109 D3
Cross Keys Cl TA2....212 A7
Cross La
  Axbridge BS26........70 A2
  Brendon EX35.......122 A4
  Long Sutton TA10....172 F4
Crossland La EX14....191 F2
Crosslands TA21......222 B8
Cross Lanes BS20......4 C4
Crossman Wlk BS21.....6 F2
Crossmead TA4.......136 E4
Cross Moor Dr BS26....70 B1
Cross Moor Dro BS26...69 E1
Cross Moor Rd BS26....70 B1
Crosspost La BA2......42 B4
Cross Rd DT9.........187 E1
Crossroads The BA9...216 C3
Cross St
  Burnham-on-S TA8...104 A7
  Keynsham BS31........24 F7
  ❸ Weston-Super-Mare
  BS23................48 E7
Cross The
  Baltonsborough BA6..158 A5
  Bradford Abbas DT9..187 E1
  Buckland Dinham BA11..100 A3
  East Harptree BS40...74 F4
  ❾ Henstridge BA8...190 A6
  Ilminster TA19......221 C3
  Milverton TA4.......167 A4
  Minehead TA24.......200 F8
  Nether Stowey TA5...134 B2

Cross The continued
  Street BA16.........207 D7
Cross View Rise TA6..208 D6
Crossway TA1.........213 C5
Cross Way DT9.......187 E1
Crossway La BA3.......96 B7
Crossways
  Coleford BA3........116 F7
  Tatworth TA20......198 D7
Crossways Cvn Pk BA2...61 F5
Crossways Rd TA6....209 B1
Crosswell Cl ❼ TA6...153 E3
Cross Wlk BS14.......23 A6
Crouds La TA10.......172 E4
Crow's Hill BA4......142 C1
Crow Castle La TA18..224 B7
Crowcombe CE Fst Sch
  TA4................151 C7
Crowcombe Heathfield Sta★
  TA4................151 B5
Crowcombe Rd TA2....212 F8
Crowcombe Wlk TA6...208 C4
Crowe Hill BA3........64 B5
Crowe La BA3.........64 B5
Crow La
  Ashill TA19.........183 C4
  Bridgwater TA7......209 E7
  Bristol BS1.........227 A2
  Broadway TA19......194 A8
  Slape Cross TA7....209 E6
  Westbury-sub-Mendip BA5..110 E6
Crown Cl TA2.........213 C6
Crowne Trad Est BA4..205 D5
Crown Gdns BA11.....119 F3
Crown Glass Pl ❺ BS48..8 E2
Crown Hill
  Bath BA1............27 C1
  West Buckland TA21..180 F7
  Winford BS40........38 A5
Crown Ho BS48.........8 C1
Crown Ind Est TA2....213 C6
Crown La
  Creech St Michael TA3..169 D6
  South Petherton TA13..220 C4
Crown Mews TA21.....180 F7
Crown Rd BA1.........27 B1
Crown Wlk TA1.......212 F3
Crowpill Cotts TA6...208 F6
Crowpill La TA6......208 F6
Crowshute Flats TA20..223 C3
Crowshute Link TA20..223 C3
Crufts Mdw TA3......169 C4
Crusader Cl TA6.....208 E6
Crusty La BS20........4 C5
Cruwy's Cross TA4...210 B7
Crypton Tech Bsns Pk
  TA6................209 B8
Cuck Hill BS25........70 E7
Cuckold's Row TA5....152 E8
Cuckoo Cnr TA1......213 B2
Cuckoo Hill
  Bruton BA10........160 D6
  Frome BA11.........119 E8
Cuckoo La
  Frome BA11.........119 F8
  High Littleton BS39...59 B3
  Thorncombe TA20....199 C7
  Wraxall BS48.........9 A6
Cuffs Mead TA20.....223 F1
Cufic La BS27.........90 C8
Culliford Cl BA16...207 D7
Culliver's Grave BA22..197 C8
Culmhead Cl TA1.....212 D1
Culmstock Prim Sch
  EX15...............179 E1
Culvercliffe Ct TA1...125 C4
Culvercliffe Rd TA23..202 D7
Culverhay BS39........41 D6
Culverhay Cl TA7....136 C4
Culverhayes TA20....223 C2
Culverhay La TA4....210 B4
Culverhay Sch BA2....44 B2
Culverhays La TA4...132 F1
Culverhill BA11......119 F3
Culver Hill TA10.....172 B7
Culver La
  Carhampton TA24....131 B4
  East Harptree BS40...74 F3
Culverlake La EX13...199 A3
Culvers Cl
  Keynsham BS31.......24 E6
  Sherborne DT9......225 C4
Culvers Rd BS31......24 E6
Culver St BS1........226 C2
Culver Street La TA5..134 A7
Culvert Dro BS27....109 B6
Culverwell Cotts BA4..140 F3
Culverwell Rd BS13....22 A4
Cumberland Basin Rd
  BS8.................11 F5
Cumberland Cl BS1...226 A1
Cumberland Ho BA1...228 A2
Cumberland Pl ❻ BS8..11 F6
Cumberland Rd BS1...226 B1
Cumberland Row BA1..228 B2
Cumberland St BS2...227 B4
Cumhill Hill BA4.....140 E3
Cumnock Cres BA7....214 C6
Cumnock Rd BA7.....214 C6
Cumnock Terr BA7....214 C6
Cunningham Ave EX13..191 B2
Cunningham Rd TA8...104 C7
Curdleigh La TA3.....181 D5
Curland Gr BS14......23 B5
Curlew Cl TA24......201 C4

Curlew Gdns BS22 . . . . **31** F1
Currells La BS40 . . . . **20** B1
Curriott Hill TA18 . . . . . . **224** B4
Curriott Hill Rd TA18 . . **224** B5
Curry Hole La BA22 . . . **197** C2
Curry La TA3 . . . . **169** E6
Curry Mallet CE Prim Sch
TA3 . . . . **183** D8
Currymead La TA10 . . . . **171** C2
Currypool La TA5 . . . . . . **134** E1
Curry Rivel CE Prim Sch
TA10 . . . . **171** D4
Currywoods Way TA10 . . **171** D4
Curtis Units BA11 . . . . . . **119** E2
Curvalion House Gdns
TA3 . . . . **169** D4
Curvalion Rd TA3 . . . . . . **169** D4
Cushuish La TA2, TA5 . . . **152** C2
Cushuish Lane Cotts
TA2 . . . . **152** B1
Custom Cl BS14 . . . . **23** A7
Custom Ho
Bristol BS1 . . . . **227** A1
Minehead TA24 . . . . . . **201** B7
Cutcombe CE Fst Sch
TA24 . . . . **129** E1
Cutcombe Cross TA24 . . **129** E1
Cutcombe Hill TA24 . . . . **129** F2
Cuthays La EX13 . . . . **198** B1
Cuthbert St TA9 . . . . **104** D3
Cutler Rd BS13 . . . . **21** F6
Cutliff Cl TA1 . . . . **212** E1
Cuts Rd TA3, TA7 . . . . . . **170** E8
Cutter's Wharf TA24 . . . **201** B7
Cutt Mill La DT10 . . . . . . **190** F3
Cut Tongue La TA20 . . . . **193** C7
Cutty Cotts BA22 . . . . . . **175** D6
Cutty La BA22 . . . . **175** D6
Cygnet Cres BS22 . . . . . . **31** F1
Cynthia Rd BA2 . . . . **44** D5
Cypress Ct
Bristol BS9 . . . . **5** D3
Somerton TA11 . . . . . . **211** E4
Cypress Dr
Puriton TA7 . . . . **136** C4
Yeovil BA20 . . . . **218** B2
Cypress Gdns BS8 . . . . . . **11** E6
Cypress Terr BA3 . . . . **78** C1
Cypress Way BA11 . . . . . . **120** C7
Cyril St W TA2 . . . . **212** E6
Cyril St TA2 . . . . **212** E6

D

Dabinett Cl TA2 . . . . **168** B5
Dafford's Bldgs BA1 . . . . . **28** C2
Dafford St BA1 . . . . **28** C2
Dagg's La BS28 . . . . **138** E8
Dagg's Lane Dro BA5,
BS28 . . . . **138** D7
Daghole BS27 . . . . **90** C8
Daglands The BA2 . . . . . . **78** E8
Dahlia Gdns BA2 . . . . **45** B7
Dairs Orch TA20 . . . . **198** C8
Dairy Cl BA5 . . . . **203** B5
Dairycroft BS2 . . . . **227** B4
Dairy Ct **3** TA18 . . . . . **224** C5
Dairy Flats DT9 . . . . **225** E5
Dairy Hill BA2 . . . . **80** B5
Dairy House La TA3 . . . . **182** E5
Dairylands TA24 . . . . **131** D4
Daisey Bank BA2 . . . . **45** B4
Daisyfield BA22 . . . . **188** A8
Dakota Dr BS14 . . . . **23** A4
Dale La BA5 . . . . **92** C3
Dale St BS2 . . . . **227** C4
Daley Cl BS22 . . . . **32** B3
Dalimores La BA11 . . . . . **143** B8
Dalleston BA3 . . . . **114** C8
Dallimore Mead BA11 . . **143** B8
Dalton Sq BS2 . . . . **227** B4
Dalwood **12** BS22 . . . . . . **32** A2
Dalwoods DT9 . . . . **225** D3
Dame Court Cl BS22 . . . . **31** F4
Dame Withycombe Villas
TA5 . . . . **135** B5
Dampier Pl BA21 . . . . . . **219** C5
Dampier St BA21 . . . . . . **219** C5
Dampiet St TA6 . . . . **208** E4
Damson Rd BS22 . . . . **49** E7
Dancey Mead BS13 . . . . . **21** F6
Dancing Cross BA9 . . . . . **176** B5
Dancing Hill TA6 . . . . **153** E4
Dancing La BA9 . . . . **216** A4
DandO's La BS28 . . . . . . **108** C4
Dandy's Mdw BS20 . . . . . . **2** E4
Dane's Lea BS28 . . . . **108** C4
Dane Rise BA15 . . . . **64** E7
Daneacre Rd BA3 . . . . **79** A3
Dane Cl BA15 . . . . **64** E7
Dane Rise BA15 . . . . **64** E7
Danesboro Rd TA6 . . . . . **208** C4
Danesborough View
TA4 . . . . **202** D3
Danesborough View E
TA4 . . . . **202** D3
Danesborough View W
TA4 . . . . **202** D3
Danes Cl EX14 . . . . **191** D7
Danesfield CE Com Mid Sch
TA4 . . . . **202** D4
Dangerfield Ave BS13 . . . **21** F6
Daniel Cl BS21 . . . . **6** F3
Daniel Mews BA2 . . . . **45** B7

Danielsfield Rd BA2 . . . **218** F2
Daniels La BA5 . . . . **111** A4
Daniel St BA2 . . . . **45** B7
Dapps Hill BS31 . . . . **24** F5
Dapwell La BS14, BS31 . . . **24** A1
Darby's Knap TA24 . . . . . **147** C5
Darby Cl SP8 . . . . **161** F1
Darby Way TA4 . . . . **151** F1
Darcis Row TA20 . . . . **223** B4
Dare Cl TA2 . . . . **213** A8
Darkey La BA10 . . . . **215** F7
Darkfield Way TA7 . . . . . **136** E3
Dark La
Backwell BS48 . . . . **19** B5
Banwell BS29 . . . . **51** C2
Berkley BA11 . . . . **120** E8
Blagdon BS40 . . . . **54** E3
Chew Magna BS40 . . . . . **38** F3
Freshford BA3 . . . . **64** B5
Hockworthy EX16 . . . . **178** B8
Holcombe BA3 . . . . **97** C1
Kilmersdon BA11 . . . . . . **98** A1
North Wootton BA4 . . . **140** C5
Sandford Orcas DT9 . . **188** C7
Seavington St Mary TA19 . **184** E1
Stoke St Gregory TA3 . . **170** F6
Stoke St Michael BA3 . . **116** C2
Upton Noble BA4 . . . . . **142** F2
Wellington TA21 . . . . . **222** D5
Witham Friary BA11 . . **143** D2
Darlick Cnr EX36 . . . . . . **145** G4
Darlington Mews BA2 . . . **45** B7
Darlington Pl BA2 . . . . . . **45** B6
Darlington Rd BA2 . . . . . . **45** B8
Darlington St BA2 . . . . . . **45** B7
Darmead BS24 . . . . **32** B1
Dartmouth Ave BA2 . . . . . **44** C5
Dartmouth Cl BS22 . . . . . **32** A2
Dartmouth Wlk BS31 . . . . **24** D4
Dart Rd BS21 . . . . **6** D1
Darwin Cl TA2 . . . . **212** B6
Dashwoods La TA4 . . . . . **132** E2
Daubeny Ct BS1 . . . . **227** A1
Daunton Cl TA9 . . . . **104** D4
David's La TA19 . . . . **184** F2
David's Rd BS14 . . . . **23** C6
Davies Cl
Bridgwater TA6 . . . . . . **208** F2
Winsham TA20 . . . . **194** E1
Davies Ct BA5 . . . . **203** B4
Davin Cres BS20 . . . . **4** C3
Davis La BS21 . . . . **16** F8
Davis St BS11 . . . . **4** B8
Davis Terr **5** BA5 . . . . . . **203** C4
Daw's La TA7 . . . . **176** A3
Dawbins Dr TA7 . . . . **136** E4
Dawes Cl BS21 . . . . **6** D1
Dawes Ct **2** BS8 . . . . . . **11** F6
Daws Cl TA6 . . . . **208** E2
Daws La TA6 . . . . **153** E3
Daws Mead TA1 . . . . **212** A3
Day Cres BA2 . . . . **43** F6
Deacon Rd TA6 . . . . **209** C6
Deacons Cl BS22 . . . . **31** E2
Deacons Cl BS22 . . . . **31** C1
Deacons La BA21 . . . . . . **187** D6
Deacon Way TA8 . . . . . . **104** B6
Deadlands La TA12, TA13 . **185** A6
Dead Maids Cross Rd
BA13 . . . . **121** E5
Deadman's Hill DT9 . . . . **176** A1
Deadmill La BA1 . . . . **28** C3
Dead Woman's Cnr BA12 **161** F8
Deal Cl TA6 . . . . **209** D5
Dean's Cross
Allerford TA24 . . . . **124** E3
Lydeard St Lawrence TA4 . **151** A4
Dean's La
Allerford TA24 . . . . **124** E3
Brompton Ralph TA4 . . **150** F4
Dean Cl
Frome BA11 . . . . **120** C6
Weston-Super-Mare BS22 . **32** B3
Deane Cl TA4 . . . . **150** D8
Deane Dr TA1 . . . . **212** B2
Deane Gate Ave TA1 . . . **213** E5
Deanery Rd BS1 . . . . **226** C2
Deanery Wlk BA3 . . . . . . **64** C6
Deanesly Way BA9 . . . . . **216** D3
Deane Way TA20 . . . . . . **198** D8
Deanhill La BA1 . . . . **27** A2
Dean La
Dunster TA24 . . . . **201** D3
Milverton TA4 . . . . **167** A6
Oakhill BA3 . . . . **115** A3
Deansley Way BA9 . . . . . **216** E3
Deans Mead BS11 . . . . **5** A8
Deans Pl **8** BA5 . . . . . . **203** D4
Deans St BS2 . . . . **227** B4
Deans The BS20 . . . . **2** B4
Dean Vale Pk TA4 . . . . . . **167** C4
Debecca's La BS20 . . . . **4** B4
De Combe Ho TA18 . . . . **224** D6
De Corcis Cl TA5 . . . . **134** A3
Decoy La TA11 . . . . **157** A2
Deep La BA12 . . . . **121** E1
Deepleigh La TA4 . . . . . . **210** C7
Deerleap
Easton BA5 . . . . **111** B6
Shipham BS25 . . . . **70** F8
Deer Mead BA5 . . . . **86** B1
Deerswood Gdns BA16 . . **207** A6
Deer View TA4 . . . . **201** C4
Delapre Rd BS23 . . . . **48** D3
Delhorn La BS24 . . . . **86** C7
Delius Gr BS4 . . . . **22** D7
Deller's Wharf TA1 . . . . . **212** F5

Dellers Ct TA1 . . . . **212** F5
Dellshore Cl TA20 . . . . . **223** D4
Dell The
Bristol, Westbury on T BS9 . . **5** F5
Minehead TA24 . . . . . . **200** E6
Nailsea BS48 . . . . **8** D2
Weston-Super-Mare BS22 . **31** E4
Delmore Rd BA11 . . . . . **119** E3
Delta Cl BA11 . . . . **119** F5
Delta Ct **1** BA11 . . . . . **119** F5
Delta Rise TA4 . . . . **151** E1
Demelza Ct BA22 . . . . . . **174** D3
De Montalt Pl BA2 . . . . . . **45** B1
Dempier Mews BA22 . . . **218** B6
Dene BS31 . . . . **24** F3
Dene Cross TA4 . . . . **167** F7
Dene Gdns TA24 . . . . **201** B4
Dene Rd
Cotford St Luke TA4 . . **167** F6
Whitchurch BS14 . . . . . . **23** C4
Dening Cl TA20 . . . . **223** C6
Denleigh Cl BS14 . . . . **23** A4
Denman's La
Barrington TA19 . . . . . **184** D5
Cannington TA5 . . . . . . **135** B2
Denmark Ave BS1 . . . . . **226** C2
Denmark Rd BA2 . . . . **44** D6
Denmark St BS1 . . . . **226** C2
Denmark Terr TA2 . . . . . **212** F7
Dennett Cl BA4 . . . . **205** E4
Denning Cl TA1 . . . . **212** B1
Denning Ct BS22 . . . . **32** B4
Dennington La
Churchinford EX14 . . . . **192** C6
Dulverton TA22 . . . . . . **163** B4
Dennor Pk BS14 . . . . **23** B7
Denny Cl BS20 . . . . **2** A5
Denny La BS40 . . . . **39** B1
Denny View BS20 . . . . **2** A5
Dennyview Rd BS8 . . . . . . **10** F8
Denston Dr BS20 . . . . **2** E4
Denston Wlk BS13 . . . . . . **22** A7
Dentwood Gr BS9 . . . . **5** B8
Denzil Cl BA22 . . . . **197** A8
Derham Cl BS49 . . . . **34** B8
Derham Ct BS49 . . . . **34** B8
Derham Pk BS49 . . . . **34** B8
Derham Rd BS13 . . . . **22** A5
Derricke Rd BS14 . . . . **23** F6
Dertfords BA12 . . . . **144** D8
Derwent Gdns BA21 . . . **219** D6
Derwent Gr
Keynsham BS31 . . . . **25** A5
Taunton TA1 . . . . **213** E4
Derwent Rd BS23 . . . . **49** A5
Derwent Way BA21 . . . . **218** C6
Devenish La BA9 . . . . . . **216** F4
Deveron Gr BS31 . . . . **25** A4
Devonia Pk TA4 . . . . **168** A1
Devonshire Bldgs BA2 . . . **44** F4
Devonshire Ct BS23 . . . . . **48** E4
Devonshire Dr BS20 . . . . . . **1** F4
Devonshire Mews BA2 . . . **44** F3
Devonshire Pl BA2 . . . . . . **44** F4
Devonshire Rd
Bathampton BA2 . . . . . . **28** E1
Weston-Super-Mare BS23 . **48** E4
Devonshire St TA6 . . . . . **209** B5
Devonshire Villas BA2 . . . **44** F4
Dewar Cl TA2 . . . . **124** A3
Dew Water La TA11 . . . . **211** D5
Dial's Gate La BA6, TA11 . **158** D4
Dial Hill Rd BS21 . . . . **6** D4
Dial La BS40 . . . . **20** D1
Diamond Batch BS24 . . . . **32** B1
Dibbens Row BA9 . . . . . . **161** A2
Dibbles La BA22 . . . . **197** A8
Dickenson's Gr BS49 . . . . **34** E3
Dickenson Rd BS23 . . . . . **48** E6
Digby Ct DT9 . . . . **225** D3
Digby Rd DT9 . . . . **225** D3
Dighton Ct **3** BS2 . . . . . **227** A4
Dighton St BS2 . . . . **227** A4
Digland La TA24 . . . . **129** F5
Dilkes La TA11 . . . . **174** C7
Dillington Farm Cotts
TA19 . . . . **221** E5
Dillington Ho TA19 . . . . . **221** D6
Dillons Rd TA24 . . . . **169** D4
Dimmer La BA7 . . . . **159** B2
Dinder BS48 . . . . **18** E8
Dinghurst Rd BS25 . . . . . . **52** E4
Dingle Cl BS9 . . . . **5** C6
Dingle Ct BS13 . . . . **21** F7
Dingle Rd BS9 . . . . **5** D7
Dingle The BS9 . . . . **5** D7
Dingle View BS9 . . . . **5** C7
Dinglewood Cl BS9 . . . . . . **5** D7
Dinhams BS49 . . . . **169** C4
Dinhay DT10 . . . . **190** F6
Dipford Rd TA3 . . . . **168** D1
Dipland Gr BS40 . . . . **54** F2
Disraeli Pl TA1 . . . . **212** D5
Ditch Furlong Rd TA7 . . **137** A2
Ditton St TA19 . . . . **221** C3
Dixon Gdns BA1 . . . . **27** F1
Dobree Pk TA21 . . . . **222** A4
Dock Gate La BS8 . . . . . . **226** A1
Doctor's Hill BA5 . . . . . . **111** B1
Dodd's Cnr BA9 . . . . **215** E1
Dodd Ave BA5 . . . . **203** F5
Dodge Cross DT9 . . . . . . **225** F5
Dodham Cres BA20 . . . . **218** F4
Dod La BA6 . . . . **206** D4
Dog Down Cross EX16 . . **178** A8
Doleberrow BS25 . . . . **52** F3

Dolebury Warren Nature
Reserve★ BS40 . . . . . . **53** A3
Dolemead La BA5 . . . . . . **90** E2
Dolemoor La
Congresbury BS49 . . . . . **34** A4
Congresbury BS49 . . . . . **34** C3
Dolling's Rd BA3 . . . . . . **181** B4
Dolling Cl TA20 . . . . **223** D6
Dolphin Sq BS23 . . . . **48** D7
Dominion Rd BA2 . . . . . . **44** A6
Dominy Cl TA20 . . . . **223** D3
Dommett's La BA11 . . . . **119** D4
Dommett Cl EX13 . . . . . **198** A2
Domus Dr BA4 . . . . **205** E4
Donald Rd BS13 . . . . **21** F7
Doniford Beach Halt
TA23 . . . . **202** E6
Doniford Dr TA4 . . . . . . **202** D3
Doniford Mdw TA23 . . . **202** F6
Doniford Orch TA23 . . . **202** F6
Doniford Rd
Watchet TA23 . . . . **202** E6
Williton TA4 . . . . **202** D4
Donne La BA22 . . . . **186** C2
Donnes Terr BA7 . . . . . . **214** B5
Donnington Wlk BS31 . . . **24** D4
Donstan Rd TA9 . . . . **104** E5
Donyatt Hill TA19 . . . . . **183** D1
Donyatt Hill Est TA19 . . **183** D1
Doone Way TA24 . . . . . . **201** B4
Dorchester Cl **6** BS48 . . . **8** D1
Dorchester Rd
Barwick BA22 . . . . **197** F7
East Coker BA22 . . . . . **197** F5
Taunton TA1 . . . . **213** A8
Yeovil BA22 . . . . **219** A1
Dorchester St BA1 . . . . . **228** C1
Dore Cl BA21 . . . . **218** C2
Dormeads View **6** BS24 . . **49** F7
Dorset Cl
Bath BA2 . . . . **44** D6
Frome BA11 . . . . **119** E5
Highbridge TA9 . . . . . . **104** E2
Dorset Ho BA2 . . . . **44** D6
Dorset Rd TA6 . . . . **209** C3
Dorset St BA2 . . . . **44** D6
Doster's La TA4 . . . . **169** C6
Double Gates Dro TA11 . **158** A3
Double Hill BA2 . . . . **79** F7
Douglas Ct **3** BS23 . . . . . **48** F5
Douglas Dr BA4 . . . . **205** B5
Douglas Rd BS23 . . . . **48** F5
Douglas Yates Ct BA3 . . **116** F7
Doulting Cl BA11 . . . . . . **120** D7
Doulting Hill BA4 . . . . . . **205** F4
Doulton Way BS14 . . . . . . **23** B5
Dovai Dr TA6 . . . . **208** E2
Dove Cots Cl BA16 . . . . . **207** C7
Dove La BS2 . . . . **227** C4
Dover Ho BA1 . . . . **228** C4
Dover Pl
6 Bath BA1 . . . . **28** A1
Bristol BS8 . . . . **226** B3
Dover Rd TA2 . . . . **213** A8
Dovers La BA1 . . . . **29** C2
Dovers Pk BA1 . . . . **29** C2
Doveswell Gr BS13 . . . . . **22** A4
Dovetail Cl **1** TA1 . . . . . **212** E3
Dovetail Dr BS23 . . . . **49** A7
Dovetons Cl TA4 . . . . . . **202** E3
Dovetons Dr TA4 . . . . . . **202** E3
Dowding Rd BA1 . . . . **28** B1
Dowell Cl TA2 . . . . **212** C6
Dowland **18** BS22 . . . . . . **32** A2
Dowland Gr BS4 . . . . **22** D6
Dowling Rd BA6 . . . . **158** A5
Dowling Rd BS13 . . . . **22** D3
Dowlish La EX13 . . . . **198** E3
Down Ave BA2 . . . . **45** A1
Down Cl BS20 . . . . **1** F4
Downclose La TA18 . . . . **196** C3
Downend Cres TA6 . . . . . **136** B4
Downend Rd TA6 . . . . . . **136** B4
Downend Terr TA6 . . . . . **136** B4
Downey Field La TA18 . . **196** D6
Downfield
Bristol BS9 . . . . **5** C7
Keynsham BS31 . . . . **24** D5
Downhall Dr TA6 . . . . . . **208** D6
Downhead La BA22 . . . . **174** C5
Down La
Bathampton BA2 . . . . . . **28** F1
Buckland Dinham BA11 . . **99** C3
Shepton Montague BA9 . . **160** B2
Sherborne DT9 . . . . **188** A3
Trent DT9 . . . . **187** F5
West Pennard BA4, BA6 . **140** C1
Downland Cl **5** BS48 . . . . **8** D1
Downlands La EX15, TA3 . **181** A2
Downleaze
Bristol, Stoke Bishop BS9 . . **5** F3
Portishead BS20 . . . . **2** A5
Yeovil BA20 . . . . **218** D2
Downleaze Rd BS9 . . . . . . **5** F3
Down Rd BS20 . . . . **1** F4
Downs Cl BS22 . . . . **31** F1
Downs Cote Ave BS9 . . . . . **5** F6
Downs Cote Dr BS9 . . . . . . **5** F6
Downside
Portishead BS20 . . . . **2** C5
Street BA16 . . . . **207** D6
Downside Abbey★ BA3 . . **96** E2

Downside Cl
Bathampton BA2 . . . . . . **28** F1
Chilcompton BA3 . . . . . . **96** D3
Downside Rd
Backwell BS48 . . . . **36** E8
Weston-Super-Mare BS23 . **48** F4
Downside Sch BA3 . . . . . **96** E2
Downslade La TA10 . . . . **172** D5
Downs Rd BS41 . . . . **21** D2
Downs Sch The BS48 . . . . **9** C8
Downs The BS20 . . . . **2** B4
Downsway BS20 . . . . **77** D6
Downton Rd BS13 . . . . . . **22** D8
Down View BA3 . . . . **97** F8
Dowry Pl **3** BS8 . . . . **11** F5
Dowry Rd BS8 . . . . **226** A2
Dowry Sq BS8 . . . . **226** A2
Dowsland Way TA1 . . . . **213** C1
Dozen's Cnr TA17 . . . . . **195** A7
Dragon Cross TA24 . . . . **131** D3
Dragonfly Chase BA22 . . **173** E2
Dragons Hill Cl BS31 . . . . **24** F5
Dragons Hill Ct BS31 . . . . **24** F5
Dragons Hill Gdns BS31 . . **24** F5
Drake's Cl TA3 . . . . **169** C4
Drake Ave BA2 . . . . **44** F2
Drake Cl
Saltford BS31 . . . . **25** D2
Staplegrove TA2 . . . . . **212** B4
Weston-Super-Mare BS22 . **31** F4
Drake Rd BA5 . . . . **203** F6
Drakes Cl TA6 . . . . **208** F5
Drakes Cres TA20 . . . . . **198** D8
Drakes Mdw
East Coker BA22 . . . . . **197** C7
Yarcombe EX14 . . . . . . **192** D3
Drakes Pk TA21 . . . . **222** D7
Drakes Pk N TA21 . . . . . **222** D7
Drakes Way BS20 . . . . **2** B5
Drang The
Coxley BA5 . . . . **139** E6
Evercreech BA4 . . . . . . **141** E1
Porlock TA24 . . . . **124** A3
Dransfield Way BA2 . . . . . **44** C4
Drapers Way TA24 . . . . . **129** D2
Drappel La BA5 . . . . **110** C3
Draycott Pl BS1 . . . . **227** A1
Draycott Ave TA2 . . . . . **213** A6
Draycott Cl **1** BA2 . . . . **208** D3
Draycott Moor Dro BS27 . **90** D1
Draycott Rd
Cheddar BS27 . . . . **90** D2
Shepton Mallet BA4 . . . **205** B6
Draycott & Rodney Stoke CE
Fst Sch BS27 . . . . **90** F3
Draydon Rd BS4 . . . . **22** D8
Dray Rd BA22 . . . . **186** C2
Drayton BS24 . . . . **49** A2
Drayton Cl BS14 . . . . **23** B8
Drayton La TA10 . . . . . . **171** D3
Drayton Rd BS9 . . . . **5** C8
Drew's La DT10 . . . . **190** B5
Drials La BA3 . . . . **94** F6
Drift Rd TA24 . . . . **201** D4
Drift The
Chard Junction TA20 . . **198** E8
Chard TA20 . . . . **194** B3
Drill Hall La BA4 . . . . **205** C5
Drimpton Cross DT8 . . . **199** F7
Dring The BA3 . . . . **78** E2
Drive The
Bristol BS14 . . . . **23** C6
Burnham-on-S TA8 . . . . . **85** A2
Churchill BS25 . . . . **52** E4
Shipham BS25 . . . . **70** E8
Stanton Drew BS39 . . . . **39** F1
Taunton TA1 . . . . **212** D1
Weston-Super-Mare BS23 . **48** F8
Woolavington TA7 . . . . **136** E4
Dropping La BA10 . . . . . **160** D5
Drove Cl DT10 . . . . **189** F2
Drove Ct BS48 . . . . **8** E3
Drove La
East Pennard BA4 . . . . . **158** E4
Shepton Beauchamp TA19 . **184** E4
Drove Rd
Congresbury BS49 . . . . . **34** C4
Stourton Caundle DT10 . **189** F2
Weston-Super-Mare BS23 . **48** F5
Drove The
Bridgwater TA6 . . . . . . **209** A4
Portbury BS20 . . . . **3** D2
Droveway TA13 . . . . **220** B5
Drove Way
Churchinford TA3 . . . . . **191** F8
Sandford BS24, BS25 . . . **51** E7
Droveway Cl BA21 . . . . . **187** C2
Druid Cl BS9 . . . . **5** C5
Druid Hill BS9 . . . . **5** C5
Druid Rd BS9 . . . . **5** D4
Druids Garth BA2 . . . . **28** D1
Druid Stoke Ave BS9 . . . . . **5** C5
Druids Wlk TA20 . . . . . . **223** C5
Druid Woods BS9 . . . . **5** C5
Druley Hill BA10 . . . . . . **161** D8
Drum Ave BA6 . . . . **206** C5
Drumhead Way The BS25 . **70** E8
Dr White's Cl BS1 . . . . . **227** B1
Dryleaze BS31 . . . . **24** E7
Drysdale Cl BS22 . . . . **31** D1
Duchess Cl TA6 . . . . **208** E7
Duchy Cl BA3 . . . . **78** E5
Duchy Rd
Clandown BA3 . . . . **78** E5
Shepton Mallet BA4 . . . **205** A4
Duck La
Chard TA20 . . . . **223** C3

Duck La continued
Churchill BS40 . . . . 53 A8
Horsington BA8 . . . . 176 E2
Ilchester BA22 . . . . 173 F1
Kenn BS21 . . . . 17 A6
Stalbridge DT10 . . . . 190 B5
Westbury-sub-Mendip BA5 110 E6
Duck Pool Dro BA6 . . . . . . 206 B7
Duckpool La TA18 . . . . 196 B8
Duck Pool La BA11 . . . . . . 102 B6
Ducks' Field Crossing
TA18 . . . . 224 C1
Ducks Hill TA10 . . . . 172 B5
Ducks La BS22 . . . . 32 A8
Duck St BS25 . . . . 52 C5
Dudley Cl BS31 . . . . 24 E4
Dudmoor TA12 . . . . 185 B7
Dudwell La BA3 . . . . 95 A5
Dugdale St TA24 . . . . 200 F6
Duke's Cl BA9 . . . . 216 E3
Duke's La
Horningsham BA12 . . . . . . 144 A1
Kilmington BA12 . . . . 161 F8
Duke Ave **7** TA5 . . . . 135 B2
Duke Ho TA1 . . . . 221 B3
Dukes Field BA4 . . . . 205 B6
Dukes Mead TA6 . . . . 209 A2
Duke St
Bath BA2 . . . . 228 C2
Bridgwater TA6 . . . . 208 E2
Frome BA11 . . . . 119 E5
Taunton TA1 . . . . 213 A4
Dull Cross TA4 . . . . 151 D3
Dulverton La TA4 . . . . 165 D7
Dulverton Mid & Com Sch
TA22 . . . . 163 D6
Dumfries Pl BS23 . . . . 48 E5
Dummis La BA5 . . . . 111 A1
Dumper's La BA3 . . . . 94 F7
Dumpers La BS40 . . . . 39 B2
Dunball Ind Est TA6 . . . . 136 B4
Dunbar Cl TA9 . . . . 104 C4
Duncan Gdns BA1 . . . . 27 A3
Duncart La BA5 . . . . 204 C7
Duncliffe Cl DT10 . . . . 190 B4
Duncombe Cl TA6 . . . . . . 209 D5
Dundas Row TA4 . . . . 167 E8
Dundry CE Prim Sch
BS41 . . . . 21 D2
Dundry La
Dundry BS41 . . . . 21 C3
Winford BS40 . . . . 38 A7
Dunedin Way BS22 . . . . . . 32 C4
Dunford Terr BA6 . . . . 158 A5
Dungarvon Rd BS24 . . . . . 49 F7
Dungeon BS28 . . . . 108 D7
Dungeon La BA5 . . . . 204 C6
Dunkerry Rd BS26 . . . . 88 C4
Dunkerton Cl BA6 . . . . . . 206 F3
Dunkerton Hill BA2 . . . . . . 61 E2
Dunkerton Rise TA2 . . . . 168 B5
Dunkery Cl BS48 . . . . .8 E1
Dunkery Rd
Bridgwater TA6 . . . . 208 D4
Weston-Super-Mare BS23 . 30 F1
Dunkery Vineyard★
TA24 . . . . 200 A1
Dunkirk Bsns Pk BA14 . . 83 D2
Dunkleys Way TA1 . . . . . 213 C2
Dunn's Hill TA21 . . . . 179 A6
Dunnings La BS28 . . . . . . 107 E7
Dunns St BS28 . . . . 108 C4
Dunsford Pl BA2 . . . . 45 B6
Dunsgreen La EX15 . . . . . 191 A8
Dunsham La TA18 . . . . . . 195 C4
Dunsley Hill EX16, EX36 . 162 D5
Dunstan Dr DT9 . . . . 225 E5
Dunstan Rd
Burnham-on-S TA8 . . . . . . 104 B7
Glastonbury BA6 . . . . 206 F4
Dunstan Way BS27 . . . . . . 90 B6
Dunster Beach Chalets
TA24 . . . . 201 F4
Dunster Castle★ TA24 . . 201 E1
Dunster Cl
Minehead TA24 . . . . 201 B4
Taunton TA2 . . . . 213 B7
Dunster Cres BS24 . . . . . . 49 A2
Dunster Ct BS25 . . . . 70 A8
Dunster Fst Sch TA24 . . 201 D2
Dunster Gdns **5** BS48 . . . .8 E1
Dunster Ho BA2 . . . . 45 A2
Dunster Rd
Bristol BS4 . . . . 22 F8
Keynsham BS31 . . . . 24 E4
Dunsters Rd BS49 . . . . 17 F1
Dunster Sta★ TA24 . . . . 201 F4
Dunster Steep
Dunster TA24 . . . . 201 E2
Porlock, Doverhay TA24 . . 124 A3
Porlock, West Porlock
TA24 . . . . 123 F4
Dunster Visitor Ctr★
TA24 . . . . 201 E2
Dunster Wood Forest Trails★
TA24 . . . . 130 D5
**Dunster Working Water
Mill★** TA24 . . . . 201 E1
Dunwear Ho **3** TA6 . . . . . 209 C4
Dunwear La TA6 . . . . 209 D3
Durban Way BS49 . . . . 17 B1
Durbin Park Rd BS21 . . . . . 6 D5
Durcott Rd BA2 . . . . 78 D8
Durham Gr BS31 . . . . 24 E4
Durham Pl **9** TA2 . . . . . . 213 A8
Durhams Cotts TA4 . . . . . 210 C5
Durkheim Dr **2** BA5 . . . . 203 C4

Durleigh Cl
Bridgwater TA6 . . . . 208 D3
Bristol BS13 . . . . 22 A7
Durleigh Hill TA5 . . . . 208 A2
Durleigh Rd TA6 . . . . 208 C3
Durley Hill BS31 . . . . 24 C7
Durley La BS31 . . . . 24 D7
Durnhill BS40 . . . . 73 F7
Durrant Cl DT9 . . . . 225 D3
Dursdon Dro
Priddy BA5 . . . . 111 C8
Wells BA5 . . . . 112 B6
Dursley Rd BS11 . . . . .4 E5
Durston BS24 . . . . 49 A2
Durston BA16 . . . . 207 C5
Durston Ho **3** BA16 . . . . 207 C5
Durston Way TA1 . . . . 212 E1
Durville Rd BS13 . . . . 22 B6
Durweston Wlk BS14 . . . . 23 C8
Dutch Rd TA9 . . . . 105 E5
Dutton Cl BS14 . . . . 23 D6
Dutton Rd BS14 . . . . 23 D6
Dutton Wlk BS14 . . . . 23 D6
Dwelly Cl TA20 . . . . 223 C3
Dyehouse Cnr TA22 . . . . 164 A6
Dyehouse Cross TA22 . . 163 F5
Dyehouse La
Bury TA22 . . . . 164 A5
Glastonbury BA6 . . . . 206 C5
Dye La BA3 . . . . 115 A3
Dyer's La TA2 . . . . 213 E5
Dyers Cl
Bristol BS13 . . . . 22 D4
Curry Rivel TA10 . . . . 171 D4
West Buckland TA21 . . . . 180 F7
Dyers Gn TA6 . . . . 153 F3
Dyers Rd TA10 . . . . 171 D4
Dyke's Way BA9 . . . . 216 B3
Dyke Hill Terr TA20 . . . . . 198 D8
Dymboro Ave BA3 . . . . . . 77 F1
Dymboro Cl BA3 . . . . 77 F1
Dymboro Gdns BA3 . . . . . 77 F1
Dymboro The BA3 . . . . . . 77 F1
Dyrham Cl TA8 . . . . 104 D7
Dyson Cl BS49 . . . . 34 B8

E

Eagle Cl
Ilchester BA22 . . . . 173 E2
Weston-Super-Mare BS22 . 49 D8
Eagle Gdns BA22 . . . . 173 E2
Eagle La **1** BA11 . . . . 119 F4
Eagle Pk BA1 . . . . 28 F5
Eagle Rd BA1 . . . . 28 F5
Eagles The BS25 . . . . 34 B8
Eames Orch TA19 . . . . . . 221 C2
Earlesfield BS48 . . . . 8 C1
Earle St BA20 . . . . 219 C5
Earlham Gr BS23 . . . . 49 A7
Earls Cl
Bridgwater TA6 . . . . 208 E7
Sherborne DT9 . . . . 225 F5
Earl St BS1 . . . . 227 A4
East Anstey Prim Sch
EX16 . . . . 162 E5
East Approach Rd TA7 . . 136 D4
East Ave TA9 . . . . 104 C4
Eastbourne Ave **15** BA1 . . 28 B1
Eastbourne Ct **13** TA1 . . 213 A4
Eastbourne Gate TA1 . . . 213 A4
Eastbourne Rd TA1 . . . . . 213 A4
Eastbourne Terr **12** TA1 . 213 A4
East Brent CE Fst Sch
TA9 . . . . 86 C4
East Bridgwater Com Sch
TA6 . . . . 209 C5
Eastbrook Terr TA3 . . . . . 168 D1
Eastbury Hill TA24 . . . . . . 131 B5
Eastbury Rd TA24 . . . . . . 131 B5
East Cl
Bath BA2 . . . . 44 A5
Haselbury Plucknett TA18 . 196 B5
East Clevedon Triangle
BS21 . . . . .6 F3
Eastcliff BS20 . . . . .2 E7
East Coker Com Prim Sch
BA22 . . . . 197 C7
East Coker Rd BA20 . . . . . 218 F2
East Coker Sawmills
BA22 . . . . 197 C7
Eastcombe Gdns BS23 . . . 30 F1
Eastcombe La BA4 . . . . . . 142 E2
Eastcombe Rd BS23 . . . . . 30 F1
East Compton Rd
Pilton BA4 . . . . 204 E1
Shepton Mallet BA4 . . . . . 205 B1
Eastcote Pk BS14 . . . . 23 B5
Eastcourt Rd BS39 . . . . . . 76 F8
Eastcroft BS40 . . . . 54 E2
Eastcroft Cl BS40 . . . . 54 E2
East Ct
Bristol BS3 . . . . 11 F3
Horrington BA5 . . . . 113 A1
Eastdown Rd BA3 . . . . 78 D5
East Dr TA9 . . . . 86 E4
East Dundry La BS41 . . . . 22 A1
East Dundry Rd BS13,
BS14 . . . . 22 F2
East End BS26 . . . . 88 D7
East End La BA3 . . . . 94 E4
Easterdown Hill
Dinnington TA17 . . . . 195 B8

Easterdown Hill continued
Seavington St Mary TA19 . 184 E1
Easter La EX35 . . . . 122 B4
Eastermead La BS29 . . . . . 51 C3
Eastern Ave TA6 . . . . 209 D4
Eastern Ho BS23 . . . . 30 E1
Eastertown BS24 . . . . 67 D1
Eastfield Bruton BA10 . . . 215 F7
29 Martock TA12 . . . . . . 185 E6
Shepton Mallet BA4 . . . . . 205 B6
Yarlington BA9 . . . . 175 F8
Eastfield Ave BA1 . . . . 27 B2
Eastfield Cl **30** TA12 . . . . 185 E6
Eastfield Gdn **12** DT9 . . . 225 B4
Eastfield Gdns BS23 . . . . . 30 F1
Eastfield La
Barrington TA19 . . . . 184 D5
Blackford BS28 . . . . 107 F5
Ditcheat BA4 . . . . 159 C7
East Chinnock BA22 . . . . 196 D8
Hambridge TA3 . . . . 184 B8
Lydford Fair Place TA11 . . 158 D3
North Perrott TA18 . . . . . 196 C4
Norton Sub Hamdon BA22 . 185 F1
Eastfield Pk BS23 . . . . 30 F1
Eastfield Rd
Hutton BS24 . . . . 49 E2
Wincanton BA9 . . . . 216 D4
East Gate **11** TA1 . . . . 213 A4
Eastgate Gdns **10** TA1 . . 213 A4
Easthams Rd TA18 . . . . . . 224 D6
Easthay La TA20 . . . . 199 A4
Easthill BA11 . . . . 120 A4
Easthill La BA4 . . . . 159 D5
East Huntspill Prim Sch
TA9 . . . . 136 E8
East La TA18 . . . . 196 B7
East Lambrook Manor Gdns★
TA13 . . . . 220 C8
East Lambrook Rd TA13 . 220 D7
Eastland Rd BA21 . . . . . . 219 C5
East Lanes BA21 . . . . 187 D6
Eastlea BS21 . . . . .6 B1
East Lea Rd BA1 . . . . 44 A8
Eastleigh Cl
Burnham-on-S TA8 . . . . . . 104 C8
Frome BA11 . . . . 120 A7
Wiveliscombe TA4 . . . . . . 210 C5
Eastleigh Rd TA1 . . . . 213 B3
Eastlyn Rd BS13 . . . . 22 B8
East Mead BA3 . . . . 78 B2
Eastmead La BS9 . . . . .5 E4
Eastmead Ct BS9 . . . . .5 E4
East Mead La
Street BA16 . . . . 207 F5
Walton BA16 . . . . 156 F6
East Mere Cross EX16 . . . 178 B2
East Mill Ct **11** DT9 . . . . . 225 E4
East Mill La DT9 . . . . 225 E4
Eastmoor La TA4 . . . . 164 E8
East Par BS9 . . . . .5 C6
East Quay TA6 . . . . 209 A6
East Quay Mews TA6 . . . . 209 A6
East Rd BA16 . . . . 207 E6
East Reach TA1 . . . . 213 A4
East Ride TA9 . . . . 86 B1
East Ridge Dr BS13 . . . . . . 21 F5
East Side La TA7 . . . . 136 F2
East St
Banwell BS29 . . . . 51 C3
Bourton SP8 . . . . 161 F1
Bristol BS2 . . . . 227 C4
Cannington TA5 . . . . 135 C2
Chard TA20 . . . . 223 D4
Crewkerne TA18 . . . . 224 D5
Drayton TA10 . . . . 171 E3
East Coker BA22 . . . . 197 B8
Ilminster TA19 . . . . 221 C4
Martock TA12 . . . . 185 E6
Milborne Port DT9 . . . . . . 217 D2
North Perrott TA18 . . . . . 196 C4
Norton Sub Hamdon TA14 . 185 F1
Shepton Montague BA9 . . 160 B2
Taunton TA1 . . . . 212 F3
Templecombe BA8 . . . . . . 176 F1
East Stoke TA14 . . . . 185 F4
East Street Dro TA12 . . . 185 E6
East Street La BA4 . . . . . . 140 A1
East Tapps La EX16 . . . . . 163 B2
East Town La TA4 . . . . . . 150 E3
**East Town La (Platterwell
La)** BA4 . . . . 141 B3
Eastville
Bath BA1 . . . . 28 B1
Yeovil BA21 . . . . 219 C5

Eastville La BS27 . . . . 90 F1
East Water La BA5 . . . . 92 F2
Eastway BS48 . . . . .8 E3
East Way BA2 . . . . 44 A5
Eastway Cl BS48 . . . . 8 D2
Eastway Sq BS48 . . . . .8 E3
Eastwell La BS25 . . . . 69 E6
Eastwick Ave TA2 . . . . . . 212 F7
Eastwick Rd TA2 . . . . 213 B7
Eastwood BA2 . . . . 45 F6
Eastwood Cl
Bridgwater TA6 . . . . 209 C4
Frome BA11 . . . . 119 C4
High Littleton BA3 . . . . . . 59 C1
East Woodlands Rd
BA11 . . . . 144 A7
East Wood Pl BS20 . . . . . . .2 E7
Eastwoods BA1 . . . . 29 B3
Eaton Cl BS14 . . . . 23 E5
Eaton Cres
Bristol BS8 . . . . 226 A4
Taunton TA2 . . . . 213 A6
Ebben La TA20 . . . . 194 F1
**Ebbor Gorge Nature
Reserve★** BA5 . . . . . . 111 D6
Ebbor Gorge Nature Trail★
BA5 . . . . 111 D5
Ebbor La BA5 . . . . 111 B5
Ebdon La BS22 . . . . 32 C5
Ebdon Rd BS22 . . . . 31 F4
Ebenezer La BS9 . . . . .5 E5
Eckweek Gdns BA2 . . . . . . 79 D8
Eckweek La BA2 . . . . 79 E8
Eckweek Rd BA2 . . . . 79 D8
Ecos Ct BA11 . . . . 119 D4
Edbrooke Rd TA24 . . . . . . 147 C5
Edbrook La TA5 . . . . 134 F3
Eddington Ct BS23 . . . . . . 48 D7
Eden Croft BA2 . . . . 49 E8
Eden Park Cl BA1 . . . . 29 A4
Eden Park Dr BA1 . . . . 29 A4
Eden Terr BA1 . . . . 28 B2
Eden Villas **4** BA1 . . . . . . 28 C2
Edford Hill BA3 . . . . 116 C6
Edgar Bldgs BA1 . . . . 228 B3
Edgarley Ct BS21 . . . . .6 C5
Edgarley Field La BA6 . . . 157 E8
Edgarley Rd
Glastonbury BA6 . . . . 139 D1
West Pennard BA6 . . . . . . 139 F1
Edgcott Rd TA24 . . . . 128 C1
Edgebury TA7 . . . . 136 E4
Edgecombe Ave BS22 . . . . 31 D2
Edgecombe Mews BA1 . . . 27 B1
Edgefield Cl BS14 . . . . 22 F3
Edgefield Rd BS14 . . . . . . 22 F3
Edgehill Rd BS21 . . . . .6 D6
Edgewood Cl BS14 . . . . . . 23 B8
Edgeworth Rd BA2 . . . . . . 44 C2
Edinburgh Pl **1** BS23 . . . 48 E8
Edinburgh Rd
Bridgwater TA6 . . . . 208 E2
Keynsham BS31 . . . . 24 E4
Edington Rd TA7 . . . . 137 D4
Edington Right Dro TA7 . 155 B7
Edington & Shapwick Sch
Burtle TA7 . . . . 137 D6
Shapwick TA7 . . . . 137 F1
Edingworth Rd BS24 . . . . 86 F7
Edith Cl TA8 . . . . 85 A2
Edithmead La TA9 . . . . . . 105 A6
Edmond's Hill TA11 . . . . . 173 D4
Edmund Hill La BA6 . . . . . 206 F4
Edmunds Way BS27 . . . . . 90 C7
Edward Cl BA22 . . . . 218 B6
Edward Ct BS31 . . . . 24 F4
Edward Rd BS21 . . . . .6 E5
Edward Rd S BS21 . . . . . . .6 E5
Edward Rd W BS21 . . . . . . .6 E5
Edward St
Bath, Bathwick BA2 . . . . . 45 B7
Bath, Lower Weston BA1 . . 44 C7
Bridgwater TA6 . . . . 209 B5
Edwin Short Cl BS30 . . . . 25 D8
Egerton Rd BA2 . . . . 44 E4
Egford Hill BA11 . . . . 119 C5
Egford La BA11 . . . . 119 C5
Egg Moor La EX13 . . . . . . 198 A7
Eggwood La TA13, TA16 . 195 B4
Eglin Croft BS13 . . . . 22 B4
Eglinton Rd BA16 . . . . . . 207 B4
Egremont Ct TA4 . . . . 202 D2
Egrove Way TA4 . . . . 202 D2
Eight Acre Dro TA7, TA9 . 137 A5
Eight Acre La
Wellington TA21 . . . . 222 E5
Wootton Courtenay TA24 . 129 F8
Eighteen Arce La BA21 . . 218 C6
Eighth Ave BS14 . . . . 23 A7
Eileen Cl BA16 . . . . 207 E5
Eirene Terr BS20 . . . . 4 D4
Elberton Rd BS9 . . . . .5 B7
Elborough Ave BS49 . . . . . 34 B8
Elborough Gdns BS24 . . . . 50 C3
Elbridge Ho **3** BS2 . . . . . 227 C3
Elderberry Wlk BS22 . . . 31 F1
Elder Cl
Chard TA20 . . . . 223 C5
Highbridge TA9 . . . . 104 D5
Eldergrove Cl TA6 . . . . . . 209 D7
Elder Ho TA8 . . . . 65 E2
Elderwood Rd BS14 . . . . . 23 B7
Eldon Pl BA1 . . . . 28 B2
Eldred Ct BS9 . . . . .5 D5
Eleanor Cl BA2 . . . . 44 A5
Eleanor Cotts BA2 . . . . . . 44 A6

Duc–Elm 245

Electric Ho TA14 . . . . 185 E3
Eleven Ct TA6 . . . . 208 E4
Elfrida Terr BA5 . . . . 203 A5
Elgar Cl
Bristol BS4 . . . . 22 D6
Clevedon BS21 . . . . .6 E1
Eliot Cl BS23 . . . . 49 A3
Eliotts Dr BA21 . . . . 218 E7
Elizabeth Cl BS24 . . . . 49 D3
Elizabeth Ct
Burnham-on-S TA8 . . . . . . 104 B6
4 Martock TA12 . . . . . . 185 E6
Elizabeth Flats BA21 . . . . 219 C6
Elizabeth Gdns **16** BA8 . 190 A6
Elizabeth Way
Bridgwater TA6 . . . . 209 C5
Chard TA20 . . . . 223 C5
Ellbridge Cl BS9 . . . . .5 D5
Ellenborough Cres BS23 . . 48 E6
Ellenborough Ct BS23 . . . 48 E6
Ellenborough Ho BS8 . . . 226 A2
Ellenborough Park Rd
BS23 . . . . 48 E6
Ellenborough Pk N BS23 . 48 D6
Ellenborough Pk S BS23 . 48 D6
Ellen Cl **8** TA6 . . . . 153 F4
Ellen Ho BA2 . . . . 44 A5
Ellersdown La TA22 . . . . . 163 E4
Ellesmere Rd
Bristol BS4 . . . . 23 D8
Weston-Super-Mare BS23 . 48 D3
Ellfield Cl BS13 . . . . 21 F6
Ellicombe La TA24 . . . . . . 201 C4
Ellicombe Mdw TA24 . . . 201 C4
Elliot Cl BA11 . . . . 119 F6
Elliots La BA11 . . . . 119 B8
Elliott's Hill BA22 . . . . . . 196 F1
Ellis's La TA5 . . . . 152 C6
Ellis Ave BS13 . . . . 22 A8
Elliscombe Pk BA9 . . . . . . 176 B6
Ellis Gr TA2 . . . . 168 B5
Ellis Pk BS22 . . . . 32 C4
Elliston Dr BA2 . . . . 44 B4
Ellworthy Ct TA11 . . . . . . 120 B4
**Ellsbridge Ho Norton
Radstock Coll** BS31 . . . 25 B5
Elm Ave TA8 . . . . 104 B6
Elmbrook BA1 . . . . 44 D8
Elm Cl
Banwell BS29 . . . . 50 E4
Broadway TA19 . . . . 183 C2
Nailsea BS48 . . . . .8 C1
Star BS25 . . . . 52 D1
Wells BA5 . . . . 203 A4
Yatton BS49 . . . . 34 B7
Elm Ct
Bristol BS14 . . . . 23 A6
Keynsham BS31 . . . . 24 C4
Elmdale Rd BS8 . . . . 226 B3
Elm Dr BA9 . . . . 216 C3
Elm Farm BS48 . . . . .9 A2
Elm Gr
Bath, Larkhill BA1 . . . . 28 C2
Bath, The Oval BA2 . . . . . 44 C4
Locking BS24 . . . . 49 F4
Minehead TA24 . . . . 201 A5
Taunton TA1 . . . . 212 E5
Elmgrove Cl TA6 . . . . 209 D7
Elmham Way TA24 . . . . . . 32 B1
Elm Hayes BS13 . . . . 21 F6
Elmhurst Ave BA21 . . . . . 219 B7
Elmhurst Est BA1 . . . . 29 A4
Elmhurst Gdns BS41 . . . . 20 F8
Elmhurst Jun Sch BA16 . 207 D6
Elmhurst La BA16 . . . . . . 207 D6
Elmhurst Rd BA24 . . . . . . 49 E2
Elmhyrst Rd BS23 . . . . . . 48 F8
Elm La
Great Elm BA11 . . . . 119 A6
Shalford BA9 . . . . 216 B7
Woolavington TA7 . . . . . . 136 F4
Elmlea Ave BS9 . . . . .5 F5
Elm Lea Cl TA7 . . . . 155 F5
Elmlea Jun & Inf Schs BS9 .5 F5
Elmleigh BA21 . . . . 218 C7
Elm Leigh BA11 . . . . 120 C6
Elmleigh Rd **21** TA12 . . . 185 E6
Elm Lodge Rd BS48 . . . . . .9 B2
Elm Pk TA1 . . . . 212 E5
Elm Pl BA2 . . . . 44 F4
Elm Rd BS39 . . . . 77 E5
Elms Cl TA1 . . . . 212 E5
Elms Est TA2 . . . . 213 F8
Elmside Cl BA16 . . . . 207 D5
Elmside Ho TA6 . . . . 208 F2
Elmside Rd TA6 . . . . 208 F2
Elms La BA2 . . . . 214 B7
Elmsleigh Rd BS23 . . . . . . 48 E4
Elmsley La BS22 . . . . 31 C5
Elms Rd TA21 . . . . 222 F5
Elm St TA20 . . . . 223 C5
Elms The
Banwell BS29 . . . . 51 A4
Bath, Lambridge BA1 . . . . 28 C2
Bath, Weston Park BA1 . . . 27 C1
Elmswood BS23 . . . . 48 F8
Elm Terr BA3 . . . . 97 C8
Elm Tree Ave
Nailsea BS21 . . . . .8 A4
Radstock BA3 . . . . 78 D1
Elm Tree Cl TA4 . . . . 155 C2
Elmtree Dr BS13 . . . . 21 F5
Elm Tree Pk BS20 . . . . 3 D3

Elm Tree Rd
Clevedon BS21 . . . . 6 D2
Locking BS24 . . . . 50 A4
Elmvale Dr BS24 . . . . . . 49 F3
Elm View
Midsomer Norton BA3 . . . . 78 B1
Temple Cloud BS39 . . . . 58 E1
Elm Way BA4 . . . . 205 A6
Elm Wlk
Portishead BS20 . . . . 2 C4
Yatton BS49 . . . . 34 B7
Elmwood Ave TA6 . . . . 208 F3
Elmwood Sch TA6 . . . . 208 F3
Elsbert Dr BS13 . . . . . . 21 E6
Elscombe La
Timberscombe TA24 . . . . 130 A4
Wootton Courtenay TA24 . . 129 F4
Elton Ho 2 BS2 . . . . . . 227 C3
Elton Rd
Bristol BS8 . . . . 226 C3
Clevedon BS21 . . . . 6 C3
Weston-Super-Mare BS22 . . 32 A4
Elton St BS2 . . . . 227 C3
Elvard Cl BS13 . . . . 22 A4
Elvard Rd BS13 . . . . . . 22 A4
Elwell La BS40, BS41 . . . 21 A1
Elworthy Cross TA4 . . . 150 C5
Elworthy Dr TA21 . . . . 222 C4
Elworthy La TA4 . . . . . 150 C5
Ely Gr BS9 . . . . 5 B7
Embankment The TA10 . 172 A5
Embercourt Dr BS48 . . . . 19 A6
Emery Gate BS29 . . . . . 51 B3
Emlet DT9 . . . . 187 E1
Emley La BS40 . . . . 54 B6
Emlyn Cl 6 BS22 . . . . . 32 B4
Emmanuel Ct BS8 . . . . 226 A4
Emmett Wood BS14 . . . . 23 B3
Empress Menen Gdns
BA1 . . . . 44 A8
Enderleigh Gdns BS25 . . 52 F4
Enfield Dr BA4 . . . . 141 E2
Enfield Rd BA4 . . . . 141 E2
Engine La BS48 . . . . 18 B8
Englands La BA22 . . . . . 174 F3
Englands Mead BA22 . . . 174 F3
Englands Rd TA24 . . . . . 124 A3
Englands Way TA20 . . . . 223 D6
Englishcombe La BA2 . . . 44 D3
Englishcombe Rd BS13 . . 22 C3
Englishcombe Rise BA2 . . 44 A3
Englishcombe Tithe Barn★
BA2 . . . . 43 F2
Englishcombe Way BA2 . . 44 E3
Enmore BS24 . . . . 49 A2
Enmore CE Prim Sch
TA5 . . . . 152 F5
Enmore Cl TA8 . . . . . . 104 C8
Enmore Rd
Bridgwater TA5 . . . . . . 153 B6
Taunton TA2 . . . . 212 F7
Ennerdale Cl BS23 . . . . . 49 A5
Enterprise Ctr The BS24 . 49 A3
Enterprise Mews BA20 . . 218 D3
Enterprise Trade Ctr BS4 . 22 F7
Entry Hill BA2 . . . . 44 F2
Entry Hill Dr BA2 . . . . . 44 F3
Entry Hill Gdns BA2 . . . 44 F3
Entry Hill Pk BA2 . . . . . 44 F2
Entry Rise BA2 . . . . 44 F1
Erin Wlk BS4 . . . . 22 D8
Erlon La BA5 . . . . 110 F4
Ermine St BA21 . . . . . . 218 D7
Ermine Way BS11 . . . . . . 4 C7
Ernest Ashman Pl TA20 . 223 D5
Ervine Terr BS2 . . . . . . 227 C4
Escott Cl TA6 . . . . 208 F6
Escott La TA4 . . . . 132 D1
Esgar Rise BS22 . . . . 31 E3
Eskdale Cl BS22 . . . . 49 D8
Esmonde Dr BA22 . . . . . 173 E2
Esmond Gr BS21 . . . . 6 D4
Esplanade
Burnham-on-S TA8 . . . . . 104 A7
Minehead TA24 . . . . 201 A4
Esplanade La TA23 . . . . 202 C7
Esplanade Rd BS20 . . . . . 2 C7
Esplanade The TA23 . . . 202 C7
Essex Cl TA20 . . . . 223 C4
Essex Ct TA1 . . . . 212 C2
Essex Dr TA1 . . . . 212 C2
Estuary Ho BS20 . . . . 2 E7
Estuary Pk TA5 . . . . . . 135 B5
Estune Wlk BS41 . . . . . . 11 A2
Esworthy Cross EX16 . . . 162 F1
Ethel St BA5 . . . . 203 C3
Ethpark Gr 1 TA2 . . . . 212 F6
Etonhurst BS23 . . . . 48 D6
Eton La BS29 . . . . 50 E7
Eton Rd TA8 . . . . 104 B6
Etsome Cl TA11 . . . . . . 211 C4
Etsome Hill TA11 . . . . . 211 C7
Etsome Rd TA11 . . . . . . 211 C5
Etsome Terr TA11 . . . . . 211 C4
Ettlingen Way BS21 . . . . . 6 F2
Eugene Flats 7 BS2 . . . 227 A4
Eugene St
Bristol, Kingsdown BS2 . . 227 A4
Bristol, St Pauls BS2, BS5 . 227 C4
Evelyn Rd BA1 . . . . 44 B8
Evelyn Terr 14 BA1 . . . . 28 A1
Evenlode Gdns BS11 . . . . 4 F5
Evenlode Way BS31 . . . . 25 A3
Evercreech CE Prim Sch
BA4 . . . . 141 E2

Evercreech Rd BS14 . . . . 23 B4
Evercreech Way TA9 . . . 104 F2
Everett Cl BA5 . . . . 112 E1
Evergreen BS25 . . . . 51 F1
Evergreen Path TA16 . . . 195 F7
Everton Rd BA20 . . . . . 219 A4
Evesham Ave BA21 . . . . 218 C6
Evesham Dr TA6 . . . . . . 209 A1
Ewart Rd BS22 . . . . 49 C8
Ewell Cl TA19 . . . . 183 C1
Exbourne 10 BS22 . . . . . 32 A2
Exbury Cl TA1 . . . . 104 C7
Excelsior St BA2 . . . . . . 45 B5
Excelsior Terr BA3 . . . . . 78 B1
Exchange Ave BS1 . . . . . 227 A2
Exebridge Ind Est TA22 . 163 F3
Exeter Cl
Burnham-on-S TA8 . . . . . 104 C7
Nether Stowey TA5 . . . . 134 B2
Exeter Rd
Portishead BS20 . . . . 2 E4
Rockwell Green TA21 . . . . 222 B5
Weston-Super-Mare BS23 . . 48 E5
Exeter Road Cvn Pk
TA21 . . . . 222 B5
Exford CE Fst sch TA24 . 128 D1
Exford Cl BS23 . . . . 48 F2
Exford Rd TA24 . . . . . . 147 C6
*Exmoor Falconry & Animal
Farm★* TA24 . . . . 124 B4
Exmoor Gdns TA22 . . . . 163 D6
Exmoor Rd BA2 . . . . 44 F2
Exmoor Way TA24 . . . . 200 E6
Exmouth Rd BS4 . . . . . . 22 F8
Express Pk TA6 . . . . . . 136 A2
Exton BS24 . . . . 49 A2
Exton Cl BS14 . . . . 23 B5
Exton La TA22 . . . . 147 E4
Eyer's La BS2 . . . . 227 C3
Eyers Rd BS24 . . . . 49 F7

F

Faber Gr BS13 . . . . 22 C4
Factory Hill SP8 . . . . . . 161 F2
Factory La
East Huntspill TA9 . . . . . 136 E8
Tatworth TA20 . . . . 198 D8
Failand Cres BS9 . . . . 5 C5
Failand La
Easton-in-G BS8 . . . . 4 A1
Portbury BS20 . . . . 3 F2
Failand Wlk BS9 . . . . 5 C6
Fairacre Cl BS24 . . . . . . 50 B4
Fairacres Cl BS31 . . . . . 24 F5
Fair Cl BA2 . . . . 81 E4
Fairclose TA20 . . . . 193 D6
Fair Cross TA23 . . . . . . 131 F2
Fairdean Rd TA9 . . . . . . 104 E4
Fairfax Cl TA6 . . . . 209 C6
Fairfax Rd TA6 . . . . 209 C5
Fairfax St BS1 . . . . 227 B3
Fairfield
Coleford BA3 . . . . 116 E8
Crewkerne TA18 . . . . . . 224 E5
Ilminster TA19 . . . . 221 A4
7 Martock TA12 . . . . . . 185 E6
Rode BA11 . . . . 82 F1
Sampford Peverell EX16 . . 178 D1
Sherborne DT9 . . . . 225 D5
Somerton TA11 . . . . 211 E4
Tunley BA2 . . . . 61 A3
Yarlington BA9 . . . . 175 F7
Fairfield Ave BA1 . . . . . . 28 A2
Fairfield Cl
Backwell BS48 . . . . 19 D7
Frome BA11 . . . . 120 A7
Marshfield SN14 . . . . 13 F8
Weston-Super-Mare BS22 . . 31 B1
Fairfield Dr TA4 . . . . . . 202 E3
Fairfield Gdns BA6 . . . . 206 D4
Fairfield Gn TA3 . . . . . . 192 A7
Fairfield Mdws BA14 . . . . 83 F3
Fairfield Mead BS48 . . . . 19 D7
Fairfield Park Rd BA1 . . . 28 A2
Fairfield Pneu Sch BS48 . . 19 C6
Fairfield Rd
Bath BA1 . . . . 28 B1
Taunton TA1 . . . . 213 B7
Fairfield Terr
Bath BA1 . . . . 28 A1
Fitzhead TA4 . . . . 166 F5
Peasedown St John BA2 . . . 79 C7
Fairfield View BA1 . . . . . 28 A2
Fairfield Way BS48 . . . . . 19 C6
Fairford Cl TA9 . . . . 104 E4
Fairford Rd
Bristol BS11 . . . . 4 D7
Highbridge TA9 . . . . 104 E4
Fair Furlong BS13 . . . . . 22 A4
Fair Furlong Prim Sch
BS13 . . . . 22 B4
Fair Hill BS25 . . . . 70 F8
Fairhouse Rd BA22 . . . . 197 F8
Fairlands Mid Sch BS27 . . 90 C7
Fairlands Way BS27 . . . . 90 C7
Fairmead Rd BA21 . . . . . 219 C8
Fairmead Sch BA21 . . . . 219 C8
Fairmont Terr 7 DT9 . . . 225 D4
Fair Pl TA11 . . . . 158 D3
Fairseat Workshops BS40 . 56 E7
Fairview
Mells BA11 . . . . 118 B7
Weston-Super-Mare BS22 . . 31 F4
Fair View BA10 . . . . . . 161 A7
Fairview Ho BS9 . . . . 5 F8

Fairview Terr
Taunton TA2 . . . . 168 D1
Yeovilton BA22 . . . . 187 A8
Fairwater Cl TA2 . . . . . 212 D6
Fairway BS4 . . . . 23 D8
Fairway Cl
Berrow TA8 . . . . 84 F4
Weston-Super-Mare BS22 . . 31 B3
Fairway Rise TA20 . . . . 223 E5
Fairways
Saltford BS31 . . . . 25 E2
Wells BA5 . . . . 203 C4
Fairways Cvn Pk TA7 . . . 136 E3
Fairways The TA1 . . . . . 212 F1
Fairway View BA21 . . . . 219 D6
Fairwood Rd BA13 . . . . 102 F5
Fairy Hill BS39 . . . . 41 D6
Falcon Cl
Bristol, Westbury on T BS9 . . 5 F8
Portishead BS20 . . . . 2 D4
Falcon Cres BS22 . . . . . . 49 D8
Falcon Ct TA1 . . . . 212 C4
Falcondale Rd BS9 . . . . . . 5 F7
Falconer Rd BA1 . . . . . . 27 A3
Falconsmead Wlk BA21 . . 219 D8
Falkland Ho 7 TA18 . . . 224 C7
Falkland Sq 6 TA18 . . . 224 C6
Falklands Rise TA24 . . . 200 D7
Fallowfield
Blagdon BS40 . . . . 54 E2
Weston-Super-Mare BS22 . . 31 F3
Falmouth Cl BS48 . . . . . . 9 A1
Fanshawe Rd BS14 . . . . . 23 A7
Faraday Rd 2 BS8 . . . . . 11 F5
Farleigh Rd 7 BS48 . . . . 20 B8
Farleigh Hungerford Castle★
BA2 . . . . 82 E8
Farleigh Rd
Backwell BS48 . . . . 19 C6
Clevedon BS21 . . . . 6 B1
Keynsham BS31 . . . . 24 D4
Norton St Philip BA2 . . . . 81 F5
Farleigh Rise BA15 . . . . . 29 E1
Farleigh View BA15 . . . . 64 F3
Farleigh Wlk BS13 . . . . . 22 A8
Farler's End BS48 . . . . . 18 F8
Farley BA11 . . . . 120 C6
Farley Dell BA3 . . . . . . 116 E8
Farmborough CE Prim Sch
BA2 . . . . 59 F6
Farm Cl
Somerton TA11 . . . . 211 B3
Westbury-sub-Mendip
BA5 . . . . 110 D6
Weston-Super-Mare BS22 . . 32 C4
Farm Ct TA13 . . . . 220 C5
Farm Dr TA11 . . . . 211 B3
Farmer Rd BS13 . . . . 21 E4
Farm Hill TA7 . . . . 156 B8
Farmhouse Cl 7 BS48 . . . 8 E2
Farmhouse Ct 1 BS48 . . . 8 E1
Farmhouse Dr BA11 . . . . 119 F7
Farm La
Buckland St Mary TA20 . . 182 A2
Coultings TA5 . . . . 134 E4
Stogursey TA5 . . . . 134 D4
Street BA16 . . . . 207 C7
Wellow BA2 . . . . 62 E1
Farm Orch DT9 . . . . . . 188 C7
Farm Rd
Bradford Abbas DT9 . . . . 187 E1
Doulting BA4 . . . . 141 E5
Hutton BS24 . . . . 49 E2
Street BA16 . . . . 207 C6
Weston-Super-Mare BS22 . . 31 B1
Farm St BA22 . . . . 186 C6
Farm View TA2 . . . . . . 168 F6
Farmwell Cl BS13 . . . . . . 22 B5
Farnaby Cl BS4 . . . . 22 C7
Farnborough Rd BS24 . . . 50 C4
Farncombe La BA9 . . . . 160 B1
Farndale Rd BS22 . . . . . . 49 D8
Farr's La BS1 . . . . 227 A2
Farr's Orch 6 TA16 . . . . 195 F7
Farrant Cl
Baltonsborough BA6 . . . . 158 A5
Bristol BS4 . . . . 22 A4
Taunton TA1 . . . . 212 A4
Farrant Rd BA11 . . . . . . 119 D5
Farriers Gn TA2 . . . . . . 213 D6
Farrington Hill La TA5 . . 134 D6
Farrington Fields BS39 . . . 77 C3
Farrington Fields Trad Est
BS39 . . . . 77 C3
*Farrington Gurney CE Prim
Sch* BS39 . . . . 77 A4
Farrington La BA4 . . . . . 141 F6
Farrington Rd BS39 . . . . 77 C5
Farrington Way BS39 . . . 77 C3
Farrow Cl TA20 . . . . . . 223 D3
Farrs La BA2 . . . . 45 B2
Farr St BS11 . . . . 4 B8
Farthing's Pitts TA21 . . . 222 C4
Farthing Combe BS26 . . . 70 D2
Farthing Down TA21 . . . 179 E7
Farthing La EX13 . . . . . 193 D1
Farthing Rd TA6 . . . . . . 208 E1
Farthing Row BA11 . . . . . 82 E1
Farthings Cl TA21 . . . . . 222 B8
Farthings Paddock BA7 . . 159 A3
Faulkland La BA2, BA3 . . . 80 C4
Faulkland Rd BA2 . . . . . . 44 D5
Faulkland View BA2 . . . . 79 E7
Faversham Dr BS24 . . . . . 49 A1
Fawcus Pl TA20 . . . . . . 223 C4
Fawn Cl BA6 . . . . 206 C3
Fayre Way BA5 . . . . . . 204 B7
Fearnville Est BS21 . . . . . 6 C2

Featherbed La
Chew Stoke BS40 . . . . . . 38 A3
Clayhanger EX16 . . . . . . 165 C1
Clutton BS39 . . . . 58 C6
Fedden Village BS21 . . . . . 1 F5
Feeder Rd BS2 . . . . 227 C1
Fellowsmead DT10 . . . . 190 F5
Felon's Oak La TA24 . . . 131 B2
Felsberg Way BS27 . . . . . 90 C7
Feltham Dr BA11 . . . . . . 120 A3
Feltham La BA11 . . . . . . 144 B8
Felton Gr BS13 . . . . 22 A8
Felton La BS40 . . . . 37 E7
Felton St BS40 . . . . 37 C7
Fender Cl TA5 . . . . 135 B5
Feniton 6 BS22 . . . . 32 A2
Fennel La BS26 . . . . 70 B2
Fennel Way BA22 . . . . . 218 A5
Fenners BS22 . . . . 32 B4
Fennington La TA2 . . . . 168 B8
Fenns La BS41 . . . . 10 E1
Fenshurst Gdns BS41 . . . . 20 F8
Fenswood Cl BS41 . . . . . . 10 F1
Fenswood Ct BS41 . . . . . 10 F1
Fenswood Mead BS41 . . . . 10 E1
Fenswood Rd BS41 . . . . . 10 E1
Fental La BA3 . . . . 116 C1
Fenton Cl BS31 . . . . 25 D3
Ferenberge Cl BA2 . . . . . 60 A6
Ferguson Cl TA5 . . . . . . 134 A3
Fermoy BA11 . . . . 120 B6
Fern Cl BA3 . . . . 78 B1
Ferndale Dr TA1 . . . . . . 168 D1
Ferndale Gdns BA21 . . . 218 E6
Ferndale Rd
Bath BA1 . . . . 28 C3
Portishead BS20 . . . . 2 D6
Ferndown Cl
Bristol BS11 . . . . 5 A7
Taunton TA1 . . . . 212 D1
Ferne Animal Sanctuary★
TA20 . . . . 193 A2
Fern Gr BS48 . . . . 18 C8
Fern Lea BS24 . . . . 67 B6
Fernlea Gdns BS20 . . . . . . 4 B4
Fernlea Rd BS22 . . . . 49 C7
Fernleigh Ave TA6 . . . . 209 A3
Fernleigh Cl BA4 . . . . . . 141 E1
Fern Lodge BS23 . . . . . . 48 D6
Fernside BS48 . . . . 19 A7
Fernsteed Rd BS13 . . . . . 21 F6
Ferry Ct BA2 . . . . 45 B6
Ferry La
Bath BA2 . . . . 45 B6
Lympsham BS24 . . . . 67 C3
Ferryman's Ct BS2 . . . . 227 B2
Ferryman Rd BA6 . . . . . 206 F7
Ferry St BS1 . . . . 227 B2
Fersfield BA2 . . . . 45 B3
Festival Units TA6 . . . . 209 B1
Feversham Ave TA6 . . . . 208 E6
Feversham Ct BA22 . . . . 173 E2
Feversham La BA6 . . . . . 206 D5
Feversham Way TA2 . . . . 213 A8
Fiddle La BA22 . . . . 174 F1
Field Cl BA3 . . . . 116 A3
Field End
Axminster EX13 . . . . . . 198 A1
Minehead TA24 . . . . 201 A5
Fielders The BS22 . . . . . . 32 B4
Fieldgardens Rd BS39 . . . 58 F1
Field Gate TA3 . . . . 183 C8
Fieldgate La TA3 . . . . . . 183 B8
Fielding's Rd BA21 . . . . . 44 C6
Fielding Ct BA21 . . . . . . 219 C6
Fielding Ho BA2 . . . . 44 A6
Fielding Path BA6 . . . . . 206 E6
Fielding Rd
Street BA16 . . . . 207 B7
Yeovil BA21 . . . . 219 C6
Fieldins BA15 . . . . 64 E7
Field La
Chewton Mendip BA3 . . . . 94 F8
Kington Magna SP8 . . . . 177 E1
Penselwood BA9 . . . . . . 161 D2
Field Marshal Slim Ct 24
BS2 . . . . 227 C3
Field Rd TA10 . . . . 156 A1
Fields End TA1 . . . . 213 C2
Fields The BS22 . . . . 32 D2
Field View BA4 . . . . 205 C5
Field View Ct BA4 . . . . . 141 E1
Fieldway BS25 . . . . 52 B4
Field Way TA9 . . . . 104 D5
**Fifehead Bsns Ctr (Manor
Farm Trad Est)** BA8 . . . 190 F8
Fifehead Hill BA8 . . . . . 190 F8
Fifth Ave BS14 . . . . 23 B7
Filer Cl BA22 . . . . 79 D8
Fillymead DT10 . . . . . . 190 F5
Filwood Broadway BS4 . . 22 E8
Finch Cl
Shepton Mallet BA4 . . . . 204 F6
Weston-Super-Mare BS22 . . 49 E8
Finches The BS20 . . . . 2 F6
Finches Way TA8 . . . . . . 85 B1
Finger Cnr DT10 . . . . . . 190 F5
Finger La DT9 . . . . 225 D3
Finmere Gdns BS22 . . . . . 32 A4
Fircliff Pk BS20 . . . . 2 D7
Fire House Mews BA9 . . . 216 C3
Firgrove La BA2 . . . . 61 B1
Fir La BS40 . . . . 72 B5
Fir Leaze BS48 . . . . 8 B1
Firs Ct BS31 . . . . 24 C4
First Ave
Axminster EX13 . . . . . . 198 A4
Bath BA2 . . . . 44 E4

First Ave *continued*
Bristol BS14 . . . . 23 A7
Portbury BS20 . . . . 3 E5
Radstock BA3 . . . . 97 C8
First Dro TA7 . . . . 155 D3
Firs The
Bath BA2 . . . . 45 B1
Langport TA10 . . . . 172 A5
Limpley Stoke BA3 . . . . . 64 A5
Wheddon Cross TA24 . . . 129 E1
First Ho BA16 . . . . 207 B6
First Sedgemoor Dro
TA10 . . . . 155 E4
Fir Tor Ave BA5 . . . . . . 203 C5
Fir Tree Ave
Paulton BS39 . . . . 77 F4
Weston-Super-Mare BS24 . . 49 E4
Firtree Cl TA5 . . . . 134 A2
Fir Tree Cl TA6 . . . . . . 209 D4
Firway Cross EX16 . . . . 164 C3
Firwood Rd BA11 . . . . . 119 E4
Fisher's Hill
Glastonbury BA6 . . . . . . 206 D4
Holywell Lake TA21 . . . . 179 D7
Fisher's La
Dinnington TA17 . . . . . . 195 A7
Mark TA9 . . . . 106 D5
Fishers Brook BA11 . . . . 120 A5
Fishers Mead TA22 . . . . 163 D6
Fisherway La TA19 . . . . 195 A5
Fishpond Bottom Rd
DT6 . . . . 199 A1
Fishwell La BA6 . . . . . . 157 D4
Fitzharding Ho 8 BS1 . . 227 A3
Fitzharding Rd BS20 . . . . . 4 E3
Fitzroy Circ BS20 . . . . . . 2 F6
Fitzroy Ho 3 BA2 . . . . . 228 C3
Fivash Cl TA1 . . . . 168 D1
Five Acres 3 BA22 . . . . 197 F8
Five Arches Cl BA3 . . . . . 78 D2
Five Ashes BA22 . . . . . . 186 C2
Five Barrows Cross
EX36 . . . . 145 B7
Five Bells TA23 . . . . . . 202 B5
Five C Bsns Ctr BS21 . . . . 6 B1
Five Cross Way TA21 . . . 180 F6
Five Cross Ways TA22 . . 162 F7
Five Dials TA19 . . . . . . 183 C1
Five Hos TA21 . . . . 222 B8
Five Lords TA5 . . . . 134 B2
Fiveways Cl BS27 . . . . . . 90 A7
Fiveways Rdbt BS21 . . . . 219 A6
Fiveways Specl Sch
BA21 . . . . 219 D6
Five Yards 3 TA4 . . . . . 167 F8
Flagstaff Rd BS26 . . . . . . 68 D7
Flamingo Cres BS22 . . . . 49 E8
Flat The BS39 . . . . 58 D5
Flatwoods Cres BA2 . . . . 45 F3
Flatwoods Rd BA2 . . . . . 45 F3
Flax Bourton CE Prim Sch
BS48 . . . . 19 F8
Flax Bourton Rd BS8 . . . . 10 B3
Flaxfield Dr TA18 . . . . . 224 C5
Flax La DT9 . . . . 187 F4
Flaxpool Hill TA4 . . . . . 151 C6
Flax Row TA18 . . . . 224 C7
Flax Way BA21 . . . . 218 C6
Fleed Cross TA4 . . . . . . 166 A6
Fleet Air Arm Mus★
BA22 . . . . 174 B3
Fletcher's La BS26 . . . . . 87 D6
Fletcher Cl TA2 . . . . . . 213 B8
Fleur De Lys Dr BA14 . . . 83 F4
Flingers La BA9 . . . . . . 216 C4
Flint Cross TA4 . . . . . . 149 C1
Flints Cl BA11 . . . . 119 D4
Florence Brown Specl Sch
BS4 . . . . 22 D8
Florence Gr BS22 . . . . . . 49 B8
Florida Fields BA7 . . . . . 214 B6
Florida St BA7 . . . . 214 C5
Florida Terr BA3 . . . . . . 78 C2
Flowerdale Rd TA23 . . . . 202 C6
Flowerdown Bridge BS22 . . 49 D7
Flowerdown Rd BS24 . . . . 50 D4
Flowerfield BA11 . . . . . . 143 B8
Flowers Hill BS4 . . . . 23 E8
Flowers Ho 1 BA20 . . . . 219 B4
Flowerstone BA3 . . . . . . 114 D7
Flowerwell Rd BS13 . . . . 22 B5
Flushing Mdw BA21 . . . . 219 E5
Foghamshire La BA11 . . . 143 D5
Foldhill Cl 25 TA12 . . . . 185 E6
Foldhill La
Ash BA22 . . . . 186 A6
Martock TA12 . . . . 185 F6
Folke La DT9 . . . . 189 A1
Folleigh Cl BS41 . . . . 11 B2
Folleigh Dr BS41 . . . . . . 11 B2
Folleigh La BS41 . . . . 11 B2
Folliott Rd BA6 . . . . . . 206 E6
Folly Cl
Cannington TA5 . . . . . . 135 B2
Midsomer Norton BA3 . . . 96 C7
Folly Dr BA4 . . . . 159 C7
Folly Dro TA19 . . . . 183 A5
Folly Farm Nature Reserve★
BS39 . . . . 58 B5
Folly Fields BA21 . . . . . 219 B6
Folly La
Buckland St Mary TA20 . . 182 A1
Kington Magna SP8 . . . . 177 F2
Nether Compton DT9 . . . 187 F4
North Wootton BA4 . . . . 140 C4
Shipham BS25 . . . . 70 E7
South Cadbury BA22 . . . . 175 D4

Folly La *continued*
Weston-Super-Mare BS23 . . 48 E1
Folly Rd TA12 . . . . 185 B7
Folly The
Cold Ashton SN14 . . . . 12 F6
Ditcheat BA4 . . . . 159 C7
Paulton BS39 . . . . 77 F6
Saltford BS31 . . . . 25 F2
Fons George TA1 . . . . 212 F2
Fons George Cl TA1 . . . . . 212 E2
Fons George Rd TA1 . . . . 212 F2
Fonthill Rd BA1 . . . . 27 E2
Font La BA22 . . . . 197 B7
Fontmell Ct BS14 . . . . 23 D7
Font Villas BA22 . . . . 197 B8
Football La BA9 . . . . 216 B4
Footlands Cl TA1 . . . . 212 F1
Forbes Fraser Hospl BA1 . 44 B8
Forche's La TA24 . . . . . . 131 D3
Forches Cnr EX15 . . . . 181 A4
Forde Abbey & Gdns*
TA20 . . . . 198 F8
Forde Pk BA21 . . . . 218 C7
Fordhay BA22 . . . . 196 E7
Fordhay Terr BA22 . . . . . . 196 E7
Ford La
Chewton Mendip BA3 . . . . . 94 D8
Pilton BA4 . . . . 140 F3
Stawell TA7 . . . . 137 A1
Yarley BA5 . . . . 139 B8
Fordmill Cross EX16 . . . . 164 D1
Ford Orch EX16 . . . . 178 D1
Ford Rd
Bampton EX16 . . . . 164 C1
Peasedown St John BA2 . . . 79 D8
Wellow BA2 . . . . 62 F1
Wiveliscombe TA4 . . . . 210 C4
Ford St TA21 . . . . 222 F4
Forefield Pl BA2 . . . . 228 C1
Forefield Rise BA2 . . . . 45 B4
Forefield Terr BA2 . . . . 45 A4
Forelands BS23 . . . . 30 B1
Fore Leaze Dro TA12 . . . . 184 E7
Fore St
9 Bampton EX16 . . . . 164 B1
Bridgwater TA6 . . . . 208 F5
Cannington TA5 . . . . 135 B2
Castle Cary BA7 . . . . 214 C5
Chard TA20 . . . . 223 C4
Dulverton TA22 . . . . 163 D6
Holcombe Rogus TA21 . . . . 178 F5
Milverton TA4 . . . . 167 A4
North Petherton TA6 . . . . . 153 E3
Othery TA7 . . . . 155 C2
Tatworth TA20 . . . . 198 D8
Taunton TA1 . . . . 212 F3
Thorncombe TA20 . . . . 199 B6
Wellington TA21 . . . . 222 D6
West Camel BA22 . . . . 174 D3
Westonzoyland TA7 . . . . . . 154 E5
Williton TA4 . . . . 202 D3
Winsham TA20 . . . . 194 E1
Forest Dr BS23 . . . . 31 A1
Forest Dro TA3 . . . . 182 F5
Forester Ave BA2 . . . . 45 B8
Forester Ct BA2 . . . . 228 C4
Forester La BA2 . . . . 45 B8
Forester Rd
Bath BA2 . . . . 45 B8
Portishead BS20 . . . . 2 D4
Foresters Cl TA4 . . . . 202 E3
Forest Hill BA20 . . . . 218 E2
Forest La TA20 . . . . 193 E8
Forest Mill La TA19 . . . . . 183 B1
Forest Rd
Frome BA11 . . . . 120 B7
Horningsham BA11, BA12 . 144 B4
Forest Wlk BA13 . . . . 121 C4
Forge Cnr
Somerton TA11 . . . . 211 C4
Stogursey TA5 . . . . 134 B6
Forge End BS20 . . . . 3 E3
Forge La
East Chinnock BA22 . . . . . . 196 E8
Zeals SP8, BA12 . . . . 161 F2
Forgotten World Mus*
BS26 . . . . 68 D4
Fortescue Rd BA3 . . . . 78 F2
Fortfield Rd BS14 . . . . 23 B5
Forth Cl BA16 . . . . 207 A4
Fortnum Pl TA19 . . . . 221 D3
Forton La
Chard TA20 . . . . 223 F1
Tatworth TA20 . . . . 194 A1
Forton Rd TA20 . . . . 223 D2
Forts Orch BA22 . . . . 186 E6
Forum Bldgs BA1 . . . . 228 C1
Forum La BA4 . . . . 205 A7
Forum The BA21 . . . . 218 C6
Forward's La TA3 . . . . 181 C5
Fosgrove La TA3 . . . . 181 E7
Fosse Barton BS48 . . . . 8 D2
Fosse Cl
Nailsea BS48 . . . . 8 C2
Yeovil BA21 . . . . 218 D7
Fossedale Ave BS14 . . . . . 23 C6
Fossefield Rd BA3 . . . . 97 B6
Fosse Gdns BA2 . . . . 62 D8
Fosse Gn BA3 . . . . 78 E4
Fosse La
Batheaston BA1 . . . . 29 A4
Blackford BS28 . . . . 107 C3
Clandown BA3 . . . . 78 D3
Nailsea BS48 . . . . 8 D2
Shepton Mallet BA4 . . . . . . 205 D4
Fosse Lane Junc BA4 . . . 205 E5
Fosse Lane Trad Est
BA4 . . . . 205 D5
Fosse Rd BA3 . . . . 115 C3
Fosse The TA3 . . . . 170 C4
Fosseway
Clandown BA3 . . . . 78 E4
Clevedon BS21 . . . . 6 C2
Midsomer Norton BA3 . . . . . 97 A5
Radstock BA3 . . . . 97 C8
Fosse Way
Nailsea BS48 . . . . 8 C2
Yeovil BA21 . . . . 218 D7
Fosseway Cl BA2 . . . . 79 C7
Fosse Way Cotts BA3 . . . . 78 D2
Fosseway Ct
Bristol BS8 . . . . 226 A2
Ilchester BA22 . . . . 173 E2
Fosse Way Est BA2 . . . . . . 44 D1
Fosseway Gdns BA3 . . . . . 78 D1
Fosseway S BA3 . . . . 97 B7
Fosse Way Sch BA3 . . . . . . 97 C8
Fosseway The BS8 . . . . . . 226 A3
Foster's Almshouses 3
BS1 . . . . 227 A3
Foster's La BA22 . . . . 175 A7
Foster Cl BA5 . . . . 112 E1
Foster Rd BA11 . . . . 120 A3
Fosters 10 DT9 . . . . 225 E4
Foundry Barton 2 BA11 . 119 F5
Foundry Cotts BA2 . . . . 60 B4
Foundry Mews
Chard TA20 . . . . 223 C4
2 Crewkerne TA18 . . . . . . 224 C5
Foundry Rd TA1 . . . . 212 F4
Foundry Sq 1 TA18 . . . . . 224 C5
Foundry The BA1 . . . . 228 C3
Fountain Bldgs 7 BA1 . . 228 B3
Fountain Ho 8 BA1 . . . . 228 B3
Fountain La BS25 . . . . 70 B7
Fountains Cl BA21 . . . . . . 218 C7
Four Acre Mdw TA6 . . . . . 208 E6
Four Acre Mead 1 TA4 . 167 F8
Four Acres
Bristol BS13 . . . . 21 E4
Shepton Mallet BA4 . . . . . . 205 C5
Fouracres Cl TA1 . . . . 213 B1
Four Acres Cl
Bristol BS13 . . . . 21 F4
Nailsea BS48 . . . . 18 E8
Four Acres Prim Sch
BS13 . . . . 21 E4
Four Elms TA21 . . . . 179 A6
Four Forks La TA5 . . . . . . 152 F7
Four Lanes TA20 . . . . 193 F6
Fourth Ave
Bristol BS14 . . . . 23 B7
Radstock BA3 . . . . 97 D8
Fourways Cl BA7 . . . . 214 D6
Fouts Cross TA19 . . . . 184 F2
Fowey Cl BS48 . . . . 19 A8
Fowey Rd BS22 . . . . 32 A4
Fowler St TA2 . . . . 212 E6
Fownes Rd TA24 . . . . 201 B5
Fox's Dro BA11 . . . . 102 C1
Foxbury Cl BA11 . . . . 119 F6
Fox Cl TA21 . . . . 222 A6
Foxcombe La DT9 . . . . 176 C1
Foxcombe Rd
Bath BA1 . . . . 44 B7
Bristol BS14 . . . . 23 B4
Foxcote BA20 . . . . 218 C2
Foxcote Ave BA2 . . . . 79 E7
Foxcote Gdns BA11 . . . . . 120 C7
Foxdon Hill TA20 . . . . 223 A7
Foxdown Hill TA21 . . . . . . 222 C4
Foxdown Ho TA21 . . . . 222 C4
Foxdown Terr TA21 . . . . . 222 D4
Foxglove Cl BS22 . . . . 32 A5
Foxglove Way
Chard TA20 . . . . 223 F5
Yeovil BA22 . . . . 218 A5
Foxhanger La TA22 . . . . . 148 A2
Fox Hill BA2 . . . . 45 A2
Foxhill Ho BA2 . . . . 45 A1
Foxhole La TA3 . . . . 169 E5
Foxholes La BA2, BA11 . . . 100 D5
Fox & Hounds La BS31 . . . 24 F5
Fox Mdws TA18 . . . . 224 D7
Fox Rd BA16 . . . . 207 A5
Fox Way TA5 . . . . 134 B2
Foxwell La BA22 . . . . 196 C7
Foye Ho BS8 . . . . 11 E6
Frampton Rd TA6 . . . . 208 F2
Francis Cl TA3 . . . . 169 D5
Francis Fox Rd 7 BS23 . . . 48 E7
Francis Ho BS2 . . . . 227 A4
Francis Reed Cl TA7 . . . . 154 F5
Francis Wlk DT9 . . . . 225 E5
Francombe Ho BS1 . . . . . 227 A1
Frankcom Ho BA2 . . . . 45 B7
Frankford Mans 7 BS23 . 30 C1
Frankland Cl BA1 . . . . 27 B1
Frankley Bldgs BA1 . . . . . . 28 B1
Frankley Terr 6 BA1 . . . . 28 B1
Franklin's Way BS49 . . . . . 17 F1
Franklin Cl TA2 . . . . 212 B7
Franklin Ct BS1 . . . . 227 B1
Franklyn Terr BS39 . . . . . . 77 A4
Frank Webber Rd TA21 . . 222 A5
Fraser Cl
Burnham-on-S TA8 . . . . 104 C7
Weston-Super-Mare BS22 . . 31 F4
Frederick Ave BA2 . . . . 79 C7
Frederick Ct BA5 . . . . 203 C4
Frederick Pl BS8 . . . . 226 B3
Frederick Rd TA6 . . . . 209 C6
Fredrick Pl 5 BA20 . . . . 219 B4
Freedom Ave BA21 . . . . . . 218 E6
Free Hill BA5 . . . . 110 E6
Freeland Pl BS8 . . . . 11 F6
Freelands BS21 . . . . 16 C8
Freeling Ho BS1 . . . . 227 B1
Freemans La BS48 . . . . 20 B2
Freemantle Ho BS2 . . . . . 227 A4
Free St BA22 . . . . 173 E1
Freeview Rd BA2 . . . . 44 A5
Freezinghill La BS30 . . . . . 12 B4
Fremantle Rd TA1 . . . . 213 B1
Frenchay Rd BS23 . . . . 48 E4
French Cl
Nailsea BS48 . . . . 8 F3
Peasedown St John BA2 . . . 79 D7
Frenchfield Rd BA2 . . . . . . 79 D7
French Weir Ave TA1 . . . . 212 E5
French Weir Cl TA1 . . . . . 212 E4
Freshford CE Prim Sch
BA3 . . . . 64 B5
Freshford La BA3 . . . . 64 A4
Freshford Sta BA3 . . . . 64 C5
Freshmoor 6 BS21 . . . . 6 F3
Frethey Rd TA1, TA4 . . . . . 168 B3
Friar Ave BS22 . . . . 31 E3
Friarn Ave TA6 . . . . 208 F4
Friarn Lawn TA6 . . . . 208 F4
Friarn St TA6 . . . . 208 F4
Friars Ave BA21 . . . . 218 D6
Friars Cl BA22 . . . . 173 D1
Friars Way TA8 . . . . 104 B6
Friary BS1 . . . . 227 C1
Friary Cl
Clevedon BS21 . . . . 6 C5
Westwood BA15 . . . . 64 E4
Witham Friary BA11 . . . . . 143 C3
Friary Rd BS20 . . . . 2 B5
Friday St TA24 . . . . 200 F7
Friendly Row BS20 . . . . 4 C5
Friendship Gr 2 BS48 . . . . 8 F2
Friendship Rd BS48 . . . . 8 F3
Friggle St BA11 . . . . 120 D1
Frithfield La BA4 . . . . 205 C6
Frobisher Ave BS20 . . . . 2 B5
Frobisher Cl
Burnham-on-S TA8 . . . . 104 D8
Portishead BS20 . . . . 2 A5
Weston-Super-Mare BS22 . . 31 E4
Frobisher Way TA2 . . . . . . 212 B6
Frog La
Bristol BS1 . . . . 226 C2
Combe St Nicholas TA20 . . 193 D6
Creech St Michael TA3 . . . . 169 F6
Dinnington TA17 . . . . 195 B8
Enmore TA5 . . . . 153 A6
Felton BS40 . . . . 37 C8
Galhampton BA22 . . . . 175 E8
Haselbury Plucknett TA18 . 196 C6
Holcombe Rogus TA21 . . . . 178 F5
Ilminster TA19 . . . . 221 C4
Kingsdon TA11 . . . . 173 D5
Langport TA10 . . . . 171 F5
North Curry TA3 . . . . 170 D5
Shepton Mallet BA4 . . . . . . 205 E4
Stoke St Michael BA3 . . . . 116 A4
Ubley BS40 . . . . 55 D1
Wanstrow BA4 . . . . 142 F4
West Camel BA22 . . . . 174 D3
Winford BS40 . . . . 37 F5
Froglands La BS27 . . . . 90 C7
Froglands Way BS27 . . . . . 90 C7
Frogmore St BS1 . . . . 226 C2
Frogs La TA21 . . . . 180 F7
Frog St
Bampton EX16 . . . . 164 B1
East Quantoxhead TA5 . . . . 133 B6
Lopen TA13 . . . . 185 A1
Frogwell Cross TA4 . . . . . 164 D6
Frome Com Coll BA11 . . . 120 A7
Fromefield BA11 . . . . 120 A6
Fromefield Ho BA11 . . . . . 120 A6
Frome Mus* BA11 . . . . . . 119 F5
Frome Old Rd BA3 . . . . 79 A2
Frome Rd
Bath BA2 . . . . 44 D1
Beckington BA11 . . . . 101 D3
Bruton BA10 . . . . 215 F7
Maiden Bradley BA12 . . . . . 144 B3
Norton St Philip BA2 . . . . . . 81 F3
Nunney BA11 . . . . 143 B8
Radstock BA3 . . . . 79 B2
Rode BA11 . . . . 101 F7
Southwick BA14 . . . . 83 F3
Wingfield BA14 . . . . 83 C5
Frome St BS2 . . . . 227 C4
Frome Sta BA11 . . . . 120 A4
Frome View BA12 . . . . 144 C2
Front St
Chapel Allerton BS26 . . . . . . 88 D1
Chedzoy TA7 . . . . 154 D8
Churchill BS25 . . . . 52 E4
Monksilver TA4 . . . . 150 B8
Frost Hill BS49 . . . . 34 D7
Frost La TA19 . . . . 183 F4
Fry's La BS40 . . . . 53 F3
Fry's Well BA3 . . . . 96 D3
Fry's Wlk BA4 . . . . 205 A5
Frys House of Mercy 11
BS1 . . . . 227 B1
Frys La TA7 . . . . 154 E8
Frys Leaze BA1 . . . . 28 B2
Frys Mews TA1 . . . . 213 C2
Fryth Ho BS48 . . . . 9 D3
Fryth Way BS48 . . . . 8 C2
Fulford Ct TA24 . . . . 200 F7
Fulford Rd BS13 . . . . 22 C5
Fulford Wlk BS13 . . . . 22 B5
Fullands Ave TA1 . . . . 168 F1
Fullands Ct TA1 . . . . 168 F1
Fullands Rd TA1 . . . . 213 B1
Fullens Cl BS22 . . . . 49 D7
Fuller Cl BA4 . . . . 205 D5
Fuller Rd BA1 . . . . 28 C2
Fullers La BS25 . . . . 70 A6
Fullers Way BA2 . . . . 62 D8
Fullwell Cl BA3 . . . . 80 D1
Fulmar Rd BS22 . . . . 31 F1
Fulwell La BA3 . . . . 80 D1
Fulwood Cl TA1 . . . . 212 D1
Furge Gr BA8 . . . . 190 A6
Furge La BA8 . . . . 190 A6
Furland Rd
Crewkerne TA18 . . . . 224 C5
Weston-Super-Mare BS22 . . 31 C2
Furland Way TA18 . . . . . . 224 C5
Furlong Cl BA3 . . . . 96 F7
Furlong Cotts EX16 . . . . . . 179 A4
Furlong Gn TA3 . . . . 168 D1
Furlong La
Curry Rivel TA10 . . . . 171 C3
Milborne Port DT9 . . . . 217 B3
Furlong Pl BS26 . . . . 70 C1
Furlongs Ave TA6 . . . . 208 E2
Furlongs The DT9 . . . . 225 D5
Furnham Cl TA20 . . . . 223 D5
Furnham Cres TA20 . . . . . 223 D6
Furnham Rd TA20 . . . . 223 D5
Furnleaze BS39 . . . . 58 E3
Furpits La TA10 . . . . 172 B6
Furringdons Cross TA18 . 195 F6
Furze Cl
Bridgwater TA6 . . . . 208 D4
Weston-Super-Mare BS22 . . 31 B2
Furzeclose La BA4 . . . . . . 142 C7
Furzehill TA20 . . . . 223 D5
Furzehill La TA24 . . . . 147 C6
Furzeland Rd TA24 . . . . . . 124 A4
Furze Rd BS22 . . . . 31 A3
Furze The BA20 . . . . 218 C2
Fylton Croft BS14 . . . . 23 B3
Fyne Court Nat Res & Visitor
Ctr* TA5 . . . . 152 E3

G

Gables Cl BS29 . . . . 51 B3
Gables The TA21 . . . . 222 C6
Gabriel Cl BA11 . . . . 120 C6
Gadd's La BS27 . . . . 90 B8
Gagley La BA5 . . . . 111 B2
Gainesmarsh La TA10 . . . 172 C5
Gainsborough DT9 . . . . . . 217 C2
Gainsborough Ct BA1 . . . . 27 B1
Gainsborough Dr
Sherborne DT9 . . . . 225 B3
Weston-Super-Mare BS22 . . 31 F3
Gainsborough Gdns BA1 . 44 C8
Gainsborough Hill DT9 . . 225 E2
Gainsborough Rd BS31 . . . 24 F5
Gainsborough Way BA21 219 E8
Gale's Dro BA6 . . . . 139 D3
Galhampton Hill BA7,
BA22 . . . . 214 C2
Galingale Way BS20 . . . . 2 F5
Gallagher Ret Pk BS23 . . . 49 A5
Galleries The BS1 . . . . . . 227 B3
Galley Batch BA3 . . . . 114 F4
Galley Batch La BA3 . . . . 114 F4
Galloping Bottom La
TA23 . . . . 149 E5
Galmington Cl TA1 . . . . . . 212 C3
Galmington Dr TA1 . . . . . . 212 C2
Galmington La TA1 . . . . . . 212 C2
Galmington Rd TA1 . . . . . . 212 C2
Gamblyn Cross TA4 . . . . . 164 F5
Gammins Cotts TA24 . . . . 129 E2
Gander Cl BS13 . . . . 22 B5
Gandstone Cross TA4 . . . 150 D2
Ganesfield BA4 . . . . 141 E6
Gange's Hill TA3 . . . . 170 F2
Ganges Cl TA3 . . . . 170 F2
Gannet Rd BS22 . . . . 31 F1
Gants Mill La BA10 . . . . . 215 D5
Gaol La BA4 . . . . 205 C6
Garamond Ct BS1 . . . . 227 B1
Garden City TA10 . . . . 172 A6
Garden Cl
Bristol BS9 . . . . 5 C5
Norton Fitzwarren TA2 . . . . 168 B4
Weston-Super-Mare BS22 . . 31 E2
Garden Ct BS8 . . . . 226 A4
Gardeners Cl
Bradford On Tone TA4 . . . . 167 F1
Cheddar BS27 . . . . 90 B8
Gardeners Wlk BS41 . . . . . 11 B1
Garden Ground BA4 . . . . . 205 C4
Gardenhurst TA8 . . . . 85 B1
Garden Hurst Cl TA8 . . . . 104 B8
Garden Plot Hill TA3 . . . . 183 E7
Gardens Rd BS21 . . . . 6 C4
Gardens The
Dulverton TA22 . . . . 163 D7
East Pennard BA4 . . . . 158 F8
Sherborne DT9 . . . . 225 C3
1 Wellington TA21 . . . . . . 222 D5
2 Wells BA5 . . . . 203 D4
Garden Terr TA21 . . . . 222 B7
Garden Way TA24 . . . . 200 D7
Garden Wlk TA6 . . . . 208 E2
Gardiners Bsns Pk TA7 . . 136 F3
Gardiners Orch BS28 . . . . 108 C4
Gardner Ave BS13 . . . . 21 F7
Gardner Rd BS20 . . . . 2 D6
Garfield Terr 1 BA1 . . . . . 28 C2
Garlandhayes La EX15 . . . 180 E2
Garland Ho 7 BS21 . . . . . . 6 C2
Garner Ct 4 BS22 . . . . 32 B4
Garonor Way BS20 . . . . 3 F5
Garre Ho BA2 . . . . 43 F5
Garrett Rd BA20 . . . . 218 D3
Garrick Rd BA2 . . . . 43 F5
Garsdale BA11 . . . . 120 A4
Garsdale Rd BS22 . . . . 49 D8
Garston Cotts BS40 . . . . . . 54 E3
Garstone La TA16 . . . . 195 F8
Garston La
Blagdon BS40 . . . . 54 E3
Frome BA11 . . . . 120 A4
Marston Magna BA22 . . . . . 174 F1
Garston Lodge 11 BA11 . . 119 F4
Garston Rd BA11 . . . . 120 A4
Garstons
Bathford BA1 . . . . 29 D2
7 Clevedon BS21 . . . . 6 B1
Wrington BS40 . . . . 35 E1
Garstons Cl
Backwell BS48 . . . . 18 F6
Wrington BS40 . . . . 35 E2
Garstons Orch BS40 . . . . . . 35 D1
Garston St BA4 . . . . 205 C6
Garstons The BS20 . . . . 2 D4
Garth Rd BS13 . . . . 22 A8
Gartons Mead BA4 . . . . . . 141 E1
Gartons Mead Rd BA4 . . . 141 E1
Garvins Rd BA6 . . . . 206 C4
Gasferry Rd BS1 . . . . 226 B1
Gashay La EX13 . . . . 199 B3
Gas La TA17 . . . . 195 D7
Gason La BA22 . . . . 174 F4
Gasper St BA12 . . . . 161 E3
Gass Cl TA9 . . . . 104 F4
Gasson's La TA11 . . . . 211 C3
Gaston's La TA12 . . . . 185 D5
Gaston Ave BS31 . . . . 24 F6
Gaston Cl BA16 . . . . 207 C4
Gastons The BS11 . . . . 5 A8
Gaswell La TA7 . . . . 155 E8
Gatchell's La TA3 . . . . 181 B5
Gatchell Gn TA3 . . . . 168 D1
Gatchell Mdw TA3 . . . . . . 168 D1
Gatchells La TA4 . . . . 132 F2
Gatcombe Farm Ind Est
BS40 . . . . 35 D3
Gatcombe Rd BS13 . . . . 22 B5
Gate Cl EX13 . . . . 198 E3
Gatehouse Ave BS13 . . . . . 22 A5
Gatehouse Cl BS13 . . . . 22 A5
Gatehouse Ct BS13 . . . . 22 B5
Gatehouse Ctr The BS13 . . 22 B5
Gatehouse Way BS13 . . . . . 22 A5
Gate La BA5 . . . . 203 D2
Gaulden Manor* TA4 . . . . 150 F2
Gaunt's La BS1 . . . . 226 C2
Gaunton Cl TA1 . . . . 212 D2
Gaunts Cl BS20 . . . . 1 F4
Gaunts Rd TA6 . . . . 135 E6
Gay's Hill BA1 . . . . 228 C4
Gay Cl TA21 . . . . 222 E6
Gay Ct BA1 . . . . 28 E3
Gay Elms Prim Sch BS13 . 22 A4
Gay Elms Rd BS13 . . . . 22 A4
Gaylard's La TA20 . . . . . . 194 B5
Gay St
Bath BA1 . . . . 228 B3
Mells BA11 . . . . 118 B7
Wellington TA21 . . . . 222 E6
Gazelle Rd
Weston-Super-Mare BS24 . . 49 B3
Yeovil BA20 . . . . 218 D3
Gefle Cl BS1 . . . . 226 B1
Geldof Dr BA3 . . . . 78 A2
Gelosia Cl TA7 . . . . 154 F6
General Higgins Ho TA9 . 104 E3
Gennes Gr BA9 . . . . 216 C4
Gentle St
Frome BA11 . . . . 119 F4
Horningsham BA12 . . . . 144 E4
Geoffrey Cl BS13 . . . . 21 E6
George's Pl BA2 . . . . 45 B6
George's Rd BA1 . . . . 28 A1
George Cl BS48 . . . . 19 D7
George & Crown Cotts
TA17 . . . . 195 C7
George La
Marshfield SN14 . . . . 13 E8
South Petherton TA13 . . . . . 220 C4
George Maher Ct TA19 . . 221 C3
Georges Bldgs BA1 . . . . . . 28 C3
Georges Ground BA11 . . . 119 E2
George Sh Ctr The TA18 . 224 C6
Georges Ho BA2 . . . . 45 B6
Georges Mews TA1 . . . . . . 213 C2
George Smith Way BA22 . 218 A6
Georges Sq BS1 . . . . 227 B2
George St
Bath BA1 . . . . 228 B3
Bath, Bathwick BA2 . . . . 45 B6
Bridgwater TA6 . . . . 208 F5
Burnham-on-S TA8 . . . . 104 A7
Charlton Adam TA11 . . . . . 173 F7
Glastonbury BA6 . . . . 206 D5
Portishead BS20 . . . . 2 C2
Sherborne DT9 . . . . 225 D4
Taunton TA2 . . . . 212 F6
Wellington TA21 . . . . 222 D6
Weston-Super-Mare BS23 . . 48 E7
George Sweetman Cl
BA9 . . . . 216 D4
George Whitefield Ct
BS1 . . . . 227 B3
George William Ct TA6 . . 208 F4
Georgian Ct BA11 . . . . 119 D3
Georgian Ho BA2 . . . . 228 C2

Georgian House (Mus)★
BS1 . . . . 226 C2
Georgian View BA2 . . . . . . 44 C2
Gerard Rd BS23 . . . . 48 F8
Gerbestone La TA21 . . . 180 E6
Gerrard Bldgs BA2 . . . . . . 45 B7
Gerrard Cl BS4 . . . . 22 D7
Geys Hill BA12 . . . . 144 D8
Giant's Grave TA20 . . . . 193 A4
Giant's Grave Rd TA20 . . 193 A7
Gibbet La BS14 . . . . 23 D1
Gibbet Rd BA9 . . . . 176 B6
Gibbs' La TA19 . . . . 184 D5
Gibbsfold Rd BS13 . . . . . . 22 C4
Gibbs Marsh Trad Est
DT10 . . . . 190 D6
Gibraltar Cotts TA24 . . . 123 E4
Giddy La BS41 . . . . 116 A4
Gielgud Cl TA8 . . . . 104 C6
Gifford Cl TA20 . . . . 223 D5
Giffords La TA18 . . . . . . 196 C5
Giffords Orch TA12 . . . . 185 A7
Giffords Pl BS13 . . . . 22 A7
Gigg La SP8 . . . . 177 C2
Gilbeck Rd BS48 . . . . 8 C2
Gilberts Cnr BA6 . . . . . . 158 A6
Gilbert Scott Ho BA5 . . 113 A1
Gilbert Scott Mews BA5 . 113 A1
Gilbert Scott Rd BA5 . . . 113 A1
Gilberyn Dr BS22 . . . . 32 A3
Gilda Cl BS14 . . . . 23 C5
Gilda Cres BS14 . . . . 23 B6
Gilda Par BS14 . . . . 23 C5
Gilda Sq W BS14 . . . . 23 B5
Giles TA10 . . . . 171 D4
Giles Farm BA5 . . . . 113 A1
Gillards TA1 . . . . 212 B4
Gillards Cl TA21 . . . . 222 B4
Gillards Mead TA3 . . . . . 192 A7
Gill Cres TA1 . . . . 212 B1
Gillebank Cl BS14 . . . . . . 23 C5
Gillingham Ct TA20 . . . . 223 D5
Gillingham Terr ❸ BA1 . . 28 B1
Gill Mews BS22 . . . . 32 B4
Gillmore Cl BS22 . . . . 31 D1
Gillmore Rd BS22 . . . . . . 31 D1
Gills La BS26 . . . . 87 B5
Gillson Cl BS24 . . . . 49 D2
Gimblett Rd BS22 . . . . . . 32 B4
Gipsy Cross TA4 . . . . . . 166 A2
Gipsy Dro TA20 . . . . 193 C4
Gipsy La
Burcott BA5 . . . . 139 E8
Frome BA11 . . . . 120 B7
Glastonbury BA6 . . . . . . 139 D1
Halse TA4 . . . . 167 B6
Sampford Arundel TA21 . . 179 D5
Staplegrove TA2 . . . . . . 212 B7
Street BA16 . . . . 207 E4
Taunton TA1 . . . . 212 C3
Wells BA5 . . . . 203 A4
Gladstone Ct BA2 . . . . . . 45 C2
Gladstone Pl BA2 . . . . . . 45 C2
Gladstone Rd
Bath BA2 . . . . 45 C2
Bristol BS14 . . . . 23 B6
Gladstone St
Midsomer Norton BA3 . . . 78 B3
Taunton TA2 . . . . 212 E6
Gladstone Terr
Minehead TA24 . . . . 201 A5
Wellington TA21 . . . . . . 222 E6
Gladstone Villas BA3 . . 115 C5
Glanfield Cl TA4 . . . . . . 167 E8
Glanfield Terr BA22 . . . . 173 F1
Glanvil Ave TA20 . . . . . . 223 C5
Glanville Dr BS39 . . . . . . 75 E6
Glanville Rd BS28 . . . . . 108 C4
Glanvil Rd BA16 . . . . . . 207 C3
Glass's Cross TA4 . . . . . 149 E1
Glass's Rocks La TA4 . . 149 D1
Glasses Mead TA1 . . . . . 212 B2
Glass House Hill DT9 . . 225 E3
Glastonbury Abbey★
BA6 . . . . 206 E4
Glastonbury Cl BS48 . . . . . 9 B1
Glastonbury Ct BA21 . . 218 D6
Glastonbury Rd
Meare BA6 . . . . 138 D4
Wells BA5 . . . . 203 B2
Glastonbury Tor★ BA6 . . 139 D1
Glastonbury Way BS22 . . 32 A2
Glaston Ho BA16 . . . . . . 207 D7
Glaston Rd BA16 . . . . . . 207 D7
Glebe Ave BS20 . . . . 2 E4
Glebe Cl BS41 . . . . 11 C2
Glebe Cotts TA3 . . . . . . 169 E2
Glebe Cres TA24 . . . . . . 200 E8
Glebe Ho
Bath BA2 . . . . 45 B5
Portishead BS20 . . . . 2 E4
Weston-Super-Mare BS22 . . 31 F3
Glebe Inf Sch The BS49 . . 34 C4
Gleband Cl TA7 . . . . 156 B8
Glebelands
❼ Merriott TA16 . . . . . . 195 F7
Minehead TA24 . . . . 200 E8
Norton Sub Hamdon TA14 . 185 F3
Nunney BA11 . . . . 143 B7
Radstock BA3 . . . . 78 D1
Glebelands BS27 . . . . 90 B6
Glebe Paddock BA5 . . . 139 E8
Glebe Rd
Bath BA2 . . . . 44 B4
Clevedon BS21 . . . . 6 C2

Glebe Rd continued
Long Ashton BS41 . . . . . . 11 C2
Portishead BS20 . . . . 2 E4
Weston-Super-Mare BS23 . . 48 E8
Glebe The
Fivehead TA3 . . . . 170 F1
Freshford BA3 . . . . 64 B4
Hinton Charterhouse BA2 . . 63 D2
Queen Camel BA22 . . . . 174 F3
Timberscombe TA24 . . . 130 B4
Timsbury BA2 . . . . 60 B3
Wrington BS40 . . . . 35 D2
Glebe Way BS27 . . . . 90 C6
Glebe Wlk BS31 . . . . 24 C4
Glebe Yd TA10 . . . . 172 E4
Glen Ave BS8 . . . . 10 F8
Glenavon Pk BS9 . . . . 5 C4
Glen Brook BS9 . . . . 5 D4
Glencairn Ct BA2 . . . . . . 45 B6
Glen Cl TA2 . . . . 168 B5
Glencoe Bsns Pk BS23 . . 49 A7
Glencoe Terr TA3 . . . . . 168 D1
Glencot La BA5 . . . . 203 A7
Glencot Rd BA5 . . . . 203 A6
Glencroft Way BS22 . . . . 31 E3
Glendale BS8 . . . . 11 F6
Glendevon Rd BS14 . . . . 23 A3
Glen Dr
Bristol BS9 . . . . 5 D5
Taunton TA2 . . . . 168 F6
Gleneagles Cl
Nailsea BS48 . . . . 9 A1
Weston-Super-Mare BS22 . 31 F3
Glenmore Rd TA24 . . . . 201 A7
Glen The
Saltford BS31 . . . . 25 F1
Weston-Super-Mare BS22 . 31 B2
Glenthorne Ave BA21 . . 219 B7
Glenthorne Nature Trail
Gate★ EX35 . . . . 122 D5
Glenthorne Rd ❾ TA2 . . 212 F6
Glentworth Ct ❿ BS23 . . 30 C1
Glentworth Rd BS8 . . . . 226 B2
Glen View BA3 . . . . 115 C7
Glenview Ho BA2 . . . . . . 79 D8
Glenville Rd BA21 . . . . . 219 D6
Glenwood Gdns TA2 . . . 212 F8
Glenwood Mans BS23 . . 30 D1
Glenwood Rise BS20 . . . . 1 F5
Glen Yeo Terr BS49 . . . . 34 C4
Globe Orch TA19 . . . . . . 196 C6
Gloucester Ho ⓫ BS2 . . 227 C4
Gloucester La ⓲ BS2 . . 227 C3
Gloucester Rd
Bath BA1 . . . . 28 C3
Bridgwater TA6 . . . . 208 F2
Burnham-on-S TA8 . . . . 104 C7
Upper Swainswick BA1 . . 28 A7
Gloucester Row ❻ BS8 . 11 F7
Gloucester St
❺ Bath BA1 . . . . 228 B3
❺ Bristol BS2 . . . . 227 B4
❽ Bristol, Clifton BS8 . . 11 F7
Taunton TA1 . . . . 213 A4
Weston-Super-Mare BS23 . 48 E8
Glovers DT9 . . . . 225 D5
Glovers Cl
Milborne Port DT9 . . . . 217 D2
❹ Stoke sub Hamdon
TA14 . . . . 185 F4
Glovers Ct BA20 . . . . . . 218 F4
Glovers Field BS25 . . . . . 70 F7
Glovers Wlk ⓲ BA20 . . 219 B4
Glynsmead TA20 . . . . . . 198 C8
Glynswood TA20 . . . . . . 223 C5
Goathill La TA4 . . . . 165 A7
Goathill Rd DT9 . . . . . . 189 B4
Godhams La TA4 . . . . . . 165 A7
Godminster La BA10 . . . 215 E6
Godminster La BA10 . . . 215 E4
Godney Dro BA5 . . . . . . 139 B6
Godney Rd BA5, BA6 . . 139 A4
Godwin Dr BS48 . . . . 8 C3
Goeffrey Farrant Wlk
TA1 . . . . 213 A5
Goes La BA7 . . . . 158 F2
Gogs Orch BS28 . . . . . . 108 C3
Gold Corner Dro TA9 . . 137 A6
Goldcrest Way BS20 . . . . 2 F6
Goldcroft BA21 . . . . 219 B6
Goldcroft Ct BA21 . . . . 219 B6
Goldenhaye La TA20 . . . 194 D3
Golden Hill
Batcombe BA4 . . . . 142 D2
Shepton Mallet BA4 . . . 205 B7
Golding's La DT9 . . . . . 217 C1
Golding Cl BA5 . . . . 203 C4
Goldney Ave BS8 . . . . . . 226 A2
Goldney Cl BS39 . . . . 58 F1
Goldney Rd BS8 . . . . . . 226 A2
Goldney Way BS39 . . . . . 58 F1
Goldsmiths La EX13 . . . 198 A4
Goldsmoor Cross EX16 . 178 E3
Gold St DT10 . . . . 190 B4
Golf Club La BS31 . . . . . 25 E2
Golf Course Rd BA2 . . . . 45 D6
Golf Links La BA3 . . . . . 114 E3
Golf Links Rd TA8 . . . . . 85 A2
Golledge El BA3 . . . . 96 C4

Gooch Cl
Bridgwater TA6 . . . . 209 B4
Frome BA11 . . . . 120 D6
Gooch Way BS22 . . . . . . 32 B3
Good's La TA5 . . . . 152 C5
Goodard Dr BS22 . . . . . . 32 B4
Goodeaves Cl BA3 . . . . 117 A7
Goodeaves Cotts BA3 . . 117 A7
Goodeve Pk BS9 . . . . 5 D3
Goodeve Rd BS9 . . . . 5 D3
Good Hill BA4 . . . . 142 E2
Goodlands La TA11 . . . . 212 F4
Goodwin Dr BS14 . . . . . 22 F4
Goodymoor Ave BA5 . . 203 B5
Goodymoor La BA5 . . . . 203 B5
Goold Cl BA2 . . . . 43 A8
Goosander Cl TA24 . . . . 201 C4
Goosard La BS39 . . . . . . 77 E8
Gooseacre Ct BA22 . . . . 197 B8
Gooseacre La
East Coker BA22 . . . . . . 197 B8
Yeovil BA22 . . . . 218 A1
Gooseham La BS49 . . . . 108 F4
Gooseham Mead BS49 . . 34 D4
Goose La
Chilton Polden TA7 . . . . 137 B3
Horton TA19 . . . . 183 C2
Gooselade BA16 . . . . . . 207 C3
Gooseland Cl BS14 . . . . 22 F3
Goose St BA11 . . . . 101 E5
Goosey La BS22 . . . . 32 C2
Gordano Bsns Pk BS20 . . 2 E5
Gordano Gdns BS20 . . . . 4 B4
Gordano Rd BS20 . . . . 3 D7
Gordano View BS20 . . . . 2 C5
Gordano Way BS20 . . . . . 3 F5
Gordon's Cl TA1 . . . . . . 213 B1
Gordon Bldgs BA3 . . . . . 79 A3
Gordon Rd
Bath BA2 . . . . 45 B5
Bristol BS8 . . . . 226 B3
Peasedown St John BA2 . . 79 D8
Taunton TA1 . . . . 213 A3
Weston-Super-Mare BS23 . 48 F7
Yeovil BA21 . . . . 219 C6
Gordon Terr TA6 . . . . . . 209 A5
Gorefield TA13 . . . . 220 D2
Gorehedge ⓮ BA11 . . . 119 F4
Gore La
Chapmanslade BA13 . . . 121 B4
Pitney TA10 . . . . 172 C2
Gore Rd TA8 . . . . 85 A1
Gores Pk BS39 . . . . 59 B2
Gore Sq TA4 . . . . 167 E8
Gorlangton Cl BS14 . . . . 23 A7
Gorlegg TA21 . . . . 179 E5
Gorpit La TA5 . . . . 134 F8
Gorse La
Bristol BS8 . . . . 226 B2
Cold Ashton BS30, SN14 . . 12 D7
Gort Rd TA2 . . . . 168 B6
Gosford Mans ❻ BS23 . . 30 C1
Goslet Rd BS14 . . . . 23 E5
Goss Barton BS48 . . . . . . 8 D1
Goss Cl BS48 . . . . 8 C1
Goss Dr BA16 . . . . 207 B3
Goss La BS48 . . . . 8 C1
Goss View BS48 . . . . 8 C1
Goswell La BA16 . . . . . . 207 C5
Goswell Rd BA16 . . . . . . 207 C5
Goulston Rd BS13 . . . . . 22 A5
Goulston Wlk BS13 . . . . 22 A5
Gournay Ct BS39 . . . . . . 77 A3
Governors Ho BA2 . . . . . 44 D6
Govier's La TA23 . . . . . . 202 C7
Grace Cl BS49 . . . . 34 B8
Grace Dr BA3 . . . . 78 A2
Grace Martin's La BA22 . 174 F3
Grace Rd BS22 . . . . 32 B4
Gradwell Cl BS22 . . . . . . 32 B3
Grafton Cl TA2 . . . . 213 A8
Graham Rd BS23 . . . . . . 48 E7
Graham Way TA4 . . . . . . 167 E6
Grainger Ct BS11 . . . . 4 E7
Grain Store The ❾ BS1 . 227 B2
Graitney Cl BS49 . . . . . . 35 A8
Granary Orch DT9 . . . . 187 F5
Granary The ❽ BS1 . . . 227 B2
Granary Way TA3 . . . . . 181 D8
Granby Hill BS8 . . . . 11 F6
Granby Rd BA22 . . . . . . 174 A2
Grand Par BA2 . . . . 228 C2
Grand Pier★ BS23 . . . . . 48 D7
Grand Western Canal
(Country Pk)★ EX16 . . 178 F2
Granfield Gdns BS40 . . . 53 A5
Grange Ave
Highbridge TA9 . . . . . . 104 C3
Street BA16 . . . . 207 B6
Grange Bsns Pk The BS24 . 33 A5
Grange Cl
Cannington TA5 . . . . . . 135 C2
Wellington TA21 . . . . . . 222 E5
Weston-Super-Mare BS23 . 48 E1
Grange Cnr DT8 . . . . . . 199 E7
Grange Dr
Bridgwater TA6 . . . . . . 208 D4
Taunton TA1 . . . . 213 A6
Grange End BA3 . . . . 97 B7

Grange Farm Rd BS49 . . 17 A1
Grangefields BA16 . . . . 207 D5
Grange Gdns TA2 . . . . . 213 A7
Grange Paddock TA9 . . 106 E4
Grange Rd
Bristol, Bishopsworth
BS13 . . . . 22 A5
Bristol BS8 . . . . 226 A4
Frome BA11 . . . . 120 A7
Huntspill TA9 . . . . 136 A8
Saltford BS31 . . . . 25 C3
Street BA16 . . . . 207 D7
Weston-Super-Mare BS23 . 48 E1
Grange The
Bath BA1 . . . . 27 C1
Bristol BS9 . . . . 5 D7
Chilton Polden TA7 . . . . 137 B2
Flax Bourton BS48 . . . . . 19 F7
Kingston St Mary TA2 . . 168 E8
Langport TA10 . . . . 171 E5
Grange Way TA6 . . . . . . 135 F5
Grant's Hill EX16, TA22 . 163 F7
Grant's La
Wedmore BS28 . . . . . . 108 D4
Wiveliscombe TA4 . . . . 210 D6
Grants Ct BA9 . . . . 216 B4
Grants La BA9 . . . . 216 C4
Granville Chapel ❺ BS8 . 11 F6
Granville Rd BA1 . . . . . . 27 E4
Granville Way DT9 . . . . 225 E6
Grasmere TA6 . . . . 208 C5
Grasmere Dr BS23 . . . . . 48 F4
Grass Meers Dr BS14 . . 23 A4
Grassmere Rd BS49 . . . . 34 B8
Grass Rd TA8 . . . . 65 F4
Grass Royal BA21 . . . . . 219 C6
Grass Royal Jun Sch
BA21 . . . . 219 C6
Gratton La EX35 . . . . . . 122 A4
Gravelands La TA3 . . . . 169 D3
Gravel Hill BS40 . . . . 56 B7
Gravel La TA3, TA19 . . . 183 C6
Gravel Pit Cross EX36 . . 145 E6
Gravel Pits DT9 . . . . . . 225 D3
Gravel Wlk BA1 . . . . 228 B3
Gravenchon Way BA16 . 207 A6
Graves ❼ TA6 . . . . 209 B4
Gray's Almshouses ⓱
TA1 . . . . 213 A4
Gray's Hill EX15 . . . . . . 180 D1
Gray's La EX15 . . . . 180 D1
Gray Hollow BS40 . . . . . 74 F4
Grayling Ho BS9 . . . . 5 F7
Grays Ave TA7 . . . . 154 E6
Grays Hill BA2 . . . . 80 B5
Grays Rd TA1 . . . . 213 B4
Grays Terr TA1 . . . . 213 B4
Great Ann St BS2 . . . . . 227 C3
Great Barton BA4 . . . . . 205 D6
Great Bedford St BA1 . . 228 B4
Great Bow Yd TA10 . . . 171 F5
Great Brockeridge BS9 . . 5 F6
Great Cnr ❺ BA21 . . . . 218 C6
Great Field La TA14 . . . 185 F4
Great Gdns BA4 . . . . . . 205 C6
Great George St
Bristol, Brandon Hill BS1 . 226 C2
Bristol, St Pauls BS2 . . . 227 C4
Great Hayles Rd BS14 . . 23 A6
Great Hill BA9 . . . . 161 D2
Great House Cl BA6 . . . 138 D4
Great House St TA24 . . . 130 B4
Great La
Knole TA10 . . . . 173 A4
Shepton Beauchamp TA19 . 184 E3
Great Mdw TA22 . . . . . 163 D6
Great Mead TA1 . . . . . . 212 B3
Great Orch BA22 . . . . . . 173 E2
Great Ostry BA4 . . . . . . 205 B6
Great Pit La BA22, DT9 . 188 B7
Great Pulteney St BA2 . 228 C3
Great Ringaton La EX36 . 162 B6
Great St TA4 . . . . 185 E2
Great Stanhope St BA1 . 228 A2
Greatstone La BS40 . . . . 37 F5
Great Western La TA11 . 211 D3
Great Western Rd
Chard TA20 . . . . 223 D5
Clevedon BS21 . . . . 6 D2
Martock TA12 . . . . 185 E7
Great Western Terr
BA21 . . . . 219 D5
Great Withy Dro BA5 . . 206 C8
Great Wood Cl TA6 . . . . 209 A2
Grebe Cl TA6 . . . . 209 B4
Grebe Ct TA6 . . . . 209 B4
Grebe Rd
Bridgwater TA6 . . . . . . 209 B4
Taunton TA2 . . . . 213 B6
Green's Dro BA6 . . . . . . 206 C7
Green's Hill TA4 . . . . . . 151 C5
Greenacre
Wembdon TA6 . . . . 208 D6
Weston-Super-Mare BS22 . 31 B2
Green Acre Rd BS14 . . . . 23 A3
Greenacres
Bath BA1 . . . . 27 B3
Bristol BS9 . . . . 5 E7
Midsomer Norton BA3 . . . 77 C1
Greenacres Pk BA21 . . . 187 A5
Greenaleigh Lower Rd
TA24 . . . . 125 C4
Greenaleigh Upper Rd
TA24 . . . . 125 C4

Greenbank Gdns BA1 . . . 27 B1
Greenbrook Terr TA1 . . 212 E4
Green Cl
Holford TA5 . . . . 133 C4
Paulton BS39 . . . . 77 E6
Sparkford BA22 . . . . . . 175 A5
Green Cotts BA2 . . . . . . 45 C2
Greendale TA19 . . . . . . 221 B3
Greenditch Ave BS13 . . 22 C5
Greenditch Cl BS13 . . . . 96 C3
Green Ditch La BA3 . . . . 96 B6
Greendown Pl BA2 . . . . . 45 A1
Green Dragon Ct ❹ TA6 . 208 F4
Green Dro TA11 . . . . 158 A4
Green Farm Ind Est
BA13 . . . . 121 C4
Greenfield Cres BS48 . . . . 8 E3
Greenfield La TA7 . . . . . 136 D2
Greenfield Pk BS20 . . . . . 2 C2
Greenfield Pl BS23 . . . . . 48 C8
Greenfield Prim Sch BS4 . 22 C4
Greenfields
Bridgwater TA6 . . . . . . 208 F3
Crewkerne TA18 . . . . . . 224 C7
Greenfields Ave BS29 . . 51 A3
Greenfield Terr TA20 . . 198 D8
Greenfield Wlk BA3 . . . . 78 A3
Greenfylde CE First Sch
TA19 . . . . 221 C3
Greengage Cl ❻ BS22 . . 49 E8
Green Gate EX16 . . . . . 178 B2
Greenham's Cross TA14 . 185 F2
Greenham Bsns Pk TA21 . 179 E7
Greenham La TA18 . . . . 199 E7
Greenham Yd TA18 . . . . 199 E7
Greenhayes BS27 . . . . . . 90 B8
Greenhays Foot EX13 . . 198 B6
Greenhill DT9 . . . . 225 D4
Greenhill Cl
Nailsea BS48 . . . . 8 D2
Weston-Super-Mare BS22 . 32 A3
Greenhill Croft BS25 . . . 52 B4
Greenhill Cross EX36 . . 162 B2
Greenhill La
Alston Sutton BS26 . . . . 88 E5
Sandford BS25 . . . . 52 B4
Greenhill Pl BA3 . . . . . . 78 A3
Greenhill Rd
Midsomer Norton BA3 . . . 78 A3
Sandford BS25 . . . . 52 B4
Yeovil BA21 . . . . 219 B6
Green Knap La TA20 . . . 193 C2
Green La
Bristol BS11 . . . . 4 B8
Brompton Regis TA22 . . 148 B1
Butcombe BS40 . . . . 55 A7
Castle Cary BA7 . . . . . . 214 F4
Chard Junction TA20 . . 198 D7
Chardstock EX13 . . . . . 198 B7
Chard TA20 . . . . 193 F1
Charlton Horethorne DT9 . 176 A2
Charlton Horethorne, Sigwells
DT9 . . . . 175 F2
Corfe TA3 . . . . 181 E7
Corsley Heath BA12 . . . 144 E7
Cricket St Thomas TA20 . 194 F3
East Chinnock BA22 . . . 196 E8
East Coker BA22 . . . . . 197 B8
Failand BS8 . . . . 10 C4
Farrington Gurney BS39 . 76 F6
Felton BS40 . . . . 37 C3
Fivehead TA3 . . . . 170 E2
Freshford BA3 . . . . 64 B3
Frome BA11 . . . . 119 D4
Hinton Charterhouse BA2 . 63 E1
Ilminster TA19 . . . . 183 E2
Kington Magna SP8 . . . 177 E2
Leigh u M BA3, BA11 . . 117 B2
Marshfield SN14 . . . . . . 13 E8
Oakhill BA3 . . . . 114 E4
Pitcombe BA7 . . . . 215 A1
Priddy BA5 . . . . 73 B7
Queen Camel BA22 . . . . 174 F3
Sampford Arundel TA21 . 179 F4
Shepton Beauchamp TA19 . 184 E3
Sherborne DT9 . . . . . . 188 E1
Southwick BA14 . . . . 83 D1
Stoke St Michael BA3 . . 116 B5
Stratton-on-f BA3 . . . . . 96 E1
Street BA16 . . . . 207 D4
Tatworth TA20 . . . . 193 D1
Winsley BA15 . . . . 64 F6
Greenland La TA24 . . . . 131 B1
Greenland Rd BS22 . . . . 31 D1
Greenlands TA1 . . . . . . 213 B2
Greenlands Rd BA22 . . . 79 C8
Green Lane Ave BA16 . . 207 C6
Green Lane End TA19 . . 184 E3
Green Lane Gate BA9 . . 176 A8
Green Mead BA21 . . . . . 218 C5
Greenmoor La BA21 . . . 187 A5
Green Ore Est BA5 . . . . 94 B1
Green Park La BA11 . . . 101 F6
Green Park Mews BA1 . 228 A2
Green Park Rd BA1 . . . . 228 B2
Green Parlor Rd BA3 . . . 79 D1
Green Pastures Rd BS48 . 9 B2
Green Pits La BA11 . . . . 143 B7
Green Pk
Bath BA2 . . . . 228 A2
Rode BA11 . . . . 101 C5
Green Quarry BA21 . . . 219 A6
Green Ride BA12 . . . . . 161 F7
Green Rise BS39 . . . . . . 58 F3
Greenridge Cl BS13 . . . . 21 E4
Greenslade Gdns BS48 . . 8 D3
Greens Pl BA5 . . . . 203 D3

Green St
Bath BA1 . . . . 228 C2
Hinton St George TA17 . . . 195 D7
Shoscombe BA2 . . . . 79 E5
Ston Easton BA3 . . . . 95 E8
Greenstalls Pk BA22 . . . . 173 F2
Green The
Backwell BS48 . . . . 19 A5
8 Barwick BA22 . . . . . . 197 F8
Bath BA2 . . . . 44 D1
Bridgwater TA6 . . . . 208 E2
Brushford TA22 . . . . 163 E4
Coleford BA3 . . . . 116 F6
Easton BA5 . . . . 111 A4
Faulkland BA3 . . . . 80 D2
Hinton Charterhouse BA2 . . 63 F1
Ilchester BA22 . . . . 173 E2
Locking BS24 . . . . 50 A4
33 Martock TA12 . . . . . . 185 E6
Pill BS20 . . . . 4 D4
Pitminster TA3 . . . . 181 E6
1 Sherborne DT9 . . . . . . 225 D4
Williton TA4 . . . . 202 D3
Winscombe BS25 . . . . 70 A7
Green Tree Rd BA3 . . . . . . 78 B3
Greenvale Cl BA2 . . . . 60 B1
Greenvale Dr BA2 . . . . 60 B1
Greenvale Rd BS39 . . . . . . 77 D5
Greenway
Bishops Lydeard TA4 . . . . . 167 E8
Faulkland BA3 . . . . 80 C1
Ilminster TA19 . . . . 221 B1
Minehead TA24 . . . . 200 D6
Monkton Heathfield TA2 . . 169 B8
North Curry TA3 . . . . 170 B3
Watchet TA23 . . . . 202 B7
Greenway Ave TA2 . . . . . 212 E6
Greenway Cl BA9 . . . . . . 216 D4
Greenway Cotts TA4 . . . . 167 E8
Greenway Cres TA2 . . . . 212 E7
Greenway Ct BA2 . . . . 44 F4
Greenway La
Barrington TA13 . . . . 184 E5
Bath BA2 . . . . 45 A4
Blagdon Hill TA3 . . . . 181 B5
Cold Ashton SN14 . . . . 12 D5
Combe St Nicholas TA20 . . 193 E6
Stoke St Mary TA3 . . . . . . 169 D2
Wiveliscombe TA4 . . . . . . 210 A5
Greenway Pk 3 BS21 . . . .6 F3
Greenway Rd
Castle Cary BA7 . . . . 214 B6
Rockwell Green TA21 . . . . 222 A5
Taunton TA2 . . . . 212 E6
Greenways BA3 . . . . 96 C2
Greenway Terr TA2 . . . . 168 D8
Greenwell La BS40 . . . . . . 53 C7
Greenwood Cl TA9 . . . . . 136 B8
Greenwood Rd
Weston-Super-Mare BS22 . . 31 E2
Yeovil BA21 . . . . 218 D7
Gregory Mead BS49 . . . . . 17 A1
Gregorys Gr BA2 . . . . 62 D8
Gregorys Tyning BS39 . . . 77 F6
Greinton BS24 . . . . 49 A2
Grenville Ave BS24 . . . . . 50 A4
Grenville Cl BA6 . . . . 157 E4
Grenville Ho TA6 . . . . . . 208 F2
Grenville Pl 7 BS1 . . . . . 11 F5
Grenville Rd TA6 . . . . . . 104 C7
Grenville View TA4 . . . . 167 E6
Grey's Cnr BA9 . . . . 161 A3
Greyfield Comm BS39 . . . 59 C2
Greyfield Rd BS39 . . . . . . 59 C2
Greyfield View BS39 . . . . 58 F1
Greyhound Cl BA9 . . . . . 216 C4
Greylands BS13 . . . . 21 F7
Greys Rd TA16 . . . . 195 F2
Greystoke Bsns Ctr BS20 . . 2 D4
Gribb View TA20 . . . . . . 199 B6
Grib La BS40 . . . . 54 F2
Griffen Cl TA6 . . . . 208 E6
Griffen Rd BS24 . . . . 49 E7
Griffin Cl
Wells BA5 . . . . 203 B6
Weston-Super-Mare BS22 . . 32 B2
Griffin Ct BA1 . . . . 228 B2
Griffin La TA3 . . . . 182 F7
Griffin Rd
Clevedon BS21 . . . . 6 E3
Hatch Beauchamp TA3 . . 182 F7
Griggfield Wlk BS14 . . . . 23 A7
Grimsey La SP8 . . . . 177 F8
Grinfield Ave BS13 . . . . . 22 C4
Grinfield Ct BS13 . . . . . . 22 C4
Groats 9 TA4 . . . . 167 F8
Grooms Orch TA21 . . . . . 222 C5
Grosvenor Bridge Rd BA1 28 C1
Grosvenor Ct BA22 . . . . . 173 E2
Grosvenor Pk BA1 . . . . . . 28 C1
Grosvenor Pl BA1 . . . . . . 28 C1
Grosvenor Rd
Bristol BS2 . . . . 227 C4
Stalbridge DT10 . . . . 190 B4
Grosvenor Terr BA1 . . . . . 28 C2
Grosvenor Villas 9 BA1 . . 28 B1
Grove Alley BA10 . . . . . . 215 E6
Grove Ave
Bristol BS1 . . . . 227 A1
Bristol, Coombe Dingle BS9 . 5 C7
Yeovil BA20 . . . . 218 F5
Grove Cl
Penselwood BA9 . . . . . . 161 E2
Watchet TA23 . . . . 202 C6
Grove Ct BS9 . . . . 5 E5
Grove Dr
Taunton TA2 . . . . 212 F8
Weston-Super-Mare BS22 . . 31 C1

Grove Hill TA7 . . . . 155 B1
Grove Ho
Bath BA2 . . . . 45 B6
Burnham-on-S TA8 . . . . . 104 A8
Grove Jun Sch BS48 . . . . 18 D8
Grove La
Faulkland BA3 . . . . 80 D2
Frome BA11 . . . . 119 E3
Knole TA14 . . . . 173 A4
North Cheriton BA8 . . . . 176 E5
Stalbridge DT10 . . . . 190 B4
West Anstey EX36 . . . . . 162 D6
Weston-Super-Mare BS23 . . 48 D8
Grove Lane Cl DT10 . . . . 190 B4
Grove Leaze BS11 . . . . 4 D6
Grove Mead BA11 . . . . . . 119 E2
Grove Orch BS40 . . . . 54 E2
Grove Park Ct BS23 . . . . . 30 D1
Grove Park Rd BS23 . . . . . 30 D1
Grove Pl TA24 . . . . 201 B4
Grove Rd
Banwell BS29 . . . . 50 E4
Blue Anchor TA24 . . . . . . 131 B6
Bristol, Coombe Dingle BS9 . 5 D8
Burnham-on-S TA8 . . . . . 104 A8
Huntspill TA9 . . . . 136 A8
Weston-Super-Mare BS23 . . 48 D8
Weston-Super-Mare, Milton
BS22 . . . . 31 C1
Groves La TA24 . . . . 131 B6
Grove St BA2 . . . . 228 C3
Groves The BS13 . . . . 22 D4
Grove Terr 8 TA2 . . . . . 212 F6
Grove The
Bath BA1 . . . . 27 C1
Bristol BS1 . . . . 227 A1
Burnham-on-S TA8 . . . . . . 85 B1
Hallatrow BS39 . . . . 77 B7
Ruishton TA3 . . . . 169 C2
Sherborne DT9 . . . . 225 D3
Winscombe BS25 . . . . 51 F1
Wraxall BS48 . . . . 9 C3
Grove Wood Rd BA3 . . . . 78 F1
Grughay La TA3 . . . . 182 E5
Grunter's La BA3 . . . . . . 114 F7
Gryphon Sch The DT9 . . . 225 E6
Guard Ave BA22 . . . . 218 B6
Guard House La 9 BA5 . . 203 D4
Gug The BS39 . . . . 59 C2
Guild CE BS1 . . . . 227 B2
Guildford Pl TA1 . . . . . . 212 F3
Guildhall La BA8 . . . . . . 108 C4
Guineagore La DT9 . . . . . 188 B4
Guinea La BA1 . . . . 228 B2
Guinea St BS1 . . . . 227 A1
Guinevere Cl BA21 . . . . . 218 D7
Gullen BA2 . . . . 80 A6
Gulliford's Bank BS21 . . . . 6 F2
Gulliford Cl TA9 . . . . 104 D4
Gullimores Gdns BS13 . . . 22 B4
Gullock Tyning BA3 . . . . . 78 B1
Gullons Cl BS13 . . . . 22 A6
Gullon Wlk BS13 . . . . 21 F5
Gulway Mead TA20 . . . . . 198 D8
Gumbrells Ct TA6 . . . . . . 209 D4
Gunners La BA22 . . . . . . 218 A5
Gunning's La TA4 . . . . . . 142 F1
Gunville La
Charlton Horethorne
DT9 . . . . 176 A2
East Coker BA22 . . . . 197 D8
Gunwyn La BA6 . . . . 206 E6
Gurney St TA5 . . . . 135 C2
Gurnville Cotts BA11 . . . 119 F2
Guthrie Rd BS8 . . . . 226 A4
Gwynne La TA1 . . . . 213 A3
Gyffarde Ct 4 TA1 . . . . . 213 A4
Gyffarde St TA1 . . . . 213 A4
Gypsy La
Cheddar BS28 . . . . 89 D6
Keynsham BS31 . . . . 42 B8
Marshfield SN14 . . . . 13 F7

H

Haberfield Hill BS8 . . . . . . 4 E2
Haberfield Ho 1 BS8 . . . . 11 F6
Hacketty Way TA24 . . . . 124 B3
Hack La
Holford TA5 . . . . 133 F2
Nether Stowey TA5 . . . . . 134 A2
Hack Mead La TA9 . . . . . 105 E1
Hackness Rd TA9 . . . . . . 136 E8
Haddon Cl TA22 . . . . 148 A2
Haddon La
Hartford TA4 . . . . 164 C7
North Petherton TA6 . . . 153 C2
Stalbridge DT10 . . . . 190 C5
Haddon View TA22 . . . . . 148 B2
Hadley Rd BA2 . . . . 45 B2
Hadrian Cl BS9 . . . . 5 C4
Hadspen Gdn★ BA7 . . . . 160 A2
Hadworthy La TA6 . . . . . 153 F4
Hagget Cl TA6 . . . . 208 F1
Hagleys Gn TA4 . . . . 151 B7
Haig Cl BS9 . . . . 5 B7
Haig Rd TA2 . . . . 168 B6
Haines Hill TA1 . . . . 212 E1
Haines La DT8 . . . . 199 D5
Haines Pk TA1 . . . . 212 E1
Hains La DT10 . . . . 190 F7
Halcombe TA20 . . . . 223 C2
Halcon Cnr TA1 . . . . 213 D4
Halcon Com Prim Sch
TA1 . . . . 213 D4
Hale La BA9 . . . . 177 C6

Halesleigh Rd TA6 . . . . . 208 E5
Hales Mdw TA1 . . . . 187 D6
Hale Way TA2 . . . . 213 D7
Half Acre TA4 . . . . 202 D2
Half Acre Cl
Bristol BS14 . . . . 23 A3
Williton TA4 . . . . 202 D2
Halfacre La BS14 . . . . 23 B4
Half Acres DT9 . . . . 225 C3
Half Moon St 6 DT9 . . . . 225 D3
Halfpenny Row BA11 . . . . 82 E1
Halfway BA22 . . . . 186 F5
Half Yd BS40 . . . . 53 D8
Hallam Cl BS11 . . . . 6 C4
Hallam Rd BS21 . . . . 6 C4
Hallards Cl BS11 . . . . 4 F8
Hallatrow Rd BS39 . . . . . . 77 C6
Hallen Dr BS9 . . . . 5 C7
Hallet Gdns BA20 . . . . . . 219 A4
Hallets Orch BA22 . . . . . 186 B6
Hallett Rd BA7 . . . . 214 B7
Halletts Way
Axminster EX13 . . . . 198 A1
Portishead BS20 . . . . 2 D5
Hall Hill EX35 . . . . 122 B5
Halliwell Rd BS20 . . . . 1 D4
Hall La BA1 . . . . 12 B3
Hall Sch The BS25 . . . . . . 70 B8
Hall Terr TA8 . . . . 104 A8
Halse Cnr TA4 . . . . 167 D5
Halse La TA24 . . . . 147 B5
Halse Manor TA4 . . . . . . 167 B6
Halston Dr BS2 . . . . 227 C4
Halsway TA6 . . . . 209 C5
Halsway Hill TA4 . . . . . . 132 F1
Halsway La
Bicknoller TA4 . . . . 133 A1
Crowcombe TA4 . . . . 151 A8
Halswell Cl TA6 . . . . 208 E4
Halswell Gdns BS13 . . . . . 22 B4
Halswell Rd BS21 . . . . 6 D1
Halt End TA6 . . . . 153 C3
Halter Path Dro TA7 . . . . 137 C7
Halves La BA22 . . . . 197 C7
Halwyn Cl BS9 . . . . 5 D5
Halyard Dr TA6 . . . . 208 E7
Halyard Pl TA24 . . . . 201 B7
Ham's La TA11 . . . . 174 D7
Hamber Lea TA4 . . . . 167 F8
Hambledon Rd BS22 . . . . 32 C4
Hambridge Com Prim Sch
TA10 . . . . 184 D8
Ham Cl BS39 . . . . 58 F1
Hamdon Cl 12 TA14 . . . . 185 F4
Hamdon Hill Country Pk★
TA14 . . . . 185 F3
Hamdon View TA14 . . . . 185 E3
Hamdown Ct TA10 . . . . . 172 B6
Ham Gn
Hambridge TA10 . . . . . . 184 D8
Pill BS20 . . . . 4 D3
Ham Gr BS39 . . . . 77 E5
Ham Hill
Coleford BA3 . . . . 116 D6
Combe St Nicholas TA20 . . 193 D8
High Ham TA10 . . . . 156 A2
Langford Budville TA21 . . 166 A1
Radstock BA3 . . . . 78 F3
Ham Hill Ctry Pk★ TA14 . 186 A3
Ham Hill Rd
Odcombe BA22 . . . . 186 C2
Stoke sub Hamdon TA14 . . 185 F4
Hamilton Ct
11 Bristol BS1 . . . . 227 A4
Taunton TA1 . . . . 213 C4
Wells BA5 . . . . 203 B4
Hamilton Ho BA1 . . . . 27 E3
Hamilton Rd
Bath BA1 . . . . 27 E2
Taunton TA1 . . . . 213 C4
8 Weston-Super-Mare
BS23 . . . . 30 C1
Hamilton Terr BA2 . . . . . 79 F5
Ham La
Bishop Sutton BS39 . . . . . 57 C5
Burnham-on-S TA8 . . . . . 104 B6
Compton Dundon TA11 . . 157 A3
Croscombe BA4, BA5 . . . 204 E7
Dundry BS41 . . . . 21 D3
Farrington Gurney BS39 . . 76 F5
Kingston Seymour BS21 . . 16 B2
Marnhull DT10 . . . . 190 F6
North End BS49 . . . . 17 A3
Paulton BS39 . . . . 77 E5
Pawlett TA6 . . . . 135 E6
Rodhuish TA23 . . . . 149 C8
Shepton Mallet BA4 . . . . 205 A4
Sherborne DT9 . . . . 188 A5
Trent DT9 . . . . 187 F5
Wraxall BS48 . . . . 9 B4
Yatton BS49 . . . . 17 A3
Ham La E BA4 . . . . 204 F7
Hamlands La TA21 . . . . . 167 D1
Hamlet The
Nailsea BS48 . . . . 9 A3
Templecombe BA8 . . . . . 176 E1
Hamley La
Buckland St Mary TA20 . . 193 B8
Combe St Nicholas TA20 . . 182 F1
Ham Link BS40 . . . . 53 F3
Hamlyn Cl TA1 . . . . 212 C1
Hamlyn Rd BA6 . . . . 206 E6
Ham Mdw DT10 . . . . 190 F6
Hammer La BA2, BA3 . . . 100 C8
Hammer St BA10 . . . . . . 161 B8
Hammet St
8 North Petherton TA6 . . 153 E3
Taunton TA1 . . . . 212 F4

Hammets Wharf 1 TA1 . 212 F4
Hammond Gdns BS9 . . . . . 5 E7
Hamp Ave TA6 . . . . 208 F3
Hamp Brook Way TA6 . . . 208 E2
Hamp Com Jun Sch TA6 . 208 F3
Hamp Green Rise TA6 . . . 209 A3
Hamp Ind Est TA6 . . . . . 209 A3
Hamp Inf Sch TA6 . . . . . 208 F3
Hampden Rd BS22 . . . . . . 31 E2
Hampton Cl
5 Barwick BA22 . . . . . . 197 F8
Bridgwater TA6 . . . . 209 D7
Hampton Cnr BS11 . . . . . . 4 E6
Hampton H BA2 . . . . 45 D8
Hampton Ho 10 BA1 . . . . 28 C1
Hampton La BS8 . . . . . . 226 B4
Hampton Rd BS6 . . . . . . 226 C4
Hampton Row BA2 . . . . . . 45 B8
Hampton View BA1 . . . . . . 28 B1
Ham Rd
Brean BS24, TA8 . . . . 66 B3
Burnham-on-S TA9 . . . . . . 85 E4
Creech St Michael TA3 . . . 169 D4
Wellington TA21 . . . . 180 D8
Hamrod La TA7 . . . . 154 E5
Hams La BS26 . . . . 68 C3
Hams Rd BS31 . . . . 24 F7
Ham St BA6 . . . . 158 B5
Hamway La TA20 . . . . . . 193 C8
Hamwood TA1 . . . . 212 B4
Ham Wood Cl BS24 . . . . . 49 B2
Hamwood Cotts TA1 . . . 212 B4
Hamwood La TA3 . . . . . . 181 B8
Hamwood Terr TA1 . . . . 212 B4
Hanbury Ct BS8 . . . . 226 A4
Hanbury Rd BS8 . . . . 226 A4
Handel Rd BS31 . . . . 24 E5
Handlemaker Rd BA11 . . 119 E2
Handy Cross TA4 . . . . . . 151 A2
Hanford Cl BS14 . . . . 23 D7
Hanger's Way TA4 . . . . . 201 D2
Hangerland La TA4 . . . . . 150 E6
Hang Hill BA2 . . . . 80 A6
Hanging Hill La TA13 . . . 184 E4
Hanglands La BA8 . . . . . 176 C2
Hanham La BS39 . . . . 77 F7
Hanham Way BS48 . . . . . . 8 B2
Hankridge Way TA1 . . . . 213 E5
Hanna Cl BA2 . . . . 44 B6
Hannah More Cl
Cheddar BS27 . . . . 90 B7
Wrington BS40 . . . . 35 E2
Hannah More Inf Sch
BS48 . . . . 18 D8
Hannah More Prim Sch
BS1 . . . . 227 C2
Hannah More Rd BS48 . . 18 D8
Hannahs La BA5 . . . . 110 E6
Hannay Rd BS27 . . . . 71 B1
Hann Cl BA5 . . . . 203 B2
Hanning Cl TA19 . . . . . . 221 F6
Hanning Pk TA19 . . . . . . 183 C1
Hanning Rd TA19 . . . . . . 183 C1
Hanny's La BS40 . . . . 39 C3
Hanover Cl
Shepton Mallet BA4 . . . . 205 A6
Weston-Super-Mare BS22 . . 32 A4
Hanover Ct
Bath BA1 . . . . 28 B2
Bristol BS1 . . . . 227 B3
Castle Cary BA7 . . . . 214 C6
Dulverton TA22 . . . . 163 D7
Radstock BA3 . . . . 79 C2
Hanover Gdns BA11 . . . . 119 D3
Hanover Ho BS20 . . . . 2 B5
Hanover Pl
Bath BA1 . . . . 45 B8
Bristol BS1 . . . . 226 B1
Hanover St
2 Bath BA1 . . . . 28 B1
2 Bristol BS1 . . . . 227 A2
Hanover Terr 5 BA1 . . . . 28 B1
Hansetown Rd TA4 . . . . . 148 F1
Hansford Cl BA2 . . . . 44 E1
Hansford Mews BA2 . . . . 44 F1
Hansford Sq BA2 . . . . 44 F1
Hanson's Way 4 BS21 . . . 6 C2
Hans Price Cl 18 BS23 . . 48 E8
Hans Price Ho 13 BS23 . . 48 E8
Hantone Hill BA2 . . . . 45 F8
Happerton La BS20 . . . . . 4 D2
Hapsburg Cl BS22 . . . . . . 32 A4
Hapsford Hill BA11 . . . . 119 C8
Harbour Cl BA21 . . . . . . 218 C5
Harbour Cres BS20 . . . . . . 2 E6
Harbour Ct TA5 . . . . 135 B5
Harbourne Cl TA8 . . . . . 104 C8
Harbour Rd
Portishead BS20 . . . . 2 D6
Sherborne DT9 . . . . 225 D1
Watchet TA23 . . . . 202 C7
Harbour Terr DT9 . . . . . 225 D1
Harbour View TA5 . . . . . 135 B5
Harbour Wall BS9 . . . . 5 B4
Harbour Way
Bristol BS1 . . . . 226 C1
Sherborne DT9 . . . . 225 C1
Harbour Wlk BS1 . . . . . . 226 C1
Harbutts BA2 . . . . 28 F1
Harcourt Cl BS31 . . . . . . 25 E2
Harcourt Gdns BA1 . . . . . 27 B2
Harcourt Mews BA11 . . . 120 A4
Harcourt St TA2 . . . . . . 212 E6
Harden Rd BS14 . . . . 23 E5
Harding's Hill TA10, TA11 172 F5

Harding's House La DT9 . 225 A6
Harding's La BA8 . . . . . . 176 D4
Harding Ct TA11 . . . . 211 D3
Harding Pl BS31 . . . . 25 B5
Hardings Cl 8 TA6 . . . . . 153 F3
Hardings Ct TA13 . . . . . . 220 C5
Hardings Dr BS31 . . . . . . 25 A2
Hardmead La BS27 . . . . . 90 E2
Hardwarden Terr BA22 . . 175 A5
Hardwick Rd BS20 . . . . . . 4 C5
Hardy Cres DT10 . . . . . . 190 B4
Hardy Ct TA18 . . . . 224 C5
Hardy Mead Dro TA9 . . . 136 B7
Hareclive Prim Sch BS13 . 22 C4
Hareclive Rd BS13 . . . . . 22 C4
Hare La TA20 . . . . 182 E2
Harepark Terr TA24 . . . . 201 A5
Hare Path TA24 . . . . 147 F8
Hare Path Cross TA24 . . . 129 D1
Harepits La BA6 . . . . 157 E3
Hare Pk TA24 . . . . 124 C4
Harestone Cross EX13 . . 198 B7
Harewell Wlk BA5 . . . . . 203 D3
Harfield Terr 10 BA20 . . . 219 B4
Harford Cl BS9 . . . . 5 C7
Harford Sq BS40 . . . . 39 B3
Hargrove La DT10 . . . . . . 190 C2
Harington Pl 2 BA1 . . . . 228 B2
Harley Ct 3 BS8 . . . . 11 F7
Harley La BS21 . . . . 7 C6
Harley Mews 2 BS8 . . . . 11 F7
Harley Pl 4 BS8 . . . . 11 F7
Harley St BA1 . . . . 228 B4
Harmony Dr BS20 . . . . 1 F4
Harnell Cl TA1 . . . . 213 C3
Harnhill Cl BS13 . . . . 22 B4
Harp Chase TA1 . . . . 213 B1
Harper's La TA23 . . . . . . 131 D1
Harper Rd TA18 . . . . 224 C5
Harpitts La SP8 . . . . 177 F2
Harp Rd
Brent Knoll TA9 . . . . 105 E6
South Petherton TA13 . . . 220 C3
Harptree BS24 . . . . 49 A2
Harptree Cl BS48 . . . . 18 D8
Harptree Hill BS40 . . . . . 74 B5
Harrier Path 3 BS22 . . . . 49 E8
Harriets Yd BS31 . . . . 24 F5
Harrington Ave BS14 . . . . 23 E6
Harrington Cl BS30 . . . . . 25 E8
Harrington Gr BS14 . . . . . 23 E6
Harrington Rd BS14 . . . . . 23 E6
Harrington Wlk BS14 . . . . 23 E6
Harris Cl EX16 . . . . 179 A4
Harris Gr BS13 . . . . 22 B3
Harris La
Abbots Leigh BS8 . . . . . . 10 F8
Curry Mallet TA3 . . . . . . 183 C8
Harrison's La TA19 . . . . . 184 E1
Harris Vale BA3 . . . . 116 F7
Hart's La
Hallatrow BS39 . . . . 77 B7
Huish Champflower TA4 . . 165 D7
Sherborne DT9 . . . . 188 A3
Hart Cl BS20 . . . . 4 E4
Hartcliffe Engineering Com
Coll BS13 . . . . 22 E8
Hartcliffe Rd BS4 . . . . . . 22 E8
Hartcliffe Way BS3, BS4,
BS13 . . . . 22 C7
Hartcliffe Wlk BS4 . . . . . 22 F8
Harter's Hill La BA5 . . . . 139 E6
Harters Cl BA5 . . . . 139 E6
Hartfield Ave BS6 . . . . . . 226 C4
Hartgill Cl BS13 . . . . 22 B3
Hartland 14 BS22 . . . . . . 32 A2
Hartley Cotts BA4 . . . . . 204 B1
Hartley Ho BA1 . . . . 228 B3
Hartley Way TA1 . . . . . . 213 D2
Hartmoor Hill SP8 . . . . . 177 E3
Hartrow Cl TA1 . . . . 212 E1
Harts Cl TA19 . . . . 221 A4
Hartsfield TA20 . . . . 223 D2
Harts Paddock BA3 . . . . . 77 F3
Hartswell TA4 . . . . 210 C3
Harvesters Dr BA16 . . . . 207 B4
Harvest La
Charlton Horethorne
DT9 . . . . 176 A2
Weston-Super-Mare BS22 . . 50 B8
Harvest Way BS22 . . . . . . 32 A5
Harvey's Rd TA13 . . . . . . 220 C4
Harvey Cl BS22 . . . . 32 A4
Harvey Way TA19 . . . . . . 183 B4
Harwood Cross TA24 . . . 130 A4
Harwood Gn BS22 . . . . . . 31 E4
Harwood La
Timberscombe TA24 . . . . 130 A4
Wootton Courtenay TA24 . 129 F4
Haselbury Gr BS31 . . . . . . 25 E2
Haselbury Plucknett CE Fst
Sch TA18 . . . . 196 C5
Haseley Ct TA1 . . . . 212 D2
Haslands BS48 . . . . 18 C8
Hassage Hill BA2 . . . . 80 E7
Hassock's La BA10 . . . . . 160 E8
Hastings Cross TA19 . . . . 183 B3
Hatch Beauchamp CE Prim
Sch TA3 . . . . 183 A7
Hatch Ct★ TA3 . . . . 183 A8
Hatcher Cl TA8 . . . . 104 D5
Hatchers Ct TA2 . . . . 212 F6
Hatchet Hill BA3, BA11 . . . 98 E4
Hatch Green La TA3 . . . . 182 F6

Hatch Mews Bsns Pk
TA3 . . . .**183** A7
Hatfield Bldgs BA2 . . . . . . **45** B5
Hatfield Rd
Bath BA2 . . . . **44** F3
Weston-Super-Mare BS23 . . **49** A8
Hathaway Ho 13 BS2 . . . . **227** A4
Hathermead Gdns BA21 . **219** D7
Haunts TA18 . . . . **196** C8
Havage Cl TA9 . . . . **104** E5
Havage Dro BS24 . . . . **51** D8
Haven Cl TA24 . . . . **201** F3
Haversham Cl BS22 . . . . . . **31** D1
Haviland Gr BA1 . . . . **27** B3
Haviland Ho 7 BS2 . . . . **227** C3
Haviland Pk BA1 . . . . **27** B2
Havory BA1 . . . . **28** C1
Havyat Rd BS40 . . . . **53** E8
Havyat Road Trad Est
BS40 . . . . **35** E1
Hawarden Terr BA1 . . . . . . **28** B1
Hawcombe View TA24 . . **124** A3
Hawk's Worth CE BA11 . . **120** C7
Hawkchurch CE Prim Sch
EX13 . . . . **198** E3
Hawkchurch Cross EX13 . **198** E2
Hawkchurch Rd EX13 . . . **198** E3
Hawker's La BA5 . . . . **112** E1
Hawke Rd BS22 . . . . **31** E4
Hawkers Cl 9 TA5 . . . . . **135** B2
Hawkfield Cl BS14 . . . . **22** D5
Hawkfield Rd BS13 . . . . . . **22** D5
Hawkfield Way BS14 . . . . . **22** D5
Hawkin's La TA4 . . . . **165** E7
Hawkins Cl
Burnham-on-S TA8 . . . . . **104** C7
Street BA16 . . . . **207** E6
Hawkins St BS2 . . . . **227** C3
Hawkins Way 2 BA21 . . . **218** C6
Hawkmoor Hill DT6, EX13 **199** B2
Hawkridge Cross TA22 . . **146** D1
Hawkridge Rd TA6 . . . . . . **208** B4
Hawksmoor St BS14 . . . . . **23** A6
Hawks Rise BA22 . . . . **218** B5
Hawksworth Dr BS22 . . . . . **32** C4
Hawksworth Rd TA24 . . . **201** B6
Hawkwell Cross EX16 . . . **162** F4
Hawley Way TA8 . . . . **104** C7
Hawthorn Cl
Bridgwater TA6 . . . . **209** D4
High Ham TA10 . . . . **156** A2
Portishead BS20 . . . .**1** F5
Hawthorn Coombe BS22 . **31** E3
Hawthorn Cres
Shepton Mallet BA4 . . . . **205** A6
Yatton BS49 . . . . **17** A2
Hawthorne Cl TA18 . . . . **224** D7
Hawthorne Rd TA21 . . . **222** F5
Hawthorn Gdns BS22 . . . . **31** D2
Hawthorn Gr BA2 . . . . **45** A1
Hawthorn Hill
Kingsbury Episcopi TA13 . **185** B6
Weston-Super-Mare BS22 . . **31** E3
Hawthorn Hts BS22 . . . . . **31** D3
Hawthorn Pk BS22 . . . . . . **31** E3
Hawthorn Rd
Frome BA11 . . . . **120** A6
Minehead TA24 . . . . **200** D7
Radstock BA3 . . . . **79** B2
Street BA16 . . . . **207** E6
Taunton TA1 . . . . **213** C1
Yeovil BA21 . . . . **219** D7
Hawthorns La BS31 . . . . . **24** E5
Hawthorns The
Clevedon BS21 . . . .**6** C3
Stalbridge DT10 . . . . **190** C4
Hawthorn Way BS48 . . . . . .**9** A2
Haxen La TA17 . . . . **195** A8
Hayboro Way BS39 . . . . . . **77** E4
Haybridge Villas BA5 . . . **203** A5
Haycombe BS14 . . . . **22** F6
Haycombe Dr BA2 . . . . **44** A4
Haycombe La BA2 . . . . **44** A3
Hayden Cl BA2 . . . . **228** A1
Hayden Cl TA1 . . . . **212** B4
Haydon Dro BA5 . . . . **113** C6
Haydon Gate BA3 . . . . **97** F8
Haydon Hill BA3 . . . . **98** A8
Haydon Hollow DT9 . . . . **189** B3
Haydon Ind Est BA3 . . . . . **97** F8
Haydon La TA1, TA3 . . . . **213** C2
Haydon Rd TA1 . . . . **213** A4
Hayesdown Fst Sch
BA11 . . . . **120** B5
Hayes End TA13 . . . . **220** D4
Hayes End Manor TA13 . **220** D4
Hayesfield Pk BA2 . . . . . . **228** B1
Hayesfield School Tech Coll
BA2 . . . . **228** A1
Hayesfield Sch Tech Coll
BA2 . . . . **44** D6
Hayes La TA11 . . . . **156** F2
Hayes Park Rd BA3 . . . . . . **77** F2
Hayes Pl BA2 . . . . **228** B1
Hayes Rd
Compton Dundon TA11 . . **156** F3
Midsomer Norton BA3 . . . . **77** F1
Hayes The BS27 . . . . **90** B8
Hayeswood Farm BA15 . . **46** F5
Hayeswood Rd BA2 . . . . . . **59** E3
Hayfield Rd TA24 . . . . . . **201** B6
Haygarth Ct BA1 . . . . **228** B4
Haygrove La TA6 . . . . **208** C3
Haygrove Pk TA3 . . . . . . **168** D1

Haygrove Rd TA6 . . . . . . **208** C3
Haygrove Sch TA6 . . . . . . **208** C4
Hay Hill
Bath BA1 . . . . **228** B3
Croscombe BA5 . . . . **204** B8
Hay La BS40 . . . . **37** D6
Hayleigh Ho BS13 . . . . **22** C4
Hayman Rd TA24 . . . . . . **200** F7
Haymarket The BS1 . . . . **227** A3
Haymarket Wlk 9 BS1 . . **227** A4
Haymoor Dro BA5 . . . . . . **139** D7
Haymoor La
Coxley BA5 . . . . **139** E6
Long Sutton TA10 . . . . . . **172** D4
Hayne Cross EX16 . . . . . . **164** B4
Hayne La TA5 . . . . **153** B7
Haynes Motor Mus★
BA22 . . . . **175** A6
Hayne Wlk TA7 . . . . **137** B2
Hay St BA3 . . . . **96** A8
Haytor Rd BS9 . . . .**5** D6
Hayward Cl BS21 . . . .**6** C1
Hayward Dr BA6 . . . . **158** A6
Haywood Cl BS24 . . . . **49** A1
Haywood Gdns BS24 . . . . . **49** B1
Haywood Rd TA1 . . . . **213** D2
Hazel Barrow BS40 . . . . . . **74** A7
Hazelbury Rd
Bristol BS14 . . . . **23** C7
Nailsea BS48 . . . .**8** D1
Hazel Cl TA1 . . . . **213** C1
Hazel Cote Rd BS14 . . . . . **23** B4
Hazel Gr
Bath BA2 . . . . **44** D4
Midsomer Norton BA3 . . . . **97** B8
Hazelgrove House (Sch)
BA22 . . . . **174** F5
Hazell Cl BS21 . . . .**6** C1
Hazel Terr BA3 . . . . **97** C8
Hazel View TA18 . . . . . . **224** D7
Hazel Way BA2 . . . . **62** D8
Hazelwell La TA19 . . . . . **221** A4
Hazelwood Ct BS9 . . . .**5** D3
Hazelwood Dr TA6 . . . . . **209** E5
Hazelwood Rd BS9 . . . .**5** D3
Hazelton Gdns BA2 . . . . . . **45** F3
Head Croft BS48 . . . . **20** B8
Head Dro
Catcott TA7 . . . . **137** D3
Othery TA7 . . . . **155** D3
Headley Ct BS13 . . . . **22** B6
Headley La BS13 . . . . **22** B7
Headley Park Ave BS13 . . **22** B7
Headley Park Prim Sch
BS13 . . . . **22** B6
Headley Park Rd BS13 . . . **22** A7
Headley Rd BS13 . . . . **22** A6
Headley Wlk BS13 . . . . **22** B7
Headon Cross TA24 . . . . **129** F8
Head St BA22 . . . . **186** B6
Headstock Cross TA20 . . **198** E6
Headstock Rd TA20 . . . . . **198** E7
Headwell TA3 . . . . **183** C8
Headwell Cl TA3 . . . . **183** C8
Headwell Hill TA3 . . . . . . **183** C8
Heal's Field EX13 . . . . . . **198** A2
Heal Cl TA8 . . . . **104** D5
Heale La TA10 . . . . **171** C4
Healeys TA24 . . . . **124** A4
Healys Mdw TA4 . . . . **167** E6
Hearn La BA22 . . . . **175** D8
Heart Meers BS14 . . . . . . **23** B5
Heath Cl BA12 . . . . **144** D8
Heathcombe Rd TA6 . . . . **208** B4
Heathcote Rd BA22 . . . . **174** A2
Heath Dr BA11 . . . . **119** F6
Heather Cl
Bridgwater TA6 . . . . **209** B3
Minehead TA24 . . . . **201** C4
Taunton TA1 . . . . **169** A1
Heatherdene BS14 . . . . . . **22** F7
Heather Dr BA2 . . . . **62** D8
Heather Rd BA21 . . . . **219** D7
Heatherton Park Ho TA4 **180** E8
Heather Way BA22 . . . . . **218** A5
Heathfield TA4 . . . . **151** E4
Heathfield Cl
Bath BA1 . . . . **27** A3
Creech St Michael TA3 . . . **169** D6
Keynsham BS31 . . . . **24** C5
5 North Petherton TA6 . . **153** F4
West Bagborough TA4 . . . **151** E4
Heathfield Com Sch TA2 **213** F8
Heathfield Cres BS14 . . . . **23** B4
Heathfield Dr TA2 . . . . . . **213** F8
Heathfield Rd BS48 . . . .**8** E3
Heathfield Way BS48 . . . . . .**8** E2
Heathgate BS49 . . . . **34** B8
Heathgates BS23 . . . . **48** D4
Heath Rd BS48 . . . .**8** F3
Heath Ridge BS41 . . . . **11** A2
Heathstock Hill TA4 . . . . **210** D5
Heathway BA12 . . . . **144** D8
Heathway La BA6 . . . . . . **138** A4
Heavitree Way TA21 . . . . **213** A6
Hebden Rd BA15 . . . . **64** F3
Heber's La TA19 . . . . **195** A5
Heckley La BA3 . . . . **115** B5
Hector Rd TA7 . . . . **137** D2
Hectors La TA3 . . . . **170** D8
Hectors Stones TA7 . . . . **136** E4
Heddon Oak TA4 . . . . **151** B8
Hedge La BA4 . . . . **141** B2
Hedgemead Ct BA1 . . . . **228** C4
Hedges Cl 3 BS21 . . . .**6** B1
Hedges The BS22 . . . . **32** C3

Hedgestocks BA4 . . . . . . **160** C8
Hedging La TA7 . . . . **170** A8
Heggard Cl BS13 . . . . **22** A5
Heights The TA19 . . . . . . **221** B4
Hele La
Langport TA10 . . . . **172** C4
South Petherton TA13 . . . **220** C4
Helena Rd BA20 . . . . **218** D1
Helens Rd BS25 . . . . **52** B4
Helland Hill TA3 . . . . **170** C3
Helland La TA3 . . . . **170** D4
Helliar's La
Curry Mallet TA3 . . . . . . **183** D8
Fivehead TA3 . . . . **170** D1
Hellier's Cl TA20 . . . . . . **223** B4
Hellier's La BS27 . . . . **89** E6
Helliers Rd TA20 . . . . . . **223** B4
Hellier Wlk BS13 . . . . **22** C3
Helling's Cross TA4 . . . . **166** A4
Helmstedt Way TA20 . . . **223** D6
Helston Rd BS48 . . . .**9** A1
Helvier's La TA4 . . . . **167** A7
Helwell Gn TA23 . . . . **202** D6
Helyar Cl BA6 . . . . **206** D5
Hembridge La BA4 . . . . . **158** E7
Hembury La BA5 . . . . **139** C7
Hemington Prim Sch BA3 **99** B3
Hemming Way BS24 . . . . . **49** E3
Hemp Gdn TA24 . . . . **200** F8
Hempitts Rd BA16 . . . . . . **156** E7
Hemplow Cl BS14 . . . . **23** D7
Hemstich Hill TA7 . . . . . **138** C1
Henacre Rd BS11 . . . .**4** F8
Henbury Hill BS9 . . . .**5** F8
Henbury Ho BA2 . . . . **45** E4
Henbury Rd BS9 . . . .**5** F8
Hencliffe Rd BS15 . . . . **23** D7
Henderson Cl TA1 . . . . . . **212** C2
Henderson Dr TA20 . . . . **223** D2
Henderson Ho 1 BS2 . . . **227** B4
Henderson Pl 5 BA5 . . . **203** D4
Hendford BA20 . . . . **219** A4
Hendford Ct BA20 . . . . . **219** A3
Hendford Gr BA20 . . . . . **219** A4
Hendford Hill BA20 . . . . **219** A3
Hendon Cl TA9 . . . . **104** E5
Hendon Cross EX16 . . . . **178** B8
Hengrove Ave BS14 . . . . . **23** B8
Hengrove Com Arts Coll
BS14 . . . . **23** B7
Hengrove La BS14 . . . . . . **23** B8
Hengrove Way BS14 . . . . . **22** E6
Henhayes La TA18 . . . . . **224** C6
Hen La BS40 . . . . **37** E3
Henley Cl EX13 . . . . **198** E3
Henley Gr TA1 . . . . **212** D4
Henley La
Butleigh BA6 . . . . **157** E4
Wookey BA5 . . . . **139** E8
Yatton BS49 . . . . **34** D7
Henley Lodge BS49 . . . . . **34** D7
Henley Pk BS49 . . . . **34** C7
Henley Rd
High Ham TA10 . . . . **156** B3
Kingsdon TA11 . . . . **173** E5
Taunton TA1 . . . . **212** D3
Henley Rise BA4 . . . . **205** D4
Henley View
Crewkerne TA18 . . . . **224** C4
Wellow BA2 . . . . **62** D1
Henley Way BA11 . . . . . . **119** F5
Henmore La BA26 . . . . **88** E6
Hennessy Cl BS14 . . . . **22** F3
Henning Way DT9 . . . . . . **217** D3
Henrietta Ct BA2 . . . . . . **228** C4
Henrietta Gdns BA2 . . . . **228** C3
Henrietta Mews BA2 . . . . **228** C3
Henrietta Pl BA2 . . . . **228** C3
Henrietta Rd BA2 . . . . . . **228** C3
Henrietta St
Bath BA2 . . . . **228** C3
Bristol BS2 . . . . **227** A4
Henry Butt Ho 11 BS23 . . **48** E8
Henry Rogers Ho 2 TA5 **135** B2
Henry St BA1 . . . . **228** C2
Hensley Gdns BA2 . . . . . . **44** E4
Hensley Rd BA2 . . . . **44** E3
Hensman's Hill BS8 . . . . **226** A2
Henson Pk TA20 . . . . **223** E5
Hensons Dr EX16 . . . . . . **179** A3
Henstridge Trad Est BA8 **190** C7
Hepburn Rd BS2 . . . . **227** B4
Herald Cl BS9 . . . .**5** D5
Herbert Ho TA20 . . . . . . **163** D6
Herbert Rd
Bath BA2 . . . . **44** D5
Burnham-on-S TA8 . . . . . **104** A8
Clevedon BS21 . . . .**6** D4
Herbert St TA2 . . . . **212** E6
Herblay BA21 . . . . **219** E6
Hereford Dr TA2 . . . . **213** A8
Heritage Cl BA2 . . . . **79** D8
Heritage Ct BA6 . . . . **206** D4
Heritage Ctyd BA5 . . . . . **203** D4
Heritage The BA2 . . . . **78** E8
Herluin Way BS22, BS23 . . **49** B6
Hermes Cl BS31 . . . . **25** D2
Hermes Pl BA22 . . . . **173** E2
Hermitage Cl BS11 . . . .**4** E7
Hermitage Hill TA10 . . . **172** D6
Hermitage Rd
Bath BA1 . . . . **27** E1
Langport TA10 . . . . **172** D6
Hermitage St TA18 . . . . **224** C5
Herne Rise TA19 . . . . **221** B2
Hern La BS48 . . . . **20** E5
Heron Cl
Minehead TA24 . . . . **201** C4

Heron Cl continued
Weston-Super-Mare BS22 . . **49** E8
Heron Ct BS21 . . . .**6** C2
Heron Dr TA1 . . . . **212** B4
Heron Gate TA1 . . . . **213** E6
Heron Gate Office Pk
TA1 . . . . **213** E5
Heron Gdns BS20 . . . .**2** E4
Heron Ho 2 TA6 . . . . **209** C4
Heron Pk TA6 . . . . **84** E8
Herons La TA4 . . . . **167** A4
Heronsmead Wlk BA21 . **219** D8
Herons Moor Prim Sch
BS24 . . . . **50** A8
Heron Way TA19 . . . . **221** C2
Herridge Cl BS13 . . . . **22** B4
Herridge Rd BS13 . . . . **22** B4
Hersey Gdns BS13 . . . . . . **21** E3
Hertford Rd BA21 . . . . . . **219** E8
Hervey Cl BS28 . . . . **108** C4
Hervey Rd
Chard TA20 . . . . **223** D3
Wells BA5 . . . . **112** E1
Hestercombe Cl TA6 . . . . **208** B4
Hestercombe House Gdns★
TA2 . . . . **169** A7
Hestercombe Rd
Bristol BS13 . . . . **22** B6
Taunton TA2 . . . . **169** A7
Hetling Ct 7 BA1 . . . . . . **228** B2
Hewett Cl TA3 . . . . **168** D1
Hewish Ct BS23 . . . . **48** E8
Hewish La
Crewkerne TA18 . . . . **224** A5
Hewish TA18 . . . . **195** D3
Hext Ct TA11 . . . . **211** D3
Hexton Rd BA6 . . . . **206** E5
Heyron Wlk BS13 . . . . **22** B4
Heywood Rd BS20 . . . .**4** C4
Heywood Terr BS20 . . . .**4** C4
Hibbs Cl SN14 . . . . **13** F8
Hicks's La BA22 . . . . **214** D1
Hidcote Mews BS24 . . . . . **49** E7
Hide Mkt BS2 . . . . **227** C3
Hidewood La EX15 . . . . . **180** F1
Higgin's Grave La TA13 . **220** B1
High Acre BS39 . . . . **77** F4
Highaton Head Cross
EX36 . . . . **162** C4
High Bank
Porlock TA24 . . . . **124** A3
Watchet TA23 . . . . **202** C7
High Bannerdown BA1 . . . **29** B4
High Bolham EX16 . . . . . **163** C1
Highbridge TA4 . . . . **202** F4
Highbridge & Burnham Sta
TA9 . . . . **104** B4
Highbridge Rd TA6 . . . . . **104** B5
Highbrooks Rd TA11 . . . . **173** B5
Highburn Cl TA8 . . . . **104** C4
Highbury Cotts
8 Bath BA1 . . . . **28** A1
Coleford BA3 . . . . **116** F7
Highbury Farm Bsns Pk
BS39 . . . . **77** A8
Highbury Par BS23 . . . . . . **30** C1
Highbury Pl BA1 . . . . **28** A1
Highbury Rd
Hallatrow BS39 . . . . **77** B2
Weston-Super-Mare BS23 . . **30** C1
Highbury St BA3 . . . . **117** A7
Highbury Terr 10 BA1 . . . **28** A1
Highbury Villas
9 Bath BA1 . . . . **28** A1
Bristol BS2 . . . . **226** C4
Highcroft
Weston-Super-Mare BS23 . . **30** F1
Woolavington TA7 . . . . . **136** E4
High Cross EX16 . . . . **164** A1
Highdale Ave BS21 . . . .**6** E3
Highdale Cl BS14 . . . . **23** B4
Highdale Rd BS21 . . . .**6** E3
High Down Jun & Inf Schs
BS20 . . . .**2** A4
Higher Actis BA6 . . . . **206** E3
Higher Backway BA10 . . . **215** E6
Higher Barton
Martock TA12 . . . . **185** D4
Trent DT9 . . . . **187** F5
Higher Beacon TA19 . . . . **221** B4
Higher Beadon TA16 . . . . **195** E7
Higher Brooks BA16 . . . . **207** C2
Higher Bullen BA22 . . . . **197** F8
Higher Burton BA22 . . . . **197** C8
Higher Cheap St 3 DT9 **225** D4
Higher Coombes TA20 . . **198** D8
Higher Cross EX16 . . . . . **179** C1
Higher Easthams La
TA18 . . . . **224** F7
Higher Farm La
Podimore BA22 . . . . **174** A4
Sparkford BA22 . . . . **175** B3
Higher Farm Trad Est
BA20 . . . . **218** C5
Higher Gunville DT9 . . . . **217** D3
Higher Heathfield TA4 . . **151** E4
Higher Kingsbury DT9 . . **217** D3
Higher Kingsbury Cl
DT9 . . . . **217** D3
Higher Kingston BA21 . . **219** B5
Higher Mead TA19 . . . . . **221** B3
Higher Millhayes EX15 . . **180** D1
Higher North Town La
BA22 . . . . **175** D7
Higher Orch
Martock TA12 . . . . **185** D4
Minehead TA24 . . . . **200** C8

Higher Palmerston Rd
TA2 . . . . **212** D6
Higher Park La TA24 . . . . **129** E2
Higher Pk TA24 . . . . **200** D5
Higher Rd
Chedzoy TA7 . . . . **154** D8
Horsington BA8 . . . . **176** D3
Shepton Beauchamp TA19 **184** E3
Woolavington TA7 . . . . . **136** E4
Higher Ream BA21 . . . . . **218** C6
Higher Rodhuish Rd
TA24 . . . . **131** B3
Higher St
Curry Mallet TA3 . . . . . . **183** C8
East Quantoxhead TA5 . . **133** B5
Martock TA12 . . . . **185** D4
Merriott TA16 . . . . **195** F8
Norton Sub Hamdon TA14 **185** E2
West Chinnock TA18 . . . . **196** B8
Higher Tolbury BA10 . . . **215** E6
Higher Town EX16 . . . . . **178** C1
Higher Westbury DT9 . . **187** E1
Higher West Hatch La
TA3 . . . . **182** D7
Higher Westholme Rd
North Wootton BA4 . . . . **140** D4
Pilton BA4 . . . . **204** A1
Highfield
Coleford BA3 . . . . **116** E8
Ilminster TA19 . . . . **221** B4
Taunton TA1 . . . . **212** A2
Taunton TA1 . . . . **212** C3
Wells BA5 . . . . **140** C7
West Chinnock TA18 . . . . **196** B8
Highfield Cl
Bath BA2 . . . . **44** B5
Somerton TA11 . . . . **211** C4
Taunton TA1 . . . . **212** A2
Highfield Cres
Chilcompton BA3 . . . . **96** C4
Taunton TA1 . . . . **212** A2
Highfield Dr BS20 . . . .**1** E3
Highfield La
Compton Martin BS40 . . . **74** B6
East Harptree BS40 . . . . . **75** A3
Highfield Rd
Keynsham BS31 . . . . **24** F2
Peasedown St John BA2 . . **79** D8
Street BA16 . . . . **207** B5
Weston-Super-Mare BS23 . . **49** A1
Yeovil BA21 . . . . **219** D3
Highfields
Barrington TA19 . . . . **184** C5
Clandown BA3 . . . . **78** E4
Midsomer Norton BA3 . . . . **78** D2
Stanton Drew BS39 . . . . . **39** F1
Highfield Terr TA12 . . . . **185** D5
Highfield Trad Est BA21 . **219** C6
Highfield View BA3 . . . . **116** E8
Highfield Way TA11 . . . . **211** C4
High Gn BA5 . . . . **111** A4
High Gr BS9 . . . .**5** B7
Highgrove TA1 . . . . **212** E1
Highgrove Cl TA6 . . . . . . **209** A2
Highgrove Wlk BS24 . . . . . **50** B8
High Ham CE Prim Sch
TA10 . . . . **156** A1
High Kingsdown BS2 . . . **226** C4
High La
Barton St David TA11 . . . **158** A2
Shapwick TA7 . . . . **155** F3
Highland Cl BS22 . . . . **31** B2
Highland Ct BA21 . . . . . . **219** C6
Highland Rd BA2 . . . . **44** B5
Highlands TA1 . . . . **212** E1
Highlands La BS24 . . . . . . **50** A8
Highlands Rd
Long Ashton BS41 . . . . . . **11** A2
Portishead BS20 . . . .**2** E3
Highland Terr BA2 . . . . . . **44** D6
High Lea BA21 . . . . **219** B8
High Littleton CE Prim Sch
BS39 . . . . **59** C3
High Mdws BA3 . . . . **77** F1
Highmead Gdns BS13 . . . . **21** E4
High Mead BS39 . . . . **57** D3
Highmore Rd DT9 . . . . . . **225** C5
High Path TA21 . . . . **222** C7
High Pk BS39 . . . . **77** D6
High Rd BA22 . . . . **175** D8
Highridge Cres BS13 . . . . . **21** F5
Highridge Gn BS13 . . . . . . **21** F6
Highridge Inf Sch BS13 . . **21** F6
Highridge Pk BS13 . . . . . . **21** F6
Highridge Rd BS13, BS41 . **21** E4
Highridge Wlk BS13 . . . . . **21** E6
High St
Aller TA10 . . . . **171** E8
Ashcott TA7 . . . . **156** B8
Axbridge BS26 . . . . **70** B2
Bampton EX16 . . . . **164** B1
Banwell BS29 . . . . **51** A4
Bathampton BA2 . . . . **28** F1
Bath BA1 . . . . **228** C2
Batheaston BA1 . . . . **28** F3
Bathford BA1 . . . . **29** D2
Bath, Twerton BA2 . . . . . . **44** B6
Bath, Weston BA1 . . . . . . **27** B1
Bishops Lydeard TA4 . . . . **167** E8
Bitton BS30 . . . . **25** E8
Blackford BS28 . . . . **107** C4
Blagdon BS40 . . . . **54** E3
Bourton SP8 . . . . **161** F2
Bridgwater TA6 . . . . **208** F5
Bristol BS1 . . . . **227** A2
Bruton BA10 . . . . **215** E6
Buckland Dinham BA11 . . **100** A3

High St continued
Burnham-on-S TA8. . . . . . . **104** A6
Butleigh BA6 . . . . **157** E4
Cannington TA5 . . . . **135** B2
Carhampton TA24 . . . . **131** A5
Castle Cary BA7. . . . . **214** C5
Chapmanslade BA13 . . . . . **121** C4
Chard TA20. . . . . **223** B4
Charlton Adam TA11 . . . . . **173** F7
Chew Magna BS40. . . . . **39** A3
Chewton Mendip BA3 . . . . . **94** F7
Claverham BS49. . . . . **17** F1
Coleford BA3 . . . . **116** F6
Congresbury BS49. . . . . **34** D4
Dulverton TA22 . . . . **163** D6
Dunster TA24 . . . . **201** E2
East Chinnock BA22. . . . . . **196** E8
East Harptree BS40. . . . . . . **74** F5
Evercreech BA4. . . . . **141** E1
Faulkland BA3 . . . . **80** D1
Freshford BA3 . . . . **64** B5
Frome BA11. . . . . **119** F5
Glastonbury BA6. . . . . **206** E4
Hardington Mandeville
 BA22. . . . . **197** A6
Henstridge BA8 . . . . **190** A6
High Littleton BS39. . . . . . . **59** D1
Hinton Charterhouse BA2 . . **63** E1
Hinton St George TA17 . . . **195** D7
Ilchester BA22 . . . . **173** E1
Ilminster TA19 . . . . **221** B4
Keinton Mandeville TA11 . . **158** A1
Keynsham BS31. . . . . **24** E6
Kingweston BA6. . . . . **157** E1
Lynford-on-F TA11 . . . . **158** C2
Maiden Bradley BA12 . . . . . **144** C2
Marshfield SN14 . . . . **13** F8
Midsomer Norton BA3. . . . . **78** B1
Milborne Port DT9. . . . . . . **217** D2
Milton Clevedon BA4 . . . . . **160** A8
Milverton TA4. . . . . **166** F5
Monksilver TA4 . . . . **150** B8
Nailsea BS48. . . . . **8** F3
North Cadbury BA22. . . . . . **175** D6
North Petherton TA6. . . . . . **153** E4
North Wootton BA4 . . . . . . **140** C4
Norton St Philip BA2 . . . . . . **81** E4
Nunney BA11. . . . . **143** B8
Oakhill BA3 . . . . **115** A3
Othery TA7. . . . . **155** C4
Paulton BS39. . . . . **77** E5
Paulton, Plummer's Hill
 BS39. . . . . **77** E6
Pensford BS39. . . . . **40** E4
Porlock TA24 . . . . **124** C4
Portbury BS20. . . . . **3** E3
Portishead BS20 . . . . **2** D5
Queen Camel BA22 . . . . . . **174** F3
Rimpton BA22 . . . . **188** A8
Rode BA11. . . . . **101** E8
Saltford BS31. . . . . **25** F3
Shepton Mallet BA4. . . . . . **205** B6
Sparkford BA22. . . . . **175** A5
Spaxton TA5. . . . . **152** E7
Stalbridge DT10. . . . . **190** B5
Stogumber TA4. . . . . **150** D8
Stogursey TA5 . . . . **134** C5
Stoke sub Hamdon TA14 . . **185** F4
Ston Easton BA3 . . . . **95** E8
Stoney Stratton BA4 . . . . . . **141** F2
Stourton BA12. . . . . **161** F5
Stourton Caundle DT10 . . . **189** F2
Street BA16. . . . . **207** C6
Taunton TA1 . . . . **212** F3
Templecombe BA8. . . . . **176** E1
Thorncombe TA20 . . . . **199** B6
Timsbury BA2 . . . . **60** B2
Wellington TA21. . . . . **222** E4
Wellow BA2 . . . . **62** D1
Wells BA5. . . . . **203** D4
West Coker BA22 . . . . **197** A8
Weston-Super-Mare BS23. . **48** B8
Weston-Super-Mare, Worle
 BS22. . . . . **31** E2
Williton TA4. . . . . **202** D2
Wincanton BA9 . . . . **216** C4
Winford BS40. . . . . **38** A7
Winsham TA20. . . . . **194** E1
Wiveliscombe TA4. . . . . . . **210** C4
Wookey BA5 . . . . **139** D8
Wookey Hole BA5. . . . . **203** A8
Woolley BA1 . . . . **27** F6
Wrington BS40 . . . . **35** D2
Yatton BS49. . . . . **34** C8
Yenston BA8 . . . . **189** F8
Yeovil BA20 . . . . **219** B4
High View BS20. . . . . **2** A4
High View Dr TA7. . . . . **156** B8
Highwall La BS14, BS31. . . . **23** F1
Highwoods Cl TA14 . . . . . . **185** F2
Higson Cl BA22 . . . . **186** D3
Hilary Rd TA1. . . . . **212** D3
Hildesheim Bridge BS23. . **48** F7
Hildesheim Cl BS23 . . . . . . **48** F6
Hildesheim Ct 9 BS23 . . . . **48** E7
Hilhouse BS9. . . . . **5** C6
Hill's La 10 TA12 . . . . **185** E6
Hill Ave BA2. . . . . **44** F1
Hillborne Gdns BA21 . . . . **218** C5
Hillbrook Ct DT9. . . . . **225** D4
Hill Brow DT9 . . . . **225** B2
Hill Cl BA9. . . . . **216** D4
Hillclose La TA19 . . . . **221** F4
Hillcote Est BS24 . . . . **67** B8
Hillcrest
 Crowcombe TA4. . . . . **151** B7
 Peasedown St John BA2. . . **79** C7
 Pensford BS39. . . . . **40** E3

Hillcrest Cl
 Nailsea BS48. . . . . **8** E1
 Yeovil BA21 . . . . **219** C7
Hillcrest Dr BA2 . . . . **44** C4
Hillcrest Rd
 Nailsea BS48. . . . . **8** E1
 Portishead BS20 . . . . **1** E4
 Templecombe BA8 . . . . . . **176** E1
Hill Crest Rd BA21 . . . . . . **219** C6
Hillcroft BS22 . . . . **31** A3
Hill Cross BA22 . . . . **196** F6
Hill Ct BS39. . . . . **77** E6
Hilldale Rd BS48. . . . . **19** B5
Hill Dr BS8 . . . . **10** C3
Hillend BS22. . . . . **31** B3
Hillfield BS27. . . . . **90** B7
Hill Gay Cl BS20. . . . . **1** F4
Hill Ground BA11 . . . . **119** E5
Hillgrove Ave BA20. . . . . . **218** F2
Hillgrove Cl TA6 . . . . **208** E5
Hillgrove Rd BA5 . . . . **93** C1
Hillgrove St N BS2 . . . . . . **227** A4
Hillgrove St BS2 . . . . **227** B4
Hillgrove Terr BS23 . . . . **48** D1
Hill Head BA6. . . . . **206** D3
Hill Head Cl
 Glastonbury BA6 . . . . **206** D3
 Taunton TA1. . . . . **213** A3
Hillhead Cotts TA2. . . . . . **212** C8
Hillhead Cross TA24. . . . . **128** D3
Hillhouse EX14 . . . . **192** D3
Hill House Cl DT9 . . . . **225** E5
Hillier's La
 Churchill BS25. . . . . **52** D4
 Yarley BA5. . . . . **139** C8
Hillingdon Ct BA21. . . . . . **218** C6
Hill La
 Bicknoller, Culverhays
  TA4. . . . . **133** A1
 Bicknoller TA4 . . . . **132** F2
 Brent Knoll TA9 . . . . **86** B3
 Carhampton TA24 . . . . **131** A4
 Chipstable TA4. . . . . **165** C6
 Clevedon BS21. . . . . **7** C4
 Draycott BS27. . . . . **90** C2
 Portishead BS20 . . . . **1** F1
 Rodney Stoke BS27 . . . . . . **91** B2
 Rowberrow BS25. . . . . **53** A1
 Shepton Mallet BA4. . . . . **205** B6
 Waterrow TA4 . . . . **165** E5
 West Quantoxhead TA4 . . **132** F4
Hill Lea Gdns BS27. . . . . . . **90** B8
Hillmead
 Churchill BS40. . . . . **53** A5
 Shepton Mallet BA4. . . . . **205** B6
Hillmer Rise BS29. . . . . **50** F3
Hill Moor BS21 . . . .**6** E2
Hillpath BS29. . . . . **51** B2
Hill Pk BS49 . . . . **34** E5
Hill Rd
 Allerford TA24 . . . . **124** E4
 Clevedon BS21. . . . . **6** D4
 Dundry BS41. . . . . **21** D2
 Minehead TA24 . . . . **125** B4
 Sandford BS25. . . . . **52** A3
 Weston-Super-Mare BS23. . **48** F8
 Weston-Super-Mare, Worle
  BS22. . . . . **31** E2
Hill Rd E BS22 . . . . **31** E2
Hillsboro TA7. . . . . **136** E4
Hillsborough BS8 . . . . **226** A2
Hillsborough Gdns TA8. . . **85** B1
Hillsborough Ho BS23. . . . **49** A4
Hills Cl BS31. . . . . **25** A5
Hills Cotts TA4. . . . . **167** A7
Hillsdon Rd BS9. . . . . **5** F8
Hillside
 Bristol BS6. . . . . **226** C4
 Chard TA20. . . . . **223** B4
 Horrington BA5. . . . . **113** A2
 Portbury BS20 . . . . **3** D3
 Puriton TA7. . . . . **136** C4
 West Pennard BA6 . . . . . . **140** B1
Hillside Ave
 Frome BA11. . . . . **119** F2
 Midsomer Norton BA3. . . . **96** F8
Hillside Cl
 Curry Rivel TA10 . . . . **171** D4
 Paulton BS39. . . . . **77** F6
Hill Side Cl BA5. . . . . **203** C5
Hillside Cres
 Midsomer Norton BA3. . . . . **96** E8
 Puriton TA7. . . . . **136** C4
Hillside Dr TA7 . . . . **136** C4
Hillside Fst Sch BS22 . . . . **31** E2
Hillside Gdns
 Bishop Sutton BS39. . . . . . . **57** C3
 Weston-Super-Mare BS22. . **31** B1
Hillside Gr TA1. . . . . **212** C1
Hillside Ho BA11 . . . . **119** F3
Hillside Rd
 Backwell BS48. . . . . **19** A4
 Bath BA2. . . . . **44** D4
 Bleadon BS24. . . . . **67** B8
 Clevedon BS21. . . . . **6** D3
 Long Ashton BS41 . . . . **11** B2
 Midsomer Norton BA3. . . . . **96** F8
 Portishead BS20 . . . . **1** D4
Hillside Terr BA21 . . . . . . **219** C5
Hillside View
 1 Barwick BA22. . . . . **197** F8
 Midsomer Norton BA3. . . . **78** A3
 Peasedown St John BA2. . . **79** C8
 Yeovil BA21 . . . . **219** D1
Hillside W BS24. . . . . **49** F2
Hills Orch 9 TA12 . . . . . . **185** E6
Hill St
 Bristol BS1. . . . . **226** C2

Hill St continued
 Stogumber TA4 . . . . **150** D8
Hill Terr TA1. . . . . **212** A4
Hill The
 Freshford BA3 . . . . **64** C5
 Langport TA10 . . . . **172** A5
Hill Top BS20 . . . . **2** A4
Hilltop La TA5 . . . . **133** D6
Hilltops TA8 . . . . **65** F6
Hillview
 Midsomer Norton BA3. . . . . **96** E7
 Timsbury BA2 . . . . **60** B1
Hill View
 Brean TA8. . . . . **65** E2
 Bristol BS8. . . . . **226** B2
 Brompton Ralph TA4 . . . . **150** C3
 Farrington Gurney BS39. . . **77** B3
 Marksbury BA2 . . . . **42** B1
 Mudford BA21. . . . . **187** D6
 Priston BA2 . . . . **61** A5
 Queen Camel BA22 . . . . . . **174** F4
 Yeovil BA21 . . . . **219** C5
Hillview Ave BS21. . . . . **6** D2
Hillview Cl TA24 . . . . **200** D7
Hill View Cl
 Ilton TA19 . . . . **183** F4
 7 Stoke sub Hamdon
  TA14 . . . . **185** F4
 West Chinnock TA18 . . . . **196** B8
Hill View Ct
 Evercreech BA4. . . . . **141** E1
 Weston-Super-Mare BS22. . **49** D8
Hillview Cvn Pk BS40. . . . . **20** B1
Hill View Gdns BS40 . . . . . **37** C8
Hill View Park Homes
 BS22 . . . . **49** D8
Hillview Rd
 Loxton BS26. . . . . **68** C4
 Minehead TA24 . . . . **200** D7
Hill View Rd
 Bath BA1 . . . . **28** B2
 Bristol BS13. . . . . **22** A8
 Carhampton TA24 . . . . **131** A5
 Weston-Super-Mare BS23. . **49** A7
Hillview Terr TA12 . . . . . . **185** D5
Hill View Terr
 Ilminster TA19 . . . . **221** B4
 Lyng TA3. . . . . **170** C7
Hill View Trad Est TA4 . . . **151** E4
Hillway TA11 . . . . **173** E7
Hillworth Ho 26 BA4 . . . . **205** B6
Hillyfield Rd BS13. . . . . **22** A6
Hillyfields
 Taunton TA1. . . . . **213** C2
 Winscombe BS25. . . . . **70** B8
Hillyfields Way BS25. . . . . **70** A8
Hilly Head TA21. . . . . **222** B5
Hilly Pk TA7 . . . . **168** B5
Hinam Cross TA22 . . . . . . **163** B7
Hinckley St TA9 . . . . **32** C4
Hincombe Hill BA4. . . . . . **142** E2
Hindhayes Inf Sch BA16 **207** D5
Hindhayes La BA16. . . . . . **207** D6
Hind Pitts BS25. . . . . **70** F7
Hine Nd TA1 . . . . **212** B1
Hinkley Point Nature Trail★
 TA5 . . . . **134** C8
Hinkley Point Visitor Ctr★
 TA5 . . . . **134** C8
Hinton BS24 . . . . **49** A2
Hinton Cl
 Bath BA2. . . . . **43** F6
 Hinton St George TA17 . . . **195** D7
 Saltford BS31. . . . . **25** E3
Hinton Cross BA22 . . . . . . **187** D7
Hinton Dr TA1 . . . . **212** E1
Hinton Hill BA2, BA3. . . . . **63** A1
Hinton La 12 BS8 . . . . **11** F6
Hinton Rd BA18 . . . . **224** B8
Hinton St George CE Sch
 TA17. . . . . **195** C7
Hinton Villas BA2 . . . . **63** E1
Hippisley Dr BS26. . . . . **70** D2
Hippisley Ho BA5. . . . . **113** A1
Hiscocks Dr BA2. . . . . **44** E4
Hiscocks La BA8 . . . . **176** E2
Hitchen TA16 . . . . **195** F7
Hitchen Cl SN14 . . . . **13** F8
Hitchen Hill BA4 . . . . **140** F3
Hitchings La TA3. . . . . **170** B7
Hitchin La BA4. . . . . **205** A5
Hither Acre TA19 . . . . **221** A4
Hither Bath Bridge BS4 . . **23** B7
Hither Gn BS21. . . . . **6** F2
Hither Green Ind Est BS21. . **6** F2
Hither Mead TA4. . . . . **167** F8
Hittsford La EX36 . . . . **162** A1
Hoare's La BA11 . . . . **98** B3
Hobart Rd BS23. . . . . **48** F3
Hobb's La BS1 . . . . **226** C2
Hobbiton Rd BS22 . . . . **32** A4
Hobbs Ct 1 BS48 . . . . **8** F2
Hobbs BS48. . . . . **20** E3
Hobbs Mead 7 TA4. . . . . . **167** F8
Hob La TA2. . . . . **168** E8
Hobwell La BS41. . . . . **11** C2
Hoccombe Ford TA4 . . . . . **150** F1
Hocken Cl TA20. . . . . **223** D6
Hockley Ct BA1. . . . . **27** D1
Hockley La BA22. . . . . **175** E5
Hockpitt La TA5 . . . . **134** A2
Hodder's Cl BA11 . . . . **119** E5
Hodges Barton TA11. . . . . **211** C4
Hodshill BA2 . . . . **62** F6
Hoecroft BA3 . . . . **96** D2
Hoecroft Gdns BA3 . . . . **96** D3
Hogarth Mews BS22. . . . . . **32** A3
Hogarth Wlk BS22 . . . . **32** A3

Hoggington La BA14 . . . . . **83** E3
Hogues Wlk BS13 . . . . **22** B4
Holbeach Way BS14. . . . . . **23** A2
Holbear TA20. . . . . **223** D2
Holbrook Cres BS13. . . . . . **22** D4
Holbrook Pk TA13. . . . . . . **220** C5
Holburne Mus & Crafts Study
 Ctr★ BA2. . . . . **45** B7
Holcombe BS14. . . . . **23** A5
Holcombe Cl BA2 . . . . **28** F1
Holcombe Gr BS31. . . . . . . **24** D5
Holcombe Hill BA3. . . . . . . **116** C7
Holcombe La
 Bathampton BA2 . . . . **28** F1
 Doulting BA4 . . . . **141** E4
Holcombe Vale BA2. . . . . . **28** F1
Holden's Way
 Curry Rivel TA10 . . . . **171** C3
 Curry Rivel TA10 . . . . **171** D3
Holders Wlk BS41. . . . . **20** F8
Holdfast La TA14. . . . . **185** D1
Holditch Court La TA20. . . **198** E5
Holditch La EX13, TA20. . . **198** E5
Holdscroft La DT6 . . . . **199** B1
Holeground Villas BA5 . . . **203** A8
Holemore Cross EX14 . . . . **191** F5
Holes La BA11 . . . . **118** B6
Holes Sq TA24 . . . . **130** B5
Holford Cl BS48. . . . . **8** E1
Holford Ct BS14. . . . . **23** B5
Holford La TA4 . . . . **151** C5
Holford Rd
 Bridgwater TA6 . . . . **208** B4
 Taunton TA2. . . . . **212** E8
Hollam Cross TA22 . . . . . . **163** E7
Hollam Dr TA22 . . . . **163** D6
Hollam La TA22 . . . . **163** D7
Holland's La TA4. . . . . **149** E1
Holland's Wash Dro
 TA20 . . . . **193** C5
Holland Ct BA16 . . . . **207** D7
Holland Rd
 Bath BA1 . . . . **28** B1
 Clevedon BS21. . . . . **6** B1
Holland St BS23 . . . . **49** A8
Holleys Cl TA20 . . . . **198** D8
Hollies Cl
 Martock TA12. . . . . **185** D5
 Middlezoy TA7 . . . . **155** B3
 Shepton Mallet BA4. . . . . **205** C6
Hollies La BA1. . . . . **29** A6
Hollies The
 Crewkerne TA18 . . . . **224** C4
 Midsomer Norton BA3. . . . **78** A1
 Yeovil BA21 . . . . **219** C2
Hollis Ave BS20. . . . . **2** C3
Hollis Cl
 Halstock BA22 . . . . **197** D3
 Long Ashton BS41 . . . . **21** A8
Hollis Cres BS20 . . . . **2** C3
Hollister's Dr BS13. . . . . . . **22** D4
Hollis Way
 Halstock BA22 . . . . **197** D3
 Southwick BA14. . . . . **83** F3
Holloway
 Bath BA2. . . . . **228** B1
 Lopen TA13 . . . . **185** A1
 Minehead TA24 . . . . **200** F7
Holloway Rd TA7 . . . . **155** B2
Holloway St TA24. . . . . . . **200** F7
Holloway Th TA21 . . . . **179** E7
Hollowbrook La BS39,
 BS40. . . . . **57** D6
Hollowell Hill
 Norton Sub Hamdon TA14,
  TA18 . . . . **185** E1
 West Chinnock TA18 . . . . **196** B8
Hollow La
 Baltonsborough BA6 . . . . . **158** B8
 Dinnington TA17. . . . . **195** B7
 Lopen TA13 . . . . **185** A1
 Montacute TA15. . . . . **186** B3
 Wembdon TA5, TA6 . . . . . **208** C7
 Weston-Super-Mare BS22. . **31** F3
Hollow Marsh La BA3,
 BS39 . . . . **76** B4
Hollowmead BS49 . . . . **34** E8
Hollowmead Cl BS49 . . . . . **34** F8
Hollow Rd
 Shepton Beauchamp
  TA19 . . . . **184** D3
 Shipham BS25. . . . . **70** F8
Hollow The
 Bath BA2. . . . . **44** B4
 Corsley Heath BA12 . . . . . **144** E8
 Dunkerton BA2 . . . . **61** D4
 Westbury-sub-Mendip
  BA5. . . . . **110** D7
Hollway Cl BS14. . . . . **23** E5
Hollway Rd BS14. . . . . **23** E5
Hollybush BA15 . . . . **64** E7
Hollybush La
 Bristol BS9. . . . . **5** E5
 Bristol BS9. . . . .**5** F4
 Leigh u M BA3. . . . . **117** A2
Holly Cl
 Bridgwater TA6 . . . . **209** E5
 Nailsea BS48. . . . . **9** A3
 7 North Petherton TA6 . . **153** F4
 Taunton TA1. . . . . **213** C1
 Weston-Super-Mare BS22. . **32** A1
Holly Ct
 Bristol BS2. . . . . **226** C4
 Frome BA11. . . . . **120** B7
Holly Dr BA2. . . . . **62** D8
Holly Gr TA18 . . . . **224** D7
Holly Hill BA4. . . . . **142** C1

Holly La
 Clevedon BS21. . . . . **6** F6
 Drimpton DT8 . . . . **199** F8
 Shepton Mallet BA4. . . . . **205** C4
Hollyman Wlk 5 BS21. . . . . **6** F3
Hollymead La BS9 . . . . **5** E4
Hollyridge BS14. . . . . **23** C6
Holly Ridge BS20 . . . . **2** A5
Holly Terr
 Chard TA20. . . . . **223** C4
 Odcombe BA22 . . . . **186** C2
Holly Tree Wlk BA20 . . . . **218** E3
Holly Wlk
 Keynsham BS31. . . . . **24** D4
 Radstock BA3 . . . . **78** E1
Holman's BA6 . . . . **157** E4
Holman Cl BA6 . . . . **206** E6
Holmbury Cl BA11 . . . . . . **120** D6
Holmbush TA24 . . . . **128** E8
Holm Cl TA8. . . . . **104** B5
Holmlea
 Portishead BS20 . . . . **2** F5
 1 Wookey BA5. . . . . **139** D8
Holmoak Rd BS31. . . . . **24** C4
Holm Oaks BA6 . . . . **157** E4
Holm Rd BS24 . . . . **49** E2
Holms Rd BS23 . . . . **49** A5
Holsom Cl BS14. . . . . **23** F6
Holsom Rd BS14 . . . . **23** F6
Holst Gdns BS4 . . . . **22** D7
Holt Ball Steep TA24 . . . . **129** D7
Holten's La BA22. . . . . **196** E6
Holt Hill DT9 . . . . **189** C1
Holt La
 Halstock BA22 . . . . **197** F3
 South Perrott DT8. . . . . . . **196** D1
 Stourton Caundle DT9,
  DT10. . . . . **189** E1
 West Pennard BA6 . . . . . . **140** D2
Holton Cross BA9 . . . . **176** C6
Holton St BA9 . . . . **176** C5
Holt Rd
 North Brewham BA11 . . . . **161** E8
 Witham Friary BA11 . . . . . **143** D1
Holtsdown La BA1. . . . . **28** F7
Holvert La TA20. . . . . **194** F1
Holway
 North Petherton TA6 . . . . . **153** F4
 Tatworth TA20. . . . . **198** D8
Holway Ave TA1 . . . . **213** B3
Holway Deane TA1. . . . . . **213** C2
Holway Gn TA1 . . . . **213** C2
Holway Hill TA1 . . . . **213** B2
Holway House Pk TA19. . . **183** E2
Holway Park Com Prim Sch
 TA1. . . . . **213** C3
Holway Rd TA1 . . . . **213** B3
Holwell Cl BS39. . . . . **77** E4
Holwell Hill BA11 . . . . **143** B7
Holwell La BS27 . . . . **89** F8
Holworthy La TA22. . . . . . **148** E2
Holy Moor Cross EX36. . . **162** C1
Holy Moor La EX36 . . . . . . **162** C1
Holyoake St TA21. . . . . . . **222** C7
Holyrood Com Sch (Lower)
 TA20 . . . . **223** C4
Holyrood Com Sch (Upper)
 TA20 . . . . **223** C5
Holyrood St TA20. . . . . . . **223** C4
Holy Tree Cross TA14 . . . **185** E3
Holy Trinity CE Prim Sch
 Taunton TA1. . . . . **213** A3
 Yeovil BA20 . . . . **218** E2
Holy Well Rd TA7. . . . . . . **137** C2
Homberg Way TA6. . . . . . **208** E6
Homeavon Ho BS31. . . . . . **24** F5
Homecanton Ho BA9. . . . **216** C4
Homecastle Ho 2 TA6 . . **208** F5
Homechime Ho BA5. . . . . **203** D3
Home Cl
 Weston-sub-Mendip
  BA5. . . . . **110** E6
 West Camel BA22 . . . . . . **174** D3
 Wrington BS40 . . . . **35** E3
Homeclose La EX13,
 TA20 . . . . **198** A8
Home Cotts TA1 . . . . **212** D5
Home Dr
 Wincanton BA9 . . . . **216** C3
 Yeovil BA21 . . . . **218** E5
Home Farm★ TA24. . . . . . **131** D6
Home Farm Cl BA2. . . . . . . **79** B7
Home Farm La BA22 . . . . . **188** A8
Home Farm Pk TA19. . . . . **183** E2
Home Farm Rd BS8 . . . . . . **11** B8
Home Farm Way TA19. . . **183** E2
Homefield
 Bishops Lydeard TA4. . . . . **167** E8
 Congresbury BS49. . . . . **34** E3
 Locking BS24. . . . . **50** A5
 Timsbury BA2 . . . . **60** C2
 Wellington TA21. . . . . **222** E4
Homefield Cl
 Beckington BA11. . . . . **101** E4
 Creech St Michael TA3. . . **169** D4
 Locking BS24. . . . . **50** A5
 Saltford BS31. . . . . **25** E3
 Winscombe BS25. . . . . **51** F1
Home Field Cl TA11. . . . . . **157** B4
Homefield Ct BA22 . . . . . . **174** F1
Homefield Ind Est BS24. . . **50** A5
Homefield Rd BS31. . . . . . . **25** F3
Homefields BA5 . . . . **110** E6
Home Fields BA4 . . . . **205** C4
Homeground BS21. . . . . **6** F2

Home Ground BS11 . . . . 4 D7
Homelea Pk E BA1 . . . . . . 44 A7
Homelea Pk W BA1 . . . . . . 44 A7
Home Mdw TA24 . . . . . . 200 D7
Homemead BA2 . . . . 43 A8
Home Mead BS4 . . . . 22 E2
Home Orch
  Chew Stoke BS40 . . . . 56 D8
  Hatch Beauchamp TA3 . . . 183 A7
Homestead BS20 . . . . 1 E3
Homestead Pk BA5 . . . . . 203 A7
Homestead The
  Clevedon BS21 . . . . 6 C3
  Keynsham BS31 . . . . 24 F2
Homestead Way BS25 . . . . 70 A8
Homeville Ho BA20 . . . . . 219 A4
Home Way Cnr BA6 . . . . . 138 B4
Hone Cross EX16 . . . . 164 F5
Hone La TA22 . . . . 147 F4
Honeycombe Rise DT9 . . . 225 B2
Honey Crock La TA7 . . . . 155 E8
Honeygar La BA6 . . . . 138 B5
Honey Garston Cl BS13 . . . 22 B4
Honey Garston Rd BS13 . . 22 B4
Honeyhall La BS49 . . . . 52 D7
Honeyhurst La BS27 . . . . 109 F8
Honeylands
  Curry Rivel TA10 . . . . . . 171 D4
  Portishead BS20 . . . . 2 C3
Honeymead
  Bristol BS14 . . . . 23 C6
  Croscombe BA5 . . . . 204 B8
Honey Mead La BA6,
  TA11 . . . . 158 B4
Honeypot La TA11 . . . . . . 158 C1
Honey Pot La BA11 . . . . . 144 A4
Honey Row La TA4 . . . . . . 132 E2
Honeysuckle Pl BS24 . . . . 50 A8
Honeywell La BA3 . . . . 94 F4
Honiton 9 BS22 . . . . 32 A2
Honiton Rd
  Clevedon BS21 . . . . 6 E1
  Taunton TA3 . . . . 168 D1
Hood Cl BA6 . . . . 206 E2
Hookedmead La BS26 . . . . 88 A1
Hook Hill TA4 . . . . 60 D2
Hook La
  Hinton Blewett BA3, BS39 . . 75 E4
  North Cheriton BA9 . . . . . 176 C5
Hooks Batch BS40 . . . . 54 C4
Hookway Hill TA24 . . . . . 123 A3
Hooper's Cl TA1 . . . . 212 B2
Hooper's La
  East Coker BA22 . . . . 197 F7
  Fordgate TA7 . . . . 154 E3
Hooper Ave BA5 . . . . 112 E1
Hooper Cl
  Burnham-on-S TA8 . . . . . 104 D5
  Highbridge TA9 . . . . 104 F4
Hooper Rd
  Bristol BS14 . . . . 23 D5
  Street BA16 . . . . 207 B5
Hoopers Barton 9 BA11 . 119 C5
Hoopers Cross EX16 . . . . 164 D3
Hopcott Cl TA24 . . . . 200 E6
Hopcott Rd TA24 . . . . . . 200 F5
Hopcott Terr TA24 . . . . . 201 A5
Hopechapel Hill 10 BS8 . . 11 F6
Hope Cl BA5 . . . . 203 C4
Hope Corner Cl TA2 . . . . 212 F8
Hope Corner La TA2 . . . . 212 F8
Hope Cote Lodge BA2 . . . 45 C1
Hope Cotts
  Highbridge TA9 . . . . 104 D3
  Kingston Seymour BS21 . . 16 B2
Hope Cross SP8 . . . . 177 D3
Hope Cl BS1 . . . . 226 B1
Hope Sq BS8 . . . . 11 F6
Hope Terr BA3 . . . . 78 B1
Hopewell Gdns BS11 . . . . . 4 F7
Hopkins Ct BA9 . . . . 216 C2
Hopkins Ho BA22 . . . . . . 218 A5
Hopkins St BS23 . . . . 48 E8
Hopton Ct BA4 . . . . 141 E1
Horesham Gr BS13 . . . . . . 22 C5
Horn's La BS26 . . . . 70 B2
Hornbeam Cl
  Bridgwater TA6 . . . . 209 D5
  Frome BA11 . . . . 120 C6
  Taunton TA1 . . . . 213 D2
Hornbeam Wlk BS31 . . . . 24 C3
Horne Cl BA3 . . . . 96 F1
Horner Nature Trails★
  TA24 . . . . 129 B8
Horner Rd TA2 . . . . 213 B7
Horningsham Prim Sch
  BA12 . . . . 144 D4
Horn La TA20 . . . . 194 B2
Hornsbury Hill TA20 . . . . 223 E8
Hornsbury Mill Mus★
  TA20 . . . . 223 E8
Hornsey La TA20 . . . . 182 B1
Horns La BA9 . . . . 160 B2
Horn St BA11 . . . . 143 B8
Hornswell DT9 . . . . 189 D4
Horrington Prim Sch
  BA5 . . . . 113 B3
Horsecastle Cl BS49 . . . . 17 A1
Horsecastle Farm Rd
  BS49 . . . . 17 A1
Horsecastle La DT9 . . . . 225 C3
Horsecastles DT9 . . . . . . 225 D3
Horse Cl BA11 . . . . 101 D5
Horsecombe Brow BA2 . . . 45 A1

Horsecombe Gr BA2 . . . . 45 A1
Horsecombe Vale BA2 . . . 45 A1
Horsecroft La TA3 . . . . . . 170 B4
Horsefair The BS1 . . . . . . 227 B3
Horseham La TA5 . . . . . . 134 E8
Horsehill La BA4 . . . . 142 D2
Horse La DT9 . . . . 176 A2
Horseland La TA24 . . . . . 131 A4
Horseleaze La BS25 . . . . . 52 D1
Horsemans Mews BA6 . . . 206 D5
Horse Mill Cross DT6 . . . 199 D3
Horse Mill La TA11 . . . . . 211 E4
Horsepark La TA24 . . . . . 130 A4
Horse Pond La TA6 . . . . . 208 F4
Horsepool Rd BS13 . . . . . . 21 E3
Horse Race La BS8 . . . . . . 10 A6
Horse Rd TA24 . . . . 130 F5
Horseshoe Cotts TA12 . . . 185 E7
Horseshoe Dr BS9 . . . . 5 C4
Horseshoe La TA20 . . . . . 199 A6
Horseshoe Wlk BA2 . . . . . 45 B5
Horsey La
  Horsey TA7 . . . . 136 C2
  Langport TA10 . . . . 172 A4
  Yeovil BA20 . . . . 219 A4
Horsey Rdbt BA20 . . . . . . 219 A3
Horsington CE Prim Sch
  BA8 . . . . 176 D3
Horsington Ho BA8 . . . . . 176 E2
Horstmann Cl 2 BA1 . . . . 44 B7
Hortmead La TA19 . . . . . 183 E3
Horton Cl BA21 . . . . 218 D6
Horton Ho BA2 . . . . 228 C4
Horton St
  Bristol BS2 . . . . 227 C3
  Frome BA11 . . . . 119 D5
Horton Way TA7 . . . . 136 E4
Horts Rd TA1 . . . . 212 C1
Horwood Rd BS48 . . . . 8 F1
Hosey Wlk BS13 . . . . 22 A5
Hoskins Cl TA10 . . . . 171 C4
Hospital La
  Sherborne DT9 . . . . 225 D4
  South Petherton TA13 . . . 220 D5
Hospital Rdbt BA20 . . . . . 219 A5
Host St BS1 . . . . 227 A3
Hot Bath St 6 BA1 . . . . . . 228 B2
Hotwell Rd BS8 . . . . 226 B1
Hotwells Prim Sch BS8 . . . 11 F6
Houlgate Way BS26 . . . . . . 70 B1
Houlton St BS2 . . . . 227 C4
Houndsmill BA8 . . . . 176 E2
Houndsmoor La TA4 . . . . 167 A4
Hound St DT9 . . . . 225 D4
Houndstone Bsns Pk
  BA22 . . . . 218 B6
Houndstone Cl BA21 . . . . 218 C5
Houndstone Cnr BA22 . . . 218 C5
Houndstone La BA22 . . . . 218 A5
Houndstone Pk BA22 . . . . 218 C5
Houndstone Ret Pk
  BA22 . . . . 218 B5
Houndwood BA16 . . . . . . 207 A6
Houndwood Dro BA16 . . . 207 A6
House's La TA20 . . . . 193 F1
House Gate Rd BA11 . . . . 143 F2
Housman Rd BA16 . . . . . 207 D5
Houston Way BA11 . . . . . 119 D5
Hoveland Cres TA1 . . . . . 212 D2
Hoveland Ct TA1 . . . . 212 C2
Hoveland Dr TA1 . . . . . . 212 D1
Hoveland La TA1 . . . . 212 C2
Howard Cl
  Burnham-on-S TA8 . . . . . 104 C7
  Saltford BS31 . . . . 25 D3
Howard Rd
  Wellington TA21 . . . . . . 222 D7
  Yeovil BA21 . . . . 219 E6
Howards Row TA20 . . . . . 223 C4
Howcroft La BS9 . . . . 5 E4
Howecroft Gdns BS9 . . . . 5 E4
Howell's La TA2, TA6 . . . . 153 D1
Howell Hill BA22 . . . . . . 174 D4
Howgrove Hill La BS40 . . . 37 C2
Howitt Way 1 BS24 . . . . . 49 F7
Howleigh La TA3 . . . . 181 C5
Hownel La TA22 . . . . 147 F2
Hoyles Cl TA21 . . . . 222 E4
Hoyles Rd TA21 . . . . 222 E4
Hozzard La BS28 . . . . 107 E2
Huckeymead La BA4 . . . . 158 F7
Huddleston St 10 BA5 . . . 203 A4
Hudson St TA8 . . . . 104 B6
Hudson Way TA2 . . . . 212 C6
Huett Cl TA8 . . . . 65 F3
Hugdole La TA7 . . . . 137 D2
Hughenden Rd BS23 . . . . . 49 A8
Hughes Cl 6 TA6 . . . . . . 209 B4
Hughes St BA11 . . . . 101 E4
Hugh Sexey CE Mid Sch
  BS28 . . . . 107 E3
Hugo St TA1 . . . . 213 A4
Huish BA20 . . . . 219 A5
Huish Ball Steep TA24 . . . 129 D7
Huish Cl
  Highbridge TA9 . . . . 104 D4
  Taunton TA1 . . . . 213 D4
Huish Cleeve TA4 . . . . . . 165 E7
Huish Ct BA3 . . . . 79 B2
Huish Episcopi Prim Sch
  TA10 . . . . 172 A5
Huish Episcopi Sch
  TA10 . . . . 172 A5
Huish Gdns 2 BA20 . . . . . 219 A5
Huish La
  Alweston DT9 . . . . 189 B2
  Washford TA23 . . . . 131 E4

Huish La continued
  Wyke Champflower BA10 . 215 C7
Huish Mdw TA24 . . . . . . 131 E4
Huish Park (Yeovil Town FC)
  BA22 . . . . 218 B7
Huish Prim Sch BA20 . . . 219 A5
Huish Rd TA11 . . . . 173 C7
Huish Row TA24 . . . . 129 A8
Hukeley Head Cross
  EX16 . . . . 164 D3
Hulk Moor Dro BA16,
  BA16 . . . . 207 C8
Hulkshay La TA6 . . . . 153 E3
Hull La DT9, BA8 . . . . . . 176 B3
Humber Gr TA1 . . . . 213 D3
Humberstan Wlk BS11 . . . . 4 E8
Humphreys Rd TA21 . . . . 222 E7
Humphry Davy Way 6
  BS8 . . . . 11 F5
Humpy La DT9 . . . . 189 A1
Hundredstone Cl BA21 . . 219 B8
Hundry La TA10 . . . . 184 D8
Hungerford Cl BS4 . . . . . . 23 E8
Hungerford Gdns BS4 . . . 23 E8
Hungerford Rd
  Bath BA1 . . . . 44 C7
  Bristol BS4 . . . . 23 E8
Hungerford Terr BA2 . . . . 62 D1
Hung Rd BS11 . . . . 4 E5
Hunstrete Rd BA2 . . . . . . 59 F7
Hunt's La BS49 . . . . 34 E8
Huntash La TA4 . . . . 167 A4
Huntenhull Gn BA13 . . . . 121 C3
Huntenhull La BA13 . . . . 121 D4
Hunter's Hill EX15 . . . . . 179 E1
Hunter's Way EX15 . . . . . 179 E1
Hunters Moon Touring Pk
  EX13 . . . . 198 F5
Hunters Rest Miniature
  Rlwy★ BS39 . . . . 59 A5
Huntham Cl TA3 . . . . 170 E6
Huntham La TA3 . . . . 170 E5
Huntham Rd TA3 . . . . . . 170 D4
Huntingham Rd BS13 . . . . 21 F4
Huntley Cl EX13 . . . . 198 A2
Huntley Gr BS48 . . . . 9 A1
Huntley La
  Chardstock EX13 . . . . . . 198 A8
  Tatworth EX13, TA20 . . . 193 D1
Hunts La TA5 . . . . 133 D5
Huntsmans Ridge BS27 . . . 90 C7
Hunts Mead DT9 . . . . . . 225 B2
Huntspill Rd TA9 . . . . . . 104 D2
Huntworth Bsns Pk TA6 . . 154 A5
Huntworth La
  Fordgate TA7 . . . . 154 C5
  North Petherton TA6 . . . 153 F4
Hurcott Cross TA19 . . . . . 184 D3
Hurcott La TA19 . . . . 184 D4
Hurd's Bldgs BA11 . . . . . 119 F4
Hurdle Way TA1 . . . . 213 A3
Hurley La TA4 . . . . 151 B8
Hurlstone Pk TA24 . . . . . 124 B3
Hurmans Cl TA7 . . . . 156 B8
Hurn Dro BA5 . . . . 139 B6
Hurn La
  Berrow TA8 . . . . 84 F7
  Keynsham BS31 . . . . 25 A3
  Pitcombe BA7 . . . . 215 A1
  Shepton Montague BA7 . . 160 A2
Hurn Rd BA5 . . . . 6 F2
Hursley Hill
  Bristol BS14 . . . . 40 D8
  Whitchurch BS14 . . . . . . 23 D1
Hursley La BS14 . . . . 23 E1
Hurst TA12 . . . . 185 D5
Hurst Dro
  Compton Dundon TA11 . . 157 A3
  Hambridge TA10, TA12 . . 184 E8
Hurst Mews TA12 . . . . . . 185 D5
Hurston Rd BS4 . . . . 22 D7
Hurst Pk TA12 . . . . 185 D5
Hurst Rd
  Bristol BS4 . . . . 22 F8
  Weston-Super-Mare BS23 . 49 A6
Hurst Wlk BS4 . . . . 22 F8
Hussey's DT10 . . . . 190 F5
Hutchin's La BA4 . . . . 160 F8
Hutchings's La TA4 . . . . . 167 D4
Hutton CE Prim Sch BS24 . 49 E2
Hutton Cl
  Bristol BS9 . . . . 5 E7
  Keynsham BS31 . . . . 25 A2
Hutton Hill BS24 . . . . 49 F2
Hutton Moor La BS22,
  BS24 . . . . 49 C6
Hutton Moor Pk BS24 . . . 49 C6
Hutton Moor Rd BS22 . . . 49 C7
Hutton Moor Rdbt BS22 . . 49 C7
Huxham La TA4 . . . . 158 F7
Hyatt Pl BA4 . . . . 204 F5
Hyatts Wood Rd BS48 . . . 19 E1
Hyde's La SN14 . . . . 13 A1
Hyde Ct BA21 . . . . 218 C6
Hyde La
  Monkton Heathfield TA2 . 169 C5
  Taunton TA2 . . . . 213 F6
Hyde Lane Cotts TA2 . . . 169 C5
Hyde Park Ave 4 TA6 . . . 153 E3
Hyde Pk 5 TA6 . . . . 153 E3
Hyde Rd
  Minehead TA24 . . . . 200 E6
  Montacute TA15 . . . . . . 186 B4
Hyde The
  Clevedon BS21 . . . . 16 C8
  Keynsham BS31 . . . . 24 F6
Hyland Gr BS9 . . . . 5 F8

Hylton Cl TA2 . . . . 212 F8
Hynicombe La TA4 . . . . . 165 D6
Hythe BS27 . . . . 89 E5

I

Iberry La TA3 . . . . 183 E8
Idwal Cl BA2 . . . . 79 C8
Iford Cl BS31 . . . . 25 E3
Iford Fields BA15 . . . . 64 E2
Iford Hill BA15 . . . . 64 E2
Iford La BA3, BA15 . . . . . . 64 C3
Ilchester Com Prim Sch (Inf)
  BA22 . . . . 173 D1
Ilchester Com Prim Sch
  (Jun) BA22 . . . . 173 E2
Ilchester Cres BS13 . . . . . 22 B8
Ilchester Mead BA22 . . . . 173 D1
Ilchester Mus★ BA22 . . . . 173 E1
Ilchester Rd
  Bristol BS13 . . . . 22 B8
  Charlton Mackrell TA11 . . 173 D1
  Chilthorne Domer BA21,
  BA22 . . . . 186 F6
  Yeovil BA21 . . . . 218 F8
Ile Ct TA19 . . . . 221 C4
Ilex Ave BS21 . . . . 6 E2
Ilex Cl
  Bristol BS13 . . . . 21 F6
  Huntspill TA9 . . . . 136 B8
Ilex La BS25 . . . . 51 F1
Ilford Ct TA1 . . . . 212 C2
Illustrious Cres BA22 . . . . 173 E2
Ilminster BS24 . . . . 49 A2
Ilminster Ave 5 BS4 . . . . 22 F8
Ilminster Avenue Prim Sch
  BS4 . . . . 23 A8
Ilminster Cl
  Clevedon BS21 . . . . 6 E2
  Nailsea BS48 . . . . 18 D8
Ilminster Rd TA1 . . . . . . 213 D4
Ilsyn Gr BS14 . . . . 23 D7
Ilton Bsns Pk TA19 . . . . . 183 D7
Imbercourt Cl BS14 . . . . . 23 B8
Immenstadt Dr TA21 . . . 222 D4
Imperial Pk BS13 . . . . 22 C6
Imperial Rd BS14 . . . . . . 23 C8
Improvement Pl 5 TA21 . 222 D5
Inchalloch 19 BA1 . . . . . . 28 A1
Incline The TA19 . . . . . . 221 B4
Inclosures The 5 BS22 . . . 49 F8
Ingleton Dr BS22 . . . . 32 A4
Ingrams Mdw TA23 . . . . 202 C6
Inkerman Ct TA1 . . . . . . 213 A3
Inman Ho BA1 . . . . 228 C4
Inn Cotts BS11 . . . . 5 A7
Inner Circ TA1 . . . . 213 D5
Inner Elm Terr BA3 . . . . . 78 C1
Inner Gullands TA1 . . . . . 212 D3
Innicks Cl BS40 . . . . 55 D1
Innox Gdns BS13 . . . . 22 A5
Innox Gr BA2 . . . . 43 F2
Innox Hill BA11 . . . . 119 E6
Innox La BA1 . . . . 28 B5
Innox Rd BA2 . . . . 44 B5
Inns Court Ave BS4 . . . . . 22 D7
Inns Court Dr BS4 . . . . . . 22 D6
Inns Court Gn BS4 . . . . . . 22 D7
Innsmead La TA7 . . . . . . 137 B1
Instow 7 BS22 . . . . 32 A2
Instow Rd BS4 . . . . 22 E8
Instow Wlk BS4 . . . . 22 E8
International Coll Sherborne
  Sch DT9 . . . . 225 D5
International Helicopter
  Mus★ BS24 . . . . 49 E5
Inverness Rd BA2 . . . . 44 C6
Inwood Rd TA6 . . . . 208 C5
Irene Cl TA6 . . . . 209 D7
Ireson Cl BA9 . . . . 216 D4
Ireson La BA9 . . . . 216 D4
Irnham Rd TA24 . . . . 201 A7
Iron Dish La TA13 . . . . . . 184 E6
Iron Mill La BA11 . . . . . . 101 A1
Ironmould La BS31 . . . . . 24 A8
Iron Post TA22 . . . . 163 B5
Irvine Ct TA2 . . . . 212 C6
Irving Cl BS21 . . . . 6 F3
Irving Ho BS1 . . . . 226 C3
Irving Rd TA11 . . . . 158 A1
Irwell La TA1 . . . . 213 D4
Isaacs Cl BA16 . . . . 207 B4
Island The BA3 . . . . 78 A1
Islemoor Dro TA3 . . . . . . 184 A8
Islemoor La TA13 . . . . . . 220 B6
Islemoor Rd TA3 . . . . . . 183 F8
Isleport Bsns Pk TA9 . . . 104 F4
Isleport Rd TA9 . . . . 104 F3
Isles La
  East Coker, Lyatts BA22 . . 197 C6
  East Coker, Sutton Bingham
  BA22 . . . . 197 D6
Ivel Ct BA21 . . . . 219 C5
Ivel Gdns BA22 . . . . 173 E1
Ivel Sq BA20 . . . . 219 B5
Ivelway TA18 . . . . 224 C5
Ivo Peters Rd BA2 . . . . . 228 A2
Ivors Way TA6 . . . . 153 E4
Ivy Ave BA2 . . . . 44 C4
Ivy Bank Pk BA2 . . . . 44 F2
Ivy Cl BS48 . . . . 8 D1
Ivy Cotts TA3 . . . . 181 C3
Ivy Cross TA21 . . . . 179 D7
Ivy Ct BS20 . . . . 1 F5
Ivy Gn TA20 . . . . 223 C3

Ivy Gr BA2 . . . . 44 C4
Ivy Grove Cl TA6 . . . . . . 209 D7
Ivy Ho
  Chard TA20 . . . . 223 B4
  Wellington TA21 . . . . . . 222 C6
Ivy House Cotts BS29 . . . 50 D7
Ivy House Pk BS29 . . . . . 169 C2
Ivy La BS24 . . . . 50 A8
Ivyleaf Rd TA11 . . . . 211 C4
Ivy Pl BA2 . . . . 44 C4
Ivythorn Cl BA16 . . . . . . 207 C4
Ivy Thorn La BA16 . . . . . 207 A1
Ivythorn Rd BA16 . . . . . 207 C4
Ivywell Rd BS9 . . . . 5 E3
Ivy Wlk
  Banwell BS29 . . . . 50 E4
  Midsomer Norton BA3 . . . 97 B8
  Yeovil BA20 . . . . 218 E3
Iwood La BS40 . . . . 35 A2

J

Jack's Dro BS28 . . . . 137 F8
Jack's La
  Croscombe BA5 . . . . 204 C7
  Frome BA11 . . . . 119 D7
Jack Price Cl BS13 . . . . . . 22 C3
Jackson's La TA5 . . . . 134 A2
Jack White's Gibbet BA9 . 176 A8
Jacob's Cl BS1 . . . . 226 C2
Jacob's La BA6 . . . . 206 E5
Jacobs Mdw BS20 . . . . 2 F4
Jacob St
  Bristol BS2 . . . . 227 B3
  Bristol BS2 . . . . 227 C3
Jagaar Ct TA7 . . . . 137 D5
Jaguar Ho 3 BA1 . . . . . . 228 B3
Jamaica St BS2 . . . . 227 B4
James's Hill BA10 . . . . . . 161 A8
James Cl
  Holcombe BA3 . . . . 116 C8
  Shepton Mallet BA4 . . . . 205 C4
James La EX14 . . . . 192 F2
James St W BA1 . . . . 228 B2
James St BS5 . . . . 227 C4
Janson Cl TA6 . . . . 209 D6
Japonica Cl TA6 . . . . 209 C5
Jarman Way TA20 . . . . . . 223 D6
Jarmany Hill BA6 . . . . . . 157 F3
Jarmyns TA1 . . . . 212 A3
Jarvis Cl DT10 . . . . 190 B4
Jarvis La TA9 . . . . 86 D4
Jarvis Way DT10 . . . . . . 190 B4
Jasmine Cl
  Crewkerne TA18 . . . . . . 224 D7
  Highbridge TA9 . . . . 104 C4
  Weston-Super-Mare BS22 . 32 A1
  Yeovil BA22 . . . . 218 B5
Jasmine Ct 8 BS23 . . . . . 48 E8
Jasmine La BS49 . . . . 17 F2
Jasmine Way BS24 . . . . . 32 A1
Jay Cl BA11 . . . . 120 B6
Jaycroft Rd TA8 . . . . 104 B6
Jay View BS23 . . . . 49 A5
Jeffreys' Way TA1 . . . . . . 212 A2
Jeffries Ct TA19 . . . . 183 C4
Jeffs Way 3 EX13 . . . . . . 198 A1
Jellalabad Ct TA1 . . . . . . 212 F3
Jellicoe Ct BS22 . . . . 31 E4
Jena Ct BS31 . . . . 25 D3
Jesmond Rd
  Clevedon BS21 . . . . 6 C3
  Weston-Super-Mare BS22 . 32 C4
Jesse Hughes Ct BA1 . . . . 28 C2
Jessop Ct BS1 . . . . 227 B2
Jessop Underpass BS3 . . . 11 F4
Jews La
  Bath BA2 . . . . 44 C6
  Churchill BS25 . . . . 52 F4
  Wiveliscombe TA4 . . . . . 210 B5
Jill's Cl BA4 . . . . 142 A6
Jim O'Neil Ho BS11 . . . . . 4 D7
Jocelin Dr BS22 . . . . 31 F4
Jocelin Rd BA6 . . . . 206 F5
Jocelyn Dr BA5 . . . . 203 B3
John Beales Hill BA4 . . . 140 F3
John Cabot Ct BS1 . . . . . 226 B1
John Carr's Terr BS8 . . . . 226 B2
John Cozens Ho 6 BS2 . . 227 C3
John Grinter Way TA21 . 222 D4
John Gunn Cl TA20 . . . . 223 C5
John St S TA6 . . . . 104 A7
John Slessor Ct BA1 . . . . 228 B4
Johnson's Ctyd DT9 . . . . 225 D3
Johnson Cl
  East Brent TA9 . . . . 86 D5
  Wells BA5 . . . . 203 F5
Johnson Flats BA21 . . . . 219 C7
John St
  Bath BA1 . . . . 228 B3
  Bristol BS1 . . . . 227 A3
  Burnham-on-S TA8 . . . . . 104 A7
  Highbridge TA9 . . . . 104 D3
Johnstone Cl BA16 . . . . . 207 B3
Johnstone St BA2 . . . . . . 228 C2
John Wesleys Chapel★
  BS1 . . . . 227 B3
Joles La BA11 . . . . 120 F1
Jones Cl BS49 . . . . 17 A1
Joselin Ct DT9 . . . . 225 D5
Joyden Ct TA20 . . . . 223 D2
Joy Hill BS8 . . . . 11 F6
Juan's La SP8 . . . . 177 E1
Jubilee Cl
  Bridgwater TA6 . . . . 209 C4

Jubilee Cl continued
Castle Cary BA7........214 C6
Chard TA20...........223 C3
Jubilee Cotts ⑩ BA11...119 F4
Jubilee Ct
  ⑧ Wellington TA21....222 D5
  Weston-Super-Mare BS23..48 F8
Jubilee Dr BS8.........10 B4
Jubilee Gdns
  Milverton TA4.........167 A4
  South Petherton TA13...220 C4
Jubilee La BS40.........53 A6
Jubilee Path BS22......31 C1
Jubilee Pl
  Bristol BS1...........227 A1
  Clevedon BS21.........6 D1
  Yeovil BA21..........218 D5
Jubilee Rd
  Axbridge BS26.........70 C2
  Radstock BA3..........78 C1
  Street BA16..........207 C4
  Weston-Super-Mare BS23..48 E7
Jubilee St
  Bristol BS2...........227 C2
  Burnham-on-S TA8.....104 B6
  Taunton TA2..........212 E6
Jubilee Terr
  Frome BA11...........119 E5
  Hemington BA3.........99 C7
  Paulton BS39..........77 E6
Jubilee Way BS22.......32 C3
Judy's Orch TA7.......154 F5
Julian's Acres TA8.....84 F4
Julian Cl
  Bristol BS9...........5 E3
  Shepton Mallet BA4....205 C4
Julian Ct BS9.........5 E3
Julian Rd
  Bath BA1.............228 B3
  Bristol BS9...........5 E3
Julier Ho BA1.........228 C4
Jumpers Combe TA23...148 E8
Junction Ave BA2......228 A1
Junction Dro TA3......170 C2
Junction Rd BA2.......228 A1
Juniper Cl
  Bridgwater TA6.......209 E4
  Yeovil BA20..........218 F3
Juniper Pl BS22........31 F4
Juniper Rd TA1........213 C2
Jurston La
  Wellington TA21......222 E6
  Wellington TA21......222 F5
Jury Hill TA22........163 E6
Jury Rd TA22..........163 E6
Justice Ave BS31......25 E3
Justice La BA11.......119 F5

K

Kale St BA4...........142 D2
Kale Street Cotts BA4..142 D2
Karen Cl BS48.........19 A4
Karen Dr BS48.........19 A5
Kaynton Mead BA1......44 B7
Keats Ho ④ BS23.......48 F4
Keats Rd
  Radstock BA3..........97 C8
  Taunton TA1..........213 C3
Kebby's Farm Cl TA4...202 A4
Keble Ave BS13........21 F5
Keeds La BS41.........10 F1
Keedwell Hill BS41....10 F1
Keel's Hill BA3........79 C8
Keen's Elm La BA16....207 E4
Keene's Way BS21......6 C2
Keens Cl BA16.........207 D5
Keens La TA7..........155 C2
Keep St BA22..........174 D3
Keep The BS22.........32 A3
Keg Store The BS1.....227 B2
Keinton Mandeville Prim Sch
  TA11.................158 A1
Kellways BS48.........19 A4
Kelson's La BS28......108 B3
Kelso Pl BA1..........44 D7
Kelso Villas BA1......44 D7
Kelston Cl BS31.......25 D4
Kelston Gdns BS22.....32 B5
Kelston Rd
  Bath BA1.............26 B1
  Keynsham BS31.........24 D5
  Weston-Super-Mare BS22..32 B5
Kelston View BA2......44 A5
Kelting Gr TA6........6 F2
Keltings TA6..........208 C6
Kelway Rd TA21........222 E7
Kember's Hill BA22, DT9.175 C3
Kemble Cl BS48........9 A1
Kemble Gdns BS11......4 F5
Kemm Cl BS27..........90 B6
Kemp's La BA11........120 F7
Kempe's Cl BS41.......11 A2
Kempe Way BS24........49 E7
Kemps La TA24.........147 B3
Kemps Way TA22.......163 D6
Ken Cl
  Chard TA20...........223 D3
  Wells BA5............140 C8
Kencot Wlk BS13.......22 B3
Kendale Rd TA6........208 E6
Kendall Cl TA3........169 D6
Kendrick Ct ❶ BA5.....203 D4
Kenilworth Cl BS31....24 D4
Kenilworth Ct BA1.....45 B8
Kenmare Rd BS4........22 E8
Kenmeade Cl BS25......70 E8

Kenmore Dr BA21.......219 B6
Kennard Cl BA6........206 F3
Kennard Moor Dro
  Butleigh BA6.........157 E7
  Glastonbury BA6......206 F1
Kennaway Rd BS21......6 E2
Kenn Bsns Pk BS21.....16 E8
Kenn Cl BS23..........49 A5
Kenn Ct BS23..........22 E7
Kennedy Cl TA9........104 E4
Kennel Batch BA5......111 D4
Kennel La
  Compton Bishop BS26...68 E3
  East Pennard BA4.....158 F8
  Langport TA10........172 A6
  West Bagborough TA4...151 D4
Kennel Lodge Rd BS3...11 E4
Kenn Est BS21.........16 E5
Kennet Gr TA1.........213 D4
Kennet Ho ⑩ BA1.......228 B2
Kennet Pk BA2.........28 E1
Kennet Rd BS31........25 A4
Kennford ⑥ BS23.......31 F2
Kennington Rd BA1.....44 B7
Kennion Cl TA20.......223 D3
Kennion Rd BA5.......203 C5
Kenn Moor Dr BS21....6 E1
Kennmoor Rd BS21.....17 A6
Kenn Moor Rd BS49....17 B1
Kenn Rd BS21..........16 F6
Kenn St BS21..........16 F7
Kensington Ct
  Bath BA1.............28 B2
  Bristol BS8..........226 A3
Kensington Fields BA14.83 F7
Kensington Gdns
  Bath BA1.............28 B1
  Bridgwater TA6.......209 D6
Kensington Gr TA24...200 E6
Kensington Pl
  Bath BA1.............28 B1
  Bristol BS8..........226 A3
Kensington Rd BS23...48 F5
Kent's Bglws TA20....198 D8
Kent's Cotts TA20....198 D8
Kent's Orch TA20.....198 D8
Kent Ave TA6..........209 A2
Kentisworth Rd DT10..190 F5
Kent La
  Shapwick TA7.........137 F1
  Shepton Mallet BA4...205 A5
Kent Rd
  Congresbury BS49.....34 D5
  Tatworth TA20........198 D5
Kents Cl TA20.........198 C8
Kentshare La BS40.....38 B6
Kents La TA20.........198 D8
Kent St BS27..........71 B1
Kent Way BS22.........32 B4
Kenwyn Cl TA1........213 D3
Keppel Cl BS31........25 D2
Kerry Croft BA11......143 C3
Kersey Ct BA11........119 C5
Kersham La TA24.......130 A1
Kestrel Cl TA6........209 C3
Kestrel Dr BS22.......31 E1
Keward Ave BA5.......203 B3
Keward Cl BA5........203 B3
Keward Mill Trad Est
  BA5.................203 B2
Keward Wlk BA5.......203 C3
Kew Rd BS21...........6 E4
Kewside BS22..........31 B4
Kewstoke Prim Sch BS22.31 B3
Kewstoke Rd
  Bath BA2.............45 A2
  Bristol BS9...........5 E4
  Weston-Super-Mare BS22..31 C3
Kew Wlk BS4...........23 C8
Keyes Path BS22.......31 F4
Keyford BA11..........119 F3
Keyford Cotts ⑮ BA11..119 F4
Keyford Ct BA11.......119 F2
Keyford Field Cotts
  BA11................119 F2
Keyford Gdns BA11....119 F3
Keyford Pl BA11.......119 F4
Keyford Rdbt BA11....197 E8
Keyford Terr BA11....119 F4
Keyhaven Bglws BS22...31 B4
Key Hill BA22.........174 A2
Keynsham By-Pass BS31.24 E7
Keynsham Hospl BS31...24 E5
Keynsham Prim Sch BS31 24 D5
Keynsham Rd BS30, BS31.25 A8
Keynsham Sta BS31....24 F6
Keyton Hill BS28.....107 E2
Kicks Hill TA7........155 B4
Kicks Hill La TA7.....155 B4
Kidd's La BA4.........205 D6
Kidder Bank BA5......203 F5
Kiddles BA21..........219 C5
Kid Gate Dro TA9, BS28..137 D8
Kidner Cl TA7.........136 E4
Kidsbury Rd TA6......208 E5
Kielder Dr BS22.......31 F3
Kilbirnie Rd BS14.....23 A3
Kildare BA2...........45 B7
Kildare Gdns TA24....200 F6
Kildare Rd BS13.......22 D8
Kilkenny Ave ⑤ TA2...212 F6
Kilkenny Ct BA11.....212 F6
Kilkenny La
  Bath BA2.............62 B8
  Wraxall BA4..........159 A6
Kilkenny Pl BS20......2 C6

Killams Ave
  Staplehay TA3.........181 F8
  Taunton TA1..........168 F1
Killams Cl TA1........168 F1
Killams Cres TA1......168 F1
Killams Dr TA1........168 F1
Killams Gn TA1........168 F1
Killams La TA1........168 F1
Killarney Ave TA8.....104 C6
Killick Way TA4.......202 D3
Kilmersdon CE Prim Sch
  BA3.................98 A6
Kilmersdon Hill BA3...98 A5
Kilmersdon Rd
  Bristol BS13.........22 B4
  Radstock BA3.........97 E8
Kilminster Rd BS11....4 D7
Kilmorie Rd TA1......212 C2
Kiln Cl TA5..........135 B5
Kiln Dr
  Evercreech BA4.......141 E1
  Highbridge TA9.......104 D3
Kiln Pk BS23..........49 A6
Kilton Cross TA5......133 E5
Kilve BS24...........49 A2
Kilve Cl TA2.........212 F7
Kilve Cres TA2........212 F7
Kilve Ct TA5.........133 C5
Kilver St BA4.........205 D6
Kilver Street Hill BA4.205 D7
Kimber Cl TA9........104 D3
Kimberley BA21........6 C2
Kimberley Terr TA6...209 B7
Kinber Cl BA1.........27 A3
Kinforde TA20.........223 C5
King's Castle Rd BA5..112 C1
King's Cnr TA22.......163 D6
King's Coll TA1.......213 B8
King's Hall Sch TA2...168 E6
King's Head La BS13...21 F7
King's Hill BA3........94 F7
King's La
  Binegar BA3..........95 E1
  Clevedon BS21........6 D5
  ⑥ Weston-Super-Mare
    BS23................48 E8
King's Mill Rd DT10...190 D3
King's Pl TA6.........208 F2
King's Rd
  Bristol BS8..........226 A3
  Clevedon BS21........6 D5
  Doulting BA4.........141 E7
  Portishead BS20......1 F4
King's Sch BA10......215 E6
King Alfred ⑧ TA6....153 F4
King Alfred Dr BA22...223 C2
King Alfred Sch The TA9 104 C5
King Alfreds Ctyd ⑦
  BA5.................203 D4
King Alfreds Mdw BS28.108 B4
King Alfred Way BA15..64 D7
King Arthur Dr BA21...218 D7
King Arthurs Com Sch
  BA9.................216 A4
King Athelstan Dr TA20.223 D2
King Ceol Cl TA20....223 C2
King Cerdic Cl TA20...223 D2
Kingcott Mill Farm Cvns
  BS48................20 B8
King Cuthred Cl TA20..223 C2
King Cuthred Dr TA20..223 C2
Kingdom BA5..........113 A4
Kingdom La TA2.......168 B4
Kingdon Mead TA3.....169 D4
Kingdown Rd BS40.....37 C5
King Edward's Jun Sch
  BA2.................45 C7
King Edward's Pre-Prep Sch
  BA1.................44 C8
King Edward's Sch BA2.45 C7
King Edward Rd BS14...23 A6
King Edward Rd
  Bath BA2.............44 D5
  Minehead TA24........201 A6
Kingfisher Cl
  Bridgwater TA6.......209 C3
  Yeovil BA20..........218 D3
Kingfisher Ct BA3.....64 C6
Kingfisher Dr BA3.....97 B8
Kingfisher Rd BS22....49 F8
King George's Rd
  Bath BA2.............44 C6
  Bristol BS13.........21 F5
King George Ave TA6...208 F2
King George Cl TA6....209 A2
King George Rd TA24...201 A6
King George St ② BA20.219 B4
King George V Pl ⑦
  BS1.................227 A2
King Ina Rd TA11......211 D4
King Ine Cl N TA20....223 C2
King Ine Cl S TA20....223 C2
King La BS39..........58 F4
Kinglake Villas TA6...209 A2
King Rd BS49..........52 E6
Kingsacre BA7.........214 B5
Kings Acre TA4........151 E5
Kings Cl
  Shepton Mallet BA4...205 B5
  Taunton TA1..........213 A2
Kingscliffe Terr TA6..209 A2
Kingscombe BA3.......114 E6
Kingscourt Cl BS14....23 A4
Kings Cres DT9.......225 D5

Kings Croft BS41.......10 E1
Kings Ct
  Bath BA1.............228 B2
  Bristol BS1..........227 A2
  ② Bristol, Withywood BS13 21 F4
  Sherborne DT9........225 D6
  Yeovil BA21..........219 C6
Kingsdon CE Prim Sch
  TA11................173 D5
Kingsdon Hill TA11....173 D5
Kingsdon Manor Sch
  TA11................173 D4
Kingsdown Cl TA6.....209 D6
Kingsdown Gr SN13....29 F3
Kingsdown Par BS6....227 A4
Kingsdown View ⑯ BA1..28 A1
Kingsdr TA7..........154 E6
Kingsfield BA2........44 C3
Kingsford Gate Cross
  TA24................145 B7
Kingsford Hill TA24...145 C7
Kingshams BA22.......173 E1
Kingshill BS48........8 C2
Kings Hill BA22.......186 E6
Kingshill CE Prim Sch
  BS48................8 D3
Kingshill Gdns BS48...8 C1
Kingshill La BS40.....56 C4
Kingsholme Ct BS23....30 E1
Kings La TA7.........156 B8
Kingsland TA23.......202 D7
Kingsland Grange ❶
  BA21................218 C6
Kingsland La TA24....148 D5
Kingsland Rd BA4.....205 B5
Kingsland Trad Est BS2.227 C3
Kings Lear TA19......183 F4
Kingsley Cl TA1......212 C1
Kingsley Ho BS2......227 C2
Kingsley Rd
  Clevedon BS21........6 D2
  Radstock BA3.........78 C1
  Weston-Super-Mare BS23..48 F3
Kingsmead BS48.......8 C2
Kingsmead Cl
  Holcombe BA3........116 C8
  Wiveliscombe TA4....210 C3
Kingsmead Com Sch
  TA4.................210 C3
Kingsmead Ct ⑧ BA1...228 B2
Kingsmead N BA1......228 B2
Kingsmead Sq BA1.....228 B2
Kingsmead St BA1.....228 B2
Kingsmead W BA1.....228 B2
Kingsmill BS9........5 D5
Kingsmoor Prim Sch
  TA7.................136 E2
Kings Oak Mdw BS39...58 E2
Kings of Wessex Com Sch
  The BS27.............90 B7
King Sq
  Bridgwater TA6.......208 F5
  Bristol BS2..........227 A4
King Square Ave BS2...227 A4
Kings Rd
  Sherborne DT9........225 D5
  Stoke sub Hamdon TA14..185 F5
  Wells BA5............140 C3
  Wrington BS40........35 D1
Kings Ride TA20......223 B6
Kings Sq BS30.........25 D8
King St
  Bridgwater TA6.......209 A5
  Bristol BS1..........227 A2
  Frome BA11...........119 E5
  Glastonbury BA6......206 D5
  Highbridge TA9.......104 D3
  Yeovil BA21..........219 B6
Kingston BA20........219 A5
Kingston Ave
  Clevedon BS21........6 E3
  Saltford BS31........25 C3
Kingston Bldgs ⑤ BA1.228 C2
Kingston Cl
  Street BA16..........207 D6
  Taunton TA1..........212 E7
Kingston Dr BS48......18 C8
Kingstone Cross TA19..221 F2
Kingstone Hill TA19...221 F2
Kingston La
  Felton BS40..........37 F8
  Maiden Bradley BA12..144 C1
Kingston Mead BA2.....37 F7
Kingston Mews ❸ TA2..212 F6
Kingston Rd
  Bath BA1.............228 C2
  Nailsea BS48.........18 C8
  Taunton TA2..........212 E7
Kingston St Mary CE Prim
  Sch TA2..............168 D8
Kingston View BA21....219 B6
Kingston Way BS48.....18 C8
Kingston Well La TA20.194 C2
Kingsway
  Bath BA2.............44 C3
  Holcombe BA3........116 C8
  Mark BS26, TA9.......87 D3
  Portishead BS20......1 F4
Kingsway Ctr BA11....119 F4
Kingsway Rd TA8......104 B7
Kingswear ❸ BS22.....32 A2

Kings Wlk BS13........21 E7
Kingswood Chase BA14..83 F6
Kingswood Prep Sch BA1 27 E1
Kingswood Rd TA18....224 C4
Kingswood Sch BA1....27 E2
Kington View BA8.....176 E1
Kingwell View BS39....59 D2
Kingweston Rd
  Butleigh BA6.........157 E3
  Charlton Mackrell TA11.173 E8
King William Ave BS1..227 A2
King William Rd TA7...137 C2
Kinsale Rd BS14.......23 C7
Kinvara Rd BS4........22 E8
Kinver Terr TA8......104 A7
Kipling Ave BA2.......44 F4
Kipling Rd
  Radstock BA3.........78 C1
  Weston-Super-Mare BS23..49 A3
Kippax Ave BS25......203 F5
Kipscombe Cross EX35..122 A6
Kirk Dr TA7..........154 E6
Kirke Gr TA2.........213 B8
Kirkham St TA11......211 E4
Kirlegate BA6........138 C4
Kissing Batch BA11...119 C6
Kit's La TA4.........166 A6
Kitchener Rd TA2.....168 A6
Kitchens La TA13.....185 A1
Kite's Nest La SP8....161 F1
Kite La BA4..........159 C6
Kites Croft BA5......110 E7
Kite Wlk ② BS22......49 E8
Kithill TA18.........224 C4
Kitley Hill BA3.......78 C4
Kitridge La TA24.....146 B7
Kitrow La TA24.......131 A6
Kitswall La TA24.....130 D5
Kitt Hill DT9........225 C4
Kitton La DT9........188 A4
Kitts TA21...........222 D4
Knacker's Hole La
  Churchinford TA3.....192 A6
  Thorncombe DT6, TA20.199 C4
Knap Hill BA3........117 B2
Knapp TA16...........195 F7
Knapp Cotts TA4......151 E1
Knapp Hill Cl BA5....113 A2
Knapp La
  Bishops Lydeard TA4..151 E1
  North Curry TA3......170 B4
Knapp Rd
  Creech St Michael TA3.169 F4
  North Curry TA3......170 A4
Knapps Cl BS25.......69 F8
Knapps Dr BS25.......69 F8
Knapps La
  Chard TA20...........194 C4
  Langport TA10........172 B5
Knapp The TA24.......130 B4
Knap The BA8.........176 E1
Knaptons Hill BA11...118 C6
Kneller Cl BS11.......5 A8
Knight's Cross TA21..181 A5
Knight's Ct BA11.....119 F4
Knight's La
  Axminster EX13.......198 A4
  Higher Chillington TA19.194 A3
Knight Cl BS22........32 A5
Knightcott BS29......50 F3
Knightcott Gdns BS29..50 F3
Knightcott Ind Est BS29.50 E3
Knightcott Pk BS29...51 A3
Knightcott Rd
  Abbots Leigh BS8.....10 F8
  Banwell BS29.........50 F3
Knightlands La TA10...172 F4
Knighton TA5.........134 B7
Knighton Dro TA10....184 D7
Knightsbridge Pk BS13.22 E4
Knightsbridge Way TA6.209 D6
Knight Shute La TA20..193 D6
Knights Rd TA21......180 D8
Knights Templar CE Meth
  Com Sch TA23........202 D6
Knightstone TA3......169 D3
Knightstone Cl
  Axbridge BS26........70 C1
  Kingsbury Episcopi TA12.185 B8
  Peasedown St John BA2..79 B8
Knightstone Cswy BS23.48 C8
Knightstone Ct
  Burnham-on-S TA8.....104 B6
  Clevedon BS21........6 D1
  Stalbridge DT10......190 B4
  Taunton TA2..........213 A6
  Weston-Super-Mare BS23..30 D1
Knightstone Gn BS23...48 E6
Knightstone Ho
  ❶ Bristol BS2........227 A4
  Weston-Super-Mare BS23..48 D8
Knightstone Hts BA11..119 F3
Knightstone Mead TA22.148 A3
Knightstone Pk ④ BS23.48 E5
Knightstone Pl
  Bath BA1.............27 B1
  ❼ Weston-Super-Mare
    BS22................31 F2
Knightstone Rd BS23...48 C8
Knightstone Sq BS23...23 C5
Knightstone Wlk BS2...226 C4
Knights Yd BA7.......214 C5
Knobsbury Hill BA3....98 D6
Knobsbury La BA3......98 C7

Knole Cswy
Knole TA10. . . . .**173** A4
Long Sutton TA10. . . . . .**172** F4
Knole Pit La TA10. . . . . .**173** A4
Knoll Ct BS9. . . . .**5** D3
Knoll Green La TA5 . . **134** F2
Knoll Hill BS9. . . . .**5** D3
Knoll Hill View BA11 . . .**143** C6
Knoll Ho **5** BA11. . . . . .**119** F4
Knoll La BA4. . . . .**142** E3
Knoll Pk TA8 . . . .**65** F2
Knoll The BS20 . . . .**2** D7
Knoll View
Burnham-on-S TA8 . . . .**104** C8
4 BA11. . . . .**119** F4
Knotcroft La TA2. . . . . . .**153** D1
Knotts Paddock DT9 . . . .**225** E4
Knowle Cross DT8 . . . . . .**199** F6
Knowle Dro
Middlezoy TA7 . . . .**155** A4
Westonzoyland TA7. . . . .**154** F5
Knowle End TA7 . . . .**136** E3
Knowle La
Chard TA20. . . . .**194** B6
Dunster TA24 . . . .**201** B1
Misterton DT8, TA18. . . .**224** E2
Shepton Mallet BA4. . . . .**204** E5
Wookey BA5. . . . .**110** E1
Knowle Moor Dro BA5 . .**110** C2
Knowle Rd TA6. . . . .**209** C6
Knowles BS21 . . . .**6** C2
Knowleyards Rd TA7 . . . .**155** B4
Kylross Ave BS14 . . . .**23** B5
Kyrle Gdns BA1. . . . .**28** F3
Kyte Rd BA4. . . . .**205** C5

L

Labbott The BS31 . . . .**24** E5
Labourham Dro BS27 . . . .**90** B5
Labourham Way BS27 . . . .**90** B6
Laburnum Cl
Bridgwater TA6 . . . .**209** D4
Frome BA11. . . . .**120** B7
Midsomer Norton BA3. . . .**96** F8
Somerton TA11 . . . .**211** D4
Laburnum Cotts **7** TA21 **222** D5
Laburnum Cres TA18. . . .**224** D7
Laburnum Ct
7 Taunton TA1. . . . .**213** A4
Weston-Super-Mare BS23 .**49** B7
Laburnum Dr TA11 . . . . .**211** D4
Laburnum Gr BA3. . . . . . .**96** F8
Laburnum Lodges TA9 . .**136** A8
Laburnum Rd
Wellington TA21. . . . .**222** E5
Weston-Super-Mare BS23 .**49** B7
Laburnum St TA1 . . . .**213** A4
Laburnum Terr
Batheaston BA1. . . . .**28** F3
Creech St Michael TA3. . . .**169** D4
Laburnum Way BA20 . . . .**218** D2
Laburnum Wlk BS31 . . . . .**24** C3
Lacey Rd BS14 . . . .**23** F6
La Ciotat Ho TA6. . . . . . .**209** A4
Ladd Cl TA9 . . . .**104** D3
Ladies Mile BS8 . . . .**5** F1
Ladman Gr BS14 . . . .**23** E6
Ladman Rd BS14. . . . .**23** E5
Ladycroft **5** BS21. . . . .**6** B1
Ladye Bay BS21. . . . .**6** D7
Ladye Wake BS22 . . . .**31** F4
Lady Harriet Acland's Dr
TA22 . . . .**164** A8
Lady Lawn TA3 . . . .**168** D1
Ladymead BS20. . . . .**2** F5
Ladymead Cl TA6 . . . . . .**208** B4
Ladymead Com Sch TA2. **168** E6
Ladymeade
Backwell BS48. . . . .**19** A7
Ilminster TA19. . . . .**221** B3
Ladymead Ho BA1 . . . . . .**228** C3
Ladymead La BS40. . . . . . .**52** F5
Ladymead Rd TA2. . . . . . .**168** F6
Lady St TA22. . . . .**163** D7
Lady Victoria's Dr TA22 . **163** E6
Ladywell BS40. . . . .**35** D2
Laggan Gdns BA1. . . . .**27** E1
Laggan Ho BA1 . . . .**27** E1
Lagger Hill TA5 . . . .**133** C5
Lahs Pl BA11 . . . .**101** E4
Lakefields BA22. . . . .**197** B8
Lakemead Gdns **3** BS13. .**21** F4
Lakemead Gr BS13 . . . . . .**21** F6
Lake Mews BA22 . . . .**219** B1
Lake Rd BS20. . . . .**2** D7
Lakeside TA4 . . . .**104** E4
Lakeside Cl BS40 . . . .**55** D5
Lakeside Ct BS24 . . . .**32** B1
Lakeside Pk
Bridgwater TA6 . . . .**209** A3
Vobster BA11. . . . .**117** E8
Lakeview Cres TA9 . . . . .**104** E3
Lake Wall TA7 . . . .**154** E4
Lambert's Hill BA4 . . . . .**204** F3
Lambert Cl DT9 . . . .**217** C2
Lambert Ct DT9 . . . .**217** D2
Lambert La TA19. . . . . . .**194** F5
Lambert Pl BS4. . . . .**22** D6
Lamberts Marsh BA14. . . . .**83** E2
Lamb La TA5 . . . .**208** F4
Lambourne Ct TA18 . . . . .**224** D7
Lambourne Way BS20 . . . . .**2** F5

Lambourn Rd BS31. . . . . .**25** A4
Lambpark Ct TA3 . . . . . .**191** F6
Lambridge **6** BA1. . . . . . .**28** C1
Lambridge Bldgs **1** BA1 .**28** C1
Lambridge Grange 6
BA1 . . . .**28** C2
Lambridge Mews **5** BA1 .**28** C1
Lambridge Pl BA1. . . . .**28** C1
Lambridge St BA1. . . . .**28** C1
Lambrok Cl BA14 . . . .**83** F6
Lambrok Rd BA14. . . . .**83** F6
Lambrook Cl TA1 . . . .**213** B4
Lambrook Gate TA13 . . . .**184** F5
Lambrook Ho BA9 . . . . . .**216** C4
Lambrook Rd
Shepton Beauchamp
TA19 . . . .**184** E4
Taunton TA1 . . . .**213** B4
Lambrook St BA6 . . . .**206** E4
Lambrook Way TA1 . . . . .**213** C4
Lambs Field DT9 . . . .**225** E5
Lamb St BS2. . . . .**227** C3
Lamington Cl BS13. . . . . . .**21** F6
Lamont Ho **7** BA1 . . . .**28** C1
Lampard's Bldgs BA1 . . .**228** B4
Lamparts Way TA19. . . . .**183** C2
Lampeter Rd BS9. . . . .**5** F7
Lampley Rd BS21 . . . .**16** D2
Lampreys La TA13 . . . . . .**220** C3
Lampton Ave BS13 . . . .**22** E3
Lampton Gr BS13 . . . .**22** E3
Lampton Rd BS41. . . . .**10** F1
Lancaster House Sch
BS23 . . . .**48** F8
Lancer Ct TA21 . . . .**222** D6
Lanch La SP8 . . . .**177** F5
Lancock St TA21 . . . .**222** A5
Lancombe La BA10. . . . . .**215** C3
Landacre La TA24. . . . . . .**146** A7
Landemann Cir BS23 . . . . .**30** E1
Landemann Path **2** BS23. **48** E8
Landlord's Hill TA21 . . . .**179** E7
Landmark Ct BS1. . . . . . .**226** C1
Landmead BA6 . . . .**206** D5
Landmoor La TA10. . . . . .**172** D4
Landsdown Mews BA11 . .**119** D5
Landseer BA8. . . . .**176** D4
Landseer Cl BS22 . . . .**31** F3
Landseer Rd BA2 . . . .**44** B6
Landshire La
Charlton Horethorne
DT9. . . . .**176** A1
Chilton Polden TA7. . . . . .**137** A3
Henstridge BA8. . . . .**190** C6
Odcombe BA22 . . . .**186** C1
Lane End TA24. . . . .**144** D8
Lane Foot TA24 . . . .**129** D7
Lane Head TA24 . . . .**123** E4
Lanesborough Rise BS14 .**23** D7
Lanes End Hill BA11,
BA12 . . . .**144** D8
Laneys Dro BS24. . . . .**49** E5
Lang's Cnr TA19 . . . .**183** B1
Langaller Hill TA22. . . . . .**163** D4
Langdon Cl TA20. . . . . . .**223** D6
Langdon Rd BA2. . . . .**44** B4
Langdons DT9 . . . .**225** E5
Langdons Way TA20. . . . .**198** C8
Langdown Ct BS14. . . . . . .**23** E5
Langer's La TA19 . . . . . .**194** E5
Langford Budville CE Prim
Sch TA21 . . . .**166** F1
Langford Cl TA1 . . . .**170** F1
Langford Ct **14** TA1 . . . . .**213** A4
Langford Ct Cotts BS40. . . .**53** E5
Langford Gate TA4. . . . . .**166** F2
Langford La
Fivehead TA3 . . . .**170** F2
Lower Langford BS40 . . . .**53** E5
Norton Fitzwarren TA2. . . .**168** C4
Langford Rd
Bristol BS13. . . . .**21** F8
Lower Langford BS40 . . . .**53** C6
Weston-Super-Mare BS23 .**49** A6
Langfords La BS39 . . . .**77** C8
Langham Dr TA1. . . . .**212** F1
Langham Gdns TA1 . . . . .**212** C1
Langham La SP8 . . . .**177** F5
Langham Pl BA11. . . . .**82** F1
Langhill Ave BS4. . . . .**22** D7
Langland's La TA9 . . . . . .**104** B1
Langland La TA7. . . . .**137** D2
Langlands **8** TA14. . . . . .**185** F4
Langleigh La TA9 . . . .**169** F2
Langley Cres BS3 . . . .**11** E1
Langley Cross TA4 . . . . . .**210** B6
Langleys Cotts BA3 . . . . . .**96** B8
Langmead Dro
Middlezoy TA7 . . . .**155** A4
Westonzoyland TA7. . . . .**154** F5
Langmead La TA7. . . . . . .**155** A4
Langmead Pl TA18. . . . . .**224** C4
Langmead Rd TA18 . . . . .**224** C4
Langmead Sq TA18 . . . . .**224** C4
Langmoor La EX13 . . . . .**198** D2
Langport Gdns BS48 . . . . .**18** E8
Langport Rd
Long Sutton TA10 . . . . . .**172** E5
Middlezoy TA7 . . . .**155** B4
Somerton TA11 . . . .**211** B4
Weston-Super-Mare BS23 .**48** E5
Lang Rd TA18 . . . .**224** C4
Langton Ho **9** BS2. . . . . .**227** C3
Langworthy Orch TA19. . .**183** C1

Lansdown Cres
2 Bath BA1. . . . .**27** F1
Timsbury BA2 . . . .**60** C2
Lansdown Ct BS23 . . . .**48** F8
Lansdowne Pl BA9. . . . . .**216** C4
Lansdowne Rd TA2. . . . . .**213** A6
Lansdown Gdns BS22 . . . . .**32** B5
Lansdown Gr BA1. . . . . . .**228** B4
Lansdown Grove Ct BA1. .**228** B4
Lansdown Grove Lodge
BA1. . . . .**228** B4
Lansdown Ho BA1 . . . .**27** F1
Lansdown Hts BA1. . . . . . .**27** F1
Lansdown La
Upton Cheyney BS30. . . . .**26** D8
Lansdown Mans BA1 . . . .**228** B4
Lansdown Pk BA1. . . . .**27** E3
Lansdown Pl
Bristol BS8. . . . .**226** A3
Frome BA11. . . . .**119** D5
High Littleton BS39. . . . . .**59** D1
Lansdown Pl E BA1 . . . . .**228** B4
Lansdown Pl W **1** BA1 . . .**27** F1
Lansdown Rd
Bath BA1. . . . .**27** E2
Bristol BS8. . . . .**226** A3
Saltford BS31 . . . .**25** E3
Lansdown View
Bath BA1. . . . .**44** C5
Faulkland BA3. . . . .**80** D1
Timsbury BA2 . . . .**60** C2
Tunley BA2. . . . .**61** B4
Lanthony Cl BS24. . . . .**50** A8
Lapwing Cl TA24 . . . .**201** C5
Lapwing Gdns BS22 . . . . . .**31** F1
Larch Ave TA20 . . . .**223** B5
Larch Cl
Bridgwater TA6 . . . .**209** D6
Churchill BS40. . . . .**53** A5
Nailsea BS48. . . . .**9** A2
Taunton TA1 . . . .**213** D2
Larch Ct BA3 . . . .**97** D8
Larches The
Nailsea BS48. . . . .**32** A3
Larchfield Cl BA11. . . . . . .**120** B7
Larchfield Trad Est TA19 .**221** B1
Larchgrove Cres BS22 . . . .**31** F1
Larchgrove Wlk BS22 . . . . .**31** F1
Larchwood Ct BA3 . . . .**79** A3
Lark Cl BA3. . . . .**97** B8
Larkhall Pl BA1. . . . .**28** C2
Larkhall Terr BA1. . . . .**28** C2
Larkhill Rd
Locking BS24. . . . .**50** B6
Yeovil BA21. . . . .**218** D7
Lark Pl BA1. . . . .**44** D7
Lark Rd BS22 . . . .**31** F1
Larks Mdw DT10 . . . .**190** C4
Larkspur Cl TA1 . . . .**213** C1
Larkspur Ct BA21 . . . .**218** D7
Larkspur Ct TA2 . . . .**212** D7
Larviscombe Cl TA4 . . . . .**202** D4
Larviscombe Rd TA4 . . . . .**202** D4
Lasbury Gr BS13 . . . .**22** C5
Lascot Hill BS28 . . . .**108** C5
Latcham Dro BS27, BS28 .**109** A4
Latches La BS27 . . . .**90** D3
Latchmoor Ho BS13 . . . . . .**22** A8
Late Broads BA15 . . . .**64** D7
Lauder Ct DT9 . . . .**217** D2
Launcherley Cross BA5. . . .**140** A6
Launcherley Rd BA4, BA5 .**140** B5
Launder Cl BA6. . . . .**206** E4
Laura Pl BA2 . . . .**228** C3
Laurel Ave TA9 . . . .**86** A2
Laurel Cl
East Coker BA22 . . . .**197** B8
Frome BA11. . . . .**120** B7
Weston-Super-Mare BS23 .**48** E2
Laurel Dr
Nailsea BS48. . . . .**8** F2
Paulton BS39. . . . .**77** E5
Weston-Super-Mare BS23 .**48** E2
Laurel Gdns
Chard TA20. . . . .**223** B5
Timsbury BA2 . . . .**60** B1
Yatton BS49. . . . .**17** B1
Laurel La BA22 . . . .**174** F3
Laurel St BA6. . . . .**140** A1
Laurels The
Churchill BS25 . . . .**52** F4
Crewkerne TA18 . . . .**224** D7
Wembdon TA6 . . . .**208** C6
Weston-Super-Mare BS23 .**48** E2
Westwood BA15 . . . .**64** F3
Laurel Terr BS49. . . . .**17** B1
Lavender Cl
Frome BA11. . . . .**120** B7
Street BA16. . . . .**207** B4
Lavender Gr TA1 . . . .**212** C3
Laver's La BA22. . . . .**198** F5
Laver's Oak TA12. . . . . . .**185** E7
Lavington Cl BS21 . . . .**6** B1
Lawfords Gate BS2. . . . . .**227** C3
Lawfords Gate Ho 17
BS2 . . . .**227** C3
Lawford St BS2. . . . .**227** C3
Law La
Drayton TA10 . . . .**171** F3
Langport TA10 . . . .**172** A3
Lawn Mdw TA3 . . . .**169** C3

Lawnmoor La TA10. . . . .**184** C6
Lawn Rd BA2 . . . .**212** C8
Lawnside BS48 . . . .**19** B5
Lawns The
Bristol BS11. . . . .**4** E7
Combe St Nicholas TA20 . **193** D6
Weston-Super-Mare BS22 . .**32** B3
Yatton BS49. . . . .**17** A1
Lawn The **1** TA21. . . . . .**222** D6
Lawpool Ct **12** BA1. . . . .**203** D4
Lawrence Cl
Burnham-on-S TA8 . . . . .**104** D5
Highbridge TA9 . . . .**104** F4
Somerton TA11 . . . .**211** D3
Weston-Super-Mare BS22 . .**31** A5
Lawrence Hayes BA9 . . . .**216** D3
Lawrence Hill BA9 . . . . . .**216** A2
Lawrence Hill Bsns Ctr
BA9. . . . .**216** B3
Lawrence Mews BS22 . . . . .**31** A5
Lawrence Rd
Coleford BA3. . . . .**116** F7
Weston-Super-Mare BS22 . .**31** A5
Wrington BS40 . . . .**35** C2
Laws Dr BS24. . . . .**49** F7
Lawson Cl
5 Martock TA12 . . . . . .**185** E6
Saltford BS31 . . . .**25** C2
Lawyer's Hill TA5 . . . .**152** C7
Lax Ct BA5 . . . .**203** B4
Laxton Cl TA1 . . . .**213** D5
Laxton Rd TA1 . . . .**213** E5
Laxton Way BA2 . . . .**79** D7
Laycock Hill DT9 . . . .**217** D7
Layfield La TA3 . . . .**170** C3
Layne Terr TA18 . . . .**196** B8
Lays Bsns Ctr BS31. . . . . . .**24** C4
Lays Dr BS31 . . . .**24** C5
Lays La BS40 . . . .**54** D4
Lays The BA11 . . . .**101** E5
Leach's Field TA2. . . . . . .**168** B4
Leach Cl BS25 . . . .**6** D1
Leaches Cl BA22. . . . .**186** B6
Leach Rd TA20 . . . .**223** D7
Lea Cl BA21 . . . .**219** B8
Lea Croft BS13. . . . .**22** A4
Leading Edge The BS8 . .**226** B2
Leadon Gr TA1. . . . .**213** D4
Leafield Cl TA2 . . . .**168** B5
Leafy Way BS24. . . . .**50** B4
Lea Grove Rd BS21. . . . .**6** C4
Leaholme Gdns BS14. . . . . .**23** A3
Lear's La TA24 . . . .**177** C6
Leat The **8** TA4 . . . .**167** F8
Leaze Cl BA11 . . . .**119** D5
Leaze Dro BA5. . . . .**139** A7
Leaze Ho BA11. . . . .**119** D5
Leaze House Mews
BA11 . . . .**119** D5
Leaze La
Blagdon BS40 . . . .**72** E8
West Chinnock TA18 . . . .**196** B8
Yeovil BA21. . . . .**219** F4
Leazemoor La TA10 . . . . .**172** B8
Leaze Rd BA11. . . . .**119** D5
Leaze The
Radstock BA3 . . . .**97** D8
Rode BA2. . . . .**82** C1
Leazeway Dro TA7 . . . . . .**155** C1
Lecher La DT8, TA18 . . . .**196** B1
Leda Ave BA5. . . . .**23** A7
Leedham Rd BS24. . . . .**50** C5
Leeford La EX35 . . . .**122** B5
Leeming Way BS11. . . . .**4** C8
Lee Pk TA21 . . . .**180** F7
Leeside BS20 . . . .**2** C5
Leet Ct DT9 . . . .**225** B2
Leeward Ct TA6 . . . .**209** C4
Leewood Rd BS23 . . . .**31** C5
Leffman Ct TA11. . . . .**211** C4
Leggar The BA5 . . . .**209** A6
Legion Rd BA21 . . . .**218** F6
Leg La BS40. . . . .**54** B3
Leg Of Mutton Rd BA6 . .**206** E6
Leg Sq BA4. . . . .**205** C6
Leg Square Ct BA4 . . . . . .**205** C6
Leigh Cl BA1 . . . .**28** A2
Leigh Court Bsns Ctr BS8 . .**5** A2
Leigh Furlong Rd BA16. . .**207** B4
Leigh La
Cold Ashton BA1 . . . .**13** B3
Crowcombe TA4. . . . .**151** A7
Halstock BA22 . . . .**197** C3
Winsford TA22 . . . .**147** C2
Winsham TA20 . . . .**199** A8
Leigh Rd
Bristol BS8. . . . .**226** B4
Leigh u M BA11 . . . .**117** C2
Street BA16. . . . .**207** C5
Taunton TA2 . . . .**213** B8
Leigh St BA3. . . . .**116** F3
Leighton Cl BA4 . . . .**141** E1
Leighton Cres BS24 . . . . . .**67** A8
Leighton La BA4 . . . .**141** E1
Leighton Lane Ind Est
BA4. . . . .**141** E1
Leighton Rd BA1 . . . .**27** A3
Leigh upon Mendip Fst Sch
BA3. . . . .**117** A3
Leigh View Rd BS20. . . . . . .**2** E7
Leighwood Dro BS48 . . . . . .**8** B1
Leigh Woods Forest Walks★
BS8. . . . .**11** A6
Leinster Ave BS4. . . . .**22** D8
Lemon La BS2 . . . .**227** C4
Lenover Gdns BS13 . . . . . .**22** B4
Lenthay Cl DT9 . . . .**225** C2

Lenthay Ct DT9 . . . .**225** C3
Lenthay Rd DT9. . . . .**225** B2
Leonard's Barton BA11. . .**119** E6
Leonard Houlden Ct 7
TA2 . . . .**213** A8
Leonard La BS1. . . . .**227** A3
Leopold Bldgs BA1 . . . . . .**228** C4
Lerburne The BA28. . . . . .**108** D4
Leslie Ave TA2 . . . .**212** E6
Leslie Rise BA15 . . . .**64** F3
Les Rosiers Gdns BA9 . . .**216** C4
Lester Dr BS22 . . . .**32** A3
Lester La DT9 . . . .**176** A2
Letham Ct TA19. . . . .**221** B4
Lethbridge Pk TA4. . . . . .**151** D1
Level La DT9. . . . .**176** A2
Level View TA10 . . . .**172** C5
Leversedge Rd BA11 . . . . .**120** A7
Lewins Mead BS1 . . . .**227** A3
Lewis's Dro BA5 . . . .**138** E7
Lewis Cres BA11 . . . .**119** F6
Lewisham Gr BS23 . . . . . . .49 A8
Lewis Rd
Bristol BS13. . . . .**22** A8
Taunton TA2 . . . .**212** E7
Lewmond Ave BA5 . . . . . .**203** F5
Leycroft Cl TA1 . . . .**213** B4
Leycroft Gr TA1 . . . .**213** B4
Leycroft Rd TA1 . . . .**213** B4
Leyland Wlk BS13. . . . .**21** F4
Leys Hill BA11 . . . .**120** A6
Leys La BA11 . . . .**119** F7
Leys The BS21 . . . .**6** B1
Leystone Cl BA11 . . . .**120** A6
Leyton Dr TA6 . . . .**209** D6
Lias Rd BA16 . . . .**207** B4
Liberty Gdns BS1 . . . .**226** C1
Liberty La BS40. . . . .**54** C2
Liberty Pl TA6 . . . .**209** B4
Liberty The BA5. . . . .**203** E5
Liddon Hill TA18 . . . .**195** C5
Liddymore La
Watchet TA23. . . . .**202** D5
Williton TA4, TA23. . . . . .**202** E4
Liddymore Rd TA23 . . . . .**202** D4
Lightermans Ct TA24 . . . .**201** B7
Lightgate TA13 . . . .**220** D5
Lightgate La TA13. . . . . .**220** D4
Lightgate Rd TA13 . . . . .**220** D4
Lilac Cl TA1 . . . .**213** C2
Lilac Ct BS31 . . . .**24** C4
Lilac Terr BA3 . . . .**78** C2
Lilac Way BS22 . . . .**32** A5
Lilian Terr BS39. . . . .**77** E5
Lillebonne Cl TA21 . . . . . .**222** F6
Lilli Batch BA11 . . . .**119** F7
Lillycombe La TA3, EX15 .**191** B8
Lillypool Cheese & Cider
Farm★ BS25. . . . .**70** F6
Lily La BA8 . . . .**176** L1
Limber Rd BA22 . . . .**218** A6
Limbers La BA5 . . . .**139** B8
Limbury **2** TA12 . . . .**185** E6
Limbury Cotts **3** TA12 . .**185** E6
Limebreach Wood BS48 . . .**8** D3
Limeburn La BS40 . . . .**38** E5
Lime Cl
Frome BA11. . . . .**120** B7
Locking BS24. . . . .**50** B4
Minehead TA24 . . . .**200** D7
Street BA16. . . . .**207** C5
Weston-Super-Mare BS23 . .**32** A1
Lime Cres TA1. . . . .**213** C2
Lime Ct BS31 . . . .**24** C4
Lime Gr
Bath BA2. . . . .**45** B6
Shepton Mallet BA4. . . . .**205** A6
Lime Grove Gdns BA2 . . . .**45** B6
Lime Kiln BA21 . . . .**218** C5
Limekiln La
Bath BA2. . . . .**45** F4
Chard, Forton TA20 . . . . .**223** D1
Chard, Lydmarsh TA20. . .**194** C3
Cricket St Thomas TA20. .**194** E2
Leigh u M BA11 . . . .**117** C3
Oakhill BA3. . . . .**114** E5
Stoke St Michael BA3 . . . .**115** F4
Tatworth TA20 . . . .**193** F1
Lime Kiln La
Castle Cary BA7. . . . .**214** E4
Clevedon BS21. . . . .**6** D3
Henstridge BA8. . . . .**190** A6
Wookey Hole BA5 . . . . . .**203** B7
Lime Kiln Rd BS1 . . . .**226** B2
Limekilns Cl BS31. . . . .**24** F5
Limepits La TA10 . . . .**172** D5
Limerick Ct DT9 . . . .**217** D2
Limerick La TA1 . . . .**101** F2
Limes Cl TA4 . . . .**202** E3
Lime St
Nether Stowey TA5 . . . . .**134** B2
Stogursey TA5 . . . .**134** C6
Limestone Hill TA5. . . . . .**135** C1
Lime Terr BA3 . . . .**78** D1
Lime Tree Ave BA20 . . . . .**218** E2
Lime Tree Cl TA6 . . . .**209** D4
Lime Tree Gr BS20 . . . .**4** D3
Limington Rd BA22 . . . . .**173** E1
Limpetshell La TA4 . . . . .**202** E3
Limpley Stoke Rd BA15. . . .**64** D6
Linch La BA4 . . . .**142** D2
Lincoln Hill TA19. . . . . . .**184** E4
Lincoln Cl BS31 . . . .**24** C4

Lincombe Rd BA3 .... 97 D8
Lincott View BA2 .... 79 C8
Linden Ave BS23 .... 49 E8
Linden Cl
  Bridgwater TA6 .... 209 C4
  Bristol BS14 .... 23 E6
  Frome BA11 .... 119 D5
  Radstock BA3 .... 97 E8
Linden Ct BS21 .... 6 D4
Linden Gdns BA1 .... 44 D8
Linden Gr TA1 .... 212 E5
Linden Hill TA21 ...... 222 A6
Linden Rd
  Clevedon BS21 .... 6 D4
  Yeovil BA20 .... 218 F5
Lindens The BS22 .... 31 E4
Lindisfarne Cl BA15 .... 64 E6
Lindsey Cl BS20 .... 1 F4
Lindsey Cres **1** TA6... 153 F3
Linemere Cl BS48 .... 19 D6
Lines Way BS14 .... 23 C3
Liney Rd TA7 .... 154 F6
Lingfield Ave BA21 .... 219 D7
Linham Rd TA6 .... 208 F6
Linhay Cl EX15 .... 179 E1
Linkhay TA20 .... 198 D8
Linkhay Cl TA20 ...... 198 D8
Link La
  Burrington BS40 .... 53 F3
  Monkton Farleigh BA15.. 46 F8
Linkmead BA3 .... 96 F2
Link Rd
  Nailsea BS48 .... 8 F2
  Portishead BS20 .... 2 C5
Links Ct BS23 .... 48 D4
Links Gdns TA8 .... 84 F3
Linkside BS21 .... 6 E6
Links Rd BS23 .... 48 C2
Link The BS27 .... 90 B8
Linley Cl
  Bath BA2 .... 44 A5
  Bridgwater TA6 ...... 209 D7
Linleys The BA1 .... 44 C7
Linne Ho BA2 .... 44 A5
Linnet Cl
  Taunton TA1 .... 212 B4
  Weston-Super-Mare BS22.. 31 E1
Linnet Gdns BS20 .... 2 E7
Linnet Way
  Frome BA11 .... 120 B6
  Midsomer Norton BA3... 97 B8
Linsvale Cl BA11 ...... 120 C5
Linsvale Dr BA11 ..... 120 C5
Lintern Cl BA4 .... 159 C7
Linton's Wlk BS14 ..... 23 A7
Lion Cl BS48 .... 8 D2
Lion D'angers TA4 .... 210 D4
Lion Ho **20** BA4 ..... 205 B6
Lion Mews TA11 ...... 211 E4
Lipe Hill La TA3, TA4... 168 B1
Lipe La TA3 .... 169 C3
Lipgate Pl BS20 .... 2 D3
Lippetts Way TA7 ..... 137 D1
Lippiat Hill BA3 .... 80 C3
Lippiatt La
  Cheddar BS27 .... 90 C7
  Shipham BS25 .... 70 F8
  Timsbury BA2 .... 60 B3
Lippiatt The BS27 ...... 90 C8
Lisieux Ct TA1 .... 213 D2
Lisieux Way TA1 ...... 213 C3
Lisle Rd BS22 .... 32 B4
Lister's Hill TA19 ..... 221 C2
Listercombe Cl TA19 .. 221 C2
Lister Gr BA15 .... 64 F3
Litfield Pl BS8 .... 11 F7
Litfield Rd BS8 .... 11 F8
Litt Hill BA3 .... 75 F2
Little Ann St BS2, BS5... 227 C4
Little Birch Croft BS14.. 23 A3
Little Bishop St BS2.... 227 B4
Littlebrook BS39 .... 77 E6
Little Brooks La BA4 .. 205 C4
Little Burrow Dro TA7.. 155 A1
Little Caroline Pl **4** BS8.. 11 F5
Little Cl TA2 .... 212 C8
Little Elm Rd TA7 ..... 155 C4
Little England TA7 .... 155 C2
Little Entry BA5 ...... 203 E5
Littlefield DT9 .... 225 B3
Littlefield Cl BA16 .... 156 E7
Littlefield La TA10 .... 172 E4
Little Field La TA5 .... 110 F7
Littlefields Ave BS29 .. 51 B3
Littlefields La TA19 ... 184 F3
Littlefields Rd BS29 ... 51 B3
Littlefields Rise BS29.. 51 B3
Little George St
  Bristol BS2 .... 227 C4
  Weston-Super-Mare BS23.. 48 E7
Little Gn BA5 .... 111 A4
Little Halt BS20 .... 1 E4
Little Ham BS21 .... 16 C8
Littleham Cotts TA3 .. 181 L6
Little Headley Cl BS13.. 22 B7
Little Keyford La BA11.. 119 E1
Little King St BS1 .... 227 A2
Little Mdw
  6 Bishops Lydeard TA4.. 167 F8
  Ilchester BA22 .... 173 E2
Little Mead TA14 ..... 185 F2
Little Mead Cl BS24 ... 49 E3

Little Meadow End BS48.. 18 E8
Little Moor Rd TA9 ... 106 F3
Littlemoor Dro TA7 .. 154 C3
Little Orch
  Cheddar BS27 .... 90 C8
  34 Martock TA12 .... 185 E6
  Street BA16 .... 207 D7
  Weston-Super-Mare BS23.. 48 D1
Little Paul St BS2 .... 226 C4
Little Pen TA8 .... 84 F5
Little Plover Cl TA7 .. 201 C5
Little Sammons BA22 . 186 E5
Little Silver Ct TA23 .. 202 C7
Little Silver La TA21 .. 222 D2
Little St TA14 .... 185 E2
Little Stanhope St BA1.. 228 A2
Little Stoke Rd BS9 .... 5 E4
Littleton Hill TA11 ... 211 E6
Littleton La
  Wellow BA2 .... 80 C7
  Winford BS40 .... 38 D5
Little Trumps BA22 .. 186 B7
Little Withey Mead BS9.. 5 F5
Little Wiveliscombe La
  TA4 .... 165 D6
Littlewood BA11 ...... 143 C4
Littlewood Cl BS14 .... 23 B3
Littlewood La BS49 .... 18 C2
Litton BS24 .... 49 A2
Liver Moor Dro TA11 . 156 E2
Livingstone Rd BA2 ... 44 D5
Livingstone Terr BA2 . 228 A1
Livingstone Way TA2 . 212 B6
Llewellyns Almshouses **6**
  BA5 .... 203 D4
Llewellyn Way BS22 ... 32 B3
Lloyd Cl TA1 .... 212 B1
Load La TA7 .... 154 E5
Load Pool TA7 .... 155 C2
Lobelia Cl TA9 .... 104 D5
Lock's Hill BA11 ...... 119 F3
Lock's La TA9 .... 216 C4
Lockemor Rd BS13 .... 22 F4
Locketts Barton TA3 . 170 D7
Lockey Rd BA4 .... 205 B4
Lock Gdns BS13 .... 21 E7
Locking Farm Ind Est
  BS24 .... 50 A5
Locking Head Dro
  Locking BS24 .... 49 F5
  Weston-Super-Mare BS24.. 50 A6
Locking Moor Rd
  Locking BS24 .... 50 B5
  Weston-Super-Mare BS22, BS23.. 49 D8
Locking Prim Sch BS24.. 50 B4
Locking Rd BS22, BS23.. 49 B7
Lockingwell Rd BS31 .. 24 D5
Locksbrook Ct **8** BA1.. 44 B6
Locksbrook Rd
  Bath BA1 .... 44 C6
  Weston-Super-Mare BS22.. 32 B3
Locksbrook Trad Est **7**
  BA1 .... 44 B6
Lockside BS20 .... 2 E7
Lockside Sq BS20 .... 2 E7
Lockswell TA7 .... 136 E4
Lockswell Cotts BA4 . 141 B1
Lockwood Ct **4** BA21 . 218 F7
Lockyer Dro TA7 ..... 156 A5
Lodes La TA4 .... 168 E8
Lodge Cl
  Taunton TA1 .... 212 A2
  Wellington TA21 ..... 222 D6
  Yatton BS49 .... 34 B8
Lodge Cotts TA3 ..... 181 D6
Lodge Ct
  Bristol BS9 .... 5 E4
  Castle Cary BA7 ..... 214 B4
Lodge Dr
  Long Ashton BS41 .... 11 C2
  Weston-Super-Mare BS23.. 31 A1
Lodge Gdns BA2 .... 44 D1
Lodge Hill
  Berkley BA11, BA13... 120 F5
  Bratton Seymour BA9.. 176 A7
  Somerton TA11 .... 211 F4
  Westbury-sub-Mendip
    BA5 .... 110 D5
  Yarlington BA9........ 175 F7
Lodge Hill Ind Pk BA5.. 110 D5
Lodge La
  Axminster EX13 ...... 198 A2
  Wraxall BS48 .... 9 B2
Lodge Pl BS1 .... 226 C3
Lodge Rd
  Horningsham BA12 ... 144 D4
  Kingsdon TA11 .... 173 D7
Lodge Rocks TA24 .... 131 D3
Lodge St BS1 .... 226 C3
Lodges The BA3 .... 96 D1
Lodway BS20 .... 4 C4
Lodway Cl BS20 .... 4 C5
Lodway Gdns BS20 ..... 4 C4
Lodwells Orch TA3 ... 170 B4
Lombardy Cl **5** BS22 . 49 E8
London Cross TA4 .... 151 E4
London Dro BA6, BA16.. 138 D7
London Ho TA4 ...... 210 C4
London Rd
  Bath BA1 .... 228 C4
  Milborne Port DT9 ... 217 E1
London Rd E BA1 ..... 29 A3
London Rd W BA1 ..... 28 E2
London Sq
  28 Martock TA12 .... 185 E6
  Portishead BS20 .... 2 E7
London St BA1 .... 228 C4

Longacre BS21 .... 16 B8
Long Acre BA4 .... 205 C4
Longacre Cl TA2 ...... 212 E7
Longacre Dro TA7 .... 154 D7
Long Acre Ho BA1 .... 228 C4
Long Acre Rd BS14 .... 23 A3
Long Acres Cl BS9 ...... 5 D7
Long Ashton Bsns Pk
  BS41 .... 11 B1
Long Ashton Rd BS41 . 11 B2
Long Ave BS21 .... 6 B2
Long Barnaby BA3 ..... 78 A2
Longbottom BS25 ...... 71 A6
Longbridge **16** BA4 .. 205 B6
Longbrook Trad Est BS3.. 11 E3
Long Cl
  Ilminster TA19 .... 221 C2
  Yeovil BA21 .... 218 C5
Long Cross
  Bristol BS11 .... 4 E8
  Doulting BA4 .... 141 F8
  Felton BS40 .... 37 D7
  Nether Stowey TA5 ... 134 A3
Long Cross Bottom
  Doulting BA4 .... 142 A8
  Stoke St Michael BA3 . 116 A1
Longdown Dr BS22 .... 32 B4
Long Dro
  Broadway TA19, TA20.. 183 A2
  Buckland St Mary TA20.. 182 F2
  Glastonbury BA5 ..... 139 E4
  Westbury-sub-Mendip
    BS27 .... 110 A4
Long Eaton Dr BS14 ... 23 B7
Longfellow Ave BA2 ... 44 F4
Longfellow Rd BA3 .... 97 C8
Longfield BA11 .... 118 A7
Longfield Cl TA4 ..... 202 E2
Longforth Rd TA21 ... 222 D6
Longforward Hill
  Dinnington TA17 ..... 195 A8
  Seavington St Mary TA19.. 184 D1
Longforward La
  Dinnington TA17 ..... 195 B8
  Seavington St Mary TA19.. 184 D1
Long Furlong La
  East Coker BA22 ..... 197 C8
  Long Sutton TA10 .... 172 E5
Long Ground BA11 .... 119 F3
Long Hay Cl BA2 .... 44 B5
Long Hill
  Clewer BS28 .... 89 D2
  Shepton Mallet BA4 .. 141 C8
Long Holcombe Cross
  EX36 .... 145 E6
Long La
  Backwell BS48 .... 19 C2
  Bourton SP8 .... 161 D1
  Cucklington BA9 ..... 177 D5
  Dinder BA5 .... 140 D7
  Felton BS40 .... 37 B5
  Fishpond Bottom DT6.. 199 B1
  Walton BA16 .... 156 A7
  Wanstrow BA4 .... 142 F5
  West Chinnock TA18 . 196 B7
  Wheddon Cross TA24.. 129 C2
  Wootton Courtenay TA24.. 129 E8
  Wrington BS40 .... 36 B2
Long Lakes TA4 ...... 202 E4
Longlands La
  East Coker BA22 ..... 197 C8
  Westbury-sub-Mendip BA5.. 110 E7
Longleat Cl BA11 ..... 119 F3
Longleat Ct BA11 ..... 119 F4
Longleat Forest Holiday
  Village★ BA12 ...... 144 F5
Longleat Ho★ BA12 .. 144 D6
Longleat La BA3 ...... 116 C8
Longleat Rd BA3 ..... 116 B8
Longleat Rly★ BA12... 144 C6
Longleat Saf Pk★ BA12.. 144 D6
Longleaze Gdns BS24 . 49 F3
Long Load Rd TA12 .. 185 E8
Longman's Lea BA4 .. 159 C7
Longmarsh La TA10 .. 172 E6
Long Mead TA4 ...... 165 E8
Long Mead BA21 ..... 218 C5
Longmead Cl
  Norton St Philip BA2.. 81 F4
  Taunton TA1 .... 212 D2
  Wellington TA21 ..... 222 B8
Longmead Cotts TA21.. 222 B8
Longmeadow Rd BS31.. 24 C4
Longmead Way TA1 .. 212 D2
Long Moor Dro TA7, TA9.. 137 A7
Long Orchard Hill TA19.. 221 E3
Longreach Gr BS14 ... 23 D6
Long Ride Dro BA6.... 157 F3
Longridge Way BS24 . 49 F7
Long Row BS1 .... 227 B2
Long Run BA22 .... 186 C3
Longrun La TA1 ...... 212 D4
Longs Field TA3 ...... 170 C4
Long St
  Croscombe BA5 ...... 204 B7
  Galhampton BA22 ... 175 E8
  High Ham TA10 ...... 156 A1
  Sherborne DT9 ...... 225 E4
  Williton TA4 .... 202 E3
Longstone Ave TA6 .. 209 C5
Longstone Cl TA5 .... 134 B2
Longstrings La TA18 . 224 C8
Long Sutton CE Prim Sch
  TA10 .... 172 E4

Long-Thorn BS48 .... 18 F6
Longthorne Pl BA2 .... 44 F2
Long Thorn La BS40 ... 55 E7
Longton Grove Rd **3**
  BS23 .... 48 E8
Longton Ind Est BS23 . 48 F6
Long Valley Rd BA2 ... 43 F5
Longvernal BA3 .... 77 C1
Longvernal Prim Sch BA3.. 77 F1
Longway Ave BS13, BS14.. 22 F4
Longwood Ho BS8 ..... 10 D4
Longwood La
  Burlescombe TA21 ... 179 C4
  Long Ashton BS8, BS41.. 10 F4
Lonsdale Ave BS23 .... 48 F4
Lonsdale Rd TA5 ..... 135 C2
Look's La BA6 .... 157 C6
Looseall La TA22 ..... 163 D8
Lopen Head TA13 .... 220 A1
Lopen La TA13 .... 220 A1
Lopen Rd TA13, TA17 . 195 D8
Lordsleaze La TA20 .. 223 D3
Lords Meadow La **5**
  EX16 .... 164 B1
Lords Way TA6 .... 208 E6
Loretto Gdns **5** EX13 . 198 A1
Loretto Rd EX13 ...... 198 A1
Lorne Pl BA5 .... 203 E5
Lorne Rd BA2 .... 44 D6
Lotment Hill TA11 ... 173 D5
Lottisham La BA4, BA6.. 158 C6
Lottisham Rd BA6 .... 158 C6
Lotts' Ave BS48 .... 19 B5
Lotus Ct BS22 .... 31 C1
Louisa Gate TA22 .... 163 F7
Louisa St BS2 .... 227 C2
Loundshay La TA4 .... 167 A4
Louvigne Cl TA8 ..... 104 C7
Love's La BA2 .... 59 F6
Love La
  Burnham-on-S TA8 ... 104 C7
  Ilminster TA19 .... 221 C3
  Marnhull DT10 .... 190 F6
  Shepton Beauchamp TA19.. 184 E4
  Wincanton BA9 ...... 216 F5
Lovelands DT2 .... 197 A1
Lovelinch Gdns BS41 . 10 F1
Lovell Dr BS39 .... 57 C4
Lovells Mead DT10 .. 190 F6
Lovells Mill BS39 ..... 57 C4
Lovells The BS20 .... 4 B4
Loveridge La TA20 ... 198 D8
Lovers' Wlk
  4 Cannington TA5 ... 135 B2
  Weston-Super-Mare BS23.. 48 D8
Lovers La BA3, BS39 ... 78 A5
Lovers Wlk BA5 ...... 203 D5
Loves Hill BA2 .... 60 A1
Loves La BA14 .... 83 C7
Lovington CE Prim Sch
  BA7 .... 158 F2
Low's Hill La DT9 .... 188 B3
Lowbourne BS14 ...... 22 F6
Lower Acreman St **3**
  DT9 .... 225 D3
Lower Actis BA6 ..... 206 E3
Lower Ansford TA7 .. 214 B7
Lower Backway BA10 . 215 E6
Lower Batch BS40 ..... 39 B3
Lower Bath Rd TA6 .. 209 B6
Lower Beadon TA16 .. 195 F7
Lower Borough Walls
  BA1 .... 228 C2
Lowerbourne Terr TA21.. 124 A3
Lower Boynton La DT9.. 188 F5
Lower Bristol Rd
  Bath BA2 .... 44 B6
  Clutton BS39 .... 58 F4
Lower Burlington Rd BS20.. 2 E7
Lower Camden Pl BA1 . 228 C4
Lower Castle St BS1 .. 227 B3
Lower Chapel Ct BA5.. 113 A1
Lower Cheriton La BA8.. 176 D4
Lower Church La BS2 . 227 A3
Lower Church Rd BS23.. 48 D8
Lower Claverham BS49.. 17 F3
Lower Clifton Hill BS8.. 226 C2
Lower College St BS1 . 226 C2
Lower Coombses TA20.. 198 D8
Lower Cross EX15 .... 179 C1
Lower Down Rd BS20 .. 2 B5
Lower East Coker Rd
  BA20 .... 218 F1
Lower East Hayes BA1.. 45 B8
Lower Fairfield TA4 .. 166 F5
Lower Fairmead Rd
  BA21 .... 219 D8
Lower Fallow Cl BS14 . 22 F3
Lower Farm La BA2 .... 43 B7
Lower Farnfield La TA19.. 184 E1
Lower Foxmoor Rd TA21.. 222 B5
Lower Gay St BS2 .... 227 A4
Lower Guinea St BS1.. 227 A1
Lower Gully Dro BS28.. 89 F3
Lower Gunville DT9 .. 217 D2
Lower Hedgemead Rd
  BA1 .... 228 C4
Lower High St BS11 .... 4 D7
Lower Holway Cl TA1 . 213 D2
Lower Hyde Rd TA15 . 186 B4
Lower Innox BA11 .... 119 E6
Lower Keyford BA11 . 119 F3
Lower Kingsbury DT9 . 217 D3
Lower Kingsdown Rd
  SN13 .... 29 F3
Lower Knowles Rd BS21.. 6 C2

Lower La
  Shepton Mallet BA4.. 205 C6
  Weston Town BA4 ... 142 E5
Lower Lamb St BS1 .. 226 C2
Lower Linden Rd BS21.. 6 D3
Lower Lodfin EX16 ... 164 B2
Lower Marshfield Rd
  TA24 .... 201 B6
Lower Maudlin St BS1.. 227 A3
Lower Mdw TA19 .... 221 A4
Lower Meadow Rd BS24.. 201 B5
Lower Middle St TA1.. 212 F4
Lower New Rd BS27 ... 90 A7
Lower Northend BA1.. 28 F5
Lower North St BS27 . 90 B8
Lower North Town La
  BA22 .... 175 D7
Lower Norton La
  Weston-Super-Mare BS22.. 31 E4
  Weston-Super-Mare, Norton
    BS22 .... 31 C4
Lower Notlake Dro BS28.. 90 C1
Lower Odcombe BA22.. 186 C2
Lower Oldfield Pk BA2.. 228 A1
Lower Orch TA24 .... 184 C5
Lower Parade Ground Rd
  BS24 .... 50 C5
Lower Park La TA24 . 129 E1
Lower Park Row BS1 . 227 A3
Lower Pk BS20 .... 200 E7
Lower Queen's BS21 ... 6 D3
Lower Rd
  Hinton Blewett BS39.. 75 E6
  Horsington BA8 ...... 176 D3
  Kingsdon TA11 ...... 173 D5
  Stalbridge DT10 ..... 190 C4
  Woolavington TA7 .. 136 E4
Lower Ream BA21 ... 218 C5
Lower Rocke's Cotts
  BA6 .... 157 D4
Lower Severalls Gdn★
  TA18 .... 196 A6
Lowerside La BA6 .... 206 D7
Lowerside Rd BA6 ... 206 E6
Lower Silk Mill BA6 . 204 F6
Lower Somerton TA11.. 211 F3
Lower St
  Buckland Dinham BA11.. 100 A2
  Carhampton TA24 ... 131 B4
  Chewton Mendip BA3.. 94 F7
  Curry Mallet TA3 ... 183 C8
  Merriott TA16 .... 195 F7
  Pilton BA4 .... 140 F3
  Rode BA11 .... 101 E8
  Upton Noble BA4 ... 142 F2
  West Chinnock TA18 . 196 B8
Lower Stoke BS2, BA3 . 64 A8
Lower Strode BS40 .... 56 A7
Lower Strode Rd BS21.. 16 A7
Lower Touches TA20 . 223 E5
Lower Town
  Montacute TA15 ..... 186 B4
  Sampford Peverell EX16.. 178 D1
Lower Turners Barn La
  BA20 .... 218 F2
Lower Vellow TA4 ... 132 C2
Lower Westholme Rd
  BA4 .... 140 D3
Lower Whitelands BA3.. 79 B3
Lower Woodcock St
  BA7 .... 214 C5
Lower Wraxhill Rd BA20.. 218 F1
Low Ham Rd TA10 .... 172 B8
Lowlands Terr TA1 ... 212 B4
Lowman Cross EX16 .. 178 C4
Lowmoor Ind Est TA21.. 222 B8
Lowsome La DT9 ..... 188 A5
Lowther Rd BA21 .... 219 F2
Lowtrow Cross TA4 .. 165 A8
Loxhams TA10 .... 156 B2
Loxleigh Ave TA6 ... 209 B4
Loxleigh Gdns TA6 .. 209 B4
Loxley Batch TA7 .... 156 A8
Loxley Gdns BA2 ..... 44 C4
Loxley Terr TA6 ..... 208 F7
Loxton Dr BA2 .... 44 B6
Loxton Rd BS23 ...... 48 F2
Loxton Sq BS14 ...... 23 A6
Lubborn La BA6 ..... 158 B5
Luckes La TA4 .... 132 E3
Luckington Cross BA11.. 98 B2
Lucklands Rd BA1 .... 27 C1
Luckley Ave BS13 .... 22 C5
Luckwells La TA24 ... 129 E2
Lucott Cross TA24 ... 128 C2
Ludbourne Rd DT9 .. 225 D3
Ludlow Ave TA2 ..... 213 A8
Ludlow Cl
  Bridgwater TA6 ..... 209 A2
  Frome BA11 .... 120 C8
  Keynsham BS31 ...... 24 D5
Ludney Cross TA19 .. 194 F7
Ludney La
  Dinnington TA17 .... 195 A8
  Ilminster TA19 ...... 194 F7
Ludwells Orch BS39 ... 77 E5
Lufton Coll of FE BA22.. 186 D4
Lufton Heights Commerce Pk
  BA22 .... 218 A7
Lufton Trad Est BA22.. 218 A7
Lufton Way BA22 .... 218 A6
Luggard's Cross BS21 . 8 C4
Lugshorn La TA11 ... 211 C8
Luke's Cl BA3 .... 78 F3
Lukes Gdn TA24 ..... 131 B4

Luke St EX16 . . . . 164 B1
Lullington La BA11 . . . . . . 101 B3
Lulsgate Rd BS13 . . . . 22 A8
Lulworth Rd BS31 . . . . 24 E4
Lundy Dr TA8 . . . . 104 B5
Luns Hill BA6 . . . . 157 F1
Lunty Mead BS48 . . . . 18 F6
Lupin Way BA22 . . . . 218 B5
Lush Path DT9 . . . . 225 E4
Lusty Gdns BA10 . . . . 215 B5
Luttrell Cl TA2 . . . . 213 B8
Luttrell Gdns TA24 . . . . . . 200 F6
Luvers La BS40 . . . . 54 D1
Luxborough Rd TA6 . . . . . . 208 B8
Lux Furlong BS9 . . . . 5 B7
Luxhay Cl TA2 . . . . 213 B8
Luxton's La BA3, BA4 . . . . 116 F1
Lyatt La BA5 . . . . 140 E8
Lyatts Hill BA22 . . . . 197 B6
Lychgate Pk BS24 . . . . 50 A4
Lyddieth Ct BA15 . . . . 64 E7
Lyddon's Hill TA22 . . . . . . 148 A1
Lyddon Cl TA21 . . . . 222 D4
Lyddon Rd BS22 . . . . 32 B3
Lyddons Mead TA20 . . . . . 223 E4
Lydeard Cross TA5 . . . . . . 152 E3
Lydeard Down Hill TA4 . . . 151 B4
Lydeard Mead TA4 . . . . . . 167 E8
Lydeard St Lawrence Com
  Prim Sch TA4 . . . . 151 A3
Lyde Ct BA21 . . . . 219 E6
Lyde Gn BA2 . . . . 81 E5
Lyde La BA21 . . . . 219 E6
Lyde Rd BA21 . . . . 219 E7
Lydon La TA4 . . . . 165 D5
Lye Cross Rd BS40 . . . . 36 C1
Lyefield Rd BS22 . . . . 31 E4
Lye Hole La BS40 . . . . 36 D2
Lye La BA4 . . . . 158 F6
Lye Mead BS40 . . . . 38 A6
Lyes The BS49 . . . . 34 D3
Lyewater TA18 . . . . 224 B6
Lyme Gdns BA1 . . . . 44 B7
Lyme Rd
  Axminster EX13 . . . . 198 A1
  Bath BA1 . . . . 44 B7
  Crewkerne TA18 . . . . 224 B4
Lymore Ave BA2 . . . . 44 C5
Lymore Gdns BA2 . . . . 44 C5
Lymore Terr BA2 . . . . 44 C4
Lympsham CE Fst Sch
  BS24 . . . . 67 B1
Lympsham Gn BA2 . . . . 62 D8
Lympsham Rd BS24 . . . . . . 67 B1
Lynbrook BS41 . . . . 10 F1
Lynbrook La BA2 . . . . 44 F3
Lynch Cl BS22 . . . . 31 F3
Lynchcombe La BA5 . . . . . 110 F6
Lynch Cres BS25 . . . . 69 F7
Lynch Hill BA3 . . . . 96 A3
Lynch La
  Cheddar BS27 . . . . 90 C8
  Hardington Mandeville
    BA22 . . . . 197 A6
  Westbury-sub-Mendip
    BA5 . . . . 110 D8
Lynchmead BS25 . . . . 70 A7
Lynch The BS25 . . . . 69 F7
Lyncombe Hall BA2 . . . . . . 45 A4
Lyncombe Hill BA2 . . . . . 228 C1
Lyncombe Vale BA2 . . . . . . 45 B4
Lyncombe Vale Rd BA2 . . . 45 A4
Lyndale Ave
  Bridgwater TA6 . . . . 208 E5
  Bristol BS9 . . . . 5 D5
Lynde Cl BS13 . . . . 22 B4
Lyndhurst Cres TA6 . . . . . 208 C5
Lyndhurst Gr TA12 . . . . . . 185 D7
Lyndhurst Rd
  Bath BA2 . . . . 44 C6
  Bristol BS9 . . . . 5 F7
  Keynsham BS31 . . . . 24 F3
  Midsomer Norton BA3 . . . . 97 B8
  Weston-Super-Mare BS23 . . 48 E4
Lyndhurst Terr BA1 . . . . . 228 C4
Lynfield Pk BA1 . . . . 27 C1
Lynfield Rd BA11 . . . . 119 D5
Lynford La TA11 . . . . 158 C1
Lyngford Cres TA2 . . . . . . 213 A7
Lyngford La TA2 . . . . 168 F6
Lyngford Park Prim Sch
  TA2 . . . . 213 B8
Lyngford Pl TA2 . . . . 213 A7
Lyngford Rd TA2 . . . . 213 A7
Lyngford Sq TA2 . . . . 213 A7
Lynmouth Cl BS22 . . . . 32 A2
Lynor Cl TA1 . . . . 213 D3
Lynton Cl BS20 . . . . 2 E4
Lynton Rd
  Burnham-on-S TA8 . . . . . 104 B6
  Midsomer Norton BA3 . . . . 97 B8
Lynwood Cl
  Frome BA11 . . . . 119 D4
  Midsomer Norton BA3 . . . . 97 A8
Lynx Cres BS24 . . . . 49 B2
Lynx Trad Est BA20 . . . . . 218 D3
Lynx West Trad Est
  BA20 . . . . 218 C3
Lyons Court Rd BS14 . . . . . 23 D7
Lyons Cl BS23 . . . . 48 F7
Lype La TA22 . . . . 147 E4
Lypstone Cl BS24 . . . . 50 A8
Lypyatt La BA6 . . . . 206 F4
Lysander Rd BA20 . . . . . . 218 B3
Lysander Ret Pk BA20 . . . 219 A3

Lysander Road Rdbt
  BA20 . . . . 218 C3
Lyster Cl BA22 . . . . 173 E1
Lyster Gdns BA22 . . . . 173 E1
Lyte's Cary★ TA11 . . . . . . 173 F5
Lytes Cary Rd BS31 . . . . . . 25 A3
Lytton Gdns BA2 . . . . 44 B4
Lytton Gr BS31 . . . . 25 A5
Lyveden Gdns BS13 . . . . . . 22 B5
Lyvedon Way BS41 . . . . . . 11 B1

M

McAdam Way BS1 . . . . 11 F5
MacAulay Bldgs BA2 . . . . . 45 C4
McCrae Rd BS24 . . . . 50 B5
McCreath Cl ❸ TA6 . . . . . 153 F3
Mc Creery Rd DT9 . . . . . . 225 D6
Macey's Rd BS13 . . . . 22 D3
Macfarlane Chase BS23 . . 49 A5
Machine Cross TA22 . . . . . 163 F6
Macies The BA1 . . . . 27 B3
McKinley Terr TA23 . . . . . 131 E4
Mackley La BA21 . . . . 81 E3
MacLeod Cl BS21 . . . . 6 A2
Macquarie Farm Cl BS49 . . 17 A1
Macrae Rd BS20 . . . . 4 E4
Madam's Paddock BS40 . . 39 B3
Madam La
  Weston-Super-Mare BS22 . . 31 F2
  Weston-Super-Mare BS22 . . 32 A3
  Weston-Super-Mare BS22 . . 32 A4
Madden Cl TA8 . . . . 104 C7
Maddocks Pk BA9 . . . . 216 C3
Maddocks Slade TA8 . . . . 104 A8
Maddox Rd BS23 . . . . 48 C8
Madeira Rd
  Clevedon BS21 . . . . 6 D3
  Weston-Super-Mare BS23 . . 30 C1
Madgeon La TA20 . . . . . . 192 E8
Madison Cl ❺ TA18 . . . . . 224 C6
Madwoman's La BS28 . . . 108 B2
Maesbury Rd BS31 . . . . 25 A2
Maesdown Cl BA4 . . . . . . 141 E4
Maesdown Cotts BA4 . . . . 141 E2
Maes Down Ho ❿ BA4 . . 205 B6
Maesdown Rd
  Doulting BA4 . . . . 141 E4
  Evercreech BA4 . . . . 141 E2
Maesknoll La BS14, BS39 . . 40 B8
Magdalana Ct BS1 . . . . . . 227 B1
Magdalene Ave BA2 . . . . . 228 B1
Magdalene Cl ❾ TA1 . . . . 212 F4
Magdalene Ct ❿ TA1 . . . . 212 F4
Magdalene Rd BA3 . . . . 79 C2
Magdalene St
  Glastonbury BA6 . . . . . . 206 D4
  Taunton TA1 . . . . 212 F4
Magdalen La BA14 . . . . 83 B7
Magdalen Rd BA2 . . . . . . 228 B1
Magdalen Way BS22 . . . . . 32 A3
Magellan Cl BS22 . . . . 31 F4
Maggs Folly BS39 . . . . 59 D2
Maggs Hill BA2 . . . . 60 B2
Maggs La
  Castle Cary BA7 . . . . 214 C7
  Whitchurch BS14 . . . . 23 C4
Maglands Rd TA23 . . . . . . 202 D6
Magna Cl BA21 . . . . 219 D8
Magnolia Ave BS22 . . . . . . 32 A1
Magnolia Cl
  Frome BA11 . . . . 120 C7
  Weston-Super-Mare BS22 . . 49 E7
Magnolia Tree Rd TA6 . . . 209 E5
Magpie Cl
  Burnham-on-S TA8 . . . . . . 85 B1
  Weston-Super-Mare BS22 . . 49 E8
Maiden Beech Mid Sch
  TA18 . . . . 224 B4
Maidenbrook La TA2 . . . . 169 A6
Maiden Croft La BA6 . . . . 139 D2
Maidenhead Cross EX16 . 179 C7
Maidenhead Rd BS13 . . . . . 22 D3
Maiden Way BS11 . . . . 4 C8
Maidstone Gr BS24 . . . . . . 49 A1
Maincombe Cl TA18 . . . . . 224 C4
Main Rd
  Brockley BS49 . . . . 18 D2
  Burrowbridge TA7 . . . . . . 154 F1
  Cannington TA5 . . . . 135 C1
  Coxley BA5 . . . . 139 E6
  Flax Bourton BS48 . . . . . . 19 F7
  Huntspill TA9 . . . . 136 B8
  Hutton BS24 . . . . 49 E2
  Kilve TA5 . . . . 133 C5
  Lyng TA3, TA7 . . . . 170 C7
  Middlezoy TA7 . . . . 155 B3
  Othery TA7 . . . . 155 B2
  Shapwick TA7 . . . . 155 F8
  Westhay BA6 . . . . 138 B5
  Westonzoyland TA7 . . . . . 154 F5
Main St
  Babcary TA11 . . . . 174 C2
  Barton St David TA11 . . . 158 A3
  Chilthorne Domer BA22 . . 186 B6
  Farrington Gurney BS39 . . . 77 A4
  Martock TA12 . . . . 185 F7
  Walton BA16 . . . . 156 D7
Mal's Mead La TA20 . . . . 194 C3
Malago Vlk BS13 . . . . 22 A5
Malden Mead BS14 . . . . . . 23 A5
Malherbie Ct TA20 . . . . . 194 B6
Mallard Pl TA9 . . . . 104 C4

Mallard Rd TA24 . . . . 201 C5
Mallard Way TA6 . . . . 209 B4
Mallard Wlk ❼ BS22 . . . . . 49 E8
Mallory Cl TA2 . . . . 212 C6
Mallow Cl BS21 . . . . 6 E2
Mall The
  Bath BA1 . . . . 228 C2
  Bristol, Clifton BS8 . . . . . . 11 F7
Malmesbury Ct ❻ BA2 . . . 218 C6
Malmesbury Way BA21 . . . 218 C6
Malta Way BA22 . . . . 174 A2
Malt Ho The TA4 . . . . 210 C4
Malthouse Cl BA9 . . . . . . 216 C4
Malthouse Ct
  Frome BA11 . . . . 119 E3
  Taunton TA1 . . . . 212 A4
Malthouse La DT9 . . . . . . 187 F5
Malthouses TA21 . . . . 167 A1
Maltings Ind Est The BA1 . 44 B6
Maltings The
  Chard TA20 . . . . 223 C3
  Frome BA11 . . . . 119 F4
  Midford BA2 . . . . 63 C5
  Sherborne DT9 . . . . 225 E4
  Weston-Super-Mare BS22 . . 31 F2
Maltlands BS22 . . . . 49 D8
Malvern Bldgs BA1 . . . . . . 28 A2
Malvern Cl TA6 . . . . 209 D6
Malvern Ct BA21 . . . . 218 D6
Malvern Rd BS23 . . . . 48 E5
Malvern Terr
  ❹ Bath BA1 . . . . 28 A1
  Taunton TA1 . . . . 212 F6
Malvern Villas ❸ BA1 . . . . 28 A1
Mamsey La TA4 . . . . 202 C3
Manchester Cotts BS22 . . . 31 E3
Mancroft Ave BS11 . . . . 4 F7
Mandarin Cl TA6 . . . . 209 B4
Mandy Mdws BA3 . . . . 77 F1
Mangle Cave Hill TA18 . . . 195 C5
Manilla Cres BS23 . . . . 30 C1
Manilla Pl BS23 . . . . 30 C1
Manilla Rd BS8 . . . . 226 A3
Manleaze Cvn Pk BA4 . . . . 205 D3
Manleys Cotts TA2 . . . . . . 168 C6
Manmoor La BS21 . . . . 7 A1
Manning's La BA3 . . . . 94 F3
Manning Cl BA5 . . . . 203 F5
Manning Rd TA4 . . . . 167 E6
Manor Barton TA14 . . . . . 185 E2
Manor Bldgs TA18 . . . . . . 196 C4
Manor Cl
  Berrow TA8 . . . . 84 F6
  Bradford Abbas DT9 . . . . 187 E1
  Chard TA20 . . . . 223 C2
  Charlton Horethorne DT9 . 176 A2
  Cossington TA7 . . . . 136 F3
  Ditcheat BA4 . . . . 159 C7
  East Brent TA9 . . . . 86 D5
  Easton-in-G BS20 . . . . 4 A4
  Farrington Gurney BS39 . . . 77 A3
  Glastonbury BA6 . . . . . . 206 D5
  Kingsdon TA11 . . . . 173 D5
  Portishead BS20 . . . . 2 A5
  South Perrott DT8 . . . . . . 196 C1
  Sparkford BA22 . . . . 175 A4
  Taunton TA1 . . . . 212 E3
  Templecombe BA8 . . . . . 189 E8
  Wellow BA2 . . . . 62 D1
Manor Cl The BS8 . . . . . . 11 A8
Manor Copse Rd BA3 . . . . 79 C2
Manor Court Prim Sch
  TA20 . . . . 223 C3
Manor Ct
  Backwell BS48 . . . . 19 A5
  Burnham-on-S TA8 . . . . . 104 B7
  Cossington TA7 . . . . 136 F3
  Easton BA5 . . . . 111 A4
  Horsington BA8 . . . . 176 D2
  Locking BS24 . . . . 50 B4
  Sherborne DT9 . . . . 225 D5
  Stawell TA7 . . . . 137 A1
  Weston-Super-Mare BS23 . . 49 A8
Manor Dr
  Bathford BA1 . . . . 29 C2
  Berrow TA8 . . . . 84 F6
  Chedzoy TA7 . . . . 154 D8
  East Coker BA22 . . . . 197 B8
  ❿ Merriott TA16 . . . . . . 195 F7
  Staplegrove TA2 . . . . 212 C7
  Taunton TA1 . . . . 212 E3
Manor Farm
  Chard TA20 . . . . 223 C3
  East Coker BA22 . . . . 197 B8
Manor Farm Barns TA7 . . 169 E8
Manor Farm Cl
  Tatworth TA20 . . . . 198 C8
  Weston-Super-Mare BS24 . . 49 B2
Manor Farm Cres BS24 . . . 49 B2
Manor Furlong BA11 . . . . 119 E2
Manor Gdns
  Farmborough BA2 . . . . . . 59 F6
  Farrington Gurney BS39 . . . 77 A3
  Ilchester BA22 . . . . 173 E1
  Locking BS24 . . . . 50 A4
  Weston-Super-Mare BS22 . . 31 B4
Manor Gn EX14 . . . . 191 F2
Manor Grange BS24 . . . . . . 67 B7
Manor Ho BS2 . . . . 226 C3
Manor House Gdns BA6 . . 206 D5
Manor House Rd BA6 . . . . 206 D5
Manor La
  Abbots Leigh BS8 . . . . 10 F8
  Wedmore BS28 . . . . 108 D5
Manor Mews TA2 . . . . 212 D8
Manor Orch TA1 . . . . 212 D2
Manor Park Cl BA3 . . . . . . 79 C2

Manor Pk
  Bath BA1 . . . . 44 B8
  Keinton Mandeville TA11 . 158 B1
  Norton Fitzwarren TA2 . . . 168 B4
  Pawlett TA6 . . . . 135 F6
  Radstock BA3 . . . . 79 C2
  Weston-Super-Mare BS23 . . 48 E1
Manor Pl TA11 . . . . 158 B1
Manor Rd
  Abbots Leigh BS8 . . . . 10 F7
  Bath BA1 . . . . 27 C1
  Bridgwater TA6 . . . . 209 C6
  Bristol, Bishopsworth BS13 . 22 A6
  Burnham-on-S TA8 . . . . . 104 B7
  Chedzoy TA7 . . . . 154 D8
  Cossington TA7 . . . . 136 F3
  Edington TA7 . . . . 137 D2
  Frome BA11 . . . . 119 E2
  Isle Abbotts TA3 . . . . 183 F7
  Kingsdon TA11 . . . . 173 D5
  Milborne Port DT9 . . . . . 217 C3
  Minehead TA24 . . . . 201 B4
  Pawlett TA6 . . . . 135 F6
  Radstock BA3 . . . . 79 C2
  Saltford BS31 . . . . 25 C2
  Staplegrove TA2 . . . . 212 C8
  Taunton TA1 . . . . 212 D3
  Weston-Super-Mare BS23 . . 49 A8
  Yeovil BA20 . . . . 219 A4
Manor Ride TA9 . . . . 86 B2
Manor St BA22 . . . . 197 A8
Manor Terr BA3 . . . . 79 C2
Manor Valley BS23 . . . . . . 31 A1
Manor View
  Crewkerne TA18 . . . . 224 C4
  Golsoncott TA23 . . . . 131 C6
Manor Villas BA1 . . . . 27 C1
Manor Way
  Berrow TA8 . . . . 84 F6
  Failand BS8 . . . . 10 C4
  Frome BA11 . . . . 119 E2
Manse La TA4 . . . . 136 C4
Mansel Cl BS31 . . . . 25 C3
Mansfield Ave BS23 . . . . . . 49 B8
Mansfield Rd TA1 . . . . 213 A3
Manship Gn BA4 . . . . 205 B4
Manston Cl BS14 . . . . 23 C7
Mantle St TA21 . . . . 222 C5
Mantle VC Rd BA22 . . . . . 174 A2
Manvers St BA1 . . . . 228 C1
Manworthy Cross TA4 . . . 166 C5
Maperton Rd DT9 . . . . 176 A2
Maple Cl
  Bristol BS14 . . . . 23 D5
  Evercreech BA4 . . . . 141 F1
  North Petherton TA6 . . . . 153 F3
  Puriton TA6 . . . . 136 C4
  Street BA16 . . . . 207 C5
  Taunton TA2 . . . . 213 A7
  Weston-Super-Mare BS23 . . 49 A8
  Wincanton BA9 . . . . 216 C2
Maple Ct
  Bridgwater TA6 . . . . 209 D6
  Bristol BS9 . . . . 5 F8
  Frome BA11 . . . . 120 A7
  ❾ Weston-Super-Mare
    BS23 . . . . 30 C1
Maple Dr
  Burnham-on-S TA8 . . . . . 104 B5
  Crewkerne TA18 . . . . 224 D7
  Radstock BA3 . . . . 78 E1
  Yeovil BA20 . . . . 218 F3
Maple Gdns BA2 . . . . 44 E4
Maple Ho BS2 . . . . 227 A4
Maple Leaf Ct BS8 . . . . . . 226 A3
Maple Rd
  Curry Rivel TA10 . . . . . . 171 D4
  Langport TA10 . . . . 172 A4
Maple Rise BA3 . . . . 79 B2
Maples The
  Nailsea BS48 . . . . 8 C1
  Shepton Mallet BA4 . . . . 205 C6
Maple Tree Ct TA7 . . . . . . 136 F3
Maple Wlk BS31 . . . . 24 D4
Mapstone Cl BA6 . . . . 206 E3
Marchant's Hill BA3 . . . . . 95 F2
Marchant-Holliday Sch
  BA8 . . . . 176 C5
Marchants Pass BA1 . . . . . 228 C1
Marchfields Way BS23 . . . . 49 A5
March La BA22 . . . . 175 D8
Marconi Cl BS23 . . . . 49 B7
Marconi Rd BS20 . . . . 1 F5
Marden Gr TA1 . . . . 213 D3
Marden Rd BS31 . . . . 25 A4
Mardi's La TA11 . . . . 158 C2
Mardyke Ferry Rd BS1 . . . 226 B1
Mare La TA13 . . . . 220 C5
Mares La BA5 . . . . 110 E2
Margaret's Bldgs BA1 . . . . 228 B3
Margaret's Hill BA1 . . . . . 228 C4
Margaret Cres TA6 . . . . . . 208 E6
Margaret Rd ❹ BS13 . . . . . 21 F4
Margery Fish Gdns★
  TA13 . . . . 220 C8
Marguerite Rd BS13 . . . . . . 21 F7
Marina Row TA6 . . . . 209 B4
Marindin Dr BS22 . . . . 32 B4
Marine Ct BA21 . . . . 219 D5
Marine Dr TA8 . . . . 104 B5
Marine Hill BS21 . . . . 6 C5
Marine Par
  Clevedon BS21 . . . . 6 C4
  Pill BS20 . . . . 4 C5
  Weston-Super-Mare BS23 . . 30 B1

Marine Par continued
  Weston-Super-Mare BS23 . . 48 D6
Mariner's Cl BS22 . . . . 31 D1
Mariner's Way BS20 . . . . . . 4 C5
Mariners' Path BS9 . . . . 5 E3
Mariners Cl
  Backwell BS48 . . . . 19 A6
  Bridgwater TA6 . . . . 209 A5
  Minehead TA24 . . . . 201 B7
Mariners Ct TA6 . . . . 209 A5
Mariners Dr
  Backwell BS48 . . . . 19 A6
  Bristol BS9 . . . . 5 D4
Mariners Way TA23 . . . . . 202 D6
Maritime Heritage Ctr★
  BS1 . . . . 226 B1
Marjoram Way BS20 . . . . . . 2 F5
Mark CE Fst Sch TA9 . . . . 106 A4
Mark Coll TA9 . . . . 106 E4
Mark Cswy TA9 . . . . 106 B4
Market Ave BS22 . . . . 32 C3
Market Cl
  ❹ Bampton EX16 . . . . . . 164 B1
  Brushford TA22 . . . . 163 E4
Market Ct
  ❽ Bridgwater TA6 . . . . . 208 F5
  ❷ Crewkerne TA18 . . . . . 224 C6
Market Gate BS2 . . . . 227 C3
Market House La TA24 . . . 200 F7
Market House Mus The★
  TA23 . . . . 202 C7
Market Ind Est BS49 . . . . . 17 B1
Market La BS23 . . . . 48 D8
Market Pl
  Burlescombe EX16 . . . . . . 179 B4
  Castle Cary BA7 . . . . 214 C5
  Frome BA11 . . . . 119 F5
  Glastonbury BA6 . . . . . . 206 D4
  Ilchester BA22 . . . . 173 E1
  Radstock BA3 . . . . 78 F2
  ❷❸ Shepton Mallet BA4 . 205 B6
  Somerton TA11 . . . . 211 E4
  Wells BA5 . . . . 203 E4
  Wincanton BA9 . . . . 216 C4
  Winford BS40 . . . . 37 F7
Market Pl The BA11 . . . . 143 B8
Market Sq
  Crewkerne TA18 . . . . 224 C6
  South Petherton TA13 . . . 220 C4
Market St
  Bridgwater TA6 . . . . 208 F5
  Crewkerne TA18 . . . . 224 C6
  Highbridge TA9 . . . . 104 E3
  Watchet TA23 . . . . 202 C7
  Wells BA5 . . . . 203 D4
  Yeovil BA20 . . . . 219 B5
Market Terr TA9 . . . . 104 E3
Mark La BS1 . . . . 226 C2
Marklands BS9 . . . . 5 E3
Mark Rd
  Burtle TA7 . . . . 137 D6
  Highbridge TA9 . . . . 105 A2
Marksbury CE Prim Sch
  BA2 . . . . 42 B2
Marks Cl TA3 . . . . 169 C4
Marksmead DT8 . . . . 199 D7
Marksview Bsns Ctr
  BA21 . . . . 219 E7
Marlborough Ave TA6 . . . . 209 A2
Marlborough Bldgs
  Bath BA1 . . . . 228 A3
  Langport TA10 . . . . 171 F5
Marlborough Cl TA6 . . . . . 209 A2
Marlborough Ct TA8 . . . . . 85 B1
Marlborough Dr BS22 . . . . 32 B2
Marlborough Flats ❽
  BS2 . . . . 227 A4
Marlborough Hill BS2 . . . . 227 A4
Marlborough Hill Pl BS2 . . 227 A4
Marlborough La BA1 . . . . . 228 A3
Marlborough La BA1 . . . . 219 E6
Marlborough St
  Bath BA1 . . . . 228 A4
  Bristol BS2 . . . . 227 A4
Marl Cl BA21 . . . . 218 E7
Marle Ground TA19 . . . . . 184 E2
Marlepit Gr BS13 . . . . 21 F6
Marley's Row TA24 . . . . . 124 A3
Marley Cl TA24 . . . . 201 A5
Marleys Way BA11 . . . . . . 119 C5
Marlfield Wlk BS13 . . . . . . 21 E7
Marling Ho TA24 . . . . 201 B7
Marl La DT9 . . . . 187 E3
Marlowe Ho ❸ BS23 . . . . . 48 F4
Marl Pits ❶ BS48 . . . . 19 A6
Marl Pits La BA11 . . . . 143 C7
Marne Cl BS14 . . . . 23 D5
Marnhull Cl DT10 . . . . 190 F6
Marriage La DT10 . . . . 190 F3
Marron Cl BS26 . . . . 70 C2
Marsden Rd BA2 . . . . 44 B3
Marshall Wlk BS4 . . . . 22 D7
Marshalsea Est DT6 . . . . . 199 C3
Marshbridge Cross TA22 . 163 C7
Marshclose Hill TA22 . . . . 146 E2
Marsh Cross TA24 . . . . . . 200 D1
Marshfield Rd TA24 . . . . . 201 B5
Marshfield Way BA1 . . . . . 28 A1
Marsh Hill BA21 . . . . 163 C8
Marsh La
  Barrington TA19 . . . . 184 E5
  Barton St David TA11 . . . 158 A3
  Bridgwater TA6 . . . . 209 B1
  Buckhorn Weston BA9 . . . 177 C4
  Cannington TA5 . . . . 135 C2
  Dunster TA24 . . . . 201 E3
  Easton-in-G BS20 . . . . 4 A4

Marsh La continued
Farrington Gurney BS39 . . . 77 A3
Henstridge BA8 . . . . 190 B7
Holcombe BA3 . . . . 116 C5
Penselwood BA9 . . . . 161 D2
Pitney TA10 . . . . 172 D7
Portbury BS20 . . . . 3 F6
South Cheriton BA8 . . . . . 176 E4
Temple Cloud BS39 . . . . 59 A1
Tintinhull BA22 . . . . 186 A5
Yeovil BA21 . . . . 218 F8
Yeovil Marsh BA21 . . . . . . 186 A5
Marsh Lane Ind Est BS20 . . . 3 F7
Marsh Pottinson Ho 🔟6
BA20 . . . . 219 B4
Marsh Rd
Bristol BS3 . . . . 11 F3
Rode BA11 . . . . 82 F1
Standerwick BA11 . . . . 102 D1
Yatton BS49 . . . . 34 B8
Marsh St
Avonmouth BS11 . . . . 4 C8
🔳 Bristol BS1 . . . . 227 A2
Dunster TA24 . . . . 201 C3
Marshway TA3 . . . . 170 D1
Marshwood CE Prim Sch
DT6 . . . . 199 C2
Marshwood Cross DT6 . . 199 E1
Marson Rd BS21 . . . . 6 D3
Marston Cl
Frome BA11 . . . . 119 D2
Taunton TA1 . . . . 212 E1
Marston La BA11 . . . . 119 D2
Marston Mead BA11 . . . . 119 D2
Marston Rd
Frome BA11 . . . . 119 D1
Nunney BA11 . . . . 143 D8
Sherborne DT9 . . . . 225 B5
Marston Trad Est BA11 . . 119 E2
Martcombe Rd BS20 . . . . 4 C2
Martha's Orch BS13 . . . . . . 21 E7
Martin's Cl TA8 . . . . 85 A3
Martindale Ct BS22 . . . . . . 49 D8
Martindale Rd BS22 . . . . . 49 D8
Martins TA3 . . . . 169 C4
Martins Bldgs 🔳 TA21 . . 222 D5
Martins Cl
Evercreech BA4 . . . . 141 E1
Wellington TA21 . . . . 222 D5
Wells BA5 . . . . 203 B3
Martins Gr BS22 . . . . 31 E2
Martins La BA4 . . . . 205 E5
Martins Paddock BA4 . . . 142 A6
Martin St BA6 . . . . 158 A5
Martins The BS20 . . . . 3 A6
Martland Cl TA7 . . . . 136 E3
Martlet Rd TA24 . . . . 200 F7
Martock BS24 . . . . 48 F2
Martock Bsns Pk TA12 . . 185 D7
Martock CE Prim Sch
TA12 . . . . 185 E6
Martock La TA12 . . . . 185 F7
Martock Rd
Keynsham BS31 . . . . 25 A3
Long Sutton TA10 . . . . 172 E4
Mart Rd TA24 . . . . 201 B7
Mart The 🔟6 BS23 . . . . 48 E7
Martyn Cl TA5 . . . . 135 B5
Marwood Cl TA8 . . . . 104 C8
Marwood Rd BS4 . . . . 22 E8
Mary Brown Davis La 🔟6
BA5 . . . . 139 D8
Marybush La BS2 . . . . 227 B3
Mary Elton Prim Sch BS21 . . 6 B1
Mary Hart Cl BA16 . . . . . . 207 B7
Mary La 🔟0 EX16 . . . . 164 B1
Mary Rd BA5 . . . . 203 C5
Mary St
Taunton TA1 . . . . 212 F3
Yeovil BA21 . . . . 219 B5
Masefield Ho BS23 . . . . 49 A4
Mason's Way BS27 . . . . 90 C7
Mason La TA15 . . . . 186 B4
Masons Way BA11 . . . . . . 119 D1
Mason Way BA4 . . . . 205 A4
Massingham Pk TA2 . . . . 213 B6
Materman Rd BS14 . . . . . . 23 E5
Matfurlong Cl TA12 . . . . . 185 D5
Matt's La TA14 . . . . 185 F4
Matthews Cl BS14 . . . . 23 F6
Matthews Rd
Taunton TA1 . . . . 212 B1
Yeovil BA21 . . . . 219 C5
Mattock's Tree Hill TA3 . 169 E1
Mattys Cross EX14 . . . . . . 191 D3
Maudlin Cross TA20 . . . . 199 C8
Maudlin La TA20 . . . . 199 C8
Maudslay Field BA22 . . . 197 C8
Maunsell Rd BS24 . . . . 49 E2
Maunsel Rd TA7 . . . . 153 F1
Max Mill La BS25 . . . . 69 C8
Maxwell Rd BA4 . . . . 205 B4
Maxwell St TA2 . . . . 212 E6
May's La BS24 . . . . 33 C3
Maybrick Rd BA2 . . . . 44 D5
Mayfair Ave BS48 . . . . 8 F1
Mayfield Ave BS22 . . . . . . 31 E1
Mayfield Cl BA22 . . . . 175 D8
Mayfield Dr TA6 . . . . 208 B4
Mayfield Rd
Bath BA2 . . . . 44 D5
Yeovil BA21 . . . . 219 D5
Mayfields BS31 . . . . 24 E5
Mayfield Terr TA4 . . . . . . 210 C4
Mayflower Cl TA6 . . . . . . 209 D5
Mayflower Gdns BS48 . . . . 9 A2

Maynard Cl
Bristol BS13 . . . . 22 C5
🔳 Clevedon BS21 . . . . 6 F3
Maynard Rd BS13 . . . . 22 C5
Maynard Terr BS39 . . . . . . 58 F3
Maypole Cl BS39 . . . . 58 E3
May Pole Knap TA11 . . . . 211 C4
Maysfield Cl BS20 . . . . 2 D3
Maysgreen La BS24 . . . . . . 33 B3
Maysmead La BS40 . . . . . . 53 C6
May Terr TA23 . . . . 131 E3
Maytree Ave BS13 . . . . 22 B7
Maytree Cl
Bristol BS13 . . . . 22 B7
Frome BA11 . . . . 120 B7
May Tree Cl BS48 . . . . 8 C1
May Tree Rd BA3 . . . . 78 E1
May Tree Wlk BS31 . . . . . . 24 C3
Mead Ave BA22 . . . . 218 B6
Mead Cl
Bath BA2 . . . . 44 E3
Bristol BS11 . . . . 4 E6
Cheddar BS27 . . . . 90 B6
East Huntspill TA9 . . . . . . 136 E8
Stoke St Michael BA3 . . . . 116 B2
Meade Cl TA6 . . . . 153 F3
Meade Ho BA2 . . . . 44 A5
Meade La TA19 . . . . 184 E1
Mead La
Blagdon BS40 . . . . 54 E3
Lydford Fair Place TA11 . . 158 C3
Saltford BS31 . . . . 25 F4
Sandford BS25 . . . . 51 E4
Stocklinch TA19 . . . . 184 C4
Wanstrow BA4 . . . . 142 F4
West Pennard BA6 . . . . . . 140 C2
Meadlands BA2 . . . . 43 B7
Meadowbank BS22 . . . . . . 31 F3
Meadow Cl
Backwell BS48 . . . . 19 B6
Chilton Trinity TA5 . . . . . . 135 F2
Farrington Gurney BS39 . . . 77 A3
Henstridge BA8 . . . . 190 B6
Highbridge TA9 . . . . 104 D4
Kingston St Mary TA2 . . . . 168 E8
Langport TA10 . . . . 172 A6
Nailsea BS48 . . . . 8 E3
Nether Stowey TA5 . . . . . . 134 A2
Stalbridge DT10 . . . . 190 B4
Street BA16 . . . . 207 B4
Wincanton BA9 . . . . 216 D3
Meadow Cotts TA24 . . . . 131 B4
Meadow Croft BS24 . . . . . 49 B2
Meadowcroft Dr TA8 . . . . 104 C8
Meadow Ct BA1 . . . . 44 A7
Meadow Dr
Bath BA2 . . . . 62 D8
Locking BS24 . . . . 50 B4
Portishead BS20 . . . . 1 F1
Meadow Gdns
Bath BA1 . . . . 27 A1
Stogursey TA5 . . . . 134 C6
Meadow Gr BS11 . . . . 4 D7
Meadow La
Bathampton BA2 . . . . 28 D1
Walton BA16 . . . . 156 E7
Meadowland BS49 . . . . . . 17 A1
Meadowlands BS22 . . . . . . 32 C2
Meadowlands Ave TA6 . . 208 E6
Meadow Pk
Bathford BA1 . . . . 29 B3
Wembdon TA6 . . . . 208 C5
Meadow Pl BS22 . . . . 32 D3
Meadow Rd
Clevedon BS21 . . . . 6 E3
Frome BA11 . . . . 119 F7
Paulton BS39 . . . . 77 F4
Yeovil BA21 . . . . 219 D4
Meadow Rise BA4 . . . . . . 205 B7
Meadow Sch The BA10 . . 215 E6
Meadowside Cl BS20 . . . . . . 1 F5
Meadows End BS25 . . . . . . 52 D4
Meadowside
Carhampton TA24 . . . . . . 131 A5
Rockwell Green TA21 . . . . 222 B5
Meadowside Cl TA1 . . . . . 212 B4
Meadowside Dr BS14 . . . . 23 A3
Meadows Prim Sch The
BS30 . . . . 25 D8
Meadow St
Axbridge BS26 . . . . 70 C2
Bristol BS2 . . . . 227 C4
Weston-Super-Mare BS23 . . 48 E7
Meadows The
🔳 Bourton SP8 . . . . 161 F1
Drayton TA10 . . . . 171 E3
Porlock TA24 . . . . 124 A3
Meadow Terr TA24 . . . . . 201 A5
Meadow View
🔳 Bampton EX16 . . . . . . 164 B1
🔳 Barwick BA22 . . . . 197 F8
East Coker BA22 . . . . 197 C8
Glastonbury BA6 . . . . 206 E3
Long Sutton TA10 . . . . . . 172 E1
Radstock BA3 . . . . 79 A1
Timberscombe TA24 . . . . . 130 B5
Meadow View Cl BA1 . . . . 44 A8
Meadow Villas 🔟4 BS23 . . 48 E8
Mead Rd BS20 . . . . 2 C2
Meads Ct TA6 . . . . 208 E3
Meads Droveway TA3 . . . 169 D5
Mead St BS3 . . . . 227 C1
Meads The DT9 . . . . 217 D2
Mead Terr BS40 . . . . 54 E2
Mead The
Clutton BS39 . . . . 58 E3
Dundry BS41 . . . . 21 D3
East Brent TA9 . . . . 86 E5

Mead The continued
Farmborough BA2 . . . . 60 A6
Henstridge BA8 . . . . 190 A6
Holcombe BA3 . . . . 116 C8
Ilchester BA22 . . . . 173 D1
Ilminster TA19 . . . . 221 B3
Paulton BS39 . . . . 77 D5
Rode BA11 . . . . 101 E8
🔟4 Shepton Mallet BA4 . . 205 B6
Shipham BS25 . . . . 70 E8
Stoke St Michael BA3 . . . . 116 B2
Stratton-on-F BA3 . . . . 96 F2
Street BA16 . . . . 207 D7
Timsbury BA2 . . . . 60 C3
Winsley BA15 . . . . 64 E7
Mead Vale BS22 . . . . 49 E8
Mead Vale Com Prim Sch
BS22 . . . . 31 E1
Meadway
Bristol BS9 . . . . 5 C6
Farmborough BA2 . . . . 60 A6
Temple Cloud BS39 . . . . . . 58 E1
Woolavington TA7 . . . . . . 136 E4
Mead Way TA2 . . . . 169 B6
Meadway Ave BS48 . . . . 8 D2
Mearcombe La BS24 . . . . . 67 F6
Meardon Rd BS14 . . . . 23 E6
Meare BS24 . . . . 48 F2
Meare Rd
Bath BA2 . . . . 45 A2
Glastonbury BA6 . . . . 206 B6
Meare Village Prim Sch
BA6 . . . . 138 D4
Meareway BA6 . . . . 138 C5
Mearn's Cross BA3 . . . . . . 94 B6
Mede Cl BS1 . . . . 227 B1
Medical Ave BS2, BS8 . . . 226 C3
Medway Cl
Keynsham BS31 . . . . 25 A3
Taunton TA1 . . . . 213 D4
Medway Dr BS31 . . . . 25 A3
Meetinghouse La BS13 . . . 18 A1
Melbourne House Mews
BA5 . . . . 203 D4
Melbourne Pl TA6 . . . . . . 209 B6
Melbourne Terr 🔳 BS21 . . . 6 D2
Melcombe Ct BA2 . . . . 44 D4
Melcombe La TA6 . . . . 153 E3
Melcombe Rd BA2 . . . . 44 D4
Mellanby Cl BA16 . . . . . . 207 D5
Mellent Ave BS13 . . . . 22 C3
Mells CE Fst Sch BA11 . . 118 A6
Mells Cl BS31 . . . . 25 A2
Mells La BA3 . . . . 79 B1
Melrose Ave
Bristol BS8 . . . . 226 B4
Wells BA5 . . . . 203 C4
Melrose Cl 🔳 BA5 . . . . . . 203 C4
Melrose Gr BA2 . . . . 44 B3
Melrose Pl BS8 . . . . 226 B4
Melrose Rd BA21 . . . . 219 B6
Melrose Terr BA1 . . . . 28 A2
Melsbury La BS13 . . . . 139 E6
Memorial Ave TA18 . . . . . 224 C5
Memorial Rd
Wrington BS40 . . . . 35 E2
Yeovil BA20 . . . . 218 B6
Mendip Ave
Shepton Mallet BA4 . . . . . 205 E4
Weston-Super-Mare BS22 . . 31 F2
Mendip Cl
Axbridge BS26 . . . . 70 D2
Frome BA11 . . . . 120 A7
Keynsham BS31 . . . . 24 D5
🔳 Nailsea BS48 . . . . 8 E1
Paulton BS39 . . . . 77 E4
Yatton BS49 . . . . 34 B7
Mendip Dr BA11 . . . . 120 A7
Mendip Edge BS24 . . . . . . 66 F8
Mendip Fields BA3 . . . . . . 96 C2
Mendip Gdns
Bath BA2 . . . . 62 D8
Frome BA11 . . . . 120 B7
Yatton BS49 . . . . 34 B7
Mendip Green Fst Sch
BS22 . . . . 31 E1
Mendip Ho TA1 . . . . 212 F3
Mendip Lea Cl BS27 . . . . . 90 F2
Mendip Lodge BS25 . . . . . 70 A8
Mendip Rd
Bridgwater TA6 . . . . 209 C4
Locking BS24 . . . . 50 D4
Portishead BS20 . . . . 2 B5
Rooks Bridge BS26 . . . . . . 87 A6
Stoke St Michael BA3 . . . . 116 A2
Weston-Super-Mare BS23 . . 49 A4
Yatton BS49 . . . . 34 B7
Mendip Rise BS24 . . . . 50 B4
Mendip Vale BA3 . . . . 116 E7
Mendip Vale Sta★ BA4 . . 205 F3
Mendip Vale Trad Est
BS27 . . . . 90 A7
Mendip View
Coleford BA3 . . . . 116 F7
Street BA16 . . . . 207 B7
Mendip Villas
Cheddar BS27 . . . . 71 A1
Compton Martin BS40 . . . . 73 F7
Emborough BA3 . . . . 95 E3
Mendip Way
Burnham-on-S TA8 . . . . . 104 B7
Radstock BA3 . . . . 78 F3
Menlea BS40 . . . . 54 D3
Mercer Rd BS24 . . . . 23 B8
Merchants' Barton 🔳
BA11 . . . . 119 F4
Merchants Almshouses 🔟6
BS1 . . . . 227 A2

Merchants Barton Ind Est
BA11 . . . . 119 F4
Merchants Ct BS8 . . . . . . 226 A1
Merchants Quay BS1 . . . . 227 A1
Merchants Rd
Bristol BS8 . . . . 226 A3
Bristol, Hotwells BS8 . . . . 226 A1
Merchants Row BS1 . . . . . 226 C1
Merchant St BS1 . . . . 227 B3
Meredith Cl BA22 . . . . . . 197 C3
Meredith Ct BS1 . . . . 226 A1
Merevale Way BA21 . . . . 218 C7
Meriden BA1 . . . . 44 D8
Meridian Pl BS8 . . . . 226 B3
Meridian Vale BS8 . . . . . . 226 B3
Meriet Ave BS13 . . . . 22 B4
Merle Cl TA6 . . . . 209 B4
Merlin Cl
Bristol BS9 . . . . 5 F8
🔳 Weston-Super-Mare
BS22 . . . . 49 E8
Merlin Dr BA5 . . . . 203 B5
Merlin Ind Pk TA2 . . . . . . 213 B6
Merlin Pk BS20 . . . . 2 A4
Merrick Ct BS1 . . . . 227 A1
Merrick Rd BA6 . . . . 206 E7
Merridge Cl TA6 . . . . 208 A4
Merridge Hill TA5 . . . . . . 152 D6
Merrifields TA4 . . . . 167 E6
Merriman Gdns BA16 . . . 207 C5
Merriman Rd BA16 . . . . . 207 C5
Merrimans Rd BS11 . . . . . . 4 D8
Merriott Fst Sch TA16 . . . 195 F7
Merriott Rd
Hinton St George TA17 . . . 195 D7
Merriott TA16 . . . . 195 F6
Merry-field BA3 . . . . 116 E8
Merryfield La
Doulting BA4 . . . . 141 F5
Ilton TA19 . . . . 183 E4
Merryfield Lane Halt★
BA4 . . . . 141 F5
Merryfield Rd BS24 . . . . . . 50 B6
Merryfields TA9 . . . . 106 D5
Merry La TA9 . . . . 136 F8
Merthyr Guest Cl BA8 . . . 176 E1
Merton Dr BS24 . . . . 50 A8
Mervyn Ball Cl TA20 . . . . 223 C5
Methwyn Cl BS22 . . . . 49 C7
Metropole Ct TA24 . . . . . 201 A7
Metropolitan The BS1 . . . 227 B1
Mews The
Bath BA1 . . . . 44 A8
🔳 Bridgwater TA6 . . . . . . 209 B4
East Coker BA22 . . . . 197 C7
Minehead TA24 . . . . 201 A7
Wiveliscombe TA4 . . . . . . 210 C4
Mewswell Dr BS27 . . . . . . 71 B1
Mezellion Pl 🔟4 BA1 . . . . 28 B1
Mianda Terr BA1 . . . . 221 C3
Michaels Mead BA1 . . . . . . 27 B2
Midas Ct TA11 . . . . 211 D3
Middle's La BA4 . . . . 140 C4
Middle Ave BS1 . . . . 227 A2
Middle Brooks BA16 . . . . 207 C3
Middlecombe Cross
TA24 . . . . 200 C6
Middle Dro
Baltonsborough BA6 . . . . . 158 B4
Compton Dundon TA11 . . . 156 F3
Glastonbury BA6 . . . . 206 B5
Hambridge TA10, TA12 . . . 184 F8
Lydford Fair Place TA11 . . 158 C3
Rodney Stoke BS27 . . . . . . 109 C6
Street BA6 . . . . 157 C7
Middlefield La
Barrington TA10 . . . . 184 D6
Norton Sub Hamdon TA13,
TA16 . . . . 185 D1
West Chinnock TA16 . . . . . 196 A8
Middle Field La DT9 . . . . . 188 B7
Middlefield Rd TA10 . . . . 172 C4
Middleford Ho BS13 . . . . . 22 C4
Middle Gate TA10 . . . . . . 172 D8
Middlegate Rd TA10 . . . . 172 C7
Middle Green Rd TA21 . . 222 E3
Middle La
Bath BA1 . . . . 28 B1
Kingston Seymour BS21 . . . 15 F4
Middle Leaze Dro TA12 . . 185 F7
Middle Leigh BA16 . . . . . . 207 C5
Middle Moor Dro TA5 . . . 134 D7
Middle Moor La BS27 . . . . 89 E7
Middlemoor Water Pk★
TA7 . . . . 136 F5
Middle Path TA18 . . . . . . 224 B5
Middlepiece La BA2, BS31 . 42 B7
Middle Rd TA7 . . . . 137 A3
Middle Ridge La DT9 . . . . 175 D1
Middleroom Dro TA3 . . . . 182 E4
Middle St
Ashcott TA7 . . . . 156 B7
Burnham-on-S TA9 . . . . . . 85 E5
East Harptree BS40 . . . . . . 74 F4
East Lambrook TA13 . . . . . 220 C8
Galhampton BA22 . . . . 175 D8
Kingsdon TA11 . . . . 173 D5
Martock TA12 . . . . 185 D4
Minehead TA24 . . . . 200 F8
Misterton TA18 . . . . 224 F3
Montacute TA15 . . . . 186 B3
North Perrott TA18 . . . . . 196 C4
Puriton TA7 . . . . 136 C4
Rimpton BA22 . . . . 188 A8
Shepton Beauchamp TA19 . 184 E3
Taunton TA1 . . . . 212 F4
Yeovil BA20 . . . . 219 B4

Middle Stoke BA3 . . . . 64 A6
Middle Stream Cl TA6 . . . 208 D2
Middleton La
Clatworthy TA4 . . . . 149 C2
Shepton Mallet BA4 . . . . . 205 B4
Middleton Rd BS11 . . . . 4 F8
Middle Touches TA20 . . . . 223 E5
Middleway TA1 . . . . 212 E2
Middle Way TA11 . . . . 157 B4
Middleway Ct TA1 . . . . . . 212 E2
Middleway Rd BA4 . . . . . . 158 E8
Middle Yeo Gn BS48 . . . . . 8 D3
Middlezoy Prim Sch TA7 . 155 B3
Midelney Rd TA10 . . . . . . 171 E2
Midford BS24 . . . . 48 F2
Midford Hill BA2, BA3 . . . 63 C5
Midford La BA2, BA3 . . . . . 63 E7
Midford Rd
Southstoke BA2 . . . . 63 B7
Taunton TA1 . . . . 213 B4
Midhaven Rise BS22 . . . . . 31 E4
Midland Bridge Rd BA1,
BA2 . . . . 228 A2
Midland Mews BS2 . . . . . . 227 C3
Midland Rd
Bath BA1 . . . . 44 D7
Bristol BS2 . . . . 227 C3
Midland St BS2 . . . . 227 C2
Midleaze DT9 . . . . 225 A3
Midney La BA9 . . . . 177 D8
Midsomer Ent Pk BA3 . . . 78 C2
Midsomer Norton Prim Sch
BA3 . . . . 78 B1
Midsomer Norton S★ BA3 97 A8
Midsummer Bldgs BA1 . . . 28 B2
Milborne Port Bsns Ctr
DT9 . . . . 217 D2
Milborne Port Prim Sch
DT9 . . . . 217 D2
Milburn Rd BS23 . . . . 48 F7
Milbury Gdns BS22 . . . . . . 31 C2
Mildmay's Rd TA10 . . . . . 155 F1
Mildmay Dr BA22 . . . . . . 174 F3
Mildred Rd BA16 . . . . 156 F7
Miles's Bldgs BA1 . . . . . . 228 B3
Miles Cl BS20 . . . . 4 E3
Miles St BA2 . . . . 228 C1
Milestone Cl TA6 . . . . 153 F4
Milestone Ct BS22 . . . . 32 C3
Mile Wlk BS14 . . . . 23 A6
Milford Inf Sch BA21 . . . 219 B7
Milford Jun Sch BA21 . . . 219 B7
Milford Pk BA21 . . . . 219 C7
Milford Pl 🔳 TA1 . . . . . . 213 A4
Milford Rd BA21 . . . . 219 C7
Milking La BS27 . . . . 90 E2
Milk St
Bath BA1 . . . . 228 B2
Frome BA11 . . . . 119 E5
Millands La TA5 . . . . 133 C6
Millands The TA11 . . . . . . 211 E4
Millard's Hill
Batcombe BA4 . . . . 142 D2
Midsomer Norton BA3 . . . . 78 C3
Millards Cl BA3 . . . . 78 B3
Millards Hill BA3 . . . . 78 B3
Mill Ave BS1 . . . . 227 A2
Millbatch BA6 . . . . 138 C4
Mill Batch Farm Ind Est
TA9 . . . . 86 F4
Mill Bay TA6 . . . . 153 E4
Millbourn Cl BA15 . . . . . . 64 D7
Millbourne Rd BS27 . . . . . 90 C7
Millbridge Gdns TA24 . . . 200 F7
Millbridge Rd TA24 . . . . . 200 F7
Millbrook BA20 . . . . 218 F1
Millbrook Cross 🔳 EX13 . 198 A1
Millbrook Ct BA2 . . . . 228 C1
Millbrook Dale EX13 . . . . 198 A1
Millbrook Gdns BA7 . . . . 214 B5
Millbrook Pl BA2 . . . . 228 C1
Mill Cl
Cannington TA5 . . . . 135 B2
East Coker BA22 . . . . 197 C8
Frome BA11 . . . . 119 F6
Nether Stowey TA5 . . . . . . 134 A2
Portbury BS20 . . . . 3 D2
Mill Cotts
Creech St Michael TA3 . . . 169 D4
Saltford BS31 . . . . 25 F2
Millcross BS21 . . . . 16 C8
Mill Cross
Halstock BA22 . . . . 197 C3
Kingston St Mary TA2 . . . . 168 E7
Mill Ct
Midsomer Norton BA3 . . . . 78 A1
Watchet TA23 . . . . 202 B7
Millennium Cl BA3 . . . . . . 116 A3
Millennium Sq BS1 . . . . . 226 C2
Miller's Hill DT9 . . . . 217 A5
Miller Cl BS23 . . . . 48 F8
Miller Ho BS8 . . . . 226 A2
Millers Cl
Bourton SP8 . . . . 161 F1
Pill BS20 . . . . 4 C4
Millers Ct BS21 . . . . 16 E8
Millers Gdns BA5 . . . . 203 E5
Millers Orch TA3 . . . . 170 F1
Millers Rise BS22 . . . . 32 A4
Millers Way 🔟 TA4 . . . . . 167 F8
Miller Way DT9 . . . . 225 E5
Miller Wlk BA2 . . . . 28 F1
Milletts Cl 🔳 TA24 . . . . . 131 A5
Mill Farm Hill TA5 . . . . . 134 F1

Millfield
Chard TA20. . . . . **223** D3
Ilchester BA22 . . . . **173** E2
Midsomer Norton BA3. . . . . **96** F8
Millfield Cl TA20 . . . . **223** D3
Millfield Ind Est TA20. . . . . **223** E3
Millfield Prep Sch BA6 . . . **139** D1
Millfield Sch BA16 . . . . **207** E5
Millford La BA4 . . . . **159** C6
Mill Gdns TA24 . . . . **201** B4
Millgreen Cl TA9 . . . . **136** B8
Millground Rd BS13 . . . . **21** F5
Millham La TA22 . . . . **163** D6
Mill Hill BA2 . . . . **62** E1
Mill Ho BS1 . . . . **227** A2
Mill House Ct BA11 . . . . . . **119** F5
Millier Rd BS49 . . . . **35** B8
Milliman Cl BS13 . . . . **22** C5
Milliner Ct BA4 . . . . **205** B5
Mill La
Alhampton BA4 . . . . **159** C5
Axminster EX13 . . . . **198** F3
Batcombe BA4 . . . . **142** C1
Bathampton BA2 . . . . **28** F2
3 Bath BA1 . . . . **44** B6
Beckington BA11 . . . . **101** D5
Bishops Lydeard TA4 . . . . **167** F8
Bitton BS30 . . . . **25** E8
Bourton SP8 . . . . **161** F1
Bradford Abbas DT9 . . . . **187** E1
Bruton BA10 . . . . **215** E6
Butcombe BS40 . . . . **55** A8
Cannington TA5 . . . . **135** B2
Chard TA20. . . . . **223** C3
Chard, Wambrook TA20 . . **193** C2
Charlton Mackrell TA11 . . **173** E7
Chew Stoke BS40 . . . . **56** D8
Clatworthy TA4 . . . . **149** E2
Compton Martin BS40 . . . . **74** A7
Congresbury BS49 . . . . **34** D4
Corfe TA3 . . . . **181** F6
Corsley Heath BA11, BA12 **144** C8
Creech St Michael TA3 . . . **169** D4
Crewkerne, Misterton
  TA18 . . . . **196** B3
Crewkerne TA18 . . . . **224** D5
Dinnington TA17. . . . . **195** B8
Dowlish Wake TA19 . . . . . **194** E7
Dunster TA24 . . . . **201** D1
East Coker BA22 . . . . **197** C7
East Coker, Holywell BA22 **197** B8
East Huntspill TA9 . . . . . . **136** D8
Exford TA24 . . . . **128** C2
Halstock BA22 . . . . **197** C3
Higher Chillington TA19 . . **194** E5
Ilchester BA22 . . . . **173** F1
Ilminster TA19 . . . . **221** B7
Kingstone TA19 . . . . **221** F1
Lopen TA13 . . . . **185** A1
Lynford-on-F TA11 . . . . . . **158** C2
Maiden Bradley BA12 . . . . **144** B3
Marnhull DT10 . . . . **190** F6
Milverton TA4 . . . . **167** A5
Monkton Combe BA2 . . . . . **63** E8
Nether Stowey TA5 . . . . . . **134** A2
North Wootton BA4 . . . . . **140** D5
Othery TA7 . . . . **155** C2
Pitcombe BA10 . . . . **215** C3
Porlock TA24 . . . . **124** A3
Portbury BS20 . . . . **3** E4
Priston BA2 . . . . **61** A7
Shapwick TA7 . . . . **155** F8
Shepton Mallet BA4 . . . . . **204** E4
Somerton TA11 . . . . **211** D2
South Petherton TA13 . . . . **220** E6
Stoke St Michael BA4 . . . . **116** B3
Stone Allerton BS26 . . . . . . **88** D4
Taunton TA3 . . . . **168** D1
Thurloxton TA2 . . . . **153** D1
Timsbury BA2 . . . . **60** B1
Trent DT9. . . . . **187** F5
Watchet TA23. . . . . **202** C7
Wedmore BS28 . . . . **108** E3
Wells BA5 . . . . **203** A1
West Monkton TA2. . . . . . **169** D8
Wiveliscombe TA4 . . . . . . **210** C4
Wrington BS40 . . . . **53** F8
Yeovil BA20 . . . . **219** B4
Mill Lane Cl TA3 . . . . **168** D1
Mill La Trad Est BA20. . . . **219** C4
Mill Leat TA5 . . . . **157** F5
Mill Leg BS49 . . . . **34** D4
Millmead Ho BS13 . . . . **22** C4
Millmead Rd BA2 . . . . **44** C5
Millmoot La TA7 . . . . **136** F3
Millpill Cl BS9 . . . . **5** D5
Mill Rd
Barton St David TA11 . . . **158** A3
Radstock BA3 . . . . **79** B2
Mill Rise
Bourton SP8 . . . . **161** F1
Staplegrove TA2 . . . . **212** B7
Mill Road Ind Est BA3. . . . . **79** B3
Mill St
Carhampton TA24 . . . . . . **131** B4
North Petherton TA6 . . . . **153** F3
Rimpton BA22 . . . . **188** A8
Watchet TA23. . . . . **202** C7
Wells BA5 . . . . **203** D4
Wincanton BA9 . . . . **216** C4
Millstream Cl TA24 . . . . . . **200** F6
Mill Stream Cl BS26. . . . . . . **70** C1
Mill Stream Gdns TA21 . . **222** B7
Mill Street Cl BA9. . . . . . . **216** C4
Millthorn Ho 2 BA16 . . . **207** C5

Millward Terr BS39 . . . . . . **77** E6
Millway
Chard TA20. . . . . **193** C2
Rodney Stoke BS27 . . . . . **110** B8
Millway Rise Ind Est
  EX13 . . . . **198** A2
Millwey Ave EX13 . . . . **198** A2
Mill Wlk TA7 . . . . **136** E3
Millwood Cl TA6 . . . . **208** E2
Milne Cl TA6. . . . . **208** F2
Milsom Pl TA4 . . . . **167** F6
Milsom St BA1 . . . . **228** B3
Milton Ave
Bath BA2 . . . . **44** F4
Weston-Super-Mare BS23. . **49** A8
Milton Brow BS22. . . . . **31** B2
Milton Cl
Nailsea BS48 . . . . **8** E3
Taunton TA1 . . . . **213** C3
Yeovil BA22 . . . . **218** C6
Milton Ct BA4 . . . . **205** B7
Milton Gn BS22 . . . . **31** C1
Milton Hill
Monkton Heathfield TA2 . . **213** E7
Weston-Super-Mare BS22. . **31** B2
Milton Ho BA21 . . . . **187** D6
Milton Jun & Inf Schs
  BS22 . . . . **31** C1
Milton La
Martock TA12. . . . . **185** E8
Wells BA5 . . . . **203** D5
Wookey Hole BA5 . . . . . . **203** B8
Milton Leaze TA10 . . . . . . **172** E2
Milton Lodge Gdn ★ BA5 **203** D7
Milton Park Rd BS22 . . . . . . **31** C1
Milton Pl TA6. . . . . **208** E4
Milton Rd
Radstock BA3 . . . . **78** C1
Taunton TA1 . . . . **213** C3
Weston-Super-Mare BS22,
  BS23 . . . . **49** B8
Milton Rise BS22 . . . . **31** C1
Miltons Cl BS13 . . . . **22** D4
Milton Terr BA5 . . . . **203** A8
Milverton BS24 . . . . **48** F2
Milverton Com Prim Sch
  TA4. . . . . **166** F4
Milverton Rd TA21 . . . . **222** B8
Milward Rd BS31 . . . . **24** E6
Minchington's Cl TA14 . . . **185** F2
Minehead First Sch
  TA24 . . . . **200** F6
Minehead Hospl TA24 . . . . **200** F7
Minehead La TA22 . . . . **164** A7
Minehead Mid Sch TA24 **201** A6
Minehead Rd
Bishops Lydeard TA4 . . . . **167** E8
Bristol BS4 . . . . **23** A8
Minehead Sta ★ TA24 . . . . **201** B7
Miners Cl BS41 . . . . **10** F2
Minerva Ct BA2 . . . . **228** C3
Minerva Gdns BA2 . . . . **44** C4
Minnows The TA20 . . . . . . **223** C3
Minster Cl TA1 . . . . **212** C1
Minster Ct TA1 . . . . **212** C1
Minster Way BA2 . . . . **45** C8
Minton Cl BS14 . . . . **23** B5
Mintons TA20 . . . . **223** B3
Mintons Orch TA20 . . . . . . **223** B3
Misbury Cl BA4 . . . . **204** F6
Misterton CE Fst Sch
  TA18 . . . . **224** F3
Mitchell's Pool TA21 . . . . . **222** E6
Mitchell's Row BA22 . . . . . **175** D6
Mitchell Gdns TA20 . . . . . . **223** B3
Mitchell La BS1. . . . . **227** B2
Mitchell St TA21 . . . . **222** C7
Mitchell Terr BA5. . . . . **112** E1
Mitchelmore Rd BA21 . . . . **219** B5
Mitford-Slade Ct BS49 . . . . **34** C7
Mitre Ct TA1 . . . . **213** B4
Mizzymead Cl 1 BS48. . . . . . **8** D1
Mizzymead Rd BS48. . . . . . . **8** E1
Mizzymead Rise BS48 . . . . . . **8** E1
Moffats Dr BA5 . . . . **113** A4
Molesworth Cl BS13. . . . . . **22** A4
Molesworth Dr BS13 . . . . . . **22** A4
Molly Cl BS39. . . . . **76** E8
Monarch Ctr TA1 . . . . **213** C4
Monday's Court La TA10. **172** E5
Money Pit La EX13 . . . . . . **193** A1
Monger Cotts BS39 . . . . **77** F4
Monger La
Midsomer Norton BA3. . . . **78** A3
Paulton BS39. . . . . **78** A4
Monington Rd BA6 . . . . . . **206** E6
Monk Barton Cl BA21 . . . . **218** C7
Monk Cross TA24 . . . . **128** D1
Monkley La BA11 . . . . **83** C1
Monks' Path TA23, TA24. . **131** E4
Monks Cl
Rooks Bridge BS26 . . . . . . **87** B5
Taunton TA1 . . . . **213** B5
Monks Dale BA21 . . . . **218** D6
Monksdale Rd BA2. . . . . **44** D4
Monks Dr TA7 . . . . **137** F1
Monks Ford BS5 . . . . **139** D8
Monksford La BA5 . . . . **139** C8
Monks Hill BS22 . . . . **31** B3
Monkstone Dr TA6 . . . . **84** F5
Monkstone Gdns 6
  EX13 . . . . **198** A1
Monksway TA23 . . . . **131** E4
Monks Way TA8 . . . . **104** B6
Monkton Ave BS24. . . . . . . **49** A2

Monkton Combe Jun Sch
  BA2. . . . . **45** C1
Monkton Combe Jun Sch
  (Pre-Prep) BA2. . . . . **45** C1
Monkton Combe Sch BA2 **45** E1
Monkton La TA5 . . . . **134** D5
Monmouth Cl
Chard TA20. . . . . **223** E4
Glastonbury BA6 . . . . **206** D5
Portishead BS20 . . . . **1** F4
Westonzoyland TA7 . . . . . **154** F6
Monmouth Ct
Bath BA1 . . . . **228** A2
Chard TA20. . . . . **223** E4
Pill BS20 . . . . **4** C5
Monmouth Dr BA11. . . . . . **120** B6
Monmouth Farm Cl TA6. **135** F5
Monmouth Paddock BA2. . **81** E5
Monmouth Pl BA1 . . . . **228** B2
Monmouth Rd
Keynsham BS31 . . . . **24** D5
Pill BS20 . . . . **4** C5
Shepton Mallet BA4 . . . . . **205** A5
Taunton TA1 . . . . **213** B5
Westonzoyland TA7 . . . . . **154** F6
Yeovil BA21 . . . . **219** D7
Monmouth St
Bath BA1 . . . . **228** B2
Bridgwater TA6 . . . . **209** A5
Montacute Cir 4 BA22 . . . **49** F8
Montacute Ho ★ TA15. . . **186** B4
Montacute Rd
Montacute TA14, TA15 . . **186** B4
Tintinhull BA22 . . . . **186** B6
Montague Ct 4 BS2 . . . . . **227** A4
Montague Flats 6 BS2 . . **227** A4
Montague Gdns BA7 . . . . . **214** B5
Montague Hill BS2. . . . . . . **227** A4
Montague Hill S 5 BS2 . . **227** A4
Montague Ho 8 BA1. . . . . . **28** C1
Montague Pl BS6 . . . . **227** A4
Montague Rd
Saltford BS31 . . . . **25** D2
Shoscombe BA2. . . . . **79** C5
Montague St BS1 . . . . **227** A4
Montague Way TA20 . . . . **223** C3
Monteclefe CE Jun Sch
  TA11 . . . . **211** E3
Montepelier BS23. . . . . **48** F8
Montgomery Ct BA11 . . . . **120** A4
Montpelier BS23 . . . . **30** F1
Montrose Cotts BA1. . . . . . . **27** C1
Montrose Rd BA21 . . . . **219** E7
Montrose Villas BS27 . . . . . **90** C7
Montsurs Cl BA3. . . . . **96** D3
Montys La TA7 . . . . **168** A6
Monument Cl TA21. . . . . . . **222** E4
Monument Rd TA21 . . . . . **222** E3
Moolham La
Ilminster TA19 . . . . **194** D7
Kingstone TA19 . . . . **221** D1
Moondown La TA3 . . . . . . **220** B2
Moonhayes Cross EX14. . **191** F4
Moon La TA7 . . . . **153** C1
Moonraker Cl 8 TA6. . . . . **209** B4
Moons Hill BA3 . . . . **116** B4
Moonshill Cl BA3 . . . . **116** A3
Moonshill Rd BA3. . . . . **116** A3
Moon St BS2 . . . . **227** A4
Moor Cl
Compton Dundon TA11. . . **156** F2
Langport TA10 . . . . **172** A6
Wincanton BA9 . . . . **216** C3
Moorclose Dro TA7 . . . . . . **137** C3
Moorclose La BA4 . . . . **158** E6
Moor Croft Rd BS24. . . . . . **49** E3
Moor Dro TA7 . . . . **155** F6
Moore's La TA5, TA6. . . . . **208** C7
Moorend Gdns BS11 . . . . **4** F2
Moor End Spout BS48. . . . . . **8** D2
Moores Yd BA14 . . . . **83** C6
Moorfield Gdn TA24. . . . . **146** C6
Moorfield Rd BS48. . . . . **19** A6
Moorfields Cl BA2 . . . . **44** D3
Moorfields Ct BS48 . . . . **8** D2
Moorfields Ho BA2 . . . . **44** D4
Moorfields Rd
Bath BA2 . . . . **44** D4
Nailsea BS48 . . . . **8** D2
Moor Gn BS26 . . . . **70** C1
Moor Gr BS11. . . . . **5** A8
Moorgrove Ho BS9. . . . . **5** C7
Moorham Rd BS25 . . . . **52** A1
Moorhouse La TA4. . . . . . . **165** A8
Moor House La TA5 . . . . . **133** E4
Moorings The
Bath BA2 . . . . **45** B6
Pill BS20 . . . . **4** C4
Moor La
Alhampton BA4 . . . . **159** C5
Backwell BS48 . . . . **18** F6
Batcombe BA4 . . . . **142** D1
Brushford TA22 . . . . **163** F4
Churchinford TA3. . . . . . . **192** A2
Clapton in G BS20 . . . . **2** E1
Clevedon BS21. . . . . **6** E2
Clevedon BS21. . . . . **7** A2
Cucklington SP8. . . . . **177** E5
Draycott BS27 . . . . **90** F1
East Coker BA22 . . . . **197** D7
Hardington Mandeville
  BA22. . . . . **197** A2
Higher Chillington TA20. . **194** F5
Hutton BS24 . . . . **49** D3
North Curry TA3. . . . . **170** B4

Moor La continued
South Petherton TA13 . . . **220** B3
Tickenham BS21 . . . . **7** F4
Walton in G BS21 . . . . **7** C6
Westbury-sub-Mendip BA5 **110** C5
Weston-Super-Mare BS24. . **49** F7
Wincanton BA9 . . . . **216** C2
Moorland Cl TA1. . . . . **213** C5
Moorland Cotts BS26. . . . . . **69** F2
Moorland Pk BS24 . . . . **33** E5
Moorland Pl TA1. . . . . **213** C5
Moorland Rd
Bath BA2 . . . . **44** D5
Bridgwater TA6 . . . . **209** D4
Street BA16 . . . . **207** B7
Taunton TA1 . . . . **213** C5
Weston-Super-Mare BS23. . **48** A4
Moorlands TA4 . . . . **167** F8
Moorlands Cl
16 Martock TA12 . . . . **185** E6
Nailsea BS48 . . . . **8** D2
Moorlands Ct TA16. . . . . . . **195** F7
Moorlands Inf Sch BA2. . . . **44** D4
Moorlands Jun Sch BA2. . . **44** D3
Moorlands Pk 18 TA12 . . . **185** E6
Moorlands Pk Sh Ctr 19
  TA12. . . . . **185** E6
Moorlands Rd TA16 . . . . . . **195** E6
Moorland St BS26. . . . . **70** C1
Moorlands The BA2 . . . . **44** D3
Moorland Way TA6. . . . . . . **209** D5
Moor Lane Cl TA3. . . . . **170** B4
Moorlay Cres BS40. . . . . **37** F8
Moorledge La BS39, BS40 . . **57** C7
Moorledge Rd BS40. . . . . . . **39** B1
Moorlinch Right Dro
  TA7 . . . . **155** D6
Moorlinch Vineyard ★
  TA7 . . . . **155** E7
Moor Park Rd TA10 . . . . . . **171** F5
Moor Pk
Clevedon BS21. . . . . **6** E2
Langport TA10 . . . . **171** F5
Moor Rd
Banwell BS29. . . . . **51** B5
Middlezoy TA7 . . . . **155** B4
Minehead TA24 . . . . **200** E8
Moorlinch TA7 . . . . **155** D7
Sutton Mallet TA7 . . . . . . **155** B8
Yatton BS49. . . . . **17** B2
Moorsfield BS39 . . . . **58** F3
Moor Sherd BS28 . . . . **110** C3
Moorside BS49 . . . . **17** B1
Moorside Ct BS21. . . . . **6** E2
Moorside Villas BS21. . . . . . . **6** E2
Moortown La TA10 . . . . . . **171** B2
Moorview Cl BA6 . . . . **138** C4
Moor Villas TA13 . . . . **220** B3
Moorway La DT9. . . . . **188** C6
Moots La TA6. . . . . **209** D4
Morangis Way TA20 . . . . . **223** B6
Moravia Cl TA6. . . . . **208** E6
Morden Wlk BS14. . . . . **23** D7
Moreton Cl BS14. . . . . **23** A4
Moreton La BS40 . . . . **56** E2
Moreton Mans 5 BS23. . . . . **30** C1
Morford St BA1 . . . . **228** B4
Morgan's La
East Harptree BS40. . . . . . . **74** F2
8 Frome BA11. . . . . **119** E5
Morgan Cl
Saltford BS31 . . . . **25** D2
Weston-Super-Mare BS22. . **50** B8
Morgan Pl BS48. . . . . **20** B8
Morgans Bldgs BS20. . . . . . . **8** F3
Morgans Hill Cl BS48. . . . . . **18** D8
Morgans Rise TA1 . . . . **212** A3
Morgan Way BA2 . . . . **79** E7
Morland Rd TA9 . . . . **104** D4
Morlands Ind Pk TA9. . . . **104** D4
Morley Terr
Bath BA2 . . . . **44** D6
Radstock BA3 . . . . **79** A3
Mornington Pk TA21 . . . . **222** E5
Morpeth Rd BS4 . . . . **22** D8
Morrell's Cross EX16. . . . . **164** A4
Morrell's La EX16 . . . . **178** B6
Morris Cl
Barrington TA19 . . . . **184** C5
Bathford BA1. . . . . **29** B3
Morris La BA1 . . . . **29** B3
Morston Ct BS22 . . . . **49** C7
Mortimer Cl
Bath BA1 . . . . **27** B2
Woolavington TA7 . . . . . . **136** E4
Mortimer Rd BS8 . . . . **226** A3
Morton's La TA10 . . . . **156** C1
Moseley Gr BS23. . . . . **48** E2
Moss Cl TA6 . . . . **209** C6
Moss La TA3 . . . . **169** C3
Mosterton Down La DT8. **196** A1
Moulton Cl BA4. . . . . **205** A4
Mound The BA6. . . . . **206** C4
Mounsdon Cl BA6. . . . . **157** E4
Mountain's La BA2 . . . . **59** E6
Mountain Ash BA1. . . . . **27** D1
Mountain Wood BA1 . . . . . **29** C2
Mountbatten Cl
Burnham-on-S TA8. . . . . . . **85** A1
Weston-Super-Mare BS22. . **31** E4
Mountbatten Ho TA6. . . . **209** C5
Mount Beacon BA1. . . . . . . **28** A1
Mount Beacon Pl 3 BA1. . **27** F1
Mount Beacon Row 1
  BA1 . . . . **28** A1
Mounter's Hill EX13,
  TA20 . . . . **193** B2
Mounters Cl DT10. . . . . . . **190** F5

Mountery Cl BA5. . . . . **203** D5
Mountery Rd BA5 . . . . **203** D5
Mountfields Ave TA1. . . . . **213** B1
Mountfields Pk TA1. . . . . . **213** B1
Mountfields Rd TA1. . . . . . **213** B1
Mount Gr BA2 . . . . **44** B3
Mount Hey TA1 . . . . **211** E3
Mount Hindrance Cl
  TA20 . . . . **223** D6
Mount Hindrance La
  TA20 . . . . **223** D6
Mount Ho TA1 . . . . **212** F3
Mount La
Charlton Horethorne
  DT9 . . . . **176** A1
Golsoncott TA23, TA24. . . **131** C1
Mount Nebo TA1 . . . . **212** E2
Mount Pleasant
Bath BA2 . . . . **45** D1
Castle Cary BA7. . . . . **214** C5
Crewkerne TA18 . . . . **224** D6
Frome BA11. . . . . **119** F2
Kilmington BA12 . . . . **161** F6
Pill BS20 . . . . **4** D4
Pilton BA4 . . . . **140** F3
Radstock BA3 . . . . **79** B2
Yeovil BA21 . . . . **219** C5
Mount Pleasant Ave BA5 **203** D5
Mount Rd
Bath BA1 . . . . **228** B4
Bath, Southdown BA2 . . . . **44** B3
Nether Stowey TA5 . . . . . **134** A2
Mountsfield BA11. . . . . **120** A2
Mount St
Bishops Lydeard TA4 . . . . **167** E8
Bridgwater TA6 . . . . **208** F5
Taunton TA1 . . . . **212** F3
Mount Terr TA1. . . . . **213** A3
Mount The
Frome BA11. . . . . **119** F2
Taunton TA1 . . . . **212** F3
Yatton BS49. . . . . **34** C5
Mount View
Bath, Beacon Hill BA1 . . . . **28** A1
Bath, Southdown BA2 . . . . **44** B3
Woolavington TA7 . . . . . . **136** E4
Mount View Terr TA6 . . . . **135** F6
Mountway TA1. . . . . **213** A3
Mountway Cl TA1 . . . . **212** C4
Mountway La TA1 . . . . **212** C4
Mountway Rd TA1 . . . . **212** C4
Movey La BA22 . . . . **173** C1
Mow Barton
Bristol BS13 . . . . **21** F6
8 Martock TA12 . . . . **185** E6
Mow Barton Rd TA11. . . . **173** D5
Mowbray Rd BS14. . . . . **23** C7
Mowcroft Rd BS13 . . . . **22** D4
Mowes La DT10. . . . . **190** F4
Mowground La TA7. . . . . . **137** A3
Mowleaze 11 BA22 . . . . . . **197** F8
Mowries Ct TA11. . . . . **211** D4
Moxham Dr BS13 . . . . **22** C4
Mucheleney Abbey ★
  TA10 . . . . **172** A3
Muchelney Hill BA6 . . . . . **158** B5
Muchelney Ho TA19. . . . . . **221** B3
Muchelney Way BA21 . . . . **218** C7
Muckleditch La TA19 . . . . **184** D3
Muddicombe Cross
  TA24 . . . . **128** B2
Muddicombe La TA4 . . . . . **151** A3
Muddy La BS22 . . . . **32** A8
Mudford Hill BA21 . . . . . . **187** C5
Mudford Rd BA21 . . . . **219** B8
Mudgley Cross Roads
  BS28 . . . . **108** C5
Mudgley Hill BS28 . . . . . . **108** E1
Mudgley Rd
Rooks Bridge BS26 . . . . . . **87** A4
Wedmore BS28 . . . . **108** E3
Mud La BS49 . . . . **17** D2
Mulberry Ave BS20. . . . . **2** E5
Mulberry Cl
Backwell BS48. . . . . **19** A6
Portishead BS20 . . . . **2** E5
Taunton TA1 . . . . **213** C2
Weston-Super-Mare BS22. . **32** A1
Mulberry Ct BA11. . . . . **120** B7
Mulberry Farm BA6 . . . . . **140** B1
Mulberry Gdns
4 Crewkerne TA18. . . . . . **224** C5
Sherborne DT9 . . . . **225** C5
Mulberry La
Bleadon BS24 . . . . **67** C6
Stoke Sub Hamdon TA14 . **186** A4
Mulberry Rd BS49. . . . . **34** E3
Mulberry Tree Cl TA6. . . . **209** D5
Mulberry Wlk BS9 . . . . **5** C8
Mullins Cl BA5. . . . . **203** B3
Mullins Way BA7 . . . . **214** B6
Mundays Mead BA9. . . . . . **216** C3
Munden's La DT9 . . . . **189** A1
Murford Ave BS13 . . . . **22** B4
Murford Wlk BS13 . . . . **22** B4
Murhill BA3 . . . . **64** C6
Muriel Terr BA5. . . . . **203** D3
Murray-Smith Dr BA22. . . **218** A6
Murray Way BA22 . . . . **216** B3
Murtry Hill La BA11 . . . . . **100** C2
Musbury Cl DT10. . . . . **190** F6
Musbury La DT10. . . . . **190** F6
Museum of South Somerset ★
  BA20 . . . . **219** B4
Musgraves TA2 . . . . **163** E6
Musgrove Rd TA1 . . . . **212** C3
Musmoor La BA22 . . . . **174** F2

Mus of Bath at Work★
  BA1................228 B4
Mus of Costume★ BA1..228 B3
Mus of East Asian Art★
  BA1................228 B3
Mutton La BS28........108 D4
Mutton St DT6.........199 D1
Mux's La TA4..........151 B3
Myrtleberry Mead BS22.. 32 A5
Myrtle Cl TA6.........209 D5
Myrtle Dr
  Bristol BS11..........4 E5
  Burnham-on-S TA8.....104 A7
Myrtle Gdns BS49....... 34 C8
Myrtle Hill BS20........4 C5
Myrtle La TA21........179 E7
Myrtle Rd
  Bristol BS2..........226 C4
  22 Martock TA12.....185 E6
Myrtles The BS24....... 49 D2
Myrtle Tree Cres BS22.. 31 A6
Myrtlle Cotts TA3.....182 D7

N

Nag's La TA18.........195 B1
Nailsea & Backwell Sta
  BS48................18 F7
Nailsea Cl BS13....... 22 A7
Nailsea Com Sch BS48....8 E1
Nailsea Moor La BS48... 17 F7
Nailsea Park Cl BS48....8 F2
Nailsea Pk BS48........8 F2
Nailsea Wall BS48..... 17 C8
Nailsea Wall La BS48... 17 E7
Naish's Cross BA3...... 96 D3
Naish's St BA11.......119 E5
Naishes Ave BA11...... 79 D7
Naish Farm BA3........ 96 D3
Naish Hill BS20........2 F1
Naish Ho BA2.......... 44 A6
Naish La BS48......... 20 D3
Naisholt Rd BA4.......204 F6
Naish Rd TA8.......... 85 A3
Nanga-gat Rd BA22.....174 A2
Nanny Hurn's La BS39... 58 A1
Napier Ct
  Bristol BS1..........226 B1
  Sherborne DT9........225 B2
Napier Miles Rd BS11....5 A8
Napier Rd BA1......... 27 A3
Naples View TA6.......208 E7
Narfords La TA20......193 C1
Narrow Plain BS2......227 B2
Narrow Quay BS1.......227 A2
Nash Barton BA22......197 C8
Nash Cl BS31.......... 25 A5
Nash Gn TA2...........212 B7
Nash La
  Dinnington TA17, TA19..195 A6
  East Coker BA22......197 C8
  Marshwood DT6........199 B2
  Yeovil BA20..........218 D2
Nates La BS40......... 35 F1
Nathan Cl BA20........218 D2
Naunton Way BS22...... 31 B2
Neale's Way BA4.......141 E2
Neathem Rd BA21.......219 C7
Neat La BA4...........204 D1
Nedge Cnr BA3......... 94 D4
Nedge Hill BA3........ 94 D3
Nedge La BA3.......... 94 C4
Needhams Patch TA4....167 E6
Nelson Bldgs BA1......228 C4
Nelson Ct
  Bridgwater TA6.......208 F5
  Weston-Super-Mare BS22.. 31 E4
Nelson Ho
  Bath BA1.............228 A3
  5 Bristol BS1........227 A4
Nelson Pl BA1.........228 C4
Nelson Pl E BA1.......228 C4
Nelson Pl W BA1.......228 A2
Nelson St BS1.........227 A4
Nelson Terr BA1.......228 C4
Nelson Villas BA1.....228 A2
Nempnett St BS40...... 55 D5
Neroche Prim Sch TA19.183 C2
Neroche View TA3......183 A4
Nerrols Dr TA2........213 C7
Neston Wlk BS4........ 22 F8
Netherclay TA1........212 A4
Netherclay La TA3.....182 E7
Nethercoombe La DT9...225 C5
Nethercott La TA4.....151 C3
Nethercott Way TA4....151 A3
Netherhay La DT8......199 F8
Nethermoor Rd TA7.....155 B3
Netherstoke La BA22...197 C3
Nether Stowey CE Prim Sch
  TA5................134 A2
Netherton Cross BA22..197 E6
Netherton La
  East Coker BA22......197 F6
  Marston Magna BA22...175 A1
Netherton Rd BA22.....219 D7
Netherton Wood La BS48. 18 A6
Netherways BS21........6 B1
Netley BA21...........218 D4
Nettlebridge Hill BA3.115 D5
Nettlecombe Hill
  Castle Cary BA7......214 F6
  Pitcombe BA7.........214 F6
Nettlecombe Ho BA5....113 A1
Nettlecombe Park Rd
  Monksilver TA4.......132 A1
  Sticklepath TA4......149 F7

Nettle Combe View BA5..113 A2
Neva Rd BS3........... 48 E6
Neville Cl 1 TA11.....173 F7
Neville Pk BA6........158 A5
Nevys La TA4..........150 E8
Newark St BA1.........228 C1
Newbarn Park Rd TA1...212 B1
Newberrys Patch TA3...192 A7
Newbery Cl 4 EX13.....198 A1
Newbery La BA22.......224 F3
New Bglws TA20........223 C3
New Bldgs
  3 Bampton EX16.......164 C1
  Dunwear TA7..........209 D1
  Frome BA11...........119 F3
  Ilminster TA19.......221 B1
  North Perrott TA18...196 C4
  Oake TA4.............135 C1
  Peasedown St John BA2.. 79 B8
New Bond St BA1.......228 C2
New Bond Street Pl BA1.228 C2
Newbourne Rd BS22..... 49 C8
Newbridge Ct BA1...... 44 B7
Newbridge Dro TA9.....105 A1
Newbridge Gdns BA1.... 44 A8
Newbridge Hill BA1.... 44 B7
Newbridge Ho BS9......5 C4
Newbridge La TA9......104 F1
New Bridge Prim Sch
  BA1................. 44 B7
Newbridge Rd BA1, BA2.. 44 B7
New Bristol Rd BS22... 31 E1
New Buildings La BA11.119 F3
Newbury BA12..........144 E4
Newbury Cotts BA1..... 28 A2
Newbury Terr 3 BA21..218 F7
Newchester Cross TA16.195 F7
New Church Rd BS23.... 48 D2
New Cl
  Bourton SP8.........161 E2
  Haselbury Plucknett TA18.196 B5
  Horrington BA5.......113 A4
  Street BA16..........207 B4
Newclose La BS40...... 56 D1
Newclose Terr TA14....185 E7
Newcombe Cvn Pk TA8...104 B8
Newcombe Dr BS9.......5 C4
Newcombe La BS25...... 70 B7
Newcombe Rd BS9.......5 F7
Newcot Cross EX15.....191 A5
New Cotts
  Milton Clevedon BA4..160 A8
  West Chinnock TA18...196 B8
New Cross TA11........211 C3
New Cross Hill
  Barrington TA12, TA13.184 F6
  Kingsbury Episcopi TA12.185 A6
New Cut BA5...........203 D7
New Cut Bow BS21...... 16 A6
Newditch La BS40...... 20 C1
Newell DT9............225 C4
Newfield TA4..........166 F4
Newfields BS40........ 72 C8
New Fosseway Rd BS14... 23 B6
New Fosseway Sch BS14. 23 B6
Newfoundland Rd BS2...227 C4
Newfoundland St BS2...227 C4
Newfoundland Way
  Bristol BS2..........227 C4
  Portishead BS20.......2 E6
New Friary Cotts BA11.143 C3
Newgate BS1...........227 B3
Newgate Cross TA22....163 D7
Newgate La TA4........210 C5
Newhaven Pl TA20......1 E4
Newhaven Rd BS20......1 D4
New Hill TA11.........211 E4
Newhouse La TA4.......165 E6
Newington Cl BA11.....119 E3
Newington Terr BA11...119 E4
New Kingsley Rd BS2...227 C2
New King St BA1.......228 B2
New La
  Bampton EX16.........163 F2
  Charlton Horethorne DT9.176 A1
  Creech St Michael TA3.169 D5
  Cricket St Thomas TA20.194 E4
  Haselbury Plucknett TA18.196 C6
  Tatworth TA20........198 C8
  Witham Friary BA11...143 C4
Newland DT9...........225 E4
Newland Cross TA24....128 B1
Newland Dr BS13....... 22 A4
Newland Flats 5 DT9...225 E4
Newland Gdn 6 DT9.....225 E4
Newland Ho BA1........ 27 F1
Newland Rd
  Bristol BS13......... 22 A3
  Weston-Super-Mare BS23.. 48 F6
Newlands Cl BS20...... 2 C5
Newlands Cres TA3.....169 C3
Newlands Gn BS21......6 E1
Newlands Gr TA3.......169 C3
Newlands Hill BS20.... 2 C4
Newlands Rd
  Keynsham BS31........ 24 D4
  Ruishton TA3.........169 C3
Newland Wlk BS13...... 22 A3
Newlyn Ave BS9........5 D5
Newlyn Cres TA7.......136 B4
Newman Cl BA6.........206 E6
Newmans La
  East Huntspill TA9...105 C1
  Timsbury BA2......... 60 B2
Newmarket Ave 9 BS1...227 A3
New Mdws TA3..........169 C3
Newnham Cl BS14...... 23 D7
New Oak Prim Sch BS14. 23 B7

New Orchard St BA1....228 C2
New Park Ho BS21......6 D5
New Pit Cotts BA2..... 60 F1
New Pk EX16...........162 E4
Newport Cl
  Clevedon BS21........6 C2
  Portishead BS20......1 F4
Newport Hill TA3......170 B2
Newport Rd BS20.......4 C5
Newquay Rd BS4........ 22 F8
New Rd
  Banwell BS29......... 50 E4
  Barwick BA22.........197 F8
  Bathford BA1......... 29 D2
  Bawdrip TA7..........136 D2
  Bridgwater TA6.......209 A5
  Burrowbridge TA3, TA7.170 E8
  Cannington TA5.......135 C1
  Carhampton TA24......131 A5
  Chapel Allerton BS26.. 88 C2
  Chard Junction TA20..198 F8
  Churchill BS25....... 52 F4
  Clevedon BS21........6 C2
  Combe St Nicholas TA20.193 D6
  Crewkerne TA18.......195 B4
  Crickham BS28........108 D8
  Draycott BS27........ 91 C3
  East Huntspill TA9...136 D8
  Freshford BA3........ 64 B5
  Frome BA11...........120 B4
  Hambridge TA12.......184 E7
  Haselbury Plucknett TA18.196 C6
  High Littleton BS39.. 59 C3
  Hinton St George TA17.195 C7
  Ilminster TA19.......221 B4
  Kilmersdon BA3....... 98 E4
  Kilmington BA12......161 E7
  Lyng TA3.............170 B6
  North Wootton BA4....140 A4
  Norton Sub Hamdon,
    Chiselborough TA14..185 F1
  Norton Sub Hamdon TA14.185 E3
  Oare EX35............122 D4
  Odcombe BA22.........186 D3
  Othery TA7...........155 C2
  Pensford BS39........ 40 D3
  Pill BS20............4 C4
  Porlock TA24.........123 E3
  Rawridge EX14........191 E1
  Redhill BS40......... 37 A4
  Seavington St Mary TA19.184 E1
  Sherborne DT9........225 E3
  Shipham BS25......... 52 E1
  South Cadbury BA22...175 E4
  Stalbridge DT10......190 B4
  Staple Fitzpaine TA3.182 D5
  Taunton TA3..........168 D1
  West Bagborough TA4..151 E4
  Weston Town BA4......142 D5
  Wiveliscombe TA4.....166 A6
  Yeovil BA22..........218 A5
New Road Gate EX35....122 D5
New Rock Ind Est BA3.. 96 D2
Newsome Ave BS20......4 C4
New Sq BA5............113 A2
New St
  Bath BA1.............228 B2
  Bristol BS2..........227 C3
  Long Sutton TA10.....172 E4
  Marnhull DT10........190 F5
  Mells BA11...........118 B7
  North Perrott TA18...196 C4
  Somerton TA11........211 E4
  Wells BA5............203 D5
New Street Flats 4 BS2.227 C3
New Thomas St BS2.....227 C2
Newton's Rd
  Weston-Super-Mare BS22.. 31 E3
  Weston-Super-Mare BS22.. 31 E3
Newton Cl
  Burnham-on-S TA8..... 85 A2
  West Harptree BS40... 74 E6
Newton Ct 14 EX16.....164 B1
Newton Gn BS48........ 18 C8
Newton La
  Bicknoller TA4.......132 E1
  Corfe TA3............181 F6
Newton Rd
  Barwick BA22.........197 F8
  Bath BA2............. 43 F6
  North Petherton TA6..153 F3
  Taunton TA1..........213 E4
  Weston-Super-Mare BS23.. 48 E6
  Yeovil BA20..........219 D3
Newton Sq 8 EX16......164 B1
Newtown TA12..........185 E7
Newtown La BA6........140 A1
Newtown Pk TA10.......172 A6
Newtown Rd
  Highbridge TA9.......104 D3
  Langport TA10........172 A6
New Way TA10..........172 B7
Nibley Rd BS11........4 E5
Nichol's Rd BS20......1 F4
Nicholas Cl TA22......163 E4
Nicholls Cl TA6.......208 D4
Nichol Pl TA4.........167 F6
Nick Reed's La EX15...180 D1
Nidon La TA7..........137 D3
Nigel Pk BS11.........4 E7
Nightingale Acre TA3..183 A7
Nightingale Ave BA11..120 B6
Nightingale Cl
  1 Bridgwater TA6.....209 C4
  Burnham-on-S TA8..... 85 B1
  Wells BA5............203 B3
  Weston-Super-Mare BS22.. 31 E1

Nightingale Ct
  16 Taunton TA1.......213 A4
  Weston-Super-Mare BS22.. 31 E1
Nightingale Gdns BS48.. 8 D2
Nightingale Gr BA4....205 C5
Nightingale La BA22...174 F6
Nightingale Rise BS20..1 F3
Nightingales TA4......167 E6
Nightingale Way BA3... 97 B8
Nile St BA1...........228 A2
Nine Acre Dro TA7.....138 B2
Nine Acre La TA3......170 C4
Nine Barrows La BA5... 92 E4
Nippors Way BS25...... 69 F8
Nithsdale Rd BS23..... 48 E4
Nixon Trad Units BS24.. 49 A3
No 1 Royal Cres Mus★
  BA1................228 B3
Noah's Hill TA2.......169 B7
Noake Rd DT9..........225 B3
Noble St TA1..........213 B4
Noel Coward Cl TA8....104 C6
Nomis Pk BS49........ 34 E2
No Place La TA5.......152 E5
Norbins Rd BA6........206 D5
Nordens Mdw TA4......210 D4
Nordrach La BS40...... 73 D5
Nore Gdns BS20........ 2 C6
Nore Park Dr BS20.....1 F5
Nore Rd BS20.......... 2 A6
Norfolk Ave BS2.......227 B4
Norfolk Bldgs BA1.....228 A2
Norfolk Cl TA6........209 C3
Norfolk Cres BA1......228 A2
Norfolk Gr BS31...... 24 C4
Norfolk Hts 10 BS2....227 B4
Norfolk Rd
  Portishead BS20......2 E4
  Weston-Super-Mare BS23.. 48 F5
Norland Rd BS8........ 11 F6
Norlet Ct BA6.........206 D5
Normandy Ave TA23..... 202 E6
Normandy Dr TA1.......213 C3
Normandy Ho BA16.....207 B6
Norman La TA7.........156 B7
Norman Rd BS31....... 25 E3
Normans The BA2....... 28 F1
Normans Way BS20......3 E7
Norrington Way TA20...223 D2
Northam Farm Cvn Pk &
  Camp Site TA8....... 65 F4
Northampton Bldgs BA1.228 B4
Northampton Ho BS48... 9 D3
Northampton St BA1....228 B4
Northanger Ct 5 BA2...228 C3
North Ave TA9.........104 C4
Northay Cross EX13....199 B3
Northay La
  Axminster EX13.......199 A3
  Combe St Nicholas TA20.193 B6
North Bank BA5........203 A8
Northbrook Dr TA7.....137 F1
Northbrook Rd
  Cannington TA5.......135 C2
  Shapwick TA7.........138 A1
  Yeovil BA21..........219 D7
North Cadbury CE Prim Sch
  BA22................175 D4
North Chew Terr BS40.. 39 B3
North Chine Dro BA5...138 D8
North Cl BS27......... 90 F3
Northcombe La TA22....163 E7
Northcote Cres BA11...120 A7
Northcote Rd BS8......5 F1
North Cres DT9........217 D3
North Croft TA4.......202 D3
North Curry CE Prim Sch
  TA3................170 B3
North Down Cl BS25.... 70 F8
North Down La BS25.... 70 F8
Northdown Rd BA3..... 78 E5
North Dro BS48........ 8 A2
North End
  Charlton Horethorne
    DT9.............176 A2
  Creech St Michael TA3.169 D5
  Midsomer Norton BA3.. 78 B2
North End Rd BS24..... 16 F3
Northern Path BS21....6 F3
Northern Way BS21.....6 F3
Northfield
  Bridgwater TA6.......208 E4
  Radstock BA3......... 79 A3
  Somerton TA11........211 C4
  Timsbury BA2......... 60 C3
  Winsley BA15......... 64 F7
Northfield Ave TA1....212 E4
Northfield Cl TA5.....134 C6
Northfield Gdns TA1...212 E5
Northfield Ho
  Bath BA1............. 27 F1
  Glastonbury BA6......206 A4
Northfield La
  Dinnington TA17......195 B8
  South Petherton TA13.220 C4
Northfield Rd
  Minehead TA24.......201 A8
  Portishead BS20......1 E3
  Taunton TA1..........212 E4
Northfields
  Bath BA1............. 27 F1
  Taunton TA1..........212 E4
Northfields Cl BA1.... 27 F1
Northfield Way TA11...211 C5
Northgate
  Bridgwater TA6.......208 F5
  Wiveliscombe TA4.....166 C5
Northgate St BA1......228 C2

North Gr
  Pill BS20.............4 C4
  Wells BA5............203 E5
North Green St 11 BS8. 11 F6
North Hill Ho BA11....120 A6
North Hill Mews BA11..119 F5
North Hill Rd TA24....200 F8
North Hills Cl BS23... 49 B2
North Hill Woodland Trail★
  TA24................125 B4
North La
  Bath BA2............. 45 D5
  Berrow TA8........... 65 F1
  Challacombe EX31, TA24.126 B4
  East Coker BA22......197 A7
  Nailsea BS48.........8 B1
  Othery TA7...........155 C2
  Stogursey TA5........134 C7
  2 Weston-Super-Mare
    BS23............... 48 E7
  Yeovil BA20..........219 B5
Northleach Wlk BS11....4 F5
North Leaze BS41..... 11 B2
Northleaze CE Prim Sch
  BS41................ 11 B2
Northleaze Ho BA16....207 C6
North Leaze La BS22... 175 C2
Northleigh Ave BS22... 31 C1
Northleigh Rd TA1.....213 B3
Northload Bridge BA6..206 C5
Northload Bridge Rdbt
  BA6................206 D5
Northload Dro BS28....109 E2
Northload La BS28.....109 D1
Northload St BA6......206 D5
Northload Terr BA6....206 D5
North Mdws TA3........ 79 E8
Northmead Ave BA3..... 77 F2
Northmead Cl BA3..... 77 F2
Northmead Dro TA3.....170 A1
Northmead Rd BA3..... 77 F2
North Mills La TA13...220 C5
Northmoor La TA3......170 C7
Northmoor Rd
  Dulverton TA22.......163 D7
  Othery TA10..........155 D1
Northover Bldgs BA6...206 B3
Northover Dr TA20.....223 B5
Northover Farmhouse
  BA6................207 D8
North Par
  Bath BA2.............228 C2
  Frome BA11...........119 F5
North Parade Bldgs 8
  BA1................228 C2
North Parade Pas 7
  BA1................228 C2
North Parade Rd BA2... 45 B6
North Perrott Rd TA18.196 C5
North Petherton Com Jun
  Sch TA6............153 F3
North Petherton Inf Sch
  TA6................153 F3
North Rd
  Banwell BS29......... 51 A3
  Bath, Bathwick BA2... 45 C6
  Bath, Combe Down BA2. 45 B2
  Charlton Horethorne DT9.176 A2
  Eastertown BS24...... 67 D2
  Leigh Woods BS8..... 11 D7
  Midsomer Norton BA3.. 78 A1
  Minehead TA24.......201 A7
  Sherborne DT9........225 E5
  Timsbury BA2......... 60 C2
  Wells BA5............203 E5
  Williton TA4.........202 D4
Northside
  Castle Cary BA7......214 C6
  Rockwell Green TA21..222 B5
North Side Rd BS48.... 36 F8
North St
  Babcary TA11.........174 C7
  Bradford Abbas DT9...187 E1
  Bridgwater TA6.......208 E4
  Bristol BS1..........227 B4
  Castle Cary BA7......214 C5
  Crewkerne TA18.......224 C7
  Drayton TA10.........171 E3
  Haselbury Plucknett TA18.196 C6
  Ilminster TA19.......221 C4
  Langport TA10........172 A5
  Martock TA12.........185 E6
  Milborne Port DT9....217 D2
  Milverton TA4........167 A4
  Nailsea BS48.........8 B1
  North Petherton TA6..153 E4
  Norton St Philip BA2. 81 F4
  Norton Sub Hamdon TA14.185 E1
  Shepton Beauchamp TA19.184 E4
  Somerton TA11........211 E4
  South Petherton TA13.220 C5
  Stoke sub Hamdon TA14.185 F4
  Taunton TA1..........212 F4
  Wellington TA21......222 D6
  Weston-Super-Mare BS23. 48 E8
  Williton TA4.........202 D3
  Wincanton BA9........216 C4
  Wiveliscombe TA4.....210 B4
North Stoke La BS30... 26 B8
North Terr BA21.......219 C6
North Town TA13.......173 D5
North Town Com Prim Sch
  TA1................212 E4
Northtown La
  North Wootton BA4....140 C4

Northtown La *continued*
  Taunton TA1 . . . . **212** E4
North Town Mews TA1 . **212** E5
Northumberland Bldgs �**1**
  BA1 . . . . **228** B2
Northumberland Pl ☐**1**
  BA1 . . . . **228** C2
North View BA3 . . . . **79** B2
North View Cl BA2 . . . . **44** B5
North View Dr BS29 . . . . . **51** A2
North Villas TA4 . . . . **167** F6
North Way
  Bath BA2 . . . . **44** A5
  Midsomer Norton BA3 . . . **78** A1
Northwick Gdns BS39 . . . . **57** D4
Northwick Rd
  Chew Magna BS39, BS41 . **39** D7
  Mark TA9 . . . . **106** B5
Northwood Cl TA2 . . . . . . **168** B4
Northwood Dro BA6 . . . . . **158** A6
Norton Cl
  Chew Magna BS40 . . . . . . **39** B3
  Shepton Mallet BA4 . . . . . **205** A5
Norton Dro TA12 . . . . **185** B8
Norton Fitzwarren CE Com
  Prim Sch TA2 . . . . **168** B5
Norton Grange BA2 . . . . . . **81** E5
Norton Hill Sch BA3 . . . . . **97** B8
Norton Ho ☐**7** BS1 . . . . . **227** B1
Norton La
  Chew Magna BS39, BS40 . **39** D5
  Wellow BA2 . . . . **81** B7
  Weston-Super-Mare BS22 . **31** C4
  Whitchurch BS14 . . . . **23** C2
Norton Radstock Coll BA3 **78** F2
Norton Rd TA14 . . . . **185** E3
Norton St Philip CE Fst Sch
  BA2 . . . . **81** E4
Norton sub Hamdon CE Prim
  Sch TA14 . . . . **185** F3
Nortons Wood La BS21 . . . **7** A5
Norville Cl BS27 . . . . **90** B8
Norville La BS27 . . . . **90** B8
Norwich Cl TA1 . . . . **212** C1
Norwich Ct TA1 . . . . **212** D2
Norwood Ave BS4 . . . . **45** E5
Norwood Farm★ BA2 . . . . **81** F7
Norwood Gr BS20 . . . . **1** F5
Notgrove Cl BS22 . . . . **31** B2
Notlake Dro BS27 . . . . **89** E4
Notting Hill Way BS26 . . . **88** D6
Nova Scotia Pl BS1 . . . . . **226** A1
Novers Cres BS4 . . . . **22** C8
Novers Hill BS4 . . . . **22** C8
Novers La BS4 . . . . **22** D7
Novers Park Dr BS4 . . . . . . **22** C8
Novers Park Rd BS4 . . . . . . **22** C8
Novers Rd BS4 . . . . **22** C8
Nowers La TA21 . . . . **222** C3
Nowhere La BS48 . . . . **9** A1
Number 15 BA21 . . . . **219** D7
Nunney Barton BA11 . . . . **119** D4
Nunney Castle★ BA11 . . . **143** B8
Nunney Catch Rbt BA11 . **143** B7
Nunney Cl
  Burnham-on-S TA8 . . . . . . **85** C1
  Keynsham BS31 . . . . **25** A2
Nunney Fst Sch BA11 . . . . **143** B8
Nunney Rd BA11 . . . . **119** D4
Nurcott La TA24 . . . . **147** C7
Nursery Cl TA5 . . . . **135** B5
Nursery Gdns TA20 . . . . . **223** E4
Nursery Rd BA20 . . . . **219** A3
Nursery Rise BA3 . . . . **96** E4
Nursery Terr TA6 . . . . **208** E5
Nursery Villas TA20 . . . . **223** E4
Nutgrove La BS40 . . . . **39** A4
Nutshole La TA20 . . . . . . **194** B2
Nut Tree Cl TA9 . . . . **136** E8
Nut Tree La TA18 . . . . . . **224** D7
Nutts La BA11 . . . . **101** F8
Nutwell Rd BS22 . . . . **31** E2
Nutwell Sq BS22 . . . . **31** E2
Nydon The TA7 . . . . **137** D3
Nye Cl BS27 . . . . **90** C7
Nye Dro BS24 . . . . **51** E8
Nye Rd BS25 . . . . **51** F5
Nyland Dro BS27 . . . . **90** B1
Nyland La BA8 . . . . **190** C8
Nyland View BS27 . . . . **90** F3
Nynehead Hollow TA7 . . . **167** C1
Nynehead Prim Sch
  TA21 . . . . **167** B1
Nynehead Rd
  Nynehead TA21 . . . . **167** C1
  Wellington TA21 . . . . **222** F8
Nythe Rd TA7 . . . . **156** A5

O

Oak's Dro BA5 . . . . **138** E8
Oak Apple Dr TA6 . . . . . . **208** D6
Oak Ave BA2 . . . . **44** C3
Oak Cl TA24 . . . . **200** D7
Oak Ct
  Bristol BS14 . . . . **23** A5
  Weston-Super-Mare BS22 . . **32** C3
Oakdale Gdns BS22 . . . . . . **31** F2
Oakdale Rd BS14 . . . . **23** A8
Oak Dr
  Crewkerne TA18 . . . . **224** C5
  Portishead BS20 . . . . **2** B4
Oake Acres TA4 . . . . **167** D4

Oake & Bradford Com Prim
  Sch TA4 . . . . **167** D4
Oake Cl TA4 . . . . **167** D4
Oake Gn TA4 . . . . **167** D4
Oak End Way TA20 . . . . . **223** C5
Oaken Ground TA21 . . . . **222** B5
Oakfield Cl
  Bath BA1 . . . . **44** D8
  Frome BA11 . . . . **119** D5
Oakfield Gr BS8 . . . . **226** B4
Oakfield Pk TA21 . . . . **222** E4
Oakfield Pl BS8 . . . . **226** B4
Oakfield Rd
  Bridgwater TA6 . . . . **208** C4
  Bristol BS8 . . . . **226** B4
  Frome BA11 . . . . **119** D4
  Keynsham BS31 . . . . **24** F2
  Street BA16 . . . . **207** B4
Oakfield Sch BA11 . . . . . . **119** D4
Oakford Ave BS23 . . . . **48** F8
Oakford La BA1 . . . . **29** A8
Oak Gr BS20 . . . . **4** C5
Oakgrove Way TA6 . . . . . **209** D6
Oakhill La BS24 . . . . **49** A2
Oakhill CE Prim Sch
  BA3 . . . . **115** B3
Oakhill Cl BS48 . . . . **9** B1
Oakhill Ct BA3 . . . . **116** E3
Oakhill Rd BA2 . . . . **44** F2
Oak Ho
  Brean TA8 . . . . **65** E2
  Bristol BS13 . . . . **22** D4
Oakhurst Rd BS23 . . . . **48** F5
Oak La
  East Anstey TA22 . . . . . . **162** E6
  Rodhuish TA24 . . . . **131** A3
  Taunton TA2 . . . . **212** F6
Oakland Ct TA12 . . . . **185** E7
Oakland Dr
  Hutton BS24 . . . . **49** E3
  Martock TA12 . . . . **185** E7
Oakland Rd TA12 . . . . **185** E7
Oaklands
  Cheddar BS27 . . . . **90** A8
  Clevedon BS21 . . . . **6** C4
  Paulton BS39 . . . . **77** E4
  Temple Cloud BS39 . . . . . . **58** E1
Oaklands Ave TA20 . . . . . **223** F4
Oaklands Rd BA21 . . . . . . **219** D7
Oakleigh BA20 . . . . **218** D2
Oakleigh Cl BS48 . . . . **19** B5
Oakley
  Bath BA2 . . . . **45** E5
  Clevedon BS21 . . . . **16** B8
Oakley Cl TA7 . . . . **154** F5
Oakley La BA22 . . . . **186** F6
Oak Lodge Cres TA24 . . . **200** F7
Oak Pk
  Nether Stowey TA5 . . . . . **134** B2
  Winscombe BS25 . . . . **70** A8
Oakridge Cl BS25 . . . . **70** B7
Oakridge La BS25 . . . . **70** C6
Oakridge Pk BA21 . . . . . . **219** A6
Oaksey Gr BS48 . . . . **9** A1
Oak St BA2 . . . . **228** B1
Oaks The
  Nailsea BS48 . . . . **9** A2
  Taunton TA1 . . . . **213** C1
  Wembdon TA6 . . . . **208** C6
  Winford BS40 . . . . **37** F7
Oak Terr BA3 . . . . **78** D1
Oak Tree Cl EX14 . . . . **191** F2
Oaktree Ct BS11 . . . . **4** E7
Oaktree Gdns BS13 . . . . . . **21** E5
Oak Tree Ho ☐**13** TA14 . . **185** F4
Oaktree Pk BS25 . . . . **49** E5
Oaktree Pl BS22 . . . . **32** C3
Oak Tree Pl TA8 . . . . **85** A3
Oak Tree Way TA5 . . . . . **135** B2
Oak Tree Wlk BS31 . . . . . . **24** D3
Oak Vale BA8 . . . . **190** A6
Oak Way BA22 . . . . **218** A7
Oatfield BS48 . . . . **19** F1
Oathill Cotts BA4 . . . . **140** E4
Oathill La
  Clapton TA18 . . . . **195** C1
  Winsham TA18 . . . . **199** E8
Oatlands Ave BS14 . . . . . . **23** A6
Oatley La TA5 . . . . **134** F2
Oborne Rd DT9 . . . . **225** F5
Obridge Cl TA2 . . . . **213** A6
Obridge Cres TA2 . . . . . . **213** A6
Obridge La TA2 . . . . **213** A6
Obridge Rd TA2 . . . . **213** A6
Obridge Viaduct TA2 . . . **213** B6
Observatory Field BS25 . . **70** B8
Observatory The BS22 . . . . **31** D3
Ocean Way BA22 . . . . **174** B3
Octagon The ☐**5** TA1 . . . **212** F4
Odcombe Hollow BA22 . . **196** E8
Odeon Bldgs BS23 . . . . **48** E7
Odins Rd BA2 . . . . **44** D1
Olands Rd TA21 . . . . **222** D6
Old Acre Rd BS14 . . . . **23** A3
Old Airfield Cvn Pk The
  TA7 . . . . **155** A4
Old Ansford Inn BA7 . . . . **214** C6
Old App BA7 . . . . **159** A3
Old Banwell Rd BS24 . . . . **50** B4
Oldbarn La
  Bampton EX16 . . . . **163** E1
  Compton Martin BS40 . . . . **56** D1
Old Barn La
  Felton BS40 . . . . **37** A5
  Hatch Beauchamp TA3 . . **182** F6
Old Barn Way BA20 . . . . **218** D3
Old Barrow Hill BS11 . . . . . **4** D7

Old Basin TA6 . . . . **209** B2
Oldberry La TA22 . . . . . . **163** D6
Old Bond St ☐**4** BA1 . . . **228** B2
Old Bowden Way DT9 . . . **217** D4
Old Bread St BS2 . . . . **227** C2
Old Brewery Ind Est The
  TA4 . . . . **210** C4
Old Brewery Rd TA4 . . . . **210** C4
Old Brewery The
  ☐**6** Frome BA11 . . . . . . **119** F4
  Rode BA11 . . . . **101** E8
Old Brewhouse The BA1 . . **27** B2
Old Bridge Cl BA22 . . . . . **206** D5
Oldbridge Rd BS14 . . . . . . **23** C3
Old Bristol Rd
  East Brent TA9 . . . . **86** E4
  Oakhill BA3, BA4 . . . . . . **114** E1
  Priddy BA5, BS40 . . . . **93** A6
  Shepton Mallet BA4 . . . . . **141** C8
  Wells BA5 . . . . **112** B5
  Weston-Super-Mare BS22 . . **32** A2
Oldbroach La TA3 . . . . . . **213** F2
Old Bull La BA4 . . . . **141** F7
Old Burnham Rd TA9 . . . . **104** D4
Old Chapel BA1 . . . . **228** C4
Old Chapel Ct TA10 . . . . . **172** A6
Old Chapel Rd TA7 . . . . . **155** B3
Old Chelsea La BS8 . . . . . . **10** C4
Old Church Rd
  Axbridge BS26 . . . . **70** C1
  Clevedon BS21 . . . . **6** E4
  Nailsea BS48 . . . . **18** D8
  Weston-Super-Mare BS23 . . **48** E8
Old Cleeve CE Sch TA23 . **131** E4
Old Coach Rd BS26 . . . . . . **69** E2
Old Combe Hill TA3 . . . . **181** F5
Old Co-op Cotts BA3 . . . **117** A7
Old Dairy Ct BS21 . . . . **6** E3
Old Dairy The BA2 . . . . . . **44** D4
Old Ditch BA5 . . . . **110** E7
Old Ditch La TA7 . . . . . . **155** C7
Old Down La BA4 . . . . **142** A6
Old Drill Hall The BS2 . . . **227** C3
Old England Way BA2 . . . . **79** E8
Old Farm DT9 . . . . **225** C4
Old Farm Cl TA24 . . . . . . **200** E6
Old Farm Ct
  Blackford BS28 . . . . **107** E4
  Queen Camel BA22 . . . . . **174** F3
Old Farm Pl TA17 . . . . . . **195** C7
Old Farm Rd
  Minehead TA24 . . . . **200** E6
  Nether Stowey TA5 . . . . . **134** B2
Old Ferry Rd BA2 . . . . **44** C6
Old Fosse Rd BA2 . . . . **44** C1
Old Frome Rd
  Bath BA2 . . . . **62** E8
  Doulting BA4 . . . . **141** E8
  Horrington BA5 . . . . **113** D3
  Oakhill BA3, BA4 . . . . . . **115** B1
Old Glove Factory The
  BA22 . . . . **186** B2
Old Gore La BA3 . . . . **95** E3
Old Green The ☐**2** DT9 . . **225** D4
Old Ham TA5 . . . . **133** D6
Old Hill
  Wincanton BA9 . . . . **216** C5
  Winford BS40 . . . . **37** D6
  Wrington BS40 . . . . **35** D4
Old Hitchen ☐**5** TA16 . . . **195** F7
Old Ho The BA3 . . . . **64** C5
Old Junction Rd BS23 . . . . **49** B5
Old King St BA1 . . . . **228** B3
Old King Street Ct BS1 . . **227** B3
Old La
  Farmborough BA2 . . . . . . **60** A6
  Nailsea BS21 . . . . **8** C4
  Porlock TA24 . . . . **124** B3
Old Main Rd TA6 . . . . . . **135** F5
Old Malt Ho BS2 . . . . **227** C4
Old Maltings The BA3 . . . **115** A3
Old Manor Est BA1 . . . . . **116** C8
Old Market ☐**6** TA12 . . . **185** E6
Old Market St BS2 . . . . . . **206** D5
Old Market Ctr TA1 . . . . . **212** F3
Old Market Mews DT10 . . **190** B4
Old Market Rd BA4 . . . . . **205** B6
Old Market Rdbt BS2 . . . . **227** C3
Old Market St BS2 . . . . . . **227** C3
Oldmead La BS26 . . . . **87** C5
Oldmead Wlk BS13 . . . . . . **21** E7
Old Midford Rd BA2 . . . . . **63** B7
Old Millard's Hill BA3 . . . . **78** B3
Old Mill Rd
  Portishead BS20 . . . . **2** D5
  Woolavington TA7 . . . . . . **136** E4
Old Mills Ind Est BS39 . . . **77** E2
Old Mills La BS39 . . . . **77** D3
Old Mill Way
  Wells BA5 . . . . **203** B2
  Weston-Super-Mare BS24 . . **50** A8
Oldmixon Cres BS24 . . . . . **49** A3

Oldmixon Prim Sch BS24 . **49** A2
Oldmixon Rd BS24 . . . . . . **49** B1
Old Mixon Rd BS24 . . . . . **49** C2
Old Newbridge Hill BA1 . . **44** D8
Old Oaks Cl TA6 . . . . **208** D5
Old Orch
  Bath BA1 . . . . **228** C3
  Chard TA20 . . . . **223** C3
Old Orchard Cl TA19 . . . . **183** F4
Old Orchards TA20 . . . . . **223** E4
Old Orchard St BA1 . . . . . **228** C2
Old Orchard The TA19 . . . **221** A5
Old Orch The TA13 . . . . . **220** C4
Old Park Hill BS2 . . . . **226** C3
Old Park Rd
  Bristol BS11 . . . . **4** D7
  Clevedon BS21 . . . . **6** E4
Old Pawlett Rd TA9 . . . . . **136** A2
Old Pit Rd BA3 . . . . **97** C8
Old Pit Terr BA3 . . . . **78** E4
Old Pk BS2 . . . . **226** C3
Old Police Station The
  BA9 . . . . **216** C4
Old Post Office Cotts
  TA7 . . . . **153** F2
Old Post Office La BS23 . . **48** D8
Old Pound Ct SP8 . . . . . . **161** E1
Old Print Works ☐**6** BA11 **119** E5
Old Priory Rd BS20 . . . . **4** B4
Old Quarry BA2 . . . . **44** D2
Old Quarry Rd BS11 . . . . . . **4** E7
Old Quarry Rise BS11 . . . . . **4** E7
Old Rd
  North Petherton TA6 . . . . **153** F4
  Odcombe BA22 . . . . **186** C2
  Pensford BS39 . . . . **40** E3
  Radstock BA3 . . . . **79** C1
  South Cadbury BA22 . . . . **175** E4
Old Rd The BA8 . . . . **189** D6
Old Rectory The TA9 . . . . . **86** C4
Oldrey La TA24 . . . . **147** C5
Old Sawmill The BA12 . . . **161** F6
Old School Cl
  Alweston DT9 . . . . **189** A1
  Ashcott TA7 . . . . **156** B8
  Churchill BS25 . . . . **52** F4
  Yeovil BA21 . . . . **218** C5
Old School Ho BA21 . . . . **219** C5
Old School Ho The
  Bath BA1 . . . . **228** B8
  Whatley BA11 . . . . **118** A3
Old School La
  Bleadon BS24 . . . . **67** C6
  Catcott TA7 . . . . **137** D2
  Lynford-on-F TA11 . . . . . **158** C2
Old School Pl
  Sherborne DT9 . . . . **225** D3
  Wells BA5 . . . . **203** E5
Old School The BA11 . . . . **119** E4
Oldshute La TA22 . . . . . . **163** C7
Old Sneed Ave BS9 . . . . **5** D4
Old Sneed Cotts BS9 . . . . . . **5** E4
Old Sneed Pk BS9 . . . . **5** D4
Old Sneed Rd BS9 . . . . **5** D4
Old St BS21 . . . . **6** E3
Old Station Cl
  Cheddar BS27 . . . . **90** A7
  Wrington BS40 . . . . **35** D1
Old Station Ct TA20 . . . . **223** D5
Old Station Gdns BA8 . . . **190** A7
Old Station La BA10 . . . . **215** C4
Old Station Rd BA20 . . . . **219** C4
Old Station Way BA20 . . . **219** C4
Old Stream Farm TA10 . . **171** E3
Old Street La BA5 . . . . . . **204** B7
Old Tannery The ☐**20** BS2 **227** C3
Old Tarnwell BS39 . . . . **40** B2
Old Taunton Rd TA6 . . . . **209** A4
Old Threshing Mill The
  BA4 . . . . **141** B2
Old Tiverton Rd EX16 . . . **164** C1
Old Tk BA2 . . . . **63** F7
Old Town TA20 . . . . **223** C3
Old Vicarage Ct BS14 . . . . **23** C4
Old Vicarage Gdns TA13 . **220** C4
Old Vicarage Gn BS31 . . . . **24** E6
Old Vicarage La TA4 . . . . **167** E6
Old Vicarage The TA21 . . **222** E6
Old Walcot Sch The BA1 . **228** B3
Old Wall BS24 . . . . **66** D5
Old Water Gdns The BS40 **54** E2
Old Way
  Chipstable TA4 . . . . **165** D6
  Stogumber TA4 . . . . **150** D8
Oldway Ho TA21 . . . . **222** F4
Oldway La TA3 . . . . **183** A8
Oldway Pk TA21 . . . . **222** F4
Oldway Pl TA9 . . . . **104** D4
Oldway Rd
  East Anstey TA22 . . . . . . **162** F5
  Wellington TA21 . . . . **222** E4
Old Wells Rd
  Bath BA2 . . . . **44** F3
  Croscombe BA5 . . . . **204** D6
  Doulting BA4 . . . . **142** A8
  Glastonbury BA6 . . . . **206** F6
  Leigh u M BA3, BA4, BA11 **117** B2
  Shepton Mallet BA4 . . . . . **205** A5
Old Weston Rd
  Congresbury BS49 . . . . **34** B5
  Flax Bourton BS48 . . . . . . **20** B8
Old Yarn Mills The DT9 . . **225** D2
Oliver's La TA19 . . . . **183** B2
Oliver Brooks Rd BA3 . . . . **96** E7

Oldmixon Prim Sch BS24 . **49** A2

Olivier Cl TA8 . . . . **104** C6
One Elm TA10 . . . . **172** B7
Onega Ctr BA1 . . . . **228** A3
Onega Terr BA1 . . . . **228** A3
Oolite Gr BA2 . . . . **44** D1
Oolite Rd BA2 . . . . **44** D1
Orange Gr BA1 . . . . **228** C2
Orange St BS2 . . . . **227** C4
Orchard Ave
  Bristol BS1 . . . . **226** C2
  Midsomer Norton BA3 . . . **77** F1
  Portishead BS21 . . . . **7** E4
Orchard Cl
  Banwell BS29 . . . . **51** B3
  Bishop Sutton BS39 . . . . . **57** C3
  Bradford On Tone TA4 . . . **167** F1
  Bristol, Westbury on T BS9 . . **5** F5
  Carhampton TA24 . . . . . . **131** B5
  Castle Cary BA7 . . . . **214** B7
  Cheddar BS27 . . . . **90** B8
  Coleford BA3 . . . . **117** A7
  Congresbury BS49 . . . . **34** D4
  Cossington TA7 . . . . **137** A3
  Coxley BA5 . . . . **139** E6
  Drimpton DT8 . . . . **199** F8
  East Brent TA9 . . . . **86** E4
  East Chinnock BA22 . . . . **196** E8
  East Huntspill TA9 . . . . . . **136** E8
  Felton BS40 . . . . **37** C8
  Flax Bourton BS48 . . . . . . **20** A8
  Frome BA11 . . . . **119** D4
  Highbridge TA9 . . . . **104** E4
  Keynsham BS31 . . . . **24** D6
  Long Sutton TA10 . . . . . . **172** E4
  ☐**3** North Petherton TA6 . **153** E3
  Odcombe BA22 . . . . **186** C2
  Portishead BS20 . . . . **2** D5
  Queen Camel BA22 . . . . . **174** F3
  Rockwell Green TA21 . . . . **222** A5
  South Petherton TA13 . . . **220** C5
  Sparkford BA22 . . . . **175** A5
  Taunton TA3 . . . . **168** D1
  Wedmore BS28 . . . . **108** C4
  West Camel BA22 . . . . . . **197** A8
  Weston-Super-Mare, Kewstoke
    BS22 . . . . **31** A3
  Weston-Super-Mare, Worle
    BS22 . . . . **31** F2
  Westwood BA15 . . . . **64** F3
  Wincanton BA9 . . . . **216** D3
  Wrington BS40 . . . . **35** E2
  Yeovil Marsh BA21 . . . . . **187** A5
Orchard Cl The BS24 . . . . . **49** F4
Orchard Cotts
  Croscombe BA5 . . . . **204** B7
  Timsbury BA2 . . . . **60** F1
Orchard Cres BS11 . . . . **4** D7
Orchard Ct
  Claverham BS49 . . . . **17** F1
  Highbridge TA9 . . . . **104** F3
  Minehead TA24 . . . . **201** B4
  Street BA16 . . . . **207** C6
  Wellington TA21 . . . . **222** E6
Orchard Dr
  Bristol BS13 . . . . **22** A6
  Sandford BS25 . . . . **52** A4
  Southwick BA14 . . . . **83** E3
  Taunton TA1 . . . . **212** A3
Orchard End BS40 . . . . **74** F4
Orchard Gdns
  Paulton BS39 . . . . **77** E6
  West Buckland TA21 . . . . **180** F7
Orchard Gn TA2 . . . . **212** F8
Orchard Ho
  Weston-Super-Mare BS22 . **31** F2
  Yeovil BA21 . . . . **219** A6
Orchard La
  Allerford TA24 . . . . **124** E8
  Bristol BS1 . . . . **226** C2
  Chewton Mendip BA3 . . . . **94** F6
  Crewkerne TA18 . . . . **224** C6
  Evercreech BA4 . . . . **141** E1
  Kingsbury Episcopi TA12 . **185** B8
  Thorncombe TA20 . . . . . . **199** B6
  Wembdon TA6 . . . . **208** D5
Orchard Lea
  Coxley BA5 . . . . **139** E7
  Pill BS20 . . . . **4** D4
  Wells BA5 . . . . **203** C5
Orchardleigh BA22 . . . . . . **196** E8
Orchardleigh View BA11 **109** D6
Orchard Lodge BA22 . . . . . **45** F8
Orchard Mead TA19 . . . . **183** C1
Orchard Paddock BA5 . . . **203** A4
Orchard Pk
  Bristol BS14 . . . . **23** D4
  West Camel BA22 . . . . . . **174** D3
Orchard Pl
  Aller TA10 . . . . **171** D4
  ☐**1** Weston-Super-Mare
    BS23 . . . . **48** E7
Orchard Rd
  Axbridge BS26 . . . . **70** C1
  Backwell BS48 . . . . **19** A6
  Carhampton TA24 . . . . . . **131** B5
  Clevedon BS21 . . . . **6** D2
  Hutton BS24 . . . . **49** E2
  Long Ashton BS41 . . . . **10** F1
  Milborne Port DT9 . . . . . **217** C2
  Minehead TA24 . . . . **200** F8
  Nailsea BS48 . . . . **8** D1
  Paulton BS39 . . . . **77** E6
  Somerton TA11 . . . . **211** B4
  Street BA16 . . . . **207** C6
Orchard Rise
  Crewkerne TA18 . . . . **224** C5
  Fivehead TA3 . . . . **170** F2
  Porlock TA24 . . . . **124** A3

Orchard Rise continued
  Ruishton TA3 . . . . .169 C4
Orchard St
  Bristol BS1. . . . . .226 C2
  Frome BA11. . . . . .119 E5
  Weston-Super-Mare BS23. . 48 E8
  Yeovil BA20 . . . . .219 A4
Orchards The
  Bristol, Shirehampton BS11 . 4 E6
  Horrington BA5. . . . . .113 A2
  Stocklinch TA19. . . . . .184 C4
Orchard Terr
  5 Bath BA2 . . . . 44 B6
  Glastonbury BA6 . . . . .206 D5
Orchard The
  Banwell BS29. . . . . 51 A3
  Bath, Combe Down BA2 . . . 45 B1
  Bath, Newbridge BA1 . . . . . 44 A7
  Corston BA2 . . . . 43 B8
  Freshford BA3. . . . . 64 C5
  Holywell Lake TA21 . . . . . .179 E7
  Locking BS24. . . . . 50 A5
  Meare BA6. . . . . .138 D4
  Pensford BS39. . . . . 40 E4
  Pill BS20 . . . . 4 C4
  Ruishton TA3 . . . . .169 C2
  Upper Stanton Drew BS39 . 40 A2
Orchard Vale
  Ilminster TA19 . . . . .221 B3
  Langport TA10. . . . . .172 A5
  Midsomer Norton BA3. . . . . 77 F1
Orchard View
  Baltonsborough BA6 . . . . . .158 B6
  Haselbury Plucknett TA18 . .196 C6
Orchard Way
  Charlton Horethorne
    DT9. . . . . .176 A2
  Cheddar BS27 . . . . 90 B8
  Keinton Mandeville TA11. . .158 A1
  Misterton TA18 . . . . .224 F3
  Peasedown St John BA2. . . 79 D7
  Shapwick TA7 . . . . .137 F1
  Taunton TA1. . . . . .213 D5
  Timberscombe TA24 . . . . . .130 B5
  Williton TA4 . . . . .202 E4
  Woolavington TA7 . . . . .136 E3
Orchard Wlk
  Churchill BS25. . . . . 52 E4
  Milborne Port DT9. . . . . . . .217 C2
Orchard Wyndham ★ TA4 132 B2
Orchid Cl TA1 . . . . .169 A1
Orchids The TA8 . . . . 85 A2
Oriel Dr BA6. . . . . .206 D4
Oriel Gdns BA1 . . . . 28 C2
Oriel Gr BA2 . . . . 44 B4
Oriel Rd BA16. . . . . .207 C5
Orme Dr BS21 . . . . 6 D5
Ormerod Rd BS9. . . . . .5 E5
Orneage Cl BA11. . . . . .101 E8
Orwell Dr BS31 . . . . 25 A4
Osborne Ave BS23 . . . . 48 F7
Osborne Gr TA1. . . . . .212 E3
Osborne Pl TA16. . . . . .195 F7
Osborne Rd
  Bath BA1 . . . . 44 B7
  Bridgwater TA6 . . . . .208 F6
  Bristol BS3. . . . . .226 C1
  Weston-Super-Mare BS23. . 48 F7
  Yeovil BA20 . . . . .219 A5
Osborne Villas BS2. . . . . . . .226 C4
Osborne Wallis Ho BS8. . . .226 A1
Osborne Way TA1. . . . . .212 E3
Osborne Wlk TA8 . . . . .104 C6
Osmond Dr BA5. . . . . .203 B3
Osmond Rd 2 BS24. . . . . 49 F7
Osprey Ct BS14. . . . . 22 D5
Osprey Gdns BS22 . . . . 31 F1
Ostlings La BA1. . . . . 29 B2
Ostrey Mead BS27 . . . . 90 B7
Otago Terr 5 BA1. . . . . 28 C2
Othery Village Prim Sch
  TA7. .155 C2
Ottawa Rd BS23. . . . . 48 F3
Otterford Cl BS14. . . . . 23 B5
Otterford Gypsy Pk TA3 .181 D2
**Otterford Lakes Nature
  Trail ★** TA3. . . . . .181 E1
Otterham La TA3. . . . . .183 F8
Otterhampton Prim Sch
  TA5. .135 B5
Otter Rd 1 BS21. . . . . .6 E1
Otter Vale Cl EX14 . . . . .191 F1
Ottery La DT9. . . . . .225 C2
**Our Lady of Mount Carmel
  RC Prim Sch** BA20 . . . . .216 C3
**Our Lady of the Rosary RC
  Prim Sch** BS11. . . . . .5 A8
Outer Circ TA1. . . . . .213 D5
Outer Gullands TA1. . . . . . .212 D2
Oval The BA2 . . . . 44 C4
Overbrook Bsns Ctr
  BS28. . . . . .107 D4
Overcombe BA8 . . . . .189 E8
Overdale
  Clandown BA3 . . . . 78 E5
  Peasedown St John BA2. . . 60 F3
Overhill BS20 . . . . 4 D4
Over Innox BA11. . . . . .119 F6
Overland La TA3. . . . . .170 C3
Overlands
  North Curry TA3. . . . . .170 C4
  Ruishton TA3 . . . . .169 C4
Overleigh
  Street BA16. . . . . .207 C3
  Street BA16. . . . . .207 C4
Overstables La BS21 . . . . 6 D3
Overton BA9. . . . . .216 D4
Owen Dr BS8. . . . . 10 B4

Owen St TA21. . . . . .222 C6
Owlaborough La EX36. . . . . .162 B2
Owl St
  South Petherton TA13 . . . . .220 B8
  Stocklinch TA19 . . . . .184 C3
Owsley Cotts TA19 . . . . .184 E4
Oxendale BA16 . . . . .207 B5
Oxen La TA3. . . . . .170 B3
Oxenpill BA6 . . . . .138 C4
Oxen Rd TA18. . . . . .224 C6
Oxford Pl
  Bath BA2 . . . . 45 C2
  19 Bristol, Clifton BS8. . . . . 11 F6
  10 Taunton TA1. . . . . .213 A4
  Weston-Super-Mare BS23. . 48 D7
Oxford Rd TA1. . . . . .219 E7
Oxford Row BA1 . . . . .228 B3
Oxford Sq BS24. . . . . 50 B6
Oxford St
  Bristol BS2. . . . . .227 C2
  Bristol, Tyndall's Park BS2 226 C4
  Burnham-on-S TA8. . . . . . . .104 B6
  Evercreech BA4. . . . . .141 E1
  Weston-Super-Mare BS23. . 48 D7
Oxford Terr 4 TA6. . . . . . . .209 B4
Oxhayes DT8 . . . . .199 F8
Oxhouse La
  Failand BS8 . . . . 10 B1
  Winford BS40 . . . . 37 D6
Oxleaze
  5 Bishops Lydeard TA4 . .167 F8
  Bristol BS13. . . . . 22 D4
Oxleaze La BS41 . . . . 21 E3
Oxley Cotts DT9. . . . . .225 C4
Ozenhay BS39 . . . . 75 E6

P

Packers' Way TA18. . . . . . . .196 B3
Pack Horse La BA2. . . . . 62 F7
Packsaddle Way BA11. . . . . .119 F7
Pacquet Ho BS20 . . . . 4 D5
Paddles La BA11. . . . . .119 D1
Paddock Cl TA3. . . . . .169 D5
Paddock Dr TA9 . . . . .104 D4
Paddock Gdn BS14. . . . . 22 F4
Paddock Pk BS22 . . . . 32 B2
Paddocks Cvn Pk The
  BS26. . . . . 87 A7
Paddocks The
  Bath BA2 . . . . 45 B1
  Ilchester BA22 . . . . .173 E1
  Sandford BS25. . . . . 52 C4
  Wellington TA21. . . . . .222 E5
  Weston-Super-Mare BS23. . 48 D2
Paddock The
  Banwell BS29. . . . . 51 A3
  Clevedon BS21. . . . . 6 D2
  Corston BA2 . . . . 43 B7
  Dulverton TA22 . . . . .163 D6
  Galhampton BA22 . . . . .175 D8
  Portishead BS20 . . . . 2 D4
  Taunton, Dowsland TA1. . . .168 F1
  Taunton, Trull TA3. . . . . . . .168 D1
Paddock Wlk DT9. . . . . .217 C2
Paddock Woods BA2. . . . . . . 45 D2
Padfield Gn BA4. . . . . .141 E6
Padleigh Hill BA2. . . . . 44 B2
Padstow Rd BS4 . . . . 22 F8
Paganel Cl TA24 . . . . .200 F6
Paganel Rd TA24. . . . . .200 F6
Paganel Rise TA24. . . . . .200 E6
Paganel Way TA24. . . . . .200 E6
Pagans Hill BS40. . . . . 38 D2
Page's Ct BS49 . . . . 34 C8
Page's Hill BA16. . . . . .207 C5
Pageant Dr DT9. . . . . .225 D3
Page La BA6. . . . . .140 A2
Pages Mead BS11. . . . . 4 C8
Paintmoor La TA20. . . . . . . .194 B4
Palace Ct BA5 . . . . .203 D3
Palace Gdns TA4. . . . . .210 C4
Palace Yard Mews BA1. . . .228 B2
Palfrey's La TA20 . . . . .193 D3
Palmer's Elm BS24. . . . . 33 B4
Palmer's End La TA2 . . . . . .184 F7
Palmer's Way BS24 . . . . 49 D2
Palmer Cl TA6. . . . . .208 F2
Palmer Row 7 BS23 . . . . 48 E8
Palmers Cl TA4 . . . . .104 D8
Palmers La BA2. . . . . 61 B3
Palmers Rd BA6. . . . . .206 D4
Palmer St
  Frome BA11. . . . . .119 F4
  South Petherton TA13 . . . . .220 C4
  Weston-Super-Mare BS23. . 48 E8
Palmerston Rd TA1. . . . . . . .212 D5
Palm Tree Cl TA6 . . . . .209 C5
Panborough Dro BA5 . . . . . .138 F8
Panoramic The BS1. . . . . . . .226 C3
Parade Nurseries BA20 . . .200 F7
Parade The
  1 Bath BA2 . . . . 44 B6
  Bristol, Bishopsworth BS13. 22 A6
  Bristol, Shirehampton BS11 . 4 E6
  Chardstock EX13 . . . . .198 A7
  Minehead TA24 . . . . .200 F7
Paradise Cres BA4. . . . . .141 E2
Paradise La
  Croscombe BA5. . . . . .204 B7
  Glastonbury BA6 . . . . .139 D2
  Langport TA10 . . . . .172 A7
  Tatworth TA20. . . . . .193 F1
Paradise Rd BA6. . . . . .206 D5
Paradise Row BS39. . . . . 41 A6
Paragon Ct 13 BS23. . . . . 30 C1

Paragon Rd BS23 . . . . 30 C1
Paragon Sch The BA2. . . . . . 45 A3
Paragon The
  Bath BA1. . . . . .228 C3
  Bristol BS8. . . . . 11 F6
Paray Dr BA5 . . . . .203 F5
Parbrook Ct BS14. . . . . 23 B5
Parbrook La BA6. . . . . .158 C7
Parcroft Com Jun Sch
  BA20. . . . . .218 F5
Parcroft Gdns BA20 . . . . . . .218 F5
Pardlestone La TA5. . . . . . . .133 C5
Parfields BA20. . . . . .218 F5
Parish Brook Rd BS48. . . . . . 8 B2
Parish Hill BA22 . . . . .175 D5
Parish Land La TA5 . . . . .152 D5
Parish Mews BA20 . . . . .218 C5
Park Ave
  Bath BA2 . . . . .228 B1
  Bridgwater TA6 . . . . .208 D4
  Castle Cary BA7. . . . . .214 B4
  Yatton BS49. . . . . 17 B1
Park Barn La TA19 . . . . .183 C4
Park Batch BS40. . . . . 54 F3
Park Bglws EX16 . . . . .179 B3
Park Cl
  Barton St David TA11 . . . . .158 A3
  Cossington TA7 . . . . .136 F3
  Keynsham BS31. . . . . 24 D5
  Paulton BS39. . . . . 77 D5
  Staplehay TA3. . . . . .181 D8
  Street BA16. . . . . .207 C5
Park Cnr
  Hambridge TA3 . . . . .184 B7
  Leigh u M BA11. . . . . .117 D3
Park Cotts TA20 . . . . .223 B5
Park Cres
  Chard TA20. . . . . .223 B5
  Cossington TA7 . . . . .136 F3
Park Ct 5 BS23. . . . . 48 E5
Park End BS29. . . . . 50 E4
Parker Cl TA21. . . . . .222 E6
Parkes Rd BS24. . . . . 50 C5
Park Farm BA6 . . . . .206 C4
Park Farm Rd BA6 . . . . .206 C4
Parkfield Cl TA6. . . . . .153 F4
Parkfield Cres TA1. . . . . .212 D2
Parkfield Dr TA1. . . . . .212 D3
Parkfield Gdns BS39 . . . . 57 D3
Parkfield Prim Sch TA1. . . .212 D3
Parkfield Rd
  Axbridge BS26. . . . . 70 D1
  Taunton TA1. . . . . .212 D3
Parkfields Orch BA6 . . . . . . .157 E4
Parkfields Residential Home
  BA6. .157 E4
Park Gate TA2 . . . . .168 F7
Parkgate La BA11. . . . . .101 E7
Park Gdns
  Bath BA1 . . . . 44 D8
  Yeovil BA20 . . . . .219 A5
Park Gr DT10 . . . . .190 B4
Park Hayes BA3. . . . . .116 F3
Park Hill
  Bristol BS11. . . . . 4 F6
  Mells BA11. . . . . .118 C7
  Pilton BA4 . . . . .140 E3
Park Hill Dr BA11. . . . . .119 F6
Park Ho BA2. . . . . 44 D7
Parkhouse La BS31 . . . . 24 C2
Parkhouse Rd TA24. . . . . . . .200 E7
Parkhurst Rd BS23. . . . . 49 A7
Park La
  Barton St David TA11. . . . . .158 A3
  Bath BA1 . . . . 44 D7
  Blagdon BS40. . . . . 54 F3
  Bristol BS2. . . . . .226 C3
  Cannington TA5. . . . . .135 B3
  Carhampton TA24 . . . . .131 A5
  Castle Cary BA7. . . . . .214 D7
  Clapton TA18 . . . . .195 B1
  Combe St Nicholas TA20 . . .193 C6
  Downhead BA4 . . . . .117 A1
  Faulkland BA3. . . . . 80 B1
  Goathurst TA5. . . . . .153 C4
  Henstridge BA8 . . . . .190 A8
  High Ham TA10 . . . . .156 D1
  Ilminster TA19 . . . . .183 E1
  Kingsdon TA11. . . . . .173 C5
  Kingston St Mary TA2 . . . . .168 C8
  Langport TA10 . . . . .171 E4
  Montacute BA22, TA15. . . . .186 B3
  North Newton TA7 . . . . .154 A3
  North Petherton TA6 . . . . . .153 F4
  Seavington St Mary TA19. . .184 C1
  Thorncombe TA20 . . . . .199 A7
  Wellington TA21. . . . . .222 C1
  West Buckland TA21 . . . . . .180 E7
  Yenston BA8 . . . . .189 F8
Parklands BS39 . . . . 59 D2
Parklands Ave BS22. . . . . 32 A4
Parklands Rd
  Bristol BS3. . . . . 11 E4
  Wellington TA21. . . . . .222 D7
Parklands Rise BA20 . . . . . .200 D7
Parklands Way TA11 . . . . . . .211 B4
Parkland Vlw TA18. . . . . .224 C4
Park Lane Cl TA24 . . . . .131 A5
Park Lodge BA20 . . . . .219 A5
Parkmead TA20 . . . . .213 E8
Park Pl
  Bath BA1 . . . . .228 A4
  Bristol BS2. . . . . .226 C4
  Bristol BS8. . . . . .226 C3
  Castle Cary BA7. . . . . .214 C4
  Weston-Super-Mare BS23. . 48 E5
Park Rd
  Bath BA1 . . . . 44 B7

Park Rd continued
  Bridgwater TA6 . . . . .208 D4
  Bristol BS3. . . . . .226 B1
  Bristol, Shirehampton BS11 . 4 F6
  Bruton BA10 . . . . .215 E5
  Chard TA20. . . . . .223 C4
  Clevedon BS21. . . . . 6 D4
  Congresbury BS49. . . . . 34 E3
  Frome BA11. . . . . .119 E4
  Henstridge BA8 . . . . .190 A6
  Keynsham BS31. . . . . 24 E4
  Paulton BS39. . . . . 77 D5
  Shepton Mallet BA4. . . . . . .205 B5
  Stalbridge DT10. . . . . .190 B4
  Street BA16. . . . . .207 C5
  Yeovil BA20 . . . . .219 B5
Park Row BS1. . . . . .226 C3
Park Sch The BA20. . . . . . . .219 A5
Parks Cotts TA2 . . . . .168 D8
Parkside Ct 1 TA6. . . . . .209 B4
Parkside Inf Sch BA1 . . . . . .228 B3
Parks La
  Brompton Ralph TA4 . . . . . .150 C3
  Minehead TA24 . . . . .200 F7
Park St
  Bath BA1 . . . . .228 A4
  Bristol BS1. . . . . .226 C3
  Castle Cary BA7. . . . . .214 C5
  Dunster TA24 . . . . .201 D1
  Exford TA24 . . . . .128 D1
  Minehead TA24 . . . . .200 F7
  Taunton TA1 . . . . .212 E3
  Yeovil BA20 . . . . .219 B4
Parks The
  Bridgwater TA6 . . . . .208 D4
  Minehead TA24 . . . . .200 E7
Parkstone Ave TA6. . . . . . . .209 A2
Park Street Ave BS1. . . . . . .226 C3
Park Street Mews BA1 . . . .228 A4
Parks View TA24 . . . . .124 A4
Parksway Ct TA24. . . . . .200 E7
Park Terr
  Chard TA20. . . . . .223 B6
  Glastonbury BA6 . . . . .206 D4
  Minehead TA24 . . . . .200 F7
Park The
  Castle Cary BA7. . . . . .214 B4
  Keynsham BS31. . . . . 24 E6
  Portishead BS20 . . . . 2 F7
  Yatton BS49. . . . . 17 B1
  Yeovil BA20 . . . . .219 A5
Park View
  Axminster EX13 . . . . .198 A3
  Bath BA2 . . . . 44 D6
  Cotford St Luke TA4. . . . . . .167 F6
  Crewkerne, Misterton
    TA18. . . . . .196 B3
  Crewkerne TA18 . . . . .224 C4
  Montacute TA15. . . . . .186 B3
  Stogursey TA5. . . . . .134 C5
Park Villas BS23 . . . . 48 D8
Park Wall BA10. . . . . .215 F5
Park Wall Dro TA7 . . . . .209 F4
Park Water La DT8. . . . . .199 F5
Parkway
  Bridgwater TA6 . . . . .209 C5
  Timsbury BA2. . . . . 60 E2
Park Way
  Bruton BA10 . . . . .215 E5
  Midsomer Norton BA3. . . . . 97 A8
  Ruishton TA3 . . . . .169 C3
  Weston-Super-Mare BS22. . 32 B1
Parkway La BA2. . . . . 60 D3
Park Wlk BS20 . . . . 4 D4
Park Wood Cl BS14. . . . . 22 F4
Parlour Ho TA1. . . . . .213 B5
Parmin Way TA1. . . . . .213 C3
Parnell Rd BS21 . . . . 6 D3
Parnell Way TA6 . . . . .104 B8
Parrett Cl TA10 . . . . .171 F7
Parrett Mead
  South Perrott DT8 . . . . .196 C1
  Taunton TA1. . . . . .213 D3
Parrett Way TA6 . . . . .209 B3
Parrett Works Cotts
  TA12. . . . . .220 F8
Parricks La EX13. . . . . .198 D3
Parrocks La TA20 . . . . .198 C8
Parry's Cl BS9. . . . . .5 E5
Parry's La BS9. . . . . .5 F5
Parry Cl BA2. . . . . 44 B4
Parrys Gr BS9 . . . . .5 F5
Parson's Batch BA4. . . . . . . .140 E3
Parson's Dro BS28 . . . . .138 C7
Parson's La TA11 . . . . .173 D5
Parson's St TA24. . . . . .124 A3
Parsonage Cl
  Langport TA10 . . . . .172 A5
  Somerton TA11 . . . . .211 E3
  Winford BS40 . . . . 37 F6
Parsonage Cotts
  Kingston St Mary TA2 . . . . .168 D8
  West Camel BA22 . . . . .174 D3
Parsonage Cres BA7 . . . . . .214 B6
Parsonage Ct
  Puriton TA7 . . . . .136 B4
  Taunton TA1. . . . . .212 A4
Parsonage Hill TA11 . . . . . .211 E3
Parsonage La
  Ashill TA19 . . . . .183 C4
  Axbridge BS26. . . . . 70 E2
  Bath BA1 . . . . .228 B2
  Charlton Musgrove BA9. . . .161 B1
  Chilcompton BA3 . . . . 96 C4
  Kingston St Mary TA2 . . . . .168 D8
  Milverton TA4. . . . . .167 A4
  Pensford BS39. . . . . 40 D6

Parsonage La continued
  Staple Fitzpaine TA3 . . . . . .182 C4
  Winford BS40 . . . . 37 F6
Parsonage Pl TA10. . . . . .171 D4
Parsonage Rd
  Berrow TA8 . . . . 84 F5
  Long Ashton BS41. . . . . 11 C2
  West Camel BA22 . . . . .174 D3
Parsons' La TA5 . . . . .152 A7
Parsons Cl
  Bicknoller TA4. . . . . .132 F2
  Long Sutton TA10. . . . . .172 F4
  Nether Stowey TA5. . . . . . . .134 A3
Parsons Gate BA7. . . . . .214 B7
Parsons Gn
  Clevedon BS21. . . . . 16 C8
  Weston-Super-Mare BS22. . 32 A3
Parsons Mead BS48 . . . . 19 F7
Parsons Paddock BS14. . . . . 23 A7
Parsons Pen BS27 . . . . 90 B7
Parsons Rd TA9. . . . . .104 C4
Parsons Way
  Wells BA5 . . . . .203 B4
  Winscombe BS25. . . . . 69 E6
Partis Coll BA1 . . . . 44 A8
Partis Way BA1 . . . . 44 A8
Partition St BS1. . . . . .226 C2
Partman's Hill BA3. . . . . . . .116 B3
Partridge Cl
  Moorlinch TA7 . . . . .155 F7
  Weston-Super-Mare BS22. . 31 F1
Partway La
  Chard Junction TA20 . . . . . .198 F6
  East Chinnock BA22. . . . . . .196 F7
Passage Leaze BS11. . . . . 4 D6
Passage St BS2 . . . . .227 B2
Pastures Ave BS22 . . . . 32 C3
Pastures The BA15. . . . . 64 E3
Patch Croft BS21 . . . . 16 C8
Pathe Rd TA7. . . . . .155 B1
Pathfinder Terr 3 TA6. . . . .209 B4
Patrick's Way TA3 . . . . .181 D8
Patrum Cl TA1. . . . . .212 B1
Patson Hill La DT9 . . . . .188 B5
Patterson Ho 8 BS1. . . . . . .227 B1
Pattinson Cl BA21. . . . . .219 D6
Pattons TA3 . . . . .169 C1
Patwell La BA10. . . . . .215 E6
Patwell St BA10. . . . . .215 E6
Paul's Cswy BS49 . . . . 34 D4
Paull's La TA19 . . . . .183 B2
Paullet EX16. . . . . .178 C1
Paulls Cl TA3 . . . . .172 A6
Paulman Gdns BS41. . . . . 20 F8
Paulmont Rise BS39. . . . . 58 E1
Pauls Rd TA11 . . . . .211 C3
Paul St
  Bristol BS2. . . . . .226 C4
  Frome BA11. . . . . .119 F5
  Shepton Mallet BA4. . . . . . .205 B6
  Taunton TA1. . . . . .212 F3
Paulto' Hill BA3, BS39. . . . . . 78 B6
Paulton Inf Sch BS39. . . . . . 77 E5
Paulton Jun Sch BS39. . . . . . 77 E5
Paulton La BA2, BA3. . . . . 78 D7
Paulton Meml Hospl BS39 77 F4
Paulton Rd
  Farrington Gurney BS39 . . . 77 B4
  Hallatrow BS39 . . . . 77 B7
  Midsomer Norton BA3. . . . . 77 F1
Paulwood Rd BS39. . . . . 58 E1
Pavement The TA3. . . . . .170 B4
Pavey Cl BS13. . . . . 22 C4
Pavey Rd BS13. . . . . 22 C4
Pavyotts La BA22 . . . . .197 E8
Pawelski Cl BA4 . . . . .142 B7
Pawlett BS24. . . . . 49 A2
Pawlett Mead Dro TA6 . . . . 136 A5
Pawlett Prim Sch TA6. . . . .135 F5
Pawlett Rd
  Bristol BS13. . . . . 22 C3
  Walpole TA6. . . . . .136 B4
  West Huntspill TA6, TA9. . . .136 A4
Pawletts Almshouses
  TA5. .134 C5
Pawlett Wlk BS13. . . . . 22 C3
Paybridge Rd BS13. . . . . 21 F4
Payne's La TA12 . . . . .185 E8
Payne Rd BS24. . . . . 49 D2
Paynes Ho 17 BS23 . . . . 48 E8
Paynes La TA7. . . . . .155 C2
Payton Rd
  Holywell Lake TA21. . . . . . .179 F7
  Rockwell Green TA21. . . . . .222 A5
Peace Cl TA6. . . . . .209 D6
Peacehay La TA21. . . . . .179 E4
Peach Tree Cl TA6. . . . . .209 E5
Peacocks Cl TA20. . . . . .180 F7
Peacocks Hill TA11. . . . . . . .158 A2
Peadon La TA5. . . . . .134 C4
Peak La
  Compton Dundon TA11. . . .157 A2
  Shepton Beauchamp TA19 .184 D3
Pear Ash La BA9. . . . . .161 E2
Pearce Dr TA9. . . . . .104 D4
Pearmain Rd BA16. . . . . .207 B4
Pearse Cl BS22 . . . . 32 B5
Pearson Ho BA21. . . . . .219 A6
Peart Cl BS13. . . . . 21 E5
Peart Dr BS13. . . . . 21 E4
Peartree La BS13. . . . . 22 B4
Pear Tree Cl
  Bridgwater TA6 . . . . .209 D4
  Westleigh EX16 . . . . .179 A4
Peartree Field BS20. . . . . 2 F5

Peartree Gdns BS24.... **67** C6
Pear Tree Ind Est BS40 ... **53** C4
Peartwater Hill TA5.... **152** D8
Peartwater Rd TA5.... **152** D7
Peasedown St John Prim Sch
BA2.................... **79** C7
Peat Moors Visitor Ctr★
BA6.................... **138** A4
Pebbles Orch TA11.... **184** E4
Pecking Mill Rd BA4.... **141** E1
Pedder Rd BS21........... **6** D1
Peddles Cl TA10.... **171** D8
Peddles La TA11.... **173** E8
Pedlars Gr
  Chapmanslade BA13.... **121** C4
  Frome BA11.......... **119** E7
Pedwell Cvn Pk TA7.... **156** A7
Pedwell Hill TA7.... **156** A7
Pedwell La TA7.... **156** A7
Peel Ct TA23.......... **202** C7
Peel St BS5........... **227** C4
Peerage Ct TA24.... **201** A6
Pegasus Ct 17 BA20 ... **219** B4
Peggy's La TA18.... **196** C5
Peile Dr TA2.......... **212** E7
Peir Cl BS20........... **2** E7
Pelham St TA6.... **209** D7
Pelican Cl BS22.... **49** F8
Pelting Dro BA5.... **92** D1
Pembroke Ave BS11....**4** E6
Pembroke Cl
  Burnham-on-S TA8.... **85** B1
  Taunton TA1.... **212** C1
  Yeovil BA21.... **219** E7
Pembroke Ct BS21.... **6** C4
Pembroke Gr BS8.... **226** A3
Pembroke Ho 1 BS23... **30** C1
Pembroke Mans BS8.... **226** A4
Pembroke Pl BS8.... **226** A1
Pembroke Rd
  Bridgwater TA6.... **209** C3
  Bristol BS8.... **226** A4
  Bristol, Shirehampton BS11 . **4** E6
  Portishead BS20........ **1** E4
  Weston-Super-Mare BS23.. **48** F4
Pembroke St BS2.... **227** B4
Pembroke Vale BS8.... **226** A4
Pemswell Rd TA24.... **200** F8
Penarth Dr BS24.... **49** A1
Penarth Rd TA6.... **208** D4
Pen Cross BA22.... **197** B6
Pendle Cl BS25.... **70** A7
Pendlesham Gdns BS23 .. **31** A1
Pendomer Rd BA22.... **197** B5
Pendragon Pk BA6.... **206** D5
Pen Elm Cotts TA2.... **168** B5
Pen Elm Hill TA2.... **168** B6
Penmore Rd BA22, DT9 .. **188** B7
Penfield BA21.... **219** C5
Pen Hill BA9.... **161** C4
Penlea Ave TA6.... **208** E2
Penlea Cl TA6.... **208** E2
Penlea Ct BS11........ **4** D7
Pen Mill Hill SP8, BA12.. **161** F2
Pen Mill Inf Sch BA21.... **219** D6
Pen Mill Sta BA21.... **219** E5
Pen Mill Trad Est BA21 .. **219** F6
Penmoor Pl TA8.... **84** F5
Penmoor Rd TA8.... **84** F5
Pennard Ct
  Bath BA2................ **44** A6
  Bristol BS14.... **23** B5
Pennard Gn BA2.... **44** A6
Pennard La BA6.... **140** A2
Penn Cl
  Cheddar BS27.... **90** C7
  Wells BA5.... **112** E2
Penn Ct BS26.... **70** C1
Penneys Piece BA11 .. **120** C6
Penn Gdns BA1.... **44** A8
Penn Hill BA20.... **219** B4
Penn Hill Pk BA20.... **219** B4
Penn Hill Rd BA1.... **27** A1
Pennine Gdns BS23.... **31** A1
Penn La BA22.... **197** A6
Pennlea BS13.... **22** C7
Penn Lea Ct BA1.... **44** B8
Penn Lea Rd BA1.... **44** B8
Pennon Rise BS1.... **226** C1
Penn Rd BS27.... **90** C7
Penn St BS1.... **227** B3
Penns The BS21........ **6** E2
Penn View BA9.... **216** D4
Penn Way BS26.... **70** C1
Penny's Meade TA19 .. **183** F4
Penny Batch La BA5.. **139** E8
Penny Cl TA21.... **222** D7
Pennycress BS22.... **49** D7
Penny Lea TA23.... **202** C6
Pennyquick BA2.... **43** D6
Pennyquick View BA2.. **43** F6
Pennywell Est 3 BS21.... **6** D2
Pennywell Rd BS2.... **227** C4
Penpole Ave BS11.... **4** E6
Penpole Cl BS11........**4** D7
Penpole La BS11.... **4** E7
Penpole Pk BS11........**4** E7
Penpole Pl BS11........**4** E6
Penrice Cl BS22.... **31** C2
Penrose BS14.... **22** F7
Penrose Sch TA6.... **208** E4
Pensford Ct BS14.... **23** D5
Pensford Hill BS39.... **40** D5

Pensford La BS39........ **40** A3
Pensford Old Rd BS39.... **40** E3
Pensford Prim Sch BS39.. **40** D4
Pensford Way BA11.... **120** D7
Pentagon The BS9........**5** B5
Pentire Ave BS13.... **22** A6
Pentridge La DT10.... **190** E2
Penzoy Ave TA6.... **209** B4
Pepperall Rd TA9.... **104** D4
Peppershells La BS39.... **41** C6
Pepys Cl BS31.... **25** D2
Pera Pl BA1.... **228** C4
Pera Rd BA1.... **228** C4
Perch Hill BA5.... **110** E6
Percival Rd BS8........ **11** F8
Percy Pl 13 BA1........ **28** B1
Percy Rd BA21.... **219** D6
Peregrine Cl BS22.... **31** F1
Perfect View BA1........ **28** A1
Periton Cross TA24.... **200** D6
Periton Ct TA24.... **200** D6
Periton La TA24.... **200** D7
Periton Mead Sch TA24.. **200** D6
Periton Rd TA24.... **200** D6
Periton Rise TA24.... **200** D6
Periton Way TA24.... **200** D6
Perkins Ct BA5.... **203** B4
Perley La TA23.... **148** D8
Perrett Ho 22 BS2.... **227** C3
Perretts Ct BS1.... **226** C1
Perrett Way BS20........**4** E4
Perridge Hill BA4.... **140** D4
Perrin Cl BS39.... **76** E8
Perrings The BS48.... **18** E8
Perrott Hill Sch TA18.... **196** B4
Perrow La BS28.... **89** C2
Perry's Cider Mills★
  TA19.... **194** E7
Perry's Cl BS27.... **90** A7
Perry Court Inf Sch BS14.. **23** A6
Perry Court Jun Sch
  BS14.... **23** A6
Perrycroft Ave BS13.... **22** A6
Perrycroft Rd BS13.... **22** A6
Perry Hill TA11.... **174** D8
Perry Hill Rd TA11.... **211** D2
Perry La TA9.... **106** F5
Perry Lake La BA5.... **139** B7
Perrymans Cl BS30.... **12** A8
Perrymead
  Bath BA2................ **45** B3
  Weston-Super-Mare BS22.. **32** B5
Perrymead Ct BA2.... **45** B4
Perrymead Pl BA2.... **45** B4
Perry New Rd TA22.... **163** F4
Perry Pl BA21.... **219** C5
Perry Rd
  Blackford TA9.... **107** A6
  Bristol BS1.... **227** A3
Perry St TA20.... **198** D8
Pesley Cl BS13.... **22** A4
Pesters La TA11.... **211** E3
Pestlefield La TA3.... **170** C1
Peter's Gore DT6.... **199** B1
Petercole Dr BS13.... **22** A6
Peterside BS39.... **76** E8
Peterson Sq BS13.... **22** C3
Peter St
  Shepton Mallet BA4.... **205** B6
  Taunton TA2.... **212** F6
  Yeovil BA20.... **219** B4
Petherton Gdns BS14 .. **23** B7
Petherton Rd
  Bristol BS14.... **23** B7
  North Newton TA7.... **153** F2
Pethick Ho BS4.... **22** F8
Peto Garden at Iford Manor
  The★ BA15.... **64** E3
Peto Gr BA15.... **64** F3
Petrel Cl TA6.... **209** D7
Petter's Way BA20.... **219** B4
Petticoat La BA4.... **205** B6
Pettitts Cl DT9.... **187** E1
Petton Cross EX16.... **165** A3
Petvin Cl BS14.... **207** D4
Petvins Ct TA18.... **196** C5
Pevensey Wlk BS4.... **22** D7
Pharmacy Flats The
  DT10.... **190** F6
Pheasant The TA19.... **184** E1
Phelps Cl TA20.... **223** D6
Philadelphia Ct BS1.... **227** B3
Philippa Cl BS14.... **23** A7
Philips Ho 2 BS2.... **227** B4
Phillip's Dro TA3.... **170** D7
Phillip Ho TA6.... **208** F2
Phillips Cl TA6.... **208** D4
Phillips Rd BS23.... **49** A6
Phillis Hill BS39.... **77** F4
Phippen St 1 BS1.... **227** B1
Phoenix Ct
  Frome BA11.... **119** D4
  Taunton TA1.... **212** F3
Phoenix Ho
  Bath BA1.... **228** B4
  Frome BA11.... **119** D4
Phoenix Rd TA6.... **209** B3
Phoenix Terr TA6.... **104** B6
Phoenix Way BS20.... **2** F6
Piccadilly Pl BA1.... **45** B8
Piccadilly Ho 13 BA4.... **205** B6
Pickeridge Cl TA2.... **213** B7
Picket La DT8.... **196** C1
Pickett La BA21.... **219** A7
Pickney La TA2.... **168** B7
Pickpurse La TA4.... **150** E8
Pickwick Rd BA1.... **28** A2

Piece TA19.... **184** E4
Piece La TA19.... **184** E4
Piece Rd DT9.... **217** C3
Piece The 2 TA16.... **195** F7
Pier Rd BS20........ **2** E7
Pierrepont Pl 9 BA1.... **228** C2
Pierrepont St BA1.... **228** C2
Piers Rd BA4.... **142** A6
Pier St TA8.... **104** A6
Piffin La TA4.... **167** E8
Pigeon House Dr BS13.. **22** D4
Pigeon La BS40.... **36** E1
Pig Hill BA22.... **197** A7
Pightley La TA5.... **152** F6
Pightley Rd TA5.... **152** F7
Pig La TA7.... **154** D8
Pig Market La TA1.... **212** F3
Pigott Ave BS13.... **22** A4
Pigs Hill La TA5.... **134** D1
Pike Cl BA6.... **206** C5
Pike Hill BA4.... **205** A7
Pike La BA4.... **205** B6
Pikes Cres
  Dunster TA24.... **201** D2
  Taunton TA1.... **212** E1
Pilcorn St BS28.... **108** C4
Pile La
  Curry Mallet TA3.... **183** C8
  Stourton Caundle DT10.. **189** F3
Piley La TA21.... **179** D8
Pilgrim's Way TA6.... **135** F5
Pilgrims Way
  Bristol BS11........ **4** C7
  Chew Stoke BS40.... **56** D8
  Lovington BA7.... **158** E2
  Weston-Super-Mare BS22.. **31** E3
Pillar La BA11.... **99** D4
Pill Bridge La BA22.... **173** D1
Pill Head La TA18.... **196** C4
Pill Mdw SP8.... **177** E2
Pillmead La BS28.... **108** D5
Pillmoor Dro BA5.... **139** F6
Pillmoor La BA5.... **139** F6
Pillmore La
  Highbridge TA9.... **105** A4
  Watchfield TA9.... **105** C4
Pill Rd
  Abbots Leigh BS8........**4** F1
  Pill BS20................**4** D4
  Rooks Bridge BS26, TA9 .. **87** C2
Pill St BS20................**4** D4
Pill Way BS21........ **6** B2
Pilots Helm TA6.... **153** E4
Pilsdon La DT6.... **199** F3
Pilton Hill BA4.... **140** C4
Pilton Manor Vineyard★
  BA4.... **140** E3
Pimm's La BS22.... **31** B2
Pimms La BS22.... **31** B3
Pimpernel Cl BA16.... **207** B7
Pince's Knap TA20.... **198** F5
Pinchay La BS40.... **38** A4
Pinckney Gn BA15.... **46** E5
Pincushion Cnr BA22.... **197** E6
Pine Ave TA20.... **223** C5
Pine Cl
  Street BS40.... **207** B3
  Taunton TA1.... **213** D2
  Weston-Super-Mare BS22.. **31** D2
Pinecroft
  Bristol BS14.... **22** F7
  Portishead BS20........ **1** F6
Pine Ct
  Chew Magna BS40.... **39** B3
  Frome BA11.... **120** B7
  Keynsham BS31.... **24** C4
  Radstock BA3.... **79** A2
Pine Hill BS22.... **31** B3
Pine Lea BS24.... **67** B6
Pine Ridge Cl BS9.... **5** C4
Pines Cl
  Chilcompton BA3.... **96** D3
  Wincanton BA9.... **216** C3
Pines Residential Site The
  BA11.... **120** D8
Pines Way
  Bath BA2.... **228** A2
  Radstock BA3.... **79** A2
Pines Way Ind Est BA2.. **228** A2
Pine Tree Ave BA20 .... **218** F3
Pine Tree Cl TA6.... **209** D4
Pinetree Rd BS24.... **50** D4
Pine Wlk BA3.... **78** E1
Pinewood TA11.... **211** D4
Pinewood Ave BA3.... **77** F1
Pinewood Dr TA11.... **211** D4
Pinewood Gr BA3.... **77** F1
Pinewood Rd BA3.... **77** F1
Pinewood Way TA8.... **65** F3
Pinford La DT9.... **188** F3
Pinhay Rd BS13.... **22** B6
Pinkham Hill TA20.... **194** B6
Pinkhams Twist BS14.... **23** A5
Pink Knoll Hollow DT9 .. **188** C8
Pinksmoor La TA21.... **179** E7
Pinkwood La BA10.... **160** F7
Pinmore BA11.... **119** E2
Pinney Cl TA1.... **212** B1
Pinnockscroft TA8.... **84** F5
Pintail Rd TA24.... **201** C5
Pinter Cl TA8.... **104** C6
Pioneer Ave BA2.... **44** F1
Pipehouse BA2.... **63** E4
Pipehouse La BA2.... **63** F4
Pipe La BS1.... **226** C2
Piper's Alley TA19.... **221** B4
Pipers Cl BS26.... **88** E6
Pipers Pl EX14.... **191** F5

Pippard Cl BA16.... **207** E5
Pippin Cl BA2.... **79** D7
Pippins The
  Portishead BS20........ **2** F5
  Wembdon TA6.... **208** D6
Pipplepen La DT8, TA18.. **196** B2
Pitchcombe Gdns BS9.... **5** D7
Pitcher's Hill TA2.... **168** F7
Pitching The
  Castle Cary BA7.... **214** C5
  Chilcompton BA3.... **96** D5
Pitch & Pay La BS9........**5** E3
Pitch & Pay Pk BS9........**5** E3
Pitcombe Hill BA10.... **215** B2
Pitcombe La TA4.... **165** B5
Pitcombe Rock BA10.... **215** C3
Pitcot La BA3.... **115** F7
Pitfield Cnr BA22.... **188** A7
Pitfour Terr BA2.... **60** B2
Pithay Ct BS1.... **227** A3
Pithay The
  Bristol BS1.... **227** A3
  Paulton BS39.... **77** F6
Pit Hill TA17.... **195** B7
Pit Hill La TA7.... **155** C7
Pit La
  Sticklepath TA23.... **149** D7
  Sutton Mallet TA7.... **155** C7
  Ubley BS40.... **55** F5
Pitman Ct BA1.... **28** C2
Pitman Ho BA2.... **44** D4
Pitman Rd BS23.... **48** E6
Pitney Hill TA10.... **172** C6
Pit Rd
  Dinnington TA17.... **195** C7
  Midsomer Norton BA3.... **78** B1
Pitsham La TA4.... **164** E6
Pitt's La BS40.... **39** B1
Pitt Ct TA10.... **171** B3
Pitten St BA3.... **116** E3
Pitt La
  Huish Champflower TA4.. **165** E8
  Porlock Weir TA24.... **123** C3
  Waterrow BA4.... **165** E1
Pitts Cl TA1.... **212** C1
Pitts La TA3.... **183** F7
Pitway BA3.... **220** D5
Pitway Cl BS39.... **76** F4
Pitway Hill TA13.... **220** D6
Pitway La BS39.... **76** E4
Pixash Bsns Ctr BS31 ... **25** B5
Pixash La BS31.... **25** C5
Pix La TA4.... **167** B4
Pixton Way TA22.... **163** E6
Pizey Ave
  Burnham-on-S TA8.... **85** A1
  Clevedon BS21.... **6** B2
Pizey Ave Ind Est BS21 .. **6** C2
Pizey Cl BS21........ **6** B2
Place Dro TA7.... **154** F4
Placket La BA20.... **218** D1
Plain Pond TA4.... **210** C3
Plain The BA2.... **81** E4
Plais St TA2.... **212** F6
Plantaganet Chase BA20 **218** D2
Plantagenet Pk BA20.... **218** E3
Platterwell La (East Town
  La) BA4.... **141** B3
Players La TA8.... **85** A1
Playfield Cl 2 BA8.... **190** A6
Playford Gdns BS11.... **4** E8
Playses Gn TA10.... **184** D8
Pleasant Pl BA1.... **29** D2
Pleshey Cl BS22.... **31** D2
Plimsoll Ho 3 BS1.... **227** B1
Plot La DT9.... **187** F5
Plott La BA8.... **190** B7
Plough Cl BA16.... **207** A4
Ploughed Paddock BS48 .. **8** D1
Plover Cl
  Milborne Port DT9.... **217** C2
  Minehead TA24.... **201** C5
  Weston-Super-Mare BS22.. **31** F1
Plover Ct BS21.... **218** D6
Plover Rd DT9.... **217** C2
Plovers Rise BA3.... **79** A3
Plowage La BA22.... **174** D3
Plox BA10.... **215** E6
Plox Gn BA10.... **215** E6
Plucknett Row BA20.... **218** D5
Plud St BS28.... **108** B3
Plumber's Barton 9
  BA11.... **119** F4
Plumers Cl 4 BS21........ **6** E1
Plum La TA6.... **209** C2
Plumley Cres BS24.... **50** A4
Plumley Ct BS23.... **48** D4
Plummer's La BA5.... **92** D5
Plum Orch DT9.... **187** F4
Plumptre Ave BA5.... **203** F5
Plumptre Cl BS39.... **77** E5
Plumptre Rd BS39.... **77** E5
Plumtree Cl BS25.... **52** A1
Plum Tree Cl TA6.... **209** E5
Plum Tree Rd BS22.... **49** E8
Plunder St BS49.... **35** B7
Plunging Dr BA6.... **206** F1
Plymor Rd TA9.... **136** A8
Poachers End TA24.... **201** C4
Pococks Yd TA10.... **171** F5
Podger's La TA19.... **183** F4
Podgers Dr BA1.... **27** B2
Podium The BA1.... **228** C2
Poets Cnr BA3.... **97** C8
Polden Bsns Ctr The
  TA6.... **136** B2
Polden Cl BS48........ **8** E1
Polden Ct TA6.... **209** B5

Polden Rd
  Portishead BS20........ **2** B5
  Weston-Super-Mare BS23.. **48** F8
Polden St TA6.... **209** B6
Polden View BA6.... **206** E3
Polden Wlk TA7.... **136** C3
Pole Rue La TA20.... **193** C6
Polestar Way BS24.... **50** A8
Polham La TA11.... **211** D3
Polkes Field TA3.... **170** F6
Pollard's La TA21.... **180** F7
Pollard Rd
  Bridgwater TA6.... **209** D6
  Weston-Super-Mare BS22.. **49** F8
Pollards Ct TA24.... **124** A3
Pollards Way TA1.... **212** E4
Polygon Rd BS8.... **226** A2
Polygon The 15 BS8.... **11** F6
Pomeroy La BA14.... **83** B6
Pomfrett Gdns BS14.... **23** E5
Pond Cl 5 BA8.... **190** A6
Pond Cotts BA3.... **80** D2
Pond Head BS20........ **4** D4
Pondhead Cross TA4.... **202** D4
Pond La TA21.... **179** D3
Pond Orch TA4.... **150** B8
Pondpool La TA3.... **170** C2
Pond Wlk DT10.... **190** B4
Ponsford Rd
  Bristol BS14.... **23** B8
  Minehead TA24.... **201** A4
Pookfield Cl BA11.... **143** B7
Poolbridge Rd BS28.... **107** C4
Pool Cl TA7.... **136** C4
Poole Hill TA22.... **163** B5
Poole Ho BA2.... **43** F5
Poolemead Rd BA2.... **43** F5
Pooles Cl TA5.... **134** A2
Pooles La TA20.... **194** E1
Poole St BS11........ **4** B8
Pooles Wharf BS8.... **226** A1
Pooles Wharf Ct BS8.... **226** A1
Pool Hill TA21.... **165** E1
Pool La BS40.... **38** A2
Poop Hill TA18.... **196** C8
Poop Hill La TA18.... **196** C8
Poor Hill TA18.... **59** F6
Poorhouse La DT6.... **199** E1
Pope's La
  Milborne Port DT9.... **217** D2
  Rockwell Green TA21.... **222** B4
Pope's Wlk BA2.... **45** B3
Pope Cl TA1.... **168** C1
Popery La TA24.... **129** E1
Popham Cl
  Bridgwater TA6.... **209** D5
  East Brent TA9.... **86** D5
Popham Flats TA21.... **222** D6
Pop La EX13, TA20.... **198** B8
Poplar Ave BS9.... **5** D6
Poplar Cl
  Bath BA2................ **44** D4
  Frome BA11.... **120** B7
Poplar Dr BA21.... **218** C7
Poplar Est TA9.... **104** D3
Poplar Farm BA5.... **111** A4
Poplar La
  Catcott TA7.... **137** D1
  Mark TA9.... **105** E3
Poplar Pl 16 BS23.... **48** E8
Poplar Rd
  Bath BA2................ **62** D8
  Bridgwater TA6.... **209** D7
  Bristol, Highridge BS13.... **21** F7
  Burnham-on-S TA8.... **104** A8
  Street BA16.... **207** C5
  Taunton TA1.... **213** D2
Poplars Cl BA21.... **187** A5
Poplars The
  Easton-in-G BS20........ **4** B4
  Porlock TA24.... **124** A3
  Weston-Super-Mare BS22.. **32** A1
Poplar Tree La BA14.... **83** C2
Poplar Wlk BS24.... **49** E5
Pople's La BA11.... **117** F8
Pople's Well TA18.... **224** B6
Poples Bow TA9.... **104** C5
Poppy Cl
  Weston-Super-Mare BS22.. **32** A5
  Yeovil BA22.... **218** B5
Porch EX13.... **198** A3
Porch Cl BA6.... **206** E3
Porchestall Dro BA6.... **206** B4
Porlock Cl
  3 Clevedon BS21........ **6** E1
  Weston-Super-Mare BS23.. **48** F2
Porlock Dr TA1.... **212** C1
Porlock Gdns BS48........ **8** E1
Porlock Hill TA24.... **123** F3
Porlock Rd
  Bath BA2................ **45** A1
  Minehead TA24.... **200** C2
Porlock Visitor Ctr★
  TA24.... **124** A3
Portal Rd BS24.... **50** D4
Portbury Comm BS20.... **2** E4
Portbury Gr BS11........ **4** D6
Portbury Hundred The
  BS20.... **3** C4
Portbury La BS20........ **9** E7
Portbury Way BS20.... **3** C4
Portbury Wlk BS11........ **4** D6
Portcullis Rd TA10.... **172** A6
Porter's Hatch BA6.... **138** D4
Portfield La TA10.... **171** F5
Portishead Bsns Pk BS20.. **2** E5
Portishead Lodge BS20.... **2** E6

Portishead Prim Sch
 Portishead BS20 . . . . 2 C5
 Portishead BS20 . . . . 2 E6
Portishead Rd BS22 . . . . . . 32 B4
Portishead Way BS3 . . . . . 11 E3
Port La TA22 . . . . 164 A5
Portland Cl
 Cannington TA5 . . . . 135 B2
 Nailsea BS48 . . . . 8 D1
Portland Ct BS1 . . . . 226 B1
Portland Dr BS20 . . . . .2 E4
Portland Grange 6 TA1. 212 E3
Portland Lofts 8 BS2 . . . . 227 B4
Portland Mans 9 BS2 . . . . 227 B4
Portland Pl
 Bath BA1 . . . . 228 B4
 Brent Knoll TA9 . . . . 86 B1
 Bridgwater TA6 . . . . 208 D5
 Frome BA11 . . . . 119 D5
Portland Rd
 Bath BA1 . . . . 228 B4
 Frome BA11 . . . . 119 D5
 Langport TA10 . . . . 172 B5
 Street BA16 . . . . 207 A4
Portland Sq BS2 . . . . 227 B4
Portland St
 Bristol, Clifton BS8 . . . . . . 11 F3
 Taunton TA1 . . . . 212 E4
Portland Terr
 Bath BA1 . . . . 228 B4
 Watchet TA23 . . . . 202 C7
Portman Cres 9 TA6. . . . . 153 F3
Portman Ct BA22 . . . . 196 E8
Portman Dr TA6 . . . . 153 E3
Portman Rd TA6 . . . . 153 E3
Portmans TA3 . . . . 170 B3
Portman St TA2. . . . . 212 F6
Portmeade Dro BS26 . . . . . 70 C1
Portmeirion Cl BS14 . . . . . . 23 B5
Portnell's La BA12 . . . . . . 161 F2
Portobello Bldgs TA20 . . . 223 B4
Portreeve Dr BA21 . . . . . . 219 B6
Port View BS20 . . . . 4 C5
Portview Rd BS11 . . . . .4 B8
Portwall Dro TA7 . . . . 209 F5
Portwall La BS1. . . . . 227 B1
Portwall La E 10 BS1 . . . . 227 B1
Portway
 Bristol, Shirehampton BS11 . 4 C6
 Bristol, Sneyd Park BS8. . . . 5 C3
 Frome BA11 . . . . 120 A4
 Holford TA5 . . . . 133 D4
 Street BA16 . . . . 207 D4
 Wells BA5 . . . . 203 C4
Port Way BA2. . . . . 100 D7
Portway Ave BA5 . . . . 203 D4
Portway Com Sch BS11 . . . .4 E7
Portway Hill
 Batcombe BA4 . . . . 142 C1
 Bruton BA4 . . . . 159 F6
Portway La
 Binegar BA3. . . . . 95 E1
 Holford TA5 . . . . 133 E4
Portway Lodge 1 BA5 . . 203 C4
Portway Rdbt BS11. . . . . . . 4 C8
Portway Villas BA11 . . . . . 120 A4
Positano Ct TA6 . . . . 208 E7
Poskitt Ho TA6 . . . . 208 F6
Post Cl TA21 . . . . 222 E4
Post La
 Malmsmead EX35 . . . . . . 122 C4
 Skilgate TA4 . . . . 164 E7
Post Office La
 Blagdon BS40 . . . . 54 D3
 Flax Bourton BS48 . . . . 19 F7
 Minehead TA24 . . . . 200 F7
 Tatworth TA20 . . . . 198 C8
Post Office Rd BS24 . . . . . . 50 C5
Post Office Yd DT8. . . . . . . 199 F7
Poston Way BA15 . . . . 64 E7
Pot La BA11 . . . . 120 F8
Potter's Cross TA4 . . . . . . 165 C2
Potters Ho 1 BA4 . . . . . . 205 B6
Potterton Cl TA6. . . . . 208 F1
Pottery Cl BS23 . . . . 49 A6
Pottery Rd TA19 . . . . 183 C1
Pottery View TA19 . . . . . . 183 C1
Pottle St BA12 . . . . 144 D3
Potts Cl BA1. . . . . 28 F3
Poulett Cotts TA17 . . . . . . 195 D7
Pound Cl
 Glastonbury BA6 . . . . 206 D5
 Stalbridge DT10 . . . . 190 B4
 Yeovil BA21 . . . . 218 C5
Pound Farm TA6 . . . . 208 D3
Poundfield Rd TA24 . . . . . 200 E6
Pound Fold BA5 . . . . 204 C7
Pound Hill TA21 . . . . 179 A5
Poundisford Cl TA1 . . . . . 212 D1
Pound La
 Bishops Lydeard TA4 . . . . 151 F1
 Buckland St Mary TA20 . . 193 A8
 Downhead BA4 . . . . 117 A1
 Easton BA5 . . . . 111 A4
 Lydford Fair Place TA11. . . 158 C3
 Martock TA12 . . . . 185 D6
 Nailsea BS48 . . . . 8 D3
 Oakhill BA3 . . . . 115 B5
 Rawridge EX14 . . . . 191 F1
 Yarcombe EX14 . . . . 192 E2
 Yarlington BA9. . . . . 175 F3
 Yeovil BA22 . . . . 218 A2
Pound Mead BS40 . . . . 37 C8
Pound Orch TA4 . . . . 151 C7
Pound Pool TA11 . . . . 211 C4
Pound Rd
 Axminster EX13 . . . . 198 F2
 Broadway TA19 . . . . 183 B2

Pound Rd continued
 Pawlett TA6 . . . . 135 F5
Poundsclose TA22 . . . . . . 163 E4
Pound Terr 3 TA21 . . . . . 222 D5
Pound The 36 D3
Pound Way TA10. . . . . 172 B3
Pounsell La TA10 . . . . 172 B5
Pow's Hill BA3. . . . . 78 D5
Pow's Orch BA3 . . . . 78 A1
Powell Cl TA3 . . . . 169 D4
Powell Ct BA5 . . . . 203 B4
Powells Acres BS21 . . . . . . .6 E3
Powis Cl BS22 . . . . 31 C2
Powlett Ct BA2 . . . . 45 B7
Powlett Rd BA2 . . . . 45 B8
Powy's Dr DT9 . . . . 225 C4
Powy's La DT9 . . . . 225 C4
Poyntz Rd BS4 . . . . 22 F8
Prankerds Rd DT9 . . . . . . 217 C2
Preachers Vale BA3 . . . . . 116 F7
Preanes Gn BS22 . . . . 32 A2
Precinct The BS20 . . . . 2 D5
Prescot Cl BS22. . . . . 31 B2
Prescott Rd EX15 . . . . 179 D1
Prestleigh La BA4. . . . . . . 141 E4
Prestleigh Rd BA4 . . . . . . 141 E2
Preston CE Prim Sch
 BA21. . . . . 218 C7
Preston Cross TA4 . . . . . . 150 E6
Preston Gr BA20 . . . . 218 F5
Preston La TA4 . . . . 150 E6
Preston Rd
 Yeovil BA20 . . . . 218 E5
 Yeovil, Houndstone BA22 . 218 B5
Preston Road Rdbt BA21 . 218 C5
Preston Sch BA21. . . . . . . 218 D5
Prestor 9 EX13. . . . . 198 A1
Pretwood Cl TA19. . . . . . . 221 C3
Prewett St BS1 . . . . 227 B1
Prey La TA3 . . . . 182 D7
Preywater Rd BA5 . . . . . . 139 D8
Prices Bldgs TA6 . . . . 209 A4
Priddles La TA20. . . . . 193 C8
Priddy Cl
 Bath BA2 . . . . 44 B5
 Frome BA11. . . . . 120 C7
Priddy Ct BS14 . . . . 23 B5
Priddy Dr BS14 . . . . 23 B5
Priddy Prim Sch BA5. . . . . 92 D3
Priddy Rd BA5 . . . . 112 E8
Priddy Veal La BA5. . . . . . 111 A5
Priest's Ho★ TA10 . . . . . . 172 A3
Priestlands DT9 . . . . 225 D5
Priestlands La DT9 . . . . . . 225 D5
Priestley Way TA8 . . . . . . 104 C5
Priest Row BA5 . . . . 203 D4
Priest St TA4 . . . . 202 C2
Priests Way BS22 . . . . 31 D2
Prigg La TA13 . . . . 220 C4
Primmerfield La BA3. . . . . . 94 C8
Primrose Hill
 Bath BA1 . . . . 27 D1
 Charlton Mackrell TA11 . . 173 F7
 East Coker BA22 . . . . 197 B7
 Nunney BA11 . . . . 143 B8
Primrose Hill Pk Homes
 TA11 . . . . 173 F7
Primrose La
 Midsomer Norton BA3. . . . . 78 B1
 Yeovil BA21 . . . . 187 D5
Prince's Bldgs 17 BS8 . . . 11 F6
Prince's Cl 11 TA14 . . . . 185 F4
Prince's Rd
 Clevedon BS21 . . . . 6 D3
 Shepton Mallet BA4 . . . . . 205 C6
 Street BA16 . . . . 207 B5
Prince's St
 Bristol BS2. . . . . 227 C4
 Clandown BA3 . . . . 78 E5
Prince Philip Cl TA20 . . . . 223 B3
Princes' La BS8. . . . . 11 F6
Princes Rd BA5 . . . . 203 D4
Princess Anne Rd BA20 . . 120 A7
Princess Cl
 Keynsham BS31. . . . . 24 E4
 12 North Petherton TA6 . . 153 F4
Princess Rd TA1 . . . . 212 D2
Princess Row BS2 . . . . 227 A4
Princess St TA8. . . . . 104 B7
Princes St
 Bath BA1 . . . . 228 B2
 Taunton TA1 . . . . 213 B4
 Yeovil BA20 . . . . 219 B5
Princess Victoria St BS8. . 11 F6
Prince St BS1. . . . . 227 A1
Prince Street Rdbt BS1. . . 227 A2
Printers Ct 32 TA12 . . . . . 185 E6
Prior's Wlk TA1 . . . . 212 F4
Prior Park Bldgs BA2 . . . . . 45 B5
Prior Park Coll BA2 . . . . . . 45 C2
Prior Park Cotts BA2. . . . . 228 C1
Prior Park Gdns BA2 . . . . . 45 B5
Prior Park Landscape Gdn★
 BA2. . . . . 45 C3
Prior Park Rd BA2 . . . . 45 B4
Priors Hill BA2. . . . . 60 A2
Priorswood Ind Est TA2 . . 213 B6
Priorswood Pl 8 TA2. . . . 213 A8
Priorswood Prim Sch
 TA2. . . . . 212 F6
Priorswood Rd TA2 . . . . . . 213 A6
Priory TA21. . . . . 222 E6
Priory Ave TA1. . . . . 213 A4
Priory Bridge Rd TA1 . . . . 213 A5
Priory Cl
 Bath BA2 . . . . 45 B2
 Cannington TA5 . . . . 135 C2

Priory Cl continued
 Castle Cary TA7. . . . . 214 B5
 Chilton Polden TA7. . . . . . 137 B2
 Ilchester BA22 . . . . 173 E1
 Midsomer Norton BA3 . . . . 78 A1
 Yeovil BA20 . . . . 218 D1
Priory Com Sch BS22 . . . . 32 B3
Priory Ct
 Bridgwater TA6 . . . . 208 F4
 9 Stoke sub Hamdon
 TA14 . . . . 185 F4
 5 Taunton TA1 . . . . 213 A4
 Wellington TA21. . . . . 222 E7
Priory Farm Trad Est BS20. 3 D3
Priory Fields TA1 . . . . 213 A5
Priorygate Ct BA7. . . . . . . 214 B6
Priory Gdns
 Bristol, Shirehampton BS11 . 4 D7
 Burnham-on-S TA8 . . . . . . 104 B6
 Easton-in-G BS20. . . . . 4 B4
 Wellington TA21. . . . . 222 E6
Priory Glade BA21 . . . . . . 218 C6
Priory Gn TA24 . . . . 201 E2
Priory Hill TA5. . . . . 134 C5
Priory Hospl BA5 . . . . 203 C3
Priory Mead BA10. . . . . . . 215 F8
Priory Mews BS23 . . . . 49 B7
Priory Path BA7 . . . . 214 C5
Priory Pl BA5 . . . . 203 D3
Priory Rd
 Bristol BS8. . . . . 226 C4
 Bristol, Shirehampton BS11 . 4 D6
 Chilton Polden TA7. . . . . . 137 B2
 Easton-in-G BS20. . . . . 4 B4
 Ilchester BA22 . . . . 173 E1
 Keynsham BS31. . . . . 24 E7
 Portbury BS20. . . . . 3 D1
 Wells BA5 . . . . 203 D3
 Weston-Super-Mare BS23 . 49 A7
Priory Sch The TA2. . . . . . 213 B7
Priory View BA7 . . . . 214 B6
Priory Villas BA9. . . . . 216 C3
Priory Way TA1 . . . . 213 B5
Priory Way Ind Est TA1 . . 213 B5
Priory Wlk
 Portbury BS20. . . . . 3 D3
 Taunton TA1 . . . . 213 A5
Priston Cl BS22 . . . . 32 B5
Priston La BA2, BA3 . . . . . . 61 A5
Priston Rd BA2 . . . . 61 D6
Pritchard St BS2 . . . . 227 B4
Private Rd
 North Brewham BA11 . . . . 161 E2
 Staplegrove TA2 . . . . 212 B7
Privet Dr BS13 . . . . 22 C5
Proctor Ho BS1. . . . . 227 B1
Prophet's La TA14 . . . . . . 185 E3
Prospect Cl
 East Brent TA9. . . . . 86 E5
 Shepton Mallet BA4 . . . . . 205 A6
Prospect Gdns BA1 . . . . . . 28 F5
Prospect Ho BS22 . . . . 31 E3
Prospect Pl
 Bath, Beacon Hill BA1 . . . . 28 A1
 Bathford BA1 . . . . 29 D2
 Bath, Weston BA1 . . . . 27 C2
 9 Weston-Super-Mare
 BS23 . . . . 48 E8
Prospect Rd BA2. . . . . 45 C4
Prospect Row TA18 . . . . . 224 F3
Prospect Terr TA1 . . . . . . 212 F5
Prospect Villas BA4 . . . . . 159 C7
Protheroes Ho BS1 . . . . . . 226 C2
Proud Cross BS40. . . . . 74 E4
Providence La BS41. . . . . . . 10 F2
Providence Pl
 Bristol BS2. . . . . 227 C4
 Bruton BA10 . . . . 215 D6
Providence Rise BS41. . . . . 10 F2
Providence View BS41 . . . . 11 A1
Provident Pl TA6. . . . . 208 E5
Prowle's Cross BA22 . . . . 197 F5
Prowse's La BS26 . . . . 70 A1
Prowse La TA9. . . . . 106 C7
Prowses Mdw TA2 . . . . . . 168 B4
Publow La BS39 . . . . 40 E5
Pud Brook DT9 . . . . 217 D1
Pudding Pie Cl BS40 . . . . . 53 A5
Pudding Pie La BS40 . . . . . 53 A6
Puddle Town TA18 . . . . . . 196 B5
Puddy's La TA9 . . . . 105 D4
Pudleigh La TA20 . . . . 223 B8
Puffin Cl
 Minehead TA24 . . . . 201 C5
 Weston-Super-Mare BS22. . 49 F8
Pullen Ct BA4. . . . . 205 B4
Pulmans La TA18 . . . . 224 C5
Pulpitsway Dro TA12 . . . . 185 A8
Pulteney Ave BA2 . . . . 45 B6
Pulteney Bridge BA2 . . . . 228 C2
Pulteney Gdns BA2 . . . . . . 45 B6
Pulteney Gr BA2 . . . . 45 B6
Pulteney Mews BA2 . . . . . . 45 B7
Pulteney Rd BA2 . . . . 45 B6
Pulteney Terr BA2 . . . . 45 B6
Pump La
 Bathford BA1. . . . . 29 B2
 Bristol BS1. . . . . 227 B1
 Redhill BS40 . . . . 36 D2
Pump Sq BS20 . . . . 4 D5
Punnet Cl BS27 . . . . 90 B7
Puppy Cross Ways BA3. . . . 94 F5
Puppy La BA3 . . . . 94 F5
Purcell Wlk BS4 . . . . 22 C7
Purdue Cl BS22. . . . . 32 B3
Purewell TA7 . . . . 136 C4
Puriton Hill TA7 . . . . 136 C3
Puriton Manor TA7 . . . . . . 136 C4

Puriton Pk TA7 . . . . 136 C4
Puriton Prim Sch TA7. . . . 136 C4
Puriton Rd
 Pawlett TA6 . . . . 136 A5
 West Huntspill TA9 . . . . . . 136 B7
Purlewent Dr BA1. . . . . 27 C1
Purley Dr TA6 . . . . 209 D6
Purn La BS24 . . . . 67 A8
Purn Rd BS24 . . . . 66 F8
Purn Way BS24 . . . . 67 B7
Purse Caundle Manor Ho★
 DT9. . . . . 189 D4
Pursey Ave BA16. . . . . 207 E5
Purving Row BS24 . . . . 67 C1
Purving Row La BS24 . . . . . 67 C1
Putham La TA24 . . . . 129 C1
Putsham Hill TA5 . . . . 133 D5
Putsham Mead TA5 . . . . . 133 D5
Putt's La DT9 . . . . 188 C3
Puttingthorpe Dr BS22 . . . 49 C7
Putts La DT9 . . . . 175 D1
Puxley Cl BS14. . . . . 23 E6
Puxton La BS24 . . . . 33 D3
Puxton Moor La BS24 . . . . 33 E2
Puxton Rd BS24 . . . . 33 C2
Pyde La TA10 . . . . 184 D6
Pye Cnr
 Churchill BS25 . . . . 52 D4
 Merriott TA16. . . . . 195 F6
 Somerton TA11 . . . . 211 D4
Pye La TA20 . . . . 198 E8
Pyleigh La TA4 . . . . 151 A1
Pyle La BA22 . . . . 174 A2
Pyles Thorne TA21 . . . . . . 222 F4
Pyles Thorne Cl TA21 . . . 222 E4
Pyles Thorne Rd TA21 . . . 222 E4
Pylewell La BS25. . . . . 52 D1
Pyle Well La TA11 . . . . 174 E8
Pylle Hill BA4 . . . . 141 A1
Pylle La BA4 . . . . 141 B1
Pylle Rd BA4 . . . . 141 A2
Pyncombe La TA4. . . . . . . 210 B3
Pyne Point BS21 . . . . 6 C3
Pynne Cl BS14 . . . . 23 F5
Pynne Rd BS14 . . . . 23 F5
Pyracantha Wlk BS14 . . . . 23 A6
Pyrland Ave TA2 . . . . 212 F8
Pyrland Pl TA2. . . . . 213 A8
Pyrland Wlk TA6 . . . . 208 B8

Q

Quab La
 Alston Sutton BS26 . . . . . . 88 F3
 Wedmore BS28 . . . . 108 A3
Quab Lane Cl BS28. . . . . . 108 B4
Quaish La BA4 . . . . 140 C4
Quaker's La TA4 . . . . 210 C3
Quakers' Friars BS1. . . . . . 227 B3
Quakinghouse La TA4. . . . 166 E5
Quantick Gdns TA24 . . . . 201 B5
Quantock Ave TA6 . . . . . . 208 D4
Quantock Cl
 Burnham-on-S TA8 . . . . . . 104 C5
 North Petherton TA6 . . . . 153 E4
Quantock Ct
 Burnham-on-S TA8 . . . . . . 104 A5
 Ilminster TA19 . . . . 221 C4
 Street BA16 . . . . 207 B5
 Williton TA4 . . . . 202 D2
Quantock Gr TA4 . . . . 202 E2
Quantock Ho TA6 . . . . 153 E4
Quantock Mdw TA6 . . . . . 208 C5
Quantock Par TA6 . . . . . . 153 E4
Quantock Rd
 Bridgwater TA5, TA6 . . . . 208 B5
 Cannington TA5 . . . . 135 C1
 Portishead BS20 . . . . 2 B5
 Taunton TA2 . . . . 212 E8
 Watchet TA23. . . . . 202 C6
 Wellington TA21. . . . . 222 D7
 Weston-Super-Mare BS23 . 48 E4
Quantock Rise
 Kingston St Mary TA2 . . . . 168 E8
 Pawlett TA6 . . . . 135 F5
Quantocks BA2 . . . . 45 A1
Quantock Terr TA6. . . . . . 209 A6
Quantock View
 Bishops Lydeard TA4 . . . . 167 F8
 Highbridge TA9 . . . . 104 D3
 Kilve TA5 . . . . 133 C6
Quantock Way
 Bridgwater TA6 . . . . 208 C5
 Kingston St Mary TA2 . . . . 168 D8
Quaperlake St BA10. . . . . 215 F7
Quarme La TA24 . . . . 147 E2
Quarr BA4. . . . . 205 C6
Quarr Cross SP8 . . . . 177 E4
Quarr Dr DT9 . . . . 225 D6
Quarr La DT9 . . . . 225 D6
Quarr Lane Pk DT9 . . . . . . 225 D6
Quarry Batch
 Street BA16 . . . . 207 A5
 Walton BA16 . . . . 156 E7
Quarry Cl
 Bath BA2 . . . . 44 F1
 Limpley Stoke BA3. . . . . . . 64 D6
 Minehead TA24 . . . . 201 B5
Quarry Cotts BA22 . . . . . . 197 F8
Quarry Hay BS40 . . . . 56 D8
Quarry Hill BA22 . . . . 175 F4
Quarry La
 Blagdon Hill TA3. . . . . 181 D4
 Bradford Abbas DT9 . . . . 187 E1
 Butleigh BA6 . . . . 157 D3
 Combe St Nicholas TA20 . 193 D6
 Kingston St Mary TA2 . . . . 168 F7

Quarrylands La BS26 . . . . . 88 B4
Quarrymans Ct BA2 . . . . . 45 B1
Quarry Rd
 Bath BA2 . . . . 45 D6
 Kingsdon TA11 . . . . 173 D5
 Portishead BS20 . . . . 2 C4
 Sandford BS25 . . . . 52 A2
 Street BA16 . . . . 207 B4
 Washford TA23 . . . . 131 F4
Quarry Rise BS24 . . . . 66 F8
Quarry Rock Gdns BA2 . . . 45 D4
Quarry Vale Cotts BA2 . . . 45 B1
Quarry Way BS48 . . . . 8 D2
Quartley Hill EX16 . . . . . . 164 E4
Quay La TA24 . . . . 201 A8
Quays Ave BS20. . . . . .2 E5
Quayside TA6 . . . . 208 F5
Quay St
 Bristol BS1. . . . . 227 A3
 Minehead TA24 . . . . 201 A8
Quays The BS1 . . . . 226 C1
Quay W TA24 . . . . 125 C1
Quebec BA2 . . . . 44 A6
Queen's Ave
 Bristol BS8. . . . . 226 B3
 Portishead BS20 . . . . 2 C5
Queen's Coll TA1. . . . . 212 D1
Queen's Coll Jun Sch
 TA1. . . . . 212 D1
Queen's Ct BS8 . . . . 226 B3
Queen's Down TA3. . . . . . 169 C4
Queen's Dr BA2 . . . . 45 A2
Queen's Par BA1 . . . . 228 B3
Queen's Rd
 Bridgwater TA6 . . . . 208 F2
 Bristol, Bishopsworth BS13,
 BS41. . . . . 21 F4
 Bristol BS8. . . . . 226 B3
 Clevedon BS21 . . . . 6 D3
 Evercreech BA4. . . . . 141 E2
 Radstock BA3 . . . . 79 B2
 Shepton Mallet BA4. . . . . 205 A5
 Weston-Super-Mare BS23 . 30 D1
Queen's Terr
 Sherborne DT9 . . . . 225 D6
 Wiveliscombe TA4 . . . . . . 210 C4
Queen's Way BS22 . . . . 31 F4
Queen Anne Ct TA6 . . . . . 209 A5
Queen Charlotte St BS1 . . 227 A2
Queen Charlton La BS14. . 23 C1
Queen Elizabeth's Hospital
 Sch BS8. . . . . 226 B3
Queen Elizabeth Ct
 Bridgwater TA6 . . . . 209 A5
 Street BA16 . . . . 207 C6
Queen Quay BS1 . . . . 227 A2
Queens Cl TA20. . . . . 223 B2
Queenscote BS20 . . . . .2 F5
Queens Cres TA14 . . . . . . 185 F5
Queens Dr TA1 . . . . 168 D1
Queens Gate BS9 . . . . 5 D5
Queens Gate Terr TA1 . . . 213 A4
Queens Gr BA9 . . . . 161 E2
Queens Par BS1 . . . . 226 C2
Queens Pl BA2. . . . . 45 B5
Queen Sq
 Bath BA1 . . . . 228 B2
 Bristol BS1. . . . . 227 A2
 North Curry TA3 . . . . 170 B4
 Saltford BS31 . . . . 25 F3
Queen Square Ave 10
 BS1 . . . . 227 A2
Queen Square Pl BA1 . . . . 228 B3
Queens Rd
 Banwell BS29. . . . . 51 A3
 Bradford Abbas DT9 . . . . 187 E1
 Frome BA11. . . . . 119 D4
 Keynsham BS31. . . . . 24 D4
 Minehead TA24 . . . . 201 A6
 Nailsea BS48 . . . . 8 D1
 Portishead BS20 . . . . 1 E4
 Somerton TA11 . . . . 211 D4
 Street BA16 . . . . 207 B5
 Wellington TA21. . . . . 222 E4
Queens Row BS27 . . . . 90 C8
Queens Sq TA9 . . . . 104 C4
Queen St
 Bath BA1 . . . . 228 B2
 Bridgwater TA6 . . . . 208 F5
 Bristol BS2. . . . . 227 B3
 Keinton Mandeville TA11 . 158 A1
 North Petherton TA6 . . . . 153 F4
 Taunton TA1 . . . . 213 B4
 Tintinhull BA22 . . . . 186 B7
 11 Wells BA5. . . . . 203 D4
 Yarlington BA9. . . . . 175 F8
Queens Terr TA1 . . . . 213 A3
Queensway
 Taunton TA1 . . . . 212 B1
 Yeovil BA20 . . . . 219 A4
Queens Way BS20. . . . . . . .1 E4
Queensway Cl TA9. . . . . . . 106 E5
Queensway Pl BA20 . . . . . 219 A4
Queensway Ctr BS22. . . . . 32 B2
Queenswood Rd TA6 . . . . 208 C4
Queenwood Ave BA1 . . . . . 28 A1
Quicksilver Rdbt BA20. . . 218 F2
Quickthorn Cl BS14 . . . . . . 23 A6
Quiet St BA1. . . . . 228 B2
Quilter Gr BS4 . . . . 22 D7
Quirke St TA24. . . . . 200 F7

R

Raby Mews BA2. . . . . **45** B7
Raby Pl BA2 . . . . **45** B7
Rackclose Gdns TA20 . . . **223** A4
Rackclose Ho TA20 . . . . . **223** A4
Rackclose Pk TA20. . . . . . **223** B4
Rackfield TA21 . . . . **222** A5
Rackfield Pl BA2. . . . . **44** B6
Rackhay BS1 . . . . **227** A2
Rackley La
 Buckland St Mary TA20 . . **182** B1
 Compton Bishop BS26 . . . **69** B2
Rackstile TA20. . . . . **223** A4
Rackvernal Cl BA3 . . . . **78** B1
Rackvernal Rd BA3. . . . . . . **78** B1
Raddon Cl BA4. . . . . **205** B6
Radford Hill
 Camerton BA2, BA3. . . . . **78** C1
 Timsbury BA2 . . . . **60** C1
Radigan La TA3, TA19 . . . **183** C5
Radlet Cl TA2. . . . . **213** B7
Radnidge La EX16. . . . . . . **162** D4
Radstock & District Mus★
 BA3. . . . . **78** F2
Radstock Rd BA3 . . . . **78** C2
Ragged Dro BA6. . . . . **158** A7
Rag Hill BA3. . . . . **79** D5
Rag La
 Babcary BA22 . . . . **174** B6
 Yarcombe EX14 . . . . **192** D2
Raglan's Cross TA4 . . . . . **202** F2
Raglan Cl
 Bridgwater TA6 . . . . **209** D7
 Chilcompton BA3 . . . . **96** C4
Raglan Ct ◳ TA2 . . . . **212** F6
Ragland La BA1. . . . . **28** A2
Ragland St BA1 . . . . **28** A2
Raglan La BS40. . . . . **37** E7
Raglan Pl ◲ BS23. . . . . . . **30** C1
Raglan Terr
 Bath BA1 . . . . **28** A2
 Yeovil BA21 . . . . **218** F7
Railford Hill BA11. . . . . . . **118** B3
Railway Arches BS2. . . . . **227** C2
Railway Cotts BA11 . . . . . **143** C8
Railway La BA2 . . . . **62** D1
Railway Pl BA1 . . . . **228** C1
Railway St
 Bath BA1 . . . . **228** C1
 Taunton TA2 . . . . **212** F6
Railway Terr BA2 . . . . **79** E4
Railway View Pl BA3 . . . . **78** B2
Rainbow La TA3 . . . . **191** C7
Rainham Ct ◲ BS23. . . . . . **30** C1
Rains Batch BS40 . . . . **72** E6
Raisey La TA20 . . . . **193** C7
Raleigh Cl
 Bridgwater TA6 . . . . **209** C5
 Saltford BS31 . . . . **25** D2
Raleigh Ct
 Sherborne DT9 . . . . **225** E4
 ◳ Weston-Super-Mare
 BS23. . . . . **48** E5
Raleigh Ho TA10 . . . . **209** C5
Raleigh Rd DT10 . . . . **190** B4
Raleigh Rise BS20. . . . .**2** B5
Raleigh Pl DT9. . . . . **225** D2
Ralph Allen Dr BA2 . . . . . **45** B3
Ralph Allen Sch BA2 . . . . **45** E2
Ralston Ct BA9 . . . . **216** C4
Rambler Way TA6. . . . . . . **208** E6
Ramon Ave TA23 . . . . **202** D7
Ramsay Cl BS22. . . . . **31** E4
Ramsay Way TA8 . . . . **104** C8
Ramscombe Forest Wlks★
 TA5. . . . . **151** E8
Ramscombe La BA1. . . . . . **28** F6
Ramsey La TA21 . . . . **179** F8
Ramshorn Cl TA1 . . . . **212** C2
Ramshorn Gn TA1 . . . . . . **212** D2
Ramshorn Pl TA1 . . . . **212** D3
Ranchways BS20. . . . .**1** F4
Randall Rd BS8 . . . . **226** B2
Randolph Ave BS13 . . . . . **22** B5
Randolph Cl BS13. . . . . . . **22** B5
Randolph Rd BA11 . . . . . . **119** F4
Ranger Rd BA6 . . . . **206** C3
Rangoon Rd TA23 . . . . . . **202** E6
Rankers La BS39 . . . . **41** C5
Rank The
 Coxley BA5. . . . . **139** F6
 Maiden Bradley BA12 . . . **144** C2
 Vobster BA3. . . . . **117** D6
Ranscombe Ave BS22 . . . . **31** D2
Ransford BS21. . . . .**6** B1
Raphael Ct BS1 . . . . **227** B1
Raps Cl TA1 . . . . **213** E5
Raps Gn TA1. . . . . **213** E5
Rashwood La BA11. . . . . . **118** B6
Ratleigh La DT9. . . . . **188** A3
Rattigan Cl TA8. . . . . **104** C6
Rattle Row TA24 . . . . **131** B4
Raven Cl BS22 . . . . **31** E1
Raven Ct BS9 . . . .**5** F8
Ravenhead Dr BS14. . . . . . **23** B8
Ravensmead TA20 . . . . . . **223** C6
Ravenswood Special Sch
 BS48 . . . .**8** D3
Ravensworth Terr TA8 . . **104** B7
Rawle's Bldgs TA24 . . . . **124** A3
Rawlings La BS26 . . . . **88** E2

Rawlins Ave BS22 . . . . **32** A5
Rayens Cl BS41 . . . . **10** F1
Rayens Cross Rd BS41. . . . **10** F1
Rayleigh Rd BS9 . . . .**5** E7
Raymar Flats TA19 . . . . . **221** A4
Raymond St TA2 . . . . **212** E6
Raymore Rise BS41. . . . . . **10** F1
Read Mead BA6. . . . . **206** E3
Reakes Cl BA5. . . . . **203** C4
Rebels Way BA4. . . . . **206** D5
Reckleford BA20, BA21 . . **219** B5
Reckleford Inf Sch BA21 **219** C5
Rector's Cl TA8 . . . . **65** F3
Rector's Way BS23 . . . . . . **48** F6
Rectory Cl
 Farmborough BA2 . . . . . . **60** A6
 ◳ North Petherton TA6 . . **153** F3
 Staplegrove TA2. . . . . . . **212** C8
 Wraxall BS48. . . . .**9** A2
Rectory Ct TA20 . . . . **193** D6
Rectory Dr
 Burnham-on-S TA8 . . . . . **104** B8
 Staplegrove TA2. . . . . . . **212** C7
 Yatton BS49 . . . . **34** C7
Rectory Farm Cl BA22 . . **174** F3
Rectory Gdns TA20 . . . . . **193** D6
Rectory Hill
 Chapel Allerton BS26. . . . **88** D2
 Pitney TA10 . . . . **172** C7
 South Cadbury BA22 . . . **175** C3
Rectory La
 Bleadon BS24 . . . . **67** C6
 Compton Martin BS40 . . . **74** B6
 Hardington Mandeville
 BA22. . . . . **197** A6
 Horsington BA8 . . . . **176** E2
 Norton Sub Hamdon TA14 **185** F2
 Shalford BA9 . . . . **216** E6
 Sparkford BA22 . . . . **175** A3
 Timsbury BA2 . . . . **60** B2
Rectory Lawn TA8 . . . . . . **104** B8
Rectory Pl TA8. . . . . **104** C8
Rectory Rd
 Ashbrittle TA21 . . . . **178** F8
 Burnham-on-S TA8 . . . . . **104** B8
 Easton-in-G BS20. . . . .**4** B3
 Norton Fitzwarren TA2 . . **168** B5
 Shepton Mallet BA4. . . . **205** B6
 Stapegrove TA2. . . . . . . **212** C8
Rectory Way
 Lympsham BS24 . . . . **66** F2
 Yatton BS49. . . . . **34** C7
Recurium Lodge BS26. . . . **70** B2
Redacre BS40. . . . . **36** D3
Red Barn La TA20 . . . . . . **193** D4
Redcliff Backs BS1. . . . . . **227** B2
Redcliffe Cl BS20 . . . .**1** E3
Redcliffe Par E BS1. . . . . **227** A1
Redcliffe Par W BS1. . . . . **227** A1
Redcliffe Way BS1 . . . . . . **227** B1
Redcliff Hill BS1 . . . . **227** B1
Redcliff Mead La BS1. . . . **227** B1
Redcliff St BS1 . . . . **227** B2
Red Cotts
 Blagdon BS40 . . . . **54** D6
 Corsley Heath BA12 . . . . **144** E8
Redcroft BS40 . . . . **36** D3
Redcross Mews ◳ BS2. . . **227** C3
Redcross St BS2 . . . . **227** C3
Redding Pit La BS40 . . . . . **37** E4
Reddings The BS40 . . . . . . **74** B7
Redfield Gr BA3 . . . . **97** A8
Redfield Rd BA3. . . . . **97** A8
Redford Cres BS13 . . . . . . **21** F3
Redford Wlk BS13 . . . . . . **21** F3
Redgate Pk TA18. . . . . . . **224** C8
Redgates Rd TA24 . . . . . . **200** E7
Redgate St TA6. . . . . **209** B4
Red Hill
 Peasedown St John BA2. . **60** E1
 Redhill BS40 . . . . **36** D2
 West Monkton TA2. . . . . **169** B7
Redhill La BA1. . . . . **95** A2
Red Hill La TA7 . . . . **155** E7
Redhole La DT9 . . . . **225** D8
Red House La BS9 . . . .**5** E6
Red House Rd TA9 . . . . . . **86** D5
Red La
 Churchinford TA3 . . . . . . **191** F7
 Hemyock EX15. . . . . **180** E3
 Seaborough DT8 . . . . . . **195** E1
 Staplehay TA3 . . . . **181** E8
Redlake Dr TA1. . . . . **213** D3
Redland Ave BS20. . . . .**3** F6
Redland La TA3. . . . . **183** C8
Redland Pk BA2 . . . . **43** F6
Redlands La TA7 . . . . **137** C2
Redlands Terr BA3. . . . . . . **96** F8
Redland Terr BA11 . . . . . . **119** F3
Red Lion Ct
 ◳ Crewkerne TA18. . . . . **224** C6
 Somerton TA11 . . . . **211** E4
Red Lodge Bsns Pk BS24. **32** D1
Redlynch Cross BA10. . . . **160** E4
Redlynch La BS31. . . . . **24** D2
Redmans Hill BS28. . . . . . **107** E4
Redpoll Dr BS20 . . . .**3** A6
Red Post
 Chard TA20. . . . . **193** D3
 Isle Abbotts TA3 . . . . . . **183** E7
 Porlock TA24 . . . . **124** B3
Red Post Cross TA11 . . . **173** D4
Red Post Ct BA2 . . . . **79** B7
Red Rd
 Berrow TA8 . . . . **85** A7
 Brean TA8 . . . . **66** A2

Redshard La BS40. . . . . . . **53** B7
Redstart Prim Sch The
 TA20. . . . . **223** C5
Redstart Rd TA20 . . . . . . **223** C6
Redway TA24 . . . . **124** A3
Red Way The BA12 . . . . . **144** F6
Redwing Dr BS22 . . . . **31** F1
Red Wing Rd DT9 . . . . . . **217** C2
Redwood Cl
 Nailsea BS48. . . . .**9** A2
 Radstock BA3 . . . . **97** E8
Redwood Ho BS13 . . . . **22** D3
Redwood La BS48. . . . . **20** C7
Redwood Rd BA21 . . . . . . **219** E8
Reed Cl
 Bridgwater TA6 . . . . **208** F2
 Chard TA20. . . . . **223** D6
 Watchet TA23. . . . . **202** D6
Reedley Rd BS9. . . . .**5** F5
Reedmoor Gdns TA6 . . . . **208** E7
Reeds Dr TA7. . . . . **136** F4
Reed Way BS22 . . . . **32** C3
Rees Way BS2. . . . . **87** E7
Reeves Cl BS27 . . . . **90** F2
Regal Rd BA4. . . . . **205** B6
Regal Way ◲ BA4. . . . . . **205** B6
Regency Cl TA8. . . . . **85** A2
Regency Ct BS5. . . . . **203** C4
Regency Wlk BA11. . . . . . **119** E4
Regent Cl BA22 . . . . **173** E2
Regent Gn TA4. . . . . **167** F1
Regent Mews TA20. . . . . **223** C3
Regent St
 Bradford On Tone TA4 . . **167** F1
 Bristol BS8. . . . . **226** A2
 Burnham-on-S TA8 . . . . . **104** A7
 Weston-Super-Mare BS23 . **48** E7
Regents The
 Cotford St Luke TA4 . . . . **167** E6
 Keynsham BS31. . . . . **24** E6
 ◳ Yeovil BA21. . . . . **218** C6
Regents Way TA24 . . . . . **200** E6
Regent Way TA6 . . . . **209** A2
Regil La BS40. . . . . **38** A6
Regil Rd BS40 . . . . **37** F3
Regina The BA1. . . . . **228** B3
Reid Ct BA5 . . . . **203** B4
Remalard Ct BA7 . . . . **214** B5
Rendcomb Cl BS22. . . . . . . **31** B2
Rennison Ct BS23. . . . . **48** E4
Reservoir La BA5 . . . . **203** C6
Retford Ho BA2. . . . . **45** E5
Retreat Cvn Pk The TA8 . . **85** A2
Retreat The
 Foxcote BA3. . . . . **79** E3
 Frome BA11. . . . . **120** B4
 Taunton TA2. . . . . **168** F6
 Weston-Super-Mare BS23 . **30** C1
Reubens Ct BS22. . . . . **31** F3
Rex's La
 Barwick BA22 . . . . **197** F8
 Yeovil BA22 . . . . **219** C1
Rex Rd BA22 . . . . **186** C2
Rexton La TA4 . . . . **150** F5
Reynald's Way
 Butleigh BA6 . . . . **157** C4
 Street BA16. . . . . **207** D1
Reynolds Cl BS31 . . . . **25** A5
Rhode Cl BS31 . . . . **25** A3
Rhode La TA6. . . . . **208** E2
Rhodes Cl TA2 . . . . **212** C7
Rhodyate BS40 . . . . **54** D2
Rhodyate Hill BS49. . . . . . **34** F6
Rhodyate La BS49. . . . . . . **35** A7
Rhodyate The BS29 . . . . . . **51** C1
Rhydderch Way TA18 . . . **224** C5
Rhyll Gate Cross TA22. . . **162** F2
Rhyne Terr BS23 . . . . **48** D2
Rhyne View BS48. . . . .**8** B1
Rich's Farmhouse Cider
 Farm★ TA9. . . . . **105** D3
Richard Beadon Cl TA4. . **210** B4
Richard Huish Coll TA1. . **213** A2
Richards Cl
 Wellington TA21 . . . . . . **222** C8
 Weston-Super-Mare BS22. . **32** A4
Richards Cres TA2 . . . . . . **169** B6
Richmond Cl
 Bath BA1 . . . . **27** F1
 Bridgwater TA6 . . . . **208** F2
 Keynsham BS31. . . . . **24** D4
 Minehead TA24 . . . . **200** E6
 Portishead BS20. . . . . **2** E5
 Sampford Peverell EX16. . **178** D1
 Sherborne DT9 . . . . **225** C3
Richmond Ct BA22 . . . . . **173** E2
Richmond Gn
 Nailsea BS48. . . . .**8** F1
 Sherborne DT9 . . . . **225** C4
 Taunton TA1. . . . . **212** D5
Richmond Hill
 Bath BA1 . . . . **27** F1
 Bristol BS8. . . . . **226** B3
Richmond Ho
 Crewkerne TA18 . . . . **224** C6
 ◳ Shepton Mallet BA4. . **205** B6
 Yeovil BA20 . . . . **219** A4
Richmond Hts
 Bath BA1 . . . . **27** F1
 Bristol BS8. . . . . **226** B3
Richmond La
 Bath BA1 . . . . **27** F1
 Bristol BS8. . . . . **226** B3
Richmond Mews BS8. . . . **226** B3
Richmond Park Rd BS8. . . **226** A3
Richmond Pk TA1. . . . . . . **212** C4

Richmond Pl BA1 . . . . **27** F1
Richmond Rd
 Bath BA1 . . . . **27** F1
 ◲ Frome BA11. . . . . **119** E4
 Sherborne DT9 . . . . **225** C3
 Taunton TA1. . . . . **212** D5
 Yeovil BA21 . . . . **219** A4
Richmond St BS23 . . . . . . **48** D7
Richmond Terr BS8. . . . . . **226** A3
Richmond Villas BA6. . . . **206** E4
Ricketts La BS22 . . . . **32** A2
Rickford La BS40 . . . . **54** A3
Rickford Rd BS48 . . . .**8** F1
Rickford Rise BS40. . . . . . . **54** A3
Rickhayes BA9. . . . . **216** B4
Rickhay Rise TA18 . . . . . . **196** B8
Ricklands The BS40. . . . . . **38** A6
Ricksey Cl TA11 . . . . **211** B3
Ricksey La TA11 . . . . **211** B3
Ricksmead Dro TA7 . . . . **155** B2
Rickyard Rd BS40. . . . . **35** E2
Ridge Cl BS20 . . . .**2** A4
Ridge Cres BS40 . . . . **74** E6
Ridge Green Cl BA2 . . . . . . **62** D8
Ridge Highway TA4 . . . . . **166** A3
Ridge Hill TA4 . . . . **210** D5
Ridge La
 Corton Denham DT9 . . . . **175** D1
 East Chinnock BA22 . . . . **196** F8
 East Coker BA22 . . . . . . **197** A7
 Pitcombe BA7, BA10 . . . . **215** A2
 Ridge BS40 . . . . **74** D5
 Shepton Mallet BA4. . . . **205** B3
Ridgemead BA20. . . . . . . **218** D2
Ridgemeade BS14 . . . . **23** B4
Ridgemount Gdns BS14 . . **23** B5
Ridge Rd
 Croscombe BA4, BA5. . . . **204** D5
 West Anstey TA22 . . . . . **162** D7
Ridge The
 Bristol BS11. . . . .**4** E7
 Porlock TA24 . . . . **124** A3
 Poyntington DT9 . . . . . . **188** F7
 Yatton BS49 . . . . **34** B8
Ridgeview BS41. . . . . **11** B2
Ridgeview Ho BS20 . . . .**2** E3
Ridgeway
 Ashcott TA7 . . . . **156** B8
 Nailsea BS48. . . . .**8** C1
 Nunney BA11 . . . . **143** C8
 Sherborne DT9 . . . . **225** B3
Ridgeway Ave BS23 . . . . . **48** E6
Ridgeway Cl BS40. . . . . . . **74** E6
Ridgeway Ct BS14. . . . . . . **23** C5
Ridgeway Gdns
 Bristol BS14 . . . . **23** C5
 Glastonbury BA6 . . . . . . **206** F5
Ridgeway La
 Bristol BS14. . . . . **23** B5
 Moorlinch TA7 . . . . **155** F7
 North Cadbury BA22 . . . . **175** D6
 Nunney BA11. . . . . **143** C8
 Shillingford EX16 . . . . . . **164** D3
 Stolford TA5. . . . . **134** E8
Ridgeway Rd BS41 . . . . . . **11** A2
Ridgeway The BS22 . . . . . . **31** B2
Ridgewood BS9. . . . .**5** D3
Ridgewood Cross EX15. . **191** B8
Ridgewood La EX15 . . . . **191** A8
Ridgway TA18 . . . . **196** B8
Ridgway Cross EX36 . . . . **145** K1
Ridings The BS13 . . . . **21** E4
Ridley Cnr TA10. . . . . **171** C5
Ridley Hill TA10 . . . . **171** E8
Riec-Sur-Belon Way
 TA19 . . . . **221** A4
Rigg La DT9 . . . . **187** B5
Rigg Lane Cotts DT9 . . . . **187** F5
Riggles Cross EX14 . . . . . **191** B3
Rimpton Hill BA22 . . . . . **188** A7
Rimpton Rd BA22 . . . . . . **174** F1
Ringdown La EX15 . . . . . **180** F2
Ringolds Way BA16. . . . . **207** B4
Ringspit La BS14, BS39. . . . **40** E8
Ring St DT10 . . . . **190** B4
Ringstone TA9 . . . . **136** B8
Ringswell Gdns BA1. . . . . . **28** B1
Ringwell BA2. . . . . **81** E4
Ringwell Hill BA12 . . . . . **185** D4
Ringwell La BA2 . . . . **81** E4
Ringwood Gr BS23 . . . . . . **31** A1
Ringwood Rd
 Bath BA2 . . . . **44** C5
 Bridgwater TA6 . . . . **209** A2
Riphay Cross TA22 . . . . . **163** E3
Rippleside BS20 . . . .**2** C5
Rippleside Rd BS21 . . . .**6** E5
Ripple The BS21 . . . .**8** D4
Risdale Rd BS3 . . . . **11** F1
Risdon Rd TA23. . . . . **202** C6
Risedale Cl TA6. . . . . **208** C5
Risedale Rd BS25 . . . . **70** A8
Risemoor Rd TA6 . . . . . . **208** E2
Ritchie Rd BA22 . . . . **218** A5
Rivendell BS22 . . . . **32** A4
Riverbed Ho TA9. . . . . . . **104** D3
River Dro TA7 . . . . **155** C4
River La TA1 . . . . **209** E1
Riverland Dr BS13 . . . . **21** F5
Riverleaze
 Bristol BS9. . . . .**5** C5
 Portishead BS20. . . . .**1** F6
River Mead BA21. . . . . **16** D8
River Pl BA2. . . . . **44** B6
River Rd
 East Huntspill TA7 . . . . . **137** B8
 Mark TA9 . . . . **106** D1

River Rd continued
 Pawlett TA6 . . . . **135** F5
 Portbury BS20 . . . .**3** F8
Riversgate BS1 . . . . **227** C2
Riverside
 Banwell BS24, BS29 . . . . . **51** B5
 Bridgwater TA6 . . . . **208** F6
 Burrowbridge TA7 . . . . . **154** F1
 Combwich TA5 . . . . **135** C5
 Dinder BA5 . . . . **140** D7
 Horton TA19. . . . . **183** C2
 Meare BA5. . . . . **138** F5
 Taunton TA1. . . . . **212** E4
 Wellington TA21 . . . . . . **222** B7
Riverside Cl
 Bristol BS11. . . . .**4** F5
 Clevedon BS21. . . . .**6** B1
 Midsomer Norton BA3. . . . **96** F7
 Weston-Super-Mare BS22. . **32** C3
Riverside Cotts BA3. . . . . . **79** A2
Riverside Ct BA2 . . . . **228** B1
Riverside Gdns
 Bath BA1 . . . . **228** B2
 Dunster TA24 . . . . **201** E3
 Midsomer Norton BA3. . . . **96** F7
Riverside Pl ◲ TA1 . . . . . **212** F4
Riverside Rd
 Bath BA2 . . . . **228** B2
 Midsomer Norton BA3. . . . **96** F7
Riverside Row TA24 . . . . **124** A3
Riverside Terr BA11 . . . . **119** F5
Riverside Wlk BA3 . . . . . . **96** F7
Rivers Rd
 Bath BA1 . . . . **228** C4
 Yeovil BA21 . . . . **219** D8
Rivers Reach BA11. . . . . . **120** A5
Rivers St BA1 . . . . **228** B3
Rivers Street Mews BA1. **228** B3
River St BS2 . . . . **227** C3
River Street Pl ◳ BA1. . . **228** B3
River Terr BS31. . . . . **24** F5
Riverton Rd TA7 . . . . **136** B4
River View
 Bridgwater TA6 . . . . **208** F6
 Combwich TA5 . . . . **135** B5
 Exebridge TA22 . . . . **163** F3
Riverway BS48. . . . .**8** F3
River Wlk BS22 . . . . **32** D2
Roachill Cross EX36 . . . . **162** C1
Road Hill
 Alcombe SN13 . . . . **29** E8
 Langford Budville TA4 . . **166** B3
Roath Rd BS20. . . . .**2** D5
Robbins Cl SN14 . . . . **13** F8
Robert Blake Science Coll
 TA6 . . . . **208** F3
Robert Ct BS8 . . . . **11** D7
Roberts Dr TA6 . . . . **209** A2
Roberts Rd TA2. . . . . **168** A6
Robert St TA4 . . . . **202** D2
Robin Cl
 Bristol BS14. . . . . **23** D6
 Midsomer Norton BA3. . . . **97** B8
 Taunton TA1. . . . . **212** B4
 Weston-Super-Mare BS22. . **49** E8
Robin Dr BS24 . . . . **49** E2
Robinia Wlk BS14. . . . . **23** A7
Robin La BS21 . . . .**6** D5
Robins Ct
 Chard TA20. . . . . **223** C5
 Frome BA11. . . . . **119** D5
Robins Dr
 Bridgwater TA6 . . . . **209** A6
 Burtle TA7 . . . . **137** D6
Robins La
 Burtle TA7 . . . . **137** C6
 Frome BA11. . . . . **119** D5
 Shepton Beauchamp TA19 **184** E4
Robinson Cl BS48. . . . . **19** A5
Robinson Hts DT10. . . . . . **190** B4
Robinson Way BS48. . . . . . **19** A5
Rob-Lynne Ct BS25 . . . . . . **69** F8
Roche Cl BA21 . . . . **218** C7
Rochester Cl BS24 . . . . . . **49** A1
Rochester Rd TA2. . . . . . . **213** A4
Rochfort Ct BA1 . . . . **45** B8
Rock's Dro BA16. . . . . **138** F3
Rock Ave BS48. . . . .**8** C2
Rock Cotts BS20 . . . .**4** E4
Rockeries Dr BS25 . . . . **69** F8
Rockeries The BS25. . . . . . **69** F8
Rocketts Cl TA3. . . . . **169** D4
Rocketts Cotts TA3. . . . . **169** C4
Rockfield Cotts TA21. . . . **179** F7
Rock Hall Cotts BA22. . . . . **45** B1
Rockhall Ho ◳ BS23 . . . . . **30** C1
Rock Hall Ho BA2. . . . . **45** B1
Rock Hall La BA2 . . . . **45** B1
Rock Hill TA3. . . . . **170** C1
Rockhill Est BS31 . . . . **24** F4
Rockingham Gdns BS11. . . .**5** A8
Rockingham Gr BS23. . . . . **31** A1
Rock La
 Bath BA2 . . . . **45** B1
 Exford TA24 . . . . **128** D1
 West Bagborough TA4 . . **151** E5
Rockleaze
 Bristol BS9. . . . .**5** E2
 Evercreech BA4. . . . . **141** E2
Rockleaze Ave BS9. . . . .**5** E3
Rockleaze Ct BS9 . . . .**5** E3
Rockleaze Mans ◲ BS23 . **30** C1
Rockleaze Rd BS9. . . . .**5** E3
Rockliffe Ave BA2 . . . . **45** B8
Rockliffe Rd BA2. . . . . **45** B8
Rock Rd
 Chilcompton BA3 . . . . **96** D2
 Keynsham BS31. . . . . **24** E5

Rock Rd *continued*
Midsomer Norton BA3.....**78** B2
Yatton BS49..............**34** C7
Rocks La BS40............**20** E1
Rocks St BA5............**204** C7
Rocks The BA4...........**142** B7
Rock Terr BA4...........**116** F6
Rockway TA3.............**170** C1
Rockwell Gate TA21.....**222** B5
Rockwell Green CE Prim Sch
TA21...................**222** B5
Rocky Hill TA11.........**173** D5
Rocky La TA23...........**131** C2
Rodber Cl BA9...........**216** B4
Rodber Gdns BA9.........**216** B4
Roddenbury Cl BA11.....**120** B5
Roddenbury View BA12..**144** D8
Rodden Rd BA11..........**120** A5
Rode Hill
Rode BA11...............**82** E1
Southwick BA11..........**83** A1
Rode Methodist Fst Sch
BA11...................**101** E8
Rodfords Mead BS14.......**23** A7
Rodhuish Cross TA24....**131** B3
Rodhuish Hill La TA24...**131** A3
Rod La TA19.............**183** F4
Rodmead La BA5.........**110** E4
Rodmead Wlk BS13........**22** A4
Rodmoor Rd BS20..........**2** D6
Rodmore Cres BA4.......**141** E1
Rodmore Rd BA4.........**141** E1
Rodney BS24..............**49** A2
Rodney Ct BA22.........**218** A5
Rodney Ho BA2...........**44** A6
Rodney Pl BS8..........**226** A3
Rodney Rd
Backwell BS48...........**19** A6
Saltford BS31...........**25** E2
Rodney Stoke National
Nature Reserve★ BS27...**91** B2
Rodway TA5.............**135** B3
Rodwell La TA13........**184** E5
Roe Ave BA22...........**218** A5
Roebuck Cl BS22.........**32** B4
Roebuck Gate La TA4....**151** B6
Roe Cl TA6.............**209** D4
Roe La BA22............**188** B4
Roemead La BA3.........**114** C5
Roemead Rd BA3.........**114** C4
Rogers Cl
Buckland Dinham BA11...**100** A3
Clutton BS39............**58** E3
North Petherton TA6....**153** F3
Rogers Wlk TA4.........**167** E6
Roland Cl TA1..........**212** E7
Roman Baths The★ BA1..**228** C2
Roman Ct BA21..........**219** D6
Roman Farm Rd BS4......**22** E7
Roman Ho BA1...........**228** C4
Roman La TA6...........**208** C3
Roman Rd
Bath BA1...............**228** C4
Bleadon BS24............**67** C8
Sandford BS25...........**51** F4
Taunton TA1............**213** C5
Roman Villas BA4.......**205** E4
Roman Way
Bristol BS9..............**5** C4
Coleford BA3...........**116** F7
Paulton BS39............**77** C6
Peasedown St John BA2...**79** E7
Watchet TA23...........**202** C7
Roman Way The BA6......**206** C3
Romney Mead TA1........**213** D4
Romsey Rd BA21.........**219** E8
Ron Jones Ho ⅜ BS1.....**227** B4
Rook's Meade La TA19...**184** E1
Rookery Cl
Puriton TA7............**136** C4
Rooks Bridge BS26.......**87** A6
Weston-Super-Mare BS22..**31** E3
Rookery La
Croscombe BA5..........**204** B7
Drimpton DT8...........**199** F6
Rookery Terr TA21......**222** C5
Rookery The BA5........**140** D7
Rookery Way BS14........**22** F4
Rook La BA11...........**119** F4
Rooksbridge Rd BS24,
BS26...................**87** B6
Rooksbridge Wlk BA4....**44** B5
Rooks La BA11..........**120** E7
Room Hill Rd TA24......**146** D7
Roper's La BS40.........**35** E3
Rope Walk Ho ⅔ BS2...**227** B4
Ropewalk The TA20......**223** B5
Rope Wk TA24...........**201** B7
Rope Wlk
Backwell BS48...........**19** A5
Bridgwater TA6.........**209** A5
Coleford BA3...........**116** E8
Evercreech BA4.........**141** E1
⅕ Martock TA12........**185** E6
Wellington TA21........**222** C4
Rope Wlk The TA23......**202** C7
Roping Rd BA21.........**219** B6
Rosary Dr TA6..........**208** B4
Rosebank Rd TA4........**167** A4
Roseberry Cotts BA3....**117** A7
Roseberry Pl BA2.......**44** C6
Roseberry Rd BA2.......**44** C6
Roseberry Terr TA1.....**212** D5
Rosebery Ave
Bridgwater TA6.........**209** B5
Yeovil BA21............**219** D6
Rosebery St TA2........**212** E7
Rosebery Terr BS8......**226** B2

Rose Cotts
Taunton TA1............**213** B3
Weston-Super-Mare BS22..**32** C2
Rose & Crown Cotts BA3 **116** F6
Rose Ct
Keinton Mandeville TA11 .**158** A1
Shepton Mallet BA4.....**205** B6
Rosedale Ave BS23......**49** A7
Rose Dale Wlk BA11.....**119** F6
Rose Gdns BS22..........**32** B4
Rose Hill
Bath BA1...............**28** C3
Spaxton TA5...........**152** F2
Rose La
Crewkerne, Misterton
TA18..................**196** B3
Crewkerne TA18.........**224** B6
Purtington TA20........**195** A3
Roseland Cl BA1........**28** C3
Roselyn Cres DT9.......**189** A1
Rosemary Cres BS20......**2** F5
Rosemary La
Dulverton TA22.........**163** D6
Freshford BA3..........**64** B4
Rosemarylane Cross
EX15..................**180** D1
Rosemary St DT9........**217** C2
Rose Meare Gdns BS13...**21** E7
Rosemont Terr BS8......**226** A2
Rosemount La BA2........**45** B4
Rosemount Rd BS48......**20** B8
Roseneath Ave TA8......**84** F4
Rose Terr
Bath BA2...............**45** C2
Bristol BS8............**226** B3
Rose Tree Paddock TA8...**84** F4
Rosette Cotts TA12.....**185** B7
Rosevean Cl TA6........**209** D7
Rose Villas TA5........**135** B2
Rosewarn Cl BA2........**44** A4
Rosewell Cl BA1........**228** B2
Rosewood Ave TA8......**104** C6
Rosewood Cl TA8.......**104** C7
Rosewood Dr TA8.......**104** C6
Roslyn Ave BS22........**31** C1
Rossendale Cl BS22.....**31** F3
Rosshayne La EX14.....**192** C4
Rossiter's Hill BA11...**119** F3
Rossiter's Rd BA11.....**119** E3
Rossiter Grange ⅚ BS13 .**21** F4
Rossiter Rd BA2.......**228** C1
Rosslyn Cl ⅐ BA1.......**44** B7
Rosslyn Rd BA1.........**44** B7
Rotcombe La BS39........**59** D2
Rotcombe Vale BS39.....**59** D2
Rotton Row TA4........**210** C4
Roughmoor TA4.........**202** E4
Roughmoor Cl TA1......**212** D5
Roughmoor Cotts TA1...**212** D5
Roughmoor Cres TA1....**212** D5
Roughmoor La BA5......**110** C7
Roundhill Gr BA2........**44** B3
Roundhill Pk BA2........**44** A4
Roundmoor Cl BS31.......**25** D3
Roundmoor Gdns BS14...**23** D7
Roundoak Gdns TA21....**167** C2
Round Oak Gr BS27......**90** A8
Round Oak Rd BS27......**90** A8
Round Pool La TA4.....**151** B7
Roundwell Cl BA4......**204** F6
Roundwell St TA13.....**220** C4
Rowacres
Bath BA2...............**44** B3
Bristol BS14...........**22** F6
Rowan Cl
Nailsea BS48.............**9** A2
Puriton TA7............**136** C4
Wincanton BA9.........**216** D2
Rowan Ct
Frome BA11............**120** B7
Radstock BA3...........**78** E1
Rowan Dr
Berrow TA8..............**84** F5
Taunton TA1............**213** D1
Rowan Ho BS13..........**22** D4
Rowan Pl BS24..........**32** B1
Rowans Cl TA6.........**209** C6
Rowans The BS20.........**2** B4
Rowan Way
Churchill BS40..........**53** A5
Yeovil BA20............**218** F3
Rowan Wlk BS31..........**24** C4
Rowbarrow Hill
Rimpton DT9...........**188** A7
Trent DT9.............**187** F6
Rowbarton Cl TA2......**212** F7
Rowberrow BS14.........**22** F7
Rowberrow La BS25......**70** F8
Rowberrow Way BS40......**8** E1
Rowcliffe Cotts TA21..**178** F8
Rowden Mill La DT10...**189** F1
Rowdens Rd BA5.........**203** D3
Rowditch La TA5........**133** D5
Rowe's Hill BA12......**144** E4
Rowe Cl TA21...........**222** A4
Row La
Keinton Mandeville TA11 .**158** A1
Laverton BA2..........**100** D8
Rowlands Cl BA1.........**29** B2
Rowlands Rise TA7.....**136** C4
Rowley Rd BA6.........**206** E5
Rowls La BA9...........**177** E6
Rowmarsh La TA10......**172** D5
Rownham Cl BS3.........**11** E4
Rownham Ct BS8........**226** A1
Rownham Hill BS8........**11** E4

Rownham Mead BS8....**226** A1
Row Of Ashes La BS40...**36** F4
Rows La EX16...........**164** A1
Rows The BS22..........**31** E2
Row The
Hambridge TA10.......**184** D8
Langport TA10.........**172** B3
Royal Ave BA1.........**228** B3
Royal Cl BA21.........**219** C6
Royal Cres
Bath BA1..............**228** A3
Weston-Super-Mare BS23..**48** D8
Royal Ct BS23.........**48** D4
Royal Fort Rd BS8.....**226** C3
Royal High Sch The BA1..**228** B4
Royal Ho ⅘ BA4.......**205** B6
Royal Hospl for Sick Children
BS2...................**226** C3
Royal National Hospl for
Rheumatic Diseases
BA1...................**228** B2
Royal Par
Bristol BS8............**226** A2
Weston-Super-Mare BS23..**48** D8
Royal Park Mews BS8...**226** A3
Royal Photographic Society★
BA1...................**228** B3
Royal Pk BS8..........**226** A3
Royal Portbury Dock Rd
BS20...................**3** E5
Royal Prom BS8........**226** B3
Royal Sands BS23......**48** D4
Royal Sch The BA1......**27** F2
Royal United Hospl BA1..**44** B4
BS8...................**226** B3
Royal York Cres BS8....**11** F6
Royal York Ho ⅞ BS8...**226** A2
Royal York Mews ⅙
BS8...................**226** A2
Royal York Villas BS8..**226** A2
Royces La TA19........**184** C5
Roynon Way BS27........**90** B7
Royston Lodge BS23.....**48** D6
Royston Rd TA3........**192** A7
Rozel Ho ⅕ BS23.......**30** C1
Rubbery La BS11.......**158** D1
Rubens Cl BS31.........**25** A5
Ruborough Rd TA6.....**209** C4
Ruckley Ford BA3.......**80** A2
Ruddock Cl BA22......**197** B8
Ruddock Way BA22.....**197** B8
Ruddymead BS21.........**6** D2
Rudge Hill BA11.......**102** D5
Rudge La
Beckington BA11.......**102** B6
Standerwick BA11.....**102** D3
Rudge Rd BA11.........**102** B2
Rudgeway Rd BS39......**77** E4
Rudgewood Cl BS13.....**22** D4
Rudleigh Ave BS20.......**4** C4
Rudleigh Rd BS20........**4** C4
Rudhall Gn BS22........**32** B3
Rudmore Pk BA1........**44** A7
Rue La
Alweston DT9..........**189** C7
Hambridge TA3........**184** B7
Ruett La BS39..........**77** B4
Rugg's Dro
Chedzoy TA7...........**154** D7
West Huntspill TA9....**136** B7
Rugg's Hill TA22......**148** E2
Rughill BS28..........**108** D8
Rugosa Dr TA8..........**84** F4
Ruishton CE Prim Sch
TA3...................**169** C3
Ruishton La TA3.......**169** C3
Ruishton Lane Cotts
TA3...................**169** C3
Runnymede Rd BA21....**219** D8
Rupert St
Bristol BS1...........**227** B4
Taunton TA2...........**212** E6
Rusham BS13............**21** F4
Rush Ash La BA3.......**116** E8
Rushgrove Gdns BS39....**57** C4
Rush Hill
Bath BA2...............**44** C2
Farrington Gurney BS39 ..**76** F3
Rush Hill La BS28.....**107** F3
Rushmoor BS21...........**6** A1
Rushmoor Gr BS48.......**19** A5
Rushmoor La BS48.......**19** A5
Rushway BS40...........**53** F4
Ruskin Cl TA1.........**213** C4
Ruskin Rd BA3..........**78** C1
Ruskway La TA10.......**184** C6
Russell's Barton BA11.**143** B8
Russell Cl BS40........**38** A6
Russell Pl
Bridgwater TA6........**208** F6
Milborne Port DT9....**217** C3
Russell Pope Ave TA20 .**223** D2
Russell Rd
Clevedon BS21...........**6** C3
Locking BS24...........**50** C6
Russell St BA1.........**228** B3
Russets The BS20........**2** F4
Russett Cl BS48........**19** B6
Russett Gr BS48........**18** C8
Russett Rd
Street BA16...........**207** C4
Taunton TA1...........**213** E5
Russet Way
Peasedown St John BA2...**79** D7
Yeovil BA20............**218** D2
Russ La BS21...........**16** E4

Russ St BS2..........**227** C2
Rusty Well BA20........**218** F3
Rusty Well Pk BA20....**218** F3
Ruthven Rd BS4.........**22** E8
Rutland Cl BS22.........**49** C8
Rutter's La TA19......**221** B4
Ryalls Ct BA21........**219** C5
Ryburn Cl TA1.........**213** D3
Rydal Ave BS24.........**50** A4
Rydal Rd BS23..........**48** F4
Rydon Cres TA5........**135** C2
Rydon La
Lopen TA13............**185** A1
South Petherton TA13...**220** A5
Taunton TA2...........**212** F8
Rye TA7...............**136** C4
Rye Cl BS13............**21** E6
Ryecroft Ave BS22......**31** E2
Ryecroft Rise BS41.....**11** B1
Ryefields Cl BA22.....**197** B8
Rye Gdns BA20.........**218** D2
Rye La TA7............**155** C2
Ryelands Farm Ind Est
TA21...................**222** B3
Ryepool TA4...........**167** F8
Ryesland Way TA3......**169** D4
Rye Water La DT2.....**197** A1
Rylands BA11..........**101** E4
Rylands Cl TA4........**202** D2
Rylestone Gr BS9........**5** F5
Rysdale Rd BS9..........**5** F6

S

Sabrina Way BS9.........**5** C4
Sackmore Gn DT10.....**190** F6
Sackmore La DT10.....**190** F5
Saco Ho BS1...........**227** B2
Sacred Heart Prep Sch
BS40..................**39** A3
Sadborow La TA20......**199** B4
Sadborow Pound TA20..**199** B5
Sadbury Cl BS22........**32** B4
Sadler St BA5.........**203** D4
Sadlier Cl BS11..........**5** A8
Saffron Cl TA1........**168** F1
Saffron Ct
Bath BA1..............**228** C4
Sherborne DT9.........**225** E4
Saffron Ho ⅒ BS23......**48** E8
Saffrons The ⅞ BS22...**32** B4
Sage's La BA3..........**94** D6
Sage Cl BS20............**1** E4
Sainsbury Cl TA24.....**200** D7
Sainsbury Rd TA24....**200** D7
St Agnes Cl BS48.........**9** A1
St Aldhelm's CE Prim Sch
BA4..................**141** E6
St Aldhelm's Cl BA11..**119** D4
St Aldhelm's Rd DT9...**225** D6
St Aldhelms Cl BA11...**119** D4
St Algars Yd BA11.....**144** A4
St Andrew's CE Jun Sch
Burnham-on-S TA8......**104** B7
Congresbury BS49.......**34** C4
St Andrew's CE Prim Sch
Bath BA1..............**228** B4
Taunton TA2...........**212** F6
St Andrew's CE Sch
EX13..................**198** A7
St Andrew's Cl
Congresbury BS49.......**34** C4
Curry Rivel TA10.......**171** D4
High Ham TA10.........**156** A4
St Andrew's Ct BA5....**203** F5
St Andrew's Dr BS21.....**6** A2
St Andrew's Par ⅐ BS23 .**48** F4
St Andrew's Rd
Burnham-on-S TA8......**104** B7
Stogursey TA5.........**134** C5
⅙ Taunton TA2........**212** F6
St Andrew's Terr BA1..**228** B3
St Andrews Cl
Castle Cary BA7.......**214** B7
Nailsea BS48............**9** A1
Weston-Super-Mare BS22..**31** F3
St Andrews Ct TA1....**200** F7
St Andrews Dr EX13....**198** A2
St Andrews La TA1....**200** F7
St Andrews Mews ⅘
BA5..................**203** C3
St Andrews Pk BA5....**203** D3
St Andrews Rd
Backwell BS48..........**19** B5
Cheddar BS27..........**90** C7
Yeovil BA20...........**218** F5
St Andrew St BA5......**203** E4
St Andrews View TA1..**200** F7
St Andrews Wlk ⅘ BA5 .**203** C3
St Ann's Cl TA2.......**212** E7
St Ann's Dr TA8........**85** A1
St Ann's Pl BA1.......**228** B2
St Ann's Way BA2.......**45** C6
St Anne's Ave BS31....**24** D6
St Anne's CE Prim Sch
BS24..................**33** B5
St Anne's Cl BA6.....**158** A5
St Anne's Ct BS31......**24** D6
St Anne's Gdns BA21..**218** E6
St Anthony's Cl BA3....**78** A2
St Antonys Sq ⅐ DT9..**225** D3
St Aubyn's Ave BS23....**48** D2
St Audries Cl TA5.....**134** C6
St Audries Ct TA23...**202** B7
St Augustine's Par BS1..**227** A2
St Augustine's Pl ⅐ BS1 **227** A2

St Augustine of Canterbury
Sch The TA2...........**213** A7
St Augustines Ct ⅐ TA1. **213** A4
St Augustine St TA1...**213** A4
St Austell Cl BS48......**19** A8
St Austell Rd BS22......**49** B8
St Barnabas CE Prim Sch
BS20....................**2** B5
St Barnabas Cl BA3.....**78** B3
St Bartholomew's CE Fst Sch
TA18..................**224** D5
St Benedict's CE Jun Sch
BA6..................**206** D4
St Benedict's Cl BA6..**206** D4
St Benedict's RC Prim Sch
BA3...................**97** C7
St Bernadette RC Prim Sch
BS14..................**23** B6
St Bernadette RC Sch
BS14..................**23** B6
St Bernard's RC Prim Sch
BS11...................**4** E5
St Bernard's Rd BS11....**4** E6
St Brandon's Sch BS21...**6** B3
St Brides Cl BA6......**206** D5
St Bridges Cl BS22.....**31** A6
St Bridges Ct BS22.....**31** A6
St Bridget's Cl TA8....**65** F5
St Cadoc Ho BS31.......**24** F5
St Catherine's Cl BA2..**45** C6
St Catherine's Cres DT9. **225** B3
St Catherine's Ct ⅒
BA11..................**119** E5
St Catherine's Mead BS20. **4** D3
St Catherine's Way DT9. **225** B3
St Catherines Hill BA10..**215** E6
St Chad's Ave BA3......**78** A1
St Chad's Gn BA3......**97** A8
St Charles Cl BA3......**78** A2
St Christopher's Ct BS21. **6** C5
St Christopher's Way TA8 **85** A4
St Christophers Cl BA2..**45** C8
St Cleer's Orch TA11..**211** C3
St Cleers TA11........**211** C3
St Cleers Way TA11...**211** C3
St Clements Ct
Bath BA1..............**27** C1
Bristol BS2...........**227** C4
Clevedon BS21...........**6** C4
Keynsham BS31..........**24** E4
⅔ Weston-Super-Mare
BS22..................**32** A2
St Clements Rd BS31....**24** F4
St Cuthbert's CE Inf Sch
BA5..................**203** C3
St Cuthbert's Lodge ⅜
BA5..................**203** D4
St Cuthbert's Villas BA5 .**203** A5
St Cuthbert Ave BA5...**203** D4
St Cuthbert St BA5....**203** D4
St Cuthbert Way BA5...**203** B5
St David's Cl
Glastonbury BA6......**206** E4
Taunton TA2...........**213** A8
Weston-Super-Mare BS22 .**31** B2
St David's Cres BA21..**219** B7
St David's Ct BS21.....**16** E8
St David's Dr EX13....**198** A2
St David's Gdns TA2...**212** F8
St Davids Cl EX13.....**198** A2
St Davids Ct TA6......**209** D3
St Davids Mews BS1...**226** C2
St Davids Pl BA10....**215** E7
St Decuman's Rd TA2 ..**202** C7
St Dubricius CE Sch
TA24..................**124** A3
St Dunstan's Com Sch
BA6..................**206** D5
St Dunstan's Pk BA6..**158** A5
St Dunstans Ct
Glastonbury BA6......**206** D5
Keynsham BS31.........**24** E6
St Edmund's Rd BA6...**206** D5
St Edmund's Terr BA3..**117** C7
St Edmund's Rd BA6...**206** E5
St Edward's St TA7....**137** B2
St Edward's Rd BS8...**226** B2
St Edyth's Rd BS9.......**5** C6
St Elizabeth's Way TA13.**220** C4
SS Peter & Paul RC Cath★
BS8...................**226** A4
SS Peter & Paul RC Prim Sch
BS8...................**226** B2
St Francis Prim Sch BS48 ..**8** F1
St Francis Rd BS31.....**24** D6
St George's Ave
Taunton TA2...........**212** B8
Yeovil BA21...........**219** B7
St George's CE Sch, Bourton
SP8...................**161** E1
St George's Cl TA24...**201** D2
St George's Cross BA11. **101** E1
St George's Hill
Bath BA1..............**45** D8
Easton-in-G BS20........**4** A3
St George's Ho BS8...**226** B2
St George's Pl ⅐ TA1..**213** F2
St George's RC Prim Sch
TA1...................**213** A3
St George's Rd
Keynsham BS31.........**24** D6
Portbury BS20...........**3** E7
St George's St TA24...**201** D2
St George CE Prim Sch
BS1...................**226** B2

St Georges Ave EX13 . . . . 198 A2
St Georges Bldgs BA1 . . . . 228 A3
St Georges Ct BA6 . . . . . . 206 E5
St Georges Mews TA1 . . . 212 F3
St Georges Pl BA1 . . . . . . 228 A3
St Georges Prim Sch
  BS22 . . . . 32 C3
St Georges Rd BS1 . . . . . . 226 C2
St Georges Sq TA1 . . . . . . 212 F3
St Georges Way TA1 . . . . 212 E2
St Gilda's Cl TA10 . . . . . . 172 A5
St Gilda's Way BA6 . . . . . 206 D4
St Gildas TA20 . . . . 223 D4
St Gildas Ct TA10 . . . . . . 172 A5
St Gildas RC Prim Sch
  BA21 . . . . 219 B5
St Gregory's CE Prim Sch
  DT10 . . . . 190 F5
St Gregory's RC Sch BA2 . 62 D8
St Helens BA22 . . . . 175 D8
St Hilary Cl BS9 . . . . 5 D5
St Ives Cl BS48 . . . . 9 A1
St Ives Rd BS23 . . . . 49 A5
St James' Barton BS1 . . . 227 B4
St James's Cl BA21 . . . . . 218 D5
St James's Par BA1 . . . . . 228 B2
St James's Pk
  Bath BA1 . . . . 228 B4
  Yeovil BA20 . . . . 218 C5
St James' Sq BA6 . . . . . . 157 D4
St James's St
  Bath BA1 . . . . 228 B4
  South Petherton TA13 . . 220 C4
St James Cl TA1 . . . . 212 F4
St James Ct
  Bridgwater TA6 . . . . . . 209 D3
  ◢ Taunton TA1 . . . . . . 212 F4
St James Mews TA13 . . . . 220 C4
St James St
  Taunton TA1 . . . . 212 F4
  Weston-Super-Mare BS23 . 48 D7
St James Terr BA22 . . . . . 197 A7
St John's Ave BS21 . . . . 6 D3
St John's Bridge ◢ BS1 . 227 A3
St John's CE Fst Sch
  BA11 . . . . 119 F4
St John's CE Inf Sch BA6 206 D4
St John's CE Jun Sch
  TA9 . . . . 104 D4
St John's CE Prim Sch
  Keynsham BS31 . . . . 24 E5
  Midsomer Norton BA3 . . 78 A1
  Wellington TA21 . . . . . . 222 E6
St John's Cl
  Peasedown St John BA2 . . 79 B7
  Skilgate TA4 . . . . 164 E6
  Weston-Super-Mare BS23 . 30 D1
St John's Cres
  Midsomer Norton BA3 . . 78 A2
  Trowbridge BA14 . . . . . . 83 F6
St John's Pl BA1 . . . . 228 C3
St John's RC Prim Sch
  BA2 . . . . 45 B6
St John's RC Prim Sch
  (Annexe) BA2 . . . . 44 D4
St John's Rd
  Backwell BS48 . . . . 19 B5
  Bath BA2 . . . . 228 C3
  Bath, Lower Weston BA1 . 44 C7
  Burnham-on-S TA8 . . . . 104 B7
  Clevedon BS21 . . . . 6 D3
  Frome BA11 . . . . 120 B5
  Taunton TA1 . . . . 212 F4
  Yeovil BA21 . . . . 219 D7
St John's Sq BA6 . . . . 206 D5
St John's Terr BA11 . . . . . 119 E3
St John & St Francis CE Prim
  Sch TA6 . . . . 209 D4
St Johns Cl TA21 . . . . 222 E6
St Johns Ct
  Axbridge BS26 . . . . 70 B2
  Bath BA2 . . . . 228 C3
  Keynsham BS31 . . . . 24 E6
  Wells BA5 . . . . 203 D3
St Johns Ho ◢ BA20 . . . 219 B5
St Johns Rd BA2 . . . . 60 B1
St Johns Ret Pk TA1 . . . . 213 B5
St John St
  Bridgwater TA6 . . . . . . 209 B4
  Wells BA5 . . . . 203 D4
St Johns Wlk BA5 . . . . . . 206 D5
St John the Evangelist CE
  Prim Sch BS21 . . . . 6 C1
St Joseph's RC Prim Sch
  Bridgwater TA6 . . . . . . 208 D4
  Burnham-on-S TA8 . . . . 104 B6
  Portishead BS20 . . . . 2 D3
St Joseph's Rd BS23 . . . . . 30 E1
St Joseph & St Teresa RC
  Prim Sch BA5 . . . . 203 D4
St Josephs Field TA1 . . . 213 A3
St Jude's Terr BS22 . . . . . . 31 C1
St Judes Ho ◢ BS22 . . . 227 C3
St Julian's CE Prim Sch
  BA2 . . . . 62 E1
St Julian's Cl BS39 . . . . . . 77 E4
St Julian's Rd BA2 . . . . 79 F5
St Juthware Cl BA22 . . . . 197 C3
St Katherine's CE Prim Sch
  BS40 . . . . 37 A7
St Katherine's Sch BS20 . . . 4 C1
St Kenya Ct BS31 . . . . 24 F5
St Keyna Rd BS31 . . . . 24 E5

St Kilda's Rd BA2 . . . . 44 D5
St Ladoc Rd BS31 . . . . 24 D6
St Laud Cl BS9 . . . . 5 D5
St Lawrence's CE Prim Sch
  BA5 . . . . 110 E6
St Leonards Ct BA20 . . . . 219 A4
St Louis RC Prim Sch
  BA11 . . . . 119 E5
St Luke's Cl TA8 . . . . 104 B7
St Luke's Rd
  Bath BA2 . . . . 44 F3
  Midsomer Norton BA3 . . 77 F2
St Lukes Mews TA4 . . . . . 167 E6
St Lukes Rd BA11 . . . . . . 101 E5
St Margaret's Cl BS31 . . . . 24 D6
St Margaret's La BS48 . . . 19 A5
St Margaret's Rd BA22 . . . 186 B6
St Margaret's Sch BA22 . . 186 B6
St Margaret's Terr BS23 . . 48 D8
St Margarets Cl BS48 . . . . 19 A5
St Margarets Cl TA10 . . . 213 B4
St Margarets La BA22 . . . 198 C8
St Mark's CE Sch BA1 . . . 228 C1
St Mark's Ecumenical CE/
  Methodist Prim Sch
  BS22 . . . . 31 F4
St Mark's Rd
  Bath BA1 . . . . 228 C1
  Burnham-on-S TA8 . . . . 104 B8
  Midsomer Norton BA3 . . . 77 F2
  Weston-Super-Mare BS22 . 32 A3
St Marks Cl
  Chedzoy TA7 . . . . 154 E8
  Keynsham BS31 . . . . 24 E6
St Marks Gdns BA2 . . . . . 228 C1
St Martin's CE Jun Sch
  BS22 . . . . 31 D2
St Martin's Cl
  Fivehead TA3 . . . . 170 F1
  Zeals BA12 . . . . 161 F3
St Martin's Ct BA2 . . . . . . 44 E1
St Martin's Garden Prim Sch
  BA2 . . . . 44 D1
St Martin's La SN14 . . . . . 13 F8
St Martin's Pk SN14 . . . . . 13 F8
St Martin's Sch TA18 . . . . 224 B6
St Martins BS21 . . . . 6 C5
St Martins Ct BS22 . . . . . . 31 E3
St Martins Hospl BA2 . . . . 44 E1
St Martins Way BA2 . . . . . 218 D2
St Mary's Bldgs BA2 . . . . 228 B1
St Mary's CE Prim Sch
  Bradford Abbas DT9 . . . 187 E1
  Bridgwater TA6 . . . . . . 208 C4
  Radstock BA3 . . . . 79 C1
  Thorncombe TA20 . . . . 199 B6
  Timsbury BA2 . . . . 60 C3
St Mary's Cl
  ◢ Axminster EX13 . . . . 198 A1
  Bath BA2 . . . . 45 B6
  Chard TA20 . . . . 223 C2
  Cossington TA7 . . . . . . 136 F3
  Timsbury BA2 . . . . 60 B2
St Mary's Cres
  Chard TA20 . . . . 223 C3
  ◢ North Petherton TA6 . 153 F4
  Yeovil BA21 . . . . 219 C8
St Mary's Ct
  ◢ Bridgwater TA6 . . . . 208 F4
  Weston-Super-Mare BS24 . 49 A1
St Mary's Gdns BS40 . . . . 53 B5
St Mary's Gr BS48 . . . . . . 18 C8
St Mary's Hospl BS8 . . . . 226 B3
St Mary's La BA4 . . . . 140 E3
St Mary's Park Rd BS20 . . . 2 C4
St Mary's Pk
  Langport TA10 . . . . 172 A5
  Nailsea BS48 . . . . 18 C8
St Mary's Prim Sch BS20 . . 3 E3
St Mary's Prim Sch
  Axminster EX13 . . . . . . 198 A1
  Bath BA1 . . . . 27 B1
St Mary's Rd
  Bristol BS11 . . . . 4 D7
  Burnham-on-S TA8 . . . . 104 B7
  Frome BA11 . . . . 120 B5
  Hutton BS24 . . . . 49 D2
  Leigh Woods BS8 . . . . . 11 D6
  Meare BA6 . . . . 138 D4
  Oxenpill BA6 . . . . 138 C4
  Portishead BS20 . . . . 2 C4
  Sherborne DT9 . . . . 225 B3
  Westonzoyland TA7 . . . 154 F5
St Mary's St BS26 . . . . 70 C2
St Mary's View BA22 . . . . 196 F7
St Mary's Wlk BS11 . . . . . . 4 D6
St Mary CE Prim Sch BA2 45 C8
St Mary Redcliffe & Temple
  CE Sch BS1 . . . . 227 B1
St Mary & St Peter's CE Fst
  Sch
  Barrington TA19 . . . . . . 184 D5
  Ilton TA19 . . . . 183 E4
St Marys Cl
  Hutton BS24 . . . . 49 D2
  Seavington St Mary TA19 184 D1
  Wedmore BS28 . . . . . . 108 C4
St Marys Ct TA6 . . . . 153 E4
St Marys Pl BA4 . . . . 142 F4
St Marys Rise BA3 . . . . . . 79 C2
St Mary St
  Bridgwater TA6 . . . . . . 208 F4
  Nether Stowey TA5 . . . . 134 B2
St Mathew's Pl BA2 . . . . . 45 B5
St Mathias Ho BS2 . . . . . 227 C3
St Matthew's Cl BS23 . . . . 30 D1

St Matthew's Field TA6 . 208 E4
St Matthew's Rd BS6 . . . 227 A4
St Matthews Gn TA6 . . . 208 E4
St Matthias Pk BS2 . . . . . 227 C3
St Medard Rd BS28 . . . . . 108 C4
St Michael's Ave
  Clevedon BS21 . . . . 6 D1
  Weston-Super-Mare BS22 . 32 A3
  Yeovil BA21 . . . . 219 C7
St Michael's CE First Sch
  TA24 . . . . 200 F7
St Michael's CE Jun Sch
  BA2 . . . . 44 A6
St Michael's Cl
  Buckland Dinham BA11 . 100 A3
  Glastonbury BA6 . . . . . 206 E3
  Nether Stowey TA5 . . . . 134 A2
St Michael's Cres TA2 . . . 213 A8
St Michael's Ct BA2 . . . . . 44 A6
St Michael's Gdns TA13 . 220 D5
St Michael's Hill
  Bristol BS2 . . . . 226 C4
  Milverton TA4 . . . . 167 A4
St Michael's Hospl BS2 . . 226 C4
St Michael's Pk BS2 . . . . 226 C4
St Michael's Pl BA1 . . . . . 228 B2
St Michael's Rd
  Bath BA1 . . . . 44 D7
  Burnham-on-S TA8 . . . . 104 B7
  Minehead TA24 . . . . . . 200 F8
  Yeovil BA21 . . . . 219 D6
St Michael's View TA15 . . 186 B4
St Michael Cl TA13 . . . . . 220 D5
St Michael on the Mount CE
  Prim Sch BS2 . . . . 226 C3
St Michael Rd TA1 . . . . . . 169 D4
St Michaels Cl
  Bawdrip TA7 . . . . 136 C4
  Walton BA16 . . . . 156 D7
  Yeovil BA21 . . . . 219 C8
St Michaels Ct
  Nether Compton DT9 . . 187 F1
  Stoke St Michael BA3 . . 116 B3
St Michaels Ct
  Bawdrip TA7 . . . . 136 C4
  Walton BA16 . . . . 156 D7
  Yeovil BA21 . . . . 219 C8
St Michaels Rd BA2 . . . . . 44 A5
St Nicholas' CE Prim Sch
  BA3 . . . . 79 A2
St Nicholas Almshouses ◢
  BS1 . . . . 227 A2
St Nicholas CE Prim Sch
  Combe St Nicholas TA20 193 D6
  Henstridge BA8 . . . . . . 190 A7
St Nicholas Chantry CE Prim
  Sch BS21 . . . . 6 E3
St Nicholas Cl
  ◢ Henstridge BA8 . . . . 190 A6
  Winsley BA15 . . . . 64 D7
  Yeovil BA20 . . . . 219 B4
St Nicholas Ct BA2 . . . . . . 28 F1
St Nicholas Pk BA20 . . . . 219 B4
St Nicholas Rd
  Bristol BS2 . . . . 227 C4
  Weston-Super-Mare BS23 . 48 D2
  Whitchurch BS14 . . . . . . 23 C4
St Nicholas St BS1 . . . . . 227 A2
St Nicholas Way BS48 . . . 18 D2
St Oswald's Ct BS13 . . . . . 22 A8
St Patrick's Ct BA2 . . . . . . 45 B6
St Patrick's Rd
  Taunton TA1 . . . . 213 A8
  Yeovil BA21 . . . . 218 D7
St Patricks Cl ◢ TA2 . . . . 213 A8
St Patricks Ct BS31 . . . . . . 24 E5
St Paul's CE Jun Sch
  BA4 . . . . 205 B5
St Paul's Ct DT9 . . . . 225 E6
St Paul's Flats DT9 . . . . . 225 E6
St Paul's Gn DT9 . . . . 225 E6
St Paul's Rd
  Bristol BS8 . . . . 226 B4
  Burnham-on-S TA8 . . . . 104 B7
  Weston-Super-Mare BS23 . 48 E5
St Paul's Terr BA5 . . . . . . 111 A4
St Pauls Ct TA13 . . . . 220 D4
St Pauls Ct TA6 . . . . 209 D3
St Pauls Pl
  Bath BA1 . . . . 228 B2
  Midsomer Norton BA3 . . 78 A2
St Paul St BS2 . . . . 227 B4
St Peter's Ave BS20 . . . . . 30 D1
St Peter's Cl
  Horton TA19 . . . . 183 C1
  Taunton TA2 . . . . 213 B7
St Peter's Ho BS8 . . . . . . 226 B2
St Peter's Rd
  Burnham-on-S TA8 . . . . 104 B7
  Radstock BA3 . . . . 97 C8
St Peter's Rise
  Bristol BS13 . . . . 22 B7
  South Petherton TA13 . . 220 D4
St Peter's Terr BA2 . . . . . . 44 D6
St Peters CE Fst Sch
  TA4 . . . . 202 E7
St Peters CE Prim Sch
  BS20 . . . . 2 D4
St Peters Cl
  Ilton TA19 . . . . 183 F4
  Staple Fitzpaine TA3 . . 182 C5
  Williton TA4 . . . . 202 D2
St Peters Ct TA6 . . . . 209 D3
St Peters Lodge BS20 . . . . 2 D4
St Peters Rd
  Portishead BS20 . . . . 2 D4
  Shepton Mallet BA4 . . . 205 A6
St Peters Terr ◢ BA4 . . . 205 B6
St Philip's CE Prim Sch
  BA2 . . . . 44 D2
St Philips Rd BS2 . . . . 227 C3

St Pias X RC Prim Sch
  BS13 . . . . 22 A5
St Quintin Pk TA2 . . . . . . 213 E6
St Rayn Hill TA17 . . . . . . 195 B4
St Saviour's Ave TA6 . . . . 209 A4
St Saviour's CE Inf Sch
  BA1 . . . . 28 B2
St Saviour's CE Jun Sch
  BA1 . . . . 28 B2
St Saviour's Rd BA1 . . . . . 28 C2
St Saviour's Terr ◢ BA1 . . 28 B1
St Saviours Way BA1 . . . . 28 C1
St Stephen's Ave ◢ BS1 . 227 A2
St Stephen's CE Prim Sch
  BA1 . . . . 27 F1
St Stephen's Cl BA1 . . . . . 27 F1
St Stephen's Ct BA1 . . . . 228 B4
St Stephen's Pl BA1 . . . . . 228 B4
St Stephen's Rd BA1 . . . . 228 B4
St Stephen's St BS1 . . . . 227 A2
St Swithin's Pl BA1 . . . . . 228 C4
St Swithin's Rd DT9 . . . . 225 E4
St Swithin's Yd BA1 . . . . 228 C4
St Swithins Cl DT9 . . . . . 225 E4
St Thomas' Ct BA5 . . . . . 203 E3
St Thomas Cross BA21 . . 219 C5
St Thomas Ct TA6 . . . . . . 209 D3
St Thomas Mews BA5 . . . 203 F5
St Thomas Pl BS1 . . . . . . 227 B2
St Thomas Rd BA3 . . . . . . 78 B2
St Thomas St E BS1 . . . . 227 B2
St Thomas St
  Bristol BS1 . . . . 227 B2
  Dunster TA24 . . . . 201 C2
  Wells BA5 . . . . 203 E5
St Thomas Terr BA5 . . . . 203 F5
St Vigor & St John CE Prim
  Sch BA3 . . . . 96 E3
St Vincent's Rd BS8 . . . . 226 A2
St Whytes Rd BS4 . . . . 22 D8
St Winifreds Dr BA2 . . . . . 45 D2
Salcombe Gdns BS22 . . . . 32 A2
Salcombe Rd BS4 . . . . 23 A8
Salerno Cl BA22 . . . . 173 E2
Sales Ho ◢ BA4 . . . . 205 B6
Salisbury Rd
  Bath BA1 . . . . 28 B2
  Burnham-on-S TA8 . . . . 104 C3
  Paulton BS39 . . . . 77 F4
  Weston-Super-Mare BS22 . 31 C1
Salisbury St TA2 . . . . 212 E6
Salisbury Terr
  Castle Cary BA7 . . . . . . 214 B5
  ◢ Frome BA11 . . . . . . 119 E3
  Weston-Super-Mare BS23 . 48 D7
Sally Hill BS20 . . . . 2 E7
Sally In The Wood BA1,
  BA15 . . . . 46 D6
Sally Lovell's La BA8 . . . 189 F8
Sally Lunn's Kitchen Mus★
  BA1 . . . . 228 C2
Sallysmead Cl BS13 . . . . . 22 B4
Salmon Par BA5 . . . . 209 A4
Saltford CE Prim Sch
  BS31 . . . . 25 E2
Saltford Ct BS31 . . . . 25 E3
Salthouse Ct BS21 . . . . 6 B2
Salthouse La BA20 . . . . . 219 A4
Salthouse Rd BS21 . . . . 6 B2
Saltings Cl BS21 . . . . 6 B2
Saltlands TA6 . . . . 208 F7
Saltlands Ave TA6 . . . . . . 208 F7
Saltlands Ho TA6 . . . . . . 208 F7
Saltry La TA24 . . . . 131 A6
Saltwell Ave BS14 . . . . . . 23 C5
Salway CI BS40 . . . . 38 E1
Salway Gdns ◢ EX13 . . . 198 A1
Samarate Way BA20 . . . . 218 D4
Sambourne La BS20 . . . . . 4 C4
Sampford Arundel Com Prim
  Sch TA21 . . . . 179 E5
Sampford Peverell CE Prim
  Sch EX16 . . . . 178 C1
Sampford Rocks TA4 . . . . 202 F1
Sampsons Rd BS13 . . . . . . 22 D4
Samuel Cl BA8 . . . . 176 F1
Samuels Ct TA2 . . . . 212 E6
Samways Ct BA22 . . . . . . 218 B5
Sanctuary Gdns BS9 . . . . . 5 D3
Sanctuary La TA22 . . . . . 148 A2
Sandbrook La BA22 . . . . . 175 D2
Sandburrows Rd BS13 . . . 21 F6
Sandburrows Wlk BS13 . . 21 F6
Sandcroft BS14 . . . . 22 F6
Sandcroft Ave BS23 . . . . . 48 D2
Sandene Cl TA2 . . . . 212 C8
Sand Farm La BS22 . . . . . 31 A6
Sandford Cl ◢ BS21 . . . . . 6 B1
Sandford Hill TA5, TA6 . . 208 A6
Sandford Orcas Manor Ho★
  DT9 . . . . 188 C3
Sandford Orcas Rd DT9 . 225 B7
Sandford Pk BA14 . . . . . . 83 F7
Sandford Prim Sch BS25 . 52 B4
Sandford Rd
  Bristol BS8 . . . . 226 A1
  Weston-Super-Mare BS23 . 49 A7
  Winscombe BS25 . . . . . . 51 F1
Sandhill La TA24 . . . . . . 131 C4
Sandhills Dr TA8 . . . . 84 F4
Sandhurst Rd BA20 . . . . 218 F1
Sanding's La
  Chapel Leigh TA4 . . . . . 167 A8
  Fitzhead TA4 . . . . 166 F8
  Lydeard St Lawrence TA4 151 A1
Sandlewood Cl BA21 . . . . 219 E8
Sandmead Rd BS25 . . . . . 52 A4

Sandown Cl
  Bridgwater TA6 . . . . . . 209 A2
  ◢ Yeovil BA20 . . . . . . 219 A5
Sandpiper Cl
  Bridgwater TA6 . . . . . . 209 A4
  Minehead TA24 . . . . . . 201 C3
Sandpiper Dr BS22 . . . . . . 31 F1
Sandpiper Rd TA6 . . . . . . 209 A4
Sandpits Rd BA6 . . . . 206 C5
Sand Rd
  Wedmore BS28 . . . . . . 108 C3
  Weston-Super-Mare BS22 . 31 B5
Sandringham Cl TA6 . . . . 209 C3
Sandringham Ct ◢ BS23 . 48 F5
Sandringham Rd
  ◢ Weston-Super-Mare
  BS23 . . . . 48 F5
  Yeovil BA21 . . . . 219 E6
Sandrocks La TA24 . . . . . 131 B3
Sandscross La BA11 . . . . 100 A3
Sand St TA4 . . . . 166 F4
Sandy's Hill La BA11 . . . . 119 E1
Sandy Cl TA9 . . . . 104 D4
Sandy Hole TA16 . . . . . . 195 F7
Sandy La
  Beckington BA11 . . . . . 101 E4
  Cannington TA5 . . . . . . 135 A3
  Easton-in-G BS8 . . . . . . 10 A8
  Failand BS8 . . . . 10 C7
  Stanton Drew BS39, BS40 . 39 E3
  Wiveliscombe TA4 . . . . 210 C3
Sandyleaze BS9 . . . . 5 E7
Sandys Moor TA4 . . . . . . 210 D4
Sandy View BA11 . . . . . . 101 E4
Sandyway Cross EX36 . . . 145 H4
Sansom's Hill TA9 . . . . . . 217 D2
Sansome's Hill DT9 . . . . . 217 D2
Sarabeth Dr BA2 . . . . 61 A4
Saracen St BA1 . . . . 228 C2
Saunder's Piece La TA18 224 A7
Saunters Ct BA9 . . . . 216 B4
Saunton Wlk BS4 . . . . 22 E8
Savernake Rd BS22 . . . . . 31 F3
Savery or Cottage Row
  TA1 . . . . 213 B3
Saviano Way TA6 . . . . . . 208 E7
Saville Cres BS22 . . . . 49 C8
Saville Gate Cl BS9 . . . . . . 5 F4
Saville Mews BS6 . . . . . . 227 A4
Saville Pl BS8 . . . . 226 A2
Saville Rd
  Bristol BS9 . . . . 5 F3
  Weston-Super-Mare BS22 . 49 C8
Saville Row BA1 . . . . 228 B3
Savoy The BS11 . . . . 4 E6
Saw Cl BA1 . . . . 228 B2
Sawmill Cotts BA11 . . . . 143 B8
Sawmill Gdns BA3 . . . . . . 96 D3
Sawpit La BA6 . . . . 140 C2
Sawpits Cl TA4 . . . . 150 D8
Sawyers Cl
  Chilcompton BA3 . . . . . 96 D3
  Wraxall BS48 . . . . 9 A2
Sawyers Ct BS21 . . . . 6 E3
Sawyers Leigh TA2 . . . . . 168 D8
Sawyers Mill EX16 . . . . . 164 E2
Saxby Cl
  Clevedon BS21 . . . . 6 B1
  Weston-Super-Mare BS22 . 32 A4
Saxon Ct
  Ilminster TA19 . . . . 221 B4
  Weston-Super-Mare BS22 . 32 A4
Saxon Gn TA6 . . . . 209 C4
Saxon Pl BS27 . . . . 90 B7
Saxon Rd
  Bridgwater TA6 . . . . . . 209 C4
  Weston-Super-Mare BS22 . 49 C8
Saxon Ridge TA23 . . . . . 202 B7
Saxon St BS40 . . . . 53 D6
Saxonvale BA11 . . . . 119 F4
Saxon Way
  Cheddar BS27 . . . . 90 B7
  Peasedown St John BA2 . . 79 E8
  Wedmore BS28 . . . . . . 108 C4
  Wincanton BA9 . . . . . . 216 B3
  Winsley BA15 . . . . 64 F7
Says La BS40 . . . . 53 B4
Scadden's La BS27 . . . . . . 91 B3
Scafell Cl
  Taunton TA1 . . . . 212 C4
  Weston-Super-Mare BS23 . 31 A2
Scamel Ho ◢ BA4 . . . . . 205 B6
Scaurs The BS22 . . . . 31 F2
School Cl
  Bampton EX16 . . . . 164 B1
  Banwell BS29 . . . . 51 B3
  Bristol, Whitchurch BS14 . . 22 F4
  Tintinhull BA22 . . . . . . 186 C6
  Watchet TA23 . . . . 202 C2
School Cotts
  ◢ East Coker BA22 . . . 197 D8
  Enmore TA5 . . . . 153 A4
  Taunton TA2 . . . . 168 F2
School Dr DT9 . . . . 225 E4
School Fields
  Cannington TA5 . . . . . . 135 C2
  ◢ North Petherton TA6 . 153 F4
School Hill
  Ashcott TA7 . . . . 156 B8
  Cucklington BA9 . . . . . . 177 D6
  Misterton TA18 . . . . . . 224 F1
  South Perrott DT8 . . . . 196 C2
  Westbury-sub-Mendip BA5 110 F6

School Hill *continued*
Wookey Hole BA5 . . . . . . .203 A8
School La
Barrow Gurney BS48. . . . . . 20 D5
Batheaston BA1. . . . . 28 F4
Blackford BS28 . . . . .107 D4
Burrowbridge TA7 . . . . . .154 F1
Chew Stoke BS40 . . . . 56 D8
Combwich TA5 . . . . .135 B5
Compton Dundon TA11. . . .157 A3
Doulting BA4 . . . . .141 E6
Draycott BS27 . . . . 90 F3
Drimpton DT8 . . . . .199 E6
Farrington Gurney BS39 . . . 77 A4
Horrington BA3. . . . . . . .113 A1
Kilmersdon BA3. . . . . 98 A6
Lopen TA13 . . . . .185 A1
7 North Petherton TA6 . .153 F4
Rowberrow BS25. . . . . 53 A1
Seavington St Michael
 TA19 . . . . .184 E2
Shapwick TA7. . . . . .137 F1
Sherborne DT9 . . . . .225 D3
Somerton TA11 . . . . .211 D6
Tatworth TA20 . . . . .198 C8
Templecombe BA8. . . . . . .176 E1
Wick St Lawrence BS22. . . . 32 B7
Woolavington TA7 . . . . . .136 E3
School of Christ the King RC
 Prim BS4. . . . . 22 E8
School Rd
Kingsdon TA11. . . . . .173 D5
Monkton Heathfield TA2 . .213 F8
Parbrook BA6 . . . . .158 C7
Westonzoyland TA7 . . . . .154 E5
Wrington BS40 . . . . 35 E2
School St
Curry Rivel TA10 . . . . . . .171 D4
Drayton TA10. . . . . .171 E3
School View BS40. . . . . . . .9 B1
Schooner Pl TA24. . . . . . . .201 B7
Scimitar Rd BA22 . . . . . . .218 B6
Scobell Rise BS39. . . . . 59 C2
Score La BS40. . . . . 54 E2
Score The BS40. . . . . 54 E2
Scornfield La BS40. . . . . . . 56 D7
Scotch Horn Cl BS48. . . . . . .8 F2
Scotch Horn Way **5** BS48. . .8 F2
Scot Cl TA6. . . . . .135 F5
Scot Elm Dr BS24 . . . . 32 D1
Scot La BS40 . . . . 38 D1
Scotland La
Axbridge BS26. . . . . .107 D8
Chapel Allerton BS26. . . . .107 D8
Rudge BA11. . . . . .102 C4
Scots Pine Ave **3** BS48. . . . .8 F2
Scott's Hill
Huish Champflower TA4. . .165 E8
Seavington St Mary TA19. .184 D1
Scott's La
Baltonsborough BA6. . . . .158 A8
Wellington TA21. . . . . . .222 E6
Scott Cl TA2 . . . . .212 C6
Scott Rd
Frome BA11. . . . . .119 F5
Highbridge TA9 . . . . . . .104 D3
Weston-Super-Mare BS23. . 49 A4
Scotts Cl BA3. . . . . .116 C8
Scotts La TA7. . . . . .137 D1
Scotts Way TA18. . . . . . . .196 B8
Scouse La EX13. . . . . .198 E2
Scrapton La TA20. . . . . . . .193 D5
Scrubbitts La TA7 . . . . . . .137 B2
Scumbrum La BS39. . . . . . . 59 C2
Seaborough View TA18. . . .224 C4
Seabrook Rd BS22 . . . . 31 D1
Sea King Rd BA20. . . . . . . .218 D3
Sea La
Carhampton TA24 . . . . . .131 A7
Dunster TA24. . . . . .201 F4
Kilve TA5 . . . . .133 C6
Watchet TA23. . . . . .132 D5
Sealey Cl BS27. . . . . 90 F3
Sealey Cres BA5. . . . . .112 E1
Sealeys Cl TA9. . . . . .136 A8
Sea Mills Inf Sch BS9. . . . . .5 C7
Sea Mills Jun Sch BS9 . . . . .5 B5
Sea Mills La BS9. . . . . .5 C5
Sea Mills Sta BS9. . . . . . . .5 B4
SeaQuarium★ BS23. . . . . . 48 D6
Searle Cres BS23 . . . . 49 A6
Searle Ct
Clevedon BS21. . . . . .6 E2
Somerton TA11 . . . . .211 D3
Seat La BA4. . . . . .142 F4
Seaton Ct BA20 . . . . .219 A4
Seaton Rd BA20. . . . . .218 F4
Seavale Mews BS21. . . . . . .6 C4
Seavale Rd BS21 . . . . .6 C4
Seaview Rd
Portishead, Redcliffe Bay
 BS20. . . . . .1 F4
Portishead, West Hill BS20. . .1 F6
Sea View Rd TA8. . . . . . . .104 A8
Seawalls BS9. . . . . .5 D2
Seawalls Rd BS9. . . . . .5 D2
Seaward Dr TA6. . . . . .208 F6
Seaward Way TA24. . . . . . .201 C6
Second Ave
Axminster EX13. . . . . . . .198 A2
Bath BA2 . . . . 44 D5
Bristol BS14. . . . . 23 B7
Radstock BA3 . . . . 97 C2
Second Dro TA7. . . . . .155 D3
Secret World★ TA9. . . . . . .136 C8
Sector Hill EX13 . . . . .198 B1
Sector La EX13. . . . . .198 A1

Sedge Cl TA6 . . . . .208 F2
Sedge Dro TA7 . . . . .137 C3
Sedge Mead BA11. . . . . . . .119 F7
Sedgemoor Cl
Nailsea BS48. . . . . 18 E8
Yeovil BA21 . . . . .219 D7
Sedgemoor Coll TA3 . . . . . .170 A2
Sedgemoor Dro
Sutton Mallet TA7 . . . . . .155 A6
Wrantage TA3. . . . . .170 A2
Sedgemoor Hill Dr TA7. . . .155 B7
Sedgemoor Manor Com Jun
 Sch TA6 . . . . .209 C6
Sedgemoor Manor Inf Sch
 TA6 . . . . .209 D5
Sedgemoor Rd
Bath BA2 . . . . 44 F2
Bridgwater TA6 . . . . .209 C3
Weston-Super-Mare BS23. . 30 F1
Woolavington TA7 . . . . . .136 E3
Sedgemoor Way
Glastonbury BA6. . . . . . .206 D5
Woolavington TA7 . . . . . .136 E3
Sedgewick Ho BS11. . . . . . . .4 E7
Seeley Cres BA16 . . . . . . .207 B3
Sefton Sq BS24 . . . . 50 A8
Selbourne Cl BA1. . . . . 44 A8
Selbourne Pl TA24 . . . . . . .200 F6
Selbourne Rd BS23 . . . . 48 E4
Selden Rd BS14. . . . . 23 E5
Sellbed Cross TA24 . . . . . .146 A8
Selley Wlk BS13. . . . . 22 A5
Selway Ct BA2. . . . . 45 B2
Selwood TA20 . . . . .223 C5
Selwood Cl BS22. . . . . 49 C7
Selwood Cres BA11 . . . . . . .120 A7
Selwood Mid Sch BA11. . . .120 B6
Selwood Rd
Frome BA11. . . . . .119 E5
Glastonbury BA6. . . . . . .206 F6
Selwood St BA11. . . . . . . .118 B7
Selworthy Cl
Bridgwater TA6 . . . . .208 F1
Keynsham BS31. . . . . 24 D5
Selworthy Gdns **4** BS48. . . .8 E1
Selworthy Ho BA2 . . . . 44 F2
Selworthy Rd
Taunton TA1. . . . . .213 B8
Weston-Super-Mare BS23. . 49 A4
Selworthy Specl Sch
 TA2 . . . . .213 A8
Selworthy Terr BA2. . . . . . . 44 F2
Semington Cl TA1. . . . . . . .213 D4
Septimus Bldgs BS14 . . . . . 22 D5
Serbert Cl BS20. . . . . .2 E5
Serbert Rd BS20. . . . . .2 E5
Serbert Way BS20. . . . . .2 E5
Sercombe Pk BS21. . . . . . . .6 E1
Serel Dr BA5 . . . . .203 B3
Serlo Ct BS22. . . . . 32 A4
Serotines The TA10 . . . . . .171 D8
Sevenacres TA11 . . . . .211 C3
Seven Acres La BA1. . . . . . . 28 F5
Seven Acres The **3** BS24. . . 49 F7
Seven Dials BA1 . . . . .228 B2
Seventh Ave BS14. . . . . 23 A7
Seven Thorns EX35 . . . . . .122 C6
Severalls Park Ave TA18. . . .224 C5
Severn Ave BS23 . . . . 48 E5
Severn Cl TA6 . . . . .209 D7
Severn Dr TA1. . . . . .213 C4
Severn Gr TA8 . . . . .104 B5
Severnleigh Gdns BS9. . . . . .5 F3
Severnmeade BS20 . . . . .1 F5
Severn Rd
Bristol BS11. . . . . .4 D6
Pill BS20 . . . . .4 C5
Portishead BS20 . . . . .2 C4
Weston-Super-Mare BS23. . 48 E5
Severn Terr TA23 . . . . .202 C7
Severn Way BS31 . . . . 25 A5
Sevier Rd BS26. . . . . 68 C3
Seville Ct
Portishead BS20. . . . . .2 E7
Taunton TA1. . . . . .212 D2
Seville Rd BS20 . . . . .2 E7
Seward Terr BA3. . . . . 79 C2
Sewell Ho BS25. . . . . 70 A8
Sexey's Hospl BA10 . . . . . .215 E6
Sexey's Hospl (Almshouses)
 BA10 . . . . .215 E6
Sexey's Rd BS28 . . . . .107 E4
Sexey's Sch BA10 . . . . . . .215 D5
Seymour Cl
Clevedon BS21. . . . . .6 E3
Wells BA5 . . . . .203 C5
Weston-Super-Mare BS22. . 31 F4
Seymour Rd
5 Bath BA1. . . . . 28 A1
Bridgwater TA6 . . . . .209 C5
Street BA16. . . . . .207 D4
Seymour St TA21 . . . . .222 C6
Shackel Cross EX15 . . . . . .191 B8
Shadow Wlk BS24. . . . . 50 C3
Shadwell La BA9. . . . . .216 C4
Shadwell La BA9 . . . . .216 C4
Shaftesbury Ave **2** BA1. . . . 44 C7
Shaftesbury Cl BS18 . . . . . . 18 D8
Shaftesbury La BA9. . . . . . .177 B6
Shaftesbury Mews **7**
 BA2. . . . . 44 D5
Shaftesbury Rd
Bath BA2 . . . . 44 D5
Henstridge BA8 . . . . .190 C8
Weston-Super-Mare BS23. . 49 B8
Shaftesbury Terr BA3. . . . . . 79 A3
Shaftgate Ave BA4. . . . . . .205 A6

Shaft Rd BA2 . . . . 45 E1
Shakespeare Ave
Bath BA2 . . . . 44 F4
Taunton TA1. . . . . .213 C3
Shakespeare Ct BS23 . . . . . 48 F3
Shakespeare Rd BA3 . . . . . 78 C1
Shaking Dro TA9. . . . . .137 B6
Shalford La
Charlton Musgrove BA9. . . .161 A2
Shalford BA9 . . . . .216 D8
Shallows The BS31. . . . . . . 25 F3
Shambles The TA3. . . . . . . .170 B4
Sham Castle La BA2. . . . . . . 45 C7
Shannon Wlk BS20. . . . . .2 F6
Shapcott La EX36 . . . . .162 C2
Shapcott Wood Hill
 EX36 . . . . .162 A2
Shaplands BS9. . . . . .5 A4
Shapway TA19. . . . . .184 F3
Shapway Cross TA19 . . . . . .184 F3
Shapway La BA4 . . . . .141 F2
Shapway Rd BA4. . . . . .141 F2
Shapwick Heath National
 Nature Reserve★ BA6. . .138 A3
Shapwick Hill TA7 . . . . . . .155 F8
Shapwick Rd BA6. . . . . . . .138 A4
Shapwick Right Dro TA7 . . .155 C6
Sharland Cl BS9 . . . . .5 E3
Sharland Gr BS13. . . . . 22 C4
Sharlands TA11 . . . . .184 C5
Sharpenton La TA7. . . . . . .155 D6
Sharpham Dro BA16 . . . . . .138 E1
Sharpham La
Glastonbury BA16 . . . . . .138 D1
Stoke St Gregory TA3. . . . .170 E5
Sharpham Rd BS27. . . . . 89 F7
Shatterwell Cotts BA9. . . . .216 C4
Shatt La TA5. . . . . .152 F3
Shatwell La
Castle Cary BA9. . . . . . . .214 F1
Yarlington BA9. . . . . .175 F8
Shaulders The TA2. . . . . . . .213 C7
Shave Cross DT6. . . . . .199 F1
Shave Hill SP8. . . . . .177 D4
Shave La
Crewkerne TA18 . . . . . . .224 A3
Donyatt TA19 . . . . .183 C1
Horton TA19 . . . . .183 C1
South Brewham BA10 . . . .161 A6
Shawford La BA11. . . . . . . .101 D7
Shaw Gdns BS14. . . . . 23 A8
Shaw Path TA8. . . . . .104 C6
Shaws Way BA2. . . . . 43 F5
Sheafhayne Cross EX14 . . . .192 E4
Shearing Cross TA20. . . . . .199 A5
Shearn La TA8. . . . . .104 B7
Shearwater Cl TA6. . . . . . . .209 D6
Shedrick Hill TA20 . . . . . . .199 B8
Sheepfair La SN14 . . . . 13 F8
Sheephouse Cvn Pk BS20. . .3 E7
Sheeplands La DT9 . . . . . . .225 B5
Sheeplands The DT9 . . . . . .225 B5
Sheeps Croft BS13. . . . . 22 A5
Sheepstealing La TA4 . . . . .150 E5
Sheepway BS20. . . . . .3 B5
Sheep Way TA19 . . . . .184 E3
Sheepway La BS20 . . . . .3 C5
Sheldon's La TA22. . . . . . . .163 A7
Sheldon Cl BS21. . . . . .6 F2
Sheldon Cl TA1. . . . . .212 E4
Sheldon Dr BA5. . . . . .203 C4
Sheldon Mill **3** BA5. . . . . .203 C3
Shelduck Cl TA24 . . . . .201 C5
Shell's La
Chard TA20. . . . . .193 A3
Shepton Beauchamp TA19. .184 E4
Shelley Ave BS21 . . . . .6 D2
Shelley Cl
Burnham-on-S TA8. . . . . . . 85 A2
Yeovil BA21 . . . . .218 D6
Shelley Dr TA8. . . . . 85 B2
Shelley Gr TA1. . . . . .213 B3
Shelley Rd
Bath BA2 . . . . 44 F4
Radstock BA3 . . . . 78 C1
Weston-Super-Mare BS23. . 49 A4
Shellthorn Gr TA6. . . . . . . .208 F2
Shelthorn Hill TA5 . . . . . . .152 F3
Shelway La TA19. . . . . .184 C4
Shepherd's Cl TA11. . . . . . .157 A4
Shepherd's Cnr TA23. . . . . .131 E4
Shepherd's Dro TA7. . . . . . .155 A3
Shepherd's Hay TA1 . . . . . .212 C2
Shepherd's Hill SP8 . . . . . .177 E4
Shepherd's La
Chard TA20. . . . . .223 B4
Frome BA11. . . . . .144 B7
Hemyock EX15. . . . . .180 F1
Shepherds Cl TA6. . . . . . . .208 D6
Shepherds Cross BA4 . . . . .176 C5
Shepherds Way BS22. . . . . . 32 C2
Sheppard's Barton **11**
 BA11 . . . . .119 E5
Sheppard's Cnr TA5. . . . . . .153 B5
Sheppards Gdns BA1. . . . . . 27 B1
Sheppards Wlk BA3. . . . . . . 96 D3
Sheppy's Cider Farm Ctr★
 TA4. . . . . .167 F2
Sheppy's Mill BS49. . . . . . . 34 D5
Shepton BS24. . . . . 49 A2
Shepton Beauchamp CE Fst
 Sch TA19 . . . . .184 E4
Shepton Mallet Com Hospl
 BA4. . . . . .204 F6
Shepton Mallet Inf Sch
 BA4. . . . . .205 C6
Shepton Mallet Mus★
 BA4. . . . . .205 B5

Shepton Old Rd
Croscombe BA5. . . . . . . .204 A6
Dinder BA5 . . . . .140 D7
Shepton Rd BA4, BA5 . . . . .204 D7
Sherborne Abbey★ DT9 .225 D3
Sherborne Abbey CE Prim
 Sch DT9. . . . . .225 B2
Sherborne Castle★ DT9 . .225 F3
Sherborne Hill DT9 . . . . . .225 E1
Sherborne Mus★ DT9 . . . .225 D4
Sherborne Old Castle★
 DT9 . . . . .225 F4
Sherborne Prep Sch
 DT9. . . . . .225 D3
Sherborne Prim Sch
 DT9. . . . . .225 E5
Sherborne Rd
Milborne Port DT9. . . . . .217 C2
Yenston BA8 . . . . .189 E6
Yeovil BA21 . . . . .219 D5
Sherborne Sch DT9 . . . . . .225 D4
Sherborne Sch for Girls
 DT9. . . . . .225 C4
Sherford Rd TA1. . . . . .212 E1
Sherford Terr TA1 . . . . .212 E1
Sheridan Cl TA6. . . . . .209 D3
Sheridan Gdns BA14. . . . . . 83 F6
Sheridan Rd
Bath BA2 . . . . 43 F5
Burnham-on-S TA8. . . . . . .104 C6
Sherlands **4** TA16 . . . . . . .195 F7
Sherlands Gdns **3** TA16. . .195 F7
Sherring Rd BA4. . . . . .205 D4
Sherrin Way BS13. . . . . 21 E3
Sherston Cl BS48 . . . . .9 A1
Shervage Ct TA6. . . . . .209 C5
Sherwood Cl BS31 . . . . 24 E5
Sherwood Cres BS22. . . . . . 31 F3
Sherwood Rd BS31. . . . . . . 24 E5
Shetland Way BS48 . . . . . . .9 A1
Shickle Gr BA2. . . . . 44 D1
Shiller's La DT9. . . . . .188 C7
Shiners Elms BS49. . . . . . . 34 B8
Shipham CE Fst Sch BS25 70 E8
Shipham Cl
Bristol BS14. . . . . 23 B5
Nailsea BS48 . . . . 18 F8
Shipham La BS25. . . . . 52 B1
Shipham Rd BS27. . . . . 71 A3
Ship La
Bristol BS1. . . . . .227 B1
Combwich TA5 . . . . .135 B5
Shiplate Rd BS24 . . . . 67 E6
Shipney La DT10 . . . . .190 C4
Shircombe La TA22 . . . . . . .147 F2
Shire Gdns BS11. . . . . .4 D8
Shirehampton Prim Sch
 BS11. . . . . .4 D6
Shirehampton Rd BS9. . . . . .5 C6
Shirehampton Sta BS11 . . . .4 D5
Shiremoor Hill TA16 . . . . . .195 F7
Shires The TA24 . . . . .201 C5
Shires Yd BA1 . . . . .228 B3
Shockerwick La BA1 . . . . . . 29 D4
Shoe La TA7 . . . . .209 E7
Shoot Hill TA17 . . . . .195 C8
Shophouse Rd BA2. . . . . 44 B5
Shop La
Pilton BA4. . . . . .140 E3
Wingfield BA14 . . . . 83 C6
Shopland Ho **8** BS21. . . . . .6 C2
Shoreditch BS40. . . . . 56 C7
Shoreditch Rd
Stoke St Mary TA3. . . . . . .169 A1
Taunton TA1. . . . . .213 B1
Shoredown La DT9, BA8. . .217 E6
Short Dro
Mudgley BS28. . . . . .138 C7
Westbury-sub-Mendip BA5,
 BS27. . . . . .110 B4
Short La
Draycott BS27 . . . . 90 E3
Litton BA3 . . . . 75 F2
Long Ashton BS41. . . . . . . 11 A2
Stone Allerton BS26 . . . . . 88 C2
Shortland La BS28. . . . . . . .108 C3
Shortmarsh La BA22 . . . . . .196 F4
Short Way BS8. . . . . 10 B4
Shortwood Rd BS13. . . . . . . 22 E3
Shortwood Wlk BS13. . . . . . 22 E3
Shoscombe CE Prim Sch
 BA2. . . . . 79 F5
Shoscombe Gdns BA11. . . .120 C7
Shovel La TA6. . . . . .153 E3
Showell Pk TA2. . . . . .212 B7
Showering Cl BS14. . . . . . . 23 D5
Showering Rd BS14. . . . . . . 23 D5
Showground Rd TA6. . . . . .209 B1
Shrewsbury Bow BS24. . . . . 50 A8
Shrewsbury Rd BA22. . . . . .218 D7
Shrubbery Ave BS23. . . . . . 30 D1
Shrubbery Cl TA8. . . . . 84 E8
Shrubbery Rd BS23 . . . . 30 D1
Shrubbery Terr **11** BS23. . . 30 C1
Shrubbery Wlk BS23. . . . . . 30 D1
Shrubbery Wlk W BS23. . . . 30 D1
Shudrick La TA19 . . . . .221 C3
Shums Ct **3** BA1. . . . . . . .228 C2
Shurtland La TA4 . . . . .150 C3
Shurton La TA5. . . . . .134 C6
Shute's La SP8. . . . . .177 E4
Shute La
Bruton BA10 . . . . .215 D6
Huish Champflower TA4. . . .165 E8
Long Sutton TA10. . . . . . .172 A4
Shute Lake La TA18. . . . . . .224 D5
Shuteleigh TA21 . . . . .222 E5
Shutemead TA1. . . . . .212 A4

Shute Row TA21. . . . . .222 E6
Shuter Rd BS13. . . . . 21 E5
Shutewater Cl TA1. . . . . . . .212 A4
Shutewater Hill TA1. . . . . . .212 A4
Shutgate Mdw TA4. . . . . . .202 D3
Shuttern **2** TA1. . . . . .212 E3
Shuttern Bridge **3** TA1. . . .212 E3
Shutwell La BA4 . . . . .140 E3
Shyners Terr **8** TA16 . . . . . .195 F7
Sidcot Dr BS25. . . . . 70 A7
Sidcot La BS25. . . . . 70 A7
Sidcot Sch BS25. . . . . 70 B7
Sideland Cl BS14. . . . . 23 E6
Sidelings The BS40. . . . . . . 73 D8
Side Wood La EX36 . . . . . . .162 A1
Sidings The DT10 . . . . .190 C4
Sidmouth Cl TA8. . . . . .104 C8
Sidney Hill Cottage Homes
 BS25 . . . . 52 E4
Silbury Rd BS3. . . . . 11 E2
Silbury Rise BS31. . . . . 25 A2
Silcox Rd BS13. . . . . 22 C4
Silk Cl BA4 . . . . .205 B7
Silk House Barton DT10 .190 B4
Silklands Gr BS9. . . . . .5 C6
Silk Mills La TA2. . . . . .212 B6
Silk Mills Rd TA1. . . . . .212 B4
Silton Rd **1** SP8. . . . . .161 F1
Silverberry Rd BS22. . . . . . . 32 A1
Silvercombe **1** BS23. . . . . . 48 E5
Silver Ct BS48. . . . . .8 C2
Silverdale Cl
Brushford TA22 . . . . .163 E4
Wembdon TA6. . . . . .208 C5
Silverdown Hill TA4. . . . . . .150 C7
Silver La BA11. . . . . .144 B7
Silverlake Cotts DT9 . . . . . .188 B2
Silverlow Rd BS48. . . . . .8 D2
Silvermead TA24. . . . . .201 B5
Silvermead Ct TA24. . . . . . .201 B5
Silver Mead BS49. . . . . 34 D2
Silver Moor La BS29. . . . . . . 50 F7
Silver Rd BA16. . . . . .207 C5
Silver Springs TA19. . . . . . .184 E3
Silver St
11 Bampton EX16 . . . . . .164 B1
Barrington TA19. . . . . . . .184 D5
Barton St David TA11. . . . .158 A3
Barwick BA22 . . . . .197 F8
Bridgwater TA6 . . . . .208 F4
Bristol BS1. . . . . .227 A3
Bruton BA10 . . . . .215 E6
Chard TA20. . . . . .223 C3
Cheddar BS27. . . . . 90 B8
Chew Magna BS40. . . . . . . 39 B3
Congresbury BS49. . . . . . . 34 D2
Crewkerne TA18 . . . . . . .196 B3
Curry Mallet TA3 . . . . . . .183 C8
Ditcheat BA4 . . . . .159 C7
East Lambrook TA13 . . . . .220 C8
Fivehead TA3. . . . . .170 F1
Glastonbury BA6. . . . . . .206 E4
Holcombe BA3. . . . . 97 C1
Huntspill TA9 . . . . .136 A8
Ilminster TA19 . . . . .221 B4
Kilmersdon BA3. . . . . 98 B5
Kingsbury Episcopi TA12 . .185 B8
Kingsdon TA11. . . . . .173 D5
Langport TA10 . . . . .172 A3
Midsomer Norton BA3. . . . 97 A7
Milverton TA4. . . . . .167 A4
Nailsea BS48. . . . . .8 D2
Portishead BS20 . . . . .1 F1
Shepton Beauchamp TA19. .184 E4
South Petherton TA13 . . . .220 D5
Taunton TA1. . . . . .213 A3
Wells BA5 . . . . .203 E4
West Buckland TA21. . . . . .180 F7
Wincanton BA9 . . . . .216 C4
Wiveliscombe TA4 . . . . . .210 C4
Wrington BS40 . . . . 35 E2
Yeovil BA20 . . . . .219 B5
Silverstone Way BS49 . . . . . 34 D3
Simbriss Rd BA3. . . . . .114 C5
Simmons Cl BA16 . . . . . . .207 D5
Simms La BS39 . . . . 77 F5
Simon's Cl BS39. . . . . 77 F5
Simons Cl BS22. . . . . 32 A2
Simons Mews
Chard TA20. . . . . .223 E4
3 Weston-Super-Mare
 BS23. . . . . 48 F7
Simons Rd DT9 . . . . .225 D5
Sinclair Ho BS8. . . . . .226 A2
Singapore Rd BS23 . . . . 48 E3
Singer's Knoll BA11. . . . . . .119 F4
Singer Ct BA11 . . . . .119 F5
Single Hill BA2 . . . . 79 F5
Singleton Ct BA5. . . . . . . .203 C5
Sion Hill
Bath BA1. . . . . 27 E1
Bristol BS8. . . . . 11 F7
Sion Hill Pl BA1 . . . . 27 E1
Sion La BS8. . . . . 11 F7
Sion Pl
Bath BA2 . . . . 45 B6
Bristol BS8. . . . . 11 F7
Sion Rd BA1. . . . . 27 E1
Sir Bevil Grenville's Mon★
 BA1. . . . . 12 A1
Sir Gilbert Scott Ct TA4 . .202 E3
Siskin Wlk BS22 . . . . 49 E8
Sisters The BA4. . . . . .205 A6
Six Acres Cl TA1 . . . . .213 C5
Sixpence BS39. . . . . 59 D2
Six Streams BA1. . . . . 27 B2

Sixteen Acre La TA20.... **193** D8
Sixth Ave BS14........... **23** A7
Sixty Acres Cl BS8 .... **10** B4
Six Ways BS21 .... **6** C4
Skillgate La TA14 .... **185** E1
Skimmerton La TA5, TA6. **208** A5
Skinner's Hill BA2....... **78** F7
Skinner's La TA14....... **185** F2
Skinners La BS25 .... **52** F4
Skitmoor Dro BS28..... **109** C2
Skylark Ave BS21 ....**1** B1
Slab Dro TA7............ **155** A1
Sladacre La BS40 .... **54** E2
Slade's Cross TA20..... **193** D7
Sladebrook Ave BA2 .... **44** C3
Sladebrook Ct BA2...... **44** C3
Sladebrook Rd BA2 ..... **44** B4
Slade Cl TA4............ **150** E8
Slade La
 Barrow Gurney BS48..... **20** C4
 Golsoncott TA23........ **131** E1
 Hawkridge TA22........ **146** D1
 Lympsham BS24 .... **67** B1
 Rimpton BA22.......... **188** A7
 Rooks Bridge BS26 ...... **87** E4
 West Anstey EX36...... **162** B6
Slade Rd BS20 .... **2** D5
Slades Ct **2** BS48........ **19** A6
Slades Hill BA8 .... **176** E1
Slades Orch TA19........ **183** C1
Slade Way TA4.......... **202** E4
Slait Hill BA4........... **142** C7
Slait La BA9 .... **216** C7
Slapes Cl TA2........... **168** F6
Slate La BS14, BS31....... **41** B7
Sleep La BS14............ **23** D3
Sleight Cl BA21......... **218** C6
Sleight La BA5.......... **140** E8
Slippery Batch TA11 .... **211** A6
Sloe Cl BS22............. **49** D8
Slopers La BA9 .... **176** D5
Slough Green Cvn Pk
 TA3 .... **182** D8
Slough Hill TA3......... **182** D6
Slough La
 Cold Ashton SN14 .... **12** F5
 Crowcombe TA4........ **151** A8
 North Wootton BA4 .... **140** B3
 Stoke St Gregory TA3.... **170** F4
 Upottery EX14 .... **191** F5
Sloway La TA6, TA9..... **136** A8
Slow Court La BA22..... **174** D3
Slowland La BA5......... **110** D8
Slugg Hill BA16......... **207** D3
Smallacombe Hill EX16,
 EX36 .... **162** D4
Smallbrook La BS39..... **41** B6
Smallcombe Cl BA3 ..... **78** E5
Smallcombe Rd BA3 .... **78** E4
Small Down End BS25... **51** F2
Small Down La BA4 .... **142** B2
Small La EX16 .... **179** B2
Small Mead Dro BA6.... **157** F4
Smallmoor Chase BA6.. **156** E7
Smallmoor Dro TA7..... **155** C3
Smallridge Rd EX13..... **198** A4
Smalls Mead **2** TA11 ... **173** F7
Small St BS1............ **227** A4
Smallway BS49........... **34** D5
Small Way La BA22..... **214** C1
Smallways La TA7....... **137** B3
Smeathy La EX15 .... **180** F3
Smeaton Rd BS1......... **11** F5
Sminhays Cnr TA23 .... **149** B5
Smith's Forge Ind Est
 BS49 .... **16** F3
Smith's Hill TA18 ...... **196** C8
Smith's La BA4 .... **159** C6
Smith's Row TA15...... **186** B4
Smith's Terr BA21 ..... **219** C6
Smithfield Rd BA16 .... **207** B4
Smithick's La BA11..... **143** E6
Smithmead BS13......... **22** B5
Smiths Cl BS27 .... **91** A1
Smith Way TA9......... **104** D3
Smithy TA1............. **212** B3
Smithyard La TA4, TA23.. **202** A3
Smithy La BA11......... **119** E4
Smokeham La TA4...... **151** D5
Smoky Hole La TA18 ... **185** F1
Smurl La TA9........... **104** C1
Smythe Croft BS14..... **23** A3
Smythes Cross EX15 ... **191** C7
Snagg La BA4........... **159** D5
Snag La BA9 .... **216** E3
Snake La BS28.......... **109** C1
Snakelake Hill BA10.... **160** C7
Snap Hill TA11......... **173** D8
Snathe Lea **4** TA4..... **167** F8
Snedden Gr TA1........ **213** B5
Snipefield La BS28..... **108** A6
Snowberry Cl BS22...... **32** A1
Snowberry Ct TA1 ..... **213** C2
Snowdon Cottage La
 TA20 .... **223** B4
Snowdon Hts TA20..... **223** B4
Snowdon Vale BS23..... **31** A1
Snowdrop Cl BS22 ...... **32** A5
Snow Hill BA1........... **28** A1
Snow Hill Ho BA1....... **228** C4
Society Rd BA4......... **205** A6
Sock's La BA10 .... **160** F8
Sock Hill BA21......... **187** C6

Sock La BA21 .... **187** C6
Soho BA21 .... **81** E5
Solomon's Hollow TA3.. **169** F2
Solon Ct BS13 .... **21** F5
Solsbury Ct BA1 .... **28** F3
Solsbury La BA1......... **28** F4
Solsbury View **17** BA1.. **28** A1
Solsbury Way BA1 ...... **28** A2
Somer Ave BA3 .... **77** F2
Somer Ct BA3 .... **78** B1
Somerdale Ave
 Bath BA2.............. **44** D2
 Bristol BS4............. **22** D8
 Weston-Super-Mare BS22.. **49** C8
Somerdale Cl BS22...... **49** C8
Somerdale Rd BS31...... **24** F7
Somerdale Rd N BS30,
 BS31................. **24** F8
Somerdale View BA2.... **44** C2
Somer Ho BA3........... **78** A1
Somer Lea BA3 .... **96** D5
Somerleaze Cl BA5 .... **203** B3
Somer Rd BA3........... **77** F2
Somerset Ave
 Taunton TA1........... **212** B2
 Weston-Super-Mare BS22,
 BS24................. **50** A8
Somerset Brick & Tile Mus★
 TA6................. **209** A8
Somerset Bridge Prim Sch
 TA6................. **209** B2
Somerset Cl
 Martock TA12.......... **185** E7
 Shepton Mallet BA4..... **205** C5
Somerset Coll of Arts & Tech
 TA1.................. **212** D4
**Somerset Coll of Arts & Tech
(Annexe)** TA1......... **212** C3
**Somerset Coll of Arts & Tech
(Bishops Hull Annexe)**
 TA1.................. **212** C3
Somerset County Mus★
 TA1.................. **212** F4
Somerset Ct BA21....... **219** A6
Somerset Cty Cricket Gd★
 TA1.................. **212** F4
**Somerset & Dorset Joint
Rly**★ BA3.............. **97** A8
**Somerset & Dorset Rlwy
Trust Mus**★ TA23...... **131** E4
Somerset Fire HQ TA2.. **169** A7
Somerset Folly BA2...... **60** B2
Somerset Gdns TA6..... **209** C3
Somerset Ho
 Bath BA2.............. **44** D3
 12 Bristol BS2........ **227** C3
Somerset La BA1........ **27** E1
Somerset Mews BS23... **48** F6
Somerset Nuffield Hospl
 TA2.................. **212** B7
Somerset Pl
 Bath BA1.............. **27** E1
 Taunton TA1........... **213** B4
 Yeovil BA20........... **219** A3
Somerset Rd
 Bridgwater TA6........ **209** C3
 Clevedon BS21........... **6** E3
 Frome BA11........... **119** E4
 Portishead BS20.........**1** F5
Somerset Rural Life Mus★
 BA6................. **206** A4
Somerset Sq
 Bristol BS1........... **227** B1
 3 Nailsea BS48......... **8** E2
Somerset St
 Bath BA1............. **228** C1
 Bristol BS1........... **227** B1
 Bristol, Kingsdown BS2.. **227** A4
Somerset Way
 Highbridge TA9........ **104** E3
 Paulton BS39........... **77** E6
Somerton BS24........... **49** A2
Somerton Bsns Pk TA11. **211** B5
Somerton Dro TA11.... **209** D4
Somerton Door Dro
 Compton Dundon TA11.. **156** E1
 Somerton TA11........ **211** A7
Somerton Dro TA11.... **156** E1
Somerton Gr 8 BS8 .... **11** F6
Somerton Gdns BA11... **120** C7
Somerton Hill
 Langport TA10......... **172** E7
 Somerton TA11........ **211** A3
Somerton Inf Sch TA11. **211** C4
Somerton Rd
 Clevedon BS21........... **6** E1
 Langport TA10......... **172** A6
 Street BA16........... **207** D4
Somervale Rd BA3....... **78** E2
Somervale Sch BA3...... **78** A1
Somerville Cl
 Saltford BS31........... **25** E2
 Shepton Mallet BA4..... **205** D4
Somerville Cotts BA5... **204** B8
Somerville Rd
 Sandford BS25........... **52** A4
 Wells BA5............. **203** C5
Somerville Way TA6.... **209** D3
Soper Gdns BS4.......... **22** D7
Sopers Field TA20...... **223** D2
Sophia Gdns BS22....... **32** B4
Southampton Row 5
 TA2.................. **213** A8
South Ave
 Bath BA2.............. **44** D5
 Highbridge TA9........ **104** C4

South Ave continued
 Portishead BS20........... **2** D6
 Sherborne DT9......... **225** B2
Southay Cross TA20.... **193** A4
Southay La TA20....... **192** F4
South Bank
 Castle Cary BA7....... **214** B3
 Wookey Hole BA5..... **203** A8
Southbourne Gdns BA1.. **28** B1
Southbourne Ho TA6... **208** E4
Southbourne Mans BA2. **228** C2
South Brent TA9 .... **85** F3
South Bristol Bsns Pk
 BS4................... **22** E7
South Bristol Trad Pk BS3 **11** F3
Southbrook TA5........ **135** C2
Southbrook Cl TA5...... **135** C2
Southbrook Cotts BA9.. **216** H4
South Cary La BA7..... **214** A5
South Cl
 Draycott BS27.......... **90** E2
 Lympsham BS24 .... **86** B8
 Walton BA16.......... **156** E7
South Combe BS24....... **67** B6
**Southcombe House (Queens
Coll)** TA3............. **168** D1
Southcombe Way BA22. **186** B6
South Common La EX13. **198** A5
Southcot Pl BA2........ **228** C1
South Croft BS25........ **51** F2
Southcroft Dr BA13.... **121** D4
South Ct DT9........... **225** B3
South Dene BS9............ **5** E6
Southdown
 Charlton Horethorne
 DT9................. **176** A1
 Weston-Super-Mare BS23.. **31** F4
Southdown Ave BA2.... **44** B3
Southdown Com Inf Sch
 BA2.................. **44** B3
Southdown Cross EX16.. **179** B2
Southdown Jun Sch BA2.. **44** B3
Southdown Rd
 Bath BA2.............. **44** B4
 Bristol BS9.............. **5** F8
South Dro
 Curry Rivel TA10...... **171** B4
 North Curry TA3....... **170** D2
Southend Gdns TA9.... **104** E5
Southend Rd BS23....... **48** E4
Southernhay BS8....... **226** B2
Southernhay Ave BS8.. **226** B2
Southernhay Cres BS8. **226** B2
Southern Lea Rd TA8... **104** C8
Southern Ring Path 4
 BS21................... **6** B1
Southern Way BS21...... **6** C1
South Espl TA8........ **104** A5
Southey Rd BS21.......... **6** D2
Southfield
 Cheddar BS27.......... **90** B8
 Norton St Philip BA2..... **81** F4
 Radstock BA3.......... **79** A2
 Southwick BA14........ **83** F2
 Wiveliscombe TA4..... **210** C3
Southfield Cl
 Nailsea BS48............ **8** E3
 Taunton TA2........... **168** F6
 Weston-Super-Mare BS23.. **48** D2
 Woolavington TA7..... **136** E3
**Southfield Farm Cvn Pk &
Camp Site** TA8......... **65** F4
Southfield Hill BA3...... **99** A6
Southfield Rd
 Nailsea BS48............. **8** F3
 Shepton Mallet BA4..... **205** A5
Southfield Rd Trad Est
 BS48................... **8** F3
Southfields
 Frome BA11........... **120** A2
 Ilminster TA19........ **183** E2
South Fields BA6....... **206** E3
Southgate
 Bath BA1............. **228** C2
 Wiveliscombe TA4..... **210** C3
Southgate Ave TA6.... **209** A3
Southgate Dr BA9...... **216** C3
Southgate Rd BA9..... **216** C3
Southgate Sh Ctr BA1.. **228** C2
South Green St **8** BS8... **11** F6
South Harp TA13....... **220** E1
South Hele Cross EX16.. **165** C1
South Hill TA5.......... **51** F2
South La
 Challacombe EX31..... **126** A3
 Nether Stowey TA5... **134** B2
Southlands
 Bath BA1.............. **27** B1
 Carhampton TA24..... **131** B5
Southlands Dr BA2...... **60** B2
Southlands Way BS49.... **34** E5
South Lawn BS24......... **49** F4
South Lawn Cl BS24..... **49** F4
South Lea Rd BA1........ **44** A8
Southleaze BS25......... **70** A6
Southleaze Orch TA7... **207** C6
Southleaze Rd BA16.... **207** B6
Southleigh BS25.......... **69** F8
Southleigh Rd
 Bristol BS8........... **226** B4
 Taunton TA1.......... **213** B3
South Mdw BA5........ **113** A1
South Mdws BS40....... **35** E2
Southmead
 West Camel BA22...... **174** D3
 Winscombe BS25........ **70** A8
Southmead Cres TA18.. **224** C5

Southmead La BA8..... **190** A6
Southmead Rd BS22.... **49** B7
Southmead Terr TA18.. **224** C5
South Molton Rd EX16. **164** B1
South Moors La TA7 ... **137** B2
Southover BA5......... **203** D3
Southover Rd BS39...... **59** D1
South Par
 Bath BA2............. **228** C2
 Chew Magna BS40....... **39** B3
 Frome BA11........... **119** E4
 Weston-Super-Mare BS23.. **48** D8
South Parade Cotts BA2. **45** C1
South Petherton Hospl
 TA13................ **220** D5
South Petherton Inf Sch
 TA13................ **220** C4
South Petherton Jun Sch
 TA13................ **220** D3
South Pk TA24......... **200** D6
South Rd
 Brean TA8.............. **65** F3
 Lympsham BS24......... **67** B1
 Midsomer Norton BA3... **78** B1
 Portishead BS20........... **2** D7
 Taunton TA1.......... **213** A2
 Timsbury BA2........... **60** B2
 Watchet TA23.......... **202** C6
 Weston-Super-Mare BS23.. **30** C1
Southridge Hts BS23..... **67** A8
South Road Villas BA9.. **216** C3
South Rock Ind Est BA3.. **96** D1
South Side BS23.......... **48** E8
Southside BS9............ **5** E8
Southside Cl BS9.......... **5** E8
Southside Cres BS22..... **31** A4
South St
 Burnham-on-S TA8..... **104** A6
 Castle Cary BA7....... **214** B4
 Crewkerne TA18....... **224** D5
 Hinton St George TA17. **195** D7
 Holcombe Rogus TA21... **178** F5
 Kington Magna SP8..... **177** E1
 Milborne Port DT9.... **217** D2
 Montacute TA15....... **186** B3
 Sherborne DT9........ **225** E3
 South Petherton TA13.. **220** D4
 Stratton-on-t F BA3..... **96** F2
 Taunton TA1.......... **213** A3
 Walton BA16.......... **156** E7
 Wellington TA21....... **222** E5
 Wells BA5............. **203** D4
 West Camel BA22...... **174** D3
 Wincanton BA9........ **216** C3
 Wiveliscombe TA4..... **210** C4
 Yeovil BA20........... **219** B4
Southstoke La BA2....... **62** F8
Southstoke Rd BA2...... **44** F1
South Terr
 Burnham-on-S TA8..... **104** B6
 Weston-Super-Mare BS23.. **48** D8
Southtown La BA6...... **158** B8
Southview TA3......... **168** D1
South View
 12 Barwick BA22..... **197** F8
 Bawdrip TA7.......... **136** E2
 Bradford Abbas DT9... **187** E1
 Broadway TA19........ **183** C2
 Clandown BA3.......... **78** E5
 Ditcheat BA4.......... **159** C6
 Horrington BA5........ **113** A1
 Lynford-on-F TA11..... **158** C1
 Monkton Combe BA2.... **45** E1
 Paulton BS39........... **77** E6
 Portishead BS20........... **2** D7
 Queen Camel BA22.... **174** F3
 Timsbury BA2........... **60** B2
 Westleigh EX16........ **179** A3
Southview Cl
 Hutton BS24............ **49** E2
 Westonzoyland TA7.... **154** F5
South View Pl BA3....... **78** E2
Southview Rd TA7...... **154** F5
South View Rd
 Bath BA2.............. **44** D6
 Milborne Port DT9.... **217** C3
South View Terr
 Taunton TA1.......... **168** D1
 Yatton BS49............ **17** B1
South Villas TA4....... **167** F6
Southville BA21....... **219** C5
Southville Rd BS23...... **48** E4
Southville Terr BA2...... **45** B4
Southway Cl BA21..... **218** F6
Southway Cres BA21... **218** F6
Southway Ct BS21......... **6** D1
Southway Dr BA21..... **218** F6
Southwell TA3......... **168** D1
Southwell Cl TA3...... **168** D1
Southwell Cres TA9.... **104** E3
Southwell St TA9...... **104** E3
Southwell St BS2...... **226** C4
South Western Bsns Pk
 DT9................. **225** D3
South Western Terr
 BA20................ **219** C4
Southwick CE Prim Sch
 BA14................. **83** F3
Southwick Ctry Pk★ BA14 **83** F5
Southwick Rd TA9..... **106** C1
Southwood BA4........ **159** D8
Southwood Ave BS9...... **5** C8
Southwood Dr BS9........ **5** B8
Southwood Dr E BS9...... **5** C8
Southwood Gr TA1..... **212** C2
Southwoods BA20..... **219** A3
Southwood Way TA3... **181** C5
Sovereign Rd TA6..... **209** D7

Sovereign Sh Ctr BS23... **48** D8
Sowden Hill TA5....... **134** D4
Spanish Hill TA6...... **153** F2
Spargrove La BA4...... **142** B5
Sparkford Hill La BA22. **175** A4
Sparkford Rd BA22.... **175** A6
Sparkhayes La TA24... **124** A3
Sparks Way TA9....... **104** D3
Sparrow Hill Way BS26.. **88** E6
Sparrow La TA24...... **146** C7
Sparrow Rd BA21..... **219** B6
Spartley Dr BS13........ **21** F6
Spartley Wlk BS13...... **21** F6
Spaxton CE Prim Sch
 TA5.................. **152** E7
Spaxton Cl TA8........ **104** C8
Spaxton Rd TA5....... **153** C7
Spearcey Cl TA3....... **181** D8
Spearcey La TA3....... **181** D8
Spearhay La TA20..... **198** F5
Spear Mead DT8....... **199** F7
Spears La TA4......... **166** A4
Specket La DT8........ **199** E5
Speckington La BA22... **174** B2
Specklemead BS39...... **77** D5
Speedwell Ind Est 1 BS21 **6** C2
Speke Cl
 Ilminster TA19........ **221** B4
 Merriott TA16......... **195** F7
 Staplegrove TA2....... **212** B6
Speke Ct TA19......... **221** B4
Spencer Ave TA2...... **212** E6
Spencer Cl TA6........ **209** D3
Spencer Dr
 Midsomer Norton BA3... **78** A2
 Weston-Super-Mare BS22.. **32** B3
Spencer Ho **6** BS1..... **227** B1
Spencers Belle Vue BA1. **228** B4
Sperring Ct BA3......... **96** F8
Sperry Cross TA4..... **149** B1
Spicer Way TA20...... **223** D2
Spillers Cl TA6........ **208** E2
Spindleberry Gr BS48.... **9** A2
Spiningmill Cotts 3
 BA11................ **119** E5
Spinners End BS22...... **32** B4
Spinners Ho **5** BA4.... **205** B6
Spinney Croft BS13..... **21** F5
Spinneyfield TA4...... **167** F7
Spinney Rd BS24........ **50** D4
Spinney The
 Ashcott TA7.......... **156** N6
 Portishead BS20........... **2** C4
 Taunton TA1.......... **212** D2
 Weston-Super-Mare BS24.. **48** F1
Spire Cross TA24...... **147** A4
Splatt La TA5......... **152** E8
Splott BS26............. **88** F6
Spoonbill Rd TA6...... **209** B4
Spratts Bridge BS40..... **39** A3
Sprigg Dr BS20............ **1** F1
Springbok Cl BA16.... **207** D7
Spring Cres BA2....... **228** C2
Springer's Hill BA3.... **116** A3
Springfield
 Ilminster TA19........ **221** B2
 Norton St Philip BA2..... **81** E4
 Peasedown St John BA2.. **79** C7
 Street BA16........... **207** B5
Springfield Ave
 Bridgwater TA6....... **208** C3
 Bristol, Shirehampton BS11. **4** D6
 Weston-Super-Mare BS22.. **31** D1
Springfield Bldgs
 Midsomer Norton BS39.. **77** D2
 Radstock BA3.......... **79** A3
Springfield Cl
 Bath BA2.............. **44** B5
 Cheddar BS27.......... **90** A8
 Cross BS26............. **69** F2
Springfield Cotts
 Upton Cheyney BS30..... **26** A3
 Winsford TA24........ **147** A6
Springfield Cres BA3.... **79** A3
Spring Field Cres DT9... **225** C3
Springfield Ct BA4..... **205** A5
Springfield Dr BS28.... **108** C3
Springfield Flats TA20.. **223** C4
Springfield Gdns BS29... **51** A3
Springfield Ho
 Bristol BS6........... **226** A4
 Portishead BS20........... **2** C4
Springfield Hts BA3..... **78** E4
Springfield Lawn BS11.... **4** D6
Springfield Pl
 Bath BA1.............. **27** E1
 Clandown BA3.......... **78** E4
 Yeovil BA21........... **218** E7
Springfield Rd
 Cheddar BS27.......... **90** A8
 Highbridge TA9....... **104** E4
 Milborne Port DT9.... **217** D3
 Pill BS20............... **4** C4
 Portishead BS20........... **2** B5
 Wellington TA21....... **222** C7
 Wincanton BA9........ **216** B4
 Yeovil BA21........... **218** E7
Springfields
 East Chinnock BA22.... **196** E8
 Stalbridge DT10....... **190** C4
Springfield Terr
 Street BA16........... **207** B5
 Tatworth TA20........ **198** C8
Spring Gardens Rd BA2. **228** C2
Spring Gdns
 Minehead TA24........ **201** B5
 Wiveliscombe TA4..... **210** C4

Spring Ground Rd BS39 . . **77** E5
Spring Hill
Bristol BS2. . . . .**227** A4
Weston-Super-Mare BS22. . **31** D2
Springhill Cl BS39 . . . . **77** C6
Spring Hill Dr BS22 . . . . **31** E1
Spring La
Bath BA1. . . . . **28** B2
Dundry BS41. . . . . **22** A1
Sandford Orcas DT9 . . . . . **188** C7
Springley Rd TA6 . . . . **209** D6
Springmead TA20 . . . . **223** B3
Springmead Sch BA11 . . . . **101** E4
Spring Rd BA11 . . . . **119** F6
Spring Rise
Portishead BS20 . . . . **2** C3
Puriton TA7 . . . . **136** C4
Wells BA5 . . . . **203** C3
Spring Terr
Frome BA11. . . . .**119** D2
Weston-Super-Mare BS22. . **31** C2
Spring Vale BA1 . . . . **28** B2
Spring Valley BS22. . . . . **31** C2
Springway Ind Est TA7 . . . . **155** A5
Spring Wood Gdns BS24. . **49** E3
Spruce Way
Bath BA2. . . . . **62** E8
Weston-Super-Mare BS22. . **49** E8
Spurwells TA19 . . . . **183** F4
Squares Rd TA5. . . . . **135** F2
Square The
Axbridge BS26. . . . . **70** C2
Banwell BS29. . . . . **51** B3
Bath BA2. . . . . **228** B1
Edington TA7 . . . . **137** C2
Maiden Bradley BA12 . . . . .**144** C2
Shipham BS25 . . . . **70** E7
Taunton TA1 . . . . **213** C2
Temple Cloud BS39 . . . . **58** E1
Wellow BA2. . . . . **62** D1
Westbury-sub-Mendip BA5 **110** E6
Winscombe BS25. . . . . **69** E6
Wiveliscombe TA4 . . . . **210** C4
Woolavington TA7 . . . . **136** E4
Squibbs Cl TA6 . . . . **209** D5
Squibbs Ho TA6. . . . . **208** F5
Squire La BS40. . . . . **55** C1
Squirrel Ct TA21 . . . . **222** D5
Stabbins Cl BS23 . . . . **32** B5
Stables The BA3 . . . . **98** B5
Stable Yd BA4 . . . . **44** D6
Stacey's Ct TA10 . . . . **171** F5
Staddlestones BA3 . . . . **96** F7
Staddonhill Rd TA24 . . . . .**146** F8
Stafford Pl BS23 . . . . **48** E8
Stafford Rd
Bridgwater TA6 . . . . **209** C3
Portishead BS20 . . . . **2** E4
Weston-Super-Mare BS23. . **48** F7
Stagman La TA7, TA16 . . . .**156** C8
Stag Mill Cross EX16 . . . . **178** B3
Stag Way BA6 . . . . **206** C4
Stainer Cl BS4 . . . . **22** D7
Staker's Cross TA20 . . . . . **195** B4
Staker's Cross La TA18,
TA20 . . . . **195** B4
Stalbridge Cl DT10 . . . . . . **190** B4
Stalbridge La
Marnhull DT10. . . . . **190** F2
Sturminster Newton DT10. **190** F1
Stalbridge Pk DT10 . . . . . .**190** A4
Stalbridge Prim Sch
DT10. . . . . **190** B5
Stalbridge Rd
Henstridge BA8 . . . . **190** A6
Stalbridge Weston DT10 . . **190** A3
Stourton Caundle DT10 . . . **189** F2
Stalcombe La BA2 . . . . **42** B4
Staling Way BA4 . . . . **205** C4
Stallards TA21 . . . . **222** C3
Stallgrove La BA16. . . . . . . **207** D3
Stall St BA1 . . . . **228** C2
Stambrook Pk BA1. . . . . **29** A5
Stammery Hill EX13 . . . . . .**198** C1
Stanchester Com Sch
TA14 . . . . **186** A4
Stanchester Way TA10 . . . **171** D4
Stancombe La
Flax Bourton BS48. . . . . **19** E7
Westbury-sub-Mendip BA5 **110** F8
Standards Rd TA7. . . . . **154** C5
Standards The TA7. . . . . . . **137** D2
Standerwick Cross BA11 **102** B3
Standerwick Orch TA19 . .**183** C2
Standfast Pl TA2. . . . . **213** C8
Standhill Rd TA10. . . . . **155** F2
Standish Ct TA1 . . . . **212** F4
Standish St TA6. . . . . **208** F7
Stane Way BS11 . . . . **4** C7
Stanford Pl BS4. . . . . **22** D7
Stanhope Pl BA1. . . . . **228** A2
Stanhope Rd BS23. . . . . **48** E3
Stanier Cl BA11. . . . . **120** D6
Stanier Rd BA2 . . . . **228** A2
Stankley View TA19 . . . . . **184** F4
Stanley Cl
Bridgwater TA6 . . . . **208** F2
Staplegrove TA2. . . . . **212** C6
Stanley Ct BA3. . . . . **78** B2
Stanley Gr BS23. . . . . **48** F7
Stanley Rd ② BS23. . . . . . . **48** F7
Stanley Rd W BA2. . . . . **44** D5
Stanley Terr BA3. . . . . **79** A3
Stanley Villas ⑫ BA1. . . . . **28** A1
Stanmoor Rd TA7 . . . . **170** F8
Stanshalls Cl BS40 . . . . **37** C8
Stanshalls Dr BS40. . . . . . . **37** C8

Stanshalls La BS40. . . . . . . **37** C8
Stanton Drew Prim Sch
BS39. . . . . **40** A2
Stanton Drew Stone Circles★
BS39. . . . . **40** A3
Stanton La BS39 . . . . **40** D4
Stanton Rd BS40. . . . . **39** B3
Stanton Wick La BS39. . . . . **40** B1
Stant Way TA20. . . . . **193** C6
Stanway Cl
Bath BA2 . . . . **44** D1
Taunton TA2 . . . . **212** D7
Staple Cl TA4. . . . . **132** E4
Staplecombe Vineyard★
TA2 . . . . **168** C6
Staplegate EX16 . . . .**178** A3
Staple Gr BS31. . . . . **24** D5
Staplegrove CE Prim Sch
Staplegrove TA2. . . . . **212** C7
Staplegrove Manor TA2 . **212** D8
Staplegrove Rd
Staplegrove TA2. . . . . **212** C7
Taunton TA1, TA2 . . . . **212** E5
Staple Hill TA3 . . . . **182** C5
Staple La TA4. . . . . **132** E4
Staples Cl BS23. . . . . **6** E1
Staples Gn BS22. . . . . **32** B3
Staples Hill BA3 . . . . **64** C4
Staples Mdw TA20 . . . . . . **198** D8
Stapleton Cl TA12. . . . . **185** E7
Stapleton Cross TA12 . . . .**185** E7
Stapleton Rd TA12 . . . . . . **185** E7
Stapley Cross TA3 . . . . **181** B1
Stapling La TA24. . . . . **130** F3
Starcross Rd BS22 . . . . **32** A2
Star La BS20. . . . . **4** D4
Starling Cl BS22 . . . . **49** E8
Starrs Cl BS26. . . . . **70** B2
Stars La BA20. . . . . **219** C4
Statham Cl
Cheddar BS27 . . . . **90** B7
Taunton TA1. . . . .**212** C2
Statham Gr TA1. . . . . **212** C2
Stathe Cotts TA7 . . . . **171** B7
Stathe Rd TA7 . . . . **171** A8
Station App
Bristol BS1. . . . . **227** C1
Frome BA11. . . . .**120** A4
Ilminster TA19 . . . .**183** E1
Pensford BS39. . . . . **40** D5
Weston-Super-Mare BS23. . **48** E7
Station Cl
Backwell BS48. . . . . **18** F7
Congresbury BS49. . . . . **34** C4
Station Lodge ⑧ BS23 . . . . **48** E7
Station Mead BA3. . . . . **96** D3
Station Path TA11. . . . . **211** D3
Station Rd
Ashcott TA7 . . . .**156** B8
Axbridge BS26. . . . . **70** C2
Backwell BS48. . . . . **19** A6
Bampton EX16. . . . . **164** B1
Bath BA1 . . . . **44** C7
Binegar BA3. . . . . **114** D7
Bishops Lydeard TA4 . . . . .**167** E8
Blagdon BS40. . . . . **54** E3
Bristol, Shirehampton BS11 . **4** D5
Bristol, Shirehampton BS11 . **4** E6
Bruton BA10. . . . . **215** F6
Burlescombe EX16. . . . . . . **179** B3
Burnham-on-S TA9. . . . . . . **85** F3
Burtle TA7 . . . . **137** D6
Castle Cary BA7. . . . . **214** B6
Chard Junction TA20 . . . . .**198** D8
Cheddar BS27 . . . . **90** B7
Clevedon BS21. . . . . **6** D3
Clutton BS39 . . . . **58** E3
Congresbury BS49. . . . . **34** C4
Cossington TA7 . . . . **136** F3
Draycott BS27. . . . . **90** E2
Dunster TA24. . . . . **201** E4
Flax Bourton BS48. . . . . **20** A8
Freshford BA3. . . . . **64** C5
Hatch Beauchamp TA3. . . .**183** A4
Ilminster TA19 . . . .**221** A4
Keynsham BS31. . . . . **24** E6
Meare TA7 . . . . **138** C1
Midsomer Norton BA3. . . . . **78** B2
Milborne Port DT9. . . . . . . **217** D4
Milverton TA4. . . . .**167** A5
Misterton TA18 . . . . **224** E4
Nailsea BS48. . . . . **8** F2
Norton Fitzwarren TA2. . . .**168** B4
Pill BS20 . . . . **4** C4
Portbury BS20. . . . . **3** E5
Portishead BS20 . . . . **2** D6
Sandford BS25. . . . . **51** F4
Shapwick TA7 . . . . **137** F2
Shepton Mallet BA4. . . . . . **205** B5
Sherborne DT9 . . . . **225** E3
Stalbridge DT10. . . . . **190** B4
Stogumber TA4 . . . . **150** D8
Taunton TA1. . . . .**212** F5
Templecombe BA8. . . . . . . **176** E1
Walpole TA6. . . . . **136** B3
Wanstrow BA4. . . . . **142** F4
Washford TA23 . . . . **131** E4
Wellington TA21. . . . . **222** C7
Wellow BA2. . . . . **62** D1
Westbury-sub-Mendip BA5 **110** E5
Weston-Super-Mare BS23. . **48** E7
Weston-Super-Mare, St Georges
BS22 . . . . **32** D2
Weston-Super-Mare, Worle
BS22 . . . . **31** F2
Williton TA4 . . . . **202** E3
Wincanton BA9 . . . . **216** C3
Wiveliscombe TA4 . . . . **210** C4

Station Rd continued
Wrington BS40 . . . . **35** D2
Yatton BS49. . . . . **17** B1
Station Rd (Blackmoor La)
BA8. . . . . **190** A7
Station Rd Ind Est BA10. **215** F6
Station Road Bsns Pk
DT10. . . . . **190** B5
Station Terr TA24 . . . . **201** A7
Station Way BA4. . . . . **141** E1
Station Wlk TA9 . . . . **104** E3
Staundle La TA3 . . . . **183** B8
Staunton Fields BS14 . . . . **23** C4
Staunton La
Minehead TA24 . . . . **201** A4
Whitchurch BS14. . . . . **23** D3
Staunton Rd TA24. . . . . . . **201** A5
Staunton Rise TA24 . . . . . **201** A5
Staunton Way BS14 . . . . . . **23** D4
Stavordale Gr BS14 . . . . . . **23** B6
Stawell Rd TA7. . . . . **137** B1
Stealmalong BA3 . . . . **183** E7
Steam Mills BA3. . . . . **96** F8
Steam Packet Terr ②
TA6 . . . . **209** B4
Steanbow Cotts BA4 . . . .**140** D3
Steart Ave TA8. . . . . **104** B6
Steart Cl TA8. . . . . **104** B6
Steart Cotts TA3 . . . . **169** C3
Steart Ct TA8 . . . . **104** A7
Steart Dr TA8. . . . . **104** A6
Steart Gdns TA8 . . . . **104** B6
Steart Hill BA22. . . . . **174** D5
Steart La
Babcary TA11. . . . . **174** B6
Wheddon Cross TA24. . . . . **129** F3
Stedhams Cl TA21 . . . . **222** D7
Steeds Terr TA1. . . . . **115** D6
Steel's La BA9 . . . . **161** D2
Steel La TA7 . . . . **137** D2
Steel Mills BS31. . . . . **24** F4
Steel Well La BA8. . . . . **190** A6
Steep La TA22. . . . . **164** C8
Steeple View BA11 . . . . . . **116** A3
Steep The TA24 . . . . **147** C5
Steevens Ho (Almshouses)
⑬ BS2. . . . . **227** C3
Stembridge Rd TA10 . . . . **156** B1
Stembridge Tower Mill★
TA10 . . . . **156** B1
Stembridge Way TA2. . . . . **168** B4
Stephen's Hill TA10 . . . . . **172** E4
Stephenson Dr BA11 . . . . . **120** D6
Stephenson Rd TA24 . . . . **201** B6
Stephen St TA1 . . . . **213** A4
Stephen Way ⑥ TA1 . . . . **213** A4
Steppes Cres ⑮ TA12 . . . . **185** E6
Steppes Mdw TA12. . . . . . **185** E6
Steps La BA22 . . . . **100** E7
Stert Dro TA5. . . . . **135** B7
Steven's Cl BA4 . . . . **205** A5
Stevens La
Frome BA11. . . . .**119** F3
Lympsham BS24 . . . . **67** C3
Stewart Ct EX13 . . . . **198** A2
Steway La BA1. . . . . **29** B6
Stibbear La TA19. . . . . **194** A8
Stiby Ct BA21 . . . . **218** F7
Stiby Rd BA21 . . . . **218** E7
Stickland BS21 . . . . **6** C1
Stickleball La BA4, BA6 . .**140** D1
Stickle Hill TA4 . . . . **151** B7
Stickle Path EX16 . . . . **165** C1
Sticklinch Rd BA6. . . . . . . **140** C2
Stilemead La BS40. . . . . **55** D1
Stiles Cl BA5 . . . . **203** B4
Stileway BA6. . . . . **138** E4
Stiling Cl TA9. . . . . **104** D4
Stillingfleet Rd BS13 . . . . . **22** C5
Stillington Cl BA5. . . . . **203** B3
Stillman Cl BS13. . . . . **21** E4
Stirling Way
Frome BA11. . . . .**120** C6
Keynsham BS31. . . . . **24** E4
Stirtingale Ave BA2 . . . . . . **44** C3
Stirtingale Rd BA2 . . . . **44** C3
Stitching La BS28 . . . . **138** C8
Stitchings La BA2 . . . . **62** F5
Stitchings Shord La BS39. **57** C4
Stoate Cl BS23. . . . . **202** C5
Stoberry Ave BA5. . . . . **203** E5
Stoberry Cres BA5 . . . . **203** E5
Stoberry Park Sch BA5. . **203** E5
Stock's La
Hatch Beauchamp TA3,
TA19 . . . . **183** B6
Leigh u M BA3. . . . .**116** B3
North Wootton BA4 . . . . . . **140** C4
Stockbridge La BA6. . . . . . **140** B2
Stockditch Rd TA12. . . . . . **185** B7
Stockers La TA4. . . . . **210** B4
Stockham Hill TA22 . . . . . **163** E8
Stock Hill BA3. . . . . **115** B8
Stockhill Cl BA3. . . . . **96** C3
Stock Hill Ct BA3 . . . . **117** B7
Stockhill Rd BA3. . . . . **96** C3
Stock La
Buckhorn Weston SP8 . . . . **177** F5
Lower Langford BS40. . . . . . **53** A7
Stockland Hill EX14. . . . . . **192** A1
Stockland Manor TA5 . . . **134** F6
Stockman La TA20. . . . . . . **198** C7
Stockmead BS40. . . . . **53** B5

Spr–Str **269**

Stones Paddock BA3 . . . . **116** C7
Stonewall Terr BA11 . . . . . **119** F2
Stonewell Dr BS49 . . . . **34** D3
Stonewell Gr BS49 . . . . **34** D3
Stonewell La BS49 . . . . **34** D3
Stonewell Park Rd BS49. . **34** D3
Stoneyard La BA3 . . . . **75** D2
Stoney Cl TA24 . . . . **129** F6
Stoneyfield Cl BS20 . . . .**4** B3
Stoneyfields BS20. . . . .**4** B4
Stoney Furlong TA2. . . . . . **213** B8
Stoney Head Cvn Pk TA3 **169** F1
Stoneyhurst Dr TA10 . . . . **171** C3
Stoney La
Bishops Lydeard TA4 . . . . .**167** E8
Curry Rivel TA10 . . . . **171** C3
East Coker BA22 . . . . **197** D6
Stocklinch TA19 . . . . **184** C4
Stones Cross EX16 . . . . . . **178** B3
Stoney Littleton Long
Barrow★ BA2. . . . . **80** C7
Stoney St TA24 . . . . **129** C7
Stoney Steep BS48. . . . . **9** A5
Stonyhead Hill TA3 . . . . . **169** F1
Stony La
Axminster EX13. . . . . **198** A1
Hawkridge TA22. . . . . **146** E3
Whatley BA11 . . . . **118** A2
Stony St BA11 . . . . **119** F5
Stoodham TA13. . . . . **220** D5
Stoodly La
North Wootton BA4 . . . . . . **140** D4
Pilton BA4 . . . . **204** A2
Stooper's Hill TA20 . . . . . **193** C6
Stopgate Cross EX14 . . . . **192** C4
Stoppard Rd TA8. . . . . **104** C6
Stopper's La BA3 . . . . **139** F6
Stormont Cl BS23. . . . . **48** F3
Stormore BA13. . . . . **121** F8
Storridge La
Axminster EX13. . . . . **198** B6
Brompton Regis TA22 . . . . **148** A1
Storridge View TA22 . . . . **148** A2
Stourhead Gdns★ BA12 . **161** F5
Stourhead Ho★ BA12 . . . **161** F5
Stour Hill SP8 . . . . **177** E1
Stour Hill Pk SP8 . . . . **177** F1
Stourton Cl BA11. . . . . **161** F6
Stourton Gdns ① BA11. . **119** E3
Stourton La BA12 . . . . **161** F6
Stourton View BA11. . . . . . **119** E3
Stourton Way BA21 . . . . . . **218** D6
Stout's Way La
Luxborough TA23 . . . . **148** F8
Rodhuish TA24. . . . . **131** A1
Stout Cross EX14 . . . . **192** C5
Stowborough Cotts BA2. . **79** C7
Stowell Hill DT9 . . . . **176** C1
Stowell La TA20. . . . . **198** D8
Stowers Row ㉛ TA12 . . . . **185** E6
Stowey Bottom BS39. . . . . **57** E5
Stowey Cross Rds BS39 . . **57** F5
Stowey La
Curry Mallet TA3 . . . . **183** E8
Fivehead TA3. . . . . **170** E1
Stowey Pk BS49. . . . . **34** D7
Stowey Rd
Pitney TA10 . . . . **172** D7
Taunton TA2 . . . . **212** E8
Yatton BS49. . . . . **34** C8
Stow Ho BS11 . . . .**4** E5
Stradling's Hill TA5 . . . . . **135** B3
Stradling Ave BS23. . . . . . . **48** F5
Stradling Cl TA7 . . . . **137** B2
Stradlings Yd BS2. . . . . **226** C4
Straight Dro
Burrowbridge TA7 . . . . **155** B1
Chilton Trinity TA5 . . . . . . **135** F2
West Huntspill TA9 . . . . . . **136** B7
Woolavington TA9 . . . . **137** A6
Straight La BA11. . . . . **101** D7
Straightmead BA3 . . . . **75** F1
Straight St BS2 . . . . **227** C2
Strap La
Ston Easton BA3 . . . . **95** F7
Upton Noble BA4, BA10. . .**143** A1
Stratford Cl BS14. . . . . **22** F3
Stratford Ct BS9 . . . .**5** F8
Stratford La BS40. . . . . **56** C1
Stratford Rd BA21. . . . . . . **218** D5
Stratheden BS8. . . . . **226** A4
Stratton Cl TA6 . . . . **209** D3
Stratton Rd
Holcombe BA3. . . . .**116** B8
Saltford BS31. . . . . **25** E3
Stratton St BS2. . . . . **227** B3
Strawberry Bank TA19 . . **221** C4
Strawberry Cl BS48 . . . . **8** D1
Strawberry Field BS26 . . . **70** D2
Strawberry Gdns BS48 . . . **18** D8
Strawberry Hill
Clevedon BS21. . . . .**6** F4
Street BA16. . . . . **207** B7
Strawberry La BS3, BS41 . **21** E3
Strawberry Way BA5. . . . . **203** C4
Strawberry Way Rdbt
BA5 . . . . **203** D3
Streaked La TA3. . . . . **170** C6
Streamcombe La TA22 . . .**163** E5
Streamcross BS49. . . . . **17** D1
Streamleaze BS40. . . . . **39** B3
Streamside
Chew Magna BS40. . . . . **39** B3
① Clevedon BS21. . . . .**6** F3
Taunton TA1. . . . .**213** C2

Street Ash La TA20......193 C8
Street Dro
　Street BA16..........207 E7
　Street, Marshall's Elm
　　BA16..............207 B1
Street End BS40........54 D2
Street End La BS40.....54 D2
Street Ho TA19........221 B3
Street La
　Odcombe BA22........186 C2
　South Brewham BA10..161 A7
Street Rd
　Compton Dundon TA11..157 A4
　Glastonbury BA6......206 D3
　Street BA6............207 D8
Street Rdbt TA6.......207 D7
Street Shoe Mus★ BA16 207 C6
Street The
　Bishop Sutton BS39....57 D4
　Chew Stoke BS40.......56 D8
　Chilcompton BA3.......96 D5
　Compton Martin BS40...74 B7
　Draycott BS27.........90 F2
　Farmborough BA2......59 F6
　Kilmington BA12......161 F6
　Radstock BA3..........78 F2
　Stowey BS39...........57 F4
　Ubley BS40............55 D1
　Wanstrow BA4.........142 F4
　West Monkton TA2.....169 C7
　Winford BS40..........37 F1
Stretcholt La TA6......135 F6
Stretford La TA19......194 F7
Stringfellow Cres TA20..223 D5
Stringfellow Mews TA20.223 C3
Stringland's La TA24....131 B2
Strode Coll BA16.......207 D6
Strode Ho ⁊ BA4......205 B6
Strode Rd
　Clevedon BS21..........6 C2
　Street BA16...........207 D6
Strode Way
　Clevedon BS21..........6 B1
　Shepton Mallet BA4....205 A5
Stroud Rd BS11.........4 E5
Stroud Way BS24........49 E2
Strowland La BS24......86 F6
Strowlands BS24, TA9...86 E6
Struthers Cl BA16......207 B7
Strutter's Hill BA10....215 D2
Stuart Ho BS23.........30 D1
Stuart Pl BA2..........44 D6
Stuart Rd BS23.........49 A5
Stuarts Cl BA5.........203 D3
Stubb's La BA11........101 D4
Studley La BA4.........142 F4
Studley Mdws BA4......142 F4
Stump Cross
　Pitcombe BA7.........215 A1
　Shepton Mallet BA4...204 D5
Sturford La BA12.......144 E7
Sturmey Way BS20........4 E3
Sturminster Cl BS14....23 D6
Sturminster Lodge BS14..23 D5
Sturminster Rd BS14....23 D7
Stutts End TA4.........167 E6
Style Flats TA4........210 C5
Style Rd TA4...........210 C5
Styles Ave BA11........120 C4
Styles Cl BA11.........120 B4
Styles Hill BA11.......120 C5
Styles Mdw BA11.......120 C5
Styles Pk BA11.........120 B4
Sub Rd BA6............157 D4
Suffolk Cl TA6.........209 C3
Suffolk Cres TA1.......212 C1
Suffolk Ct TA1.........212 C1
Sugg's La TA19.........183 C2
Sulis Manor Rd BA2.....62 D8
Sullivan Cl BS4........22 D6
Sully Cl TA6...........209 D6
Sumerleaze Cres TA2....213 C8
Sumerlin Dr BS21........6 F3
Summer Ct BS8........226 B3
Summerfield BS22.......32 A3
Summerfield Ave TA21..180 D8
Summerfield Cl TA7.....154 F5
Summerfield Ct TA1.....212 E4
Summerfield Rd BA1.....28 A1
Summerfields BA8......190 A7
Summerfields Rd TA20..223 C3
Summerfield Terr BA1...28 A1
Summerfield Way TA21..180 D8
Summerhedge Cres TA7..155 C2
Summerhedge Rd TA7....155 C1
Summer Hill
　Frome BA11...........119 F3
　Hinton St George TA17.195 D7
Summerhill Rd BA1......27 D1
Summerhouse BS21........8 D4
Summer House Terr
　BA20................219 B4
Summerhouse View
　BA21................219 C6
Summer La
　Banwell BS29..........50 E5
　Chard TA20...........194 D4
　Hinton St George TA13,
　　TA17..............195 C8
　Monkton Combe BA2....63 D8
　Weston-Super-Mare BS22,
　　BS24...............32 B1
　Weston-Super-Mare BS29..50 C8
　Weston-Super-Mare BS29..50 D7

Summer La N BS22.......32 A2
Summerland Ave TA24...201 A7
Summerland Pl TA24....200 F7
Summerland Rd TA24...200 F7
Summerlands
　Backwell BS48.........19 B5
　Yeovil BA21..........218 E6
Summerlands Hospl
　BA21................218 F6
Summerlands Park Ave
　TA19................221 B4
Summerlands Park Cl
　TA19................221 B4
Summerlands Park Dr
　TA19................221 B4
Summerlands Rd BS23...49 B8
Summer Lane Cvn Pk
　BS29.................50 E3
Summer Lane Park Homes
　BS29.................50 E4
Summerlays Ct BA2......45 B6
Summerlays Pl BA2......45 B6
Summerlea BA2..........61 A5
Summerleaze BS31.......24 E7
Summerleaze Cres TA2..213 C7
Summerleaze Pk BA20...218 F5
Summer Shard TA13.....220 C4
Summers Hill La BA4...204 C2
Summerville Terr TA8...104 B6
Summerway TA24.......129 E1
Summerway Dro TA7....209 E4
Summerwood Rd BA16...207 B4
Sun Batch BS27.........91 A3
Sunderland Pl BS8......226 B3
Sunderland St ❷ BA2...228 C3
Sundew Cl TA1.........213 C1
Sunfield Rd BS24.......49 E3
Sunningdale BS8.......226 B4
Sunningdale Cl BS48......9 A1
Sunningdale Rd
　Weston-Super-Mare BS22..31 F3
　Yeovil BA21..........219 C6
Sunnybank BA2.........45 B4
Sunny Bank TA4.......150 B8
Sunnybank Ct BS24......32 B1
Sunnybank Rd TA6.....208 E2
Sunnybank Way BS24....32 B1
Sunnybrow Cl ❿ TA6...153 F4
Sunny Cl TA9..........136 B8
Sunny Hill
　Bristol BS9............5 C7
　Pitcombe BA10.......215 C4
Sunnyhill Dr BS11.......4 E6
Sunnyhill Ho E BS11....4 E6
Sunnyhill Ho W BS11....4 E6
Sunny La BA10.........215 C4
Sunnymead
　Bridgwater TA6.......208 E2
　Keynsham BS31........24 F3
　Midsomer Norton BA3...77 F2
　Oakhill BA3..........114 F3
　Stratton-on-t F BA3....96 F2
Sunnymeade BA6.......138 C4
Sunnymeade Rd BS48......8 D3
Sunnyside
　Barrington TA19......184 C5
　Bristol BS9............5 E5
　Burlescombe EX16.....179 C2
　Clatworthy TA4.......149 F1
　Clutton BS39..........59 B4
　Farrington Gurney BS39..77 B3
　Frome BA11...........119 F3
Sunnyside Cotts TA19...129 A8
Sunnyside Cres BS21.....6 D3
Sunnyside Farm Trad Est
　BS20.................4 C2
Sunnyside Gdns BA2.....60 B2
Sunnyside Pl BA11.....119 F3
Sunnyside Rd
　Clevedon BS21..........6 D3
　Weston-Super-Mare BS23..48 E5
Sunnyside Rd N BS23....48 E5
Sunnyside Terr ❻ DT9..225 E4
Sunnyside View BA2.....79 C7
Sunnyvale
　Camerton BA2..........78 E8
　Clevedon BS21..........6 B1
Sunridge Cl BA3........96 F8
Sunridge Pk BA3........96 F8
Sunset Cl BA2..........79 C7
Sun St BA11...........119 E5
Suprema Ave TA7......137 C2
Suprema Est TA7.......137 D2
Surrey St BS2.........227 B4
Susanna's Cross BA3...116 B2
Sussex La BA3.........116 C2
Sussex Ave TA6........209 B3
Sussex Cl TA6.........209 B3
Sussex Lodge TA1......212 F5
Sussex Pl BA2.........228 C1
Sutherland Ave TA8....104 B6
Sutherland Cl TA1.....212 C1
Sutherland Ct TA1.....212 C1
Sutherland Dr BS24....49 D2
Sutton Cl
　Frome BA11...........120 B7
　Weston-Super-Mare BS22..49 E8
Sutton Cross TA10.....172 F4
Sutton Grange BA21....218 C6
Sutton Hill
　East Coker BA22......197 D6
　Long Sutton TA10....172 E3
Sutton Hill Rd BS39....57 D4
Sutton La
　Redhill BS40..........36 F1
　Walton BA16..........156 D6
Sutton Pk BS39.........57 D4
Sutton St TA11........211 C2

Sutton St BA2..........45 B7
Sutton View TA10......172 E2
Swains TA21...........222 D4
Swains La TA21........222 D4
Swain St TA23.........202 C7
Swainswick BS14........22 F6
Swainswick CE Prim Sch
　BA1..................28 B5
Swainswick Gdns BS10...28 C2
Swainswick La BA1......28 D4
Swallow Cl BA3.........97 B8
Swallowcliffe Ct ❺
　BA20................219 A5
Swallowcliffe Gdns
　BA20................219 A5
Swallow Ct
　Bristol BS14..........23 F6
　Sampford Peverell EX16..178 F1
Swallow Dr BA11.......120 B6
Swallow Gdns BS22......49 E8
Swallow Hill TA10.....172 A6
Swallow St BA1.......228 C2
Swallows The BS22.....49 D7
Swan Cl BA20..........49 E8
Swancombe
　Blagdon BS40..........54 E2
　Clapton in G BS20......8 E8
Swan Down TA20.......194 E4
Swane Rd BS14.........23 F6
Swan Hill TA18........196 C5
Swan Ho ❸ BA4.......205 B6
Swanmead Com Sch
　TA19................221 C3
Swan Prec TA19.......221 C3
Swanshard La BA5.....139 D6
Swans La BS27.........90 F2
Swan Yd DT9..........225 D4
Swedish Hos TA13.....220 D1
Sweetgrass Rd BS24....50 A8
Sweethay Cl TA3.......181 D8
Sweethay Cross TA3....181 C8
Sweethay La TA3.......181 C8
Sweetleaze BA3........116 A2
Swell Cl TA9..........136 B8
Swell La TA3..........171 A2
Swiddacombe La EX36...162 C7
Swift Cl BS22..........31 F1
Swift Lodge BA20......219 A4
Swifts TA21...........166 F1
Swillbridge Cvn Pk TA23.202 F6
Swingbridge TA2.......213 E2
Swiss Dr BS3..........11 F2
Swiss Rd
　Bristol BS3...........11 F1
　Weston-Super-Mare BS23..48 F7
Sycamore Cl
　Bridgwater TA6.......209 D5
　Burnham-on-S TA8.....104 A5
　Nailsea BS48............8 C2
　Shipham BS25..........70 E8
　Taunton TA1..........213 C2
　Weston-Super-Mare BS23..49 A8
　Weston-Super-Mare, Locking
　　BS24...............49 E5
　Westonzoyland TA7....154 E5
Sycamore Ct TA20......223 C5
Sycamore Dr
　Crewkerne TA18......224 D7
　Frome BA11...........120 B7
　Langport TA10........172 A6
　Yeovil BA20..........218 F2
Sycamore Rd
　Minehead TA24.......200 D7
　Radstock BA3..........79 B2
Sycamores BS23.........30 E1
Sycamore Sq TA20......223 C5
Sycamore Wlk TA3......169 D4
Sydenham Bldgs BA2....228 A2
Sydenham Cl
　Bridgwater TA6.......209 C6
　Porlock TA24.........124 B4
Sydenham Rd
　Bath BA2............228 A2
　Bridgwater TA6.......209 C6
Sydenham Terr BA2.....45 C1
Sydling Rd BA21.......219 D6
Sydnalls La BA12......144 E8
Sydney Bldgs BA2.......45 B6
Sydney Ho BA2.........45 B7
Sydney Mews BA2.......45 B7
Sydney Pl BA2.........45 B7
Sydney Rd BA2.........45 B7
Sydney Row BS1.......226 B1
Sydney Wharf BA2......45 B7
Sylvan Rd TA21.......222 E5
Sylvan Way
　Bristol BS9............5 B7
　Monkton Heathfield TA2.213 E8
Symes Ave BS13.........22 C4
Symes Cl
　Chard TA20...........223 C4
　North Perrott TA18....196 C4
Symes Pk BA1..........27 A2
Symons Way
　Bridgwater TA6.......209 A6
　Cheddar BS27..........90 C7
Syndercombe La TA4,
　TA23................149 D2

T

Tabernacle La ❹ BA20..219 B4
Tadhill La BA3........116 D2
Tadwick La BA1.........28 A6
Tail Mill TA16........195 F7
Tailor's Ct ⁊ BS1.....227 A3
Talbot Cl TA9.........104 D3

Tallis Gr BS4..........22 D6
Tallowood BA4.........205 D5
Tamar Ave TA1........213 B1
Tamar Dr BS31.........24 E4
Tamar Rd BS22.........32 A2
Tamblyn Cl BA3.........79 A3
Tamsin Ct BS31.........24 F5
Tamworth Rd BS31......24 E4
Tancred St TA1.......213 A4
Tangier TA1..........212 E4
Tankard's Cl BS8......226 C3
Tankey's Cl BA11......120 A7
Tan La SP8...........161 F2
Tanner's Hill TA4.....165 E2
Tanners La SN14........13 F8
Tanners Wlk
　Bath BA2.............43 F5
　Marshfield SN14.......13 F8
Tannery Cl BA16.......207 C5
Tannery Ct TA18.......224 C7
Tanorth Cl BS14........23 A3
Tanorth Rd BS14........22 F3
Tansee Hill TA20......199 B6
Tansey BA4...........142 A4
Tansy La BS20...........2 F5
Tanyard
　Broadway TA19.......183 C2
　Nether Stowey TA5....134 B2
Tanyard Cotts TA24....131 A5
Tanyard La
　Langport TA10........172 A5
　North Wootton BA4....140 C4
　North Wootton, Lower
　　Westholme BA4......140 D3
Tan Yard La TA13.....184 F5
Tanyards BA10........215 F7
Tanyard The BA16......207 C5
Tape La BA3..........114 F7
Taphouse La DT6.......199 E1
Tapmoor Rd TA7.......155 C8
Tappers La ❷ BA2.....153 E3
Tapps La TA7.........136 E4
Tapstone Rd TA20.....223 D4
Taranto Hill BA22.....173 E2
Taranto Way BA22.....174 A2
Target La TA12........185 D4
Tarnock Ave BS14.......23 A7
Tarnwell BS39..........40 A2
Tarrant La BA20.......218 F1
Tarratt La
　East Coker BA22......197 E8
　Yeovil BA20, BA22....219 A1
Tarratt Rd BA20.......218 F1
Tarr Post TA22........146 C1
Tarr Stps★ TA22......146 E3
Tarr Water Cotts TA23..148 E8
Tatham Ct TA1........212 D4
Tatworth Prim Sch TA20.198 C8
Tatworth Rd BA22......223 C2
Tatworth St TA20......198 C8
Tauntfield Cl TA1.....213 A3
Taunton Rd
　Ashcott TA7.........156 B7
　Bishops Lydeard TA4..167 F7
　Bridgwater TA6.......209 A3
　North Petherton TA6..153 F4
　Thurloxton TA6.......153 E2
　Wellington TA21......222 F2
　Weston-Super-Mare BS22..32 B4
　Wiveliscombe TA4.....210 D4
Taunton Sch TA2......212 C4
Taunton & Somerset Hospl
Musgrove Pk TA1......212 C3
Taunton Sta TA1......212 F5
Taunton Trad Est TA2..212 A7
Taunton Vale Pk TA2...213 F8
Taunusstein Way ⓬
　BA20................219 B4
Taveners Wlk BS48.......8 F3
Taverner Cl BS4........22 D7
Taverners Cl ❻ BS23...48 F4
Tavistock Rd BS22......32 A2
Tawny Way BS22........49 F8
Taylor's Meade TA20..193 D6
Taylor's Orch TA14...185 E1
Taylor Cl TA2........168 B5
Taylor Ct
　Bridgwater TA6.......209 A5
　Weston-Super-Mare BS22..32 B4
Taylor Gdns BS13.......21 F4
Taylor Ho TA19.......221 B3
Tayman Ridge BS30.....25 D8
Teagle Cl BA5........203 F5
Teak Cl TA6..........209 D6
Teal Cl
　Bridgwater TA6.......209 A4
　Weston-Super-Mare BS22..31 F1
Tealham Moor Dro BS28.137 E8
Teal Rd TA1..........201 C5
Teals Acre ❽ TA5.....135 B2
Teapot Lane (Worms Lane)
　BA6.................158 B6
Teasel Wlk BS22........49 D7
Technical St TA8......104 B6
Teck Hill TA6.........153 E2
Teckhill La TA6.......153 E2
Teddington Cl BA2......44 C4
Teesdale Cl BS22.......49 D8
Teeside BA14...........83 F4
Teign Ct BS14.........156 D7
Teignmouth Rd BS21.....6 E3
Telephone Ave BS1.....227 A2
Telford Ho
　Bath BA2.............44 D3
　Leigh Woods BS8.......11 E7

Temblett Gn TA6......208 C5
Templars Barton BA8...176 E1
Templars Ct
　Long Sutton TA10....172 E1
　❶ Weston-Super-Mare
　　BS22..............49 D7
Templars Pl BA8......176 E1
Templars Way BS25.....70 E7
Temple Back BS1......227 B2
Temple Back E BS1....227 C2
Temple Bridge Bsns Pk
　BS39.................76 F7
Temple Circus Giratory
　BS1.................227 C1
Templecombe La SP8...177 C3
Templecombe Sta BA8..176 E1
Temple Ct BS31........24 E5
Temple Field TA23....202 C6
Temple Gate BS1......227 B1
Temple Inn La BS39....58 E1
Temple La BA8........176 E1
Templeland Rd BS13....21 C5
Temple of Harmony★
　TA5.................153 B5
Temple Prim Sch BS31..24 F6
Temple Rose St BS1...227 B2
Temple St
　Bristol BS1..........227 B2
　Keynsham BS31........24 F5
Temple Way BS2.......227 B2
Temple Way Underpass
　BS2.................227 C3
Tenby Rd BS31.........24 D4
Tengore La TA10.......172 C6
Tennis Corner Dro BA11.102 D2
Tennis Court Ave BS39..77 D5
Tennis Court Rd BS39...77 D5
Tennyson Ave BS21......6 E2
Tennyson Cl BS31......24 F6
Tennyson Rd
　Bath BA1.............44 D7
　Weston-Super-Mare BS23..49 A3
Tenterk Cl BS24........67 B6
Tents Hill BA11.......118 B6
Terhill La TA4........151 F3
Termare Cl BA22......218 B6
Terrace The
　Minehead TA24.......201 A5
　Shipham BS25.........70 E8
Terrace View DT9......225 E5
Terrace Wlk BA1......228 C2
Terrell St BS2.......227 A4
Terry Hill BA3.........98 D8
Terry Ho BS1.........226 C3
Tetbury Gdns BS48......9 A1
Tetton Cl TA6........208 B4
Teviot Rd BS31.........25 A4
Tewkesbury BA21......218 D6
Tewther Rd BS13.......22 D3
Teyfant Com Sch BS13...22 E4
Teyfant Rd BS13........22 E4
Teyfant Wlk BS13......22 E4
Thackeray Ave BS21.....6 E4
Thackeray Ho BS23.....49 A5
Thackeray Rd BS21......6 E4
Thames Dr TA1.......213 D4
Thatcham ❷ BA21.....218 F7
Thatcham Ct ❶ BA21..218 F7
Thatcham Pk BA21.....218 F7
Thatch Cotts TA20....194 E1
Thatcher Cl BS20.......2 D4
Thatch The TA11......211 C4
Theaks Mews TA1.....213 A3
Theatre Royal BS1....227 A2
Theillay Cl TA5......134 A3
There-and-Back-Again La
　BS1.................226 C3
Theynes Croft BS41....11 B1
Thicket Mead BA3......78 A2
Thickthorn Cross TA19.183 C3
Thimble La DT9.......217 D2
Third Ave
　Bath BA2.............44 D5
　Bristol BS14..........23 B7
　Radstock BA3..........97 D7
Thirlmere Rd BS23.....49 A4
Thistledoo Vine TA7..136 F2
Thistle Pk TA6.......209 B1
Thomas Cl BS29.......51 A3
Thomas Ct BS1.......227 B2
Thomas La BS1.......227 B2
Thomas Lane Apartments
　BS1.................227 B2
Thomas St
　Bath BA1............228 C4
　Bristol BS2.........227 B4
　Taunton TA1.........212 F6
Thomas Way BA6......206 B4
Thomas Way Ind Est
　BA6.................206 B4
Thompson Cl TA6.....209 D6
Thompson Rd BS14.....23 E6
Thomson Dr TA18......224 D5
Thong La TA10.........184 D6
Thornash Cl TA2......213 F8
Thornbank Ct DT9.....225 E4
Thornbank Pl BA2.....228 A1
Thornbury Dr BS23.....48 D2
Thornbury Rd BS23.....48 C2
Thornbush Cross TA4...150 F3
Thorn Cl BS22.........32 A3
Thorncombe Cres TA6..209 C6
Thorncombe Thorn
　TA20................199 B6
Thorndale BS8........226 A4
Thorndale Cl BS23.....49 A5
Thorndale Cl BS22.....49 D8
Thorndale Mews BS8...226 A4

Thorndun Park Dr TA20 223 D6
Thorne Cross BA22 218 B7
Thorne Cross Way TA21 178 D8
Thorne Gdns BA21 218 C7
Thorne La
Wheddon Cross TA24 147 C8
Winsford TA24 147 C8
Yeovil BA21 218 C8
Thorne Pk TA8 104 B5
Thorneymoor La TA10 172 A3
Thorney Rd TA12 185 B8
Thornhill Dro TA12 173 A1
Thornhill Rd DT10 190 B4
Thorn La TA3 169 D2
Thornton Rd BA21 218 D7
Thornwell La BA9 216 D3
Thornwell Way BA9 216 C3
Thorny La BA21 187 E8
Thornymarsh La BA7 175 B8
Three Ashes DT8 199 D7
Three Ashes La TA11 157 B4
Three Corner Mead
BA21 218 C5
Three Gates Cross TA22 163 C6
Three Hill View BA6 206 E5
Three Horse Shoes Hill
TA5 152 C4
Three Oaks Cross TA19 183 C4
Three Queens' La BS1 227 B2
Three Ways Sch Lime Grove
Site BA2 45 B6
Threeways Sch Summerfield
Site BA1 27 D1
Three Wells Rd BS13 21 F4
Thrift Cl DT10 190 C4
Throgmorton Rd BS4 22 F8
Throop Rd BA8 176 F1
Thrubwell La BS40 37 B4
Thrupe La BA5 114 A2
Thrush Cl 4 BS22 49 E8
Thumb La BA4 158 E7
Thurlbear CE Prim Sch
TA3 182 C8
Thurlestone BS14 23 A6
Thurlocks BA22 186 B6
Thyme Cl BS20 2 F5
Thynne Cl BS27 90 B6
Tibbott Rd BS14 23 D5
Tibbott Wlk BS14 23 D5
Tichborne Rd BS23 30 E1
Tickenham CE Prim Sch
BS21 7 F4
Tickenham Hill BS48 8 E4
Tickenham Rd BS21 7 A4
Tide Gr BS11 5 A8
Tides Reach TA24 125 C4
Tiffany Ct BS1 227 B1
Tiledown BS39 58 E1
Tiledown Cl BS39 58 F1
Tile Hill BA10 161 A7
Tile House Rd
East Huntspill TA7 137 B8
Mark TA9 106 C1
Tilery EX14 192 D3
Tilham St BA6 158 B6
Tilley Cl
Farmborough BA2 60 A5
Keynsham BS31 25 A2
Tilley La BA2 60 A5
Tilleys Dro BA5 138 F7
Tilsey La TA4 150 C5
Tilton Ct 5 DT9 225 D3
Timberscombe CE First Sch
TA24 130 B5
Timberscombe Way TA6 208 B4
Timberscombe Wlk BS14 23 C5
Timbers The BA3 97 B7
Timberyard TA7 137 F1
Timewell Hill EX16 164 C4
Timsbury Rd
Farmborough BA2 60 B5
High Littleton BS39 59 D1
Timsbury Village Workshops
BA2 59 F3
Tin Bridge Rdbt BA6 139 D3
Tinker's La
Compton Martin BS40 74 B7
Cucklington BA9 177 D7
Halse TA4 167 C6
Kilmersdon BA11 98 B1
Tinneys La DT9 225 E4
Tintagel Cl BS31 24 D4
Tintagel Rd BA21 218 D7
Tintern BA21 218 C6
Tintinhull Gdn★ BA22 186 C6
Tintinhull Rd BA21 186 F5
Tipcote Hill 17 BA4 205 B6
Tipnoller Hill TA4 210 F7
Tippacott La EX35 122 A4
Tiptoft 3 TA14 185 F4
Tirley Way BS22 31 B2
Titan Barrow BA1 29 C2
Tithe Barn Cross EX15 179 D2
Tithe Ct BA20 218 D5
Tithe Mdw TA4 167 A7
Tithill La TA4 167 F7
Titlands La BA5 203 A7
Tiverton Gdns BS22 32 A2
Tiverton Rd
Bampton EX16 164 C1
2 Clevedon BS21 6 E1
Tivington Cross TA24 129 F8
Tivoli Ho BS23 48 E8
Tivoli La BS23 48 E8
Toghill La BS30 12 A8
Tolbury La BA10 215 D6
Tolbury Mill BA10 215 E6
Tolland BS24 49 A2
Tolland Cross TA4 150 E3
Toll Bridge Rd BA1 28 E3
Tolley's La TA20 194 C3
Toll Gate TA4 210 C4
Toll House Rd 1 TA5 135 B2
Toll Rd
Porlock TA24 124 A3
Weston-Super-Mare BS23 66 F8
Toms Cl TA20 223 B3
Tomtit's La TA11 211 C3
Tonedale Bsns Pk TA21 222 B7
Tonedale Ind Est TA21 222 B8
Tone Dr TA6 209 B3
Tone Gn TA4 167 E2
Tone Hill TA21 222 B8
Tone Rd BS21 6 D1
Toneway TA2 213 C6
Toose The BA21 218 C6
Top Hill BA4 142 F2
Top La
Gasper BA12 161 E4
Mells BA11 118 B6
Top Rd
Charlton Adam TA11 173 F7
Cheddar BS27 90 E5
Shipham BS25 70 F7
Westbury-sub-Mendip BA5 110 E6
Top St
Kingsdon TA11 173 D5
Pilton BA4 140 F3
Top Wood BA3 116 B7
Torbay Cl BA7 214 B5
Torbay Rd BA7 214 A5
Torbay Road Ind Est
BA7 214 A5
Torbay Villas BA7 214 A5
Tor Cl BS22 32 A2
Torhill La BA5 203 F4
Torhole Bottom BA3 94 A4
Tormynton Rd BS22 31 E3
Torre Cider Farm★ TA23 131 E3
Torre Rocks TA23 131 E2
Torre The BA21 218 C6
Torridge Mead TA1 213 D4
Torridge Rd BS31 25 A4
Torrington Ave BS4 22 F8
Torrington Cres BS22 32 A3
Tor St BA5 203 E4
Tor View
Cheddar BS27 90 C7
Woolavington TA7 136 E4
Tor View Ave BA6 206 D3
Tor Wood View BA5 203 E5
Totnes Cl BS22 32 A2
Totney Dro BS28 137 E8
Totshill Dr BS13 22 E4
Totshill Gr BS13 22 E4
Tottenham Pl BS8 226 B3
Totterdown La
Pilton BA4 204 B1
Weston-Super-Mare BS24 49 A1
Totterdown Rd BS23 48 F4
Touches La TA20 223 E5
Touches Mdw TA20 223 E5
Touching End La SN14 13 F8
Touch La TA10 156 C1
Touchstone Cl TA20 223 B4
Touchstone La TA20 223 B4
Tout Hill BA9 216 C3
Tout La BA22TA11 174 A6
Tovey Cl BS22 31 E4
Tower Cl
Cheddar BS27 90 B6
Stoke St Michael BA3 116 A3
Towerhead Rd BS29 51 D3
Tower Hill
Bristol BS2 227 B3
Bruton BA10 215 D6
Holcombe Rogus TA21 178 D5
Horsington BA8 176 E2
Locking BS24 50 D4
Stogursey TA5 134 B5
Stoke St Michael BA3 116 A3
Williton TA4 202 E2
Tower Hill Rd TA18 224 B5
Tower House La BS48 9 A4
Tower La
Bristol BS1 227 A3
Taunton TA1 212 E4
Towerleaze BS9 5 D3
Tower Rd
Kilmington BA12 161 D6
Portishead BS20 2 A4
Stawell TA7 137 B1
Yeovil BA21 219 C8
Tower St
Bristol BS1 227 B2
Taunton TA1 212 E4
Tower The BS1 227 B2
Tower View
Frome BA11 119 F2
South Cheriton BA8 176 D3
Wanstrow BA4 142 E4
Tower Wlk BS23 30 D1
Town Barton BA2 81 F4
Town Cl
North Curry TA3 170 B4
Stogursey TA5 134 B6
Town End BA2 81 F4
Townend Villas TA14 185 F2
Town Farm TA3 170 B4
Townhall Bldgs BA5 203 E4
Town Hill EX36 162 C6
Town La BA4 205 C6
Town Marsh TA22 163 D7
Townrise 15 BA20 219 B4
Townsend
East Harptree BS40 75 A5
Townsend *continued*
Ilminster TA19 221 D3
Marston Magna BA22 174 F1
Middlezoy TA7 155 C3
Montacute TA15 186 B3
Shepton Mallet BA4 205 B5
Westonzoyland TA7 154 F5
Williton TA4 202 E3
Townsend Cl
Bristol BS14 23 F5
Bruton BA10 215 F7
Townsend Cotts TA24 147 C5
Townsend Gn 10 BA8 190 A6
Townsend La
Chilton Polden TA7 137 B2
Emborough BA3 95 B2
Theale BS28 109 A2
Townsend Orch
Merriott TA16 195 F8
Street BA16 207 B5
Townsend Pk BA10 215 F7
Townsend Rd
Bristol BS14 23 F5
Minehead TA24 201 A6
Townsend Rise BA10 215 F7
Townshend Rd BS22 32 B5
Town St BA4 205 B6
Town Tree Farm Nature
Trail★ TA12 185 C8
Town Tree La TA10, TA12 185 D8
Tracey Cl TA7 209 E8
Trackfordmoor Cross
TA22 163 B3
Tracy Cl BS14 22 F7
Trafalgar Rd BA1 27 B1
Traits La BA22 174 E4
Trajan's Way BA4 205 E5
Tramshed The BA1 228 C3
Transform Ind Est TA6 209 A6
Transom Ho BS1 227 B2
Transom Pl TA24 201 B7
Travers Cl BS4 22 D6
Trawden Cl BS23 31 A1
Treasure Ct TA8 85 A1
Treasurer's Ho★ TA12 185 E6
Treborough Cl TA2 213 B8
Treefield Rd BS21 6 D2
Tregarth Rd BS3 11 F1
Tregelles Cl TA9 104 C4
Tregonwell Rd TA24 201 A7
Trelawn Cl BS22 32 D2
Trelissick Gdns 3 BS22 49 F8
Trellech Ct 3 BA21 218 C6
Tremes Cl SN14 13 F8
Tremlett Mews 3 BS22 32 B4
Trenchard Rd
Locking BS24 50 D4
Saltford BS31 25 D3
Trenchard St BS1 226 C3
Trendle La
Bicknoller TA4 132 F2
Stoney Stoke BA9 160 E3
Trendle Rd TA1 212 B1
Trendle St DT9 225 D3
Trendlewood Way BS48 9 A1
Trenleigh Dr BS22 32 A2
Trent Cl BA21 219 E8
Trent Ct TA1 213 D4
Trent Gr BS31 25 A4
Trent Mdw TA1 213 E4
Trent Path La DT9 225 A5
Trent Youngs CE Prim Sch
DT9 187 F5
Tresco Spinney BA21 218 C6
Trescothick Cl BS31 24 E6
Trevanna Rd BS3 11 F1
Trevelyan Rd BS23 48 F7
Trevett Rd TA1 212 C2
Trevithick Cl BA11 120 C6
Trevor Rd TA6 209 C6
Trevor Smith Pl TA1 213 A3
Trewartha Cl BS23 48 F8
Trewartha Pk BS23 48 F8
Trewint Gdns BS4 22 F8
Triangle Ct 2 BA2 44 D5
Triangle Ctr The BS21 6 D3
Triangle E BA2 44 D5
Triangle N BA2 44 D5
Triangle S BS8 226 B3
Triangle The
Castle Cary BA7 214 C5
Clevedon BS21 6 D3
North Curry TA3 170 A4
Paulton BS39 77 E6
Portishead BS20 2 B5
Somerton TA11 211 D4
Wrington BS40 35 D2
Triangle Villas 1 BA2 44 D5
Triangle W
Bath BA2 44 D5
Bristol BS8 226 B3
Tribunal & Lake Village
Mus★ BA6 206 D4
Trickey Warren La TA3 181 C1
Trim Bridge 3 BA1 228 B2
Trim St BA1 228 B2
Trinder Rd BS20 4 B4
Trindlewell La TA18 196 C4
Trinity Bsns Ctr TA1 213 A3
Trinity CE Fst Sch BA11 119 C4
Trinity Cl
Bath BA1 228 B2
Blackford BS28 107 D4
Burnham-on-S TA8 85 A1
Wellington TA21 222 C5
Trinity Coll BS9 5 E4
Trinity Ct
Bridgwater TA6 208 F6
Trinity Ct *continued*
Nailsea BS48 8 C1
13 Yeovil BA20 219 B4
Trinity Gate TA1 213 A3
Trinity Mews 15 BS2 227 C3
Trinity Pl
3 Bristol BS8 226 A2
4 Weston-Super-Mare
BS23 30 C1
Trinity Rd
Bath BA2 45 B2
Nailsea BS48 8 D1
Taunton TA1 213 B3
Weston-Super-Mare BS23 30 C1
Trinity Rise TA8 85 A1
Trinity Row
Frome BA11 119 E5
Wellington TA21 222 C5
Trinity St
Bath BA1 228 B2
Frome BA11 119 E5
Taunton TA1 213 B3
Trinity Way
Bridgwater TA6 208 E6
Minehead TA24 201 B7
Trinity Wlk
Bristol BS2 227 C3
Frome BA11 119 E5
Trin Mills BS1 227 A1
Tripps Cnr BS49 34 D7
Tripps Dro BA5 139 A6
Tripps Row BS41 11 A1
Triscombe Ave TA6 208 D4
Triscombe Gate TA24 147 D8
Triscombe Ho TA4 151 D5
Triscombe Rd TA2 212 E8
Tristram Dr TA3 169 D4
Tropical Bird Gdn★ TA8 47 F2
Tropiquaria Wildlife Pk★
TA23 131 F4
Trossachs Dr BA2 45 D8
Trotts La TA19 183 B2
Trottsway Cross TA24 129 C2
Trowbridge Cl TA9 104 D4
Trowell La TA4 165 E4
Trow La BA12 144 C2
Truckwell La TA4 150 D4
Trull CE Prim Sch TA3 168 D1
Trull Green Dr TA3 168 D1
Trull Rd TA1 212 E2
Trumps Cross EX16 178 E3
Truro Cl TA8 104 C7
Truro Rd BS48 9 A1
Trym Bank BS9 5 D7
Trym Cross Rd BS9 5 C5
Trymleaze BS9 5 C5
Trym Side BS9 5 C5
Trymwood Par BS9 5 D6
Tucker's Cross DT9 188 A4
Tucker's La
Baltonsborough BA6 157 F6
Ubley BS40 73 E8
Tucker's Moor Cross
EX16 162 F3
Tuckers La BA7 214 B7
Tucker St
Bristol BS2 227 C3
Wells BA5 203 C4
Tuckerton La TA7 153 F1
Tuckingmill La BS39 41 E5
Tuckmarsh La BA11 143 E7
Tuckmill BS21 6 B1
Tudballs TA24 128 D1
Tuddington Gdns BA5 203 B4
Tudor Ct
Chard TA20 223 C6
Yeovil BA20 219 A4
Tudor Rd
Portishead BS20 2 E4
Weston-Super-Mare BS22 32 A4
Tudor Way TA6 209 A1
Tudway Cl BA5 203 C4
Tufton Ave BS11 5 A8
Tugela Rd BS13 21 F7
Tuggy's La BA2 63 E1
Tulip Tree Rd TA6 209 E5
Tulse Hill BA12 161 F2
Tunbridge Cl BS40 39 B2
Tunbridge Rd BS40 39 B2
Tuncombe La TA18 195 D4
Tunley Hill BA2 60 E2
Tunley Rd BA2, BA3 61 D5
Tunnel La BA3 96 F5
Tunnell La 14 TA14 185 F4
Tunnel The TA24 128 B2
Tunscombe La BA4 142 D8
Tunstall Cl BS9 5 E4
Turkey Ct 5 TA1 212 E3
Turnbury Ave BS48 9 A1
Turnbury Cl BS22 31 F3
Turner's Barn La BA20 218 F2
Turner's Court La BA3 114 D8
Turner's La DT6 199 B2
Turner's Twr BA3 80 A1
Turner Cl
Bridgwater TA6 209 A4
Keynsham BS31 25 A5
Turner Ct
Wells BA5 203 D3
Weston-Super-Mare BS22 31 F3
Turner Rd TA2 212 E7
Turner Way BS21 6 B1
Turn Hill TA10 155 F2
Turnhill Rd TA10 156 A2
Turnpike
Milverton TA4 167 A4
Sampford Peverell EX16 178 C1
Turnpike Cl TA18 196 B3
Turnpike Cnr BA3 95 B8
Turnpike Cross TA14 185 E2
Turnpike Cvn Pk TA20 193 A4
Turnpike Gn TA18 196 B3
Turnpike La BA4 142 B6
Turnpike Rd
Cross BS26 69 E1
Shipham BS25 70 E8
Turstin Rd BA6 206 F6
Turtlegate Ave BS13 21 E4
Turtlegate Wlk BS13 21 E4
Tut Hill DT9 189 C1
Tutton Way BS21 6 D1
Tuttors Hill BS27 71 C1
Tuxwell La TA5 152 C8
Tweed Rd BS21 6 C1
Tweed Rd Ind Est 2 BS21 6 C1
Tweentown BS27 90 B8
Twelve Acre Post TA22 163 A4
Twerton Farm Cl 2 BA2 44 B6
Twerton Inf Sch BA2 44 A5
Twinell La TA5 152 D7
Twines Cl BA22 175 A5
Twinhoe La BA2 62 E2
Twistgates La EX14 192 A4
Twitchen Ball Cnr EX36 145 G3
Twitchens La BS27 90 F2
Two Acres Cvn Pk BS21 1 B1
Two Acres Rd BS14 23 A7
Two Ash Hill TA20 193 F1
Two Ash La TA20 194 A1
Two Elms BA21 187 E8
Two Tower La BA22 219 B2
Two Trees BS40 72 E8
Twyford Pl TA21 222 D5
Tydeman Rd BS20 2 F5
Tyler's La TA4 167 A7
Tyler Gn 2 BS22 32 B4
Tylers End TA9 104 F3
Tyler Way TA9 104 D3
Tyndall's Park Rd BS8 226 C4
Tyndall Ave BS8 226 C4
Tyndall Ho 5 BS2 227 C3
Tyndalls Park Mews BS2 226 C4
Tyne Gr BS20 2 F6
Tyne Pk TA1 213 D3
Tyning Cl BS14 23 A7
Tyning Cotts BA3 116 C7
Tyning End BA2 45 B5
Tyning Hill
Hemington BA3 99 C8
Radstock BA3 79 B3
Tyning La BA1 28 B1
Tyning Pl BA2 45 C2
Tyning Rd
Bathampton BA2 28 F2
Bath BA2 45 C2
Peasedown St John BA2 79 D7
Saltford BS31 25 E2
Winsley BA15 64 E7
Tynings BS39 58 D3
Tynings La BA5 203 C8
Tynings Mews BS23 48 E4
Tynings Rd BA16 207 B4
Tynings The
Clevedon BS21 6 A1
Portishead BS20 1 F1
Tynings Way
Clutton BS39 58 E3
Westwood BA15 64 F3
Tyning Terr 15 BA1 28 A1
Tyning The
Bath BA2 45 B5
Freshford BA3 64 B4
Tynte Ave BS13 22 E3
Tynte Rd TA6 209 D6
Tyntesfield Rd BS13 22 A8
Tyrone Wlk BS4 22 E8
Tytherington La BA11 143 E8
Tythe St BA6 206 E3
Tythings Com Ctr The
BA9 216 C3
Tythings Ct TA24 200 F7
Tything Way BA9 216 D3

U

Ubley CE Prim Sch BS40 55 D1
Ubley Dro BS40 73 B7
Ullcombe La EX14 191 F4
Ullswater Cl BS23 49 A4
Ullswater Dr BA1 28 A2
Uncombe Cl BS48 19 D7
Underbanks BS20 4 D4
Underdown BA21 219 F5
Underdown Ho BS1 227 A1
Underdown Hollow
Bradford Abbas DT9 187 E2
Yeovil BA21 219 F4
Underdown La DT9 225 F6
Underhill
Gurney Slade BA3 114 E7
Hambridge TA10 184 D8
Penselwood BA9 161 D1
Underhill Ave BA3 77 F2
Underhill Cl BA16 207 B5
Underhill Dr BS23 48 D1
Underhill La
Midsomer Norton BA3 77 F2
Staple Fitzpaine TA3 182 B4
Underhill Rd BA16 207 B5
Under Knoll BA2 79 E8
Under La BS40 36 D1
Underleaf Way BA2 79 [illegible]

Undertown BS40 . . . . 74 A7
Undertown La BS40 . . . . . 74 A7
Under Way TA20 . . . . 193 D6
Underwood Ave BS22 . . . . 31 B1
Underwood End BS25 . . . . 52 A4
Underwood La TA10. . . . . 172 C8
Underwood Rd
　Glastonbury BA6 . . . . 206 D4
　Kingsdon TA11. . . . . 173 D5
　Portishead BS20 . . . . 2 C3
Union Dro TA10. . . . . 172 B6
Union La BA4 . . . . 202 E4
Union Pas BA1. . . . . 228 C2
Union Pl BS23 . . . . 48 D7
Union St
　Bath BA1 . . . . 228 C2
　Bridgwater TA6 . . . . 209 B6
　Bristol BS1 . . . . 227 B3
　Cheddar BS27 . . . . 90 B7
　Dulverton TA22 . . . . 163 D6
　Nailsea BS48 . . . . 8 C1
　Wells BA5 . . . . 203 D4
　Weston-Super-Mare BS23 . . 48 D7
　Yeovil BA20 . . . . 219 B4
Unite Ho BS1 . . . . 226 C2
Unity Ct BS31. . . . . 25 A5
Unity Rd BS31. . . . . 25 A6
Unity St BS1 . . . . 226 C2
University Cl BS9 . . . . 5 F4
University Rd BS8. . . . . . 226 C3
University Wlk BS8. . . . . 226 C3
Univ of Bath BA2 . . . . 45 E5
Univ of Bristol BS8. . . . . 226 C3
Univ of Bristol Dept of Ed
　BS8 . . . . 226 C3
Univ of Bristol Dorothy
　Hodgkin Bldg BS1 . . . . . 227 A4
Univ of Bristol Langford
　House Sch of Veterinary
　Science BS40. . . . . 53 B6
Univ of Bristol Sch of
　Veterinary Science
　BS2. . . . . 226 C4
Univ of the West of England
　BS3 . . . . 11 E4
Upcot Cres TA1 . . . . 212 B2
Upcott La
　Bicknoller TA4 . . . . 132 F1
　Winsford TA24 . . . . 147 D7
Upcott Rd TA1, TA4 . . . . . 168 B3
Uphill Dr BA1 . . . . 28 B2
Uphill Farm Cvn Pk BS23 . 48 E1
Uphill Prim Sch BS23 . . . . 48 D2
Uphill Rd N BS23. . . . . 48 D4
Uphill Rd S BS23 . . . . 48 D2
Uphills BA10. . . . . 215 E7
Uphill Way BS23 . . . . 48 D1
Upjohn Cres BS13. . . . . . . 22 D3
Uplands
　Bratton Seymour BA9 . . . . 176 B8
　Mark TA9 . . . . 106 A4
Uplands Cl BA2 . . . . 63 F7
Uplands Dr BS31. . . . . 25 F2
Uplands Rd BS31. . . . . 25 F2
Uplands Terr BA22 . . . . . 197 B8
Uplands The BS48. . . . . . . 18 C8
Uplowman CE Prim Sch
　EX16 . . . . 178 B2
Upottery Prim Sch EX14. 191 F2
Upper Belgrave Rd BS8 . . . . 5 F1
Upper Berkeley Pl BS8 . . 226 B3
Upper Bloomfield Rd BA2 44 D1
Upper Borough Walls
　BA1 . . . . 228 C2
Upper Breach BA5 . . . . . . 113 A2
Upper Bristol Rd
　Bath BA1 . . . . 44 D7
　Clutton BS39 . . . . 58 D3
　Weston-Super-Mare BS22. . 31 B1
Upper Byron Pl BS8 . . . . . 226 B3
Upper Camden Pl BA1. . . 228 C4
Upper Church La
　Bristol BS2. . . . . 226 C3
　Hutton BS24 . . . . 49 D2
Upper Church Rd BS23 . . . 30 D1
Upper Church St BA1 . . . 228 B3
Upper Crannel Dro BA6 . 139 C4
Upper East Hayes BA1. . . . 28 B1
Upper Farm Cl BA2 . . . . . . 81 F4
Upper Flowerfield BA11 . 143 B7
Upper Furlong 60 B3
Upper Green La BS40 . . . . . 55 B7
Upper Hedgemead Rd
　BA1 . . . . 228 B4
Upper High St
　Castle Cary BA7. . . . . 214 C5
　Taunton TA1. . . . . 212 F3
Upper Holway Rd TA1. . . 213 C2
Upper Kewstoke Rd BS23. 30 B1
Upper Lambridge St BA1 . 28 C2
Upper Lansdown Mews
　BA1 . . . . 27 F1
Upper Maudlin St BS2. . . 227 A4
Upper Merrifield BA3 . . . 116 E8
Upper Merryfield BA3 . . . . 97 E1
Upper Mount Pleasant
　BA3 . . . . 64 A4
Upper Myrtle Hill BS20. . . . 4 C4
Upper New Rd BS27. . . . . . 90 A8
Upper North St BS27. . . . . 90 B8
Upper Oldfield Pk BA2 . . 228 A1
Upper Pitching BA3 . . . . . . 96 D5
Upper Rd BS39 . . . . 75 E6

Upper Stanton BS39. . . . . 40 A2
Upper Strode BS40. . . . . . 55 F7
Upper Town La BS40 . . . . . 37 C8
Upper Wells St BS1 . . . . . 226 C2
Upper Whatcombe BA11 119 E6
Upper Wood St TA1. . . . . 212 E4
Upper York St BS2 . . . . . . 227 B4
Upton BS24. . . . . 49 A2
Upton Cotts BS41 . . . . 38 F8
Upton La
　Dundry BS41. . . . . 39 A8
　Seavington St Michael
　TA19 . . . . 184 E2
Upton Noble CE Prim Sch
　BA4. . . . . 142 F2
Urchinwood La BS49 . . . . . 34 F4

V

Vagg Hill BA22. . . . . 186 E5
Vagg La BA22. . . . . 186 F5
Vagg Pk BA22 . . . . 186 F5
Valda Rd BS22. . . . . 31 C2
Vale Cl TA18. . . . . 224 C4
Vale Cres BS22 . . . . 32 C2
Vale Ct BS8. . . . . 226 A4
Vale End BS48 . . . . 8 D1
Vale La BS3 . . . . 22 C8
Vale Mill Way BS24 . . . . . . 49 F8
Vale View BA1 . . . . 28 F3
Valentine Cl BS14. . . . . . . 23 B5
Valentines TA22 . . . . 163 E6
Vale Rd
　Stalbridge DT10. . . . . 190 B4
　Yeovil BA21 . . . . 219 E6
Valerian Cl BS11. . . . . 4 F6
Vale St BA8. . . . . 190 A6
Valetta Cl BS23 . . . . 48 F3
Valetta Pl TA6 . . . . 208 F5
Vale View
　Aller TA10 . . . . 171 E8
　Henstridge BA8 . . . . 190 A7
　Radstock BA3 . . . . 79 A2
　Wincanton BA9 . . . . 216 F5
Vale View Cotts TA4 . . . . . 151 E4
Vale View Gdns BA9 . . . . 216 C2
Vale View Pl BA1. . . . . 28 B1
Vale View Terr BA1 . . . . . . 28 F3
Valley Cl
　Nailsea BS48 . . . . 8 E2
　Wells BA5 . . . . 203 C4
Valley Ct BS20. . . . . 1 B3
Valley Gdns BS48 . . . . 8 E2
Valley Line Ind Pk BS27 . . 90 A7
Valley Rd
　Bristol, Bedminster Down
　BS13 . . . . 22 A8
　Clevedon BS21. . . . . 6 F5
　Crewkerne TA18 . . . . 224 C4
　Leigh Woods BS8. . . . . 11 C7
　Portishead BS20 . . . . 2 A2
　Taunton TA1. . . . . 213 C5
Valley View
　Axminster EX13 . . . . 198 A1
　Chilcompton BA3 . . . . 96 D3
　Clutton BS39 . . . . 58 E3
　Frome BA11. . . . . 119 D6
　Millmoor EX15 . . . . 179 E1
　Moreton EX16 . . . . 164 B3
Valley View Cl BA1. . . . . . . 28 B3
Valley View Rd
　Bath BA1 . . . . 28 C3
　Paulton BS39 . . . . 77 E6
Valley Way Rd BS48 . . . . . . 8 E3
Valley Wlk BA3 . . . . 78 B2
Vallis Cl TA1 BA11. . . . . . 119 E5
Vallis Fst Sch BA11 . . . . . 119 E5
Vallis Rd BA11. . . . . 119 D5
Vallis Trad Est BA11. . . . . 119 D5
Vallis Way BA11. . . . . 119 E5
Van Diemen's La BA1 . . . . 27 F2
Vandyck Ave BS31. . . . . . . 24 F6
Vane St BA2. . . . . 45 B7
Vanguard Ct BA22 . . . . . . 218 A5
Varsity Way BS24 . . . . 50 B6
Vaughan Ct BA5 . . . . 203 B4
Veales DT10 . . . . 189 F2
Veale The BS24 . . . . 67 C6
Veal La
　Horrington BA5 . . . . 113 B2
　Walton BA16 . . . . 156 E6
Vedal Dro TA10. . . . . 172 D4
Vee La BS40 . . . . 37 D8
Vellore La BA2. . . . . 45 C7
Vellow Rd TA4 . . . . 150 D8
Vellow Wood La TA4 . . . . 132 D1
Vemplett's Cross TA3 . . . 131 E1
Venford Hill
　East Anstey TA22 . . . . 162 E8
　Hawkridge TA22. . . . . 146 D1
Venland Bsns Pk TA24 . . 201 B6
Venland Ind Pk TA24 . . . . 201 A6
Venn Cl TA4 . . . . 167 E6
Venn Cross TA4 . . . . 165 D3
Venn Hill DT6, TA20. . . . . 199 C6
Venniford Cross TA24 . . . 129 F8
Vennland Way TA24 . . . . . 201 A6
Venns Cl BS27 . . . . 90 B7
Venns Gate BS27. . . . . 71 A1
Venture 7 BA20 . . . . 218 C3
Venture 20 BA20. . . . . 218 C3
Venture Eleven The TA2 . 213 B6
Venture Way TA2 . . . . 213 B6
Venus La BS39 . . . . 58 E3
Venus St BS49 . . . . 34 E2
Vera St TA2 . . . . 212 F7
Verbena Way BS22 . . . . . . 32 A1

Verdun Terr TA23 . . . . 131 E4
Vereland Rd BS24. . . . . . . 49 E3
Verlands BS49 . . . . 34 E5
Vernal La BA11. . . . . 119 D6
Vernalls Rd DT9 . . . . 225 D5
Vernham Gr BA2. . . . . 44 C1
Vernon Cl BS31. . . . . 25 D3
Vernon La BS26. . . . . 69 B3
Vernon Pk BA2 . . . . 44 C6
Vernon Terr BA2. . . . . 44 C6
Vernslade BA1. . . . . 27 A2
Verriers TA6 . . . . 153 E3
Verrington Hospl BA9. . . 216 B4
Verrington La BA9 . . . . . . 216 B5
Verrington Park Rd BA9. 216 B4
Vesey's Hole Hill SP8 . . . 177 E4
Vestry Cl BA16. . . . . 207 C5
Vestry Ct BA16 . . . . 207 C5
Vestry Rd BA16 . . . . 207 C5
Vian End BS22 . . . . 31 F4
Vicar's Cl BA5 . . . . 203 E5
Vicar's La TA12 . . . . 184 F1
Vicarage Cl
　Chard TA20. . . . . 223 C3
　Coxley BA5. . . . . 139 E6
　Creech St Michael TA3. . . . 169 D4
　Frome BA11 . . . . 119 F4
　Stogursey TA5 . . . . 134 C6
　Weston-Super-Mare BS22. . 32 A3
　Westonzoyland TA7 . . . . . 154 F5
Vicarage Ct
　Burnham-on-S TA8. . . . . . 104 A7
　Timberscombe TA24 . . . . . 130 B5
Vicarage Gdns BA2 . . . . . . 79 B7
Vicarage Hill
　Combe St Nicholas TA20 . . 193 D6
　Dulverton TA22 . . . . 163 D6
Vicarage La
　Barrow Gurney BS48 . . . . . 20 C6
　Compton Bishop BS26 . . . . 69 B3
　Compton Dando BS39 . . . . 41 D6
　Creech St Michael TA3. . . . 169 D4
　Draycott BS27 . . . . 90 F3
　Mark TA9 . . . . 106 E5
　Norton St Philip BA2 . . . . . 81 E4
　Pawlett TA6 . . . . 135 F5
　Shapwick TA7 . . . . 137 F1
　Wookey BA5 . . . . 139 D8
Vicarage Lawns TA3 . . . . 169 D4
Vicarage Rd
　Bristol, Bishopsworth
　BS13 . . . . 22 A6
　Carhampton TA24 . . . . . . 131 B5
　Leigh Woods BS8. . . . . 11 D6
　Minehead TA24 . . . . 200 F8
　Stogursey TA5 . . . . 134 C6
　Wookey BA5 . . . . 139 E8
　Woolavington TA7 . . . . . . 136 E4
Vicarage St
　Burnham-on-S TA8. . . . . . 104 A7
　Frome BA11. . . . . 119 F4
　Tintinhull BA22 . . . . 186 C6
　Yeovil BA20 . . . . 219 B4
Vicarage Wlk BA20. . . . . . 219 B5
Vicars La TA6. . . . . 208 D5
Vickery Cl
　Bridgwater TA6 . . . . 208 D3
　Curry Rivel TA10 . . . . 171 D4
Victoria Art Gall The★
　BA2 . . . . 228 C2
Victoria Ave TA20 . . . . . . 223 D4
Victoria Bldgs
　Bath BA2 . . . . 44 D6
　Glastonbury BA6 . . . . 206 E4
Victoria Bridge Ct BA1 . . 228 A3
Victoria Bridge Rd BA1,
　BA2 . . . . 228 A3
Victoria Bsns Pk TA20 . . 223 D4
Victoria Cl
　Bath BA2 . . . . 44 C5
　Portishead BS20 . . . . 2 D5
　Yeovil BA21 . . . . 219 D6
Victoria Cotts BA2 . . . . . . 62 F7
Victoria Ct
　Castle Cary BA7. . . . . 214 B5
　Chard TA20. . . . . 223 D4
　Frome BA11. . . . . 120 A4
　Ilminster TA19 . . . . 221 C4
　Portishead BS20 . . . . 2 D5
Victoria Gate TA1. . . . . . . 213 B4
Victoria Gdns
　Batheaston BA1 . . . . 28 F3
　Castle Cary BA7. . . . . 214 B6
　Henstridge BA8 . . . . 190 A6
Victoria Gr BA4 . . . . 205 D5
Victoria Ho
　Bath BA1. . . . . 44 D8
　Keynsham BS31. . . . . 24 F4
Victoria Hospl BA11. . . . . 119 E4
Victoria Jubilee Homes
　BS40 . . . . 53 C6
Victoria La BA4 . . . . 141 E1
Victoria Lodge BS22 . . . . . 31 E2
Victoria Mews BA7. . . . . . 214 B5
Victoria Park Bsns Ctr
　BA1. . . . . 44 D7
Victoria Pk
　Castle Cary BA7. . . . . 214 B5
　Weston-Super-Mare BS23. . 30 D1
Victoria Pl
　Bath, Combe Down BA2 . . 45 C1
　Bath, Lambridge BA1. . . . . 28 C1
　Chardstock EX13 . . . . 198 A7
　Highbridge TA9 . . . . 104 D3
　Paulton BS39 . . . . 77 D5
　Weston-Super-Mare BS23. . 48 D8
Victoria Quadrant BS23 . . 48 E8

Victoria Rd
　Avonmouth BS11 . . . . 4 B7
　Bath BA2. . . . . 44 D6
　Bridgwater TA6 . . . . 208 E5
　Castle Cary BA7. . . . . 214 B5
　Clevedon BS21. . . . . 6 C3
　Frome BA11. . . . . 120 A4
　Minehead TA24 . . . . 201 A5
　Saltford BS31 . . . . 25 D3
　Yeovil BA21 . . . . 219 D6
Victoria Sh Mews TA18 . 224 C6
Victoria Sq
　Bristol BS8. . . . . 226 A3
　Crewkerne TA18 . . . . 224 B6
　Evercreech BA4 . . . . 141 E1
　Portishead BS20 . . . . 2 D5
　Weston-Super-Mare BS23. . 48 D7
Victoria St
　Bristol BS1. . . . . 227 B2
　Burnham-on-S TA8. . . . . . 104 A7
　Taunton TA1. . . . . 213 B4
　Wellington TA21. . . . . 222 D6
Victoria Terr
　Bath BA2 . . . . 44 D6
　Bristol, Clifton BS8. . . . . . 11 F6
　Bristol, Redland BA8 . . . . . 190 A6
　Paulton BS39 . . . . 77 E6
Victoria Way TA5 . . . . 152 E7
Victory Rd TA2. . . . . 213 A4
Vigor Rd BS13 . . . . 22 B5
Viking Cl TA23 . . . . 202 D7
Vilberie Cl TA2 . . . . 212 A7
Village Rd TA3. . . . . 182 F6
Villa Rosa BS23 . . . . 30 C1
Villes La TA24 . . . . 124 A4
Villice La BS40. . . . . 74 A7
Vincent Cl TA8. . . . . 104 C7
Vincent Pl BA20. . . . . 219 B5
Vincents Cl DT9. . . . . 189 A1
Vincent St BA20. . . . . 219 B5
Vine Gdns
　Frome BA11. . . . . 119 F6
　Weston-Super-Mare BS22. . 32 A2
Vine Gr BA8 . . . . 176 E1
Vine House Gdns TA20 . . 223 C3
Vinery The BS25 . . . . 70 A7
Vine St BA8. . . . . 176 E1
Viney's Yd BA10 . . . . 215 F6
Vineyards BA1 . . . . 228 C3
Viney La EX14 . . . . 191 F1
Viney St TA1 . . . . 213 B3
Vining's Hill BA4. . . . . . . 142 D1
Vinney La BA11 . . . . 143 F8
Violet La DT9 . . . . 176 A2
Virginia Cl BA8. . . . . 190 A6
Virginia Orch TA3 . . . . . . 169 C3
Viscount Sq TA6. . . . . 208 E7
Vivary Ct TA1. . . . . 212 E3
Vivary Gate TA1. . . . . 212 E3
Vivary Hts TA1 . . . . 212 E2
Vivary Rd TA1 . . . . 212 E3
Vivien Ave BA3 . . . . 78 A2
Vixen Cl BA22. . . . . 174 A3
Vobster Cross BA3 . . . . . . 117 D7
Vobster Hill BA3 . . . . 117 D7
Vole Rd
　Brent Knoll TA9 . . . . 86 D1
　Mark TA9 . . . . 106 B7
Volis Cross TA5. . . . . 152 F1
Volis Hill TA2 . . . . 168 F8
Vowell Cl BS13 . . . . 22 B4
Vowles Cl BS48 . . . . 9 A3
Vulcan Ho BA2. . . . . 228 C1
Vulcan Rd BA22 . . . . 201 B6
Vynes Cl BS48 . . . . 9 A1
Vynes Ind Est BS48. . . . . . . 9 A3
Vynes Way BS48 . . . . 9 A1
Vyvyan Rd BS8. . . . . 226 A3
Vyvyan Terr BS8 . . . . 226 A3

W

Wadbrook Cross EX13 . . . 198 C4
Wade Cl TA7. . . . . 154 E6
Wadeford Hill TA20 . . . . . 193 D5
Wade St BS2 . . . . 227 C3
Wadham's Almshouses
　TA19 . . . . 183 E4
Wadham Cl
　Bridgwater TA6 . . . . 209 D6
　Ilminster TA19 . . . . 221 A4
Wadham Cross
　Knowstone EX36 . . . . 162 A2
　West Anstey EX36 . . . . . . 162 A4
Wadham Hill EX36 . . . . . . 162 A2
Wadham Sch TA18 . . . . . . 224 D7
Wadham St BS23 . . . . 48 D8
Wagg Dro TA10. . . . . 172 B5
Waggs Plot EX13 . . . . 198 B4
Wagon & Horses Hill
　BA4 . . . . 141 B8
Wagtail Gdns BS22. . . . . . 49 E8
Wains Cl BS21 . . . . 6 C2
Wainwright Cl BS22 . . . . . 32 B4
Wainwright Ct BA4. . . . . . 205 B4
Wainwright Dr BA11 . . . . 120 C7
Waits Cl BS29. . . . . 50 F3
Wakedean Gdns BS49 . . . . 17 A1
Walcombe La BA5 . . . . . . 203 E6
Walcot Bldgs
　Bath BA1. . . . . 45 B8
　Bath BA1. . . . . 228 C4
Walcot CE Inf Sch BA1 . . 228 C4
Walcot Gate BA1 . . . . 228 C4
Walcot Ho BA1 . . . . 228 C4
Walcot Par BA1. . . . . 228 C4

Walcot St BA1 . . . . 228 C3
Walcot Terr BA1 . . . . 228 C4
Waldegrave Rd BA1. . . . . . 27 E1
Waldegrave Terr BA3 . . . . 79 A3
Walden Rd BS31 . . . . 25 A4
Waldock Barton TA13 . . . 220 B4
Waldron's Cross TA21. . . 165 E1
Wales La BS22 . . . . 174 E3
Walford Ave BS22. . . . . . . 32 C3
Walford Cross Roads
　TA2 . . . . 169 D7
Walker Rd BA11 . . . . 120 A3
Walkers Dr BS24 . . . . 49 F7
Walkers Gate TA21. . . . . . 222 D5
Walker St BS2 . . . . 226 C4
Walk La TA13 . . . . 184 F1
Wallace La BS40 . . . . 74 E3
Wallace Rd BA1. . . . . 28 B1
Wallace Wells Rd TA8. . . 104 D5
Wallbridge BA11. . . . . 120 A4
Wallbridge Ave BA11. . . . 120 A4
Wallbridge Gdns BA11 . . 120 A4
Wallbridge Ho BA11. . . . . 120 A4
Wallbridge Ind Est BA11. 120 A4
Wall Ditch La TA16. . . . . . 196 A4
Wallenge Cl BS39 . . . . 77 F6
Wallenge Dr BS39. . . . . . . 77 F6
Walley La BS40 . . . . 57 B7
Wall Gn BS26 . . . . 70 C4
Wallingford Rd BS4 . . . . . 22 D7
Wallington Way BA11 . . . 119 D6
Walliscote Grove Rd TA11
　BS23. . . . . 48 E7
Walliscote Prim Sch BS23 48 E7
Walliscote Rd BS23 . . . . . 48 D6
Walliscote Rd S BS23 . . . . 48 D4
Walls La BS28 . . . . 108 B8
Walls The TA7 . . . . 137 C2
Wall The TA9 . . . . 106 C5
Wally Court Rd BS40 . . . . 56 E8
Walmsley Terr BA1. . . . . . 28 B1
Walnut Bldgs BA3. . . . . . . 79 A3
Walnut Cl
　Axbridge BS26. . . . . 70 B1
　Cheddar BS27 . . . . 90 B7
　Easton-in-G BS20. . . . . 4 A3
　Keynsham BS31. . . . . 24 C4
　Nailsea BS48 . . . . 18 E8
　Puriton TA7 . . . . 136 C4
　Rode BA11 . . . . 101 E8
　Weston-Super-Mare BS24. . 49 E8
Walnut Dr
　Bath BA2 . . . . 44 E4
　Bridgwater TA6 . . . . 209 D4
　Somerton TA11 . . . . 211 D4
Walnut Gr BA4. . . . . 205 C4
Walnut La TA7 . . . . 136 F3
Walnut Rd TA10. . . . . 172 A4
Walnuts The TA7 . . . . 137 B2
Walnut Tree Cl
　Ubley BS40 . . . . 55 D1
　Wells BA5 . . . . 203 C5
Walnut Tree Cnr TA23. . . 131 E4
Walnut Tree Ct BS49 . . . . 34 D4
Walnut Tree Dr TA24. . . . 131 A4
Walnut Wlk
　Bristol BS13. . . . . 22 A6
　Frome BA11. . . . . 120 B7
　Keynsham BS31. . . . . 24 C4
Walridge Cross TA4. . . . . 166 E4
Walrond's Pk TA3. . . . . . . 184 B7
Walrond Ct TA19. . . . . . . 221 B3
Walrow TA9 . . . . 104 E3
Walrow Ind Est TA9 . . . . 104 F2
Walrow Terr TA9 . . . . 104 E3
Walscombe Cl TA14 . . . . . 185 F4
Walsh Ave BS14. . . . . 23 A7
Walsh Cl BS24 . . . . 49 B2
Waltham End BS24 . . . . . . 50 A8
Walton BS24. . . . . 49 A2
Walton Bay House Park
　Homes BS21 . . . . 1 B1
Walton CE Prim Sch
　BA16. . . . . 156 E7
Walton Cl
　Bridgwater TA6 . . . . 209 D5
　Keynsham BS31. . . . . 24 D4
Walton Cres BS40. . . . . . . 37 E8
Walton Cross BS21. . . . . . . 7 B7
Walton Ct TA24 . . . . 201 A7
Walton Dro BA16. . . . . . . 156 D5
Walton Rd
　Bristol BS11. . . . . 4 D6
　Clevedon BS21. . . . . 6 F4
Walton St
　Portishead BS21 . . . . 1 A1
　Walton in G BS21. . . . . 7 A8
Walwyn Cl BA2 . . . . 44 A4
Walwyn Gdns BS13. . . . . . 22 C3
Wambrook Cl TA1 . . . . . . 212 E1
Wansbeck Gn TA1 . . . . . . 213 D3
Wansbeck Rd BS31. . . . . . 25 A4
Wansbrough Rd BS22 . . . . 32 B4
Wansdyke Bsns Ctr BA2. . 44 D4
Wansdyke Ct BS14 . . . . . . 23 B5
Wansdyke Prim Sch BS14 22 F4
Wansdyke Rd BA2 . . . . . . 44 D1
Wansdyke Sch BA2 . . . . . . 62 E8
Wansdyke Workshops
　Keynsham BS31. . . . . 25 A6
　Peasedown St John BA2. . . 79 D6
Wapping Rd BS1. . . . . 227 A1
Warden Rd TA24 . . . . 200 F6
Ward La TA7. . . . . 154 E8
Wardleworth Way TA21 . 222 C7
Wardour Rd BS4 . . . . 22 E8
Wareham Cl BS48. . . . . 8 D1

Wareham Cross EX13 . . . . . **198** E1
Wareham Rd EX13 . . . . . **198** E2
Wares La TA6 . . . . **208** D6
Waring Ho BS1 . . . . **227** A1
Warleigh Cl BA11 . . . . . . **119** D4
Warleigh Dr BA1 . . . . . . **29** A3
Warleigh La BA1 . . . . . . **46** C5
Warleys La BS24 . . . . . . **32** C1
Warman Cl BS14 . . . . . . **23** F6
Warman Rd BS14 . . . . . . **23** C8
Warmington Rd BS14 . . . **23** C8
Warminster Rd
  Beckington BA11 . . . . . **101** E4
  Claverton BA2, BA3 . . . **46** B5
  Frome BA11 . . . . **120** B4
Warne Pk BS23 . . . . **49** A6
Warner Cl BS49 . . . . **35** A7
Warne Rd BS23 . . . . **49** A6
Warren's Cl BS27 . . . . . . **71** B1
Warren Cl
  Bridgwater TA6 . . . . . . **208** F6
  Bruton BA10 . . . . **215** E6
  Charlton Horethorne DT9 . **176** A2
  Hutton BS24 . . . . **49** D2
Warren Farm Cvn Pk & Camp
  Site TA8 . . . . **65** F5
Warren Gdns BS14 . . . . . **23** F5
Warren La BS41 . . . . **20** E8
Warren Rd
  Brean TA8 . . . . **65** F6
  Minehead TA24 . . . . . . **201** B7
Warrens Hill BS27 . . . . . **71** B1
Warrens Hill Rd BS27 . . . **71** D4
Warren St TA21 . . . . **222** A4
Warrens Way BA5 . . . . . . **113** A1
Warren The BA16 . . . . . . **207** A5
Warres Rd TA2 . . . . **213** C8
Warrilow Cl BS22 . . . . . . **32** B5
Warrior Ave BS24 . . . . . . **218** B6
Warry Cl BS48 . . . . **9** B2
Warth La BS22 . . . . **32** A8
Warwick Ave TA6 . . . . . . **209** C3
Warwick Cl BS31 . . . . . . **49** C8
Warwick Gdns
  Burnham-on-S TA8 . . . . **85** B1
  Clutton BS39 . . . . **58** D3
  Taunton TA1 . . . . **213** C2
Warwick Rd
  3 Bath BA1 . . . . **44** B7
  Keynsham BS31 . . . . . . **24** D4
  Taunton TA2 . . . . **213** A8
Washcross La TA19 . . . . . **184** E3
Washford Cross TA23 . . . **131** D1
Washford Hill TA23 . . . . . **202** A5
Washford Sta TA23 . . . . . **131** E4
Washingpool DT9 . . . . . . **188** E7
Washing Pound La
  Bristol BS14 . . . . **23** B4
  Nailsea BS48 . . . . **8** B4
Washington Gdns TA6 . . . **208** E5
Washington Terr TA20 . . . **223** B5
Wash La TA15 . . . . **186** B4
Washpool La BA2 . . . . . . **43** F2
Wassail Cl **5** TA24 . . . . **131** A5
Wassail View TA2 . . . . . . **168** B4
Watchet Boat Mus★
  TA23 . . . . **202** C7
Watchet Sta TA23 . . . . . . **202** C7
Watch House Pl **2** **2** E7
Watch House Rd BS20 . . . **4** D4
Watchill Ave BS13 . . . . . . **21** F6
Watchill Cl BS13 . . . . **21** F6
Watchwell Dro TA10 . . . . **157** D7
Waterbridge Rd BS13 . . . **21** F4
Watercombe Hts BA20 . . **218** D2
Watercombe La
  Yeovil BA20 . . . . **218** C2
  Yeovil, Preston Plucknett
    BA20 . . . . **218** D5
Watercombe Pk BA20 . . . **218** D3
Watercress Cl BS48 . . . . . **9** B2
Waterfield Cl TA1 . . . . . . **212** B3
Waterfield Dr TA1 . . . . . . **212** B3
Waterford Beck BA14 . . . **83** F6
Waterford Cl TA6 . . . . . . **209** A2
Waterford Pk BA3 . . . . . . **78** C1
Waterfront Ho BA2 . . . . . **228** B1
Water Hill TA4 . . . . **150** F7
Waterhouse La BA2 . . . . . **63** F8
Water La
  Bristol BS1 . . . . **227** B2
  Butleigh BA6 . . . . **157** E4
  Charlton Horethorne DT9 . **176** A2
  Crowcombe TA4 . . . . . . **151** A7
  Frome BA11 . . . . **119** E3
  Horningsham BA12 . . . . **144** D4
  Keenthorne TA5 . . . . . . **134** C1
  Lopen TA13 . . . . **185** A1
  Nether Stowey TA5 . . . . **134** A1
  Paulton BA3, BS39 . . . . **78** A4
  Pill BS20 . . . . **4** C4
  Somerton TA11 . . . . . . **211** C3
  Stogumber TA4 . . . . . . **150** F7
Waterlake DT10 . . . . **190** B4
Waterlake Rd TA20 . . . . . **198** D4
Waterlands La TA18 . . . . **224** C8
Waterleaze TA2 . . . . **213** D7
Waterlip BA4 . . . . **141** F7
Waterloo
  Frome BA11 . . . . **119** F5
  Puriton TA7 . . . . **136** C4
Waterloo Bldgs **4** BA2 . . **44** B6
Waterloo Cotts TA1 . . . . . **212** B4
Waterloo Cres DT9 . . . . . **176** A1
Waterloo Ho BS20 . . . . . **4** D5

Waterloo La
  Stalbridge DT10 . . . . . . **190** A1
  Yeovil BA20 . . . . **219** A4
Waterloo Pl **19** BS2 . . . . **227** C3
Waterloo Rd
  Bristol BS2 . . . . **227** C3
  Radstock BA3 . . . . **79** A2
  Shepton Mallet BA4 . . . **205** B7
  Wellington TA21 . . . . . . **222** C6
Waterloo St
  Bristol BS2 . . . . **227** C3
  9 Bristol, Clifton BS8 . . **11** F7
  Weston-Super-Mare BS23 . **48** E8
Waterloo Terr TA19 . . . . . **225** F4
Watermans Mdw TA6 . . . **208** E6
Watermead TA20 . . . . . . **198** D8
Watermead **9** BA1 . . . . **228** B2
Water Path TA21 . . . . . . **222** A5
Waters Edge BS20 . . . . . **2** E7
Waterside Cres BA3 . . . . **78** D1
Waterside La BA3 . . . . . . **98** A6
Waterside Pk BS20 . . . . . **1** D4
Waterside Rd
  Radstock BA3 . . . . **78** D1
  Wincanton BA9 . . . . . . **216** C4
Waterside Way BA3 . . . . . **97** D8
Waters La BS27 . . . . **90** C8
Watersmeet Cl
  Golsoncott TA23 . . . . . **131** D1
  Rooks Bridge BS26 . . . . **87** B5
Water St
  Barrington TA19 . . . . . . **184** D5
  Curry Rivel TA10 . . . . . **171** C4
  East Harptree BS40 . . . . **74** F4
  East Lambrook TA13 . . . **220** C8
  Hambridge TA10 . . . . . **171** C4
  Lopen TA13 . . . . **185** A1
  Martock TA12 . . . . **185** D5
  Seavington St Michael
    TA19 . . . . **184** E1
Watery Combe BA3 . . . . . **94** E7
Watery La
  Axminster EX13 . . . . . . **198** A3
  Bath BA2 . . . . **44** A6
  Broadway TA19 . . . . . . **194** B8
  Charlton Horethorne DT9 . **176** A2
  Clatworthy TA4 . . . . . . **149** C2
  Coultings TA5 . . . . **134** E3
  Doynton BS30 . . . . **12** A8
  Halstock BA22 . . . . **197** D3
  Hewish TA18 . . . . **195** D3
  Langford Budville TA4,
    TA21 . . . . **166** C2
  Minehead TA24 . . . . . . **200** F7
  Nailsea BS48 . . . . **8** B2
  North Petherton TA6 . . . **153** E4
  Spaxton TA5 . . . . **152** F4
  Stogursey TA5 . . . . **134** C5
  Stratton-on-t F BA3 . . . **97** A3
  Williton TA4 . . . . **202** E4
  Winford BS40 . . . . **38** B4
  Wiveliscombe TA4 . . . . **210** C6
Watling St BA1 . . . . **218** D7
Watling Way BS11 . . . . . . **4** D7
Watsons La TA5 . . . . **209** A5
Watts's Quarry La TA10,
  TA11 . . . . **173** A5
Watts's Rd TA7 . . . . **137** D8
Watts La TA4 . . . . **151** E4
Wavering Down Rise
  BS26 . . . . **70** A3
Waverley TA11 . . . . **211** C4
Waverley Cl
  Frome BA11 . . . . **120** C6
  Somerton TA11 . . . . . . **211** C4
Waverley Rd
  Backwell BS48 . . . . **19** A7
  Bridgwater TA6 . . . . . . **208** F6
  Bristol, Shirehampton BS11 . **4** E6
  Weston-Super-Mare BS23 . **48** F4
Waverly Ct BS49 . . . . **34** D3
Waverney Cl TA1 . . . . **213** D3
Wayacre Dro BS24 . . . . . **66** E6
Wayclose La BA9 . . . . **177** D5
Waycroft Prim Sch BS14 . **23** E5
Waydown Cross TA24 . . . **130** A4
Waydown La TA24 . . . . . . **130** A4
Wayfield Gdns BA1 . . . . . **28** F4
Wayford Cl BS31 . . . . . . **25** A3
Wayford Hill TA18 . . . . . **195** C1
Wayland Rd BS22 . . . . . . **31** E3
Waysdown La TA4 . . . . . . **149** D1
Wayside
  Staplehay TA3 . . . . **181** D8
  Weston-Super-Mare BS22 . **31** D2
Wayside Cl BA11 . . . . . . **120** C6
Wayside Dr BS21 . . . . . . **6** E5
WCA Ho BS1 . . . . **227** A2
Weacombe Rd
  Bridgwater TA6 . . . . . . **209** C5
  Taunton TA2 . . . . **212** F7
Weal Terr BA1 . . . . **27** B2
Weal The BA1 . . . . **27** C2
Weare CE Fst Sch BS26 . . **88** D7
Weare Ct BS1 . . . . **226** A1
Weares La TA7 . . . . **137** D2
Weatherley Dr BS20 . . . . **1** F3
Weatherly Ave BA2 . . . . . **44** D2
Weaver's Reach TA21 . . . **222** B7
Weavers Cl
  Crewkerne TA18 . . . . . **224** D5
  Shepton Mallet BA4 . . . **205** D4
Weavers Ct BA11 . . . . . . **119** E4
Weavers Orch BA2 . . . . . **62** D1
Weavers The BA11 . . . . . **101** E4
Webb's Cl BA5 . . . . **203** D3
Webb's Hill BA11 . . . . . . **119** B5

Webber Rd BA4 . . . . **205** D4
Webbers TA4 . . . . **167** F7
Webber CE Prim Sch
  TA21 . . . . **178** F5
Webbers Cl TA21 . . . . . . **222** E4
Webbers Way TA7 . . . . . . **136** B4
Webbington Rd BS26 . . . **69** C3
Webbs Mead
  Beckington BA11 . . . . . **101** E4
  Chew Stoke BS40 . . . . . **56** D8
Wedgwood Cl BS14 . . . . **23** B5
Wedgwood Rd BA2 . . . . . **44** A5
Wedlakes TA23 . . . . **202** C6
Wedlands TA2 . . . . **212** F7
Wedlock Way BS3 . . . . . . **11** F3
Wedmore Cl
  Bath BA2 . . . . **44** A3
  Burnham-on-S TA8 . . . . **104** C8
  Frome BA11 . . . . **120** C7
  Weston-Super-Mare BS23 . **48** F2
Wedmore Fst Sch BS28 . . **108** B4
Wedmore Pk BA2 . . . . . . **44** A3
Wedmore Rd
  Cheddar BS27 . . . . **90** A7
  Clevedon BS21 . . . . . . **6** B1
  Nailsea BS48 . . . . **18** E8
  Saltford BS31 . . . . **25** D4
Weekesley La BA2 . . . . . . **60** D1
Weekes Mdw TA21 . . . . . **179** E6
Week La TA22 . . . . **147** D4
Weetwood Rd BS49 . . . . **34** E5
Weind The BS22 . . . . **31** D2
Weirfield Gn TA1 . . . . . . **212** D5
Weirfield Rd TA1 . . . . . . **201** A8
Weir Head Cotts TA22 . . . **163** D7
Weir La
  Abbots Leigh BS8 . . . . . **10** F5
  Marshfield SN14 . . . . . **13** F8
  Pilton BA4 . . . . **140** E3
  Yeovilton BA22 . . . . . . **174** A1
Weir Rd BS49 . . . . **34** E3
Welbeck Rd BA21 . . . . . . **219** E7
Welland Cl TA1 . . . . **213** D4
Welland Rd
  Keynsham BS31 . . . . . . **24** F4
  Yeovil BA21 . . . . **219** D7
Wellard Cl **1** BS22 . . . . **32** B4
Well Cl
  Long Ashton BS41 . . . . . **11** B1
  Weston-Super-Mare BS24 . **49** B2
  Winscombe BS25 . . . . . **70** A8
Wellesley Ct TA1 . . . . . . **212** C1
Wellesley Gn BA10 . . . . . **215** E6
Wellesley Park Prim Sch
  TA21 . . . . **222** E4
Wellesley Pk TA21 . . . . . **222** D4
Wellesley St TA2 . . . . . . **212** F6
Wellesley Way TA3 . . . . . **192** A7
Wellfield Hill DT6, EX13 . . **199** B2
Well House Cl BS9 . . . . . **5** E3
Wellhouse La BA6 . . . . . . **206** F4
Wellings Cl TA21 . . . . . . **198** C8
Wellington Bldgs BA1 . . . **27** B2
Wellington Cottage Hospl
  TA21 . . . . **222** D5
Wellington Ct BS21 . . . . . **6** C5
Wellington Flats BA20 . . . **219** A4
Wellington Hill TA21 . . . . **222** F2
Wellington Jun Sch
  TA21 . . . . **222** E5
Wellington Mews BS11 . . . **4** D5
Wellington Mus TA21 . . . **222** E5
Wellington New Rd TA1 . . **212** B3
Wellington Pl
  Cheddar BS27 . . . . **90** B7
  Weston-Super-Mare BS23 . **48** D7
Wellington Rd
  Bridgwater TA6 . . . . . . **209** B5
  Bristol BS2 . . . . **227** C4
  Taunton TA1 . . . . **212** D4
Wellington Sch TA21 . . . **222** E5
Wellington Sq TA24 . . . . **200** F7
Wellington Terr
  18 Bristol BS8 . . . . . . **11** F6
  Clevedon BS21 . . . . . . **6** D5
  Wiveliscombe TA4 . . . . **210** C5
Well La
  Banwell BS29 . . . . **50** E3
  Purse Caundle DT9 . . . . **189** D4
  Timberscombe TA24 . . . **130** A5
  Yatton BS49 . . . . **34** C8
Wellow Brook Ct BA3 . . . **78** B3
Wellow Brook Mdw BA3 . . **78** B2
Wellow Dr BA11 . . . . **120** C7
Wellow La
  Hinton Charterhouse BA2 . . **63** D1
  Norton St Philip BA2 . . . **81** D5
  Peasedown St John BA2 . . **79** C6
  Shoscombe BA2 . . . . . . **79** E6
Wellow Mead BA2 . . . . . . **79** B7
Wellow Rd BA2 . . . . **80** B8
Wellow Tyning BA2 . . . . . **79** D7
Well Pk BS49 . . . . **34** E4
Wells Cathedral★ BA5 . . . **203** E4
Wells Cathedral Jun Sch
  BA5 . . . . **203** D5
Wells Cathedral Sch
  BA5 . . . . **203** E5
Wells Central CE Jun Sch
  BA5 . . . . **203** C3
Wells Cl
  Bristol BS14 . . . . **23** C5
  Burnham-on-S TA8 . . . . **104** C1
  Nailsea BS48 . . . . **9** B1
  Taunton TA2 . . . . **213** A8
Wells & District Hospl
  BA5 . . . . **203** F5
Wellsea Gr BS23 . . . . . . **49** B7

Wellshead La TA24 . . . . . **128** A3
Wells Mus★ BA5 . . . . . . **203** E4
Wellsprings Prim Sch
  TA2 . . . . **212** F8
Wellsprings Rd TA2 . . . . . **212** F7
Wells Rd
  Bath BA2 . . . . **228** B1
  Bristol BS14 . . . . **23** C7
  Chilcompton BA3 . . . . . **96** F4
  Clevedon BS21 . . . . . . **6** D1
  Corston BA2 . . . . **43** B7
  Dundry BS40, BS41 . . . . **38** F7
  Glastonbury BA6 . . . . . **206** E6
  Glastonbury, Southway
    BA6 . . . . **139** D4
  Hallatrow BS39 . . . . . . **77** B7
  Norton St Philip BA2, BA3 . . **81** C3
  Priddy BA5 . . . . **92** E2
  Radstock BA3 . . . . **78** E2
  Rodney Stoke BS27 . . . . **91** B1
  Shepton Mallet BA4 . . . **204** E6
  Theale BS28 . . . . **109** B1
  Westbury-sub-Mendip BA5 **110** E6
  Wookey Hole BA5 . . . . . **203** A7
  Yarley BA5 . . . . **139** C8
Wells Road Trad Est BA6 . **206** F7
Wells Sq BA3 . . . . **78** D1
Wellsway
  Bath BA2 . . . . **44** F3
  Keynsham BS31 . . . . . . **24** F3
Wells Way BS28 . . . . **107** F3
Wellsway Pk BA2 . . . . . . **62** D8
Wellsway Sec Sch BS31 . . **25** A5
Well The TA21 . . . . **222** B5
Welsford Ave BA5 . . . . . . **203** C5
Welsford Cl BA5 . . . . **203** B5
Welsh Back BS1 . . . . **227** A2
Welsh Ct BA5 . . . . **203** B4
Welshmill La BA11 . . . . . **119** F5
Welshmill Rd BA11 . . . . . **119** F5
Welton Gr BA3 . . . . **78** B3
Welton Prim Sch BA3 . . . **78** C2
Welton Rd BA3 . . . . **78** C2
Welton Vale BA3 . . . . . . **78** B2
Wembdon Ct TA6 . . . . . . **208** E4
Wembdon Hill TA6 . . . . . **208** C6
Wembdon Orch TA6 . . . . **208** C6
Wembdon Rd TA6 . . . . . . **208** C6
Wembdon St George's CE
  Prim Sch TA6 . . . . **208** C6
Wemberham Cres BS49 . . **17** A1
Wemberham La BS49 . . . **33** E8
Wendick Dro TA10 . . . . . **171** E3
Wentwood Dr BS24 . . . . . **49** A1
Wentworth Cl BS22 . . . . **32** A3
Wentworth Rd BA21 . . . . **219** E7
Werren Cl TA23 . . . . **202** B7
Wesley Ave BA3 . . . . **78** C1
Wesley Cl
  Brean TA8 . . . . **65** F3
  Frome BA11 . . . . **119** F4
  Southwick BA14 . . . . . . **83** E2
  Taunton TA1 . . . . **212** C1
  Wanstrow BA4 . . . . **142** F4
Wesley Ct BS23 . . . . **48** F8
Wesley Dr BS22 . . . . **32** A3
Wesley La BA14 . . . . **83** E2
Wesley Mews BS27 . . . . . **90** B7
Wesley Rd BA3 . . . . **78** D1
Wesley Slope **13** BA11 . . **119** F4
Wesley Villas
  Coleford BA3 . . . . **116** F6
  12 Frome BA11 . . . . . **119** F4
Wessex Bldgs TA11 . . . . **211** B5
Wessex Bsns Ctr BS27 . . **90** A7
Wessex Ct
  Bridgwater TA6 . . . . . . **209** C4
  Chard TA20 . . . . **223** C2
  Street BA16 . . . . **207** C6
Wessex Ct **4** DT9 . . . . . **225** D3
Wessex Dr BS22 . . . . . . **187** E1
Wessex Fields BA11 . . . . **119** D2
Wessex Fields Ret Pk
  BA11 . . . . **119** D2
Wessex Ho **10** BS2 . . . . **227** C4
Wessex Pk TA11 . . . . . . **211** B5
Wessex Rd
  Stalbridge DT10 . . . . . . **190** C4
  Taunton TA1 . . . . **168** E1
  Weston-Super-Mare BS24 . **49** B2
  Yeovil BA21 . . . . **218** D8
Wessex Rise TA11 . . . . . . **211** E3
Wessex Way BA9 . . . . . . **216** B3
Westacre BA16 . . . . **207** A4
Westacre Cl BS27 . . . . . . **90** B8
Westacre Rd BS27 . . . . . **90** B8
West Anstey School Cross
  EX36 . . . . **162** C5
West Approach Rd TA7 . . **136** D4
West Ave
  Bath BA2 . . . . **44** C5
  Highbridge TA9 . . . . . . **104** C4
Westaway Cl BS49 . . . . . **34** C7
Westaway Pk BS49 . . . . . **34** D7
West Bank BA5 . . . . **203** A4
Westbourne Ave
  Clevedon BS21 . . . . . . **6** B2
  Keynsham BS31 . . . . . . **24** E5
Westbourne Cl BS20 . . . . **218** E5
Westbourne Cres BS21 . . **6** B2
Westbourne Gr BA20 . . . . **218** E5
Westbourne Ho BA2 . . . . **228** C4
Westbourne Pl BS8 . . . . . **226** B3
West Bourton Rd SP8 . . . **177** D8
West Bow Ho TA6 . . . . . . **208** A4
West Bow La TA5 . . . . . . **153** C2
Westbridge Pk DT9 . . . . . **225** B4
West Brook BA21 . . . . . . **218** D6

Westbrook Ct BA4 . . . . . **141** E1
Westbrooke Ct BS1 . . . . **226** A1
Westbrook Pk BA1 . . . . . **27** A2
Westbrook Rd
  Bristol BS4 . . . . **23** D8
  Evercreech BA4 . . . . . . **141** E1
  Weston-Super-Mare BS22 . **31** D1
Westbrook Vale BA4 . . . . **141** E1
West Buckland Com Prim
  Sch TA21 . . . . **180** F7
West Buckland Rd TA21 . . **180** D7
Westbury
  Bradford Abbas DT9 . . . **187** E1
  Sherborne DT9 . . . . . . **225** D3
Westbury Court Rd BS9 . . **5** F7
Westbury Cres BS23 . . . . **48** F2
Westbury Gdns BA22 . . . **186** C2
Westbury La BS9 . . . . . . **5** C7
Westbury Terr
  Dunkerton BA2 . . . . . . **61** E3
  2 Sherborne DT9 . . . . **225** D3
Westbury View BA2 . . . . **79** E8
West Camel Farm BA22 . . **174** E3
West Camel Rd BA22 . . . **174** E3
West Charlton TA11 . . . . **173** E7
West Chinnock CE Prim Sch
  TA18 . . . . **196** B3
West Cl
  Bath BA2 . . . . **44** A5
  Dunster TA24 . . . . **201** D2
West Coker CE Prim Sch
  BA22 . . . . **197** A8
West Coker Rd BA20 . . . . **218** E2
Westcombe BA8 . . . . **176** E1
Westcombe Hill BA4 . . . . **142** C2
Westcombe Rd
  Evercreech BA4 . . . . . . **141** F2
  Westcombe BA4 . . . . . . **142** A2
Westcombes EX13 . . . . . **198** B7
Westcombe Trad Est
  TA19 . . . . **183** E1
West Compton La BA4 . . . **204** E3
West Coombe
  Bristol BS9 . . . . **5** D6
  Yeovil BA22 . . . . **218** D6
West Coombe La TA4 . . . **165** D8
West Cornmoor Dro
  TA9 . . . . **136** D7
Westcott Cl BA11 . . . . . . **120** C6
Westcott Cross TA23 . . . **130** D1
Westcott La TA4 . . . . . . **148** F2
West Cotts TA24 . . . . . . **127** A2
West Cres TA19 . . . . **221** B2
West Croft
  Blagdon BS40 . . . . **54** E2
  Clevedon BS21 . . . . . . **6** B2
West Ct
  Horrington BA5 . . . . . . **112** F1
  Portishead BS20 . . . . . **2** D4
  Templecombe BA8 . . . . **176** E1
West Dene BS9 . . . . **5** E6
West Dro TA7 . . . . **137** D4
West Dundry La BS41 . . . **21** E2
West End
  Bristol BS3 . . . . **226** C1
  Bristol, Kingsdown BS2 . . **227** A4
  Frome BA11 . . . . **119** F5
  Lower Weare BS26 . . . . **88** D2
  Marston Magna BA22 . . **174** E1
  Somerton TA11 . . . . . . **211** C4
  Street BA16 . . . . **207** B5
  Wedmore BS28 . . . . . . **108** C3
West End Cl
  Somerton TA11 . . . . . . **211** C4
  South Petherton TA13 . . **220** B4
West End Ct
  Chedzoy TA7 . . . . **136** D1
  South Petherton TA13 . . **220** B4
West End Farm Cvn Pk
  BS24 . . . . **49** E4
Westend La BA11 . . . . . . **143** C6
West End La BS48 . . . . . . **18** A8
West End Trad Est BS48 . . **8** B1
West End View
  Barrington TA19 . . . . . . **184** C5
  South Petherton TA13 . . **220** B4
West End Way TA13 . . . . **220** B4
Westerkirk Gate TA2 . . . . **212** C7
Westerleigh Rd
  Bath BA2 . . . . **45** B1
  Clevedon BS21 . . . . . . **6** B2
Westerly Ct TA19 . . . . . . **221** B4
Western Approaches
  BA22 . . . . **174** A2
Western Ave BA21 . . . . . **218** B6
Western Ct
  Clevedon BS21 . . . . . . **6** D3
  Shepton Mallet BA4 . . . **205** B6
Western Dr BS14 . . . . . . **22** E6
Western Gate TA10 . . . . **172** C7
Western La
  Minehead TA24 . . . . . . **200** F7
  Ridge BS40 . . . . **74** C3
Western Retreat BA5 . . . . **203** B5
Western St DT9 . . . . **187** E4
Western Way
  Bridgwater TA6 . . . . . . **208** F7
  Winsham TA20 . . . . . . **194** E2
Westex Ho BS23 . . . . . . **49** B5
Westfield
  Bruton BA10 . . . . **215** D5
  Clevedon BS21 . . . . . . **16** D8
  Curry Rivel TA10 . . . . . **171** C3
  Shepton Mallet BA4 . . . **205** A6
  Sherborne DT9 . . . . . . **225** B2

Westfield Ave BA21 . . . . . . **218** E6
Westfield Cl
　Backwell BS48 . . . . **19** A6
　Bath BA2 . . . . **44** E3
　Bridgwater TA6 . . . . **208** E4
　Burnham-on-S TA8 . . . . . . **104** B8
　Keynsham BS31 . . . . **24** C5
　Weston-Super-Mare BS23 . . **48** D2
West Field Cl TA1 . . . . . . **212** A2
Westfield Com Sch BA21 **218** E6
Westfield Cres
　Banwell BS29 . . . . **51** A3
　Yeovil BA21 . . . . **218** F6
Westfield Ct TA8 . . . . **104** B8
Westfield Dr
　Backwell BS48 . . . . **19** A6
　Burnham-on-S TA8 . . . . . . **104** B8
Westfield Est BA3 . . . . . . **161** F2
Westfield Gr BA21 . . . . . . **218** E6
Westfield Ho
　Bath BA2 . . . . **44** E3
　Bridgwater TA6 . . . . **208** E4
Westfield Ind & Trad Est
　BA3 . . . . **97** C7
Westfield Inf Com Sch
　BA21 . . . . **218** E6
Westfield La
　Curry Rivel TA10 . . . . **171** C3
　Draycott BS27 . . . . **90** E3
　North Curry TA3 . . . . **170** C3
　Rodney Stoke BS27 . . . . . **110** C8
　Street BA6, BA16 . . . . **207** E2
Westfield Pk BA1 . . . . **44** A7
Westfield Pk S BA1 . . . . . . **44** A7
Westfield Pl
　Bristol BS8 . . . . **11** F7
　Yeovil BA21 . . . . **218** E6
Westfield Prim Sch BA3 . . **97** C8
Westfield Rd
　Backwell BS48 . . . . **19** A6
　Banwell BS29 . . . . **51** A3
　Burnham-on-S TA8 . . . . . . **104** B8
　Frome BA11 . . . . **119** D3
　Wells BA5 . . . . **203** C4
　Weston-Super-Mare BS23 . . **48** D2
　Yeovil BA21 . . . . **218** F6
Westfields BS23 . . . . **48** D2
Westfield Terr BA3 . . . . . . **78** D1
Westford Cl TA21 . . . . . . **222** A5
Westford Ct TA21 . . . . . . **222** A5
Westford Dr TA21 . . . . . . **222** A5
West Garston BS29 . . . . . . **51** A3
Westgate BS1 . . . . **226** B1
Westgate Bldgs BA1 . . . . . **228** B2
Westgate St
　Bath BA1 . . . . **228** B2
　4 Taunton TA1 . . . . **212** E3
Westhall Rd BA1 . . . . **44** D7
West Harptree Rd BS40 . . **74** F5
West Hatch La TA3 . . . . . **182** F8
Westhaven Cl BS48 . . . . . . **19** A6
Westhaven Sch BS23 . . . . . **48** D2
Westhay Broad Dro TA7 . **137** E6
Westhay Cross EX13 . . . . **198** F3
Westhay Moor Dro BA5,
　BA6 . . . . **138** D6
Westhay Rd BA6 . . . . **138** C4
West Hay Rd BS40 . . . . . . **35** C3
West Hendford BA20 . . . . **218** F3
West Hill
　Milborne Port DT9 . . . . . **217** D2
　Nailsea BS48 . . . . **9** A5
　Portishead BS20 . . . . **2** B5
　Wincanton BA9 . . . . **216** B4
West Hill Ct BS20 . . . . **2** C6
Westhill Gdns BS20 . . . . . . **2** C5
West Hill Gdns
　Radstock BA3 . . . . **78** D1
　Radstock BA3 . . . . **78** E1
Westhill La TA9 . . . . **105** C2
West Hill Rd BA3 . . . . **78** D1
Westholm Rd TA11 . . . . . **211** B4
West Howetown La
　TA24 . . . . **147** D5
West Huntspill Com Prim
　Sch TA9 . . . . **104** C1
West La
　Alhampton BA4 . . . . **159** C5
　Alweston DT9 . . . . **189** A2
　Barrington TA13 . . . . **184** F5
　Croscombe BA5 . . . . **140** F8
　Felton BS40 . . . . **37** C8
　Lynford-on-F TA11 . . . . . **158** D2
　Sherborne DT9 . . . . **188** F1
Westlake Cl TA7 . . . . **155** C2
Westland Rd BA20 . . . . . . **218** F4
West Lea Rd BA1 . . . . **27** A1
West Leaze BA16 . . . . **207** B6
Westleigh Gdns BA4 . . . . **205** A6
West Leigh Inf Sch BS48 . **19** A6
Westleigh Pk BS14 . . . . . . **23** B8
Westleigh Rd TA1 . . . . . . **213** B3
West Links BS23 . . . . **48** D2
West Links Cl BS22 . . . . . . **31** B3
West Littleton Rd SN14 . . **13** F8
West Lodge BA4 . . . . **205** A5
West Lynne BS27 . . . . **90** B8
West Mall BS8 . . . . **11** F7
Westmans Est TA8 . . . . . . **104** C7
Westmarch Way BS22 . . . . **32** A4
Westmead BA3 . . . . **96** D3
Westmead Gdns BA1 . . . . . **27** A2
West Mendip Com Hosp
　BA6 . . . . **139** D3

Westmere Cres TA8 . . . . . **104** C8
West Mill La
　Marnhull DT10 . . . . **190** D6
　Sherborne DT9 . . . . **225** C2
Westminster BA21 . . . . . . **218** C7
Westminster Bldgs DT10 **190** B4
Westminster Cotts DT10 . **190** B4
Westminster St BA20 . . . . **219** A4
West Monkton CE Prim Sch
　TA2 . . . . **213** F8
Westmoor Dro TA10,
　TA12 . . . . **184** E7
Westmoor La TA10 . . . . . **184** D8
Westmoreland Dr BA2 . . **228** A1
Westmoreland Rd BA2 . . **228** A1
Westmoreland St BA2 . . . **228** A1
Westmoreland Station Rd
　BA2 . . . . **228** A1
Weston All Saints CE Prim
　Sch BA1 . . . . **27** A2
Weston Bsns Pk BS24 . . . . **49** E5
Weston Cl
　Bristol BS9 . . . . **5** C7
　East Chinnock BA22 . . . . **196** E8
Weston Coll
　Nailsea BS48 . . . . **8** E2
　Weston-Super-Mare BS23 . **48** D8
Weston Coll (Westcliff)
　BS23 . . . . **30** B1
Weston Ct BS23 . . . . **49** B3
Weston Dro BS20 . . . . **7** F8
Weston Euro Pk BS24 . . . . **49** B4
Weston Farm La BA1 . . . . **27** D1
Weston Gateway Tourist Pk
　BS24 . . . . **32** C1
Weston General Hospl
　BS23 . . . . **48** E2
Weston Hill SP8 . . . . **177** D3
Westonia BS22 . . . . **31** E2
Westonian Ct BS9 . . . . **5** C4
Weston Ind Est BS24 . . . . **49** B2
Weston La
　Bath BA1 . . . . **44** C8
　Christon BS26 . . . . **68** C7
　East Coker BA22 . . . . **197** E5
　Halstock DT2 . . . . **196** F1
Weston Lock Ret BA2 . . . . **44** C6
Weston Lodge BS23 . . . . . . **48** D8
Weston Milton Sta BS22 . . **49** C7
Weston Miniature Rly★
　BS23 . . . . **48** D5
Weston Park Ct BA1 . . . . . **27** D1
Weston Park Prim Sch
　BS11 . . . . **4** F8
Weston Pk BA1 . . . . **27** C1
Weston Pk E BA1 . . . . **27** D1
Weston Pk W BA1 . . . . **27** C1
Weston Rd
　Bath BA1 . . . . **44** D8
　Brean TA8 . . . . **66** A5
　Congresbury BS49 . . . . **34** B5
　East Brent BS24, TA9 . . . . **86** D6
　Failand BS8 . . . . **10** C3
　Long Ashton BS41 . . . . **20** D8
　Weston Ret Pk BS23 . . . . . **49** A6
Weston Sixth Form Coll
　BS23 . . . . **48** F2
Weston St
　Buckhorn Weston SP8 . . . **177** D3
　East Chinnock BA22 . . . . **196** E8
Weston-Super-Mare Sta
　BS23 . . . . **48** E2
Weston Town BA4 . . . . . . **141** E1
Weston Way BS24 . . . . **49** F2
Weston Wlk BA11 . . . . . . **119** C6
Weston Wood Rd BS20 . . . . **2** C3
Westonzoyland Prim Sch
　TA7 . . . . **154** F5
Westonzoyland Pumping
　Sta★ TA7 . . . . **154** D3
Westonzoyland Rd TA6,
　TA7 . . . . **209** E4
Westover
　Frome BA11 . . . . **119** D4
　Nunney BA11 . . . . **143** B7
Westover Ct BA11 . . . . . . **119** D4
Westover Gdns BS9 . . . . **5** F8
Westover Gn TA6 . . . . **208** E4
Westover Green Com Sch
　TA6 . . . . **208** E4
Westover La
　Crewkerne TA18 . . . . **224** B7
　Martock TA12 . . . . **185** F8
Westover Trad Est TA10 . **171** F5
Westover View TA18 . . . . **224** C7
Westowe Hill TA4 . . . . . . **151** A3
West Par BS9 . . . . **5** C7
West Park Cl TA24 . . . . . . **200** E7
West Pennard CE Prim Sch
　BA6 . . . . **140** B1
West Pk
　Bristol BS8 . . . . **226** B4
　Butleigh BA6 . . . . **157** E4
　Castle Cary BA7 . . . . **214** B6
　Minehead TA24 . . . . **200** E7
　Yeovil BA20 . . . . **218** F5
Westport La TA3, TA10 . . **184** B7
West Quay TA6 . . . . **208** F5
West Rd
　East Brent BS24, TA9 . . . . **86** B7
　Lympsham BS24 . . . . **67** B1
　Midsomer Norton BA3 . . . **78** A3
　Yatton BS49 . . . . **34** B7

Westridge DT9 . . . . **225** C3
Westridge Way TA4 . . . . . **167** E7
West Rocke Ave BS9 . . . . . . **5** D6
West Rolstone Rd BS24 . . **33** A1
West Sedgemoor Nature
　Reserve★ TA3 . . . . **170** F3
West Sedgemoor Rd
　TA3 . . . . **170** D3
West Shepton BA4 . . . . . . **205** A5
West Somerset Com Coll The
　TA24 . . . . **201** B5
West Somerset Rly
　Crowcombe TA4 . . . . **151** C4
　Stogumber TA4 . . . . **150** F7
West Somerset Rural Life
　Mus★ TA24 . . . . **124** C4
West St
　Ashcott TA7 . . . . **156** B8
　Axbridge BS26 . . . . **70** B2
　Bampton EX16 . . . . **164** B1
　Banwell BS29 . . . . **51** A3
　Banwell BS29 . . . . **51** B3
　Bishops Lydeard TA4 . . . . **167** E8
　Bridgwater TA6 . . . . **208** E4
　Bristol BS2 . . . . **227** C3
　Carhampton TA24 . . . . . . **131** B4
　Crewkerne TA18 . . . . **224** B6
　Dunster TA24 . . . . **201** D1
　Hinton St George TA17 . . **195** C7
　Ilchester BA22 . . . . **173** E1
　Ilminster TA19 . . . . **221** B4
　Kington Magna SP8 . . . . **177** E1
　Martock TA12 . . . . **185** E8
　Minehead TA24 . . . . **200** E6
　Seavington St Mary TA19 . **184** D1
　Somerton TA11 . . . . **211** D4
　South Petherton TA13 . . . **220** B4
　Stoke sub Hamdon TA14 . **185** E3
　Templecombe BA8 . . . . . . **189** E8
　Watchet TA23 . . . . **202** B7
　Wells BA5 . . . . **203** C3
　Weston-Super-Mare BS23 . **48** D8
　Wiveliscombe TA4 . . . . . . **210** C4
　Yarlington BA9 . . . . **175** F7
　Yeovil BA20 . . . . **218** F4
West Terr BA2 . . . . **82** C1
West Town Gr BS4 . . . . . . **23** D8
West Town La
　Baltonsborough BA6 . . . . **157** F5
　Bristol BS4, BS14 . . . . **23** C8
West Town Pk BS4 . . . . . . **23** D8
West Town Rd
　Backwell BS48 . . . . **19** A5
　Bristol BS11 . . . . **4** C7
West Tyning BA2 . . . . **42** B1
Westview BS39 . . . . **77** C5
West View
　Creech St Michael TA3 . . **169** D5
　Long Sutton TA10 . . . . . . **172** E4
　Milborne Port DT9 . . . . . **217** D3
　Queen Camel BA22 . . . . . **174** F4
　South Cadbury BA22 . . . . **175** D4
　West Monkton TA2 . . . . . **169** D8
West View Cl TA7 . . . . . . **155** B4
Westview Orch BA3 . . . . . . **64** B5
West View Rd
　Batheaston BA1 . . . . **29** A3
　Keynsham BS31 . . . . **24** E5
West Villas TA4 . . . . **167** F6
Westville BA21 . . . . **219** C5
Westward BS41 . . . . **11** B2
Westward Cl BS40 . . . . **35** D2
Westward Dr BS20 . . . . **4** C4
Westward Gdns BS41 . . . . **11** B2
Westward Rd BS13 . . . . . . **21** F7
Westway
　Nailsea BS48 . . . . **8** E2
　Street BA16 . . . . **207** B6
West Way BS21 . . . . **6** C3
Westway Ctr BA11 . . . . . . **119** F5
Westway La BA4 . . . . **205** B4
West Ways BA22 . . . . **196** E8
West Well La BS28 . . . . . . **109** C1
West Wick BS22 . . . . **32** C1
West Wick Rdbt BS22,
　BS24 . . . . **50** B8
Westwood BA2 . . . . **45** E6
Westwood Ave BS39 . . . . . **59** C2
Westwood Cl 2 BS22 . . . . **31** F2
Westwood Cotts BA8 . . . . **176** E1
Westwood Dr BA11 . . . . . **119** C4
Westwood Dro TA11 . . . . **158** C3
Westwood Rd
　Bridgwater TA6 . . . . **209** D7
　Bristol BS4 . . . . **23** D8
Westwoods BA1 . . . . **29** B3
Westwood with Iford Prim
　Sch BA15 . . . . **64** F3
Wetherell Pl BS8 . . . . **226** B3
Wet La BS27 . . . . **90** F2
Wetlands La BS20 . . . . **2** C3
Wetlands & Willows Visitor
　Ctr★ TA3 . . . . **170** D5
Wetmoor La
　Langport TA10 . . . . **172** C2
　Westbury-sub-Mendip BA5 **110** E1
Wexford Rd BS4 . . . . **22** D8
Weycroft Ave EX13 . . . . . **198** A2
Weylands La BA11 . . . . . . **119** E6
Weymont Cl TA7 . . . . **155** B3
Weymouth Ct BA1 . . . . . . **45** B8
Weymouth Rd
　Evercreech BA4 . . . . **141** E1
　Frome BA11 . . . . **119** E4
Weymouth St BA1 . . . . **45** B8
Whaddon Hill BA10 . . . . . **160** C2
Wharf Cotts TA21 . . . . . . **222** B8
Wharf Ho TA19 . . . . **221** B4

Wharf La
　Ilminster TA19 . . . . **221** B3
　Portbury BS20 . . . . **3** B5
Wharfside BS24 . . . . **66** E3
Wharncliffe Cl BS14 . . . . . **23** B5
Wharncliffe Gdns BS14 . . . **23** B5
Whatcombe Rd BA11 . . . . **119** E6
Whatcombe Terr BA11 . . . **119** E6
Whatley TA10 . . . . **171** F5
Whatley Cross TA20 . . . . **194** C1
Whatley La
　Buckland St Mary TA20 . . **192** D7
　Langport TA10 . . . . **172** A5
　Tatworth TA20 . . . . **194** C1
　Winsham TA20 . . . . **199** A8
Whatley Mews TA10 . . . . **171** F5
Whatley Vineyard & Herb
　Gdn★ BA11 . . . . **118** D4
Wheatfield Dr BS22 . . . . . . **32** A5
Wheatfield La BA3 . . . . **95** A6
Wheathill Cl
　Keynsham BS31 . . . . **24** D5
　Milborne Port DT9 . . . . . **217** D2
Wheathill La DT9 . . . . **217** E3
Wheathill Way DT9 . . . . . **217** D2
Wheatleigh Cl TA1 . . . . . . **212** C2
Wheatley Cres TA1 . . . . . . **213** B5
Wheatstones 10 TA4 . . . . **167** F8
Wheeler Gr BA5 . . . . **203** B4
Wheelers Cl BA3 . . . . **78** C2
Wheelers Dr BA3 . . . . **78** C2
Wheelers Rd BA3 . . . . **78** C2
Wheel House La TA20 . . . **199** B7
Wheelwright & Gypsy Mus★
　BS26 . . . . **68** D4
Whellers Mdw TA12 . . . . **185** E7
Whetham Mill Cross
　DT8 . . . . **199** F5
Whetham Mill La DT8 . . . **199** F6
Whetstones Almshouses
　TA19 . . . . **183** F4
Whippington Ct BS1 . . . . **227** B3
Whirligig La 15 TA14 . . . . **185** F4
Whirligig La TA1 . . . . **212** F4
Whirligig Pl 7 TA1 . . . . . **212** F4
Whistley La BS40 . . . . **74** F6
Whitbourne Moor BA12 . . **144** E6
Whitbourne Springs
　BA12 . . . . **144** F7
Whitchey Dro TA9 . . . . . . **137** A5
Whitchurch District Ctr
　BS14 . . . . **23** A5
Whitchurch La
　Bristol, Bishopsworth
　　BS13 . . . . **22** B5
　Bristol, Hartcliffe BS13 . . . **22** C5
　Bristol, Whitchurch BS14 . . **22** E5
　Dundry BS41 . . . . **22** C1
　Henstridge BA8 . . . . **190** A7
　Yenston BA8 . . . . **189** F8
Whitchurch Prim Sch
　BS14 . . . . **23** C4
Whitchurch Rd BS13 . . . . . **22** A6
Whitcombe Farm La
　DT9 . . . . **175** D2
Whitcross 10 BA22 . . . . . **197** E8
White's Dro BA5 . . . . **138** F7
White's La TA4 . . . . **133** A1
White Ash La TA20 . . . . . **193** A5
Whitebeam Cl TA6 . . . . . **209** D5
Whitebrook La BA2 . . . . . . **79** A8
Whitebrook Terr TA21 . . **178** F5
White Cats Cotts BA8 . . . **176** E3
Whitechapel La BA11 . . . **101** C1
Whitecroft TA4 . . . . **202** E4
White Cross
　Brent Knoll TA9 . . . . **105** C8
　Exford TA24 . . . . **128** B1
Whitecross Ave BS14 . . . . **23** C6
White Cross Gate BS39 . . . **76** F6
Whitecross La
　Banwell BS29 . . . . **51** A4
　Minehead TA24 . . . . **200** E7
Whitecross Rd
　East Harptree BS40 . . . . . . **74** F4
　Weston-Super-Mare BS23 . . **48** E6
Whitecross Way TA24 . . . **200** E7
Whitedown Cross EX15 . . **191** B4
Whitefield Cl BA1 . . . . **29** B4
Whitefield Cross EX36 . . . **162** D3
Whitefield La TA19 . . . . . **184** D4
Whitefield Rocks TA4 . . . **150** B1
Whitegate Cl
　Bleadon BS24 . . . . **67** B6
　Minehead TA24 . . . . **201** A6
Whitegate Rd TA24 . . . . . **201** A6
Whitegates Gdns TA24 . . **200** F6
Whitehall
　Taunton TA1 . . . . **212** F5
　Watchet TA23 . . . . **202** B7
Whitehall Cl TA13 . . . . . . **220** D4
Whitehall Ct TA18 . . . . . . **224** C7
White Hart La TA21 . . . . **222** D6
White Hill
　Langport TA10 . . . . **172** A7
　Shoscombe BA2 . . . . **79** F6
White Hill Dro TA20 . . . . **193** C5
Whitehole Hill BA3 . . . . . **116** E4
White Horse Dr BA11 . . . **120** C6
White Horse La BS28 . . . . **138** D8
White Horse Rd BA15 . . . . **64** E7
Whitehouse Ctr (PRU)
　BS13 . . . . **22** C5
Whitehouse La
　Litton BA3 . . . . **75** D3
　Wraxall BS48 . . . . **9** A6
White House La
　East Huntspill TA9 . . . . . **136** E7

White House La continued
　Loxton BS26 . . . . **68** A3
Whitehouse Rd BS49 . . . . . **34** F8
White House Rd TA5,
　TA6 . . . . **135** D5
Whiteladies Rd BS8 . . . . . **226** B4
Whitelands BA3 . . . . **79** B3
Whiteleaze La
　Thurloxton TA2 . . . . **153** C1
　West Monkton TA2 . . . . . **169** D8
White Lodge Pk BS20 . . . . . **2** D6
White Mead BA21 . . . . **218** D6
Whitemill La BA11 . . . . . . **119** C3
Whitemoor Hill TA20 . . . **194** C4
Whitemoor La TA4 . . . . . . **150** F3
Whitemore Ct BA1 . . . . . . **29** A4
Whiteoak Way BS48 . . . . . **18** D3
White Oxmead La BA2 . . . **61** E1
White Ox Mead La BA2 . . **61** E1
White Post
　Midsomer Norton BA3 . . . **97** B6
　Twitchen EX36 . . . . **145** K2
Whitepost Gate DT9 . . . . **188** D6
Whites Cl TA6 . . . . **208** E2
Whitesfield Cl BS48 . . . . . . **8** D2
Whitesfield Rd BS48 . . . . . **8** D1
Whitesome's Dro BS27 . . **109** C6
White St
　Bristol BS5 . . . . **227** C4
　Creech St Michael TA3 . . **169** E4
　Horningsham BA12 . . . . . **144** E4
　North Curry TA3 . . . . **170** C4
Whitestaunton Cross
　TA20 . . . . **193** B5
Whitestone Rd BA11 . . . . **120** B6
Whitewall Cnr TA3 . . . . . **181** B4
Whiteway TA20 . . . . **193** E6
Whiteway Rd BA2 . . . . **44** A3
Whitewell Pl BA11 . . . . . . **119** C3
Whitewell Rd BA11 . . . . . **119** C3
Whitewells Rd BA1 . . . . . . **28** A2
Whitewick La TA5 . . . . . . **134** F8
Whitfield Rd TA6 . . . . **209** D6
Whitford Hill
　Corfe TA3 . . . . **182** A4
　Pitminster TA3 . . . . **181** F5
Whitford La TA3 . . . . **182** A4
Whithys The BA16 . . . . . . **207** C2
Whiting Cl BA4 . . . . **205** C4
Whiting La 1 TA6 . . . . . . **153** E3
Whiting Rd
　Bristol BS13 . . . . **22** A4
　Glastonbury BA6 . . . . **206** F5
Whiting Way BA5 . . . . . . **203** D4
Whitland Ave BS13 . . . . . . **22** B5
Whitland Rd BS13 . . . . . . **22** B5
Whitley La BA16 . . . . **156** D7
Whitley Rd TA7, BA16 . . . **156** C8
Whitling St BS40 . . . . **38** A2
Whitmead Gdns BS13 . . . . **22** C4
Whitmore La TA2 . . . . . . **212** D3
Whitmore Rd TA2 . . . . . . **212** E3
Whitnage La EX16 . . . . . . **178** C2
Whitnell Cnr BA5 . . . . **113** F6
Whitnell La
　Binegar BA3 . . . . **114** B3
　Keenthorne TA5 . . . . **134** C2
Whitney Hill TA19 . . . . . . **193** F8
Whitson Ho 1 BS2 . . . . . **227** C4
Whitson St BS1 . . . . **227** A4
Whitstone Cl BA4 . . . . . . **205** C5
Whitstone Cnr BA4 . . . . . **205** D1
Whitstone Ct BA4 . . . . . . **205** D5
Whitstone Hill BA4 . . . . . **204** C1
Whitstone La BA4 . . . . . . **205** E1
Whitstone Rd BA4 . . . . . . **205** D4
Whitstone Rise BA4 . . . . . **205** D4
Whitswood Steep TA24 . . **130** D4
Whittakers Ho 6 BA4 . . . **205** B6
Whitting Rd BS23 . . . . **48** E4
Whittington Dr BS22 . . . . **31** D2
Whittock Rd BS14 . . . . . . **23** D6
Whittock Sq BS14 . . . . . . **23** D7
Whittox La BA11 . . . . **119** E5
Whitwell Rd BS14 . . . . . . **23** B8
Whitworth Rd
　Frome BA11 . . . . **119** F2
　Minehead TA24 . . . . **200** D7
Wicketsbeer Rd BA22 . . . **197** C6
Wickfield BS21 . . . . **6** C2
Wickham's Cross or Beggar's
　Grave BA6 . . . . **157** C3
Wickham Ct BS21 . . . . **6** C3
Wickham Rise BA11 . . . . **119** C6
Wickham Way
　East Brent TA9 . . . . **86** D6
　Shepton Mallet BA4 . . . . **205** A6
Wick Hill
　Charlton Horethorne
　　DT9 . . . . **176** A3
　Milborne Port DT9 . . . . . **217** B6
Wickhill Rd TA10 . . . . . . **171** D5
Wick Hollow BA6 . . . . . . **206** F5
Wick House Cl BS31 . . . . . **25** D3
Wick La
　Burnham-on-S TA9 . . . . . . **85** E6
　Glastonbury BA6 . . . . **139** E2
　Lympsham BS24 . . . . **66** E1
　Peasedown St John BA2,
　　BA3 . . . . **60** F1
　Pensford BS39 . . . . **40** D3
　Upton Cheyney BS30 . . . . **26** A8
Wicklow Rd BS4 . . . . **22** E8
Wick Moor Dro TA5 . . . . **134** C2
Wick Rd
　Bishop Sutton BS39 . . . . . **57** C3
　Lympsham BS24 . . . . **66** D2

Wick Rd *continued*
Milborne Port DT9 . . . . . . **217** C4
Wick St Lawrence BS22. . . . **32** B7
Widcombe BS14 . . . . **23** A6
Widcombe CE Jun Sch
  BA2. . . . . **45** B5
Widcombe Cres BA2 . . . . . . **45** B5
Widcombe Hill BA2 . . . . **45** C4
Widcombe Inf Sch BA2. . . . . **45** B5
Widcombe Par BA2 . . . . . . **228** C1
Widcombe Rise BA2 . . . . . . **45** B5
Widcombe Terr BA2 . . . . . . **45** B5
Wideatts Rd BS27. . . . . **90** A7
Widmore Gr BS13 . . . . **22** B5
Wigeon Cl TA24. . . . . **201** C5
Wight Row BS20 . . . . **2** F6
Wigmore Gdns BS22 . . . . . . **31** D2
Wiindsor Cres TA20 . . . . . . **223** B3
Wilbye Gr BS4 . . . . **22** D7
Wildcountry La BS48. . . . . . **20** E6
Wilde Cl TA8 . . . . **104** C6
Wilder Ct BS2 . . . . **227** B4
Wilderness Dro BA16. . . . . **138** E2
Wilderness The **9** DT9. . . . **225** E4
Wilder St BS2 . . . . **227** B4
Wildmoor La TA21 . . . . **180** F6
Wild Oak Ho TA3. . . . . **168** D1
Wild Oak La TA3 . . . . **168** D1
Wilfred Rd TA1 . . . . **213** A4
Wilfrid Rd BA16. . . . . **207** D6
Wilkins Cl TA20. . . . . **223** D4
Wilkins Rd TA6 . . . . **209** D5
Willcocks Cl **6** TA21 . . . . **222** D5
Willcox Cl BA6. . . . . **206** E5
Willet's La BA3 . . . . **94** D6
Willet Cl TA9 . . . . **104** C4
Willett Hill Cross TA4 . . . . **150** D5
Willey Rd TA3 . . . . **170** E6
Willia m Daw Cl BS29. . . . . **50** F3
William Herschel Mus★
  BA1. . . . . **228** B2
William Reynolds Ho
  BA16 . . . . **207** D7
William St
  Bath BA2 . . . . **228** C3
  Taunton TA2 . . . . **212** F6
Williamstowe BA2 . . . . **45** C1
Willie Gill Ct TA1 . . . . **212** E4
Willinton Rd BS4. . . . . **22** F8
Willis's La TA18. . . . . **196** C4
Willis Hay DT9 . . . . **225** D3
Williton Cres BS23 . . . . **48** F3
Williton & District Hospl
  TA4 . . . . **202** D3
Williton Sta TA4 . . . . **202** F4
Will La TA4 . . . . **151** A3
Willmott Cl BS14. . . . . **22** F3
Willmotts Cl TA7. . . . . **137** B2
Willoughby Cl BS13 . . . . . . **22** B7
Willoughby Pl TA20. . . . . . **223** D3
Willoughby Rd TA6 . . . . . . **208** C4
Willowbank TA24 . . . . **130** B4
Willow Cl
  Bath BA2 . . . . **62** E8
  Clevedon BS21. . . . . **6** E3
  East Huntspill TA9 . . . . . . **136** E7
  Langport TA10 . . . . **172** A6
  Long Ashton BS41 . . . . . . **10** F1
  Portishead BS20 . . . . **2** C4
  Radstock BA3 . . . . **78** E2
  Taunton TA1. . . . . **213** D1
  Weston-Super-Mare, St Georges
    BS22 . . . . **32** D2
  Weston-Super-Mare, Uphill
    BS23 . . . . **48** E2
  Westonzoyland TA7 . . . . . **154** E5
  Williton TA4 . . . . **202** E3
Willow Ct TA6 . . . . **209** D5
Willowdown BS22. . . . . **31** E4
Willow Dr
  Bleadon BS24 . . . . **67** C6
  Hutton BS24 . . . . **49** E2
  Shepton Mallet BA4. . . . . **205** A6
  Weston-Super-Mare BS24. . **49** E5
Willowfalls The BA1 . . . . . . **28** E3
Willow Gdns BS22 . . . . **32** D2
Willow Gn
  Bath BA2 . . . . **44** D4
  Chedzoy TA7. . . . . **154** D8
Willow Gr TA23 . . . . **131** E4
Willow Ho BS13. . . . . **22** D4
Willow La EX15 . . . . **180** F2
Willow Rd
  Street BA16. . . . . **207** B3
  Yeovil BA21 . . . . **218** F6
Willows The
  Brent Knoll TA9 . . . . **86** A2
  Nailsea BS48. . . . . **8** F3
Willow The BA3. . . . . **96** F2
Willow Tree Cl BA22 . . . . . **174** A4
Willow Vale BA11 . . . . **119** F5
Willow Way TA18 . . . . **224** D7
Willow Wlk
  Bridgwater TA6 . . . . **209** C4
  Keynsham BS31. . . . . **24** D4
Wills Ind Est TA6. . . . . **209** A4
Wills Rd TA6. . . . . **208** F1
Wills Way BS4 . . . . **22** D6
Willway St BS2 . . . . **227** C3
Wilmots Way BS20 . . . . **4** D4
Wilsham Cross EX35 . . . . . **122** A5
Wilsham La EX35 . . . . **122** A5
Wilson Pl BS2 . . . . **227** C4
Wilson Cl TA5 . . . . **134** B2
Wilson St BS2 . . . . **227** C4
Wilton Cl
  Burnham-on-S TA8 . . . . . **104** C8
  Street BA16 . . . . **207** D5

Wilton Cl *continued*
  Taunton TA1. . . . . **212** E3
Wilton Ct BS23 . . . . **48** D7
Wilton Gdns BS23. . . . . **48** D7
Wilton Gr TA1 . . . . **212** E3
Wilton Orch
  Street BA16 . . . . **207** D5
  Taunton TA1. . . . . **212** E2
Wilton Rd BA21 . . . . **219** E8
Wiltons BS40 . . . . **35** D2
Wilton St TA1. . . . . **212** E3
Wiltown TA10. . . . . **171** D3
Wiltown La EX15. . . . . **180** F3
Wiltshire Ct TA1 . . . . **212** C2
Wiltshire Cl TA1 . . . . **212** C2
Wiltshires Barton **4**
  BA11. . . . . **119** E5
Wiltshire Way BA1 . . . . **28** A2
Wilway La BA3 . . . . **163** C6
Wimblestone Rd BS25. . . . . **51** F2
Wimborne Cl TA1. . . . . **213** D3
Wimborough La BA22 . . . . **196** F6
Winash Cl BS14. . . . . **23** D7
Wincanton Bsns Pk BA9. **216** B3
Wincanton Cl BS48. . . . . **9** B1
Wincanton Prim Sch
  BA9 . . . . **216** C3
Wincanton Town Mus★
  BA9. . . . . **216** C4
Winchcombe Cl BS48 . . . . . **19** A8
Winchcombe Gr BS11 . . . . . **4** F5
Winchester Cotts TA19. . . . **184** E1
Winchester Gdns TA1 . . . . **219** C7
Winchester Ho **2** TA1. . . **213** A4
Winchester Rd
  5 Bath BA2 . . . . **44** D5
  Burnham-on-S TA8. . . . . **104** C7
Winchester St TA1 . . . . . . **213** A4
Windball Hill TA22 . . . . . . **163** B7
Windcliff Cres BS11. . . . . . . **4** E7
Wind Down Cl TA6 . . . . . . **208** C4
Windermere Ave BS23 . . . . **48** F4
Windermere Cl BA20 . . . . . **218** F2
Windmill TA3. . . . . **170** F5
Windmill Bsns Pk BS21. . **16** E8
Windmill Cl TA9 . . . . **105** B7
Windmill Cotts TA15 . . . . . **186** C4
Windmill Cres TA7. . . . . . . **136** E3
Windmill Hill
  Hutton BS24 . . . . **50** A2
  Wrantage TA3 . . . . **170** A2
Windmill Hill La
  Ashill TA19 . . . . **183** B3
  Westbury-sub-Mendip
    BA5. . . . . **110** D4
Windmill Hill Rd BA6. . . . . **206** E5
Windmill La
  Langport TA10 . . . . **172** C5
  Montacute TA15 . . . . **186** C4
  West Pennard BA6 . . . . . **140** C1
Windmill Rd
  Clevedon BS21. . . . . **16** E8
  High Ham TA10 . . . . **156** A1
Windmill Rise TA18 . . . . . . **224** C7
Windrush Cl BA2. . . . . **43** F4
Windrush Gn BS31. . . . . **25** A4
Windrush Rd BS31 . . . . **25** A4
Windsbatch Hill BA11 . . . . **101** C1
Windsbatch La BA11 . . . . . **101** B1
Windsor Ave BS31 . . . . **24** E4
Windsor Bridge Rd BA1,
  BA2 . . . . **44** D7
Windsor Castle BA1. . . . . . **44** D7
Windsor Cl
  Burnham-on-S TA8 . . . . . . **85** B1
  Clevedon BS21. . . . . **6** D2
  Minehead TA24 . . . . **200** E6
  Taunton TA1. . . . . **212** C1
Windsor Cres BA11 . . . . . . **120** A5
Windsor Ct
  4 Bath BA1 . . . . **44** C7
  13 Bristol, Clifton BS8. . . **11** F6
Windsor Dr
  Bridgwater TA6 . . . . **209** D7
  Nailsea BS48. . . . . **8** E2
Windsor Hill La BA4. . . . . . **141** B8
Windsor Ho BS9. . . . . **209** C5
Windsor La TA14. . . . . **186** A4
Windsor Pl
  5 Bath BA1 . . . . **44** C7
  Bristol, Clifton BS8 . . . . . **11** F6
Windsor Rd
  Bridgwater TA6 . . . . **209** D7
  Weston-Super-Mare BS22. . **31** C2
Windsor Terr
  Bristol, Clifton BS8 . . . . . **11** F6
  17 Henstridge BA8 . . . . . **190** A6
  Paulton BS39. . . . . **77** E5
Windsor Villas **3** BA1. . . **44** C7
Windway Hill TA4 . . . . **164** D6
Windwhistle La
  Sticklepath TA4 . . . . **149** F6
  Weston-Super-Mare BS23. . **48** E3
Windwhistle Prim Sch
  BS23. . . . . **48** F3
Windwhistle Rd BS23 . . . . . **48** F3
Windy Ridge TA17 . . . . **195** D7
Windyridge La TA11 . . . . . **211** B1
Wine St
  Bath BA1. . . . . **228** C2
  Bristol BS1. . . . . **227** A3
  Frome BA11 . . . . **119** F4
  Yeovil BA20 . . . . **219** B4
Winford CE Prim Sch
  BS40 . . . . **37** F7
Winford Cl BS20 . . . . **2** E4
Winford Gr BS13 . . . . **22** A8

Winford La BS41 . . . . **21** C1
Winford Rd BS40. . . . . **38** F3
Winford Rural Workshops
  BA22 . . . . **197** A2
Winford Terr
  Bridgwater TA6 . . . . **209** B6
  Bristol BS41. . . . . **21** C5
Wingard Cl BS23 . . . . **48** D2
Wingard Ct **6** BS23 . . . . . **48** E5
Wingate Ave BA21 . . . . . . **219** C7
Wingfield CE Prim Sch
  BA14 . . . . **83** C6
Wingfield Rd DT9 . . . . **225** C3
Winifred's La BA1 . . . . **27** E1
Winifred Cliff Ct **1** EX16 **164** B1
Winkworth La TA1, TA2 **213** A5
Winnibrook La TA24 . . . . . **131** A5
Winnowing End BS25 . . . . . **52** A3
Winpenny La TA2 . . . . **168** E8
Winsbeer La
  Rockwell Green TA21. . . . **222** A6
  Runnington TA21 . . . . . . **179** F8
Winsbury View BA2 . . . . . . **42** B1
Winscombe Cl BS31. . . . . . **24** D6
Winscombe Ct BA11 . . . . . **120** B5
Winscombe Dro
  Shipham BS25. . . . . **70** D6
  Winscombe BS25. . . . . . . **70** A5
Winscombe Hill BS25. . . . . **69** F5
Winscombe Rd BS23 . . . . . **49** A7
Winscombe Woodborough
  Prim Sch BS25. . . . . **70** A8
Winsham Cl BS14 . . . . **23** B5
Winsham Prim Sch TA20 **194** E1
Winslade Cl TA1 . . . . **213** B7
Winsley CE Prim Sch
  BA15 . . . . **64** E7
Winsley Hill BA3. . . . . **64** B6
Winsley Rd BA15. . . . . **64** F7
Winsors La TA24 . . . . **131** A5
Winstitchen Cross TA24. . . **127** C2
Winstitchen La TA24 . . . . . **127** C2
Winston Cl TA2 . . . . **212** E6
Winston Dr BA21. . . . . **218** F8
Winstone Ct BS2. . . . . **226** C3
Winter's La TA4. . . . . **150** C3
Winterfield TA18. . . . . **196** B5
Winterfield Pk BS39. . . . . . **77** E4
Winterfield Rd BS39 . . . . . **77** E5
Winterhay La TA19 . . . . . . **221** A5
Winter La DT9 . . . . **188** C8
Winters Cross TA4 . . . . . . **165** C8
Winters Field TA1. . . . . . . **213** A5
Winters Hill La BA4 . . . . . **204** C3
Winters La BS40 . . . . **36** D6
Winters Orch TA3. . . . . . . **169** C1
Winterstoke Commercial Ctr
  BS23. . . . . **49** A6
Winterstoke Rd
  Bristol BS3. . . . . **11** F3
  Weston-Super-Mare BS23,
    BS24 . . . . **49** B4
Winterstoke Underpass
  BS3 . . . . **11** F4
Winterwell La BA4 . . . . . . **141** F4
Wint Hill BS29. . . . . **51** B2
Winyards View TA18 . . . . . **224** D4
Wireworks Est The TA6. . . **136** E4
Wirral Park Rd BA6 . . . . . **206** C3
Wirral Park Rdbt BA6 . . . . **206** C3
Wishford Mews BA3 . . . . . . **78** C2
Wisley Wlk BS22 . . . . **49** F7
Wisteria Ave BS24 . . . . **49** D2
Wisteria Cl BA22 . . . . **218** B5
Wiston Cross EX36 . . . . . . **162** C6
Witches Wlk TA6 . . . . **208** E2
Witch Hazel Rd BS13. . . . . . **22** E3
Witcombe Dro TA12. . . . . . **172** F1
Witcombe La TA12 . . . . . . **185** F8
Witham Cl TA1. . . . . **213** D3
Witham Rd BS31. . . . . **25** A3
Withey Cl E BS9 . . . . **5** F6
Withey Cl W BS9. . . . . **5** F5
Witheys The BS14 . . . . **23** C4
Withial Hill BA4. . . . . **158** D8
Withiel Dr TA5. . . . . **135** B2
Withiel Hill TA24. . . . . **148** F6
Withies La BA3 . . . . **97** A8
Withies Pk BA3 . . . . **96** F8
Withmoor Dro TA10 . . . . . **172** E4
Withybed La BA9 . . . . **177** E6
Withy Cl BS48 . . . . **8** F3
Withycombe Cross TA24. . **131** C4
Withycombe Hill TA5. . . . . **135** A5
Withycombe Hill Gate
  TA24 . . . . **130** F4
Withycombe La TA24. . . . . **131** B5
Withy Cotts BA3 . . . . **115** C5
Withyditch La BA2. . . . . **61** C4
Withy Gr TA7 . . . . **136** C7
Withy Grove Cl TA6 . . . . . **209** D7
Withy Hays Rd **3** TA11 . . **173** F7
Withy La
  Barton St David TA11. . . . **158** A3
  Clatworthy TA4 . . . . **149** B2
  Hemyock EX15. . . . . **180** B1
  Oakhill BA3 . . . . **115** C5
Withypool Cross
  Hawkridge TA22. . . . . . . **146** C2
  Twitchen EX36. . . . . **145** J4
Withypool Gdns BS14 . . . . **23** B5
Withy Rd TA9 . . . . **136** C7
Withys The BS20. . . . . **4** D4
Withywine La TA24 . . . . . . **162** C5
Withywood Com Sch
  BS13. . . . . **22** A5
Withywood Gdns **1** BS13. **21** F4
Withy Wood La BA4 . . . . . **142** C5

Withywood Rd BS13. . . . . . **21** F4
Witney Cl BS31 . . . . **25** D3
Witney La
  Chard TA20. . . . . **223** B8
  Tatworth TA20 . . . . **193** F1
Wittey's La TA20 . . . . **199** B6
Wiveliscombe Prim Sch
  TA4 . . . . **210** B5
Wivenhoe Cl BA11 . . . . . . **120** C6
Woburn Rd BA21. . . . . **219** E7
Wolfester Terr BA22 . . . . . **174** F4
Wollens Cl BA6. . . . . **206** C4
Wolmer Cl TA6 . . . . **208** E2
Wolsey Cl BA5 . . . . **203** B3
Wolverlands BA22 . . . . **175** A6
Wolvershill Ind Units
  BS29. . . . . **50** C6
Wolvershill Pk BS29. . . . . . **51** A3
Wolvershill Rd BS29. . . . . . **50** E6
  Banwell BA4. . . . . **79** C4
  Winscombe BS25. . . . . . . **69** F8
Woodburn Cross EX16 . . . **162** F2
Woodburn Hill EX16 . . . . . **162** F2
Woodburn Water Cross
  EX16 . . . . **162** F1
Woodbury Ave BA5 . . . . . **203** F5
Woodbury Cl BA5. . . . . . . **203** F5
Woodbury Rd TA6 . . . . . . **208** D4
Wood Cl BA5 . . . . **203** B4
Woodcliff Ave BS22 . . . . . . **31** C1
Woodcliff Rd BS22 . . . . **31** C1
Wood Close La TA17 . . . . . **195** A8
Woodcock St BA4. . . . . . . **214** C5
Woodcock Way EX13 . . . . **198** B7
Woodcombe Brake
  TA24 . . . . **200** D7
Woodcombe Cotts TA24. . **200** C8
Woodcombe La TA24. . . . . **200** C8
Woodcote BA20 . . . . **218** D2
Woodcroft BS39 . . . . **57** C3
Woodcroft Mdws TA20 . . **192** E7
Wooddene BS25. . . . . **70** A8
Wood Dro TA10. . . . . **171** E8
Wood End TA4. . . . . **167** D6
Wood End Wlk BS9 . . . . **5** C6
Wood Farm Cotts TA5. . . . **134** E4
Woodfield Cl TA4. . . . . **104** C5
Woodford Cl BS48 . . . . **9** A1
Woodford Cotts TA4 . . . . . **132** A1
Woodford Ct **2** BS23 . . . . **48** E5
Woodford La
  Coxley BA5 . . . . **139** F6
  Wells BA5 . . . . **203** B1
Woodford Rd BA5. . . . . . . **140** A6
Woodfords Gn BA7. . . . . . **214** B6
Woodhayes BA8 . . . . **190** A6
Woodhayes Ct **18** BA8 . . . **190** A6
Woodhayes Ho **12** BA8 . . **190** A6
Woodhayes Rd BA11 . . . . **120** C6
Woodhenge BA22. . . . . . . **218** B5
Woodhill BS49 . . . . **34** E6
Woodhill Ave BS20. . . . . **2** D6
Woodhill Ct BS20 . . . . **2** D7
Wood Hill Pk BS20 . . . . **2** D7
Woodhill Terr TA3 . . . . **170** F6
Woodhill Views BS48. . . . . . . **8** F3
Woodhouse Cross SP8 . . . **177** E6
Woodhouse La
  Axminster EX13 . . . . **198** D1
  Chard TA20. . . . . **194** B6
  Marston Magna BA22 . . . **175** B1
  Montacute TA15 . . . . **186** C3
Woodhouse Rd
  Axminster EX13 . . . . **198** D1
  Bath BA2 . . . . **44** A6
Woodhurst Rd BS23. . . . . . **49** A7
Woodington Rd BS21. . . . . . **6** C1
Wood Kilns The BS49 . . . . **17** A1
Wood La
  Axbridge BS26 . . . . **70** D2
  Blue Anchor TA24 . . . . . . **131** C6
  Butleigh BA6 . . . . **157** C4
  Carhampton TA24 . . . . . . **131** B4
  Chapmanslade BA13 . . . . **121** D4
  Clapton in G BS20 . . . . **8** E8
  Crowcombe TA4 . . . . **151** C7
  Drimpton DT8 . . . . **199** E7
  High Ham TA10 . . . . **155** E1
  Marnhull DT10. . . . . **190** F2
  Moorlinch TA7 . . . . **155** E8
  Rodney Stoke BS27. . . . . . **91** B1
  South Cheriton BA8 . . . . **176** C4
  Stalbridge DT10. . . . . . . **190** B4
  Stawell TA7 . . . . **137** A1
  Stogumber TA4 . . . . **150** D7
  Weston-Super-Mare BS23. . **30** F1
Woodland Ave TA7. . . . . . **154** F5
Woodland Cl
  6 Carhampton TA24. . . **131** A5
  Failand BS8 . . . . **10** B4
Woodland Cotts BA3 . . . . . **64** D6
Woodland Glade BS21. . . . . **6** E5

Wic–Woo **275**

Woodland Gr
  Bath, Bushey Norwood
    BA2 . . . . **45** E5
  Bath, Weston Park BA1 . . **27** C1
  Bristol BS9. . . . . **5** D6
  Yeovil BA20 . . . . **219** B4
Woodland Pl BA2 . . . . **45** D5
Woodland Rd
  Bristol BS8. . . . . **226** C4
  Frome BA11. . . . . **119** F4
  Nailsea BS48. . . . . **8** E3
  Taunton TA2 . . . . **213** A7
  Watchet TA23 . . . . **202** C6
  Weston-Super-Mare BS23. . **48** D4
Woodlands
  Axbridge BS26. . . . . **70** D2
  Wellington TA21. . . . . . . **222** F3
  Weston-Super-Mare BS23. . **30** D1
Woodlands Bsns Pk
  EX16 . . . . **179** C3
Woodlands Ct BS11. . . . . **4** E5
Woodlands Dr
  Ruishton TA3 . . . . **169** C3
  Winsley BA3 . . . . **64** B6
Woodlands La
  Holcombe BA3. . . . . **116** B7
  Isle Abbotts TA3 . . . . **184** E6
Woodlands Mead DT10. . . **190** F6
Woodlands Pk BA1. . . . . . . **28** C2
Woodlands Rd
  Baltonsborough BA6. . . . **158** A8
  Clevedon BS21. . . . . **6** C4
  Portishead BS20 . . . . **2** D8
Woodlands The
  Peasedown St John BA2. . **60** F3
  Shepton Mallet BA4. . . . . **205** D5
Woodland Way BS8 . . . . . . **10** B4
Woodleaze BS9 . . . . **5** B6
Woodleigh Gdns BS14. . . . . **23** C6
Woodmarsh Cl BS14 . . . . . . **23** A4
Woodmead Gdns BS13 . . . . **22** C4
Woodmill BS49 . . . . **17** A1
Woodmill Cl DT10. . . . . . . **190** B5
Woodpecker Ave BA3 . . . . . **97** B8
Woodpecker Dr BS22 . . . . . **49** E8
Woodram La TA3 . . . . **181** E5
Wood Rd
  Ashill TA19 . . . . **183** B4
  High Ham TA10 . . . . **172** A8
Woodridge Mead TA4 . . . . **167** E8
Wood Rock EX36. . . . . **162** C5
Woodrush Cl TA1 . . . . **213** C1
Woods Batch BA16. . . . . . **207** B6
Woods Cnr TA11. . . . . **173** E8
Woodside
  Bristol BS9. . . . . **5** D3
  Midsomer Norton BA3. . . **77** B8
Woodside Ave TA24 . . . . . . **49** B2
Woodside Cl TA24. . . . . . . **200** D7
Woodside Ct BS23 . . . . **49** A8
Woodside Gdns BS20 . . . . . . **1** E5
Woodside Rd BS21. . . . . **6** E5
Woodspring Ave BS22. . . . . **31** B3
Woodspring Cres BS22. . . . **31** A3
Woodspring Mus★ BS23. . **48** E8
Woodspring Priory★
  BS22 . . . . **14** C1
Woods Rd BA16. . . . . **207** A6
Wood St
  Bath BA1 . . . . **228** B2
  Bath, Beechen Cliff BA2 . . **228** B1
  Milverton TA4. . . . . **166** F5
  Taunton TA1. . . . . **212** E4
Woodstock Rd
  Taunton TA1. . . . . **212** E5
  Weston-Super-Mare BS22. . **49** B8
  Yeovil BA21 . . . . **219** C7
Woodview
  Chilcompton BA3 . . . . **96** E5
  2 Clevedon BS21. . . . . . . **6** F3
  Paulton BS39. . . . . **77** C5
  Weils BA5 . . . . **203** E5
Woodview Cl BS11 . . . . **4** E7
Woodview Dr BS49. . . . . . . **35** B8
Woodview Rd BS27 . . . . . . **90** C7
Woodview Terr
  Nailsea BS48. . . . . **8** F2
  Weston-Super-Mare BS23. . **49** A6
Wood Way BS35 . . . . **122** D4
Woodwell Rd BS11. . . . . **4** E5
Wookey Cl BS48 . . . . **18** F8
Wookey Hole Cave★
  BA5. . . . . **111** E5
Wookey Hole Papermill &
  Mus★ BA5 . . . . **203** A8
Wookey Hole Rd BA5. . . . . **203** B5
Wookey Prim Sch BA5 . . . **139** D8
Woolavington Hill TA7. . . . **136** E3
Woolavington Rd TA7 . . . . **136** D4
Woolavington Right Dro
  TA7 . . . . **154** D6
Woolavington Village Prim
  Sch TA7 . . . . **136** E4
Woolcott La SP8 . . . . **161** E1
Wooler Rd BS23 . . . . **48** E8
Wooley La TA19, TA20. . . . **194** C6
Woolhayes La TA20 . . . . . **223** A8
Woollard La
  Bristol BS14, BS39 . . . . . . **41** A7
  Whitchurch BS14. . . . . . . **23** E1
Woollen La BA22. . . . . **174** F1
Woolley La BA1 . . . . **28** A4
Woolley Rd BS14. . . . . **23** E5
Woolpit La TA24 . . . . **146** B7

Woolshed Cl TA24 ...... 129 E1
Woolstone La TA5 ...... 134 F7
Woolston Rd BA22 ...... 175 E6
Woolvers Way BS24 ...... 50 B6
Wooton Hill BA6 .... 157 C5
Wootton Cross EX13 .... 198 F1
Wootton Gr DT9 .... 225 E5
Wootton St BA6 .... 157 C6
Wootton Vineyard★ BA4 140 C5
Worberry La BA3 .... 95 B7
Worcester Bldgs BA1 .... 28 B2
Worcester Cl BA2 .... 79 D7
Worcester Cres BS8 ..... 226 A4
Worcester Ct BS8 .... 226 A4
Worcester Gdns BS48 .... 18 C8
Worcester Pk BA1 .... 28 B2
Worcester Pl BA1 .... 28 B2
Worcester Rd BS8 .... 226 A4
Worcester Terr
  Bath BA1 .... 28 B2
  Bristol BS8 .... 226 A4
Wordsworth Ave TA6 .... 208 E6
Wordsworth Cl TA8 ...... 85 B2
Wordsworth Dr TA1 ..... 213 B3
Wordsworth Rd
  Clevedon BS21 .... 6 C2
  Weston-Super-Mare BS23 .. 49 A3
World's End La BS31 ..... 25 C5
Worldwide Butterflies &
  Lullingstone Silk Farm★
  DT9 .... 187 A3
Worlebury CE Fst Sch
  BS22 .... 31 B3
Worlebury Cl BS22 ...... 31 B3
Worlebury Hill Rd BS22,
  BS23 .... 31 B2
Worlebury Park Rd BS31 A2
Worle Ct BS22 .... 31 F3
Worle Ind Est BS22 ...... 32 B2
Worle Moor Rd BS24 .... 49 E7
Worle Sta BS22 .... 32 B1
Wormcliff La SN13 ...... 29 F3
Worminster Batch BA4 . 140 D5
Worston La TA8 .... 104 C5
Worston Orch TA4 ...... 104 E4
Worston Rd TA9 .... 104 E5
Worthings The BS22 .... 67 B1
Worthington Cl BS28 ... 108 D5
Worth La TA22, TA24 .... 146 C4
Worthy Cres BS24 .... 67 B1
Worthy La
  Creech St Michael TA3 .. 169 D5
  Pilton BA4 .... 140 F3
  5 Weston-Super-Mare
  BS23 .... 48 E8
  West Pennard BA4, BA6 . 140 D1
Worthy Pl **4** BS23 ..... 48 E8
Worthy Toll Rd TA24 .... 123 D4
Wouldham Rd TA23 .... 202 D6

Wrangcombe La TA21 .. 180 A4
Wrangcombe Rd TA21 . 180 A4
Wrangle Farm Gn BS21 .. 6 E2
Wrangle The **5** BS24 .... 49 F7
Wrangway Rd EX15 ..... 180 A3
Wraxall Cross Rds BA4 . 159 A7
Wraxall Gr BS13 .... 22 A8
Wraxall Hill
  Ditcheat BA4 .... 159 A8
  Wraxall BS48 .... 9 C5
Wraxall Rd BA4 .... 159 B7
Wraxhill Cl BA16 .... 207 D5
Wraxhill Rd
  Street BA16 .... 207 C5
  Yeovil BA20 .... 218 E1
Wreath La TA20 .... 194 B3
Wren Cl
  Frome BA11 .... 120 B6
  Taunton TA1 .... 212 C4
  Weston-Super-Mare BS22 .. 49 D8
Wrenmoor Cl TA6 ...... 209 C3
Wrington CE Prim Sch
  BS40 .... 35 E2
Wrington Cres BS13 .... 22 A7
Wrington Hill BS40 ..... 35 F5
Wrington La BS49 ...... 34 E5
Wrington Mead BS49 ... 34 E5
Wrington Rd BS49 ..... 34 F4
Wristland Rd TA23 .... 202 D7
Writhlington Ct BA3 ... 79 C2
Writhlington Sch BA3 .. 79 C1
Writh Rd DT9 .... 189 B1
Wroughton Dr BS13 .... 22 D4
Wroughton Gdns BS13 . 22 D4
Wry La TA4 .... 149 F2
Wyatt's Cl BS48 .... 8 D2
Wyatt Ave BS13 .... 21 F5
Wyatt Cl BS13 .... 21 F5
Wyatts Ct TA17 .... 195 C7
Wyatts Field TA3 ...... 168 D1
Wyatts Way TA19 ...... 183 C4
Wych Ct EX13 .... 198 E3
Wych Elm Rd BA11 .... 120 C6
Wydford Cl DT9 .... 225 B3
Wydon La TA24 .... 124 F3
Wye Ave TA6 .... 209 D3
Wyedale Ave BS9 .... 5 C7
Wyke Rd
  Wyke Champflower
  BA10 .... 215 A5
  Wyke Champflower BA10 215 A6
Wyke Rd
  Castle Cary BA7, BA10 . 214 E7
  Wyke Champflower BA10 215 C6
Wylds Rd TA6 .... 209 A7
Wyllie Ct BS22 .... 32 A5
Wymbush Cres BS13 ... 22 C5
Wymbush Gdns BS13 .. 22 C5
Wyndeats La TA5 ...... 134 B5
Wyndham's TA4 .... 210 C4

Wyndham Cres BS20 ..... 4 B4
Wyndham Ct BA21 ..... 219 C5
Wyndham Rd
  Bridgwater TA6 .... 209 C6
  Taunton TA2 .... 212 E7
  Watchet TA23 .... 202 C6
Wyndham St BA20 ..... 219 C5
Wyndham View BA21 .. 219 D5
Wyndham Way BS20 ..... 2 E5
Wyndham Way Ret Pk
  BS20 .... 2 D5
Wynford Rd BA11 ...... 120 B5
Wynnes Cl DT9 .... 225 C3
Wynnes Rise DT9 ...... 225 C3
Wynsome St BA14 ...... 83 F3
Wynter Cl BS22 .... 32 A3
Wyrral Cl BA6 .... 206 D3
Wytch Gn EX13 .... 198 E3
Wythburn Rd BA11 .... 120 C5
Wyvern Cl
  Bruton BA10 .... 215 F7
  Weston-Super-Mare BS23 . 48 F7
  Yeovil BA20 .... 218 C1
Wyvern Com Sch BS23 .. 48 F5
Wyvern Ct TA18 .... 224 C6
Wyvern Mews **5** BS23 .. 48 F7
Wyvern Rd TA1 .... 168 E1
Wyville Rd BA11 .... 120 C6

Y

Yadley Cl BS25 .... 70 A7
Yadley La BS25 .... 70 A6
Yadley Way BS25 ...... 70 A7
Yallands Hill TA2 ...... 213 E8
Yanel La BS25 .... 52 B5
Yanhey Hill TA5 .... 162 E4
Yanleigh Cl BS13 .... 21 D6
Yanley La BS41, BS13 ... 21 C7
Yarbury Way BS24 ...... 32 B1
Yarde Pl TA1 .... 212 F4
Yard La
  Marshwood DT6 ...... 199 F3
  Wiveliscombe TA4 .... 210 C6
Yardleigh Cross EX13 . 198 D4
Yard The BA11 .... 143 C4
Yardwall Rd TA9 ...... 106 A3
Yarley Cross BA5 ...... 139 C8
Yarley Field La BA5 ... 139 B7
Yarley Hill BA5 .... 139 C7
Yarlington Cl TA2 ..... 168 B4
Yarnbarton BA8 .... 176 E1
Yarn Barton BA20 ..... 219 A4
Yarrow Ct BS22 .... 32 A5
Yarrow Rd TA20 .... 106 D3
Yatton Cl BS13 .... 21 F8
Yatton Jun & Inf Schs
  BS49 .... 34 C8
Yatton Sta BS49 .... 17 A1
Yeabsleys Way BA7 .... 214 C6
Yealscombe La TA24 .. 128 B2
Yeamen's Ho BS1 ..... 227 B1

Yeap's Dro BA5 .... 139 A7
Yearmoor La TA5 ...... 134 F8
Yearnor Mill La
  Oare TA24 .... 122 F5
  Porlock Weir TA24 ... 123 B5
Yeates Ct BS21 .... 6 E3
Yeatman Cl BS39 .... 57 D4
Yeatman Hospl DT9 ... 225 D4
Yellingmill La BA4 .... 141 C8
Yellowcombe La TA24 . 147 C5
Yellow Rose Cvn Pk
  TA20 .... 193 D6
Yellow Way Rd
  Maiden Bradley BA11,
  BA12 .... 144 A3
  Witham Friary BA11 .. 143 F3
Yellow Wood Cross TA4 132 D2
Yenston Hill BA8 ...... 189 F8
Yeo Bank La BS21 ...... 15 F1
Yeo Cl
  Cheddar BS27 .... 90 B6
  Weston-Super-Mare BS23 . 49 A5
Yeo Ct
  Clevedon BS21 .... 6 C2
  Congresbury BS49 ..... 34 D4
Yeo La
  Bridgwater TA6 .... 209 B2
  Long Ashton BS41 ..... 10 F1
Yeolands Dr BS21 .... 6 B1
Yeo Mill Cross EX36 .. 162 C5
Yeo Moor BS21 .... 6 E2
Yeo Moor Dro BS27,
  BS28 .... 109 D3
Yeo Moor Inf Sch BS21 . 6 E2
Yeo Moor Jun Sch BS21 . 6 E2
Yeo Rd TA6 .... 209 B2
Yeo Valley **2** BA22 .. 197 F8
Yeo Valley Way BS48 .... 9 B2
Yeovil Bsns Ctr BA21 . 219 F7
Yeovil Coll BA21 ...... 219 A6
Yeovil District Hospl
  BA21 .... 219 B5
Yeovil Junction Sta
  BA22 .... 219 E1
Yeovil Marsh Pk BA21 . 187 A5
Yeovil Rd
  Crewkerne TA18 ...... 224 E7
  Halstock BA22 .... 197 D3
  Montacute TA15 ...... 186 B3
  Sherborne DT9 .... 225 C4
  Tintinhull BA22 ...... 186 C6
  Yeovil BA22 .... 218 F1
Yeovil Small Bsns Ctr
  BA22 .... 218 B6
Yeovil Trinity Foyer **7**
  BA20 .... 219 B4

Yeoward Rd BS21 .... 6 E1
Yeo Way BS21 .... 6 B2
Yet Mead La BS27 ..... 110 B7
Yewcroft Cl BS14 .... 23 A4
Yewtree Batch BS40 .... 37 A1
Yew Tree Cl
  Bishop Sutton BS39 .... 57 D4
  Lower Langford BS40 .. 53 E6
  Nailsea BS48 .... 8 C1
  Yeovil BA20 .... 218 E2
Yew Tree Cotts BS40 ... 54 E3
Yew Tree Ct BS14 ...... 23 B5
Yew Tree Dr BS22 ...... 50 B8
Yew Tree Gdns
  Nailsea BS48 .... 8 C1
  Pill BS20 .... 4 C4
  Sandford BS25 .... 52 A4
Yew Tree La
  Compton Martin BS40 . 74 A7
  Kingston Seymour BS21 . 16 B1
  Taunton TA2 .... 213 E6
Yew Tree Pk BS49 ...... 34 D3
Yomede Pk BA1 .... 44 A7
Yonder Dro TA10 ..... 184 E8
Yonder Hill Cotts TA20 198 E7
Yonder Mead TA4 ..... 167 F7
York's La BA3 .... 94 B6
York Bldgs TA6 .... 208 F5
York Cl
  Axminster EX13 ...... 198 A1
  Weston-Super-Mare BS22 . 32 A4
York Ct BS2 .... 227 B4
York Gdns BS8 .... 11 F6
York Lodge **4** BA20 .. 219 A5
York Pl
  Bath BA1 .... 45 B8
  Bristol, Brandon Hill BS1 226 C2
  Bristol, Victoria Park BS8 226 B3
  Yeovil BA20 .... 219 A5
York Rd
  Bridgwater TA6 ...... 208 F2
  Bristol BS2 .... 227 C1
  Taunton TA1 .... 213 C5
York St
  Bath BA1 .... 228 C2
  Bristol BS2 .... 227 B4
  5 Frome BA11 ..... 119 E5
  Weston-Super-Mare BS23 . 48 D7
Youngwood La BS48 ... 18 D2

Z

Zeals Rise BA12 .... 161 F2
Zembard La TA20 ..... 223 C4
Zeta Cl TA7 .... 209 E8
Zig Zag BS21 .... 6 D4
Zion Hill
  Midsomer Norton BA3 . 96 B7
  Oakhill BA3 .... 115 A3
  18 Shepton Mallet BA4 .. 205 B6

NH	NJ	NK		
NN	NO	NP		
NS	NT	NU		
NX	NY	NZ		
SC	SD	SE	TA	
SH	SJ	SK	TF	TG
SN	SO	SP	TL	TM
SS	ST	SU	TQ	TR
SX	SY	SZ	TV	

Any feature in this atlas can be given a unique reference to help you find the same feature on other Ordnance Survey maps of the area, or to help someone else locate you if they do not have a Street Atlas.

The grid squares in this atlas match the Ordnance Survey National Grid and are at 500 metre intervals. The small figures at the bottom and sides of every other grid line are the National Grid kilometre values (**00** to **99** km) and are repeated across the country every 100 km (see left).

To give a unique National Grid reference you need to locate where in the country you are. The country is divided into 100 km squares with each square given a unique two-letter reference. Use the administrative map to determine in which 100 km square a particular page of this atlas falls.

The bold letters and numbers between each grid line (**A** to **F**, **1** to **8**) are for use within a specific Street Atlas only, and when used with the page number, are a convenient way of referencing these grid squares.

Example   The railway bridge over DARLEY GREEN RD in grid square B1

Step 1: Identify the two-letter reference, in this example the page is in **SP**

Step 2: Identify the 1 km square in which the railway bridge falls. Use the figures in the southwest corner of this square: Eastings **17**, Northings **74**. This gives a unique reference: **SP 17 74**, accurate to 1 km.

Step 3: To give a more precise reference accurate to 100 m you need to estimate how many tenths along and how many tenths up this 1 km square the feature is (to help with this the 1 km square is divided into four 500 m squares). This makes the bridge about **8** tenths along and about **1** tenth up from the southwest corner.

This gives a unique reference: **SP 178 741**, accurate to 100 m.

Eastings (read from left to right along the bottom) come before Northings (read from bottom to top). If you have trouble remembering say to yourself Along the hall, THEN up the stairs !

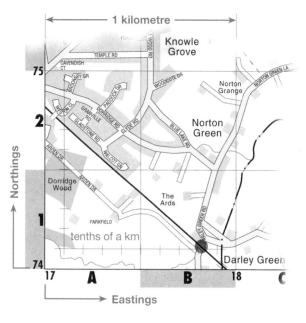

PHILIP'S MAPS

the Gold Standard for drivers

◆ **Philip's street atlases cover every county in England, Wales, Northern Ireland and much of Scotland**

◆ Every named street is shown, including alleys, lanes and walkways

◆ Thousands of additional features marked: stations, public buildings, car parks, places of interest

◆ Route-planning maps to get you close to your destination

◆ Postcodes on the maps and in the index

◆ Widely used by the emergency services, transport companies and local authorities

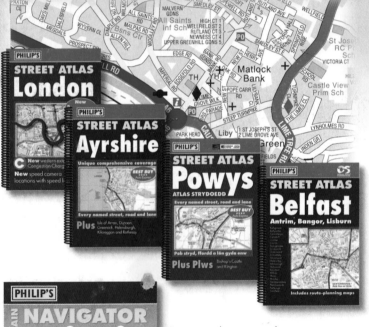

For national mapping, choose **Philip's Navigator Britain** the most detailed road atlas available of England, Wales and Scotland. Hailed by Auto Express as 'the ultimate road atlas', the atlas shows every road and lane in Britain.

'The ultimate in UK mapping'
The Sunday Times

Street atlases currently available

England
Bedfordshire and Luton
Berkshire
Birmingham and West Midlands
Bristol and Bath
Buckinghamshire and Milton Keynes
Cambridgeshire and Peterborough
Cheshire
Cornwall
Cumbria
Derbyshire
Devon
Dorset
County Durham and Teesside
Essex
North Essex
South Essex
Gloucestershire and Bristol
Hampshire
North Hampshire
South Hampshire
Herefordshire Monmouthshire
Hertfordshire
Isle of Wight
Kent
East Kent
West Kent
Lancashire
Leicestershire and Rutland
Lincolnshire
Liverpool and Merseyside
London
Greater Manchester
Norfolk
Northamptonshire
Northumberland
Nottinghamshire
Oxfordshire
Shropshire
Somerset
Staffordshire
Suffolk

Surrey
East Sussex
West Sussex
Tyne and Wear
Warwickshire and Coventry
Wiltshire and Swindon
Worcestershire
East Yorkshire Northern Lincolnshire
North Yorkshire
South Yorkshire
West Yorkshire

Wales
Anglesey, Conwy and Gwynedd
Cardiff, Swansea and The Valleys
Carmarthenshire, Pembrokeshire and Swansea
Ceredigion and South Gwynedd
Denbighshire, Flintshire, Wrexham
Herefordshire Monmouthshire
Powys

Scotland
Aberdeenshire
Ayrshire
Dumfries and Galloway
Edinburgh and East Central Scotland
Fife and Tayside
Glasgow and West Central Scotland
Inverness and Moray
Lanarkshire
Scottish Borders

Northern Ireland
County Antrim and County Londonderry
County Armagh and County Down
Belfast
County Tyrone and County Fermanagh

How to order
Philip's maps and atlases are available from bookshops, motorway services and petrol stations. You can order direct from the publisher by phoning **0207 531 8473** or online at **www.philips-maps.co.uk**
For bulk orders only, e-mail philips@philips-maps.co.uk